Edgar Allan Poe

EDGAR ALLAN POE

A Life

RICHARD KOPLEY

UNIVERSITY OF VIRGINIA PRESS
Charlottesville and London

The University of Virginia Press is situated on the traditional lands of the Monacan Nation, and the Commonwealth of Virginia was and is home to many other Indigenous people. We pay our respect to all of them, past and present. We also honor the enslaved African and African American people who built the University of Virginia, and we recognize their descendants. We commit to fostering voices from these communities through our publications and to deepening our collective understanding of their histories and contributions.

University of Virginia Press
© 2025 Richard Kopley
All rights reserved
Printed in the United States of America on acid-free paper

First published 2025

1 3 5 7 9 8 6 4 2

Library of Congress Cataloging-in-Publication Data
Names: Kopley, Richard, author.
Title: Edgar Allan Poe : a life / Richard Kopley.
Description: Charlottesville : University of Virginia Press, 2025. | Includes bibliographical references and index.
Identifiers: LCCN 2024041125 (print) | LCCN 2024041126 (ebook) | ISBN 9780813952239 (hardcover) | ISBN 9780813952246 (ebook)
Subjects: LCSH: Poe, Edgar Allan, 1809–1849. | Authors, American—19th century—Biography. | LCGFT: Biographies.
Classification: LCC PS2631 .K66 2025 (print) | LCC PS2631 (ebook) | DDC 818/.309 [B]—dc23/eng/20240906
LC record available at https://lccn.loc.gov/2024041125
LC ebook record available at https://lccn.loc.gov/2024041126

Frontispiece: Frontispiece: Daly daguerreotype of Poe, ca. 1847. (Special Collections, Fine Arts Library, Harvard College Library)
Cover art: Raven's wings, AI generated by pham. (stock.adobe.com, 87288062)
Cover design: Cecilia Sorochin

For Amy, with love

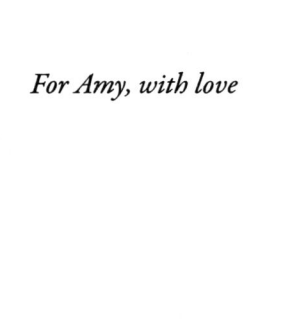

Contents

List of Abbreviations ... ix

Introduction · "The Mystic Empire and High Power" ... 1

1. "No Tie More Strong" · 1809–1811 ... 5
2. "From Childhood's Hour" · 1811–1815 ... 16
3. "The Flap of Its Wings in My Ear" · 1815–1820 ... 28
4. "With Many Cares and Toils Oppress'd" · 1820–1825 ... 43
5. "Mistakes for Manhood to Reform" · 1826 ... 67
6. "Abroad on the Wide Earth" · 1827 ... 81
7. "In the American Army" · 1827–1829 ... 89
8. "Irrecoverably a Poet" · 1829–1830 ... 97
9. "I Am a Cadet" · 1830–1831 ... 111
10. "I Am Poor" · 1831–1834 ... 128
11. "Nothing Would Give Me Greater Pleasure" · 1834–1835 ... 152
12. "A Fair Prospect of Future Success" · 1835–1837 ... 163
13. "A Flattering Invitation" · 1837–1838 ... 196
14. "I Shall Remain in Philadelphia Perhaps for a Year" · 1838–1840 ... 205
15. "Fortune & Fame Must Go Hand in Hand" · 1840–1842 ... 230
16. "As Regards Myself—I Will Probably Succeed Too" · 1842 ... 262
17. "I Would Say to You, Without Hesitation, Aspire" · 1843–1844 ... 286

18.	"A Certainty of Success" · 1844–1845	307
19.	"It Will Be a Fortune to Me If I Can Hold It" · 1845–1846	331
20.	"There Is a Sweet *Hope* in the Bottom of My Soul" · 1846–1847	351
21.	"Then My Heart It Grew Ashen and Sober" · 1847–1848	370
22.	"I Feel I Am Now a Prophet" · 1848	388
23.	"The Passionate Throbbings of My Heart" · 1848–1849	411
24.	"All May Yet Go Well" · 1849	433
25.	"Hope for a Wretch Like Me" · 1849	453
	Conclusion · "A Dream within a Dream"	473
	Acknowledgments	481
	Notes	485
	Index	665

Illustrations follow page 308

Abbreviations

DLC-EA   Library of Congress, Ellis & Allan Papers

H   *Complete Works of Edgar Allan Poe.* Edited by James A. Harrison. 17 vols. 1902. New York: AMS, 1965.

L1   *Eureka.* Edited by Stuart Levine and Susan F. Levine. Urbana: University of Illinois Press, 2004.

L2   *Critical Theory: The Major Documents.* Edited by Stuart Levine and Susan F. Levine. Urbana: University of Illinois Press, 2009.

M   *Collected Works of Edgar Allan Poe:* vol. 1, *Poems;* vol. 2, *Tales and Sketches, 1831–1842;* vol. 3, *Tales and Sketches, 1843–1849.* Edited by T. O. Mabbott. Cambridge, MA: Belknap Press of Harvard University Press, 1969, 1978. Reprint, Urbana: University of Illinois Press, 2000.

O   *The Collected Letters of Edgar Allan Poe.* 3rd ed. Edited by John Ward Ostrom, Burton R. Pollin, and Jeffrey A. Savoye. 2 vols. New York: Gordian, 2008.

P   *Collected Writings of Edgar Allan Poe:* vol. 1, *The Imaginary Voyages.* Boston: Twayne, 1981; revised and corrected, New York: Gordian, 1994; vol. 2, *The Brevities;* vol. 3, *The Broadway Journal: Text;* vol. 4, *The Broadway Journal: Annotations;* vol. 5, *The Southern Literary Messenger.* Edited by Burton R. Pollin and (for vol. 5) Joseph V. Ridgely. New York: Gordian, 1985–97.

Introduction
"The Mystic Empire and High Power"

POE BELIEVED IN HIS OWN GENIUS. Whatever his faults and his failures, he had complete confidence in his genius. He wrote in his early poem "Tamerlane" of "The mystic empire and high power / Giv'n by the energetic might / of Genius, at its natal hour" (M 1:32). And he was true to that genius throughout his life. Through all his struggles—with his foster father, with drink, with poverty, with disappointment, with depression, with the loss of those he loved—he remained faithful to his sense of himself. This biography, recounted chronologically, tells the dramatic story that was prompted by his passionate certainty—a certainty that ultimately transformed the "mystic empire" into an enduring literary one.

Poe made substantial mistakes in his life and ultimately caused his own downfall, but he bravely sought—and sometimes attained—the greatness that he knew was his. Aspiring high, he wrote beautiful lyric poems, compelling tales of terror, extraordinary tales of ratiocination, a wonderful novel, discerning criticism, and prescient cosmology. Remarkably—and repeatedly—he was able to turn his suffering into great literature: the death of his childhood friend's mother Jane Stith Stanard into the classic poem "To Helen," the death of his older brother Henry into the novel *The Narrative of Arthur Gordon Pym*, the death of his young wife Virginia into the haunting poem "Ulalume." His most celebrated poem, "The Raven," itself honors "*Mournful and Never-ending Remembrance*" (L2 70). And it was not just grief that Poe could transmute. When he was attacked in the newspapers by

Thomas Dunn English, he was able to turn his anger at the insult and humiliation into one of the great tales of revenge, "The Cask of Amontillado." There is a heroism here.

This volume is a critical biography, a presentation of the life with an analysis of the work. And life and work inevitably illuminate each other. Poe saw biography as a possible key to literature; he praised Barthold Georg Niebuhr's "Essay on the Allegory in the First Canto of Dante" (P 5:96), which states of Dante's work that "everything must be explained by his life, and the peculiarities connected therewith."[1] I draw on Poe's life to help clarify his work. If disintegration is sometimes his theme,[2] integration of his life in his work is often his method. But I also consider a variety of Poe's works—letters, tales, poems, reviews—to help gain insight into his life. Poe expressed a belief in what we would call "close reading": "The analysis of a book is a matter of time and of mental exertion. For many classes of composition there is required a deliberate perusal, with notes, and subsequent generalization" (H 11:3). Poe was an artist of inordinate care—as the poet Richard Wilbur has said, "I think that if he's read word by word, he turns out, at his best, to be a very rich and intentional writer."[3] I attend to a range of aesthetic concerns, from allegory and allusion to verbal patterning and verisimilitude. Even as there were multiple levels to Poe's life, there are often multiple levels to his work. And sometimes they shed important light on the man.

I also consult others' writings about Poe and his work—contemporary comments, later reminiscences, and scholarly studies, biographical and otherwise, published and unpublished. Meriting particular mention here are the two most important biographies of Poe: Arthur Hobson Quinn's 1941 *Edgar Allan Poe: A Critical Biography* and Kenneth Silverman's 1991 *Edgar A. Poe: Mournful and Never-ending Remembrance*. Also invaluable is Dwight Thomas and David K. Jackson's *The Poe Log: A Documentary Life of Edgar Allan Poe, 1809–1849*.[4] (I offer elsewhere a consideration of a range of Poe biographies and an overview of Poe scholarship.)[5] The essential Poe editions are James A. Harrison's *Complete Works of Edgar Allan Poe,* Thomas Ollive Mabbott's *Collected Works of Edgar Allan Poe,* Burton R. Pollin's *Collected Writings of Edgar Allan Poe,* Stuart and Susan F. Levine's *Eureka* and *Critical Theory,* and John Ward Ostrom, Burton R. Pollin, and Jeffrey A. Savoye's third edition of *The Collected Letters of Edgar Allan Poe*. I rely on these works throughout this book.

Unique to this volume is engagement with the revealing correspondence of the stepdaughter of Poe's best friend to her distant relative who planned to write a Poe biography. Flora Lapham Mack, stepdaughter of John H. Mackenzie, wrote extensively about Poe—especially Poe in Richmond—to William Lanier Washington. Some of the letters are owned by the Poe Museum;[6] others are in my collection.

The background may be briefly stated. Mack's great-grandparents William Simmons and Tabitha Hobbs were Washington's great-great-grandparents. John H. Mackenzie and his first wife, Louisa Lanier (granddaughter of Simmons and Hobbs), married in 1827 and took into their household in 1833 Louisa's cousins when they were girls, including Mack's mother, Mary Mattox. In 1849, after the cousins had grown up and moved out, John and Louisa took into their household Louisa's nieces when they were girls (after their mother had died), including Washington's mother, Jane Britney Lanier. Many years later, in 1872 (Louisa had died in 1870), John H. Mackenzie married his wife's cousin, now a widow, Mary Mattox Lapham. Her daughter Flora Lapham therefore became Mackenzie's stepdaughter. And Flora Lapham married John Graham Mack in 1874. Flora Lapham Mack offers in her letters to William Lanier Washington hitherto unknown accounts of Poe from the Mackenzie family of Richmond. Mack provides new access to the private man.[7]

Diarist Mary Chesnut lamented about the Evacuation Fire in Richmond of April 3, 1865, "Everything lost in Richmond, even our archives."[8] What she doubtless did not know was that the Poe archives of bibliophile Thomas G. Mackenzie (one of John's brothers) were lost, as well.[9] When the Confederate army destroyed the city to prevent the Union from acquiring Richmond's tobacco and other goods, it also destroyed, unintentionally, part of the South's literary heritage. Mack's correspondent, Washington, perhaps dissatisfied with his own work, later destroyed the five hundred pages that he had written based on Mack's letters.[10] However, the informative letters themselves survive. They tell an inside story, one about Poe in Richmond from early boyhood to final days, prompting sometimes delight, sometimes dismay. Mack's chief source was "Cousin John"—John H. Mackenzie, Poe's lifelong friend. He knew all of Poe's flaws but loved Poe just the same. Mack's other sources included her mother, Mary Mattox Lapham; John's mother, Jane Scott Mackenzie; his wife, Louisa Mackenzie; and his brothers, Thomas and Richard Mackenzie.

Mack tells new stories about Poe, stories that she was singularly well situated to know. She occasionally gets a fact wrong, inadvertently—she was not a scholar and did not have rich scholarly resources at her disposal. When possible, I have checked the passages of hers that I offer here. Sometimes, however, she is the sole authority. She is sometimes highly critical of Poe—far more severely than her stepfather. But she also conveys John H. Mackenzie's devotion to Poe and adds insight into Poe's life with his wife, Virginia. Mack's letters refine, enrich, and intensify our previous understanding of Poe.

Distinguishing this biography further is inclusion of recent scholarly discoveries—both those of others and those I have made. Online resources have also been a significant help. My interest is not just to present Poe's life but also to bring Poe to life.

I will argue in these pages that even as Poe often examined that which was disturbing, he ultimately sought to express that which was consoling. He achieved literary consolation most extraordinarily through memory and religion at the end of *The Narrative of Arthur Gordon Pym* and through memory and reverie at the end of *Eureka: A Prose Poem*. If there was no "balm in Gilead," Poe would provide it in his art.

I intend this biography to be accessible to all. Since Poe enjoys so broad an audience, I write for the general reader, the aficionado, and the scholar. He clearly wished for an international readership: he wrote, "the world at large" is "the only proper stage for the literary *histrio* [actor]" (L2 39; see also P 2:508). My goal is to get as close to Poe as I can for as many readers as I can. His great aspiration, his deft integration of his life in his work, and his poignant efforts at consolation in his writings will be woven throughout this book.

Poe rewards both initial attention and renewed attention. When I was organizing the First International Conference on Edgar Allan Poe in Richmond, Virginia, in 1999, I received a session proposal for "Teaching Poe to the Nineties." This did not concern Poe in the 1990s, but, rather, Poe for people in their nineties. The proposer, Albert E. Millar Jr., taught in an Elderhostel program, and his students, who remembered reading Poe in their youth, had asked that he teach a course on Poe so that they could see what they thought of this fascinating writer after so many years. As I wrote this book, I bore in mind those young people just beginning to think about Poe—he is often the first great writer whom they really *get*—and those coming back to him. My hope and expectation is that even years after people first encounter Poe, they will find their return to him a rich and satisfying experience.

And it is not just that we need him. As we think through his struggles, we may come to feel that he needs us.

1

"No Tie More Strong"

1809-1811

EDGAR ALLAN POE AS A young man confided to a correspondent, the editor and novelist John Neal, "There can be no tie more strong than that of brother for brother—it is not so much that they love one another, as that they both love the same parent—their affections are always running in the same direction—the same channel—and cannot help mingling" (O 1:47). Edgar had one brother, two years older, whose name was William Henry Leonard Poe; he was known as Henry. And the parent whom they both loved was their mother, Eliza Poe.

On Wednesday, March 19, 1806, at the Richmond New Theatre in Richmond, Virginia, the audience witnessed "*Between the Play and the Farce, an entire new* OLIO, *Consisting of Song, Dance and Dialogue.*" Included in this confection—an interlude of various entertainments—was "An ALAMANDE by Mrs. Hopkins and Mr. Poe," a formal dance of elegant embrace.[1] Perhaps those attending—or at least those in the company—knew the moment of this moment. For Mr. Poe had signed his marriage bond to Mrs. Hopkins five days earlier, on Friday, March 14.[2] Three weeks after the alamande, on Wednesday, April 9, Mrs. Hopkins was listed as Mrs. Poe.[3]

The opening of the theater, a brick building near Capitol Square, had been announced for January 17, 1806, and apparently this new venue was then still a work in progress: "The Theatre, although not completed, already exhibits taste and elegance; and no pains have been omitted in rendering it comfortable for the accommodations of the visitors."[4] However, an actor there would later consider it "not only the worst-constructed theater on the company's tour but the worst he had ever performed in."[5] Eliza Poe—born Eliza Arnold in England—was an experienced actress who had been performing since 1796, when she was nine years old.[6] A miniature shows her to have grown to be a beautiful young woman with large eyes and lustrous dark curls.[7] She was the widow of the actor Charles Hopkins, who had died in 1805. Her new husband, David Poe Jr., had been performing since 1803, when he was nineteen.[8] He had an attractive appearance, but he was not as talented as his wife, and reviews of his acting would often be disparaging.

David and Eliza Poe continued at the Richmond Theater through the spring of 1806. In the summer, they appeared in Philadelphia and New York,[9] and in October, having made their way from one city of seven hills to another, from the James River to the Charles River, they began a three-year stint at the Boston Theatre. As noble and impressive as was Thomas Jefferson's white neoclassical Capitol Building in Capitol Square in Richmond, so, too, was Charles Bulfinch's copper-domed State House on Beacon Hill in Boston. Bulfinch was the architect for many other Boston buildings, as well, including the expanded Faneuil Hall and the Boston Theatre, on Federal Street, in the Financial District. This theater, built in 1794, burned down in 1798; the second Boston Theatre, also designed by Bulfinch and built in 1798, was a two-story brick structure considered "of unparalleled elegance."[10]

In the fall of 1806, Eliza Poe earned largely positive notices—for instance, as Miss Blandford in Thomas Morton's *Speed the Plough* she was said to have had "a flattering promise of very handsome ability in the lines of *naivete* comedy and the opera," and as Priscilla Tomboy in Isaac Bickerstaffe's *The Romp*, she gave "an excellent performance." About her appearance as Miss Jenny in John Vanbrugh and Colley Cibber's *The Provoked Husband,* one critic wrote, "The hoyden is Mrs. Poe's forte."[11] Her husband prompted a less auspicious response. Although he occasionally won positive notices, others were cautionary: as Frederick in Elizabeth Inchbald's *Lovers' Vows,* "Mr. Poe must learn to elevate his voice and dignify his gestures. They are oftentimes laughable when he wishes to be serious; and generally are tame when he strives to be energetic." As Frank Rochdale in George Colman the Younger's *John Bull,* "Mr. Poe, as he did not appear to aim at, so he did not attain much celebrity." And regarding Count Basset in *The Provoked Husband,* "We would advise Mr. Poe to leave off, upon the stage at least, the manner he has, of constantly looking at, no doubt admiring his *pretty person*—we would also recommend to this gentleman, not to be continually striking his fists into his sides, for all the world as if he was waiting for a pugilistic antagonist."[12] The divergence in the husband's and wife's reputations would continue.

Notable at this time was a December 30, 1806, newspaper advertisement, titled "Young Roscius," for a book about Master Betty, the renowned boy actor who had so charmed British audiences.[13] Master Betty's full name is given: William Henry West Betty. Mrs. Poe was then eight months pregnant, and a month later, on January 30, 1807, she gave birth to a son whom she and her husband named William Henry Leonard Poe.[14] Their naming of their firstborn may well have been aspirational.

In March 1807, the magazine *Polyanthos* was becoming strident. Joseph T. Buckingham wrote of Mr. Poe as Barnwell in George Lillo's *George Barnwell*, "We expected little satisfaction, and of course were not disappointed." And he was severe with regard to Mrs. Poe's playing Little Pickle in *The Spoiled Child* (the character was "*hermaphroditical*," as suggested by "the uncouthness of his costume") and about her performing as Cordelia in William Shakespeare's *King Lear* (Mrs. Poe was "totally inadequate to [the character's] representation").[15] David Poe may have recalled that his friend Luke Noble Usher had warned critics against writing about the acting of his wife, Harriet Ann L'Estrange Usher: one of those critics had explained, "Of Mrs. USHER, we shall be silent, as Mr. U. has menaced with death, any audacious scribbler who shall dare to introduce her name into any gazette!"[16] Mr. Poe threatened no murder, but he did threaten punishment. Years later, Buckingham remembered, "Mr. Poe—the father of the late Edgar A. Poe,—took offense at a remark on his wife's acting, and called at my house to 'chastise my impertinence,' but went away without effecting his purpose. Both he and his wife were performers of considerable merit, but somewhat vain of their personal accomplishments."[17] Another critic was kinder about Mrs. Poe's performance as Cordelia, noting that "[Mrs. Poe's] amiable timidity evidently betrayed her own apprehension, that she had wandered from the sphere of her *appropriate* talent; while her lovely gentleness pleaded strongly for protection against the rigid justice of criticism."[18] And yet a third praised her performance, but with a qualification: "Mrs. Poe, as Cordelia, has once received our approbation, and has again deserved it. But we notwithstanding prefer her comedy."[19]

Meanwhile, David Poe continued to provoke criticism. An outraged theatergoer reported that at an April 6, 1807, performance of *Julius Caesar*, after Thomas Caulfield "*read badly* the part of Cassius," an impotent yet impudent servant of the publick, dared to obtrude himself upon them and interrupt the performance, in a manner more obnoxious and insulting than ever has yet been witnessed even in this Theatre. Had this been an occurrence before any other audience he would sooner have been "*hacked to silence*" and not suffered to quit their presence, without a *more humble* apology. This was Mr. Poe, whom the audience will not suffer to appear on the Boards again without the recollection of his insolence. Mrs. Poe still continues a favourite of the publick.[20]

The disparity between the reputations of husband and wife was growing vast.

Of later literary significance is mention in the *Polyanthos* of one of the new plays recently produced at the London theater: "*Tekeli,* a Melo-Drama in three acts, by Mr. Hook."[21] Theodore Hook's play, which ran for "fifty-two nights at Drury Lane,"[22] would be widely produced, including in December 1807 in New York and in October 1809 in Boston.[23] Mrs. Poe would eventually perform in it, and her son would later use it importantly in his fiction.

David and Eliza Poe continued to appear at the Federal Street Theatre; while she was criticized for her voice, he was hissed.[24] An article on a March 1808 benefit for the couple focused on "the talents of Mrs. Poe."[25] (A "benefit" provided the profits of an evening's performance to a specific performer or to specific performers.) A comment for an April benefit revealed further the differing standings of husband and wife: Mrs. Poe is "the favorite of the public, and the delight of the eye," but Mr. Poe is considered only "an improving performer."[26]

Sometime that year, Eliza Poe painted a watercolor sketch, titled *Boston Harbour Morning 1808*.[27] The image, no longer extant, would probably have included many anchored American ships since this was the time of the increasingly unpopular Jefferson embargo of trade with Great Britain.[28] It was a difficult period for Boston, but Mrs. Poe was thriving. She would later provide the painting for her second son, writing on its back that Boston was where she had found "her *best* and *most sympathetic* friends."[29]

When Eliza Poe became pregnant with her second son, the name selected may again have been drawn from the stage. Repeatedly through 1807 and 1808, she performed as Cordelia in *King Lear,* and even while this character is the daughter who genuinely loves her father, King Lear, Edgar is the son who genuinely loves his father, the Earl of Gloucester. In the softened Elizabeth Inchbald version of the play, probably used in the production in which Eliza played Cordelia, Lear regains the throne, and Cordelia marries Edgar.[30]

Regarding this son (played in this Boston production by Thomas Caulfield), one critic of the time asserted, "As a champion in the last act he was greeted with deserved approbation; and we know of no character more calculated to influence an audience in favor of an actor than that of Edgar."[31] It may be that David and Eliza Poe named their second son after the devoted son of the Earl of Gloucester.[32] If so, then the naming of their second son was also aspirational. But it would be his mother rather than his father to whom this son was devoted.

The last performance of Eliza Poe for nearly a month was on January 13, 1809; she gave birth to Edgar on January 19.[33] Poe later wrote of his brother's birth and his own through allegory, a literal story implying a figurative one. The allegory appeared first in the serial publication of "Arthur Gordon Pym" in the January and February 1837 issues of the *Southern Literary Messenger*. This publication comprised what would become three chapters and part of the fourth chapter of the coming novel. The allegory appeared again, with only very minor changes, in the 1838 novel *The Narrative of Arthur Gordon Pym*. In the first chapter, the Edgar-like Arthur relays the account of the Henry-like Augustus, who was submerged after the wreck of the *Ariel:* "Upon his first attaining any degree of consciousness, he found himself beneath the surface, whirling round and round with inconceivable rapidity, and with a rope wrapped in three or four folds tightly about his neck. In an instant afterwards he felt himself going rapidly upward, when, his head striking violently against a hard substance, he again relapsed into insensibility" (P 1:63). In the second chapter, Arthur is trapped in the hold of the *Grampus*. He later tells his own story: following "the guidance of the whipcord" toward "the trapdoor" (P 1:69, 74), "I struggled forward by slow degrees, dreading every moment that I should swoon amid the narrow and intricate windings of the lumber, in which event I had nothing but death to expect as the result. At length, upon making a push forward with all the energy I could command, I struck my forehead violently against the sharp corner of an iron-bound crate" (P 1:74). Both passages suggest a boy's emerging from the womb, with the umbilical cord attached, and each boy's hitting his head, presumably on his mother's pelvic bone. Thus, years afterward, the births of Henry and Edgar were subtly recounted.

Eliza Poe began to perform again on February 10; the *Boston Gazette* warmly announced, "We congratulate the frequenters of the Theatre on the recovery of Mrs. Poe from her recent confinement."[34] But David Poe evidently traveled to Baltimore and brought the baby to his parents, David

Poe Sr. and Elizabeth Poe, for six months.[35] He also made a side trip to Stockerton, Pennsylvania, in the Lehigh Valley, visiting his cousin George Poe Jr. on February 22, 1809, to ask for money. This cousin later wrote to a brother-in-law that he had no interest in the struggling actor, whom he sarcastically termed "young Roscius," and he included a copy of David Poe's "impertinent note," received after the applicant had missed a planned meeting on February 23. This note reflects a mix of arrogance, pride, resentment, and discouragement. It reads, in part, "Your answer by the bearer will prove whether I yet have 'favour in your eyes' or whether I am to be despis'd by (as I understand) a rich relation because when a *wild boy* I join'd a profession which I then thought and now think an honorable one. But which I would most willingly quit tomorrow if it gave satisfaction to your family provided I could do *any thing* else that would give bread to mine." George Poe Jr. commented, in part, "For the fu[ture] I desired to hear not from him or of him—so adieu to Davy."[36]

Soon Jefferson's embargo ended, and at the Federal Street Theatre on March 17, 1809, the characters in a "Martial Dance" displayed "in transparent letters, the emphatic words, COMMERCE RESTORED!"[37] And in April, John Howard Payne—the real American "young Roscius"—made a series of appearances with the troupe, playing, among other roles, Romeo to Mrs. Poe's Juliet, Hamlet to Mrs. Poe's Ophelia (and Mr. Poe's Laertes), and Edgar to Mrs. Poe's Cordelia (and James Fennell's King Lear).[38] Eliza Poe won high acclaim: announcing a benefit for Mrs. Poe, the *New England Palladium* stated, "In their performances generally, few take precedence of this pleasing actress; and for their assiduity and unassuming deportment, none."[39]

The season closed on May 12, 1809; by August, David and Eliza Poe must have picked up their son Edgar in Baltimore,[40] and the family settled in New York City for performances at the Park Theatre. It was here that David Poe's career would come to an end.

The Park Theatre stood at the intersection of Park Row and Broadway, across from the park where City Hall would be built. Constructed in 1797, with a capacity of two thousand people, it was New York's "first fully appointed and elegant theatre."[41] Just prior to the 1809–10 season, its interior—boxes, columns, lobby, lighting—was richly renovated. A critic praised the new look: "Indeed, the alterations throughout are most judicious, and the *tout ensemble* airy and beautiful."[42]

Eliza Poe's performances in tragedies (opposite Thomas Cooper) were criticized ("Mrs. Poe is too light for Ophelia," "Mrs. Poe is very unequal to

Desdemona"), but her performances in comedies were lauded ("*mrs. Poe's Tomboy* [in *The Romp*] gave surety of succeeding fame and favoritism," "In the afterpiece [*John Bull at Fontainbleau*], mrs. Poe was excellent").[43] However, the same critic mercilessly mocked her husband. Mr. Poe's pronunciation of the name "Dandoli" was incorrect, prompting the disparaging name "Dan Dilly." He had no *gravitas*: "This man was never destined for the high walks of the drama;—a footman is the extent of what he ought to attempt." His appearance was unprepossessing: he had a "muffin face." And his acting skills were inadequate: "Poor *Dan* is fated to spoil whatever he undertakes, and like a millstone round the neck of a goose, he will be sure to drag it to the bottom in spite of all its buoyant properties." Noting Mr. Poe's having taken "some of our former remarks very much in dudgeon," the critic sarcastically commented on "his amiable *private character* and high *professional standing*."[44] A pseudonymous author even wrote a poem lampooning David Poe by way of a pun on his last name: "Sur un *Poe* de Chambre."[45] An editorial defense was not encouraging: Mr. Poe's talents "*if he would take pains*" are "by no means contemptible."[46] Later in the season, one Nemo Nobody, of Boston, also defended the ridiculed actor.[47] But it was too late—he was gone.

David Poe's absence from the stage on October 20, 1809, was attributed to "a sudden indisposition."[48] Nemo Nobody admitted, "We are well aware of the errors of this gentleman, but we *know* that such errors have frequently been introduced by unfeeling criticism."[49] We may infer the nature of the "indisposition," the "errors": David Poe was drinking. Evidently he had been drinking in Boston, too. Exactly what he did after giving up his short acting career is not known.

Eliza Poe continued at the Park Theatre in the winter and spring of 1810. Of particular note is that when she played Ophelia to Payne's Hamlet on March 7, one critic wrote, "Mrs. Poe, in the character of Ophelia, did great credit to herself."[50] But her voice was still occasionally an issue: a pseudonymous correspondent in New York for a Philadelphia magazine later opined, "Mrs. Poe is a pleasing actress, with many striking defects. She should never attempt to sing."[51] Still, a July 2, 1810, letter to the editor about that night's benefit refers to "the well-known merits of Mrs. *Poe*" and makes a personal appeal to the "lovers of theatrical performance": "Let this be a stimulant to every exertion on their part, to give aid to a female who has taken a benefit for the purpose of extricating herself from embarrassments occasioned by having two small children to support out of the scanty pittance of her weekly wages. To those that are mothers, this appeal will really be unnecessary; as the calling of infants in distress will always bring to their aid a mother."[52] Mr. Poe is not mentioned.

Having completed her long New York run in July, Eliza Poe appeared in several productions in Richmond in August and September, culminating with her September 21, 1810, benefit at the Richmond Theater. The bill included Hannah Cowley's *Belle's Stratagem* and James Kenney's *Matrimony, or the Test of Love*. During the first play, Mrs. Poe sang and again danced an alamande—this time with manager Alexander Placide.[53] A writer for the *Virginia Patriot* paid tribute to her and invited theatergoers' generosity: "The feast is spread by the fair hand of Mrs. Poe whose dramatic excellence as well as long exertions in the cause of the public will certainly ensure her that liberal compensation, which she so justly deserves."[54] A writer for the *Richmond Enquirer* offered a more extensive and effusive tribute, wishing "to take aspiring genius by the hand and help it from obscurity." This encomiast wrote, in part, "If it be excellent to satisfy the judgment and delight the heart, then Mrs. Poe is excellent. If it be the perfection of acting to conceal the actor, Mrs. Poe's name is a brilliant gem in the Theatrick crown. In a word, as no one has received more than she of the public applause, no one is better entitled to the public liberality."[55] This may have been the peak of her professional acclaim.

There is no record of Eliza Poe's performing in Richmond in 1810 after her benefit. The company performed *Tekeli* on November 6, 1810,[56] but we do not know if Eliza was among the players. We do know, however, that she was pregnant: on December 20, in Norfolk, she gave birth to her daughter Rosalie.[57] In coming years, rightly or wrongly, people would wonder about the girl's paternity.[58]

The letter to the editor about Mrs. Poe, from July 2, 1810, had noted, "It is a circumstance truly to be lamented, that New York is shortly to lose this entertaining actress, as she is shortly to embark for Charleston, to revive hilarity on their festive boards."[59] The *Charleston Courier* reported that Placide's theater troupe—including "Mrs. Poe, a lady of much celebrity"—would be performing toward the end of December.[60] The company commenced its Charleston run on January 7, 1811.[61] Eliza Poe began performing at the Charleston Theatre—a place considered a "combination of elegance and novelty"[62]—a month after Rosalie's birth, on January 23, 1811. She appeared in *The Castle Spectre* and *The Romp*—no doubt, in the latter, again contributing hilarity as Priscilla Tomboy.[63] And she played many other light roles, including Lady Teazle in Richard Sheridan's *School for Scandal*, Lydia Languish in his *The Rivals*, and Mopsa in Shakespeare's *The Winter's Tale*.[64] She also appeared in a variety of other parts, ranging from a nymph in George Graham's *Telemachus* to a Grace in *Cinderella*.[65]

And she performed in Charleston in Theodore Hook's melodrama *Tekeli; or, The Siege of Montgatz*. The play conveys the triumph of Count Tekeli and his Hungarian soldiers over the threatening Austrians. Especially relevant, as will later become clear, is that Eliza Poe played a bride named Christine. *Tekeli* was scheduled for March 22 but was delayed to the following day, March 23, because of "the bad appearance of the weather."[66] Mrs. Poe's benefit was on April 29; after the players' final performance in Charleston that season on May 20, 1811, the troupe traveled to Norfolk.[67]

In that city, Eliza Poe had another benefit, this time with another actress, on July 26. The benefit was anticipated by a pseudonymous letter to the editor of the *Norfolk Herald*, acknowledging the beauty of Mrs. Poe: "She was said to be one of the handsomest women in America; she was certainly the handsomest I had ever seen." The letter attested to her past great successes: she used to win "involuntary bursts of rapture from the Norfolk audience." And the letter noted her current difficulties: "Misfortunes have pressed heavy on her. Left alone, the only support of herself and several young children—Friendless and unprotected, she no longer commands that admiration and attention she formerly did,—Shame on the world that can turn its back on the same person in distress, that it was wont to cherish in prosperity. And yet she is as assiduous to please as ever, and tho' grief may have stolen the roses from her cheeks, she still retains the same sweetness of expression, and symmetry of form and feature."[68] It may be that Eliza Poe was already sick. Her coming performances in Richmond would be her last.

Mrs. Poe's appearances at the Richmond Theater in September and October 1811 were only occasional. She began as one of the "Graces" in *Cinderella; or, the Little Glass Slipper* on September 20; may have taken part in Nathaniel Lee's *Alexander the Great* or George Colman the Younger's *Love Laughs at Locksmiths* at her own benefit on October 9; and gave her final performance in August von Kotzebue's *The Stranger* on October 11.[69] One Richmond theater historian considers it likely that Edgar, approaching his third birthday, would have been one of the "Little Masters" appearing as "Cupids" in *Cinderella* and as one of the "Hunters" in the children's ballet *The Hunters and the Milkmaid*, especially when it was performed at his mother's benefit.[70]

On November 2, Samuel Mordecai—later the author of *Richmond in By-Gone Days*—wrote to his sister, "A singular fashion prevails here this season—it is—charity—Mrs. Poe, who you know is a very handsome woman, happens to be very sick, and (having quarreled and parted with her husband), is destitute. The most fashionable place of resort, now is—her chamber.... It is a very laudable fashion and I wish it may last long."[71] On November 29, the managers at the Richmond Theater announced another benefit for her, and a *Richmond Enquirer* notice invited readers' consideration: "TO THE HUMANE OF HEART, On this night, *Mrs. Poe*, lingering on the bed of disease and surrounded by her children, asks your *assistance*, and *asks it perhaps for the last time*.—The generosity of a Richmond Audience can need no other appeal."[72]

Doubtless all three children were initially with their mother. Henry later wrote a poem about three locks of hair in a pocketbook; the second stanza concerns one of these locks:

> My Mother's, too!—then let me press
>   This gift of her I loved so well,—
> For I have had thy last caress,
>   And heard thy long, thy last farewell.[73]

But when two kindly young married women, Jane Scott Mackenzie and Frances Allan, visited Mrs. Poe, Henry had already been taken away to his paternal grandparents, in Baltimore. Flora Lapham Mack, whose source of information was the Mackenzie family, wrote about the two "devoted friends & most excellent and charitable women": "Being told in December of that year that a young actress was dying in distress and poverty they went together to visit her and relieve her necessities. And they spoke with her. She told them she had recently been widowed, and her husband's family, the Poes, of Baltimore had taken her older son Henry, promising to provide for him."[74]

Mrs. Poe was very worried about the future of Edgar and Rosalie: "She was agonizing over the fate of her younger son and her baby and her distress so appealed to these good women, that they determined to adopt them at once."[75] Mrs. Mackenzie had a son, John Hamilton, and a daughter, Mary Gallego, at the time,[76] but her friend had no children. Mrs. Allan "was much more attracted to the boy, who was very handsome and bright than to the delicate unattractive baby girl and Mrs. Mackenzie readily allowed her to take her choice."[77]

David Poe had died in Norfolk, "after months of suffering & privation," of "the great white plague"—that is, tuberculosis.[78] Eliza Poe was cared for by Jane Scott Mackenzie: "Mrs. Mackenzie who ministered to his [Poe's] mother during her last hours told me 'she was a sweet gentle tender creature' and [']very winsome' even in her last hours."[79]

Eliza Poe left Edgar a gathering of her letters and two pictures she had made, including the watercolor with the inscription about Boston on the back, beginning, "For my little son Edgar."[80] She died in Richmond, at the age of twenty-four, on December 8, 1811, and was buried in the graveyard of St. John's Church on December 10.[81] The *Richmond Enquirer* stated, "By the death of this Lady the Stage has been deprived of one of its chief ornaments— And, to say the least of her, she was an interesting Actress; and never failed to catch the applause and command the admiration of the beholder."[82] Poe would later declare in a theater review, "The writer of this article is himself the son of an actress—has invariably made it his boast—and no earl was ever prouder of his earldom than he of his descent from a woman who, although well-born, hesitated not to consecrate to the drama her brief career of genius and of beauty" (P 3:176). And he would also later confide to a friend "that he owed to his Mother 'every good gift of his intellect, & his heart.'"[83]

Edgar and Rosalie were taken to the Mackenzies' home, and then he was taken alone to the Allans' home.[84] Frances Allan wanted the boy, but her husband, merchant John Allan, did not—he only wished to please his wife. Jane Scott Mackenzie told Mack, "It was just this way. Mr. Allen [*sic*] never wished to take Edgar at first. Mrs. Allen Mr. Mackenzie and myself just persuaded and insisted so that he could hardly help it. He said to me the first night they took him home 'I don't want the boy my self but if I were sure it would be for my wife's happiness I would not be so reluctant but it is an experiment just an experiment.'"[85] And so, with uncertainty, Edgar Poe's new life began.

2

"From Childhood's Hour"

1811–1815

According to Flora Lapham Mack, Edgar moved, in December 1811, from "the spacious nursery of Mrs. Mackenzie" to the "lonely Allan nursery." (The Allans lived above the Ellis & Allan store at Richmond's Main and Thirteenth Streets.) He was cared for by "a new black Mammie" and adored by his delicate and lovely foster mother, Frances Allan, and her sister Nancy Valentine, who "fell fathoms deep in love with him at once petting and caressing him constantly."[1] Yet Mack was told that "for quite a while . . . he had a strange cat-in-a-garrety-air a vague unrest and disquietude a what-next-I-wonder query in his solemn beautiful dark grey eyes that worried Mrs. Allan and made her think him home sick and perhaps not really happy in spite of all they were doing for him." So Mrs. Allan sent Edgar over to Mrs. Mackenzie's to see baby Rosalie and to play with the children.[2] It was John Hamilton Mackenzie who would become his particular friend.

John Allan, Frances Allan, and her sister Nancy Valentine took Edgar "for the Christmas holidays" to the Bowler Cocke plantation on Turkey Island, south of Richmond on the James River.[3] Cocke, a close friend of John Allan and a customer of his firm Ellis & Allan, had in October 1811 invited him to visit: "I hope when the weather gets cold you'll come & take a hunt with me."[4]

On the night of December 26, 1811, in Richmond, five-year-old John Hamilton Mackenzie was waiting to see his mother before she and his father went to the theater.[5] He would later tell his stepdaughter Flora that "the greatest treat that could be promised him as the reward of good behavior when he was a child was that he should be allowed to stay awake and have his mother come in to kiss him good night after she was dressed for a ball or an evening entertainment." He still remembered the "wonderful dress of yellow brocade satin with neckline lace flowers in which she had arrayed herself to attend the theater on the night of the memorable fire." While waiting, "[h]e was indulging in wild gymnastics" on his new high bed, and he fell and "broke his right arm in two places." Mrs. Mackenzie quickly gave the couple's two theater tickets to her nephews, the Grays of Norfolk,[6] and attended to her injured son. Mack refers to her stepfather here and elsewhere as "Cousin John" since he was, by marriage, her mother's cousin: "Cousin John's arm was hardly set when the fire broke out & in a few moments the boys rushed in sobbing 'Oh Aunt Jane: every body but our selves are burned to death.'"

This was the "Overwhelming Calamity" so painfully reported in the black-bordered December 28, 1811, issue of the *Richmond Enquirer:* the disastrous conflagration at the Richmond Theater.[7] Eliza Poe used to perform at this theater. Charles Ellis, John Allan's partner, attended the December 26 performance but happened to leave early; when he heard the alarm and saw the light of the fire, he returned to assist with the rescue.[8] According to Ellis's son Thomas, "It is not improbable that Mr. and Mrs. Allan would have been present on that occasion" had they not been at the Bowler Cocke plantation.[9] Thomas H. Ellis was correct: Allan wrote to White Matlock Jr. on January 3, 1812, "You have heard of the Horrible & fatal Catastrophe which befel[l] our poor City on the Evening of the 26th ult. [last month]. Fortunately my family & myself were at Bowler Cocke[']s or we might also have been numbered with the rest."[10] Matlock responded, "How fortunate that yourself & Family were out of Town."[11] Of the 648 people at the theater that night, 72 were soon identified as having perished, including the governor of Virginia.[12] The cause of the catastrophe was the raising of a candelabrum above the stage with one of its candles still lit: the flame caught the backdrop, and the fire spread. Especially at risk were those people in the boxes, including many women, who jumped from windows or tried the narrow staircase. People were burned, crushed, and suffocated.[13] But there were numerous heroic rescues from the burning building. In one instance, a powerful blacksmith, an enslaved man named Gilbert Hunt, caught women who were dropped from a high window by Dr. James McCaw.[14]

Mack wrote, "Cousin John said that he could never forget that terrible night; he suffered untold agony with his arm & his father and mother who sat up all night with him were in the deepest grief and anxiety over the fate of their many dear friends and neighbors who had perished in the flames."[15] Joseph Gallego, owner of the Richmond flour mills and "a very intimate friend of the Mackenzies"—indeed, godfather to John and his sister Mary[16]—lost his wife, Mary, and his niece Sally Conyers in the fire; he "never recovered from that loss."[17]

John later hurt his arm again "when he fell down the steps in a gallant scuffle to kiss little Isabelle Ritchie." Because of the even more severe injury, "he was forbidden to play with any children of his own size." He was allowed, however, to play with little Edgar Poe. Mack states, "It was at this point and under these conditions that his lifelong intimacy with and friendship for Edgar Poe commenced and was cemented." She continues, "Cousin John began to play with and talk to the beautiful and bright little boy and found him a most interesting and entertaining companion. Edgar was equally pleased with the amiable sweet-tempered jolly big boy and always delighted to stay with him as long as permitted."[18]

Their game at this time involved competing with one another to tell the best fairy tale. Mack describes how the competition began: "Cousin John said one day he began to tell Edgar a fairy tale and he had hardly finished when Edgar began to tell it back again to him most eagerly & with such amusing exaggerations and wonderful embellishments that he was greatly amused and on its completion told Edgar another improbable fairy story which he purposely stretched as wildly and wonderfully as possible and Edgar responded immediately; it was completed by going him one better in the most ingenious and interesting way possible."[19] Here we have the earliest evidence of Poe's wonderful imagination. Perhaps that imagination was enriched not only by the fairy tales Edgar had heard but also by those he had seen. After all, on April 26, 1811 (in Charleston), and on September 20, 1811 (in Richmond), Eliza Poe had performed as a Grace in *Cinderella* (with Edgar possibly playing a Cupid in the latter production).[20] And, notably, "The Grand Drama of the *Forty Thieves*" was performed in Richmond on September 9, 1811.[21]

Mack states that John and Edgar's competing in telling fairy tales "became their constant amusement, afterwards considered through their walks together and their hours at home during the months of his [John's] enforced quietude due to the badly broken arm." And evidently there was a progression from the literary to the personal: "Edgar soon told him [John] all his troubles, finding him such a sympathetic and satisfying listener and confidant that he never again failed to go to him with every trouble & sorrow of his life." The connection of five-year-old John and nearly three-year-old Edgar led to a close and lasting friendship: Mack reports, "Cousin John always after this time because of this early companionship & mutual admiration & of his loyal affectionate helpful disposition never again failed to love advise comfort & help Edgar Poe as long as he lived."[22] Only at the very end of Poe's life, as Mack reveals in another letter, did the two friends have a tragic falling-out.

The relationship between Edgar and his foster father, John Allan, was initially a warm one: Mack, relying on John's mother, Jane Scott Mackenzie, states that Allan "seemed to grow quite fond" of Edgar.[23] Indeed, old Richmonders remembered "that he loved Poe most tenderly." One old friend reported, "Mr. Allan made Poe his companion, walked with him, read with him, and took him wherever he went."[24] And in one of his later plaintive letters to Allan, Poe recalls "the love you bore me when I sat upon your knee and called you father" (O 1:72). Edgar's foster mother, Frances Allan, "fairly idolized" her young son.[25] Thomas H. Ellis, son of John Allan's partner, Charles Ellis, asserts that "Mr. and Mrs. Allan entertained the greatest admiration for their precocious, highly gifted, and very handsome little adopted son, and were in all outward manifestations as devoted to him as if he had been their own and only child."[26] However, Edgar was not adopted, and that fact would come to make a difference in later years.

Evidently Edgar was sick in late May 1812, but he readily recovered: John Allan wrote, "Edgar has got quite well."[27] In early June, the Allans and Edgar again visited Bowler Cocke.[28] And the boy would continue to thrive during his family's visit to a mountain retreat, White Sulphur Springs.

In the summer of the year, after the United States had finally declared war against Great Britain for not respecting its neutrality (thereby beginning the War of 1812), John and Frances Allan first took Edgar to White Sulphur Springs, in the Virginia mountains. They would take him there also for the summers of 1813 and 1814.[29] This elite southern resort was advertised in Richmond as able "to entertain comfortably, upwards of one hundred persons, with their servants" (that is, including the enslaved). It boasted new buildings—"seventeen neat lodging houses" and "a very spacious dining house"—as well as expanded stables, which could accommodate "upwards of an hundred horses." The southern gentry were cordially invited to a "FOUNTAIN OF HEALTH!"[30] J. K. Paulding wrote of the resort, "It is situated in a pretty little glen, surrounded by hills on all sides; the air is too often loaded with fogs to be altogether to my liking, and the evenings and the dog-days are cool and refreshing. The visitors live in cabins built of square logs, whitewashed, and disposed in a range just on the skirts of a little lawn, so that they have all the air of a rural village."[31]

Eugene Didier wrote expressively of Edgar at White Sulphur Springs: "There are several persons now living in Richmond, who remember seeing him there in those years. They describe him as a lovely little fellow, with dark curls and brilliant eyes, dressed like a young prince, and charming every one by his childish grace, vivacity, and cleverness. His disposition was frank, affectionate, and generous, and he was very popular with his young companions."[32] Edgar was a lively and endearing boy.

While in Staunton, Virginia, in early September 1812—perhaps on the family's return to Richmond from White Sulphur Springs—John Allan received a letter from his niece Rosanna Dixon, the daughter of Frances Allan's half-sister Sarah Valentine and Frances's guardian John Dixon Jr., about family matters, including Poe's sister, Rosalie, who was then seriously ill. (She recovered.) Rosanna Dixon, at the time about eleven years old, writes toward the end of her letter, "Tell Edgar, Tib [a large tabby cat] is very well, also the Bird and Dog," and she closes, "Kiss Edgar for me." (A postscript laments, "Poor Tib is lost; that is to say, cannot be found.")[33]

As a foster father, Allan was "quite fond" of his young charge. And as a merchant, he would have seemed solid and steady. But he did have his uneasy moments: he was soon shaken by an unexpected business reversal. The Non-Intercourse Act, which had replaced the Embargo in 1809 to protect American shipping from Great Britain and France,[34] threatened the prosperity of Ellis & Allan. In October 1812, the ship *Newburyport*—bound from Liverpool with the goods of Ellis & Allan and its customers—was seized by the collector of the port of New London, Connecticut, for violation of that Non-Intercourse Act. Ellis & Allan did eventually recover the ship and its cargo, which were owned by Americans, and the court eventually ruled in the company's favor.[35] Still, Allan's initial response to the dire news from his partner, Charles Ellis, gives a hint of his vulnerability, his fear: "I received yours of the 12th last night I assure you after a perusal of it I felt a degree of chagrin mortification disappointment that I don't often feel. I will however be patient although your letter certainly opens new causes of dread."[36]

Throughout 1812, the city of Richmond was trying to recover from the enormous tragedy of the theater fire. To honor those who had lost their lives, the city leaders planned the construction of the Monumental Church on the site of the disaster; its cornerstone was laid on August 1. The most generous contributor was the grieving Joseph Gallego. John Allan and Charles Ellis also contributed. One Richmond resident asked that the one-year anniversary of the disaster, December 26, 1812, be marked by "humiliation and prayer."[37] Charles Ellis tried to help the city return to ordinary pleasures, serving as a manager of a ball, held on January 20.[38] The church continued to be built through 1813.

David Poe's sister Elizabeth Poe, from Baltimore, had sought to honor the Allans in a letter to Frances Allan in July 1812; it may never have arrived, but she sent another on February 8, 1813. "Tis the Aunt of Edgar that addresses Mrs. Allan for the second time," she begins. Having concluded that the first letter was never received, she goes on, "[P]ermit me my dear madam to thank you for your kindness to the little Edgar—he is truly the Child of fortune to be placed under the fostering care of the amiable Mr. and Mrs. Allan, Oh how few meet with such A lot—The Almighty Father of the Universe grant that he may never abuse the kindness he has received and that from those who were not bound by any ties except those that the feeling and humane heart dictates." Toward the close, Elizabeth Poe conveys the warmth of the Poe family: "[G]ive my love to the dear little Edgar and tell him tis his Aunt Eliza who writes this to you. My Mother and family desire to be affectionately remembered to Mr. Allan—and yourself—Henry frequently speaks of his little Brother and expresses A great desire to see him, tell him he sends his very best love to him and is greatly pleased to hear that he is so good as also so pretty A Boy as Mr. Douglas represents him to be." She signs the letter "with the greatest respect Eliza Poe" and adds, "Mrs. Allan the kind Benefactress of the infant Orphan Edgar, Allan, Poe."[39] The commas lend an emphasis to each of his names and a regard for both of his families. We do not know if Frances Allan replied.

Frances Allan's cousin Margaret Keeling Nimmo wrote on February 20, 1813, from Richmond, to her brother James Nimmo in Norfolk, "Kiss my dear little Mucius [her nephew] for me, and tell him that little Edgar Allan Poe sends his love to him."[40] Meanwhile, the British navy was blockading Norfolk, and British forces were gathering.[41] The war was at the edge of the lives of the Allans and young Edgar.

The boy had some of the usual childhood diseases—whooping cough in May, measles in July.[42] The fury of the war, on the other hand, was becoming unusual; in June, the enemy, unable to take Norfolk, occupied the town of Hampton in the battle for Craney Island and raped women there.[43] There was, of course, great outrage. But Frances Allan's calm prompted her husband's pride: "my wife very cool[l]y making some Bounce [a cherry cordial]."[44] Weeks later, there was some relief—at least in Virginia. For it became clear that there would be no attack on Richmond: the British forces left the

Norfolk area in July and sailed toward Baltimore.[45] It may have been at this time that the Allan family returned to White Sulphur Springs.

There was soon cause for celebration in Richmond, as elsewhere in the country, for Oliver Hazard Perry's great triumph over the British ships on Lake Erie in September 1813. John Allan wrote from Richmond to his partner, Charles Ellis, "The Guns have been roaring their Gratitude for the signal Victory obtained by Gen. Perry over the British fleet on Lake Erie on the 18th Inst. [of this month]." And a month later Richmond celebrated another American military success, William Henry Harrison's defeat of the British near the Thames River in Upper Canada. Allan, who was recovering from an illness, wrote again from Richmond to his partner, "We had a general & splendid illumination last night in honor of Harrison's Victory over [Henry] Procter."[46] Doubtless young Edgar would have heard the cannon and seen the fireworks.

And Charles Ellis had had some good news of his own; he wrote to John Allan in August, "The Gods I am sure must begin to envy the happiness of your friend, The lovely Margaret has with that Frankness and candor which she is capable of given me her whole soul."[47] Allan's partner was to marry Frances Allan's cousin, Margaret Keeling Nimmo. Ellis paid tribute to his friendship with Allan, concluding, "I believe our heart is the same."[48] Margaret herself closed a letter to another cousin, "Remember me to the two Nancy's [presumably Frances's sister Nancy Valentine and friend of the family Nancy Smith], little Edgar, and all enquiring friends."[49] The marriage took place in Norfolk on November 13; Ellis reported, "My earthly cup is overflowing."[50] Allan wrote admiringly to a correspondent, "Our Charles has just taken to himself a wife a fine Blooming Girl." But congratulating Charles himself, Allan also cautioned his older partner, perhaps having learned from his own marriage: "[Y]ou are however not to expect that your happiness will remain free from those alloys to which we are all subject they will come, the mixture of greif [sic] and joy of pain & pleasure seem to be pretty equal[l]y balanced."[51]

Edgar turned five in January 1814; John Allan was already providing for his education.[52] And Allan could be protective of his young charge. Edgar had explored a vegetable garden next to his school, and when his teacher punished him by hanging a vegetable from his neck, Allan upbraided the woman.[53] But Allan could also be punitive. Allan threatened a whipping for Edgar's running in the rain, and he administered a real whipping when Edgar, encouraged by Frances Allan's cousin Edward Valentine Jr. to pull out a chair from a boy sitting down, pulled out a chair from a woman sitting down.[54] In one version of the latter story, Frances Allan consoled the punished boy. According to Jane

Scott Mackenzie, as reported by Flora Lapham Mack, Edgar was to cause "an atmosphere of unrest and strain" in the Allan household. He would come to be, Mackenzie said, "extravagant, not at all obedient and impatient of all restraint."[55] Probably John Allan's occasional severity would have aggravated the situation.

Poe remembered Allan's indulgence and his severity. The biography in the *Saturday Museum* of February 1843, which Poe wrote either with Henry B. Hirst or by himself, stated of Allan, "He treated his young *protégé* with as much kindness as his gross nature permitted."[56] And Sarah Helen Whitman, whom Poe later courted, reported that Poe had told her that Allan was "a man of a gross & brutal temperament, though *indulgent* to *him* & at *times* profusely lavish in the matter of money—at others, penurious & parsimonious."[57] Poe's later praise of a passage in T. S. Arthur's novel *Insubordination* may well be relevant: "[A] passage where Jimmy, an ill-treated orphan, relates to the only friend he has ever found, some of the poignant sorrows of his childhood, embodies a fine theme, handled in a manner which has seldom been excelled. Its pathos is exquisite."[58] Consulting the passage in the book, we learn that it concerns Jimmy's having been beaten.[59] Doubtless young Edgar was mischievous, but Allan was the adult. Perhaps the judgment by Edgar's childhood playmate Mary Jane Poitiaux Dixon is a fitting summing up: "His [Edgar's] misfortune was in being subjected in early life to the alternate petting and punishing caressing and scolding of ordinary children, while his sensitive nervous organization, like a fine string instrument, needed gentle handling and a most judicious touch."[60]

Richmond's long-awaited Monumental Church was consecrated in the spring of 1814. A four-sided white marble monument in the front porch of the church honored the victims of the theater fire; the names listed included Mary Gallego and Sally Conyers. The pews had been purchased by many of the leading citizens of Richmond. William Mackenzie (John H. Mackenzie's father) had Pew 54, Charles Ellis had Pew 76, and John Allan had Pew 80. Mrs. Allan and Edgar often attended.[61] In the summer, John and Frances Allan and their foster son visited "The Grove," the estate of James Penn, near Lynchburg,[62] and returned to White Sulphur Springs. The young boy was evidently enough of a familiar presence—whether at home or at the Ellis & Allan office or at church or on the family's travels—that one customer wrote to John Allan, "I will thank you to send me blue cashemire sufficient to make 2 suits of cloathes for a boy the size of Edgar."[63]

It may have been at this point that, on a horseback ride with Edward Valentine Jr., little Edgar read the newspaper aloud to the country folk and wrestled with little African American boys.[64] At home, he is said to have offered a toast and recited poetry, including from Sir Walter Scott's "Lay of the Last Minstrel."[65]

James Nimmo—the brother of Margaret Keeling Nimmo, now Margaret Ellis—wrote to John Allan on August 17, 1814, about the growing British fleet in the Chesapeake Bay, concluding, "I think there is little doubt they will make an attack on Washington."[66] The American defense was not effective; on August 24, the British forces took the city and burned the Capitol.[67]

There was fear in Richmond. John Allan bought a pair of horses and a carriage and drove his family northwest, to the mountains, to the city of Staunton.[68] Margaret Ellis wrote to her brother James on September 1 from the Clover Green plantation of Robert Hunter, eighty miles south of Staunton, in Concord, Campbell County, "Mr. Allan and Cousin [Frances] started for Staunton the day that we left Richmond; I believe there is scarcely a family left in the city."[69] Mrs. Ellis gave birth to her first child, Thomas H. Ellis, on September 6; he would become a playmate of Edgar's.[70] Allan returned to Richmond and wrote to his wife that the city was safe. She addressed "My Dear Husband" in her letter of September 11, trying to reassure him (and perhaps herself), "I shall endeavor to take you[r] advices [sic] as to my fears."[71]

The British headed toward Baltimore and on September 13 and 14 attacked Fort McHenry, sentinel for Baltimore's inner harbor. This time, the Americans triumphed, and Francis Scott Key, observing the battle, wrote the poem that would become the national anthem, "The Star-Spangled Banner."[72] John Allan, then thirty-five, wrote to John H. Cocke—Bowler Cocke's brother and commander of a battalion at White Oak Swamp—professing "no fear" and offering to serve. Cocke invited Allan to visit camp but did not take him up on his offer: "[T]he enemy will be too cautious to attempt Richmond by a Land march of any length in the face of the force we have now prepared to bring against him."[73] On October 14, John Allan wrote to James Nimmo that the Allan family had returned home, acknowledging that the trip had been "not, as you well know, from choice, but from compulsion."[74] And he wrote two weeks later to William Burgess, "For the present, the storm has blown over and all the old women have returned from the fastnesses of the mountains, amongst the rest my family, and we are now enjoying a state of comparative ease & security, eating Bacon and greens."[75]

The Treaty of Ghent, committing to "a firm and universal peace" between England and the United States, was signed by the delegates on December 24, 1814.[76] The war continued; Andrew Jackson won a great victory at the Battle of New Orleans.[77] But on February 16, 1815, the United States Senate ratified the treaty.[78] John Allan (or his partner, Charles Ellis) reported to British merchants from Richmond that "here the expression of joy is warm and universal"; "[N]ever did any event cause such heartfelt demonstrations of joy. It might be said that our whole continent has been & will be in one great blaze of illumination."[79] So once again—and this time more lastingly—commerce was restored. John Allan was considering going to England.[80]

In February, Allan bought "a pair [of] trammaels for Edgar"—a toy that made ellipses (two-dimensional oval shapes)—as well as a variety of books, including a collection of moralistic children's stories, *Evenings at Home*. This work, written by British physician John Aikin and his sister Anna Letitia Barbauld, appears to have had a lasting influence on Poe. It offered, for example, a tale of detection focused on windows, a tale that exculpated the innocent and identified the guilty (anticipating "The Murders in the Rue Morgue"). And it featured an explanation and demonstration of the "emblematical" (anticipating "The Raven" and "The Philosophy of Composition"). Remarkably, an account of a young man's incurring "a *debt of honour*" at the university and therefore possibly "embarrassing his father's affairs" is suggestive of Poe's later life.[81]

In March, Allan bought Edgar schoolbooks—*Murray's Reader* and *Universal Spelling Book*.[82] Edgar's teacher was William Ewing, who then kept school in an "excellent, spacious, and commodious room, on the principal upper floor" of a house on E. Street (later Main Street).[83] Ewing inquired after his former pupil two years later, in November 1817: "I trust Edgar continues to be well and to like his School as much as he used to when he was in Richmond. He is a charming boy and it will give me great pleasure to hear how he is, and where you have sent him to school, and also what he is reading." He closed by acknowledging Mrs. Allan and her sister and adding, "[D]o not forget to mention me to their august attendant Edgar."[84] Evidently, Ewing remained impressed and interested. Allan responded to Ewing in March 1818, "Edgar is a fine Boy and I have no reason to complain of his progress."[85]

The initial prompt for Ewing's letter was Allan's debt for the tuition of Edward Collier.[86] Allan agreed to pay what was owed, but no more.[87] Poe scholars have taken Collier to have been Allan's illegitimate son.[88] And there would be other illegitimate children.

By late May 1815, to increase business, Allan "had finally concluded to go to London."[89] He inquired about a possible voyage and booked passage on a vessel headed from Norfolk to Liverpool, the *Lothair*, bearing ten hogsheads (large barrels) of his own firm's tobacco.[90] He decided to sell his household goods: the sale, taking place on June 7, yielded more than three thousand dollars.[91] He bought Edgar "A great Coat" and shortly thereafter heard from Moses Myers & Sons that he and his family should be ready to leave for England on June 20.[92] Friends of the Allans, the Poitiauxs, threw a "farewell dinner," and the children "played at marrying him [Edgar] to my [Mary I. Dixon's] little sister [Catherine Elizabeth Poitiaux] whom he called his 'sweetheart.'"[93]

On June 22, 1815, from Norfolk, Allan wrote to his partner, asking him to sell several of those he enslaved.[94] Allan reports, "The Lothair & Steam Boat went off together today at 10 a.m. The Boat moved off handsomely and with the tide." He and his family would board the following morning. And he adds, "Frances & Nancy evince much fortitude, it has been a sore trial to them, thier [sic] spirit is good, Ned [Edgar] cared but little about it, poor fellow." Writing from the *Lothair* the following afternoon, Allan states, "Frances & Nancy & the qualmish Edgar & myself well." Then, at "1/2 p. 5 p.m." on Friday, June 23, "We are now abreast of the Light House and are off, F & Nancy sick Ed. & myself well."[95] So began Edgar's only voyage abroad.

Allan had not been dissuaded from traveling by the approaching war between the British and the French. And he did not yet know that on June 18 the Duke of Wellington had defeated Napoleon Bonaparte at the Battle of Waterloo. But if the military news was to be good, the eventual economic news was to be very bad. Allan had no idea that his stay in England would yield "new causes of dread," far worse than any he had known.

The transatlantic trip involved a common difficulty—"Frances and Nancy were very sick but are now perfectly Hearty. Edgar was a little sick but soon recovered." And it also involved a less common one—a "too close and niggardly captain." He was, evidently, controlling and stingy.[96] The Allans arrived in Liverpool on Friday, July 28.[97] They made their way to Allan's extended family in Kilmarnock, in Scotland, his native land. Allan notes in a letter to Charles Ellis of September 21, "Edgar says Pa say something for me say I was not afraid coming across the Sea." And he adds at the end, "Edgar's love to Rosa [his sister Rosalie] and Mrs. Mackenzie."[98]

Edgar had entered John Allan's home-world. But he carried within him his own. He was, after all, a boy who had lost his mother—he would have had before him the image of Eliza Poe, with her large eyes and lustrous dark curls. He would later write on a piece of paper that he had placed on the back of his miniature portrait of her, "My adored Mother!"[99] She was, he would acknowledge, "a string to which my heart fully responds" (O 1:116). It would surely have been Eliza Poe foremost of whom he wrote that "[f]rom Childhood's hour . . . all I lov'd—*I* lov'd alone" (M 1:146).

And if his life without his mother was sometimes without luster—"the dull reality / Of waking life" (M 1:68)—he still had the world he could create, as intimated in his early poem "Dreams":

> But should it be—that dream eternally
> Continuing—as dreams have been to me
> In my young boyhood—should it thus be given,
> 'Twere folly still to hope for higher Heaven!
> For I have revell'd, when the sun was bright
> In the summer sky; in dreamy fields of light,
> And left unheedingly my very heart
> In climes of mine imagining—apart
> From mine own home, with beings that have been
> Of mine own thought—what more could I have seen? (M 1:68)

And perhaps Edgar, now six years old, would have carried within him not only an enduring memory and an intense imagination but also an inchoate sense of what he later termed in *Tamerlane,* "The mystic empire and high power / Giv'n by the energetic might / Of Genius, at its natal hour" (M 1:32). Beneath his charm and his mischief, his willingness and his willfulness, would eventually grow a conviction that would defy all else: he would be great.

3

"The Flap of Its Wings in My Ear"

1815-1820

THE TRIP FROM LIVERPOOL WAS an ambitious one. Sometime after August 6, 1815, John Allan took Frances, Nancy, and Edgar to his family in Scotland, stayed a few weeks, and then made a circuit of towns and cities in Scotland and England, arriving in London after a journey of what must have been seven hundred miles, on October 7.[1]

The first stop was Irvine, Allan's birthplace, where the four visited Allan's sisters Mary and Jane. Edgar briefly attended the Old Grammar School there and visited the old church and its churchyard, up the hill. The marbles game in Poe's "The Purloined Letter" later reminded one Irvine resident of "an old Irvine game."[2] The next stop was seven miles east, Kilmarnock, where the Allans stayed with Allan Fowlds and his wife, John Allan's sister, Nancy. Edgar was said to have enjoyed traveling by "red riding carts." He was later remembered by two former playmates in Kilmarnock—one of these, James Anderson, said that Edgar was "much petted by the Allans, and a 'curmudgeon,' or forward, quick-witted boy, but self-willed." Allan wrote to Ellis & Allan from Kilmarnock on August 22, stating that he intended to go to Glasgow shortly (where he did indeed go, by himself) and that "Frances is not as well pleased with Scotland as with England."[3] And then the Allans traveled north to Greenock; it was there that Allan wrote the September 21 letter to Charles Ellis, conveying Edgar's fearlessness on their recent voyage. And, he reported, Frances was "bewildered with wonders" in Scotland though complaining of the cold and the rain.[4]

John Allan wrote to Charles Ellis from London on October 10, "I arrived here on the Evg of the 7th from Kilmarnock by way of Greenock Glasgow Edinburg New Castle Sheffield Leeds and Nottingham."[5] (Perhaps, given the southward direction of the latter part of this journey, the sequence was Edinburgh, Newcastle, Leeds, Sheffield, and Nottingham.) The Allans stayed at Blake's Hotel, on Jermyn Street, near Piccadilly.[6] Allan stated that Frances had "a bad cold & sore throat" and "the rest of us are well but cursedly dissatisfied." Yet he was impressed by London—to a second correspondent in Richmond, he wrote, "This is a wonderful City—A stranger is seized with a kind of confused stare upon entering it, that he is scarcely himself my amazement is beginning to subside."[7] By October 30, the Allans were settled on a middle-class Bloomsbury street: "[B]y a snug fire," Allan writes, "in a nice little sitting parlour in No 47 Southampton Row Russell Square where I have procured lodgings for the present with Frances & Nancy Sewing & Edgar reading a little Story Book I feel quite in a comfortable mood for writing."[8]

In early November, everyone was sick—"The Doctor says we must all have a seasoning"—but a week later, everyone was doing better: "[W]e are all nearly well & over our seasoning."[9] Little Thomas H. Ellis, in Richmond, was also recovering from sickness: Allan wrote, "Glad to hear my little Thomas is getting better and none more delighted than Edgar."[10] The tobacco markets were giving Allan reason to become uncomfortable since the disparity between the Richmond market and the London one was growing: "[D]amp the prices," Allan warned Ellis on October 30 and "[Di]scourage high prices" on November 20; however, the letters from London to Richmond were not arriving in a timely way, and Ellis wrote Allan from Richmond on November 21, "I have caught a little of the mainac [mania]"—that is, the tobacco mania.[11] The tobacco market would soon fall, and "great expectations" for it would prove to have been, as Allan wrote, "*real[l]y Dangerous.*"[12] His new firm, London's Allan & Ellis (as opposed to Richmond's Ellis & Allan), would be at risk.

Because of Allan's wishes, Edgar apparently returned to Irvine, perhaps toward the end of 1815, with James Galt, who reported that the boy maintained "an unceasing fuss all the way over." Edgar again attended the Old Grammar School there, unhappily, and threatened to travel to London on his own. The family then gave up on efforts to educate him in Irvine, and Edgar was taken back to the Allans in London.[13]

Late in the year, Ellis wrote Allan hopefully, "Xmas will be here tomorrow week when I shall drink all your healths in the merry moode of the season."[14] And the Allans welcomed to 47 Southampton Row a young Richmond art student, Edward Peticolas, who later wrote Allan from Paris, "[N]othing can make me forget the comfort of your cheerful fireside—where I experienced so much happiness during my stay in London."[15]

The weather, however, was not so cheerful—by late January 1816, Allan was writing to his uncle in Richmond, William Galt, "Frances is complaining a little, this is such a Muddy, Dirty Cold Damp & Cloudy place, she cannot get out to exercise, It's a rarity to see the sun."[16] And the economy was darkening. Galt warned Allan of the "speculative Market" and faulted Allan's "calculations" as "Eronious," but Ellis continued to buy tobacco at high prices, confident that these prices would rise further.[17] Finally, on February 3, Allan wrote to Ellis that one of their British customers, William Holder, couldn't pay his bill for the excessively expensive tobacco. Allan discouraged further buying—"I dislike to be in a state of fear and alarm."[18] Still Ellis bought more, not receiving many of Allan's letters until March 13. He later acknowledged that he might not have purchased as much if he had known of Allan's warnings, but he still was sure that tobacco prices would rise. And he stated on March 18 that he would stick with his plan to buy.[19] His confidence, however, was unwarranted—he eventually experienced "extreme anguish" about the Holder purchases; he was "all but mad."[20] Tobacco prices fell, and Allan visited Holder in Bristol, then writing to Ellis on April 23, "Tobacco rushing in from all Quarters. I am so much distressed in mind, that I can hardly do any business" and adding on May 4, "This will prove a sad year. . . . [S]evere losses must be the consequence."[21] Ellis wrote to Allan on April 19 with regard to the Holder debacle, "I cannot collect myself so as to enable me to say what ought to be done," and he added plaintively on May 4, "God help us out and deliver us from perdition."[22]

Seven-year-old Edgar may have been aware to some degree of his foster father's distress. And he may have become aware of his foster mother's own distress, as well, caused not only by her having been frequently ill but also by her not having her own biological child. News of a Virginia friend's pregnancy made her "almost crazy."[23] Fortunately for the family's calm, by mid-March Allan secured a counting-room, 18 Basinghall Street, and a clerk, one George Dubourg.[24] And in April Edgar was enrolled in a boarding school, that of George's sisters, the Dubourgs, at 146 Sloane Street. His first quarter lasted until midsummer 1816.[25]

We know from "Masr Allan's School Account to Midsumr" that Edgar had his own bed, a place in church, school supplies, and any needed medicine. He had both teachers and servants. And he had a spelling book, a geography book, a prayer book, a church catechism, and an English history catechism. The cost for the quarter was twelve pounds, two shillings.[26] We also know from an advertisement for the auction of Miss Dubourg's household effects from 146 Sloane Street in October 1819 that the school had not only the expected beds and linen, tables and chairs, but also "a very excellent large reflecting telescope."[27] If this had already been at the school two or three years earlier, then it may well have been Edgar's first telescope—an instrument worthy of note for the boy who would grow up to become the author of his own cosmology, the 1848 volume *Eureka: A Prose Poem*.

On May 18, 1816, little Catherine Poitiaux wrote from Richmond to John Allan, "Give my love to Edgar and tell him I want to see him very much." Also, "Josephine and all the children want to see him very much." And she speculated, "I expect Edgar does not know what to make of such a large City as London."[28] Doubtless this was so, but John Allan would have been an able guide. Allan had taken Edgar around Richmond; when Edgar was home at Southampton Row, Allan would probably have taken him around London, too. And Allan would no longer have been "seized with a kind of confused stare"; he had grown familiar with navigating the city. He wrote in August 1816, "I have become a perfect pedestrian, London is so large, and the places where I have business so remote from each other the Streets so crouded [*sic*] with Carts Waggons Gigs Coaches etc that besides saving expence I save time by walking." In all likelihood, when Edgar was home, especially in the warmer months, Allan would have walked with him around Bloomsbury, where they lived, including to the British Museum, only three blocks away, or southwest to Chelsea, where the Dubourgs had their school, or southeast to central London, where Allan had his countinghouse.[29] It is possible that Allan and his sister-in-law and his foster son went to coffeehouses: brother-in-law Allan Fowlds wrote to Allan in September, "I am happy also to find that Miss Valentine [Frances Allan's sister] little Edgar and yourself are become Gourmandizers."[30] As past Poe biographers have suggested, Edgar's walks with Allan might have contributed to Poe's later writing his classic 1840 short story "The Man of the Crowd."[31]

Regardless of his gourmandizing, Edgar was "thin as a rasor," "growing and of course thin." The family was healthy, and William Galt later wrote from Richmond, "I am glad to hear that you are all well & getting all fatt except Edgar."[32] Edgar's new quarter at the Dubourgs' school began on July 22, 1816; John Allan paid twenty-three pounds, sixteen shillings, presumably for two quarters, on December 28.[33] One of the brothers of the Dubourg sisters, C. S. Dubourg, then wrote to Allan on January 30, 1817, from Sloane Street, asking the merchant to provide his younger brother George, Allan's clerk, with a salary, and offering an encouraging postscript: "Your Son I am glad to say is well & happy—& I sincerely hope you will find his Improvement at the end of the half year equal to your Expectations."[34]

Allan was beginning to feel some sense of hope financially, writing to his uncle in October 1816, "I think I have weathered the storm, and feel as easy as a man can do under the recollection of a very bad year[']s business"; "I jog on pretty well among the Cockneys, and have no fears of weathering the Storm safely." Galt responded in late December, "I am very glad to hear that you have weathered the storm, it no doubt blowed a Hurricane."[35]

But another danger emerged. Galt wrote on April 5, 1817, "I observe you were in a great Confusion during the riot I have no doubt but it was very alarming & I can readily imagine Frances situation it was almost as bad, as the Ringing the Bells in Richmond I suspect, nor indeed is it surprising that such Riots should cause great Alarm."[36] The riot may have been the Spa Fields Riot of December 2, 1816, prompted by growing economic unrest in England.[37] And the ringing of the bells in Richmond may have been—at least in part—an allusion to the never-to-be-forgotten Richmond Theater Fire of 1811.[38]

Edgar continued at the Dubourg school in the spring and summer; receipt for Allan's payment of Edgar's account was made on August 28.[39] Allan continued at his countinghouse, at one point visited there not only by Frances Allan but also by Jane Mackenzie, who would become increasingly significant in Edgar's life. She was John H. Mackenzie's aunt (his father William's sister) and would start a girls' school in Richmond at which Poe's sister, Rosalie, would later teach penmanship and to which his young wife, Virginia, would later go.[40] And the Allans continued to welcome friends to 47 Southampton Row—H. W. Tabb, the brother of P. E. Tabb, wrote to Allan, "I shall not soon forget the many pleasant hours which I have spent in your most pleasant and hospitable mansion."[41] In the summer, Allan rented 39 Southampton Row, but it wouldn't become available until the fall.[42] Economic problems still threatened: Allan's Richmond friend John Richard wrote Allan, "[W]here great deficiency exists, it must ultimately show itself," and Charles Ellis observed that tobacco prices were falling and added, "God only knows what are [is] to become of us poor Imposters."[43] He had evidently come to doubt his market judgment. Buying high and selling low was clearly unsustainable.

In early August, John and Frances Allan and Nancy Valentine traveled to the spa town of Cheltenham, nearly one hundred miles west of London, for Frances's health. They stayed at the Stiles Hotel.[44] Apparently the spa was helpful; John Allan wrote to his clerk George Dubourg, "Mrs. Allan has been using the waters and they agree verry [sic] well with her."[45] And George Dubourg served as the Allans' intermediary with Edgar. "Edgar is quite well," he wrote, and, later, "Edgar is quite well & desires his love [to be passed on]." (Dubourg then reassured Mrs. Allan that he would take care of the expected parrot.) Later he wrote, "Edgar is perfectly well." Allan conveyed Mrs. Allan's love to their foster son—"Mrs. Allan desires her love to Edgar"—and Dubourg, responding to John Allan's writing to Edgar, advised, "Edgar is quite well, & will I Dare say be quite delighted at receiving your Letter." Allan directed Edgar to write to his mother (if he writes) since he himself will be returning to London.[46] And then Allan took Edgar back with him to Cheltenham.[47] This elite health resort would probably have seemed a small-town British version of White Sulphur Springs.[48]

On September 26, Allan wrote, "I have just returned from Cheltenham." And he noted, "Mrs. Allan has benefited greatly but still not Hearty."[49] Waiting for 39 Southampton Row to become available, Allan reported to his uncle from his temporary nearby lodging, "Frances recovered at Cheltenham but London has made her sick again. The Typhus Fever is in our neighborhood & has carried off many persons which alarms her I do not think there is any danger or I should leave it Nancy & Edgar are quite well."[50] William Galt counseled, "I hope if the fever ap[p]roaches your neighborhood that you will move from it."[51] This infectious disease often caused a rash, sometimes death; perhaps Edgar's memory of the typhus fever fears would have contributed to his one day writing "The Masque of the Red Death." The Allans did not leave; they moved in to 39 Southampton Row, which Poe later mentions in "Why the Little Frenchman Wears His Hand in a Sling" (M 2:464). Edgar may well have been back at the Dubourg school; Allan paid a school bill on December 18, 1817.[52] But this would have been the end of Edgar's time there. F. W. Thomas later reported that "Poe told him that his school days in London were sad, lonely and unhappy."[53] In 1841, Poe would obliquely acknowledge the Dubourg school: he names the laundress who offered a deposition in "The Murders in the Rue Morgue" "*Pauline Dubourg*" (M 2:538).

In 1818, the Allans were well settled at 39 Southampton Row; John Allan had committed to the house for five years at one hundred guineas per year, and he was "furnishing it plainly and cheaply."[54] Frances would become "quite pleased with her residence in London."[55] During the workday, Allan was busy at 18 Basinghall Street; he described himself as "confined as I am within Brick walls scarcely conscious that the Heavens forms [sic] a Canopy above my head and but seldom blessed with the Heart cheering Beams of the Sun."[56] And Edgar was now attending the Manor House School, just north of London in the village of Stoke Newington.

Allan first paid tuition for the school to its headmaster, Reverend John Bransby, on July 24, 1818.[57] Edgar boarded at the Manor House School but came home on weekends.[58] Allan was proud of Edgar's accomplishment; on January 22, he wrote, "Edgar is a fine Boy & reads Latin pretty sharply." On March 21, he wrote the comment to William Ewing, "Edgar is a fine Boy and I have no reason to complain of his progress."[59] It may be that Edgar's first letters were written at this time: on January 22, "John Allan paid postage for Edgar Poe."[60] And there seems to have been a haunting avian experience in the school's village: reportedly Poe told Cornelius Mathews many years later at the Park Theatre in New York City, regarding "a raven, bird of ill omen," "Do you know, that bird, that imp bird pursues me, mentally, perpetually; I cannot rid myself of its presence; as I sit here, I hear its croak as I used to hear it at Stoke Newington, the flap of its wings in my ear."[61]

Regarding the school at Stoke Newington and the Reverend John Bransby, the February 25, 1843, *Philadelphia Saturday Museum* biography of Poe, written by either Poe and Henry B. Hirst or by Poe alone, asserted, "A faithful description of this school and its principal, is introduced in Mr. Poe's tale of 'William Wilson.'"[62] The story was prompted by a work by Washington Irving, "An Unwritten Drama of Lord Byron," which describes an immoral young man plagued by his moral double; the evil twin slays the interfering good one and thereby kills himself (M 2:423–24). Poe elaborated this tale brilliantly, offering an allegory of the "bi-part soul" (M 2:425). Poe's description is probably partly "faithful," but the actual building has been said to be a Queen Anne building (rather than an Elizabethan one), and Poe's rendering evocative of another building, Stoke Newington's Fleetwood House, and the schoolroom has been said to represent one at the Old Grammar School at Irvine.[63] The figure of Reverend Bransby has been characterized as a blend of Bransby, Dr. Brown of Irvine Grammar School, and Reverend George Gaskin of St. Mary's Church, Stoke Newington.[64]

The story invites us to see William Wilson as having some resonance with Poe—indeed, Wilson and his narrator double were born on January 19, Poe's birthday, and, in one version, in the correct year, 1809. Poe modifies his age in other versions, substituting the year 1811 and that of 1813 (M 2:432). Certain comments in the story, independent of plot and setting, seem suggestive of Edgar's actual experience. Poe writes, for example, "The teeming brain of childhood requires no external world of incident to occupy or amuse it" (M 2:430), "In childhood I must have felt with the energy of a man what I now find stamped upon memory in lines as vivid, as deep, and as durable as the *exergues* of the Carthaginian medals" (M 2:430), and "If there is on earth a supreme and unqualified despotism, it is the despotism of a master-mind in boyhood over the less energetic spirits of its companions" (M 2:431). Especially notable, in light of a thematic pattern already observed in his life, is mention of corporal punishment—a behavior attributed to the composite principal but perhaps also a reminder of that of John Allan: "This reverend man, with countenance so demurely benign, with robes so glossy and so clerically flowing, with wig so minutely powdered, so rigid and so vast—could this be he who, of late, with sour visage, and in snuffy habiliments, administered, ferule in hand, the Draconian Laws of the academy? Oh, gigantic paradox, too utterly monstrous for solution!" (M 2:428–29). A defender of Bransby did not deny his flogging students but rather asserted its appropriateness: "Undoubtedly he was a strict disciplinarian, but I never remember him flogging a boy who did not deserve it, or more than he deserved."[65]

Bransby said of his former student, "Edgar Allan was a quick and clever boy and would have been a very good boy if he had not been spoilt by his parents, but they spoilt him, and allowed him an extravagant amount of pocket-money, which enabled him to get into all manner of mischief—still I liked the boy—poor fellow, his parents spoilt him!" And he also observed, "Allan was intelligent, wayward, and willful."[66]

At home, at 39 Southampton Row, Frances was sometimes sick ("with a nervous attack," with "the croup," with "catarrh"), and her sister Nancy Valentine served as her nurse.[67] Frances sometimes improved. And the Allans sometimes had company. Jane Galt and Allan's sister Mary visited.[68] Dr. Thomas Nelson probably also visited—he wrote to Allan from Richmond, "I think of No. 39 Southampton Row every day," and he conveyed his "salutations more than one to Mrs. Allan & Miss Valentine & Edgar."[69] There was a lighthearted moment on one occasion when John and Frances Allan went out—he wrote of "the first frolic I have had for a long time" at "a grand Dinner Party" on board the ship *Philip Tabb* in June 1818, when "Mrs. Allan was in great spirits and raced the Ladies up & down the Decks."[70] In August, John and Frances Allan traveled to the Isle of Wight for her health.[71] In October, Frances went with merchant George Elwall and his wife to Devonshire, and Elwall wrote to Allan that Frances wasn't really sick—she just needed exercise.[72] When Allan suggested such a view to Frances, she responded sharply: "[Y]ou are determined to think my health better contrary to all I say."[73] He speculated a week later, "I often think her religious Habits taints [sic] her mind with melancholy, affecting her spirit & injurious to her Health."[74]

Edgar continued at the Manor House School. He took, in addition to the regular course of studies, French, dancing, drawing, and music. He was assigned John Bigland's *Letters on English History, for the Use of Schools.* He injured his hand, and he was treated. He was provided with a pair of shoes.[75] Sometimes he would visit London: Mary Allan wrote, "Edgar is at School at Stock [Stoke] Newington about four miles from London he is quite well he was in town for a day this week."[76]

The chief ongoing problem for the family was financial. Allan wrote to Charles Ellis in August 1818, "I hope my early & steady friend will be as ready to forgive as he expects to be forgiven & let him & the rest of my Friends rely hereafter that I will redeem any unfavourable impressions they may have formed of me as a Salesman we are all liable to err.—You shall not have your head on that a/c [account] hereafter but don't mention it again I am quite sensitive on that subject." He had been having difficulty selling what was left of the enormous amount of tobacco that had been shipped to William Holder. He wrote, "The difficulty I have experienced with these remnants it always appears to me like giving them away."[77] Frances Allan returned to the family in London in better health by late October.[78] By late December, John Allan would write to Charles Ellis, "Dull & distressing as the times are we had a few friends Xmas eve & Drank all your Health in a Bowl of Egg Nog & trusting that the same Good Providence who has guided us in safety through this year will continue his kindness to us through the next."[79] He would later admit that Christmas 1818 was spent "with heavy heart & unavailing regrets."[80] And safety was not to continue. The firm of Campbell and Bowden collapsed. John Allan wrote to Charles Ellis on January 9, 1819, "The effect of such an unsuspected House as this giving way is tremendous. It destroys all confidence between man and man for no one can well say he is safe & its effect on the tobacco market will be sensibly felt and we fear even a farther depression. I never saw things look more gloomy in my life."[81]

And they would get worse. In 1819, "fear and alarm" would become hopelessness: the firm of Allan & Ellis would collapse.

Christmas vacation ended for Edgar on January 25, 1819, and he returned to the Manor House School in Stoke Newington.[82] John and Frances Allan and Nancy Valentine remained at 39 Southampton Row. Frances had a "nervous head ache" but got better.[83] John Allan's worries, however, were growing; he wrote to Charles Ellis in February, "You may think me desponding & so I am." In another letter, he confessed, "I have a good share of fortitude certainly but there is a shaking point which I look to with *Horror!!!*"[84] The "shaking point" was coming. Perhaps, on his visits home, Edgar felt some of the foreboding.

Tobacco prices continued to fall; losses continued to mount on both sides of the Atlantic. Allan's despairing state was clear in his letters to Ellis of March and April: without payment "we must give up, it is impossible to go on," "*all my resources is [sic] exhausted, what am I to do, I know not,*" "Pray you to send every farthing you can," "The times are truly awful."[85] In late April, a fellow merchant hanged himself.[86] In May and June, the plummeting continued, and Allan acknowledged that tobacco could fall even further.[87] He attended the Parliament in late May when the House of Lords was discussing the requirement that banks pay bullion (gold and silver) for paper money, thereby tightening the money supply.[88] That requirement was approved. There was a moment when Allan seemed to catch his breath: on June 8, he wrote to William Galt, "We will hope the worst is now past & at all events we can see our way now clearly." And he wrote to Ellis on June 17, using Galt's earlier metaphor, "I think we shall not only ride out the Hurricane with God[']s assistance & our exertions, it has been a destructive period it looked as if one fell swoop would engulf us all."[89]

The Allans attended a wedding in Irvine in late June and, perhaps wisely, given the times, John and Frances left Edgar there until September. He was regarded well by the family there, remembered as "a bright attractive boy, a favorite with them all."[90] Returned to London, Allan wrote to Ellis, "I hope we shall yet survive the storm." But, he added, "If we are doomed to fall let us fall like men."[91] Companies continued to founder, one after the other, unable to pay their bills.[92] And on July 17, 1819, Allan & Ellis succumbed, too. "We have this day stopped payment," Allan wrote to Ellis. He closed his letter, "We have hardly a shilling left to bless ourselves with here & though my poor wife knows it, she bears herself wonderfully. If you can send a little Bill to her to keep us from starving altogether you will make her glad for she is verry [sic] economical." The return address marked the arrival of that much-feared "shaking point": "John Allan 17th July 1819 Day of Suspension."[93]

Allan met with his British creditors on July 27 at the Baptist's Head Coffee House and secured a "Deed of Inspection" that allowed Allan & Ellis twelve months to pay back its debts. And the deed was a "License to go on without danger of arrest—or Process of any kind."[94] But still, Allan was concerned whether these creditors would allow him to return to the United States—and perhaps after five years away he would, as an "Alien Citizen," lose his citizenship and, most critically, his ability to inherit real estate after the loss.[95] He may have already anticipated an eventual inheritance from his wealthy uncle William Galt. Meanwhile, he admitted in a letter's postscript, "I am without funds."[96] And he feared for "the distress of mind" of his partner, Charles Ellis, whom Galt characterized to Allan as "a tender man."[97] Allan sometimes blamed his financial difficulties on nonpaying customers in Virginia and sometimes on bankers, but he did confide to Ellis, "The truth is our pride & vanity had perhaps carried us beyond the bounds of Prudence."[98] In October Allan considered himself "held as a Hostage for the concern." And he continued to ask Ellis for money. The British creditors, apparently annoyed that Richmond creditors had been compensated early on, would nonetheless eventually relent in early December and allow Allan to return to America.[99]

Edgar was back at 39 Southampton Row sometime in September 1819 and continued at the Manor House School. Allan wrote to his uncle on September 28, "Edgar is growing wonderfully & enjoys a good reputation as both able & willing to receive instruction."[100] Two months later, Allan offered additional praise: "Edgar is in the Country at School he is a very fine Boy & a good scholar."[101] Perhaps it was at this time that, as Poe recalled later, "we first learned to grow serious over Robinson Crusoe! . . . we first found the spirit of wild adventure enkindling within us, as, by the dim fire light, we labored out, line by line, the marvelous import of those pages" (P 5:98). And despite the financial crisis, the family was doing well; Allan wrote, "I am happy to say that Mrs. Allan's health has recently improv'd so much that she is no longer like the same person & promising to become quite fat & hearty. Ann Valentine, as usual fat, active & bustling. Edgar is also well & I am perfectly so."[102] Jane Mackenzie left London for Richmond in September—"[S]he's a delightful woman," Allan wrote to Charles Ellis, "one that you & Margaret will be greatly pleased with"—and the Allans were soon discussing their possible departure.[103]

When Edgar returned home in September, the leading political issue was the August 16 attack by the Manchester Yeomanry against the men, women, and children in St. Peters Field in Manchester who were protesting the poor economy and inadequate suffrage—the "Peterloo massacre." Eleven people died; approximately four hundred people were injured.[104] The poet Percy Bysshe Shelley wrote in his poem "England in 1819" of "A people starved and stabbed in th'untilled field."[105] Allan deplored the attack repeatedly in his letters.[106] Edgar would surely have heard of this event—and as a grown man, he may later have been referring to it in his 1844 detective story "The Purloined

Letter." There, the detective, seeking a distraction from his planned appropriation of the eponymous letter, had hired "a man with a musket," who "fired it among a crowd of women and children," causing "a series of fearful screams, and the shoutings of a mob" (M 3:992). And other details in the story Poe would draw from Regency England, the decade (1811–20) when the Prince of Wales served as regent in place of his father, King George III, who was insane.

On Christmas Eve 1819, the Allan family would again share the traditional eggnog.[107] John Allan, if less observant and fervent than his wife, was nonetheless devout—he had written to William Galt in late September, "[W]e are all firm believers in the Divine Character & Doctrines of Our Lord, Jesus Christ. However much from the frailties & corruption of our nature we may fall short in the Practice."[108] And he wrote to his uncle in late December that the family "had a Bowl of Egg Nogg on X Mass Eve by way of Drinking the Health & remembrance of our old Friend," keeping what he termed "the old Custom" and thereby also commemorating "by decent joy & grateful Hearts to this Giver of all Good Gifts & this most especial Manifestation of the Birth of our Redeemer bringing Peace and Good will to Man."[109] Earlier, on December 23, Allan shared with Ellis in a letter marked "Private," "Should I get a Glass of Egg Nog tomorrow Evg I shall not fail to recollect my old Friends in Richmond & the days of other Years & though the Tear at present dims my Eyes I pray God to Bless you all & that we may through His Kind Providence live to see many returns of the Season growing in Grace as time rolls on, having our Lamps well trimmed & supplied, watching patiently for the Bridegroom to call us to the Marri[a]ge Supper."[110]

Here Allan alludes to the book of Revelation 19:9 ("Blessed are they which are called unto the marriage supper of the Lamb") and to the idea of the ultimate union of Christ, the Bridegroom, and the Church, his Bride, according to Christian eschatology. It is a form of consolation, perhaps especially needed after such a difficult year. And it is a form of consolation to which the grown Edgar, after many difficult years, would covertly return at the close of his 1838 novel *The Narrative of Arthur Gordon Pym*. And he would do so through the image of his beloved mother. If the source of solace later shifted for him from religion to cosmic reverie, it was still consolation that Poe would seek at the close of his 1848 volume *Eureka*.

The year 1820 was the Allans' final one in London. Edgar was at school, and John Allan was winding down his business. The British firm Allan & Ellis had fallen; Allan would return to the United States to assist with the Richmond firm Ellis & Allan. Edgar may have forgotten many people back home, but not all. Allan reassured William Galt, "You are among the few that Edgar recollects perfectly"; "Uncle Galt" is one of "his old Friends."[111] Allan wrote his partner Charles Ellis regarding Jane Mackenzie, now in Richmond, "Tell Miss McKenzie that all her Friends are well. I have just called at Roderick[']s. They are much surprized at not hearing from her." Roderick Mackenzie was Jane's older half brother.[112] (Because of the 1839 short story "The Fall of the House of Usher," the name "Roderick" would come to seem a Poe property.) Allan paid Edgar's tuition, and the family continued to think about their return. He reported that his wife Frances was eager to see her friends in Richmond but fearful of the voyage—"6 or 8 Inches between her & Davy Jones's Locker though last not least." And, he added, "The Sea Sickness she suffers severely."[113] Allan and his wife had "severe colds" in late February; in March Allan had "A Billious Pleurisy" that kept him in his room twenty-eight days and delayed the voyage home. Frances and Nancy nursed him well, but "the fatigue was too much for poor Frank [Frances]."[114]

George III died on January 29; Allan wrote about his death, the people's response, his son the regent—now George IV—and the new queen, Caroline. The former Prince and Princess of Wales had long been disaffected from one another; Caroline had been living in Italy for several years. With the death of her father-in-law, she would dramatically make her way back to England to be crowned queen. But Allan was correct in his assessment: "One great difficulty occurs with respect to the Princess of Wales now Queen consort. King George IV will never allow her to be crowned."[115] Queen Caroline's return would be carefully followed by the people and the press.

Allan finally got back to the countinghouse on April 3; his primary focus was his overextended tobacco customer William Holder.[116] Meanwhile, at home, he reported, "Frances complains a good deal & Ann & Edgar are quite well."[117] Allan paid Edgar's last Manor House bill on May 26.[118] A former student of Reverend Bransby, who had known the principal in later years, reported, "That he [Poe] profited under Dr. Bransby's care is shown by the fact that when he entered the school he was very backward with his studies, not having had any regular instruction, and that when he left it he was able to speak the French language, construe any easy Latin author, and was far better acquainted with history and literature than many boys of a more advanced age who had had greater advantages than he had."[119] On May 31, Allan asked for accommodations on the ship *Martha,* which sailed from Liverpool.[120] Perhaps then the Allan family visited Allan's sisters in Irvine.[121] By June 8, they were in Liverpool.[122]

Allan wrote from Liverpool to Charles Ellis, "Mrs. Allan is in better health than usual Ann is quite well so is Edgar & for myself I never was better." He noted that the ship *Martha,* with Captain Sketchly, would not leave before June 14.[123] That ship was listed in the newspaper as "coppered and copper-fastened"—a description that Poe would later use in *Pym* for the ship *Penguin* (P 1:62).[124] And the newspapers were full of stories about the queen. Allan wrote about her, "The arrival of the Queen [in London] produced an unexpected sensation few thought she would return, but the bold & courageous manner by which she effected it has induced a vast number to think her not guilty She was received with immense acclamations & the Populace displaced her Horses drew her past Carlton House [where George IV lived] & thence to Alderman Woods House South Audley St The Same day the King made a communication to the House of Lords charging her with High Treason a certain offence being committed by the Queen is High Treason (aduly)."[125] Whether or not Caroline was guilty of adultery, the people loved her and despised her spendthrift estranged husband.

On June 16, 1820, the *Martha* set sail from Liverpool to New York City. The voyage took thirty-six days; the seas were "very rough," and the passengers endured "heavy cold foggy weather." Frances Allan and Nancy Valentine were "very Sea Sick."[126] The conversation on board must have involved, in part, the accused queen. Edgar would surely have remembered the story. Years later, he would adapt a story about Caroline from a book titled *Death-Bed Confessions;* she would become the threatened female royal in "The Purloined Letter."

The Allans arrived in New York City on July 21, and Mrs. Allan was ill, delaying their return home. On July 28, they took a steamboat to Richmond by way of Norfolk.[127] The family arrived back in Richmond—from the Thames to the James—on August 2, 1820.[128] The Allans moved into the Ellis house, on the southwest corner of Franklin and Second Streets, seven blocks west of Capitol Square.[129] Charles Ellis, in Richmond, writing to his wife, Margaret, in the country, referred to "Mr. & Mrs. Allan who are at our home receiving the congratulations of their friends" and described Mrs. Allan at the time as "even tempered" and "accomidating" [*sic*]—apparently uncharacteristically so.[130] Ellis continued, a few days later, "Our Friends Mr & Mrs Allan Nancy & Edgar are very well & you would be surprise[d] to see what health and colour Mrs A has, they are quite well satisfied at our house, and I make out pretty well altho not as well as you would do, They are a little Englishised but it will soon wear off."[131]

In May 1821, Doctor Neil Arnott would write to John Allan from London, "You know that I have Master Edgar still inhabiting one of my rooms. Your not asking for him with these other things makes me hope that you do mean to come back again."[132] The inhabitant was in all probability a portrait of Edgar. So Edgar had not entirely left England. And certainly England had not entirely left Edgar. Perhaps he did not so fondly remember his five years in England, but that time would prove to be important and influential in his later work.

4

"With Many Cares and Toils Oppress'd"

1820-1825

JOHN ALLAN KNEW THAT THERE had been significant changes in his Richmond world. William Galt, Allan's uncle and patron, had adopted as his son a distant relative, young William Galt, who had emigrated from Irvine, Scotland, in 1817; the elder Galt employed the younger one in business. And young William Galt had written to Allan in 1818 about important city news. Joseph Gallego, who had long suffered from his losses in the Richmond Theater Fire, had died. There was later a fire at his mills. And the city was expanding. Young William Galt—now William Galt Jr.—reported on the new dock, the new courthouse, the new theater, and the new hotel.[1] There had followed the Panic of 1819, resulting in greater indebtedness and declining property values.[2] But Allan was also interested in what hadn't changed, including, he hoped, his old friends. Charles Ellis explained to his wife, Margaret, shortly after his partner's return, "I find Mr. Allan can't do much yet as it will take some time to obtain a knowledge of our affairs & he is engaged in seeing his old friends." Evidently Allan was reassured: he wrote in late 1820, "I am happy to find my former Friends; Friends still."[3]

And Edgar would have found John H. Mackenzie a friend still. We do not know if they resumed their early storytelling competition, but Susan Archer Weiss recounts Mackenzie's memories of his escapades with Edgar and other boys.[4] Mackenzie said of Edgar, in part:

He delighted in playing practical jokes, masquerading, and making raids on orchards and turnip-patches. Oh, yes; every schoolboy liked a sweet, tender, juicy turnip; and many a time after the apple crop had been gathered in, we might have been seen, a half dozen of us, seated on a rail-fence like so many crows, munching turnips. We didn't object to a raw sweet potato at times—anything that had the relish of being stolen. On Saturdays we had fish-fries by the river, or tramped into the woods for wild grapes and chinquepins [chestnuts]. It was not always that Mr. Allan would allow Edgar to go on these excursions, and more than once he would steal off and join us, though knowing that he would be punished for it.[5]

In one instance, Edgar thoughtfully included the younger, less robust Robert Sully in the Saturday adventure, encouraging him to ride in the wagon. "Now, that showed his consideration," Sully commented, "he knowing that I could not walk the long distances that most boys could, and therefore seldom went on one of their excursions."[6]

And then there was Thomas H. Ellis, Charles Ellis's first son, only a baby when Edgar had left in 1815, a six-year-old boy when Edgar returned in 1820. He was the one whose recovery from illness had prompted John Allan to write, "None more delighted than Edgar."[7] Now Edgar could include him in his exploits. A great admirer of the older boy when they were young, Thomas H. Ellis later wrote of the one whipping that he knew John Allan had administered to Edgar "for [his] carrying me out into the fields and woods beyond Belvidere, one Saturday, and keeping me there all day and until after dark, without anybody at home knowing where we were, and for shooting a lot of domestic fowls."[8]

Beginning anew to develop his group of friends in Richmond, Edgar also began anew to attend school there. He went to Joseph H. Clarke's academy, at Broad and Fifth Streets, over a store.[9] This school has been taken to be the one that Poe mentions at the beginning of *Pym*, "Mr. E. Ronald's academy on the hill" (P 1:57, 218).[10] Clarke was a classicist from Trinity College, Dublin, who later remembered Edgar's having read in his school (through 1822) "Ovid, Caesar, Virgil, Cicero, and Horace in Latin, and Xenophon and Homer in Greek." He noted of Edgar that "[a]s a scholar, he was ambitious to excel, and although not conspicuously studious, he always acquitted himself well in his classes."[11] A fellow student recalled him as "very ambitious in his classes"; he "hated a rival" and in scanning Horace "was always the first in the school."[12]

Edgar was recognized at the school particularly for his poems. Clarke described them as "written *con amore*." Yet when John Allan visited to ask the schoolmaster's advice regarding Edgar's wish that his poetry be published as a book, Clarke recommended against publication: "I told him that Edgar was of a very excitable temperament, that he possessed a great deal of self-esteem, and that it would be very injurious to the boy to allow him to be flattered and talked about as the author of a printed book at his age." The poems were written to Richmond girls whom Edgar had especially liked.[13] John H. Mackenzie's mother, Jane Scott Mackenzie, disparaged the poems as "worthless imitations of Byron . . . blended with some original nonsense."[14] (Though, for the most part, Edgar's early poems to Richmond girls have not survived [M 1:4], there may have been one exception, as will be argued here.) The Allan-Clarke anecdote tends to confirm the report of James Galt, William Galt Sr.'s second adopted son, that "Poe was fully imbued in his early youth with an idea that he would one day become a great writer, and was impatient to have his writings published, for a try to become famous."[15] Edgar was clearly sure of his own genius.

The Allans returned to Pew 80 at the Monumental Church.[16] In early September the family enjoyed good health, but soon John Allan became sick, and Frances Allan was sick on and off from their return to Richmond through the end of the year.[17] According to Thomas H. Ellis, John Allan had brought back with him from England a telescope; apparently Allan acquired a dog and bought Edgar a knife.[18] Also according to Ellis, the Allans stayed at his parents' house "for nearly a year," but Susan Archer Weiss contends that they moved to "the corner of Clay and Fifth streets at the end of 1820."[19] Wherever the Allans were living, they doubtless spent Christmas Eve there with their friends the Ellises, whom Allan had been toasting with eggnog in past years in London. We have no letter attesting to his maintaining the tradition this year in Richmond, but we do see that on December 24, 1820, Allan paid $1.50 for "4 doz Eggs."[20]

As the new year began, Edgar was thriving at school. Joseph H. Clarke later wrote, "At 12 years old he was master of Horace and Livy and was reading in the 13th book of Homer[']s Iliad."[21] The teacher commented, as well, on Edgar's personality:

> He was remarkable for self-respect, without haughtiness. In his demeanor toward his playmates, he was strictly just and correct, which made him a general favorite, even with those who were older than he was. His natural

and predominant passion seemed to me to be an enthusiastic ardor in everything he undertook. In any difference of opinion which occurred between him and his fellow students, he was very tenacious in maintaining his own views, and would not yield until his judgment was convinced. He had a sensitive and tender heart, and would do anything to serve a friend. His nature was entirely free from selfishness, the predominant quality of boyhood.[22]

Elsewhere Clarke noted, "I don't think Edgar Poe was a beautiful boy, although he had a sweet disposition. He had very pretty eyes and hair and a rather effeminate face. He was always cheerful, brimful of mirth and a very great favorite with his schoolmates. He was not remarkable for his application to study, but he was naturally very smart and always knew his lessons. I never had occasion to say a harsh word to him while he was at my school, much less to make him do penance."[23] Perhaps Edgar found with Clarke the "gentle handling" and "most judicious touch" that Mary Jane Poitiaux Dixon had noted the boy needed.[24] If, as seems likely, there were tensions at home, Allan did not yet let on; in April 1821, George Murn wrote to Allan, "I am happy to hear so good an account of Edgar."[25]

Allan's business situation was still troublesome. His agent Morgan Utz was trying to collect on old debts for the firm of Ellis & Allan in January, and Ellis himself then rode by horseback inland to recover funds in late March and early April.[26] But already the original Deed of Inspection that had granted time for the payment of the British creditors had run out. Fortunately, by May 1821, the creditors agreed to offer an extension of a year or a year and a half.[27] Some of the creditors, however, were impatient; another "shaking point" was yet to come. And Frances Allan's condition remained worrisome: Allan wrote in March, "Mrs Allan still continues in poor health Miss Valentine Edgar & myself pretty well." His wife was soon "rather better," and Ellis wrote encouragingly in early April, "Mrs. Allan will no doubt get better as the weather gets warmer, if it should near do so."[28]

Among the new friends whom Edgar made in Richmond was Ebenezer Burling, whom he would have met at Clarke's school and at the Monumental Church and who taught him to swim and to take part in a variety of athletic activities.[29] Edgar evidently passed on his skills: Thomas H. Ellis later recalled that Edgar "taught me to shoot, to swim, and to skate, to play bandy [similar to ice hockey] etc."[30] (When Poe was editor at *Burton's Gentleman's Magazine* in 1840, he included a piece about three-wheeled skates that would function on the ice and on the ground and commented, "[I]n our boyhood we used a pair of skates made as above described.")[31] Ellis went on to give an indication of Poe's coaching ardor: "I ought to mention that he once saved me from drowning—for having thrown me into the falls headlong, that I might 'strike out' for myself, he presently found it necessary to come to my help, or it would have been too late."[32] Edgar's excess of enthusiasm and his mistaken confidence in his friend's skill yielded to concern and quick action.

Increasingly important for Edgar was Sarah Elmira Royster. As a middle-aged widow, Elmira Royster Shelton would later write that she first knew Edgar "at a very early period of my life." Edward M. Alfriend, whose father, Thomas, had been a friend of the Royster family, stated that "He [Poe] knew Miss Royster as a little girl, and grew up loving her." (She was born in 1810 or 1811 [M 1:539n].) Those who remembered Elmira in her youth agreed that she was "a beautiful girl."[33] As an older woman, she would recall, "We lived opposite to Poe on 5th. I made his acquaintance so." This must have been at the Fifth and Clay location, for Shelton said in an interview with John J. Moran (Poe's doctor at his death), "We spent much of our time together when we were children. A few years after Mr. Allan built a large mansion farther up the street."[34] Indeed, after leaving Fifth and Clay for Fourteenth Street and Tobacco Alley, Allan would move "farther up the street"—Fifth Street—to "a large mansion" (one already built) at Fifth and Main. And as the years passed, the childhood friendship of Edgar and Elmira—"Myra," as he referred to her—would become an adolescent romance.[35]

Summer for the Allans brought socializing with "Miss [Jane] Mackenzie [William Mackenzie's sister from England] & her friends": "we often see each Other, & she enjoys herself much & seems quite contented with Virginia."[36] The family participated in the "Sociable Barbecue Club" and acquired a piano, a tub, and a turtle. The Allans were, for a while, all healthy. Charles Ellis asked his partner to protect the Ellis family while he was in the country. And John Allan went out one evening "a Birding"—that is, in all probability, bird-hunting.[37] Despite the financial uncertainties, the Allans were trying to live a life of normalcy.

Some news from England must have seemed remote—for instance, the coronation of King George IV and the death of Queen Caroline.[38] But the claims of the British creditors must have seemed immediate and disturbing. At one point, Ellis requested that Ellis & Allan's British agent George Elwall forgive a recent letter from Allan about their hugely overextended and non-paying debtor William Holder: "Our Mr Allan may have been agitated and vexed when he wrote the letter alluded to."[39] Soon began a series of insistent, unrelenting letters to Ellis & Allan from William J. Shepherd, of Petersburg, Virginia, representing the Sheffield, England, firm of Furniss, Cutler, and Stacey, which wanted the money that Ellis & Allan owed.[40] The firm's terms were not accepted by the trustees for Ellis & Allan, John Forbes and John Richard, who very likely would have preferred to deal with the agents for all the creditors, William Taylor and Arthur Saltmarsh, but Ellis & Allan did not then come to terms with these agents either.[41]

Edgar continued at Clarke's school in the fall, doing well.[42] He was growing; Allan bought him a new "coat and pantaloons."[43] Edgar assisted and protected his friend Robert Sully, who recalled, "I was a dull boy at school . . . and Edgar, when he knew that I had an unusually hard lesson, would help me out with it. He would never allow the big boys to teaze [sic] me, and was kind to me in every way. I used to admire and in a way envy him, he was so bright, clever and handsome."[44] Perhaps it was at this time that Edgar won the prize for declamation. As Thomas H. Ellis remembered, "There was not a brighter, more beautiful and graceful, or more attractive boy in the city than Edgar Allan Poe."[45]

But as Edgar ascended, John Allan descended. Furniss, Cutler, and Stacey initiated a suit against Ellis & Allan in the United States Fifth Circuit and Eastern District of Virginia. The amount to be paid back was $9,749.33 (approximately $265,000 in 2023).[46] The Allans' presumptive Christmas Eve with the Ellises must have been an anxious one.

And then, on January 24, 1822, John Allan and Charles Ellis were arrested.[47] The bail was set at $12,000. Allan and Ellis did not go to jail, but imprisonment was threatened. Allan or Ellis immediately wrote a letter—probably Allan, given the letter's tone—to the agents for the British creditors, Taylor and Saltmarsh: "[I]n Novr next judgement will be obtained an Execution will instantly follow it will be returned no effects then against our Bodies, we must to jail for ten days after which Swear Out, for we venture to say they will not get a cent."[48] On January 28, Allan or Ellis—again, probably Allan—wrote of the arrest, "To minds of any sensibility how mortifying & to men whose only error is the misfortunes of others & who without a solitary condition have placed all their Estate & Effects in the hands of Gentlemen of undoubted integrity for the general benefit of their Creditors. Should Honesty meet this reward? What more could be done to us if we were villains?"[49]

Charles Ellis, as the agent for the Ellis & Allan trustees Forbes and Richard (the "Gentlemen of undoubted integrity"), provided to the agents of the creditors, Taylor and Saltmarsh, the power of attorney and authorized the distribution of money to the creditors—except to litigious Furniss, Cutler, and Stacey.[50] On April 24, the British creditors of Allan & Ellis (the British branch of Ellis & Allan that John Allan had run) met again at the Baptist's Head Coffee House, and they wrote a "Memorandum" stipulating the distribution of some funds and the request for the books of Allan & Ellis (which were later sent).[51] As a result of his attending this meeting, John R. Furniss wrote to Ellis & Allan, "I must sincerely wish if you value your reputation that you will immediately meet the expectations of the meeting and for fifteen Shillings in the Pound (not less) I have no doubt you may receive a general discharge, but the sooner this is done the better."[52] (Since there were twenty shillings to the pound, this arrangement required payment of three-quarters of the debt.) And a letter from Furniss, Cutler, and Stacey also stipulated payment of "altogether fifteen Shillings in the Pound," adding "in consequence of which we are induced to withdraw our Suit for the present."[53] The issue dragged on, with a judgment against Furniss, Cutler, and Stacey in the Circuit Court of the United States in May, though they could try again, which they apparently intended to do, for they threatened depositions in Sheffield, England, in October.[54] It was not until November 16 that Ellis & Allan could report that Furniss, Cutler, and Stacey had told William Shepherd to dismiss the suit in federal court—and yet another suit remained.[55] And there continued to be differences between Ellis & Allan and its British creditors.[56]

Allan's financial and legal problems are important here insofar as they may have affected his relations with others. He may have been "agitated and vexed" not only in correspondence but also in person. Allan's own partner, Charles Ellis, complained in late August 1822 of Allan's making a demand and a threat: "[Y]our proposition made to day hurt me exceedingly, being made in stile & mode accompanied with a threat, which neither could serve our ends at getting clear of our difficulties or serving your honor, that I least expected from you, I mean particularly the bearing of that hart [*sic*] when you named a sum so large for your expence as you supposed would about balance our a/cs [accounts], and if I did not accede to it you would wipe off the whole by taking the Insolvent Oath."[57] Allan was becoming difficult with a friend; he may have become more difficult with thirteen-year-old Edgar, as well.

We do have some insight about John Allan and Edgar offered by the boy's best friend, John H. Mackenzie, as recounted by Susan Archer Weiss. Mackenzie recalled, "Mr. Allan was a good man in his way . . . but Edgar was not fond of him. He was sharp and exacting, and with his long, hooked nose and small keen eyes looking from under his shaggy eyebrows, always reminded me of a hawk. I know that often, when angry with Edgar, he would threaten to turn him adrift, and that he never allowed him to lose sight of his dependence on his charity."[58] In light of the severe difficulties that Allan was enduring in 1822, including threats of jail and reminders of indebtedness, he may have been even more likely to threaten Edgar and remind him of his own indebtedness.

Of course, Edgar also actively made John Allan angry. John Bransby had said that Edgar was "intelligent, wayward, and willful"; according to Flora Lapham Mack, Jane Scott Mackenzie said that Edgar was "extravagant not at all obedient and impatient of all restraint." Mrs. Mackenzie reportedly added, "He never liked Mr. Allen [sic] at all because he tried to manage him and he did not seem to care how much trouble he occasioned Mrs. Allen though I think he was really fond of her."[59] No doubt Edgar was a challenge, especially for the strict and increasingly stressed John Allan. And his wife would take Edgar's side, Mrs. Mackenzie noted, deceiving Allan "constantly in small ways to screen & indulge Edgar." Mack later asserted that Mrs. Mackenzie tried to intercede with Edgar, but to no avail.[60] The "experiment," as Allan had once characterized his taking in of Edgar Poe, was not working. And the relationship of foster father and foster son would grow worse.

Still, Edgar distinguished himself at Clarke's school. According to J. T. L. Preston, a classmate two or three years younger than Edgar, the older boy was proficient at "capping" Latin verses—that is, reciting from memory a Latin verse beginning with the same first letter as the verse just recited had begun—and at "double capping," or reciting a Latin verse beginning with the same first letter and ending with the same last letter as the verse just recited had begun and ended. Edgar used to enjoy reciting the Odes of Horace. And he excelled in French. Often he would write his own verses, and Preston was sufficiently impressed that he brought Edgar home and his mother read the work, praising it "very highly."[61] Poe's teacher himself later recalled, "One summer [Edgar] wrote me a complimentary letter in verse, which I afterwards showed to Rev. Mr. Damphoux, of St. Mary's College, in Baltimore, who said to me that the composition would do honor and credit to the best educated professor in his college."[62]

Preston remembered Edgar not only as a student but also as an athlete. He was "a swift runner, a wonderful leaper, and what was more, a boxer, with some slight training." He was also a strong swimmer. For his marked skill as a runner, Edgar was chosen by the students of the school to represent them in a footrace in Capitol Square in May. Edgar lost but competed ably.[63]

Poe's character was memorable—as were the reservations of his peers. "Edgar was," his classmate recalled, "self-willed, capricious, inclined to be imperious, and though of generous impulses, not steadily kind or even amiable; and so what he would exact was refused to him." Furthermore, there was the matter of caste: "Of Edgar Poe it was known that his parents [the Poes] were players, and that he was dependent upon the bounty that is bestowed upon an adopted son. All this had the effect of making the boys decline his leadership; and on looking back on it since, I fancy it gave him a fierceness he would otherwise not have had."[64] Contrary to this comment, Poe was never adopted, but the gist of the passage is very telling. Fierceness would become an especially strong trait of Poe; others' doubts of his status must have intensified his sense of his own genius and his aspiration to prove it.

The Allan family moved after May 1822 from the house at Clay and Fifth to a house at Fourteenth Street and Tobacco Alley, which, according to Thomas H. Ellis, was a gift from Allan's uncle William Galt.[65] Evidently also in 1822, Miss Jane Mackenzie, whom John Allan had met in London and with whom he socialized in Richmond, began her school for young ladies. Working with her sister-in-law Mrs. Jane Scott Mackenzie, Miss Mackenzie, "a most highly cultured English lady," created, according to Flora Lapham Mack, "her very fashionable expensive & exclusive school." The location was Franklin Street between Fifth and Sixth Streets, not far from Clarke's school and the Ellis house. Perhaps it was near here that Edgar would run toward a group of schoolgirls as if to hug them all, causing the girls to run away with screams of mock fear.[66] Poe's sister Rosalie would later teach handwriting at the Mackenzie school, and Poe's young bride, Virginia, would later attend the school.

In July and August 1822, *Timour the Tartar* was performed at the Richmond Theater. If Edgar saw or heard about the play, it may have later influenced the poem "Tamerlane."[67]

The last recorded payment for Edgar's attending Joseph H. Clarke's school is for the quarter ending December 11, 1822.[68] His classmates chose Edgar to give the farewell ode to their teacher, and he "did so with grace and satisfaction to all."[69] Clarke, said to have been "a hot-tempered, pedantic, bachelor Irishman,"[70] married in September 1821 in Washington and would soon be moving to Baltimore.[71] He would later recall his devoted student fondly: "As a boy Edgar was open-hearted, cheerful and good, while as a man he was loving and affectionate to me. He would never forget to come and visit me when he came to Baltimore, and when he became editor of Graham's Magazine he sent it to me regularly."[72]

On April 1, 1823, Edgar began to attend William Burke's school,[73] and he continued to do well. A classmate, Creed Thomas, later acknowledged, "Poe was one of our brightest pupils. He read and scanned the Latin poets with ease when scarcely thirteen [fourteen] years of age. He was an apt student and always recited well, with a great ambition to excel in everything."[74] And, notably, unlike other students, Edgar was never whipped at school. He was "a quiet, peaceful youngster, and seldom got into a difficulty with his schoolmates. He was as plucky as any boy at school, however, and never permitted himself to be imposed upon." Provoked by one boy's insults, Edgar got into a fight: he first allowed himself to be beaten for a while, and then, when his opponent ran out of breath, he "administered a sound whipping" (H 1:27–29).[75]

But there was a distinct change in his general demeanor. Probably because of the difficult regime at home, Edgar became withdrawn: "He was not at all popular with his schoolmates, being too retiring in disposition and singularly unsociable in manner." And while he had a few friends at school, he never invited anyone home (H 1:28). John H. Mackenzie, not a classmate at Burke's school but certainly the boy's best friend, would later refuse to go home with Edgar: "[He] could never be persuaded to visit Edgar at his home, so strict was the etiquette observed at table and in general behavior."[76] As much as John Allan's financial life was out of his control, he tried in his domestic life to exert control.

Allan was still unable to secure acceptable terms and release from his British creditors; he felt "shackled and bound down." And his wife, Frances, was "never clear of some cause of complaint." He reported that "Miss Valentine is well Edgar & myself are also well," but he also admitted that he himself had a limp.[77] Edgar was trying not to feel constrained by his foster father's management of him: he would go swimming; he would visit the Mackenzies (calling Mrs. Mackenzie "Ma"); and, over Allan's objections, he joined the Thespian Society, taking part in performances with his classmates, once even reciting his poems.[78] Then, unexpectedly, Edgar found solace and relief in a visit to his classmate Rob Stanard's home, at Ninth Street near Franklin,[79] where he met his friend's mother, Jane Stith Stanard.

It was a moment of bliss. She was, Poe later wrote, "The first, purely ideal love of my soul" (O 2:694). Poet Sarah Helen Whitman described what Poe must have described to her before: "This lady, on entering the room, took his hand and spoke some gentle and gracious words of welcome, which so penetrated the sensitive heart of the orphan boy as to deprive him of the power of speech, and, for a time, almost of consciousness itself. He returned home in a dream, with but one thought, one hope in life—to hear again the sweet and gracious words that had made the desolate world so beautiful to him, and filled his lonely heart with the oppression of a new joy."[80] Edgar must have felt both braced and embraced. He returned repeatedly; Poe's aunt (and future mother-in-law) Maria Clemm wrote, "When he was unhappy at home, (which was very often the case) he went to her for sympathy, and she always consoled and comforted him."[81] Whitman noted, "The lady afterwards became the confidant of all his boyish sorrows, and her's [*sic*] was the one redeeming influence that saved and guided him in the earlier days of his turbulent and passionate youth."[82] Stanard would later be the inspiration for Poe's tribute to the return to one's spiritual home, the classic and classical poem "To Helen." Edgar had found in Jane Stith Stanard a mother—and a muse.

John Allan and Charles Ellis continued to wait for satisfactory terms and release from the British creditors, Allan working at the office and Ellis trying to collect debts in the countryside. Notably, Allan wrote to Ellis arguing against working hard for children who would then disdain hard work. With Thomas Ritchie, the editor of the *Richmond Enquirer,* Allan oversaw the "Clark's Spring Sociable Club."[83] And in early August, the Richmond penitentiary burned. What is significant about this event for our purposes is that many prisoners were saved by Gilbert Hunt, the same enslaved blacksmith who had caught women dropped from a second-story window in the burning Richmond Theater back in December 1811.[84] Hunt may have been the model for an important character in Poe's 1838 novel *The Narrative of Arthur Gordon Pym,* as will be discussed. In early September, Alexander Fulton of Mount Erin died.[85] (It was to Fulton's house, Mount Erin, overlooking Richmond from the south, that John H. Mackenzie would bring his bride, Louisa Lanier, in 1827.) In November 1823, Allan & Ellis did finally receive a "Deed of Conditional Release."[86]

Edgar must have continued to hold to his dream of unconditional release—into poetic eminence. As we know, he had written a collection of poems "to his young female friends," but Joseph H. Clarke had recommended to Allan against their publication as a book. T. O. Mabbott has stated, "Not one of these poems addressed to schoolgirls has been preserved" (M 1:4). But as James Galt recalled, Edgar was impatient for publication, and it may well be that a subsequent poem of his to a young female friend was in fact published. In December 1823, when Edgar was living at "the corner of 14th Street and Tobacco Alley"—which was between Main and Franklin Streets—the office of a new newspaper opened on the same block, Fourteenth between Main and Franklin. The newspaper was the *Richmond Phenix*. It was named after the mythical bird that is born again from its own ashes (an image featured in the paper's banner).[87] Perhaps the unusual name of the paper attracted the young poet's attention. The editor and proprietor Samuel Crawford wrote that "the Phenix rises from the ashes of 'The Va. Times,'" his previous paper, which had been appropriated by printer William Ramsay.[88] The *Phenix* was short-lived—it lasted from December 1823 through May 1824 (under another proprietor)—and, as Samuel Mordecai noted, it was one phoenix "from whose ashes no other was hatched."[89] Yet it may have offered Edgar an opportunity. More than fifty years later, Elmira Royster Shelton did not believe that Edgar had "addressed any poems to me," but she may well have been mistaken.[90] We may note that she was the subject of several of Poe's poems, including "Tamerlane" and "Song." And "To—" is thought to be "To [Elmira]" (M 1:132).

"To Myra" appeared on Monday, December 22, 1823, in the second issue of the *Richmond Phenix*. It is headed on the upper right "FOR THE PHENIX"— this was no reprint from another paper. The poem, arguably Edgar's first publication, warrants reprinting here.

TO MYRA
I saw thee start with feign'd surprise,
    When madly whispering in thy ear;
I told the love which these fond eyes
    Too plainly proved not insincere.

How could you call the hours too few,
    Which gave my captive heart to thee!
Oh! he that looks but once on you,
    Thy victim and thy slave must be.

How could you laugh, and coldly chide,
    And swear I only *acted* well,
The love which prudence could not hide,
    The passion folly dared to tell!

Oh! if too long I linger'd there
    To beg the idle rose you wore,
Forgive the crime, if crime it were,
    Since I shall never see thee more.

No, I will never weakly sue
    To win thy smile or sooth thy pride;
Glory alone my soul shall woo,
    And fame shall be my only bride.[91]

This seems to be Edgar's work. It offers familiar elements such as the openings "I saw thee" (see "Song" [M 1:66] and the second "To Helen" [M 1:445]) and "How could" (see "Tamerlane F" [M 1:48] and "Politian" [M 1:254]); resonant phrases such as "feign'd surprise" (see "feign'd journey" in "Tamerlane A" [M 1:36]), "fond eyes" (see "fond breast" in "Tamerlane A" [M 1:34]), and "dared to tell" (see "dared to stir" in the second "To Helen" [M 1:445]); and the line "Since I shall never see thee more," a seeming foreshadowing of Poe's signature refrain in "The Raven," "Nevermore." Notably, "victim" and "slave" are elsewhere also applied to a man enthralled to his beloved (see the former word in "Fanny" [M 1:226] and the latter in the second "To Helen" [M 1:446]). Even the moving lines of aspiration, "Glory alone my soul shall woo, / And fame shall be my only bride," seem echoed later, through inversion, in "Politian," "Fame awaits thee—Glory calls" [M 1:268]. (Unlike the speaker of this poem, Politian resists.) The form—five quatrains with ABAB rhyme—is characteristic of Poe early on, as in the first version of "A Dream" (M 1:79–80) and "To M—" (M 1:136–37) and "To—" (M 1:224).

And thematically, the poem touches on probable vital elements of Edgar's life at the time. The ardency of the romantic love expressed seems likely for the intensely romantic Edgar—and Elmira Royster Shelton later remembered, "He was as warm and zealous in any cause he was interested in, very enthusiastic and impulsive, I was about 15 & 16 when he first addressed me and I engaged myself to him."[92] We may readily suppose that as friendship first shifted to courtship, Elmira might have seen Edgar's ardency as performance. And Edgar's anticipating yielding his romantic love for his abiding quest for literary greatness seems wholly likely, consistent with his account of the conflict of love and ambition in "Tamerlane." The essence of the poem is also consistent with Poe's later short essay "Byron and Miss Chaworth," in which the mature poet pays tribute to "[t]he boyish poet-love," "earnest" but "born of the hour, and of the youthful necessity to love." He sees it as emerging from the poet's power: "the magnetism of *his* actual presence," "the necromancy of *his* words of fire." Miss Chaworth was the embodiment of Byron's ideal, a love shaped by his romantic imagination and therefore not destined to last (M 3:1122–23). We may well read here Poe's reflecting on his own remembered "boyish poet-love" of Myra.

Edgar continued to do well at Burke's school, and another student, Andrew Johnston, who began attending in October 1823, later offered a reminiscence of the older boy through 1825: "Poe was a much more advanced scholar than any of us; but there was no other class for him—that being the highest—and he had nothing to do, or but little, to keep his headship of the class. I dare say he liked it well, for he was fond of desultory reading, and even then wrote verses, very clever for a boy of his years, and sometimes satirical. We all recognized and admired his great and varied talents, and were proud of him as the most distinguished school-boy of the town." Johnston observed, too, "In dress he was neat but not foppish. His disposition was amiable, and his manners pleasant and courteous." Johnston characterized Edgar physically as "well made, active, sinewy, and graceful."[93] And John Allan, admitting that his wife's health was "none of the best," stated in a letter to his brother in Scotland, "Miss Valentine is as fat as usual Edgar & myself cannot enjoy better health."[94]

Edgar did occasionally go to the Ellis & Allan shop, and he had a "fondness for the upper floor of the building," where the literary magazines were kept.[95] He also visited the Ellis home. At the latter, Thomas H. Ellis recalled, a ghost once appeared at the "Gentleman's Whist Club": approached by Dr. Philip Thornton, "the ghost was 'larruping' him over the shoulder with the long cane which he carried in one hand, while with the other he was struggling to keep from being tripped by the sheet which enveloped his body. When finally forced to surrender and the mask was taken from his face, Edgar laughed as heartily as ever a ghost did before."[96] Edgar clearly enjoyed a practical joke, as he would later relish a literary hoax. He was naturally fun-loving, but not when overly constrained—or devastated. And devastation was soon to come.

In January 1824, William Galt Sr. told John Allan what his struggling nephew must have suspected—that he would inherit a portion of his uncle's estate. But, given the complicated financial situation that Allan was a part of, he could not say anything yet.[97] Also then, the agents for the British creditors, Saltmarsh and Taylor, provided Ellis & Allan with a new deed, dated December 31, 1823, which stipulated a six-month further payment period.[98] And the firm of Ellis and Allan was preparing to be dissolved.[99]

In March 1824, Allan was using Edgar as a runner for the business.[100] Especially noteworthy in Richmond at the end of the month and the beginning of April was a series of lectures on astronomy, offered at the new theater by

Robert Goodacre of Nottingham, England. Employing advanced and varied equipment to illustrate his descriptions, Goodacre was on a twenty-four-city tour in North America; he had recently been in Philadelphia, Baltimore, and Washington. Former Virginia governor William H. Cabell reported to Thomas Jefferson that Goodacre had given his lectures "with so much applause in the principal cities of the United States." The eight lectures in Richmond were available to those over twelve years old for five dollars; each individual lecture cost one dollar. Cabell attended the series of lectures "with much pleasure & profit." The introductory lecture, held on Thursday, March 25, was free; tickets might be obtained at the city's bookstores. This lecture was attended by "an overflowing assembly," "a crowd of near 1000 spectators." We do not know if fifteen-year-old Edgar was present at this lecture or at any of the subsequent eight lectures. But given his access to Allan's telescope—and, perhaps earlier, to the telescope at the Dubourg school—and his intellectual curiosity, he might well have attended, at least the free introduction. Whether he attended or not, he must have known at the time about this remarkably popular series. We may later recall his surely knowing of Goodacre's lectures on astronomy—and perhaps attending—when, in 1848, Poe delivered his own lecture on the universe.[101]

Meanwhile, difficulty with John Allan would have continued. Perhaps it was at this time that Allan complained to Mrs. Mackenzie that Edgar "did not know the meaning of the word *gratitude*"; she suggested that Edgar, like her foster daughter Rosalie (Edgar's sister), was too young to appreciate the need to express gratitude.[102] But even Rosalie came to see the need for Edgar to express gratitude to the Allans—Flora Lapham Mack reports that she heard from the Mackenzie family that when Edgar "began to be so wild and wayward and give Mr. and Mrs. Allan so much trouble and distress she [Rosalie] was bitterly indignant at him and ashamed of his ingratitude."[103]

Of course, Rosalie may not have known the extent of the problematic relationship of Edgar with John Allan at home. And Edgar may well have been grateful to another—his maternal confidant, Jane Stith Stanard. But her health was failing—she was, in fact, depressed and becoming insane. Maria Clemm wrote that Edgar "only saw her once when she was ill, which grieved him greatly."[104] And on April 28, Jane Stith Stanard died.[105] Years later, John H. Mackenzie would remember that "when Mrs. Stanard died," his friend Edgar—usually "bright and full of fun and high spirits"—"appeared for some time grieving and depressed."[106] Her death was a severe blow: he had lost his beautiful consoler. Mrs. Stanard was buried in Shockoe Hill Cemetery. Maria

Clemm added, mentioning Mrs. Stanard's son and Edgar's friend, "Robert has often told me, of his, and Eddie's visits to her grave." And Edgar also went there alone.[107] Poe would later write, in an early poem titled "A Dream," "That holy dream—that holy dream, / While all the world were chiding, / Hath cheered me as a lovely beam / A lonely spirit guiding" (M 1:79).

As John Allan looked forward to the resolution of his business affairs in England, he served as the secretary for the Amicable Society and the treasurer for the "Clark's Spring Barbecue Club."[108] Then, in June, the dissolution papers of Ellis and Allan noted the "Deed of Release," and the trustees Forbes and Richard, in light of the new arrangement, celebrated the coming end of their trusteeship.[109] The financial problems were easing. John Allan and his friend Doctor Thomas Nelson catered the July 31 barbecue.[110]

Edgar, perhaps then unable to overcome his grief and depression, could still meet another challenge. He accepted a wager, and on a hot June day swam six miles down the James River from Ludlam's Wharf to Warwick Bar, against the tide. Thomas G. Clarke watched from the wharf; other boys followed in boats, along with teacher William Burke, who could rescue Edgar if the boy had any difficulty. Schoolmate Robert Mayo swam with Edgar but went only three miles, either because of the intense sun or Edgar's intense wish to go it alone. Edgar did not have any difficulty, swam the entire distance, and, badly sunburned, walked back to town. Poe was very proud of his achievement, probably aware that it might recall Byron's famously having swum the Hellespont, and years later he diminished Byron's feat by comparison to his own more difficult one. He concluded his comment with characteristic bravado, "I would not think much of attempting to swim the British Channel from Dover to Calais" (O 1:84).[111]

And Edgar continued to write. In his first extant manuscript, he offered an also characteristic languid sorrow:

—Poetry. By. Edgar. A. Poe—
Last night, with many cares and toils oppress'd
Weary, I laid me on a couch to rest—(M 1:6)

Allan repurposed the leaf, turning it over and marking it "Money due in July & June [1824]," reassuring himself, after some figuring, that he had thirty thousand dollars "available in any emergency."[112] Edgar's "cares and toils" at this time would have included, foremost, the loss of Mrs. Stanard, but also the weight of John Allan. Mrs. Jane Scott Mackenzie later said that "[s]he often heard him [Edgar] express the wish that he had been adopted by Mr.

Mackenzie instead of by Mr. Allan."[113] He was still struggling with Allan's severity at home. And perhaps by age fifteen, Edgar might have understood that John Allan was involved in occasional amorous improprieties. Regarding the boy's antipathy to his foster father, it may be telling that a work that Edgar then chose to declaim was a speech by Cassius to Brutus from act 1, scene 2 of Shakespeare's *Julius Caesar*.[114] It is easy to imagine Edgar intoning, with appropriate "scorn, contempt and anger," "Now in the names of all the gods at once, / Upon what meat doth this our Caesar feed / That he is grown so great?" (1.2.148–50).[115]

In late October, Edgar enjoyed a public role during the visit of General Lafayette to Richmond—he served as lieutenant of the Richmond Junior Volunteers, a group of local boys.[116] Lafayette, the hero of Yorktown at the end of the Revolutionary War, was on a farewell tour from New York (where, in Brooklyn, he kissed a baby boy named Walter Whitman) through eastern cities, including Baltimore (where he asked for his friend and supporter David Poe—Edgar's grandfather—and, learning that he had died, visited with David Poe Sr.'s widow).[117] Lafayette was received with great acclaim in Richmond, as he was everywhere.[118] Edgar's role was to help guard the marquee created in Capitol Square for the general's reception. Edgar's military group was irregular, and so, too, was Edgar: one of the boys present later remembered, "There was some trouble about the watch one night; and Edgar, the Officer of the day, to smooth matters, at the suggestion of his comrades, put the clock two hours ahead."[119] His playful expedience was clearly at odds with reliability and decorum. Still, Edgar's role in the great celebration was recognized and valued: his friend Thomas H. Ellis later wrote, "[N]ever was I prouder of him."[120]

John Allan was anything but proud of Edgar. He revealed his highly critical view in a November 1, 1824, letter to Edgar's older brother Henry. He begins by noting Henry's October 25 letter to Edgar and adding that he, Allan, is "much afflicted that [Edgar] has not written you." But, of course, only a week had passed, during which time Edgar had been occupied with the Richmond Junior Volunteers (though Allan claims he "has had little else to do" than write). Then, not mentioning his whipping Edgar, his threatening Edgar, his reminding Edgar of his dependency (and never adopting him), Allan goes on to assert, "[F]or me he does nothing & seems quite miserable, sulky & ill-tempered to all the Family. How we have acted to produce this is beyond my conception[;] why I have put up so long with his conduct is little less wonderful. The boy possesses not a spark of affection for us not a particle of gratitude for all my care and kindness towards him."[121] Allan focuses only on his own needs, not Edgar's. But he was the grown-up; he had the advantage of maturity over his foster son. And Edgar was later to write to him, "I have heard you say (when you little thought I was listening and therefore must have said it in earnest) that you had no affection for me" (O 1:10).

A bit further on in his letter to Henry, Allan adds about Edgar, "I fear his associates have led him to adopt a line of thinking & acting very contrary to what he possessed when in England." (Perhaps he was thinking, in part, of Ebenezer Burling, who, Mrs. Shelton later said, was "very intimate with Mr. Poe"; she added that the two "used to visit our house together a great deal" and that Burling was "rather inclined to dissipation.") Allan's complaint about one brother to another certainly seems unseemly. Then Allan flatters Henry by comparison to Edgar and later, mentioning "your poor Sister Rosalie," brings forth the stigmatizing attack on Eliza Poe that he must have leveled to Edgar—and against which the boy would have been unable to respond: "At least [Rosalie] is half your Sister & God forbid my dear Henry that we should visit upon the living the Errors & frailties of the dead."[122] Even if the implied accusation against Eliza Poe of an illicit affair were true, it was hardly the sort of thing that a loving foster father would bring up to his foster son—or his foster son's brother. Henry and Edgar loved their mother, but they responded to the charge against her in different ways. Henry apparently accepted it, writing in a poem about locks of hair from his father, mother, and sister, "My Rosa's! pain doth dim my eye, / When gazing on this pledge of thine—/ Thou wer't a dream—a falsity—/ Alas!—'tis wrong to call thee mine!"[123] But Edgar rejected the charge. Marie Louise Shew Houghton later acknowledged that Poe had confided to her "[t]hat it was the regret of his life, that he had not vindicated his mother to the world, as pure, as angelic and altogether lovely, as any woman could be on earth."[124] There was much about John Allan to distress Edgar, but the charge against his mother's virtue would probably have been the most intolerable of his foster father's acts. It would certainly have helped to turn the boy against him.

At the time, Edgar very likely knew nothing of John Allan's letter to Henry. He would have been more focused on his service with the Richmond Junior Volunteers during Lafayette's visit—indeed, he wrote two letters asking for permission to keep the arms that were used. (These letters are the first and second in the edition of Poe's letters [O 1:3–5].) Doubtless the year 1824 ended for Edgar with the usual Christmas celebration of the Allans and the Ellises. Presumably the families continued their tradition of an eggnog toast.

It may have been at this gathering that Edgar appropriated one of the presents, a toy snake, to scare Thomas Ellis's little sister Jane.[125]

The year 1825 was Edgar's final full year living with the Allans. It was the year of William Galt's death, John Allan's inheritance, Henry's second visit, and Edgar's presentation of a long satirical poem, for which we have a long-unknown extended account. Edgar would continue to see Elmira until he went to the university.

In March Edgar left Burke's school to prepare for the University of Virginia, which had just opened.[126] And momentously for John Allan, his devoted uncle, mentor, and patron William Galt died on March 26. The funeral was held on March 28, and "hundreds attended his remains to their last abode." Edgar may well have been among that number. Galt's will specified, for most of the estate, "an equitable distribution" among nephew Allan and Galt's two adopted sons, William Galt Jr. and James Galt. Allan inherited "three landed estates, named the 'Byrd,'" "with the slaves, stocks and property of all kinds belonging thereto."[127] Only three years earlier Allan had been arrested for indebtedness; now he was a rich man. But in all likelihood he had long expected this development. Accused of having exerted influence on Galt's writing the will to his own benefit, Allan denied the charge and stated that he would have inherited more had there been no will. Galt was reported to have considered his estate to be worth $750,000. (In 2023 dollars, that is $23,258,000. Ten years later, Edgar estimated John Allan's estate alone to be worth $750,000 [O 1:100].) And, though in 1825 Edgar probably thought of himself as heir to Allan's estate, that he would never be.[128]

On June 28, 1825, Allan paid $14,950 for "Moldavia," a home named for Molly and David Meade Randolph, who had had it built in 1800. The stately brick building, on the southeast corner of Main and Fifth Streets, had once been occupied by Joseph Gallego. And the Mackenzies lived next door. (Nancy Valentine would later write a letter to John Allan from Moldavia in which she mentioned observing through a window William Mackenzie's moving his plants on a rainy day.) Edgar had a corner room on the second floor, facing north and east; he could see the Capitol and the James River. There was a second-floor portico, on which Allan had a telescope (probably the one he had brought from England). (If there had been one at the Dubourg school when Edgar was there, then this telescope would have been his second.) Moldavia was an impressive home, commensurate with Allan's new status.[129]

The summer of 1825 was also the occasion of the second visit of older brother Henry to younger brother Edgar in Richmond. (We do not know the date of the first visit.) Henry, born in Boston like Edgar, had been brought up by his grandfather General David Poe and his grandmother Elizabeth Cairnes Poe of Baltimore. And he had been educated by his godfather, Henry Didier.[130] According to the earlier-cited comment from Edgar's October/November 1829 letter to John Neal—"There can be no tie more strong than that of brother for brother—it is not so much that they love one another, as that they both love the same parent" (O 1:47)—the two boys would have been close because of their shared love for their mother. Certainly, the boys would have discussed her; perhaps Henry, who had been nearly five when she died, would have shared his more ample memories with Edgar, who had been nearly three. Probably Henry would have discreetly relayed to his brother John Allan's caustic comments in the aforementioned November 1, 1824, letter, and Edgar would have expressed his great hostility to his foster father. And probably Edgar would have shared his poems in manuscript with Henry. Perhaps Henry then had his own literary ambitions—both brothers would publish in 1827.[131]

We know that Elmira encountered Henry: she said in an interview, "I have seen his [Edgar's] brother Henry Poe who was in the Navy."[132] Edgar and Henry may have visited her at her home. Also, Henry may have visited or stayed with Edgar at Moldavia. And we may imagine that Edgar and Henry visited their sister (or half sister) Rosalie at the Mackenzies' home, next door. But we cannot be sure of most of the boys' activities. Whatever these were, we may infer an intensity of mutual interest between the two long-separated brothers. In the future, they would both be part of the household of their aunt (David Poe Jr.'s sister) Maria Clemm in Baltimore.

John Allan continued to execute his new responsibilities, including visiting the Byrd.[133] But Edgar later stated, "The vast amount of wealth nearly turned his brain, and, worse, confirmed him in habits of habitual drunkenness" (O 1:185). Allan's wife Frances continued to be ill, with Doctor Joseph Trent visiting her frequently.[134] The Allans' niece Rosanna Dixon married William Galt Sr.'s first adopted son, William Galt Jr., on September 15.[135] And Frances remained sick: Allan reported in early October 1825, "Frank is in her old way complaining & far from being well."[136]

Edgar was writing not only the romantic poetry that would be featured in *Tamerlane* but also satirical poetry. Childhood friend R. C. Ambler remembered that Edgar, who belonged to a debating society, had written a satire of it, and the lines were "circulated in manuscript among the boys."[137] This poem is no longer extant—but another satirical poem by Edgar from this period has survived: "Oh, Tempora! Oh, Mores!" Mocking a young social climber, Edgar demonstrated his allegiance to social distinction. He was serving—or at least probably thought he was serving—his social set, for whom the perceived presumptuous fellow had become "a nuisance & an incubus."[138]

Flora Lapham Mack relates the story behind "Oh, Tempora! Oh, Mores!" as told to her "a hundred times" by John H. Mackenzie.[139] Edgar, she writes, "simply could not tolerate anything common or unclean or plebeian in his associates at this period of his life." However, one Robert Pitts, a dry goods clerk, longed for acceptance by the aristocratic young people of Richmond. He was, Mack states, "of very plebeian birth, and defective education, but the possessor of a fine person & handsome face and a great, but misdirected ambition to rise above his origin and surroundings." The young clerk worked his way into the gatherings of the privileged youth, but, Mack adds, "Edgar Poe had taken to him the most intense aversion and had determined on his downfall and banishment from the society he frequented. He declared he could not breathe in such an atmosphere." Edgar's comrades also objected to the interloper "but submitted to his enforced society more good naturedly than Poe did."[140]

Finally, as a result of a fox hunt, the unendurable would no longer be endured. Edgar and his peers usually did not see the fellow during their morning sport, for Pitts had to work and had no horse. But one day the clerk managed to get the morning off—and to secure a "hard looking jade," as well. The response to the intruder was muted. Mack relates, "Edgar Poe was at white heat, but he said not a word. The boys were indignant & felt this to be the last straw." After the hunt, Edgar called on these boys and invited them to the house of the daughter of Pitts's employer, at 6:00 p.m. for "a little fun" and sent notes to the girls inviting them there likewise "for a good time." And he invited Pitts, as well. The plan was a mystery. Edgar retreated for the afternoon—to write.[141]

He then appeared at the house, shaking hands with everyone he had invited but the unsuspecting Pitts. There was an uncertainty about the singular proceedings. Then, Mack writes, "The door bell rang, and the butler brought in a missive on a silver tray which he handed [the merchant's daughter], who excused her self, broke the seal and said 'Why this is poetry, that is in your line Edgar, here read it to us' and that played exactly into his hands and he began to read." With an inadequate firelight in a darkening room, Edgar read what he had just written.[142] And when he finished, he gave the manuscript to his friend John H. Mackenzie. Mack recalled the poem imperfectly, but her correspondent William Lanier Washington later sent her the version published in 1889 in *No Name Magazine* (subsequent to the version published in the 1868 *Southern Opinion*), and she wrote to him that this was "printed exactly as Cousin John used to repeat it" and added "I am really glad to have a perfect & correct version of the familiar old poem."[143] That version of the poem is the one that appears as the first substantial work in T. O. Mabbott's 1969 scholarly edition of Poe's poetry (M 1:9–12).[144]

The poem features eight stanzas of from eight to eighteen lines, comprising in their entirety ninety-two lines—forty-six heroic couplets (that is, each of them two rhymed lines of iambic pentameter). The title alludes to Cicero; the mocking manner echoes eighteenth-century satirical poetry, perhaps especially Samuel Butler's *Hudibras*.[145] The first half of the work is laconic; the second half offers increasingly sharp derision. In his wide traveling, the speaker says, he has never met "So pat, agreeable and vastly proper / As this for a neat, frisky counter-hopper."[146] The speaker elaborates on the clerk's opportunistic shift from shop floor to dance floor: the ambitious assistant would "Complete at night what he began A.M. / And having cheated ladies, dance with them; / For at a ball what fair one can escape / The pretty little hand that sold her tape, / Or who so cold, so callous to refuse / The youth who cut the ribbon for her shoes." Then offering false praise, the speaker subsequently focuses on the site of the clerk's thought: "Ah yes! his little foot and ankle trim, / 'Tis there the seat of reason lies in him; / A wise philosopher would shake his head, / He then, of course, must shake his foot instead" (M 1:10–12).[147] And finally the speaker moves to the poem's withering climax:

> At me in vengeance shall that foot be shaken—
> Another proof of thought, I'm not mistaken—
> Because to his cat's eyes I hold a glass
> And let him see himself a proper ass?
> I think he'll take this likeness to himself,
> But if he won't *he shall*, the stupid elf,
> And lest the guessing throw the fool in fits,
> I close the portrait with the name of *Pitts*. (M 1:12)

Mack writes in her letter to Washington, "The door opened and closed and Pitts was gone."[148]

Yes, the poem and its presentation were harsh. But if we limit our response to this, we are missing much. Edgar probably would have seen himself not only as expressing his scorn but also as protecting his coterie, as using his wit and learning to defend social distinction against exasperating and unwarranted incursion. He was part of a community, and he was standing up for it. And perhaps, as classmate J. T. L. Preston concluded, the occasional questioning of Edgar's status—for his parents' having been actors, for his dependency on John Allan—made the boy fierce. The threats and demoralizing accusations and reminders from John Allan would have contributed to the fierceness. Edgar's inclination to shield his cherished group would therefore have been all the greater. And it may be that Edgar's poem and its presentation were vital matters of self-definition. Socially insecure—and perhaps threatened by one whose tenuous status might hint at his own—Edgar may have tried to assert his belonging—and his poetic genius.[149]

The response of those present was mixed. Mack writes that the merchant, his daughter, and her friend "were very indignant and told Poe so in plain language he not caring at all for what they said. The boys thought it pretty hard treatment but were glad to be rid of the fellow on any terms." Edgar had set the terms and succeeded. Mack closes, "They were rid of him [Pitts] forever for he left Richmond next day."[150] Edgar was, in all likelihood, from his own perspective—and perhaps from that of some of the boys in the group—a champion.[151]

"Oh, Tempora! Oh, Mores!" anticipated later work by Poe, from his satirical West Point poems (represented by "Lines on Joe Locke") to such satirical fictions as the "Folio Club" introduction, "Lionizing," and "The Literary Life of Thingum Bob, Esq." It also anticipated a celebrated work of vengeance, the tale "The Cask of Amontillado," Poe's annihilation of Thomas Dunn English (M 3:1252–53). And it significantly anticipated some of Poe's most discerning reviews: while this poem disparaged a pretender to a social elite, a number of the reviews disparaged pretenders to the literary elite. Poe was committed to the defense of distinction. What was sometimes seen in his critical work as severity may also be seen as his upholding aesthetic standards. And time has tended to validate his judgments. We may readily relate his sometimes fervent critical analysis to this early poem.

As for Elmira, Edgar continued to see her; she later recalled, "Our acquaintance was kept up until he left to go to the University." Flora Lapham Mack wrote that Edgar would often visit Elmira with John H. Mackenzie and that she was "gay coquettish and very pretty." According to Mack, her stepfather asserted "[t]hat she [Elmira] was a bright laughing pretty girl & he [John H. Mackenzie] liked to go to her home with Poe with whom she was a great favorite, and that they were all real good friends."[152] But everything would soon change.

We may infer that the year 1825 closed out with Edgar continuing to prepare for the university and continuing to write. In all probability, the Allan and the Ellis families drank eggnog together on Christmas Eve. Edgar turned seventeen on January 19, 1826. And he was soon off to Charlottesville to attend Thomas Jefferson's University of Virginia, an institution now in its second year. There is some difference of opinion as to whether Edgar maintained a correspondence with Elmira. Flora Lapham Mack wrote that Elmira "always claimed that her father intercepted Edgar's letters & thinking him [Edgar] faithless and negligent she married Mr. Shelton." Indeed, Mrs. Shelton had asserted in an interview, "[D]uring the time he was at the University he wrote to me frequently, but my father intercepted the letters because we were too young—no other reason. . . . I was not aware that he wrote to me until I was married to Mr. Shelton when I was 17."[153] (Elmira married Alexander Shelton on December 6, 1828 [M 1:65].) But John H. Mackenzie had his doubts. Mack wrote, "Cousin John did not believe Edgar wrote her any letters but that he made up the story of writing them & being wounded at receiving no replies when he went courting her just before his death. Then she jumped at the conclusion that her Father who was then dead had intercepted them because he disapproved of Edgar & wished her to marry Mr. Shelton."[154] It is difficult to resolve these views; I tend to trust Mackenzie's account. What seems clear, however, is that Edgar did have a "boyish poet-love" for Elmira before he went to the university and she loved him in return. His early love for her would soon find expression in *Tamerlane*. More than twenty years later, Edgar's relationship with the widow Elmira Royster Shelton would become the cause of a major rift between John H. Mackenzie and his lifelong friend.

J. H. Whitty records that a servant (presumably one of the people enslaved by Allan) who took a letter that Edgar had written to Elmira (perhaps the only such letter), reported that "Edgar and Mrs. Allan were sad at heart the day he left for the University, and on the way Poe intimated a desire to break away from Allan, and seek his own living."[155] Edgar spent only ten months at the university; he would soon afterward achieve his wish to break away from his foster father.

Meanwhile, the new session at the university began on February 1, and Edgar matriculated on February 14.[156] He would meet the academic challenge, but Allan's inadequate financial support and his own imprudent gambling would lead to the end of his college career.

5

"Mistakes for Manhood to Reform"

1826

EDGAR MADE MANY MISTAKES AT the University of Virginia, as he would later admit. Some may have been attributable to his youthful willfulness, some to John Allan's unfortunate tight-fistedness. Of course, Allan had had uncertainty about Edgar from the beginning, when taking in the boy was only "an experiment." And he'd had growing criticism as expressed in his 1824 letter to Henry. Perhaps we should also observe Allan's having written to his partner, Charles Ellis, more generally, in 1823, "It is realy [sic] a spectacle worth contemplating to behold a Father Delving, Dredging, begrudging himself of the Comforts of Life to give his children a handsome set out in Life or make them Rich at his Death, those same children afterwards boasting of no occasion to labour[,] despising every one who does[,] born Gent[m] [Gentlemen] etc. etc. one might ask to what does all this foolerie & nonsense tend, had I begun my subject at the right end I could write for an hour on this field of boundless extent."[1] Perhaps Allan feared being taken advantage of by his foster son, who clearly considered himself a genius.

Poe later wrote to Allan that he had sent him to the university with $110 when immediate payment for board ($50) and tuition ($60) amounted to as much, and immediate payment for rent ($15), bed ($12), and furniture ($12) was another $39. Poe blamed Allan's "mistaken parsimony" and added that he wrote a letter to Allan in the first week at the university asking "for some more money, and for books," and Allan had responded "in terms of the utmost abuse," sending $40, thereby leaving him one dollar (O 1:59–60).

Though Allan disputed Poe's letter (O 1:63), there is little reason to disbelieve the financial detail. Edgar attended the classes of two professors, and, according to the advertisement for the university at the time, the cost for tuition for two professors was $30 apiece, totaling indeed $60. Board was $100, half of which was payable in advance, indeed $50.[2] And even as he had to pay the fees he enumerated, Edgar still had to buy books. So began his indebtedness during his time at the University of Virginia, and it would grow greater.

Edgar lived in Jefferson's "academical village." Facing the Lawn were two parallel lines of two-story pavilions, with varied facades, joined by one-story dormitories, the whole with protective arcades in front and termed East and West Lawn. The pavilions were for the professors, the dorms for the students. Behind these pavilions were East and West Range, facing away. These additional two parallel lines of buildings included student dorms and "hotels," or dining buildings. At the head of these parallel pavilions, on the north, was the Rotunda, to which the university's library was moved when the building was ready, during Edgar's time there. Jefferson was deeply learned in classical architecture and interested in the ideas of others also knowledgeable of the tradition. The model for the pavilions was the work of sixteenth-century classically influenced Andrea Palladio, and that for the Rotunda was Rome's renowned domed classical temple, the Pantheon. Edgar lived first in one of the Lawn rooms and moved later to 13 West Range (which is still preserved today as his room). And he certainly would have visited the library in its original location in a pavilion and later in the Rotunda.[3]

Edgar signed up for two of the schools at the university, Ancient Languages and Modern Languages. (He later wrote that "I had no means of attending the mathematical lectures" [O 1:60].) The professor for Ancient Languages was George Long; that for Modern Languages was George Blaetterman. Long's classes were held from 7:30 to 9:30 a.m. on Mondays, Wednesdays, and Fridays; Blaetterman's were held at the same time on Tuesdays, Thursdays, and Saturdays. The teaching involved mainly lectures, with exams and written work, as well. Lectures concerned Latin and Greek in the Ancient Languages class and French, Spanish, and Italian in the Modern Languages one.[4]

Nearly fifty years later, Professor Long remembered the name of Poe only slightly and therefore concluded "he could not be among the worst, and perhaps not among the best." Fellow student Robert Hunter remembered that Long had challenged those in his class to translate into English hexameter (lines with six feet, six units of meter) ten lines from satirical Roman poet Juvenal. Edgar, a capable Latinist, competed but did not win—and the student who did win was suspected by Long of plagiarism (though the professor could not prove it).[5] Here we have an early instance of the subject of plagiarism in Poe's life, a subject that would concern him repeatedly through his career.

Edgar's attendance in his Modern Languages class was recalled by a fellow student, William Wertenbaker, as "tolerably regular." Wertenbaker also remembered that Professor Blaetterman had recommended that his students translate into English lines from the Italian blank verse of Torquato Tasso's "Jerusalem Delivered" and that only Edgar had taken the prompt: "At the next lecture in Italian the professor inquired if any of the class had complied with his suggestion. No one responded but Edgar Poe, who arose from his seat and proceeded to read line after line of Tasso, translated just as he had directed. The professor expressed his regrets that no one but Poe had profited by his advice, and complimented him upon the rare poetical talent and extraordinary powers of application he had evinced by his difficult performance."[6] In future years, in the novel *Arthur Gordon Pym*, it would be Jerusalem destroyed—and the New Jerusalem prophesied—that would occupy Edgar's talent. Wertenbaker, who became librarian at the university, also remembered Edgar's seeking books that would have related to the Modern Languages class: "During the year 1826, there used to come into the Library a handsome young student, perhaps eighteen years of age, in search of old French books, principally histories: that young man, even the little I chanced to see of him, made a deep impression on me, and, in fact, I am sure I will always tenderly cherish my recollections of Edgar Allen [*sic*] Poe."[7]

Student life at the University of Virginia in its early years was characterized by drinking, gambling, fighting, and generally defying authority. Jefferson had sought to impose stronger rules in the first year, but they had not succeeded. Apparently John Allan visited Edgar at the university and later sent him clothing; Edgar, in a letter of May 26, 1826, expressed his appreciation for the clothes—"The coat is a beautiful one & fits me exactly"—and went on to describe the consequence of the latest "disturbances," which included a grand jury, a sheriff's list of sanctioned students, students retreating to the mountains, a faculty proclamation, and suspensions and expulsions. And there were also student fights (O 1:5–6).[8] There is no evidence that Edgar was involved in the widespread challenge to university authority. Indeed, Wertenbaker asserts that university records show that "at no time during the session did he fall under the censure of the Faculty."[9] Still, Edgar did sometimes succumb, sufficiently unobtrusively, to the all-too-available twin temptations, liquor and cards. But at other times he was bookish and highly imaginative.

Library records, cited by Wertenbaker, show Edgar borrowing a variety of works from June through November, including John Marshall's biography of George Washington and two volumes of Voltaire.[10] Douglas Sherley, relying on the recollection of Edgar's classmate Thomas G. Tucker, wrote that the two young men spent time in the library "engaged in reading the histories of Lingard and Hume; while to them the whole field of English poetry from Chaucer to Scott was perfectly familiar."[11] Edgar also requested a copy of Tacitus from John Allan (O 1:6), presumably for his class in Ancient Languages. Peter Pindar Pease, an assistant in a harness-making shop in Charlottesville, remembered that Edgar visited the shop and wanted to purchase a book of Hogarth prints, for which the young clerk was paying installments. The work of the satirical artist would naturally have appealed to the sometimes satirical poet. Edgar invited Pease to his room with the book and there proposed gambling for it—if Pease won the toss of the dice, Edgar would pay for it, but if Edgar won the toss, Pease would pay for it and give it to him. Edgar lost the toss and somehow paid for the book.[12] Another book purchase worked out better. Fellow student Thomas Bolling later recalled that he and Edgar bought "a beautiful copy of Byron." The celebrated British Romantic poet was a model for Edgar, as he later acknowledged in a letter to Allan (O 1:30). Doubtless the young American Romantic poet expected that he would awake one morning and find himself famous. Attracted in particular by the engravings, Edgar made a crayon copy of one of them on the ceiling. He eventually drew profusely throughout the room, and Bolling and others considered the images "more ornamental and attractive than any fresco."[13]

Of course, Edgar's creative work at the university also involved writing poetry and fiction. Classmate James A. Clarke remembered, "The first poetic effusion I knew Poe to write was suggested by some trouble occurring between Poe and a roommate. It was written and posted in a conspicuous place, and I remember the incident as clearly as if it happened yesterday." (The incident was probably the "boyish freak," the "mere boyish affair," recalled by Edgar's pugilistic opponent [though not his roommate], Miles George.)[14] Bolling remembered that Edgar would challenge himself intellectually, "trying to see if he could divide his mind, carry on Conversation, and write sense on a different subject." Bolling states that Edgar would "reply to the point" even as he wrote; the impressed former classmate adds, "several times on such occasions, [Edgar] handed me some verses he had written, and all I remember about them, they rhymed pretty well."[15]

Douglass Sherley wrote that Thomas G. Tucker recalled that Edgar would read to him "those early productions of his youth—productions that his critical hand afterwards destroyed, thinking them unfit for publication." Edgar would occasionally read to others, as well, at 13 West Range, pieces that Tucker had particularly lauded—"mostly stories and characterized by that same weirdness of style, graphically picturing horrible scenes and incidents, that so strongly marks all of his published writings." Sherley recounted Tucker's memory of an incident that reveals Edgar's abiding sensitivity:

> On one occasion Poe read a story of great length to some of his friends, who, in a spirit of jest, spoke lightly of its merits and jokingly told him that his hero's name, Gaffy, occurred too often. His proud spirit would not stand such, as he thought, open rebuke; so in a fit of anger, before his friends could prevent him, he had flung every sheet into a blazing fire, and thus was lost a story of more than ordinary parts, and, unlike the most of his stories, was intensely amusing, entirely free from his usual somber coloring and sad conclusions merged in a mist of impenetrable gloom. He was for a long time afterwards called by those in his particular circle "Gaffy" Poe, a name that he never altogether relished.[16]

And Edgar could readily shift from reading his writing aloud to drawing on the walls. Miles George, who visited Edgar in both his West Lawn and West Range rooms, remembered "many happy hours spent therein" and added, "Poe ... was fond of quoting poetic authors and reading poetic productions of his own, with which his friends were delighted & entertained, then suddenly a change would come over him & he would with a piece of charcoal evince his versatile genius by sketching upon the walls of his dormitory, whimsical, fanciful & grotesque figures, with so much artistic skill, as to leave us in doubt whether Poe in future life would be Painter or Poet."[17] The very strong visual quality of Poe's writing reflects his early talent in drawing.

Edgar's demeanor fluctuated—George recalled that "He was very excitable & restless, at times wayward, melancholic & morose, but again—in his better moods frolicksome, full of fun & a most attractive and agreeable companion." Evidently the naturally buoyant manner of his boyhood was sometimes overcome by sadness—we can imagine his thinking of the death of his mother or the death of Mrs. Stanard or the oppressive disapproval of John Allan. To Bolling, there seemed to be an inaccessibility about him: "My impression was and is that no one could say he *knew* him. He wore, I may say, a sad, melancholy face always, and even a smile, for I don't remember his ever having laughed heartily, seemed to be forced." Poe participated well in athletic contests—running and leaping in one instance twenty feet—but without enthusiasm: "Poe, with that same sad face, appeared to participate, in what was amusement to others, more as a task." He could seem to his professors "sober, quiet and orderly," with the "deportment" of "an intelligent and polished gentleman," but some of his classmates could see intimations of a darker side.[18]

Intensifying his sadness were his money concerns. Classmate Henry Tutwiler wrote, "I only knew him as belonging to a set of students who were regarded as somewhat wild and dissipated." Poe later acknowledged as much in his January 3, 1831, West Point letter to John Allan. He maintained there that Allan's inadequate support led him to borrow money, for not only did he need books, but also, "I was obliged to hire a servant, to pay for wood, for washing, and a thousand other necessaries. It was then that I became dissolute, for how could it be otherwise?" (O 1:60). Remarkably, Poe alludes, consciously or not, to a book that Allan had sent him at the university and later deprecated, Alain René Le Sage's comic novel *Gil Blas,* the first volume of which, as a cadet, Poe read or reread under Professor Claudius Berard.[19] Gil Blas writes about the time he spent with a group of profligate actors, "I was shocked at their faults, but unhappily too well pleased with their way of life; so that I plunged into debauchery. How could it be otherwise?"[20]

Poe elaborated in his letter to Allan, "I could associate with no students, except those who were in a similar situation with myself—altho' from different causes—They from drunkenness, and extravagance—I, because it was my crime to have no one on Earth who cared for me, or loved me." And he went on to defend himself: "I call God to witness that I have never loved dissipation—Those who know me know that my pursuits and habits are very far from any thing of the kind. But I was drawn into it by my companions[.] Even their professions of friendship—hollow as they were—were a relief" (O 1:60). It was drinking that Edgar yielded to—and gambling. And it was gambling that ended his time at the university.

William Wertenbaker reported that "He at no time was addicted to drinking" and stated, "He certainly was not habitually intemperate but he may occasionally have entered into a frolic. I often saw him in the Lecture room and in the Library, but never in the slightest degree under the influence of intoxicating liquors."[21] Others discussed what Wertenbaker characterized as "a frolic." Miles George wrote that Edgar drank "[t]o calm and quiet the excessive nervous excitability under which he labored."[22] Thomas G. Tucker noted that "It was not the *taste* of the beverage that influenced him; without a sip or smack of the mouth he would seize a full glass, without water or sugar, and send it home at a single gulp. This frequently used him up; but if not, he rarely returned to the charge."[23] Of course, drinking itself at the University of Virginia in the early years was altogether typical. Professor Long, though he could not recall Edgar distinctly, did remember that "Drinking was the common vice."[24] And, likewise, as Sherley writes, relying on Tucker, "Gaming during the first two or three sessions of the University was very prevalent."[25] It was Edgar's intensity that was striking.

Wertenbaker asserted that while at the university Edgar "had an ungovernable passion for card-playing" and "his practice of gaming did escape detection." Douglass Sherley, relying on Edgar's classmate Thomas G. Tucker, maintained, "Poe was also particularly fond of playing cards—seven-up and loo being his favorite games. He played in such an impassioned manner as to amount to almost an actual frenzy. All of his card playing and drinking he did under a sudden impulse." And he later added, "he could play cards and drink *peach and honey* for hours with those who were thrown in his way by matter of circumstance." Classmate William M. Burwell wrote, "The particular dissipation of the university at this period was gaming with cards, and into this Poe plunged with a recklessness of nature which acknowledge [*sic*] no restraint."[26] Poe's eponymous character William Wilson, from the 1839 short story, in some ways resonates with Edgar, but in some ways serves as an alter-Edgar—that is, he is a gambler who cheats and inevitably wins. Yet in imagining how Wilson's friends mistakenly thought of the young swindler, Poe may have been idealizing his remembered self as an impassioned cardplayer: "the gay, the frank, the generous William Wilson—the noblest and most liberal commoner at Oxford—him whose follies (said his parasites) were but the follies of youth and unbridled fancy—whose errors but inimitable whim—whose darkest vice but a careless and dashing extravagance" (M 2:440). Edgar's "careless and dashing extravagance" during his student days at the University of Virginia would lead to immense financial losses and the end of his stay there.

Midway through Edgar's ten months at the university, its founder and rector, Thomas Jefferson, died. The date was, appropriately enough, July 4, 1826. (John Adams died on the same date, shortly afterward.) We do not know whether Edgar had met Jefferson, but Andrew K. Smith wrote, "Among the students present at the funeral, I recollect seeing Edgar A. Poe, a high-minded and honorable young man, though easily persuaded to his wrong."[27] Poe did later indirectly honor Jefferson. In his March 19, 1827, letter to John Allan on leaving his house, he seems to echo, through his iteration of Allan's offenses (O 1:10–11), Jefferson's listing of King George III's offenses in the Declaration of Independence.[28] And though Poe would allegorically disparage the development of American democracy as run by the despot "*Mob*" in his 1845 satire "Some Words with a Mummy," he praised the founding of the United States: "Thirteen Egyptian provinces determined all at once to be free, and so set a magnificent example to the rest of mankind. They assembled their wise men, and concocted the most ingenious constitution it is possible to conceive. For a while they managed remarkably well" (M 3:1194).

Perhaps also during the summer of 1826 Edgar would have hiked through the Ragged Mountains, southwest of Charlottesville.[29] He would later draw on this region for his evocative 1844 work "A Tale of the Ragged Mountains," in which a doctor's writing induces his patient's mesmeric trance. And it would seem that Edgar would later draw on his newspaper reading of this time. On July 15, 1826, the *Saturday Evening Post* featured a poem by John Lofland, "The Bride," which opens, "I saw her on the bridal day," perhaps anticipating the first line in Poe's 1827 poem "Song," "I saw thee on thy bridal day." And on the same date, a Charlottesville newspaper, the *Central Gazette,* offered a prize-winning poem by Lydia Sigourney, "Greece," which begins "Hail holy clime! Where science rear'd her throne," perhaps anticipating the first line of Poe's 1831 poem "The Doomed City" (later "The City in the Sea"), "Lo! Death hath rear'd himself a throne."[30]

On September 21, 1826, Edgar wrote the second of two extant letters to John Allan from the University of Virginia. Perhaps this was the point at which he'd begun his "reformation": he wrote in his angry January 3, 1831, West Point letter, "Had you let me return [to the university], my reformation had been sure—as my conduct the last 3 months gave every reason to believe—and you would never have heard more of my extravagances" (O 1:59). Edgar's concern in September was clearly the coming examination. He stated, "I have been studying a great deal in order to be prepared, and dare say I shall come off as well as the rest of them, that is—if I don't get frightened" (O 1:8). The examination was held between December 4 and 15. Those from the university's Board of Visitors who were present were James Madison, James Monroe, John H. Cocke, Chapman Johnson, and Joseph C. Cabell. The exam was written rather than oral.[31] And Edgar did very well—he was listed in both Latin and French as one of the students "who excelled."[32]

But despite his academic success, he was doomed by what he would later term his "infamous conduct" (O 1:20). It was already too late.

In December 1826, Edgar not only took his exam but also bought some clothing and, later in the month, testified to the university faculty that he had no knowledge of "hotel keepers playing cards or drinking with students."[33] There was, however, he later acknowledged, some backsliding during his "reformation": he wrote in his January 3, 1831, letter to Allan that the hundred dollars that his foster father had provided toward the end of his time at the university was insufficient "to be of any service in extricating me from my difficulties," that James Galt had turned down a request for funds, and that "I then became desperate, and gambled—until I finally i[n]volved myself irretrievably" (O 1:60). Poe wrote to Allan in 1829, "I never meant to offer a shadow of excuse for the infamous conduct of myself & others at that place"—but then added, "I say again I have no excuse to offer for my [con]duct except the common one of youth[fulnes]s" (O 1:20). The later angry West Point letter would make clear that he blamed Allan's inadequate funding and his own dissolute companions. Doubtless these were all views that he held at one time or another—but the evidence closest to the time suggests self-reproach. His classmate William Wertenbaker, who was with Edgar in his room at the university on his final night there, recalled, "[H]e spoke with regret of the amount of money he had wasted and the debts he had contracted during the session." These debts totaled $2,000. Another source suggests they may have been as much as $2,500.[34] The 2023 equivalent for $2,000 in 1826 is more than $62,000 and for $2,500 more than $77,000—in each case, an exorbitant amount of money.[35] Regret may have been very difficult for Edgar to express to his accusatory foster father, but he could confide it to a sympathetic fellow student. The later public record, on the other hand, seemed to require a degree of shading. In the 1843 *Saturday Museum* biography of Poe, written by Poe and Henry B. Hirst—or by Poe alone—there is acknowledgment of "a natural disgust" growing out of the young man's dissoluteness at the university—but nowhere does the piece admit regret—or guilt—or shame.[36] And certainly the heavy blame he would experience from Allan and those back in Richmond would probably diminish considerably any willingness Edgar might have had to admit it himself.

Jane Scott Mackenzie said of Allan, according to Flora Lapham Mack, "He had never regarded him [Edgar] as a son tho' Mrs. Allen [sic] tried hard to make him do so but the final straw that 'broke the camel's back[']' was those university debts. Mr. Allen never pretended to care for him at all after that time."[37] Edgar had told William Wertenbaker that "though they were gaming debts, he was earnest and emphatic in the declaration, that he was bound by honor to pay at the earliest opportunity, every cent of them."[38] And according to Poe in his January 3, [1831], West Point letter to Allan, "You would not let me return because bills were presented you for payment which I never wished nor desired you to pay" (O 1:59). However, Mrs. Mackenzie said, according to Mack, that "Edgar resented most bitterly the fact that Mr. Allan had refused to pay his debts of honor as he called them. He used to rave about it at my house and say that nothing mattered now, his future was blighted and he had to go through life with the stigma of this disgrace attached to his name and then he would abuse Mr. Allan calling him a parsimonious dotard."[39] At forty-seven, Allan was no dotard, but he does seem to have been parsimonious. Probably, considering Allan's wealth, Edgar did want his financial help in getting out from under his overwhelming debt—though his own reckless gambling had precipitated it.

Edgar's inadequate funding at the university was not part of the story that was told of him in Richmond. Poe later wrote to Allan in his January 3, 1831, letter, "These circumstances were all unknown to my friends when I returned home—They knew I had been extravagant—but that was all" (O 1:60). He went on, "I had no hope of returning to Charlottesville, and I waited in vain in expectation that you would, at least, obtain me some employment" (O 1:60–61). He made this same point earlier, in the March 19, 1827, letter declaring his independence: "You . . . are continually upbraiding me with eating the bread of Idleness, when you yourself were the only person to remedy the evil by placing me to some business" (O 1:10). (T. H. Ellis later wrote that Edgar worked in the Ellis & Allan counting room; if this is true, Edgar was probably not paid.)[40] Edgar's treatment in front of others in Richmond was especially galling: "You take delight in exposing me before those whom you think likely to advance my interest in this world." And Edgar added, "You suffer me to be subjected to the whims & caprice, not only of your white family, but the complete authority of the blacks" (O 1:10–11). The prodigal son had returned to an unforgiving foster father.

This was a troubled time for Edgar. Allan had paid some of his debts, but others, including the gambling debts, remained.[41] And clearly Edgar's path to professional success was cut off. The young man wrote to Allan, "Since I have been able to think on any subject, my thoughts have aspired, and they have been taught by *you* to aspire, to eminence in public life—this cannot be attained without a good Education, such a one I cannot obtain at a Primary school—A collegiate Education therefore was what I most ardently desired, and I had been led to expect that it would at some future time be granted—but in a moment of caprice—you have blasted my hope because forsooth I disagreed with you in an opinion, which opinion I was forced to express" (O 1:10). What that opinion was we do not know, but we may guess that it was Edgar's reluctant expression of a fault with his foster father. Edgar clearly aspired to literary eminence, but what he had at this time was general disgrace. He later wrote to Allan of "how much I had to suffer upon my return from the University," "the taunts & abuse that followed it [his conduct] even from those who had been my warmest friends" (O 1:20).

Edgar spent some time at Allan's Byrd Plantation. It does seem that he wrote notes to a young woman who was visiting Mrs. Juliet J. Drew.[42] Perhaps he briefly saw Elmira Royster—T. O. Mabbott speculates that Edgar was at a party celebrating her engagement to Alexander B. Shelton (M 1:65). And, presumably, although humiliated and angry at his position and situation, Edgar continued to work on his poetry.

According to one account about Edgar at the Allan home at this time, when he overheard Frances Allan tell of his extravagant spending and his gambling at the university, Edgar appeared and remarked, "I went to college to see how much of the old man's money I could spend, and I have done it."[43] If this account is true, then it would seem that the proud, angry young man was hiding his earlier expressed regret for his out-of-control gambling and the consequent losses by suggesting a deliberate vengefulness as his motive for having gone to the University of Virginia in the first place. Such a motive for the intellectually ambitious Edgar would have been manufactured for the bitter situation. In later years, Poe would again occasionally revise matters after the fact to make his failure seem like cunning (as with regard to the October 1845 Boston Lyceum episode). Of particular interest in this account is Edgar's having allegedly referred to Allan as "the old man." Frances Allan had used this epithet affectionately in an October 1818 letter ("dear old man").[44] But Allan (born September 10, 1779) would have been only thirty-nine years old in October 1818 and only forty-seven years old in early 1827. Poe's applying to Allan the phrase "old man" may be relevant to our later consideration of Poe's short story "The Tell-Tale Heart," which repeatedly refers to the "old man" (O 3:792–96).

A notable event took place in Richmond in early March 1827, one that Edgar might have attended and about which he certainly would have heard. Jeremiah N. Reynolds, the young disciple of John Cleves Symmes (the advocate of the hollow Earth theory), gave a public lecture on March 2. One newspaper provided this engaging announcement:

> *Mr. Reynolds.*—This highly intelligent gentleman, by permission of the Speaker, lectures this evening in the Hall of Delegates, on what is popularly called, Symmes' Theory of the Earth. We have the pleasure of a personal acquaintance with Mr. Reynolds, and we confidently promise high gratification to those who may attend. His philosophy, sustained by many profound arguments, has made converts of many of the soundest and most unimaginative heads in the United States, and shaken the incredulity of all who have heard of him.[45]

Reynolds later gave three additional lectures.[46] He had—by contrast with Edgar's own disgrace—the much-sought eminence. We will later see Poe praising Reynolds in the *Southern Literary Messenger* and mentioning him and relying on his work in *The Narrative of Arthur Gordon Pym*. And when Poe lay dying, he called the name "Reynolds."

During his time at home in Richmond in 1827 Edgar would have continued reading. Of particular note is that the *Richmond Enquirer* of March 13, 1827, included the poem "Stanzas on a View of the Sea," for its line "Thy sandy shore is like a jewelled sky"[47] may have later influenced Poe's writing in his classic "Sonnet—To Science" about the poet "wandering / To seek for treasure in the jewelled skies" (M 1:91).

Meanwhile, Edgar's situation with John Allan was becoming intolerable, and, finally, on March 18 and 19, the inevitable blowup took place. In his Declaration of Independence letter, beginning, "Sir," Edgar writes, "After my treatment on yesterday and what passed between us this morning, I can hardly think you will be surprised at the contents of this letter. My determination is at length taken—to leave your house and indeavor [*sic*] to find some place in this wide world, where I will be treated—not as *you* have treated me." Then follow the grievances against Allan, including that he had denied Edgar a college education, that he had confided to another that he did not love his foster son, that he had blamed Edgar for not working but provided no employment, that he had humiliated Edgar in front of others, and that he had permitted Edgar's subordination to others. (He does not mention Allan's not having paid his gambling debts, though he would later do so in a not-always-reliable memorandum to Rufus Wilmot Griswold [H 1:345].) Edgar states in his letter to Allan, "[T]hese grievances I could not submit to; and I am gone." Doubtless this was just the result that Allan desired. Edgar asks for his trunk and some money: "As the last cal[l] I shall make on your bounty, To prevent the fulfillment of the Prediction you this morning expressed, send me as much money as will defray the expences [sic] of my passage to some of the Northern cit[i]es & then support me for one month." What was that "Prediction"? Perhaps Allan saw only poverty and failure for Edgar. The young man expresses his intention to work and to save and to return to the university. He closes, "If you fail to comply with my request—I tremble for the consequence." He adds, in a postscript, "It depends upon yourself if hereafter you see or hear from me" (O 1:10–11).

Beginning likewise, "Sir," Allan responds to his foster son by recalling his "parental solicitude & affection over your tender years," contending that "Don Quixote, Gil Blas, Jo: Miller & such works" do not make possible "eminence in Public Life" and that his goal was "to urge you to perseverance & industry in receiving the classics, in perfecting yourself in the mathematics, mastering the French etc." Perhaps at the heart of Allan's objection was Edgar's sense of himself: "For one who had conceived so good an opinion of himself & his future intentions I hesitate not to say, that you have not evinced the smallest disposition to comply with my wishes." (Of course, Allan is not mentioning Edgar's having achieved academic excellence at the university in both Latin and French.) Probably alluding to his foster son's susceptibility to drinking and gambling, Allan contends that he "had good reason to fear for you, in more ways than one." He adds, "I should have been justly chargeable, in reprimanding you for faults had I had any other object than to correct them." And he closes with mockery: "Your list of grievances require no answer the world will reply to them—& now that you have shaken off your dependence & declared for your own Independence—& after such a list of Black charges—you Tremble for the consequences unless I send you a supply of money."[48] There is not only a lack of sympathy here but also what seems a self-righteous disdain.

Edgar wrote on March 20, as well—he has not received his trunk or any money. He declares, "I am in the greatest necessity, not having tasted food since Yesterday morning. I have no where to sleep at night, but roam about the Streets—I am nearly exhausted." He asks for his trunk and the loan of money so he can make his way to Boston. He closes, "Give my love to all at home—" and adds after his signature, "I have not one cent in the world to provide any food." "Pretty Letter," Allan writes on the reverse of the pitiful plea (O 1:12–13). Former Richmond mayor Joseph Mayo later told John R. Thompson "that public sentiment at the time of the unfortunate occurrence was strongly in favor of Poe, and the impression prevailed in the community that he had been harshly dealt with."[49]

On Saturday, March 24, 1827—we may imagine with his trunk and some money from some source—Edgar voyaged to Norfolk and then north, ultimately bound for the city of his birth. We do not know exactly the vessel that Edgar took or the schedule that it followed. Perhaps he began on a coal vessel.[50] He may well have traveled partway with his friend Ebenezer Burling. Burling is mentioned in the 1843 *Saturday Museum* essay, written by Poe and Hirst or by Poe alone, but then the piece veers to Poe's made-up tale of travel to Greece and Russia.[51] Flora Lapham Mack later writes, "He [Edgar] was never Cousin John [John H. Mackenzie] declared too far away to be the beneficiary of all the help Mrs. Allan & Miss Nancy Valentine could give him until he came home from Fortress Monroe a few days after Mrs. Allan's funeral [in March 1829]. The story [of his travel abroad] was all false and born of his imagination."[52] But John Allan speculated on March 27, "I'm thinking Edgar has gone to sea to seek his fortune." And Allan identifies him as "alias Henri Le Rennet."[53]

There is a possibility that Edgar briefly stopped in Baltimore—after all, his brother Henry lived there. Henry had already begun his publishing career, with such poems as "Jacob's Dream" and "Psalm 139th" appearing in the *Saturday Evening Post*.[54] It may have been at this time that Edgar wrote a short composite poem in the album of Margaret Bassett, of Baltimore—the work, titled "To Margaret," comprises humorous transformations of classic lines (M 1:14–16). He wrote out another poem in the album of Octavia Walton, who seems to have been visiting Baltimore at the time, but the poem was not by Poe but by Horace Smith.[55]

According to one source, by late March Edgar was in Boston.[56] Perhaps he was seeking there the consolation of an association with his mother, who had given him her watercolor of Boston Harbor in 1808, inscribed, "For my little son Edgar, who should ever love Boston, the place of his birth, and where his mother found her *best,* and *most sympathetic* friends."[57] He probably had the watercolor with him. And he would have had, as well, a sheaf of his poems. He wanted his first book published—he wanted to prove his genius.

# 6
"Abroad on the Wide Earth"
1827

IT WAS NINETEEN YEARS SINCE Eliza Poe had painted *Boston Harbour Morning 1808*. In late March or early April 1827, her eighteen-year-old son Edgar Allan Poe returned to the city of his birth by way of Boston Harbor. Remaining about eight months, young Poe struggled in the commercial world, then joined the army, serving at Fort Independence, at the mouth of the harbor. Though certain of his genius, he was uncertain of his future. He wrote in an untitled poem soon to appear in his first book, *Tamerlane and Other Poems:*

> A wilder'd being from my birth
>   My spirit spurn'd control,
> But now, abroad on the wide earth,
>   Where wand'rest thou my soul? (M 1:80)

Arriving in Boston, Poe would have seen a bustling harbor of sailing vessels (by contrast to the relatively still harbor of anchored vessels during the Jefferson Embargo [1807–9]). At the center of the array of wharves were Long Wharf and Central Wharf. Slightly to the right of these was the newly expanded Faneuil Hall, by then including Quincy Market. Up State Street from Long Wharf, at Washington Street, was the Old State House, and beyond was Common Street (today Tremont Street), which led left to the Boston Common. Up Park Street from Common Street was the commanding domed State House. Alternatively, up Milk Street from Central Wharf was the Federal Street Theatre, where Poe's mother and father had performed. Boston was dense and, surely for this young stranger, daunting.[1]

Peter Pindar Pease, with whom Poe had thrown dice for a volume of Hogarth prints back in Charlottesville, was, remarkably enough, working on the waterfront in Boston when he saw "a pale, rather stoop-shouldered clerk, emerging from a mercantile house hard by." It was Poe. Avoiding a public greeting, "Poe hurriedly pushed him [Pease] into an alleyway and begged him not to speak his name aloud, giving for his reason that 'he had left home to seek his fortune, and until he had hit it hard he preferred to remain incognito.'" Poe appeared "very tired" and though "very poorly clad was scrupulously neat." He briefly related his troubles in Boston: his employer at a "wholesale merchandise house," "a man of brutal and unscrupulous character," had largely avoided paying him; his landlady, unimpressed with his writing at night, had thrown him out; his subsequent employer, the owner of an "obscure paper" and "a man of shady reputation," had incurred debt and ended the enterprise. Poe had decided to join the army since "his resources were utterly exhausted, and he was determined not to write to former friends for help."[2] He was, evidently, much buffeted but proud and perhaps bitter. Poe would hide this period of his life, preferring the romantic fiction that he had gone off to fight in Greece and later gotten into trouble in St. Petersburg.[3] But he would later admit to Pease that at this time in Boston "he felt desperate enough to 'do anything except cut his throat.'"[4]

Thomas H. Ellis asserted that Poe had performed in Boston in 1827: "The occasional letters which he wrote home were dated 'St. Petersburg', but were written while he was on the stage in Boston, or an enlisted soldier in the Army."[5] It is possible that Poe appeared onstage there, but there is no conclusive evidence.[6] However, it seems very likely that he would have visited the Federal Street Theatre. Perhaps, too, he would have visited Washington Gardens, a site for indoor and outdoor entertainment on Common Street, north of West Street—also the site of the Usher mansion.[7] What we can be sure of is that sometime before May 26 (when he enlisted), Poe met with the printer Calvin F. S. Thomas. Through Thomas, the aspiration that had been denied in Richmond in 1820 would be fulfilled. Poe would publish his first book.

Thomas himself was a young man, only nineteen years old. His office was upstairs at 70 Washington Street, at the corner of State Street, up from Faneuil Hall, near the Old State House. Although Poe may have had connections that led him to Thomas, it seems likelier that he would have just come upon him at so central a location. And the block, like the street, was a bastion of print. Next door, at 72 Washington Street, was the bookstore of Bowles & Dearborn, above which were the offices of the *Christian Examiner.* At 74 Washington Street were the offices of the *North American Review* and the *United States Review and Literary Gazette.* Poe may well have looked for employment at such places. Perhaps, too, he ventured across the street to 79 Washington Street to visit the booksellers Robert P. and Charles Williams, as well as the bookseller Jonathan P. Peaslee. Thomas's advertisement at the back of Poe's little book elaborates the nature of his work:

> Printing.
> CALVIN F. S. THOMAS
> CONTINUES TO EXECUTE
> BOOK & JOB PRINTING
> IN ALL ITS BRANCHES,
> INCLUDING
> Books, Pamphlets, Catalogues, Cards,
> Show Bills, etc. etc.
> ON THE MOST REASONABLE TERMS

We may imagine Poe's entering Thomas's shop hopefully, with a slender sheaf or portfolio of poems. We do not know the terms of the printing; we know only that Poe and Thomas came to terms. *Tamerlane and Other Poems* would appear in June or July 1827.[8]

Meanwhile, Poe was struggling to make a living. He had confided to Pease that he would join the army because "his resources were utterly exhausted," and Colonel James House of the First Artillery confirms this, stating in an 1829 letter that Poe "became reduced to the necessity of enlisting into the service and accordingly entered as a soldier in my Regiment, at Fort Independence in 1827."[9] Poe's enlistment was on May 26, 1827, perhaps at Broad Street, close to Rowes Wharf, and the would-be incognito Poe enlisted as "Edgar A. Perry" (a name perhaps drawn, as has been suggested, from a former University of Virginia classmate, Sidney A. Perry). He claimed he was twenty-two years old and gave his birthplace as Boston, his occupation as clerk, his height as five feet eight inches, his eyes as gray, his hair as brown, and his complexion as fair. He joined Battery H of the First Artillery at Fort Independence on Castle Island. He later omitted mention of his time in the army, but his new position at least afforded him a means of survival.[10]

As Private Perry, Poe had descended dramatically in social status. Other soldiers at his rank wouldn't have had anything like his upbringing or education.

"Abroad on the Wide Earth" · 83

Fortunately, by July 1 Poe was made company clerk, managing paperwork and relaying messages. And apparently Colonel House, who had once been a portrait painter and was devoted to literature, was relatively lenient as a disciplinarian.[11] Furthermore, though he may have found much routine in army life, Private Perry had a private solace: the publication of *Tamerlane*.

It was a small book, not quite six and a half inches by not quite four and a half inches—a duodecimo with just twenty leaves, forty pages. Scholars have estimated that forty to two hundred copies were printed, probably priced at 12½ cents apiece. (Today there are only twelve extant copies; the little volume is widely considered the ultimate American literary treasure.) The title on the front wrapper and the title page, "Tamerlane and Other Poems," is followed by the then-opaque phrase "By a Bostonian." Poe had been born in Boston and had returned to Boston and probably sought the favor of Boston readers and critics. And as he had acknowledged to Pease, he was not ready to reveal himself. The book's epigraph, William Cowper's couplet "Young heads are giddy, and young hearts are warm, / And make mistakes for manhood to reform," intimates both tender age and poignant error (M 1:21).[12]

The preface claims that the poems "were written in the year 1821–2" (M 1:21), but they were probably of a somewhat later date—T. O. Mabbott suggests, plausibly, 1825 to 1827. Poe declares that the short poems "perhaps savour too much of Egotism" and that "Tamerlane" reveals "the folly of even *risking* the best feelings of the heart at the shrine of Ambition" (M 1:21–22). The Poe scholar Paul Lewis rightly notes that Poe diminishes Ambition in fulfilling his Ambition. The poet states that even if his book fails, he will follow a "resolution already adopted"—to pursue his literary vocation. He closes, "This is challenging criticism—let it be so. *Nos haec novimus esse nihil* [I myself know the unimportance of all this]" (M 1:22; for the translation, see M 1:21). The Latin tag offers both self-protective self-deprecation and an assertion of privilege. And so Poe began his literary ascent.[13]

The title poem, "Tamerlane," adapts the dark Romanticism of Lord Byron (perhaps especially that in "Manfred" and "The Giaour") for Poe's autobiographical purposes. The eponymous hero lies on his deathbed confessing to a friar what seems an allegory of Poe's young life. Tamerlane acknowledges his long-felt sense of "self supremacy": "The soul which feels its innate right—/ The mystic empire and high power / Giv'n by the energetic might / Of Genius, at its natal hour" (M 1:32). He recalls that early on he knew "the lovely summer sun / Of our boyhood" (M 1:39), but a poisonous "mountain dew" (M 1:28) disturbed his innocence, and Ambition came to dominate. Yet there was a woman—"I have no words, alas! To tell / The lovliness of loving well" (M 1:29). Indeed, he states, "I saw no Heav'n, but in her eyes" (M 1:30). Furthermore, the "kindling thought" of ambition might have passed had not "the beam / of Beauty, which did guide it through / The livelong summer day, oppress / My mind with double loveliness" (M 1:33). In these varied lines we seem to have both Elmira Royster and Jane Stith Stanard (who, in "A Dream," "Hath cheered me as a lovely beam / A lonely spirit guiding" [M 1:79]). Tamerlane speaks to his beloved Ada (presumably Myra)—but obscurely—"of power and pride" (M 1:33). And he imagines his great triumphs and his returning, a conqueror, to take her as his queen. So he forsakes her to follow his "high fate" (M 1:34), to seek "fame" and "glory" (M 1:27, 35). Here we have a rough allegory of Poe's past—or at least of Poe's Romantic idea of his past. He conveys his sense of his own genius, his life in nature, his young love and wise guidance, and his aspiring, above all. Then, Poe elaborates an allegory of his future. With both fame and glory attained—as well as "shame" (M 1:27)—Tamerlane returns home, "my home no more," to find his beloved "long dead" and himself heartbroken (M 1:39). Having chosen to follow what Tamerlane terms "the fickle star within" (M 1:30), Poe meditates on the choice he has made. He offers a slight consolation in a note—the "day flower" that dies at night "lives again in the morning" (M 1:39n). Still, the tone of the close is preponderantly melancholy. Poe has lent a tragic and darkly Romantic cast to the as-yet unknown consequences of his life so far.

However, the caution so earnestly offered by Tamerlane is belied by Poe's having written "Tamerlane." His allegiance was, and always would be, to follow his "high fate." He even comments in the poem (and in a note) on how difficult it was for people to recognize the greatness of one whom they know (M 1:34–35). Perhaps it was satisfying for Poe, in "Tamerlane," to explore regret—maybe even displaced regret. But his "boyish poet-love" (M 3:1122) was behind him. We may recall that John H. Mackenzie thought that Poe had never written Elmira any letters from the university.[14] As Poe in all likelihood had written, in "To Myra," "Glory alone my soul shall woo, / And fame shall be my only bride."

"Tamerlane" is followed by nine "Fugitive Pieces." The first, "To — —," begins, "I saw thee on thy bridal day," recalling the 1826 John Lofland piece beginning, "I saw her on the bridal day." The two blanks of the title, Mabbott conjectures, represent "Elmira Royster." Though Elmira did not marry Alexander B. Shelton until December 6, 1828, the poem may concern, Mabbott speculates, Elmira's engagement party (M 1:65–67).[15] The poem "Dreams" honors

Poe's visionary boyhood—"For I have revell'd when the sun was bright / In the summer sky, in dreams of living light."[16] Here is Poe in a Wordsworthian tone. By contrast, "Visit of the Dead" (M 1:71–72) is a sepulchral meditation, resonant of the Incantation of Byron's "Manfred" and perhaps suggestive of Poe's boyhood visits to the grave of his beloved Jane Stith Stanard.[17] With "The Evening Star," as has rightly been observed, Poe is in dialogue with Thomas Moore's "When Gazing on the Moon's Light"; the American poet prefers the warm light of Venus to the cold light of the moon. This slight poem anticipates the later mournful masterpiece "Ulalume," in which the warmth of Astarte is preferred to the cold of Dian.[18]

The lines in Poe's poem "Imitation," "With a wild, and waking thought / Of beings that have been" (M 1:75), suggest lines from Byron's "The Dream," and, as Mabbott notes, the debt to Byron clarifies the poem's title (M 1:76). The sense of "mystery" about Poe's "early life" seems to foreshadow "The mystery which binds me still" (M 1:146) in Poe's similarly Byron-inflected 1829 poem "From Childhood's Hour," known as "[Alone]." We may conjecture Edgar's early dark responsiveness emerging after the death of his mother. "In Youth Have I Known One" ("[Stanzas]") is another Wordsworthian piece, concerning Poe's early visionary response to Nature. The work is a tribute, Richard Wilbur persuasively writes, to "poetic intuition."[19] The untitled poem beginning, "A wilder'd being from my birth," would later be titled "A Dream," and the first stanza would be eliminated, perhaps because it was too explicit. The "joy departed," the "holy dream" that cheered and guided, intimates Jane Stith Stanard, who offered young Poe her sympathy and her belief in him.[20] "The happiest day—the happiest hour" has been diversely interpreted; the apostrophe of the third stanza suggests that the poem is Poe's lament over the consequences of his own pride. Yet Poe seems to write this proudly.[21] The final poem, "The Lake," recalls the poet as a boy, responding with "tremulous delight" to a dark lake, corresponding as it did to his own "darken'd mind," his "dark imagining." Mabbott suggests that this is the Lake of the Dismal Swamp (M 1:83). The final words, "that dim lake" (M 1:85), suggest that the poem may owe something to Thomas Moore's "I Wish I Was by That Dim Lake." We may readily link "The Lake" to the earlier "Imitation." It is suggestive to see that the lake could bring "solace" since it is solace, consolation, that Poe would repeatedly seek in later literary works.[22] Poe had written that the short poems in *Tamerlane* might "savour too much of Egotism," but he also defended the pieces since "they were written by one too young to have any knowledge of the world but from his own breast" (M 1:21–22). Readers may savor that very egotism—an emotional openness, however poetically clothed, that invites even as it challenges.

Tamerlane and Other Poems was listed in August 1827 in the *United States Review and Literary Gazette* and in October in the *North American Review*. It was also mentioned in 1829 in Samuel Kettell's *Specimens of American Poetry* (M 1:21). When the lead poem was published in a revised form in 1829 in *Al Aaraaf, Tamerlane, and Minor Poems,* an advertisement preceding it stated, "This poem was printed for publication in Boston, in the year 1827, but suppressed through circumstances of a private nature."[23] No evidence of suppression has been found; probably Poe was noting that *Tamerlane* was not widely distributed or circulated. Poe must have sent a copy to his brother Henry (William Henry Leonard Poe) in Baltimore since "The Happiest Day" and "Dreams" were reprinted over the initials "W. H. P." in Baltimore's *North American*—the former poem appeared on September 15, 1827, and the latter on October 20, 1827.[24] On October 27, 1827, W. H. P. contributed "The Pirate," supposedly transcribed from his logbook. The pirate is Edgar-Leonard, who relates the story of his having stabbed to death his beloved Rosalie, who was about to marry another. Henry blends elements of "Tamerlane" and "To———," using his sister's name. The issue of who betrayed whom may vary; in his life and in "Tamerlane," Poe left Elmira for his "high fate."[25]

Meanwhile, Poe endured his more modest fate as a clerk at Fort Independence.[26] Sometimes, surely, he would have been allowed to go to the city. Probably he would have visited the office of his printer, Calvin F. S. Thomas, and the nearby bookish places. It is interesting to note that bookstore Bowles and Dearborn, which sold Thomas Green Fessenden's *New England Farmer's Almanack, for 1828,* would in all likelihood have sold, as well, Fessenden's well-known monthly *New-England Farmer*. For this magazine featured on its front page in the August 31 and September 7 issues "Remarks on the Scarabæus Roseus, or Rose-Bug," a plausible prompt for "The Gold-Bug," a story that Poe would set in his next location, Sullivan's Island, near Charleston, South Carolina.[27] We do not know if Poe was able to attend either of the lectures of J. N. Reynolds on an "Antarctic Expedition," presented in Boylston Hall (at Boylston and Washington Streets) on November 1 and 3, but he certainly would have read about them.[28] Poe's time in Boston was soon to come to an end; his company would voyage from Fort Independence to Fort Moultrie on Sullivan's Island, near Charleston, South Carolina.[29]

Before Poe left Boston, an important event took place in Virginia. Although Poe was striving to be incognito, his whereabouts were known by his friend John H. Mackenzie: Flora Lapham Mack reports that Mackenzie told her that "he had always known where he [Poe] was under all circumstances through out his entire life."[30] Whether Poe heard of the development in his friend's life at this time is a matter of speculation. But he would come to know—and it would make a significant difference for him—that Mackenzie had taken a bride. On October 9, 1827, in Petersburg, John H. Mackenzie married the beautiful young Louisa Lanier.[31] In years to come, in times of crisis and times of joy, the couple would be especially close to Poe.

On November 6, the ship *Waltham* picked up the soldiers of the First Regiment of Artillery at Fort Independence, bound for Charleston: "Brig Waltham, [Captain] Webb, which is to take the garrison of Fort Independence to Charleston to make a transfer with one there, was lying at the fort yesterday."[32] After a difficult voyage, including "drifting on a lee shore, off the shoals of Cape Cod," the vessel arrived in Charleston on November 18.[33] At Fort Moultrie, Poe would continue his army career, as well as his writing.

7

"In the American Army"

1827–1829

Fort Moultrie—in 1827, the third iteration of the fort at the entrance to Charleston Harbor—was built of brick and stone. As constructed in 1808 and 1809, it was "enclosed by 15-foot high brick walls with a spacious brick magazine, 40 guns, and quarters for three companies of soldiers, present[ing] a stout three-sided battery along the seafront."[1] From this site, on November 18, 1827, officers from the First Regiment of Artillery (H. W. Griswold and Joshua Howard, lieutenants, and James Mann, assistant surgeon) offered the captain of the ship *Waltham*, George Webb—on behalf of themselves, their families, and their men—their "most unfeigned thanks" for his "kind attention," his "nautical abilities," and his "good management." They were grateful, especially, for his having saved the drifting ship "from most imminent danger" off Cape Cod.[2] Poe no doubt shared the officers' gratitude and, for a while anyway, appreciated his new haven. For a time, he was to be unbuffeted.

Poe would have continued, in the early months at Fort Moultrie, as a private, serving as company clerk. As he had at Fort Independence, he would have done necessary paperwork, including, in all likelihood, the creation of payrolls and muster rolls and the writing of dictated letters.[3] Fort Moultrie was located on Sullivan's Island, a setting that Poe would later use in "The Gold-Bug" and "The Balloon Hoax."[4] Even as he continued his routine military duties, Poe would surely have explored the beach nearby, as well as the city of Charleston itself. He would probably have met conchologist Dr. Edmund Ravenel of Sullivan's Island and Colonel William Drayton of Charleston.[5]

Of particular note is that T. O. Mabbott, discussing a source for Poe's later classic poem "Annabel Lee"—a poem titled "The Mourner," appearing in the *Charleston Courier* of December 4, 1807—states, "it is not at all improbable that he [Poe] glanced through a file [of the *Charleston Courier*] when stationed near Charleston, or even had a copy of the paper" (M 1:471). Robert Adger Law, who discovered the source, wrote that files of the newspaper were available at the Charleston Chamber of Commerce, the Charleston Library, and the College of Charleston. Perhaps another file was available at the *Charleston Courier* office. As Law observes, what would have been of special interest to Poe would have been any evidence of his parents' performances in Charleston.[6] Decidedly important would have been his mother's 1811 performances there, before her final few appearances in Richmond. Edgar had been only two years old when he and his brother and sister accompanied their mother to Charleston. Whatever Poe may have dimly remembered or been told by his brother Henry, he could now read a Charleston newspaper of the time to learn more. It is possible that he even returned to the Charleston Theatre, where his mother had performed.

A perusal of early 1811 issues of the *Charleston Courier* reveals that Mrs. Poe had had a variety of roles from January through May.[7] It is salient that she performed as the bride Christine in Theodore Hook's play *Tekeli* on Saturday, March 23. Significantly, the play had been scheduled for performance on Friday, March 22, but bad weather interfered. Our later consideration of Poe's novel, the 1838 *The Narrative of Arthur Gordon Pym*, will return us to the March 22 listing of *Tekeli*. His mother's performance as the bride Christine would prove critical for Poe's imagination.[8]

Surely Poe continued his own writing, as he had done in Charlottesville and Boston. And surely he continued to aspire to fulfill his genius. He was working toward a second book of poetry, which would indeed be published in 1829, titled *Al Aaraaf, Tamerlane, and Minor Poems*. T. O. Mabbott states, "Poe presumably composed 'Al Aaraaf' while in the army" (M 1:97). Perhaps it was begun in Boston after the publication of *Tamerlane*—Poe said that he wrote it "as the only alternative for relief"[9]—and then continued it in Charleston. Mabbott notes that "To M—," from the 1829 volume, exists in a manuscript of "about 1828" (M 1:136). Mabbott also mentions that Poe copied out excerpts from Shakespeare and Milton while he was in the army (M 1:540)—perhaps he did so while he was at Fort Moultrie.[10] Poe would have been doing his writing in his spare time; he continued to serve as a soldier, and with success. On May 1, 1828, he was promoted to "artificer."

An artificer was a soldier whose expertise was in the making of bombs and shells. This was an important position in Company H and in the First Artillery. Notably, as a result of the promotion, Poe's pay increased (from five dollars to ten dollars per month), and, presumably, his status increased, as well. William F. Hecker writes, "As an artificer, Poe occupied a technical realm. His daily business concerned the weights and measures of ores and chemicals. His value to his artillery battery became, in many ways, correspondingly technical. . . . Through this promotion, Poe's officers now publicly endorsed his value to the organization by relying upon him to produce the unit's artillery rounds."[11]

We may read with much interest an article titled "Fourth of July," appearing in the *Charleston Courier* of July 7, 1828:

> The fifty-second Anniversary of the Independence of the United States, was celebrated in this city on Friday last [July 4].
>
> A salute was fired at day-light, by a detachment of the Regiment of Artillery, which was repeated at meridian by the garrison at Fort Moultrie.[12]

It may well be that the artificer and poet Edgar Allan Poe, of the First Artillery at Fort Moultrie, helped salute the anniversary of American independence for the Fourth of July celebration in Charleston in 1828.

There was yellow fever in Charleston in the summer of 1828, as there had been the year before. The peak for yellow fever cases and other fever cases in Charleston in 1827 had been September; perhaps this was again the case in 1828. There is no evidence that Poe was infected, but he may well have seen people who were. Symptoms of yellow fever were reported to be "the dark mahogany colour of the skin" and, in some cases, "the black vomit." And Poe would surely have seen some who were escaping the epidemic since Sullivan's Island was a retreat from the disease.[13] He may have been reminded of the typhus fever outbreak in London in 1817. We might later recall both the typhus fever in London and the yellow fever in Charleston when we consider Poe's classic short story "The Masque of the Red Death."

On October 31, 1828, Battery H of the First Artillery was ordered up the coast to Fortress Monroe, Old Point Comfort, Virginia (H 1:70). This was only eighty miles southeast of Richmond, which Poe had left in such anger little more than a year and a half earlier. Poe's debts were, of course, still remembered. John Allan's partner, Charles Ellis, received on June 28, 1828, an inquiry regarding Poe's debt for clothing, incurred at the university in December 1826. Also, the tenuous health of Poe's foster mother, Frances Allan, continued to be an issue. Allan wrote to Ellis on September 7 from Warm Springs, "Mrs. Allan has received less benefit from the use of the Bath than I had hoped but yet many of her painful sensations have either been removed or greatly mitigated." And Poe's friend John H. Mackenzie and his new wife, Louisa, were now living at Mount Erin, a "fine old house" overlooking the city from Fulton Hill, to the south.[14]

Meanwhile, by the fall of 1828, probably prompted by his ambition, Poe had come to want a discharge from the army. He spoke to his commanding officer, Lieutenant Joshua Howard, who offered the condition that Poe resolve matters with his foster father. Howard wrote a letter to Allan, delivered by John O. Lay, and Allan responded, recommending that Poe complete his five-year enlistment. Poe followed up with a letter on December 1 (addressed "Dear Sir"), attempting both to reconcile with Allan and to secure his approval for the desired discharge. Countering what he considered Allan's belief that he was "degraded and disgraced," Poe wrote, "At no period of my life, have I regarded myself with a deeper Satisfaction—or did my heart swell with more honourable pride." Poe tried to reassure Allan, asserting, "I feel that within me which will make me fulfill your highest wishes." He was attentive in this letter to his foster parents' health, expressing concern over Allan's "indisposition" and stating, "Let me know how my Ma preserves her health." He added, "My dearest love to Ma—it is only when absent that we can tell the value of such a friend—I hope she will not let my wayward disposition wear away the love she used to have for me." And he closed, "Yours respectfully & affectionately" (O 1:13–15). Poe received no reply.

The ship *Martha,* carrying Battery H of the First Artillery, sailed north from Charleston on December 11, arriving at Fortress Monroe, Old Point Comfort, on December 15. This was the largest of American forts, enclosing sixty-three acres, featuring six sides, and protecting Hampton Roads and Norfolk, the James River, the York River, and the Chesapeake Bay in general. Poe was soon assigned to the office of the adjutant.[15] Not certain that his earlier letter had been received, Poe renewed his request of Allan on December 22, amplifying on an earlier comment: "You yourself cherished the cause of my leaving your family—Ambition. If it has not taken the channel you wished it, it is not the less certain of its object. Richmond & the U. States were too narrow a sphere & the world shall be my theatre." And he predicted rightly, "I will be an honor to your name." His confidence in his literary future was firm. He again expressed his feeling for Frances Allan, sending "my dearest love," "my best love," and yet again "my dearest love." And he closed, "I am Your affectionate son" (O 1:16–18). Again, he received no reply.

On January 1, 1829, Poe was promoted to regimental sergeant major.[16] He was sick for a time in the military hospital, where he was treated by the surgeon Dr. Robert Archer, the uncle of a young Susan Archer Talley, who would become a poet and who would meet Poe in Richmond in 1849.[17] And the newly promoted soldier continued to try to win his foster father's favor and support. On February 4, 1829—he was now twenty years old—Poe wrote to Allan that John H. Mackenzie had written to him and "seemed to take an interest in my welfare." Poe had asked Mackenzie to meet with Allan and request his advocacy for an appointment for Poe as a cadet to West Point. And Poe made the case to Allan for the appointment, clarifying the steps he might take. Poe referred to his "infamous conduct" at the university and the "taunts & abuse" at home. He added that on Allan's response "depend a great many of the circumstances of my future life." He returned to his foster mother—"Give my love to Ma"—and closed, "I am Yours affectionately" (O 1:19–20). We do not know if Allan replied to this letter. But Poe and Allan were soon to be brought together by a mutually sorrowful event: on February 28, 1829, Frances Allan died of asthma.[18]

Her funeral began at Moldavia on Monday, March 2, at noon, and her burial took place at Shockoe Hill Cemetery. Given the wide social circle of the Allans, the funeral must have been well attended—indeed, Thomas Willis White, later the publisher of the monthly *Southern Literary Messenger,* printed three hundred tickets. Her epitaph states, in part, "This monument is erected / by John Allan her husband. / In testimony of his gratitude / for her unabated affection to him / the zeal to discharge her domestic duties; and the / fervor she manifested / both by precept and example / in persuading all to trust in the promises of the Gospel." Those who knew the Allan family well would have known that she also had an unabated affection for the wayward Edgar. And late in his life Poe spoke of her "with the tenderest affection." He regretted having been away when she died and wrote to Allan, in 1831, by way of caustic contrast, "She I believed loved me as her own child." The young soldier obtained a leave from Fortress Monroe and returned to Richmond on March 2, 1829, "the night after the burial" (O 1:61). Disaffected though Poe and Allan were, the two did then have a brief rapprochement. Allan bought Poe his mourning clothes.[19]

Poe was in Richmond for a week, apparently staying in Allan's house, Moldavia. The young man's letter on his return to Fortress Monroe opened, "My dear Pa," and closed, "I am, dear Pa, Yours affectionately." Things had changed. Poe notes that "in the morning of my departure I went to your room to tell you good-bye—but, as you were asleep, I would not disturb you" (O 1:21–22). There is a gentleness here. But in later years, Poe's treatment of the "old man" asleep in bed, "The Tell-Tale Heart," would suggest enduring hostility. For now, however, there was an easing between foster son and foster father.

Certainly Poe would have seen his aunt, Nancy Valentine, who lived in Allan's home. And he would have seen many old friends and associates who would have visited Moldavia and gone to the cemetery for the funeral, including William Galt's adopted sons, William and James, who had inherited the Galt fortune with John Allan. Poe would have seen Charles and Margaret Ellis, as well as their children, including his friend Tom, now fifteen, and nearly two-year-old Frances, who had been named for Frances Allan.[20] And it is very likely that Poe saw John H. Mackenzie and his wife, Louisa, who would surely have paid a condolence call and might have invited Edgar to visit them at Mount Erin. Critically, the brief time at home yielded Allan's support for Poe's getting discharged from the army and seeking a cadet's appointment.

Back at Fortress Monroe, Poe was anticipating his discharge, hoping for the cadetship, and preparing for possible entrance exams for West Point. He wrote to Allan on March 10, 1829, "[I] am anxious to retri[ev]e my good name wi[th my] [frie]nds & especially yo[ur] good opinion" (O 1:22). Poe apparently had a second chance.

On March 30, Colonel James House wrote to the commanding general of the Eastern Department, asking for his permission to discharge "Edgar A. Perry" (Poe) from the army. House stated that "Perry" and his foster father had achieved "an intire [sic] reconciliation"; he asserted that "Mr. Allen" (Allan) "reinstates him [Poe] into his family & favor" and that Allan had written a letter requesting the discharge if a substitute is secured.[21] On April 4, Major General Edmund P. Gaines, through R. Lowndes, ordered the discharge of "Sergt. Major Edgar A. Perry" (and another soldier) providing that each would secure "an acceptable substitute without expense to the Government."[22] And on April 15, Poe was discharged from the army.[23]

Poe's substitute—"An experienced Soldier & approved Sergeant," according to House—was Samuel Graves.[24] Poe explained to Allan in letters of June 25 and July 26, 1829, that he had promised to pay the standard twelve dollars for his substitute, not realizing that in the temporary absence of Lieutenant

Howard and Colonel House, the cost would climb to seventy-five dollars. He wrote that he had paid Graves twenty-five dollars and given him a note for the remaining fifty dollars, which he subsequently redeemed, relying on a portion of the hundred dollars that he had received from Allan in May (O 1:33, 36–37). If this was the case, apparently there was still another debt to Graves that Poe could not pay, and his indiscreet response to Graves's letter nearly a year later, May 3, 1830—including his statement that "Mr A is not very often sober" (O 1:54)—would cause him irreparable harm with his foster father.

Poe stayed at Fortress Monroe a few days beyond his discharge to obtain letters of recommendation. They were very encouraging. Lieutenant J. Howard wrote on April 20, 1829, that Poe's conduct had been "unexceptionable" and his "duties" "promptly and faithfully done," and he closed, "his habits are good, and intirely [sic] free from drinking." Captain H. W. Griswold added that Poe had been promoted to sergeant major of the First Artillery and that his "deportment" was "exemplary" and his "discharge of his duties" "prompt & faithful"; he was "highly worthy of confidence." Lieutenant Colonel W. J. Worth concurred, asserting that "his [Poe's] deportment has been highly praise worthy & deserving of confidence." He stated, "His education is of a very high order and he appears to be free from bad habits." He concluded, "I unhesitatingly recommend him as promising to acquit himself of the obligations of that station [of a cadet] studiously and faithfully."[25] Bearing encomia from these men, Poe would have returned to Richmond with much pride. And he would have carried other documents of considerable consequence—his manuscripts of new poems.

Other letters of support for Poe's cadetship followed. On May 6, Speaker of the House Andrew Stevenson wrote a letter to Secretary of War John H. Eaton, "He [Poe] will be an acquisition to the service & I most earnestly recommend him to yr especial notice & approbation." And Major John Campbell declared, "I unite with great pleasure with Mr. Stevenson & Col. Worth in recommending him [Poe] for a place in the Military Academy at West Point." On May 13, Colonel James P. Preston—whose son had been Poe's school friend—added his own ample endorsement, mentioning Poe's early difficulties, his writing, his time at the university, and his character: "I know Mr. Poe and am acquainted with the fact of his having been born under circumstances of great adversity. I also know from his own productions and other undoubted proofs that he is a young gentleman of genius and talents—I believe he is destined to be distinguished, since he has already gained reputation for talents & attainments at the University of Virginia—I think him possessed of feelings & character peculiarly intitling [sic] him to public patronage."[26]

Of particular interest are John Allan's mixed comments on Poe. To the secretary of war, on May 6, Allan referred to Poe's gambling at the university and acknowledged his good grades there, as well, and then wrote confidingly, "Frankly Sir, do I declare that He is no relation to me whatever; that I have many [in] whom I have taken an active Interest to promote thiers [sic]; with no other feeling than that, every man is my care, if he be in distress." We may recall Allan's initial reservation about taking in young Edgar in 1811—"it is an experiment just an experiment." Having established his distance from Poe in this letter to Eaton—perhaps as a cool reminder to Poe, to whom he might have shown it—Allan went on, "I do request your kindness to aid this youth in the promotion of his future prospects."[27] However, his grudging tone disappeared when Allan wished to brag to his longtime correspondent John H. Cocke, who was a wealthy planter, a former battalion commander, and a member of the University of Virginia's Board of Visitors. Following personal and religious reflections on the recent deaths he had experienced, Allan closed his letter of May 22 with a self-satisfied postscript: "I am sure you will be pleased to hear that my Protegé Edgar A. Poe has restored himself to well earned favour by two years admirable & praise worthy conduct in the artillery of the U. States & has gone on to Washington with the warmest testimonials to get a Cadetship in the Military Academy of West Point & with a fair prospect of success."[28] The foster son who sixteen days earlier had been "no relation to me whatever" became "my Protegé." Allan advanced Poe's interests with reservations but took some credit for his recent achievements without any.

Poe must have presented the April 20 and May 6 letters to John H. Eaton in Washington. After all, Allan had begun his May 6 letter to Eaton, "The youth who presents this, is the same alluded to by Lt. Howard Capt. Griswold Colo. Worth our representative & the speaker the Hon'ble Andrew Stevenson, and my Friend Majr Jno. Campbell,"[29] and he wrote in his May 22 letter to Cocke that Poe "has gone on to Washington with the warmest testimonials." Poe then traveled to Baltimore, where, while waiting for news about his cadetship, he would continue writing poetry and secure publication of his second book.

8

"Irrecoverably a Poet"

1829-1830

I<small>N 1827, P<small>RESIDENT</small> J<small>OHN</small> Q<small>UINCY</small> A<small>DAMS</small></small>, acknowledging the Battle Monument and the Washington Monument, famously termed Baltimore "the monumental city." As Poe approached Baltimore from Washington, by land or by water, on May 7 or 8, 1829, he would have seen, on a hill toward the west, above the schooners and steamships, and the brick buildings and spired churches, the still-not-completed Washington Monument, perhaps still surrounded by scaffolding. Poe arrived with his manuscript complete, but unpublished. Toward the end of the year, the final piece of the statue at the top of the 188-foot Washington Monument would be put in place, and Poe's second book of poetry would be published. And *Al Aaraaf, Tamerlane, and Minor Poems,* too, would ascend high.[1]

Poe had significant family connections to Baltimore. David Poe Sr., Poe's paternal grandfather, had been assistant deputy quartermaster general for Baltimore and had won the friendship of Lafayette. His son David Poe Jr., born in Baltimore, appeared on the stage in Baltimore in 1805, as had Eliza Arnold (later Eliza Arnold Poe), from 1799 through 1802. In early 1809, when Poe's parents were living in Boston, David Poe Jr. left baby Edgar with David Poe Sr. and his wife, Elizabeth, in Baltimore. When Eliza Arnold Poe died in Richmond in 1811, Edgar's brother Henry was taken by their grandparents in Baltimore. And Poe's aunt Elizabeth Poe (David Poe Jr.'s sister) had written to the Allans from Baltimore about Edgar in 1813. When Poe arrived in Baltimore in May 1829, he found his family: "I have succeeded in finding Grandmother &

my relations," he wrote to John Allan on May 20 (O 1:24). (David Poe Sr. had died in 1816.) But there is no definitive evidence that he stayed in their household at this time. Indeed, he wrote on July 15 that "Grandmother is not in a situation to give me any accomodation [*sic*]" and on August 10, "My grandmother is extremely poor & ill (paralytic)[.] My aunt Maria [David Poe Jr.'s sister, mother of Virginia Clemm] if possible still worse & Henry [Poe's brother] entirely given up to drink & unable to help himself, much less me" (O 1:35, 43). He may have stayed with a cousin, Mrs. Beacham.[2]

Soon after his arrival in Baltimore, Poe eagerly sought interest in his poem "Al Aaraaf." On May 11, he visited William Wirt, writer, lawyer, and former attorney general—and an acquaintance of John Allan's (O 1:19, 24). Poe's poem elicited a thoughtful response from Wirt, who deprecated his own judgment of poetry, suggested that more traditional readers might not respond to the work, and noted that younger readers might. Poe took the day-boat to Philadelphia to see the editor Robert Walsh, whom Wirt had recommended that Poe consult.[3] Walsh assured Poe of a review of his book in the *American Quarterly Review*. Poe then submitted the poem to the publisher Isaac Lea, extensively describing the poem and terming himself "irrecoverably a poet" (O 1:26–27).[4] Poe stated in a May 29 letter to John Allan that he was encouraged by the responses of Wirt and Walsh, though he acknowledged that both men had observed that it was difficult to publish poetry in the United States. But, he added, "the *difficulty* should be no object, with a proper aim in view." And Poe solicited financial support from Allan to cover possible loss to Carey, Lea, and Carey, up to one hundred dollars, if the publishing firm published his book, adding "I shall wait anxiously for your answer" (O 1:29–31). The aspiring young writer also shared his poem with William Gwynn, editor of the *Federal Gazette and Baltimore Advertiser*, and selections from the end of the work appeared in that newspaper on May 18.[5] Clearly, Poe was not only an ardent poet but also an ardent advocate of his poetry.

Allan did not welcome Poe's request for his covering possible loss due to publication. Writing on the reverse of Poe's May 20 letter, Allan had totaled his recent support of his foster son as two hundred dollars, but writing on the final page of Poe's May 29 letter, Allan noted "replied to Monday 8th June 1829 strongly censuring his conduct—refusing any aid."[6] Poe responded with great concern on June 10 and 25 and July 15, seeking Allan's approval, forgiveness, and understanding (O 1:32–35). He wrote in that third letter, "I am very anxious to return home thro Washington," "I am sure no one could be more anxious," "I am anxious to abide by your directions," "You would relieve me from a great deal of anxiety by writing me soon" (O 1:35). It is not likely that his anxiety diminished when Allan responded on July 19, sending Poe money (O 1:36). For according to Poe's subsequent letter, Allan had mocked his foster son by stating "that men of genius ought not to apply to [my] aid," had expressed various "accusations & suspicions," and had warned him away by declaring, "I am not particularly anxious to see you" (O 1:36, 38). Poe offered explanations for various money-related situations (his securing a substitute, his having been robbed) and proudly related his walking to Washington and seeing Secretary of War John Eaton in Washington with regard to his possible appointment as a cadet. Poe recurred to past troubles, noting, "I am conscious of having offended you formerly—greatly—but I thought *that had been forgiven*. at least you told me so." Poe then made the publication of his poems contingent on Allan's "entire approbation." And he acknowledged, toward the letter's close, "I will wait with great anxiety for your letter" (O 1:38). What seems certain about Poe's personal predicament was his profound uncertainty.

Perhaps it was at this time that Poe offered his cousin Elizabeth Rebecca Herring an acrostic poem in her album and, later in the year, another. The first letters of the lines of these poems spell, respectively, "Elizabeth Rebecca" and "Elizabeth" (M 1:148–50). Poe also wrote in the album of Lucy Holmes a poem he titled "Original," but which the editor and author Eugene L. Didier later titled "Alone" (M 1:146–47). Though Poe claimed to John Allan, "I have long given up *Byron* as a model" (O 1:30), "Alone" is inflected with Byron— both "Manfred" (especially a passage about the hero's abiding difference from others) and "The Prisoner of Chillon" (especially a passage about the captive's observing a single ominous cloud). If Poe was writing in "Alone" about his mysterious estrangement, he seems also to have been intimating his connection with another poet, his part in a literary fellowship, a kind of solace.[7]

We know that Poe and his friend John H. Mackenzie corresponded when the young poet was at Fortress Monroe (O 1:19); it would seem likely that the correspondence continued when Poe was in Baltimore. Although there are no extant letters between them from the time, Flora Lapham Mack has explained that, after Poe's death, John H. Mackenzie gave his letters from Poe to his brother Thomas G. Mackenzie, who was planning to write a biography. These and other valuable Poe materials in Thomas's collection were destroyed in the April 1865 burning of Richmond. We may reasonably conjecture that John would have written to Poe in Baltimore, especially after the death of his father William on June 7, 1829. William Mackenzie had shifted from the tobacco business to real estate speculation in the western portions of Richmond and had lost a great deal. Mack contends, "He was so mortified & discouraged by his failure that he soon died." His son John apparently thought that "it was building in his lots fine houses which broke him." John at this time would have still been living with his wife, Louisa, at Mount Erin. And he probably would have had other news for his friend. Working backward from later events, we may infer that Louisa either had already had her baby boy or was soon due. John and Louisa named him Edgar Poe Mackenzie.[8]

By July 28, 1829, Poe's manuscript was accepted for publication by Hatch & Dunning, of Baltimore. On that date, the young writer requested the return of his manuscript from Carey, Lea & Carey (O 1:39–40), acknowledging, "I should have been proud of having your firm for my publishers & would have preferred publishing, with your name, even at a disadvantage had my circumstances admitted of so doing." Perhaps financial concerns were critical here. But Poe was clearly pleased, referring to his "[h]aving made a better disposition of my poems than I had any right to expect." He noted, leaving matters open, "Perhaps, at some future day, I may have the honor of your press, which I most sincerely desire" (O 1:39–40). (Poe would publish *Tales of the Grotesque and Arabesque* with Lea and Blanchard in 1840.)

On August 4, not having heard from his foster father since the letter of "accusations & suspicions," Poe gave up the opening "Dear Pa" for "Dear Sir," the latter last used before Frances Allan's death (O 1:41, 19). He asserted his recent effort to secure a position at West Point (unwisely also blaming Allan) and returned to past difficulties: "If you have not forgiven me for my former conduct—that is a different thing—but you told me that you had." He noted that he is "anxious" to return home and closed, "Perhaps the time may come when you will find that I have not deserved 1/2 the misfortunes which have happened to me & that you suspected me unworthily" (O 1:41–42). Allan responded, with additional funds, and Poe returned to his previous salutation, "Dear Pa," on August 10. But the anxiety remained: "I am not so anxious of obtaining money from your good nature as of preserving your good will—I am extremely anxious that you should believe that I have not attempted to impose upon you." Still hopeful that he could repair the breach, he concluded, "I remain / Dear Pa / Yours affectionately / Edgar A. Poe" (O 1:42–44). Allan sent an additional fifty dollars (O 1:45).

Probably it was also in August 1829 that Poe wrote to the editor of the *Yankee,* John Neal, providing some of his soon-to-be-published poetry. With that passionate and controversial poet, critic, and novelist, Poe found a champion.

Neal, who had returned to Portland, Maine, after years in Baltimore and then London, was the thirty-six-year-old author of, most recently, *Rachel Dyer*, concerning the Salem witchcraft frenzy, and a keen promoter of American literature.[9] He wrote in the September 1829 issue of the *Yankee*, "If E.A.P. of Baltimore—whose lines about 'Heaven,' though he professes to regard them as altogether superior to any thing in the whole range of American poetry, save two or three trifles referred to, are, though nonsense, rather exquisite nonsense—would but do himself justice, might make a beautiful and perhaps a magnificent poem. There is a good deal here to justify such a hope." And Neal provides two extracts from "Heaven" (soon retitled "Fairy-Land"), a delicate and evocative poem about fairies descending to Earth and ascending from Earth in tents of the light of the moon. For the second extract, Neal italicized the alluring conceit "Oh deep! / Is the passion of their sleep!"[10] Poe writes at the close of the poem about the fairies as "those butterflies / of Earth, who seek the skies" and bring down with them "a specimen [from their tents of moonlight] / Upon their quivering wings," thus fulfilling his later characterization of Poetry as "a wild effort to reach the beauty above" (H 11:72).

Neal's appreciation prompted in October or November a letter of elation and aspiration from Poe, which began, "I am young—not yet twenty—*am* a poet—if deep worship of all beauty can make me one—and wish to be so in the more common meaning of the word. I would give the world to embody one half the ideas afloat in my imagination" (O 1:47). It was in this missive that Poe confided, "[T]here can be no tie more strong than that of brother for brother." Neal published the letter in the December 1829 *Yankee*, along with excerpts from "Al Aaraaf," "Tamerlane," and "To — —." And he commented, in part, "[I]f the remainder of 'Al Aaraaf' and 'Tamerlane' are as good as the body of the extracts here given—to say nothing of the more extraordinary parts, he will deserve to stand high—very high—in the estimation of the shining brotherhood."[11] Here was a response to Poe perhaps equal to that of Jane Stith Stanard so many years ago in Richmond. He was, once again, recognized.

Meanwhile, Baltimore was thriving. On August 8, citizens celebrated the city's centennial, honoring the last surviving signer of the Declaration of Independence, Charles Carroll of Carrollton. Also, the first stone of the Baltimore and Susquehanna Railroad was laid. In September, a new theater opened and new schools were begun; in October, a temperance society was planned.[12] Poe was still struggling, trying to persuade John Allan of his serious effort to gain a cadetship at West Point and lamenting, "I am sorry that your letters to me have still with them a tone of anger as if my former errors were not forgiven—if I knew how to regain your affection God knows I would do anything I could" (O 1:45–46). Having sent his poetry to another editor, N. P. Willis of the *American Monthly* in New York City, Poe would have been distressed to see from Willis's piece in the November issue that "Fairy-Land" was apparently consigned to the flames.[13] He wrote to his foster father on November 12 that he was "almost without clothes" and had been without money since mid-August (O 1:49–50); on November 18 he acknowledged with gratitude having received eighty dollars and asked for a piece of linen with which his aunt Maria Clemm might make him some clothing. And he noted that Hatch & Dunning would print his second book of poetry and that he would receive 250 copies. Mr. Dunning, traveling to Richmond, would bring the book to Allan (O 1:50–51).

At this time, on behalf of Maria Clemm, Poe apparently facilitated the sale of an enslaved man named Edwin for forty dollars to one Henry Ridgway, evidently also a "person of colour," for nine years.[14] Poe was a southerner seeking to be a helpful nephew to his impoverished aunt. When he later became an editor and critic, he evidenced what has been fairly termed an "average racism."[15] And, notably, in *Arthur Gordon Pym*, he depicted a dark-skinned hero, as we shall see. Poe was no abolitionist, but he was no pro-slavery zealot either.

On November 25, the last piece of the statue on the Washington Monument in Baltimore was secured. And some time before December 29, Poe's *Al Aaraaf, Tamerlane, and Minor Poems* was published.[16] The slender volume was roughly eight inches tall and five inches wide; it comprised seventy-one pages and provided the two long poems and ten short ones.

"Al Aaraaf" offers, on the "Messenger Star," an imagined refuge for the lover of the beautiful. Its introductory sonnet (later titled "Sonnet" or "Sonnet—To Science") is termed "illegitimate" by Poe (O 1:27)—perhaps for its irregular meter, rhyme, rhyme scheme, and thematic development—but it legitimately and compellingly prepares the way for the author "To seek a shelter in some happier star." The prompt passage, an English translation of Saint-Pierre's "Pleasures of Ignorance," critiques science for excluding divinity; Poe critiques science for excluding imagination.[17] In Poe's apostrophe, Science preys on the Promethean poet, suppresses the Icarian poet, and (in a transformation of the language of Saint-Pierre) expels mythic beings from their worlds, as well as Poe himself from his vision. What Poe cherishes is "wandering / To seek for treasure in the jewell'd skies," "The summer dream beneath shrubbery."[18] He reverences reverie—and the poem "Al Aaraaf" will do it honor.

The poem features two parts. In the first of these, the lovely Nesace—maiden, queen, angel, goddess—rules Al Aaraaf, which is conceived as a wandering star, now near the constellation Cassiopeia, a star that was discovered by Tycho Brahe in 1572 and would disappear from sight in 1574. Al Aaraaf is neither Heaven nor Hell but rather a home to Beauty. Nesace sings to God, "Who livest—*that* we know / In Eternity—we feel," for whom she is "the favour'd one" and a "messenger" to "other worlds." The voice of God bids her ascend with her angel attendants and bear the message that will protect against "the guilt of man."[19] Then, in the second part, Nesace alights at her palace on Al Aaraaf and sings to all "Bright beings" to arise from their sleeping and dreaming, asking Ligeia to awaken them. A myriad of these beings comply, but two do not, preferring love to duty: "a maiden-angel and her seraph-lover," Ianthe and Angelo.[20] In dialogue with Ianthe, Angelo—Michelangelo (O 1:27)—looks at Earth, remembers his death at the Parthenon when Al Aaraaf was near, and yearns to return. Ianthe protests, contending for Al Aaraaf. And the two lovers passionately discuss the two worlds, never ascending with Nesace because of their attachment to their love. According to one of Poe's notes, on Al Aaraaf the consequence of their choice will be "final death and annihilation." Yet perhaps "Sweet was their death—with them to die was rife / With the last extacy of satiate life."[21]

The language and imagery of the poem are rich—consider, for example, "'Twas a sweet time for Nesace—for there / Her world lay lolling on the golden air." The lush sensory detail is sometimes blended, yielding an effect known as "synesthesia," as in "fairy! to whose care is given / To bear the Goddess' song, in odours, up to Heaven." There is a profusion, an opulence, a spilling over, a reaching for pleasure after pleasure, as, for instance, in the lines, "The Sephalica, budding with young bees, / Uprear'd its purple stem around her [Nesace's] knees—/ And gemmy flower, of Trebizond misnamed—/ Inmate of higher stars, where erst it sham'd / All other loveliness: its honied dew / [The fabled nectar that the heathen knew] / Deliriously sweet, was dropp'd from Heaven, / And fell on gardens of the unforgiven / In Trebizond."[22] The sources are varied, ranging from Thomas Moore to John Milton to George Sale's Koran. And the narrative seems to suggest a second Fall—in Genesis, Adam and Eve in Eden fell through their seeking knowledge, arguably "the guilt of man"; here Angelo and Ianthe fall on "Al Aaraaf" through their yielding to passion, producing guilt yet again, since the quest for the divine through Beauty has been forsaken, causing their death. There appears to be no Fortunate Fall here. Poe's reverie has led to both the transcendent and the tragic. And the theme of beauty as a path to transcendence will reemerge in varied forms in Poe, starting with "Letter to B—" and progressing on to "The Poetic Principle."[23]

The dedication for "Al Aaraaf" is a literary quotation—purportedly John Cleveland's "Who drinks the deepest?—here's to him"—but that for the revised "Tamerlane" is personal—"TO / JOHN NEAL / THIS POEM / IS / RESPECTFULLY DEDICATED."[24] Apparently Poe had proposed dedicating the entire volume to Neal, but Neal had demurred, thinking that such a dedication might hurt sales.[25] So Poe provided this dedication for the one poem. The new "Tamerlane" is significantly shorter than the original, without notes and sometimes without the terms that had elicited the notes. Some of the original sections are trimmed or broken up or omitted. The poem seems slightly less Byron-linked—there is no "chamois," no "Ada." There is new material, especially toward the end. But despite the changes, this tighter version of the poem still suggests, in rough allegory, Poe's life, still presents the conflict of Ambition with Love.

Of the ten "Miscellaneous Poems," four are revisions of "Fugitive Pieces" that had appeared in *Tamerlane and Other Poems*: the second "To — —" ("I saw thee on thy bridal day"), "The Lake — To — " (formerly "The Lake"), "Spirits of the Dead" (formerly "Visit of the Dead"), and "A Dream" (formerly without title). Six are new: "Preface" (later "Romance"), the first "To — —" (with a slight debt to "Imitation"), the third "To — —," "To the River —," To M—," and "Fairyland." Poe was very proud of "Preface," writing to Neal on December 29, 1829, that the first five lines of the second stanza "have never been surpassed." He adds, "'It is well to think well of one's self'—so sings somebody" (O 1:52). This poem again pays tribute to reverie—"Romance," shadowed forth by the reflection of a "painted paroquet" in his childhood, survives, even in "late eternal Condor years," as "an hour with calmer wings," "That little time with lyre and rhyme."[26] The first "To — —" mourns loss and asserts defiance; the third "To — —" offers ambiguity and apparent chastisement.[27] "To the River —" is a paean to a beloved, the river reflecting the woman and signifying the poet's mind, which also reflects this woman. "To M—" conveys a bitterness, an alienation, yet still the need for another. And "Fairyland," which we have discussed, concerns the moonlight-borne fairies. Perhaps, as Floyd Stovall has argued, these "butterflies / Of Earth" that bring back "a specimen" of the moonlight are emblems of poets.[28] This was the poem that Neal had praised and Willis had claimed to have burned.

And Neal continued his praise. He wrote in one notice that Poe was "evidently a fine genius"; he predicted in a review, "If the young author now before us should fulfill his destiny . . . he will be *foremost* in the rank of *real* poets" and reiterated, "Our author, if he be just to his peculiar gift, (for it *is* a gift here,) will be distinguished among the *most* distinguished."[29] An unidentified reviewer declared of *Al Aaraaf, Tamerlane, and Minor Poems*, "Throughout, there runs a rich vein of deep and powerful thought, clothed in language of almost inimitable beauty and harmony."[30] Poe's second cousin Neilson Poe—whose grandfather was the brother of Poe's grandfather—concluded in January 1830, "*Our* name will be a great one *yet*."[31] But John Hill Hewitt, in the *Baltimore Minerva,* termed the poems in *Al Aaraaf* "a pile of brick-bats" and offered his readers a bemused noncomprehension.[32]

Poe sent a copy of *Al Aaraaf* to John Neal with his December 29, 1829, letter; he also gave a copy to Elizabeth Herring, inscribed "For my cousin Elizabeth—E. A. Poe."[33] It must have been at this time that Poe competed with John Lofland, "the Milford Bard," to write the most verses in a given period. There is some disagreement as to who provoked the competition, but there is agreement that Poe lost.[34] Meanwhile, the anxious foster son must have gained some easing of what he had termed in July 1829 Allan's "prohibition to return" (O 1:38), for in early January 1830 Poe did indeed return to Richmond.

He would again have been living at Moldavia. And he had a story to tell of distress and achievement. Thomas Bolling, who had met Poe at John Allan's house before going to the University of Virginia and who had known Poe at the university, visited Poe at Allan's again when his former classmate came back from Baltimore. Bolling remembered his visit well:

> I happened there the second night after he got back—when he gave me a history of all he had experienced while away, how he had suffered and shifted to live, when finally as the only alternative for relief, he wrote the Alaura-af [*sic*]—that Sanky [R. D. Sanxay]—who kept a book store in Rich^d at that time, had it for sale—to call on him for as many copies as I wished and should I meet with any of our old College mates, that would like to see it, give him one, as coming from *me* not Poe—The next day, he went with me, gave me a copy, leaving the above instructions with Sanxy—I never called again for I could make neither *head or tail* of it.[35]

Presumably these were Poe's own copies, provided by Hatch & Dunning, and therefore available for his largesse. Probably Poe was trying to win back his reputation. But at least in the case of Bolling, the challenge of the poems' language and tone was evidently too much. Sanxay did advertise the book, using a passage from an early John Neal encomium, which Poe might well have provided.[36]

Poe must have hoped that, while living at Moldavia, he could get back into John Allan's good graces and thereby be—as he had long expected to be—his foster father's heir. But though Allan occasionally provided for Poe incidentally,[37] he had other views. Flora Lapham Mack's account of the comments of Jane Scott Mackenzie—John H. Mackenzie's mother—about Allan and Poe is clarifying. According to this account, Allan had been distressed about Edgar's having interfered with his happiness with his wife, Frances:

> They [John and Frances] had been a very happy & devoted couple before they took Edgar to live with them but he soon inaugurated an atmosphere of unrest & strain that was some thing entirely new in that household. Mr. Allan bitterly resented this and also the fact that his wife whom he passionately loved should deceive him constantly in small ways to screen & indulge Edgar. He often told me it was a dark day for their happiness when Edgar crossed their threshold. He had never regarded him as a son tho Mrs. Allen [sic] tried hard to make him do so but the final straw that broke the camel's back was those university debts. Mr. Allen never pretended to care for him at all after that time.

Allan also thought that Edgar had been "so ungrateful to his beloved wife & caused her so much sorrow & unhappiness."[38]

Poe saw Allan as too severe—threatening, grudging, and punitive; Allan probably thought he hadn't been severe enough. And Frances had often been a buffer for Edgar. Jane Scott Mackenzie's recollection makes plain Allan's attitude toward Poe after Frances's death. Mack states:

> He was one of the men she said who could not endure with any degree of patience the idea of his wife deceiving him in the slightest particular about any thing & he ferreted out Mrs. Allen's [sic] every attempt to screen Edgar or supply his constant demands for money and hotly & bitterly reproached her with it. Then after her death he brooded so deeply over the unhappiness this had caused between them thinking of how harmonious & affectionate & peaceful their life together had been up to the time of Poe's adoption [sic] and he grew to resent it bitterly that an alien & a stranger whom he had taken in & befriended in every way produced such a condition of affairs between them & he had determined to rid him self of him for ever before he married again.[39]

John H. Mackenzie and his wife, Louisa, evidently confirmed this account. And while Poe had acknowledged some fault to Allan ("I am conscious of having offended you formerly—greatly" [O 1:38], and similar later comments), we are not aware that Allan ever had acknowledged any fault of his own to Poe. No doubt Poe had been a difficult foster son—but also without doubt, Allan had not been up to the challenge. Indeed, at times, he had aggravated matters through his severity.

And despite Allan's idealization of his love for Frances, there was a problem: there is reason to believe that Poe's foster father had been unfaithful. As has been noted, Edward Collier has been taken to have been Allan's illegitimate son. And Arthur Hobson Quinn states, in commenting on the will of Poe's foster father, that he had had an affair with Elizabeth Wills while he was married to Frances, and Wills had given birth to a daughter. And the relationship continued after Frances's death—in July 1830, Wills had twin boys by Allan. The wealthy man tried to provide for these children of Mrs. Wills in his will.[40] He did wish to marry again, and Allan turned to Frances's sister Ann ("Nancy"). Flora Lapham Mack conveyed what Jane Scott Mackenzie had remembered: "She said Mr. Allen [sic] had wanted to marry Miss Nancy Valentine his wife's older sister & that if she had married him Edgar would have occupied just the same position he had done before the 1st Mrs. Allen's death because Miss Nancy was equally devoted to him."[41] Unfortunately for Poe, Miss Nancy must have turned Allan down. Allan would eventually meet Louisa Gabriella Patterson, from Elizabethtown, New Jersey, and she would become his second wife.

There was progress in early 1830 in Poe's effort to secure a cadetship at West Point. On March 13, in response to a letter from Poe, Powhatan Ellis—the younger brother of Charles Ellis and then a United States senator from Mississippi—wrote to Secretary of War John H. Eaton supporting Poe's application: "I am not personally acquainted with Mr. Poe—but from information I would say his capacity & learning eminently qualify him to make in a few years a distinguished officer." On March 31, in response to an appointment letter for Poe from Eaton, Allan identified himself as Poe's "Guardian" and gave his permission for Poe's "signing articles by which he [Poe] shall bind himself, to serve the United States for five years."[42] So the way was clear, and Poe would eventually leave Richmond in mid- to late May and arrive at West Point in late June.

Poe's activities in Richmond from January to May 1830 are very slightly known. But we may infer that Poe probably attended Monumental Church, probably visited the graves of Jane Stith Stanard and Frances Allan at Shockoe Hill Cemetery, and probably regularly visited the bookstores, including Sanxay's. Perhaps he attended the wedding of William Galt Jr. to Mary Bell Taylor (Galt's first wife, Rosanna Dixon, having died in 1828).[43] Surely Poe visited friends such as the Ellises. He may well have heard more about Miss Jane Mackenzie's School since daughters Jane and Elizabeth Ellis were enrolled there.[44] And he would very likely have visited the Mackenzies.

He would probably have visited Jane Scott Mackenzie, living in the western area of Richmond—she would one day build the celebrated Duncan Lodge there.[45] His sister Rosalie would have still been living with her. And over the course of nearly five months he would almost certainly have visited John H. Mackenzie and his wife Louisa, and her mother, Mary Simmons Lanier, at Mount Erin, in the town of Fulton. Flora Lapham Mack states that the area "was then semi country & still surrounded by fields." The house, overlooking Richmond from the heights of Fulton Hill or Powhatan Hill (in the East End, south of Church Hill), was built by James Alexander Fulton for his wife, Elizabeth Bland Mayo Fulton. He died there in 1823. John and Louisa lived there from their marriage in October 1827 to their move to a farm outside of Richmond in 1833 or 1834. Edward V. Valentine later considered the site to have been that of the native chief Powhatan's town. An 1852 diagram of the property shows, off the Williamsburg Stage Road, a long entrance lane, a barn ahead, the mansion down the avenue to the left, with a hothouse to its right, and, behind the house, the gardens and a woodland. If Poe did visit Mount Erin in the winter and spring of 1830, he would surely have met his namesake, Edgar Poe Mackenzie. Flora Lapham Mack recalled, "She [Louisa Mackenzie] said she had always liked Edgar very much indeed & she had allowed cousin John to name their baby Edgar Poe after him."[46]

Poe would have continued to write poetry and to read. And he would have been attentive to current events. He would have learned of large political matters—for instance, the Virginia Constitutional Convention in Richmond and the growing schism over states' rights in Washington.[47] But local newspapers would also have provided more focused pieces, often drawn from other venues. And some of these pieces anticipate Poe's later fiction. The *Richmond Enquirer,* for example, reprinted items about the shocking murder of wealthy Captain Joseph White in Salem, Massachusetts. Daniel Webster's later prosecutorial speech regarding the murder would help prompt Poe's short story "The Tell-Tale Heart." And editor Thomas Ritchie's triweekly paper also reprinted a squib on exploration: "We learn that the

American discovery brigs, Seraph and Annawan, under the command of Captains Pendleton and Palmer, left a post in the vicinity of Cape Horn, the middle of January last, all well, and proceeded Southward for Palmer's Land and the South Pacific."[48] On the voyage was J. N. Reynolds, the advocate for the expedition. And accompanying the brigs was a schooner, the *Penguin*.[49] Its name would engage Poe's imagination in his novel *The Narrative of Arthur Gordon Pym*.

Meanwhile, the difficult state of things between Poe and Allan in the spring of 1830 becomes evident in two letters—one of these from Poe to his substitute, Samuel Graves, from Richmond, on May 3, 1830 (O 1:53–54), and the other from Poe to Allan, from West Point, on January 3, 1831 (O 1:58–62). Graves had written to Poe twice regarding money that Poe owed him—presumably different from the money that Poe had paid for Graves's having served as a substitute. One of these letters did not reach Poe, but the other did. Poe assures Graves that he intends to pay him. He states, with a tone of disrespect for his foster father, "I have tried to get the money for you from Mr A a dozen times—but he always shuffles me off." And, worse, he notes, in passing, "Mr A is not very often sober" (O 1:54). Whether this was true or not, Poe's stating so was the height of indiscretion. (Years later, Poe would write of Allan's "habits of habitual drunkenness" [O 1:185].) Graves later wrote to Allan, apparently enclosing Poe's letter, and Poe, in an angry letter responding to Allan, wrote:

> As regards Sergt. Graves—I *did* write him that letter. As to the truth of its contents, I leave it to God, and your own conscience.—The time in which I wrote it was within half an hour after you had embittered every feeling of my heart against you by your abuse of my *family*, and myself, under your own roof—and at a time when you knew that my heart was almost breaking. (O 1:61)

So, in all likelihood, on May 3, 1830, Allan had returned to asserting the accusation against Poe's mother that he had made to Poe's brother Henry on November 1, 1824: "At least She [Rosalie] is half your Sister & God forbid my dear Henry that We should visit upon the living the Errors & frailties of the dead."[50] If this was the abuse that Poe wrote of, then the provocation was great—and though Poe's statement against Allan in his letter to Graves was a serious error, his loyalty to his assailed and beloved mother was wholly admirable. And Allan was, quite simply, cruel. If we consider Allan's infidelities, then his repeated accusation about Eliza Poe seems also deeply hypocritical.

Poe left Richmond sometime after Allan's verbal attack on May 3, and no later than May 20, since Allan wrote to him, in Baltimore, on May 21 (O 1:55). From Baltimore, Poe would continue north, to West Point. He would succeed academically for his one term there, but Allan's inadequate support and evident hostility would lead Poe to neglect his duties and thereby cause his own court-martial and dismissal.

9
"I Am a Cadet"
1830-1831

In Baltimore, Poe presumably saw his family, and he also visited Nathan C. Brooks, a teacher, poet, and editor, to whom he promised to send a poem for an annual. Brooks later remembered his friend as "a man inspired by noble and exalted sentiments."[1] Poe must not have stayed in Baltimore very long—the May 21, 1830, letter from John Allan had to be forwarded by brother Henry to Poe at West Point. Poe arrived at the U.S. Military Academy by late June (O 1:55).

The site of the Military Academy is a bold promontory high above the Hudson River, fifty miles north of New York City. It features an extensive plain, where the cadets drill. A fortification was built in 1778, a military academy proposed in 1783, and the school itself established in 1801. In its early years, the school was "like a foundling, barely existing among the mountains and nurtured at a distance out of sight and almost unknown to its legitimate parents." But the Military Academy expanded in 1812, developed a course of studies in 1816, engaged Sylvanus Thayer as superintendent in 1817, and elaborated a system of regulation in 1821. By the time Poe arrived in 1830, the U.S. Military Academy was no foundling but a proudly recognized son. Poe's own status, however, vis-à-vis his foster father, continued to be questionable.[2] Indeed, in his first letter of three letters to John Allan from West Point, that of June 28, 1830, Poe had to defend himself against accusations of theft: "As to what you say about the books etc. I have taken nothing except what I considered my own property" (O 1:55).

This letter, still addressed "Dear Pa," indicates that Poe had presented his recommendations and had been welcomed by Ethan A. Hitchcock (captain of the infantry) and Edward C. Ross (instructor of mathematics). He subsequently took and passed his admission examination. He was, at the time of writing the letter, taking part in the summer encampment on the Plain, sharing a tent with three other cadets (O 1:55–56). Poe was formally admitted to West Point on July 1. The encampment was called "Camp Eaton," after Secretary of War John H. Eaton, and one of Poe's tentmates was Eaton's nephew. Poe would have been involved there in extensive drills with various weapons, as well as guard duty and twice-daily parades. There was a celebration on July Fourth involving the cadets' marching on the Plain and listening to a reading of the Declaration of Independence in the chapel. And there was a "Grand Fancy Ball," with costumed participants, on August 24. (Notably, $4.25 was deducted from a cadet's account for "4th July Dinner & Fancy Ball.") When the tents were struck at the end of encampment, the cadets moved to their barracks. Poe's new home was South Barracks, at the south end of the Plain, east of the Mess House and the Academy.[3]

Poe shared a second-story room, number 28, with two other cadets, Thomas W. Gibson and Timothy Pickering Jones.[4] South Barracks rooms were approximately eleven feet by eleven feet and featured three cots; these rooms were reportedly very cold.[5] A cadet's day was prescribed from reveille to taps. As a first-year student—a member of the "fourth class"—Poe studied mathematics (including trigonometry, geometry, and algebra) and French; his schedule involved recitations and study in both subjects, for approximately eight hours a day. He also took part in roll calls and parades.[6]

He apparently had a good start in his academic work—he and Henry B. Hirst (or Poe alone) wrote in the 1843 *Saturday Museum* biography (or autobiography), "At first he was delighted with everything, busied himself in study, and 'headed' every class." And Timothy Pickering Jones supported this view, stating, "At first he studied hard and his ambition seemed to be to lead the class in all studies."[7] Poe reported to Allan in his second letter from West Point, that of November 6, 1830, "I have a very excellent standing in my class—in the first section in every thing and have great hopes of doing well." He asked, in particular, for "a Box of Mathematical Instruments" and a mathematics textbook, or money for them (O 1:57). French would have been welcome for Poe given his background in the language at the University of Virginia, but math may have proven less appealing. Jones said, "He was an extraordinary scholar in all branches except mathematics, for which he seemed to have an aversion," later asserting that Poe "boldly declared [that mathematics] had no place in the brain of an intellectual man—too dull and commonplace."[8] Jones's comments tend to be corroborated by a contemporary letter—cadet David E. Hale wrote about Poe to his mother, the editor Sarah Josepha Hale, on February 10, 1831, "He is thought a fellow of talent here but he is too mad a poet to like Mathematics."[9] Former cadet George Washington Cullum later stated that Poe "preferred making verses to solving equations."[10] Still, if he did not especially care for mathematics, Poe did have "a wonderful aptitude for [it]."[11] Later works of his would certainly involve solving for x.

Poe's demeanor at West Point was reported by some to be shy and sensitive. He was also characterized as occasionally "a victim to the blues," as having "a worn, weary, discontented look."[12] Although he did well in his academic work, he was not at ease with the rigors of military discipline. "His great fault," former classmate A. B. Magruder later stated, "was his neglect of and great contempt for military duties." An unnamed former cadet asserted, "His mind was off from the matter-of-fact routine of the drill, which in such a case as his seemed practical joking, on some etherial [sic], visionary expedition."[13] Poe was dedicated to the lyrical, not the logistical.

And for his fellow cadets, he would engage, as well, in the satirical, mocking their military superiors. One instance of his comic mode at West Point endures, a send-up of barracks inspector Joseph Locke, whom Poe is reported to have "hated . . . with a holy hatred":[14]

> As for Locke, he is all in my eye,
>   May the d—l right soon for his soul call.
> He never was known to lie—
>   In bed at a *reveillé* "roll call."
>
> John Locke was a notable name;
>   Joe Locke is a greater; in short,
> The former was well known to fame,
>   But the latter's well known "to report." (M 1:151)

Poe was also reading much—"He was a devourer of books"—and offering firm, sometimes imperious, literary critical judgments.[15] He was preparing for a career—just not a military one.

And, much to his misfortune, he was drinking. Classmates Gibson, Cullum, and Jones later attested to this.[16] A vital source for liquor for the cadets was Benny Havens's nearby tavern, which Poe visited and where he talked with its proprietor.[17] Gibson tells of a hoax that Poe formulated, one that recalls Poe's boyhood appearance as a ghost at Charles Ellis's whist party. In late November 1830, the cadets in 28 South Barracks, at Poe's suggestion, drew straws for the needed foray to the tavern to obtain drink. Gibson got the short straw and made his way through the cold wet night to Benny Havens, carrying candles and Poe's blanket for a trade. Returning with a bottle of brandy and a bloody beheaded gander, Gibson was met on the way by Poe, who, seeing his classmate's bloodied shirt and face and hands, concocted a ruse. The bird was tied up, a knife was daubed, and then Poe returned to the barracks room, where "Old P" (perhaps Timothy Pickering Jones) and a visitor from North Barracks remained. Poe was followed by a seemingly intoxicated Gibson, covered in blood. Poe expressed simulated distress, and Gibson spoke of K — —, Old K — —!" To Poe's seemingly earnest questioning, Gibson replied, "He won't stop me on the road any more!" then displayed the bloodied knife, and added "I have killed him!" Finally, to Poe's expression of performed disbelief, Gibson responded, "I didn't suppose you would believe me, . . . so I cut off his head and brought it into barracks. Here it is!" And he threw the gander at the single candle, causing darkness, fright, and the panicked escape of the visitor from North Barracks, who related the shocking horror to other cadets. The bird was then cooked and eaten "in effigy."[18]

As Mary E. Phillips has noted, "Old K" himself was probably Zebina J. D. Kinsley. He was an unpopular West Point instructor of tactics of the time, who was remembered by John H. B. Latrobe as doing his duty "too zealously." Latrobe referred to him as "old Zeb" and "our old detestation." Albert E. Church recalled that Kinsley "could call everyone present by name and was therefore never at a loss, whom to report for the least violation of regulations, where ever occurring." This instructor had also been "foremost" in the temperance movement at West Point.[19] Perhaps that was why he would have been particularly likely to be stopping cadets—or at least thought to be stopping cadets—on the road between the barracks and Benny Havens's tavern.

Poe would have thoroughly enjoyed the dramatic deception that had been practiced with the bloody gander—his imagination had surpassed reality with the ultimate (we may venture) in fowl play. And even as the event harked back to Poe's earlier performance as a ghost, it also anticipated Arthur Gordon Pym's performance as a bloodied corpse in the 1838 novel.[20]

But with more sensitive matters, Poe was doubtless circumspect. It may well be that his fellow cadets (with the possible exception of David E. Hale) did not know of his early book publications or of the reprinting in the fall of his recent sonnet.[21] And he probably shared with none of them his ongoing stressful relationship with his foster father. His anxiety would have increased when Allan married for a second time on October 5, in New York City. The new wife was thirty-year-old Louisa Gabriella Patterson, whom fifty-one-year-old Allan had met through the Mayo family (H 1:78). Although, in his November 6 letter to Allan, Poe wrote, "Please give my respects to Mrs A," he also lamented Allan's not having visited on his recent trip: "I was greatly in hopes you would have come on to W. Point while you were in N. York, and was very much dissapointed [sic] when I heard you had gone on home without letting me hear from you," and later "Mr Cunningham was also on here some time since, and Mr J. Chevalie [acquaintances from Richmond] and I was indeed very much in hopes that the beauty of the river would have tempted yourself and Mr and Mrs Jas Galt to have paid us a visit" (O 1:57–58). By this time, Poe may have feared that Allan would forsake him altogether. We do not know if Allan had replied to his June 28 letter; certainly Poe's return on November 6 to the address "Dear Sir" suggests another falling off between them—though not yet the final falling out.

Poe tried to balance the positive and the negative—"I have spent my time very pleasantly hitherto—but the study requisite is incessant, and the discipline exceedingly rigid." He notes, further, "I have seen Genl [Winfield] Scott here since I came, and he was very polite and attentive—I am very much pleased with Colonel [Sylvanus] Thayer, and indeed with every thing at the institution," but "my more necessary expenditures have run me into debt" (O 1:57). Poe may have been ambivalent about West Point or just trying to put a good face on an increasingly trying situation. Scott, a longtime family friend, later became a devoted advocate of Poe.

It was perhaps in late 1830 or early 1831 that there was a tragedy back in Richmond—Poe's namesake, Edgar Poe Mackenzie, died at Mount Erin in a fall. Flora Lapham Mack writes, "He fell from a high old tester bed on his head while leaning over in baby glee to try to see his nurse who in playing with him had run under the bed to hide. He was picked up in convulsions and died in a few hours."[22] Mack noted that the baby was eighteen months old at the time, though John and Louisa's niece Jane Mackenzie Byrd Miller (daughter of Martha Mackenzie Byrd) stated that he was ten months old.[23]

This was the Mackenzies' only biological child. But the couple would bring up six girls in the coming years.

Poe continued his studies at West Point, with no doubt diminishing enthusiasm. He took his exams on January 3, 1831, and received the results on January 9: in a class of eighty-five, he was third in French and seventeenth in mathematics.[24] So he had clearly excelled. But his tenuous relationship with his foster father was strained to its limit, and Poe's January 3, 1831, letter—beginning "Sir,"—reveals that John Allan had written to Poe, stating his wish for "no further communication" (O 1:58–59, 61). Allan had learned of Poe's May 3, 1830, letter to Samuel Graves asserting, "Mr A is not very often sober" (O 1:61; see 1:54 for the original). Evidently Graves had sent it to Allan (O 1:55n). Allan's second marriage had probably been threatening to his foster son, but it would have been Allan's letter cutting off communication—and, presumably, inheritance—that would have most agitated Poe. Now plainly cast out by his outraged foster father, Poe wrote vehemently in his third and final letter to him from West Point.[25]

Poe reviewed Allan's assuming financial responsibility for him and then providing inadequately at the University of Virginia and preventing his returning. He maintained that he never wanted Allan to pay the contentious bills, the gambling debts, and explained his gambling in terms of his indebtedness, noting that at the end of his time at the university he was well on his way to reformation. He added, "I am not about to proclaim myself guilty of all that has been alledged against me, and which I have hitherto endured, simply because I was too proud to reply." And he asserted that Allan repeated his stingy behavior with him regarding the United States Military Academy: "You sent me to W. Point like a beggar." He observed, "The same difficulties are threatening me as before at Charlottesville—and I must resign." He admitted writing the letter to Samuel Graves, explaining its provocation—"your abuse of my *family*." He mentioned "the fatigues of this place," "the inconveniences which my absolute want of necessaries subject me to," and he requested written permission for the resignation so that he would be provided with travel costs. He closed by promising, "From the time of writing this I shall neglect my studies and duties at the institution" (1:58–62). And he did.

If the fault was not entirely Allan's, it does seem that it was largely his— that what Poe termed "your own mistaken parsimony" led to problems at the University of Virginia, as well as at West Point. And Poe's accusation of Allan to Samuel Graves—unwise even if true—had been significantly provoked. But Allan was, predictably, unsympathetic. He wrote on Poe's letter on January 13, "I rec^d this on the 10th, & did not from its conclusion deem it necessary to reply. I make this note on the 13th & can see no good Reason to alter my opinion, I do not think the Boy has one good quality. He may do or act as he pleases, tho' I w^d have saved him but on his own terms & conditions since I cannot believe a word he writes, His letter is the most barefaced one sided statement" (O 1:63). The view that Poe had not "one good quality" seriously calls into question Allan's judgment. How Allan would have saved Poe we do not learn. Poe wrote a letter to John H. Mackenzie asking his friend to try to persuade Allan to grant permission to resign, and Mackenzie obliged, but Allan refused Mackenzie's entreaty: "He said he was tired of fooling with Edgar & intended to wash his hands of him for good and all."[26] With or without Allan's permission, Poe's West Point career was about to come to an end.

On January 23, 1831, Poe was "placed in arrest." On the following day, a warrant from the War Department arrived. And on February 8, Poe's court-martial took place. The first charge was "Gross neglect of duty." According to the first specification of this charge, Poe had missed evening parade six times, reveille roll-call seven times, class parade six times, church parade once, and guard mounting once. According to the second specification, Poe had not met his academic obligations, missing mathematics recitation ten times. The second charge was "Disobedience of orders." The first specification of this charge indicated that Poe had not followed an order to attend church; the second specification maintained that Poe had similarly not followed an order to attend the Academy. "The Prisoner" pleaded not guilty to the first specification of the first charge and guilty to the remaining specifications. The court judged him guilty of the first specification of the first charge, accepted his guilty plea for the other specifications, and dismissed him from military service. Several other cadets, including Poe's friend Thomas W. Gibson, were tried at this court-martial for lesser offenses. Poe's punishment was therefore the most severe: "Cadet Edgar A. Poe will be dismissed [from] the service of the United States and cease to be a Member of the Military Academy after the 6 of March."[27] An order of February 18 released Poe from arrest. And an order of February 20 stated, "The name of cadet Poe will be dropped from the records of the Academy from and after the 6 of March."[28] The name was dropped from subsequent West Point records but never from West Point history. And a memorial arch pays tribute to Poe in West Point's library.[29]

"The strict discipline, the mathematical requirements of the military school, kept my friend in an unhappy frame of mind," recalled Timothy Pickering Jones. This perception was supported by Poe's aunt and mother-in-law

Maria Clemm, who later stated that Poe found the discipline "too severe," and by poet Sarah Helen Whitman, who later noted (as had been related to her by a classmate) that he found the "routine uncongenial."[30] Surely the rigors of the U.S. Military Academy contributed to Poe's deliberately not performing his duties. Also significant would have been Poe's growing financial problems. He later wrote, "The army does not suit a poor man—so I left W. Point abruptly, and threw myself upon literature as a resource" (H 1:345). There is one report that some classmates disdained this child of actors, this dependent foster son.[31] But it would seem most likely that the precipitating cause for Poe's prompting his own court-martial was his having been, in effect, renounced by his foster father. Given up on by John Allan, Poe gave up on pleasing him through his performance at West Point.

We do have an account of Poe's final time there. His roommate Timothy Pickering Jones, who had already been dismissed, years later described Poe's confiding in him and weeping—"as we talked the tears rolled down his cheeks."[32] We may be reminded of Poe's last night at the University of Virginia with William Wertenbaker. The ninety-year-old Jones, looking back, said, "Poe had his faults, but I loved him."[33]

Poe left West Point on February 19, for New York (O 1:64). He wrote to his brother Henry (the letter is now lost) and then to John Allan. His tone to his foster father is pathetic, his situation dire. He is sick, with a bad cold and an ear infection. He is without funds. And he is angry. He declares to Allan, "I have been *dismissed*—when a single line from you would have saved it." He adverts to his "standing and reputation for talent." Presumably referring to his indiscreet remark to Samuel Graves, he closes "Please send me a little money—quickly—and forget what I said about you—/ God bless you—/ E A Poe" (O 1:63–64). There is no evidence of a response. Then, a desperate and bitter Poe decided to confront John Allan personally. So he returned to Richmond.

There has been some disagreement about this visit. For instance, Susan Archer Weiss asserted that it took place, but George E. Woodberry first denied it and later stated that it took place in the summer.[34] Flora Lapham Mack, a frequent critic of Weiss, here agreed with her. The timing of the visit would seem to be late February, when Poe was fervent and indignant. Poe's New York letter to Sylvanus Thayer of March 10, 1831, suggests that by then he was resigned to the situation with Allan, referring to himself as "Having no longer any ties which can bind me to my native country—no prospects—nor any friends" (O 1:65). His 1831 encounter in New York with Peter Pindar

Pease is focused on his later imminent book rather than on his troubles in Richmond.[35]

Mack relates the story as told to her years later by Jane Scott Mackenzie, John H. Mackenzie's mother. In 1831, Mrs. Mackenzie was living in the western suburbs of Richmond; Mack calls her home there "Duncan Lodge," but this was not the famous home by that name where Mrs. Mackenzie lived from 1843 to 1853.[36] John H. Mackenzie was living at Mount Erin with his wife, Louisa, and her mother, Mrs. Lanier. "Rose" was Poe's sister Rosalie. Jane Scott Mackenzie states that after Allan turned down John H. Mackenzie's request for him to intercede for Poe,

> Edgar behaved so badly they sent him away from West Point and before we knew he was in Richmond he came rushing in at Duncan Lodge one day perfectly incoherent with excitement and anger. I never understood precisely what had occurred[.] Edgar was in no condition to tell, Indeed he was in such state that he was really ill for several days afterwards but I at last found out he had gone straight from the depot to Mr Allan's house, "determined to assert his rights" he said by which I suppose he meant that he intended to assume that he was still the presumptive heir to Mr Allen's [sic] fortune and act accordingly, but in an interview with Mrs. Allen which occurred immediately after his arrival in the house whether with or without provocation I don't know he had insulted her so unpardonably that he had been ordered off of the premises & told to never return. He raved for a while like a madman and I had to send for John who had been married for 2 or three years & was living in the country to come in & try to quell him John was very fond of him and had more influence with him than anyone else always. I had a house full of company as I always had at Duncan Lodge and Edgar was irritated beyond expression by poor Rose. She was almost on the verge of hysterics herself and hovered round him condoling lamenting & trying to console him in her tactless way so when John proposed to take him home with him in his buggy I was glad he consented to go. He was in a perfect state of collapse when he got there and Mrs. Lanier and Louisa had to nurse him for nearly a week just as if he had had a spell of fever or some illness of that kind. I think he still had some hope that Mr. Allen would relent & send for him but this was the end of everything between them. And when he realized this he concluded to leave the city. He was penniless and we raised what money we could for him & he left for Baltimore.[37]

What happened between Poe and Mrs. Allan? According to Poe's second cousin Neilson Poe, "the trouble arose from the fact that Edgar looked upon the young wife as an intruder into the family, who was pushing him out & that he made his feelings known very distinctly, as we might expect from his impulsive nature."[38] Presumably he would have been particularly sensitive to any felt usurpation since his position with John Allan had come to be so fraught. Susan Archer Weiss offered a fuller account, crediting as her sources the Mackenzies and Mrs. Julia Mayo Cabell, who had heard it from her husband, who had heard it from Poe. The gist is that Mrs. Allan had had Poe's things moved from what had been his room in Moldavia to a room that had been that of "Mrs. Allan's maid." When Poe arrived, he was taken aback at the new arrangement and would not have his carpetbag taken to the lesser room. He expressed his unhappiness to Mrs. Allan, who defended her decision, explaining that she had never been told that the room that became the new guest room should be considered Poe's room, and referred to his dependent status, whereupon Poe intimated that perhaps Mrs. Allan had married for money. She was outraged and contacted her husband; from his business office John Allan ordered Poe out of the house. John Allan returned to the house as Poe departed (according to Poe himself), and Poe left, despite Allan's withdrawn purse.[39] There was a new dispensation at Moldavia—but Poe could not dispense with his pride.

And so, John H. Mackenzie drove his buggy east from his mother's home—starting probably on Broad Street (then called "H Street")—across Richmond, past Church Hill, taking the Williamsburg Stage Road to his home on Fulton Hill or Powhatan Hill, Mount Erin, accompanied by his very distraught friend Edgar. Briefly, Poe had found a refuge.

Mack wrote of Mount Erin, "It was here Cousin Lou came to live a bride. Here Edgar Poe Mackenzie her son was born and died. . . . Here Edgar Poe came from Duncan Lodge about that time to be nursed back to life & hope after the crushing blow of being ordered to leave the Allan home forever."[40] Mrs. Lanier (also known as "Aunt Pollie") and her daughter Louisa attended to Poe, seeking to soothe him, to calm him down. "They were very fond of him," Mack maintains; "he seemed to have the art of making all the women fond of him and Cousin John did everything he could to brace him up when he was at home."[41] They had to help him surrender his sense of Moldavia as his home, as well as the expectation, which had been encouraged in him as a boy, of inheritance. They had to assure Poe somehow that his loss of a claim to John Allan's fortune was a difficulty that could be overcome. Perhaps the extraordinary view of the city from Mount Erin might have provided some serenity. Perhaps the nearby woods, garden, and hothouse would have fostered a degree of tranquility.[42] Perhaps the Mackenzies' home itself was for Poe a kind of hothouse—a place that would nurture and sustain the young man at his most vulnerable and fragile. As the days passed, the Mackenzies "finally decided he must go to work at some thing and that he had nothing to hope from Mr. Allen [sic] and as he decided that he preferred to go to Baltimore[,] [t]he Mackenzies fixed him up nicely gave him what money they could spare & sent him to that city."[43] He would settle in Baltimore in May, but first he would go to New York City, probably to pursue the publication of a third book of poetry.

Poe's official dismissal from West Point took place on March 6, 1831. On March 10, from New York City, Poe wrote to Sylvanus Thayer, superintendent of West Point, asserting that he had "no longer any ties which can bind me to my native country—no prospects—nor any friends" and asking therefore for a statement of his standing at the Military Academy so that he could perhaps secure, through the good offices of the Marquis de Lafayette, a position in the Polish army (then fighting a war with Russia). Attaining such a position, he claimed, was his "only feasible plan of procedure" (O 1:65–66). Poe's request, not surprisingly, came to naught. But there was another "feasible plan"—the publication of the poems that Poe had been writing since *Al Aaraaf*. Peter Pindar Pease, who had met Poe in Charlottesville and Boston, met him again in New York City, "where Poe had gone, he said, to secure the publication of a book of his poems by Harpers." Poe was newly hopeful—at least in conversation with Pease: "He claimed, almost boisterously, that he had 'hit it hard' (evidently a favorite expression with him), meaning that his fortune was made. He told Pease that he was living in the vicinity of Madison Square, that he loved to walk beneath the elm trees there, and invited Pease to go with him for a refreshment." Pease declined the invitation but remembered the encounter.[44] Poe would not publish with the Harpers for another seven years, but Elam Bliss, of New York—who, by one account, had met with Poe at West Point[45]—agreed to publish *Poems*.

The volume was another modest book—nearly nine inches by nearly four inches, with 124 pages—identified on its title page as the "Second Edition." Yet it is sufficiently distinct from the 1829 *Al Aaraaf* to be considered a first edition. It was published after March 10—in either March or April 1831. After the printer's imprint (Henry Mason, 64 Nassau Street) appears a page stating, "TO / THE U. S. CORPS OF CADETS / THIS VOLUME / IS RESPECTFULLY

DEDICATED." The contents include one essay, "Letter to Mr. — —"; five revised poems, "Introduction," "Fairy Land," "[Sonnet—To Science]," "Al Aaraaf," and "Tamerlane"; and six new poems, "To Helen," "Israfel," "The Doomed City," "Irene," "A Paean," and "The Valley Nis." The essay and the new poems are of primary interest.[46]

The letter begins with a place and time: "West Point,——1831." Since Poe had left West Point on February 19, it would seem that he wrote this essay—his first published prose work—while deliberately neglecting his military and academic duties or even while serving time in the guardhouse.[47] Regarding the "B" of the address "Dear B——," General George W. Cullum, who had known Poe at West Point, stated, "While at the Academy he [Poe] published a small volume of poems, dedicated to Bulwer [the English author Edward George Bulwer-Lytton] in a long rambling letter."[48] (Of course, Poe had the volume published after he left West Point.) Stuart and Susan Levine write, "It is not really clear why an essay on poetry should have been put in the form of a letter to a novelist, but Mabbott felt that General Cullum's testimony 'cannot be lightly dismissed'" (L2 12). It should be added that Bulwer had written two books of poetry: *Ismael; An Oriental Tale. With Other Poems* (1820) and *Weeds and Wild Flowers* (1826). Other suggested identities for "B" are the publisher Elam Bliss and the poet William Cullen Bryant (L2 12–13).

The essay conveys Poe's confidence, his comic style, and his critical judgment. Faulting William Wordsworth, Poe mostly praises Samuel Taylor Coleridge, whose *Biographia Literaria* he has been reading. The vital point—stated by Coleridge (in chapter 14) and restated nearly verbatim by Poe (after his praise of Coleridge)—is that the purpose of poetry is pleasure.[49] Poe elaborates on the importance of indefinite pleasure and compares such pleasure in poetry to that of music. This is in contrast to what he construes to be Wordsworth's view, that the purpose of poetry is instruction. Later, Poe would call this view "the heresy of *The Didactic*" (L2 182). Of particular interest in this essay, given Poe's 1838 novel *The Narrative of Arthur Gordon Pym*, is the honoring of the tenets of Christianity—"the principles of our divine faith—that moral mechanism by which the simplicity of a child may overbalance the wisdom of a man."[50]

Remarkably, for a poet of twenty-two years of age, three of his six new poems—"To Helen," "Israfel," and "The Doomed City" (later titled "The City in the Sea")—were to become canonical. "To Helen," though not yet perfected, is already, in its initial version, a beautiful hymn to one's spiritual home—an "etherial, visionary expedition." And as we know from Poe's

October 1, 1848, letter to Sarah Helen Whitman, this poem was inspired by "the first, purely ideal love of my soul—to the Helen Stannard [sic] of whom I told you" (O 2:694).

We may find in Poe's treatment of Jane Stith Stanard in his early poetry the consistent theme of guidance. Poe writes in "Tamerlane" that his ambition might have vanished "did not the beam / Of Beauty, which did guide it through / The livelong summer day, oppress / My mind with double loveliness" (M 1:33). He writes in "A Dream," "That holy dream—that holy dream, / While all the world were chiding, / Hath cheered me as a lovely beam / A lonely spirit guiding" (M 1:79). And the theme of guidance continues in the elegant "To Helen":

> Helen, thy beauty is to me
>   Like those Nicean barks of yore,
> That gently, o'er a perfum'd sea,
>   The weary way-worn wanderer bore
>   To his own native shore.
>
> On desperate seas long wont to roam,
>   Thy hyacinth hair, thy classic face,
> Thy Naiad airs have brought me home
>   To the beauty of fair Greece,
>   And the grandeur of old Rome.
>
> Lo! in that little window-niche
>   How statue-like I see thee stand!
>   The folded scroll within thy hand—
> A Psyche from the regions which
>   Are Holy land![51]

And a comment by Sarah Helen Whitman is consonant with this understanding of the place of Mrs. Stanard in Poe's poetry: "The lady afterwards became the confidant of all his boyish sorrows, and her's [sic] was the one redeeming influence that saved and guided him in the earlier days of his turbulent and passionate youth."[52] Poe transformed her guidance of him as a boy—presumably to believe in himself and in his gift—into a poem celebrating spiritual guidance itself. "To Helen" is a poem of calm vision and high tribute.

And Poe, so inspired, aspired. The extraordinary "Israfel" conveys his impossible aspiration—to ascend to the song of an angel. He concludes, so bittersweetly, in his final stanzas:

> Yes, Heaven is thine: but this
> Is a world of sweets and sours:
> Our flowers are merely—flowers,
> And the shadow of thy bliss
> Is the sunshine of ours.
>
> If I did dwell where Israfel
> Hath dwelt, and he where I,
> He would not sing one half as well—
> One half as passionately,
> And a stormier note than this would swell
> From my lyre within the sky.[53]

Perhaps we may hear an echo of the close of Coleridge's poem "Kubla Khan." But the critical point to be made here is that there seems to have been a visceral basis for Poe's reaching. He later wrote in "The Poetic Principle" about "an ecstatic prescience of the glories beyond the grave"; he states, "We are often made to feel, with a shivering delight, that from an earthly harp are stricken notes which *cannot* have been unfamiliar to the angels" (L2 184). It is that "shivering delight," a physical response to a beautiful sound, that promises a heavenly beauty—as the lyre of Israfel even more powerfully intimates what Poe terms "The extacies above."[54] The pleasure of that "shivering delight" is only momentary—and therefore there is sorrow: great poetry or music may yield what Poe termed "a certain, petulant, impatient sorrow at our inability to grasp *now*, wholly, here on earth, at once and for ever, those divine and rapturous joys, of which *through* the poem, or *through* the music, we attain to but brief and indeterminate glimpses" (L2 184). To use a word associated with the Roman critic Longinus, it is "transport" that Poe seeks—and it is his seeking it to which readers respond.

Poe descends to despair in "The Doomed City." This poem of the sinking of a destroyed city in the Dead Sea shows Poe's range—and his felt darkness: "And when, amid no earthly moans, / Down, down that town shall settle hence, / Hell rising from a thousand thrones / Shall do it reverence" (M 1:200).[55] It is curiously satisfying to see Poe acknowledging, in his pseudonymous "A Reviewer Reviewed," his debt for these lines to Lydia Sigourney's "Musing Thoughts" (M 3:1385). He seems also to have been indebted for the first line of his poem ("Lo! Death hath rear'd himself a throne") to the first line of Sigourney's "Greece" ("Hail holy clime! Where science rear'd her throne"), a poem appearing in Charlottesville's *Central Gazette* when he was at the University of Virginia.[56] Again brilliantly transforming earlier texts, Poe will return to the theme of the destroyed city, imagining mysteriously and most pleasurably the recovery of one destroyed city, Jerusalem, in *Pym*.

Two of the remaining three new poems, "Irene" (later "The Sleeper") and "A Paean," hold a particular interest because they are treatments of Poe's well-known theme of the death of a beautiful woman (later discussed in "The Philosophy of Composition" [L2 65]). Irene lies peacefully until she is no longer mourned. It has been suggested that she may represent Jane Stith Stanard or Frances Allan,[57] but we do not know for sure. The Christian reference, the moon's humming, "'Lady, awake! lady awake! / 'For the holy Jesus' sake!'" has been traced by Mabbott to a poem by John Wilson (M 1:181–82); Poe does not repeat the reference in his 1836 *Southern Literary Messenger* version of "Irene," perhaps to diminish his debt. Like "Irene," "A Paean" (later fully revised as "Lenore") expresses a concern for the disrespectful treatment of the dead—offensive "light laughter" in "Irene" is a nameless "wrong" in "A Paean": "Or that my tone should be / Tun'd to such solemn song / So mournfully—so mournfully, / That the dead may feel no wrong." Whether Poe had in mind Jane Stith Stanard or Frances Allan or another woman—or no specific woman at all, as Killis Campbell has suggested—there is a fear of slighting the person who is now gone. Sarah Helen Whitman later wrote of Poe's works offering "a lingering pity and sorrow for the dead;—an ever-recurring pang of remorse in the fear of having grieved them by some involuntary wrong of desertion or forgetfulness."[58] There is a delicacy, a sensitivity, in the wish for a death-defying devotion, which does honor to the man. The final new poem in this volume, "The Valley Nis" (later revised as "The Valley of Unrest"), offers an evocative landscape of death and loss. Mabbott suggests, most plausibly, a Scottish background to it all, perhaps drawn from Poe's boyhood time in Scotland (M 1:190–91). Poe may have been using that which was known but remote, a subjective correlative perhaps, to convey that which was near—an abiding sense of bereavement.

"THE U. S. CORPS OF CADETS" subscribed to Poe's *Poems*. Poe's account had been settled by West Point for $36.72 on March 16; sometime in March or April, 135 cadets (of 232) allowed $1.25 to be deducted from their accounts for the purchase of Poe's *Poems*. Some of these included Thomas W. Gibson, David E. Hale, John E. Henderson, A. B. Magruder, and Philip St. George Cocke, son of Allan's correspondent John Hartwell Cocke. One person who contributed has not been identified. The total was $170, and on April 23 a check was provided to Poe, which he endorsed "EAPoe."[59] We do not know if Poe paid for the publication of the book, either with some of the Mackenzie money or with the cadets' subscription money. But, regardless, when the cadets received copies of the volume, they were annoyed. Thomas W. Gibson reported that there was "a general expression of indignation at the inferior quality and condition of the book," and A. B. Magruder stated that there was "a general expression of disgust" at the "puny volume," which offered none of the expected satirical poems. George W. Cullum declared that the cadets thought Poe's poems "ridiculous doggerel."[60] The critics' views were more varied.

In May, one critic wrote a mixed review for the *New-York Mirror*. Quoting from "The Doomed City" and "Fairy Land," the writer complains of the opacity of the work. He writes, memorably, "Every thing in the language betokens poetic inspiration, but it rather resembles the leaves of the Sybil when scattered by the wind." Another critic in May, responding to Poe's expressed hope in the first paragraph of "Letter to Mr. — —" that the poems "may have some chance of being seen by posterity," offered a discouraging prediction: "Posterity and these poems will scarcely make acquaintance."[61] Poe sent or had sent a copy of the book to admiring editor John Neal: "Mr. John Neal, with the author's best wishes."[62] And in July, Neal provided favorable comment in the *Morning Courier and New York Enquirer*, quoting from "Irene" and the entirety of "To Helen" and "[Sonnet—To Science]." He opens by asserting Poe's "fine genius" and closes by maintaining of Poe, "He has a fine genius, we repeat it, and may be distinguished, if he will not mistake oddity for excellence, or want of similitude to all others, for superiority over them."[63]

Having had his third book of poetry published, Poe followed his preference of returning to Baltimore, as he had indicated to the Mackenzies at Mount Erin. Perhaps he arrived in the city by May 1. He wrote a letter to the editor William Gwynn, inquiring about a job, on May 6. He notes, "I no longer look upon Richmond as my place of residence" and acknowledges in a postscript that he has "a severe sprain in my knee" (O 1:66–67). He also asked Nathan C. Brooks for a teaching position.[64] But in neither instance did Poe obtain employment. Where Poe stayed at first we do not know, but he came to live with his aunt Maria Clemm. Flora Lapham Mack writes, "Cousin John had helped him frequently during this sad time always responding to his appeals generously and in replying to his letters Edgar told him of his wonderful aunt who had searched & found him out and taken him into her own home giving him the loving care of a tender mother and of her pretty little girl who from the first had seemingly twined herself around his heartstrings."[65] That home was at Mechanics Row, Wilks Street;[66] that "pretty little girl" was his eight-year-old cousin Virginia. Also in the household were Maria Clemm's mother, Elizabeth Cairnes Poe; her son Henry; and Poe's brother Henry, who was probably by this time seriously ill.

10

"I Am Poor"

1831-1834

THE HOUSEHOLD THAT POE HAD entered in the spring of 1831 was a struggling one. Nearly two years earlier, Poe had written to John Allan, "My grandmother is extremely poor & ill (paralytic)[.] My aunt Maria if possible still worse & Henry entirely given up to drink & unable to help himself, much less me" (O 1:43). The family must still have been desolate. Indeed, a begging letter from about this time from Poe's aunt Maria Clemm (sister of David Poe Jr. and widow of William Clemm Jr.) refers to her "continual ill health" and states that she and her children are "enduring every privation."[1] Nonetheless, Edgar, who may himself have then been ill, was welcome. His "wonderful aunt" was a resourceful housekeeper and seamstress, as well as the caregiver for her sick mother, Elizabeth Cairnes Poe. The elderly Mrs. Poe, the widow of David Poe Sr., received a small pension. Mrs. Clemm's children, Virginia and Henry, eight and twelve, may have brought some lightness to the home. Poe's brother Henry was twenty-four, and he would not live much longer. Poe had acknowledged to John Allan a few months earlier, from New York City, "I have written to my brother—but he cannot help me" (O 1:64). Henry had apparently once been "a dashing gay cavalier," but those days were long gone.[2]

Edgar and Henry were close. Not only did Edgar later write, "There can be no tie more strong than that of brother for brother" (O 1:47), but also Henry used brotherhood as a standard of closeness: he wrote, about meeting fellow Americans abroad for fifteen minutes, "we were almost as well acquainted as if we had been brothers."[3] Henry had visited Edgar in Richmond; Edgar had visited Henry in Baltimore and had sent him a copy of *Tamerlane*. Henry treated his brother in such short stories as "The Pirate" and "Recollections" and even published his brother's poetry over his initials (all appearing in the *Baltimore North American*).[4] In the impoverished household of Maria Clemm, the two brothers may have shared the same room.

The editor of the *Baltimore Minerva,* John Hill Hewitt, met Henry once and recalled, "He was a young man of fine appearance—prepossessing countenance and an intellectual forehead. A phrenologist at a glance would pronounce his head a fine one—though the animal propensities greatly overbalanced the moral and intellectual. He was a young man of loose habits, of a sanguine temperament and a poet of no mean order. He sent in to the *Minerva,* a literary weekly which I conducted, a number of contributions, only two of which I have been able to save from oblivion."[5]

Hervey Allen and Thomas Ollive Mabbott, who saved other works by Henry Poe, reasonably conjectured about the brothers in Maria Clemm's household, "Edgar must have spent much of his time nursing his elder brother."[6] It is true that Edgar would later sometimes need nursing himself, but he could care for another who was in difficulty. For instance, when he was editing the *Broadway Journal,* in August 1845, he attended an eighteen-year-old clerk who had fainted. This clerk, Alexander T. Crane, remembered, "When I recovered consciousness I was stretched out on the long table at which I had been at work and Poe was bending over me bathing my wrists and temples in cold water. He ministered to me until I was able to stand up, and then he sent me home in a carriage."[7] Doubtless Edgar was ministering to his dying brother in May, June, and July, and on August 1, the day Henry died. According to the editor of the *Minerva,* "He died of intemperance."[8] Henry's funeral was held on August 2, and his burial took place on the following day.[9] Poe's memory of the death of his brother would powerfully endure.

Poe was continuing to write—and, increasingly, fiction. He had written fiction as early as his time at the University of Virginia, as the recollection of his tossing into the fire the mocked comic tale of "Gaffy" attests. A striking work of fiction, "A Dream," which appeared in Philadelphia's *Saturday Evening Post* on August 13, 1831, has been tentatively attributed to Poe by Killis Campbell and Thomas Ollive Mabbott. Lambert A. Wilmer, who would soon become Poe's close friend, then worked at this weekly (and Henry had published two biblically themed poems there in 1827). The brief tale is an imagining of the Crucifixion, with an especially vivid treatment of the emergence of the dead from their graves afterward (based on Matthew 27:52–53). The piece is signed "P." and offers a mix of reverence and horror. The language of this story—"I heard a muttered groan," "the fearful thought stole over me that the day of retribution had come," "The veil . . . was now rent," "The fire . . .'twas lost in utter darkness," "A column of light shot athwart the gloom," "There was an opening in the vast arch of heaven's broad expanse" (M 2:8)—resonates with language later used in an allegorically similar moment in Poe's *Pym* (P 1:182–83). I believe that Campbell and Mabbott were correct: this is Poe's work. And in light of the funeral of Poe's brother eleven days before this story's publication, it is interesting to see reference in the short work to "a mantle of crape," "the badge of mourning," "the habiliments of sorrow," "the sables of mourning" (M 2:7–8).[10]

The editor who would have published Henry Poe's two poems in the *Saturday Evening Post* back in 1827 was Morton McMichael, and he took on Philadelphia's *Saturday Courier* in 1831. He would come to have a significant connection with Edgar Allan Poe. The *Saturday Courier* announced a contest for the "best AMERICAN TALE," with a premium of one hundred dollars, on May 28, and offered the rules repeatedly, beginning on July 9. Poe did submit five tales to the contest, the deadline for which was December 1. These were "Metzengerstein," "The Duke de L'Omelette," "A Tale of Jerusalem," "A Decided Loss," and "The Bargain Lost."[11] Precisely when Poe began to elaborate the larger design for these related tales is not known—probably 1831 or 1832—but four of the five, or revisions of them, would help to make up the eleven-story collection "Tales of the Folio Club" in 1833.[12]

Despite his catastrophic last visit to John Allan, Poe did not utterly give up on his foster father. He wrote four letters to him from mid-October to late December 1831. An October 16 letter, addressed, "Dear Sir," asked for no support and offered an expression of regret: "When I look back upon the past and think of every thing—of how much you tried to do for me—of your forbearance and your generosity, in spite of the most flagrant ingratitude on my part, I can not help thinking myself the greatest fool in existence—I am ready to curse the day when I was born." And he was, he added, "wretchedly poor" but "*out of debt*" (O 1:68). This letter of contrition evidently had a short-term effect, for the letter of November 18 begins, "My Dear Pa." It also asserts that he does not wish to "apply to you again after your late kindness" and closes, "Yours affectionately." Presumably Allan had written to Poe and sent him money. But, nonetheless, Poe is now "in the greatest distress" because he has been arrested for a debt that he and Henry had taken on, and he asks for eighty dollars. He adds an injudicious additional pressure—"if you refuse God only knows what I shall do, & all my hopes & prospects are ruined forever." Still, he reassures, "I have made every exertion but in vain" (O 1:69–70). With no response from Allan to Poe for two weeks, Maria Clemm interceded for Edgar in a letter to Allan of December 5, begging for assistance and adding that her nephew is "extremely distressed at your refusal to assist him" and "has been extremely kind to me as far as his opportunities would permit."[13]

Then, still not having heard back, Poe wrote again to Allan on December 15, addressing him as "Dear Pa." Stating that "I have offended you past all forgiveness," he implored his foster father's assistance "in the name of God," "for the sake of Christ." Poe is no longer proud but abased: "If you wish me to humble myself before you I am humble—Sickness and misfortune have left me not a shadow of pride. I own that I am miserable and unworthy of your notice, but do not leave me to perish without leaving me still one resource" (O 1:70–71). His desperation is painful to read. Allan noted on the letter that he had directed John Walsh, on December 7, "to procure his liberation & to give him $20 besides to keep him out of farther difficulties." Perhaps Allan had recalled his own arrest in January 1822. However, he did not send his letter to Walsh until January 12 (O 1:72). Returning to "Dear Sir," Poe wrote again to Allan on December 29, asserting that "I have no claim upon your generosity" but beseeching "for the sake of what was once dear to you, for the sake of the love you bore me when I sat upon your knee and called you father do not forsake me this only time—and god will remember you accordingly" (O 1:72). This is Poe's penultimate letter to John Allan. There was no response.

On December 31, 1831, the *Saturday Courier* announced that the judges had determined the winner of its tale contest to be Delia S. Bacon's "Love's Martyr." This work was published on January 7.[14] Poe's five stories would nonetheless also be published in the *Saturday Courier* in 1832—but anonymously and probably without payment. The first of these was "Metzengerstein"; it appeared on January 14, 1832. The tale elaborates "metempsychosis," typically the travel of a soul upon the death of its body to another body, but here the travel of a soul to an apparition. In the story, Wilhelm, Count Berlifitzing, is burned alive trying to save his horses in a stable fire that his enemy Frederick, Baron Metzengerstein, caused, and the soul of the count migrates to an enormous horse fantastically escaped from the baron's tapestry. That horse is ridden by Baron Metzengerstein—eventually into his burning castle to his death. Even this early, Poe showed a mastery of the Gothic genre, which includes here such elements as a dark prophecy and an ancient aristocratic rivalry. Animating the latter portion of the work are the baron's terror and the count's search for vengeance—eventually attained. Accordingly, this story may be seen thematically as an early antecedent of "The Cask of Amontillado." The brief depiction of the baron's mother, "The beautiful Lady Mary," who died young of consumption, suggests Poe's mother, Eliza Poe.[15]

Poe's larger project, which he later called "Tales of the Folio Club," was a series of satires of literary modes and men. Poe offered, in his 1833 manuscript introduction to this never-to-be-published collection, a series of pseudonyms for the authors of the tales. The author of "Metzengerstein"—a work later revised and subtitled "A Tale in Imitation of the German" (M 2:18)—has been fairly inferred to be "Mr. Horribile Dictû, with white eyelashes, who has graduated at Gottingen" (M 2:205). Poe would have been exposed to the Germanic tradition of the short story, usually the gothic genre, when he was a boy visiting upstairs at the offices of Ellis & Allan in Richmond and reading the British magazines. And British novels might also have served as influences, including Horace Walpole's *Castle of Otranto* and Benjamin Disraeli's *Vivian Grey* (M 2:16–17). The Folio Club itself had a variety of models, but the most immediate would have been the Delphian Club of Baltimore, no longer extant but still remembered in Poe's time there.[16]

Also in January 1832, Lambert A. Wilmer, author of *Merlin*, moved from Philadelphia to Baltimore to edit a new weekly, the *Baltimore Saturday Visiter*. Wilmer and Poe became good friends; Poe later wrote in a review (using the editorial "we") that "we are very proud in being ranked" among Wilmer's "circle of *private* friends" (P 5:116), and Wilmer referred to Poe in a later poetic tribute to him as "thou dear friend." According to Wilmer, they had an "intimate acquaintance" in Baltimore and later in Philadelphia, from 1832 through 1844.[17] Poe was, in appearance, Wilmer recalled, "delicate and effeminate" and "fashionably neat," and "[h]is time appeared to be constantly occupied by his literary labors." Still, Poe and Wilmer did make regular excursions: "My intercourse with Poe was almost continuous for weeks together. Almost every day we took long walks in the rural districts near Baltimore, and had long conversations on a great variety of subjects. . . . He did not monopolize the discourse, but seemed to be quite as willing to listen as to talk." Apparently Poe denigrated Shakespeare and Milton but lauded Alfred Tennyson and Benjamin Disraeli. On one occasion, Wilmer recounts, when he and Poe and Poe's cousin Virginia were wandering through Baltimore, they came upon a graveyard and encountered a funeral at a gravesite. First Virginia wept, and then Edgar wept, as well. Defending Poe against charges of constant drinking,

Lambert nonetheless mentions Maria Clemm's chastising Poe "for coming home intoxicated on the preceding evening." Though Lambert was not aware that such an incident recurred, it unfortunately would happen again.[18]

The second tale by Poe published in the *Saturday Courier,* "The Duke de L'Omelette," appeared on March 3, 1832. Even while he was no longer able to be a "Gourmandizer," as he had been as a boy with John Allan and Nancy Valentine in London, Poe could satirize epicures such as the editor N. P. Willis and the protagonist in Benjamin's Disraeli's 1830 novel *The Young Duke,* the Duke of St. James. The object of interest in Disraeli's novel and Poe's tale is an apparently delectable bird, the ortolan. Disraeli's duke writes of the bird that has been served, "All Paradise opens! Let me die eating ortolans to the sound of soft music." Poe writes in his tale, "The door opens to the sound of soft music, and the most delicate of birds [the ortolan] is before the most enamoured of men!" But, comically, Poe's duke "expired in a paroxysm of disgust," for the bird is without feathers and without its paper coverings (for its legs). And Paradise does not open. Three days later, the duke is the birdlike potential victim: he is told by the devil to strip and, after refusing (but unable to leave), he takes "a bird's eye view of his whereabout," the devil's chamber. Realizing that Hell is outside, he plays cards with the devil for his soul and, by cheating, wins. As with "Metzengerstein," Poe seems to tell a tale of the triumphant soul—either the unconsumed ortolan in the first section or the duke's fraudulently saved soul in the second.[19]

The pseudonymous author of "The Duke de L'Omelette" in the introduction to "Tales of the Folio Club" is "the host, Mr. Rouge-et-Noir, who admired Lady Morgan" (M 2:205), perhaps N. P. Willis. "Rouge et Noir," or Red and Black, was a card game; Lady Morgan was a French author who focused on aristocratic pursuits; and Willis praised her. Notably, the tale of Mr. Rouge-et-Noir "was condemned at the previous monthly meeting." He is the host at this meeting since "[t]he father of the tale held . . . to be least meritorious, is bound to furnish the dinner and wine at the next similar meeting of the Society" (M 2:204–5). Perhaps Poe is thereby mocking not only Willis's writing but also his own mocking tale, which, though fascinating, is not as strong as some of the other pieces.[20]

In Richmond at this time, John Allan was "confined to his room," "quite unwell"; he put up his Richmond property for sale and worked on revising his will. At West Point, cadet James Ellis was accumulating demerits, and his father, Charles Ellis, who had previously offered him helpful advice, now offered him bank shares as incentives for good behavior. James was appropriately appreciative. Charles Ellis's supportive treatment of his faltering son at the Military Academy contrasts starkly with John Allan's negligent, even cruel, treatment of his foster son when he was there.

In Baltimore, Poe visited Coale's Book Store on Calvert Street and Widow Meagher's Oyster-place on Pratt Street. The widow reportedly referred to him as "Bard."[21] And he was continuing to write, and his work continued to be published in the *Saturday Courier*. "A Tale of Jerusalem" appeared there on June 9, 1832. It is a supposedly comic tale about the Romans providing to the besieged Jews of Jerusalem, in a basket lowered over the wall, a pig—an animal forbidden, of course, according to Jewish dietary law. This is a slight, not-quite-funny work, based upon a story by Horace Smith in his 1829 novel *Zillah, a Tale of Jerusalem*.[22] Yet the piece is important in that Poe later allegorizes it in his 1838 novel *The Narrative of Arthur Gordon Pym*. There, the tale of the siege of Jerusalem fits well, for it is the destruction of Jerusalem that is ultimately allegorized. "A Tale of Jerusalem" is sometimes considered a Folio Club tale, the one written by the pseudonymous caricatured author "Chronologos Chronology who admired Horace Smith, and had a very big nose which had been in Asia Minor" (M 2:205). However, Alexander Hammond reasonably contends that the 1833 tale "Epimanes," which is also linked to Horace Smith, replaced "A Tale of Jerusalem" in the collection.[23]

Poe had seen some young women in Baltimore—for instance, Kate Bleakley and his cousin Elizabeth Herring.[24] Of particular note is that about this time, Poe began to see his neighbor Mary Starr, also known as Mary Devereaux. Later, as an elderly woman, "Poe's Mary" told her nephew, Augustus Van Cleef, the story of Poe's yearlong courtship of her, and that story is worth drawing on here.[25]

It was "[o]ne summer afternoon" that Mary first met Poe. The year must have been 1832, as Mary's nephew tentatively suggested, since Poe's cousin Virginia, who was born August 15, 1822, was "about ten years of age" and Poe had "recently come to live with his aunt, Mrs. Clemm, after leaving West Point," but the 1831 death of Poe's brother Henry is not mentioned. Mary lived on Exeter Street, and Poe around the corner, on Wilks Street. The elderly former Mary Starr remembered that when Poe was introduced to her and sat beside her on her stoop, "He told me I had the most beautiful head of hair he ever saw, the hair that poets always raved about." So began their relationship, and she recalled, "From that time on he visited me every evening for a year."

Mary offers a fine description of Poe ("Eddie") at that time: "He was handsome, but intellectually so, not a pretty man. He had the way and the power to draw any one to him. He was very fascinating, and any young girl would have fallen in love with him." Noting his "black hair," his "piercing" "eyes," and his "clear, beautiful olive" "skin," she adds, "He had a sad, melancholy look. He was very slender when I first knew him, but had a fine figure, an erect military carriage, and a quick step. But it was his manner that most charmed. It was elegant. When he looked at you it seemed as if he could read your very thoughts. His voice was pleasant and musical, but not deep." After describing his clothing, including his "black frock-coat buttoned up," she closes by commenting, "Affectionate! I should think he was; he was passionate in his love." She confirms the accounts of his forlornness and his intensity that we have encountered before. And she notes, "We had no definite engagement, but we understood each other."

And Mary relates further telling details. Poe's cousin Virginia used to bring his notes to her at her home. Once, when Poe visited Mary, he told of his having just carried a young woman across a flooded street. Poe and Mary would frequently walk in the evenings to the hills outside the city. On one occasion, when they were returning to her home, he suddenly suggested going to a nearby minister and getting married. (She ran home.) He could get very jealous, as when she played on the piano his favorite song, "Come rest in this bosom," for another man, and Poe threw the sheet music on the floor. He admired her name and recited Burns to her—perhaps "Highland Mary" or "Mary Morison." He once showed her a letter from John Allan; according to Mary, Poe's foster father "said, referring to me, that if he [Poe] married any such person he would cut him off without a shilling." Of course, even without the marriage, John Allan would leave Poe nothing, but the threat would find its way into Poe's *Pym*. Acutely, Mary said of Allan, "He had no business to treat Eddie as he did, to educate him as he did, and then throw him over." The romance of Poe and Mary Starr would last through the summer of 1833.[26]

Meanwhile, Poe continued to write fiction, and his friend Lambert Wilmer lauded a sheaf of his tales, unpublished works that would presumably also be part of "Tales of the Folio Club." A squib in the August 4, 1832, *Baltimore Saturday Visiter* states:

> Mr. Edgar A. Poe, has favoured us with the perusal of some manuscript tales written by him. If we were merely to say that we had *read* them, it would be a compliment, for manuscripts of this kind are very seldom read by any one but the author. But we may further say that we have read these tales every syllable, with the greatest pleasure, and for originality, richness

of imagery and purity of the style, few American authors in our opinion have produced any thing superior. With Mr. Poe's permission we may hereafter lay one or two of the tales before our readers.[27]

However, there was very little time "hereafter," for Wilmer was being pushed out at the *Saturday Visiter* in favor of John Hill Hewitt. Wilmer sued the publishers, won a five-hundred-dollar settlement, and left Baltimore in October. In 1834 or 1835, Poe wrote to Wilmer to suggest that they edit together "a monthly magazine of a superior intellectual character," but the proposed venture came to nothing since Poe was soon thereafter offered a position on the *Southern Literary Messenger* in Richmond. Poe's effort to have his own high-quality literary magazine was to become his lifelong quest.[28]

By the summer of 1832, cholera had reached Baltimore from the northern cities. John Allan, in White Sulphur Springs, Virginia, wrote a letter to Charles Ellis on August 10, anticipating that cholera would reach Richmond. In fact, on August 12, Poe's old friend Ebenezer Burling died of cholera there. Poe, in Baltimore, may well have been reminded of the typhus fever in London in 1817 and the yellow fever in Charleston in 1828. The dread of an epidemic would later inform his elegant but ominous short story "The Masque of the Red Death."[29]

Two more Poe stories would be published by Morton McMichael in the *Saturday Courier* toward the end of the year: "A Decided Loss" on November 10 and "The Bargain Lost" on December 1. The former concerns the narrator's losing his breath—suggesting both his potency and his soul. The unfortunate protagonist undergoes a series of insults and abuses, culminating in his being tossed out of a coach and run over by that vehicle, having his nose bitten off by cats, and then being hanged as a mail-robber, eviscerated by a doctor, and finally electrified by an apothecary with a galvanic battery. The tale was revised for "Tales of the Folio Club" as "Loss of Breath," in which the narrator, Lackobreath, recovers his breath (his potency, his soul) from Windenough (his wife's suitor, perhaps her lover), who had appropriated it. The devil, it is intimated, assisted in the pneumatic transfer.

The tale later appeared in the *Southern Literary Messenger* with the subtitle "A Tale a la Blackwood" (M 1:61n), and Poe would refer to it in a letter as a satire "of the extravagancies of Blackwood" (O 1:125). Poe undoubtedly had studied *Blackwood's Edinburgh Magazine,* which he had known from his days on the upper floors of Ellis & Allan. The pseudonymous author of "Loss of Breath" in "Tales of the Folio Club" is clearly "Mr. Blackwood Blackwood who had written certain articles for foreign Magazines" (M 2:205). Characteristic of many *Blackwood's* stories was the blend of the sensational and the learned, to appeal to the many and the few. "A Decided Loss" and "Loss of Breath" possess just that blend. Later commenting to his employer at the *Messenger*, Thomas W. White, on types of popular magazine articles, Poe refers to "the ludicrous heightened into the grotesque" (O 1:84). Certainly this is an apt description of "A Decided Loss" and "Loss of Breath," each of which is a literal *jeu d'esprit*.[30]

And yet another is Poe's last tale published in the *Saturday Courier* in 1832, "The Bargain Lost." Philosopher Pedro Garcia, perfecting his manuscript, imminently to be published, is visited by a stranger—the devil. Realizing the identity of his guest, Pedro also realizes that his soul is at risk, and he begins to drink wine—Sauterne—to excess. After all, Pedro is "by no means, a fool" (M 2:90), and the devil confides parenthetically, "(and a pickled spirit is *not* good)" (M 2:92). At the close, "the metaphysician prostrated by the downfall of the lamp" is not disappointed by the devil's rejection of his soul but rather, we may infer, quietly triumphant that his deliberate inebriation has protected it. The Duke De L'Omelette beat the devil by cheating at cards; Pedro Garcia enjoys such a victory by becoming intoxicated. Not incidentally, Poe provided his characters victory through his own incipient vulnerabilities, gambling and drinking.

Poe revised "The Bargain Lost" to "Bon-Bon" for "Tales of the Folio Club." The philosopher Pedro Garcia becomes the bargain-obsessed philosopher-chef Pierre Bon-Bon, and the text becomes considerably longer and more involved. But the contest and its outcome remain the same. Scholars have suggested, fairly, that the author of this comic piece is "De Rerum Naturâ, Esqr., who wore a very singular pair of green spectacles," as mentioned in the introduction to "The Folio Club" (M 2:205). De Rerum Natura is appropriate since it was the title of a work by a philosopher, Lucretius, and the devil in "Bon-Bon" did indeed wear "[a] pair of green spectacles" (M 2:103). It has been fittingly concluded, then, that the author, De Rerum Natura, is the devil himself. He is generously narrating a tale of his own defeat.[31]

Notably, of the five *Saturday Courier* tales, four—"Metzengerstein" seriously and "The Duke de L'Omelette," "A Decided Loss," and "The Bargain Lost" comically—concern the soul.[32] Poe will return to that focus in later work.

Poe did correspond with John H. Mackenzie during this period. Flora Lapham Mack wrote that "[Poe] had often written to Cousin John of Mrs. Clemm & her lovely little daughter during his dark days in Baltimore succeeding his break with the Allans." Whatever were the many letters exchanged between Poe and his lifelong friend, the correspondence may have been interrupted in late 1832 and early 1833. For Mackenzie and his wife Louisa were headed west. Persuaded that they had the right to western lands for which her father and grandfather had made a long but unsuccessful legal fight, the couple decided to travel west and to renew that fight. Mack states, "They went in pioneer fashion in one of those long covered wagons called prairie schooners, carrying a woman to cook and a man to drive and their bedding provisions & cooking utensils etc." Their destination was, according to Mack, "some where Southwest near the Mississippi river." And Allan clarifies the matter in a February 27, 1833, listing of debts that he must collect: "John McKinzie Richmond gone to Kentucky [$]4.63." However, the cost of the Mackenzies' initiating the suit again was too great, and John and Louisa returned to Richmond. In later years, Mack writes, "Cousin John always alluded to it as their trip to 'the Western Country.'"[33]

On February 2, 1833, Poe published the poem "Enigma [on Shakespeare]" in the *Baltimore Saturday Visiter*. Despite Wilmer's telling of his disdaining Shakespeare, Poe here celebrated the playwright, using the first letter of nine hinted authors' names to spell Shakespeare's name (Spenser, Homer, Aristotle, Kallimachos, Shelley, Pope, Euripides, Akenside, Rogers, and Euripides) (see M 1:220–22). Elsewhere Poe wrote out excerpts from Shakespeare and made frequent references and allusions to him.[34]

About this time, Poe moved to Maria Clemm's new home at 3 Amity Street, going from East Baltimore to the developing western section of the city. Living with Mrs. Clemm in the household were also her mother, Elizabeth Cairnes Poe, and her daughter, Virginia. The narrow building (still extant) offered a parlor on the first floor, two bedrooms on the second floor, and a bedroom in the attic. Probably this last was Edgar's. While he lived at this home, Poe would eventually find his writing gaining greater attention—and his affection for his cousin growing into love.[35]

By April, John and Louisa Mackenzie were back at their Mount Erin home outside Richmond. But there was then a double loss in Louisa's family. Her aunt, Susan Simmons, of Prince George County, had lost her husband, Robert Mattox, on March 26. And Susan Simmons herself died on April 7. (She was the sister of Louisa's mother Mary, also known as Aunt Polly or Aunt Pollie.) So John and Louisa quickly decided to take in the three orphan girls of Robert Mattox and Susan Simmons—Louisa's cousins—Ann, Mary, and Eliza. From Susan Simmons's funeral, the Mackenzies brought the three girls to live with them at Mount Erin. The girls were enrolled in the school of John's aunt, Miss Jane Mackenzie.[36]

Of special note is the second daughter, Mary Mattox, almost ten years old at the time. For she would later become a friend of Poe's young wife Virginia. She would marry Benjamin Byrene Lapham, with whom she had children, one of whom was Flora Lapham Mack. And many years later, after John's wife had died and Mary's husband had died, John would marry Mary, making Flora his stepdaughter.[37]

In Baltimore, on April 12, Poe wrote his last letter to his foster father John Allan, futilely seeking support. There is no salutation or close—only a paragraph of desolate entreaty, reading in part, "If you will only consider in what a situation I am placed you will surely pity me—without friends, without any means, consequently of obtaining employment, I am perishing—absolutely perishing for want of aid. And yet I am not idle—not addicted to any vice—nor have I committed any offence against society which would render me deserving of so hard a fate. For God's sake pity me, and save me from destruction" (O 1:73). He signs his plea "E A Poe."

On the same day, in Richmond, Allan penned his final judgment of his foster son on the letter that Poe had written to him after leaving West Point, from New York City, on February 21, 1831. Allan declares, "[I]t is now upwards of 2 years since I received the above precious relict of the Blackest Heart & deepest ingratitude alike destitute of honour & principle every day of his Life has only served to confirm his debased nature—suffice it to say my only regret is in Pity for his failings—his Talents are of an order that can never prove a comfort to their possessor" (O 1:65). This absolute condemnation of a foster son by a foster father is difficult to read. Had Allan looked beyond Poe's justifiably angry letter of February 21, he would have seen Poe's October 16, 1831, letter, acknowledging Allan's "forbearance and . . . generosity" and "the most flagrant ingratitude on my part," causing Poe to think himself "the greatest fool in existence" (O 1:68). He also could have read Poe's November 18, 1831, letter, referring to Allan's "late kindness" (O 1:69). Though Allan provided belated funds in response to Poe's December 15, 1831, letter, he did not take the opportunity, as the foster father, to counter with magnanimity his foster son's assertion "that I have offended you past all forgiveness" (O 1:70) or his December 29, 1831, assertion "that I have no claim upon your generosity" (O 1:72). Unlike Poe, Allan never accepted any fault for the problematic relationship of foster father and foster son. Like Poe, Allan admired Shakespeare—he termed him "a tolerable judge"[38]—but he could not or would not remember or take sufficiently seriously Portia's caution in *The Merchant of Venice,* "The quality of mercy is not strain'd" (4.1.184).

Poe published on April 20, in the *Baltimore Saturday Visiter,* the love poem "Serenade," a rendering of communion as the speaker's gentle words enter his beloved's dream (M 1:222–23). And he would soon afterward publish there two other poems, "To——," a tribute to a sleeping woman, and "Fanny," a recollection of a romantic rejection in his boyhood.[39] And sometime during 1833 he wrote his first draft of what would later be titled "To One in Paradise," a sorrowful poem of loss, which initially included the phrase "never more" (M 1:215).[40] But Poe's most extended effort during the first half of 1833 was another Folio Club tale, "Epimanes."

Poe wrote out this comic tale in a simulated print style, embedding it in his May 4, 1833, letter of submission to Joseph T. Buckingham and his son Edwin, editors of the *New England Magazine.* The young writer was aiming high, for this periodical was then considered "the head of the American monthlies."[41] Poe introduces the tale as one of "Eleven Tales of the Arabesque." He clarifies, "[O]riginality more than any thing else has been attempted." He offers for publication the story alone or the entire collection and adds, after the tale, the postscript, "I am poor" (O 1:77). The work was not accepted; we do not know if there was any letter of response.[42]

"Epimanes" is a mockery of the egomaniacal—insane—Syrian king Antiochus IV Epiphanes—or Epimanes ("madman"). Dressed as a "cameleopard" (M 2:125)—a giraffe—he leads a large adulatory procession through the city of Antioch, in celebration of his killing "a thousand chained Israelitish prisoners" (M 2:124). Epimanes is chased to the Hippodrome by wild animals, which are insulted by his costume. The tale is a political allegory—a mocking of President Andrew Jackson and his administration and his followers. It ultimately anticipates Poe's 1845 tale "Some Words with a Mummy," in which the eponymous ancient speaker recalls supposed Egyptian history: "Thirteen Egyptian provinces determined all at once to be free," but later the enterprise devolved into "the most odious and insupportable despotism that ever was heard of upon the face of the Earth"—"it was *Mob*" (M 3:1194).[43]

The pseudonymous author of the tale is "Chronologos Chronology who admired Horace Smith, and had a very big nose which had been in Asia Minor" (O 2:205). The tale is told in the style of Horace Smith's *Tales of Early Ages.* And Chronologos Chronology also suggests Mordecai M. Noah, a prominent Jewish supporter of Jackson, who then shifted his political allegiance. In later years, Noah would importantly vouch for Poe.[44]

Meanwhile, John Allan was causing a problem for the Ellis family. Thomas, a student at the University of Virginia, wrote to his father, Charles Ellis, about Allan on May 6, "Besides, he has, as you say, widely mistaken the disposition of your son, if he thinks any kind of labor would be disrelished by him when it is to relieve you of the burden so long & so gallingly supported—No No! however time will show." Presumably Allan had shared with his former partner his view of the children of hard-working fathers "boasting of no occasion to labour despising every one who does," expressed in 1823. Allan continued to keep track of those who owed him money, including "John McKinzie Richmond [$]4.63." During the summer, Allan had increasing health problems because of the heat, and he traveled to his Byrd Plantation and White Sulphur Springs.[45]

On June 15, 1833, a literary contest was announced in the *Baltimore Saturday Visiter*, one that would prove a critical opportunity for Poe. The publishers, Charles F. Cloud and William P. Pouder, offered fifty dollars for the best tale and twenty-five dollars for the best poem. (Alternatively, they would provide a goblet for either competition.) The eminent judges would be the lawyer and novelist John P. Kennedy, lawyer and architect John H. B. Latrobe, and Doctor James H. Miller. The deadline for the competition was September 30. The announcement of the contest was repeated in the newspaper through September 7. There was a risk for Poe if he entered the contest, for if he lost, his work could still be published, with no remuneration, as had occurred with the *Saturday Courier*.[46] But believing in his work and no doubt hoping to prove himself the genius that he knew himself to be, Poe would submit to this contest both fiction and poetry.

Poe's yearlong courtship of Mary Starr came to an end in the summer of 1833. Decades later, the elderly woman recalled to her nephew "[o]ur final lovers' quarrel." Poe, who "had been drinking," was late in visiting her, and she was crying. Speaking to her through her parlor window, he explained that he'd had "supper and champagne" at a hotel with old West Point friends. (Here he repeated the gist of his excuse to Maria Clemm in 1832, about falling in with friends and having dinner and drinks, as Lambert Wilmer later recalled.) Poe's Mary remembered, "A glass made him tipsy. He had more than a glass that night. As to his being a habitual drunkard, he never was as long as I knew him." Then, sitting on the front stoop, the two had an argument that the elderly woman preferred not to elaborate. Perhaps he was seeking greater intimacy or, again, marriage. She ran to her mother in a back room, and Poe followed. Then, at her mother's direction, Mary went upstairs. Her mother took charge, blocking Poe from the door to the stairs. He claimed, according to Mary, by way of her nephew, "She is my wife now in the sight of Heaven," but Mary's mother told him to go home—and he did.[47]

This sodden episode reflects no credit on Poe. And it had distressing consequences. Mary broke up with Poe. He was unwelcome at her house, and his initial letters were unopened. When she did finally open a letter, she found that he "upbraided me in satiric terms for my heartless, unforgiving disposition." He also published in a local newspaper an accusatory poem about Mary (a poem that has not been recovered). Without telling Mary, her uncle James wrote Poe "a very severe, cutting letter." Insulted, Poe purchased a cowhide and flogged her uncle at his store. Poe later declared his action to Mary's father (James's brother) and cast the cowhide itself at Mary's feet. Rex Bowman and Carlos Santos have commented, in another context, that "[h]orsewhipping itself was a violent though acceptable form of insult under the gentleman's code of honor." But Poe's behavior still seems egregious. What is remarkable is that in later years there came to be a kind of closeness between Poe and Mary—she was with him and his seriously ill wife at the Fordham cottage in January 1847 the day before Virginia died.[48]

From June 15 to September 30, 1833, the publishers of the *Baltimore Saturday Visiter* received short stories and poems for its two contests, and John Hill Hewitt, the editor, provided these works to the judges, who met at John H. B. Latrobe's Mulberry Street house on October 7. It was an afternoon of wine and cigars and good fellowship, with Latrobe unwrapping the packages and reading the submissions aloud to Kennedy and Miller. Reviewing the stories first and finding nothing that he and the others considered worthy of the prize, Latrobe then observed an entry of unusual appearance—"a small quarto-bound book." And so he read, in their entirety, six hand-printed tales, which included "MS. Found in a Bottle," "Lionizing," and "The Visionary." As he read them, his fellow judges remarked, at various moments, "Capital!" "Excellent!" "How odd!" Latrobe recalled in 1875, "There was genius in everything they listened to," and earlier, in 1852, "The prize was recognized, and given, as the right of *Genius*." He commented that the book "was so far, so very far, superior to anything before us, that we had no difficulty in awarding the first prize to the author. Our only difficulty was in selecting from the rich contents of the volume. We took the 'MS. Found in a Bottle.'" Latrobe then withdrew from the envelope the note with the name of the author. This was Poe's moment: he was indeed who he thought he was.[49]

Of the submitted manuscript poems, two earned the judges' approval—"The Coliseum," in the now-familiar print of Poe, and "The Song of the Winds," whose accompanying envelope later identified the author as "Henry Wilton," a pseudonym for editor John H. Hewitt (a fact perhaps not yet known to the committee). Latrobe later recalled, "I am not prepared to say that the committee may not have been biased in awarding the fifty [twenty-five] dollar prize to Mr. Hewitt by the fact that they had already given the one hundred [fifty] dollar prize to Mr. Poe. I recollect, however, that we agreed that, under the circumstances, the excellence of Mr. Hewitt's poem deserved a reward, and we gave the smaller prize to him with clear consciences."[50]

The *Baltimore Saturday Visiter* published the results of the competitions on October 12. The judges explained that they had "no ground for doubt" in selecting a work from "The Tales of the Folio Club"—tales of "a wild, vigorous and poetical imagination, a rich style, a fertile invention, and varied and curious learning"—and they chose "MS. Found in a Bottle" "by the originality of its conception and its length." The author, they reported, was "Edgar A. Poe, of Baltimore." Furthermore, they maintained that "the writer owes it to his own reputation, as well as to the gratification of the community to publish the whole volume." By contrast, the selection of the winning poem was not so clear: "There were several others of such a degree of merit as greatly to perplex our choice and cause us some hesitation in the award we have made." The winner was "The Song of the Winds," and its author was "Henry Wilton, of Baltimore."[51]

Even as Poe was pleased to have won the short story prize, he was annoyed that he had not won the poetry prize. Merit, he clearly believed, should have triumphed rather than a generous but misguided impulse to share. He later wrote to Thomas W. White, proprietor of the *Southern Literary Messenger*, "One fact I would wish particularly noticed. The Visiter offered two Premiums—one for the best Tale & one for the best Poem—*both* of which were awarded to me. The award was, however, altered and the Premium for Poetry awarded to the second best in consideration of my having obtained the higher Prize. This Mr Kennedy & Mr Latrobe told me themselves" (O 1:96). Poe was also irritated that the winning poem had not been attributed to its actual author. Hewitt later acknowledged, "I thought it would not look well for me to be a competitor, being editor of the journal which offered the premium; and I used a false name, thus allowing the production to stand entirely upon its own merits."[52] In the coming days, Poe would visit the judges to thank them—and he would confront Hewitt in the street.

"MS. Found in a Bottle" was published in the *Baltimore Saturday Visiter* on October 19, 1833. Its narrator recounts, with compelling detail, a terrible shipwreck and the subsequent overwhelming of the destroyed vessel by a huge black ship. This is the *Flying Dutchman,* the legendary ship that reportedly must sail forever because of a crime committed by those on board. Flung from the wreck to the ghost ship, the narrator encounters the aged and impervious captain and crew, no doubt dead and still doomed.[53] As the narrator contemplates his situation, an uncanny event takes place:

> An incident has occurred which has given me new room for meditation. Are such things the operations of ungoverned chance? I had ventured upon deck and thrown myself down, without attracting any notice, among a pile of ratlin-stuff and old sails, in the bottom of the yawl. While musing upon the singularity of my fate, I unwittingly daubed with a tar-brush the edges of a neatly-folded studding-sail which lay near me on a barrel. The studding-sail is now bent upon the ship, and the thoughtless touches of the brush are spread out into the word DISCOVERY. (M 2:142).[54]

This paragraph is a resonant one for Poe's readers who seek discovery. Perhaps its only equal for the theme is John Keats's sonnet "On First Looking into Chapman's Homer."

Finally, the *Flying Dutchman* approaches a fearful southern whirlpool—the hole at the pole that Poe might well have heard of from J. N. Reynolds's lecture on Symmes's Hollow Earth theory in Richmond in March 1827. The narrator inserts his tale in a bottle and throws the bottle in the sea as the ship is swallowed:

> Oh, horror upon horror!—the ice opens suddenly to the right, and to the left, and we are whirling dizzily, in immense concentric circles, round and round the borders of a gigantic amphitheatre, the summit of whose walls is lost in the darkness and the distance. But little time will be left me to ponder upon my destiny! The circles rapidly grow small—we are plunging madly within the grasp of the whirlpool—and amid a roaring, and bellowing, and shrieking of ocean and of tempest, the ship is quivering—oh God! and—going down! (M 2:146)[55]

And so, mystery yields to disaster, and a rush of vivid language renders vortex and inevitable death.

The pseudonymous author of this extraordinary tale is "Mr. Solomon Seadrift who had every appearance of a fish" (M 2:205). This author is perhaps a parodic version of Adam Seaborn, the pseudonymous author of the 1820 novel *Symzonia: A Voyage of Discovery,* about a vessel's passage through the hole near the South Pole to the center of the Earth. The actual author of *Symzonia* was either John Cleves Symmes or someone who knew his work well. Poe would use the idea of the hole near the South Pole at the conclusion of his 1838 novel *The Narrative of Arthur Gordon Pym.* Also critical in this tale is Edward John Trelawney's 1831 narrative *The Adventures of a Younger Son.*[56]

According to Latrobe, after the publication of "MS. Found in a Bottle," Poe visited contest judge John P. Kennedy first. Kennedy had published his own novel *Swallow Barn* with Carey, Lea & Blanchard and would serve for Poe as a conduit to that firm and, later, to the *Southern Literary Messenger.* Kennedy stated in his journal on November 2, "The volume ["Tales of the Folio Club"] exhibits a great deal of talent, and we [the contest judges] advised him to publish it. He has accordingly left it in my possession, to show it to Carey in Philadelphia." Then Poe visited contest judge Latrobe, in his office, who recalled that Poe stopped by (on Monday, October 21) "to thank me, as one of the committee, for the award in his favor." Though Poe's clothing was worn, "*Gentleman* was written all over him." Poe had a solemn expression, except when he began to talk.[57] Especially charming is Latrobe's account of Poe's telling him the story that he was then working on, of Hans Pfaall and his voyage to the moon:

> [B]ecoming more and more animated, he described his sensation, as he [as Hans Pfaall] ascended higher and higher, until, at last, he reached the point in space where the moon's attraction overcame that of the earth, when there was a sudden bouleversement of the car and a great confusion among its tenants. By this time the speaker had become so excited, spoke so rapidly, gesticulating much, that when the turn-up-side-down took place, and he clapped his hands and stamped with his foot by way of emphasis, I was carried along with him, and, for aught to the contrary that I now remember, may have fancied myself the companion of his aerial journey. The climax of the tale was the reversal I have mentioned. When he had finished his description he apologized for his excitability, which he laughed at himself.[58]

Here we have a sense of Poe at his best, imaginatively engaged and readily sharing his pleasure in his work. Melancholy gave way to mirth, and Poe was at ease and appreciated. Especially notable is that climactic "bouleversement," for turnaround was sometimes characteristic of his imaginative work. The moment of symmetrical force upon the car by the Earth and the moon would have especially appealed to Poe, who later commented in *Eureka* that symmetry "is the poetical essence of the Universe" (L1:96). Poe's writings would sometimes exhibit a notable symmetry, including that of language, a verbal bouleversement.

Poe's visits of gratitude were complemented by a meeting of anger. According to Hewitt, a defiant Poe soon confronted him outside the *Saturday Visiter* office (at the corner of Baltimore and Gay Streets). With an "ominous scowl," Poe claimed that Hewitt had used "underhanded means" to win the poetry prize, employing a pseudonym. (However, the judges had already selected "The Song of the Winds" before they knew the pseudonym, let alone the author's actual name.) Poe went further, contending that Hewitt had "tampered with the committee." (He had not, but the judges had evidently "tampered" with their original judgment regarding the prize poem in the interests of broader prize distribution.) Then came the inevitable final exchange: Hewitt asserted, "The committee are gentlemen above being tampered with, sir; and if you say that you insult them," whereupon Poe replied, "I agree that the committee are gentlemen, but I cannot place *you* in that category." A resentful Poe, feeling cheated of the poetry prize, had deliberately and publicly insulted Hewitt. The provoked editor struck Poe—"a blow which staggered him"—and fortunately friends interceded, preventing another contest altogether. Hewitt lived a long life and maligned Poe years after Poe had died.[59] Poe expressed his lasting antagonism toward Hewitt in an 1842 letter to the new editor of the *Baltimore Saturday Visiter,* Joseph E. Snodgrass: "I have often thought, of late, how much better it would have been had you joined me in a Magazine project in the Monumental City, rather than engage with the 'Visiter'—a journal which has never yet been able to recover from the *mauvais odeur* [sic] imparted to it by Hewitt" (O 1:339).

In the *Baltimore Saturday Visiter* of October 26 appeared the poem "The Coliseum." Poe would have known varied treatments of the subject, from such a canonical work as Lord Byron's 1817 *Manfred* to such a fugitive work as an anonymous writer's 1832 *New-York Mirror* poem "The Coliseum." In these works, the effort was to wrest from the ruin of man's labor the reassurance of a lasting force.[60] Poe offers that reassurance in his blank verse poem through a parallel exchange between his narrator and the "Echoes" of the Coliseum regarding the obvious elements of deterioration: "These stones—alas! these gray stones—are they all—/ All of the great, and the colossal left / By the corrosive Hours to Fate and me?" "'Not all'—the Echoes answer me—'not all!'" The "Not all" turnaround provides the shift away from the evidence of ruin to the assertion of an abiding dominion:

> "We rule the hearts of mightiest men—we rule
> "With a despotic sway all giant minds.
> "We are not desolate—we pallid stones.
> "Not all our power is gone—not all our fame—
> "Not all the magic of our high renown—
> "Not all the wonder that encircles us—
> "Not all the mysteries that in us lie—
> "Not all the memories that hang upon
> "And cling around about us now and ever,
> "And clothe us in a robe of more than glory."[61]

The Echoes offer a consoling response to the narrator's fear. And consolation will emerge again from ruin in *The Narrative of Arthur Gordon Pym*.

In the same issue of the *Baltimore Saturday Visiter*, an announcement titled "The Folio Club" was published. It may well have been written by Poe himself and probably concerned the eleven-tale version of the collection.[62] Readers are invited there to subscribe to the forthcoming book, for its tales "are all characterized by a raciness, originality of thought and brilliancy of conception which are rarely to be met with in the writings of our most favored American authors." Noting that the author has experienced "the opposition of the press" and "the lukewarmness of the public in appreciating American productions," the writer of the announcement exhorts, "[L]et us give him something more substantial than bare praise." But a week later the newspaper reports that Poe will not publish his Folio Club tales by subscription in Baltimore; rather he will have them published in Philadelphia (presumably by Carey, Lea & Blanchard). However, "Tales of the Folio Club" would never be published by that firm or any other.[63]

Back in Richmond, John Allan was heartened by his better health; he wrote to Charles Ellis, "I feel so much improved that a few days of good weather will permit me to go out fearless of danger." But he soon wanted to settle his affairs, writing Ellis, "My Health is perhaps as good now as it ever will be while therefore I can attend to these matters it were wise to do it."[64] Poe's foster father, who was fifty-four years old, had previously been sick, and his good health would prove to be only temporary. His hostility toward Poe, however, was permanent.

The January 1834 issue of Sarah Josepha Hale's prominent monthly *The Lady's Book* (later to become *Godey's Lady's Book*) featured the unattributed tale "The Visionary," one of the works that Poe had submitted for the *Baltimore Saturday Visiter* short story prize. This is a rich tale, comprising two sections. In the first section, the narrator, in a gondola in Venice, approaches the Bridge of Sighs, between the prison and the palace. He hears the scream of the Marchesa Bianca, whose child, who had been in her arms, has fallen from a window into the canal below. Efforts at rescue are unsuccessful, until a stranger, whom the marchesa observes closely, jumps from the prison side into the water, emerges with the infant, and presents it to its mother. The child is taken from her—presumably at the direction of her elderly husband Mentoni—and she says to the stranger, "'Thou hast conquered,' . . . 'thou hast conquered, one hour after sun-rise—let it be.'"[65] In the second section of the tale, the narrator takes the stranger to his (the stranger's) apartment, returning the next morning, at the stranger's invitation, to the home of extravagance and luxuriance, a gallery of the gorgeous and otherworldly. The narrator finds in the pages of a tragedy a handwritten lover's lament—clearly that of the stranger—a light revision of Poe's manuscript poem of 1833 that would become "To One in Paradise." It includes the incantatory stanza, "And all my hours are trances, / And all my nightly dreams / And where thy dark eye glances—/ And where thy footstep gleams / In what etherial dances, / By far Italian streams!"[66] The stranger shows the narrator an extraordinary painting of the marchesa and then drinks several goblets of wine. A panicked servant arrives to say that Marchesa Bianca has been poisoned—and the narrator finds the stranger dead. He suddenly realizes "the entire and terrible truth."[67]

What has happened? The marchesa and the stranger have poisoned themselves, thereby consummating their suicide pact, which was accepted by the lady earlier, after the baby (probably the stranger's own) was rescued ("thou hast conquered, one hour after sun-rise—let it be"). Evidently the stranger had proven something to the marchesa through the rescue, which legitimated the pact. We may infer the ultimate significance of that rescue by considering Poe's referring in an 1845 review of Elizabeth Barrett Barrett's *The Drama of Exile, and Other Poems* to "the metaphor of a person leaning from a window so far that finally he falls from it—the person being the soul, the window the eye" (P 3:7).

So, the rescue of the baby that has fallen from the window is the rescue of the marchesa's soul. The stranger has demonstrated figuratively personal resurrection, and the marchesa is therefore willing to die simultaneously with her lover, with confidence in their union in the afterlife. In its focus on the soul, "The Visionary" is akin to Poe's earlier tales "Metzengerstein," "The Duke de L'Omelette," "Loss of Breath," and "The Bargain Lost."

Details regarding the stranger—"a very young man, with whose name the greater part of Europe was then ringing"[68]—reveal that he is Lord Byron. The marchesa is a composite of Byron's loves Mary Chaworth and the Countess Guiccioli, and the narrator is the early Byron biographer Thomas Moore. "The Visionary" is a Folio Club tale; Moore is represented by the pseudonymous "Mr. Convolvulus Gondola, a young gentleman who had travelled a good deal" (M 2:205).[69]

It is interesting that Poe here evokes in language regarding Byron's beloved his own early beloved, Jane Stith Stanard. "[H]er classical head in curls like the young hyacinth"[70] recalls, from "To Helen," "Thy hyacinth hair, thy classic face,"[71] and "that statue-like form" and "a scroll which lay at her feet"[72] recall from the same poem "How statue-like I see thee stand! / The folded scroll within thy hand—."[73] The Marchesa Bianca may well be Poe's renewed intimation of "the first, purely ideal love of my soul" (O 2:694), the consoling Mrs. Stanard, recovered in this tale through death.

It would be fourteen months before Poe would publish another tale—he was awaiting a decision from Carey, Lea & Blanchard on publication of "Tales of the Folio Club" as a book. On January 1, 1834, John Pendleton Kennedy, who had submitted the Poe manuscript, wrote to Henry C. Carey, asking about the work's status.[74] Months would pass before the matter was resolved.

In the eleven-tale version of the collection, five already-written tales had not yet been published in any form by early 1834: "Epimanes" (previously discussed), "Siope—A Fable," "King Pest," "Raising the Wind," and "Lionizing." Though never to be published in the proposed book collection, or the proposed expanded collection, all these tales would be published individually. "Siope" is a biblically cadenced tale of despair, describing an enormous rock with the word "DESOLATION," later changed to "SILENCE," atop which is a mysterious and troubled man (M 2:195–98). The critical source is Edward Bulwer-Lytton's short work "Monos and Daimonos, A Legend" (M 2:193). The imagined author of "Siope" is probably the one characterized in the "Folio Club" introduction as "a very little man in a black coat with very black eyes" (M 2:205)—in all likelihood, Bulwer-Lytton or Poe himself or a blend of the two.[75] "King Pest" is a dark tale of two inebriated seamen, Legs and Hugh Tarpaulin, who are threatened by a group of misshapen drinkers in an undertaker's shop in a disease-ridden neighborhood in London. Interpreted, alternatively, as political or venereal, the tale is certainly what Poe would later term "the ludicrous heightened into the grotesque: the fearful coloured into the horrible" (O 1:84). An important source was an incident in Benjamin Disraeli's 1826 novel *Vivian Grey*. The author of "King Pest" seems to be "a stout gentleman who admired Sir Walter Scott" (M 2:205), probably suggesting Washington Irving.[76]

"Raising the Wind; or, Diddling Considered as One of the Exact Sciences" offers spirited elaborations of various ruses and cons. The story, apparently intended as the first in the Folio Club collection, appeared in the *Philadelphia Saturday Courier,* but in 1843. It has been reasonably argued that its imagined author is "Mr. Snap, the President, who is a very lank man with a hawk nose, and was formerly in the service of the Down-East Review" (M 2:205). The reference is to the Maine novelist, former editor of the *Yankee,* and Poe advocate, John Neal.[77] Finally, "Lionizing" is a spoof of the fashion of adulation of writers, mocking, in particular, the author of *Vivian Grey,* Benjamin Disraeli, and perhaps the editor N. P. Willis, as well. This is arguably the last tale to appear in the collection, written by the unhappy narrator, the newest member, whose work has been voted the worst of the evening.[78] Hence the opening to the "Folio Club" introduction: "The Folio Club is, I am sorry to say, a mere Junto of *Dunder-headism.* I think too the members are quite as ill-looking as they are stupid. I also believe it their settled intention to abolish Literature, subvert the Press, and overturn the Government of Nouns and Pronouns. These are my private opinions which I now take the liberty of making public" (M 2:203). Indeed, in a letter commenting on the expanded version of the collection, Poe later wrote that the author of the tale voted worst would publish all the stories and appeal to the public for vindication (O 1:163).

Poe had clearly been very productive during his early years in Baltimore, writing all the pieces in the eleven-tale Folio Club collection. These tales suggest that he already strove for a market-savvy breadth, along with complexity and often a personal dimension. He clearly had confidence in his genius and was resolved in his aspiration. And he would continue to write fiction in his final years in Baltimore. Poe would comment on his tales in 1836, "Most of them were *intended* for half banter, half satire" (O 1:125), but of the original collection, "Metzengerstein," "MS. Found in a Bottle," "Siope," and "The Visionary" were serious. "Tales of the Folio Club" invites questions. Was the literary marketplace unreliable, as in the "Folio Club" introduction, or would it fairly treat work of great literary merit? Would Poe's reading public be more like the rabble of "Epimanes" or, alternatively, more like the public whose judgment the author of "Lionizing" was willing to trust? And, to shift from the material to the immaterial, would Poe be able to overcome his own "DESOLATION" and "SILENCE"? Could he save his own soul? And how would he approach the ultimate "grasp of the whirlpool"?

11

"Nothing Would Give Me Greater Pleasure"

1834-1835

How exactly Poe learned that his foster father had worsened we do not know. Perhaps there was a letter from John H. Mackenzie or someone else who knew well the Allan household. According to Thomas H. Ellis, relying on an account he had heard, Poe visited shortly before Allan's death—therefore, probably early or mid-March 1834. Leaving Baltimore for Richmond, Amity Street for enmity at Moldavia, Poe may have been seeking, however unrealistically, some word of forgiveness. This was his last chance. He rang the bell of his former home, the imposing brick mansion on Fifth Street and Main (earlier E Street), and Louisa Allan answered. Poe asked if he could see Mr. Allan, but Mrs. Allan stated that his illness was such that visitors were forbidden. The determined foster son pushed in nonetheless, ascended the stairs with Mrs. Allan behind, and stepped into the sick chamber. This was in all likelihood the same room about which Poe had written nearly five years earlier, "I went to your room to tell you good bye—but, as you were asleep, I would not disturb you" (O 1:22). Allan was not now asleep, and he was truly disturbed. Afflicted with "dropsy"—edema, a retention of fluid—Allan would have been seated in a chair. Ellis writes of Allan and Poe, "Mr. Allan raised his cane, and threatening to strike him if he came within his reach, ordered him out; upon which Poe withdrew; and that was the last time they ever met." Poe returned to Baltimore, repulsed and unforgiven.[1]

Charles Ellis, who was traveling in New York City and Philadelphia, learned the news of his business partner's failing condition by letter. His wife reported on March 19 that "Mr. Allan was very sick, the Dr has put a large blister plaster on his side." On the following day, Thomas H. Ellis wrote to his father that "Uncle Allan has been quite unwell all this week," though "He is now rather better." Finally, on March 27, Charles Ellis Jr. wrote to his father, "I seat myself to inform you of Uncle Allan's Death, which took place today at 11 o'clock, very suddenly; he was sitting in his Easy Chair by himself; and had not Mrs. Allan been called in by the cries of one of the children, who got hurt, he would not have been known to be dead for some time; when she went in he was laid back, and she noticed the difference in his appearance directly, and brought several persons to her assistance by her screams." Thomas followed up on March 29, writing, "Uncle Allan was buried this morning at 12 o'clock. His death has created much sensation & his family appear deeply distressed." Allan was interred beside his first wife, Frances, in Shockoe Hill Cemetery.[2]

The *Richmond Enquirer* referred to Allan as "one of the worthiest citizens of Richmond." But from West Point, James N. Ellis wrote to his brother Charles Jr. on April 15, "I have just heard the particulars of Uncle Allan's death. It was indeed a sudden call to one who has not although the papers say so, spent his time in a proper way. But peace be to his ashes for he was ever kind and affectionate to all and all his sins were against himself."[3] Perhaps James had in mind as "sins . . . against himself" Allan's drinking. (As already noted, Poe had indiscreetly described Allan in that letter to Samuel Graves as "not very often sober" [O 1:54] and later referred to Allan's "habits of habitual drunkenness" [O 1:185].) Yet there were also sins against others, including Allan's infidelity to his wife Frances. And then there was the question of his treatment of his foster son.

Mack writes, in Allan's defense, "[B]oth Cousin John and Mrs. Mackenzie his mother told me that no one in the world could blame Mr. Allan for *any thing* that had happened in his intercourse with Edgar Poe. That for the sake of his idolized & beautiful wife the 1st Mrs. Allan he had exercised towards Edgar a patience forbearance & generosity entirely foreign to his nature and disposition which Edgar repaid by dislike disobedience and a reckless disregard of any and all obligations toward him."[4] Yet there is another view. Frances Allan had felt the need to protect Edgar from her husband. Her sister Ann Valentine had sympathized with Edgar. And we know of Allan's whipping Edgar, reminding Edgar of his dependency, threatening Edgar, accusing Edgar, humiliating Edgar, never adopting Edgar, impugning Edgar's mother to his brother for an alleged affair, insulting Edgar's family to Edgar himself, and inadequately supporting Edgar at the University of Virginia and at West Point. The *Richmond Enquirer* obituary mentioned Allan's "devotion to his family,"[5] but Allan's difficult relationship with his foster son was not Edgar's fault alone.

Allan's complicated will, probated on May 8, 1834, was objectionable to his widow, and she renounced it. Probably she did not care for its mention of the daughter and twin sons of his former mistress, Elizabeth Wills. Louisa Allan relied on the intestate process. But either way, Edgar Allan Poe was never named.[6]

According to the 1843 *Saturday Museum* biography of Poe, written by Henry B. Hirst and Poe, or by Poe himself, Mrs. Allan declined to allow Poe to have Allan's books: "His widow even refused him possession of his library—a valuable one. To be sure, he never treated this lady with a whit more respect than that to which he thought her, as a woman, entitled."[7] And Louisa Allan refused to receive Poe at Moldavia after her husband's death.[8] Ann Valentine, who lived in the Allan home, is reported to have sided with the foster son over the second wife, "taking Edgar Poe's part against Mrs. Allan, she [Ann Valentine] maintaining that the former had been 'more sinned against than sinning.'"[9] There is conflicting evidence about the conflict. Thomas H. Ellis quotes the second Mrs. Allan as writing, "I never influenced Mr. Allan against him [Poe] in the slightest degree; indeed, I would not have presumed to have interfered or advised concerning him. Poe was never spoken of between us." Yet there is a record of a letter from Louisa Allan to Poe, written after John Allan died, acknowledging her culpability. This letter would be brought out and shared by Poe's wife Virginia as she lay dying in 1847.[10]

Detail for Poe in mid-1834 in Baltimore is sparse. He would have continued to live on Amity Street with Maria Clemm; her mother, Elizabeth Cairnes; and her daughter, Virginia. While he waited to hear from Carey, Lea & Blanchard regarding his Folio Club manuscript, he must have continued to write, perhaps one of the two tales he published in early 1835, the horrific "Berenice" or the haunting "Morella" (see M 2:208, 224). Meanwhile, in Richmond, all possibility of inheritance had ended, but a means to greater reputation was just beginning: Thomas W. White's new periodical, the *Southern Literary Messenger*.

White was hardworking and ambitious. At the age of forty-six, he had accomplished much—he had risen from printer's apprentice to printer to "Printer and Proprietor" of a promising magazine. It was he who had printed the three hundred tickets for Frances Allan's funeral in 1829. He also printed books, including, in 1828, James E. Heath's Revolutionary War–era plantation novel, *Edge-Hill*. White was apparently an affable man, with many friends.

The prospectus for his *Southern Literary Messenger* was printed on May 1, 1834; the first issue appeared in August. One of the encomia on the first page of the magazine was by the lawyer and writer John P. Kennedy, a supporter of White and, since the *Baltimore Saturday Visiter* contest, a mentor and advocate of Poe. Poe might have seen the magazine's prospectus or encountered early issues in Baltimore, but his personal connection with White and the *Messenger* would begin in early 1835.[11]

In the fall previous, Poe was working as a laborer. Though the writer's ambitions were empyrean, a former West Point classmate learned that "*Poe was then working in a brick-yard in Baltimore, being engaged in wheeling clay in a wheel-barrow.*"[12] He was evidently doing what he could to contribute to his aunt Maria Clemm's impoverished household.

This was clearly not enough, and Poe wrote to Kennedy on about November 19, 1834, explaining that he had no inheritance and requesting that Kennedy ask for "a small sum" from publisher Carey & Lea, which still had his Folio Club manuscript (O 1:79). One month later, he renewed his request (O 1:81). Kennedy had already been in touch with Henry C. Carey, and he conveyed to Poe the gist of Carey's response in a letter of December 22. Although Carey planned to publish the book, he did not expect to make a profit from a short story collection. However, he suggested that individual tales be sold to the annuals, and Kennedy had agreed, so Carey sold a tale to the editor Eliza Leslie. Kennedy received from Carey fifteen dollars, which he invited Poe to pick up from him (H 17:3). The tale chosen was the already-published "MS. Found in a Bottle," and, despite Poe's wish that something new be selected, the prize-winning tale would appear in *The Gift: A Christmas and New Year's Present for 1836* (M 2:134).[13]

It was Kennedy who advised Poe to seek a connection to the *Southern Literary Messenger*. Kennedy wrote to White in April 1835 that Poe had talent but was "*very* poor," and then acknowledged, "I told him to write something for every number of your magazine, and that you might find it to his advantage to give him some permanent employ." There was a passing allusion to Poe in a piece titled "The Doom" in the January 1835 issue of the *Messenger* (appearing around February 10); his contributions would begin in the March issue (appearing April 17).[14]

Poe, in Baltimore, still struggled financially. He asked Kennedy for his help in obtaining an advertised teaching job (O 1:82–83); we don't know if Kennedy obliged, but Poe certainly did not get the job. Kennedy did invite Poe to visit him for dinner, and the destitute writer confessed embarrassedly that he was unable to come because of his "personal appearance," and he asked for a loan, which would enable him to visit on the following day (O 1:83). Kennedy later recalled, "It is many years ago, I think perhaps as early as 1833 or '34, that I found him [Poe] in Baltimore in a state of starvation. I gave him clothing, free access to my table and the use of a horse for exercise whenever he chose; in fact brought him up from the very verge of despair."[15] This was a dark time for Poe; Kennedy's assistance must have been invaluable. And his making the connection of Poe with White was to be invaluable, as well.

In the March 1835 issue of the *Messenger* appeared the weird and shocking tale "Berenice," which is still anthologized today.[16] This is the one about the teeth—indeed, it was titled "The Teeth" in the planned collection "Phantasy-Pieces" (M 2: between pp. 474 and 477). An obsessive young man, Egaeus, becomes maddened by the allure of the teeth of his betrothed, his cousin, the once-beautiful, now diseased Berenice. He seeks in these teeth solace, calm, reason. Afflicted by a cataleptic seizure, the withered woman is perceived to have died, and, alone with her apparent corpse, the monomaniacal Egaeus sees what he most fears and yearns for: "The livid lips were wreathed into a species of smile, and, through the enveloping gloom, once again there glared upon me in too palpable reality, the white and glistening, and ghastly teeth of Berenice." Later, after having "done a deed," he finds refuge in the library where he was born, and he is told by a terrified servant "of a violated grave—of a disfigured body discovered upon its margin—a body enshrouded, yet still breathing, still palpitating, still alive!" Directed to look at his bloodied clothes and the nearby spade, Egaeus rushes to a small ebony box, which he drops, and "from it, with a rattling sound, there rolled out some instruments of dental surgery, intermingled with many white and glistening substances that were scattered to and fro about the floor." He now knows—in a frenzy, he has wrenched the teeth from the mouth of the entombed, but still vital, Berenice.[17]

For sheer horrific intensity, this is a masterpiece. However, admitting its strengths, the editor James E. Heath nonetheless had reservations, stating "there is too much German horror in his subject."[18] Thomas W. White seems to have had reservations, as well, and Poe responded on April 30, 1835: "A word or two in relation to Berenice. Your opinion of it is very just. The subject is by far too horrible, and I confess that I hesitated in sending it you especially as a specimen of my capabilities." Acknowledging that the work was prompted by a bet that he could not write successfully a serious tale about so unusual a topic, Poe went on to offer White his rationale for such a work, revealing his considerable analysis of the magazine marketplace:

The history of all Magazines shows plainly that those which have attained celebrity were indebted for it to articles *similar in nature—to Berenice—* although, I grant you, far superior in style and execution. I say similar in *nature*. You ask me in what does this nature consist? In the ludicrous heightened into the grotesque: the fearful coloured into the horrible: the witty exaggerated into the burlesque: the singular wrought out into the strange and mystical.

He added, shortly, "To be appreciated you must be *read,* and these things are invariably sought after with avidity." (Notably, on April 22, Charles Ellis Jr. had written, "Picked up the last no. of S.L. Messenger, and saw a very fanciful piece by Edgar Poe.")[19] Toward the close of his letter, Poe admitted, "In respect to Berenice individually I allow that it approaches the very verge of bad taste— but I will not sin quite so egregiously again." He stated his intention to send White every month a tale of the sort he has described, but each one nonetheless differing from every other one. And he contended that the virtue of the tales should be evident by their effect upon circulation (O 1:84–85).

Clearly in "Berenice" it is "the fearful coloured into the horrible" that Poe has provided. He has transformed a fascination with the trivial into an ultimately violent fixation. The tight focus and building momentum and elegant and ominous language and syntax create for the reader what Poe terms a "unity of effect" (H 8:75), a phrase drawn from Friedrich Schlegel (H 8:126). But even as Egaeus asks, "How is it that from Beauty I have derived a type of unloveliness?"[20] we may invert the question and observe that Poe created from unloveliness a type of Beauty. And that is evident on our consideration of the unity of design. For even as the narrator loses control, the artist exerts control. "Berenice" is an early instance of a Poe tale that rewards analysis of structure. It is not just a narrative but an object.

We may recall the "bouleversement" in Poe's oral account of "Hans Pfaall," a result of the symmetrical force on the car of the Earth and the moon. As stated, Poe would later write in *Eureka* that symmetry "is the poetical essence of the Universe" (L1:96). We may investigate the symmetry of "Berenice." The tale comprises four sections—separations are noted by a line of asterisks. Poe writes, at the beginning of the third section, the critical central passage: "The shutting of a door disturbed me, and, looking up, I found my cousin had departed from the chamber. But from the disordered chamber of my brain, had not, alas! departed, and would not be driven away, the white and ghastly *spectrum* of the teeth."[21] The pattern "departed . . . chamber / chamber . . .

departed" is an instance of verbal inversion, sometimes referred to as the pattern ABBA. The name for the pattern is "chiasmus," suggested by the name "chi" for the Greek letter X. We may readily see the X by linking the like terms:

    departed   chamber
                X
    chamber   departed

Framing the central X is symmetrical language. The first half, made up of the first two sections, feature "a memory like a shadow—vague, variable, indefinite, unsteady," "a species of epilepsy," "I sat, and sat, as I thought alone, in the inner apartment of the library. But uplifting my eyes Berenice stood before me," "the thin and shrunken lips" and "the teeth."[22] The second half, composed of the second two sections, features similar language in reverse: "The teeth!—the teeth! . . . with the pale lips writhing about them," "I arose hurriedly from my seat, and, throwing open one of the doors of the library, there stood out in the antechamber a servant maiden," "epileptic fit," and "Yet its memory was rife with horror—horror more horrible from being vague, and terror more terrible from ambiguity."[23] There is an architecture to Poe's art that is impressive and satisfying. And the formal pattern of "Berenice" will be repeated in later Poe tales.[24]

 Still impoverished in Baltimore, Poe had the new hope of a position with the *Southern Literary Messenger.* He was submitting short stories and writing criticism. And he apparently had been tutoring his twelve-year-old cousin Virginia: Flora Lapham Mack writes, "[S]he [Virginia] had never been to school & had been taught most desultorily & imperfectly principally by Edgar himself during his residence with Mrs. Clemm."[25] Perhaps by April 1835, the friendly relationship between Poe and Virginia was becoming something closer, especially in light of a letter to Maria Clemm four months later, in which he passionately declared his love for his cousin.

 The April 1835 issue of the *Southern Literary Messenger* appeared about May 14, featuring Poe's tale "Morella" and more than a dozen of his reviews and notices. "Morella," like "Metzengerstein," "The Duke de L'Omelette," "Loss of Breath," "The Bargain Lost," and "The Visionary," is a tale of the soul. Like "Metzengerstein," in particular, it is a tale of metempsychosis. The narrator is enthralled by (though not in love with) the immensely learned Morella and marries her. He studies with her, particularly concerned with the question of the endurance of identity. But he gradually loses his fascination and impatiently awaits her death. The dying Morella prophesies the birth of their daughter, Morella, and his own sorrow. She dies, and their daughter is born, whom he does love, but who is increasingly like her mother. At her long-delayed baptism, the narrator names her "Morella." The daughter eventually dies, and her father carries her to the tomb of her mother, which is now empty. Evidently, the soul of the mother had entered the body of her daughter; in this case, identity does survive death through maternal metempsychosis, perhaps as a means of vengeance on an unloving husband.[26]

Poe brilliantly transformed an earlier text, Henry Glassford Bell's "The Dead Daughter," which had appeared in the *Edinburgh Literary Journal* (M 2:222–24). Again praising Poe's work, including its "terrific beauty," editor Heath again faulted it, as well: "[W]e cannot but lament that he [Poe] has drank so deep at some enchanted fountain, which seems to blend in his fancy the shadows of the tomb with the clouds and sunshine of life."[27] Understandably, when Poe reprinted Heath's high praise of "Morella" in the second volume of a later collection, *Tales of the Grotesque and Arabesque,* he omitted the objectionable censure.[28]

In Poe's reviews and notices in the April issue of the *Messenger,* most telling are his highly favorable comments, in reviews of the *North American Review* and the American edition of the *London Quarterly Review,* on the lately deceased British poet Samuel Taylor Coleridge (P 5:6).[29] Of special significance is Poe's praise for Coleridge's *Table Talk,* for that work would prove a prompt for the novel *The Narrative of Arthur Gordon Pym*:

> Coleridge's Table Talk is highly interesting, as every authentic fragment of his sentiments and opinions must be. The work reviewed in this article, is published by Mr. Henry Coleridge, a near relative of the departed philosopher and poet, and is made up from notes of numerous conversations, taken down by the publisher immediately after their occurrence. They bear the impress of Coleridge's mind, will be read with interest by all classes, and probably do more to make the general reader acquainted with him and his opinions, than all else that has been written. (P 5:6)

A positive review of the April issue of the *Messenger* appeared in the *Baltimore Republican and Commercial Advertiser* of May 14; it commented, in part, "A striking feature in this Magazine, and one which cannot be too highly recommended, is the variety of critical notices of New Works: embracing nearly all of any consequence which have appeared in this country since the publication of the last number." The author of this review was Poe himself.[30]

In May, Poe was working on a review of Kennedy's novel *Horse-Shoe Robinson,* but he was sick and therefore unable to do the job he wanted to do.

He wrote to White, "I seriously feel ashamed of what I have written.... I am vexed about the matter, for Mr K has proved himself a kind friend to me in every respect, and I am sincerely grateful to him for many acts of generosity and attention" (O 1:88–89). He suggested his reviewing the *Messenger* in the *Baltimore American*. And he expressed his contentment with White's treatment of him: "You ask me if I am perfectly satisfied with your course. I reply that I am—entirely. My poor services are not worth what you give me for them" (O 1:89).[31] Poe was ably building his rapport with White.

On June 11, 1835, the May issue of the *Southern Literary Messenger* was published.[32] Featured there was the humorous "Lion-izing. A Tale," the final Folio Club tale, the new member's poorly received work. It was well received by the new editor of the *Messenger*, Edward V. Sparhawk (who replaced James E. Heath): "'*Lion-izing*,' by Mr. Poe, is an inimitable piece of wit and satire: and the man must be far gone in a melancholic humor, whose risibility is not moved by this tale."[33] Poe himself, in the *Baltimore Republican*, anonymously termed "*Lionizing*, a tale by Edgar A. Poe," "an admirable piece of burlesque, which displays much reading, a lively humor, and an ability to afford amusement or instruction, according to the direction he may choose to give his pen, which should not be suffered to lie unemployed, and will not, we trust, be neglected."[34] Poe was kinder to this tale than the members of his Folio Club had been.

Poe's discussion of Kennedy's *Horse-Shoe Robinson*, though not a "thorough review" (O 1:88), offers thoughtful commentary with evident commendation, concluding, "[W]e prophecy that *Horse-Shoe Robinson* will be eagerly read by all classes of people, and cannot fail to place Mr. Kennedy in a high rank among the writers of this or of any other country."[35] Owing to illness, Poe did not "examine it [the novel] in detail" in this "hasty sketch" (O 1:88–89), and he criticizes reviewers for a too-revealing analysis, which he would himself object to "should we ever be so lucky as to write a book." His reference to "that connecting chain which unites into one proper whole the varied events of the novel" is memorable in light of the novel he would soon write.[36] As an unnamed reviewer, Poe elsewhere praised this review of *Horse-Shoe Robinson*.[37] A filler in the May issue titled "Swimming" quotes from Poe's April 30 letter to White about his childhood feat (O 1:84).[38] And comments on Poe's "Morella" appearing on the wrappers of the May 1835 *Messenger* acknowledge his power but fault his gloom.[39]

Poe continued to correspond with White, presumably hoping for what Kennedy had termed "permanent employ." On June 12, Poe reassured White that he was now well, touched on various particular *Messenger* matters, and closed, generously, "What I can do farther to aid the circulation of your Magazine I will gladly do—but I must insist on your not sending me any remuneration for services of this nature. They are a pleasure to me & no trouble whatever." He added his congratulations on White's having hired Sparhawk as editor (O 1:91). Ten days later, Poe wrote White again, offering advice regarding the magazine and a willingness to be responsive, and commenting thoughtfully on a poem in honor of White's deceased son. The possibility of a position must have been tentatively noted by White in his letter of June 18, and Poe wrote, "You ask if I would be willing to come on to Richmond if you should have occasion for my services during the coming winter. I reply that nothing would give me greater pleasure." He avoids presuming that a job is his, expressing an interest in moving to Richmond and obtaining "a situation likely to suit me." Toward the close, he intimates his professional aspiration: "What you say, in the conclusion of your letter, in relation to the supervision of proof-sheets, gives me reason to hope that possibly you might find something for me to do in your office" (O 1:93). Poe's eventual 150-mile trip from Baltimore to Richmond would make possible his early national reputation. But first came a trip to the moon.

"Hans Phaall—A Tale" appeared in the June 1835 *Southern Literary Messenger*, which came out before July 10.[40] The balloon ascent to the moon, which Poe had recounted to Latrobe in October 1833, was later fully written down in what Poe described as "a fortnight[']s hard labour" (O 1:96). Sources included encyclopedia entries, magazine and journal articles, and John Herschel's *Treatise on Astronomy* (P 1:369–72). The published work is a tour de force of science fiction, offering compelling verisimilar detail, including an ingenious atmosphere condenser and a hydraulic alarm clock. And, like any April 1 extravaganza, it eventually reveals its hoaxical underpinnings. As editor Sparhawk wrote in his introductory comments, "Mr. Poe's story is a long one, but it will appear short to the reader, whom it bears along with irresistible interest." Poe's hard labor made for easy reading. Poe anonymously lauded his tale in the *Baltimore Republican*, terming it "a capital burlesque upon balloonings."[41]

Several of Poe's reviews in the June 1835 *Messenger* invite brief attention. His review of *Outre-Mer*, by Henry Wadsworth Longfellow, is notable for its positive attitude toward a later foe. That of *Voyage of the United States Frigate Potomac*, by J. N. Reynolds, is significant for its characterization of the author or compiler as "the associate of Symmes in his remarkable theory of the earth, and a public defender of that very indefensible subject." Nonetheless, Poe's reliance on the holes-at-the-poles theory is evident in "Hans Phaall" and would be apparent in *Pym*, where Poe also leaned on passages in

Reynolds's *Voyage*. The review of *The History of Ireland*, by Thomas Moore, praises Moore's biography of Byron, and the review of *Pencil Sketches*, by Eliza Leslie, announces the forthcoming annual *The Gift . . . for 1836*, which, not incidentally, will include Poe's "MS. Found in a Bottle." Poe mentions "a host of *stellæ minores*" in the annual—of which he would be one (P 5:20–21).[42]

Poe's paternal grandmother, Elizabeth Cairnes Poe, died on July 7 and was buried on the following day.[43] Her daughter Maria Clemm had cared for her "with a Christian & martyr-like fortitude," according to Poe (O 1:99). The straitened Clemm household would now no longer have the small Revolutionary War pension of David Poe Sr. In all likelihood, Poe was still writing—perhaps finishing his review of the second edition of John Marshall's *Life of George Washington* (O 1:91). But on July 20, responding to White's two recent letters, Poe expressed his keen disappointment that his Marshall review would not appear—apparently because the judge had lately died. Poe's final extant letter to White touches on a variety of topics, including White's health, "Hans Phaall," the *Baltimore Saturday Visiter* competition, and Poe's payment for his work for the *Messenger* (O 1:95–97).

The July issue of the magazine appeared following August 7.[44] Poe contributed a revised version of the Folio Club tale "The Visionary" (now "The Visionary—A Tale"). He also provided a short new poem, "To Mary," reportedly addressed to Mary Winfree, who had visited him in Baltimore from Virginia (M 1:236–37). Poe, from his "Sad path," finds in dreams of Mary "solace," "An Eden of sweet repose." The poem's second stanza recalls the solace of Jane Stith Stanard in the opening of "To Helen."[45] Also, White features praise of Poe's previous *Messenger* work, including John Hampden Pleasants's comment that there is "much sublimity" in "Hans Phaall."[46]

Sometime before August 14, 1835, Poe finally left Baltimore for Richmond, perhaps by steamboat.[47] The next eighteen months would be a time of contrasting intensities. He would carry on literary sprints and drinking sprees, serious lucubration and self-destructive lubrication. He would sometimes ruin his hard-won domestic contentment with his overriding susceptibility. Yet even in this time of repeated alcoholic lapses, there was the occasional delight—even the glorious leap. It was during this very difficult time that Poe would find moments of extraordinary happiness.

12

"A Fair Prospect of Future Success"

1835-1837

O N AUGUST 18, 1835, THOMAS W. WHITE, publisher of the *Southern Literary Messenger*, wrote to his friend and advisor Lucian Minor, "Mr. Poe is here also.—He tarries one month—and will aid me all that lies in his power."[1] Poe's power was great, but unsteady, for he was sometimes drinking.

Once again in Richmond, Poe lived initially at Mrs. Poore's boardinghouse on Bank Street, opposite Capitol Square.[2] Also living there were her daughter and son-in-law, Thomas W. Cleland. A short walk east was the *Southern Literary Messenger* building, a three-story brick structure at the southeast corner of Fifteenth and Main (or E) Streets; the editorial office was on the second floor. (Next door, along Fifteenth, was the warehouse of Ellis & Allan.) The proprietor of the *Messenger* was of benign countenance: he appears in a contemporary portrait as red-cheeked, curly-haired, and nearly smiling. His previous editors had been James H. Heath and Edward V. Sparhawk. Working in his office was a staff of about eleven, including foreman William Macfarlane and "printer's devil" John W. Fergusson. For a year, beginning at the end of March 1835, a young Boston newspaperman and former *Messenger* subscriber, Edward G. Frothingham, served as "a proofreader and corrector."[3] He would leave, in part, because of the horrors of slavery. Poe, raised in the South, was not adamant on either side. But he would shortly depict a dark-skinned character who would prove to be lifesaving.

Even as he began at the *Messenger*, Poe applied for a teaching job at the Richmond Academy, unsuccessfully. As he worked on the August issue of the magazine, he was clearly concerned with his family back in Baltimore. He responded to a second cousin in Georgia, banker William Poe, elaborating family history and requesting support for his aunt Maria Clemm, whose financial situation was particularly bleak without her mother's small annuity (O 1:100). And he expressed to Mrs. Clemm his anguish about his possible loss of his now beloved Virginia.

It was August 29. Poe had received a letter from Mrs. Clemm asking his advice about an offer from Neilson Poe, of Baltimore, to take into his household her daughter Virginia. "N. Poe," as Poe referred to him, was the husband of Josephine Clemm, the daughter of Mrs. Clemm's husband William by his first marriage. The possibility of Virginia's accepting the offer devastated Poe. He wrote, in obvious pain, in response to Maria Clemm:

> I am blinded with tears while writing thi[s] letter—I have no wish to live another hour. Amid sorrow, [*MS torn*] and the deepest anxiety your letter reached—and you well know how little I am able to bear up under the pressure of grief. My bitterest enemy would pity me could he now read my heart—My last my last my only hold on life is cruelly torn away—I have no desire to live and *will not*. But let my duty be done. I love, *you know* I love Virginia passionately devotedly. I cannot express in words the fervent devotion I feel towards my dear little cousin—my own darling.

Countering the advantages that Neilson Poe might provide, Poe states, "I had procured a sweet little house in a retired situation on [ch]urch hill—newly done up and with a large garden and [eve]ry convenience—at only $5 per month. I have been dreaming [*MS torn*] every day & night since of the rapture I should feel in [havi]ng my only friends—all I love on Earth with me there, [and] the pride I would take in making you both comfor[table] & in calling her my wife." He goes on, "Are you sure she would be more happy. Do you think any one could love her more dearly than I?" He declares, "She will have far—very far better opportunites [*sic*] of entering into society here than with N. P. Every one here receives me with open arms." He closes, "Ask Virginia. Leave it to her. Let me have, under her own hand, a letter, bidding me *good bye*—forever—and I [m]ay die—my heart will break—but I will say no more." Still, he does add, "Kiss her for me—a million times[.]" And to Virginia herself, Poe writes, "For Virginia, My love, my own sweetest Sissy, my darling little wifey, thi[nk w]ell before you break the heart of your cousin. Eddy" (O 1:102–04). Poe could aspire, but he could also despair. He would wait for his aunt's letter back with "anxiety & dread" (O 1:104). The loss of Virginia, whom he loved and needed, would have been a very great blow.

Of those in Richmond who received him "with open arms," foremost would have been the Mackenzies. He would have been welcomed by Jane Scott Mackenzie, still living in the western section of Richmond, where she would later build Duncan Lodge. Poe's admiring sister Rosalie still lived there with her (O 1:100). And he would have been warmly received by Mrs. Mackenzie's oldest son, Poe's lifelong friend John, and his wife Louisa—they would have been glad to see him, but perhaps also, with good reason, somewhat worried about him.

John and Louisa no longer lived at Mount Erin; they had moved. With Louisa's mother, Mrs. William Sturtevant Lanier (also known as Aunt Polly or Aunt Pollie), and Louisa's cousins Ann, Mary, and Eliza Mattox, the couple had relocated to a farm seven miles south of Richmond, known as Darby Town. John was regularly in Richmond for his tobacco business and his dray business, and he could readily provide Poe a buggy ride to his family's new home, soon to be an important landscape in Poe's life and imagination.[4] And Darby Town would become memorable for Virginia, as well.

The August issue of the *Messenger* must have appeared by September 4 since Poe wrote to John Neal then, providing a copy of the issue, seeking an exchange with his correspondent's publication (O 1:105–6). Neal, to whom Poe had dedicated "Tamerlane" in 1829, was coeditor (with H. Hastings Weld) of the *New England Galaxy,* a weekly Boston newspaper. An exchange ensued, for Poe quoted Neal's published praise of the August issue in the September issue.[5] The August 1835 *Messenger* featured Poe's short story "Bon-Bon—A Tale," which was a rewriting of "The Bargain Lost," and his poem "The Coliseum," now titled "The Coliseum. A Prize Poem." Poe wrote the criticism; most interesting here are his high praise for Theodore Hook, author of the short story collection *Magpie Castle* (P 5:29) and, years earlier, the play *Tekeli,* and his high expectations for Eliza Leslie's forthcoming volume of *The Gift,* with its "galaxy of talent" (P 5:31)—which included himself. This issue of the *Messenger* concludes with "To Readers and Correspondents," concerning Poe and the *Baltimore Saturday Visiter* competition. Consistent with his letter to White of July 20 (O 1:96), the editorial piece (probably written by Poe) states that he had won both the fiction and poetry contests and includes the tribute to Poe from judges John P. Kennedy, John H. B. Latrobe, and James H. Miller (P 5:31).

We do not know precisely how long it took Maria Clemm to reassure Poe about Virginia. And he would have been drinking. Taverns were plentiful in 1835 Richmond—across Main Street from the *Messenger* building was the Bell Tavern, and in various locations in the city were the Washington Tavern, the Swan Tavern, the Shockoe Hill Tavern, and the Court House Tavern.[6] Of course, there was also the possibility of drinking at inns and private homes. White wrote to Lucian Minor on September 8, "Poe is now in my employ— not as Editor. He is unfortunately rather dissipated,—and therefore I can place very little reliance upon him. His disposition is quite amiable. He will be some assistance to me in proof-reading—at least I hope so."[7]

Drinking was in all likelihood a symptom of other problems. There was the uncertainty of his life with Virginia. There was the tenuousness of his employment at the *Messenger* (O 1:109). And it may well have been that there was something even more, something profound and essential. He wrote to his champion John P. Kennedy, on September 11, confessing "a depression of spirits such as I have never felt before" and stating that "I have struggled in vain against the influence of this melancholy." He confides, "I am wretched, and know not why." He directs his friend and mentor, "Console me—for you can. But let it be quickly—or it will be too late. Write me immediately. Convince me that it is worth one's while——that it is at all necessary to live, and you will prove yourself indeed my friend" (O 1:107). This was another dark time for Poe, one that may well have contributed to the depth of his future writing—and to his concern with literature's power of consolation.

Kennedy replied encouragingly, on September 19, noting Poe's growing reputation and counseling, "Rise early, live generously, and make cheerful acquaintances and I have no doubt you will send these misgivings of the heart all to the Devil" (H 17:19). Poe later acknowledged the "great influence" of this letter (O 1:120), but its influence was not in time to forestall White's giving Poe notice as editor. White wrote to Minor on September 21, "Poe has flew [*sic*] the track already. His habits were not good.—He is in addition the victim of melancholy. I should not be at all astonished to hear that he had been guilty of suicide."[8] Poe had left Richmond for Baltimore. He had to regain his sobriety, shake his depression, and win his adored Virginia.

Poe wooed and won his young cousin. On September 22, 1835, a marriage license was granted to the couple. There has been disagreement among scholars as to whether the two were then married in Baltimore—Thomas Ollive

Mabbott and Kenneth Silverman give the marriage credence, but Arthur Hobson Quinn dismisses it.[9] What can be added here is that Flora Lapham Mack wrote of Poe's comments at the time to the Mackenzies, "[Poe] often spoke to them most affectionately of Mrs. Clemm & Virginia saying that he loved them dearly & was unhappy without them & he was going to bring them to Richmond to live with him soon but I never heard of his hinting ever that there was a suspicion of a marriage between them."[10]

Poe must have asked White for his job back, for the publisher wrote his former assistant a letter of caring advice on September 29, agreeing to take him on again if he would stop drinking. He wrote, in part, "You have fine talents, Edgar,—and you ought to have them respected as well as yourself. Learn to respect yourself, and you will very soon find that you are respected. Separate yourself from the bottle, and bottle companions, for ever! Tell me if you can and will do so—and let me hear that it is your fixed purpose never to yield to temptation" (H 17:20–21). Poe must have agreed that this was indeed his fixed purpose, for he was rehired. Owing to the kindness of White, Poe would have another chance. But so, too, would temptation.

The September issue of the *Southern Literary Messenger*, the last number of the first volume, came out toward the end of the month.[11] Included were Poe's tale "Loss of Breath," an expansion of "The Bargain Lost"; his tale "King Pest the First. A Tale Containing an Allegory"; his short tale "Shadow. A Fable"; and his short poem "Lines Written in an Album," formerly addressed to Elizabeth Rebecca Herring and now, evidently, to White's daughter Eliza.[12] The seven critical notices were Poe's. Of particular interest are the review of Robert Folkestone Williams's *Mephistopheles in England*, for its mention of Byron's poem "English Bards and Scotch Reviewers" and its extended quotation about the extraordinary dancing of Marie Taglioni (P 5:37), and the review of Eliza Leslie's *The Gift . . . for 1836*, for its declaring, "Never had Annual a brighter galaxy of illustrious literary names in its table of contents" (P 5:41)—among which were Paulding, Irving, Simms, and Poe. Largely positive comments on the *Messenger*, including Neal's, were offered in this issue.

Poe, Virginia, and Maria Clemm arrived in Richmond on Saturday night, October 3, and they would remain there for the next fifteen months. They lived at first at Mrs. James Yarrington's boardinghouse.[13] Mrs. Clemm, who was sick, was very appreciative of Poe's efforts; she wrote in a letter to William Poe (her cousin, the son of Poe's great-uncle William), "Here, myself & daughter know that we have someone to love & care for us, there [Baltimore] we had no one. We are boarding and it takes nearly all he can make to answer that demand, but poor fellow he is willing to do all in his power for us." And she adds later, "My daughter Virginia is with me here and we are entirely dependent on Edgar. He is indeed a son to me and has always been so."[14]

Poe returned to Thomas W. White at the offices of the *Southern Literary Messenger*, working on the first issue of the second volume, for December 1835. He wrote the critical notices, read proofs, and helped conduct correspondence, including letters soliciting submissions. Nonetheless, White asked his friend and contributor Lucian Minor to write an introductory comment not referring to Poe as editor. That comment, following White's request, states that "the intellectual department of the paper is now under the conduct of the Proprietor, assisted by a gentleman of distinguished literary talents." However, Minor (on behalf of White) was willing to name Poe as an author possessing a "uniquely original vein of imagination, and of humorous, delicate satire." White's not-quite-editor—or, more accurately, his de facto editor—was apparently then a steady employee: even as late as December 25, White wrote that Poe, "I rejoice to tell you, still keeps from the Bottle."[15]

The December 1835 issue of the *Messenger* appeared around November 26.[16] Three scenes of the "tragedy" that Kennedy had mentioned that Poe was working on, in his April 13, 1835, letter to White, were featured here.[17] Two more scenes would be published in the January 1836 issue. The story was based on "the Kentucky tragedy," Jeroboam O. Beauchamp's killing of Colonel Solomon P. Sharp, who had seduced and abandoned Ann Cook before Beauchamp married her. The sensational story would have intrigued Poe, perhaps especially for the character of the wronged woman. He set the story in sixteenth-century Rome; Beauchamp is represented by Politian, Sharp by Castiglione, and Ann Cook by Lalage. In light of the plaintive question (drawn from Jeremiah 8:22) that is asked in Poe's classic 1845 poem "The Raven"—"Is there—*is* there balm in Gilead?" (M 1:368)—it is poignant that Lalage requests "The Holy Evangelists" (Matthew, Mark, Luke, and John), saying "If there be balm / For the wounded spirit in Gilead it is there!" Whatever the source, whether religion (in *Pym*) or cosmic reverie (in *Eureka*), the possibility of "balm in Gilead" was very much Poe's concern.[18]

Also in the December 1835 issue of the *Messenger* were a version of "MS. Found in a Bottle" and a variety of book reviews, a preponderance of them by Poe. Most celebrated—or notorious—of these reviews was Poe's critique of the novel *Norman Leslie*, which had been written by an editor of the *New-York Mirror*, Theodore S. Fay. The plot is "a monstrous piece of absurdity and incongruity"; the style is "unworthy of a school-boy"; the whole is "the most inestimable piece of balderdash with which the common sense of the good people of America was ever so openly or so villainously insulted" (P 5:62). The final paragraph, mocking and sharp, is still laugh-out-loud funny, a "blistering" conclusion. Fay's book, remembered today only for Poe's treatment of it, was based in part on the actual 1799 murder of Gulielma Sands—later to be a source for one of Poe's Dupin tales, "The Mystery of Marie Rogêt."[19] Worthy of comment in the other Poe reviews are his praise of Sir Walter Scott in his review of Robert Montgomery Bird's novel *The Hawks of Hawk-Hollow* (P 5:50); his ongoing encomium for J. N. Reynolds in his review of Reynolds's edited *A Life of George Washington, in Latin Prose,* by Francis Glass (P 5:58); and his favoring Edward Lord Bulwer-Lytton's novel *Pelham* in his review of F. W. Thomas's novel *Clinton Bradshaw* (P 5:74).[20]

Poe soon received discerning and pointed encouragement from White's correspondent and supporter Nathaniel Beverly Tucker. Writing to White, Tucker acknowledged Poe's genius but offered caution about humor in criticism (regarding the review of *Norman Leslie*) and the sensational and the vulgar in fiction (regarding "MS. Found in a Bottle"). He advised that "[Fancy] must be made the minister of higher faculties." He also mentioned that "I remember his beautiful mother when a girl."[21] White read Tucker's letter to Poe, who clearly appreciated the thoughtful and well-intended criticism, and responded not only to the literary but also, revealingly, to the personal: "In speaking of my mother you have touched a string to which my heart fully responds. To have known her is to be an object of great interest in my eyes. I myself never knew her—and never knew the affection of a father. Both died (as you may remember) within a few weeks of each other. I have many occasional dealings with Adversity—but the want of parental affection has been the heaviest of my trials" (O 1:116).

Another who recognized Poe's genius, John Neal, went on to praise the *Southern Literary Messenger* beyond the August 1835 issue: "We have heartily recommended this work upon the strength of two numbers. Having now seen the whole [the first volume], instead of seeing reason to qualify what we then said, we are rather inclined to say more—much more in its favor." Commenting on the January 1835 issue, he terms the *Messenger* "a journal worthy of decided, warm and general encouragement." Later, deploring the absorption of the *New England Magazine* by New York's *American Monthly Magazine,* he proposes for New England "a respectable and independent journal—the foundation we might say, of *Independence in our Literature.*" He suggests that the periodical might be sustained by a thousand subscribers for five years for five dollars a year.[22] Poe would have read Neal's words since he received the *New England Galaxy* in exchange. And he had already imagined something akin to the "independent journal" that Neal described—according to Lambert A. Wilmer, before Poe was offered his position at the *Southern Literary Messenger,* "He proposed to join with me in the publication of a monthly magazine of a superior intellectual character, and he had written a prospectus, which he transmitted to me for examination."[23] Neal's views would have reinforced Poe's own views. Poe would later write, "[B]efore quitting the Mess:, I saw, or fancied that I saw, through a long & dim vista, the brilliant field for ambition which a Magazine of bold & noble aims presented to him who should successfully establish it in America" (O 1:467). Whether he quit the *Messenger* or was let go (in early 1837), Poe would always cherish—and fight for—his dream of owning an elite and fearless literary magazine.

During the Christmas/New Year's period of 1835/36, Poe may well have had more time to spend socially with the Mackenzies. Flora Lapham Mack leaves us a hitherto-unknown description of Poe, as remembered by her mother's cousin, John H. Mackenzie, and her mother, at that time young Mary Mattox:

> Cousin John and my mother have often attempted to describe Poe's appearance to me. They both said he was one of the most graceful persons they ever saw never assuming by accident an attitude or making a gesture that did not seem to harmonize with his lithe slender but perfectly proportioned figure. Cousin John said he always appeared to be taller than he really was, he was so erect & he carried himself so well & he said he was a much stronger man physically than his appearances indicated. His hair was very black & slightly wavy & of a silken sheen & fineness. His forehead very high & broad and very white. There was nothing very remarkable about any of his other features, except his beautiful expressive eyes. They were of the brownish grey color some times called agate & some times a dark hazel. Very large & expressive and never just alike two minutes together some times they seemed black & some times brown. As they burned and glowed with the brilliancy of his changing thoughts—again they were just as beautiful with a soft dreamy faraway expression as if they were seeing visions never seen by man before. They both agreed more beautiful eyes they had never seen. There was a delicacy & refinement in the entire make up of his mobile and changeable countenance.

> He rarely ever laughed aloud. His teeth were rather singular when seen through the parting of the thin wide cut lips. They were dazzlingly white very sharp pointed & small & narrow. (Mother said like rat's teeth.) His hands & feet were small & well shaped. With just a half or third of a chance he gave you the impression always of being extremely well groomed & dressed. When you came to examine his garments closely however you were often surprised to find them well worn and thread bare. He wore them with such an easy perfect grace & carried himself so well & proudly you rarely thought of his clothes at all in admiring his physique. Cousin John used to say Edgar was always unmistakably a gentleman in his appearance when sober.[24]

There is an elegance and nobility here, with the exception of the surprising comment on his teeth. The final caveat, "when sober," intimates troubles past and troubles to come.

The January 1836 issue of the *Messenger* featured another portion of "Scenes from an Unpublished Drama," revised versions of the poem "A Paean" and the tale "Metzengerstein," and additional critical notices. Here Poe praised Barthold George Niebuhr's "Essay on the Allegory in the First Canto of Dante" (in the review of Francis Lieber's *Reminiscences of an Intercourse with Mr. Niebuhr* [P 5:96]), which argues, about Dante's writing, as noted earlier, "everything must be explained by his life, and the peculiarities connected therewith."[25] And here Poe admired a new edition of Daniel Defoe's novel *Robinson Crusoe*, highlighting in particular "the potent magic of verisimilitude" (P 5:98), the writer's skill in conveying incidents, through well-chosen detail, as seemingly authentic and believable. Personal allegory and verisimilar prose will be characteristic of the fictional work that Poe will begin in 1836, *The Narrative of Arthur Gordon Pym*. Finally, an eight-page "Supplement" in the January issue offers an array of responses to the December 1835 issue; the review of *Norman Leslie* was especially controversial, lauded as independent and lambasted as in bad taste. The *Lynchburg Virginian* asked a broad question that would surely have been a provocative one to Poe: "[W]hy does Mr. Poe throw away his strength on shafts and columns, instead of building a temple to his fame?"[26]

Poe's correspondence at this time indicates an improvement in his situation and his state of mind. In order to introduce a request to Maria Clemm's cousin George Poe Jr. for support for her opening a boardinghouse, Poe states that he is now the editor at the *Southern Literary Messenger*, earning an annual salary of eight hundred dollars (O 1:118). Poe's correspondent did indeed provide a hundred dollars (W 17:376). In order to introduce a question about a possible inheritance by Maria Clemm's two children, Virginia and Henry, Poe writes to John P. Kennedy, with gratitude, "Although I have never yet acknowledged the receipt of your kind letter of advice some months ago, it was not without great influence. I have, since then, fought the enemy manfully, and am now, in every respect, comfortable and happy. I know you will be *pleased* to hear this. My health is better than for years past, my mind is fully occupied, my pecuniary difficulties have vanished, I have a fair prospect of future success—in a word all is right. I shall never forget to whom all this happiness is in great degree to be attributed. I know that without your timely aid I should have sunk under my trials." Recalling his recent "circumstances of absolute despair," he adds, "you will see how great reason I have to be grateful to God—and to yourself" (1:120–21). Kennedy was not able to secure any inheritance for Mrs. Clemm's children (H 17:32–33), but he was delighted with Poe's recovery: "Your letter assures me that you have entirely conquered your late despondency. I am rejoiced at this" (H 17:28).

On February 13, the third number of the second volume of the *Messenger* was published.[27] Poe, whom White had come to consider "[m]y right hand man,"[28] contributed much. Among his pieces in the February issue were a revised version of "The Duc de L'Omelette"; an essay titled "Palaestine"; a revised version of "The Valley Nis"; fillers; additional reviews; and the first installment of "Autography," an analysis of writers' handwriting. What warrants remark about the synthetic nonfiction piece "Palaestine" in light of Poe's coming work on *Pym* is the closing mention of Titus's destruction of Jerusalem (P 5:107).[29]

We find, among the reviews, Poe's discussion of plagiarism in his mockery of Morris Mattson's novel *Paul Ulric,* his repeated praise of verisimilitude in his commendation of Lambert A. Wilmer's novel *The Confessions of Emilia Harrington,* and his expression of high regard for Edward Lord Bulwer-Lytton in his acclaim of the novel *Rienzi, The Last of the Tribunes.* Most important in Poe's reviews in the February 1836 issue of the *Messenger* is his treatment of Henry F. Chorley's collection *Conti the Discarded: With Other Tales and Fancies.* Here Poe writes of "the *Art Novels*—the Kunstromanen—books written not so much in immediate defence, or in illustration, as in personification of individual portions of the Fine Arts—books which, in the guise of Romance, labor to the sole end of reasoning men into admiration and study of the beautiful, by a tissue of *bizarre* fiction, partly allegorical, and partly metaphysical" (P 5:119). *The Narrative of Arthur Gordon Pym* would be one of these books.[30]

The crucial prompt, I believe, came a few days after the publication of the February 1836 issue of the *Messenger* in the form of an article in the newspapers the *Norfolk Beacon* of February 18 and the *Norfolk Herald* of February 19 concerning the wreck of the *Ariel,* a Norfolk vessel, from which two men survived.[31] Here we have a suggestion of the story that Poe would soon begin to write, in the first chapter of *Pym,* about two boys in a boat named the *Ariel,* experiencing wreck and rescue. The additional attraction of the newspaper story of the wreck of the *Ariel* would have been that it presented a solution to a problem that Samuel Taylor Coleridge had admitted he could not solve, recorded in *Table-Talk,* a book that Poe had esteemed in an April 1835 review. Coleridge said, "The destruction of Jerusalem is the only subject now remaining for an epic poem.... I schemed it at twenty-five; but, alas! *venturum expectat.*" And he added later about this subject, "Yet, with all its great capabilities, it has this one great defect—that, whereas a poem, to be epic, must have a personal interest,—in the destruction of Jerusalem no genius or skill could possibly preserve the interest for the hero from being merged in the interest for the event. The fact is, the event itself is too sublime and overwhelming."[32] Poe even quoted Coleridge, in a June 1836 review, with regard to his plan for "the epic poem on—what still appears to me the one only fit subject remaining for an epic poem—Jerusalem besieged and destroyed by Titus" (P 5:212). The wreck of the *Ariel* as it appeared in the Norfolk newspapers provided Poe with a means to prove his "genius or skill"—to show that he could do what Coleridge could not: he could use the wreck of the *Ariel* to convey the destruction of Jerusalem allegorically, thereby preserving "personal interest." For, as Poe would have known as a student of the Bible, the name "Ariel" signifies Jerusalem: "Woe to Ariel, to Ariel, the city where David dwelt! add ye year to year; let them kill sacrifices. / Yet I will distress Ariel, and there shall be heaviness and sorrow: and it shall be unto me as Ariel" (Isaiah 29:1–2).[33]

Poe's success with the *Messenger* continued—Maria Clemm wrote to George Poe Jr., the son of Poe's great-uncle George Poe Sr., on February 21, "Myself & daughter are under the protection of Edgar—he is the Editor of the Southern Literary Messenger and bids fair to be an honour to our name" (H 17:376). But Poe did not succeed with "Tales of the Folio Club": rejected by Carey, Lea & Blanchard, it was also rejected by Harper and Brothers. J. K. Paulding informed T. W. White in March that the latter publishers were concerned because the tales would be both too familiar (having already appeared in the *Messenger*) and too arcane. Paulding conveyed the Harpers' recommendation "that if he [Poe] will lower himself a little to the ordinary comprehension of the generality of readers, and prepare a series of original Tales, or a single work, and send them to the Publishers, previous to their appearance in the 'Messenger,' they will make such arrangements with him as will be liberal and satisfactory."[34] Harper and Brothers reiterated the two objections directly to Poe in June but also discouraged "detached tales and pieces," preferring "works (especially fiction) in which a single and connected story occupies the whole volume, or number of volumes, as the case may be." *Pym* would be that "single and connected story," but a small portion of it would have already appeared in the *Messenger,* and some of it would remain what Harper and Brothers termed "too learned and mystical."[35] Nonetheless, the publishers would accept the book, perhaps because they recognized a sea novel, but not an Art Novel.

After March 26, the March number of the *Messenger* appeared; it included Poe's short story "Epimanes," lightly revised; his poem "To Helen"; and his five critical notices.[36] The issue had been held up to accommodate Thomas Dew's very lengthy "Address," which, toward its close, ardently defended slavery. The proofreader Edward G. Frothingham—a Yankee journalist and a friend of John Greenleaf Whittier and William Lloyd Garrison—would surely have found this piece extremely objectionable. Because of his antipathy to slavery, doubtless intensified by what he saw in Richmond, including a slave auction, he declined a second year with the *Messenger* and returned home to Boston.[37] However, Poe was a Virginian (as he later declared [O 1:287]) and, in the words of Terence Whalen, "an average racist." Whalen shows that he tried to avoid partisanship in his writing and strove to win readers North and South.[38] Still, of particular note is that in the novel that Poe had perhaps already begun to plan, the diabolical "other," the character Dirk Peters, was to become salvific. There may well have been a historical model.

It is intriguing to see, on the inside rear wrappers of the March 1836 issue, that one of the magazine's subscribers was Dr. James D. McCaw, he who had rescued women from the burning Richmond Theater on December 26, 1811, by dropping them down to the enslaved blacksmith Gilbert Hunt. In 1836, Hunt was no longer enslaved—he had bought his own freedom—but he remained a blacksmith in Richmond. True, it was already twenty-five years since the catastrophe, but as quoted in the *Messenger* of February 1835, "Long will that mournful event be remembered by those who survived or witnessed its horrors!"[39] Soon after the tragic fire, Edgar had returned to Richmond with the Allans; he would doubtless not have forgotten the stories that he had heard about it.

During March 1836, in the evening, Poe made "frequent visits to the exhibition of Maelzel" (P 5:161)—that is, to the supposed "automaton chess-player" displayed at the Museum, on nearby Capitol Square.[40] He observed the apparatus carefully and wrote an essay for the April 1836 *Messenger*, "Maelzel's Chess-Player," showing that the work of the automaton, observed "by the citizens of Richmond a few weeks ago" (P 5:157), was actually performed by a man concealed in the cabinet or trunk.[41] Though Poe often drew for this piece on David Brewster's *Letters on Natural Magic*, there is occasional original material, including reference to "mirrors in the interior of the trunk," intended "to multiply to the vision some few pieces of machinery within the trunk so as to give it the appearance of being crowded with mechanism" (P 5:161).[42] Poe's use of mirrors to "multiply to the vision" some critical element would be characteristic of his long nautical narrative *Arthur Gordon Pym*.

Poe also provided for the April 1836 *Messenger*, published after April 28, a light revision of his 1832 Folio Club piece "A Tale of Jerusalem," as well as a few critical notices.[43] The most important of these is Poe's review of Joseph Rodman Drake's *The Culprit Fay, and Other Poems* and Fitz-Greene Halleck's *Alnwick Castle, with Other Poems*. Poe begins by defending himself against charges of critical severity, then comments on the work of Drake and Halleck, which he argues does not reach the heights of "the Faculty of Ideality," "the sentiment of Poesy." He clarifies, "This sentiment is the sense of the beautiful, of the sublime, and of the mystical. Thence spring immediately admiration of the fair flowers, the fairer forests, the bright valleys and rivers and mountains of the Earth—and love of the gleaming stars and other burning glories of Heaven—and, mingled up inextricably with this love and this admiration of Heaven and of Earth,—the unconquerable desire—*to know*. Poesy is the sentiment of Intellectual Happiness here, and the Hope of a higher Intellectual Happiness hereafter. Imagination is its soul" (P 5:166). Here he recalls the heavenward seeking of "Israfel" and anticipates later poems, as well as critical comments, such as in his 1842 review of Henry Wadsworth Longfellow and his posthumous essay "The Poetic Principle." He writes in the last piece of "*an elevating excitement of the Soul*," an earthly frisson signifying "the Human Aspiration for Supernal Beauty" (L2:198). Such "elevating excitement" is characteristic of Poe's work at its best.

And it was the love of Virginia that made for Poe's life at its best. Flora Lapham Mack contested Susan Archer Weiss's claim that John H. Mackenzie had alleged the negative effect on Poe of his marriage; she wrote rather, "[T]he truth is he [Mackenzie] died regarding Virginia as almost an angel and Poe's tender love & care for her as the most beautiful thing in his life."[44] On Monday, May 16, 1836, at the parsonage of the Presbyterian minister and editor Amasa Converse, Poe married his cousin Virginia. Fame was not his only bride.

Relying on her mother, Mary Mattox Lapham; her father, Benjamin Byrene Lapham; and her stepfather, John Hamilton Mackenzie; Flora Lapham Mack reported that, at the time of her marriage, Virginia "was a roly poly plump dimpled baby-faced little girl very attractive & winsome in her appearance with the most childlike ways and tastes."[45] She had short black hair and black eyes, Mack noted, and "[t]heir expression was peculiar having by turns an appealing pathetic softness and a sort of wide open innocent surprised wondering glance[,] which was very attractive." Mack elaborated on Virginia's white dimity dress: "The white dimity was intended for her Sunday dress when made Mrs. Clemm said and was her 'wedding' dress. She wore it with a necklace of baby coral around her white neck. It was made in empire style with the neck cut low elbow sleeves very short waist an exceedingly narrow 'skinnity' skirt only coming to the ankles."[46]

The printed document for the wedding bond stated that the bride was twenty-one years old, but she was actually thirteen. Today we would wholly disapprove the marriage of so young a bride, but Mack, citing several examples of other young brides, stated, "[I]t was not unusual at all but the customary thing at that time for girls to marry while yet children."[47] Among those present, in addition to Poe, Virginia, Maria Clemm, and the minister, were *Messenger* proprietor Thomas W. White, his daughter Eliza, *Messenger* foreman John McFarlane, *Messenger* assistant John W. Fergusson, Thomas W. Cleland (son-in-law of Poe's former boardinghouse owner, Mrs. Poore) and his wife (her daughter), Mrs. James Yarrington (Poe's present boardinghouse owner), and Jane Foster, a small young girl who witnessed the wedding in a mirror and marveled at Virginia's not changing in appearance after the brief ceremony. The company celebrated with wine and a wedding cake made by Mrs. Clemm and Mrs. Yarrington.[48]

Though it is sometimes argued that Poe and Virginia left then for Petersburg,[49] there is another version of the story, involving their staying in Richmond that night. Mack asserts, "Edgar came around on the morning after the 16th of May & announced [presumably to Mrs. Jane Scott Mackenzie, who lived in the western section of town] the fact that he had been married the night before at the Presbyterian parsonage by Rev Mr Converse." Mack goes on, "This was the very first intimation that the Mackenzies had that he had any idea of marrying his little cousin." She adds,

> Cousin John [John H. Mackenzie] said he had heard the news[,] had time to get over his first surprise & to conclude that perhaps it would make Edgar who had been leading a very wild and dissipated life for some time past do better with these two very sweet and interesting women to care for before he saw him & so he first cordially congratulated him & called by their boardinghouse and congratulated Virginia & Mrs. Clemm telling them how fond he was & had always been of Edgar & that they must come soon and often to Darby Town and let your [Mack's correspondent, William Lanier Washington's] Great Grandmother [Mrs. William Sturtevant Lanier, a.k.a. Aunt Polly] & Aunt [Mrs. John H. Mackenzie, Louisa Lanier] add their congratulations. He offered to send the carriage [*sic*] for them at any time and said it was always in town Monday morning & Friday afternoon & entirely at their service.

And then came an extraordinary moment: "He said Virginia put up her sweet little face to be kissed as he told her goodly [goodbye] & completely won his heart by her confidence and innocence."[50]

We may wonder about Poe's "very wild and dissipated life." After all, White had written in late December that Poe was avoiding drink. Also, Poe still had his job. And White was at the wedding. Perhaps Poe was able to hide his drinking, for a time, from his employer. Indeed, the young assistant at the *Messenger,* John W. Fergusson, later remembered, "[L]ike others in his day Poe was addicted to periodical sprees, but they did not interfere to any extent with his writings."[51] And if they did interfere with his editorial work, Poe apparently sometimes had help. R. M. T. Hunter recalled:

> Here [at the *Messenger*] his habits were bad and as White did not appreciate his literary excellences I had hard work to save him from dismissal before it actually occurred. During a part of the time I was in Richmond, a member of the Legislature [the General Assembly of Virginia met from December of one year through March of the next], and frequently volunteered to correct the press when pieces were being published with classical quotations. Poe was the only man on White's staff capable of doing this and when occasionally drinking (the habit was not constant) he was incapacitated for work. On such occasions I have done the work

more than once to prevent a rupture between his employer and himself. He was reckless about money and subject to intoxication, but I was not aware of any other bad habit that he had.[52]

Hunter's kind intercession evidently extended Poe's tenure on the *Messenger*.

Poe and Virginia did subsequently travel to Petersburg, twenty-four miles south of Richmond, for their honeymoon, enjoying the hospitality of the editor Hiram Haines and his wife, and others.[53] Doubtless the groom continued to express his "tender love & care" for his bride, but there is a question as to whether there was then a sexual relationship, given her age. Bardwell Heywood, brother of Annie Richmond (a woman whom Poe would come to love after Virginia died), wrote in 1848, based on Poe's own words, that after his marriage to Virginia, Poe "did not for two years assume the position of husband." The poet and novelist Elizabeth Oakes Smith later wrote, "His wife was hardly fourteen at the time of his marriage[;] he did not claim her for two years."[54]

Within a week they returned to Richmond. Poe continued to work at the *Messenger*, and Virginia occasionally attended Miss Jane Mackenzie's School, at Fifth and E (or Main) Streets, where Poe's sister Rosalie, living with Jane Scott Mackenzie, was a teacher of handwriting, and where Louisa Mackenzie's cousins Ann, Mary, and Eliza Mattox, living at Darby Town, were students. (This was the school where, many years earlier, "Poe's amatory verses, addressed to the young ladies, disturbed the discipline of the seminary.")[55] Flora Lapham Mack wrote, "Miss Jane [sister-in-law of Jane Scott Mackenzie] seemed singularly drawn toward Virginia & was most anxious even after the marriage to supplement the very rudimentary and erratic education she had received from busy Mrs. Clemm & Edgar with a more systematic a[nd] practical course at her school but she [Virginia] did not avail herself of the opportunity except to take lessons in the guitar & vocal lessons for a little while & to try to paint & draw a little." Virginia's mother wanted her daughter at home and, along with Mrs. Lanier, didn't think it appropriate for a married woman to attend school. Mack recalled that according to her own mother, Mary Mattox Lapham, "Virginia enjoyed the companionship of the school girls and the games at recess quite as much as she [Mary Mattox] did & would have dearly loved to have been allowed to come regularly to school with her & her sisters & mingle with the scholars." But Mrs. Clemm was strict: "Cousin John [John H. Mackenzie] & Mother would often tell me how after a feat of running or jumping or of laughing immoderately at some of their girlish jokes & pranks she [Virginia] would check her self suddenly & exclaim 'Oh Mere (she always called he[r] mother so) will just have a fit if she sees me or hears me.'"[56] Apparently Virginia was being directed to grow up more quickly than she was ready to.

Poe's former girlfriend, Elmira Royster, now twenty-six and married (since 1828) to merchant Alexander B. Shelton, apparently still had feelings for the poet. She later recalled to Mrs. Clemm, "I remember seeing Edgar, & his lovely wife, very soon after they were married—I met them—I never shall forget my feelings at the time—They were indescribable, almost agonizing—'However in an instant,' I remembered that I was a married woman, and banished them from me, as I would a poisonous reptile."[57] Years later, Elmira would return to Poe's life in a significant way.

On about May 27, the May issue of the *Messenger* appeared.[58] Notable is Poe's inclusion of the sonnet that had introduced "Al Aaraaf" in 1829 (later "Sonnet—To Science") and the revised "Irene" from 1831 (later revised further to "The Sleeper"). The reviews by Poe feature extensive extracts but also occasional salient comments, as, for example, one comment on friendship and another on biography. With regard to Alexander Slidell's *Spain Revisited*, Poe writes that if the compliments offered in the dedication are a matter of form, "we feel, at once, a degree of righteous indignation at the profanation to so hollow a purpose, of the most sacred epithets and phrases of friendship" (P 5:188). And regarding J. K. Paulding's *A Life of Washington*, Poe states, "The rich abundance of those delightful anecdotes and memorials of the private man which render a book of this nature invaluable—an abundance which has hardly more delighted than astonished us—is the prevailing feature of Mr. Paulding's Washington" (P 5:194).

While Poe was working at the *Messenger*, Virginia and Mrs. Clemm would repeatedly accept the invitation of Poe's friend John H. Mackenzie to his Darby Town farm, especially on weekends. And Poe would sometimes join them. (The farm was near what is today the Richmond International Airport.) The carriage—probably Mackenzie's barouche, a four-wheeled vehicle that could accommodate the driver and four passengers—would travel seven miles south from Richmond on Darby Town Road. The family that founded Darby Town was the Enroughtys. In 1836, Mackenzie didn't yet own his Darby Town property—perhaps he rented or leased it from the Montagues. (He would buy it from the Sharpes in 1844.) Although he was occasionally listed as a farmer, he was not: he sold vehicles in the city and operated a tobacco warehouse. A daguerreotype, perhaps from the 1840s, shows him to have had a thick, at-times-solemn, bearded face. The farm—or plantation—was run by his mother-in-law, Mary Simmons Lanier (Mrs. William Sturtevant Lanier, "Aunt Polly"), and his diminutive, fine-featured wife, Louisa Lanier Mackenzie, both of whom had requested that he take it on in the first place. John H. Mackenzie had an overseer, named Andrews, and, in 1836, seven enslaved people, whose names are not known. Mrs. Lanier had additional slaves. Mack writes, "The numerous negroes belonging to the united families worked the farm & garden & waited in the house[,] some of the men being employed by cousin John in his ware house & stables as drivers etc."[59]

Slavery was, of course, characteristic of plantations in the South at this time. Notably, Abraham Lincoln said in Peoria, Illinois, nearly twenty years later, in 1854: "I think I have no prejudice against the Southern people. They are just what we would have been in their situation. If slavery did not now exist among them, they would not introduce it. If it did now exist among us, we should not instantly give it up."[60] The Civil War would eventually change "their situation" and lead to the freeing of the slaves, including those of John H. Mackenzie. Meanwhile, the indefensible continued to be defended.

Flora Lapham Mack described Poe's wife and cousin Virginia at Darby Town as a delightful girl: she "lov[ed] dearly to play with the kittens and puppies trotting round after Aunt Pollie of whom she was exceedingly fond, to feed the peafowls (you know they always raised hundreds of them at their big plantation as well as every other feathered thing) and having a perfect passion for sweets which kept her constantly nibbling one of Aunt Pollie's tea cakes while she was playing at Darby Town or Enroughty Town as it was properly called." As for her relationship to Edgar, Mack declared, "Virginia gave him a perfect love. He was the sun in whose rays she lived caring for nothing else cold, heat, privation nothing mattered so long as she was near him. She was not stupid not insensible to comfort or discomfort. She was a lovely child and she was absolutely happy near him." And Mack reported on the appraisal by John H. Mackenzie of Edgar's relationship to Virginia: "He said he thought Edgar loved her as much as he could have loved any one and delighted in her soft shy sweet manners lisping speech and rounded dimpled prettiness that he loved to have her caress him & talk to him and sit on his lap & rub her cheek against his own and was always gentle and affectionate to her and respectful and loving to Mrs. Clemm under all circumstances." She also noted, "Cousin John thought that as nearly as possible he [Poe] found the woman best suited to him as a wife in Virginia." Of Maria Clemm, Mack wrote, "She never gave Edgar a cross or unkind word or look under the most trying circumstances."[61]

And there would be very trying circumstances. In fact, they had probably simply continued into Poe's married life.

Following a failed attempt for Poe, Virginia, and Maria Clemm to share a new house bought by Thomas W. White (O 1:145–46), Mrs. Clemm rented what Susan Archer Weiss termed "a cheap tenement on Seventh street."[62] Once (Flora Lapham Mack writes), when the Mattox girls were returning from Miss Jane's School to Darby Town on a Friday afternoon, and they were waiting for Virginia to dress, Mrs. Clemm invited them inside:

> They were invited in by Mrs. Clemm & she [Mary Mattox, Flora's mother] thought their sitting room beautiful. It & the whole house was [sic] as spotlessly clean as hands & soap & water would make it and Mrs. Clemm had done such wonderful things with packing boxes & with nails & hammer & paint and bits of muslin & chintz drapery in the way of manufacturing a book case a couch a dressing stand ottomans a window seat etc. that she was entirely independent of the cabinet-maker for any thing save a cheap snowy white bed and a chair or two. She always had her windows filled with thrifty flowering plants and English Ivy flowers always grew well for her and a pet or two a bird & a cat prefferably [sic] were always there and these with some strips of rag carpet made the prettiest cheeriest most home like room she remembered seeing in her childhood.[63]

Mary Mattox Lapham remembered that on other occasions Mrs. Clemm "sewed & cleaned & knitted & cooked and washed and ironed continuously & always uncomplainingly." Mrs. Clemm taught her "all kinds of fancy knitting," and Virginia did such knitting, as well, and "eyelet & other beautiful embroidery," which was sold at local shops. Mack wrote that Virginia was "always cheerful and gay with a bright sweet perfectly patient & amiable disposition never complaining never blue or out of sorts[,] singing sweetly all the while she was at work and laughing joyously on the smallest provocation." The family's beautiful sitting room doubled as Edgar and Virginia's bedroom; if Maria Clemm could secure boarders, she slept in a cot in the kitchen.[64] Mrs. Clemm's gift for homemaking was evidently well appreciated by her son-in-law; Mack noted, "He delighted in Mrs. Clemm's orderly comfortably kept rooms, often saying he could not rest amid disorder."[65] The disorder in Poe's life would be of his own making.

Poe was back at work on the *Messenger* in June, soliciting contributions from a variety of well-known writers (O 1:139–52).[66] He stated in his letter to John P. Kennedy—which also requested a loan, needed because of the unsuccessful housing prospect with the Whites—"Our Messenger is thriving beyond all expectation, and I myself have every prospect of success" (O 1:146). After June 16, 1836, the June number of the *Messenger* appeared.[67] Worthy of particular mention are Poe's quoting Coleridge on the fall of Jerusalem (in his review of *Letters, Conversations and Recollections of S. T. Coleridge* [P 5:212]); his commentary on his practice of close reading (in his review of William Leete Stone's *Ups and Downs in the Life of a Distressed Gentleman* [P 5:215]); and his consideration of "unity of effect," which "is indispensable in the 'brief article,' and not so in the common novel" (P 5:218). Of course, *The Narrative of Arthur Gordon Pym* would be no common novel.

On June 19, Harper & Brothers rejected Poe's expanded Folio Club collection. Their thoughtful letter reiterated some of what J. K. Paulding had already reported, as mentioned earlier—that the firm had reservations about the tales' previous publication and difficulty of comprehension—and the letter notes, as well, the publisher's preference for a single narrative. In the coming months, this advice may well have encouraged Poe to continue to work out the design of his novel and to begin to write it. In the short term, however, this letter may have seriously set him back. He had been trying to publish his short story collection for three years, without success.

We cannot know precisely the dates of Poe's sprees in Richmond in 1836. But they unquestionably took place. Poe admitted this himself in a letter to Joseph E. Snodgrass of 1841. Defending himself against the charge of intemperance, made evidently by William E. Burton, Poe denied that he had ever been "in the *habit* of intoxication" but acknowledged, "[F]or a brief period, while I resided in Richmond, and edited the *Messenger*, I certainly did give way, at long intervals, to the temptation held out on all sides by the spirit of Southern conviviality. My sensitive temperament could not stand an excitement which was an everyday matter to my companions. In short, it sometimes happened that I was completely intoxicated. For some days after each excess I was invariably confined to bed" (O 1:263–64). Still, there is far more to say.

Messenger assistant John W. Fergusson said, "Poe was a fine gentleman when he was sober. He was ever kind and courtly, and at such times every one liked him. But when he was drinking he was about one of the most disagreeable men I have ever met."[68] And Flora Lapham Mack provides detail regarding the consequences of Poe's excesses. "Cousin John," she writes, "was very much outdone at Edgar's behavior at this time, he drank, he gambled, he staid [sic] a way from home coming back only when worn out with disappation [sic] to be nursed back to health by Mrs. Clemm."[69] She writes elsewhere:

> After a space he [Poe] would drag himself home an apparent wreck physically & mentally all the spring & elasticity gone from his step his shoulders drooping his eyes lacking luster & of an almost olive green shade of color. Every bit of vitality gone from mind & body & there he would lie prone & almost lifeless loathing food & light & companionship of any kind except Mrs. Clemm for days. It required the most careful nursing & watchfulness to revive and restore him after one of those break downs. And Mrs. Clemm had learned to be an adept in this task. With love & tenderness & unfailing patience she ministered to his body & mind stimulating & encouraging him until he was fitted to take up the battle of life again. Cousin John said he owed his life to her time & again for there were often times when in his awful depressions & abject misery & despair he was tempted to kill him self. Then she never relaxed her vigilant watch night or day and almost exhausted herself to the verge of illness by spending many sleepless nights & weary days together in constant attendence [sic] on him, pleading coaxing & commanding by turns, until he was him self again.[70]

Mrs. Clemm was clearly a valiant caregiver. And to confide in someone, she would turn not to her young daughter or to Poe's sister,[71] but to stalwart, sympathetic John H. Mackenzie.

The bond was that they both loved Edgar—to Maria Clemm he was her dear nephew and son-in-law and to Mackenzie he was his lifelong friend, "a most lovable brilliant & interesting person." Mack expands on their connection:

> Both he [Mackenzie] and Mrs. Clemm seem to have agreed at least tacitly that they must take him just as he was and condone and accept his faults & failings as best they might, loving him dearly because they must. It was because she understood & rejoiced in this attitude of John Mackenzie's toward Edgar, recognizing in it a duplicate of her own feeling toward him[,] that Mrs. Clemm came to rely on & confide in him as she did no one else[,] not even his wife[,] whom she tenderly sheilded [sic] as much as possible[,] taking the burden on her own shoulders[.] For this reason[,] this poor care burdened creature often sought the office of John Mackenzie's warehouse to unburden her heart & consult with him as to the complex worries & sorrows of her hard & joyless life. And she always found in him a faithful & helpful friend & a safe confident [confidant].[72]

Maria Clemm and John H. Mackenzie were fortunate to have each other—as was Poe to have both of them.

With regard to Edgar's relationship to Mrs. Clemm and Virginia, Mackenzie believed "that with all that was best & purest in his nature Edgar loved them both[;] he loved to have them near him & touch him tenderly & often[;] their caresses were never ill timed or unwelcome but sought invited whenever he came near them." But Poe's good friend was outraged by Edgar's sprees, and privately he admonished his friend. Mack relates Mackenzie's response:

> [E]ven in the first months of his marraige [sic][,] he [Poe] neglected them [Virginia and Mrs. Clemm][,] spending his money in rioting & carrousing [sic] & leaving them to live as best they could[,] as irresponsible & improvident toward them as possible & yet always dragging himself home half dead despondent & despairing to be nursed petted and carressed [sic] back to a point where he could take up the burden of life again. After every prolonged debauch[,] Cousin John told him in great indignation his opinion of his behavior in the plainest terms time & again & was promised each time he would do better. He declared he was ashamed of him self & he wished he was dead etc.[,] but it wrought no permanent change for the better[;] in a little while he had gone back to his same old habits[,] & Cousin John[,] loving him tenderly through it all despite his sympathy and affection for Mrs. Clemm & Virginia[,] declared that he did not beleive [sic] Edgar could help it though he beleived he really & honestly tried to and was sincerely ashamed of his conduct.[73]

Could Poe have helped it? Certainly a family predisposition, evident in his father and brother, worked against him. And today's best authorities regard alcoholism not as a moral failing but as a disease. *Facing Addiction in America: The Surgeon General's Report on Alcohol, Drugs, and Health* states:

> Scientific breakthroughs have revolutionized the understanding of substance use disorders. For example, severe substance use disorders, commonly called *addictions*, were once viewed largely as a moral failing or character flaw, but are now understood to be chronic illnesses characterized by clinically significant impairments in health, social functions, and voluntary control over substance abuse. Although the mechanisms may be different, addiction has many features in common with disorders such as diabetes, asthma, and hypertension. All of these disorders are chronic, subject to relapse, and influenced by genetic, developmental, behavioral, social, and environmental factors. In all of these disorders, affected individuals may have difficulty in complying with the prescribed treatment.[74]

According to this report then, John H. Mackenzie was right: Poe could not help it. What remains remarkable is that despite his susceptibility—which ultimately led to his death—Poe was able so long to persevere. With the help of those who loved him, including Maria Clemm and John H. Mackenzie, Poe could return from desperation to aspiration. And he could do so with increasing resonance in his writing and, on occasion, with a noble effort to attain consolation. Poe would eventually be defeated by his affliction—but until then, he would manage to win varied and enduring victories.

Despite whatever lapses may have occurred, the July 1836 *Messenger* appeared on time, after July 13.[75] The issue included Poe's lightly revised "Letter to Mr. —— ——," now titled "Letter to B——." Of great importance, in light of Poe's symbolic treatment of memory in *The Narrative of Arthur Gordon Pym* (to be discussed), is his comment in his review of Lydia H. Sigourney's *Letters to Young Ladies,* "Few subjects are more entirely misapprehended than that of the faculty of Memory" (P 5:228). Poe defends himself against the *Newbern Spectator* in the "Supplement" and provides numerous, mostly favorable reviews. Especially significant is the last review, on the inside back wrapper, taken from the first issue of the *Philadelphia Saturday News and Literary Gazette* (July 2, 1836), published by Louis A. Godey and edited by Morton McMichael (who had published Poe's tales in the *Philadelphia Saturday Courier*) and Joseph C. Neal. One or the other editor—or perhaps both editors—wrote that the *Southern Literary Messenger* "from its commencement, has been an especial favorite with us" and acknowledged "the bold, independent tone of its criticism."[76] It was the *Saturday News,* in 1838, that would prove a rich source of material for Poe's first detective story, the 1841 "The Murders in the Rue Morgue."

In late July and early to mid-August, Poe was carrying on correspondence for the *Messenger* and working on the August 1836 issue, which he hoped would feature work by "all the first pens in the land" (O 1:139). Thomas W. White wrote on August 5, "I have had a great deal of sickness in my office among my best hands, and since the 4th July,"[77] but Poe was writing letters on behalf of the magazine on July 4, 16, and 30, as well as on August 19 (O 1:152–57). It is clear from an August 25 letter from White that Poe was active at the *Messenger:* "Courtesy to Mr. Poe whom I employ to edit my paper makes it a matter of etiquette with me to submit all articles intended for the Messenger to his judgment and I abide by his dicta."[78]

John H. Mackenzie was involved with his own work, seeking a partner for his dray business on August 9.[79] Since it was late summer, Virginia was probably not at Miss Jane's School—she and Maria Clemm would have been spending a significant amount of time at Darby Town. And Poe and Mackenzie would have spent time there, as well, especially on weekends. At Darby Town, with his wife and mother-in-law and best friend, Poe would probably have had no "bottle companions" (as White had called Poe's fellow drinkers).

On August 22, 1836, the August *Messenger* was published[80]—it was, according to Poe, "the best number, by far, yet issued" (O 1:156). It did indeed include some of "the first pens in the land," including Lydia H. Sigourney, William Gilmore Simms, Joseph Hopkinson, Francis Lieber, James K. Paulding, Robert Montgomery Bird, Matthew Carey, and Sarah Josepha Hale. Works by Poe were the lightly revised "Israfel" and "The City in the Sea" (now "The City of Sin"), as well as a gathering of short miscellaneous pieces, "Pinakidia," and an analysis of writers' handwriting, "Autography." Among the most significant elements of the "Critical Notices" are Poe's asserting, "The Etymology is placed distinctly by itself for the convenience of hasty reference" (P 5:250; regarding Charles Richardson's *A New Dictionary of the English Language*); his maintaining "that gentleman [J. N. Reynolds] has been appointed to the highest civil situation in the expedition; a station which we know him to be exceedingly well qualified to fill" (P 5:256; regarding *Report on the Committee on Naval Affairs*); and his listing the contents of N. P. Willis's *Inklings of Adventure*, including the short story "The Cherokee's Threat" (concerning one St. John and his beloved Nunu). Poe set great store by his review of *Inklings of Adventure*, suggesting to Hiram Haines that it be copied (O 1:156) and writing about Willis in "Autography," "Mem. Mr. Messenger should do him justice. [Mem. by Mr. Messenger. I have.]" (M 2:280). Etymology, J. N. Reynolds, and a character named Nunu[81] would figure notably in *Arthur Gordon Pym*, which Poe had assuredly been planning and, perhaps by now, begun writing.

In early September, Poe penned a letter to the editor of the *Richmond Compiler*, defending himself against the accusation of "cutting and slashing" (O 1:157–59), and another to the printer Harrison Hall, seeking publication of a seventeen-tale version of his Folio Club collection (O 1:162–64). But, in his effort to maintain high standards and to engage his readers, Poe was occasionally severe in his criticism.[82] And his Folio Club collection would never be published.

A note at the end of the September issue of the *Messenger*, appearing after September 24, reported, "The illness of both Publisher and Editor will, we hope, prove a sufficient apology for the delay in the issue of the present number, and for the omission of many promised notices of new books" (P 5:277). Poe's illness may have been related to his drinking; White later acknowledged that he had considered letting his editor go at this time.[83]

Poe's recklessness with money was also a problem—on occasion, the young editor gambled, indulged in extravagance, borrowed from friends, and requested credit from merchants. John H. Mackenzie told Flora Lapham Mack that "he [Edgar] was his lifelong friend and he loved him & he was perfectly welcome to every penny he had ever loaned him or lost by him." But others may have felt differently. Poe's December 19, 1842, bankruptcy papers list substantial Richmond debts.[84]

Poe's critical contributions to the September issue were modest. Meriting special attention was his review of Robert Montgomery Bird's novel *Sheppard Lee,* a narrative of serial metempsychosis that Poe termed "a very clever, and not altogether unoriginal, *jeu d'esprit*" (P 5:285). Poe intimates that the work may have been somewhat derivative—perhaps he recalled a children's tale of serial metempsychosis, "The Transmigrations of Indur," which had appeared in a book that John Allan had given him many years ago, *Evenings at Home.*[85] Poe's preferring "the infinity of arts which give verisimilitude to a narration" (P 5:286) to the explanatory dream of *Sheppard Lee* is consistent with his work in progress.

Meanwhile, the three Mattox sisters (Flora Lapham Mack's mother, Mary, and Ann and Eliza) would be driven on Mondays from Darby Town to Miss Jane Mackenzie's School, where they boarded, and back on Fridays from the school to Darby Town, frequently with Virginia and Mrs. Clemm, who would visit for the weekend. Mrs. Lanier—Aunt Polly—would provide the Poe household with eggs, butter, fruit, and vegetables. On occasion, Virginia and her mother would stay at the farm for weeks, and John and Edgar would ride out and back every day. On Sundays, by carriage and buggy, the Mackenzies and the Mattox girls drove into town to attend church.[86] It is possible that Edgar, Virginia, and Maria Clemm might sometimes have joined them.

While living in Richmond and yielding to intermittent bouts of drinking, Poe evidently found Darby Town a safe place. Flora Lapham Mack has left us a vivid description of his time there with his wife and the three Mattox girls:

> They, my mother [Mary Mattox], her sisters [Ann and Eliza], Virginia & Edgar would always go out walking or go for nuts wild grapes persimmons or something of the kind[,] roaming through the feilds [*sic*] & woods together. Edgar was always at his very best in these expeditions[,]

gay & bright telling them gay stories or weird ghost tales as they walked or rested in mossy dells or sunny fields or grassy knolls and Edgar the immortal climbing the trees for fruit[,] shaking down the nuts & gathering the nuts & honey shucks[,] whistling gayly an accompaniment to the songs they sang as p[a]eans of praize [sic] for the very joy of living[;] he walked always hand in hand with Virginia & carried her in his arms over the logs thrown across the branches & brooks for bridges which she was timid about trusting herself upon & she was perfectly & radiently [sic] happy.[87]

This wonderful time may well have been the basis for Poe's extraordinary tale of love in the "Valley of the Many-Colored Grass," "Eleonora."

Flora Lapham Mack continued, describing Edgar and Virginia and the Mattox girls returning to the Darby Town home of the Mackenzies:

Then as evening approached they came happily homeward bearing their spoils & singing as they came to assemble those dear people the seeing of whom once more & greeting joyously forms my sweetest visi[o]n of heaven. Your great grandmother [Mrs. Lanier][,] my kind benignant well remembered & beloved aunt[,] your Aunt Louise [Louisa Mackenzie] a frail delicate little woman whom I also loved very much.[,] my own dear mother, her sisters[,] Dear old Cousin John[,] Mrs. Clemm[,] Edgar Poe & little Virginia. Think of this group assembled in the old huge square reception Hall of Darby Town on an Autumn Evening just as they were so often gathered there together.[88]

The memorable hall, the scene of such gladness, is detailed affectionately:

The old Hall I remember so well. It was a huge apartment with its polished well wax[ed] floor[.] Its two long long old hair cloth sofas. Its mahogany tables & "secretary" or escritaire [escritoire] & bookcase. Its cosy armchairs & rockers. The firelight flickers over the brass fender & andirons (I have the same fender as a souvenir still) is reflected in the old polished mahogany furniture on every side & almost make the light of the four candle[s] in their tall brass candle sticks seem an impertinence. Two of these are situate on the ends of [the] carved tall mantlepeice [sic] the carving of which was my childish delight to look at & study representing Pharoes [Pharaoh's] host being drownded [sic], and two on the candlestand which in the daytime is folded flat and set against the wall.

Well! they are all passed away now peace to their ashes[,] but then and for many years afterward they were more alive than most.[89]

And, thanks to Flora Lapham Mack, we have a delightful moment imminent for which we might well pause. Poe's life was famously full of sorrow, so it is satisfying to encounter an instant of elation, one that we have not known before. Mack writes, with evident pleasure, about Poe's remarkable caper into the Mackenzies' parlor and the joyous activities that followed:

> Cards[,] music & dancing were a part of the evening program at Darbytown & little Virginia loved to dance about as well as the rest of them. Cousin John often told me how a great danseuse (Elselier I think it was [Fanny Elssler]) had just visited Richmond at this time and Edgar to their delight and amusement would imitate her grand Entré opening wide the doors which led from the Entrance Hall through a short entry in to the parlour where they had all assembled now with Virginia at the piano[.] He would come with a sort of running leap in to the parlour & landing on the toes of his right foot twirl rapidly around for a moment & then he would dance most gracefully & rhythmetically [sic] an intricate a[nd] Spanish fandango. Then they would all dance square dances a while and then Cousin John & Virginia would sing together. He sang well as long as he lived & loved Moore's [Irish] Melodies[,] Burns['s] songs etc. and she & he loved to sing together to her simple self taught accompaniment ["]Bonnie Mary of Argyle[,"] ["The Auld] Ingleside[,"] ["]The last rose of summer[,"] etc.[90]

Poe's fantastic leap is well worth remembering, especially when we reach those familiar moments of suffering and tragedy. For Poe was part of a small social world in Richmond in which he was respected and loved. He was as profoundly at home here at Darby Town as he ever was anywhere.

It had not been Fanny Elssler whom Poe had seen since she did not tour in the United States until 1840.[91] But clearly Poe was familiar with other celebrated dancers, and he was himself, as this passage reveals, a skilled dancer.[92] The popular songs mentioned at the end are all sentimental—all too appropriate for this moment that was about to be lost by the Poes. The latter two songs honor old times—"auld lang syne"—"the days that are gane" ("The Old Ingleside"), the loss of "love's shining circle" ("The Last Rose of Summer"). And it was not just the Poes who would lose the old times. For eventually the Civil War would come, and, with justice, this world of the Mackenzies would vanish. Much as they might have celebrated the drowning of their enemies,

Pharaoh's host, the Mackenzies themselves would turn out to be Pharaoh's host, themselves suffering because of the very institution that had undergirded their world, slavery.

However, that all lay many years in the future. For now, in the fall of 1836, friends and family were gathered at Darby Town in an enchanted warmth. Flora Lapham Mack offered the view of her mother, Mary Mattox Lapham: "My mother always said she thought that Virginia must in afterlife have looked back on the Saturday evenings she spent at Darbytown during this time[, t]hose evenings when Edgar came out to stay a day or two, as the happiest times of her whole life."[93]

The October 1836 issue of the *Southern Literary Messenger* appeared late, after November 8. The delay was attributed (perhaps by Poe) to "sickness in our office, the difficulty of obtaining workmen at short notice in the South, and other causes unforeseen."[94] Poe's first review, that of Susan Rigby Morgan's *The Swiss Heiress,* is severe, but the next review, that of S. A. Roszel's *Address,* includes the mild comment, "a fellow-feeling has taught us to be lenient" (P 5:296). Poe may even have been strategically favorable, terming Saunders & Otley "publishers of the highest respectability" in his review of *Memorials of Mrs. Hemans* (P 5:304), since they had expressed an interest in his tales.[95] Introducing the notices of the *Messenger,* White excuses Poe from any self-serving involvement, stating that the publisher was responsible for this feature. The notices are mostly favorable—indeed, sometimes exceptionally so: the *New York Messenger* states, "One thing we do know assuredly, that this Magazine would do honor to any part of the world."[96]

Even as he worked on the final issue of the second volume, that for November, Poe was probably also working on the early chapters of *The Narrative of Arthur Gordon Pym.* He would have already determined the form and crafted the final image of the novel, toward which the whole would be tending. It is apposite here to quote Poe's comment at the beginning of his 1846 essay "The Philosophy of Composition" (about the writing of "The Raven"): "Nothing is more clear than that every plot, worth the name, must be elaborated to its *dénouement* before anything be attempted with the pen. It is only with the *dénouement* constantly in view that we can give a plot its indispensable air of consequence, or causation, by making the incidents, and especially the tone at all points, tend to the development of the intention" (L2 60).

In late 1836, there were growing problems at the *Messenger:* White reported on November 24, returning from a trip, "When I reached home I found my wife very ill in bed, and all my office affairs in great confusion." The

November 1836 issue would come out, on December 10, but shortly thereafter, White wrote further, "[M]y Printing is nearly suspended, in consequence of as ruinous as a foolish strike of the young men Printers."[97] And it may be that White was again seeing incontrovertible evidence of Poe's drinking. Therefore, as indicated in his September 29, 1835, letter to Poe (H 17:20–21) and in his apparent warning in September 1836,[98] all his obligations to him would come to an end.

Poe's contributions to the November 1836 issue of the *Messenger* were slender. Most important was his review of Charles Dickens's *Pickwick Club*, featuring, as it did, an excerpt from "A Madman's MS." There are parallels between this tale and Poe's "Ligeia," "The Imp of the Perverse," and "The Tell-Tale Heart."[99] At the close of the issue appears this statement: "A press of business connected with some necessary arrangements for Volume the Third, has prevented us from paying, in this Messenger, the usual attention to our Critical Department. We have many books now lying by us which we propose to notice fully in our next. With this number we close Volume the Second" (P 5:316).

In mid- and late December 1836, Poe would have been working on the January 1837 issue of the *Messenger*. Perhaps he understood that his time at the magazine was coming to a close. He might then have been imagining his establishing his own literary magazine (O 1:467). And he might well have been continuing to write the early chapters of his sea novel.

According to Flora Lapham Mack, John H. Mackenzie said that Poe had given Virginia "an occasional box of candy or extract of violets[,] of both of [which] she was inordinately fond," but never the thing she desired most, "a musical instrument to accompany her voice[,] prefferably [sic] a piano of her very own." Poe would make excuses, but Miss Jane Mackenzie heard of Virginia's wish and took matters into her own hands: she sent Virginia a guitar for Christmas. And Miss Mackenzie invited Virginia to come to her school and take guitar and voice lessons. "This she did," Mack reports, "and the guitar became the greatest joy of her life." Mack continues, "She carried it lovingly with her from the [sic] Richmond in her arms[,] swathed in a green baize bag. Cousin John said that he often found the little creature[,] when Mrs. Clemm sent for him to come & see Edgar in one of his 'bad spells[,]' sitting at a window in the lower hall busily embroidering[,] with the guitar leaning against the sill beside her and as she talked with him in passing[,] her fingers would nois[e]lessly & carresingly [sic] touch the strings. She always brought it with her to Darbytown when she came after its acquisition & played very sweetly accompaniments on it to their [the Mackenzies'] songs."[100]

Virginia enjoyed also the generosity of both Aunt Polly, who gave her Anne Mattox's outgrown "nice mazerine [mazarine] blue merino" dress, and John's sister Mary, who gave her her own "brown silk dress with a gay roman striped plaid check." Mrs. Clemm modified the dresses for Virginia, and the much-beloved girl was very attractive. Mack writes, "'Virginia really looked exceedingly nice' Mother said in her new (?) blue merino or her handsome plaid silk with her Tuscan straw bonnet trimmed with a dark red plaid ribbon & her hair thick heavy & black coiled low on her neck behind, and she was much delighted with her new clothes."[101]

Poe must have been charmed by Virginia's appearance and her delight. But his own situation was increasingly tenuous. Given his likely absences from work after a spree, Poe had clearly not been discreet about his indiscretions. Given White's latest warning, in September 1836, Poe must have recognized that because of his repeated lapses, his tenure at the *Messenger* would soon lapse.

On December 27, 1836, White wrote to his friend Beverly Tucker, "Highly as I really think of Mr. Poe's talents, I shall be forced to give him notice, in a week or so at farthest, that I can no longer recognize him as editor of my Messenger." He intimates that Poe had been drinking—"certain conditions" (presumably staying sober) "he has again forfeited." And he complains of having been "cramped by him in the exercise of my own judgment."[102] Nearly a month later, White wrote to his friend William Scott, "Mr. Poe retired from the editorship of my work on the 3d inst [the third of the present month, January 3, 1837]."[103] He repeats this in the January 1837 issue of the *Messenger* (appearing after January 26): "Mr. POE, who has filled the editorial department for the last twelve months, with so much ability, retired from that station on the 3d inst." Poe wrote, after his notices in the January issue, "Mr. Poe's attention being called in another direction, he will decline, with the present number, Editorial duties of the Messenger" (P 5:325). White was generous to state that Poe had "retired," to allow Poe to state that he "will decline" his duties. It is clear that Poe's intemperance had led to his termination. And White would have been relieved to be rid of Poe's occasionally excessively harsh criticism—he wrote to Beverly Tucker on January 24, "The Messenger is safe. It shall live—and it shall outlive all the injury it has sustained from Mr. Poe's management."[104] Of course, even as Poe's critical severity could be a problem, his incisive analyses enlivened the periodical. His involvement with the magazine, as a contributor and as an editor, did vitally contribute to its success and has been the primary reason for all the attention that the *Messenger* has received since.

Poe remained in Richmond from late December through January. He notified his old friend, the editor and poet Lambert A. Wilmer, of the available position at the *Messenger*. And despite his equivocal status after January 3, he wrote a letter to his old West Point friend Allan B. Magruder regarding his submission to the *Messenger* on January 9 (O 1:169–70). He apparently wrote out his poem "Irene" in the album of a Richmond friend, John Collins McCabe (M 1:182–83). According to Benjamin B. Minor, Poe asked to be reinstated at the *Messenger*, but the long-suffering White turned him down.[105] On January 17, White promised to provide him with some funds (H 17:41–42); two days later (Poe's twenty-eighth birthday), White wrote Beverly Tucker, "Poe feels his situation at last—I see but little of him—but I hear a great deal about him and from him."[106] By January 31, White was very impatient: "Poe pesters me no little—he is trying every manoeuvre to foist himself on some one at the North—at least I believe so.—He is continually after me for money. I am as sick of his writings, as I am of him,—and am rather more than half inclined to send him up another dozen dollars in the morning, and along with it all his unpublished manuscripts."[107]

Poe later claimed that he was "induced to abandon" the *Messenger* by Francis Hawks of the *New York Review*, who sought the services of his "*broad-axe*."[108] There would be no job waiting for Poe at the *Review*—though he did write one lengthy piece—but Poe, Virginia, and Maria Clemm would make their way to New York City in early February 1837. Mack reports, "Cousin John told Mrs. Clemm at parting to write to him in any emergency without fail and he would always do all that he could for her & for Virginia but that henceforth only through her should he attempt to succor Edgar as he was convinced that was the only way to do them any good[,] & he[,] though he never saw her again[,] kept his word faithfully & always responded to her appeals as generously as he could afford to do & did it willingly & gladly."[109]

Before Poe and his wife and mother-in-law left, the January 1837 issue of the *Southern Literary Messenger* appeared. The most important of the Poe pieces in this issue was the first of two installments of "Arthur Gordon Pym," early chapters of Poe's only novel, which, as will be suggested, was to be one of Poe's greatest achievements. This installment is titled on the inside front wrapper (and similarly in White's editorial note [P 5:325]) as "Arthur Gordon Pym, a Sea Story, No. 1."[110] It begins simply (and now, famously), "My name is Arthur Gordon Pym." There were other Poe contributions—two fine poems about lost love, "Ballad" and "Sonnet. To Zante," as well as five reviews, including notices of works that were sources for the novel, Washington Irving's

Astoria and J. N. Reynolds's *Address,* and Poe's gracious farewell[111]—but it was "Arthur Gordon Pym" that was the most consequential contribution. White disparaged it and complained that though he ostensibly paid Poe three dollars a page for "Pym," he was really paying him twenty dollars a page.[112] He was also perplexed as to the work's meaning. He wrote to Beverly Tucker on January 31, "Tell me candidly what you think of his Pym (Marryatt's style I suppose) and his poetry."[113] And he would later write to William Scott, "Tell me, when you write what Poe is driving at—that is, if you know—but do not put yourself out to gratify perhaps an idle curiosity. I have not heard from him since he left here."[114]

Pym reads best in full, but the first installment holds its rewards. Perhaps some in Richmond—John H. Mackenzie or his mother, Jane Scott Mackenzie, for instance—recognized some of the personal elements in those four pages. Arthur Gordon Pym was Edgar Allan Poe, and his friend Augustus Barnard—two years older and a drinker, who told him tales of his travels—was Henry Poe. Relevant to the two boys was that "[i]t is probable indeed that our intimate communion had resulted in a partial interchange of character." Pym's maternal grandfather was John Allan; his frantic mother was Frances Allan. And "Mr. E. Ronald's Academy on the hill" was probably Joseph H. Clarke's school, and, as Richard Wilbur first noted, an anagrammatical reference to Poe's mother, Eliza Arnold. Augustus's emerging from the water, with a rope around his neck, and hitting his head, suggests, as stated earlier, Henry's birth.

The story of the boys' survival from the boat *Ariel,* wrecked by the ship the *Penguin,* was an adaptation of the actual wreck of the Norfolk vessel the *Ariel,* one employed here to begin to suggest the destruction of Jerusalem. The boat's location near "the lumber-yard of Pankey & Co." intimates that the *Ariel* is "the key to it all."[115]

Here are the beginnings of two allegories—one of these autobiographical and the other biblical and historical. As out of control as Poe's life could sometimes be, his literary work was utterly in control. Here we have the first chapter and a portion of the second chapter of Poe's Art Novel, which "labor[s] to the sole end of reasoning men into admiration and study of the beautiful, by a tissue of *bizarre* fiction, partly allegorical, and partly metaphysical" (P 5:119).

Many years later, Poe scholar J. H. Whitty found in Poe's *Southern Literary Messenger* desk a fragment of Poe's poetry, which may have been prompted in part by a poem appearing on the reverse side of the paper. The three lines, now called "Spiritual Song," are "Hark, echo!—Hark, echo! / 'Tis the sound / Of archangels, in happiness wrapt" (M 1:304).[116] Doubtless there were moments in Richmond in 1836, particularly with his lovely child-bride Virginia, that Poe was "in happiness wrapt." But the underlying darkness remained, tragically addressed through his drinking—and brilliantly addressed, and expressed, through his writing. Without analyzing the completed novel here, we may at least highlight Poe's having written to Maria Clemm on August 29, 1835, "[Y]ou well know how little I am able to bear up under the pressure of grief" (O 1:102). It was, I would propose, "the pressure of grief" at the loss of his brother Henry that prompted the extraordinary *Narrative of Arthur Gordon Pym*, and the novel's goal would be a mysterious but triumphant consolation. Through his literary genius, Poe was able to offer both beauty and balm.

13

"A Flattering Invitation"

1837-1838

THE TWIN BANES OF POE'S life, drinking and gambling, seem to have abated when he and his family moved to New York City in February 1837. He later claimed, in the April 1841 letter in which he admitted to his drinking in Richmond, "[I]t is now quite four years since I have abandoned every kind of alcoholic drink" (with one exception, involving cider, during his early time in Philadelphia) (O 1:264). There is no evidence to contradict his assertion. His twelve or fifteen months in Manhattan in 1837 and 1838 were relatively quiet. He published only modestly—two tales and an essay—but he made significant progress on the manuscript of his novel.

Poe, Virginia, and Maria Clemm moved to an apartment on Sixth Avenue, close to Waverly Place (near what is now Washington Square Park). The Poe family shared their space with a boarder, William Gowans, the bookman who had published Plato's *Phaedon* and a collection titled *The Phenix,* which included works by Confucius and Zoroaster. Gowans conducted his book auction business about thirty blocks south, at the Long Room, 169 Broadway, near Cortlandt Street. He later left an appreciative recollection of Poe at this time in his commentary on a British first edition of *Pym* (1838):

> For eight months, or more, "one house contained us, us one table fed." During that time I saw much of him, and had an opportunity of conversing with him often, and I must say I never saw him the least affected with liquor, nor even descend to any known vice, while he was one of

the most courteous, gentlemanly, and intelligent companions I have met with during my journeyings and haltings through divers divisions of the globe; besides, he had an extra inducement to be a good man as well as a good husband, for he had a wife of matchless beauty and loveliness, her eye could match that of any houri, and her face defy the genius of a Canova to imitate; a temper and disposition of surpassing sweetness; besides, she seemed as much devoted to him and his every interest as a young mother is to her first born.[1]

Thomas C. Latto reported that Gowans said that Poe "was uniformly quiet, reticent, gentlemanly in demeanour, and during the whole period he lived there, not the slightest trace of intoxication or dissipation was discernible in the illustrious inmate, who was at that time engaged in the composition of 'Arthur Gordon Pym.'"[2] This was, then, a period of comparative calm for Poe, his wife, and his mother-in-law. Perhaps, with regard to his personal habits in this new city, he was trying to start over.

Despite what Poe later termed "a flattering invitation" from the proprietors of the *New York Review*,[3] no job materialized for him. The family might have been destitute, but fortunately they were aided by the generosity of John H. Mackenzie: "[H]e (Cousin John)[,] soon after they went to New York after his [Poe's] marraige [sic][,] began to send what he could afford to give to Mrs. Clemm instead of Edgar[,] knowing she would expend it to the best advantage for the mutual benefit of the three."[4] So there would have been a respite for Poe—and he would have had time to write.

A letter written in Baltimore to Poe, on January 30, was sent to Richmond and then forwarded to New York—and on February 28, Poe responded to the editors of the prospective *Baltimore Book* regarding their invitation to furnish a contribution. He responded favorably, asking for further information (O 1:173–74) and eventually provided the short, compelling, unpublished Folio Club tale of spiritual terror "Siope—A Fable" (later "Silence—A Fable"). The piece was published in the fall of the year.

Sometime after March 3, the February 1837 issue of the *Southern Literary Messenger* appeared.[5] Nearly eight pages comprised the second installment of "Arthur Gordon Pym," corresponding to the fourth paragraph in the second chapter of the book through the third paragraph in the fourth chapter. On the ship *Grampus*, captained by his father, Augustus Barnard helps Arthur Gordon Pym stow away in the hold. However, Pym is trapped there for a week, suffering hunger and thirst, seasickness and fever. Augustus tries to warn him with a note affixed to Pym's dog, Tiger. But subsequently, overwhelmed by the poisonous atmosphere in the hold, Pym becomes dazed and delirious, and the dog becomes maddened and dangerously threatening. Intending to visit Pym when he is awake, Augustus is constrained by a mutiny. So, the series of nautical horrors continues.

And the autobiographical allegory is sustained: Pym tells us that, seeking the trapdoor from the hold and guided by a whipcord, he crawled through "the narrow and intricate windings of the lumber" and then "upon making a push forward, with all the energy I could command, I struck my forehead violently against the sharp corner of an iron-bound crate."[6] Leaning perhaps on the robbers' cavern passage in Alain-René Lesage's novel *Gil Blas,* Poe renders a second birth, his own. As noted, this follows the earlier allegorical birth of his brother Henry, rendered through Augustus's coming up from the water, with a rope encircling his neck, and then banging his head.[7]

Pym's maternal grandfather, Mr. Peterson, again suggests John Allan. Augustus's note to Pym, "*blood—your life depends upon lying close,*" intimates the possibility of the two brothers' (Henry and Edgar's) sharing the same bed in Mrs. Clemm's impoverished Baltimore apartment (as Augustus and Arthur shared the same bed at the Barnards' home). And the use of such proper names as "Goddin" and "Vredenburg" may be indebted to the list of subscribers to the *Southern Literary Messenger,* including John Goddin and Isaac A. Goddin, as well as Otis Vredenburgh.[8] This second installment of "Arthur Gordon Pym" was the last; the full novel would appear in sixteen months.

Poe's time in New York City in 1837 and 1838 seems to have been relatively subdued and modest, but there was one extraordinary and extravagant event in which he took part, the March 30, 1837, Booksellers' Dinner. Diarist Philip Hone wrote, "This was the greatest dinner I was ever at, with the exception perhaps of that given to Washington Irving on his return from Europe" (held on May 30, 1832).[9] Probably invited by William Gowans, Poe attended this grand celebration of the New York book world at the popular City Hotel.

This five-story building was far south on Broadway, past Gowans's Long Room, between Cedar and Thames Streets, just short of Trinity Church and Wall Street. The ample hall for the dinner featured, on this occasion, busts of William Shakespeare, John Milton, Benjamin Franklin, Sir Walter Scott, and Washington Irving (who was there). Also among the 277 men dining that evening were William Cullen Bryant, Fitz-Greene Halleck, Charles Fenno Hoffman, George Pope Morris, Mordecai Noah, James K. Paulding, and N. P. Willis. The master of ceremonies was the publisher George Dearborn.

The gathering was, we are told, "a brilliant assembly, and such a one as rarely occurs." Those attending enjoyed a memorable evening of bookish good fellowship.

The menu was prodigal, from "Trouffled Pates" to "Stewed Terrapins"; from "Saddles of Mountain Mutton" to "Robins," "Larks," and "English Snipe"; from "Wild Geese" to "Fricando Veal." Desserts included "Plum Puddings," "Madeira Jellies," "Blanc Mange," "Peach, Plum, and Apple Pies," and "Ice Cream." Among the drinks were "Chateau Margaux" claret, "Star, oeil de perdrix" champagne, and "East India, red seal" madeira. The profusion would have satisfied the most discriminating gourmandizer. Poe must have been fairly astounded—and perhaps, as a would-be epicure, profoundly at ease.

The program for the evening included orchestra music and singing, as well as a series of speeches and toasts saluting literary and journalistic attainments. Among those offering the lengthiest addresses, followed by toasts, were John Keese and W. L. Stone. Shorter speeches were given by Harrison Gray, James Harper, Charles King, Mordecai Noah, Philip Hone, J. W. Francis, Washington Irving, and J. K. Paulding. Many gave individual toasts, and, notably, three of the men honored women. One of them, for example, publisher George P. Putnam, graciously toasted "The Female Intellects of our country—Brilliant luminaries in its literary horizon."

The publisher Fletcher Harper, presumably standing and raising his glass, toasted "Booksellers—Generous individuals who kindly assist Authors to obtain an immortality in which they do not themselves participate." And the aspiring Poe, who must also have risen, with a glass in hand, toasted "The *Monthlies* of Gotham—Their distinguished Editors, and their vigorous *Collaborateurs*." As one who would soon publish in New York's *American Monthly Magazine* and the *New York Review,* he was himself to be a vigorous collaborator. Also, he would publish in the following year with the Harpers—and eventually obtain an immortality.

The evening ended late, and those at the remarkable gala are said to have departed "evidently highly gratified." We may well imagine Poe to have departed impressed and ever more ambitious for the acclaim of New York's literary world.[10]

Gowans gives us an impression of Poe's appearance at this time: "Poe had a remarkably pleasing and prepossessing countenance, what the ladies would call decidedly handsome." And he also characterizes Poe's library: "Poe[,] the most original of all the American poets, had a library made up of newspapers, magazines bound and unbound, with what books had been presented to him from time to time by authors and publishers. He had no very high opinion of the modern generators of books, especially those so employed around him, and hence many of these gifts found an early transfer into the possession of some second-hand dealer at wonderfully reduced prices."[11] Poe would have been continuing to write *Pym* in the spring of 1837, thereby continuing, as we shall see, to mourn his brother Henry. And he worked on a short story, "Von Jung, the Mystific," soon to be submitted to the *American Monthly Magazine*, edited by Charles Fenno Hoffman and Park Benjamin and published in New York by George Dearborn.

If this was a relatively calm period for Poe personally, it was not to be for the city and country economically, for on May 10 New York banks refused to honor paper money with gold or silver ("specie"), and the Panic of 1837 began.[12] There were repercussions for Poe. His novel, whose title was copyrighted on June 10, would not be published for another year.[13] And despite John H. Mackenzie's generous support of the Poe family, there was still financial need. It was, after all, the midst of hard times. Poe's bankruptcy documents of December 19, 1842, list seven creditors from New York City. It was probably sometime in 1837 that Poe incurred personal debts to J. N. Reynolds, William Cullen Bryant, and J. K. Paulding (all of whom he may then have met personally), as well as rent debts and other debts.[14] Though evidently not drinking or gambling, Poe was beginning to be financially challenged again.

Probably it was a rent debt that led Poe and his family to move a few blocks southwest to a simple two-story wooden house, 113½ Carmine Street, near Varick Street. As their boarder, Gowans may well have accompanied them. One source describes Poe and Virginia walking in St. John's Burying Ground, which was south on Varick Street, as well as Virginia watching her husband from a window.[15] Virginia would probably have continued to knit and to embroider. And perhaps she brought her much-loved guitar from Richmond—if so, she might have played it and sung popular songs, as at Darby Town of yore. No doubt Maria Clemm remained an exemplary housekeeper and the manager of their all-too-slender funds.

On May 27, Poe wrote to the classicist Charles Anthon, seeking the translation of biblical verses for the review he would write of John Lloyd Stephens's *Incidents of Travel in Egypt, Arabia Petræa, and the Holy Land*. Anthon responded on June 1, providing the translation of the specified passage from Isaiah, about desolation (H 17:42–43). Poe worked on his long review of Stephens's book, which would appear in the October issue of the *New York Review*.

Among the "magazines bound and unbound" that Gowans mentioned in Poe's library may well have been issues of the *American Monthly Magazine*. Of particular interest to Poe would have been reviews of Stephens's *Incidents of Travel* in the April and May issues and a much-shortened version of the *New York American*'s account of the Booksellers' Dinner in the May issue. Poe's short story "Von Jung, the Mystific," a satire on dueling, was published in the June 1837 issue.

The narrator of this tale relates an anecdote concerning the brilliant Baron Ritzner Von Jung, proficient in "the science of *mystification*." Seeming to share the obsession with dueling of the foolish Hermann, Von Jung actually mocks him. He appears to observe a fine code of honor and baits Hermann with a singular attack—throwing a decanter of wine at a mirror that reflects Hermann and shattering the mirror. Encouraged by Von Jung to accompany the properly insulted man, the narrator listens as Hermann quotes from an obscure book that Von Jung had given him. The narrator brings Von Jung the anticipated letter of challenge from Hermann, and the "mystific" responds with a letter that apparently satisfies Hermann with its reference to a passage in that obscure book. The narrator learns that Hermann could not fathom that passage, one that was apparently meaningless, and therefore acquiesced rather than admit his lack of comprehension. Yet an understanding of the secret to reading the text—"leaving out every second and third word alternately"—enabled Von Jung to read to the narrator a burlesque of dueling, "a most horribly grotesque account of a duel between two baboons." The book was, in fact, "a series of ludicrous quizzes upon the duello."[16] Von Jung's knowledge is suggestive with regard to our reading the work that Poe was then finishing, *The Narrative of Arthur Gordon Pym*, for recognition of a hidden pattern may yield otherwise unattainable meaning. Poe was a hermetic writer—even as he sought to engage the many, he also sought to encode for the few. Fortunately for all readers of Poe, the pattern in *Pym* is not arbitrary and may be ascertained through close reading.

Hard times continued in New York City, but there was still a July Fourth celebration, which Poe probably heard during the day and surely heard and saw in the evening. Lamenting eight years of President Andrew Jackson and other causes of a loss of independence, diarist Philip Hone wrote of a noontime tolling, "The bells [of St. Paul's Church] were ringing a merry peal in honor of the day. Their sound proclaimed the liberty and independence of my country; but now, for the first time, there seemed to me mockery in those sounds. The glory seems to have departed." Then he offered a description of the later "grand display of fireworks": "The evening was dark, dry, and clear, and it seemed as if the whole population of New York has been seized with a pyrotechnicmania, and were determined to make up for the slender celebrations of the day by a universal display of rockets, blue lights, and Roman candles. The shores were illuminated up and down the river, and the reports more or less loud in every direction would have led one to fancy that the city was undergoing a vigorous siege."[17] Yet one need not have been fanciful to realize that there actually was a siege, an economic one, in 1837 New York City. The fireworks were, of course, an effort to maintain tradition but perhaps also an effort to rally the spirits of a dispirited people.

During the summer of 1837, Poe was writing the review of John L. Stephens's *Incidents of Travel;* he may also have been futilely seeking regular work. It is possible that his attacks in the *Messenger* on Theodore S. Fay's novel *Norman Leslie* and works by other New York City writers set some Gotham editors against him.[18] In any case, money was tight in the city and in his household. John Ward Ostrom estimates that Poe was paid $14 for "Siope" and $12 for "Von Jung, The Mystific." His review would pay $26.[19] Poe's income was meager at best. Maria Clemm, who would have received money from boarder William Gowans and perhaps from her (and Virginia's) sewing, knitting, and embroidery, would very likely have continued to receive money from the ever-generous John H. Mackenzie. And it would seem likely that Mackenzie would have written a note or letter to accompany each contribution. Perhaps, then, Poe would have thereby learned of significant family news.

The younger brother of Mackenzie's wife Louisa, William Lewis Lanier, married Lucy Eliza Virginia Armistead on September 17, 1837. Poe would probably have remembered the young man from his recuperative time with the Mackenzies at Mount Erin in 1831. William Lewis Lanier and his wife Lucy, who would live in northern Mississippi in Holly Springs, would have three daughters; these sisters (Louisa's nieces) would be taken in by the Mackenzies at Darby Town when their mother died, in March 1849. The oldest of these girls, Jane Bretney Lanier, remembered Poe from his stay in Richmond in 1849 and spoke of him to her son (William Lewis Lanier's grandson) William Lanier Washington. Washington would later be the correspondent of John H. Mackenzie's stepdaughter Flora Lapham Mack.[20]

Evidently even as John H. Mackenzie would write to Maria Clemm, sometimes Maria Clemm would write to him. And sometimes Poe would write, as well. But despite Mackenzie's having saved the letters received from the two of them, most of these letters are no longer extant. As noted earlier, this is because of their incineration during the burning of Richmond. Flora Lapham Mack explains that many of "the letters that passed between Edgar Poe Mrs. Clemm & John H. Mackenzie during their lifelong friendship & intimacy" were given to Thomas G. Mackenzie (John's brother) for a biography of Poe and subsequently destroyed in the Evacuation Fire of April 1865. Thomas lost "all his Poe papers & pictures and the manuscript of his book already prepared."[21] These Poe papers might have shed much light upon this relatively little-known period in his life—indeed, upon much of Poe's life away from Richmond.

The October 1837 issue of the *New York Review* included Poe's anonymous review of J. L. Stephens's *Incidents of Travel in Egypt, Arabia Petræa, and the Holy Land* (where Poe employed the translation by Charles Anthon). Relying in part on Alexander Keith's *Evidence of the Truth of the Christian Religion, Derived from the Literal Fulfilment of Prophecy,* Poe argues that biblical prophecies are indeed literally fulfilled. The purpose of the prophecies and their fulfillment was to advance Christian belief. Poe explains that the obscurity of the prophecies was needed to preclude the doubters' claiming that the prophecies, through Christian readers, caused their own fulfillment. He asserts that understanding the prophecies is possible only upon their fulfillment. And he defends Keith, in a note, against the charge of plagiarism (H 10:1–25). The particular prophecy that no one shall pass through Idumea (in Isaiah and Ezekiel) is considered characteristically hyperbolic and actually fulfilled inasmuch as it is considered "only to predict the general desolation and abandonment of the land" (H 10:19).

There are, I think, three takeaways from this review. First, Poe seems to offer the devout view of a traditional millennialist. His language certainly appears pious: "the Book of Books" (H 10:1), "the providence of the Deity" (H 10:2), "the infallibility of the Divine word" (H 10:6), "the ends of Providence" (H 10:8), "a remarkable curse of the Divinity" (H 10:9), "the providential plan of the Deity" (H 10:9), "the providence of God" (H 10:10), "the darkness of the veil shall be uplifted" (H 10:11), and "a strict prohibition on the part of the Deity" (H 10:19). Perhaps, it might be argued, he was only trying to please his audience, including *New York Review* editor Reverend Caleb S. Henry;[22] his correspondent Francis L. Hawks; and J. L. Stephens's publisher (and his own), the Methodist Harper brothers. But the detail and intensity of the review and Poe's typical critical unyieldingness suggest otherwise.

Second, Poe asserts a conviction that only a single point of view will permit comprehension: "[M]ost of the predictions become intelligible only when viewed from the proper point of observation—the period of fulfillment" (H 10:10). As open to interpretation as his own works are, he himself thought in terms of the one entry, the one perspective, the one key (as we may recall from Von Jung's arcane book and as we will see in the Dupin tales and "The Gold-Bug" and Poe's pieces on secret writing in general). For Poe, decoding and encoding presumed a single correct solution. He lived in the Age of Newton, not Heisenberg. Regarding language, it was the Age of Champollion, the decipherer of Egyptian hieroglyphics. The possibility of the multiplicity of accurate solutions would have diminished Poe's authority and the virtue of discovery—and it would have undercut the beauty of a hermetically designed work of art.

Third, Poe had been thinking about the matter of biblical desolation. Indeed, he had a particular preoccupation, owing probably to Coleridge's self-acknowledged failure to write the great epic about the destruction of Jerusalem: the desolation of the Holy City. All three points relate to his coming novel.

It was probably sometime in 1837, according to Burton R. Pollin, that Poe saw the play *The Poor Gentleman,* featuring actor William E. Burton as the comical apothecary Dr. Ollapod. Poe refers to Ollapod in his later work "How to Write a Blackwood Article" but changes the name (to Dr. Morphine) when he is working on Burton's periodical, then changes the name back when he is no longer associated with *Burton's Gentleman's Magazine.*[25] Late in the year, *The Baltimore Book* appeared, including Poe's haunting piece "Siope." And we have a report, later confirmed, that in the severe winter of 1837, Poe visited a clinic, the Northern Dispensary (located at Waverly Place and Christopher Street), to treat a cold.[24]

This early stay in New York City was successful in terms of Poe's writing but not in terms of his income. Early in 1838, Poe, Virginia, and Maria Clemm moved to Philadelphia, where they would remain six years. Soon *Pym* would be published. And Poe would write a variety of classic short stories, including "The Fall of the House of Usher," "The Tell-Tale Heart," "The Black Cat," as well as the three Dupin tales, which constitute the beginnings of the modern detective story. He would also edit two literary magazines, *Burton's Gentleman's Magazine* and *Graham's Magazine.* Still, Poe would have to declare bankruptcy. And accompanying his ongoing financial failure was a devastating personal tragedy: Virginia would become seriously ill.

14

"I Shall Remain in Philadelphia Perhaps for a Year"

1838–1840

SEVEN OF THE EIGHT PLACES in the United States that claim Poe as their own—Boston, Charleston, Richmond, Charlottesville, West Point, Baltimore, and New York City—are referred to, explicitly or implicitly, in his novel *The Narrative of Arthur Gordon of Nantucket*.[1] One of the narrative's two allegories is clearly autobiographical. The eighth place that claims him, Philadelphia, is where Poe lived when *Pym* was published.

Precisely when Poe, Virginia, and Maria Clemm moved to Philadelphia is not known. John H. Ingram, relying on a letter from Thomas C. Latto to Sarah Helen Whitman, reports that the bookseller William Gowans left the Poe family "when the household was broken up." But we don't know exactly when Gowans began living with the Poes, and he was not sufficiently specific when he wrote that he was with them for "eight months, or more."[2] I would conjecture that the Poes moved in late April or early May 1838, after Poe had drawn on J. N. Reynolds's "Leaves from an Unpublished Journal" (which appeared in the April 21, 1838, *New York Mirror*) for a late passage in *Pym*.[3] (The June 10, 1837, copyright of the novel's title does not necessitate our concluding that Poe wrote no more of the work after that date—J. V. Ridgely has Poe making changes even as the book was going to press [see P 1:32, as well as 35–36].) According to J. H. Whitty, the move of the Poe family from New York City to Philadelphia was facilitated by the Philadelphia writer and editor James Pedder.[4] As Dwight Thomas has noted, the Poes settled into the boardinghouse of Mrs. C. Jones at 202 Arch (or Mulberry) Street, not far west of Fourth Street.[5]

Philadelphia was built on the grid plan, with the axis comprising Broad Street, running north-south, and High (or Market) Street, between the Delaware River and the Schuylkill River, running east-west. Many of the offices of the magazines and newspapers of Philadelphia were clustered south of the east end (the Delaware River end) of High Street, in the center of the Old City, on Chestnut Street and Walnut Street; on the intersecting cross streets, Second Street and Third Street; and on a street angled southeast off Third, Dock Street. This periodicals district, conveniently a few blocks east of Independence Square and west of the New York and Baltimore steamboats, was analogous to the Washington Street area in Boston and the Nassau Street area in New York City. Poe's boardinghouse was a short walk away; Arch was on the north side of High.[6]

The periodicals district would naturally have been important for Poe the magazinist: it was here that he would come to meet the literary and journalistic men of the city; edit two magazines, *Burton's Gentleman's Magazine* and *Graham's Magazine;* and submit his own work. But it may well have been here, too, that, in the spring and summer of 1838, Poe endured what he termed in a July 17, 1838, letter from Philadelphia to his supporter J. K. Paulding, now secretary of the U.S. Navy, a "miserable life of literary drudgery" (O 1:175). It was for Poe a time of continued struggle. He sought from Paulding "the most unimportant Clerkship in your gift—*any thing, by sea or land*" (O 1:175), but without success.

We have little detail about Virginia and Maria Clemm at this time. Perhaps they brought in meager money from their sewing (supplemented by John H. Mackenzie's occasional support). Regarding Virginia, we may only conjecture that, by the spring of 1838, she and Edgar would have consummated their marriage, given the comments of Bardwell Haywood and Elizabeth Oakes Smith about the two-year waiting period.[7] We may note that in the autobiographical tale "Eleonora," the narrator's cousin was "at the close of the third lustrum of her life"—that is, fifteen—when the narrator and she "had drawn the God Eros from that wave" (M 2:640). And Virginia was, in May 1838, fifteen.

We may be uncertain about this tender matter but absolutely sure about a harsh historical one: not far from the Poes' home, the ongoing antislavery struggle was dealt a severe blow. On May 17, Pennsylvania Hall, newly built as a venue for abolitionism, but unprotected, was burned by a pro-slavery mob. The building's location—between Cherry Street and Sassafras Street on Sixth—was only blocks from Mrs. Jones's boardinghouse. Perhaps Poe,

Virginia, and Mrs. Clemm saw the ascending flames, even smelled the acrid smoke. This might be remembered on consideration of Poe's later writing in the final version of "The Bells" of "the deaf and frantic fire, / Leaping higher, higher, higher, / With a desperate desire / And a resolute endeavor / Now— now to sit, or never, / By the side of the pale-faced moon" (M 1:436). On May 18, the mob tried to destroy an African American orphan asylum, but the building and its residents were bravely defended by Alderman Morton McMichael, an ally of Poe's, former editor of the *Philadelphia Saturday Courier*, present coeditor of the *Philadelphia Saturday News*, and one day to become the mayor of Philadelphia. McMichael's "courage and eloquence," we are told, "alone prevented the second sacrifice"; "His powers as a speaker helped him to defy the mob."[8]

Meanwhile, ninety miles north, in New York City, Poe's novel was finally approaching publication. The book was announced as forthcoming in the May 1838 *Knickerbocker*, and the date "May, 1838" appeared on the page that was bound ahead of the title page, "Important Works Just Published by Harper & Brothers, New-York" (P 1:36, 51). The *New York American* of July 31 lists the volume as having been published on July 30; the copyright document indicates that it was deposited for copyright on August 1.[9] We may analyze this ambitious work, an Art Novel, probably first imagined after Poe read the newspaper articles about the destruction of the vessel the *Ariel* in February 1836. We may consider the literal plot and then the double allegories, the stories behind the story. In so doing, we may also recognize the secret design of the novel. This is an extraordinary work, one of Poe's greatest achievements, offering excitement in its entanglements and in its possibility of disentanglement.

Poe provided a preface to the novel, supposedly by A. G. Pym, to explain why the *Southern Literary Messenger* chapters had been attributed to himself: Pym had been concerned that the story would not be believed, so he allowed Poe to write it in his own words, but the story was believed, so Pym took on its authorship. Poe thereby increased the verisimilitude, for Pym was now evidently an actual person. Poe revised elements of the *Messenger* chapters, including making Pym and his friend Augustus two years older (sixteen, not fourteen) and providing a transitional sentence, in chapter 1, and changing the time sequence in chapters 2 and 4. (To see all variants, compare the text of the first edition with that of the *Messenger* [P 1:57–86 and 211–14].) However, the essential plot of the two *Messenger* installments remained the same in the book: the *Penguin* crashed into the *Ariel*, destroying it, and Pym and Augustus were saved; later, Augustus hid Pym in the hold of the *Grampus*, where the stowaway suffered a variety of privations, and Augustus himself, in his stateroom and on deck, experienced a violent mutiny.

The rest of the plot, tightly related in the book's subtitle, may be summarized more fully here. Despite the mutiny, Augustus manages to warn Pym with a note tied around the dog Tiger. Augustus does finally make his way into the hold and rescues his despairing friend. Upon deck, the seemingly terrifying Dirk Peters (son of a Native American woman and a white man) turns out to be a friend to Augustus and Pym, wanting to take back the ship. The countermutiny succeeds through Peters's engaging the drunken, superstitious mutineers in conversation about their recent violence, words designed to prick their conscience, after which Pym appears disguised as the bloody figure of a crewman who had recently been poisoned. Most of the stricken company is quickly dispatched; only one of them, Parker, survives. However, Augustus has been stabbed seriously in his right arm. Now a storm threatens the ship, and the four endure, tied down through the tempest, and subsequently they undergo great hunger and thirst. An apparent rescue ship is actually a horrifying vessel of the dead, presumably the *Flying Dutchman*. After repeated futile dives into the cabin of the *Grampus* to retrieve food or drink, Parker, Peters, and Augustus, and a reluctant Pym agree that cannibalism is the only alternative—Parker draws the short straw, and he is stabbed to death and eaten. Eventually, olives, wine, ham, and a tortoise are recovered from the storeroom, but sharks threaten the men. Augustus, whose arm has mortified and who has become pathetically debilitated, dies, and his decaying body is thrown to the sharks. Surviving on the barnacles of the upended vessel, Pym and Peters are finally rescued by the ship *Jane Guy*.

The two men recover, and the *Jane Guy*, buffeted by a storm, explores South Sea islands. On Kerguelen's Island, a rookery of penguins and albatrosses is observed. With encouragement from Pym, Captain Guy voyages south, across the Antarctic Circle. The vessel arrives at the island of Tsalal, a place of strange animals, peculiar water, and deceitful natives. These natives come on board the ship, and their chief, Too-wit, collapses in the cabin at the sight of himself between two facing mirrors. Pym and Peters and ten others from the *Jane Guy* head inland with the natives to their village of Klock-Klock, where the men from the ship refuse an unappetizing meal of the entrails of a hog. Subsequently, as the ship's men walk through gorges, the natives cause a landslide, trapping Pym and Peters in a crevice and killing their companions. The natives destroy the *Jane Guy*, which explodes, killing many Tsalalians. Pym and Peters encounter mysterious figures in the fissures they explore; then

Peters descends a steep precipice, and Pym follows, but falls, into the arms of the rescuing Peters. Killing several natives, the two men secure a canoe, identical in bow and stern, and, with the native Nu-Nu, head south from Tsalal after destroying a remaining canoe. The ocean water becomes warm and milky and the men torpid as their canoe speeds toward a cataract. The fascinating final journal entry reads:

> *March* 22. The darkness had materially increased, relieved only by the glare of the water thrown back from the white curtain before us. Many gigantic and pallidly white birds flew continuously now from beyond the veil, and their scream was the eternal *Tekeli-li!* as they retreated from our vision. Hereupon Nu-Nu stirred in the bottom of the boat; but, upon touching him, we found his spirit departed. And now we rushed into the embraces of the cataract, where a chasm threw itself open to receive us. But there arose in our pathway a shrouded human figure, very far larger in its proportions than any dweller among men. And the hue of the skin of the figure was of the perfect whiteness of the snow. (P 1:205–6)

A note following this climax is both suggestive and mystifying.

What did critics of Poe's time make of this narrative? They tended to be split, some considering the work a concoction of lies, others seeing it as a remarkable work of imagination. Poe's future employer William E. Burton, for instance, termed the novel "a mass of ignorance and effrontery," while Morton McMichael wrote that "it abounds in the wild and wonderful, and it is apparently written with great ability."[10] The general reader would offer similar disparate views—one, for example, labeled *Pym* "a base fabrication," while another wrote, "Centuries may elapse ere another such story is written. Future generations will appreciate the genius of its gifted but erratic author."[11]

Today, through close reading—what Poe termed "deliberate perusal" (H 11:3)—we may decode Pym's much-contested account. Our examination of this example of one of the Art Novels—what Poe had termed in his review of Henry F. Chorley's *Conti the Discarded* as offering "a tissue of *bizarre* fiction, partly allegorical, and partly metaphysical"—may indeed yield "admiration and study of the beautiful" (H 8:231; P 5:119). If our analysis slows down our narrative briefly, it will also, I believe, enrich it.

We may see Poe integrating his life in his fiction through his autobiographical allegory. Though he sometimes faulted allegory, he allowed for it if sufficiently subtle: "Where the suggested meaning runs through the obvious one in a *very* profound under-current so as never to interfere with the upper one without our own volition, so as never to show itself unless *called* to the surface, there only, for the proper uses of fictitious narrative, is it available at all" (H 13:148). We have already "*called* to the surface" the allegories of the births of brothers Henry and Edgar. That Henry is two years older than Pym, later tells Pym tales of his travels, drinks excessively, becomes sick, and dies on August 1 strengthens the correspondence between Pym's friend and Poe's brother. Perhaps the adventure of the *Ariel* involved memories of sailing not only with Ebenezer Burling but also with brother Henry. Poe wrote, as we have earlier noted, "There can be no tie more strong than that of brother for brother—it is not so much that they love one another, as that they both love the same parent—their affections are always running in the same direction—the same channel—and cannot help mingling" (O 1:47). We should therefore not be surprised to see Eliza Arnold Poe recur in the novel, beyond the birth allegories—initially, anagrammatically, through reference to "Mr. E. Ronald's academy on the hill" (P 1:57). And she will appear again, importantly, in that final journal entry. We may see others in Poe's life, as well, including John Allan, represented by Pym's admonishing "maternal grandfather," Mr. Peterson (P 1:57, 66, 67).

Furthermore, reference to "absolute mountains of ragged ice" (P 1:164) recalls the Ragged Mountains near Charlottesville, where Poe attended the University of Virginia. Pym's escape on the *Grampus* recalls Poe's escape from Richmond, perhaps by coal vessel, in 1827. And Pym's appearing as a dead man on the *Grampus* recalls Poe as a ghost at a whist game at the Ellis home and later Poe's bedaubed friend Gibson as the bloodied murderer of a hated professor at West Point.[12]

In light of the autobiographical basis of Arthur Gordon Pym and Augustus Barnard, we may conjecture briefly about Dirk Peters. It is possible, of course, that his origins were literary. But the critical passage in which the dark-skinned "other" catches the falling Pym (P 1:197–98) calls to mind a Richmonder of Poe's time well known for having caught people—the enslaved blacksmith Gilbert Hunt. He had caught ten or twelve women dropped by Dr. James D. McCaw from the second story of the burning Richmond Theater on December 26, 1811. Though Edgar, then nearly three years old, was not in Richmond at the time, he would have heard of Hunt's heroic feat soon, when the Allan family returned to the city. Later, as a fourteen-year-old, he would have been reminded of that feat when he heard of, or read of, Hunt's rescuing prisoners at the burning penitentiary on August 8, 1823. Notably, Hunt was respected and, indeed, celebrated in Richmond. The salvific Dirk

Peters might have been suggested in part by the salvific Gilbert Hunt. A photograph of an older Gilbert Hunt, who had bought himself out of bondage, reveals a man of proud, striking visage. It is possible that Dirk Peters is Poe's subversive tribute to this remarkable man.[13]

Interpreting the autobiographical elements in *Pym* will be deepened by examining intently Poe's greatest passage, that final mysterious journal entry, which Poe had probably imagined before he wrote the book: the March 22 paragraph concerning the large white "shrouded human figure." Here we have the hermetic Poe at his most brilliant—and personal.[14]

We may track backward, by language, the "shrouded human figure" (P 1:206) to the "human figure" in the chasm (P 1:195) to the penguin that resembles a "human figure" in the rookery. Poe wrote, "These birds [the penguins] walk erect, with a stately carriage. They carry their heads high, with their wings drooping like two arms, and, as their tails project from their body in a line with the legs, the resemblance to a human figure is very striking, and would be apt to deceive the spectator at a casual glance or in the gloom of the evening" (P 1:151). (The final portion of this passage diverges from the relevant passages in the Benjamin Morrell source, *A Narrative of Four Voyages*.) On reading of the "human figure" that is a penguin, we may recall the ship the *Penguin* in the first chapter (P 1:61, 62) and realize that the "human figure" at the close of the novel is the unseen ship the *Penguin* at its opening, a vessel that will again destroy the small vessel and rescue the two men. Poe is employing symmetry (as he had in "Berenice")—his book, like the earlier canoe, is "modelled with the bow and stern alike" (P 1:200): it begins and ends with a penguin.

Why a penguin? For the autobiographical level of the novel, Poe helps us by stating what his Morrell source does not: "In short, survey it as we will, nothing can be more astonishing than the spirit of reflection evinced by these feathered beings" (P 1:153). Poe is, of course, suggesting thoughtfulness, but he is also suggesting, more subtly, a mirror. And so we realize that the two penguins forming two mirrors constitute part of the design of the novel, a design intimated in miniature by the overwhelmed native chief Too-wit "in the middle of the cabin" of the *Jane Guy*, caught between two facing mirrors—he who Pym feared "would expire upon the spot" (P 1:169–70). (There was only one mirror in Poe's Morrell source. We may also recall the "mirrors in the interior of the trunk" in Poe's "Maelzel's Chess-Player" [P 5:161].) Who, then, corresponds to the centrally positioned Too-wit in *The Narrative of Arthur Gordon Pym*? It is Augustus. The novel offers twenty-five chapters, the central one of which, chapter 13, covers two weeks and twenty-two paragraphs. After one week, in the eleventh paragraph, on August 1, Poe's friend Augustus dies:

> *August* 1. A continuance of the same calm weather, with an oppressively hot sun.... We now saw clearly that Augustus could not be saved; that he was evidently dying. We could do nothing to relieve his sufferings, which appeared to be great. About twelve o'clock he expired in strong convulsions, and without having spoken for several hours. (P 1:142)

With this central passage, we are back with Poe at his brother Henry's deathbed, in Maria Clemm's Baltimore apartment, on August 1, 1831.

The effect of two facing mirrors on a person midway between them is an infinite reflection—hence Too-Wit's utter bewilderment. Similarly, the death of Augustus—Henry Poe—is infinitely reflected in the penguin mirrors at either end of the work. What is represented here is Poe's infinite memory of the death of his brother—what he later termed, with regard to "The Raven" in "The Philosophy of Composition," "*Mournful and Never-ending Remembrance*" (L2:70). Poe uses the popular genre of the nautical adventure in *Pym* to convey, in its covert design, a private experience. On August 29, 1835, he had written to Maria Clemm, in part, "[Y]ou well know how little I am able to bear up under the pressure of grief" (O 1:102). Poe transformed the unbearable "pressure of grief" for the death of Henry to the emotional prompt for his Art Novel, a coded memorial to his lost brother.

And there was also the professional prompt—Coleridge's lamenting that he could never write that much-desired epic about the destruction of Jerusalem. With his abundant artistic pride, Poe may well have been eager to prove that he could succeed where Coleridge had failed. The February 18 and 19, 1836, Norfolk newspaper articles about the destruction of the *Ariel*, we may infer, provided Poe with the solution to Coleridge's problem—the destruction of Jerusalem could be allegorized, for Ariel was also the name of the destroyed holy city (Isaiah 29:1–2). And the second allegory could be the twin of the first, for they both concern loss—loss for the beloved brother, loss for the beloved city.

The wreck of the *Ariel* by the *Penguin* in the first chapter of *Pym* is repeated in the wreck of the canoe—the *Ariel* equivalent—by the inferred *Penguin* in the last chapter of the novel. The destruction of the *Ariel* and of its equivalent suggest the destruction of Jerusalem (both 65 BC and AD 70). The importance of the vessel is emphasized by Poe's placing it, in that first chapter, "at the old decayed wharf by the lumber-yard of Pankey & Co." (P 1:58)—"Pankey" suggests "the key to it all." The destruction of Jerusalem is anticipated in chapter 19 of *Pym* by the allegorical siege of Jerusalem—that is, the twelve shipmates from the Jane Guy who are offered the entrails of a hog as the natives press in and around their tent (P 1:175–76) correspond to the twelve tribes of Israel besieged by the Romans (in 65 BC) and taunted with forbidden food—a story that Poe had told earlier, with apparent comic purpose, in "A Tale of Jerusalem." And the natives' landslide is yet another instance of the destruction of Jerusalem. The critical words are "stakes" and "cords," as in Isaiah 33:20: "Look upon Zion, the city of our solemnities: thine eyes shall see Jerusalem a quiet habitation, a tabernacle that shall not be taken down; not one of the *stakes* thereof shall ever be removed, neither shall any of the *cords* thereof be broken" (emphasis added). Poe inverts biblical prophecy, writing of the landslide with the repeated use of the words "stakes" and "cords":

> In several spots along the top of the eastern ridge of the gorge (we were now on the western) might be seen *stakes* of wood driven into the earth.... *stakes* similar to those we saw standing had been inserted, at not more than a yard apart, for the length of perhaps three hundred feet, and ranging at about ten feet back from the edge of the gulf. Strong *cords* of grape vine were attached to the *stakes* still remaining on the hill, and it was evident that such *cords* had also been attached to each of the other *stakes*.... There can be no doubt that, by the continuous line of *stakes*, a partial rupture of the soil had been brought about, probably to the depth of one or two feet, when, by means of a savage pulling at the end of each of the *cords* (these *cords* being attached to the tops of the *stakes*, and extending back from the edge of the cliff), a vast leverage power was obtained, capable of hurling the whole face of the hill, upon a given signal, into the bosom of the abyss below. (P 1:184–85; emphasis added)

Undergirding the destruction of Jerusalem in Poe's novel is a corresponding tragedy, the crucifixion of Christ. We have regular allusions, including "the blessed sun" (P 1:117), "A heavy cross sea" (P 1:149), the drawing of lots (P:133–35), the "cross questioning" (P 1:176), the native cries of "*Lama-Lama!*" (P 1:168, 174–75, an exclamation echoing Christ's asking "Eli, Eli, lama sabachtani," "Father, father, why hast thou forsaken me?"), the application of vinegar to the wounds of Augustus (P 1:141), and the cataclysm after the crucifixion ("a concussion resembling nothing I had ever before experienced, and which impressed me with a vague conception ... that the whole foundations of the solid globe were suddenly rent asunder, and that the day of universal dissolution was at hand" [P 1:181–82]). Relevant here is Poe's 1831 short story "A Dream," concerning, as well, the events after the crucifixion (M 2:8–9).

From February 1836, I believe, Poe was working out and writing his double allegory (personal and biblical), through the remaining year in Richmond and the subsequent year in New York City. And he provided the resolution of the two allegories in that ever-amazing final journal entry.

Critics have linked the biblically cadenced passage about the white "shrouded human figure" with "The Vision of the Seven Candlesticks" in the first chapter of Revelation, concerning "one like unto the Son of man," whose "head and his hairs were white like wool, as white as snow" (Revelation 1:13–14). We must return, again, to that which the "shrouded human figure" represents, the ship the *Penguin*. And we may recall in this regard Poe's mentioning etymology in his review of Charles Richardson's *New Dictionary* in the August 1836 *Southern Literary Messenger* (P 5:250). Consulting the dictionaries of Samuel Johnson and Noah Webster, we learn that the origins of the word "penguin" are Welsh, signifying "white head." ("Guin," as in Guinevere, conveys white, and "pen," head.) So, finally, we may realize why Poe chose the bird the penguin in the first place—it could serve as a coded reference to the white head of Jesus, in the Vision of the Seven Candlesticks. Jesus has come to prophesy the coming of the New Jerusalem (Revelation 3:12). What has been lost may be found, according to Christian eschatology—the holy city of Jerusalem, and also, presumably, one's lost loved ones.

We may be aided in more fully understanding that final journal entry by considering the date, March 22, and the cry of the white birds (very likely albatrosses), "*Tekeli-li!*" (P 1:206). For as Poe would have known, probably from consulting issues of the *Charleston Courier* when he was stationed near Charleston at Fort Moultrie, Eliza Poe performed in *Tekeli* on March 23, 1811—but was scheduled originally for March 22. And her part was that of the bride Christine—she would have been dressed all in white. And now we may deduce why Poe chose to allude to this play of all the plays in which his mother had appeared: her role, that of the bride Christine, unites both the Bride, the Church, and the Bridegroom, Christ. She represents the prophesied wedding of Christ and the Church at the end of time.

It is to the Christian promise of this ultimate wedding that a financially ruined John Allan had referred in a private letter to his partner, Charles Ellis, on December 23, 1819: "Should I get a Glass of Egg Nog tomorrow Evg I shall not fail to recollect my old friends in Richmond & the days of others Years

& though the Tear at present dims my Eyes I pray God to bless you all & that we may through His Kind Providence live to see many returns of the Season growing in Grace as time rolls on, having our Lamps well trimmed and supplied, watching patiently for the Bridegroom to call us to the Marri[a]ge Supper."[15] It is to this Christian promise that a still-bereft Poe was building in *Pym*. Through his extraordinary Art Novel—both allegorical and metaphysical—Poe was providing, however covertly, beauty and much-needed consolation. In *Pym*, at least, there was balm in Gilead.

It is true that the nature of Poe's belief is sometimes difficult to ascertain. But we may recall his October 1837 review of J. L. Stephens's *Incidents of Travel in Egypt, Arabia Petræa, and the Holy Land*, touching on divine providence, suggesting, at least at this time, a degree of faith. And years later, Flora Lapham Mack's correspondent, William Lanier Washington, conveyed John H. Mackenzie's view of Poe and religion:

> Of Edgar Poe Mr. MacKenzie has said, he was also [like his sister Rosalie] an avowed Episcopalian & attended the services in that church [Monumental Church] whenever he was within going distance on Sundays—Poe and Mr. MacKenzie had many discussions upon the subject of religion and the life to come & Poe was firm in his belief as to the hereafter & in his religious principles despite the many conflicting phases of his character and the general opinion held of him in this particular.
>
> Mr. MacKenzie is [the] authority for what has been stated concerning this matter.[16]

Poe will again build toward a religious (though not explicitly Christian) consolation at the close of his later long work, the 1848 prose-poem *Eureka*.

The Morton McMichael review of *Pym* (stating that "it abounds in the wild and wonderful") appeared in the August 4, 1838, issue of the *Philadelphia Saturday News & Literary Gazette*, a weekly newspaper whose praise, in its first issue, of Poe's *Southern Literary Messenger* was included in the Supplement to the July 1836 *Messenger*. The *Saturday News* was owned by Louis A. Godey, of *Godey's Lady's Book;* the two publications shared the same office, first at 100 Walnut Street and then, after July 1837, at 211 Chestnut Street, below Seventh Street and two doors above the Marshall House.[17] Doubtless Poe visited the Chestnut Street office in 1838. The editors were Morton McMichael and Joseph C. Neal; Poe mentioned the *Saturday News* in his November 1841 "Autography" piece on Neal (H 15:199). What is especially striking about the August 4 issue of the newspaper is that adjacent to

McMichael's review of *Pym* is a piece titled "Dreadful Murder in Broadway at Midday," one of a series of sources in the *Saturday News* for Poe's 1841 "The Murders in the Rue Morgue," the first modern detective story.[18] Perhaps, as he saw that *Pym* was not well understood, Poe wished to dramatize the nature of careful reading and so created Monsieur C. Auguste Dupin.

It is heartening to see that, in the August 15 issue of the *Saturday Evening Post*, Poe's achievement as a writer was recognized. "Horace in Philadelphia"—really Lambert A. Wilmer in Baltimore—wrote the paean "Ode XXX.—To Edgar A. Poe," two stanzas of which will convey Wilmer's high regard:

> But the same wind whose angry tones
> Sends small dull craft to Davy Jones,
> Is but an impulse to convey
> The nobler vessel o'er the sea;—
> So thou dear friend, shalt haply ride
> Triumphant through the swelling tide
> With fame thy cynosure and guide.
>
> So may it be.—tho' fortune now
>   Averts her face, and heedless crowds
> To blocks, like senseless Pagans, bow;—
>   Yet time shall dissipate the clouds,
>   Dissolve the mist which merit shrouds,
> And fix the laurel on *thy* brow.[19]

Poe's genius, Lambert anticipated, would eventually be known.

Writing on September 4 to Nathan C. Brooks, editor of Baltimore's *American Museum of Literature and the Arts* (where the short story "Ligeia" would soon appear), Poe acknowledges payment, declines an invitation to write a review on Washington Irving, discloses having "gotten nearly out of my late embarrassments," and states "I am just leaving Arch street for a small house" (O 1:177–78). This small house is generally considered to have been near Locust on Sixteenth Street (although another location has been mentioned). The Poe family would remain at this house—in one instance termed "a pretty little rose-covered cottage"—for four years.[20]

Also on September 4, Louis A. Godey and Morton McMichael were fêted by distinguished New Yorkers at the American Hotel in New York City.[21] It is easy to imagine conversation at that event turning to Poe, who had recently left New York City and published a novel there. That *Pym* remained a current topic for Godey and McMichael (and Neal) is indicated by an allusion to that novel's reputation for exaggeration in a comment on the circulation of *Godey's Lady's Book* in the September 15 issue of the *Saturday News:* "We dare not mention what is the present circulation of this work, lest we should be suspected to be of the Arthur Gordon Pym school."[22]

On September 11, Poe wrote to John C. Cox, who resided at Mrs. Jones's boardinghouse on Arch Street, "I am busily and profitably employed, and the future looks well. For this I have to thank only your kindness." Poe apparently owed him thirty dollars and asked for the remaining twenty dollars (of an offer of fifty dollars) because his family might otherwise "have to suffer many serious privations." A year later, Poe was still unable to pay Cox, though he had paid Mrs. Jones (O 1:180–81, 204–5).

In October, *Pym* was published by Wiley & Putnam in London.[23] However, the critical climactic March 22 journal entry was omitted. Poe's British readers would therefore be at a great disadvantage in trying to interpret the work. In the same month, "Ligeia" appeared in the first issue of Baltimore's *American Museum.*

It was a dream, Poe noted, that led him to write "Ligeia"—"a dream," according to J. H. Ingram, "in which the eyes of the heroine produced the intense effect described in the fourth paragraph of the work."[24] Perhaps these were the full eyes of Poe's much-mourned mother, revealed in his miniature of her. With the prompt of his dream, Poe returned to familiar territory, metempsychosis, often motivated by vengeance. In "Metzengerstein," the soul of Count Berlifitzing, who had died in a stable fire set by Baron Metzengerstein, migrates to the body of the horse escaped from Metzengerstein's tapestry and causes the baron to enter his own burning palace, to his death. In "Morella," the soul of the narrator's wife, Morella, migrates to the body of her daughter, thereby wreaking vengeance upon her unloving husband. And in "Ligeia," the soul of a deceased woman of passion, beauty, and learning, assisted by her loving former husband's efforts at magic and seeming magic, migrates to the body of his unloved second wife, Lady Rowena Trevanion of Tremaine, gaining vengeance on her successor and on Death itself, proving the power of man's will, however temporary. The beauty of Ligeia to her husband (the narrator) seems to be that of "beings either above or apart from the earth."[25] In this work, aspiration and consolation appear again to unite. Sarah Helen Whitman links the tale to what Poe termed in one of his marginalia, "*a glimpse of the spirit's outer world.*"[26]

Poe offered a satire of the tale of sensation in the November issue of the *American Magazine,* providing Mr. Blackwood's advice to the writer Psyche Zenobia in "The Psyche Zenobia" and then her use of that advice, involving a description of her own beheading in "The Scythe of Time." These pieces are grotesques in Poe's 1840 *Tales of the Grotesque and Arabesque.* And the two works were later titled "How to Write a Blackwood Article" and "A Predicament."

Meanwhile, intermittently, from September through December of 1838, the *Saturday News* featured stories that Poe would later adapt, along with "Deliberate Murder in Broadway, at Midday," for "The Murders in the Rue Morgue"—including "A Mischievous Ape" (a piece titled "Orang-Outang" had already appeared), "Deaths in New York," "Mohametan Worship," "Appalling Accident," and "Humorous Adventure—Picking up a Madman."[27] We do not know if, as Gowans had reported in New York City, Poe had a library of newspapers and magazines at home in Philadelphia. Perhaps he had, but, alternatively, he may have read the issues of this newspaper at the office of the *Saturday News* or that of its successor, *Atkinson's Evening Post and Saturday News,* or in someone else's collection.[28] We should note that in February 1840 he wrote in a review of "looking over a file of newspapers, not long ago" (H 10:72).

Probably it was in the winter of 1838/39 that Poe, Virginia, and Mrs. Clemm did suffer "many serious privations." He acknowledged in his later letter to Cox that he had been able to pay his former landlady Mrs. Jones, around Christmas 1838, "only with the most painful sacrifices" (O 1:204). Poe was in all likelihood at this time unemployed, and he was certainly without savings and paid poorly for his literary productions. James Pedder recalled that his daughters Anna and Bessie "aided the family of Poe when he was literally suffering for want of food, and Poe himself had not clothes enough to keep him warm." Bessie said that the Poe family "often have lived on bread and molasses for weeks together." A year later, in December 1839, Poe expressed his gratitude to the sisters with a gift of a copy of his *Tales of the Grotesque and Arabesque,* inscribed, "For Miss Anna and Miss Bessie Pedder, / from their most sincere friend, / The Author."[29]

The *Saturday News* ceased publication on January 5, 1839. It may be that by then Poe was already beginning to think about creating a tale involving elements of that newspaper. His magazine pieces of the winter and spring appeared, like his last three stories, in Baltimore's *American Museum*—in January and February, two installments of "Literary Small Talk," one of these critical of Bulwer-Lytton, the other of Edward Gibbon (H 14:90–94), and in April, a remarkable poetic allegory about a man's loss of reason, "The Haunted Palace."

In response to Poe's mid-February query, Harper & Brothers reported disappointing news: "We are inclined to think that 'Pym' has not succeeded or been received as well in this country as it has in England."[30] William Gowans later reported that *Pym* was "the most unsuccessful of all his [Poe's] writings"; despite its publication by the Harper & Brothers, "it did not sell."[31] But many moneymaking books that the Harpers published at the time are forgotten today while *Pym* has endured.

On April 20, 1839, the *Philadelphia Saturday Courier* offered brief comment on *The Conchologist's First Book,* a textbook about shells. The book was chiefly by Thomas Wyatt, who had tried to avoid copyright infringement on his earlier, fuller book on shells, published by Harper & Brothers, by asking Poe to assume authorship and to write the preface and introduction, which he did, perhaps in the fall of 1838 (see H 14:95–100). Poe was paid fifty dollars, which he surely badly needed. In 1846, Poe was accused of plagiarism by the *Saturday Evening Post,* but Poe defended himself to his correspondent George W. Eveleth, asserting that "I wrote the Preface and Introduction, and translated from Cuvier" and clarifying that it had been a collaborative effort with Thomas Wyatt and [Henry] McMurtrie, "my name being put to the work, as best known, and most likely to aid its circulation" (O 2:619). According to two who later spoke to Wyatt, William Whitelock and John Gould Anthony, Wyatt acknowledged the book to be his own and explained his use of Poe's name to circumvent copyright concerns. In 1874, Sarah Helen Whitman recalled a visit from Wyatt, who had for Poe "a most affectionate & friendly sympathy & regard." Dwight Thomas and David K. Jackson assert, "While it [*The Conchologist's First Book*] contained some original material, it was largely compiled from various European sources, like most American textbooks and scientific manuals of the time."[32]

The date of an advertisement at the beginning of *The Gift for 1840,* "May 1st, 1839" (M 2:425), suggests that Poe had already written his contribution for the volume, a tale of the double, "William Wilson." Perhaps by now he was working on, or had completed, "The Fall of the House of Usher." He published a satire of conventionality, "The Devil in the Belfry. An Extravaganza," in the *Philadelphia Saturday Chronicle* in mid-May. But his financial situation had not improved. In fact, according to John Ward Ostrom, "Without a steady job for two and one-half years, he apparently earned a total of only

$143.50 or 16¢ a day."[33] This was a pittance, and a supplement from Virginia and Mrs. Clemm's sewing and John H. Mackenzie's occasional contribution would probably still have been inadequate.

Poe needed a job, and he wrote to William E. Burton, proposing to work on his monthly, *Burton's Gentleman's Magazine.* The actor-cum-publisher responded on May 11, offering Poe ten dollars a week for what would be supposedly two hours of work a day, accepting Poe's more liberal terms for 1840, presumably fifty dollars a month, noting that all was contingent on Poe's not working for any periodical that might compromise the success of the *Gentleman's Magazine.*[34]

Poe replied in a letter, no longer extant, that must have resonated with his despairing September 11, 1835, letter to John Pendleton Kennedy ("I am suffering under a depression of spirits such as I have never felt before" [O 1:107]), for Burton replied by noting Poe's feelings of "morbid tone," his mind of "melancholy hue." Even as Kennedy had begun, "I am sorry to see you in such plight as your letter shows you in" (H 17:19), Burton began, "I am sorry that you thought [it] necessary to send me such a letter as your last." Even as Kennedy had responded by referring to "these villainous blue devils" (H 17:19), Burton responded by referring to "the foul fiend, care."[35] Poe must have been suffering continued "depression of spirits," fighting it as he could, managing to write in spite of the darkness, yet also, probably, writing informed by that darkness. Poe would state, later in the year, in his introduction to *Tales of the Grotesque and Arabesque,* "I maintain that terror is not of Germany, but of the soul" (M 2:473).

Burton warned Poe against harshness in criticism, and though Poe would have had reservations about the editor's critical laxity, the two did come to terms; Poe was listed as "Assistant Editor" in the June issue of *Burton's Gentleman's Magazine.*[36] Poe's working at *Burton's,* on Dock Street across from the Mercantile Exchange, brought him in touch with a variety of Philadelphia literati, including Thomas Dunn English, who later introduced him to Henry B. Hirst.[37] His relationship with English, in particular, would eventually become hostile.

There is a question as to whether Poe was drinking during his year at *Burton's* (June 1839 through June 1840). In April 1841 he maintained that he hadn't drunk since his *Southern Literary Messenger* days, and John Ward Ostrom accepted his assertion (O 1:263–65). Poe later declared that his drinking resumed with the January 1842 illness of his wife (O 2:641). Yet there is some evidence that he did occasionally lapse during the *Burton's* period.[38] The publisher Charles Alexander referred to his "unfortunate failing" but noted that this did not affect his work on the magazine. Furthermore, characterizing Poe as possessing a "uniform *gentleness of disposition* and kindness of heart," Alexander commented on Poe's weakness, "[H]e alone was the sufferer."[39]

Poe's first issue of *Burton's,* that for July 1839, included two of his poems, "To Ianthe in Heaven" and "Spirits of the Dead," which were revisions of earlier work, and several reviews, the last two of which warrant particular mention. Poe acknowledges, in his piece on Thomas Wyatt's *A Synopsis of Natural History,* "personal knowledge, and the closest inspection and collation," suggesting his possible involvement with the volume. And he extracts, in his piece on Henry Lord Brougham's *Sketches of Public Characters, Discourses, and Essays,* a clever retort to the claim that a man over forty "is always either a fool or a physician," "Mayn't he be both, Doctor!"[40] Brougham and the quoted exchange are featured in Poe's final tale about Monsieur Dupin, "The Purloined Letter."

A July 4 letter shows Burton trying to manage his magazine—and his assistant editor—from afar. (He was then performing in New York City.) Doubtless the series of directives would have been unwelcome by Poe.[41] Welcome, by contrast, was a letter from George W. Poe (son of George Poe Jr., a cousin of Poe's father), to which Poe responded with extensive (if not always accurate) genealogical information. And he added near the close, "I shall remain in Philadelphia perhaps for a year—but Richmond is my home" (O 1:185).

The August issue of *Burton's* offered three earlier poems—"Fairyland," "To—" (formerly "To Elizabeth"), and "To the River—"—several reviews, and a new short story, the satirical jeu d'esprit "The Man That Was Used Up." The name of the main character, Brevet Brigadier General John A. B. C. Smith, may have been drawn from the name of a subscriber to the *Southern Literary Messenger* during Poe's time there, Colonel John B. D. Smith.[42] The mysterious and much-admired general is actually composed entirely of an assemblage of fashioned parts, including a mechanism for speech. We have in Poe's 1836 essay "Maelzel's Chess-Player" and his 1839 story "The Man That Was Used Up" inverted doubles of debunking—in the former, a man inhabits a mechanical invention, and in the latter, a mechanical invention inhabits a man. What is consistent between the two works is Poe's discerning exposure of fraud.

Also in the summer of 1839, Poe offered his keen critical analysis in a review and an essay in E. Burke Fisher's Pittsburgh periodical the *Literary Examiner and Western Monthly Review.*[43] Especially notable in his review of N. P. Willis's play *Tortesa, the Usurer* is the lament, "Most certain it is that, in America especially, we are sadly given to undervalue the effect of patient thought and careful elaboration." Similarly warranting attention in Poe's essay on American criticism in general is a quotation from Thomas Browne's *Urn-Burial*, which states that the mysteries of the Syrens' song and Achilles's assumed name "are not beyond all conjecture"—a quotation that Poe would employ again at the close of the first modern detective story, "The Murders in the Rue Morgue."[44]

One of the greatest of all Poe's short stories, "The Fall of the House of Usher," appeared in the September 1839 issue of *Burton's*. Poe's reviews in this issue are of interest, of course—especially those of Henry Lord Brougham's *Historical Sketches of Statesmen Who Flourished in the Time of George III* and John Galt's *Continuation of the Diary Illustrative of the Times of George IV* (in light of "The Purloined Letter") and the rapturous critique of de la Motte Fouqué's *Undine: A Miniature Romance* (in which a soulless river sprite attains, through marriage, a soul). But it is "Usher" that enthralls the reader, offering an inexorable intensity of terror.

"Usher" is part of a long-term enterprise, Poe's fictional treatment of the soul. He had already explored the migration of the soul ("Metzengerstein," "Morella," "Ligeia"), the saving of the soul ("The Duke de L'Omelette," "The Bargain Lost" [later "Bon-Bon"], and "The Visionary" [later "The Assignation"]), the recovery of the soul ("Loss of Breath"), and the preexistent soul ("Berenice"). He now explored an instance of the shared soul. With the assistance of the narrator, a visiting friend, the neurasthenic aesthete Roderick Usher temporarily places the apparently dead body of his cataleptical twin sister, Madeline, in a temporary tomb in the depths of the Usher mansion. However, still alive, she later returns from the crypt and falls, dying, upon her anguished brother, also dying, causing the end of the House of Usher—the final descendants and their ancient home. Transforming a range of literary sources, from Edward Bulwer-Lytton's novel *Pelham* (for the opening) to Sir Walter Scott's novel *Ivanhoe* (for *The Mad Trist* at the close), as well as personal details, from the name of the couple who performed with his parents on the Boston stage to elements of his own sensitive nature, and employing his earlier allegorical poem "The Haunted Palace" at the tale's center, Poe created the culmination of the tales of *Blackwood's Edinburgh Magazine* that he had read as a boy, the ultimate exemplar of the Gothic genre. This work of disintegration is also an instance of Poe's integration of his life in his writing. "The Fall of the House of Usher" is a classic, a memorable consequence of "patient thought and careful elaboration."[45]

Later in the month, "William Wilson. A Tale" appeared in *The Gift for 1840*, and Poe continued his fictional elaboration of the shared soul. Prompted by an essay by Washington Irving (O 1:199), and including detail drawn from his time in Stoke Newington, Poe offered the confession of a condemned man. The eponymous William Wilson, an increasingly immoral youth, is afflicted by his interfering double. Whether cheating at cards or trying to seduce a married woman, William Wilson is frustrated by his whispering counterpart. At the tale's climax, the infuriated William Wilson murders his double— and, therefore, himself. Poe's allegory of the triumph of conscience is both relentless and masterful.

His letters indicate that this was a time of great promise. In response to the September issue of *Burton's* that Poe had sent him, Washington Irving had spoken "with enthusiasm" of "Usher" (O 1:193, 195). Poe would then send him the October issue, seeking Irving's accolade for the reprint there of "William Wilson," "my best effort" (O 1:199), again winning his approval (O 1:202).[46] Furthermore, Poe would soon publish with Lea & Blanchard a two-volume collection, *Tales of the Grotesque and Arabesque* (O 1:190, 194, 199). And, finally, Poe was planning to realize the dream of his *Messenger* days and even earlier, publishing his own magazine (O 1:194). Poe was doing well: he wrote to Joseph E. Snodgrass, "I think you will be pleased to hear of my well-doing" (O 1:202).[47]

The three remaining issues of *Burton's* for 1839 offer an array of Poe's contributions. The October issue featured the republication of "William Wilson"; a piece on gymnastics; and reviews, including a negative assessment of Henry Wadsworth Longfellow's novel *Hyperion, a Romance*, and positive appraisals of *The Gift for 1840* and *Opinions of Lord Brougham*. In faulting Longfellow's work, Poe specifies what is missing (and presumably what he admires and engages in himself), "the unremitting toil and patient elaboration which, when soul-guided, result in the beauty of Unity, Totality, Truth" (H 10:40).[48] The November issue furnished a revision of "Morella," as well as reviews, including a mixed assessment of William Gilmore Simms's novel *The Damsel of Darien*. (Also appearing here is an Elizabeth Barrett Barrett sonnet that would have engaged Poe, "Consolation.") Finally, the December issue supplied Poe's first angelic dialogue, "The Conversations of Eiros and Charmion," concerning an apocalyptic comet, and reviews, embracing, in part, an estimate of John A. Clark's *The Christian Keepsake and Missionary Annual for 1840* (with an allegation of plagiarism), an approbation of Charles Dickens's novel *The Life and Adventures of Nicholas Nickleby*, and a laudation of Joseph R. Chandler's *An Address, Delivered before the Goethean and Diagnothian Societies of Marshall College*. Regarding the last, Poe wrote of "the inspiration of the light of revelation," "the elevated knowledge of a *futurity* of existence," and "the glowing and burning hopes to which that knowledge of futurity gives rise"—"just such a *turn* as the man of genius might be led to give to a discourse upon an occasion of the kind, and such as *only* the man of genius would have given" (H 10:58).[49]

In early December 1839, Lea and Blanchard published, in two volumes, Poe's short story collection *Tales of the Grotesque and Arabesque*. Seven hundred and fifty copies were printed of which twenty copies were provided to Poe.[50] The twenty-five tales that were included ranged in time of original publication from the five *Saturday Courier* tales, of 1832, to "William Wilson," of the just-published volume *The Gift for 1840*. Solely for the comical tale "Why the Little Frenchman Wears His Hand in a Sling," the previous publication venue remains unknown (M 2:463).[51] The terms "grotesque" and "arabesque" were drawn from Sir Walter Scott's essay "On the Supernatural in Fictitious Composition"[52]—in the context of this collection, "grotesque" suggests the comical, and "arabesque" the serious. Poe closes his brief preface to the collection by declaring his "matured purpose and very careful elaboration" (M 2:474). And he appends previous personal and editorial encomia at the end of the second volume, closing with a comment from the *St. Louis Commercial Bulletin:* "With an acuteness of observation, a vigorous and effective style and an independence that defies control, he [Poe] unites a fervid fancy and a most beautiful enthusiasm. His is a high destiny."[53]

The recipients of Poe's copies of *Tales of the Grotesque and Arabesque* included his wife Virginia, friends Anna and Bessie Pedder, Colonel William Drayton (to whom the collection is dedicated), creditor John C. Cox, Baltimore editors Joseph E. Snodgrass and John L. Carey, writer Philip Pendleton Cooke, and former president of the Second Bank of the United States Nicholas Biddle.[54] (Subsequently, Poe sent a copy to John Wilson ["Christopher North" of *Blackwood's Edinburgh Magazine*] in the hope of securing a review [O 1:190, 231] and to Charles Dickens in the hope of securing British publication of the collection.)[55] The reviews were frequently positive—summative comments included, "Poe follows in nobody's track,—his imagination seems to have a domain of its own to revel in"; "On the whole, we think these tales highly creditable to the literature of our country"; and "These volumes present a succession of richly-coloured pictures in the magic lantern of invention."[56] There was occasional criticism—of improbability, of Germanism, for instance—but a later report noted that when a British publisher reprinted two tales ("Why the Little Frenchman Wears His Hand in a Sling" and "The Fall of the House of Usher"), American periodicals that had initially faulted the collection reprinted these tales, as well.[57]

The November 20, 1839, issue of *Alexander's Weekly Messenger* and the December issue of *Burton's* advertised both a coming long narrative, "The Journal of Julius Rodman," and a coming thousand-dollar premium scheme. "Julius Rodman" was Poe's effort to take advantage of popular interest in western exploration; the contest was William E. Burton's effort to take advantage of writers. Regarding this contest, Poe confided to Joseph E. Snodgrass on December 19, 1839, "The tru[th is,] I object, in toto, to the whole scheme" (O 1:208). In the early months of 1840, the narrative unfolded and the contest collapsed.[58]

On December 18, Poe began publishing short pieces in *Alexander's Weekly Messenger*. He invited substitution ciphers—one letter replacing another—in "Enigmatical and Conundrum-ical," thereby prompting a spate of puzzles to be solved. But not all of his contributions there involved codes—some concerned his work, his life, and his friends. He wrote in this same issue, for instance, about James Pedder in "[Article on Beet-Root]." Generally, Poe's work in *Alexander's Weekly Messenger* was a light complement to his reviews and other nonfiction pieces in *Burton's Gentleman's Magazine*.

The first couple of issues of *Burton's* in 1840 featured the commencement of the unsigned "Julius Rodman" serial. Working from a variety of sources throughout, including Washington Irving's *Astoria* and Meriwether Lewis and William Clarke's *History of the Expedition,* Poe offered a supposedly edited version of Rodman's journal. The January number of the magazine provided the introduction, concerning the origins of the manuscript and the history of discovery in the region; the February number related the 1791 voyage of a pirogue and a keelboat up the Missouri River to the Platte River. The chief purpose of the party of fifteen was hunting and trapping, but the protagonist of the title had a yearning to push up the river beyond where any white men had reached before, and others came to share his desire.

To the January issue of *Burton's,* Poe also contributed reviews, most importantly a review of Thomas Moore's *Alciphron, a Poem,* which states that "All novel conceptions are merely unusual combinations." Commenting on Samuel Taylor Coleridge's distinction between "Fancy" and "Imagination," Poe asserts that the latter is distinguished by a "*mystic*" or "*suggestive*" quality that "lifts" the "*fanciful* conception" into the "*ideal,*" intimating "a far more ethereal beauty *beyond.*"[59] And to the February issue, Poe also provided the comical story "Peter Pendulum the Business Man" and several reviews, including the censorious review of Henry Wadsworth Longfellow's book of poems *Visions of the Night*. It was not just that, again, the poet had "no combining or binding force," "absolutely nothing of unity," but also that he had plagiarized Alfred Tennyson's "The Death of the Old Year" in "Midnight Mass for the Dying Year": "[N]early all that is valuable in the piece of Tennyson is the first conception of personifying the Old Year as a dying old man, with the singularly wild and fantastic *manner* in which that conception is carried out." If Poe's charge could be argued, Longfellow's access to Tennyson's poem could not.[60] Poe's articles in *Alexander's Weekly Messenger* in the same period of time addressed primarily puzzles but also touched on his work (*Tales of the Grotesque and Arabesque, Burton's Gentleman's Magazine,* "The Journal of Julius Rodman," "Peter Pendulum," and the Longfellow review) and his life (his black cat, his boyhood swimming feat). According to a later letter, in his editorial capacity at *Burton's*, Poe was also proofreading, overseeing the printing office, preparing manuscripts, and compiling articles (O 1:219).

It was in 1840 in Philadelphia that "social meetings" took place among the literati, which eventually grew into a group called "Our Club." Listed members included Joseph R. Chandler, Morton McMichael, Joseph C. Neal, William E. Burton, Richard Penn Smith, eight others, "& occasionally Edgar A. Poe."[61] McMichael later said that "Edgar Allan Poe was a great genius, but that he was of very nervous temperament, and too sensitive."[62] A story about the group related by Smith's son Horace Wemyss Smith does mention Poe's drinking.[63] In later years, Poe would refer to the "Philad[elphia]. clique—Neal, Chandler, McMichael, Godey, Smith, Brown, Mitchell."[64] Perhaps Poe also attended gatherings at the Falstaff Hotel and spent time with Henry B. Hirst, Andrew Scott, and Horace Wemyss Smith at John Upton's place near Dock Street.[65] We cannot be certain of either, but Poe was a sociable person and, with or without a glass, would doubtless have welcomed good fellowship. Notably, he responded positively to an invitation from his doctor, John Kearsley Mitchell, for the evening of February 29, perhaps to examine Maelzel's Chess-Player, which Mitchell had bought or would soon buy (O 1:214).[56] Even as Poe sought "a far more ethereal beauty *beyond*," he lived in the world.

In the installment of Poe's serial in the March issue of *Burton's*, Julius Rodman and the others pushed on for three weeks, marveling at the beauty of the scenery, observing the work of a colony of beavers, and fearing the Sioux Indians, who, they were told, planned to kill them. In the April installment,

Rodman fired a cannon preemptively against the threatening Sioux, killing six and wounding more, and then he and his party headed farther up the river and established their winter encampment. This installment features an image of a figure said to be the leader of the Sioux party, allegedly drawn later by Poe's character Thornton, but recognizable as *A Sioux on Horseback* from the June 1836 issue of Nathaniel Hawthorne's *American Magazine of Useful and Entertaining Knowledge*.[67] Poe's nonfictional contributions to the March issue include comments on trans-Atlantic ballooning and on the Rosetta Stone in "A Chapter on Science and Art," as well as a review of Henry Duncan's *Sacred Philosophy of the Seasons*, with renewed attention to the matter of the fulfillment of prophecy, earlier considered in the *New York Review* (H 10:81–85). Poe's nonfictional pieces in the subsequent issue include words on school days in "Omniana" and "A Chapter on Science and Art," as well as a thoughtful discussion of the absence of international copyright. Also present is Poe's "Silence. A Sonnet," which had earlier appeared in the *Saturday Courier*.

The highest drama of the March and April issues was intimated on the inside front cover. The thousand-dollar premium scheme that Burton had loudly hyped was failing—at first, the deadline was postponed; then the contest was canceled. Burton lamented that he had received too few submissions, perhaps because writers mistrusted competitions.[68] But Poe later revealed privately to Joseph E. Snodgrass that Burton did have Snodgrass's submitted essay (though Burton denied it) and "a pile of other M.S.S. sent for premiums," and Poe contended "that it was never his [Burton's] intention to pay one dollar of the money offered" (O 1:229–30). Evidently the bogus competition was merely a means for Burton to obtain new material for his magazine. Poe would have been especially annoyed since, as one of the editors of *Burton's*, he would have been perceived to be involved in the scheme. When Burton later sold his magazine to George R. Graham, he sold the submissions, as well, though he had no right to them. *Graham's* editor Charles J. Peterson wrote to one of the participants in the alleged competition, "Believe me *such* a piece of (I must say it) fraud I could not knowingly countenance." The deceived contestant was none other than poet James Russell Lowell.[69]

Poe closed out his contributions to *Alexander's Weekly Messenger* in March and April and one issue in May. He furnished again a series of pieces on puzzles, as well as an article touching his own work (on *Burton's Gentleman's Magazine*), his life (on long leaps), and his friends (Hiram Haines and Henry B. Hirst). Also of particular interest, in light of the later story "The Tell-Tale Heart," is an essay on the calm manner of an insane man.

On March 24, 1840, Hiram Haines, in Petersburg, Virginia, probably grateful for Poe's good words about him in *Burton's*, offered to give Poe's wife Virginia a fawn. Poe was later appreciative but unable to accept the gift because of the difficulty of transportation (O 1:215). On April 30, in Danville, Virginia, Louisa Mackenzie's cousin Mary Mattox married Benjamin Byrene Lapham. Mary was one of the sisters whose parents had died in 1833 and whom John H. Mackenzie and Louisa had taken in and raised as their own daughters at Mount Erin and later Darby Town. In 1850, the Laphams would have a daughter, Flora, who would one day write her revealing letters about Poe, drawing largely on what she had been told by her mother's cousin—later her stepfather—John H. Mackenzie.[70]

In the May issue of *Burton's*, Julius Rodman and the others continued their upriver travel. The group reached the Yellowstone River, experiencing the illness of Rodman's close friend Thornton (who recovered), the loss of three of their men (who then escaped from their Sioux captors during an antelope melee), the drowning of a herd of buffalo, and the fascination of some friendly Assiniboins with Toby, the slave of Rodman's partner Pierre Junôt. In the final installment, that of June 1840, the men continued west on the Missouri River, through the Black Hills, hoping to reach the Rocky Mountains, which Rodman and two others did glimpse in the distance. The narrative closes with the confrontation of Rodman and two of his comrades with two huge brown bears on a cliff overlooking the river—one of the two bears was killed, and the other, trapped on a ledge, would inevitably die.[71] The men then returned to camp. But, because of his disagreement with Burton, Poe never returned to his story, which supposedly would have followed the men over the Rocky Mountains to the Yukon and eventually back home (P 1:508–9). The incomplete narrative is sometimes very promising, sometimes derivative and plodding—it does not seem to have the suggestive undercurrent that would lift it beyond. Yet we cannot be sure since Poe never wrote the second half of the work.

Remarkably enough, a United States Senate document of 1840 referred to Rodman's narrative as if it were authentic. And, perhaps more knowingly, an 1849 book on seamanship included passages about a ship's stowage from *Pym*, not identifying the source as fiction.[72]

Among the most interesting nonfiction pieces that Poe provided in the May issue were "A Notice of William Cullen Bryant," "The Philosophy of Furniture," and a review of *Memoirs and Letters of Madame Malibran*. There was, however, a falling off in the June issue—Poe's "Some Account of Stonehenge, the Giant's Dance, A Druidical Ruin in England" was largely derivative, and the few reviews modest.[73] With this issue, featuring the final episode of "Julius Rodman," the reader reaches the "END OF THE SIXTH VOLUME"[74]—and Poe the end of his career at *Burton's*.

Poe had been biding his time. He had disclosed in September 1839, "As soon as Fate allows I will have a Magazine of my own—and will endeavor to kick up a dust" (O 1:194). It was in May 1840—a time when Poe was meeting new friends Frederick W. Thomas and Jesse E. Dow and attending a William Henry Harrison rally—that Fate finally allowed. On May 21, William E. Burton, who had been having a new theater built, opaquely listed *Burton's Gentleman's Magazine* for sale. Poe, who had not been informed but who recognized what was going on, could anticipate the end of *Burton's*, and he therefore arranged for the printing of a prospectus for his planned "Penn Magazine." On May 30, having learned of the prospectus for the new magazine, which might undercut the value of his old magazine, Burton fired Poe.[75]

Poe responded to Burton's letter of dismissal, attributing his employer's unfriendly attitude and behavior to the concern Burton had about a negative review he had written of *Pym*. With great detail, Poe disputed the hundred-dollar debt that Burton claimed he owed, stating that the amount due was only sixty dollars. And Poe charged Burton with having made an unfair and ominous reduction in his salary, having regularly disparaged him to others, and having withheld the information about the planned sale of the magazine. Poe was standing up for himself, reasonably enough. He wrote to Burton, "The opportunity of doing something for myself seemed a good one—(I was about to be thrown out of business)—and I embraced it." Responding to what must have been Burton's query about "Julius Rodman," Poe wrote, "I can give you no definitive answer (respecting the continuation [of] Rodman's Journal,) until I hear from you again" (O 1:217–20). There was no resolution of the conflict. Poe was out of a job, and Rodman was permanently stranded at his camp near the Missouri River.

At the time, Poe evidently thought that his future prospects depended on his prospectus. He sent it out to individuals and periodicals, but the proposed magazine would never be published. However, through his writing, Poe would still manage "to kick up a dust."

15

"Fortune & Fame Must Go Hand in Hand"

1840-1842

Poe now had time. He took great care with the prospectus for the "Penn Magazine," a bold declaration of purpose. He committed to expressing "an honest and a fearless opinion" and to pleasing his readers through "versatility, originality and pungency," sometimes providing "the enkindling of the imagination" (L2 23–25). His aspiration was high—he sought to gain editorial independence—indeed, to master the literary marketplace. His vehicle would be a high-quality, five-dollars-per-year monthly. The prospectus brochure was folded vertically; the text appeared within on the right, and his own handwritten personal comments would appear within on the left (L2 22). He paid for the publication of the prospectus in the *Saturday Evening Post* and the *Spirit of the Times,* where it was presented on June 6 and June 12, 1840, respectively.[1] He sent it out to Philadelphia editors and to a range of friends and allies and potential allies, including the Portland writer John Neal, Baltimore editor Joseph E. Snodgrass, Philadelphia poet Charles W. Thomson, and the corresponding secretary of Gettysburg College's Philomathean Society, A. S. Cummings (O 1:227–35). Poe was ready; he was confident, or trying to be: he wrote to Snodgrass, "If there is any impossibility about the matter, it is the impossibility of *not* succeeding" (O 1:230). He built his growing list of possible subscribers and contributors.[2] His "mystic empire" would become a practical one.

By August, he moderately revised the prospectus. He promised "a criticism self-sustained; guiding itself only by the purest rules of Art," lamented "those organized *cliques* . . . hanging like nightmares upon American literature," and declared his allegiance to "the general interests of the republic of letters, without reference to particular regions; regarding the world at large as the true audience of the author" (L2 25–27). And he continued sending out his prospectus, to his Georgia relatives William Poe and Washington Poe; the Charlottesville lawyer Lucian Minor; Cincinnati watchmaker Joseph B. Boyd; Jackson, Tennessee, postmaster John Tomlin; Frankford, Pennsylvania, physician and poet Pliny Earle, novelist and political speaker Frederick W. Thomas (O 1:235–46, 248–50), and Georgia poet Thomas Holley Chivers.[3] Writing to William Poe, he acknowledged the need for five hundred subscribers by December 1 and offered a phrase from John Milton that would probably have appealed to family pride: "If I fully succeed in my purposes I will not fail to produce some lasting effect upon the growing literature of the country, while I establish for myself individually a name which that country 'will not willingly let die'" (O 1:236–37). We may be reminded of Poe's assuring his foster father, John Allan, years earlier, "I will be an honor to your name" (O 1:17).

Even as Poe was devoting himself to the creation of a new magazine, he was also developing significant friendships with two contemporaries visiting Philadelphia, Frederick W. Thomas and Jesse E. Dow. In the spring of 1840, Thomas, who had been a friend of Poe's brother Henry, was furnishing his third novel, *Howard Pinckney,* to Lea & Blanchard; Dow, a writer from Washington, D.C., was testifying at the court-martial trial of Commodore Jesse Elliott. Poe met Thomas and later introduced him to Dow. On May 19, 1840, Poe wrote in Alexander's *Daily Chronicle* about Thomas, "He has the true soul of genius," and about Dow, "He has true and peculiar talent, and as a man there is no one whom we more highly respect."[4] That evening, Poe attended a rally for William Henry Harrison, Whig candidate for president. (Poe would likely have then remembered the fireworks in Richmond in October 1813 for Harrison's military triumph over British forces in Canada.) Thomas spoke at this rally (as did Thomas Dunn English); issues in the campaign were largely economic, given the Panic of 1837 and that of 1839. And the Whigs were then advocating a reform of the bankruptcy laws.[5] Some of those at the rally supported Harrison's opponent, incumbent Democratic candidate Martin Van Buren, and disrupted the proceedings. Thomas wrote to Poe, "I . . . got pelted by the people as you remember—or rather by the Locos" (H 17:99). The "Loco-Focos" were then considered the Democrats, latter-day Jacksonians, and they hurled "brickbats and stones" at the Whig speaker.[6]

Poe, Thomas, and Dow became a sociable trio for a while in May and June—they enjoyed a camaraderie. Poe would later write to Thomas, referring to the three witches of Shakespeare's *Macbeth* (1.1.1), "I would give the world to see you once again and have a little chat. Dow you & I—'when shall we three meet again?'" (O 1:322).[7] Thomas had moved to Washington, D.C., and Dow had returned there. Their presence and the possibility of a political appointment would lead Poe to visit the capital in 1843, much to his misfortune.

Among those who later commented on the Poe family at home around this time were Thomas Dunn English, Mary Starr, and an unnamed philanthropic lady of Philadelphia. English recalled that "Mrs. Poe was a delicate gentlewoman, with an air of refinement and good breeding, and Mrs. Clemm had more of the mother than the mother-in-law about her."[8] Mary Starr remembered that after a chance encounter with the Poe family on the street in Philadelphia, she and her cousin were invited back to the Poe home, where Edgar asked her to sing again his favorite, "Come Rest in This Bosom." She obliged, intoning Thomas Moore's lyric of consolation (which begins, "Come rest in this bosom, My own stricken deer, Tho' the herd have fled from thee, Thy home is still here"). She added, "We spent a pleasant evening, and Mr. Poe accompanied my cousin and myself back to her house."[9] Amanda Bartlett Harris offers us the reminiscence from the unnamed philanthropic lady, who was "in some way connected with an association intended to assist in a delicate manner those in reduced circumstances who had been accustomed to a life of refinement and perhaps luxury." The mutual devotion of Poe and Virginia was evident: "Poe was very proud and very fond of her, and used to delight in the round, child-like face and plump little finger, which he contrasted with himself, so tall and thin and half-melancholy looking; and she in turn idolized him." The recollection makes clear that Poe did somehow eventually get Virginia the piano she wanted but that their later poverty took it away from her: "She [Virginia] had a voice of wonderful sweetness, and was an exquisite singer, and in some of their more prosperous days, when they were living in a pretty little rose-covered cottage on the outskirts of Philadelphia, she had her harp and piano. But these articles disappeared, with all the luxuries of house and of wardrobe, being disposed of one after another for the necessities of life, until when they left that place [by May 25, 1842] they had scarcely anything."[10] Poe's friend Lambert A. Wilmer later wrote about the piano, "He [Poe] kept a piano to gratify her [Virginia's] taste for music, at a time when his income could scarcely afford such an indulgence."[11] Perhaps it was the purchase of this piano to which his later employer, George R. Graham, was referring when he wrote, "[*T*]*wice* only, I remember his purchasing some rather expensive luxuries for his house, and then he was nervous to the degree of misery until he had, by extra articles, covered what he considered an imprudent indebtedness."[12]

In the summer of 1840, Poe was out of work but still expecting things to work out. He was, as so often in his adult life, struggling. He admitted to William Poe, by way of excusing his delay in responding, "I have been overwhelmed by worldly cares, which left me scarce a moment for thought" (O 1:235). And he stated to Washington Poe, "You are aware that hitherto my circumstances, as regards pecuniary matters, have been bad." But he believed that the new magazine would save him—"If I succeed in the present attempt ... fortune & fame must go hand in hand" (O 1:239). He received varied responses to his outreach—sometimes discouraging, sometimes encouraging: John Tomlin sent the names of nine possible subscribers (O 1:243). Meanwhile, Poe was probably then beginning to work on a new short story, "The Man of the Crowd," which would appear in a transitional issue of *Graham's Magazine.*

On October 20, 1840, George R. Graham, who already owned the *Casket,* bought *Burton's Gentleman's Magazine* from William E. Burton, paying $3,500 for 3,500 subscribers. He merged the magazines, creating the most popular magazine of its time. There is little likelihood that Burton advocated Poe to Graham given Poe's contested debt and Burton's recent published reference to Poe's "infirmities." And certainly Poe was still hostile to Burton, asking about him mockingly in a letter to Frederick W. Thomas: "Have you heard that that illustrious graduate of St John's College, Cambridge, (Billy Barlow,) has sold his Magazine to Graham, of the 'Casket'?" (O 1:249). (The Ostrom edition of Poe's letters quotes Kenneth Silverman that "Billy Barlow" was "the stage name of a low comedian who had committed suicide" [O 1:250].) But there seems to have been no animus between Poe and Graham. We may recall that in June Poe had published the prospectus for the "Penn Magazine" in the *Saturday Evening Post,* a newspaper that Graham owned.[13]

Around this time, Poe began an important friendship with the engraver John Sartain. This contemporary of Poe's later wrote, "It was at the period of the transfer of Burton's Magazine to Graham that I first met Poe, already of much fame as a poet. He became one of my dearest friends. His memory I cherish and honor."[14] It was at this time, too, that Poe received a letter from young Richard Henry Stoddard, an aspiring poet who must have been requesting a manuscript; Poe responded on November 6, sending a handwritten copy of the sonnet "To Zante" (O 1:246–47). Stoddard would in later years be critical of Poe.

Poe continued to plan for the "Penn Magazine"—he wrote to John Tomlin in September, Pliny Earle in October, and Frederick W. Thomas in November about his publishing, or wanting to publish, their work in his first number (O 1:244, 245, 249), and he mentioned to Thomas his reviewing *Howard Pinckney* there, as well (O 1:248). He confided to Thomas that "the first sheet" of the magazine would go to press in early December (O 1:249). Poe had promised that the "Penn Magazine" would first appear on January 1, 1841 (L2 25, 27). He would have been cheered by notices about the anticipated "Penn Magazine" in newspapers, including those from out of town, which he read at the Philadelphia Merchants' Exchange (O 1:248). One of these notices, for instance, evidently mentioned by Thomas, stated memorably, "Mr. Poe is not only a man of genius and a ripe scholar, but he has an upright, a downright, and an outright honesty and fearlessness of purpose, which will guide his pen in the critical department of his work, without fear or favor."[15]

In late November, the *Casket* and the *Gentleman's Magazine* of December 1840 appeared, newly designated as *Graham's Magazine*. The transitional issue featured Poe's haunting tale "The Man of the Crowd."[16] The work's narrator is a convalescent observer in a London coffeehouse, who at first catalogues the different strata of humanity, from high to low, and then becomes fascinated by—and follows—an enigmatic old man who walks throughout the evening, the night, and the following day and evening, evidently seeking to be amid people. This pedestrian is anything but pedestrian—he conveys to the narrator "the ideas of vast mental power, of caution, of penuriousness, of avarice, of coolness, of malice, of blood-thirstiness, of triumph, of merriment, of excessive terror, of intense, of supreme despair."[17] Yet despite persistent pursuit of the old man, the narrator gains no insight and concludes that "the singular being" is "the type and the genius of deep crime";[18] he is like a particular German book—"[I]t does not permit itself to be read."[19]

The darkness and mystery of Poe's tale compel interest. The tale comprises two halves, the first of these concerning the types of urban walkers, the second concerning the old man. Patterns of language contribute to a symmetrical structure, as we have seen in Poe's work as early as the 1835 "Berenice." Such language as "The Man of the Crowd," "momently increased," "absorbed in contemplation," and "eyes rolled quickly" is mirrored by "eyes rolled wildly," "momently increasing," "absorbed in contemplation," and "*the man of the crowd."* The center is a line of inversion and parallelism: "As the night deepened, so deepened to me the interest of the scene."[20]

Poe's immediate source for the epigraph, La Bruyère's "Ce grand malheur, de ne pouvoir etre seul,"[21] is Edward Bulwer-Lytton's novel *Pelham;* a translation of the full passage is "Every evil that befalls us comes from not being able to be alone; from this comes gaming, luxury, dissipation, wine, women, ignorance, slander, envy, forgetfulness of self and of God."[22] Poe omits this abundant detail. It is "dissipation, wine" that seems most germane here.

We may work toward an interpretation of the tale when we note in the first half the catalogue of "drunkards" and in the second half the old man's approach to "one of the huge suburban temples of Intemperance—one of the palaces of the fiend, Gin."[23] Furthermore, source passages for "The Man of the Crowd" from Charles Dickens's "The Drunkard's Death" and "Gin-Shops," Edward Bulwer-Lytton's *Pelham,* and Washington Irving's "Rip Van Winkle" all concern drinking. It may be that Poe, in this work, is covertly confessing his own unfortunate susceptibility. He may be reaching toward what Bulwer-Lytton referred to in *Pelham* as the "*heart laid bare*"—a phrase Poe later used in "Marginalia" (P 2:322–23). And we may relevantly anticipate that Poe would one day confide to a correspondent (here reversing La Bruyère), "The desire for society comes upon me only when I have become excited by drink" (O 2:648).[24]

At the end of December, Poe wrote to the poet Lewis J. Cist of Cincinnati that he had had "a severe illness" and had been "confined . . . to bed for the last month"; the launch of the "Penn Magazine" would have to be delayed until March 1 (O 1:251; see also O 1:253, 256). While he was sick, there were several salient developments. Whig candidate William Henry Harrison was elected president, making likely a reform of the bankruptcy law.[25] Furthermore, the first issue of *Graham's Magazine* appeared, featuring John Sartain, Jesse E. Dow, and Thomas Dunn English; this periodical would soon become Poe's professional home.[26] Finally, a dinner party honoring Harrison's victory, at Thomas Evans's Hotel, would include toasts from English, Robert Morris, and Rufus Wilmot Griswold.[27] The last, a journalist lately arrived from New York City—where he had worked with Horace Greeley on the weekly *New-Yorker* and had edited the forthcoming *Biographical Annual*—had come to Philadelphia to edit the Whig newspaper the *Daily Standard*. And he also probably sought to approach and negotiate with the publisher Carey & Hart regarding his anthology of American poetry.[28] Both *Graham's Magazine* and *The Poets and Poetry of America* would be great successes. Graham himself would become a good friend to Poe, but Griswold would become an antagonist and, eventually, the author of a vicious and still-notorious obituary.

As he recovered from his illness, Poe renewed his correspondence concerning his cherished magazine—he wrote to the author John Pendleton Kennedy (O 1:252–53), former bank president Nicholas Biddle (O 1:253–54), editor Joseph E. Snodgrass (O 1:256–58), and playwright Robert T. Conrad (O 1:260–61). Declaring to Snodgrass in a letter of January 17, 1841, his commitment to originality in the "Penn Magazine," Poe added, "I have one or two articles of my own in statu pupillari [in a pupil, or early, state] that would make you stare, at least, on account of the utter oddity of their conception. To carry out the conception is a difficulty which—may be overcome" (O 1:257). One of these "articles" may have been "The Murders in the Rue Morgue"— Poe referred in the tale's opening paragraphs to their "prefacing a somewhat peculiar narrative."[29] The work, which would appear in *Graham's* in March, would be something new—indeed, something foundational: the first modern detective story. Intended, presumably, for the magazine that never started, it created a genre that has never ended.

Prospects for the "Penn Magazine," which were "*glorious,*" according to Poe in mid-January (O 1:256), were doubtful in early February. The problem was the economy—on February 4, as a result of an ongoing crisis of credit and confidence, banks refused to redeem paper money with "specie," gold and silver.[30] Poe later acknowledged the difficulty in a letter to Joseph E. Snodgrass—the "unexpected bank suspensions"—but, relying on a phrase from *Macbeth* (3.2.13), he wrote, "The *Penn,* I hope, is only 'scotched, not killed.'" He noted, "Mr. Graham has made me a liberal offer, which I had great pleasure in accepting. The *Penn* project will unquestionably be resumed hereafter" (O 1:264). Apparently Graham had promised to support the "Penn" in six months or a year provided that Poe could secure as contributors most of those on a list of high-quality writers (O 1:278–79, 346–47). Graham himself, in his *Saturday Evening Post* on February 20, asserted Poe's former fine prospects for the "Penn" but supported his cessation of efforts on the magazine, necessitated by the financial turbulence of the times. And Graham went on, "It is with pleasure we add, that we have secured the services of Mr. Poe as one of the editors of Graham's Magazine. As a stern, just and impartial critic Mr. Poe holds a pen second to none in the country, and we have the confident assurance, that with such editorial strength as the Magazine now possesses, the literary department of the work will be of the very highest character." Poe began his work on *Graham's* on the April 1841 number.[31]

During the year that Poe worked at *Graham's*, the periodical was located at SW Third and Chestnut.[32] Graham's office was on the top floor of the building of the highly successful penny newspaper the *Public Ledger*. Also located at that address was his *Saturday Evening Post, and News*. Across the street at NW Third and Chestnut was the penny newspaper the *Spirit of the Times*, edited by John S. Du Solle, soon to be assisted by George Lippard. Within a few blocks were the offices of other magazines, including *Godey's Lady's Book*, *Burton's Gentleman's Magazine*, and James Pedder's *Farmer's Cabinet*. Many other newspapers, including Benjamin N. Matthias's *Saturday Chronicle* and Francis J. Grund's *Daily Standard*, were also nearby.[33] Poe was again in the thick of Philadelphia's publishing world.

He was evidently paid $800 a year for his work as book review editor for *Graham's* and additional sums for his literary contributions—for example, $56 for "The Murders in the Rue Morgue," John Ward Ostrom estimates (presumably fourteen pages at what Poe later termed "the old price [$4 per page])" (O 2:632).[34] Remarkably, when the manuscript of that story was printed and proofed, it was thrown away but then fortunately retrieved by a printer's apprentice (H 4:295–96). It survived fires and smoke and endures today in the Rare Book Department of the Free Library of Philadelphia.

The singular narrative, no longer "in statu pupillari" but fully matured, appeared by March 26 in the April issue of *Graham's Magazine* with the final line "Philadelphia, March, 1841."[35] Its unnamed narrator is the sometimes-incredulous admirer of the keenly analytical C. Auguste Dupin. (Poe drew the name from a letter he had received the previous September regarding a candidate for a French teaching position, C. Auguste Dubouchet.)[36] The setting is Paris. The problem is the mysterious and gruesome murder of the L'Espanayes, an old woman and her daughter. The former had had her head nearly cut off, her body thrown out the window; the latter had been choked to death, her body stuffed up the chimney, upside down. The room in which the murder took place is locked and in complete disarray. But nothing, including gold coins, was taken. The police are utterly bewildered, and they arrest an innocent man, Adolphe Le Bon. Dupin and his friend, reading of the murders in the newspaper, visit the scene of the crime, and Dupin, through careful ratiocination, infers the solution. He states that no person could have committed these murders, which involved inordinate strength and agility and no ascertainable human motive—but, given the disagreement of witnesses about the language spoken, the print of the hand on the young woman's neck, the tuft of hair in her hand, and a copy of Cuvier, he determines that an escaped orangutan, wielding a razor, had entered the apartment by the fire escape and shutter and, becoming upset by the screams of the old lady, killed the two women. The nail that had seemed to keep one of the windows closed was actually broken; a secret spring had enabled the raising and closing of the window. Dupin confirms his inference about the orangutan through the testimony of the animal's owner, lured to the apartment of Dupin and his friend and eager to confess the truth. Le Bon is freed, and the orangutan is captured.

And the reader is amazed. The editor Frederick W. Thomas wrote in response to Poe's April 1 query, "I think it ["The Murders in the Rue Morgue"] the most ingenious thing of the kind on record—It is managed with a tact, ability and subtlety that is wonderful." The future editor and reformer Thomas Wentworth Higginson, as a Harvard College student, wrote on May 7, 1841, of staying up late one night reading "a splendid account of tracing circumstantial evidence in a Paris murder, by E A Poe." When the lightly revised story was published in 1843, it was probably the editor Robert Morris who wrote, "'The Murders in the Rue Morgue' is one of the most enchaining, finished, and powerful fictions that we have for a long time read."[37] And later writers in the detective fiction genre that Poe created, from Arthur Conan Doyle to Jorge Luis Borges, have taken inspiration from the work.

Reviewing Bulwer-Lytton's novel *Night and Morning* in the same issue of *Graham's Magazine* in which "Rue Morgue" appeared, Poe discusses at length "the expedient of writing his [Bulwer's] book backwards."[38] That this expedient was employed with regard to "Rue Morgue" is clarified in a review of the 1845 collection *Tales* by the *Aristidean* editor Thomas Dunn English, informed by Poe—or by Poe himself—or by both of them: "The incidents in the 'Murders in the Rue Morgue' are purely imaginary. Like all the rest, it is written backwards." And English or Poe or both stated, "The author, as in the case of 'Murders in the Rue Morgue,' the first [of the Dupin tales] written, begins by imagining a deed committed by such a creature, or in such a manner, as would most effectually mislead inquiry. Then he applies analysis to the investigation."[39] Perhaps impatient with what he considered the disproportionate presence of ratiocinative tales in his 1845 collection *Tales,* Poe self-deprecatingly confirmed the order of his composing in a letter to the poet Philip Pendleton Cooke: "In the 'Murders in the Rue Morgue' . . . where is the ingenuity of unravelling a web which you yourself (the author) have woven for the express purpose of unravelling? The reader is made to confound the ingenuity of the supposititious Dupin with that of the writer of the story" (O 1:595; for Cooke to Poe, see H 17:262–64). Nonetheless, Poe's weaving has continued to impress. Mark Twain once wrote, "What a curious thing a 'detective' story is. And was there ever one that the author needn't be ashamed of, except 'The Murders in the Rue Morgue'?"[40]

Many sources for the story have been identified, from Voltaire to Sir Walter Scott to Edward Bulwer-Lytton.[41] But I would highlight here the stories from the 1838 *Philadelphia Saturday News*—some of the "component parts" (to use Poe's language) that Poe shaped into the "purely imaginary" "griffin" (H 10:62; see also P 3:16). One of the critical prompts, I would argue, is the August 4, 1838, story "Deliberate Murder in Broadway, at Midday," appearing, unmissably, next to Morton McMichael's review of *Pym*. Edward Coleman, a Black man, slit the throat of his wife, Ann, whom he suspected of adultery. Anticipating language in "Rue Morgue," the *Saturday News* story refers to an "atrocious murder," Coleman's "nearly severing her head from her body with a razor" and then "dropping her upon the pavement," and his later offering responses "of the most *outre* kind." A subsequent *Saturday News* piece on Coleman describes the weapon, "the razor, upon the blade and handle of which there was a great quantity of congealed blood." Among the other *Saturday News* pieces of 1838 that would have caught Poe's attention for his later story are an account of an orangutan; another of an escaped ape; yet another about the deaths of an older woman and a younger woman, her daughter, in "a small upper room" whose door had to be broken in; and still another about a "madman" "recently escaped from an insane Hospital," described as "a wild-looking object, holding on the window shutters outside of the house, and peering into the room," one who is "swinging upon the window shutters during the night" and later "grinning like a yellow monkey." (Perhaps Poe intimated this last source when the narrator concludes that "[a] madman . . . has done this deed—some raving maniac escaped from a neighboring *Maison de Santé*," and Dupin replies, "In some respects . . . your idea is not irrelevant.") The blending of detail involving a Black man and an ape—perhaps encouraged by the *Saturday News* phrase "the hideous Negro with ourang-outang face"—is clearly racist and deplorable, but it was not uncharacteristic of the time.[42] Some of those who read the *Saturday News* stories in 1838 would also have read "The Murders in the Rue Morgue" in 1841, but perhaps (to use Poe's words in the tale) they "[found] themselves upon the brink of remembrance, without being able, in the end, to remember."[43]

Poe assembled and adapted all his source material into the plot elaborated, concerning thought dramatized, with a symmetry of language in four parallel groupings, framing the central opening of a window, itself featuring a symmetry of language: "I now carefully replaced this head portion [of the nail] in the indentation whence I had taken it, and the resemblance to a perfect nail was complete. I gently raised the sash for a few inches; the head went up with it, remaining firm in its bed. I closed the window, and the semblance of the whole nail was again perfect. The riddle, so far, was now unriddled."[44] The center of the locked-room mystery is, ironically, an open window. We shall see the ironic center in the later Dupin tales, as well.

We may interpret the story variously—I will focus on the hermeneutic and the personal. Perhaps guiding readers who were challenged by *Pym,* Poe offers a protagonist, Dupin, a master analyst, who speaks of the importance of identification ("the analyst throws himself into the spirit of his opponent, identifies himself therewith"), attention to sources ("a comprehension of *all* the sources [whatever be their character] from which legitimate advantage may be derived"), shrewd observation of detail ("The necessary knowledge is that of *what* to observe"), and consideration of that which is especially unusual ("But it is by these deviations from the plane of the ordinary, that reason feels its way, if at all, in its search after the true)."[45] Through Dupin, Poe elaborates the method of a close reader.

And the personal may be inferred. The *Saturday News* source "Deliberate Murder in Broadway, in Midday" offers a hint, which will reappear in sources for "The Mystery of Marie Rogêt" and "The Purloined Letter": a woman of uncertain reputation. Ann Coleman was suspected of a sexual impropriety, as Poe's mother had been, accused by John Allan and others of having had an affair (that resulted in the birth of Rosalie).[46] As mentioned earlier, Poe told Marie Louise Shew Houghton "[t]hat it was the regret of his life, that he had not vindicated his mother to the world, as pure, as angelic, and altogether lovely, as any woman could be on earth."[47] He would, in the Dupin tales, repeatedly turn to a source about a woman of uncertain reputation—and in the last of these tales, "The Purloined Letter," he would, through Dupin, finally save her.

Poe wrote in the aforementioned review of Bulwer's *Night and Morning,* parenthetically and revealingly, about "the brief tale" as "(a species of composition which admits of the highest development of artistical power in alliance with the wildest vigor of imagination)."[48] Perhaps this characterization might be applied to his "brief tale" that appeared only a few pages earlier.

The other article "in statu pupillari" to which Poe was referring in his January 17 letter may have been "Eleonora" (M 2:637). He sent this lush, tragic, yet ultimately ameliorative tale of romantic love to *The Gift for 1842*, and it was now at the printer.[49]

Poe's work at *Graham's Magazine* evidently was going well. Graham remembered, after Poe died, "For three or four years I knew him intimately, and for eighteen months saw him almost daily, much of the time writing or conversing at the same desk, knowing all his hopes, his fears, and little annoyances of life, as well as his high-hearted struggle with adverse fate; yet he was always the same polished gentleman, the quiet, unobtrusive, thoughtful scholar, the devoted husband, frugal in his personal expenses, punctual and unwearied in his industry, *and the soul of honor* in all his transactions." Graham added, well aware of Poe's later difficulties, "This, of course, was in his better days, and by them *we* judge the man" (H 1:404).

Meanwhile, the new presidential administration started—and stopped. Inaugurated as president on March 4, William Henry Harrison died of pneumonia on April 4. The vice president, John Tyler (of "Tippecanoe and Tyler Too"), succeeded Harrison, but he defied many of the Whig positions. Fortunately, however, for Poe and other debtors, Tyler did later sign the Bankruptcy Act of 1841.[50]

With the May issue of *Graham's Magazine* nearly finished by April 1, Poe wrote revealing letters to Joseph E. Snodgrass and Thomas Wyatt. To Snodgrass he made a persuasive case against his former employer William E. Burton, and he defended himself against accusations of drunkenness, though acknowledging indiscretions in Richmond. The questionable absoluteness of his assertion "My sole drink is water" may have been prompted by Snodgrass's temperance views (O 1:263–64).[51] To Wyatt, with whom he had worked on *The Conchologist's First Book,* Poe wrote, intriguingly, "We have had Rose (my sister) on to spend a week with us, since I saw you. John Mc K. came with her, and left her with us while he went to Boston" (O 1:266). "John Mc K." was Poe's old friend John H. Mackenzie. The scholar Joseph J. Moldenhauer wrote, "Poe's reference to him as 'John Mc.K.' in the present letter implies that Wyatt was more familiar with MacKenzie than with Rosalie, whom Poe felt it necessary to identify in parentheses."[52] Poe had known Wyatt since late in 1838 or early in 1839; it is therefore possible that Poe had introduced "John McK." to him then. This possibility may lead to an interesting speculation regarding "The Fall of the House of Usher." It may be that before—or when—Poe was writing in this tale about the narrator visiting "one of my boon companions in boyhood" (M 2:398), John H. Mackenzie had been—or was—visiting Poe. In light of the focus on sister and brother, Madeline Usher and Roderick Usher, in "The Fall of the House of Usher," it is suggestive that John H. Mackenzie's aunt, schoolmistress Jane Mackenzie, was half sister to Roderick Mackenzie.[53] Of course, the link is only conjectural, but it need not be ruled out. The real-life Ushers (M 2:393) may not have been the only family with a connection to this classic tale.

The May issue of *Graham's Magazine* included Poe's tale "A Descent into the Maelström." It offers a blend of sublime terror at approaching destruction in a giant whirlpool and shrewd observation of a vortex-defying barrel, leading to the imperiled seaman's securing himself to a cask and thereby surviving. Poe's narrator refers to "an abyss penetrating the globe,"[54] an idea he considers attractive in imagination but unbelievable in fact. Poe thus recalls his previous fictions with the Symmes-Reynolds "Hollow Earth" motif—"MS. Found in a Bottle," in which the narrator succumbs to the whirlpool, and *The Narrative of Arthur Gordon Pym,* in which he is rescued from the edge of the vortex. Repeatedly describing that edge, Poe repeatedly visits "the brink of eternity" (M 2:143).

Poe later criticizes his tale—responding to the praise of Joseph E. Snodgrass, Poe states, "It was finished in a hurry, and therefore its conclusion is imperfect" (O 1:297). Also, Poe subsequently called into question a supposedly validating footnote he had added in the 1845 *Tales* (M 3:1382–83).[55] But "A Descent into the Maelström" has remained a buoyant work, a much-anthologized favorite Poe tale.

Also in the May issue of *Graham's* was Poe's review of Charles Dickens's *The Old Curiosity Shop, and Other Tales* and *Master Humphrey's Clock.* The discerning critic praised *The Old Curiosity Shop* in particular, writing chiastically of Dickens versus Bulwer, "Mr. Bulwer, through art, has almost created a genius. Mr. Dickens, through genius, has perfected a standard from which Art itself will derive its essence, in rules."[56] This review, valuable in itself, is valuable, too, for its detail relating to future Poe works—for example, its passage on inertia, redeployed in "The Purloined Letter,"[57] and its lauding Dickens's "Confession Found in a Prison in the Time of Charles the Second," a likely source for "The Tell-Tale Heart" and perhaps for "The Black Cat," as well.[58] A related piece, appearing in the *Saturday Evening Post* of May 1, was Poe's review of Dickens's novel in progress *Barnaby Rudge.* Here Poe predicted correctly that Barnaby Rudge was the son of the murderer. He also wrote about Barnaby's pet raven, contending, somewhat generously, that its "croakings are to be frequently, appropriately, and prophetically heard." It seems very probable that Dickens's raven helped suggest Poe's own.[59]

At the *Graham's Magazine* office, Poe would regularly see Graham and his associate Charles J. Peterson, and on occasion the talented engraver for the magazine, John Sartain. Probably it was early May when Poe visited John A. Jones's Union Hotel, at 152 Chestnut Street, to meet the editor of the *Daily Standard*, Rufus W. Griswold. Poe would probably have known that the Whig journalist had secured Carey & Hart as his publisher for his anthology in progress, "The Poets and Poetry of America." Not finding Griswold home, Poe left him two letters of introduction. The ambitious assembler and compiler visited Poe the next day, presumably at his office, and the two discussed literary issues relating to the anthology. The young Griswold was later ably described by editor Harry Morford: "He was a man of rather small figure, a very intelligent face, with the eyes deep-set, good forehead showing an early inclination to the loss of front hair, sharp and trenchant nose, short, full beard and mustache (adopting the European fashion in advance of most other Americans), and a habit of holding down the head a trifle and looking keenly out from beneath the overhanging brows, not a little impressive when he was very much in earnest."[60] Inclusion in Griswold's anthology would have been of great interest to Poe; Poe's critical approval would have been of great interest to Griswold.

Probably also in early May, Poe delivered a note to Griswold, requesting a book to review (O 1:270–71), and in late May he sent a letter to Griswold, now editor of the *Boston Notion*, with some of his own poems for consideration for the anthology and a brief, not altogether reliable biography (O 1:272–74; H 1:344–46).[61] (Poe may well have already seen Griswold's May 22 negative comment on his recently published June 1841 *Graham's* review of Pliny Earle's poetry.)[62] Poe would be in the anthology, but his relationship with Griswold would be, for both of them, one of mixed tenuous respect and disdain. And the lesser writer would get his revenge on the greater.

Since Poe was working for Graham, some of his correspondence represented him as editor rather than as author. For example, a May 3 letter requested a contribution to the magazine from Longfellow (O 1:268–70). Perhaps Poe was irritated to appeal to a man whom he considered a plagiarist (an allegation he conveyed to Griswold [O 1:272]); alternatively, perhaps he would have been proud to overcome his critical reservation to achieve an editorial purpose. And he did admire some of Longfellow's work. The Cambridge poet declined, graciously, on May 19, responding to Poe's self-deprecating comment, "You are mistaken in supposing that you are not 'favorably known to me.' On the contrary, all that I have read from your pen has inspired me with a high idea of your power; and I think you are destined to stand among the first romance-writers of the country, if such be your aim."[63]

Poe heard other encouraging words at this time from his friend Frederick W. Thomas, who invited him to come to Washington, D.C., to seek a clerical position. The life that Thomas imagined for Poe would surely have astounded the long-struggling writer:

> How would you like to be an office holder here at $1500 per year payable monthly by Uncle Sam who, however slack he may be to his general creditors, pays his officials with due punctuality. How would you like it? You stroll to your office a little after nine in the morning leisurely, and you stroll from it a little after two in the afternoon homeward to dinner, and return no more that day. If during office hours you have anything to do it is an agreeable relaxation from the monstrous laziness of the day. You have on your desk everything in the writing line in apple-pie order, and if you choose to lucubrate in a literary way, why you can lucubrate. (H 17:85)

Though a sinecure was never a sine qua non for Poe, it would have had its charm. But Poe would ruin whatever chances for it that he may have had.

By May 22, the June issue of *Graham's* was published, leading with Poe's sketch "The Island of the Fay."[64] It accompanied a plate by John Sartain, based on a drawing by the English artist John Martin. Sartain may well have modified his work in accordance with Poe's wishes.[65] And Poe modified his "Sonnet—To Science" for the epigraph, providing in its penultimate line "the dainty *fay*."[66]

The subject, the death of a fairy, is delicate, but the structure is firm. The sixth paragraph of eleven paragraphs—the center of the work, featuring a modified couplet from "The City of Sin" (formerly "The Doomed City")—offers such markers as "midway" and "mirror-like" to confirm what its position suggests:

> About midway in the short vista which my dreamy vision took in, one small circular island, fantastically verdured, reposed upon the bosom of the stream.
>
> So blended bank and shadow there,
> That each seemed pendulous in air—

so mirror-like was the glassy water, that it was scarcely possible to say at what point upon the slope of the emerald turf its crystal dominion began.[67]

This passage is symmetrically framed in the tale by the "dainty *fay*," the narrator's contemplative analogies, the eastern and western ends of the island, in the first half, and then, "mirror-like," the western and eastern ends of the island, the narrator's additional contemplative analogies, and "the fay" herself, in the second half.

The fairy's eventual repeated circling of the island, itself "circular," in the second half, echoes the first half: "As we find cycle within cycle without end—yet all revolving around one far-distant centre which is the God-head, may we not analogically suppose, in the same manner, life within life, the less within the greater, and all within the Spirit Divine?"[68] The sketch anticipates the end of Poe's prose poem *Eureka*.

An engaging resonance prompts a hypothesis here. The background is that "The Island of the Fay" appeared in the first volume of Griswold's edition of Poe, which (with the second volume) was published on or soon after January 10, 1850, when Herman Melville, living in New York City, was soon to begin *Moby-Dick*.[69] Given especially the keen interest then in the recently deceased Poe and his writings, it would not have been unlikely for Melville to consult the volume in the collection of his friend Evert Duyckinck or elsewhere, or perhaps even to borrow or to purchase it. Poe's phrasing at the center of this tale—"About midway," "one small circular island," and "in air"—seems transformed at the close of the first chapter of Melville's new book: Ishmael sees in his mind "endless processions of the whale, and, *midmost* of them all, *one* grand hooded phantom, like a snow hill *in the air*" (emphasis added).[70] It may be that the reverie of Poe's narrator lent itself to that of Ishmael.

Poe's review of Thomas Macaulay's essays in the June issue of *Graham's* discusses the valuable use of analogy, suggested by science, concerning matters beyond proof, such as God and immortality. Clearly, despite the use of "Sonnet—To Science" in "The Island of the Fay," Poe had by this time developed a growing respect for science. Another Poe review, of T. S. Arthur's novel *Insubordination*, offers the reference, mentioned earlier, to a passage regarding a boy's having been beaten. A third Poe review, that of Pliny Earle's *Marathon, and Other Poems*, praises Earle and his work, prompting the sharp attack by Griswold, who disdained Earle's volume.[71] Earle was one who had expressed interest in Poe's "Penn" (O 1:245–46), but Poe could certainly criticize someone he liked, as he did on the same page of *Graham's* regarding J. H. Ingraham.[72] (Hearing of Ingraham's "high dudgeon," Poe wrote of wishing to avoid "dishonor to my own sense of truth" [O 1:287].) So Poe's stated admiration of Earle may well have been genuine. But here was an instance in which Poe "the tomahawk man" was faulted for excessive praise. Griswold, who had condemned Earle's book in the May 15 issue of the *Boston Notion*, reviewed the June 1841 issue of *Graham's* in the May 22 issue of the newspaper, extracting the positive early portion of Poe's review of *Marathon, and Other Poems*, and avowing, "[W]e never saw anything more ineffably senseless and bombastic, than these verses so lauded by the editor of *Graham's Magazine*." Poe's comparison of Earle to poet Fitz-Greene Halleck provoked Griswold to write, "[Earle's] 'Marathon' reminds one of Halleck about as much as Shales [a reputedly poor actor] does of Edmund Kean, or Kemble, or Cooke; or a monkey with a tin sword and chapeau of Washington or Napoleon."[73] Poe probably saw the review and obliquely responded to it on several occasions.[74] So began the troubles between Poe and Griswold. Poe later wrote in his December 1841 "A Chapter on Autography" that Griswold's handwriting suggests "a certain unsteadiness of purpose."[75] Knowing what we do about Griswold's treatment of Poe in the obituary and "Memoir," we may wish that the vindictive and envious anthologist had had less steadiness of purpose.

In June 1841, Poe was working on the July issue of *Graham's*, but he was ambivalent about his future. On one hand, he continued his work on the magazine and made inquiries, on behalf of Graham and himself, with regard to the rescheduled "Penn Magazine," approaching Washington Irving, John Pendleton Kennedy, Henry Wadsworth Longfellow, Fitz-Greene Halleck, and James Fenimore Cooper (O 1:274–85, 289–91), as well as William Cullen Bryant, James K. Paulding, and N. P. Willis (letters to them unrecovered but inferred [O 2:1199]). Poe anticipated a January 1, 1842, publication date and requested an exclusive arrangement for one year (O 1:274–85, 289–91). On the other hand, he was growing impatient with his position at *Graham's*—he would later assert his "disgust with the namby-pamby character of the Magazine" (O 1:333)—and he remembered F. W. Thomas's enticing description of a job in Washington, D.C. Sending a copy of the July 1841 issue of *Graham's* on June 26, Poe wrote to Thomas, who had just obtained a government job, "For my own part, notwithstanding Graham's unceasing civility, and real kindness, I feel more & more disgusted with my situation. Would to God, I could do as you have done. Do you seriously think that an application on my part to [President John] Tyler would have a good result?" (O 1:287). Undoubtedly,

Poe sought the time to "lucubrate" that he believed that Thomas had obtained. Perhaps the Virginian Tyler might be responsive. Poe went on, "My claims, to be sure, are few. I am a Virginian—at least I call myself one, for I have resided all my life, until within the last few years, in Richmond. My political principles have always been as nearly as may be, with the existing administration, and I battled with right good will for Harrison, when opportunity offered. With Mr. Tyler I have some slight personal acquaintance—although this is a matter which he has possibly forgotten. For the rest, I am a literary man—and I see a disposition in government to cherish letters. Have I any chance?" (O 1:287). Poe underscored his interest at the close of the letter, "I am *really* serious about the office" (O 1:288). He would come to pursue both options—first, staying with *Graham's* for another nine months, and then, eleven months later, traveling to Washington, D.C., for a possible job, with disastrous results. And throughout the period—and, indeed, beyond it—Poe would maintain his commitment to establishing an independent magazine.

Poe's chief contribution to the July 1841 issue of *Graham's* was the essay "A Few Words on Secret Writing," which would be followed by three supplements in the August, October, and December issues. Poe adverted in the July essay to his invitation in *Alexander's Weekly Messenger* for alphabetical substitution ciphers and the ample response (later confirmed by the publisher Charles W. Alexander in the *Philadelphia Daily Chronicle* of July 13). Poe refuted the claim that he had made up the ciphers himself: "[T]he ciphers were all written in good faith, and solved in the same spirit." In fact, he claimed, somewhat more modestly than originally, "[H]uman ingenuity cannot concoct a cipher which human ingenuity cannot resolve."[76]

Having offered a new challenge for ciphers in his review of R. M. Walsh's translation *Sketches of Conspicuous Living Characters of France* in the April 1841 issue of *Graham's*,[77] Poe received a letter from one "S. D. L." from Stonington, Connecticut, with two encoded messages. (The researcher Michael J. Bielawa has worked out that "S. D. L." was Samuel [Davis] Longworthy.)[78] Poe decoded both messages (about cryptography) in "A Few Words on Secret Writing," indicating the key phrase for each of them.[79] He probably relied on the *Encyclopaedia Britannica* for some of the detail in this essay, but he did not explain his decoding method until he published, in 1843, "The Gold-Bug," which elaborated the letter frequency pattern that facilitated the decryption there.[80]

Of the ten critical reviews and notices in the July 1841 issue of *Graham's*, nine were by Poe (the exception is the review of Bolingbroke—see the postscript to Poe's letter to William Landor [H. B. Wallace] [O 1:296]). The review of *Powhatan; A Metrical Romance, in Seven Cantos,* by Seba Smith (a.k.a. Jack Downing), is a good instance of Poe's acerbic humor. For example, criticizing Smith's/Downing's oversharing, Poe writes, "Powhatan never did anything in his life, we are sure, that Mr. Downing has not got in his poem. He begins at the beginning, and goes on steadily to the end—painting away at his story, just as a sign-painter at a sign; beginning at the left hand side of his board, and plastering through to the right. But he has omitted one very ingenious trick of the sign-painter. He has forgotten to write under his portrait,—'*this is a pig,*' and thus there is some danger of mistaking it for an opossum."[81] Elsewhere in this review there may be a touch of Griswold's caustic words on the poetry of Pliny Earle: while Griswold had written, "[W]e never saw anything more ineffably senseless and bombastic," Poe wrote of Smith/Downing, "We never saw any one so uncommonly bad."[82] Poe's review of *Powhatan* would elicit an angry response from the editor of the weekly New York newspaper *Brother Jonathan,* H. Hastings Weld, and the conflict would finds its way into Poe's correspondence and his next Dupin tale, "The Mystery of Marie Rogêt."

Also worth mentioning is Poe's notice of James Bermingham's *A Memoir of the Very Reverend Theobald Mathew. With an Account of the Rise and Progress of Temperance in Ireland,* which includes P. H. Morris's essay "The Evil Effects of Drunkenness Physiologically Explained." The notice offers a wisdom that in coming years Poe could not put into practice. He begins, "It is scarcely too much to say that the Temperance Reformation is the most important which the world ever knew." He later states, "The temperate man carries within his own bosom, under all circumstances, the true, the only elements of bliss." And commenting particularly on the essay, Poe closes, "Through the influence of the physical, rather than of the moral suggestions against alcohol, the permanency of the temperance reform will be made good. Convince the world that spirituous liquors are poison to the body, and it will be scarcely necessary to add that they are ruin to the soul."[83] Poe's problems with alcohol, which would increase in the future, were certainly not due to a failure of understanding.

But it may be that in July 1841 Poe was himself a temperate man. He seems to have been working capably, attending to his criticism, his cryptographic analysis, and his short fiction. Regarding his tales, he was maintaining his generic virtuosity: having recently composed another angelic dialogue ("The Colloquy of Monos and Una," to appear in the August issue of *Graham's*), he turned again to satire ("Never Bet Your Head. A Moral Tale," to appear in the September issue of the magazine). At the same time, he was looking to the future, still cherishing his plans for his own magazine (with Graham's support) and encouraging F. W. Thomas, in Washington, D.C., to make an inquiry for him regarding a government job (O 1:292–94).

Graham recalled Poe's devotion to Virginia and Maria Clemm: "I shall never forget how solicitous of the happiness of his wife and mother-in-law he was, whilst one of the editors of Graham's Magazine—his whole efforts seemed to be to procure the comfort and welfare of his home." And perhaps it was at this time that Poe was welcomed as a guest at Graham's elegant home on Arch Street. Graham later selected as an epigraph for his reminiscence of Poe lines from Shakespeare's *King Henry VIII* originally concerning Cardinal Wolsey, which closed, "Lofty, and sour, to them that loved him not; / But, to those men that sought him, sweet as summer" (4.2.53–54).[84]

On July 26, H. Hastings Weld wrote an indignant response to Poe's review of Seba Smith's *Powhatan* for *Brother Jonathan*.[85] This newspaper was a popular publication in Philadelphia—a local correspondent had written in June 1840, "In my walks through the streets, I often observe the familiar visage of 'Brother Jonathan';—I should say that he is unrivalled among the weeklies in the estimation of our citizens."[86] Weld declared, with evident pique, "A more capricious, unjust, and ridiculous affair, purporting to be a review, we never happened upon than is the notice of Powhatan, in Graham's Magazine."[87] On August 14, Poe wrote a relatively businesslike letter to Weld, requesting his autograph (for "A Chapter on Autography"), but he closed by conveying his own sense of mistreatment: "Should you grow weary, at any time, of abusing me in the 'Jonathan' for speaking what no man knows to be truth better than yourself, it would give me sincere pleasure to cultivate the friendship of the author of 'Corrected Proofs'" (O 1:303).[88] The matter would not be fully resolved.

On July 28, Mary Rogers, a young woman who had worked in a cigar store in New York City, was found dead in the Hudson River. Her death prompted extensive and sensational coverage in the New York newspapers, including *Brother Jonathan,* and the ongoing mystery would eventually prompt Poe's second Dupin tale, "The Mystery of Marie Rogêt," in which Poe would subtly hint at his rift with *Brother Jonathan*'s editor.

The August 1841 issue of *Graham's* included what Poe termed to Joseph E. Snodgrass "a paper ... which will please you" (O 1:297): "The Colloquy of Monos and Una," an imagining of life after death. Guided by analogy with sleep, dreaming or half-dreaming, and waking, Poe conceives what is inconceivable. The hypnagogic state becomes a path to the afterlife, in which a sense of being is succeeded by a sense of place and time. Here is an ultimate reaching, as in *Pym* and *Eureka,* but, in this instance, more quiescent and calm.

Poe anticipated the lead review in this issue in the same letter to Snodgrass: "Among the Reviews (for August) I have one which will, at least, surprise you. It is a *long* notice of a satire by a quondam Baltimorean L. A. Wilmer. You must get this satire and read it—it is really good—good in the old-fashioned Dryden style. It blazes away, too, to the right & left—sparing not. I have made it the text from which to preach a fire-&-fury sermon upon critical independence, and the general literary humbuggery of the day" (O 1:297).[89] Wilmer, who had so praised Poe in the 1838 poem "Ode XXX: To Edgar A. Poe," now mocked a range of authors in *The Quacks of Helicon,* from William Cullen Bryant to N. P. Willis. Poe faults Wilmer's excesses but admires "the talent, the fearlessness, and especially the *design* of this book."[90] Clearly for Poe, the literary assault was satisfying.

Poe closed the issue with the first supplement to "A Few Words on Secret Writing," titled simply "Secret Writing." He presents the cryptograph of F. W. Thomas's friend Charles S. Frailey, stating that he has solved it and challenging his readers to solve it, as well, with a promised award of a year's subscription to *Graham's* and another to the *Saturday Evening Post.* Though Poe does not present the solution, he does append a portion of a letter from Frailey confirming that he has indeed solved it. Poe would provide the solution in the October issue of the magazine.[91]

Probably bolstered by the response to his fiction in *Graham's,* Poe proposed to Lea & Blanchard on August 13 a new edition of his tales. It would have included *Tales of the Grotesque and Arabesque* and eight additional tales: in all likelihood the previously published "The Business Man," "The Man of the Crowd," "The Murders in the Rue Morgue," "A Descent into the Maelström," "The Island of the Fay," "The Colloquy of Monos and Una," and the imminent "Never Bet Your Head. A Moral Tale" and "Eleonora" (O 1:301–2). Poe suggested the very modest former terms of twenty complimentary copies. But the publisher, still not having made a profit on the original volumes, cordially and respectfully declined (H 17:101–2).

Attending to New York City newspaper treatments of the suspicious death of Mary Rogers—especially those of the August 14, 21, and 28 *Brother Jonathan*—Poe must have begun to think about having Monsieur Dupin resolve the matter. "The Mystery of Marie Rogêt" would be a long tale that would require extensive time to write.

Poe seems to have accommodated himself to his situation, writing to F. W. Thomas on September 1, "I am still jogging on in the same old way, and will probably remain with Graham, even if I start the 'Penn' in January." There is perhaps a mix of pride and envy in his noting, "Our success (Graham's I mean) is astonishing—we shall print 20,000 copies shortly. When he bought Burton out, the joint circulation was only 5000." And Poe still had high hopes for his own magazine: "I have had some excellent offers respecting the 'Penn' and it is more than probable that it will go on" (O 1:305).

He tried to help others professionally when he could. He obliged Griswold, newly returned from Boston to oversee the publication of *The Poets and Poetry of America*, by seeking biographical information from Thomas (O 1:304–5). He would also oblige Thomas, by inquiring about—and securing—the publication of his new song in Philadelphia (H 17:103; O 1:311–12). Griswold, of course, would be considering Poe's poems for his anthology, and Thomas would be trying to help Poe with regard to that imagined job in Washington (H 17:102).

Meanwhile, President Tyler—to be termed "His Accidency"—was about to veto the contentious bank bill, but first, on August 10, he signed the bankruptcy bill.[92] Poe would probably have been aware of this, and the bankruptcy bill would later provide him with much-needed relief. For now, though, he had regular employment. Shortly, the September issue of *Graham's* would be published.

It was here that appeared, for the first time, a lightly revised version of "To Helen" with the famous couplet "To the glory that was Greece—/ To the grandeur that was Rome."[93] Poe's reworking this poem ten years after its first publication is clear evidence of his patient artistry. It was here, too, that appeared Poe's burlesque "Never Bet Your Head. A Moral Tale," a send-up of the convention that literature must have a moral. (This work would itself be revised in future years.) Through his narrator, Poe mock-cautions against a current expression, "betting your head," by literalizing it. Comic protagonist Toby Dammit, who has made the unusual wager of his head, attempts to leap a turnstile from within a covered bridge and is decapitated by a horizontal support beam. The devil gathers up Toby's head and, presumably, his soul. H. Hastings Weld reprinted the piece in the September 4 issue of *Brother Jonathan*.[94]

Poe commented on this tale to Joseph E. Snodgrass on September 19, regarding his mention of the Transcendentalist magazine the *Dial,* "My slaps at it [the *Dial*] were only in a 'general way.' The tale in question is a mere Extravaganza levelled at no one in particular, but hitting right & left at things in general" (O 1:309). It was a "jeu d'esprit," involving the main character's "perte d'esprit."

The several reviews offer astute critiques. Perhaps most memorably, Poe states, "The successful novelist must, in the same manner [like the dramatist who provides a chorus], be careful to bring into view his *private* interest, sympathy, and opinion, in regard to his own creations."[95] This assertion may readily be applied to Poe's novel *Pym*—and to a number of his tales, as well, including "Eleonora," which was finally published at this time in *The Gift for 1842*.[96]

This tale richly relates the lives of the narrator Pyrros, his cousin Eleonora, and her mother in "the Valley of the Many-Coloured Grass." Poe writes, entrancingly:

> Hand in hand about this valley, for fifteen years, roamed I with Eleonora, before love entered within our hearts. It was one evening at the close of the third lustrum of her life, and of the fourth of my own, that we sat, locked in each other's embrace, beneath the serpent-like trees, and looked down within the waters of the River of Silence at our images therein. We spoke no words during the rest of that sweet day; and our words upon the morrow were tremulous and few.
>
> We had drawn the god Eros from that wave.[97]

Poe's "*private* interest" regarding "Eleonora" seems clear: he is telling of his life with his cousin Virginia and her mother, Maria Clemm, and the transformation of the two cousins into lovers. Though he could not explicitly render sexual love, he could offer its symbolic equivalent, the radiant metamorphosis of their sequestered world: the bursting "star-shaped" flowers, the springing "ruby-red asphodel," the "tall flamingo" of "scarlet plumage," the "golden and silver fish," and the "vast and voluminous cloud" of "crimson and gold."[98] The raptures of Pyrros and Eleonora are conveyed through their transformed surroundings.

But the "exceeding delicacy of her frame" and "the hues of her cheek" intimate her death, presumably by consumption. She reveals her fear that he will marry another, and he promises that he never will. Promising to watch over Pyrros, Eleonora then dies peacefully. And so ends the narrator's well-remembered first era. But his second era is uncertain, probably because Poe hadn't lived it. (We may remember a similar pattern in "Tamerlane.") Pyrros eventually leaves "the Valley of the Many-Coloured Grass" and meets, in the court of "a strange Eastern city," a maiden "from some far distant and unknown land," the beautiful Ermengarde, an imagined woman, a woman of fantasy. Pyrros falls in love, defies his vow to Eleonora, and marries Ermengarde. And Eleonora speaks to Pyrros from Heaven: "Sleep in peace; for the spirit of Love reigneth and ruleth; and in taking to thy passionate heart her who is Ermengarde, thou art absolved, for reasons which shall be made known to thee in Heaven, of the vows unto Eleonora."[99]

We may be mystified, yet the early reference by Pyrros to the riddle of the Sphinx encourages us to think that there is a solution. Perhaps Poe was inverting the idea "that two separate souls were enshrined within her"[100]— that is, that Eleonora and Ermengarde themselves shared one soul (as had, for instance, Roderick and Madeline Usher). So, in Heaven, Pyrros would learn that he had not betrayed Eleonora but rather loved her in another form.[101] This reading may be strengthened by evident linkings between the two women, suggestive of some kind of equivalence. Eleonora was "slender even to fragility," she had "naturally-waving auburn hair," "[t]he grace of her motion was surely ethereal. Her fantastic step left no impress upon the asphodel," and she had "alternate moods of melancholy and of mirth."[102] And similarly, Ermengarde was "a fair-haired and slender maiden," Pyrros admired "the wavy flow of her auburn tresses," he was enamored of "the fantastic grace of her step," and he remarked on "the radical transition from tears to smiles that I had wondered at in the long-lost Eleonora."[103] If the narrator thinks his love for Ermengarde is greater than that for Eleonora, he is only showing that he does not yet know, at the time of his second love, the secret that Eleonora will reveal (and that his language suggests)—that he has been faithful to the spirit of Eleonora, for Ermengarde is an embodiment of Eleonora, perhaps even sent to him by her. If—as we cannot know—Poe already feared for the health of his wife in early 1841, then perhaps "Eleonora" offered an advance consolation, one that eased the author in his fears of the loss of the love of his life. And, fittingly, Eleonora—Virginia—had the last word. Notably, despite soon writing that the tale was "not ended so well as it might be," Poe did not modify Eleonora's final reassurance in his subsequent revision (M 2:645).[104]

And it would seem that Poe was offering Virginia an easing, as well. The beautifully imagined setting of the story has been related to the Amity Street home in Baltimore where Poe, Virginia, and Mrs. Clemm once lived and to the nearby valley of Gwynn's Falls where Poe and Virginia may once have walked,[105] but it seems likelier that the model was John H. Mackenzie's farm south of Richmond, Darby Town. For it was here where Edgar and

Virginia, with the Mattox sisters, would go "roaming through the fields & woods together," where "he walked always hand in hand with Virginia." Flora Lapham Mack's mother, Mary Mattox Lapham, had said, after all, "that Virginia must in afterlife have looked back on the Saturday evenings she spent at Darbytown during this time[,] those evenings when Edgar came out to stay a day or two, as the happiest times of her whole life."[106] It may well be that, through "Eleonora," Poe was once again integrating his life in his work and thereby recovering for Virginia the "happiest times" and celebrating their love. This tale, appearing in *The Gift*, may well have been a gift for his wife—both a work of art and a work of love.

Through the fall of 1841, Poe kept "jogging on in the same old way." He remained with Graham, still hoping for "The Penn" and for Graham's support. He wrote in mid-September, "It is not impossible that Graham will join me in The 'Penn'" (O 1:309), and in late October, "Graham holds out a hope of his joining me [in the 'Penn'] in July" (O 1:313). Jesse E. Dow and Frederick W. Thomas encouraged Poe's plan for the monthly, the former writing about Poe in the newspaper the *Index*, of Alexandria, Virginia, "We trust that he will soon come out with his Penn Magazine," and the latter declaring to Poe in a letter, "I believe you can make the best Magazine extant."[107] Thomas also kept alive the possibility of Poe's securing a government job.[108]

Poe wrote in mid-September of his work on *Graham's*, "I merely write the Reviews, with a tale monthly, and read the last proofs" (O 1:307). But his routine could vary. He acknowledged in the same letter that he had been "absent from the city for some time" (O 1:306); indeed, a note in the October issue of *Graham's* reported, "Owing to the temporary absence of Mr. Poe, the reviews in this number are from another hand." It went on, "That department is exclusively under the control of Mr. Poe. C. J. Peterson, his coadjutor, has the charge of the other departments of the work."[109] The items by Poe in this issue were only two—a slightly expanded version of the poem "Israfel" and the second of his three supplements to "A Few Words on Secret Writing," again titled "Secret Writing." Here he solved a cipher of one "Timotheus Whackemwell" and another, which he had mentioned in the August essay, by Dr. Charles S. Frailey—according to William K. Wimsatt Jr., "the most difficult which Poe ever solved."[110] Clearly, Frailey did not strictly follow the rules of a substitution cipher, nor did he eschew obfuscation. (His decoded message began, "In one of those peripatetic circumrotations I obviated a rustic whom I subjected to catechetical interrogation respecting the nosocomical characteristics of the edifice to which I was approximate.")[111] But Poe worked out the cipher and its key phrase, "*But find this out and I give it up,*" and he printed Frailey's entire validating letter.[112] Back at *Graham's,* after his absence, Poe focused on continuing his two lively "Autography" pieces from the February 1836 and August 1836 *Southern Literary Messenger,* analyses of the handwriting of various literati. And he continued with his reviews. The November 1841 issue of *Graham's* was ready before October 19.[113]

"A Chapter on Autography" comprised two installments, appearing in the November and December 1841 issues of *Graham's Magazine,* followed by an appendix in the January 1842 issue. The first installment included forty-one autograph facsimiles, with comment; the second, sixty-seven, with comment, as well. Poe gathered the assorted autographs to show what he could gather from them. His judgments of the autographs easily slid into judgments of authors and their works. There was a confident confidentiality that could intrigue or antagonize. A sampling of his lively remarks in this installment would include his assessment of N. P. Willis—"It has been the fate of this gentleman to be alternately condemned *ad infinitum,* and lauded *ad nauseam*—a fact which speaks much in his praise"; his appraisal of Henry Wadsworth Longfellow—"His good qualities are all of the highest order, while his sins are chiefly those of affectation and imitation—an imitation sometimes verging upon downright theft"; and his estimate of John Neal—"Any one, from Mr. Neal's penmanship, might suppose his mind to be what it really is—excessively flighty and irregular, but active and energetic."[114] A reader might consider Poe's judgments to be candid and discerning or arrogant and obnoxious. They were genuine, yet also designed to stir things up, which they did.

Seven reviews followed, all perceptive. The review of Samuel Warren's novel *Ten Thousand a Year* is especially noteworthy since here Poe writes, "It appears to us that a main source of the interest which this book possesses for the mass, is to be referred to the *pecuniary* nature of its theme. From beginning to end it is an affair of pounds, shillings, and pence—a topic which comes home at least *as* immediately to the bosoms and business of mankind, as any which could be selected."[115] He may be beginning to think about trying the topic himself—and he would provide an exceptional treatment in his 1843 tale "The Gold-Bug."[116]

Back home, Virginia was "very anxious" to see a copy of F. W. Thomas's new song ["Oh! Blame Her Not"] since his earlier work "'Tis Said That Absence' &c" ["Conquers Love" (H 17:98)]—about the endurance of love despite absence—"is a great favorite with her," according to Poe (O 1:312–15).

Apparently, Poe wrote later that, having seen the new piece, Virginia was not pleased with the music. Thomas graciously commented, "I am sorry that your lady likes not the music to which my song is married.... I like 'Virginia's' frankness [presumably, given the quotation marks, Poe's own], my dear friend, as I have always liked yours."[117]

At the office, Poe was working on the December issue and, as usual, reading the periodical press, including "Three Thursdays in a Week" in the *Public Ledger*. He also solicited a poem from Lydia H. Sigourney (O 1:315–16) and an article from N. P. Willis. (Sigourney agreed to provide the poem, but Willis declined to provide the article, owing to his commitment to Louis A. Godey.)[118] And Poe received letters regarding cryptographs from Richard Bolton and W. B. Tyler, responding at least to Bolton, acknowledging his correspondent's solution of the Frailey cryptograph (which Poe acknowledged in the December *Graham's,* as well, though contesting the solution privately in a letter to Thomas [O 1:318–22]).[119] According to Poe's letter to Bolton, dated November 18, the December issue "has been quite ready for ten days" (O 1:318); it is noticed as early as November 25.[120]

Poe offered in that issue the second installment of "A Chapter on Autography," claiming in the introduction that "no Magazine paper has ever excited greater interest than the one now concluded." He contended that "[t]o all readers it has seemed to be welcome—but especially to those who themselves dabble in the waters of Helicon [i.e., poets]:—to those and their innumerable friends."[121] Despite favorable notices, this judgment was to prove incorrect. Poe was faulted by Edwin P. Whipple for favoring those associated with his magazine—"[I]t is well to know that the path to immortality lies through Graham's Magazine."[122] And Poe lamented that he did yield to Graham's occasional urging to be gentler (O 1:325). Poe concluded, "Know better next time. Let no man accuse me of leniency again" (O 1:326).[123] But Poe was also accused of harshness. For instance, the poet Thomas Holley Chivers wrote to Poe, evidently complaining of Poe's treatment of him in "A Chapter on Autography" (O 1:349). (Poe had begun, "Dr. Thomas Holley Chivers, of New York, is at the same time one of the best and one of the worst poets in America.")[124] And, probably unknown to Poe, one "T," writing in the *Hampshire Gazette* (of Northampton, Massachusetts), defended the renowned New England poet John Greenleaf Whittier against the charge that he was "remarkably deficient" "in *imagination*," arguing rather that "[t]he conceited ignorance, and flippant dandyism of the article, place the intellectual and literary character of the writer [Poe] beyond all doubt."[125] The very strengths of "A Chapter on Autography"—its "vinegar and sweet sauce,"[126] as Jesse E. Dow had it—were its very clear vulnerabilities.

The subsequent reviews reveal Poe's usual critical skill, but the piece on secret writing suggests limits to his cryptographic skill, at least in the time available. Poe declined to solve W. B. Tyler's two cryptographs in his letter because "[o]ur time is much occupied." Tyler, who termed Poe "the king of 'secret readers,'" presented his two ciphers to challenge Poe's view that all ciphers may be solved. It would seem that presenting Tyler's ciphers and not solving them did not serve Poe's purpose, but the young editor presented the ciphers anyway, inviting his readers to solve them.[127]

One hundred and fifty years later, Terence Whalen solved the first Tyler puzzle. He solved for the word "the," worked out the other letter substitutions, reversed the decoding, and presented the solution, concerning the immortality of the soul.[128] John A. Hodgson also solved this puzzle and recognized the passage to have been drawn from Joseph Addison's play *Cato*. He argued—persuasively, I think—that W. B. Tyler was not Poe.[129] And 159 years later, a Toronto software expert, Gil Broza, worked out the text of the second Tyler puzzle, an excessively florid piece with a remaining mystery. Discovery of earlier newspaper versions of the piece helped clarify the closing double pun. A young woman asks her lover not to pull the curtain against the sun for she would prefer "a little sun than no air at all." The newspaper versions italicize "sun" and "air," making absolutely clear what Tyler had made absolutely unclear: the passage concerns the desire for a son, an heir.[130] Poe had written of the cipher, "of its impenetrability we are by no means sure."[131] It turns out that his doubt was fully justified.

The December 1841 issue of *Graham's* closed with "The Closing Year," but there were actually many weeks left to go. Poe was working on the January 1842 number and had "made a definite engagement with Graham for 1842" (O 1:313). Despite his salary, he incurred a debt of $104, due in three months, to a local tailor.[132] Later bankruptcy papers suggest that Poe was spending too freely.

Probably at this time he was still planning "The Mystery of Marie Rogêt." And on November 27, he published in the *Saturday Evening Post* the comic tale "A Succession of Sundays." The idea (based on "Three Thursdays in a Week")[133] was that for different people—several staying home, one man having circumnavigated the world west and returned after a year (Pratt), and one man having circumnavigated the world east and returned after a year (Smitherton)—Sunday would be considered three different days. Poe used this anomaly as the means of fulfilling the arbitrary demand of grudging, curmudgeonly great-uncle Rumgudgeon for the marriage of his daughter and her cousin to take place.

What is particularly interesting here is Poe's again embedding his life in his work. We may readily identify the "little, pursy, pompous, passionate, semicircular somebody, with a red nose, a thick scull, a long purse, and a strong sense of his own consequence," he who has a "repugnance to 'the humanities,'" as John Allan. The narrator tells us that, having been given to Rumgudgeon by his dying parents, "I had lived with the old gentleman all my life." He reviews his upbringing: "From my first year until my fifth he obliged me with very regular floggings. From five to fifteen he threatened me hourly with the House of Correction. From fifteen to twenty not a day passed in which he did not swear a round oath that he would cut me off with a shilling." With this last detail, Poe may well have been alluding to Allan's response to Poe's possibly marrying Mary Starr. Furthermore, "[M]y own inkling for the Muses excited his entire displeasure."[134] There is no doubt humorous exaggeration in the narrator's comments, but they must have been prompted for Poe by the old, enduring pain of his foster father's conduct toward him. The weight of John Allan had not been lifted by his death.

From the fall of 1841 through April 1842, Poe's defender John S. Du Solle—"well known," Poe had written, "through his connection with the 'Spirit of the Times'"[135]—employed a nineteen-year-old assistant editor, George Lippard, who then published a series of articles against the banking system and another against Dickens-mania. The reform-minded young man, later the author of popular novels, became a friend to Poe, praising his work, corresponding with him, and, in July 1849, crucially assisting him on his sad final visit to Philadelphia. Lippard would be considered by Poe as a possible subscriber or contributor to his long-planned magazine. Notably, Lippard would write admiringly about Poe in the newspaper the *Citizen Soldier,* "He is, perhaps, the most original writer that ever existed in America."[136]

By early December 1841, Poe was probably finishing work on the January 1842 issue of *Graham's,* which came out shortly before the end of the year.[137] All his contributions were nonfiction. He closed out the "Autography" series with "An Appendix of Autographs," maintaining with regard to his judgments, "[T]he voice of him who maintains fearlessly what he believes honestly, is pretty sure to find an echo (if the speaker be not mad) in the vast heart of the world at large."[138] Notably, however, the public also responded to Ralph Waldo Emerson, of whom Poe wrote, "Mr. Ralph Waldo Emerson belongs to a class of gentlemen with whom we have no patience whatever—the mystics for mysticism's sake."[139]

The introduction to the reviews, now titled "Exordium," warned against subservience to England on one hand and nationalism on the other. Deprecating generality in criticism, Poe advised (as noted earlier), "The analysis of a book is a matter of time and of mental exertion. For many classes of composition there is required a deliberate perusal, with notes, and subsequent generalization."[140] He was recommending no theoretical approach but a traditional concentration on the text, a close reading. He argued at the conclusion for a critic to possess "a talent for analysis and a solemn indifference to abuse."[141] Of the twelve reviews and notices, the first of these, the review of Henry Cockton's novel *Stanley Thorn,* is the most important, in large part because of the angry attack it provoked. Poe would surely need "a solemn indifference to abuse."

Poe stated that *Stanley Thorn* did not warrant critical attention because it was shallow and derivative—not "literature," not a work of art, not "*suggestive*," not "thoughtful"—merely, for some, a conventional amusing amalgam. Poe wrote, with his usual boldness, "It [*Stanley Thorn*] not only demands no reflection, but repels it, or dissipates it—much as a silver rattle the wrath of a child."[142] But Poe's maintaining fearlessly what he believed honestly could provoke wrath. On January 3, 1842, an unidentified reviewer for New York's *Evening Tattler,* unaware (or pretending to be unaware) of the identity of the *Graham's* writer, defended "that excellent and very popular novel 'Stanley Thorn,'" terming its condemner "a critical jack ass," "some atrocious blockhead," "a fool and a coxcomb," imagined to be "an envious, disagreeable, and inordinately conceited person, who, being disappointed in earning a reputable distinction for himself; turns round and expectorates the gall of his malice upon successful genius or talent wherever he can find it," "rather in the likeness of a hag than a man," like "an excited blue bottle fly ... on the horn of a rhinoceros." He went on to label the *Graham's* writer "a nincompoop," "the noodle," and added, relying on *Macbeth* (3.4.78), "Beyond doubt the Philadelphian is a living miracle, for is it not written that when the brains are out the man will die." Notwithstanding the heaping of insults here, the justice of Poe's critical opinion seems fair, and, not surprisingly, *Stanley Thorn* has long been forgotten. Indeed, it is Poe's critical opinion that endures.[143]

This may be a good moment to pause, before the onset of Virginia's illness. There were certainly significant tensions in Poe's life—between his high aspiration and his actual attainment, between his dream magazine and the fripperies of *Graham's*, between financial independence and his modest means and real indebtedness. And, of course, Poe carried painful memories of loss—and of his foster father's mistreatment of him. Still, he was successful as a magazine editor, notably increasing the reputation of *Graham's*—and his own, as well. He was writing admired tales and had a promising work in progress, the second Dupin tale, "The Mystery of Marie Rogêt." His criticism was acute, if sometimes controversial, arguably effectively upholding standards for American letters. He provided his regular pay from *Graham's* to Maria Clemm, who ran the Poe household, and he devoted himself to the well-being of his wife and her mother. He was impatient but had hopes—perhaps Graham would join him in "The Penn"; perhaps Thomas would help him secure a government position. And, as far as we know, Poe at this time was limiting his drinking. Somehow, he seems to have been managing to manage. But he would soon be unable to do so.

In December 1841 and early January 1842, Poe would have been writing critical pieces for the February issue of *Graham's*. In mid-January, he received correspondence—from Richard Bolton and Frederick W. Thomas. On January 19, Poe turned thirty-three. And on or near January 20, his wife, while singing one evening, coughed blood. According to one account, she "nearly bled to death on the spot."[144] So began Virginia's repeated dire health crises, over a five-year period, culminating in her death. The cause was consumption—tuberculosis.

On February 3, Poe confided to his friend Frederick W. Thomas what had happened: "My dear little wife has been dangerously ill. About a fortnight since, in singing, she ruptured a blood-vessel, and it was only on yesterday that the physicians gave me any hope of her recovery. You might imagine the agony I have suffered, for you know how devotedly I love her. But to-day the prospect brightens, and I trust that this bitter cup of misery will not be my portion" (O 1:324). Poe seems to be avoiding the word "consumption" or "tuberculosis," but he knew, nonetheless, the seriousness of her condition. Nearly a year after her death in 1847, Poe returned to the events of early 1842—the beginning of "the terrible evil"—in a letter to his inquiring correspondent George W. Eveleth: "Six years ago, a wife, whom I loved as no man ever loved before, ruptured a blood-vessel in singing. Her life was despaired of. I took leave of her forever & underwent all the agonies of her death. She recovered partially and I again hoped" (O 2:641). Amanda Bartlett Harris remembered what she had been told about the calamitous situation in the Poes' cottage: "[T]he room where she lay for weeks, hardly able to breathe except as she was fanned, was a little place with the ceiling so low over the narrow bed that her head almost touched it. But no one dared to speak—Mr. Poe was so sensitive and irritable; 'quick as steel and flint,' said one who knew him in those days. And he would not allow a word about the danger of her dying—the mention of it drove him wild."[145]

There is a story about Virginia's later halting recovery in Philadelphia that has been considered apocryphal, but given the nature of the symptoms of her illness and Flora Lapham Mack's account of "Edgar the immortal climbing the trees for fruit" at Darby Town, it seems credible and worth mentioning. A little girl from Poe's neighborhood in Philadelphia witnessed a relapse: "Passing the house one day she saw Poe in a cherry tree in the garden, throwing down cherries to Virginia, who was dressed in white. Suddenly while she was laughing and stretching her arms, Virginia had a hemorrhage. The child, terrified, ran home without pausing to see any more."[146]

The bitter cup of misery was, indeed, to be Poe's portion.

16

"As Regards Myself—
I Will Probably Succeed Too"

1842

For a while longer, Poe stayed with *Graham's*. His contributions to the February 1842 issue—doubtless written well before the onset of Virginia's illness—included incisive analyses of John G. C. Brainard's *Poems* and Cornelius Mathews's *Wakondah*, and, more appreciatively, Charles Dickens's *Barnaby Rudge*. Poe quotes in the Dickens review his May 1, 1841, piece on *Barnaby Rudge* from the *Saturday Evening Post*, and he returns to his focus on the raven itself, stating, "Its croakings might have been *prophetically* heard in the course of the drama."[1]

Even as Barnaby's raven must have been suggestive for Poe, so, very likely, was the language of a poem by James Russell Lowell appearing in the February issue of *Graham's*, "Rosaline." (Burton R. Pollin and Jeffrey A. Savoye have observed connections, as well [O 1:369].) The work conveys the abiding guilt of the speaker, who plaintively apostrophizes the woman of modest means whom he married and evidently murdered. Especially notable are two late couplets: "Thine eyes are shut. they nevermore / Will leap thy gentle words before" and "Thy voice I nevermore shall hear, / Which in old times did seem so dear."[2] The word "nevermore" appeared in a variety of literary works, but its appearance twice in "Rosaline" in a magazine that Poe helped edit would certainly have contributed to his coming use of the word in "The Raven." This conjecture tends to be supported by Poe's positive mention of the poem in his criticism, in his correspondence, and in his conversation.[3]

After the initial recovery of Virginia, Poe must have remained "sensitive and irritable." He later acknowledged, "I am constitutionally sensitive—nervous in a very unusual degree" (O 2:641). Any symptom of her illness would have shaken him. His employer, George R. Graham, later recalled, "His love for his wife was a sort of rapturous worship of the spirit of beauty which he felt was fading before his eyes. I have seen him hovering around her when she was ill, with all the fond fear and tender anxiety of a mother for her first-born—her slightest cough causing in him a shudder, a heart-chill that was visible."[4] And perhaps there was a resonance with a time Graham wouldn't have known—Poe's tending his sick brother Henry in the summer of 1831.

Just when Poe returned to drink we do not know—perhaps his regular employment made possible some resistance. But neither his employment nor his resistance would last.

Poe's February 3 letter to Frederick W. Thomas reveals his concerns beyond Virginia's health, including finances (Graham wouldn't advance his salary despite his having helped increase the magazine's circulation), the "Penn Magazine" (perhaps Robert Tyler would support it), and *Barnaby Rudge* (he had anticipated its plot) (O 1:324–27). Charles Dickens had arrived in Boston on January 22 and was grandly fêted there and in New York. While Philadelphia made big plans for his arrival and George Lippard attacked the widespread Dickens obsession, Poe featured Dickens-related material in *Graham's* and probably had already resolved to request an interview.[5]

The March issue of *Graham's* offered Poe's poem "To One Departed" (formerly "To Mary"), as well as several reviews. Poe shows the inadequacy of Charles Lever's popular but ordinary novel *Charles O'Malley*, the merits of Henry Wadsworth Longfellow's *Ballads and Other Poems* (even with its objectionable didacticism), and the problems with *The Critical and Miscellaneous Writings of Henry Lord Brougham* (though the brilliance of Brougham himself). This last point is important in light of the man's significance in "The Purloined Letter." The notices are not notable, except for the brief mention of Nathaniel's Hawthorne's children's book *Famous Old People*. A comment there deserves attention for its promise of criticism to come: "Hereafter we shall endeavor to speak of his tales with that deliberation which is their due."[6]

Meanwhile, Poe wished to speak of his own tales with the visiting lion, Charles Dickens. He wrote a letter of inquiry, accompanied by books and papers—presumably including the two-volume *Tales of the Grotesque and Arabesque* and his reviews of Dickens. The British writer, staying at the United

States Hotel, invited the American writer to visit: "I shall be very glad to see you whenever you will do me the favor to call," suggesting "between half-past eleven and twelve" (H 17:107). It was probably Monday, March 7, that the two men met for what Poe later termed "two long interviews" (O 1:450). Dickens was barely thirty and already at the peak of literary fame. Poe, older by three years, was still seeking such eminence. We may only imagine the genial, elegant host and his intense, self-possessed guest. From later documents, we may infer that they discussed American poetry: Poe apparently brought a prepublication copy of Griswold's *Poets and Poetry of America;* he read to Dickens a poem by Ralph Waldo Emerson, "To the Humble-Bee," a paean to that "Voyager of light and noon / Epicurean of June."[7] The two men would likely have discussed international copyright; Poe probably invited Dickens to contribute to *Graham's.* Clearly Poe asked him to try to secure a British publisher for *Tales of the Grotesque and Arabesque*—or, even likelier, an expanded version of those volumes. And Dickens agreed.[8]

Poe later followed up with a letter in early June, before the British writer's departure from New York to England. Five months later, without having placed Poe's book and with his obligation apparently weighing on him, Dickens asked his publisher Edward Moxon for a letter to send to Poe, one that would make possible "absolution for my conscience in this matter."[9] Moxon furnished such a letter, and Dickens sent it on to Poe with his own gracious letter, explaining that he had failed in his effort and closing thoughtfully, "Do not for a moment suppose that I have ever thought of you but with a pleasant recollection; and that I am not at all times prepared to forward your views in this country, if I can" (H 17:125). Though the meeting of Poe and Dickens did not yield Poe's object, a British edition of his tales, it did apparently provide brief literary fellowship.

Probably by the time of Dickens's visit to Philadelphia, Poe would have completed his work on the April number of *Graham's;* during March he would have been working on "The Mask of the Red Death," "The Pit and the Pendulum," and several reviews for the May number.[10]

The April 1842 issue of *Graham's Magazine* was well received. The *New Orleans Time-Picayune* stated of it on March 27, "Its contents, in a literary point of view, are of a superior order," and the *New York Tribune* concurred on April 2: "The literary contents of this number are unusually good." On the same day, the *Baltimore Saturday Visiter* characterized the April issue as "admirable." And both the *Tribune* and the *Saturday Visiter* praised Poe's work in particular.[11]

Poe's tale in the April issue was "Life in Death" (later titled "The Oval Portrait"). The two-page Gothic work recounts a wounded man's settling into the turret of an elaborately appointed mansion, taking opium, and contemplating paintings as he reads a book of commentary about them. Upon seeing one painting, which had been in the dark, the narrator/protagonist closes his eyes and then opens them. And he looks again upon the portrait of a woman, rendered with singular "*life-likeliness* of expression,"[12] and reads of the artist's painting his lover and thereby taking her life.

It was evidently a painting by Poe's friend Robert M. Sully that had suggested the tale.[13] And Poe's having recently written about Virginia in "Eleonora" and her having become seriously ill bear a rough resonance with the artist's portraying his bride in a painting and her dying. Clearly there is a great sadness in the subject. But there is also a beauty in the symmetry of the form. That symmetry is suggested by Poe's use of such words and phrases as "half filled," "half and half," "half-slumber," "half sitting, half reclining," and "half-parted."[14]

The symmetrical frame is subtle but discernible. The critical phrases and clauses in the first half are "Life in Death," "prevented me from perceiving," "remote turret of the building," "a small volume . . . which purported to criticise and describe them" ["these pictures"], "The position of the candelabrum displeased me," and "the portrait of a young girl." The mirroring phrases in the second half are "The portrait, I have already said, was that of a young girl," "I replaced the candelabrum in its former position," "the volume which discussed the paintings and their histories," "high turret-chamber," "he *would* not see," and "indeed *Life*" and "indeed Death."[15]

At the center, in the fourth paragraph of seven paragraphs, the narrator/protagonist closes and opens his eyes: "I glanced at the painting hurriedly, and then closed my eyes" and "In a very few moments I again looked fixedly at the painting."[16] Here we may be reminded of the opened and closed window at the center of "The Murders in the Rue Morgue." Again there is irony, for a tale about seeing is built around not seeing.

The narrator/protagonist articulates the purpose of his closed eyes: "It was an impulsive movement to gain time for thought—to make sure that my vision had not deceived me—to calm and subdue my fancy for a more sober and more certain gaze."[17] Here, it may be, Poe is intimating his own interior state: he is trying to understand and to come to terms with what he has seen. We may infer, however, that it is not the "*life-likeliness* of expression" of a young girl that had such power for Poe (as it did have for his narrator) but rather the possibility of his young wife's death. The implicit becomes explicit by the tale's end. And the balance of the painter's rendering life and his taking life is reflected by the balance of the tale's language.

A critical triumph for Poe in the April 1842 issue was his second and longer review of Longfellow's *Ballads and Other Poems*. Here, to provide the basis for his judgment of the poems, Poe elaborates his sense of poetry as a response to a "burning thirst": "This burning thirst belongs to the *immortal* essence of man's nature. It is equally a consequence and an indication of his perennial life. It is the desire of the moth for the star." Poe alludes thus to Percy Bysshe Shelley's poem "To—" ("One word is too often profaned"). And he continues his ascent:

> It is not the mere appreciation of the beauty before us. It is a wild effort to reach the beauty above. It is a forethought of the loveliness to come. It is a passion to be satiated by no sublunary sights, or sounds, or sentiments, and the soul thus athirst strives to allay its fever in futile efforts at *creation*. Inspired with a prescient ecstasy of the beauty beyond the grave, it struggles by multiform novelty of combination among the things and thoughts of Time, to anticipate some portion of that loveliness whose very elements, perhaps, appertain solely to Eternity. And the result of such effort, on the part of souls fittingly constituted, is alone what mankind have agreed to denominate Poetry.[18]

We may recall, perhaps, "The extacies above" from Poe's "Israfel" (M 1:174) and "the Hope of a higher Intellectual Happiness hereafter" from Poe's Drake-Halleck review (P 5:166). And if we also recall from our own reading experience any momentary frisson, what Poe later terms in "The Poetic Principle," regarding music, "A shivering delight" (L2:184), then we may gain a hint of Poe's sense of the purpose of poetry.

Poe returns to Longfellow in the longer review of *Ballads and Other Poems* by way of the old ballads and those of Thomas Moore. Perhaps here Poe was remembering Virginia and John H. Mackenzie's singing Moore's "The Last Rose of Summer" at Darby Town. He discusses thoughtfully Longfellow's poems "The Village Blacksmith," "The Wreck of the Hesperus," and "The Skeleton in Armor" and closes movingly with Longfellow's treatment of a valiant mountain-climber's ascent to his death, the poem "Excelsior":

> It depicts the *earnest upward impulse of the soul*—an impulse not to be subdued even in Death. Despising danger, resisting pleasure, the youth,

bearing the banner inscribed "*Excelsior!*" (higher still!) struggles through all difficulties to an Alpine summit. Warned to be content with the elevation attained, his cry is still "*Excelsior!*" And, even in falling dead on the highest pinnacle, his cry is *still "Excelsior!"* There is yet an immortal height to be surmounted—an ascent in Eternity. The poet holds in view the idea of never-ending *progress*.[19]

There is a keenness of appreciation here. Longfellow has conveyed in this poem a version of the very yearning to which, according to Poe, poetry responds.[20]

It is not surprising that young Charles J. Peterson, fellow editor at *Graham's*, wrote to Lowell on April 1, 1842, "By the Bye read Poe's review on Longfellow. It is, in my opinion, the most masterly critique, as a whole, I ever saw from an American pen."[21] And the reaching that Poe so values is not necessarily confined to poetry—we need only recall or reread the final journal entry of *Arthur Gordon Pym*.

A suggestion of additional critical esteem appears in a short review of *Twice-Told Tales,* by Nathaniel Hawthorne. Poe closes, "Upon the whole we look upon him as one of the few men of indisputable genius to whom our country has as yet given birth. As such, it will be our delight to do him honor; and lest, in these undigested and cursory remarks, without proof and without explanation, we should appear to do him *more* honor than is his due, we postpone all farther comment until a more favorable opportunity."[22] Perhaps the crisis in Virginia's health had helped prompt Poe's literary rising. Perhaps it had vitally intensified both his aspiration and his quest for consolation—and his recognition of both in other writers.

On March 31, 1842, Poe received $58, his last payment for his editorial work at *Graham's*. And on April 1, he stepped down from his position.[23] He explained to his friend Thomas, on May 25, "My reason for resigning was disgust with the namby-pamby character of the Magazine—a character which it was impossible to eradicate—I allude to the contemptible pictures, fashion-plates, music and love tales. The salary, moreover, did not pay me for the labor which I was forced to bestow. With Graham who is really a very gentlemanly, although an exceedingly weak man, I had no misunderstanding" (O 1:333). He subsequently noted to the poet and postmaster Daniel Bryan that Graham had not fulfilled his promise to support the "Penn Magazine." Faulting Graham's "want of faith" and his own "folly," Poe clarified, "In fact, I was continually laboring against myself. Every exertion made by myself for the benefit of 'Graham', by rendering that Mag: a greater source of profit, rendered its owner, at the same time, less willing to keep his word with me" (O 1:346–47). Still, there is also the possibility that Poe's drinking may have contributed to his departure. His friend and later partner Thomas Cottrell Clarke wrote about that departure, "His unfortunate habit led to a separation."[24]

Whatever the reason or combination of reasons, Poe, already significantly in debt, was now without his monthly editorial income. For the rest of 1842, according to John Ward Ostrom, Poe earned from his freelance writing a mere $121.25.[25] He was in trouble.

After that April 1 break with *Graham's,* Poe did initially write—he seems to have composed "The Landscape-Garden" at this time (M 2:701). We cannot be sure if Poe returned to drink immediately.

The May issue of *Graham's,* Poe's last, featured "The Mask of the Red Death. A Fantasy"—one of Poe's most popular tales, all-too-relevant in recent years, given COVID-19. It concerns the effort of Prince Prospero and his thousand friends, during a plague, to revel in place. This is a tale of hubris defeated, for the Red Death enters the supposedly inviolable abbey and vanquishes both revel and revelers: "And Darkness and Decay and the Red Death held illimitable dominion over all."[26]

This work might have been suggested, in part, by disease in cities where Poe had lived—typhus fever in London in 1817, yellow fever in Charleston in 1828, and cholera in Baltimore in 1832. And literary works surely played a role, as well, including the Bible, the sixteenth letter of N. P. Willis's "Pencillings by the Way" (M 2:668), and Nathaniel Hawthorne's "Howe's Masquerade" and "Lady Eleanore's Mantle."[27] What Poe achieved in his transformative tale is extraordinary. He brilliantly conveys, through diction and cadence and sound, through motion and color and tone, a sense of apocalyptic inevitability. And notably, the phrases "Red Death" frame the parallel passages about the seven colored rooms, which frame the central phrases "other apartments," appearing at the end of the seventh paragraph and the beginning of the eighth paragraph in a tale of fourteen paragraphs. The characteristic symmetrical form effectively fortifies Poe's sleek chronicle of ruin, his sublime warning.[28]

This classic tale in the May issue is complemented by a classic review—the second and fuller treatment of Hawthorne's *Twice-Told Tales.* Poe does make a misstep when he considers "Howe's Masquerade" derivative of "William Wilson"—Hawthorne's tale came first—and Poe's reading of "The Minister's Black Veil" seems questionable, but the review is otherwise compelling for its delineation of the power of the tale, its commentary on many Hawthorne tales, and its tribute to Hawthorne, culminating in a series of accolades: "The style is purity itself. Force abounds. High imagination gleams from every page. Mr. Hawthorne is a man of the truest genius."[29] Poe recognized his literary brother.

By late May, the Poe family had moved to northeast Philadelphia, to what he later described as "a very pretty and convenient house, just built, in Coates Street, not far from Fairmount." A photograph shows it to be a three-story brick building.[30] The dampness of the earlier house, after the rains, had prompted the family to leave.[31] Poe wrote to his friend Frederick W. Thomas on May 25, "I am rejoiced to say that my dear little wife is much better, and I have strong hope of her ultimate recovery" (O 1:333–34).[32] But by early June, she was sick again.

Poe wrote to James Herron, a civil engineer whom he may have known in Richmond, "You have learned, perhaps, that I have retired from 'Graham's Magazine'. The state of my mind has, in fact, forced me to abandon for the present, all mental exertion. The renewed and hopeless illness of my wife, ill health on my own part, and pecuniary embarrassments, have nearly driven me to distraction. My only hope of relief is the 'Bankrupt Act', of which I shall avail myself as soon as possible." He closes by returning to Virginia's illness: "Mrs. Poe is again dangerously ill with hemorrhage from the lungs. It is folly to hope" (O 1:335–36).

Promised a position at the Custom House and evidently then without the means to seek bankruptcy (O 1:336), Poe would not make the necessary petition until December. But, meanwhile, the consequences of his near-distraction were clear. *Graham's* editor Charles J. Peterson wrote to James Russell Lowell on May 31, "I suppose you know Poe has left us. He's a splendid fellow, but 'unstable as water.'" In other words, Poe was drinking.[33]

Poe was always susceptible. Whatever restraint he had been able to muster was overcome by Virginia's precarious health and his precarious finances. He later wrote to George W. Eveleth that Virginia's repeated illness—and his own "horrible never-ending oscillation between hope & despair"—drove him insane, leading to drink, "God only knows how often or how much" (O 2:641). And his poverty was a torment, as well—especially when he had no job. George R. Graham asserted, "[W]hen he was fairly at sea, connected permanently with no publication, he suffered all the horrors of prospective destitution, with scarcely the ability of providing for immediate necessities; and at such moments, alas! the tempter often came." Graham observed, as well, "Pride, self-reproach, want, weariness, drove him to seek excitement, perhaps forgetfulness, in wine; and the least drop of wine, to most men a moderate stimulus, was to him literally the cup of frenzy."[34] Perhaps it was at this time, the late spring or early summer of 1842—or in the months soon following—that Thomas Dunn English came upon a drunken Poe in the street.[35]

In 1836, after a spree in Richmond, Poe would reply to John H. Mackenzie's "indignation" by saying that "he was ashamed of himself & he wished he was dead." Doubtless, shame would follow a spree in Philadelphia, as well. Graham acknowledged of Poe, "[I]n his better moods, he was afflicted with fits of utter disconsolateness, despondency, penitence, and self-abasement." Poe's addiction was a terror equal to some of the terrors in his fiction. Fortunately, his love and Virginia's and Maria Clemm's sustained the family, even through the grimmer times.[36]

Poe was succeeded at *Graham's Magazine* in May by Rufus Wilmot Griswold, whose *Poets and Poetry of America* had been published by Carey & Hart in April. The volume included Poe's "The Coliseum," "The Haunted Palace," and "The Sleeper." The anthology was very successful, but Poe was unimpressed: he wrote to the *Baltimore Saturday Visiter* editor Joseph E. Snodgrass, "It is a most outrageous humbug, and I sincerely wish you would 'use it up'" (O 1:341). Regarding the addition of Griswold to the *Graham's* staff, Charles J. Peterson wrote Lowell, "A more suitable person we could not have obtained."[37] But he would come to change his mind. By contrast, Jesse E. Dow, editor of the newspaper the *Index,* wrote, "We would give more for Edgar A. Poe's toe nail, than we would for Rueful Grizzle's soul, unless we wanted a milk-strainer. Them's our sentiments."[38]

On June 4, Poe wrote queries regarding the possible publication of "The Mystery of Marie Rogêt." Probably in light of his surreptitious criticism of H. Hastings Weld in that tale, he sought to avoid cities where Weld had particular friends, New York (where Weld had edited *Brother Jonathan* and the *Evening Tattler*) and Philadelphia (where Weld would soon be invited to edit the *Saturday Evening Post*). So Poe wrote to George Roberts of the *Boston Notion,* the aforementioned Joseph E. Snodgrass of the *Baltimore Saturday Visiter,* and perhaps Thomas W. White or Matthew F. Maury of Richmond's *Southern Literary Messenger* (O 1:337–43; 2:1206–7). However, his overtures were not successful. Poe decided to try again an earlier effort, to interest a publisher in an expanded collection of his tales. This collection would be called "Phantasy-Pieces."[39]

The book was never published, but the handwritten title page and table of contents may be found in Poe's annotated copy of the first volume of *Tales of the Grotesque and Arabesque.* The title page shows that the set was initially imagined to comprise three volumes and was then shifted to two. It also shows that Poe added thirteen recent tales to the earlier collection: "The Murders in the Rue Morgue," "A Descent into the Mäelström," "The Colloquy of Monos and Una," "The Business Man," "The Mask of the Red Death," "Never Bet Your Head," "Eleonora," "A Succession of Sundays," "The Man of the Crowd," "The Pit and the Pendulum," "Life in Death," "The Island of the Fay," and "The Mystery of Marie Rogêt." But he then crossed out the titles of the as-yet-unpublished "The Pit and the Pendulum" and "The Mystery of Marie Rogêt." And he revised a few of the old titles toward clarity and vividness—for example, "Metzengerstein" became "The Horse-Shade," "A Tale of Jerusalem" became "A Pig Tale," and "Berenice" became "The Teeth."[40]

Poe traveled to New York City on or shortly before June 24 to obtain a job and to place "Phantasy-Pieces," but he failed in both efforts.[41] He may have succeeded in selling "The Mystery of Marie Rogêt" to Robert Hamilton of Snowden's *Ladies' Companion*.[42] But, as he later acknowledged to his friend Frederick W. Thomas, he was drinking.[43] He apparently spent time with a Kentucky poet then living in New York, William Ross Wallace. When, on July 18, from Philadelphia, he submitted his sketch "The Landscape-Garden" to James and Henry G. Langley, publishers of John O'Sullivan's *Democratic Review*, he seems to have been seeking a light touch to mask his embarrassment over his recent visit: "Will you be kind enough to put the best possible interpretation upon my behavior while in N-York? You must have conceived a *queer* idea of me—but the simple truth is that Wallace would insist upon *the juleps,* and I knew not what I was either doing or saying" (O 1:353).[44]

It was probably after his stay in New York that Poe traveled to Jersey City to visit Mary Starr, whom he had courted in Baltimore in 1832 and 1833. She remembered that during his visit, "on one of his sprees," he asserted that she loved him, not her husband. He had tea with Mary and her sister, and he asked Mary to sing for him. She obliged with "his favorite song," presumably the consolatory "Come Rest in This Bosom." Maria Clemm, in Philadelphia, distressed for herself and for Virginia, visited Mary, seeking her son-in-law; Poe was later located "in the woods on the outskirts of Jersey City," according to Mary, "wandering about like a crazy man." Perhaps, it has been suggested, if he was north of Jersey City, near Hoboken, he was exploring an area near the site of the death of Mary Rogers. In any case, his long lapse concluded with Mrs. Clemm's bringing him home on June 29.[45]

Poe offered to his cousin Elizabeth Tutt a version of his return to Virginia, omitting the interlude of intemperance, emphasizing his wife's concern:

"As Regards Myself—I Will Probably Succeed Too" · 271

About ten days ago . . . I was obliged to go on to New York on business which absolutely required my personal attendance, and no sooner had I turned my back than she began to fret. It so happened that I could not get back as soon as I had promised, and because she did not hear from me twice a day, she became nearly crazy, and in spite of all Muddy [Maria Clemm] could do, she would neither eat nor sleep, but spent her whole time in watching for me out of the windows, although it rained heavily a great portion of the time. The result was, that upon my return, I found her again *ill,* with her cough as bad as ever, and so emaciated that I was shocked to see her. By dint of coaxing and petting, however, she is now once more recovering her health and good looks; but she has extracted from me a solemn promise, that I will never leave her again, as long as I live, for more than six hours at a time. What it is to be pestered with a wife![46]

Perhaps, we may infer, this patronizing account of his anxious, loving wife, was a defense against his guilt for his repeated failing and its consequence. Virginia had, of course, good reason to be worried. And Poe was probably, ultimately, pleased to be so missed and grateful to be so "pestered"—as his cousin Elizabeth would likely have understood.

She would have appreciated his various chatty details, most notable of which was his report that his sister Rosalie and his old friend John H. Mackenzie, among others, had been converted to Methodism "by Mr. Maffitt's preaching"—that is, by a sermon of the "charming," "soothing" evangelist, John Newland Maffitt. Poe's particular surprise about Mackenzie's conversion—"(would you believe it?)"—was probably owing to its unexpectedness given Poe's many conversations with his friend about religious matters.[47]

Thanking James Herron on June 30 for sending a check for twenty dollars and the assurance of a Custom House position in Philadelphia from Robert Tyler, the president's son, Poe offered his own assurance: "Your own brilliant prospects *must* be realized; for it is not Fate which makes such men as yourself. You make your own Fate. There is such a thing as compelling Fortune, however reluctant or averse. As regards myself—I will probably succeed too. So let us both keep a good heart" (O 1:345).

Trying to compel Fortune, Poe made significant efforts: he attempted again to establish the "Penn Magazine," despite Graham's nonsupport, planning a January 1, 1843, publication date (O 1:346–47, 349–50); he submitted his sketch "The Landscape-Garden" to the *Democratic Review* (O 1:353); he wrote a long, invited review of Rufus W. Griswold's *Poets and Poetry of*

America for the *Boston Miscellany;* and, probably toward summer's end, he began to write a major new tale, "The Gold-Bug."[48]

In late August and early September, Poe continued his correspondence with his *"true friend"* (O 1:333) Frederick W. Thomas, and therein revealed uncertainty—Virginia's health was fluctuating, as was Poe's confidence in his obtaining the Custom House appointment (O 1:356, 358, 360). Thankful for Thomas's "kind offices in the matter of the appointment," Poe reiterated on September 12 the friendship he had expressed earlier (O 1:334): "I would give the world to clasp you by the hand & assure you, personally, of my gratitude. I hope it will not be long before we meet" (O 1:358). Thomas had tried to visit Poe in Philadelphia in late June, but Poe had then been in New York.[49] However, Thomas did visit Poe at his Coates Street home on Saturday, September 17.

Thomas later remembered the poverty of the family and the illness of Poe's wife:

> His house was small, but comfortable inside for one of the kind. The rooms looked neat and orderly, but everything about the place wore an air of pecuniary want. Although I arrived late in the morning Mrs. Clemm, Poe's mother-in-law, was busy preparing for his breakfast. My presence possibly caused some confusion, but I noticed that there was delay and evident difficulty in procuring the meal. His wife entertained me. Her manners were agreeable and graceful. She had well formed, regular features, with the most expressive and intelligent eyes I ever beheld. Her pale complexion, the deep lines in her face and a consumptive cough made me regard her as the victim for an early grave. She and her mother showed much concern about Eddie, as they called Poe, and were anxious to have him secure work.[50]

Thomas recalled, as well, both Poe's love for his wife and his continued drinking: "When Poe appeared his dark hair hung carelessly over his high forehead, and his dress was a little slovenly. He met me cordially, but was reserved, and complained of feeling unwell. His pathetic tenderness and loving manners towards his wife greatly impressed me. I was not long in observing with deep regret that he had fallen again into habits of intemperance."[51]

The two friends "visited the city together"—presumably the lame Thomas holding "a stout cane"—with Poe confessing his "uneasiness" concerning the Custom House position (O 1:371) and the two men probably talking about Charles Dickens and his recent visit, as well as Rufus W. Griswold and his anthology.[52] Thomas had written to Poe only two weeks earlier, "I hope ere long to see you in Philadelphia, and have a long talk about old times,"[53] so perhaps these companions also reminisced about Poe's brother Henry, with whom Thomas had once competed in a love affair, and about Mary Starr, to whom Poe had once wished to be married.[54] Another meeting of Poe and Thomas was planned for the next morning at Congress Hall, but Poe was unable to make it—either because, as he wrote, he had been sick (O 1:361–62) or because he had been drinking or suffering from the effects of drinking. Thomas would later be characterized as "distinguished for the encouragement he always held out to authors,"[55] and he certainly continued to offer encouragement to Poe.

Sometime in mid-September, "The Pit and the Pendulum" appeared in *The Gift for 1843*.[56] In this formidable tale of terror, the narrator, condemned by the Spanish Inquisition, is entombed in a crypt and subject to unrelenting mortal dangers: a rat-infested pit, a descending sharp-edged pendulum, and heated compressing walls. Despite the narrator's fortunate tripping at the edge of the pit and his ingenuity as he lay bound beneath the approaching pendulum, the Inquisition's steady deadly purpose prevails—until the coming of the French and the rescue of the narrator.

The tale was probably written in March 1842, at roughly the same time that Poe was writing his second review of Hawthorne's *Twice-Told Tales*. Poe states in the review that after a poem, "the prose tale" "should best fulfil the demands of high genius"—that is, "the short prose narrative, requiring from a half-hour to one or two hours in its perusal." He adds, "During the hour of perusal the soul of the reader is at the writer's control." Asserting that the tale is more suitable than the poem for "terror, or passion, or horror," he defends "those *tales of effect* many fine examples of which were found in the earlier numbers of Blackwood."[57] Poe may well have been thinking of his "The Pit and the Pendulum," which had sources in earlier numbers of *Blackwood's*: the 1821 "The Man in the Bell," the 1821 "Singular Recovery from Death," the 1830 "The Iron Shroud," and the 1837 "The Involuntary Experimentalist."[58] (Notably, "The Man in the Bell" and "The Involuntary Experimentalist" were mentioned in Poe's satirical 1838 "How to Write a Blackwood Article" [M 2:340].) Poe achieved in "The Pit and the Pendulum" the intense terror that he so "relished" in the *Blackwood's* tales; in fact, his tale has become exemplary of the Gothic genre.[59]

The tale features not only the requisite unity of effect but also a unity of form. Scholars have noted the symmetry of the opening and closing phrases "indeterminate hum" and "discordant hum."[60] Observable within are additional symmetries. Even as the condemned narrator's body is carried "down—down—still down" in the first half, the pendulum swings down, as well: "Down—steadily down it *crept*"; "Down—certainly, relentlessly down!"; and "Down—still unceasingly—still inevitably down!" in the second half.[61] Within this symmetry, the phrase "right angles to the wall" corresponds to the later phrase "right angles to my length."[62] Farther in is the symmetry "the doom which had been prepared for me" and "the doom prepared for me."[63] Closer to the middle is a symmetry of two pairs of clauses, "I gazed directly upward" and "Its [the pendulum's] sweep was brief" and then "I again cast my eyes upward" and "The sweep of the pendulum had increased."[64] And then appears the halfway marker, regarding the time between the narrator's looking down and his looking up: "It might have been half an hour, perhaps even an hour (for I could take but imperfect note of time)."[65]

There may well be a hint of the reader's reading the text in the text. The condemned narrator's stating that "I must have returned upon my steps"[66] seems to suggest the reader's retracing the language of the first half in the second half. And the central phrase "half an hour, perhaps even an hour" seems to recall Poe's writing in his second review of Hawthorne's *Twice-Told Tales* about "the short prose narrative, requiring from a half-hour to one or two hours in its perusal." The recessed symmetries of the tale may well frame the amount of time it takes to read the tale. We may recognize in both effect and form what Poe termed "the one pre-established design" and thereby gain "a sense of the fullest satisfaction."[67] Even as the narrator of "The Pit and the Pendulum" may finally be decrypted, so may the text, as well.

On September 21, Poe was "still very unwell" (O 1:362), owing either to illness or the after-effect of drinking, but he also still held out hope for the Custom House job. Indeed, for two months, between mid-September and mid-November, he made no commitment, anticipating that the government position would come through (O 1:370–72). He neither accepted Graham's offer to return nor petitioned for bankruptcy. Ironically—or perhaps fittingly—he continued to work on "The Gold-Bug," a tale of seeking and finding great treasure. And he planned for the "Penn Magazine": encouraged by receiving the names of four potential subscribers from poet Thomas H. Chivers, he invited the affluent poet to support his endeavor (O 1:363–65). Convinced that he would receive the Custom House appointment, he wrote to John Tomlin that the magazine would appear on January 1 (O 1:367). However, Philadelphia Custom House prospects were still on hold; the deeply indebted Poe was holding on.

Poe's sketch "The Landscape-Garden" appeared, by late September, in the October 1842 issue of Snowden's *Ladies' Companion*.[68] The writer imagines here one Ellison, a man of immense wealth—$450 million—who dedicates his fortune to the creation of a transcendently beautiful landscape garden, one that suggests "the sentiment of *spiritual* interference."[69] Ellison wishes to design a garden that seems the product of the angels. Poe in this work is speaking again of the nature of the quest for the supernal. Appropriately, the characteristic symmetry—a pair of references to the four elements needed for a life of Bliss and a pair of phrases regarding the garden's "adaptation to the eyes which were to behold it upon earth"—frames the center, "the fulfillment of [Ellison's] destiny as Poet."[70]

Those four elements for a life of Bliss are "free exercise in the open air," "the love of woman," "the contempt of ambition," and "an object of [unceasing] pursuit."[71] And Ellison adds that "other things being equal, the extent of Happiness was proportioned to the spirituality of this object."[72] So Poe is again declaring his aspiration—a desire to reach, through art, an intimation of the divine. This is an essential pattern in Poe's work—in "Al Aaraaf," in "Israfel," at the ending of *Arthur Gordon Pym*. Repeatedly, Poe reaches toward something akin to the soul's home.

He clearly anticipated "The Landscape-Garden" in his April 1842 review of Longfellow's *Ballads*. The "first element" of "Poesy," he writes, is "the thirst for supernal BEAUTY—a beauty which is not afforded the soul by any existing collocation of earth's forms." The "second element" is "the attempt to satisfy this thirst by *novel* combinations among those forms of beauty which already exist."[73] And he would keep reaching for the supernal throughout his life, as in the expansion of "The Landscape-Garden," "The Domain of Arnheim," and in his metamorphosis of elements of his Longfellow review, "The Poetic Principle." Even his sometimes-materialist cosmology *Eureka* will yield to the immaterial, the lyrical longing for the divine. It was a spiritual transport that Poe was after—for himself and for his readers.

Poe continued with his criticism, deprecating the poetry of Rufus Dawes in the October 1842 *Graham's* and mixing regard with reservation concerning the anthology of Rufus W. Griswold in the November 1842 *Boston Miscellany*. The review of *Poets and Poetry of America*, invited by Griswold, was carefully modulated: though seen by the editor Henry J. Raymond as "a good puff," it did assert disagreement with some of Griswold's literary judgments.[74] Nonetheless, the review offers no demonstration that the work was what Poe had privately termed "a most outrageous humbug" (O 1:341). He exercised a critical restraint, describing the anthology as "so vast an improvement upon those of a similar character which have preceded it," "*the most important addition which our literature has for many years received.*"[75] But Poe would have known that any censure would have been intolerable to the sensitive Griswold, who indeed wrote, to publisher James T. Fields, on August 12, 1842, "I care not a fig about the publication of the criticism as the author and myself not being on the best terms, it is not decidedly as favorable as it might have been."[76] Poe's praise was not faint, and there was no damning—and only moderate darning—but the imperious and insecure reverend was still offended. We may imagine that Poe would have been pleased.[77]

In early October, Poe had written to Robert Hamilton, whom he had probably seen in New York in June, "I am straight as judges—somewhat more straight indeed than some of our Phil: dignitaries—and, what is more, I intend to keep straight" (O 1:366). It was fortunate that Poe had the intention (if he kept to it), for he needed great forbearance at this time: he was being encouraged in bad faith regarding the Custom House job by the new collector, Thomas S. Smith. During five visits between October 12 and November 19, Poe had to put up with Smith's false promises on several occasions, his absence on one occasion, and his ultimate rejection. Poe asserted fairly to his friend Thomas, "[H]e has treated me most shamefully," and he asked Thomas if he could approach Robert Tyler to ask his father the president to intercede. Poe added, "I could have forgiven all but the innumerable and altogether *unnecessary* falsehoods with which he insulted my common-sense day after day." Poe closed, "I would write more my dear Thomas;—but my heart is too heavy. You have felt the misery of hope deferred & will feel for me" (O 1:370–72). He thus alluded to Proverbs 13:12, "Hope deferred maketh the heart sick."

The two months' wait—a moratorium on other practical efforts—had been costly: he confided in Thomas, "You cannot imagine the trouble I am in, & have been in for the last 2 months—unable to enter into any literary arrangements—or in fact to do anything—being in hourly expectation of getting the place" (O 1:371–72). Poe had tried, patiently and perseveringly, but Fortune remained uncompelled.

Poe's second Dupin tale, "The Mystery of Marie Rogêt," appeared in three installments, in the November and December 1842 and February 1843 issues of Snowden's *Ladies' Companion*.[78] In light of the proximity of the issues in which the installments were published and the unity of the whole, I will treat the three sections together.

The sequel to "The Murders in the Rue Morgue" again takes place in Paris and again features detective C. Auguste Dupin and his admiring friend, who is again the narrator. The sequel again draws on recent newspaper articles. However, whereas the mystery of "Rue Morgue" was created by Poe, that of "Marie Rogêt" already existed in New York's popular press of the time. The narrator of "Marie Rogêt" offers an account parallel to that of the deceased "cigar girl," Mary Rogers—Poe stated in a letter and in a subsequent introduction that he intended the solution to the Paris mystery to illuminate the New York one (O 1:337–38; M 3:723).

In the first installment, the Paris prefect secures Dupin's assistance regarding the investigation of the death of the "perfumery girl," Marie Rogêt, whose body was found in the Seine. The narrator presents reported detail and several newspaper judgments, and Dupin critiques *L'Etoile,* in particular, questioning its inferences (regarding, for instance, the amount of time that must pass for a drowned body to rise and the possibility that Marie Rogêt was still alive). In the second installment, Dupin continues with his challenge of the reasoning of *L'Etoile* and faults, as well, that of *Le Commerciel* and *Le Soleil.* He also provides six extracts from additional papers, arguing against the theory that a gang had attacked Marie Rogêt and suggesting the culpability of a "secret lover," a "naval officer." In the third and final installment, Dupin contends that evidence found in a thicket was deliberately placed there and that letters suggesting the guilt of a gang were written by the guilty individual or individuals. He finally asserts that Marie Rogêt was killed by one man—a "naval officer"—whose identity may be determined by examining the handwriting of the letters to the newspapers, by questioning those who had seen him, and by investigating the rudderless boat mentioned in the sixth newspaper extract. The tale closes with a facetious disavowal of the necessity that the story of Marie Rogêt must illuminate that of Mary Rogers.[79]

Influenced, no doubt, by additional press reports and perhaps by what he later learned when he moved to New York, Poe subsequently modified his view of the cause of Mary Rogers's death, revising the tale in 1845 to accommodate the possibility of an abortion.[80] Poe explained in a letter to his inquiring correspondent George W. Eveleth in January 1848, "The 'naval officer' who committed the murder (or rather the accidental death arising from an attempt at abortion) *confessed* it; and the whole matter is now well understood" (O 2:641).

That the matter might still be better understood is suggested by the abundance of scholarly responses to the case of Mary Rogers.[81] Clearly, however,

Poe did effectively challenge erroneous contemporary journalistic judgments. We may elaborate here the tale's context, note the work's familiar structure, and suggest a personal connection in "Rue Morgue" and "Marie Rogêt" that will reappear in "The Purloined Letter."

Poe's resource—and that of his narrator and Dupin—was an assortment of newspapers of the time (M 3:723).[82] Even Dupin's sixth newspaper extract, which has been termed "invented," "fabricated,"[83] was closely based on an actual newspaper piece—from Mordecai Manuel Noah's *New York Times and Evening Star* (not the "N.Y. Standard," which Poe had given for "Le Diligence" in the 1845 version [M 3:754]).[84] Perhaps Dupin's contending that the guilty party had blamed the innocent one may owe something to Theodore S. Fay's 1835 novel *Norman Leslie* and its 1799 historical antecedent, the murder of Gulielma Sands—both of which were referred to in James Gordon Bennett's *New York Herald*.[85] The newspaper that Poe's narrator gives predominant attention is *L'Etoile*, which Poe later correctly termed *Brother Jonathan* (M 3:731).

What is especially illuminating here is the personal connection, for Poe had already had a conflict with its editor, H. Hastings Weld. As noted, Poe had humorously savaged Seba Smith's *Powhatan,* which he considered "uncommonly bad," and the *Brother Jonathan* editor had faulted Poe's mockery: "A more capricious, unjust, and ridiculous affair, purporting to be a review, we never happened upon than is the notice of Powhatan, in Graham's Magazine." Poe had responded privately to Weld in a letter of August 14, 1841, quoted earlier, "Should you grow weary, at any time, of abusing me in the 'Jonathan' for speaking what no man knows to be the truth better than yourself, it would give me sincere pleasure to cultivate the friendship of the author of 'Corrected Proofs'" (O 1:303). But Weld did not desist, accusing Poe in April 1842 of "hypercriticism" and of being "too much after the precedent of Draco." Clearly Poe genuinely objected to the reasoning of the editor of *Brother Jonathan* regarding Mary Rogers, but Weld's assaults on him may well have contributed to Poe's motive for attacking first and at length the editor of the French stand-in for *Brother Jonathan, L'Etoile.* Dupin's stating that "[t]he editor of L'Etoile had no right to be offended at M. Beauvais' unreasoning belief" may concern, in part, Weld's being offended at Poe's justifiable review of *Powhatan*.[86] It might be added that Poe's covert attack on H. Hastings Weld in "Marie Rogêt" anticipates Poe's covert attack on Thomas Dunn English in "The Cask of Amontillado": Poe immures here with argument as he immures later with stones and mortar.[87]

Poe's customary symmetrical structure may be observed in "Marie Rogêt," as well. A selection of the elements will suffice. A cluster of phrases at the beginning, including "*parallel,*" "the Calculus of Probabilities," "*coincidences,*" and "the late murder of MARY CECILIA ROGERS" is found, too, at the end, including "coincidences," "the fate of the unhappy Mary Cecilia Rogers," "parallel," and "the very Calculus of Probabilities to which I have referred."[88] Framing passages within concern Marie Rogêt's clothing and the site in which it was found, the thicket.[89] Approaching the center are the framing phrases "[t]he question of identity" and two questions about a newspaper, "And what . . . do you think of the opinions of Le Commerciel?" and "And what are we to think . . . of the article in Le Soleil?"[90] In the central paragraph, concerning Marie Rogêt's walking through Paris, is framing language regarding "personal acquaintance" and "proceeded upon a route," within which is the central sentence: "In this case, granting the personal acquaintances to be equal, the chances would be also equal that an equal number of personal rencounters would be made."[91] And so, ironically, in this tale of parallels appears a central chiasmus:

personal acquaintances   equal
                    X
equal   personal rencounters[92]

Discussion of the tale may conclude here by noticing a link between "Rue Morgue" and "Marie Rogêt." The former has a source, "Deliberate Murder in Broadway, at Midday," about a young woman, Ann Coleman, suspected of infidelity. The latter has sources about a young woman, Mary Rogers, suspected of sexual impropriety. We may make a further inference upon reaching a source about another woman of uncertain reputation for the third and final Dupin tale, "The Purloined Letter."

In the fall of 1842, Virginia remained sick, declining and improving and declining over time. Margaret E. Wilmer later recalled her father Lambert A. Wilmer's observing of Virginia and Edgar, "Her husband watched over her with devoted solicitude, and neglected no means which affection could suggest, to restore her health or to promote her comfort." And Poe remained what Wilmer himself described as "one of the most hard-working men in the world."[93] He was working on several short story masterpieces—beginning "The Gold-Bug" in the late summer of 1842 and writing "The Tell-Tale Heart" and "The Black Cat" toward the end of the year.

Perhaps having determined that the "Penn Magazine" would not appear on January 1, 1843—he did not, after all, fulfill his promise to announce in mid-October its coming publication (O 1:363, 367)—Poe initially targeted *Graham's Magazine* for "The Gold-Bug" and the *Boston Miscellany* for "The Tell-Tale Heart." Graham, who read the manuscript of "The Gold-Bug" aloud, accepted the work,[94] but Henry T. Tuckerman, who had just succeeded Nathan Hale Jr. as editor of the *Boston Miscellany*, rejected "The Tell-Tale Heart," probably, as James Russell Lowell posited, recalling Poe's uncomplimentary words on Tuckerman in "A Chapter on Autography" (H 17:125).

Poe knew Lowell through his publications and probably from former colleague Charles J. Peterson, who corresponded with Lowell and with Lowell's friend and future contributor William Wetmore Story. Poe began his own correspondence with Lowell on November 16, offering to write something for each issue of his new magazine, the *Pioneer*. Lowell offered Poe "*carte blanche* for prose or verse as may best please you," though cautioning against harsh criticism, like the Rufus Dawes piece. He wanted, particularly, "good stories (imaginative ones)" and indicated that something sent soon could be included in the first issue, already in press. Poe had asked that the editor of the *Boston Miscellany*, if he were to decline "The Tell-Tale Heart," pass it on to Lowell, and Poe suggested to Lowell, on November 24, that he inquire after the piece. On December 17, Lowell wrote to Poe with good news: "Your story of 'The Telltale Heart' will appear in my first number." That story would later be considered, by N. P. Willis, "the only thing in the number that most people would read and remember."[95] But before enjoying his triumph with "The Tell-Tale Heart," Poe finally took the step that he had long been putting off—on Monday, December 19, 1842, he petitioned for bankruptcy.

Prompted by the Panic of 1837 and that of 1839, the Whig-supported Bankruptcy Act of 1841 began on February 2, 1842, and lasted until March 3, 1843. Humane but controversial, it allowed the insolvent to petition for bankruptcy, often resulting in a complete expunging of debt. The thirteen-month period of the act was wryly named "The Jubilee of the Bankrupts."[96]

Poe's bankruptcy document reveals the woeful state of his finances.[97] "Schedule A" shows an indebtedness of more than $2,000. His creditors were from Philadelphia, Richmond, and New York. Many of the debts were outright loans, ranging from $150 from his friend Robert Stanard Jr., of Richmond, to $10 from the celebrated writer and lecturer J. N. Reynolds, of New York. Some of the debts were promissory notes ("Note of Hand") or ledger figures ("Book Debt"), indications of indebtedness for goods or services rendered. Amounts were as high as $169.10 ("Note of Hand"), to tailor J. W. Albright, and as low as $4.00 ("Book Debt"), to the printer Charles Alexander, both of Philadelphia. Some of the indebtedness was for rent (in Philadelphia and New York); some was for his wife Virginia: "Med. Attendance," "Piano Hire," "Music Lesson." Poe's contested debt of $100 to William E. Burton was included in the list.

Poe's excesses in Richmond, his unemployment in New York and Philadelphia, and his occasional drinking during his time in Philadelphia must have seriously damaged his financial situation. And certainly he was not always a responsible manager of money. But it is also true that the literary marketplace of the day just adequately rewarded his editorial work and very meagerly his literary work. Also, it was because the years since 1837 had been so challenging financially for many that the Bankruptcy Act of 1841 was created in the first place.

"Schedule B," intended to reveal a debtor's property, outdid Schedule A in Poe's case with its remorseless statement, "The Petitioner is possessed of no Property, real, personal or mixed, beyond his wearing apparel and a few printed Sheets, of no use to any one else, and of no value to anyone."[98] There was evidently no need to worry about the $300 worth of property that a bankrupt was allowed to possess.[99]

The bankruptcy document was signed by Poe—"Edgar A. Poe"—and by Oliver Hopkinson—"O. Hopkinson"—Commissioner in Bankruptcy.[100] As high as were Poe's aspirations, so low was his actual condition. Perhaps he felt humiliated, perhaps relieved—probably both. In any case, "Edgar A. Poe Late Editor" had done what he needed to do. Now, he could only wait for the response.

On the following day, December 20, the *Public Ledger* listed Poe as one of the previous day's eleven petitioners for bankruptcy. On the same day, the first issue of the *Pioneer* came out, featuring Poe's "The Tell-Tale Heart."[101] As a petitioner under the Bankruptcy Act of 1841, Poe was one of more than forty-one thousand.[102] As a writer, he was one of a kind.

"The Tell-Tale Heart" is brief and unrelenting. The first-person narrator, disturbed by what he considers the "Evil Eye" of the old man, resolves on murder. Apparently confident of his own sanity—given his calm, given his deliberateness—he tries, as he tells his story, to convince his doubting readers, as well. At midnight, over the course of eight days, the narrator slowly opens the door of the old man's bedroom and puts his head within, shining his lantern on the offending eye. For seven nights the eye is closed, but on the eighth night, since the old man has been awakened, it is disturbingly open. And so, the provoked intruder, distressed as well by the sound of the old man's heart, waits as long as he can bear and then rushes upon the terrified old man, smothering him with his bed. He dismembers the body and hides its parts beneath the floorboards. Police arrive, and the ecstatic murderer, at first believing himself to be persuasively self-assured, begins to reveal himself as he hears the old man's heart—or his own—beating increasingly louder. Unable to tolerate the merciless sound and his growing conviction that the police actually know what he has done, he ultimately confesses all.

A classic of obsession, violence, and guilt, "The Tell-Tale Heart" was inspired in part by a speech by Daniel Webster concerning the murder of Captain Joseph White, in Salem, quotation from which appeared in *Brother Jonathan* on August 21, 1841 (M 3:789–91). A variety of other prompts included *Macbeth,* a tale by Bulwer-Lytton, tales by Dickens, and a sketch by Hawthorne.[103] The central chiasmus, in the ninth of eighteen paragraphs, is "open—wide, wide open"—the *X* describing the old man's eye, the "damned spot" (a phrase that recalls the guilt of Lady Macbeth).[104] The work is both cathartic and beautiful.

It does seem that Poe in "The Tell-Tale Heart" was relying on his own life, integrating his animus toward John Allan in his fiction.[105] The nervousness of the narrator was characteristic of Poe—not only did he later admit that he was "nervous in a very unusual degree" (O 2:641), but also the coming biographical sketch of him referred to his "marked nervousness."[106] The narrator's visit to the old man's bedroom calls to mind, by contrast, Poe's writing to John Allan in March 1829, "[I]n the morning of my departure I went to your room to tell you good bye—but, as you were asleep, I could not disturb you" (O 1:22). And, unforgettably, Poe's final visit to his foster father in his bedroom resulted in John Allan's threatening his foster son with a cane. Perhaps Poe was using his enduring anger with Allan—and his guilt—to intensify his writing of this story.

And, given Poe's comparing the old man's beating heart to a muffled watch, it is interesting to add that the writer partially paid his large debt to the tailor J. W. Albright with his own engraved pocket watch.[107]

Horace Greeley termed "The Tell-Tale Heart" "strong and skilful" but "overstrained and repulsive." However, Willis's commenting that it was "very wild and very readable" seems closer to the mark.[108] And defending "Berenice" to Thomas W. White years earlier, Poe had asserted, fairly, "To be appreciated you must be *read*" (O 1:85). Notably, "The Tell-Tale Heart" was twice reprinted in the weeks after its initial publication.[109] And the work's power may be inferred by Frederick Douglass's deft allusion to it in his 1845 *Narrative of the Life of Frederick Douglass*. Douglass writes of Master Hugh Auld, "He raved, and swore," even as Poe's narrator in "The Tell-Tale Heart" stated, "I raved—I swore!" And Douglass declares that his master "thought I was never better satisfied with my condition than at the very time during which I was planning my escape" even as Poe's narrator maintained, "I was never kinder to the old man than during the whole week before I killed him." Poe understood well oppressive patriarchy. And Douglass evidently recognized this.[110]

Poe did positively review the January issue of the *Pioneer* anonymously in the *Philadelphia Saturday Museum*, mentioning Lowell, himself, and Neal. It is particularly interesting that he wrote, "The Reviews are good and just" (except for the review of Cornelius Matthews's novel *Puffer Hopkins*). For among those "good and just" reviews was one—presumably by Lowell—of the anonymous 1842 novel *The Salem Belle*, which would prove to be a vital prompt for a work Poe did not live to see, Hawthorne's 1850 masterpiece, *The Scarlet Letter*.[111]

There was, in early 1843, a very hopeful turn in Poe's situation. On January 13, his petition for bankruptcy "passed decree." Poe was one of sixty-two listed—one of the more than 33,000 petitioners who were approved under the Bankruptcy Act of 1841.[112] Additionally, around this time he found a backer for his proposed literary magazine, now called "The Stylus": Thomas C. Clarke, the modest, kindly editor of the recently established newspaper the *Philadelphia Saturday Museum*. Clarke would oversee the practical process while Poe would perform the literary work. Poe later confided to Thomas, in less than kind terms, "I have managed, *at last*, to secure, I think, the great object—a partner possessing ample capital, and, at the same time, so little self-esteem, as to allow me entire control of the editorial conduct. He gives me, also, a half interest, and is to furnish funds for all the business operations—I agreeing to supply, for the first year, the literary matter" (O 1:381). Plans were developing for an illustrator for the magazine—by month's end, Poe and Clarke would sign a contract with Felix O. C. Darley (H 17:126–27).[113] And no doubt Poe was beginning to work on his new prospectus.

Furthermore, Clarke was planning a series in the *Saturday Museum* titled "The Poets and Poetry of Philadelphia," which would include a biographical sketch of his new partner. Poe was seeking the help of Frederick W. Thomas in the writing of the piece; perhaps by this time the daguerreotype—from which a woodblock image would be made to complement the sketch—had already been made.[114] Poe would certainly have enjoyed Henry B. Hirst's attack on Griswold's *Poets and Poetry of America* in the January 28 issue of the *Saturday Museum* (unless he himself wrote it).[115]

And the February 1843 issue of the *Pioneer*, arriving probably by January 26, would have been very satisfying, not only for the publication of Poe's poem "Lenore," the reprint of his review of the January issue, and the reprint of Willis's review of the January issue (including his praise of "The Tell-Tale Heart"), but also for Nathaniel Hawthorne's piece "The Hall of Fantasy." For in that tale Poe was included in the contemporary literary pantheon, along with Ralph Waldo Emerson, Washington Irving, James Fenimore Cooper, and Henry Wadsworth Longfellow. We may well conceive that Poe would have been delighted to read Hawthorne's stating, "Mr. Poe had gained ready admittance for the sake of his imagination, but was threatened with ejectment, as belonging to the obnoxious class of critics."[116] For Poe was, after all, proud of what he considered his critical rigor (and he later included the comment in the *Saturday Museum* account of his life and work).[117] Finally, he would already have been anticipating a visit to friends Frederick W. Thomas and Jesse E. Dow in Washington, D.C., where he would seek a government position.[118]

Much was going right for Poe at this time. At the end of January 1843, he signed a letter to Thomas, signaling his disposition: "In high spirits, / Yours truly, / E. A. Poe" (H 17:128).

17

"I Would Say to You, Without Hesitation, Aspire"

1843-1844

FREDERICK W. THOMAS was elated at Poe's upbeat tone—"[N]othing gives me greater pleasure than to know that you are well and doing well" (H 17:128)—but declined to write the biography,[1] for which Poe turned to Henry B. Hirst. During the first few months of 1843, Poe asked Graham to return "The Gold-Bug"—perhaps at this time, for inclusion in "The Stylus," or perhaps after March 29, to submit to the *Dollar Newspaper*'s short story contest.[2] And Poe was continuing to submit work to the *Pioneer*—the essay "Notes upon English Verse," which would appear in the March issue, the third and last, and the poem "Eulalie," which would appear in 1845 in the *American Review*.[3]

In the February 18 issue of the *Philadelphia Saturday Museum*, the initial installment of the series "The Poets and Poetry of Philadelphia" appeared, concerning Dr. James McHenry. The February 25 issue featured the next installment, on Poe; it appeared, as well, in the March 4 issue. This was the first extensive prose treatment of Poe, and though he attributed it to Hirst, the language, attitude, and detail suggest that Poe was himself an author.[4]

The front page of the March 4, 1843, issue of the *Saturday Museum* presents the Poe biography in its entirety, with a commanding woodcut portrait of Poe at the top. The writer is formally dressed and seated, in a posture of staunch repose; he has a firm, fixed mien, framed by trim muttonchops. The image conveys judgment, authority, even indomitableness. The imperviousness of the figure in the woodcut contrasts with what seems the permeability of the figure in the first daguerreotype of Poe, the McKee daguerreotype, from about 1842.[5] But it was the McKee image—or another daguerreotype made at the same sitting—from which the unyielding image in the woodcut was taken. The concluding sentence in the *Saturday Museum* essay—"Our portrait conveys a tolerably correct idea of the man"—may have been by Hirst or even Clarke; John S. Du Solle agreed with this judgment, but Joseph E. Snodgrass did not.[6] Certainly the "somewhat slender" figure of the biography has been replaced by a nearly paunchy one. Poe wrote of what he considered the "caricature," "I am ugly enough God knows, but not *quite* so bad as that" (O 1:381). And he wrote some months later that the newspaper portrait was "particularly false": "It does not convey the faintest idea of my person. No one of my family recognised it" (O 1:413).[7]

Even as the woodcut tends toward the resolute, the essay tends toward the romantic. Poe had told Thomas that the *Saturday Museum* account of his life "was intended to help the magazine project."[8] Understandably, then, it offers a blend of engaging youthful exploits—notable accomplishments of swimming and leaping, dissolute achievement at the university, deliberate court-martial at West Point, and fabricated problems abroad—with incomparable brilliance in fiction, poetry, and criticism. A variety of tributes to Poe's imaginative tales enhance the account, as do sample poems and instances of cryptographic acumen.[9] Nowhere is there mention of literary failure (the unpublished "Tales of the Folio Club," the incomplete and derivative "Journal of Julius Rodman") or personal problems (alcoholism, depression, poverty, bankruptcy, his wife's illness). The *Saturday Museum* biography was Poe's enthusiastic advertisement for himself. If not always true in fact, it is true in spirit. And the vaunted success celebrated there is all the more impressive for the unacknowledged sorrow that lay behind it.[10]

As Poe admitted, the primary purpose of the sketch was to increase interest in "The Stylus." The biography notes, "By reference to another page of our paper, it will be seen that he [Poe] has issued the prospectus of a Monthly, to be entitled 'THE STYLUS,' for which, it is needless to say, we predict the most unequivocal success." A secondary purpose was to promote that elusive new edition of his short fiction. The sketch asserts, "A complete collection of his Tales is a *desideratum* in our Literature."[11] If we recall "The Landscape-Garden," we may note that Poe had no contempt for ambition, but he certainly had objects of unceasing pursuit.

The epigraph about truth in Poe's new prospectus for "The Stylus"— which states, "Lo! This is writ / With the antique *iron pen*" (L2 28)—is by

"*Launcelot Canning*," a pseudonym for Poe that is familiar from "The Fall of the House of Usher" (M 2:413–15, 422; see also M 1:328–29).[12] Poe switched the title of the publication from "The Penn Magazine" ("too local") to "The Stylus" but reiterates points he has made in the "Penn" prospectus, including the importance of a single editorial vision and the virtue of critical fearlessness. Again, the price will be five dollars a year, and Poe states that the periodical will commence on July 1, 1843. Though he no longer snipes at "cliques," he does derogate "the most pompous or Puritanical way." Recalling Clarke's series "The Poets and Poetry of Philadelphia" (which might have been a Poe invention), he proposes a series titled "*Critical and Biographical Sketches of American Writers*" (L2 28–32). Doubtless he wished to challenge the judgment of Rufus W. Griswold in *The Poets and Poetry of America*. The genealogy for Poe's proposed magazine may be tracked backward at least as far as John Neal's December 1835 advocacy for a five-dollar-a-year periodical, "a respectable and independent journal" (albeit one of New England)—an advocacy made in the *New England Galaxy*, which three months earlier Poe had requested in exchange for the *Southern Literary Messenger* and where Neal had then praised Poe as "*emphatically* a man of genius."[13] Even earlier that year, in Baltimore, Poe had proposed to Lambert Wilmer that they coedit a monthly magazine.[14] Poe also seems to have approached Joseph E. Snodgrass (O 1:339).

Assuredly, Poe would go to the *Saturday Museum* office at 101 Chestnut Street (also the address of *Godey's Lady's Book*) in early 1843, and probably he visited Clarke's home at Twelfth Street and Walnut (where he had visited in earlier times).[15] Perhaps it was at this time that Maria Clemm would seek out Clarke to locate her errant son-in-law.[16] Mrs. Clemm could try to intervene with Poe's drinking or at least to cope with its after-effects as quickly as possible if Poe was somewhere nearby, as when they lived in Richmond or now in Philadelphia. But she could do nothing until much after the fact if he was elsewhere—as, recently, in New York, or as, imminently, in Washington, D.C.

Poe's long-held wish to go to Washington (O 1:292) to promote his interests was probably encouraged by the U.S. Senate's rejection, on March 3, of his nemesis, Thomas S. Smith, as Philadelphia's collector.[17] Seeking funding for the trip from James Russell Lowell's partner on the *Pioneer*, Bostonian Robert Carter, on March 7 (O 1:384), Poe then left for Washington before he could have heard back, on March 8, probably supported by Clarke, for Poe was to seek "Stylus" subscribers. Not incidentally, he would also try to win support for his own place in the Custom House.

The eight-day Washington episode was a disastrous one. Arriving at Fuller's City Hotel on March 8, Poe found his friend Thomas sick and unable to help, beyond writing a letter of introduction for Poe to Robert Tyler, the president's son. Had Thomas been well, he could have been Poe's all-too-necessary minder. Poe drank port wine in the evening, becoming "somewhat excited" (according to Jesse E. Dow) but managed to maintain sobriety on March 9, writing to the scientist J. K. Townsend (O 1:385–86) and securing new subscribers to "The Stylus." On March 10, however, presumably under great pressure in a strange city, with both his new magazine and his possible new government position on the line, Poe began to drink and to excess. During his extended spree, he wore his cloak inside out, failed to pay his barber, and insulted various people. On March 11, Poe wrote to Clarke to say that he was doing well (though the handwriting suggested otherwise) and to ask for money (O 1:386–88). Perhaps it was also at this time that a "woe-begone" Poe encountered John Hill Hewitt on Pennsylvania Avenue and asked for money.[18]

On March 12, as the spree continued intermittently, Jesse E. Dow wrote to Clarke out of genuine concern, noting that Poe had been drinking and thereby enabling his political enemies (probably Thomas Dunn English, in particular, who had influence with President Tyler). Dow asked Clarke to come to Washington and to accompany Poe back to Philadelphia. And he implored Clarke not to tell Virginia about the fiasco until Poe was home. In light of later tragic events, it is especially disturbing to read, "Should you not come, we will see him on board the cars bound to Phila., but we fear he might be detained in Baltimore and not be out of harm's way."[19]

As usual after a binge, Poe was sick, and he was cared for by Thomas's physician, Dr. Lacey. On March 15, Poe took the train to Baltimore and then to Philadelphia, where he was met by the ever-protective Maria Clemm. Poe returned home in the late afternoon, had a bath and ate dinner, and then visited Clarke, who was presumably at home, given the time of day. Poe joked to Thomas and Dow in a letter the following day, "I never saw a man in my life more surprised to see another. He thought by Dow's epistle that I must not only be dead but buried & would as soon have thought of seeing his great-great-great grandmother" (O 1:388). And he apologized to both Thomas and Dow for his inconsiderate and erratic behavior (O 1:389–90).

Thomas later knowingly commented on this letter, "I have seen a great deal of Poe, and it was his excessive, and at times morbid sensibility which forced him into his 'frolics,' rather than any mere morbid appetite for drink, but if he took but one glass of weak wine or beer or cider the Rubicon of the cup was passed with him, and it almost always ended in excess and sickness" (H 17:137). Thomas noted, "[H]e fought against the propensity as hard as ever Coleridge fought against it"; "His was one of those temperaments whose only safety is in total abstinence. He suffered terribly after any indiscretion." And he closed, "[T]here is a great deal of heartache in the jestings of this letter" (H 17:138). Poe was embarrassed and ashamed, as he had been with John H. Mackenzie in Richmond seven years earlier. He confided to Thomas and Dow, "I blame no one but myself" (O 1:389). But perhaps the problem was simply beyond his control.[20]

Virginia was very upset. Poe wrote in his letter to Thomas and Dow, "Virginia's health is about the same—but her distress of mind has been even more than I had anticipated" (O 1:389). She loved her husband, and she suffered.

Clarke did not give up on Poe. He published reprints or revisions of Poe's work—"Original Conundrums," "The Destruction of the World" (formerly "Conversation of Eiros and Charmion"), and "The Business Man,"[21] as well as the prospectus. On March 27, Poe wrote to Lowell that though he was not editing the *Saturday Museum,* he did enjoy "the privilege of inserting what I please editorially" (O 1:394). He probably still saw Clarke at home. It may have been at this time that, because of tensions between Thomas Dunn English and Poe, and perhaps between English and Henry B. Hirst, too, the three visiting writers were placed in separate rooms in Clarke's house: Poe in the dining room, Hirst in the library, and English in the parlor.[22] And friends in Washington did not give up on Poe either. Thomas reassured Poe that President Tyler and his sons remained favorable toward him; he closed his March 27 letter, "I trust to see you an official yet." And Robert Tyler, responding to Poe's request for "a reiteration of my former recommendation of you," offered it clearly and unmistakably (H 17:140–41).

Seeking and receiving encouragement regarding a government position, Poe also sought assistance with "The Stylus." He tried, in his March 27 letter to Lowell, to obtain for the new magazine a poem from him and a tale from Hawthorne. He also inquired about securing images of the two men for prospective biographical sketches and sought information on Lowell himself (O 1:394–95). Additionally, Poe made inquiries of others regarding the possible purchase of the subscription list of the *Southern Literary Messenger.* The magazine's founder and publisher (and Poe's former employer), Thomas W. White, had recently died, and there was, for a while, uncertainty regarding the list's disposition. Thomas G. Mackenzie, fifteen years younger than his brother John H. Mackenzie and "a man of letters and great culture & literary taste,"²³ wrote to Poe regarding the *Messenger*'s subscription list (according to Poe himself) "that the heirs had not made up their minds respecting it" (O 1:397). To pursue the possible purchase of the list, Poe wrote on March 24, 1843, to the Richmond printer (and White son-in-law) Peter D. Bernard (O 1:392), then on April 22 to Thomas G. Mackenzie (O 1:396–97), and then to his old friend John H. Mackenzie (O 1:398). If there were responses to Poe's letters, they have not survived. His effort to secure the list was not successful: Benjamin Blake Minor obtained the magazine in July 1843.²⁴

On March 29, the *Dollar Newspaper* offered a hundred-dollar first prize for its short story contest. "The Gold-Bug" would be Poe's entry.²⁵

It was probably in April that the Poe family moved east, within Philadelphia, from Coates Street in Fairmount to 234 North Seventh Street in Spring Garden. They were thereby moving away from an area not far from the Schuylkill River, between the Philadelphia and Columbia Railroad and the Fairmount Water Works on one side and the State Penitentiary on the other, to a quiet suburban neighborhood of Quakers, less distant from the center of the city and from the Delaware River.²⁶ The Poes' new residence was remembered by a frequent guest, the young writer Mayne Reid, as a three-room wooden "lean-to," set against the grand brick home of a wealthy Quaker.²⁷ A fifteen-year-old neighbor, Lydia Hart Garrigues, frequently saw a serious-looking Poe walking past her father's house on North Seventh Street, toward the center of the city, wearing "a Spanish cloak."²⁸ One girl, who used to walk to school and back in Spring Garden, recalled Virginia and Maria Clemm watering their flowers and Virginia sewing. All was evidently not unrelieved sorrow: this girl commented, "They seemed always cheerful and happy, and I could hear Mrs. Poe's laugh before I turned the corner."²⁹

By mid-May of 1843, Poe had evidently written to his second cousin William Poe, of Augusta, Georgia, of "many recent reverses," among which were Virginia's illness and his own "sickness & despondency," and probably his lamentable visit to the capital. (He wrote to Lowell on June 20, citing "sickness and domestic affliction" [O 1:400].) Having written back to Poe and heard nothing, Cousin William, visiting Baltimore, wrote again in mid-June, encouragingly and reassuringly (as John Pendleton Kennedy had done in 1835). He asked, with kind concern, "Ought you ever to give up in despair when you have such resources as yr well stored mind to apply to? let me entreat you then to persevere, for I hope the time is not far distant, when a change will take place in yr affairs & place you beyond want in this world." And he warned against drink, "a great enemy to our family" (17:145–46). (We may readily recall Poe's father and Poe's brother.) He took an interest in Poe's projected "Stylus" but did not know that, in late May or early June, Poe had experienced another reverse: Clarke had declared in the *Saturday Museum* that he would no longer support Poe's magazine.[30]

Financial problems probably contributed to his decision: Clarke, who had three different business partners in only a few months, acknowledged his "difficulties" in the newspaper.[31] Perhaps Poe's critical severity weakened Clarke's commitment.[32] It is also possible that Poe's drinking played a part; Clarke, a temperance man, may have finally just lost patience (as Thomas W. White had done before him). Certainly Poe's reputation was damaged—Lambert Wilmer wrote about Poe to John Tomlin on May 20, "Poor fellow! he is not a teetotaler by any means, and I fear he is going headlong to destruction, moral, physical and intellectual."[33] Poe was angry at Clarke for his decision, writing to Lowell on June 20, "alas! my Magazine scheme has exploded—or, at least, I have been deprived, through the imbecility, or rather through the idiocy of my partner, of all means of prosecuting it for the present" (O 1:401).[34] And he was angry at Wilmer, too—"a reprobate of the lowest class"—and obtained the offending letter from Tomlin (O 1:404–5; H 17:152). Notably, though, both Clarke and Wilmer, admitting Poe's drinking, defended Poe in later years. Clarke characterized him as "kind hearted, affectionate, refined and amiable"; Wilmer referred to his "years of patient toil and heroic effort."[35]

Owing Clarke for his financial support for "The Stylus," Poe left him a manuscript story, originally intended for the magazine. And an obituary of Clarke states that he owned "unpublished" pieces, "some of the most powerful satires ever written by Poe." These manuscripts have never been found.[36]

Furious as Poe was at Clarke's withdrawal from "The Stylus," he would have been delighted to learn, by June 14, that the hundred-dollar first prize in the short story contest of the *Dollar Newspaper* had gone to "The Gold-Bug." He had composed the story in 1842, reportedly writing it backward.[37] He had submitted it to *Graham's* and then withdrawn it, perhaps anticipating its publication in "The Stylus" and later entering it in the *Dollar Newspaper* competition. The illustrator F. O. C. Darley later recalled that Poe had read it aloud to him from a self-fashioned roll, comprising individual pieces of paper, each of them affixed to the next.[38]

The judges for the competition were the playwright Robert T. Conrad (whom Poe had earlier ranked as having "the first place among our Philadelphia *literati*"), physician Henry Street Patterson, and *Public Ledger* editor Washington L. Lane.[39] The *Dollar Newspaper* published the first half of the

"The Gold-Bug" on June 21 and the entire story on June 28, followed by several reprintings. Prints of two drawings by Darley—of finding and showing the treasure—accompanied the story.[40]

The immediately popular adventure story concerns pirates, buried treasure, and secret writing—a compelling, even exhilarating, combination. One cold October evening, the narrator visits his friend William Legrand, who lives in a hut on Sullivan's Island, off Charleston, South Carolina, with his servant Jupiter, who had earlier been freed from slavery by Legrand's family. Legrand is excited about a beetle he has found and briefly lent, so he draws a picture of it and passes that picture to his guest, who is seated near a vigorous fire in the fireplace. Legrand's Newfoundland dog arrives and playfully jumps upon the familiar figure in the armchair. When Wolf settles down, Legrand's visitor settles into a study of the picture, which looks to him more like a death's head than a beetle, and he returns the document to his host, who is at first insulted, then mystified, then fascinated. A month later, a worried Jupiter visits the narrator, in Charleston, to deliver an enigmatic missive from Legrand, requesting his friend's return on a matter "of the *highest* importance."

The narrator does return, with Jupiter, to the hut, and believing that his friend has lost his mind about his singular beetle, reluctantly accompanies Legrand and Jupiter to the mainland, to a large tulip tree in a remote hilly area. At his master's request, Jupiter climbs the tree, finds a skull nailed to a branch, and drops the gold-bug, attached to a string, through what he thinks is the skull's left eye socket. Legrand measures fifty feet from the tree, through the point to which the gold-bug was dropped, and the three men then dig at the indicated location, but in vain. Understanding, with a mix of anger and relief, the error with regard to the eye socket used, Legrand marks a point three inches from the original one and measures fifty feet from the tree through this new point. The three men dig a new hole, and they find Captain Kidd's treasure chest, with gold and jewels worth well over the initial estimate of $1.5 million.

The remainder of the story involves the explanation of the extraordinary detection of Legrand, beginning with his realizing that the parchment sheet on which he had drawn the beetle had heat-sensitive markings, which had begun to become visible through proximity to the fire, when Wolf had jumped on the seated visitor. These markings include the death's head (the seal of pirates), an image of a kid (a pun on Captain Kidd), and, between the two, a code. Legrand, possessing the cryptographic skills of his author, relies on patterns of alphabetic frequency to decipher the directions. Then, through local exploration and inquiry, he is able to clarify the meaning of puzzling locations in these directions. And so, with the narrator and Jupiter, Legrand finds and unearths the pirate treasure.[41]

The remarkable story has a variety of likely literary sources, among them Washington Irving's 1824 short story "Wolfert Webber," featuring a Dutchman, a German doctor, a "black fisherman," and buried treasure, as well as Robert Montgomery Bird's 1836 novel *Sheppard Lee*, featuring an old slave, his master, and the master's digging for Captain Kidd's buried treasure (M 3:800). Another probable literary source, for Jupiter in particular, is William Gilmore Simms's 1839 short story "The Lazy Crow," which includes a superstitious slave, Scipio, who speaks in a lively, purportedly comical Gullah dialect. Poe could not have missed this work by his renowned southern contemporary Simms since it appeared in *The Gift of 1840*, the same volume in which his "William Wilson" also appeared.[42] Despite the claim, made in 1845, that Jupiter is not a caricature, he clearly is. We can acknowledge the stereotype even as we study the story further.[43]

If we seek the treasure of the buried form of "The Gold-Bug," we are readily rewarded. The first half of the symmetrical frame includes such language as, "a large Newfoundland . . . leaped upon my shoulders" (M 3:809), "a death's-head" (M 3:809), "the beetle" (M 3:810), "He . . . was about to crumple it [the parchment], apparently to throw it in the fire" (M 3:810), "Fastening one end of this [a tape measure] at that point of the trunk of the tree which was nearest the peg, he unrolled it till it reached the peg, and thence farther unrolled it . . . for the distance of fifty feet" (M 3:822), and "'my lef eye' . . . his *right* organ of vision" (M 3:824). The second half of the symmetrical frame includes similar language, in reverse: "'de lef eye' . . . his right eye" (M 3:824), "Taking, now, the tape-measure from the nearest point of the trunk, as before, and continuing the extension in a straight line to the distance of fifty feet (M 3: 824–25, with variant "the trunk to the peg, as before"), "I was about to crumple it [the parchment] up and throw it angrily in the fire" (M 3:828, with variant "into the fire"), "death's-head" (M 3:829), "the beetle" (M 3:829), and "the Newfoundland . . . leaped upon your shoulders" (M 3:832).[44] At the framed center, Jupiter is ascending from a kneeling position: he "looked, mutely, from his master to myself, then from myself to his master" (M 3:824). If "master" is A and "myself" is B, then we have the central chiastic ABBA:

master		myself
myself	X	master

X does indeed mark the spot.[45]

Underscoring the symmetry of the tale is the palindromic phrase "sanguine . . . enigma" (M 3:842) and, in a later version, another such phrase, "ominous insignium" (M 3:843). The phrase "death's head" is a near palindrome, as one of my former students, Wesley McMasters, noted, and even "gold-bug" is, according to one scholar, Henri Justin, "slightly palindromic."[46] Poe's later contention in *Eureka* that "the sense of the symmetrical . . . is the poetic essence of the Universe" (L1 96) was embodied in Poe's own fiction as early as the 1835 "Berenice" and is evident again in this celebrated—and beautifully elaborated—tale.

Poe's integration of his life in "The Gold-Bug" is both evident and subtle. Clearly, Poe is recalling through the setting his time at Fort Moultrie on Sullivan's Island in 1827–28—he even twice mentions the fort at the story's beginning (M 3:807, 808). It is notable that before Poe was stationed at Fort Moultrie, when he was still in Boston in 1827, he would likely have encountered, next door to Calvin F. S. Thomas's shop, in the Bowles and Dearborn bookstore, Thomas Green Fessenden's magazine *New England Farmer*. For this periodical featured a first-page article in two successive issues (August 31 and September 7) titled "Remarks on the Scarabaeus Roseus, or Rose-Bug." Of course, Poe had gone to Boston in the first place because of his March 1827 falling out with his foster father, John Allan.[47]

There are suggestive allusions in "The Gold-Bug" to overcoming a problematic father figure. The narrator's concluding about Legrand, just after the tale's midpoint, "Here my friend, about whose madness I now saw, or fancied that I saw, certain indications of method, removed the peg" (M 3:824) recalls Polonius's remarking about Hamlet, "Though this be madness, yet there is method in't" (2.2.205–6). Through his narrator, Poe intimates Hamlet, the detective-hero son seeking to displace the objectionable uncle, Claudius. Similarly, the narrator's referring to Captain Kidd's writing his encrypted directions, "When, in the course of his composition" (M 3:840), recalls Thomas Jefferson's beginning the Declaration of Independence, "When in the course of human events." Through his narrator, Poe hints at the son seeking to displace an objectionable father, King George III. And, significantly, Poe had already relied on the Declaration of Independence in his March 19, 1827, letter of grievances to the objectionable John Allan (O 1:10–12).[48]

Unlike the Dupin tales, this ratiocinative tale does not relate to a woman of uncertain reputation—Poe's mother—but, rather, through allusions to *Hamlet* and the Declaration of Independence, to a callous king—Poe's foster father. Like the impoverished Legrand, seeking reinstatement to his lost riches through Captain Kidd's treasure, the impoverished Poe seeks reinstatement to his rightful place of affluence and high regard through his writing. Like Prince Hamlet, like Thomas Jefferson, Poe is another son resentful of cruel male authority—or, to employ the language of the tale's center, another self trying to become master.[49]

The judges of the short story contest of the *Dollar Newspaper* considered "The Gold-Bug" to be "a capital story." George Lippard in the *Citizen Soldier* stated, "It is one of the best stories that Poe ever wrote." And Thomas Cottrell Clarke in the *Saturday Museum* noted, "[It] has been very justly designated as the most remarkable 'American work of fiction that has been published within the last fifteen years,'" commenting, "The period might very safely have been extended back to a period much more remote," and remarking, too, "It is the unique work of a singularly constituted, but indubitably great intellect."[50] Two objections were soon resolved: Francis H. Duffee, alleging fraud on June 27, settled with Poe, retracting his accusation on July 24; and John S. Du Solle, alleging plagiarism on July 1, retracted his accusation on July 15.[51]

The popular response to "The Gold-Bug" was great. The story was repeatedly reprinted, and the *Public Ledger* fulsomely characterized readers' responses: "All who have read it through, so far as we have heard it spoken of, pronounce it superior to any American production that they ever before read."[52] Poe later wrote to Lowell, in 1844, "Of the 'Gold-Bug' (my most successful tale) more than 300,000 copies have been circulated" (O 1:441). Scholars have not considered this an exaggeration.[53] Poe clearly had a hit on his hands. There was even a play of "The Gold-Bug" performed in Philadelphia, but unlike the original work, it was not a success.[54]

The writer—and a good friend—Mayne Reid evidently continued to stop by Poe's Spring Garden home; he later recalled Virginia's beauty and modesty, Poe's genius and originality, and Maria Clemm's devotion and vigilance. Poe, he wrote, was "a generous host, an affectionate son-in-law and husband." One incident suggests a summer call—Virginia's removing the skins from fresh peaches and, mixing the fruit with cream and sugar, offering the sweet concoction to visitors. But, of course, Reid knew that Virginia had consumption, and Poe later acknowledged having had "domestic and pecuniary troubles" (O 1:407).[55]

Poe's professional achievement continued. On or about July 18, George R. Graham's brother William H. Graham published *The Prose Romances of Edgar A. Poe,* comprising "The Murders in the Rue Morgue" and "The Man

That Was Used Up." The edition was well received; one review in the *Saturday Courier* closed, "For learning, uniqueness and originality—we unhesitatingly say that Edgar A. Poe, in his own country, stands entirely alone."[56] Furthermore, having sharply critiqued Thomas Ward in *Graham's Magazine* of March 1843, Poe offered a pointed assessment of William Ellery Channing in the August issue.[57] And before August 18, the *United States Saturday Post* (more typically titled the *Saturday Evening Post*) published Poe's classic short story "The Black Cat."

This is another tale of metempsychosis—the transmigration of souls—harking back to such early Poe tales as "Metzengerstein" and "Morella." As was the case with "The Gold-Bug," he wrote it on a self-fashioned roll and read it aloud to Felix O. C. Darley.[58] A brief plot summary will be useful: The narrator, condemned to die, confesses from his prison cell the sins he has committed. In the first half of the tale, inebriated, he gouges out the eye of his black cat, and later, in a fit of perverseness, he hangs the cat—the murder revealed by a plaster bas-relief in the wall. In the second half, the narrator, fearful of a second black cat (suggestive of the first) and enraged at his wife's protecting it, axes his wife to death—this murder later revealed by the cry of the second cat, entombed with the corpse of the wife, behind the freshly plastered wall. The white breast of this one-eyed black cat had taken the shape of a gallows—and the murderer is indeed to be hanged. Notably, the second half of the tale is parallel to the first.

The narrator recalls his wife's linking a black cat with a witch—she considered "all black cats as witches in disguise" (M 3:850)—a linking that Poe himself made in the 1840 "Instinct vs Reason—A Black Cat": "black cats are all of them witches" (M 2:479).[59] As Brett Zimmerman has noted, the nature of the killing of the cat in the first half—hanging—is appropriate given the well-known punishment for supposed witches in Salem. And the connection of the black cat with witchcraft is hinted in the second half with reference to the black cat's "craft" (M 3:859; see also 857).[60] Poe observes the logic of the fantastic to embody the logic of the human mind. Though he would object to "the heresy of *The Didactic*" (L2 182), he is keenly interested in employing the otherworldly to dramatize what he considers psychological truth.

Whatever prompts the narrator—whether alcohol or perverseness or fear—his sense of his own sin will prevail. He admits that his explanation of the mysterious and accusative bas-relief of the hanged cat—that the animal had been thrown through a window and fixed into the fresh plaster—did not satisfy his conscience (M 3:853). Indeed, it is conscience itself that must be satisfied (however ostensibly repressed it is), as it will be through the supernatural, the metempsychosis of the first cat to the second, and the eventual revelation and confession.

In an earlier Poe tale of guilt, "The Tell-Tale Heart," a critical allusion is to a conscience-stricken character in *Macbeth*—the guilty Lady Macbeth, recalled through the phrase "the damned spot" (M 3:795; see *Macbeth* 5.1.35).[61] Similarly, in "The Black Cat," a critical allusion is to another conscience-stricken character in that play—the guilty Macbeth himself, recalled through the phrase "to render doubly sure their assurance" (M 3:858; see *Macbeth* 4.1.83).

The black cat in both its forms is an emblem of conscience—a kind of feline William Wilson. As the novelist Marilynne Robinson has observed, "The Black Cat," among several Poe tales, speaks to "a perfect justice." It is one of Poe's "moral parables."[62]

Sources for the tale included the *Baltimore Monument*'s 1836 "The Black Cat," as well as Charles Dickens's 1840 "The Clock-Case: A Confession Found in a Prison in the Time of Charles the Second" (in *Master Humphrey's Clock*) and the *Public Ledger*'s 1842 "Mysterious."[63] And there were autobiographical connections with regard to some of the sins of the narrator of Poe's tale. As a child, Poe is reported to have killed a pet of his foster mother's: "The first Mrs. Allan had a pet fawn, and to spite her once, in a fit of resentment, he cut the little animal's throat."[64] Removing the context, Poe made the horrible even more horrible. Furthermore, as a man, Poe certainly yielded repeatedly to "the Fiend Intemperance"—later acknowledged to be a "disease" (M 3:851). Again Poe integrated his life in his work. Some of the guilt was probably his own. And he had already acknowledged, in 1840, the personal nature of his work, discouraging too much focus on Germanic origins: "If in many of my productions terror has been the thesis, I maintain that terror is not of Germany, but of the soul" (M 2:473).

Late August and early to mid-September 1843 may have been when Poe visited the Barhyte Farm in Saratoga Springs, New York. Apparently, James Barhyte, son of John Barhyte, the owner, and his, wife Ann, heard, while rowing home from a fishing outing, the repeated word "Nevermore." Rowing closer, the boy saw a familiar guest, Poe, pacing in a clearing in the woods, reciting a poem about a bird, with the recurrent "Nevermore." Landing, James declared to Poe, "Oh! What a name for a bird! Who ever heard of a bird named 'Nevermore'?" And Poe replied, "I have it. Just the thing. That will make the very stanza I need to complete the poem."[65] (This would have been stanza 9 [M 1:366–67].) Poe biographer George E. Woodberry doubted the Saratoga story in 1885 but was more accepting in 1909, proposing that the version of the poem referred to was an early draft of the well-known work, the same as the one that George R. Graham later rejected after Poe read it out loud. The critical model for the metrics of "The Raven" as we know it was Elizabeth Barrett's "Lady Geraldine's Courtship," not published until 1844. Poe's contemporary Peter Pindar Pease attested to E. M. Murdock's stating that Poe visited Saratoga in 1843.[66]

Poe's correspondence from Philadelphia soon after his return gives us a sense of his state at the time. The writer remained in straitened circumstances, despite his contest victory—he sought the ten dollars that Lowell owed him, and he tried to sell property on behalf of Maria Clemm, whom he characterized as "in indigent circumstances" (O 1:407, 409). Yet he also remained hopeful, as is clear from his encouraging letter to a young farmer-poet from South Attleboro, Massachusetts. Abijah M. Ide Jr. had reached out to Poe on October 1, seeking literary fellowship (H 17:153–55), and Poe replied warmly on October 19, "You ask me for my hand in friendship. I give it with the deepest sincerity." Furthermore, Poe offered heartening advice: "I would say to you, without hesitation, aspire. . . . Be bold—read much—write much—publish little—keep aloof from the little wits, and fear nothing." He went on to refer to "a very bold and comprehensive enterprise"—presumably his planned literary magazine, "The Stylus" (O 1:410–11). Poe could be kind and optimistic, responsive to another's needs. And he did not give up.[67]

In the fall of 1843, Poe published two minor pieces: the essay "Raising the Wind; or, Diddling Considered as One of the Exact Sciences" and the sketch "Morning on the Wissahiccon." The former appeared in October in the weekly *Philadelphia Saturday Courier,* where five Poe tales had appeared in 1832. The latter, prompted by a picture by J. G. Chapman, appeared in early November in the 1844 volume of the annual *The Opal,* where "A Chapter of Suggestions" would appear in the 1845 volume. "Raising the Wind" concerns a variety of grifts, and "Morning on the Wissahiccon"—a tribute to a tributary—depicts a dreamy drift. Though these are modest works, they highlight a considerable range. And probably sometime in the fall, Poe was writing the more ambitious "A Tale of the Ragged Mountains."[68] He was also writing a review of Cooper's novel *Wyandotté,* published in the November issue of *Graham's,* and another of Robert Tyler's poem "Death," published in the December issue.[69] And he worked on a lecture on American poetry.

On October 21, the *Philadelphia Public Ledger* advertised the new season of the William Wirt Institute Lectures and Debates, to be held at the Julianna

Street Church, three blocks east of North Seventh Street, between October 1843 and February 1844. Listed third (among ten dates) was: "November 21, 1843—Lecture, by Edgar A. Poe, Esq Subject—American Poetry." This would be the first documented lecture of more than a dozen lectures that Poe would give over the next few years. His growing fame was such by then that he could command an audience. Other speakers in the series of this season included the newly elected sheriff Morton McMichael on "The Past and Present Social Condition of Women" and the lawyer and playwright David Paul Brown on "Immortality of the Soul."[70] On November 15, George Lippard announced Poe's lecture in the *Citizen Soldier,* stating, "Poe was born a poet, his mind is stamped with the impress of genius. He is, perhaps, the most original writer that ever existed in America." Praising, in particular, Poe's *Arthur Gordon Pym* and his work on *Graham's Magazine,* Lippard stated, "We can promise the audience a refined intellectual repast in the lecture of Edgar Allan Poe."[71] The *Public Ledger* and the *Pennsylvania Inquirer* published brief announcements of Poe's lecture, with the latter declaring, "A large and intellectual audience will no doubt be in attendance."[72]

Approximately 1,100 people crowded the Julianna Street Church on Tuesday, November 21, to attend Poe's lecture on American poetry. Hundreds had to be turned away. Poe spoke forcefully and eloquently, criticizing those he considered faux authorities, including Rufus W. Griswold, and censuring the practice of "puffing" inferior work. He was sometimes severe, even personally so. He also praised poetry that he admired by two Philadelphia writers, both of whom had spoken in earlier seasons of the William Wirt Institute series, Robert T. Conrad and Robert Morris. He spoke in particular of Conrad's "Sonnets on the Lord's Prayer," which he read aloud, creating "a marked sensation." And he lauded the poetry of Morris. Notably, neither Conrad nor Morris had been included in Griswold's anthology *Poets and Poetry of America.* The audience was thoroughly responsive, offering the speaker much applause. The lecture was later deemed to have offered "good sense and good judgment"; it was described as "one of the most brilliant and successful [lectures] of the season," indeed "one of the best ever delivered in this city."[73] The evening was a sheer triumph.

It is relevant to add that Griswold's standing in Philadelphia at the time was not strong. According to Poe in September 1842, Graham "is not especially pleased with Griswold" (O 1:358), an editor at *Graham's Magazine.* And according to Lippard in August 1843, Graham had "discharged" Griswold from the magazine. Graham is later reported to have said that Griswold had anonymously attacked fellow editor Charles J. Peterson.[74]

When Poe gave the same lecture on November 28, 1843, to the Franklin Lyceum in Temperance Hall in Wilmington, Delaware, he did not soften his critique. George R. Graham later wrote of Poe, "Literature with him was religion; and he, its high-priest, with a whip of scorpions scourged the money-changers from the temple."[75] The *Spirit of the Times* considered the talk to be "Good, but rather severe."[76] Poe's earning the enmity of Griswold would prove to have rather severe consequences.

Thomas Cottrell Clarke had commissioned Thomas Dunn English to write a temperance novel for the *Saturday Museum*, and though it was ready in June, its publication was delayed because of the unfinished illustrations. *The Doom of the Drinker* began to appear in installments in the *Cold Water Magazine* in October and then in the *Saturday Museum* on November 25. The third installment, published on December 9, featured English's rendering of Poe, "a pale, gentlemanly looking personage, with a quick piercing, restless eye, and a very broad and peculiarly shaped forehead." Acknowledging this gentleman's brilliance, including his analytical skills, English mentions the character's susceptibility to wine. More problematically, he contends that the gentleman is guilty of theft, betrayal, and deceit. English's biographer, William H. Gravely, attributes English's hostility to Poe during their time in Philadelphia to Poe's critical strictures and his drinking (evidence of which English saw in Philadelphia and Washington, D.C.). Resentment and self-righteousness are a potent combination. Gravely sees the portrait as evidence of English's "revengeful feeling toward Poe." And English's writing about Poe would become even more virulent in New York City, prompting a libel suit.[77]

Poe continued lecturing. It had been rainy for ten days in Newark, Delaware, and there was mud. Poe reportedly fell stepping down from his stagecoach and needed to borrow a coat, which was too tight, but he appeared, at his lecture at Newark Academy on December 23, "a dignified and well-bred gentleman." (There is disagreement as to whether or not Poe had earlier been drinking.) Perhaps owing to the recent weather, the audience was small, but it included students and teachers from Newark Academy and Delaware College, as well as interested local residents. For nearly two hours, Poe "charmed" those in attendance.[78]

Poe censured puffing and mocked the elliptical language of the Transcendentalists. He treated Griswold and his anthology "in not the most gentle manner" and again observed the omission of Conrad and Morris from the book. He faulted Griswold's selection of poets and of their works. He discussed and assessed individual poets, women and men. And he concluded, objecting to didacticism in poetry, focusing on "the true end and province of poetry"—presumably, as we know from his April 1842 *Graham's* review of Longfellow's *Ballads,* "a wild effort to reach the beauty above . . . a forethought of the loveliness to come." This was, according to the writer of the sketch of the event, "one of the most interesting and instructive lectures I have ever had the pleasure of hearing." We may well imagine that by lecture's end, even as the boots of Poe's listeners were caked with mud, their minds were considering "the desire of the moth for the star."[79]

Back in Philadelphia, Poe was doubtless writing. He was probably making progress on—or finishing—"A Tale of the Ragged Mountains," and perhaps he had begun "The Spectacles." His review of James Fenimore Cooper's biography *Ned Myers* and his notice of R. H. Horne's poem *Orion* appeared in the January 1844 issue of *Graham's Magazine,* and he may well have been preparing critical work for the March issue.

On December 29, three representatives of the Mechanics Institute of Reading invited Poe to lecture, but their letter languished in the Philadelphia post office for two months (O 1:426). Poe did lecture again in Philadelphia, this time at the Philadelphia Museum, on January 10, 1844. George Lippard anticipated the event with enthusiasm, writing, in part, "Mr. Poe is rapidly adding to his towering fame as Poet, Author, Critic, in his new capacity of lecturer; and all friends of a correct and healthy national literature hail with delight, the appearance of an able and eloquent advocate of the right and caustic censor of the wrong." Yet, again, Poe's sharp criticism was not always approved. After his January 31 lecture on American poetry in Baltimore, the editor Joseph E. Snodgrass wrote of Poe, in part, "He was witheringly severe upon Rufus W. Griswold."[80]

Sometime in late 1843 or early 1844, the artist A. C. Smith made a watercolor portrait of Poe. The image was an amiable and refined one, but Poe stated, "It scarcely resembles me at all" (O 1:431). Yet this almost ingratiating rendering would have an impact, for it was to be engraved and included in *Graham's Magazine* of February 1845.[81] And in late January 1844, Thomas Dunn English effectively parodied Poe's tale "The Black Cat" with "The Ghost of the Grey Tadpole" in the *Irish Citizen.*[82]

Meanwhile, Poe was planning a change. His two cherished Philadelphia prospects—editing "The Stylus," in partnership with Clarke, and working in the Custom House—had vanished. On February 18, he described himself as "[b]eing upon the point of quitting Philadelphia for some weeks" (O 1:425). Philadelphia and New York had long been the axis of American publishing, but New York was gaining ascendancy in the 1840s.[83] Probably Poe sought new and greater opportunities in Gotham.

Ready for his departure, Poe was still writing. It is likely that by early February he had begun his third and final Dupin tale, "The Purloined Letter," and a simulated journalistic account, "The Balloon Hoax." He also soon wrote a revealing letter to his friend George Lippard, suitable for publication, closing with advice about dealing with enemies and concluding, "*I have never yet been able to make up my mind whether I regard as the higher compliment, the approbation of a man of honor and talent, or the abuse of an ass or a blackguard. Both are excellent in their way—for a man who looks steadily up*" (O 1:423–24). (Poe did offer his permission to Lippard to publish the letter, and Lippard shortly did so.) And Poe remained interested in lecturing—he inquired of James Russell Lowell about the possibility of giving a talk in Boston. In a letter of March 6, Lowell discouraged him regarding the present year but suggested that something might develop in the following year (H 17:158–60).[84]

In mid-February, the March issue of *Graham's Magazine* was published, including remarkable reviews by Poe of R. H. Horne's *Orion* and James Russell Lowell's *Poems*.[85] Elaborating the argument in the April 1842 review of Longfellow's *Ballads,* both reviews offer some criticism and exceptional praise. Though disparaging didacticism, false knowing, and opaque language,[86] Poe extols what he considers the extraordinary poetry of Horne's myth-focused work. He provides generous extracts, commenting after one of these, concerning an enshadowed elk drinking at a stream at dusk, "There is nothing more richly—more weirdly—more chastely—more sublimely imaginative—in the wide realm of poetical literature. It will be seen that we *have* enthusiasm—but we reserve it for pictures such as this." The poem is, Poe judges, "one of the noblest, if not the very noblest poetical work of the age."[87] Poe's critique was itself soon extolled by John S. Du Solle in the *Spirit of the Times* as "a rare production—one of those strong, thoughtful, intelligible, and truth-telling papers, which only come across us about once in a century."[88]

Poe's review of Lowell's *Poems,* shorter than the *Orion* review and unsigned, offers similar intense accolades.[89] Poe considers Lowell to be "*at the very head of the poets of America*" and views "A Legend of Brittany"—a poem of seduction and murder, guilt and heavenly entreaty—"as by far the finest poetical work, of equal length, which the country has produced." Esteeming a concern for truth and human welfare, though faulting their presence in poetry, Poe goes on to acclaim, in particular, the climactic portion of the poem, concerning a church organ: "The description of the swelling of the organ . . .

surpasses, in all the loftier merits, any similar passage we have seen. It is truly magnificent. . . . We know not where to look, in all American poetry, for any thing more richly ideal, or more forcibly conveyed." (Perhaps, through such an encomium, Poe indirectly contributed to Nathaniel Hawthorne's transforming this very passage at the climax of *The Scarlet Letter*.) Poe closes by asserting of Lowell, "[H]e has given evidence of at least as high poetical genius as any man in America—if not a loftier genius than any."[90] Poe has found in the poetry of Horne and Lowell that hint of otherworldly beauty that he so ardently sought.

At this time, the 1844 New York edition of Goold Brown's *The Institutes of English Grammar* appeared, with quoted praise by Poe, drawn from his "Notes upon English Verse" in the March 1843 *Pioneer*: "A work perhaps the very best of its kind, and of which the accuracy is far more than usual." It is telling that Poe's words appear here with those of teachers, principals, and superintendents. He was evidently considered not just an author, but also an authority. But Poe had taken issue, in "Notes upon English Verse," with Brown's definition of "versification."[91]

On March 1, Poe picked up from the Philadelphia post office the December 29, 1843, letter from John C. Myers, Samuel Williams, and William Graeff Jr. of the Mechanics Institute of Reading, Pennsylvania. They were inviting Poe to present his lecture on American poetry in Reading (O 1:426–27). Poe responded immediately with interest and on March 7 agreed to the proposed date of March 12 (O 1:428). Probably Poe took the train from Philadelphia to Reading. He spoke at Academy Hall and, according to one account, quoted from N. P. Willis and Philip Pendleton Cooke and attacked Rufus W. Griswold.[92] He probably also read aloud Thomas H. Chivers's "The Heavenly Vision," for he would write to Chivers four months later, in July 1844, "I have been lately lecturing on 'American Poetry' and have drawn profuse tears from large and intellectual audiences by the recital of your 'Heavenly Vision'— which I can never weary of repeating" (O 1:453). Poe had seen this poem as a submission to *Graham's Magazine* in 1842; had passed it on to the new editor, Griswold; and had seen it again in its published form in the June 1842 issue of the magazine. He had written to Chivers in July 1842 that his "Heavenly Vision" (and another poem, about Shelley) were "the finest [poems] I have *ever read*" (O 1:349).[93] It is easy to imagine Poe's responding fully to "The Heavenly Vision," a poem of consolation, one offering solace from the spirit of a lost beloved.[94] We need only remember the departed Eliza Arnold Poe and Jane Stith Stanard, the ending of *Pym* and the poem "To Helen."

The *Baltimore Sun* commented on Poe at Academy Hall, "He was greeted by a large and respectable audience, and they testified their approbation of the lecture by repeated bursts of applause."[95] He had done very well in his lectures on American poetry in Philadelphia, Wilmington, Newark, Baltimore, and Reading. Ahead of him lay additional speaking engagements—of great success and of great disappointment.

By late March, close to the end of his stay in Philadelphia, Poe may well have already submitted "The Purloined Letter" to the next volume of *The Gift*. And two new tales appeared: "A Tale of the Ragged Mountains" in *Godey's Lady's Book* of April 1844 and "The Spectacles" in the *Dollar Newspaper* of March 27.

The former work was an Oriental tale, about mesmeric or magnetic influence. In an 1827 trek through the Ragged Mountains, west of Charlottesville, the sickly Bedloe experiences the 1780 uprising in Benares even as his physician, Doctor Templeton, is writing about the event. Having joined the smaller, defensive force, Bedloe experiences death from a snakelike arrow to his head even as Templeton writes of the death of his old friend Oldeb in the uprising from a poisoned arrow to his head. After his trance, Bedloe does in fact die, reportedly because of a poisonous snakelike creature, mistakenly applied as a leech to his head by the doctor. Bedloe's trance had repeated the earlier death and presaged the later one. Doctor Templeton evidently believes that the soul of Oldeb had migrated to the body of Bedloe. Thus, Poe has returned to his favored theme of metempsychosis.[96]

A variety of sources has been identified, including Charles Brockden Brown's novel *Edgar Huntly*, T. B. Macaulay's review of G. R. Gleig's *Memoirs of the Life of the Right Hon. Warren Hastings*, and the Gleig work itself (M 3:936–38).[97] A symmetrical design is evident, elements of which are, "I bent my steps immediately to the mountains," "the sun could not be seen," and "in . . . fearful agitation" in the first half and "in furious agitation," "the sun had never been able to shine" and "I . . . bent my steps eagerly homewards'" in the second half. The significant center is a pair of parallel sentences in the seventeenth and eighteenth paragraphs of this thirty-four-paragraph story: "You arose and descended into the city" and "I arose, as you say, and descended into the city."[98] A tale of a double again involves doubled halves.

The integration of Poe's life in his work is betokened by the tall, slender, ill Bedloe as his brother Henry, and the cherished Oldeb, long dead and represented in a watercolor portrait, as his mother, Eliza Arnold Poe. Through Templeton's belief in metempsychosis, Poe conveys the deep connection he felt between the two. Poe echoes in this tale the autobiographical resonance of brother and mother that he earlier intimated in *Pym*.[99]

By contrast, the latter tale, "The Spectacles," is a long, labored, unfunny farce about supposed "love at first sight." A young man with poor vision is captivated by the image of a woman in the audience at the opera, one Eugénie Lalande. He pursues her, proposes to her, and marries her, only to discover, by putting on her spectacles, that she is a very old woman—indeed, she discloses, his great-great-grandmother. She and his friend Talbot and a clergyman (with the aid of an antique miniature) had duped him; fortunately, the marriage ceremony had been a fraud. He does marry her young friend Stephanie Lalande—and stands to inherit the estate of his aged ancestor. If the story is unspectacular, it does sharpen our appreciation of Poe's willingness to take risks in the interest of demonstrating the breadth of his literary skill. And again he explores the limits of perception.

On March 30, Poe sent a copy of the March 27 issue of the *Dollar Newspaper*, with "The Spectacles" in it, to James Russell Lowell. His having done so suggests some degree of pride in the work, though he acknowledges, "I fear it will prove little to your taste" (O 1:431).[100] Poe reveals in this final letter of his six-year residence in Philadelphia that he was "positively idle," that he considers himself "at a sad loss for a Biographer," and that he continues to aspire to edit an elite literary magazine, perhaps funded through silent investors from the literary world (O 1:431–33).

A week later, on the morning of Saturday, April 6, Poe and Virginia were finally leaving for New York. They arrived early at the Walnut Street Wharf to take a vessel to the Camden and Amboy Railroad. Poe had their trunks stowed (limit of fifty pounds of baggage per passenger), and in a nearby hotel they glanced at several local newspapers. The two boarded at 7:00 a.m., presumably paying the full fare of three dollars apiece. They began their trip, Poe reported in a cheery letter to Maria Clemm, "in good spirits" (O 1:437).[101] They were, after all, en route to new possibilities. And, at his best, Poe was indeed "a man who looks steadily up."

18

"A Certainty of Success"

1844-1845

ARRIVING BY STEAMBOAT FROM AMBOY, New Jersey, to a wharf on the North River (Hudson River) side of Lower Manhattan, Poe and Virginia separated, she remaining on board, and he buying an umbrella and walking steadily up Greenwich Street. Poe quickly found a boardinghouse, on the west side of the street, just short of Cedar, and brought Virginia back to their agreeable new lodging. That night, missing her mother and their cat Catterina, Virginia had "a hearty cry" (as Poe wrote in a letter to Mrs. Clemm in Philadelphia [O 1:438]). But the Poes had found abundance—for dinner, ham and veal and cakes "in the greatest profusion," and for breakfast, veal cutlets and ham and eggs. Poe wrote with evident pleasure, "I never sat down to a more plentiful or a nicer breakfast." He added, "Sis [Virginia] is delighted, and we are both in excellent spirits" (O 1:438). Commenting on their bountiful board, Poe comically mentioned Catterina: "I wish Kate could see it—she would faint" (O 1:437).

True, there were serious money concerns—he had only $4.50—but he would soon borrow a few dollars for a couple of weeks. And his writing would bring in more. He recurred, reassuringly, "[I]t is impossible we could be more comfortable or more at home than we are" (O 1:438). Virginia was coughing only slightly, and Poe was not drinking. This was an auspicious start.

In the next few days, Poe made his way several blocks north and east (or east and north) to 91 Nassau Street, the southwest corner of Nassau and Fulton Streets, the home of Moses Y. Beach's *New York Sun*. Nassau Street was the bustling publishing center of New York, akin to Chestnut Street in Philadelphia and Washington Street in Boston. The *Sun* was the celebrated penny daily that had featured, in 1835, Richard Adams Locke's "Moon Hoax." In Philadelphia, Poe had been working up more "breaking news," a faux account of a balloon voyage from North Wales, across the Atlantic, to Charleston, South Carolina. He sold the new sensation to the *Sun* for fifty dollars. The joke was apparently very practical.[1]

Relying on Monck Mason's *Account of the Late Aeronautical Expedition from London to Weilburg, accomplished by Robert Hollond, Esq., Monck Mason, Esq., and Charles Green, Aeronaut* and an article, drawn from Mason's *Remarks on the Ellipsoidal Balloon* [...], titled "Another Aerial Machine"—perhaps its appearance in the *Pictorial Times*—Poe fashioned a document of verisimilar detail and dramatic journal entries.[2] On April 6, 1844 (according to this document), a balloon named the *Victoria*, managed by screw and rudder, and bound for Paris with eight people in its wicker car, encountered adverse east winds. Monck Mason, encouraged by some passengers, altered his course to the west, over the Atlantic Ocean, to North America. The balloon landed, after seventy-five hours of flight, on April 9, on the beach of Sullivan's Island, near Fort Moultrie (Poe's old posting). Whether this imagined achievement was truly "the most stupendous, the most interesting, and the most important undertaking, ever accomplished or even attempted by man" (M 3:1082) is another matter.

The hoax was published in an April 13 extra of the *Sun*. Unquestionably there was a crowd. But there are two different accounts of what ensued. According to Poe in the May 25, 1844, issue of the *Columbia Spy*, "[T]he 'Balloon-Hoax' made a far more intense sensation than anything of that character since the 'Moon-Story' of Locke." The announcement of the coming "extra" in the morning paper produced a great throng around the *Sun* office, and the item itself, available shortly before noon, was in such demand that it sold for as much as fifty cents, and Poe himself could not obtain a copy. The newsboys "made a profitable speculation beyond doubt."[3] (It was probably Poe who later wrote in an introductory note to the story, "The rush for the 'sole paper which had the news,' was something beyond even the prodigious.")[4] With regard to the balloon account's credibility, Poe judged, "[T]he more intelligent believed, while the rabble, for the most part, rejected the whole with disdain."[5]

Thomas Low Nichols asserted what Poe had not: that an intoxicated Poe had appeared before the *Sun* building and declared the report to be a hoax

Portrait miniature of Eliza Poe, Poe's mother. (Courtesy of The Free Library of Philadelphia, Rare Book Department)

Photograph of portrait of John Allan, Poe's foster father. (Courtesy of the Edgar Allan Poe Museum, Richmond, Virginia)

Painted portrait of Frances Keeling Valentine Allan, Poe's foster mother. (Courtesy of the Edgar Allan Poe Museum, Richmond, Virginia)

Photograph of Moldavia, Poe's childhood home in Richmond.
(Courtesy of the Edgar Allan Poe Museum, Richmond, Virginia)

Oil painting of Jane Scott Mackenzie, foster mother of Poe's sister Rosalie Mackenzie Poe. (Courtesy of the Edgar Allan Poe Museum, Richmond, Virginia)

Daguerreotype of John H. Mackenzie, Poe's friend and foster brother/legal guardian of Poe's sister Rosalie Mackenzie Poe. (Courtesy of the Edgar Allan Poe Museum, Richmond, Virginia)

Ambrotype of Louisa Mackenzie, first wife of John H. Mackenzie. (Author's collection)

Photograph of daguerreotype of Maria Clemm, Poe's aunt and mother-in-law. (Courtesy of the Edgar Allan Poe Museum, Richmond, Virginia)

Painting of Thomas W. White, founder of the *Southern Literary Messenger* and Poe's employer. (Courtesy of the Edgar Allan Poe Museum, Richmond, Virginia)

Engraving of William E. Burton, publisher of *Burton's Gentleman's Magazine*. (Courtesy of the Edgar Allan Poe Museum, Richmond, Virginia)

Print of engraving of George R. Graham, publisher of *Graham's Magazine*. (Courtesy of the Edgar Allan Poe Museum, Richmond, Virginia)

Painting of Rufus Wilmot Griswold, Poe's literary executor. (Courtesy of the Edgar Allan Poe Museum, Richmond, Virginia)

Brennan family farmhouse, where "The Raven" was written.
(New-York Historical Society)

Painted portrait of poet Frances Sargent Osgood, by Samuel S. Osgood, ca. 1835. (New-York Historical Society)

Painted portrait of Poe, by Samuel S. Osgood, 1845.
(New-York Historical Society)

Picture of N. P. Willis and George Pope Morris. (Edgar Allan Poe Art Collection, 77.22.84, Harry Ransom Center, The University of Texas at Austin)

Poe cottage at Fordham. (Courtesy of The Bronx County Historical Society Collection, The Bronx, New York)

Print of painting of Virginia Poe (deceased). (Courtesy of the Edgar Allan Poe Museum, Richmond, Virginia)

Painted portrait of Sarah Helen Whitman, 1838, by C. Giovanni Thompson. (Providence Athenaeum)

Annie Richmond. (Lowell Historical Society)

Ultima Thule daguerreotype of Poe.
(American Antiquarian Society)

Photograph of Duncan Lodge (home of Mrs. Mackenzie). (Courtesy of the Edgar Allan Poe Museum, Richmond, Virginia)

Daguerreotype of Elmira Royster Shelton. (Courtesy of the Edgar Allan Poe Museum, Richmond, Virginia)

Rosalie Mackenzie Poe tintype. (Courtesy of the Edgar Allan Poe Museum, Richmond, Virginia)

and the author to be himself. Accordingly, both the crowd and its demand dramatically diminished.[6]

Poe's account seems wholly plausible. And though Nichols's version has not been confirmed by any contemporary evidence, it is not wholly implausible.

Two days later, the *Sun* acknowledged with regard to its report of the *Victoria* that "the intelligence is erroneous" but not naming Poe (M 3:1067–68). And a competitor of the *Sun*, the *New York True Sun*, a few blocks north at 162 Nassau Street, stated, also on April 15, "Beach's Balloon Humbug hoaxed nobody so much as the poor newsboys. We saw several late on Saturday night with bundles of the unsaleable 'extras' under their arms, crying bitterly. This hoaxing little ragged boys out of their pennies is rather a small business."[7] Presumably the *True Sun* editor S. DeWitt Bloodgood wrote this, and it was probably he who added on the following day, "Crowds rushed to the True Sun office to obtain the *true* account, a compliment which we fully appreciate. But as humbug is no part of our system of doing business, we had no extras to sell, no marvels to communicate."[8] The *True Sun* followed up with a mocking poem, "Recipe for a Hoax," and a compilation of a dozen disapproving newspaper responses (none of them mentioning Poe). According to one of these responses, from the *Philadelphia Daily Chronicle*, "The expression of all that we heard speak of it, (and there were hundreds reading it at our bulletin board,) was, that it was the paltriest effort ever attempted."[9]

With or without Poe's alleged public avowal, his account of transatlantic flight was not generally believed. But Poe did prompt excitement—as he had done as a boy, appearing as a sheeted ghost at a whist game, and again as a young man, concocting a scheme in which a bloody beheaded gander became the supposed head of a supposedly murdered professor. Perhaps for Poe, creating the excitement was enough. Through James Russell Lowell's 1845 biography of him, Poe did first acknowledge in print his authorship of "The Balloon Hoax." He was surely proud. And if the account of the transatlantic voyage was not well regarded as journalism, it is—like the earlier "Hans Pfaall"—an important early example of science fiction.

With his earnings from his provocative flight of fancy, Poe would have been able to bring Maria Clemm (with Catterina) to New York. His mother-in-law had been busy settling matters in Philadelphia—unfortunately also selling a borrowed volume of the *Southern Literary Messenger* that Poe had asked her to return—and it was time for her to rejoin her family, which she did.[10] Perhaps Poe briefly moved to Ann Street to make room for her on Greenwich Street.[11]

Poe soon began a series of topical letters from New York to Eli Bowen and Jacob L. Gossler, the editors of a Pottstown, Pennsylvania, newspaper, a weekly characterized by George Lippard as "that respectable and popular sheet, the old established *Columbia Spy*."[12] The seven letters appeared in issues from May 18 through July 6, 1844 (not including the issue from June 22). The letters offer wandering and pondering, with Poe ranging "Mannahatta" from the reservoir at Forty-Third Street and Fifth Avenue to the Bowling Green Fountain, rowing around Blackwell's Island (today's Roosevelt Island), and even venturing to a "villa" in Brooklyn. He admires the picturesque, deplores the squalid or tasteless, and laments the anticipated effects of "[t]he spirit of Improvement." Along the way, he offers varied commentary—for instance, decrying the "street-cries" and contending for the relevance of the seemingly irrelevant. Poe's *Columbia Spy* letters are engaging for their jaunts and their jaunty manner.[13]

Poe regularly returned in these letters to literary matters—the merits of Bulwer versus Dickens, the poetry of Willis, the significance of the poets Richard H. Horne and William Wallace, the insignificance of "the great Seatsfield"—and to journalistic ones—the newspapermen James Gordon Bennett, Thomas Low Nichols, Moses Y. Beach, and Horace Greeley, as well as the magazinist John Inman.[14] A touch of indignation is evident on occasion in Poe's *Columbia Spy* letters with regard to the inadequate recognition of great men—Horne, Wallace, and J. N. Reynolds. Perhaps most revealing is Poe's writing of Wallace, "The Kentucky poet, being that odious viper, a poor man and friendless, was in exceedingly bad odor with the small *literati* of this country; and they lost no time in chuckling over what they styled his 'insult,' and endeavored to believe his degradation."[15] Poe may well have been intimating his own chagrin about not having yet attained the reputation he believed he deserved. But he also went on to acknowledge that Wallace later won much regard.

Poe did recur in his *Columbia Spy* letters to his own work. In one case, he playfully acknowledged a piece as his own (the biography of Robert Conrad in *Graham's* of June 1844); in another he discussed a work without acknowledging it as his own ("The Balloon Hoax"); and in yet another, he obliquely hinted at a work of his own by referring to its venue, *The Gift for 1845,* as the new volume of an annual that "will bear away the palm" ("The Purloined Letter").[16]

Poe seemed ready to continue the *Columbia Spy* letters. At the close of the seventh and last letter, he anticipated his writing about the latest issues of magazines in "my next." Proud of his generic variety—and always in need of pay—Poe could turn to the ostensibly casual, even the seemingly ephemeral.[17] We do not know why his *Columbia Spy* letters ceased, but four years later Eli Bowen, then editor of the *Miner's Journal,* invited Poe to renew his epistolary effort, and Poe responded, "I am willing to accept your offer about the Correspondence, and will commence whenever you think proper" (O 2:705). Poe's career as a correspondent did not begin again, but Poe had been open to the possibility.

Meanwhile, he maintained a significant personal correspondence. Remarkably, even as Poe wrote *about* N. P. Willis in his second *Columbia Spy* letter, on May 21, 1844—denying him genius but honoring his fine private qualities[18]—he wrote *to* Willis on the same day, submitting new work and expressing respect and affection (O 1:439–40). Notably, in that letter of May 21 to the *Columbia Spy,* Poe uses John Milton's phrase for Hell in *Paradise Lost,* "darkness visible," with reference to Third Avenue unlit,[19] and that phrase takes on a new suggestiveness upon considering that Poe states, in his personal letter of May 21 to Willis, that he would have visited but was "ill in health and wretchedly depressed in spirits" (O 1:439). Perhaps Poe was recovering from a bout of drinking. Perhaps he was afflicted by both perceived professional neglect and his recurrent melancholy. Poe privately praised Willis's poem "Unseen Spirits" (O 1:439), and he termed it "the best of *all* the author's poems" in his final *Columbia Spy* letter, reprinting this work about "*Peace*" and "*Honor*" accompanied by "*Want*" and "*Scorn.*"[20] It was perhaps Poe's own "darkness visible" that yielded a resonant humanity.

Having earlier written to James Russell Lowell, "I am at a sad loss for a Biographer" (O 1:431), Poe acknowledged, in a letter to him of May 28, his pride that Lowell would write the new biography, and he listed recent and forthcoming tales and enclosed the *Philadelphia Saturday Museum* biography (O 1:441–42). And on July 2—by which time he and Virginia and Maria Clemm were living at the Brennan farmhouse, north of the city (near what is now West Eighty-Fourth Street), not far from the Hudson River—he offered, in another letter to Lowell, a revealing view of himself (O 1:448–52). He discussed his eager roaming in nature, fervent writing, lack of ambition, conviction of human vanity, belief in the divinity of "unparticled matter" (O 1:449), sense of the impermanence of the temporal, and intense responsiveness to music and some poetry. He wrote, "My life has been *whim*—impulse—passion—a longing for solitude—a scorn of all things present, in an earnest desire for the future" (O 1:450). The letter provides clarity and insight, but, probably because it was written to inform a biography, it avoids quotidian difficulties—illness, poverty, sorrow, depression. And the very ambition of Poe's elaboration of the nature of the universe belies his claim to be without ambition. Indeed, his ambition was great.

The eager roaming (though not for "whole months") and fervent writing ("a mania for composition") were spoken of by his landlady Mary Brennan, who reported that even as, on some days, Poe would sit on a large rock called "Mount Tom," observing the river, "Other days he would roam through the surrounding woods, and, returning in the afternoon, sit in the 'big room,' as it used to be called, by a window and work unceasingly with pen and paper, until the evening shadows." Brennan also attested to Poe's sobriety during his time at the farmhouse, as well as his attention to Virginia: "He was the gentlest of husbands and devoted to his invalid wife. Frequently when she was weaker than usual, he carried her tenderly from her room to the dinner-table and satisfied every whim."[21] Here we may be reminded of Poe's carrying Virginia over logs and brooks at John H. Mackenzie's Darby Town farm back in 1836.

These early months in the country—what would become New York's Upper West Side—were evidently for Poe steady and productive. He characterized himself to poet Thomas H. Chivers on July 10 as "in strict seclusion, busied with books and [ambiti]ous thoughts, until the hour shall arrive when I may come forth with a certainty of success" (O 1:453). And in his first letter to Frederick W. Thomas since immediately after the Washington spree, that of September 8, 1844, Poe assured his friend of his recovery by alluding to an added line in *Richard III:* "Thank God! Richard (whom you know) is himself again."[22] He stated that he had been "playing hermit in earnest—nor have I seen a living soul out of my family," and he added, "I am working at a variety of things (all of which you shall behold in the end)—and with an ardor of which I did not believe myself capable" (O 1:457–58). In the summer of 1844, in the big room at the Brennan farmhouse, Poe was writing and gathering strength. His aspiration had found a welcome bower.

Recent compositions were beginning to appear—short pieces for the *Public Ledger* on the omnibus, the cab, and cats were published in mid-July. Some pieces that Poe had listed as finished but unpublished in his May 28 letter to Lowell (O 1:441) were also appearing—a tale of terror, "The Premature Burial," was published in the *Dollar Newspaper* at the end of July; a tale of metaphysical exploration, "Mesmeric Revelation," was published in the *Columbian Magazine* of August; and a tale of misreading, "The Oblong Box," was published in *Godey's Lady's Book* of September.

The first tale, recalling a passage in *Pym* (P 1:182), builds upon recorded cases of burial alive in the first half to offer an apparent personal case in the second half. Between the two halves, parallel phrases—"Fearful indeed the suspicion—but more fearful the doom!" (M 3:961)—signal the shift. Toward the end of the tale, the narrator, mistakenly thinking himself buried alive, undoes the reassurance of John 14:16, 26 concerning the coming Comforter, stating instead, "And now the Comforter fled for ever" (M 3:967). The second of the three tales anticipates passages in Poe's July 2 letter to Lowell (O 1:449–50) and his July 10 letter to Chivers (O 1:453–54) on the materiality of spirit, an idea that would emerge again in Poe's 1848 cosmology, *Eureka*. And the third of these tales draws on John C. Colt's transporting the dead body of the man he had murdered, one Samuel Adams, on a ship, in a wooden box filled with salt.[23]

Poe was working, in all likelihood, on the comic tale "The Angel of the Odd" in the summer of 1844, and he may have begun the "[Preface to] Marginalia" and "Some Words with a Mummy." Probably he was trying to imagine how to revise the poem he had recited near the Barhyte farm and at the *Graham's Magazine* office. He was still planning to establish "The Stylus" (O 1:453). And he could occasionally be attentive to an imminent publication. He asked to correct the proof of "The Purloined Letter" (O 1:444–45), which he termed "perhaps, the best of my tales of ratiocination" (O 1:450). This final Dupin tale appeared by mid-September in *The Gift for 1845*.[24]

Again, as in "The Murders in the Rue Morgue" and "The Mystery of Marie Rogêt," the admiring unnamed narrator relates a tale of the brilliance of his friend C. Auguste Dupin. The problem here is not a killing, whether deliberate or accidental, but a blackmailing. A brief plot summary will serve here: A female royal—whether princess or queen—is in her boudoir reading a letter from her amour when her husband enters the room. She quickly places the letter face down upon the table, and though the prince or king does not understand her compromised situation, the visiting Minister D— does, and he deftly steals the incriminating missive. The prefect of police, unable to find the letter despite exhaustive and thorough investigation of Minister D—'s apartment, consults with Dupin, who infers that the shrewd minister must have hidden the letter in an obvious—and therefore unexamined—location. Indeed, on visiting Minister D—, Dupin identifies the disguised letter, hidden in plain sight, in a "card-rack,"[25] and on a return visit he deftly recovers it. He thereby earns a great reward and protects the reputation of the threatened royal.

The tale was well appreciated—reprinted, abridged, translated. The reviewer of Poe's *Tales* in the *American Review* of September 1845 wrote about Dupin's method in "The Purloined Letter," "This identification of the reasoner's mind with that of his adversary, so as to discover what course of action he would in all probability pursue in given circumstances, is, of course, an exercise of imagination, just as much as the delineation of an imaginary character. No force or acuteness of mere understanding, could do the office of the imagination in such a case."[26] In the mid-twentieth century, the Poe scholar T. O. Mabbott asserted, "For absolute preëminence one may name *The Purloined Letter*, surely unsurpassed in detective fiction and perhaps unequaled."[27]

A variety of sources for elements of the tale have been identified, from Richard Gooch's jest book *Nuts to Crack* to Horace Binney Wallace's novel *Stanley*, but the primary prompt was a story in the 1822 volume *The Death-Bed Confessions of the Late Countess of Guernsey, to Lady Anne H********.[28] This involves Britain's Princess Caroline, estranged wife of the prince regent, who, on the death of his insane father, George III, in 1820, would become George IV. In 1813, according to this story, the princess wrote a letter to the prince appealing for his sympathy, and a supposed friend of hers, seeking increased salary, took the letter from the desk of the princess's secretary and had it printed in the newspaper. He thereby won the favor of a powerful minister, secured the position he wanted, and provoked the prince against his consort. Evidently pleased with the success of his guile, "The man in office met that day his *confreres* at——, and, after dinner, amused them with an account of the purloined letter."[29]

Perhaps young Edgar would have heard of Princess Caroline as he was growing up in London, and he certainly would have heard of the princess—now the queen—on the death of her father-in-law in early 1820 and her return from Europe to be crowned. This was the dominant story in the newspapers at the time, and John Allan discussed the royal couple in his letters. Poe later wrote favorably about Queen Caroline and negatively about King George IV, and at some point he must have encountered the critical sensational volume *Death-Bed Confessions*, which was published in Philadelphia as well as London. It is also possible that Poe's Minister D—was drawn from the ambitious Henry Lord Brougham.[30]

Poe's tale based on the Princess Caroline story has an extraordinary design. Poe again offered a work of symmetrical framing, with much corresponding language from "arose . . . sat down" to "get up . . . come down" at either end of the work to "accurate admeasurement" and "accuracy . . . admeasured" close to the center. And he again provided a parallel center: Dupin tells the prefect, "[Y]ou may as well fill me up a check for the amount mentioned. When you have signed it, I will hand you the letter," and the narrator states of the prefect, "[H]e . . . finally filled up and signed a check for fifty thousand francs, and handed it across the table to Dupin." The verbs—"fill," "signed," and "hand," and then "filled," "signed," and "handed" make the central parallelism clear.[31] Again the center of a Dupin tale is ironic. In "The Murders in the Rue Morgue," the center featured an open window in a locked-room mystery. In "The Mystery of Marie Rogêt," the center offered a chiasmus in a work of parallels. And in "The Purloined Letter," the center concerns a purchase in a tale of theft. But there is even more to the tale's structure.

Poe provides us with a hint of its further complexity through Dupin's analogy for hiding something in plain sight: eluding an opponent who will seek a specified name on a map—and who will often look at the tiny names—by specifying an enormous name, appearing over the breadth of the entire map. We may thereby infer Poe's creating a design, beyond symmetry, over the breadth of his entire story.[32]

An emblem of that design, the mise en abîme, is the game of marbles. A gifted schoolboy is able to determine whether his classmate is holding one or two marbles in his closed hand by identifying with him. He is thereby able to win all his classmates' marbles. Playing a less intelligent classmate, the gifted student guesses wrongly "Odd," and then, thinking that his opponent would shift from even to odd, guesses "Odd" again and wins. However, playing a somewhat more intelligent classmate, he guesses wrongly "Odd," and then, imagining that his more skilled competitor would stay with even, guesses "Even" and wins. Here, in this latter example, we have the remarkable structure of the two halves of "The Purloined Letter."[33]

The gifted schoolboy's first answer to the more intelligent classmate, "Odd," is the key word of the first half—it appears five times (and never the word "Even"): "odd notions," "every thing 'odd,'" "oddities," "excessively *odd*," and "Simple and odd."[34] His second answer to that classmate, "Even," is the key word of the second half—it appears three times (and never the word "Odd"): "even the truths," "To be even with him," and "even, as it seemed."[35] The gifted schoolboy's responses to the more intelligent classmate figure Poe's responses to his readers—and, ultimately, to us. That schoolboy has won the marbles, and Poe has won the literary victory, but we readers may recognize the pattern and thereby attain a victory of our own.[36]

Language about Minister D—'s hiding place for the letter reflects on the tale itself. The "trumpery fillagree card-rack of pasteboard" indicates Poe's victory in a hand of cards—he has the trump card, a piece of pasteboard with a filigree on its back. Furthermore, the word "card-rack" is a near palindrome—its symmetry reflects the symmetry of the tale. The place of concealment for "the purloined letter" serves as a representation of "The Purloined Letter."[37]

Poe's final Dupin story is an exceptionally brilliant literary effort—engaging on its surface level and tremendously satisfying at its deeper level, in which Poe hints in the work (through the map game, the marbles game, and the implicit card game) at the design of the work itself. The "repleteness"[38] of the tale—the subtle working together of its myriad elements—is a marvel, an artistic triumph. We may, in this context, turn to the critic F. O. Matthiessen, who, though he neglected Poe in *American Renaissance,* later stated of the writer, "He stands as one of the very few great innovators in our literature."[39]

And what of the personal in "The Purloined Letter"? The source figure offers an answer. Like Ann Coleman for "Rue Morgue" and Mary Rogers for "Marie Rogêt," Princess Caroline—later Queen Caroline—for "The Purloined Letter" was a woman of uncertain reputation. The intimation is Poe's own mother, accused of an extramarital affair leading to the birth of Poe's sister Rosalie. We have seen that John Allan himself made the accusation in a letter to Henry and probably in hurtful speech to Edgar. As earlier noted, Marie Louise Shew Houghton maintained about Poe "[t]hat it was the regret of his life, that he had not vindicated his mother to the world, as pure, as angelic and altogether lovely, as any woman could be on earth."[40] Certainly in the first two Dupin tales, he did not, through Dupin, save the characters whose source figures were women of questionable reputation—both the l'Espanayes and Marie Rogêt died. However, in "The Purloined Letter," the threatened female royal, whose source figure was a woman of questionable reputation, is indeed saved—the compromising letter is recovered. In the final Dupin story, Poe succeeded in addressing "the regret of his life": through Dupin, he was "a partisan of the lady concerned," his mother. Poe again integrated his life in his work, becoming finally the protective son that he wished to be.[41]

Meanwhile, his protective mother-in-law was working on his behalf. Walking or taking the omnibus or the ferry, fifty-four-year-old Maria Clemm traveled the nearly seven miles from the Brennan farm to Nassau Street to inquire for employment for "Eddie." She was, as Mayne Reid had described her in Philadelphia, "A woman of middle age, and almost masculine aspect," "the ever-vigilant guardian of the house," "the sole servant," and "the sole messenger."[42] Her message in this instance was that of entreaty—probably at Poe's suggestion, she visited the elegant literary lion and journalist N. P. Willis, one of the editors of the new two-cent newspaper the *New York Evening Mirror*, at the southeast corner of Nassau and Ann (103 Nassau Street), to ask for a job for her son-in-law. She explained that he was sick, that her daughter was infirm, and that the family's need was great. Willis wrote, after Poe's death, with much admiration for Mrs. Clemm: "The countenance of this lady, made beautiful and saintly with an evidently complete giving up of her life to privation and sorrowful tenderness, her gentle and mournful voice urging its plea, her long-forgotten but habitually and unconsciously refined manners, and her appealing and yet appreciative mention of the claims and abilities of her son, disclosed at once the presence of one of those angels upon earth that women in adversity can be."[43]

And so, Willis hired Poe. The job of "mechanical paragraphist" had little allure or prestige, but Poe performed well. According to Willis in an 1858 letter to his former partner George Pope Morris, Poe sat at a desk in the corner, responsive to various editorial requests, "everything but the writing of a 'leader,' or constructing any article upon which his peculiar idiosyncrasy of mind could be impressed." Willis commented with fondness, "[Y]ou remember how absolutely and how good-humoredly ready he was for any suggestion, how punctually and industriously reliable, in the following out of the wish once expressed, how cheerful and present-minded in his work when he might excusably have been so listless and abstracted. We loved the man for the entireness of fidelity with which he served us—himself, or any vanity of his own, so utterly put aside."[44] By any standard, Willis's encomium sounds like today's "Exceeds expectations."

Willis and Morris were the senior editors of the *New York Evening Mirror*, but there was a junior editor, Hiram Fuller. The contract signed by the three, dated October 7, 1844, stipulates that Fuller would contribute five thousand dollars within ninety days.[45] Fuller would later clarify the division of duties—Willis was responsible for the content of the paper, Morris for business matters, and he himself for the book publication endeavor, the Mirror Library.[46]

Notably, according to Thomas Dunn English, "Fuller . . . hated Poe almost as much as he did me."[47] An initial reason for Fuller's antagonism may well have been Poe's reputation for drinking—after all, in 1838, when Fuller was teaching in Providence (with Margaret Fuller, no relation), he said "that he had rather hear of his father[']s death, than that he had become intemperate."[48] And there would be other reasons for hostility.

October 7, 1844, was also the day of the first issue of the *Evening Mirror*, a paper that had been prompted, in part, by the exorbitant postage that had been required for the now-defunct magazine, the *New Mirror*. Selections from the *Evening Mirror* would comprise the *New York Weekly Mirror*. On October 8, Willis mentioned Poe in an essay: "There will doubtless be criticism by Lowell and Poe—each in a very different spirit from the other, but Damascene as to its temper of the weapon—of a certain new book, just published by the Langleys." That book, appearing on October 4, was Elizabeth Barrett Barrett's *A Drama of Exile, and Other Poems*.[49] Its poem "Lady Geraldine's Courtship" would be an influence on Poe's coming revision and elaboration of what would be his most famous poem, "The Raven."

Willis adverted to Poe again on October 10—on behalf of an "author's crusade," "we solemnly summon Edgar Poe to do the devoir of Coeur de Lion—no man's weapon half so trenchant."[50] And he referred to Poe as "[o]ne of the regular allies of the Mirror, a man of a very humorous critical vein," offering Poe's whimsical "The Swiss Bell-Ringers," which claimed that the seven well-synchronized musicians were actually an automaton manipulated by some covert technician (M 3:1118–20).[51] (We may well recall Poe's revealing the mechanical to be human [in "Maelzel's Chess-Player"] and the human to be mechanical [in "The Man That Was Used Up"].) A reader soon encouraged Willis to feature Poe: "I'm glad to see that Edgar Poe is in your clearings. He is a man of the finest ideal intellect in the land—carries a nasty tomahawk as a critic—bitter as gall to the literary flies who have been buzzing around his windows. Do give Poe a corner (or a column, or ten o' 'em) in your 'Strong-ly' Mirror, and let him fire away at the humbugs of our literature."[52] Yet in a letter published two weeks later, the pseudonymous Philadelphian W. Penn-onas asked with some dismay, "Where is Poe? Is the tomahawk buried?"[53]

Although a variety of *Evening Mirror* pieces from this time have been attributed to Poe, many are questionable.[54] And unquestionably, as Willis recalled, Poe was not writing full articles in his distinct manner for the *Evening Mirror*. If his tomahawk was not buried, it was at least lowered. But it would be raised again.

Meanwhile, Poe was a walker in the city. It was perhaps in early October 1844, or even earlier, at actor Gabriel Harrison's general merchandise shop at Broadway and Prince Street, nearly twenty blocks north of the *Evening Mirror*, that a sad-looking gentleman—"a small man with a large head"—visited, taking an interest in the Virginia leaf tobacco sold there. He didn't buy any tobacco, but Harrison gave him some. On a subsequent occasion, in response to Harrison's effort to write a political song for his White Eagle Club, which supported Democrat James K. Polk for president, the visiting stranger quickly penciled five stanzas set to the tune of "The Star-Spangled Banner." Harrison later remembered one of these stanzas:

> See the White Eagle soaring aloft to the sky,
> Wakening the broad welkin with his loud battle cry;
> Then here's the White Eagle, full daring is he,
> As he sails on his pinions o'er valley and sea. (M 1:341–42).

The songwriter accepted a bag of coffee for his effort. Asked his name, he responded that it was Thaddeus K. Peasley. The White Eagle Club did employ the song of this mock-pompous stranger in the 1844 campaign, perhaps even including it during the Democratic torch-lit procession of November 1. Finally, a friend of Harrison's, the poet Fitz-Greene Halleck, recognized Peasley one day and identified him to Harrison as Edgar Allan Poe. Harrison and the putative Peasley became good friends, and in later years the former actor and shop owner wrote and spoke with appreciation of his long-ago companion.[55]

Back home at the Brennan farmhouse, Poe would have been continuing to do what he could for his wife Virginia, whose health he had lately described as "excessively precarious" (O 1:457). He would also have been reading, including, in all likelihood, the new American edition of Elizabeth Barrett Barrett's *A Drama of Exile, and Other Poems,* which he would review in the *Broadway Journal.* And he was again planning his much-hoped-for literary magazine "The Stylus." Writing to James Russell Lowell on October 28, Poe renewed the proposal in his March 30 letter (O 1:431–32) that literary men secretly contribute their funds and their work to establish the magazine (O 1:462–64). Writing to the classicist Charles Anthon before November 2, he requested—with some anxiety, given his extensive revisions—his correspondent's assistance in securing a contract for a book of his tales with the Harpers, the success of which would lead to his envisioned magazine (O 1:465–71). To both men, Poe wrote of a monthly magazine featuring 128 pages per issue and requiring annual subscription rates of five dollars from twenty thousand subscribers. Poe had done the math, but the magazine would remain mythical.

Anthon approached the Harpers, without success. He wrote to Poe, "They have *complaints* against you, grounded on certain movements of yours, when they acted as your publishers some years ago" (perhaps regarding *Pym,* from

1838, or perhaps regarding *The Conchologist's First Book,* from 1839, a competitor with one of their own volumes).[56] Anthon encouraged Poe to visit the Harpers himself. Lowell did not respond to Poe's magazine scheme but instead offered an introduction to Charles F. Briggs, who was beginning a new weekly, the *Broadway Journal,* and mentioned, as well, having praised Poe to George H. Colton, who was editing a monthly, the *American Review*.[57] Poe would follow up on both of Lowell's kindly intended contacts.

In the fall of 1844, Poe published plentifully in venues other than the *Evening Mirror.* "The Angel of the Odd," appearing in the October *Columbian Magazine,* constitutes an inversion of his usual critique of credulity—here Poe plays with the incredulity of a vulnerable drinker, who is punished, both awake and asleep, for his hubristic vow not to be believe anything odd. "Thou Art the Man," appearing in the November *Godey's Lady's Book,* offers a narrator-detective who ironically assumes the view of the mistaken public while secretly working out the innocence of the accused and the guilt of the accuser. With its heroic rescue and climactic explanation of a much-discussed mysterious death (real or supposed), this tale resembles to some degree a Hawthorne tale that Poe admired, "Mr. Higginbotham's Catastrophe" (H 11:111). And "The Literary Life of Thingum Bob, Esq.," appearing in the December *Southern Literary Messenger,* serves as a satirical extravaganza about the literary/journalistic world. It mocks plagiaristic, talentless, self-infatuated authors and obtuse, vitriolic, penurious editors, and it is still funny today. For instance, Poe's narrator writes of a review in the imagined periodical *Daddy-Long-Legs,* "We all know what is meant by 'damning with faint praise,' and, on the other hand, who could fail seeing through the covert purpose of the 'Daddy'—that of glorifying with feeble abuse?" (M 3:1139). Poe would soon be listed in an advertisement for *Graham's Magazine* of 1845 as one of the authors of "Comic and Humorous Sketches."[58] But by the late fall and early winter of 1844, Poe was assiduously revising a serious and sorrowful work, a dark and solemn poem that would propel him to the peak of his fame.

A grade-school teacher once told me that Poe is the first great writer that a child really *gets*. It is therefore particularly apt that a boy, James Barhyte (son of the owner of the Barhyte farm), witnessed Poe reciting an early version of "The Raven." Similarly, a girl, Martha Susannah Brennan (daughter of the owner of the Brennan farm), witnessed Poe revising "The Raven." Seated, he placed finished pages face down on the floor, and lying below, she turned them face up and ordered them according to their page numbers. The

Brennan farmhouse was years later demolished and the plaster bust of Pallas Athena lost, but the mantelpiece—on which Poe had scratched his name—survives at the Rare Book and Manuscript Library of Columbia University's Butler Library. Although Martha's mother, Mary Brennan, was annoyed with his signature upon her mantelpiece, she must have been gratified—and perhaps a bit amazed—when he read to her, before the poem was submitted for publication, what would become his signature achievement.[59] With this work, he would "come forth with a certainty of success."

Poe remained in the background in the pages of the *Evening Mirror,* implicit in the November 28, 1844, issue when Willis responded to Amelia B. Welby (who had quoted a version of the poem "Lenore" incorrectly attributed to the *Evening Mirror* editor) by denying his authorship of the stanzas ("These are not ours—we wish they were!"). And Poe was again implicit in the December 18 issue, when Willis praised "our indefatigable sub-Editor" for catching two errors in the *New York Express.*[60]

Willis and Morris's partner Hiram Fuller was, unfortunately, not in the background. According to an item copied in the *Evening Mirror* of November 29, "A Strange Tale," and then thoughtfully discussed, a man had punched a woman at the Park Theatre—in fact, as Willis (and perhaps Morris) obliquely acknowledged, that woman was the wife of junior editor Hiram Fuller.[61] Evidently her father had been so outraged about his daughter Emilie Louise Delaplaine's having recently married Fuller that John F. Delaplaine took out his anger publicly, with his new son-in-law nearby. This sensational and embarrassing incident becomes relevant, as will be seen, since Poe later cites it in a confidential letter (O 1:579) and alludes to it in an abbreviated fashion in the course of his later literary feud with Thomas Dunn English.

English was then planning a new monthly magazine, the *Aristidean;* its first issue, that for March 1845, would appear in late February. And Charles F. Briggs was planning the new weekly magazine the *Broadway Journal;* he and John Bisco signed a contract on December 23, 1844 (P 4:xv–xvi n15), and the first issue appeared by January 4, 1845. The magazine's office was at 135 Nassau Street. Lowell, in his letter of December 12, 1844, had introduced Poe to Briggs, giving his address at 1 Nassau Street, and Poe visited the editor, arranging to contribute a review of Elizabeth Barrett Barrett's *A Drama of Exile, and Other Poems.* Lowell had also mentioned George H. Colton, the editor of the *American Review,* and Poe submitted "The Raven" to him. The magazine's office was nearby at 118 Nassau Street. In early January, Lowell's biography of Poe, with the engraving of the A. C. Smith watercolor portrait, finally appeared, in the February 1845 issue of *Graham's*.[62] Poe's professional ascent was clearly accelerating.

In that January 4 issue of the *Broadway Journal*, and in its successor, Poe acknowledged his great admiration of Elizabeth Barrett Barrett and offered his incisive, extended evaluation. He faulted her work's occasional mysticism, melodrama, and moralizing, but praised its beauty, insight, and passion. Through the course of the piece, he challenged the critic who had earlier written on the same collection in *Blackwood's Edinburgh Magazine*—presumably John Wilson, a.k.a. Christopher North. Regarding "Lady Geraldine's Courtship," Poe considered it to have "the fiercest passion" and "the most ethereal fancy" of any poem except Alfred Tennyson's "Locksley Hall," of which, he asserted, it was an imitation. Still, while noting the artistry of Tennyson's piece, he also lauded the narrative focus of Barrett's. Plainly, Poe had striven for both of these strengths in his soon-to-be-published "The Raven."[63] And though he preferred the rhythm and rhyme scheme of "Locksley Hall" to those of "Lady Geraldine's Courtship," both poems offer versions of trochaic octameter—lines of eight two-syllable feet, each of which feet has the emphasis on the first syllable. This is the meter that Poe employs in "The Raven." And it is "Lady Geraldine's Courtship" that features the line "With a rushing stir, uncertain, in the air, the purple curtain," probably helping to suggest Poe's line in "The Raven," "And the silken, sad, uncertain rustling of each purple curtain."[64]

The February issue of *Graham's Magazine* was published very early, received by some newspapers on January 7. The lead piece was Lowell's five-page critical/biographical essay on Poe, accompanied by an engraving of the A. C. Smith portrait of an amiable Poe, right arm over chair back, a near-smile inviting approach. Lowell offers a treatment that is a tribute, with occasional qualification. He writes, "Mr. Poe is at once the most discriminating, philosophical, and fearless critic upon imaginative works who has written in America." But Lowell asserts that "he sometimes seems to mistake his phial of prussic-acid for his inkstand." Lowell's marquee encomium is "Mr. Poe has that indescribable something which men have agreed to call *genius*." According to the Cambridge poet/critic, although the highest genius has not yet been achieved, it is well promised. Identified as elements of Poe's genius, appropriately enough, are his analysis and his imagination. As Lowell honors the extraordinary in Poe's fiction, he praises, also, the order in his work. He contends, "Even his mystery is mathematical to his own mind. To him x is a known quantity all along." And Lowell encourages practical steps. He suggests offering Poe his own magazine, comparing him favorably with

Christopher North. Furthermore, he recommends gathering Poe's tales and collecting his essays. With discernment and distinction, Lowell heralds Poe's arrival. Poe had built the reputation of *Graham's Magazine;* here, *Graham's Magazine* builds the reputation of Poe.[65]

The immediate reception of Lowell's profile of Poe was largely positive (though response to the portrait varied). Margaret Fuller declared, "This article is frank, earnest, and contains many just thoughts, expressed with force and point." Charles F. Briggs referred to "the fine sketch of Mr. Poe's genius." And Evert A. Duyckinck graciously stated, "We cordially give a welcome to this distinct recognition of Mr. Poe's merits. Whenever his name is mentioned it has been with the comment that he is a remarkable man, a man of genius."[66] And Lowell's piece offered not only recognition but also augury, very soon to be fulfilled.

At the *Evening Mirror,* Poe's role was about to change. Perhaps this was in part because the "mechanical paragraphist" had been hailed as a genius. Perhaps this was also in part because the ninety-day period, in which the new partner (and temperance man) Hiram Fuller had contracted to pay Willis and Morris five thousand dollars, had expired—the money must have been paid. So, presumably, Poe need no longer have been relatively muted on behalf of the senior editors, his friends. On January 6, Briggs wrote to Lowell, "Poe is going to assist Willis in the Mirror." Willis would still refer to Poe as his "Sub-Editor," but the *True Sun* considered him "one of the associate editors of the Mirror," and the *Saturday Emporium* went so far as to call him "one of the editors of the Evening Mirror."[67] In any case, on January 8 and over the subsequent weeks, Poe would contribute characteristically to the *Evening Mirror,* enlivening the newspaper and causing some difficulty.

Now allowed to have his say, Poe wrote primarily on literary topics.[68] He began by arguing briefly for a "proper" critical review for New York, in part to defend the city against "the East," Boston. He was implicitly making the case for a monthly like his proposed "Stylus." (Willis would soon write, "We wonder, by the way, that, with so fine a critic at command for an editor, some New York publisher does not establish a Monthly Review, devoted exclusively to high critical purposes." And Poe himself would inform Abijah M. Ide, "I shall very soon establish a Magazine in the city—'The Stylus'" [O 1:479].) With his tomahawk raised, Poe again attacked the critic of *Blackwood's Edinburgh Magazine*—ostensibly unsure if it was Christopher North—for the review of Elizabeth Barrett Barrett's *A Drama of Exile.* And he faulted the imitativeness of American drama.[69]

Poe's first *Evening Mirror* review concerned Lowell's *Conversations on Some of the Old Poets*. Here the astute critic acknowledged Lowell's "*poetic* genius," praising "A Legend of Brittany" (as he had done in the March 1844 *Graham's*) and specific excerpted passages. But he disputed the view that simplicity in art is more powerful than technical skill, valuing above all the union of theory and practice. Poe's objections would precipitate a critical response from a *New York Tribune* writer, possibly Margaret Fuller, which would itself yield a response from Poe.[70]

His second *Evening Mirror* review was a two-part piece concerning Henry Wadsworth Longfellow's *The Waif: A Collection of Poems*. Poe admired, in the first part, great British writers who were included and praised Longfellow's "Proem" ("The Day Is Done"), extracting three stanzas of "*poetic* beauty." But he alleged (incorrectly) that the poems attributed to "Anonymous" were Longfellow's own, and he challenged a tautological simile and questioned the absence of author names from the beginning of each work. Poe extolled, in the second part, Thomas Hood's poem "Bridge of Sighs," quoting from it at length, and he commended several other works featured. He added that another piece by Hood in Longfellow's collection, "The Death-Bed," had been plagiarized for a poem in Griswold's collection—James Aldrich's "A Death-Bed." (Poe would later repeat this claim in the July 1846 installment of "The Literati of New York City" [H 15:62].) He closed, most provocatively, by asserting that *The Waif* "is infected with a *moral taint*—or is this a mere freak of our own fancy?" He suggested the possibility that Longfellow had deliberately avoided including American writers who might be competitors of his and whom he imitated. Certainly only five of the poets named in *The Waif* were living American poets, and only one of them, Ralph Waldo Emerson, was a poet of the first rank. Poe's tentative accusation was sharp, but not singular. William Gilmore Simms wrote, "I think Longfellow's 'Waif' a poor compilation. I had almost said a dishonest one."[71]

Willis defended Poe in the *Evening Mirror*, terming him "an able though very critical hand." He also published a defense of Longfellow by the Boston lawyer and friend George S. Hillard, as well as Poe's response. Willis later offered another defense of Poe in the *Evening Mirror*, but he also published Charles Sumner's defense of Longfellow. Privately, Willis wrote to Sumner about the matter, "I mean to let Poe make a feature of his own in the Mirror, & be recognized as the author of criticisms there, and I am obliged, (to have anything good from him) to give him somewhat free play. Tell Longfellow he should never suffer 'in the long run' from me or mine."[72] Poe's review of *The*

Waif and the initial response to it commenced what Poe later labeled "the Little Longfellow War" (H 12:41; P 3:28).

Poe's fiction continued to appear. Seeking attention for a recent work, the unmuted critic asked in the *Evening Mirror* who had written "The Literary Life of Thingum Bob, Esq." And his "The Thousand-and-Second Tale of Scheherazade" was published a few days later in *Godey's Lady's Magazine*. Here Poe again mocks incredulity, but not as in "The Angel of the Odd," by way of the narrator's drinking and dreaming but, rather, by way of remarkable scientific inventions.[73] His "Some Words with a Mummy," lately accepted in the *Columbian Magazine,* would be included in the *American Review* in the spring (M 3:1177).

Poe had been planning his return to the city (O 1:475); on January 20, 1845, Willis reported that "Mr. Poe is now residing in New York,"[74] and on January 25, Poe wrote, from the city, "I am now living here" (O 1:478). With his wife and mother-in-law, he apparently returned to Greenwich Street—this time, Number 154 (O 1:500). On January 14, 1845, with Poe reemerging in the *Evening Mirror* and about to reenter the city, sometime-target Rufus W. Griswold wrote Poe a confidential letter, acknowledging the rift between them but requesting information for his forthcoming *Prose Writers of America* (H 17:197–98). Poe responded confidentially, blaming himself, mentioning "a hope of reconciliation," and expressing an interest in meeting with Griswold (O 1:477). And the two men did indeed meet (O 1:487). Notably, "Dear Griswold" in January became "My Dear Griswold" in February (O 1:477, 487). Poe may well have misconstrued a professional overture for a personal one. But even the professional overture was later suppressed by the deceitful compiler and Poe's February 24 letter distorted.[75]

In mid- to late January, Poe published in the *Evening Mirror,* in addition to items already mentioned, two responses to Evert A. Duyckinck (one regarding Barrett, the other regarding a newspaper misidentified), an essay on stylistic extremes, and a four-part series on the pay of American authors.[76] Meanwhile, during the run-up to the publication of "The Raven," Poe had a verbal run-in with his friend William Ross Wallace. Having read the poem aloud, Poe was annoyed with Wallace's response that the verses were "fine, uncommonly fine," asserting, rather, "[I]t's the greatest poem that was ever written." Poe would no doubt have been more satisfied with George H. Colton's comment after the editor read the unpublished poem aloud in his office: "[T]hat is amazing—amazing!"[77]

Finally, on January 29, Willis published in the first column of the back page of the *Evening Mirror* a slight variant of the poem in the forthcoming February issue of the *American Review,* Poe's "The Raven," with the author's name.[78] He introduced the work appreciatively, observing, "In our opinion, it is the most effective single example of 'fugitive poetry' ever published in this country; and unsurpassed in English poetry for subtle conception, masterly ingenuity of versification, and consistent, sustaining of imaginative lift and 'pokerishness.' It is one of those 'dainties bred in a book' which we *feed* on. It will stick to the memory of everybody who reads it." And on February 1, Colton featured the poem—attributed to one "Quarles"—over three pages of his distinguished monthly. He termed it "one of the most felicitous specimens of unique rhyming which has for some time met our eye."[79] Perhaps the subsequent commentary on prosody was Poe's or influenced by Poe. But Colton's earlier response would prove more characteristic of the response of other readers to the poem. They were amazed. Poe's moment had arrived.

"The Raven" is a narrative poem of eighteen stanzas, 108 lines, lulling and alarming. The narrator, a student seeking solace in his books for the loss of his cherished Lenore, falls asleep reading at midnight, only to be awakened by the visit of an otherworldly black bird, which lights on a bust of Pallas Athena. Learning its single and singular response, "Nevermore," the student asks questions regarding heavenly comfort and reunion to which that answer will elicit a thrilling pain. Finally, on hearing apparent confirmation that he will never again hold his beloved, the grieving student succumbs to the dominion of the unintending prophet.

Poe's technique is masterful. He blends incantatory trochaic octameter, and its variants, with end-of-line rhyme, internal rhyme, alliteration, a minor refrain ("nothing more") and a major refrain ("Nevermore"). The famous first stanza may illustrate Poe's virtuosity:

> Once upon a midnight dreary, while I pondered, weak and weary,
> Over many a quaint and curious volume of forgotten lore,
> While I nodded, nearly napping, suddenly there came a tapping,
> As of some one gently rapping, rapping at my chamber door.
> "'Tis some visiter," I muttered, "tapping at my chamber door—
>   Only this, and nothing more."[80]

As the poem builds, the reader—or rereader—is carried along by its unceasing flow. Listening to the speaker slide from reason to rage, veering between nameless fear ("fantastic terrors never felt before") and seemingly futile intimations of religious faith ("By that Heaven that bends above us—by that God we both adore—"), the reader rushes upon the torrent ("'Be that word our sign of parting, bird or fiend!' I shrieked, upstarting") to the calm of surrender ("And my soul from out that shadow that lies floating on the floor / Shall be lifted—nevermore!"). And even as the reader has found catharsis, he or she has also found the inevitable question of interpretation.

The contemporary reception to "The Raven" was predominantly favorable—the work was described as "a poem which would have enriched Blackwood," "a grand poem," "a wild and *shivery* poem."[81] And amid the responses were very thoughtful glosses of the central image. The writer Charles Fenno Hoffman, after reading the poem aloud, said of the iconic bird, "It is despair brooding over wisdom." Editor James Brooks in the *Morning Express*, who termed the poem "a wonder," wrote that the raven was a personification of "deep settled grief, bordering on sullen despair."[82] Poe eventually assisted with interpretation in his April 1846 *Graham's Magazine* essay "The Philosophy of Composition."

Poe was generous in giving us something resembling the backstory of the creation of "The Raven," however streamlined and incomplete. He exaggerated to make his point—that there is a deliberateness to the writing of a poem, a method, a thinking through, a careful craft. Acknowledging early on the false starts and second thoughts, he takes us step by step from intention (to write a poem appealing to the general reader and the critical one) to length (about one hundred lines, suitable for one sitting) to effect (the stirring of the soul through Beauty) and to tone (melancholy)—and then on to compelling special feature (a refrain whose meaning would vary) to choice of a particular refrain ("Nevermore") to speaker of the refrain (a parrot, then a raven) to theme (the death of a beautiful woman)—and yet still on to dynamic (a bereft lover making increasingly sensitive inquiries to a repetitive raven) to meter (trochaic octameter and variants presented in stanza form) to setting (the lover's chamber) to striking contrasts (the storm with the chamber, the fantastic with the serious, the marble with the feathers) and to climax (the much-sought suffering of the lover, whose desire for pleasurable pain regarding his lost love is satisfied by responses to his anxious queries of the assured negative of the raven). Poe elides sources, even Dickens's *Barnaby Rudge* and Barrett's "Lady Geraldine's Courtship" (though he later dedicates *The Raven and Other Poems* to Barrett).[83] And he nearly elides personal significance until, at the close of the essay—perhaps planned from the beginning—he comments that the metaphorical expression at the end "'Take thy beak from out *my heart,* and take thy form from off my door' / Quoth the Raven 'Nevermore'" inclines the reader to infer something further, and, on reading the final stanza, he or she may come to see the raven as "emblematical of *Mournful and Never-ending Remembrance*" (L2 70).

So, this poem that "will stick to the memory of everybody who reads it" is itself about memory. Poe, having recovered the poet's achievement through a detailed but somewhat fanciful account of inevitable forward motion—an account acknowledged elsewhere to be not wholly accurate[84]—offers at the close an ascertainable backward motion, a hint of his own private relation to the work.

We might return to 1815, when John Allan gave six-year-old Edgar a copy of John Aikin and Anna Laetitia Barbauld's *Evenings at Home,* with its essay "On Emblems," which repeatedly refers to the "emblematical." Surely this was one of Poe's first books, offered at a critical transition time—when the boy was learning to read, when he was traveling from the United States to England (from Richmond to Irvine, Kilmarnock, and London). "On Emblems" may have introduced the boy—or helped introduce the boy—to encoded visual equivalences. The "emblematical" in this early volume may well be related to the "emblematical" raven. (And a few years later Poe did experience a raven nearby in Stoke Newington.) Poe's attributing "The Raven" in the *American Review* to one "Quarles" tends to underscore the importance of Poe's use of the term "emblematical," for Francis Quarles was the author, most notably, of the 1635 *Emblems*.[85]

For the sorrowful remembrance in "The Raven," we might return to 1836, when Poe would have first planned the structure of *The Narrative of Arthur Gordon Pym*. As I have argued earlier, the symmetrical appearances of the penguin, possessing the "spirit of reflection," represent facing mirrors, at the center of which is Augustus (Poe's brother Henry), dying. That is, as with Too-wit midway between facing mirrors in the cabin of the *Jane Guy,* Poe offers an image of the infinite. Poe had written the year before to his aunt Maria Clemm, with whom he had lived in Baltimore when Henry died, "[Y]ou well know how little I am able to bear up under the pressure of grief" (O 1:102). With *Pym*, Poe symbolically fashioned his infinite memory of the sorrowful death of his brother. Poe embodied in *Pym,* years before the publication of "The Raven," "*Mournful and Never-ending Remembrance.*" It is notable that Susan Archer Weiss asserted that Poe had told her that the poem "had lain for more than *ten years* in his desk unfinished"[86]—that is, since roughly the time of his beginning *Pym* or before.

Still, given the focus of the poem on the lost Lenore, on the death of a beautiful woman, we should call up Poe's other memories of grief—the loss of his mother; the loss of "the first, purely ideal love of my soul" (O 2:694), Jane Stith Stanard; and the loss of his foster mother, Frances Allan. As public a triumph as "The Raven" was, it had its private weight. As with *Pym,* Poe transmuted the unbearable into art, ceaseless memories of sorrow into a masterpiece. The novel and the poem seem to be thematic doppelgängers.

Of course, in other ways they vary greatly. The genres, plots, characters, settings, and language are wholly different, and whereas *Pym* is hermetic, "The Raven" is not. Furthermore, in *Pym,* Poe offered consolation through the visionary final journal entry—specifically, the consolation of an intimation of divinity, which, I have argued, is a Christian theophany conveying the union of Christ and the Church in the New Jerusalem, a hereafter in which lost loved ones will be reunited. And there is repeated mention in *Pym* of consoling and of efforts at consoling—"Tiger . . . desirous by his caresses, of consoling me in my troubles" (P 1:76), "Augustus . . . endeavoured to console himself" (P 1:88), Dirk Peters used "language of a consolatory nature" (P 1:100), "We endeavoured . . . to console ourselves" (P 1:120), and "neither of us attempting to offer consolation to the other" (P 1:145). But there is no offer of consolation in "The Raven." And yet . . .

Poe scholar Adam C. Bradford has argued that when seen in the context of the culture of mourning and memorializing of its day, "The Raven" *is* consoling in that it provides for a community of grief. The student's need for "balm in Gilead" (with phrasing drawn from Jeremiah 8:22) would have been shared by grieving readers—Poe's poem may well have opened a space for impassioned and empathic mourning in defiance of the raven's instilled negative. Bradford's investigation of contemporary reader response to the poem tends to support his reading.[87] In this view, the merciless "Nevermore" is a prompt to a merciful working through of sorrow with an assurance of the fellow feeling of others who have suffered loss. "*Mournful and Never-ending Remembrance*" may have acted to encourage resilience and, with a sense of communal sharing, relief.

It might be argued further that a beautiful and definitive rendering of ultimate bleakness may itself assuage. Abraham Lincoln used to read some of the darkest passages in Shakespeare, including the desolating soliloquy of *Macbeth* (5.5.19–28):

> Tomorrow, and tomorrow, and tomorrow,
> Creeps in this petty pace from day to day,
> To the last syllable of recorded time;
> And all our yesterdays have lighted fools
> The way to dusty death. Out, out brief candle!
> Life's but a walking shadow, a poor player,
> That struts and frets his hour upon the stage,
> And then is heard no more. It is a tale
> Told by an idiot, full of sound and fury,
> Signifying nothing.

Of this somber passage, Lincoln said, "I cannot read it like [Edwin] Forrest, but it comes to me to-night like a consolation." Years earlier, when on the court circuit, Lincoln "[c]arried Poe around the Circuit—read and loved the Raven—repeated it over & over." Perhaps Poe's poem, also an articulation of ultimate bleakness—"Nevermore"—may have served "like a consolation," as well.[88]

With the publication of "The Raven," Poe became the lion of lions—fascinating, mysterious, and much celebrated. He would enjoy his fame, but even as he had won it, in part, by offering his reader something beyond, he would find that what he still sought was beyond him. He would still need consolation himself.

19

"It Will Be a Fortune to Me If I Can Hold It"

1845–1846

WHILE POE'S RAVEN REMAINED PERCHED upon a bust of Pallas, his poem swooped through the periodical press in 1845, perching in innumerable and varied venues, from the *Alexandria Gazette* to the *Vermont Phoenix*.[1] The poem perched also in books—the second edition of George Vandenhoff's *A Plain System of Elocution* and eventually Poe's own *The Raven and Other Poems*.[2]

And the poem became a steady part of Poe's New York experience. At the theater, the author heard "Nevermore" effectively inserted in a play. At Dr. John W. Francis's home, he appeared, solemnly introduced by the physician as "The Raven." At receptions, he recited "The Raven." At the *Broadway Journal* office, Poe provided the manuscript of the poem to the celebrated actor James E. Murdock, who recited the work to those gathered around, including the young office boy Alexander Crane, for whom the dramatic reading was "the most cherished memory of my life." Reading New York newspapers and magazines, Poe would have repeatedly encountered reprints and parodies of "The Raven." And visiting the home of friends in Brooklyn, where he was regularly implored by a seven-year-old boy, who was leaning against his chair or sitting on his knee, to recite "the Raven," Poe always obliged, offering "Nevermore" as a question, as an exclamation, as a whisper, as a shriek, thus providing a "most weird experience," which was remembered decades later. Poe had reached a new level of fame and acclaim, and he was clearly responsive to it.[3] As he would later write of "The Raven" compared with an earlier triumph, "The bird beat the bug, though, all hollow" (O 1:505).

The coming months would yield their share of "sweets and sours" (to recall "Israfel"). Meanwhile, in February 1845, even as he began to enjoy his extraordinary growing renown, Poe had to make a decision.

He continued with the *New York Evening Mirror*, walking daily from Greenwich Street to Mirror Corner. On Tuesday, February 4, he would likely have been trudging there, for there was a major snowstorm—more than a foot of snow fell that day, with drifts of five or six feet. On the following day, he might have detected lingering ash in the air, for there had been a fire overnight in the *New York Tribune* building. He might well have trudged the two blocks north from the *Mirror* to witness the damage. No one had been seriously hurt, but William H. Graham and his assistant had jumped from a second-story window to the cushioning snow in the middle of the night, and all of the publisher's stock had been destroyed. This may account for the rarity of *Prose Romances*, which Graham had published in 1843 in Philadelphia.[4]

Poe continued to contribute to the *Evening Mirror*, most notably with literary pieces. He faulted the moralistic poetry of the Transcendentalists (recalling his March 1844 *Graham's* review of *Orion*) and elaborated further objections to plagiarism. He also addressed specific periodicals—the *American Review* and the *Aristidean*—and specific writers—Nathaniel Hawthorne (whose *Twice-Told Tales* was out of print) and Robert T. Conrad (who was very ill).[5] Still, Poe had to make a choice.

The *Town* reported, "Mr. EDGAR A. POE, has it in contemplation to publish a new five dollar Magazine"—presumably "The Stylus."[6] Though this was his goal, he did not immediately pursue it, probably because of inadequate funds. At this time, Charles F. Briggs's three-dollar newspaper, the *Broadway Journal*, which had been publishing Poe's work, was gaining recognition. The *New York True Sun* described it as the "clever, witty, well written, well edited Journal."[7] And Poe praised it in the *Evening Mirror*, terming the February 8 issue (which featured "The Raven") "in all respects . . . an excellent number," and he provided for the next issue the excoriating "Some Secrets of the Magazine Prison-House." Poe would have been attracted to the *Broadway Journal* by the increased responsibility and potential profit. Briggs valued revenue from book advertisements, so he wanted Poe to enhance the newspaper's literary focus through his criticism (P 4:xix). Poe did soon make up his mind. N. P. Willis later wrote, "With a prospect of taking the lead in another periodical, he, at last, voluntarily gave up his employment with us."[8]

On February 21, Poe signed a contract with the publisher John Bisco to join the *Broadway Journal* to assist Briggs as one of the weekly's editors and to share in one-third of its profits (though without any salary).[9] The weekly's office was nearby at 153 Broadway. Poe's affiliating with the *Broadway Journal*—along with Henry C. Watson for the music department—was announced the following day.[10] The *Town* could barely keep up with Poe's career—the periodical announced on February 22 that Poe was "one of the editors" of the *Evening Mirror*, then added a postscript that in fact "EDGAR has since gone into the Broadway Journal."[11]

And a dozen blocks north of the office of the *Broadway Journal*, in the dignified Greek Revival building of the New York Society Library, at the corner of Broadway and Leonard Street, Edgar soon spoke on American poetry. Willis admiringly described his friend addressing two or three hundred literati in the lecture hall on the evening of Friday, February 28: "He becomes a desk,—his beautiful head showing like a statuary embodiment of Discrimination; his accent drops like a knife through water, and his style is so much purer and clearer than the pulpit commonly gets or requires, that the effect of what he says, besides other things, pampers the ear."[12]

Poe pampered and he pummeled. He attacked the practice of unwarranted praise of literary works—the aforementioned "puffing"—and the controlling literary cliques, especially the literary establishment of Boston and the Transcendentalists. He faulted the work of several women writers, including Lydia Sigourney and Lucretia and Margaret Davidson, though offering favorable comment on the work of Amelia Welby, Frances Sargent Osgood, and Elizabeth Oakes Smith. He considered a variety of male poets, including the five featured on the frontispiece of Griswold's *Poets and Poetry of America* ("the Copperplate Five"), calling out William Cullen Bryant for his narrowness, Henry Wadsworth Longfellow for his plagiarism, Charles Sprague for his diluted imitation of Alexander Pope, and Richard Henry Dana Sr. for his ineffective meter, extolling without qualification only Fitz-Greene Halleck. He closed by discussing the purpose of poetry and reading three poems he esteemed and thought neglected—N. P. Willis's "Unseen Spirits" (on suffering women), Philip Pendleton Cooke's "Florence Vane" (on a lost unrequited love), and again Thomas Holley Chivers's "The Heavenly Vision" (on an otherworldly assurance from a lost love).[13]

Poe boldly spoke his truth to literary power—as he had written it as early as his *Norman Leslie* and Drake-Halleck reviews in the *Southern Literary Messenger*. He declared in a letter to the *Broadway Journal*, appearing on

March 8, "Could I, at the moment, have invented any terms *more* explicit, wherewith to express my contempt of our general editorial course of corruption and puffery, I should have employed them beyond the shadow of a doubt." He expected and accepted the censure of those he had censured, commenting that without it "I should at this moment have been looking about me to discover what sad blunder I had committed" (O 1:491). Writing to a fellow editor about his recent lecture, Poe mentioned the good attendance, the presence of "the most intellectual & refined portion of the city," and the high commendations of "the leading journalists of the City." He attributed the negative response of the *New York Tribune* (edited by Horace Greeley) and the *Boston Atlas* and *Boston Evening Transcript* to his critical views of Boston and its purported Transcendentalism. And he closed with the ultimate evidence of his success: "So well was the Lecture received that I am about to repeat it" (O 1:496–97). His repeat performance was scheduled for the Society Library on April 17. It would never take place.

Of particular note is that, unlike his lecture on American poetry in Philadelphia, Wilmington, Newark, and Reading, the New York version of the lecture did not involve an attack on Griswold. Poe even called Griswold's attention to this fact (O 1:503; see also O 1:477). In the case of the anthologist, Poe was evidently trying to effect a rapprochement. But he would fail.

Shortly after the February 28 lecture, in the drawing room of the imposing block-long, five-story Astor House, Willis introduced Poe to the beautiful poet Frances Sargent Osgood. Poe had sought the meeting, and Osgood was interested; she had read "The Raven" (courtesy of Willis on behalf of Poe) and had heard that Poe had praised her work in his lecture, reading one of her poems. She recalled her first encounter with Poe vividly: "With his proud and beautiful head erect, his dark eyes flashing with the elective light of feeling and of thought, a peculiar, an inimitable blending of sweetness and hauteur in his expression and manner, he greeted me, calmly, gravely, almost coldly; yet with so marked an earnestness that I could not help being deeply impressed by it." She wrote that in the coming year he would turn to her "for counsel and kindness in all his many anxieties and griefs." (Here we may recall Edgar and the consoling Jane Stith Stanard.) Virginia encouraged the connection between the two, believing, rightly, that Osgood would never tolerate Poe's drinking. Poe's friendship with Osgood would prove important to both, but the literary flirtation would become a source of gossip, damaging to Poe and Virginia, as well as to Osgood herself, and intolerable to the ever-vigilant Maria Clemm.[14] (Flora Lapham Mack later stated that Mrs. Clemm had warned both Poe and Osgood. But Osgood asserted that Poe had sought her, not the reverse, and blamed Mrs. Clemm for her comments.)[15]

Willis, who introduced Poe to Osgood, also introduced to his readers—in the very issues of the *Evening Mirror* (March 1) and the *Weekly Mirror* (March 8) in which he praised Poe's lecture—a challenger to Poe's claim of plagiarism against Longfellow: the pseudonymous "Outis" (Nobody). Willis had maintained his allegiance both to Poe and to Longfellow and his friends, and he referred to the Outis piece as an "admirable article" for which "we meant to have thanked and complimented the author."[16] Briggs termed Outis "[s]omebody in Boston . . . whose name I forget." The identity of Outis remains a mystery in Poe studies; he has been considered to be Harvard professor C. C. Felton, New York editor Lawrence Labree, and even Poe himself.[17] This last possibility seems an improbability, resonant with the refuted identification of the encrypter W. B. Tyler with Poe.[18] But regardless of the writer's identity, it is clear that Poe took Outis's argument very seriously. Beginning with the March 8 issue of the *Broadway Journal,* for which his name first appeared on the masthead as one of the editors, Poe responded to Outis with an analytical five-part series.

Poe offered in this series the "sincere and unbiased opinions" promised in the broadside for the Briggs/Poe/Watson *Broadway Journal.*[19] Reviewing the recent controversy, beginning with his own January 14 *Evening Mirror* review of Longfellow's *The Waif* and the subsequent defenses of Longfellow, Poe reprinted, from the *Evening Mirror* of March 1, Outis's essay "Plagiarism." Then bemusedly—perhaps even gleefully—Poe dismantled Outis's argument, employing, on occasion, deft analogy and imagined interior monologue. What he argued in essence in the first four installments is that even as coincidences exist, so does plagiarism (typically by a well-known writer of a less-known writer); that Outis's specious apparent allegations of plagiarism against "The Raven" amounted to nothing; that a charge of plagiarism should be based not simply on the number of parallels but also on the nature of these parallels and their occurring over a specified expanse of text; and that, based on this premise, Longfellow (and James Aldrich, implicitly, too) might well be fairly accused of plagiarism. But surprisingly, in the fifth and final installment, Poe offered not a coup de grace, but a coda of graciousness: he granted that what may seem plagiarism may be only a poet's naturally absorbing the beauties he has encountered in his reading and, over time, feeling them inevitably to be his own, forgetting their origin, and later employing them in some fashion in his work.[20]

In the midst of the series, one critic opined, "We think Mr. Poe has the best of the argument, and he promises to pursue it."[21] Poe's argument seems well reasoned, with detail and wit, and, at the close, generosity.

The authorship of a subsequent harsh piece on Longfellow in the April 1845 issue of the *Aristidean,* edited by Thomas Dunn English, is not altogether clear. The work was listed in the magazine's index as by "E. A. P." But Poe somewhat disavowed it, writing, "It is, perhaps, a little coarse, but we are not disposed to call it unjust; although there are in it some opinions which, by implication, are attributed to ourselves individually, and with which we cannot altogether coincide" (P 3:108). Still, he later referred to the work as his (O 2:735). The evidence is ambiguous; I tend to think that the review was a cooperative effort by Poe and English.[22]

During the Outis period, Poe published much else in the *Broadway Journal.* Among the pieces of particular interest are his two-part notice of Francis Fauvel-Gouraud's *Phreno-Mnemotechny; or The Art of Memory* (a book intended to enable man to control memory, contrasting to memory's controlling man in "The Raven"); his brief treatment of Margaret Fuller and his briefer one of Nathaniel Hawthorne; and his comments on Frances Sargent Osgood and his inclusion of her poems.[23] Poe also featured revisions of his own "Lionizing" and "Berenice." Meanwhile, he was going to the theater, maintaining his correspondence, and publishing a new short story in the *American Review,* "Some Words with a Mummy," a work of social criticism that he mentioned in the *Broadway Journal* (P 3:87). And his earlier offering of selected short stories to editor Evert A. Duyckinck (O 1:486) yielded Wiley and Putnam's commitment to a new book, *Tales.*[24]

What Poe may well have anticipated for his New York lectures was the double triumph he had had in Philadelphia in November 1843 and January 1844. However, although the February 1845 talk had gone well, the turnout for the April one was severely limited by "a most dismal rain." Addressing the Society Library audience—which was reported "to have made up, in discrimination and respectability in taste and judgment, what it lacked in numbers"—Poe announced that the second talk would be postponed and money refunded.[25] But the canceled April 17 New York lecture on American poetry was never rescheduled.

Alexander Crane, the office boy at the *Broadway Journal* who later remembered Poe as "the gentlest, truest, tenderest and knightliest man I ever knew," recalled of that bleak night, "I was one of those present, as Poe had given me a complimentary ticket to the lecture, and badly as I was disappointed, I could see upon his face that my master was much more so. It was a little thing, it is true, but he was a man easily upset by little things." Poe had lost a moment of glory, of ascent. "The next morning" Crane continued, "he came to the office, leaning on the arm of a friend, intoxicated with wine."[26] The expected verbal quickening had been replaced by an artificial one.

Poe recovered and returned to his obligations. His route to work changed, for he moved from 150 Greenwich Street to 195 East Broadway, and his office from 153 Broadway to 135 Nassau Street.[27] But his routine—which was anything but routine—remained demanding. On May 4, he explained to his friend Frederick W. Thomas his not having written for a long while (since January 4), "For the last three or four months I have been working 14 or 15 hours a day—hard at it all the time" (O 1:504). The work must have intensified when he joined the *Broadway Journal*—writing the regular reviews and criticism and editorial comments for his portion of the sixteen-page weekly, as well as revising his short stories for renewed publication there. He would also have been preparing his lecture and correcting proof for *Poets and Poetry of America* (O 1:502–3) and perhaps *Tales*. He might have begun his new literary analysis, "American Parnassus" (O 1:512). And he was sometimes holding forth: William H. Starr, then associated with the *Broadway Journal,* remembered, "Often have I seen him, while he was editing the Broadway Journal, seated at the little side desk he used in the office in Nassau street, with a circle of literary friends gathered around his chair, completely entranced by his eloquence; his impassioned utterances and magnetic fascination, his words, and often full sentences, sparkling and glowing with a more than diamond radiance: and this even when his mind was shadowed by trouble and despair."[28]

And yet, through all his efforts, he had only prospects—no salary—and he confided, "The Devil himself was never so poor" (O 1:505). He could not keep it up.

On June 27, Charles F. Briggs wrote to his friend James Russell Lowell about Poe, "[H]e has lately got into his old habits and I fear will injure himself irretrievably." On July 16, Briggs stated, "I believe that he had not drunk anything for more than 18 months until within the past 3 months, but in this time he has been very frequently carried home in a wretched condition."[29] It was in the period after his canceled lecture, then, that Poe was once again defeated by his old enemy. Anne C. Lynch's June 27 response to an unlocated Poe letter intimates an underlying and long-extant dynamic: "I am exceedingly pained at the desponding tone in which you write. Life is too short & there is too much to be done in it, to give one time to *despair*. Exorcise that devil, I beg of you, as speedily as possible" (H 17:258; O 2:1230). Lynch echoes similar cautions that Poe had received—in 1835 from John Pendleton Kennedy (about "these villainous blue devils" [H 17:19], what Poe had termed his "depression of spirits" [O 1:107]); in 1839 from William E. Burton (about Poe's "morbid tone," its "melancholy hue"); and in 1843 from William Poe (who had asked, "Ought you ever to give up in despair when you have such resources as yr well stored mind to apply to?" [H 17:146]).[30] Frederick W. Thomas recalled, "[I]t was his excessive, and at times morbid sensibility which forced him into his 'frolics,' rather than any mere morbid appetite for drink" (H 17:137). It would seem that depression, "darkness visible," contributed to Poe's sometimes drinking alcohol, which, given his constitution, would often triumph.

The drinking was intermittent; Poe still contributed to the *Broadway Journal*. He wrote a variety of essays and reviews, including a mostly commendatory piece on William Bolles's *An Explanatory and Phonographic Pronouncing Dictionary of the English Language* and a condemnatory piece on William W. Lord's *Poems*. He followed up on a brief poem to Frances Sargent Osgood appearing on April 26, "Impromptu: To Kate Carol," with another on May 24, "To [Violet Vane]." The latter, a response to Osgood's "To——," proposed "A love which shall be passion-free": "We both have found a life-long love / Wherein our weary souls may rest, / Yet may we not, my gentle friend / Be each to each the *second best?*"[31] He also revised previous stories and poems for reprinting in the *Broadway Journal*, as he had recently revised selected stories for *Tales*. Furthermore, he published his final angelic dialogue, "The Power of Words," in the May issue of the *Democratic Review*. And he wrote occasional correspondence.

But hints of Poe's great vulnerability appeared in the *Town* in late April, ironically crediting Poe with "a treatise on 'Aqua Pura.'"[32] And subsequent personal accounts by James Russell Lowell make clear that Poe had again been defeated. Lowell recalled to John H. Ingram his visit to Poe (probably in late May), when he observed the after-effects of inebriation: "I went by appointment & found him a little tipsy, as if he were recovering from a fit of drunkenness, & with that over-solemnity with which men in such cases try to convince you of their sobriety. I well remember (for it pained me) the anxious expression of his wife." He revisited his visit to Poe in a letter to George E. Woodberry: "His manner was rather formal, even pompous, but I have the impression he was a little soggy with drink—not tipsy—but as if he had been holding his head under a pump to cool it." Maria Clemm, who also witnessed the meeting, must have shared Virginia's anxiety; she later wrote to Lowell,

"How much I wish I could see you, how quickly I could remove your wrong impression of my darling Eddie. The day you saw him in New York *he was not himself.* Do you not remember that I never left the room."[33]

Understandably, Briggs lost patience with Poe's drinking—like employers before him—and he wrote to Lowell in that letter of June 27 that he would "haul down Poe's name" from the masthead of the *Broadway Journal*.[34] Evidently Poe had already decided to leave; on June 26, Poe wrote to his friend Duyckinck, "I have resolved to give up the B. Journal and retire to the country for six months, or perhaps a year, as the sole means of recruiting my health and spirits" (O 1:512). But unfortunately, he did not keep to this resolution. Perhaps he believed that, despite his evident infirmity, he could still make his own Fate.

In late June, Thomas Holley Chivers—who had recently discussed literature with Poe at his East Broadway home and met Virginia and Maria Clemm—saw Poe at Nassau Street near Ann Street, "coming along the pavement, tottering from side to side." Ignoring one man's loudly declaring him the "*Shakespeare of America*," Poe insisted that Chivers visit again, but, upon seeing Lewis Gaylord Clark, he confronted the *Knickerbocker* editor about his mocking comments in the July issue concerning an unsigned Poe piece ("Magazine-Writing—Peter Snook") in the June 7 issue of the *Broadway Journal*, perhaps seeking (but failing) to provoke a fight. Also, Poe maintained that he had just been invited by a woman in Providence (Frances Sargent Osgood) to visit her. Later he asserted that the visit was intended to obtain her testimony about a false forgery allegation against him—but he supposedly boasted of "the d——dst amour you ever knew a fellow to be in in all your life" (though he denied it the following day). (William H. Gravely challenges Chivers's account here.) Chivers wrote that when Poe finally approached his home, "he was so far gone—staggering from side to side of the Pavement—that it was with the greatest of difficulty I could keep him from falling prostrate in the Street." Virginia, seeing her husband through the window, locked herself in her room. Chivers took Poe upstairs, and Maria Clemm put her son-in-law to bed. He remained there, avoiding a commitment to present a poem to the Philomathean and Eucleian Societies of New York University.[35] The *Town* reported his absence in a short piece titled "POH!" with an illustration of an exclaiming raven clutching a dagger in each hand.[36]

Chivers would later write to Poe, "*What would God think of that Angel who should condescend to dust his feet in the ashes of Hell?*" Poe responded (in late summer), "I have not touched a drop of the 'ashes' since you left N.Y.—&

I am resolved not to touch a drop as long as I live" (O 1:524). And Chivers answered, with relief, "*That's a man.* For God's sake, but *more* for your own, never touch another drop."[37]

In the midst of this very fraught time in Poe's life, on June 25, Wiley and Putnam published, in its series Library of American Books, his second collection of short fiction, *Tales*. Although Poe was not entirely pleased with the limited range of works that had been chosen, he did present copies of the book to John Bisco, Anne Lynch, and Mary Gove, and later Sarah Helen Whitman.[38] And *Tales* elicited some notably positive reviews. Margaret Fuller commented in July in the *New York Daily Tribune*, "His narrative proceeds with vigor, his colours are applied with discrimination, and where the effects are fantastic they are not unmeaningly so." An unidentified writer for the *New-York Commercial Advertiser* wrote in August that Poe's tales are "very extraordinary and clever specimens of the wild and wonderful." Evert A. Duyckinck, who selected the tales, asserted in August in the *American Review*, "[I]t [the volume] evinces a quickness of apprehension, an intensity of feeling, a vigor of imagination, a power of analysis, which are rarely seen in any compositions going under the name of 'tales.'" And William Gilmore Simms stated in December in *Southern and Western Magazine*, "[H]e [Poe] is an acknowledged master—a Prospero, whose wand is one of wonderful properties."[39] There was, of course, some dissent. Charles Anderson Dana remarked on the book in July in the *Harbinger*, "Its tales are clumsily contrived, unnatural, and every way in bad taste. There is still a kind of power in them; it is the power of disease; there is no health about them, they are alike in the vagaries of an opium eater." Also in July, an unidentified reviewer for the *National Intelligencer* termed *Tales* "a marvelously bad collection of visions of some one to whom Fancy only comes in a fit of the nightmare."[40] However, the popular readership tended to want Prospero's wand—the volume sold 1,500 copies in the first few months.[41] Featured among its dozen pieces were "The Gold-Bug," "The Black Cat," "The Fall of the House of Usher," "The Murders in the Rue Morgue," "The Purloined Letter," and "The Man of the Crowd." Poe's *Tales* is one of the great short story collections in American literature.

Also in late June, Poe's tale "The Imp of the Perverse" was the lead-off piece in the July 1845 issue of *Graham's Magazine*. Illuminating man's "overwhelming tendency to do wrong for the wrong's sake,"[42] the work offers an extended account culminating in confession, which for the narrator exemplifies perverseness, but which for the reader suggests—as in "The Black Cat" and "The Fall of the House of Usher"—the power of conscience.

As Chivers had intimated, Poe traveled to Providence in early July. According to Sarah Helen Whitman years later, Poe had told Frances Sargent Osgood that he had wandered the hills on the east of Providence and seen Whitman that moonlit night, wearing white, walking near her house (on Benefit Street).[43] Poe also recalled, in a letter to Whitman, that he had declined to visit her with Osgood, believing that the Providence poet was happily married (O 2:694). (In fact, she had lost her husband in 1833.) He would pay tribute to his first sight of Sarah Helen Whitman in an 1848 poem that began, "I saw thee once—once only—years ago" (M 1:445).

Poe traveled to Boston, as well. He evidently returned to the area of Washington Street—where he had once found Calvin F. S. Thomas, who printed *Tamerlane*—and was "agreeably surprised at the number of intrinsically valuable works on the counters of 'the trade,'" lamenting that there was not a greater dissemination of these works in New York. Having a few months earlier deplored the fact that Hawthorne's *Twice-Told Tales* was out of print, he was pleased to see it published again (the second issue of the second edition) by James Munroe and Company. He mentioned forthcoming publications from Ticknor and Company, not noting what he might have seen in the local newspaper, that Ticknor was then advertising his own *Tales*. Poe's brief piece on Boston books, appearing in the August 23 issue of the *Broadway Journal*, would reveal none of the criticism of Boston that had been in his February 28 lecture or that he would suggest in October at his Boston Lyceum presentation and express in no uncertain terms afterward.[44]

However, there was, on occasion, an ominous animus in the Boston press. Perhaps it was one of the editors of the satirical weekly the *Jester* who, in the June 14 issue, offered "The Turkey," a parody of "The Raven" featuring an inebriated narrator, with an illustration of a besotted fellow by a lamppost.[45] And it was presumably the editor Cornelia Wells Walter who, in the July 14 issue of the *Boston Evening Transcript*, characterized the second verse of Poe's recently published poem "Eulalie" as "somewhat weak and silly in expression." She quoted the lyrical and incantatory lines, a tribute to a woman's beauty, and then invoked Longfellow, sarcastically asking, "Who will read *Excelsior* after this?"[46] Her mockery would increase after Poe's Boston Lyceum lecture.

Meanwhile, Poe's return to New York went surprisingly well. The merchant who had alleged forgery against Poe (in the presence of Frances Sargent Osgood), Edward J. Thomas, recanted his charge in a letter to Poe of July 5 (H 17:251). On July 10, Poe, with Henry T. Tuckerman and W. D. Snodgrass, judged student writing at the Rutgers Female Institute; Poe read aloud the winning composition by Louisa Olivia Hunter on the following day. And Charles F. Briggs, who had intended to let Poe go from the *Broadway Journal,* found that publisher John Bisco was asking for more money than he was willing to pay to assume control. The second volume of the magazine commenced one week late, on July 12, with Briggs's name hauled down from the masthead. The remaining editors were Poe and Watson.[47] And Bisco clarified, "The editorial conduct of 'The Broadway Journal' is under the sole charge of EDGAR A. POE—Mr. H. C. WATSON, as heretofore, controlling the Musical Department." Poe signed a new contract on July 14 that stated that he was "the sole editor."[48]

In July and August 1845, Poe continued to write criticism for the *Broadway Journal,* proceeding from Henry H. Hirst's *The Coming of the Mammoth, and Other Poems* to Thomas Hood's *Prose and Verse.* He also provided revisions of tales, progressing from "The Masque of the Red Death" to "William Wilson," and revisions of poems, from "Sonnet—To Zante" to "The City in the Sea." He offered editorial comments, as well as an advertisement for an investor in the newspaper. And he made occasional professional comments—on his coming book of poems, on the publication history of "The Fall of the House of Usher"—and occasional personal comments—on his mother as an actress, on his recent visit to Boston. Even with his recurrent debility, Poe was a dedicated editor, trying to make the *Broadway Journal* a success.[49] And he began to contribute marginal notes to *Godey's Lady's Book.*

But he had lost allies. The departed *Broadway Journal* editor Charles F. Briggs, probably resentful, described Poe to William Page as "a drunken sot, and the most purely selfish of human beings." James Russell Lowell, probably remembering a not-quite-sober Poe, described him to Briggs as "wholly lacking in that element of manhood which, for want of a better name, we call *character,*" and Briggs agreed, referring to "Poe's characterless character."[50] The two men were, at least in part, taking a medical problem for a moral one. And Poe also lost a potential ally. In a better moment, at his home, he reassured young Richard H. Stoddard that his "Ode on a Grecian Flute" would appear in the *Broadway Journal,* but in a lesser moment, under the influence in his office, he alleged that the work was not by Stoddard at all. Stoddard later acknowledged that the work was derivative.[51]

Unquestionably, Poe could be difficult. Under great stress, both personal and financial, and occasionally drinking, he could be more than usually abrasive and absolute. Yet he had his moments, as well. It was on a steamy afternoon in August that the *Broadway Journal* office boy Alexander Crane fainted—and awoke, he later recalled, lying on his long work table, with Poe "bending over me bathing my wrists and temples in cold water." Crane added, "He ministered to me until I was able to stand up, and then he sent me home in a carriage." And he commented, with gratitude, "This act of kindness, coupled with his uniform gentle greetings, when he entered the office of a morning, together with frequent personal inquiries and words of encouragement, made me love and trust my editor."[52]

Also at this time, Poe was on congenial terms with the booksellers John Russell Bartlett and Charles Welford, proprietors of Bartlett and Welford at 7 Astor Place, a gathering place for literary New York. It was remembered years later by one patron as "that cozy nook under the Astor House." The shop was an elite and refined sanctuary for Poe. According to Bartlett, Poe was "sometimes daily" in the shop and "held long conversations on literary subjects with Wellford [sic], with whom he was on terms of familiar intercourse." Two titles that the Bartlett and Welford bookshop advertised in the spring of 1845— Charles Wilkes's *Narrative of the United States Exploring Expedition,* about the celebrated voyage initially proposed by J. N. Reynolds, and *The Works of William Hogarth,* recalling the volume that Poe had admired and gambled for in Charlottesville—might well then have been topics of conversation between Poe and Bartlett or Welford or both. Perhaps, too, Poe discussed his own recently published *Tales,* which might have been for sale in the shop. Also, Poe visited Bartlett at his residence at 1 Amity Place, and he would stop by daily when Frances Sargent Osgood was visiting there. Bartlett recalled Poe's great appreciation of his coffee.[53]

Poe saw Osgood not only at Bartlett's home but also at the literary salons, and she was rapt. She recalled, "[F]or hours I have listened to him, entranced by strains of such pure and almost celestial eloquence as I have never read or heard elsewhere." In the summer of 1845, her literary flirtation with Poe shifted from poetry to fiction with "Ida Grey." Quoting "The Raven" in that short piece, Osgood goes on to describe her eponymous coquette's meeting "a remarkable looking man, whose face once seen could never be forgotten, so wonderfully spiritual was its expression." The language Osgood then uses ("singular earnestness," "cold and calm") echoes her account of her actual first meeting with Poe. We may even wonder if the name "Ida Grey" conveys covertly, through an embedded anagram, "Edgar." And Osgood would subsequently write additional Poe-focused pieces.[54]

Frances Sargent Osgood was distant from her husband, Samuel S. Osgood, as hinted in her poem ["Yes! 'lower to the level'"], published in the

Evening Mirror in December 1844. Presumably he understood the "literary alliance" of his wife and Poe. And Poe had written in "To [Violet Vane]" that the relationship could be "passion-free," that each of them had already "found a life-long love," that his "gentle friend" could be *second best.*" Samuel S. Osgood was apparently sufficiently unperturbed by the relationship that he painted Poe's portrait. The image is, as Michael Deas has observed, "a benign and somewhat idealized likeness of Poe." It seems to intimate, on the part of the painter, sympathy rather than suspicion. According to Deas, the painter's niece later asserted, "There never would have existed a portrait of the poet from my uncle's brush had there not been a kindly feeling between them."[55]

In this busy time, dominated by work on a weekly newspaper, Poe still held to his dream of his own monthly magazine, as is clear from his letters. On August 8, he proclaimed somewhat dubiously to his second cousin, Neilson Poe, "'The B. Journal' flourishes—but in January I shall establish a Magazine" (O 1:516). A few days later, asking for a loan of fifty dollars from Thomas Holley Chivers for the *Broadway Journal,* he boasted, tenuously, "My prospects about 'Maga' are glorious" (O 1:519). Poe's statements were exaggerated, but his ongoing aspiration was real.

Poe persevered with his *Broadway Journal* work in the late summer and early fall, writing incisive reviews of such books as John Wilson's (Christopher North's) *Genius and Character of Burns,* Rufus Wilmot Griswold's *Prose Works of John Milton,* and William Gilmore Simms's short story collection *The Wigwam and the Cabin.* He offered columns of "Editorial Miscellany," discussing such matters as John Greenleaf Whittier and plagiarism, William Jones on "American Humor," and Thomas Dunn English's poem "Ben Bolt." He also featured revised versions of various tales, including "Diddling," "Ligeia," and "MS. Found in a Bottle," and various poems, including "To the River," "To——," and "Fairyland." He continued to contribute to *Godey's* and *Graham's,* and he wrote "Our Book-Shelves" for the September issue of English's *Aristidean.*[56] Early in September, he submitted poems to Evert A. Duyckinck for the anticipated book of his poems with Wiley and Putnam (O 1:525). In the middle of October he corrected the last proofs for the volume.[57] Consolidating his work in *Tales* and *The Raven and Other Poems,* he was also consolidating his reputation. And amid all the activity of this period, Poe, Virginia, and Maria Clemm made another move—sometime in September, they took an apartment at 85 Amity Street, just one block south of Washington Square. From this location, Poe could easily continue his visits with the bookseller John Russell Bartlett at home at nearby 1 Amity Place, where Frances Sargent Osgood would also visit.[58]

By mid-September, Poe was invited to speak at the Boston Lyceum. (In early 1844, he had written to Lowell about the possibility of a speaking engagement in Boston, and the Cambridge poet had reported that the secretary of the Boston Lyceum had been encouraging about the following year [H 17:159].) Poe accepted the invitation, but, as had apparently been the case with the Philomathean and Eucleian Societies, he could not compose an original poem. This time, rather than drink or stay in bed, he sought the advice of Thomas Dunn English—who recommended that he delay the engagement until he had written the poem—and evidently asked for the aid of Frances Sargent Osgood.[59]

We cannot know precisely Poe's request of her; our only source, the unreliable Griswold, later claimed that Poe had written to Osgood, "You compose with such astonishing facility . . . that you can easily furnish me, quite soon enough, a poem that shall be equal to my reputation. For the love of God I beseech you to help me in this extremity."[60] Probably some appeal was made, however it may have been worded. Osgood may have offered some portion of her poem "Lulin; or the Diamond Fay," but this work of sentimental Fancy would not serve.[61] Poe decided to present the 1829 "Al Aaraaf," his early work about an imagined home to Beauty, which could effectively challenge what he later termed "the heresy of *The Didactic*" in poetry (L2 182), a characteristic misconception, he believed, of the Bostonians.

The Boston Theatre, where Poe's parents had performed, had been refashioned and renamed the "Odeon." It was "densely crowded at an early hour" that Wednesday evening, October 16. At 7:30, Caleb Cushing began his disquisition, comparing Great Britain with the United States, and he went on for more than two hours. When Cushing finished, Poe arose, to applause, and offered an apology—really a mock apology—for not having written a didactic poem. And then he delivered "Al Aaraaf." The poem, literally otherworldly and difficult to understand on first reading, would have been challenging to many on first hearing (although it was claimed that one attendee was comfortably following along in his copy of the 1831 *Poems*). Twenty-one-year-old Thomas Wentworth Higginson, present in the Odeon that evening—who had read *Tales of the Grotesque and Arabesque* and recognized its author's "original genius"—later wrote that that night Poe had "the look of over-sensitiveness" and that his "persistent, querulous" intoning of an "apology for his poem, and a deprecation of the expected criticism of the Boston public" was "nauseous flattery." Apparently the first section of the poem had no distinct impact, but the second section, offering the angel Nesace's rhapsodic apostrophe to Ligeia, the spirit of music, was compelling: "[H]is [Poe's] voice seemed attenuated to the finest golden thread; the audience became hushed, and, as it were, breathless; there seemed no life in the hall but his; and every syllable was accentuated with such delicacy, and sustained with such sweetness, as I never heard equalled by other lips." Poe had wrought his magic. Higginson and his friends, returning to Cambridge, "felt that we had been under the spell of some wizard." But Poe's lovely reaching did not yield appreciation from all. While some were ravished, others were bewildered.[62]

Some people walked out. Cornelia Wells Walter noted that some left after the introduction: they "finally commenced the noisy expedient of removing from the hall." Some left during the poem: "The audience now thinned so rapidly and made so much commotion in their departure that we lost the beauties of the composition." If we don't entirely trust the antagonistic Walter, we may trust Joseph T. Buckingham, who admired the writer's "elegant and classic production" but reported, "That it was not appreciated by the audience, was very evident, by their uneasiness and continual exits in numbers at a time." Some left after the recitation, "fatigued at its close, both by the length of the preface, and the oppressive beauties of the poem"—this despite the announced reading of "The Raven."[63] And then Poe aggravated the situation afterward by stating that in his reading of "Al Aaraaf" he had been bantering ("quizzing") his Bostonian listeners (P 3:291). We cannot be sure if this was indeed the case or if his claiming this was a defensive strategy, either preplanned or improvised after the fact. It seems likelier that the claim was defensive.

Back in New York, Poe came to terms with the publisher John Bisco to purchase the *Broadway Journal* for fifty dollars cash—available perhaps from payment from the Boston Lyceum or from a loan from Horace Greeley—and a promissory note for debts, due in three months. The masthead of the October 25 issue read "EDGAR A. POE, EDITOR AND PROPRIETOR." Seeking loans for his new enterprise from his adversary Rufus Wilmot Griswold and his friend John Pendleton Kennedy, Poe wrote to both regarding the *Broadway Journal*, "It will be a fortune to me if I can hold it" (O 1:529, 531).[64]

Predictably, some journalists, led by Cornelia Wells Walter, attacked Poe's performance at the Odeon. The new proprietor of the *Broadway Journal* defended himself in two lengthy pieces in the issues of November 1 and November 22 (including, early on, in the former of the two pieces, supportive published comments by Mordecai Noah, and in the latter, such comments by William Gilmore Simms). Poe contended that given the impossibility of pleasing the Boston "*clique,*" he had decided to offer only a "juvenile poem." Most of the audience had given his reading of "Al Aaraaf" "respectful and profound attention," with frequent applause, but some of his implacable Boston foes had walked out and later assailed him in the press. He had hoaxed them, he maintained, for the poem was "bad," "wretched," and he had written and published it at the age of ten. No doubt angry, Poe seems to have been willing to take some liberties for the sake of insult. Certainly Higginson and his friends would have been surprised to hear such deprecation of the work of "delicacy" and "sweetness." And those familiar with Poe's early career would have known that "Al Aaraaf" was written probably when the poet was in the army, at age nineteen, and was published in the Monumental City when he was twenty. Very likely, some of those whom the *Broadway Journal* representative William Fairman termed Poe's "great many friends" in Baltimore and Washington would have seen that Poe's response to the attacks itself contained an element of hoax. Continuing to convey his low estimate of Walter and of a Boston audience, Poe soon wrote that on his return to "Frogpondium" he would read "a fine poem that we wrote at seven months."[65]

In late October through mid-November, Poe continued to write criticism for the *Broadway Journal,* including reviews of Mary L. Hewitt's *The Songs of Our Land and Other Poems,* Sarah Josepha Hale's *Alice Ray: A Romance in Rhyme,* and Charles Lamb's *Specimens of English Dramatic Poets,* and continued to revise his own work, publishing versions of "The Thousand-and-Second Tale of Scheherazade," "Some Words with a Mummy," and "The Devil in the Belfry." (And he published the new tale "The System of Doctor Tarr and Professor Fether" in *Graham's Magazine.*) In the November 1 issue of the *Broadway Journal,* Poe mentioned his forthcoming book of poems; in the November 8 issue, Wiley and Putnam began listing Poe's collection *The Raven and Other Poems* in its advertisement. The firm published the book, volume 8 in the Library of American Books, on November 19.[66]

The ninety-one-page volume is dedicated "TO THE NOBLEST OF HER SEX," Elizabeth Barrett Barrett, and prefaced by self-deprecatory remarks, in which Poe rues that "Events not to be controlled have prevented me from making, at any time, any serious effort in what, under happier circumstances, would have been the field of my choice." What poetry Poe might have otherwise written we cannot know, but the works gathered here are extraordinary, from "The Raven" (leading off the first section, poems published since 1831) to "To Helen" (closing the second section, "Poems Written in Youth," poems published until 1831).[67] The critical response to the book, however, was mixed.

Not surprisingly, the city that Poe had mocked had its say. An unnamed reviewer for the *Boston Post* termed the book "a parcel of current trash," and Timothy Dwight in Brook Farm's *Harbinger* characterized the work as offering "the beauty which springs from no feeling."[68] And Poe's longtime enemy in New York, Lewis Gaylord Clark, found fault, as well. Still, Poe's friend George Pope Morris wrote in response to *The Raven and Other Poems* in the *Evening Mirror,* "We feel dream-land to be more and more touching than the actual life we had left," and an unnamed reviewer in the *Baltimore Daily Commercial* closed his favorable piece, "We commend the volume to the lovers of song." Freeman Hunt concluded sympathetically in the *Merchant's Magazine and Commercial Advertiser,* "[W]e regret Mr Poe should do aught else than write poetry."[69]

Despite his remarks in the preface, Poe took pride in the volume, providing copies to John Bisco and Thomas Holley Chivers, and copies bound with *Tales* to Elizabeth Barrett Barrett and, later, Sarah Helen Whitman. And he kept a copy of *The Raven and Other Poems,* bound with *Tales,* for himself, revising his work in his remaining years.[70]

Great credit goes to Evert A. Duyckinck, who had assisted with both *Tales* and *The Raven and Other Poems.* He understood Poe's susceptibility, confiding it to his notebook and to William Gilmore Simms, who responded that "the care of the circle in which he [Poe] moves" should be "to control his infirmities with a moral countenance which coerces while it soothes & seems to solicit."[71] Just before the publication of *The Raven and Other Poems,* Poe acknowledged, in a letter to the editor, both his own condition and Duyckinck's great support: "For the first time during two months I find myself entirely myself—dreadfully sick and depressed, but still myself. I seem to have just awakened from some horrible dream, in which all was confusion, and suffering—relieved only by the constant sense of your kindness, and that of one or two other considerate friends." Finances were the immediate concern, so Poe asked if the money that Wiley and Putnam owed him could be secured ahead of time (O 1:533–34). And Poe sought loans from others—the remaining $45 from Chivers (O 1:535), $200 from second cousin George Poe (O 1:537), and $100 from Fitz-Greene Halleck (O 1:542). (This last amount was provided.)

Not yet all-out enemies with Thomas Dunn English—who had recently written with some sympathy about the Lyceum event—Poe sought his advice in late November regarding the *Broadway Journal*'s falling circulation. And he took that advice. Poe signed a contract on December 3 with Thomas H. Lane, publisher of the *Aristidean*. Poe gave Lane a half interest in the *Broadway Journal* but retained his position as sole editor; Lane agreed to pay debts up to $40, assist with expenses, and manage business matters. This new arrangement worked only briefly.[72]

There is a sorrowful reminiscence of Poe from the fall of 1845. Richard H. Stoddard, then only twenty, saw him waiting beneath an awning during an intense rain. The young man thought of offering his umbrella for the walk home—but did not. Poe remained, "pale, shivering, miserable." Though no friend of Poe, Stoddard came to have his regrets: "There I still see him, and always shall,—poor, penniless, but proud, reliant, dominant. May the gods forgive me! I can never forgive myself."[73]

The *Broadway Journal* moved from 135 Nassau Street to 304 Broadway, and Poe continued with the weekly for a few weeks more.[74] He reviewed a range of works, including Caroline M. Kirkland's *Western Clearings,* Frances Sargent Osgood's *Poems,* and William H. Prescott's *Biographical and Critical Notices,* and included revised versions of such works of short fiction as "The Spectacles," "A Tale of the Ragged Mountains," and "Four Beasts in One—The Homo-Cameleopard." He featured a piece on the Cheney Family Singers as exemplary of genuine American music—"Art-Singing and Heart-Singing"—by one "Walter Whitman," and he added, "It is scarcely necessary to add that we agree with our correspondent throughout."[75] (Whitman later visited Poe at the *Broadway Journal* and remembered him as "very cordial in a quiet way" and "very kindly and human, but subdued, perhaps a little jaded.")[76] Poe also published in the November *Aristidean* a composite essay on American poetry, in the December *American Review* a verisimilar tale of a mesmerist's holding off death in "The Facts in the Case of M. Valdemar" (reprinted in the *Broadway Journal*), and in the January 1846 *Arthur's Ladies' Magazine* (appearing in mid-December) a seemingly fearsome tale of misperception, "The Sphinx."[77]

Poe announced in the December 20 issue of the *Broadway Journal,* "A NEW VOLUME of the Broadway Journal, will commence on Saturday, the tenth of January next."[78] He apparently still believed in—or at least would have others believe in—the viability of the weekly. But there would be no new volume. He had written of the *Broadway Journal* that "It will be a fortune to me if I can hold it," but he could not hold it—and he could not hold it together.

Poe was drinking again. And the December 27 issue was incomplete. Thomas Dunn English provided a couple of additional pieces, and Thomas H.

Lane tried to help Poe recover from his recent bout, but without success.[79] We may think back to similar failings over the years, even nine years earlier, when Poe edited the *Southern Literary Messenger*. John H. Mackenzie would chastise his friend repeatedly, and Poe would be abject and contrite yet would eventually go on another spree. Perhaps Mackenzie's conclusion for 1836 would apply as well to 1845: "[H]e [John H. Mackenzie] did not beleive [*sic*] Edgar could help it though he beleived he really & honestly tried to and was sincerely ashamed of his conduct."[80] And more than in Richmond in 1836, Poe in New York in late 1845 was under great pressure. He was under stress at home, where his wife was slowly dying of consumption, and at the office, where his underfunded weekly was losing subscribers. And he was in considerable debt. Poe must have felt overwhelmed. Clearly, in this circumstance and in this condition, he could not withstand his underlying addiction.

Lane decided to end the *Broadway Journal* with the second volume. The December 27 issue featured Poe's critical work, including some telling comments—for example, regarding Longfellow's *Hyperion*, "This book does not go *beyond itself*," and regarding atheism, "Men deny a God only with their lips." And it contained, as well, a revised version of "Mystification."[81] The final issue of the *Broadway Journal*, that of January 3, 1846, apparently overseen by Lane and his foreman, offered critical comment and a revised version of "Loss of Breath." And Poe offered a dignified, if opaque, "Valedictory": "Unexpected engagements demanding my whole attention, and the objects being fulfilled, so far as regards myself personally, for which 'The Broadway Journal' was established, I now, as its editor, bid farewell—as cordially to foes as to friends. Mr. Thomas H. Lane is authorized to collect all money due the Journal."[82]

Poe would never edit a periodical again—but not for lack of trying. He would not give up on his life's dream, to edit the long-imagined five-dollar-per-year literary monthly "The Stylus."

And there would be additional problems very soon for Poe and his family.

20

"There Is a Sweet *Hope* in the Bottom of My Soul"

1846-1847

POE ACCOMMODATED THE FAILURE OF the *Broadway Journal*—he wrote to the editor Sarah Josepha Hale on January 16, 1846, "The B. Journal had fulfilled its destiny—which was a matter of no great moment. I have never regarded it as more that a temporary adjunct to other designs" (O 1:559). The preeminent of these designs was the establishment of "The Stylus"; he now anticipated the commencement of the magazine in January 1847. He also sought the publication of a second volume of his *Tales* (O 1:550–51), and he wrote a new magazine series, to appear in *Godey's Lady's Book,* "The Literati of New York City." Without the burden of the *Broadway Journal,* he could focus on several literary efforts. And he could continue to enjoy his great success at the city's literary evenings.

Poe was, at these evenings—at the homes of John R. Bartlett, Orville Dewey, Anne C. Lynch, and James Lawson—"the observed of all observers." At the peak of his fame, he piqued great interest and curiosity. The much-celebrated author of "The Raven," with his "captivating" smile, was alluringly mysterious. Furthermore, "His manners at these reunions," Elizabeth Oakes Smith relates, "were refined and pleasing, and his scope of conversation that of the gentleman and the scholar." Clearly, she later states, he "delighted in the society of the superior of the sex [women]." He sometimes came with his wife Virginia, and at other times he spoke with warm regard of her. Anecdotes tell of his respectful attitude toward the poet William Cullen Bryant, as well as his defense of a writer criticized by Margaret Fuller.

Perhaps his place among the elite literary men and women in New York City in 1845 and early 1846 resonated for him with his place among the elite young people in Richmond back in 1824 and 1825. Impoverished though he was, he would likely have relished a sense of belonging to a social and intellectual aristocracy.[1]

Poe's welcome at the literary soirees was augmented by other indications of respect. George W. Eveleth, a medical student from Phillips, Maine, wrote to Poe on December 21, 1845, that "Mr. Poe is the one I have selected from all the writers of whom I know any thing, for my especial favorite" and followed up on January 5, 1846, commenting that if "The Facts in the Case of M. Valdemar" is a work of the imagination, "[Y]ou are a genius of wonderfully curious fancies, I must confess."[2] The Eveleth-Poe correspondence would become an important source for knowledge about Poe. And the increasingly famous writer also received a request for the solution to a cryptograph (O 1:549) and another for the securing of his autograph (O 1:552). It was probably in early 1846 that Poe visited the studio of the artist John A. McDougall, who painted an engaging miniature portrait of his distinguished guest: the writer appears in the watercolor as both elegant and penetrating.[3] Poe also visited the "Poughkeepsie Seer," the spiritualist Andrew Jackson Davis, who wrote of him, "He is, in spirit, a foreigner. My sympathies are strangely excited." Davis left an affecting description of Poe, arriving and departing, with "a perfect *shadow* of himself in the air in front of him, as though the sun was constantly shining behind and casting shadows before him, causing the singular appearance of one walking into a dark fog provided by himself."[4]

Without a business office, Poe was working from home at 85 Amity Street. Mary Starr visited the Poes at Amity Street.[5] And his devoted *"second best,"* Frances Sargent Osgood, who admittedly "never could resist her [Virginia's] affectionate summons," visited them there, as well.

Poe was "unusually gay and light-hearted," Osgood later remembered, during one of her visits "towards the close of his residence in this city"— probably sometime in January 1846. Virginia, who considered Osgood a good influence on her husband, had sent her "a pressing invitation to come to them." The occasion was what Osgood termed Poe's "just completing" "The Literati of New York City," his series of casual appraisals of New York writers (actually continued through May or later). Poe wrote each of these appraisals on rolls—the aforementioned slender sheets affixed one to another and rolled up tidily. With "laughing triumph," Poe proposed to determine (what he already knew)—the extent of his regard for each of the various authors based on the length of the respective author's rolls. "Come, Virginia, help me!" Poe entreated, and he threw open to her successive rolls, culminating in his tossing to his laughing wife, from one corner of the room to the opposite one, the lengthiest appreciation. Alluding to John Milton's "L'Allegro," Osgood asked, "And whose lengthened sweetness long drawn out is that?" And a gleeful Poe responded, "Hear her! just as if her vain little heart didn't tell her it's herself!"[6]

The unqualified pleasure of this moment may be allowed to linger—the troubles will come soon enough. We may think back to Poe's infinite delight at Virginia's singing "Mrs. Poe" with neighborhood girls in the couple's Spring Garden home and, farther back, to his walking hand in hand with Virginia at John H. Mackenzie's Darby Town farm. We may savor these moments here, treasuring Poe's occasional elation, which will intensify our coming sense of his bitter loss.

It was very likely the poet Elizabeth F. Ellet, featured by Poe in the *Broadway Journal*, who, according to Elizabeth Oakes Smith, "fell in love with Poe and wrote a love-letter to him."[7] Poe sometimes shared with Virginia letters that he had received, and Ellet happened to come to the Poes' home when Virginia and Frances Sargent Osgood were laughing over her missive. And she tore it away from them. Ellet was probably not only hurt and angry but also jealous of Osgood, her rival in literary flirtation with Poe.[8] Poe later confided his developing antipathy, "I scorned Mrs. Ellet, simply because she revolted me" (O 2:777). This minor incident is a telling prequel to the unfortunate scandal that followed.

Again it involved Ellet. On a subsequent visit to the Poes, she saw a letter from Osgood to Poe that supposedly compromised Osgood. Presumably some expression of affection was taken as evidence of impropriety. Osgood was concerned and agreed that Margaret Fuller and Anne C. Lynch would visit the Poes to retrieve her letters. Indignant at the implied accusation by the two women, Poe unwisely warned that Ellet should be concerned about her own letters to him. He knew immediately that he had gone too far: he later wrote to Sarah Helen Whitman, "When in the heat of passion—stung to madness by her [Ellet's] inconceivable perfidy & by the grossness of the injury which her jealousy prompted her to inflict upon *all of us*—upon both families [the Poes and the Osgoods]—I permitted myself to say what I should not have said—I had no sooner uttered the words, than I *felt* their dishonor. I felt, too, that although *she* must be damningly conscious of her own baseness, she would still have a right to reproach me for having betrayed, under *any* circumstances, her confidence" (O 2:731). Clearly here, conscience, which Poe had repeatedly dramatized in his fiction, deeply disturbed him in his life. Fuller and Lynch departed with Osgood's letters, and Poe collected Ellet's letters and placed them at her door. Unquestionably, he had made a serious mistake. But, as Sarah Helen Whitman later wrote, it was Ellet who was "the acknowledged *instigator* & Grand Inquisitor of the movement." So began Ellet's campaign of persecution.[9]

Aiding Ellet was her brother William M. Lummis, who demanded the letters (which had already been returned) and threatened violence. Poe later wrote, "The position in which she [Ellet] thus placed me you may imagine. Is it any wonder that I was driven *mad* by the intolerable sense of wrong?" (O 2:732). Poe sought a pistol from Thomas Dunn English, who refused, and the two men fought. Apparently then Poe wrote an apologetic letter to Ellet, suggesting that he may have been mad. But her efforts continued, through anonymous letters to Virginia, who was "continually tortured" (O 2:732). Such letters were Ellet's characteristic method—she subsequently sent anonymous letters, over three years, to persecute Rufus Wilmot Griswold through his friends and associates.[10]

Poe was devastated and disgraced by the Ellet-Osgood scandal. He was certainly no longer welcome at the literary evenings, and he no longer saw Osgood. Yet his regard for her remained: He wrote a progressive acrostic valentine to her (her name spelled out in the first letter of the first line, the second letter of the second line, and so forth), sending a copy for reading to Anne C. Lynch's February 14, 1846, Valentine's party. He also praised her in the March issue of *Godey's Lady's Book*. But, as noted, Maria Clemm came to have little tolerance for her son-in-law's relationship with Osgood. According to Flora Lapham Mack, Clemm indicated to Poe and Osgood "that there was a limit even to her forbearance & they had reached it."[11]

We sometimes have no direct evidence for Virginia's voice on matters, but here we are fortunate to have two significant pieces of direct evidence. Poe's wife characterized the recent time as "this brief period in which this wretch's [Ellet's] insinuations drove me *mad*."[12] She thereby anticipated Poe's language. And cherishing her time together with Edgar, she wrote a tender, yearning acrostic valentine to her husband. (The first letters of the thirteen lines spell his name.) With this poem, we have a prospect from which we may view the past ten years of the Poes' marriage and the coming remaining year. Alluding to the scandal, Virginia expressed her wish to find with her beloved a haven:

Ever with thee I wish to roam—
Dearest my life is thine.
Give me a cottage for my home
And a rich old cypress vine,
Removed from the world with its sin and care
And the tattling of many tongues.
Love alone shall guide us when we are there—
Love shall heal my weakened lungs;
And Oh, the tranquil hours we'll spend,
Never wishing that others may see!
Perfect ease we'll enjoy, without thinking to lend
Ourselves to the world and its glee—
Ever peaceful and blissful we'll be. (M 1:524)

With attention to both the acrostic and the balance of tetrameter and trimeter, and despite her husband's faults, Virginia tellingly expressed her love for, and her devotion to, Edgar—or, as she called him, "Eddy." Perhaps when he read this valentine by Virginia—"Sissy"—his delight was once again infinite.[13] We may be reminded correspondingly of John H. Mackenzie's considering "Poe's tender love & care for her [Virginia] as the most beautiful thing in his life."[14]

Shortly after Virginia wrote her earnest poem, the Poes left the fraught city for a temporary refuge near the East River. She was ill, but maybe the couple could find there some "tranquil hours."[15]

They moved near Turtle Bay (now the site of the United Nations in the East Forties). Neighborhood children, twelve-year-old Sarah F. Miller and her nine-year-old brother James L. Miller, later recalled the Poes. Sarah remembered Poe's rowing in her father's boat and going for a swim (in the East River, near Blackwell's Island, now Roosevelt Island), as well as Maria Clemm's tearfully confiding their straitened circumstances to her mother. James, who was scared of Poe, admitted that "he was a great swimmer and I well remember some of his antics in the water." We may be reminded of Poe in Richmond's James River and later on Philadelphia's Schuylkill River. James left a reminiscence of a touching moment involving the ailing Virginia: she reportedly said to her sometimes-wayward husband, "'Now, Eddie, when I am gone I will be your guardian angel, and if at any time you feel tempted to do wrong, just put your hands above your head so,'—she placing her hands in that position—'and I will be there to shield you.'"[16] However, unshielded, Poe journeyed south in March 1846 to Baltimore.

We have a privileged view of Poe in Baltimore from one who was then a young journalist and a fellow customer in a tavern—Robert D'Unger, in Guy's Coffee House, at Monument Square and Fayette Street. Poe spoke with John H. Millington, foreman of the *Baltimore Patriot,* about Virginia's poor health, acknowledging that "there was a slight improvement in her condition." Poe had a large whiskey, and he was joined by Millington and D'Unger. The older newspaperman teased the younger one, then a suitor, and Poe cautioned D'Unger, "My young friend—don't hurry yourself to a marriage. It has its joys, but its sorrows overbalance these." This was the "morose, melancholy, glum" Poe, candid among fellow drinkers, worn down by Virginia's tuberculosis and the certainty of her coming death, admitting his misery.[17]

D'Unger, who seems a reliable source, saw Poe again in the next few years. He left a revealing comment about Poe's drinking:

> The trouble with him was that he *"worked himself down"* and then became despondent. Drink was induced by this despondency, and he kept up the "drunk" as long as he had money; but without getting beastly drunk. He drank until his nerves were shattered, poured it down until he was actually sick. He ate very little whilst indulging. I suppose he told me a hundred times that *he was going to quit the habit,* and I am sure he was sincere in his wish to do so. All his drunks were followed by a weakening diarrhoea. That was what carried him off.[18]

D'Unger here confirms F. W. Thomas's comment, "[I]t was his excessive, and at times morbid sensibility which forced him into his 'frolics,' rather than any mere morbid appetite for drink" (H 17:137). And we may readily remember John H. Mackenzie's recollections of an abject Poe after his sprees.

Mary E. Hewitt, a friend of Frances Sargent Osgood and an admirer of Poe, wrote to him on April 14, "*We* were all exceedingly sorry to hear of your illness in Baltimore, and glad when we heard that you had so far recovered as to be able to return to our latitude."[19] Without mentioning his trip to Baltimore, Poe wrote to Philip P. Cooke on April 16, "I have been living in the country for the last two months (having been quite sick)." And he asked Cooke to update the Lowell biography of him, adding, "If you are willing to oblige me—speak frankly above all—speak of my *faults,* too, as forcibly as you can" (O 1: 563, 565). Subsequently, on April 28, Poe referred to his "serious, and, I fear, permanent ill health" (O 1:568).

Nonetheless, in late April or perhaps sometime in May, Poe was able to take Virginia to the village of Fordham, to see a possible retreat, "half-buried in fruit trees, which were then all in blossom." And Sarah F. Miller recalled that in the midst of Maria Clemm's friendship with her mother, "[T]hey [the Poes] came and told us they were going to move to a distant place called Fordham, where they had rented a little cottage, feeling sure the pure country air would do Mrs. Poe a world of good."[20] Even as they knew the inevitable outcome, they managed to seem hopeful. And so began the final months of Edgar's life with Virginia.

In recent months, Poe's publications had continued. Among them were Wiley and Putnam's composite volume, comprising both *Tales* and *The Raven and Other Poems,* in February, and the essay on the writing of "The Raven," "The Philosophy of Composition," in *Graham's* in April. Poe's six-part series "The Literati of New York City" began in mid-April in the May issue of *Godey's Lady's Book.*

Distinguishing the "quacks" from the "men of genius" and popular reputation from private judgment, Poe promises his "honest opinions" of various New York writers (H 15:1–2).[21] Each piece would be not so much an analysis as an entertainment, even an exposé, with an attention to both personality and person. The first installment treats George Bush, George H. Colton, N. P. Willis, William M. Gillespie, Charles F. Briggs, William Kirkland, and John W. Francis. Poe's manner is lively and fresh; his tone sometimes appreciative, sometimes critical. The sketches were clearly designed to engage curious readers with unfiltered disclosure. The conspicuously negative entry here is that for Briggs. Poe veers into vitriol toward his former employer: "Mr. Briggs has never composed in his life three consecutive sentences of grammatical English. He is grossly uneducated" (H 15:22).[22] Poe's characteristic inclination to deprecate those he deems objectionable—going back to Robert Pitts, as well as other targets in his reviews and lectures—would inevitably antagonize. Lewis Gaylord Clark, Poe's longtime enemy, attacked the first installment of the "Literati" series, but Louis A. Godey responded by attributing the "insane attack" to Clark's "perfect agony of terror" about Poe's coming treatment of him in a subsequent installment.[23]

The occasionally all-too-candid nature of the "Literati" doubtless contributed to its great popularity, the "commotion" that Godey anticipated. Indeed, he referred appreciatively to "the public, who have expressed distinct and decisive approbation of the articles in that unmistakable way which a publisher is always happy to recognize."[24] The publisher ran out of the May issue and included its installment of the "Literati" in the June issue. And the second installment featured Anna Cora Mowatt, George B. Cheever, Charles

Anthon, Gulian C. Verplanck, Freeman Hunt, Piero Maroncelli, and Laughton Osborn. These pieces are generally more temperate, even good-natured. The Anthon piece is especially interesting for the light it sheds on Poe's view of the making of a textbook (and therefore on *The Conchologist's First Book*). No particular foe is included in this installment. But Poe would attack again in the third installment of the "Literati" in the July issue.

The move to Fordham probably took place in May 1846 or perhaps early June. John Valentine had bought the property on Kingsbridge Road for one thousand dollars and charged the Poes one hundred dollars a year in rent. Poe would write to Thomas H. Chivers on July 22, "I am living out of town about 13 miles, at a village called Fordham, on the rail-road leading north. We are in a snug little cottage, keeping house, and would be very comfortable, but that I have been for a long time dreadfully ill" (O 1:591). Maria Clemm considered it a "sweet sequestered spot." Mary Gove Nichols later remembered Poe's new home as "a little cottage at the top of a hill," with velvety grass and impressive cherry trees, which cast generous shade. Inside the modest white frame structure were "a kitchen, a sitting-room, and a bed-chamber over the sitting-room." The home was not far from the Bronx River, High Bridge, and St. John's College. Poe would later elaborate his Fordham dwelling, with romantic touches, in "Landor's Cottage." He would write, in part, "In fact, nothing could well be more simple—more utterly unpretending than this cottage. Its marvelous *effect* lay altogether in its artistic arrangement *as a picture*" (M 3:1335). Although Virginia did not get her cypress vine, she did have a cottage for her home.[25]

But, as Poe admitted to Chivers, he was enduring "dreadful poverty" (O 1:591). One visitor to Fordham, Charles E. West, recalled that Poe had stated that he and his family had only a loaf of bread to eat (M 1:397). There was distress in that little cottage.

In the spring of 1846, Poe had invitations from the University of Vermont and Dickinson College, as well as letters from Elizabeth Barrett Barrett and Nathaniel Hawthorne. Frances Sargent Osgood followed her "Ida Grey" with "Ida's Farewell," probably intimating a wish for eventual reunion with Poe in the afterlife.[26] Meanwhile, Poe was true to his *first best*. Offered an interview that required travel from Fordham, he wrote a note to Virginia (on June 12), the only one of his notes to his wife solely[27] for which the text survives:

> My Dear Heart. My dear Virginia! Our mother will explain to you why I stay away from you this night. I trust the interview I am

promised will result in some *substantial good* for me, for your dear sake, and hers—keep up your heart in all hopefulness, and trust yet a little longer—In my last great disappointment, I should have lost my courage *but for you*—my little darling wife. You are my *greatest* and *only* stimulus now, to battle with this uncongenial, unsatisfactory, and ungrateful life—I shall be with you tomorrow P.M. and be assured until I see you, I will keep in *living remembrance* your *last words* and your fervent prayer!

Sleep well, and may God grant you a peaceful summer with your devoted

Edgar (O 1:578)

Poe was trying to comfort his wife even as she must often have tried to comfort him.

And there was trouble coming. The early "Literati" sketches provoked varied attacks—a poetic assault by "Mustard Mace" and a vicious parody by Hiram Fuller, now sole editor of the *Evening Mirror*. Poe asked Joseph M. Field, of the *St. Louis Daily Reveillé,* to respond to Fuller's diatribe (O 1:579–81), and Field adapted Poe's letter for publication. A full-blown crisis emerged with Godey's June 20 publication in the July issue of the *Lady's Book* of the third installment of the "Literati." The treatment by Poe of Thomas Dunn English—prompted no doubt by their fight during the Ellet scandal—yielded a protracted literary and legal struggle.[28]

That third installment included largely positive assessments of Fitz-Greene Halleck and Evert A. Duyckinck, mixed commentaries on Ann S. Stephens and Mary Gove, impatient critiques of Henry Cary and Christopher Pearse Cranch, and a partially condemnatory, partially indulgent judgment of James Aldrich (the indulgent portion drawn from Poe's final reply to Outis). The treatment of Thomas Dunn English, however, was harsh, from an accusation of "downright plagiarism," without excuses, to a characterization of his subject as "a man without the commonest school education" to a presumptuous recommendation of "private instruction" to an evident snub, "I do not personally know Mr. English" (H 15:64–66).[29] So began the literary brawl.

English roughly handled Poe. He asserted in the June 23 *Morning Telegraph* and *Evening Mirror* that Poe had deceitfully borrowed money and committed forgery. He discussed the NYU incident, the Lyceum lecture, and the Ellet scandal, and repeatedly mentioned Poe's drinking. He returned the accusation of plagiarism. And English claimed about Poe, "He is not alone thoroughly unprincipled, base and depraved, but silly, vain and ignorant—not alone an assassin in morals, but a quack in literature."

On June 27, Poe returned the vituperation—for instance, comparing English's face to "that of the best-looking but most unprincipled of Mr. Barnum's baboons." Poe elided some of the specific events recounted, but did acknowledge his drinking, terming it "a calamity," not "a crime," and suggesting that there was an "extenuation" (implicitly, Virginia's illness [see O 2:641]). He referred to the accusation of plagiarism, calling it "what all the world knows to be *especially* false." And with regard to the charges of deceitful borrowing and forgery, Poe denied both and promised a lawsuit. Poe closed with an attack on the editor of the *Evening Mirror*, which had published English's diatribe, but forbore to assert what had been reported, that at the theater Hiram Fuller had not defended his wife as her father attacked her. Instead, he stated sarcastically that he pitied Fuller for, among other things, "the unwavering conjugal chivalry which, in a public theatre—but I pause. Not even in taking vengeance on a Fuller can I stoop to become a Fuller myself."[30]

Though annoyed that his reply was not published in *Godey's Lady's Book*—it appeared (for ten dollars) in the *Spirit of the Times,* on July 10—Poe was pleased with his work. He wrote to Godey, "I have never written an article upon which I more confidently depend for *literary* reputation than that Reply. Its merit lay in being *precisely* adapted to its purpose. In this city I have had, upon it, the favorable judgments of the best men" (O 1:588).[31]

English ostensibly welcomed Poe's planned lawsuit in a response in the *Evening Mirror* of July 13. By July 16, Poe had enlisted the lawyer E. L. Fancher to conduct the libel suit, which, on July 23, would seek payment of five thousand dollars from Hiram Fuller and Augustus A. Clason Jr., co-owners of the *Evening Mirror,* where English's attack on Poe had appeared. But the damage to Poe's reputation for his free-for-all with English would obviate any advantage to possible legal damages. And Poe had been in New York City drinking again, according to a disdainful piece by Hiram Fuller on July 20. Poe's visit to the city may have been in connection with his initiation of the lawsuit. The *Morning News* commented, in thoughtful defense, "Mr. Poe is a man of talent but he is, notwithstanding, flesh, and possesses frailties with which a great portion of the human family is afflicted."[32]

Poe confided to Thomas H. Chivers in his July 22, 1846, letter his illness and his poverty and added, "I have been driven to the very gates of death and a despair more dreadful than death, and I had not even *one* friend, out of my family, with whom to advise. What I would not have given for the kind pressure of your hand!" He reported, less than truthfully, "It has been a long while since any artificial stimulus has passed my lips," adding, "I am done forever with drink—depend on that—but there is much more in this matter than meets the eye." And he closed his personal comments, "Do not let anything in this letter impress you with the belief that I *despair* even of worldly prosperity. On the contrary although I feel ill, and am ground into the very dust with poverty, there is a sweet *hope* in the bottom of my soul" (O 1:591–92). We may recall Poe's encouraging Virginia, "[K]eep up your heart in all hopefulness." Even after all his troubles, Poe still had a surprising resilience.

In the early summer of 1846, Poe's sister Rosalie stayed at the Fordham cottage. According to Susan Archer Weiss, Rosalie later remembered that Poe had initially been sick but, nursed by Maria Clemm, had then improved. And she remembered that Virginia had been cheerful and (perhaps speaking with some irritation) that her sister-in-law had been "petted . . . like a baby" by Poe and her mother. But Poe's ailing wife certainly understood her situation—she had her own resilience. According to Elizabeth Oakes Smith, Virginia said, "I know I shall die soon; I know I can't get well; but I want to be as happy as possible, and make Edgar happy."[33]

Rosalie returned to Richmond sometime in July. She would never see Virginia again. Poe's sister delivered a letter from Maria Clemm to John H. Mackenzie, seeking financial aid.[34] Doubtless Clemm would have remembered her conversations with Mackenzie at his tobacco warehouse ten years earlier, during which the two of them had shared their love for Poe and their acceptance of him as he was. Doubtless, too, Poe's old friend would have provided assistance. Edgar and John would renew their lifelong friendship during Edgar's visits to Richmond in 1848 and 1849. But ultimately, they would have a sad falling-out.

Among others who first visited the Poes in Fordham that summer were the reformer Mary Gove and her fourteen-year-old daughter Elma Mary Gove. Mary Gove (later Mary Gove Nichols) remembered Poe's keeping a bobolink in a cage for the bird's beautiful song, his showing her a recent admiring letter from Elizabeth Barrett Barrett, and his later confessing to her his passion for fame. She recalled of Virginia, "Her pale face, her brilliant eyes, and her raven hair gave her an unearthly look. One felt that she was almost a disrobed spirit, and when she coughed it was made certain that she was rapidly passing away." And Maria Clemm, Mary Gove recollected, was "a stalwart and queenly woman," "a sort of universal Providence for her strange children."[35] Daughter

Elma Mary Gove (later Elma Mary Gove Letchworth) remembered seeing "the beautiful chi[l]d-wife lying on her white bed and fading away." And she went on, "Great dark eyes, a sweet pale face, and masses of dark hair remain in my memory. Everything white save the eyes and the hair." She also listened to Poe talk, after lunch, about literary matters, including Longfellow and Barrett.[36] Both mother and daughter fondly recalled Poe's voice: "Poe's voice was melody itself"; "[T]he great charm of Poe was his voice."[37]

Augustine O'Neil, who later recalled Poe at the Fordham train station, also remembered him with Virginia: "I once saw him and his wife on the Piazza of their little cottage at Fordham. There was much quiet dignity in his manner."[38] Poe was seeking—but not always achieving—that "peaceful summer."

The fourth installment of Poe's "Literati" series appeared in late July in the August issue of *Godey's*. Poe treated there Margaret Fuller, James Lawson, Caroline M. Kirkland, Prosper M. Wetmore, Emma C. Embury, and Epes Sargent (H 15:73–93). The lengthy piece on Fuller was the most remarkable in the group, an earnest tribute and appreciation. Interestingly, though considering Fuller's book *Woman in the Nineteenth Century* "nervous, forcible, thoughtful, suggestive, brilliant, and to a certain extent scholar-like," Poe objected to her thesis on the basis of design—"the intention of the Deity as regards sexual differences."[39] The application of the argument from design to sexual differences clearly does not resonate with today's views, but the argument from design for divine will does endure. And the appeal to "the intention of the Deity" was characteristic of Poe, evident as early as his April 1836 Drake-Halleck review (H 8:281; P 5:165).

It is telling to see Poe's sensitively responding to another's loss, presumably remembering his own loss of Jane Stith Stanard, his brother Henry, and his foster mother Frances Allan. He wrote to his friend Frederick W. Thomas on August 24, 1846, about the loss at sea of Thomas's sister, nephew, and niece, "I dare not say one word, dear friend, on the final topic of your letter just received. For sorrows such as this there is no consolation but in unrestrained grief." And he added, "May God bless you" (O 1:599).[40] Significantly, having sought consolation for death in *Pym*, Poe would return to an effort to find such consolation through his writing, as will become evident at the end of his cosmological prose poem *Eureka*.

In late July, William Gilmore Simms warned Poe, in a heartfelt and sympathetic letter, "[Y]ou are now perhaps in the most perilous period of your career," and advised, with circumspection, against drinking and public controversy.[41] Poe may have resented the admonition, but he was clearly then thinking about his serious work. He wrote to Philip Pendleton Cooke on August 9 about "The Stylus" as "the one great purpose of my literary life" (O 1:597). And by late summer, he may well have been writing the compelling short story "The Cask of Amontillado."[42]

The penultimate installment of Poe's "Literati" was published in late August in the September issue of *Godey's*. Five of the six sketches—on Frances Sargent Osgood, Lydia Maria Child, Elizabeth Bogart, Catherine M. Sedgwick, and Anne C. Lynch—were in some measure positive, and the sketch on Lewis Gaylord Clark, which might have been scathing, was only moderately negative. The stand-out piece was, not surprisingly, that on Osgood, the original of which was the manuscript roll that Poe had flipped open to Virginia back in January. Poe celebrates Osgood's work, focusing on its grace: "It is this irresoluble charm—in *grace*—that Mrs. Osgood excels any poetess of her country—or, indeed, of any country under the sun" (H 15:98).[43] Poe's great esteem for Osgood would continue for the rest of his life.

Meanwhile, Poe's lawsuit proceeded, but slowly. On August 4, Fuller and Clason pled not guilty, but, with the strong allegation of libel, a trial date was set—initially for September 7, and then, owing to the court's crowded schedule, for February 1. By year's end, English had moved to Washington, D.C.[44]

The sixth installment of Poe's "Literati," which appeared in late September in the October issue of *Godey's*, concerned Charles Fenno Hoffman, Mary E. Hewitt, and Richard Adams Locke. The last piece is of greatest interest since, in discussing Locke's "Moon Hoax," Poe touches on his "Hans Pfaall."[45] With this installment, "The Literati of New York City" ceased. It is possible that Godey may have been pressured, as Poe alleged, but the final decision appears to have been Poe's. On February 21, 1847, George W. Eveleth reported to Poe that Godey had written to him "saying that he *did* not know" why the "Literati" series had ended, and Eveleth responded by quoting a portion of Poe's explanation (of December 15, 1846), which was "I was forced to do so [to terminate the series], because I found that people insisted on considering them elaborate criticisms when I had no other design than critical *gossip*." Poe acknowledged to Eveleth "haste, inaccuracy, or prejudice" in the series and stated his plan for "a *book* on American Letters generally" (O 1:602). Poe would work on notes for the book in late 1846 and early 1847; he considered his submitted review of Hawthorne and his essay "The Rationale of Verse" as illustrative of that book (O 1:602).[46]

Between July and November 1846, the *Evening Mirror* and the *Weekly Mirror* featured serially the novel *1844, or, the Power of the "S.F."* The anonymous author was Thomas Dunn English, who included repeated attacks on a character representing Poe—attacks that were largely extraneous to the plot. The novel has been forgotten, except for its Poe connection.[47] By contrast to English, Poe drew on the literary conflict of the past year to create one of the great revenge tales of all time, "The Cask of Amontillado." It followed the last installment of "The Literati of New York City," appearing in the November 1846 issue of *Godey's Lady's Book*.

The tale's narrator, Montresor, famously begins, "The thousand injuries of Fortunato I had borne as I best could, but when he ventured upon insult I vowed revenge."[48] During "the carnival season," Montresor lures the vain and inebriated Fortunato, dressed as a fool, to the vaults under the city, ostensibly so that the self-infatuated man might judge supposed Amontillado, but actually to chain him within a recess and wall up the opening with tiers of brick. Entombed and now aware of his situation, Fortunato cries, "*For the love of God, Montresor!*" and Montresor replies darkly, "Yes, . . . for the love of God!"[49]

It is neatly and leanly done, a perfect immuring yielding the single effect of inestimable terror. As Richard Dilworth Rust has persuasively argued, Poe elaborated the story, in part, by alluding to English's *1844*, from the theme of revenge to the setting of an underground vault. Poe's tightly controlled work defeats English's amalgam, offering in plot, tone, character, symbolism, and unity an artistry missing from the lengthy assemblage.[50]

And Poe has returned, in his one masterpiece of 1846, to his own life: he has integrated his recent literary battle into his work, yielding an enduring triumph. Recalling the encoded language sometimes typical of Poe, we might even wonder about the central word "*im*bedde*d*" and the subsequent words "*d*escend*ed . . . d*escending" (emphasis added)—it is, after all, "Eddy" who is behind it all.[51] This inference is consistent with T. O. Mabbott's assessment: "That 'The Cask of Amontillado' . . . was the working out of his [Poe's] immediate emotions can hardly be doubted" (M 3:1253).

By contrast to having sought revenge on his enemy, Poe sought relief for his ailing wife. Mary Gove recounts that in the fall, as it became cold, the dying Virginia had chills and fever: "She lay on the straw bed, wrapped in her husband's great-coat, with a large tortoise-shell cat on her bosom. The wonderful cat seemed conscious of her great usefulness. The coat and the cat were the sufferer's only means of warmth, except as her husband held her hands, and her mother her feet."[52] Poe and Maria Clemm did what they could to assuage and alleviate. And they must have supported each other, as they would have done as Henry lay dying fifteen years earlier.

They did soon have help: Mary Gove brought back to the Fordham cottage the compassionate Marie Louise Shew, the daughter of a doctor.[53] She lovingly ministered to Virginia and then to Edgar. With kindness and devotion, she eased and she calmed.

It is also possible that an actual doctor visited. In May 1848, Poe would offer a recommendation of one "Doctor Freeman," who, he wrote, had "attended my family for the last two years" (O 2:668). In all likelihood, this was Dr. Alfred Freeman, a former neighbor of the Poes on East Broadway, who was later remembered as having "sympathy with the afflictions of others."[54]

During the final months of 1846, Poe did manage to write. He extended the 1842 sketch "The Landscape-Garden" to "The Domain of Arnheim," providing thereby the realization of Ellison's vision. Probably he also concluded his Hawthorne review and "The Rationale of Verse." He worked on "Literary America" (O 1:606). And in mid- and late December, he maintained his correspondence, including regarding "The Murders in the Rue Morgue" in Paris (O 1:608) and the question of the genuineness of "The Facts in the Case of M. Valdemar" (H 17:268–69 and O 1:609–11).

And Poe visited nearby St. Johns College. One priest recalled "a startling pallor" that attested, in part, to "the agony of his fears for the flickering of life in the little home on the hill." Reverend Edward Doucet said, "I knew him well. . . . In bearing and countenance, he was extremely refined. His features were somewhat sharp and very thoughtful. He was well informed on all matters. I always thought he was a gentleman by nature and instinct."[55]

But the agony continued; the lives of the Poes were grim. And word got out. The *Morning Express* reported on December 15 that Poe and his wife were "dangerously ill with the consumption" and were "so far reduced as to be barely able to obtain the necessaries of life." The writer of the piece closed, "At least, his friends say that the publishers ought to start a movement in his behalf."[56] N. P. Willis responded in the *Home Journal* of December 26. Referring to the *Morning Express* paragraph, the admiring editor wrote, "Here is one of the finest scholars, one of the most original men of genius, and one of the most industrious of the literary profession of our country, whose temporary suspension of labour, from bodily illness, drops him immediately to a level with the common objects of public charity." Willis advocated generous aid to Poe and his family. And, acknowledging attacks on Poe, he commented,

"To blame, in some degree, still, perhaps he is. But let charity for the failings of human nature judge of the degree."[57] With deferential uncertainty, Willis sent his editorial to Poe (H 17:272).[58]

Poe responded to the *Morning Express* paragraph and what he considered Willis's "kind and manly comments" on December 30. He wrote of Virginia's illness and the painful anonymous letters to her, as well as his own illness and recent published abuse of him. He hopefully anticipated his "new prosperity." He admitted his poverty but not his inability to endure it. And he asserted that he had many friends. He closed with a bold determination: "I do not think, my dear Willis, that there is any need of my saying more. I am getting better, and may add—if it be any comfort to my enemies—that I have little fear of getting worse. The truth is, I have a great deal to do; and I have made up my mind not to die till it is done" (O 1:611–12).[59]

Newspapers commented sympathetically and otherwise to Poe's letter to Willis, which was published in the *Home Journal* of January 9 (an issue that Poe sent to Chivers and Eveleth). The *Washington Union* replied to the letter's final sentence, "May it be so, Mr. Poe; but alas! how many a brave and true spirit has passed away on the threshold of just such confident projects and resolves!"[60] For Poe, however, the "alas!" was premature. He would get to do at least some of what he hoped to do in his few remaining years.

Meanwhile, friends and admirers did rally on his behalf, and monies were provided through Mary Louise Shew, the poet Mary E. Hewitt, Willis, the editor George H. Colton, and perhaps others.[61] We may well imagine that the support—which Poe had not sought—was wholly heartening. And Poe would need whatever heartening would be offered, for Virginia was soon to die. And, Shew later wrote, he had endured "extreme suffering of mind and body, (actual want and hunger and cold, being borne by this heroic husband to supply food medicine and comforts to his dying wife)."[62]

Among those who visited the Poes in Fordham at this time were not only Mary Gove and Marie Louise Shew, but also Mary Starr, as well as the daughter of Poe's former employer Thomas W. White, Eliza White; Poe's cousin Elizabeth Herring; and the poet Sarah Anna Lewis and her husband, the lawyer Sylvanus D. Lewis.[63]

Mary Starr later remembered a tender scene with Virginia and Edgar: "The day before Virginia died I found her in the parlor. I said to her, 'Do you feel any better today?' and sat down by the big arm-chair in which she was placed. Mr. Poe sat on the other side of her. I had my hand in hers, and she took it and placed it in Mr. Poe's, saying, 'Mary, be a friend to Eddie, and don't forsake him; he always loved you—didn't you Eddie?'"[64] Virginia would surely have recalled that when she was a ten-year-old girl in Baltimore, she had delivered her cousin Edgar's love notes to Mary Starr. And Mary Starr had visited the Poe family in Philadelphia, singing for Edgar "Come Rest in This Bosom." Later Edgar (under the influence) had visited her in Jersey City; she was married to a Mr. Jenning. She had subsequently visited the Poes at their Amity Street home in New York. And now she had come to Fordham. Virginia, anticipating her own death, would have seen Mary Starr as a woman whose devotion and affection might console her desolated husband.

Also, from her bed in a small first-floor bedroom, and with her husband present, Virginia conveyed her profound appreciation to Marie Louise Shew, who was about to leave the Poe cottage "to make some arrangements for her [Virginia's] comfort." Kissing a portrait of Poe that she had withdrawn from beneath her pillow, Virginia gave it to Shew. And the dying woman removed from her workbox a jewel case that had once belonged to Poe's mother Eliza and gave it to Shew, as well. And then Virginia honored the kind woman by sharing with her a private family matter. She passed to her husband a letter from Louisa Allan—John Allan's second wife—that Poe read "weeping heavy tears" before passing it to the loyal nurse to read. Sometime after John Allan's death in March 1834, Mrs. Allan had confessed in this letter her own guilt and exonerated Poe: "It [the letter] expressed a desire to see him, acknowledged that she alone had been the cause of his adopted Father's neglect, out of jealousy that Mr. Poe really was a relative by blood to her husband."[65] Doubtless Poe had borne some responsibility for his difficult relationship with his foster father, but certainly John Allan himself—and evidently Louisa Allan, as well—had borne significant responsibility. Bringing out this revealing correspondence, Virginia was also bringing her loving caregiver further into the family. And perhaps surmising that Marie Louise Shew would continue as caregiver to Poe, Virginia was encouraging commiseration and understanding for him.

After Shew left, Poe wrote to her, with ample thankfulness, "Kindest—dearest friend—My poor Virginia still lives, although failing fast and now suffering much pain. May God grant her life until she sees you and thanks you once again! Her bosom is full to overflowing—like my own—with a boundless—inexpressible gratitude to you. Lest she may never see you more—she bids me say that she sends you her sweetest kiss of love and will die blessing you[.]" And he implored, "But come—oh come to-morrow!" and added, "Yes, I *will* be calm—everything you so nobly wish to see me" (O 2:617–18).

Virginia died of tuberculosis, on Saturday, January 30, 1847. She was twenty-four.

Poe had promised to be calm, but, whatever his efforts, he couldn't have wholly succeeded. In August 1835, he had written to Maria Clemm, presumably about his brother Henry's death, "[Y]ou well know how little I am able to bear up under the pressure of grief" (O 1:102). And in August 1846, he had written to his friend Frederick W. Thomas about Thomas's losses, "For sorrows such as this there is no consolation but in unrestrained grief" (O 1:599). Poe must have given way.

Yet there must have been sad relief, as well, for Virginia was no longer in pain; her five-year struggle was over. And what Poe later termed to George W. Eveleth his own "horrible never-ending oscillation between hope & despair" was ended. He concluded to Eveleth, "In the death of what was my life, then, I receive a new but—oh God! how melancholy an existence" (O 2:641). Robert D'Unger, Poe's Baltimore coffeehouse companion, commented, "The loss of his wife was a sad blow to him. He did not seem to care, after she was gone, whether he lived an hour, a day, a week or a year. She was 'his all.'"[66]

In the hours after the death of Virginia, an unknown artist made a watercolor portrait of her. The image is beautiful but leaden—all too peaceful—the living Virginia had laughed and loved and suffered.[67] Marie Louise Shew did return to the Poe cottage and took a stagecoach with Mary Starr to the city. She continued her much-needed support of the family—she purchased Virginia's coffin, as well as her linen burial garment, so important to Mrs. Clemm. With Mary Starr's assistance, Shew purchased Poe's mourning clothes. She dressed Virginia's body, and the daughter of landlord John Valentine assisted in laying it out. An obituary that appeared in the *New York Herald, New York Tribune, New York Evening Post,* and *New-York Commercial Advertiser* on February 1 announced Virginia Poe's funeral at 2:00 p.m. on the following day—those people attending from Manhattan could take a noon train from City Hall and board a 4:00 p.m. train back.[68]

The funeral took place in the living room (the "sitting-room") of the Poe cottage. There were flowers; there was the scent of cologne. Among those gathered besides Poe and his mother-in-law were Marie Louise Shew, Mary Starr, John Valentine's daughter Mary, the writer Ann S. Stephens, Sylvanus D. Lewis and, in all likelihood his wife Sarah Anna Lewis, cousin Elizabeth Herring, the journalist Richard H. Stoddard ("with green goggles over his eyes"), and Poe's devoted friends N. P. Willis and George Pope Morris. At the close of the service, Mary Starr remained, and probably Maria Clemm, as well. Others walked in the cold to the Old Dutch Reformed Church, where Virginia's body was interred in the vault of the Valentine family.[69]

A few days later, Willis noted the death of Virginia in "Death of Mrs. Edgar A. Poe" in the *Home Journal:* "Among the deaths, last week, we regret to notice that of Mrs. Poe, who fell a victim to pulmonary consumption. Mrs. Poe was an estimable woman and an excellent wife. Her loss is mourned by a numerous circle of friends."[70]

21

"Then My Heart It Grew Ashen and Sober"

1847–1848

T HE WEEKS FOLLOWING THE DEATH of Virginia were a dark time for Poe. He acknowledged in March having been "overwhelmed by a sorrow so poignant as to deprive me for several weeks of all power of thought or action" (O 2:624). It was probably even worse than this. According to his friend Charles Chauncey Burr, "Many times after the death of his beloved wife, was he found at the dead hour of a winter's night, sitting beside her tomb, almost frozen in the snow."[1] Such behavior would certainly have been worrisome, but it was also loving. And it was consistent with Poe's response to an earlier loss. When the much-cherished Jane Stith Stanard died in Richmond in April 1824, Poe went to her grave at Shockoe Hill Cemetery not only with his friend, her son, Rob Stanard, but also by himself at night. He told Sarah Helen Whitman "that on stormy & dreary nights he went most often—that he could not endure to think of her lying there forsaken & forgotten."[2]

Every other day, Marie Louise Shew nursed the grieving and feverish Poe, thereby fulfilling her promise to Virginia, and Maria Clemm took care of him when Shew was away. Shew had also promised Virginia that she would listen to Poe's sorrows, and doubtless she did listen, also consoling as she could. Furthermore, she counseled her patient "that nothing would, or could, save him from a sudden death, but a prudent life, of calm with a woman fond enough—and strong enough to manage his work and its remunerations for his best good." Notably, Shew had provided Virginia with wine—without which, Mrs. Clemm suggested, there would have been "no last words, no loving messages, *no sweet farewells*"—and Poe asked that the remaining wine be returned for the sake of an ailing artist friend of Shew.³

Poe's compassionate nurse later wrote, "I saved Mr. Poe's life at this time."⁴ It was surely her having done so to which her grateful patient referred in his Valentine's Day 1847 tribute to her, published in the *Home Journal* a month later as "To M. L. S—." He spoke of those who bless her

> Hourly for hope—for life—ah! above all,
> For the resurrection of deep-buried faith
> In Truth—in Virtue—in Humanity—

and went on, at the framed center, to speak

> Of all who, on Despair's unhallowed bed
> Lying down to die, have suddenly arisen
> At thy soft-murmured words, "Let there be light!"
> At the soft-murmured words that were fulfilled
> In the seraphic glancing of thine eyes—

He closed, exaltingly, that he, "[t]he truest—the most fervently devoted" of those who are so thankful to her, "thrills to think / His spirit is communing with an angel's" (M 1:400).

With Marie Louise Shew's help, Poe began to recover. Meanwhile, members of New York's Union Club, including General Winfield Scott, provided Poe with funds after Virginia's death. Scott, who would have remembered Poe from West Point and from Richmond before that, contributed five dollars (wishing he could have given five hundred) and spoke with much respect. Shew later wrote, "He believe[d] Poe to be very much belied, that he had noble and generous traits which belonged to a gentleman of the old and better school." Moreover, she added, "It was his [Poe's] manner and bearing and grateful heart that Scott admired; and the pride and strength of intellect came in to make up the rest."⁵

On February 17, Poe won his libel suit against Hiram Fuller and Fuller's brother-in-law Augustus H. Clason and was awarded $225.⁶ (Poe later designated Maria Clemm to receive the money [O 2:629].) And on February 20, the *Columbian Magazine* of March 1847 featured Poe's "The Domain of Arnheim," an extravagant expansion of "The Landscape-Garden" offering the attainment of Ellison's "object of unceasing pursuit," a "Paradise of Arnheim":

There is a gush of entrancing melody; there is an oppressive sense of strange sweet odor;—there is a dream-like intermingling to the eye of tall slender Eastern trees—bosky shrubberies—flocks of golden and crimson birds—lily-fringed lakes—meadows of violets, tulips, poppies, hyacinths and tuberoses—long intertangled lines of silver streamlets—and, upspringing confusedly from amid all, a mass of semi-Gothic, semi-Saracenic architecture, sustaining itself as if by miracle in mid air; glittering in the red sunlight with a hundred oriels, minarets, and pinnacles; and seeming the phantom handiwork, conjointly, of the Sylphs, of the Fairies, of the Genii, and of the Gnomes. (M 3:1283)

Poe subsequently confided that this sketch "expresses *much of my soul*" (O 2:712). The work was warmly praised at the time: "The reader will be much pleased with Mr. Poe's gorgeously imaginative article—'The domain of Arnheim.' It is written with the vivid coloring of his best productions, rivaling even that of Beckford's 'Caliph Vathek.'"[7]

And Poe returned to his correspondence. Writing to George W. Eveleth on February 16, Poe defended *The Conchologist's First Book* against the charge of plagiarism, noting its acknowledgment of Cuvier and citing common practice regarding making schoolbooks (O 2:618–20). Writing to Horace Greeley on February 21, Poe asked the editor to distance himself from accusations made in the *Tribune*—accusations of Poe's not having paid his debts and his not having written in response to English's attack (O 2:620–23). (Poe owed Greeley $50, money he had borrowed to take on the *Broadway Journal*—and it was very likely Greeley who had made the accusations. The editor did not respond to Poe's request and later published Griswold's malicious obituary of Poe.)[8]

Poe's recovery was slow. On March 10 and 11, the still-infirm writer mentioned his continuing poor health in three additional letters—one of them to Jane E. Locke regarding her poem about him ("Being still too unwell to leave my room" [O 2:623]), another in response to George W. Eveleth ("I am still quite sick and overwhelmed with business" [O 2:626]), and yet another to J. F. Reinman and J. H. Walker, concerning an honorary membership in a literary society ("Very serious illness has hitherto prevented me from replying" [O 2:628]).

It was probably sometime late in the month that Poe traveled with Marie Louise Shew by closed carriage to visit Dr. Valentine Mott, who lived at 1 Depau Row, on Bleecker Street. Shew offered the famed doctor her own diagnosis of Poe—that his irregular pulse was due to a lesion of the brain. And it was perhaps in April that Poe wrote a poem about this visit. Shew bought the poem from Poe, not wanting Poe's praise of her to be misunderstood as her marriage approached. Although the manuscript of the poem has been lost, Shew later offered some lines, commenting to John Ingram, "You can imagine it was a perfect thing as he revised it afterwards."[9] Mabbott reprints the eleven lines of the poem that Ingram had gathered, apparently from several Shew letters, including three lines about the author's never forgetting her. Poe wrote of this poem in his June 1848 letter to Shew, "I place you in *my esteem* in all *solemnity* beside the friend of my boyhood [Jane Stith Stanard], the mother of my school fellow, of whom I told you, and as I have repeated in the poem the 'Beloved Physician,' as the truest, tenderest, of this world's most womanly souls, and an angel to my forlorn and darkened nature" (O 2:679).

Marie Louise Shew soon offered to her patient a particularly congenial employment: she asked him to assist her uncle in choosing furniture for the music room and library of her new house on Tenth Street.[10] Poe responded, in a letter of May 1847, with continued deep gratitude, praising her taste, anticipating "so much pleasure in thinking of you & yours, in that Music Room & Library," and promising that "I know I can please you in the purchases." He made himself available to her uncle "any or every day this week" (O 2:630). Poe had already given the matter of interior decoration much thought, as is evident from his piece in the May 1840 *Burton's Gentleman's Magazine*, "The Philosophy of Furniture," where he was keenly attentive to detail, prizing "keeping" (tastefulness, harmony) and "*Repose.*" Especially notable there is his description of an exemplary room, featuring, in part, "a piano-forte—also of rose-wood, and without cover" and "light and graceful hanging shelves" holding "two or three hundred magnificently-bound books."[11] With Shew's commission, Poe could fashion something akin to that room, an interior Arnheim. His nurse—now his patron—later told John H. Ingram that when Poe took on the project, "[M]y uncle said he had never seen him so cheerful and natural—'quite like other people.'"[12] Poe was enjoying another sort of composition.

We have varied accounts of Poe in the coming time, both at home and in New York City. In Fordham, perhaps in early or mid-June, Poe enjoyed the visit of a small group—the elocutionist Cotesworth P. Bronson, his thirteen-year-old daughter Mary Elizabeth Bronson, and others, including several women. Mary Elizabeth—later LeDuc—recalled her first seeing Poe, "a very handsome and elegant-appearing gentleman, who welcomed us with a quiet, cordial, and graceful politeness that ill accorded with my imaginary sombre poet." The visitors encountered Maria Clemm and entered the cottage, "a model of neatness and order." Poe observed that a portrait of a young girl displayed on the wall was not "the lost Lenore" and acknowledged that some people expected a raven above his door.

After a meal, the guests accompanied Poe along the Bronx River and eventually gathered, some sitting, beneath a canopy of trees, where the men discussed literature. Poe spoke on his own work and that of others, offering special praise for the poetry of Frances Sargent Osgood.

And then, as he spoke, there was a moment of impromptu tribute: "In one of the pauses in this pleasant talk, one of the ladies placed on the head of the poet an oak-leaf wreath; and as he stood beneath the tree, half in the shade, the sun's rays glancing through the dark-green leaves, and lighting up his broad white forehead, with a pleasant, gratified smile on his face, my memory recalls a charming picture of the poet, then in his best days."[13] Poe had long ago imagined that he could be great, and here a sweet wordless gesture assured him that indeed he was.

However, another visit to Fordham, involving the editors Cornelius Mathews and Evert A. Duyckinck, did not go so well. Matthews offered the more temperate recollection. Guests had been surprised by the "supper-room" of the impoverished Poes—"the floor laid with a brand-new rag carpet, an ample table, sumptuous with delicacies, and Mrs. Clemm at the head of the table, decanting, from a new silver-plated urn, amber coffee, which glowed as it fell in the light of the setting sun." Mathews inferred, reasonably, that the monies recently received from Hiram Fuller had contributed to the décor and the bounty. During an after-meal walk, he found Poe's conversation to be objectionably "abstract" and "analytic."[14]

Duyckinck, writing in his diary, was downright condemnatory: "At night the whole agreeable impression of the afternoon reversed by dreams, into which it might have been supposed Poe had put an infusion of his Mons Valdemar with the green tea, the probable cause of them. All the evil I had ever heard of him took bodily shape in a series of most malignant scenes."[15] This account is frustratingly opaque. Was Poe insufferably egotistical? Was he drinking? Was he belligerent? Did he have words with Maria Clemm or their guests? Was there any sort of provocation? We do not know. Presumably, Duyckinck, writing for himself, was confident that he would remember and did not need to provide unpleasant detail. But we may wonder—if Poe's behavior was so egregious, why didn't Matthews mention it? It is unclear.

Duyckinck later wrote an undiscerning, unsympathetic, Griswold-influenced sketch of Poe in the Duyckincks' *Cyclopaedia of American Literature*.[16]

Poe's few visits to New York City at this time were similarly divergent. His visits to his friends the Bronsons were entirely amiable; his visit to his enemy Hiram Fuller was, not surprisingly, anything but.

Mary Elizabeth Bronson LeDuc recounted the daylong visit of Poe and Maria Clemm, during which the girl's coral necklace prompted Poe to comment on women's adornments. (Perhaps he would have been reminded of Virginia's coral necklace.) On another visit, Poe responded to the girl's interest in collecting daguerreotypes by going to a daguerreotypist with her father and providing Mary Elizabeth with a likeness of himself. This image, considered by Poe "the most natural-looking he had ever seen of himself," might well have been the one now known as the Daly daguerreotype. This is the first image of Poe with a moustache, as we typically remember him. He appears in a black suit, a white shirt and collar, and a black cravat—"a very handsome and elegant-appearing gentleman." He seems calm, kempt, and composed—trim and self-assured.[17]

By contrast to Mary Elizabeth Bronson LeDuc, Hiram Fuller—recently found guilty of libel and obliged to pay damages—offered a bitter response to Poe's unwise visit to the *Evening Mirror* office. Fuller's June 7, 1847, piece—recalling his similarly bitter July 20, 1846, diatribe—asserted that Poe's black suit had probably been bought with "the money so infamously obtained" and that Poe had conducted himself so badly that the aggrieved *Evening Mirror* editor had had to call the police. Doubtless Poe had been drinking—but Fuller chose to publish with vitriol and contempt as Poe did not choose his difficulty with alcohol. And, as Sarah Helen Whitman fairly judged, "Fuller of *course* is not" "a man to understand Poe."[18]

Poe visited New York City again on June 30, when he met Rufus W. Griswold in the street and was, according to the anthologist, "extremely civil."[19] And Poe soon traveled south to Washington, D.C., and Philadelphia. In the capital, he may have visited his friends Frederick W. Thomas and Jesse E. Dow and the bureaucrat Charles Eames.[20] With a group of friends, Poe attended an outdoor graduation ceremony at Episcopal High School, six miles south of Washington, near Alexandria, Virginia. Recognized as he stood near the stage, he became "the object of universal attention." Poe was then invited to recite "The Raven" to those gathered, and he did so "to the delight of all who were present."[21] It was a rich moment, and it seems to anticipate generations of students and teachers responding to Poe's work in so many middle school and high school English classrooms over the years.

Poe's experience in Philadelphia was, by contrast, unfortunate. Staying at William Arbuckle's Western Hotel on High Street, Poe met with the editors Louis A. Godey and George R. Graham, and he encountered (under unidentified problematic circumstances) the poet, editor, and lawyer Robert T. Conrad (whom he had previously praised in "A Chapter on Autography" [H 15:232–33] and the lecture "American Poetry").[22] Godey later confided to George W. Eveleth that although Poe had been sober when visiting him, "I have heard from him elsewhere, when he was not so."[23] And Poe subsequently wrote to Conrad that, sometime after seeing him, he had been "exceedingly ill" (O 2:632). Probably the trouble, which must have been dire, had involved Poe's drinking. Perhaps Conrad had found Poe in an intoxicated state and rescued him, and Poe had then experienced the adverse after-effects. Poe expressed his appreciation to Conrad in a letter from August 10: "Permit me to thank you, in the first place, very sincerely, for your considerate kindness to me while in Philadelphia. Without your aid, at the precise moment and in the precise manner in which you rendered it, it is more than probable that I should not now be alive to write you this letter" (O 2:632). Also, Poe apparently owed Conrad money and awaited his decision regarding several pieces submitted ("The Rationale of Verse" was very likely one of them). By virtue of Conrad's unspecified "kindness" (see also the August 31 letter [O 2:634]), Poe returned to Fordham, but his reputation had been further damaged: Godey wrote to Eveleth, "Mr. Poe has been on here—but it were better for his fame to have staid away."[24]

In September 1847, Cotesworth P. Bronson and his daughter returned to New York City. Mary Elizabeth Bronson LeDuc later stated, "I learned then that Mr. Poe was in straitened circumstances, and that all of his projects had proved unsuccessful."[25] The Poe scholar John Ward Ostrom considered Poe's income in 1847 to have been "grossly inadequate" and concluded, "The expenses of Virginia's final illness and death and of Poe's necessities and comforts, as one might expect, seem largely to have been paid by friends."[26] Probably among these friends, most from New York and Philadelphia, would have been one friend from Richmond: John H. Mackenzie, to whom Maria Clemm had appealed by a letter delivered by Rosalie Poe in July 1846. Mackenzie would have known to send the money directly to Mrs. Clemm, not to Poe. Virginia's death would very likely have renewed Mackenzie's generosity.

The Bronsons soon visited Poe again at his home. LeDuc recalled that on their return to Fordham, Maria Clemm was anxious and Poe nervous. Cotesworth P. Bronson understood that money was an issue and suggested that Poe write a poem that could be readily performed, with varied intonation. LeDuc reported, "He [her father] recited to the Poet in illustration Collins' Ode to the passions and assured Poe that he would gain both fame and profit for any suitable poem of this kind. Ulalume, Anabell [sic] Lee, and The Bells were written as the result of this suggestion and subsequent encouragement" (M 1:410).[27] Poe would draw for his next poem on the agonized time of Virginia's death and her burial.

In mid-October, Poe's review of Hawthorne's *Mosses from an Old Manse* appeared in the November issue of *Godey's Lady's Book*.[28] Poe had relied, in part, on his 1842 review of *Twice-Told Tales,* but he also inferred a cliqueishness in the work at hand (perhaps because of "The Old Manse") and conveyed a newly sharp tone, arguing that Hawthorne "is *not* original in any sense" but, rather, "peculiar." Criticizing Hawthorne's inclination to allegory—and allegory itself—Poe did offer his important exception for unobtrusive allegory, appearing in "a *very* profound under-current."[29] He thus provided an important light on *Arthur Gordon Pym* and others of his works.

October 1847 was the time of a British boarder at the Poe cottage, the writer Anna Blackwell. Mary Gove—under whose direction Blackwell had undergone the water cure treatment—had suggested the arrangement to both her former patient and Maria Clemm.[30] The new resident, thirty-one years old and "in very delicate health at the time," stayed with the Poes two or three weeks. Sarah Helen Whitman recalled of Blackwell, "She was charmed with the exquisite neatness & quiet of the household & the delicious repasts, prepared for her by Mrs. Clemm." Though she did not get to know Poe, she remembered him as "courteous & gentlemanly."[31] Whitman later related that Blackwell said that Poe had made two pine tables for the parlor, tables that he had "very neatly & tastefully covered" with "fine green baize."[32] (We may be reminded of Virginia's green baize guitar bag.) Also, Poe evidently took pleasure in his caged tropical birds and his flower garden. Whitman added that Blackwell recollected (most memorably), "A favourite cat, too, enjoyed his friendly patronage, and often when he was engaged in composition it seated itself on his shoulder, purring as in complacent approval of the work proceeding under its supervision."[33] Poe's great work of this period was the strange and powerful poem "Ulalume."

Maria Clemm told Mary Elizabeth Bronson that her son-in-law had composed "a beautiful poem—better than anything before." Poe invited Cotesworth P. Bronson to Fordham, with his daughter, in part so that the elocutionist might respond to the poem that he had prompted (O 2:634–36), but since the Bronsons were unable to come, Poe visited them. The father was away, but the daughter was there, and Mary Elizabeth had as privileged an experience of "Ulalume" as Mary Brennan had once had of "The Raven." Years, later, as Mary Elizabeth Bronson LeDuc, she remembered seeing the manuscript and listening to Poe read the poem:

> I asked if I might read it. He not only assented, but opened the roll, which consisted of leaves of paper wafered neatly together, and I noticed then and afterward that the writing was beautifully distinct and regular, almost like engraving. It was the "Ballad of Ulalume." He made one or two remarks in regard to the ideas intended to be embodied, answering my questions while he read it to me, and expressing his own entire satisfaction with it.[34]

Subsequently, Poe offered the manuscript poem to the editor Caroline M. Kirkland for publication in the new *Union Magazine,* but she turned it down. She had consulted with the poet Richard H. Stoddard, who had said that "he could not understand it."[35] Stoddard was a particularly unsuitable choice to vet Poe's work not only because of his animus toward Poe but also because of his limited range. He later admitted to Sarah Helen Whitman, "The fact is that the more I read about Poe the less I understand him. I am too commonplace a person to understand unusual developments of genius."[36] On Poe's behalf, Maria Clemm delivered the manuscript poem to the editor of the *American Review,* George H. Colton, who had admiringly published "The Raven."

Around this time, several friends visited Poe at Fordham. Mary Gove Nichols remembered that there had been a leaping contest, probably proposed by Poe. He and two or three other men competed, and Poe, with a "grand leap," triumphed. But there was a cost: as a consequence of that leap, his "gaiters" "burst." His guests did not have either the money needed for the shoes or the temerity to risk injuring Poe's pride by offering such money. Maria Clemm took Mary into the kitchen and asked that she approach the man to whom she herself (Clemm) had brought the manuscript of "Ulalume." After all, "Eddie says it is his best." And payment for the poem could provide payment for the shoes. Gove couldn't understand the poem—and George H. Colton seems to have been one of Poe's leaping competitors ("The reviewer had been actively instrumental in the demolition of the gaiters"). But Gove approached Colton, and he agreed to publish the work. And so, one of Poe's more otherworldly poems yielded a much-needed worldly benefit.[37]

Poe also was then making a literary "grand leap"—a figurative one that would, like his literal one, cause unintended damage. He was planning a book about the nature of the universe. It would be called *Eureka*.[38] And he would soon be writing the satirical tale "Mellonta Tauta," which he then adapted for *Eureka*.[39]

In late November, he submitted a sonnet to a magazine, another progressive acrostic, this one honoring Sarah Anna Lewis. She, with her husband, Sylvanus D. Lewis, had visited and supported the Poes, including financially, and the Poes in turn had visited them, in Brooklyn. Poe expressed his gratitude to Mrs. Lewis in a letter of November 27 (O 2:636–37). But his actual view was more mixed: his gratitude was doubtless genuine, but so was his impatience with her—even intolerance for her—as one of the "*Literary bores.*"[40]

While the December 1847 number of the *American Review* was in press, the twenty-nine-year-old editor, George H. Colton—who had been sick for more than a month (presumably since his visit to Fordham)—died of typhus fever.[41] Although Poe hadn't had a high opinion of Colton as an editor or a poet, he had liked him as a person: "I always liked him and I believe he liked me" (O 2:648).[42] George W. Eveleth, who had been in correspondence with Colton, responded to Poe, "*I* think Colton liked you, as a writer and as a friend."[43] The late editor had clearly respected Poe's work, publishing a number of pieces by him, including the short stories "Some Words with a Mummy" and "The Facts of M. Valdemar's Case." And, indeed, it had been Colton who, on reading "The Raven" aloud before he published it in the *American Review*, had said, "[T]hat is amazing—amazing!"[44]

The December number appeared, in its usual dark buff wrappers, by December 7—Poe referred to it as "just issued" as he sent it to N. P. Willis on December 8.[45] "Ulalume" appeared without its author's name, and Poe asked Willis to reprint it in the *Home Journal* and to wonder about its author's identity (O 2:638).

The portentous opening lines entrancingly invite entrance:

The skies they were ashen and sober;
   The leaves they were crispèd and sere—
   The leaves they were withering and sere;
It was night in the lonesome October
   Of my most immemorial year.

The eerie and alluring ballad offers ten stanzas, each of them of nine to thirteen lines, with similar incantatory rhyme schemes. The anapestic trimeter (with some substitutions) is both delicate and firm. The story is evident—on that "night of all nights in the year," Halloween, the narrator and his soul, Psyche, wander in a dark and mysterious landscape. Though the narrator is cheered by the light of Astarte (Venus), Psyche considers the light unreliable, even dangerous. As they wander, the two find a tomb, that of the narrator's lost beloved, Ulalume—and the speaker remembers all. Perhaps, the two imagine, friendly "ghouls" called forth the planet to distract them from the somber site.

"Ulalume" is the third of Poe's three great indirect renderings of memory. *Pym* treated it through form—the facing mirrors infinitely reflect the center. "The Raven" treated it through emblem—the black bird itself signifies "*Mournful and Never-ending Remembrance*" (L 2:70). "Ulalume" treats it through opposition—persistent forgetting gives way to recovered memory. Whatever his literary approach, Poe gets to the same essential matter—the powerful memory of the precious dead—still grieved, still cherished.

The drama of the poem is the shift from forgetting to remembering. The speaker acknowledges that it is his "most immemorial year" and that "Our memories were treacherous and sere." He goes on,

> For we knew not the month was October
>   And we marked not the night of the year—
>   (Ah, night of all nights in the year!)
> We noted not the dim lake of Auber—
>   (Though once we had journeyed down here)—
> We remembered not the dark tarn of Auber,
>   Nor the ghoul-haunted woodland of Weir.

And he refers with seeming longing to the mythological river of forgetfulness—"the Lethean peace of the skies." But eventually, as he and his soul walk on, they reach a tomb, and peregrination yields to peripeteia. Poe writes, as the speaker addressing his soul,

> And I said—"What is written, sweet sister,
>   On the door of this legended tomb?"
> She replied—"Ulalume—Ulalume—
> 'Tis the vault of thy lost Ulalume!"

And so comes the turn, the reversal, the recovery of memory:

Then my heart it grew ashen and sober
  As the leaves that were crispèd and sere—
  As the leaves that were withering and sere,
And I cried—"It was surely October
  On *this* very night of last year
  That I journeyed—I journeyed down here—
  That I brought a dread burden down here—
  On this night of all nights in the year,
  Oh, what demon has tempted me here?
Well, I know, now, this dim lake of Auber—
  This misty mid region of Weir—
Well I know, now, this dank tarn of Auber,
  In the ghoul-haunted woodland of Weir."[46]

Here, unlike in *Pym* and "The Raven," memory is not fixed: it fails—then prevails. The speaker has returned to the place, he now knows, where a year earlier he buried his wife.

Various literary sources have been suggested,[47] but ultimately it was Poe's life that was the basis for the poem. Sarah Helen Whitman commented in *Edgar Poe and His Critics*—prompted by the close of "Eleonora" (an anticipation of "Ulalume," its dark inverse)—about Poe's "lingering pity and sorrow for the dead;—an ever-recurring pang of remorse in the fear of having grieved them by some involuntary wrong of desertion or forgetfulness. This haunting remembrance—this sad, remorseful pity for the departed, is everywhere a distinguishing feature in his prose and poetry."[48] Also, she contended that the origin of the poem "Ulalume" was "simply historical," including "the poet's lonely midnight walk."[49] She wrote to Maria Clemm, "I have heard Edgar speak of the circumstances under which he composed the poem of Ulalume. It purports to have been suggested on a midnight walk on the Anniversary of a burial—but it is my impression that he told me it *was* so written. But Virginia died in January, did she not?—And the poem was professedly written in *October*—Perhaps the correspondence in *time* was purely *ideal*—I know he described the emotions themselves as *real*."[50] Poe's use of "October" instead of "January" may have been owing not only to the "night of all nights in the year," but also to the former word's rhythm and potential for rhyme, far more fitting for "Ulalume."

Years later, John H. Ingram wrote to Whitman that Virginia was buried in "the family vault of a neighbor [John Valentine] who allowed her to be interred there." He notes, "This is interesting as corresponding with the terms of 'Ulalume.'"[51] Subsequently Whitman commented to him on the last stanza of the poem—which she had once persuaded Poe to delete—that its reference to "the spectre of a planet" intimates that Venus is "a mirage of the fancy," overcome by the discovery of "the sepulchre wherein his Virginia lay entombed." And she added, "Then, overwhelmed with that remorseful sorrow that seems always to have visited him when his thoughts reverted from some dream of present happiness to the memory of a lost love, he explains, 'Oh what demon has tempted me here?' In this view of the theme of the poem, is not the last verse, however obscure, necessary to its elucidation?"[52]

Remembering his dead—in *Pym,* in "The Raven," in "Ulalume"—no matter how painful, may assure Poe that he is not guilty of "some involuntary wrong of desertion or forgetfulness." These three are works of great aspiration, providing the integration of Poe's life in his writing and perhaps even an integration of self, yielding an alleviation of "remorseful pity," "remorseful sorrow"—a kind of personal consolation.

And sometimes, especially for one who reads the full poem "Ulalume" aloud, the long-delayed understanding (on learning that this was the tomb of his lost love)—"Then my heart it grew ashen and sober"—may offer a hint of that "shivering delight" (L2 184) that Poe wrote of in "The Poetic Principle." With "Ulalume," again, Poe movingly transformed mourning.

Poe continued his "Marginalia" installments in *Graham's Magazine.* Significantly, the installment in the January issue (appearing by December 21) included an item about the impossibility of writing a book titled "My Heart Laid Bare." The source for the phrase is a passage about vengeance in Bulwer-Lytton's novel *Pelham.* In that work, "[T]he secrets of one passionate and irregulated heart laid bare" relate to the presence of romance whereas in "Marginalia" "My Heart Laid Bare" relates to the impossibility of taking "the road to immortal renown" with a book so titled because of its unwritability.[53] For Poe, in late 1847, literary ambition was resurgent.

At this time, he probably continued to write his projected book "Literary America." He probably also wrote another tribute to Marie Louise Shew, "To Marie Louise."[54] He certainly worked on his new prospectus for his still-projected literary magazine "The Stylus," which would include "Literary America" (L2 33).[55] And most significantly, Poe made progress on his new cosmology.

A remarkable interlude took place at a Christmas Eve service at midnight in the Twentieth Street Free Church in Manhattan. Accompanying Marie Louise Shew and another woman, Poe initially participated with evident facility and familiarity: "He went with us," Shew recalled, "followed the service like a 'churchman,' looking directly towards the chancel, and holding one side of my prayer book, sang the psalms with us, and to my astonishment struck up a tenor to our sopranos and, got along nicely during the first part of the sermon, which was on the subject of the sympathies of our Lord, to our wants." Then, as the Episcopal priest Dr. William Augustus Muhlenberg proceeded with his sermon, Poe was stirred by the treatment of a passage in Isaiah 53:3, "He was a man of sorrows and acquainted with grief"—and he left the pew: "He begged me to stay quiet that he would wait for me outside, and he rushed out, *too excited to stay.*" After the sermon, Poe returned from the rear of the sanctuary to Shew: "I looked back and saw his pale face, and as the congregation rose to sing the Hymn, 'Jesus Saviour of my soul,' he appeared at my side, and sang the Hymn, without looking at the book, in a fine clear tenor. He looked inspired! And *no wonder. He imagined* he would have made a successful orator, and priest—I did not dare to ask him why he left, but he mentioned after we got home, that the subject '*was marvelously handled,* and ought to have melted many hard hearts.'"[56]

We may infer that Poe had identified with the "man of sorrows . . . acquainted with grief" and that he also understood that this Old Testament figure was considered, from a Christian perspective, a type of Jesus. And the focus of the sermon, "the sympathies of our Lord, to our wants," was clearly affecting. Shew remembered that Virginia had once confided that Edgar considered Dr. Muhlenberg "a true and inspired teacher of the Gospel." The hymn, "Jesus Saviour of My Soul," known to Poe from his early boyhood, offered abiding protection.[57] In the midst of his cosmological aspirations, Poe was responsive to religious consolation. Nine years earlier he had offered such consolation himself (however encoded) at the ending of *Pym.*

Poe returned to Fordham and kept on with his work on *Eureka.* Maria Clemm later talked about his writing that book. Eugene Didier remembered, "Mrs. Clemm told me that while engaged upon this extraordinary prose poem, he would walk up and down the porch in front of the cottage, in the coldest nights of December, with an overcoat thrown over his shoulders, contemplating the stars, and 'pondering the deep problems' of the universe, until long after midnight."[58] R. E. Shapley recalled her saying, "When he was composing 'Eureka,' we used to walk up and down the garden, his arm around me, mine around him, until I was so tired I could not walk. He would stop every few minutes and explain his ideas to me, and ask if I understood him." And Richard H. Stoddard recollected, "[S]he [Maria Clemm] . . . told me of the long winter nights in which Poe often used to talk with her about the 'Problem of the Universe,' while it was in progress, and how one winter night in particular they passed hours together under the glittering starlight, walking up and down the little piazza of their cottage at Fordham, he explaining the 'Cosmos' to her, and she, I gathered, shivering with cold, though she would not for worlds have owned the fact."[59] Presumably, for Poe, the exhilaration of confronting the ultimate mystery mitigated the cold.

Even as Poe worked on his cosmological treatise, several of his professional initiatives came to fruition. His April and August 1846 letters reaching out to Philip Pendleton Cooke to write a "P.S." to Lowell's biographical sketch (O 1:565, 595–96) led to a piece in the January 1848 issue of the *Southern Literary Messenger*. Lauding more recent works, including "The Raven" and "The Facts in the Case of M. Valdemar," Cooke noted, "I believe Mr. P. has been for some time ill—has recently sustained a heavy domestic bereavement—and is only now returning to his literary labors." He commented encouragingly, "The public will doubtless welcome the return of so favorite an author to pursuits in which heretofore he has done so much and so well" (H 1:387). Poe's December 1847 request to N. P. Willis to reprint "Ulalume," with a question as to who wrote it, led to both the reprint and the query, under the heading "Epicureanism in Language" in the *Home Journal*. Willis characterized the poem as an "exquisitely piquant and skilful exercise of rarity and niceness of language," "a curiosity, (and a delicious one, we think,) in its philologic flavor."[60] And Poe published the second prospectus for "The Stylus," the fourth prospectus for the literary magazine that he had been striving for since 1840, earlier called "The Penn." Poe promised, in this prospectus, the work "Literary America," "that great desideratum, a *faithful* account of the literary productions, literary people, and literary affairs of the United States" (L2 33).

After the failure, five years earlier, of the first effort to launch "The Stylus," under the auspices of partner and publisher Thomas C. Clarke, Poe had written about the magazine to James Russell Lowell in June 1843, "Under better auspices I may resume it next year" (O 1:401). Now, in January 1848, he finally resumed his effort, but under his own auspices: "I am resolved to be my own publisher," he wrote to George W. Eveleth. He went on, "To be controlled is to be ruined. My ambition is great. If I succeed, I put myself (within 2 years) in possession of a fortune & infinitely more" (O 2:641–42). Perhaps he had in mind the financial success of George R. Graham.

Poe wrote in his full and upbeat January 4, 1848, letter to Eveleth, "My health is better—best. I have never been so well" (O 2:639–40). And he asserted his bold and promising plan: to go on a lecture tour in the South and the West, collecting subscriptions from friends for the new magazine. To begin the periodical, he would need *"a list of at least 500 subscribers"* (O 2:641–42).[61] He wrote to Henry D. Chapin that to fund the tour he had first thought of visiting John Neal in Portland and giving a lecture there that might raise a hundred dollars. (Neal had been an early supporter of Poe's—and had proposed a five-dollar-per-year literary magazine in 1835, albeit one with a thousand subscribers, who would pay ahead for five years. Lowell had visited Neal before publishing the *Pioneer*.)[62] But, Poe continued, he had decided, after having talked to Chapin, to rely on friends in New York and to raise the money needed to begin the tour by giving a lecture at the New York Society Library (where he had earlier spoken on American poetry). He asked Chapin for fifteen dollars to secure the lecture room, which could accommodate the three or four hundred people he expected. The anticipated date of the lecture was "the *first Thursday in February*" (O 2:644–45)—that is, February 3, 1848, just beyond the year of mourning for Virginia. Poe also shared his plan with N. P. Willis, clarifying that he already had almost two hundred of the needed five hundred subscribers and that on his tour he would reach out to "my personal and literary friends—old college and West Point acquaintances."[63] And he revealed his subject. Intimating his ostensible wish to avoid controversy, he wrote, "[T]hat there may be no cause of *squabbling,* my subject shall *not be literary* at all. I have chosen a broad text—'The Universe.'" Poe sought Willis's "aid," his "tact and generosity" for this endeavor (O 2:646–47). The step-by-step plan—to give the New York lecture to support the lecture tour to build subscriptions to launch the new magazine—seemed reasonable and plausible.

Although the shift from a literary subject to a cosmic one was new, Poe had had an early familiarity with astronomy, perhaps having had access to a telescope at the Dubourgs' school in London, certainly having had access to a telescope at his home with the Allans in Richmond, and probably having heard Robert Goodacre lecture on astronomy in Richmond, in 1824. For the poem "Sonnet—To Science," Poe did question the value of science—"Vulture, whose wings are dull realities"—and relied, for rhetorical questions about the interference of science, on a passage hostile to science in Saint-Pierre's "Pleasures of Ignorance" (M 1:90–91). And, for the poem "Al Aaraaf," he offered an additional negative view of science—"ev'n with *us* the breath / Of Science dims the mirror of our joy" (M 1:111).[64] However, he gradually altered his view, writing fiction with scientific themes, including "The Unparalleled Adventures of Hans Pfaall," "A Descent into the Maelström," and "Mesmeric

Revelation," and writing nonfiction about automata, conchology, cryptology, daguerreotypy, mnemonics, optical effects, the United States Exploring Expedition, and other scientific topics, with great interest. He had become, after all, a magazinist. And perhaps he came to feel that science was not so dull if it could enable, rather than restrain, the poet. Perhaps he came to believe that if science would yield to his imagination, he would yield to science.[65]

Eveleth promised to subscribe to "The Stylus" and to promote it in Maine. Poe did secure the lecture room of the New York Society Library—perhaps with Chapin's assistance. And Willis wrote about Poe's coming lecture in the *Home Journal,* "The subject is rather a broad one—'The Universe;' but from a mind so original, no text could furnish any clue to what would probably be the sermon. There is but one thing certain about it, that it will be compact of thought, most fresh, startling, and suggestive." Most other announcements of Poe's coming talk were similarly auspicious. But the announcement in Thomas Dunn English's *John-Donkey* was, not surprisingly, an outlier, closing, "Some of our friends say that they hope he will not disappoint his auditors, as he did once before. We suspect he will, whether he delivers his lecture or not."[66]

Even as Poe's ambition was great, so was his conviction regarding his argument. And his effort suggests that he still believed in man's effort to shape his life. As he had written in 1842, "You make your own Fate. There is such a thing as compelling Fortune, however reluctant or averse" (O 1:345). Despite all the troubles of his life, he would give it his all. And perhaps he would do so, in part, because of all those troubles.

The weather on the night of February 3, 1848, was not as bad as that on April 17, 1845, when Poe had had to cancel his lecture on American poetry.[67] But still, conditions were unsettled enough to depress the number of people attending. Maunsell B. Field was in the attenuated audience, and he recalled the event vividly: "It was a stormy night, and there were not more than sixty persons present in the lecture-room. I have seen no portrait of POE that does justice to his pale, delicate, intellectual face and magnificent eyes. His lecture was a rhapsody of the most intense brilliancy. He appeared inspired, and his inspiration affected the scant audience almost painfully. He wore his coat tightly buttoned across his slender chest; his eyes seemed to glow like those of his own raven, and he kept us entranced for two hours and a half."[68] The weather did not depress the speaker—he evidently elaborated his argument with fervor. He was reaching as high as he possibly could. This was for Poe an "Excelsior" moment, illustrating what he had termed in his review of Longfellow's poem "the *earnest upward impulse of the soul*" (H 11:84–85).

The press response to Poe's lecture ranged from the *Philadelphia Saturday Gazette*'s concluding that Poe was half-crazy to the *New York Morning Courier*'s characterizing the talk as "a nobler effort than any other Mr. Poe has yet given to the world." The *New York Daily Herald,* referring to recent lectures, including Poe's lecture on the universe, asked, "Will no one get up, and give a lecture on common sense?" And the *New-York Commercial Advertiser* described a recent positive review of Poe's lecture in the *New York Morning Express* as "Hyperbolic Nonsense."[69]

Poe described that positive review as "[t]he only report of it [the lecture] which approaches the truth," though "only my general idea" (O 2:649), and he sent on copies of it to correspondents George W. Eveleth and George Isbell (O 2:649, 659). Perhaps the author of the report, John Henry Hopkins Jr., had been taking notes at the lecture, for his piece, though relatively short, was still detailed and dense. Hopkins sketches Poe's argument, from the deductive portion, descending from God, to the inductive portion, ascending from Earth. He recounts Poe's contending for the "irradiation and diffusion" of the original matter, formed by God, to the "attraction and condensation" of all diffused matter—the universe—back into the original unity. And he notes, among a variety of the assertions made, Poe's assertion of the power of intuition. Hopkins introduces his thoughtful summary by terming Poe's talk "the most elaborate and profound effort we ever listened to in the shape of a lecture," and closes by stating, "The conclusion of this brilliant effort was greeted by warm applause by the audience, who had listened with enchained attention throughout."[70] The piece thoroughly and unqualifiedly extolled Poe's talk. But a later judgment by Hopkins would cause Poe a serious problem.

Poe's own sense of his achievement is evident in his letter to Eveleth of February 29. (This was, after all, a leap year.) Poe wrote, "As to the Lecture. I am very quiet about it—but, if you have ever dealt with such topics, you will recognize the novelty & *moment* of my views. What I have propounded will (in good time) revolutionize the world of Physical & Metaphysical Science. I say this calmly—but I say it" (O 2:650). Eveleth responded, in part, "Wouldn't you do well to give your lecture in other places, and to publish it one of these months? I should really like to see it."[71] *Eureka: A Prose-Poem* would be published in July 1848. Poe would consider it his greatest work.

22

"I Feel I Am Now a Prophet"

1848

After his loss of Virginia and his subsequent despair, Poe may well have felt somewhat steadied by his writing and presenting his new cosmology. And his fair hope for the eventual publication of the work may have contributed to a growing sense of triumph, however temporary. The modestly attended lecture probably hadn't provided the funds needed to support his travel to Richmond to begin his tour for "The Stylus," but he still planned to make the trip, and he still revised the magazine's prospectus. And through it all, he was still grateful for the devotion of Marie Louise Shew. The approaching Valentine's Day prompted a new tribute—and a new possibility.

Poe revised his 1846 progressive acrostic valentine to Frances Sargent Osgood, including correcting the spelling of her middle name ("Sergeant" to "Sargent"). Now dated "Valentine's Eve, 1848" (M 1:387), the poem, though then submitted, was not published until 1849. But Poe also wrote an entirely new Valentine's Day poem, yet another to Shew, in December 1847 or January 1848. He published one version of this poem ("To — — —") in the March issue of the *Columbian Magazine* (appearing before February 23), and he sent another version ("To Marie Louise") to Shew herself.[1] Both versions of the poem diminish his "mad pride of intellectuality" about the power of words by contrast to his vision of the woman who had so lovingly cared for him. The private version included then-unpublished words:

> Ah, Marie Louise!
> In deep humility I own that now
> All pride—all thought of power—all hope of fame—
> All wish for Heaven—is merged forevermore
> Beneath the palpitating tide of passion
> Heaped oe'r my soul by thee. (M 1:406–7)

The tenderness of this version is evident, further, in Poe's placing Marie Louise among "clouds of glory," an allusion to that phrase in Wordsworth's celebration of early childhood, the Intimations Ode.

Meanwhile, at the Valentine's Day party at the home of Anne Lynch, those gathered heard a poem titled "To Edgar A. Poe." This ten-stanza work, addressing Poe as his own "grim and ancient Raven"—"a nobler sight" than the white doves representing Juliet[2]—closes with a caution that seems a teasing invitation: "Not a bird that roams the forest / Shall our lofty eyrie share!" (M 1:442–43). Poe was not present at Mrs. Lynch's home—he was still out of favor because of the Ellet incident—but he received a manuscript copy of the poem by way of Lynch and Osgood. And on March 2 he responded to his admirer, the work's author, the Providence poet Sarah Helen Whitman, by tearing out from his copy of *The Raven and Other Poems* the page with the final poem, the 1831 "To Helen," and sending that page to her (as he fervidly explained in his October 1 letter to her [O 2:694–96]).[3] So began an intense literary romance, sometimes performative, and, finally, emotionally costly for both of them.

Besides working on the revised and final prospectus for "The Stylus" in February, Poe also wrote a "Marginalia" installment in February or March, long unpublished in its entirety.[4] Another "Marginalia" installment did appear in the March issue of *Graham's Magazine,* and his "Sonnet" (later titled "An Enigma"), a progressive acrostic honoring Sarah Anna Lewis, appeared in the March issue of the *Union Magazine*.[5]

At the end of February, Poe wrote an extensive letter to George W. Eveleth, responding to his of January 11. He asserted that he would travel to Richmond on March 10 (in fact, he would leave more than four months later, in July). He noted, among other matters, that indeed his habits had been, as described, "shockingly irregular," but he maintained that they were now "rigorously abstemious." He added, "[T]he causes which maddened me to the drinking point [Virginia's intermittently dire condition] are no more, and I am done drinking, forever" (O 2:648). Poe elaborated for the remainder of the letter the ideas of his recent lecture, offering also a lengthy, highly technical postscript. And Poe wrote on the same day to George S. Isbell, who had included with his letter a review of Poe's talk that observed links to the book *The Vestiges of Creation*. Employing his latest prospectus for stationery (O 2:661), Poe denied that he had read the book, though he had seen extracts, and he offered a concise summary of his February 3 argument.[6] Poe continued to think about his cosmology, considering revision of the manuscript for book submission.

Especially interesting from this time is a poem that Poe lightly edited, presumably in February—Harriet B. Winslow's "To the Author of 'The Raven'"—which appeared in mid-March in the April 1848 issue of *Graham's Magazine*.[7] The dialogic dynamic between "The Raven" and "To the Author of 'The Raven'" is anticipated by that between Winslow's most famous poem, initially published anonymously, "To the Unsatisfied" (also published anonymously as "Why Thus Longing?" in Longfellow's *The Waif*) and "To the Authoress of The Unsatisfied."[8] "To the Unsatisfied" proposed that the near-at-hand be cherished, but its antithetical poem advocated valuing Beauty as a token of heaven. Similarly oppositional, "The Raven" rendered the bird as evil, but "To the Author of 'The Raven'" presented it as friendly, perhaps even angelic. Most memorably, the latter poem links the benign raven, in one stanza, with the African American:

> Though he be a sable brother, treat him kindly as another!
> Ah, perhaps the world has scorned him for that luckless hue he wore,
> No such narrow prejudices can *he* know whom Love possesses—
> Whom one spark of Freedom blesses. Do not spurn him from thy door
>   Lest Love enter nevermore![9]

The Poe scholar Paul Lewis writes astutely, "Poe's willingness to assist Winslow suggests that—though he expressed frustration with some abolitionist arguments—he was open to both Winslow's love-based repudiation of racial bias and her alternative reading of 'what the ominous bird of yore / Meant in croaking "Nevermore."'"[10] Poe's attention to Winslow's poem may indicate a degree of sympathy for the Black man.

Poe continued to work on his analysis of the nature of the universe, and by sometime in March it was ready for transcription. Eliza Kurtz Starr, chosen from almost one hundred applicants for a position as amanuensis (for the sake of her clear handwriting), copied the manuscript at the Fordham cottage.[11]

Poe must have still appreciated John H. Hopkins Jr.'s thoughtful review of his talk "The Universe," for on March 30 he asked Marie Louise Shew to invite Hopkins to visit him in Fordham: "When you see Mr. Hopkins I wish you would say to him that I would take it as an especial favor if he would pay me a visit at Fordham next Sunday. I have something to communicate to him *of the highest importance,* and about which I need his advice. Won't you get him to come—& come with him to show him the way?" (O 2:662). Clearly, Shew had shown Poe the way through Virginia's illness and death and his own illness and sorrow. And clearly Hopkins had bolstered Poe in the understanding review. But even as Poe could be sustained by both Shew and Hopkins, he could also be utterly crushed.

Shew and Hopkins did visit Poe in Fordham—perhaps on the day that he had specified, Sunday, April 2. Hopkins later recalled for Shew (then Marie Louise Shew Houghton) his discussion with Poe about the February 3 lecture, which Poe was "thinking of printing . . . in book form." Hopkins wrote:

> I did all I could to persuade him to omit the bold declaration of Pantheism at the close, which was not necessary to the completeness or beauty of the lecture. But I soon found that *that* was the dearest part of the whole to him; and we got into quite a discussion on the subject of Pantheism. For some time his tone and manner were very quiet, though slowly changing as we went on; until at last, a look of scornful pride worthy of Milton's Satan flashed over his pale, delicate face & broad brow, and a strange thrill nerved and dilated for an instant his slight figure, as he exclaimed, "My whole nature utterly *revolts* at the idea that there is any Being in the Universe superior to *myself!*"[12]

Here was the crux of the problem. Poe was relying on an inner sense, beyond standard religious precept or empirical demonstration. He had termed it in "Tamerlane" "self supremacy" (M 1:32). Yet he was suggesting in *Eureka* not solely the felt "self supremacy" of his own soul but also that of everyone's soul. He wrote eventually in the published book,

> No thinking being lives who, at some luminous point of his life of thought, has not felt himself lost amid the surges of futile efforts at understanding, or believing, that anything exists *greater than his own soul*. The utter impossibility of any one's soul feeling itself inferior to another; the intense, overwhelming dissatisfaction and rebellion at the thought;—these, with the omniprevalent aspirations at perfection, are

but the spiritual, coincident with the material, struggles towards the original Unity—are, to my mind at least, a species of proof far surpassing what Man terms demonstration, that no one soul *is* inferior to another—that nothing is, or can be, superior to any one soul—that each soul is, in part, its own God. (L1 104)

This sounds more like Walt Whitman than Satan. But, in any case, the theology student Hopkins considered Poe's views pantheistic and heretical—perhaps much as John Winthrop of the Massachusetts Bay Colony had once objected to the "inner light" of Anne Hutchinson and John Wheelwright—and he eventually felt compelled to break with Poe and to encourage Marie Louise Shew to do the same. Hopkins would not betray traditional religious views. But Poe would not betray his private sense of the essence of man.

It was probably toward the end of April 1848 that a critical meeting took place at a publisher's office on Broadway. Years later, George P. Putnam remembered the Saturday afternoon visit by "a gentleman with a somewhat nervous and excited manner" who wished to speak on a matter "of the highest importance." Edgar Allan Poe had come to propose the publication of *Eureka*. Putnam recounted, a touch ironically, Poe's grand contentions: "Newton's discovery of gravitation was a mere incident compared to the discoveries revealed in this book. It would at once command such universal and intense attention that the publisher might give up all other enterprises, and make this one book the business of his lifetime. An edition of fifty thousand copies might be sufficient to begin with, but it would be but a small beginning. No other scientific event in the history of the world approached in importance the original developments of this book." Fixed by Poe's gaze, which he later compared to that of the Ancient Mariner, Putnam was "really impressed but not overcome." He offered Poe a loan and the assurance of a determination by Monday. Whether he then rose a sadder and a wiser man we do not know, but Putnam did commit to publishing five hundred copies of Poe's cosmology.[13]

Unfortunately, though Poe had succeeded with his proposal, he would succumb to twin foes, alcohol and Rufus Wilmot Griswold. Apparently he had gone to secure payment from a periodical and then to have dinner with the untrustworthy reverend. Marie Louise Shew recalled, "The only time I ever knew of his [Poe's] being intoxicated during the years I knew him, *was after dining with Mr. Griswold,* in an Eating house. whatever was given him, he became insane and unmanageable and he told the servant who tried to turn him out, (after the departure of this man, or fiend, Griswold) that his friends lived at 47 Bond St." Informed of the disturbance, Shew asked Roland S. Houghton (her future husband) and John H. Hopkins Jr. to help out. They found Poe under the influence—"crazy-drunk in the hands of the police," according to Hopkins. Houghton and Hopkins brought Poe back safely to Fordham to Maria Clemm. Shew commented, "I afterwards learned the circumstances of his [Poe's] condition, during an illness which followed, and altho Mrs. Clemm knew it was true, she over looked this in Griswold, thinking it was unintentional, but I always believed (*and so said Mr. Poe*) that he would have been home with his hard-earned money *but for Griswold*." We are left to infer that somehow Griswold encouraged or facilitated Poe's partaking of what the envious anthologist knew would lead to catastrophe. The situation seems to have involved Griswold's enabling disguised as camaraderie.[14] Shew reported that though Poe had pledged to Maria Clemm to be civil to Griswold, "Mr. Poe told me clearly that Griswold was his enemy," that when he was with Griswold he "always felt he was in the presence of a viper, who would sting him the first chance he got."[15]

Soon thereafter, it was to 47 Bond Street that Poe turned again, not this time inebriated and infuriated but, rather, languid and dull. Shew remembered, "Mr. Poe wrote the Bells at my house. He came in and said, 'Marie Louise, I have to write a poem. I have no feeling, no sentiment, no inspiration.'" She offered him tea in the conservatory and then a piece of paper. The room, situated close to a church, had open windows. A bell sounded, which Shew thought "very jolly and sharp," but Poe responded, "I so dislike the noise of bells tonight. I cannot write. I have no subject. I am exhausted."

And Marie Louise Shew again showed the way. He watched her write, with his pen, "The Bells. By E. A. Poe." And then she introduced lines, and he completed them—first about "the little silver bells," then "The heavy iron bells." With deftness and sensitivity, she roused his dormant creativity. The seventeen-line poem—only the first version of the work—read:

> The bells!—ah, the bells!
> The little silver bells!
> How fairy-like a melody there floats
>   From their throats—
>   From their merry little throats—
>   From the silver, tinkling throats
> Of the bells, bells, bells—
> Of the bells!

> The bells!—ah, the bells!
> The heavy iron bells!
> How horrible a monody there floats
>   From their throats—
>   From their deep-toned throats—
>   From their melancholy throats!
>   How I shudder at the notes
> Of the bells, bells, bells—
> Of the bells! (M 1:434)

Completing the poem, the enlivened Poe told Marie Louise, "What a pity you had not been educated. You are a genius. You can wake the dead." Poe then slept at her house for twelve hours.[16]

Shew, who had formerly taken Poe to see Dr. Valentine Mott, now called in her neighbor Dr. John W. Francis, who stated that Poe had heart disease. (Poe later denied this, claiming he had a "[l]ong–continued nervous disorder" [O 2:699].) She later drove Poe back home in her carriage.[17]

At this time, Poe was trying to heed her warning that he needed a woman "fond enough" to take care of him.[18] He corresponded with Jane Ermina Locke, of Lowell, Massachusetts, a mill town thirty miles northwest of Boston. In 1846, she had written a sympathetic poem about him, forwarded to him by Willis. Poe tried discreetly to determine if Locke were a widow (O 2:666). (She was not—she was married, with children.) His epistolary relationship with her would lead to her visiting him in Fordham and to his visiting her in Lowell, giving a lecture, and meeting Annie Richmond, whom he would truly love.

In May, Poe's book manuscript was steadily making its way closer to publication. Writing to Poe on May 15, Hopkins stated that he had been "glancing over" the manuscript at Putnam's (presumably that transcribed by Eliza Kurtz Starr in March and April). He criticized the argument and promised to attack the section that he considered pantheistic if Poe did not delete it. (Poe kept it, and Hopkins did attack.) Writing to Locke on May 19, Poe mentioned that he was involved in "the proof-reading of a work of scientific detail" (O 2:665). On May 22, he signed a contract with Putnam for *Eureka*, which promised 10 percent royalties once the publisher's expenses were recouped. On the following day, he signed for an advance or loan from Putnam of fourteen dollars, promising not to ask for another advance; the document was countersigned by Maria Clemm and Marie Louise Shew. (Putnam later contended that when the text of the book was in type, Poe, who was unhappy with having had his request for an additional advance denied, threatened to offer the work to another publisher.) Word of the approaching publication of the book was getting out: M. Harbin Andrews wrote on May 28, in the first issue of *The Empire Ladies and Gentleman's Magazine*, "Edgar A. Poe at present resides at Fordham, N.Y., where he enjoys his *otium cum dignatate* [leisure with dignity], as every worthy author should, amid buds and blossoms and those scenes of nature which call forth *poe*-tical; and philosophical associations. His last great effort—his 'Lecture on the Universe'—has been carefully revised, and, we understand, will be shortly published. It is, indeed, a magnificent prose poem, which should be possessed by the *literati* generally." A manicule at the left called attention to this generous advance encomium.[19]

Yet one former champion of Poe's had become an adversary. The close of *Eureka,* stating that the "Heart Divine" is "*our own*" (L1 103), had earned Poe the hostility of Hopkins, who shared his concern with Shew, eventually persuading her to relinquish her friendship with Poe. She wrote him a letter declaring an end to their relationship. Poe stated in his June 1848 reply that he had known he was losing her, recalled her distant manner during her recent visit to Fordham with Hopkins, and asked—futilely, he knew—"Why sacrifice your angelic prerogative for a commonplace nature? Why turn your soul from its true work for the desolate, to the thankless and miserly world!" The profundity of her aid to him is clear when he asked, "How can I believe in Providence when *you* look coldly upon me. Was it not you who renewed my hopes and faith in God? . . . & in humanity." Perhaps suggesting that he was learning from his pain, he asserted, "Why I was not a priest is a mystery, for I feel I am now a prophet." He consoled his consoler: "[Y]ou must know and *be assured,* of my *regret,* my *sorrow,* if aught I have ever written has hurt you! My *heart never wronged you!*" He compared her to the much-loved solace of his boyhood, Jane Stith Stanard. And he closed with restraint and appreciation, "I will try to overcome my grief for the sake of your unselfish care of me in the past, and in life or death, I am ever yours gratefully & devotedly" (O 2:677–79).[20] There is a noble resignation here.

Later, Marie Louise Shew—as Marie Louise Shew Houghton—confided to John H. Ingram her remorse for forsaking Poe: "Mr. Poe always treated me with respect and I was to him a friend in need, and a friend indeed, but he was so excentric [sic], and so unlike others, and I was also, that I had to define a position, I was bound to take, and it hurt his feelings, and after he was dead I deeply regretted my letter to him, as we all do, often to [sic] late."[21]

Poe predicted in his June letter to Shew (echoing her earlier warning), "[U]nless some true and tender and pure womanly love saves me, I shall hardly last a year longer, alone!" (O 2:678). He sought such love, reaching out to Sarah Helen Whitman in Providence and welcoming Jane Ermina Locke to Fordham.

Whitman was the subject of a conversation between Poe and Maria J. McIntosh, perhaps in May. Having responded to Whitman's "To Edgar A. Poe" by sending the published poem "To Helen" to the Providence poet in March—and enduring what he later termed to Whitman "an indefinable sorrow in your silence" (O 2:695)—he sent the unsigned, unpublished poem, the second "To Helen," to her in late May or early June. This work paid tribute to his first seeing her, "all in white," when he was walking in Providence with Frances Sargent Osgood in July 1845 (M 1:445). And he focused intently and intensely on her eyes—"They fill my soul with Beauty (which is Hope)" (M 1:446). He wrote the poem, he later asserted, with great love for her and a sense of the possibility of her love for him (O 2:695–96).[22]

Furthermore, having heard from Jane Ermina Locke and responded in May, he welcomed her to his home for a day in June. Earlier, when she received his letter, she wrote her second poem about him, "The True Poet." She would subsequently arrange for his lecture "The Poets and Poetry of America" in Lowell and serve as his hostess during his visit.[23]

And even as Poe earnestly sought "pure womanly love," he sought, as well, much-needed financial support. He appealed for a loan to the young writer Charles Astor Bristed (a grandson of John Jacob Astor). Bristed, associated with the *American Review*, had earlier provided Poe with money—ten dollars—through editor George H. Colton (O 2:617). Poe, in one of his "Marginalia" installments, had later faulted Bristed for his views on metrics, but he had also termed the young classicist "a gentleman, well known for his scholarship" (P 2:317). Poe had evidently once left his black-bordered calling card for Bristed, a neighbor of Shew's at 32 Bond Street, asking on the card, "Will Mr Bristed honor Mr Poe with a few minutes' private conversation?" Writing to Bristed on June 7, 1848 (in a letter delivered by Maria Clemm), Poe acknowledged Bristed's "former kindness" and stated that he was "desperately circumstanced—in very bitter distress of mind and body." He asked to borrow money so that he could travel to Richmond to see someone: "My last hope of extricating myself from the difficulties which are pressing me to death, is in going personally to a distant connexion [*sic*] near Richmond, Va, and endeavoring to interest him in my behalf" (O 2:669). That "distant connexion near

Richmond, Va" was doubtless none other than John H. Mackenzie. Poe may not have seen him since Mackenzie's visit to Philadelphia in 1841, and he certainly had not been to Mackenzie's farm near Richmond, Darby Town, since 1836 or early 1837. But clearly Maria Clemm would have remembered well Mackenzie's devotion to Poe and might have encouraged this journey back, to see him. We may understand that, for Poe, his old friend from boyhood and youth would seem his "last hope." And, indeed, Poe would soon visit Mackenzie at Darby Town.[24]

Still in Fordham, he awaited publication of *Eureka,* due out by June 15.[25] He inquired of Anna Blackwell about Mrs. Whitman, submitted the second "To Helen" to the *Union Magazine,* and praised Sarah Anna Lewis for her *Child of the Sea* (O 2:671–77). A later story, "Landor's Cottage," suggests that Poe at this time may have made a walking tour of northern counties, near the Hudson River (M 3:1328).

And Jane Ermina Locke visited Poe. She would soon organize Poe's July 10 talk in Lowell. While there, Poe stayed with Jane and her husband John at Wamesit Cottage near the Concord River. She was, we are informed by Annie Richmond, "deeply in love with Mr. Poe."[26] Indeed, her August poem "Ermina's Tale" declares "I felt as in the presence of a god!" But the encounter was followed by her "deep despair."[27] Critically for Poe, Jane Ermina Locke introduced him to Annie Richmond—Nancy Locke Heywood Richmond, the wife of Charles B. Richmond.[28]

The Lowell talk was a great success. In the upstairs lecture hall of the new Wentworth Building, Poe spoke on Monday, July 11, about "The Poets and Poetry of America." Of course, he had given a lecture on American poetry in Philadelphia, Wilmington, Newark, Baltimore, Reading, and New York between 1843 and 1845. (It had even been called the "Poets and Poetry of America" in Reading and New York.)[29] In Lowell he treated, among other writers, Sarah Anna Lewis, Anne Lynch, Frances Sargent Osgood, and Sarah Helen Whitman. He evidently again critiqued the puffing system. And he presumably read "The Raven," as advance notices said that he would. The audience was engaged—a review stated that the lecture "was deservedly listened to with much attention."[30] Annie Richmond's brother Bardwell Heywood wrote of the talk, "'Twas a brilliant affair in the course of which he recited specimens of the best poetry America ever produced, paying a passing tribute to their respective authors." Annie Richmond's sister Susan H. Heywood remembered, "Everything was rendered with pure intonation and perfect enunciation, marked attention being paid to the rhythm. He almost *sang* the more musical versifications. I recall more perfectly than anything else the undulations of his smooth baritone voice as he recited the opening lines of Byron's 'Bride of Abydos,'—'Know ye the land where the cypress and myrtle / Are emblems of deeds that are done in their clime,'—measuring the dactylic movement perfectly as if he were scanning it. The effect was very pleasing." And she commented, "His manner was quiet and grave."[31]

That evening and the following day, Poe spent time at the home of the Richmonds. Bardwell Heywood wrote to fellow teacher Annie Sawyer, on October 2, that Poe had recounted his life story. Despite occasional inaccuracies (whether of Poe's telling or Heywood's remembering or both), the remembered narrative is significant. Of greatest interest is Heywood's recollection of Poe speaking about Virginia—that they initially shared "a brotherly and sisterly affection" and that after their marriage "he did not for two years assume the position of husband." Heywood recalled of Poe, "He spoke of his wife in a most eloquent and touching manner, the tears running down his cheeks in torrents." Memory must have quickened Poe's grief. And Heywood added, "Spoke of her as beautiful beyond description, as lovely beyond conception, and my sister [Annie Richmond], who has since visited his mother [his mother-in-law Maria Clemm] in N.Y., says she (Virginia) is represented as being almost an angel on earth."[32]

Poe was home at Fordham by Friday, July 14, when he wrote a letter to Thomas H. Chivers, inviting him to visit and not mentioning *Eureka*. Poe noted his having come back from Lowell and his planning to leave for Richmond on Monday, July 17 (O 2:681). Review copies of the delayed book seem to have been released, but the official publication date was now July 15.[33] On this day, Poe sent copies of the book to Mary Osborne, of Fordham, and Mary McIntosh, of Providence (O 2:682). The slim duodecimo was elegant and dignified.

The title page announces "EUREKA: A PROSE POEM. BY EDGAR A. POE." The dedication, "with very profound respect," is to the distinguished cosmologist Alexander von Humboldt. And the "Preface" intimates the earnestness of the author:

> To the few who love me and whom I love—to those who feel rather than to those who think—to the dreamers and those who put faith in dreams as in the only realities—I offer this Book of Truths, not in its character of Truth-Teller, but for the Beauty that abounds in its Truth; constituting it true. To these I present the composition as an Art-Product alone:—let us say as a Romance; or, if I be not urging too lofty a claim, as a Poem.

> *What I here propound is true:*—therefore it cannot die:—or if by any means it be now trodden down so that it die, it will "rise again to the Life Everlasting."
>
> Nevertheless it is as a Poem only that I wish this work to be judged after I am dead.
>
> E. A. P. (L1 5)[34]

The subject of Poe's book is science, but the subtext is soul.

"Eureka: An Essay on the Material and Spiritual Universe" (L1 7) offers no chapters, but there are discernible sections—I will identify fifteen. Poe writes self-reflectively later in the work, "If then I seem to step somewhat too discursively from point to point of my topic, let me suggest that I do so in the hope of thus the better keeping unbroken that chain of *graduated impression* by which alone the intellect of Man can expect to encompass the grandeurs of which I speak, and, in their majestic totality, to comprehend them" (L1 78).

The introduction (paragraphs 1–10) asserts his thesis: "*In the Original Unity of the First Thing lies the Secondary Cause of All Things, with the Germ of their Inevitable Annihilation*" (L1 7). Attentive to a unique, all-inclusive "individual impression," he offers an image of our spinning at the top of Mount Aetna—"a mental gyration on the heel" (L1 7–8) that permits a single effect, comprehensive, presumably to be provided by this book. Poe then proceeds to an imagined letter from the year 2848 (pars. 11–25)—drawing from the yet-to-be-published "Mellonta Tauta"—in which one Pundita mocks the approaches of deduction and induction, advocating "seemingly intuitive *leaps*": For centuries, "[n]o man dared utter a truth for which he felt himself indebted to his soul alone" (L1 10). She speaks for "the Soul which loves nothing so well as to soar in those regions of illimitable intuition which are utterly incognizant of '*path*'" (L1 14). And she mentions the value of "*Consistency*" as indicative of "*Truth*" (L1 15). She imagines Johannes Kepler saying of "the machinery of the Universe," "I grasped it with *my soul*—I reached it through mere dint of *intuition*" (L1 15). Pundita then pokes fun at an idea that Poe later accepts—that intuition results from a combination of unseen deductions and inductions (L1 15–16; see also L1 22 and O 2:688–89).

Now Poe elaborates two reverse sections—one of these concerning deduction, from the general to the specific, from the intuited Simplicity of the Godhead to the particle (pars. 26–57); the other concerning induction, from the specific to the general, from the Gravity of Earth to the intuited

Unity of all (pars. 60–73). Poe is bolstered by his habit of mind, reversibility, so evident in his work in terms of action, language, expectation, and interpretation.[35]

Poe lays out his cosmic narrative in these two sections. Relying on intuition, he declares that God created from nothing *"Simplicity"* (L1 22)—a particle. Furthermore, that particle, diffused into space, formed the Universe. When the diffusion was complete, the varied atoms accumulated into masses, repelled from each other by electricity (an intuited spiritual force). But the completed Divine Action will ultimately yield to the inevitable reaction—the return of Matter to Divine Oneness again. Attraction (Gravity) and Repulsion (Electricity) are the great forces animating the dynamic. Poe's discussion of Gravity—the attraction of every atom to every other atom—is born of "unthoughtlike thoughts—soul reveries" (L1 33). The diffused atoms were, after all, once One. Poe returns us, then, to his original intuitions of Simplicity and Unity.

Poe clarifies that he offers an interpretation of *"Godhead"* not *"in itself,"* but in its design (L1 21; see also O 2:690). Although the narrator of the tale "The Imp of the Perverse" challenges inferences about God's design based on human characteristics (M 3:1219–20), Poe himself, in his criticism, repeatedly argues for God's design, evident in human reverence and the sense of the beautiful, as well as in sexual differences and the limits of human progress. He also infers God's design from biblical prophecy.[36] And he does give a hint of his direction in *Eureka* when he quotes Jacob Friedrich Bielfeld, "We know absolutely *nothing* of the nature or essence of God—in order to comprehend what he is, we should have to be God ourselves" (L1 21). Poe wonders "if this our present ignorance of the Deity is an ignorance to which the soul is *everlastingly* condemned" (L1 22).

He offers a brief review (pars. 74–79) and then moves on to the phenomenon of radiation, which permits the diffusion of the original particle (pars. 80–111). Relying on the analogy of radiation from the center of a hollow glass sphere, Poe argues for intermittent radiation, of a finite duration, yielding evenly distributed atoms. This process allows for the completion of the Divine Act and the ultimate reaction, Gravity—the return to Unity. Poe refutes opposing views (pars. 112–26) and summarizes (pars. 127–33), arguing for the parallel development of Gravity and Electricity and concluding, "Thus the two Principles Proper, *Attraction* and *Repulsion*—the Material and the Spiritual—accompany each other, in the strictest fellowship, forever. Thus *The Body and The Soul walk hand in hand*" (L1 54, repeated L1 63).

He then addresses specifically our solar system (pars. 134–73). Poe draws on and modifies the "Nebular Hypothesis" of Pierre Simon Laplace, discussing the spinning off of the planets from the condensing Sun and the rings and moons from the condensing planets. He infers an analogy between the multiple circles of Laplace's theory and the multiple circles of his own theory of radiation. He then contends that the solar system is just one instance that makes evident the divine design, the fullest interrelatedness of diverse matter.

Poe proceeds in his discussion to the Galaxy, the Milky Way (with some debt to Humboldt's *Cosmos*), and then to the Universe, and he eventually conjectures that there may be other universes, each of which has its own God, its own origin, and its own laws (pars. 174–88). In the course of his larger argument, he considers the fact that the sky is not completely illuminated (Olbers' Paradox), noting his conviction that the stars are not limitless and the possibility that some are so far away that their light has not yet reached Earth.

At this point, Poe expands upon expanse—the vast distances of the Universe (pars. 189–213). He borrows, on occasion, from Thomas Dick's *Christian Philosopher*. Poe progresses from the 237,000 miles from Earth to the moon, to the 28 hundred million miles from the Sun to Neptune, to the 61 trillion miles from the Earth to the star 61 Cygni. He is intimating sublimity, concluding, "In a word, the events which we behold now—at this moment—in those worlds [distant nebulae]—are the identical events which interested their inhabitants *ten hundred thousand centuries ago*. In intervals—in distances such as this suggestion forces upon the *soul*—rather than upon the mind—we find, at length, a fitting climax to all hitherto frivolous considerations of *quantity*" (L1 87). The immensity of space evidently speaks poetically to the soul.

Poe turns briefly to the "the complete *mutuality* of adaptation" (L1 88), "an absolute *reciprocity of adaptation*" (L1 89), suggesting the apparent reversibility of cause and effect in Divine design (as opposed to in human design) (pars. 214–18). He relies here on one of his November 1844 marginalia (P 2:127–28; see also H 13:44–46). Then, though acknowledging the critical importance of analogy and symmetry, he nonetheless resists the idea, expressed by Johann Heinrich von Mädler, of a central star in the universe (pars. 219–45). Accordingly, Poe distinguishes between what he terms "the symmetry of mere surface" and the more profound "symmetry of *principles*" (L1 99)—exemplified by the Original Unity diffusing to heterogeneity and returning to Original Unity again.

Poe reiterates in his penultimate section (pars. 246–54) his controlling narrative, from past through present and future, focusing on "the great End," "[t]he inevitable catastrophe" (L1 100). Developing the idea of the "absolute *reciprocity of adaptation*" (L1 101), he infers that the very Electricity—here termed a "spiritual Ether" (L1 101)—whose force of repulsion served to prevent the immediate collapse of matter is itself served by that matter, which eventually may attain *"Thought,"* "Conscious Intelligence" (L1 101). And he describes matter's return to Unity, now immaterial and etherless—he writes, "God would remain all in all" (L1 101, 103).

And so begins Poe's great lyrical conclusion to *Eureka,* in which the soul reverie that underlies the work most powerfully emerges (pars. 255–66). Poe considers the possibility—his wish—that the dynamic of Divine creation and return to Original Unity will recur endlessly, "that the processes we have here ventured to contemplate will be renewed forever, and forever, and forever; a novel Universe swelling into existence, and then subsiding into nothingness, at every throb of the Heart Divine." And then he adds (regardless of the objection of John H. Hopkins Jr.), "And now—this Heart Divine—what is it? *It is our own*" (L1 103).

It is Poe himself who speaks now, not Poe mediated through science. He tells of "spiritual shadows," *"Memories* of a Destiny more vast—very distant in the by-gone time, and infinitely awful" (L1 103). In our youth, he writes, we feel ourselves to exist forever, from the beginning to the end of time. This is taken for granted, challenged only with the coming of "a conventional World Reason" (L1 104), which calls into question our sense of eternal existence. And here he offers the aforementioned assertion of the felt supremacy of man's soul—evidence, he believes, that God exists in us. He adds that "the regathering of this diffused Matter and Spirit will be but the re-constitution of the *purely Spiritual* and Individual God" (L1 104). Striving, as embodiments of God, for greater joy—however unsuccessfully—we may understand the resulting sorrow, part of God's expansion and contraction, the Divine narrative in which we have a part.

The final two paragraphs—Poe's final ascent—articulate memories that endure even until manhood. These memories concern a Divine Being who, though unable to increase his own joy, may vary it through his diffusion of his divinity through all matter, animate and inanimate, and his eventual contraction again. The happiness of all is the happiness of this Divine Being. We enjoy a sense of our own identity, as well as our identity with God. Inevitably, over eons, our self-identity will fade, and our divine identity will intensify. Poe closes, "Think that the sense of individual identity will be gradually merged in the general consciousness—that Man, for example, ceasing imperceptibly to feel himself Man, will at length attain that awfully triumphant epoch when he shall recognize his existence as that of Jehovah. In the meantime bear in mind that all is Life—Life—Life within Life—the less within the greater, and all within the *Spirit Divine*" (L1 106).

We have been here before. The ecstatic conclusion, involving union with the Divine, was present in the climax of *The Narrative of Arthur Gordon Pym*, ten years earlier. Poe has parallelled his covertly Christian narrative with a scientific and spiritual one. In *Pym,* the protagonist's loss of union with his mother and his brother and his eventual recovery of that union according to Christian eschatology, at the time of the wedding of Christ and his Church, finds a correspondence here in the loss of Original Unity and the eventual return to that Unity, the divine dynamic in which, according to Poe, we all participate. In both cases, we have "the symmetry of *principles*" that Poe has extolled (L1:99). Poe has offered a learned treatise in *Eureka,* a series of abstractions, which, in their larger contours, recall his highly personal tale. And hints of the original may be inferred in such language as "brotherhood" and "common parentage" (L1 33), as well as "brothers" (L1 86) and "lost parent" (L1 34). Poe's two great master narratives are, I would argue, in their essence, resonant—themselves brothers.

We may also reach backward to an 1829 Poe poem, later titled "Sonnet" and "Sonnet—To Science," in which the speaker asks Science rhetorically about the attitude of the poet, "How should he love thee—or how deem thee wise / Who wouldst not leave him, in his wandering, / To seek for treasure in the jewell'd skies / Albeit, he soar with an undaunted wing?"[37] Poe echoes this in an aforementioned passage in the Pundita section of *Eureka,* "[T]he Soul . . . loves nothing so well as to soar in those regions of illimitable intuition which are utterly incognizant of '*path*'" (L1 14). The soaring soul is evident in some of Poe's greatest works, including *Pym* and *Eureka*. An encoded Christianity, in the novel, and far-reaching science, in the cosmology, are the mediums through which that soul ascends.

The conclusions of *Pym* and *Eureka* offer consolation, and the consolation of the latter is emphasized in Poe's 1849 penciled note in the Hurst-Wakeman copy (in the Susan Jaffe Tane Collection): "The pain of the consideration that we shall lose our individual identity, ceases at once when we further reflect that the process, as above described, is, neither more nor less than that of the absorption, by each individual intelligence, of all other intelligences (that is, of the Universe) into its own. That God may be all in all, *each* must become God" (L1 106).

The contemporary reviews of *Eureka*, predictably mixed, included the expected assessment by John H. Hopkins Jr., in the *Literary World*, "All this is extraordinary nonsense, if not blasphemy, and it may very possibly be *both*," and the unexpected appreciation by an unknown critic of the *New York Daily Tribune*, "The tenacity with which he [Poe] pursues the subject along the farthest brink of finite knowledge, and the daring with which he throws aside all previous systems of philosophers and theologians, constitute the chief merit of the book." It was probably Epes Sargent who alleged, in the *Boston Evening Transcript*, that in reading the preface, "the knowing reader, if he be one of the vulgar, will be apt to reply by placing his forefinger on the side of his nose, and ejaculating humph!" And it was Poe's enemy Thomas Dunn English who imagined in the *John-Donkey* that the "ponderosity" of copies of *Eureka* had destroyed the shelves of Wiley and Putnam and that the volumes were sought by the Canal Bank of Albany as "dead-weight.'" Still, Freeman Hunt in his *Merchant's Magazine* praised the work fulsomely, "As a work of the imagination, it teems with the highest beauty of view and glorious thought." And it was probably Poe's friend Henry B. Hirst who wrote, in a previously uncollected review from Philadelphia's *Illustrated Monthly Courier*, that, although the validity of Poe's argument may be determined only in the afterlife, "The subject . . . contains an immensity of interest, and Mr. Poe has treated it in a bold, logical, and mathematical manner. He has urged many strange things, strange because new, things which will seize at once upon the imagination, and perhaps do a world of philosophic good. We commend this very original work to general perusal."[38]

With *Eureka* published—and with or without assistance from Charles Astor Bristed—Poe finally made his way to Richmond, perhaps on July 17, as he had planned (O 2:681). He would stay for about seven weeks, welcomed by John H. Mackenzie and his family. When Poe wrote to Maria Clemm on August 5, "I am still out at John's—although I have been to Mrs. M's & am going back in a day or two to stay some time" (O 2:683), he was referring to the two Richmond-area Mackenzie homes, Darby Town and Duncan Lodge.

Poe's return to Darby Town, John H. Mackenzie's farm seven miles south of Richmond, must have been, at least in part, bittersweet: this had been the site of Virginia's greatest happiness, and she was gone. The girls who had accompanied Edgar and Virginia on their joyous expeditions and who would have remembered—Louisa's cousins Mary, Ann, and Eliza—had grown up, married, and moved away.[39] But John was still there and still Poe's warm friend. And John's wife Louisa would have been gracious and amiable—Poe wrote of her to Maria Clemm, "I think she is the sweetest creature in the world and makes John the best of wives. She is hardly changed in the least. You know how often I have spoken to you of her heavenly smile" (O 2:683). Surely Poe remembered that the only child of John and Louisa, who had died in infancy, had been named Edgar Poe Mackenzie.

The 193-acre farm, in July and August, would have had full and abundant crops—perhaps the herd grass and clover, chard, grapes, and strawberries described in a later year. There would have been horses and sheep, cows and pigs, and a variety of fowls. The farm was managed by Louisa and her mother, Mary Lanier, with the assistance of the overseer named Andrews. (John worked in the city in the tobacco warehouse.)[40]

Clearly, the hard work of the farm was done by enslaved labor. According to tax records, John H. Mackenzie "owned" eleven slaves at this time. We may wonder if Poe believed that they were also part of the "Heart Divine." As a child of the antebellum South, Poe was doubtless, in the aforementioned phrase of Terence Whalen, "an average racist." But we may consider that Poe had written in his Drake-Halleck review in the April 1836 *Southern Literary Messenger* that the instinct of veneration "becomes perverted from its principal purpose [veneration of God], and although, swerving from that purpose, it serves to modify the relations of human society—the relations of father and child, of master and slave, of the ruler and the ruled" (P 5:165). Poe certainly knew the perversion of the instinct of veneration in the relation of father and child. Perhaps he could see it in the relation of the Mackenzies and those they enslaved. We do not know. We do know, however, that the mantelpiece at the Darby Town farm, depicting the drowning of Pharoah's host, ironically anticipated the family's eventual fall. Their slaves—not they—would prove to be the Israelites.[41]

Nearly a mile west of Richmond, out on Broad Street (H Street) to Turnpike Road, close to the recently founded Richmond College, was the other Mackenzie home, Duncan Lodge. Poe saw it for the first time on this visit— the stately two-story brick house had been built in 1843. It was set on twenty-eight acres, which offered a stream near one corner, and a variety of fruit trees near the house. The building itself was grand—fifty feet by forty feet, with sixteen rooms (counting the garret). The interior featured elegant Empire furniture and a variety of paintings, including a portrait of the much-beloved Mary Gallego, who had died in the 1811 Richmond Theater fire.[42]

This was the house of John's mother, Jane Scott Mackenzie, then sixty-five. In 1811, with Frances Allan, she had visited the dying Eliza Poe and agreed to take her baby daughter Rosalie; Poe's sister still lived with Mrs. Mackenzie. Also living there were John's surviving siblings: Tom (lately graduated from Thomas Jefferson Medical College in Philadelphia), Dick, and Martha ("Mat," soon to be married to William P. Byrd). John's sister Mary had died in childbirth, with her infant, four years earlier, but her husband, Caleb Jones, was also at Duncan Lodge. Poe, Caleb Jones, and other men evidently played leapfrog outside the Mackenzie home. (Unlike the slender Poe, the hefty Jones took a fall.)

Flora Lapham Mack, who would be born to Louisa's cousin Mary Mattox Lapham in 1850 and who would know the Mackenzies all her life, wrote to her distant cousin William Lanier Washington in 1909 concerning an article in an issue of the *Richmond Times* that she had sent him, "You of course noticed Duncan Lodge and saw what a beautiful house it was when the Mackenzies were living there on their heyday of fortune. Such a joyous happy generous family as they were and then Edgar was a welcome and honored guest always and Rose a daughter of the house." There is even a story that, in the summer—perhaps in 1848, perhaps in 1849, perhaps both—Poe would write at a round table in the center hall of Duncan Lodge, enjoying the breeze from the front door to the rear door.[43]

There were enslaved people at Duncan Lodge, too,[44] but another sort of breeze was distantly blowing, which would, a dozen years after Poe's death, become the prolonged gale of the Civil War.

One evening during the late summer of 1848, the "welcome and honored guest" offered the Mackenzie family and friends a private recitation. One who was there, Parke Vanparke, later provided a vivid reminiscence:

> [T]he great poet was in one of his "fine frenzies," and pacing the spacious hall back and forth, and repeating, at our request, some passages from his inimitable poetry. He repeated "Ulalume," as he alone could repeat it. The manner, the mellow voice, and rythmical [sic] cadences of the bard had, I noticed, a magical effect on the good Mrs. McKenzie. When he concluded, the lady wiped her eyes, and remarked, rather upbraidingly, "Mr. Poe, why *don't* you write so that any body can understand you?" The poet wheeled his fine, poetical person upon his heel, directly facing the lady, stopped short, and with an expression of great gravity on his beautiful face, remarked, "Madam, I make it a special point—a *very* special point, to write so that *any body cannot* understand me."

Poe was protecting his poetic privilege. Yet there may have been those there who did understand—perhaps Rosalie, perhaps John if he were visiting—that, through his lyric opacity, Poe was mourning his lost wife, Virginia. Even Jane Scott Mackenzie, who evidently did not know the meaning of the poem, still knew enough to cry.[45]

Poe gave other private readings in Richmond that summer. Jane Clark later remembered that she had met him at the Mackenzies. She was then thought to be like Virginia, and, she commented, "It may have been that that fact made him my friend." He visited her frequently at the Park House, across from Capitol Square—"daily, sometimes two or three times a day." She noted, "He came there as he said to rest." Perhaps he was on his way to Darby Town, south, or Duncan Lodge, west, or visiting the office of the *Southern Literary Messenger* or the *Richmond Whig*. If there were others present, he would often recite poetry—sometimes his own work. On one occasion, he visited with Rosalie and "one or two of the Mackenzies," and by the light of an astral lamp in an otherwise darkened room, with a few others gathered as well, he read "The Raven." Mrs. Clark recalled, "Poe had a wonderful voice, rich, mellow and sweet. He read that piece in a sort of rapt monotone."[46]

And she offered insight into her old friend: "They say he was morbid and conceited. I don't know. Why do they quarrel with a man's nature? If he was morbid, he hurt mostly himself, and himself suffered most. I do not think his conceit, if conceit it was, had in it contempt of his kind. It was more a defiant effort to be something—a justification of himself to his inner self—and a consciousness of weakness."[47] It is Poe's "defiant effort to be something" that seems so touching even all these years later, especially given his "consciousness of weakness."

Meanwhile, he was waiting. He was waiting for a response to the manuscript poem he had sent back in late May or early June to Sarah Helen Whitman. But she did not reply. He later confided to her, "Oh God! how long—*how long* I waited *in vain*—hoping against Hope—until at length I became possessed with a spirit far sterner—far more reckless than Despair" (O 2:696).

Poe apparently did see another, the girl he had courted in his youth, Elmira Royster, now the wealthy widow Elmira Royster Shelton. Sarah Helen Whitman wrote to Julia Deane Freeman in 1859 and to Richard H. Stoddard in 1872 that Poe visited Elmira Shelton in the summer of 1848 and was "received with great kindness." Whitman also wrote to Maria Clemm in 1859 about her conversation with Poe in the fall of 1848: "He spoke of having thought of renewing with her [Elmira Shelton] an earlier attachment previous to visiting Providence, etc. etc. But at that time I think he told Mr. Pabodie [a friend of Whitman's] that the years of their separation had greatly changed the tastes & idiosyncrasies of both and that there seemed but little chance of happiness for either in a renewal of their earlier relations" (H 17:424). Despite his reservations, however, he was evidently considering courting her again.[48]

The warm fellowship of the Mackenzies and their friends for Poe was firm, but there was much that was tentative about his life. Personally, there was not only the receptive Elmira Shelton and the unresponding Sarah Helen Whitman, but also the unattainable (married) Annie Richmond, whom he had met in Lowell in July. Poe sought a woman in his life, but who it might be was unclear. Professionally, he was still not able to support himself and Maria Clemm adequately through his writing. And his most cherished idea, the prospective literary magazine "The Stylus," ostensibly depended on his going on a lecture tour in the South and West to build his subscription list.[49] But, clearly, such a tour would be arduous and wearing and not guaranteed of success. Poe had much to worry about that summer in Richmond.

Poe had written to George W. Eveleth in February, "[T]he causes which maddened me to the drinking point are no more, and I am done drinking, forever" (O 2:648). Yet, as he had acknowledged to Joseph E. Snodgrass in 1841, he had been drinking in Richmond when he was editing the *Southern Literary Messenger* (O 1:263–64)—and this was well before Virginia became sick. Doubtless in Richmond in 1848, there was still "the temptation held out on all sides by the spirit of Southern conviviality" (O 1:263). And personal and professional uncertainties abounded. Poe was to be defeated again.

John R. Thompson, then editor of the *Southern Literary Messenger*, is our source for accounts of Poe's drinking at this time. He wrote a letter on October 17, stating that Poe had been "horribly drunk and discoursing 'Eureka' every night to the audiences of the Bar Rooms." Friends had been unsuccessful in their efforts to help him.[50] Thompson's two later recollections are not altogether consistent, however, and seem to blend events from 1848 and 1849. Poe was evidently on a binge in a disreputable area of Richmond, Rocketts, but Thompson failed to find him there. According to his 1849 account, Poe walked to the house of John H. Mackenzie (Darby Town) and reappeared the next day at the *Messenger* office with Mackenzie. But according to his 1860 account, Poe showed up at the *Messenger* office ten days later, by himself.[51] What is clear is that Poe had been on a spree again and had been holding forth at the taverns on the nature of the universe, revealing both mastery and an utter lack thereof. Thompson offered in his 1860 account his own considered judgment: "Poe was not what is called 'a regular drinker,' but he was what is worse, a most irregular one, the desire for stimulants seeming to seize him like an attack of madness which he was powerless to resist."[52] Perhaps this was what Poe meant by a spirit "far more reckless than Despair."

Poe's occasional drinking continued. Thompson, who had earlier accepted Poe's extended poetic treatise "The Rationale of Verse" and his review of Sarah Anna Lewis's *The Child of the Sea and Other Poems*, sought other contributions, but without success.[53] And presumably for some perceived insult—"probably," Thomas and Jackson suggest, "related to Poe's problems with alcohol and money"—Poe challenged the editor of the *Richmond Examiner*, John M. Daniel, to a duel. Fortunately, there was no satisfaction—the duel was never fought.[54]

Poe's impasse was finally resolved by a poem sent from the city of Providence. Sarah Helen Whitman, having been "gratified & charmed" by Maria J. McIntosh's report of Poe's comments about her, decided that she must seem "very ungracious" in not responding for two months to Poe's poem to her. So she wrote a two-stanza poem, a "gracious & playful acknowledgment" of his earlier poem, and sent the unsigned piece to him at Fordham.[55] Maria Clemm picked up the letter at the West-Farms Post Office and forwarded it to Poe in Richmond. The sign of understanding that Poe had been seeking lay in the final couplet of Whitman's poem, in a quotation from Poe's poem: "And, gazing on Night's starry cope, / I dwell with '*Beauty which is Hope.*'" And so—Poe finally knew that she knew that he was the author of the adoring "Lines to Helen."[56] This indication was what Poe later termed to her "some faint token ... giving me to understand that the source of the poem is known and its sentiment comprehended even if disapproved" (O 2:696). And perhaps, he must have wondered, it was not entirely disapproved.

In the late summer of 1848, about to leave on his lecture tour (O 2:696), Poe gave it up when he received Whitman's poem. He needed what he had termed in June "some true and tender and pure womanly love" that would save him (O 2:678). He needed a woman's consoling and embracing devotion to feel at ease in the world. He needed a forgiving communion, which was described so well in the Thomas Moore song that he loved so much—that he had repeatedly requested from Mary Starr—that he would praise and quote in his lecture, and later his essay, "The Poetic Principle"—"Come Rest in This Bosom":

Come, rest in this bosom, my own stricken deer,
Though the herd have fled from thee, thy home is still here;
Here still is the smile that no cloud can o'ercast,
And a heart and a hand all thy own to the last.

Oh! what was love made for, if 'tis not the same
Through joy and through torment, through glory and shame?
I know not, I ask not, if guilt's in that heart,
I but know that I love thee, whatever thou art.

Thou has called me thy angel in moments of bliss,
And thy angel I'll be, 'mid the horrors of this,—
Through the furnace, unshrinking, thy steps to pursue,
And shield thee, and save thee,—or perish there too! (L2 191)

Poe returned to New York and on September 5 sent a pretend request for an autograph to Sarah Helen Whitman (signing it Edward S. T. Grey).[57] He was trying to determine that she was indeed in Providence (O 2:687). If so, then he would go to her there. Perhaps, he must have imagined, she would be his angel.

And then there was also Annie Richmond...

23

"The Passionate Throbbings of My Heart"

1848-1849

IN LATE SEPTEMBER 1848, POE made his first of five visits to Sarah Helen Whitman, a widowed poet in Providence, bearing with him a letter of introduction from his acquaintance—Whitman's friend—Maria J. McIntosh.[1] This was the first time he actually met Whitman, whom he had so long imagined. His first impression, he later wrote to her, suggested "the existence of spiritual influences altogether out of the reach of the reason" (O 2:696).

He visited her two-story Benefit Street home, where she lived with her mother and sister, for three nights in a row, September 21, 22, and 23, and he later characterized his response to her as "all-Heavenly delight" (O 2:697). Also, he met her friends, including William J. Pabodie. Perhaps it was then, at the gathering of her friends at her house, that he embraced and kissed Whitman. During the day, he and she visited the Providence Athenaeum, where he acknowledged his authorship of "Ulalume," signing the poem in the December 1847 issue of the *American Review,* and they made their way to Swan Point Cemetery, where he declared his love and proposed marriage.[2]

It would seem likely that it was during this visit that he gave her the bound volume of *The Raven and Other Poems* and *Tales,* inscribed "To Mrs. Sarah Helen Whitman—from the most devoted of her friends," as well as two volumes of the *Broadway Journal,* with a number of pieces marked by Poe with a "P." He also showed her the manuscript of his July lecture in Lowell.[3] And he told her the story of his life. It may well have been on this visit that he read "Ulalume" aloud. She later wrote to John H. Ingram, "How I wish you could have heard Poe's voice! To have heard his reading of 'Ulalume' or 'The Bridal Ballad' is a never-to-be-forgotten memory!"[4]

Whitman commented tellingly about Poe, "There was often fervor & intensity, but always mingled with an almost supernatural calmness of eye & gesture."[5] She remembered his first visit, many years later, with clarity—evidently she had not been convinced that she could be the angel he needed: "During this visit he endeavored... to persuade me that my influence and my presence would have power to lift his life out of the torpor of despair which had weighed upon him, and give an inspiration to his genius, of which he had as yet given no token. Notwithstanding the eloquence with which he urged upon me his wishes and his hopes, I knew too well that I could not exercise over him the power which he ascribed to me."[6] She did not declare her love for him; rather, she promised to respond more fully in a letter, after he departed. Poe's ardent entreaty had met with a not-unsympathetic, but prudent, reluctance.

They parted on September 24; he went to the cemetery by himself on September 25—perhaps savoring the memory of their closeness—and left in the evening by train to New York City (O 2:713). His fraught courtship of Sarah Helen Whitman would last through the end of the year.

We know from Poe's October 1 letter to Whitman that she had objected to his blandishments, in her letter to him, on the basis of her changing appearance, her age, and her health. Refuting her concerns, Poe responded with a torrent of effusion, avowing his spiritual love, asserting his sense of the fatedness of their union, and imploring her own expression of love. He acknowledged his poverty and his "late errors and reckless excesses" but directed her to search "into the soul of my soul, and see if you can discover there one taint of an ignoble nature!" (O 2:698–99). His writing is literary, allusive, not surprising for one poet pleading with another. Clearly, Poe was writing for effect, seeking a victory, but this fact does not prove insincerity. Perhaps her family's affluence was already not without appeal, but this does not appear to have been the essence of the matter. He seems, at this time, to have been a fervent and intense suitor who believed in his own emotion. But he would change.

He added a postscript to his October 1 letter on October 3 (O 2:700), mailing the missive that day. It may have been in this letter's envelope that he included a lock of his hair.[7]

The response of Whitman to Poe's letter may be inferred from his subsequent letter to her, of October 18. She acknowledged his love but did not offer her own—she declared, rather, her admiration. She also quoted other people to the effect that he had "*no* principle—*no* moral sense" (O 2:707) and asked for his explanation of such a view.

Poe was, of course, very hurt. He conveys this in his October 18 letter, defending himself against the quoted accusation, asserting that "my soul is incapable of dishonor" but admitting "occasional follies and excesses which I bitterly lament, but to which I have been driven by intolerable sorrow." To demonstrate his sense of honor, he is not entirely truthful, as when he claims that he "married, for another's happiness, where I knew that no possibility of my own existed" (O 2:708). (His letter of August 29, 1835, makes clear his love for Virginia [O 1:102–4].) He explains others' enmity by reference to his success as a writer and his honesty as a critic. And returning to the pervasive theme of his unrequited love, he turns to the song that so warmly imparts what he seeks, "Come Rest in This Bosom."

Discussing this work in "The Poetic Principle," Poe writes, "There are two of the lines in which a sentiment is conveyed that embodies the *all in all* of the divine passion of love—a sentiment which, perhaps, has found its echo in more, and in more passionate, human hearts than any other single sentiment ever embodied in words" (L2 190). But he quotes the entire piece and does not identify the two lines. However, he does identify them in his October 18 letter to Whitman:

Tell me, *darling!* To *your* heart has any angel ever whispered that the very noblest lines in all human poetry are these—hackneyed though they be?

I know not—I ask not if guilt's in thy heart:—
I but know that *I love thee* whatever thou art.[8] (O 2:710)

He goes on, "When I first read your letter I could do nothing but shed tears, while I repeated, again and again, those glorious, those all-comprehensive verses, till I could scarcely hear my own voice for the passionate throbbings of my heart" (O 2:710). It is the forgiving, consoling expression of love—exemplified early on for Poe by Jane Stith Stanard—that he profoundly needs. Thomas Moore's song, simple and empathic, assuages the troubled Poe and yields relief.

Poe adds that his hopes for the realization of "divine dreams" with Whitman have vanished because of both her recent letter and his learning that she is "*comparatively rich while I am poor.*" This knowledge, he states, "opens between us *a gulf*—a gulf, alas! which the sorrow and the slander of the

World have rendered forever impassable—by *me*" (O 2:712). He seems to be inviting her to contradict his gloomy conclusion.

Even as Poe maintained his intense correspondence with Whitman at this time, he attended to professional matters. On October 18 also, he wrote to Eli Bowen, editor of the *Miner's Journal* of Pottstown, Pennsylvania (and formerly of the *Columbia Spy*), agreeing to contribute to his current publication (O 2:704–5), and he wrote to Thomas L. Dunnell, agreeing to lecture in Providence (O 2:706). Sometime in early or mid-October, he wrote to both Jane Locke and Annie Richmond, of Lowell, introducing to them Sarah Anna Lewis (O 2:715–17), a minor poet to whom he and Maria Clemm were grateful for financial support.[9] Poe would soon return to Lowell to give a lecture. En route, on October 20, he stopped in Providence to visit Whitman. He asked her "to forgive his waywardness & his reproaches" and to agree to delay her response to his proposal by a week and to write to him in Lowell.[10]

Soon after his October 20 visit in Providence, Poe again stayed with Jane Ermina Locke and her husband John at Wamesit Cottage in Lowell. But he did not give his lecture because of the focus at the time on the presidential election, to be held on November 7. Notably, the Illinois congressman Abraham Lincoln had visited Lowell on September 16 to campaign for the Whig candidate, Zachary Taylor, who did indeed win the contest.[11]

There was another more private contest then taking place—that between Jane Ermina Locke and Annie Richmond. According to Whitman, "Mrs. L[ocke] introduced him [Poe] to Mrs. R[ichmond], and the two ladies apparently vied with each other in attentions to their brilliant [visitor?]."[12] Poe later explained to Annie Richmond that the Lockes had insulted her and her husband Charles—they had claimed that "through their patronage alone, you were admitted into society" and that her husband "was everything despicable." Therefore, Poe wrote, since he "sincerely & most purely loved" her and "had every reason to like & respect" Mr. Richmond, "I arose & left their house & incurred the unrelenting vengeance of that worst of all fiends, 'a woman scorned'" (O 2:775–76). So began for Poe an interlude with Annie Richmond and her family.

Poe stayed first at the Ames Street home of Annie and her husband, where the writer had visited in July, after his lecture. Annie had, since his first visit to Lowell, visited Maria Clemm in Fordham—whether Poe was there at the time, we do not know.[13] Annie was, at the time of Poe's first and second visit to Lowell, twenty-eight years old. Poe limns her in "Landor's Cottage," noting her "*modest decision* of step altogether indescribable" and "*enthusiasm*," focusing on her eyes: "So intense an expression of *romance,* perhaps I should call it, or of unworldliness, as that which gleamed from her deep-set eyes, had never so sunk into my heart of hearts before" (M 3:1338–39). A photograph of Annie Richmond, taken some years later, conveys the depth of her eyes—eyes that Poe describes as "spiritual gray" (M 3:1338–39).

Invited by Annie's brother Bardwell Heywood, Poe continued his visit with the Richmond family for three days at the home of Annie's parents, the Heywoods, in Westford, nine miles southwest of Lowell. Sister Sarah recalled Poe's walking "to look at the hills" in the day; sitting silently before the fireplace "holding the hand of a dear friend" (Annie) at dusk; and reciting his own work, as well as that of Willis and Byron, to the local reading club at night.[14] Bardwell recalled Poe's offering both "The Raven" and "Ulalume," as well as his debating matters with Reverend John B. Willard. Bardwell noted that much as Poe admired Prospect Hill's vista, he imagined and described improvements.[15] Poe clearly had the habit of mind of the visionary Ellison in "The Landscape-Garden" and "The Domain of Arnheim."

But it is the silent time, Poe's holding hands with Annie before the fire, that is the most suggestive. Something was happening. Even as he was awaiting Sarah Helen Whitman's much-delayed letter,[16] he seems to have been finding with Annie a degree of solace. Poe would eventually write to her, on November 16, "I know that you *felt* too deeply the nature of my love for you" (O 2:721). And he signed this letter with the familiar name, "Eddy" (O 2:723). But what of Annie herself? She later admitted to John H. Ingram (several years after her husband's death), her "*wonder & admiration*" regarding Poe—"[H]e was incomparable."[17] She cherished "the bit of *Romance* that found its way into the 'web & woof' of my life in the days of 'auld lang syne'"—and she confessed, most revealingly, that she was interested in the "vindication of a name *dearer to me than any other in the world.*"[18] She confided this again, appreciating Ingram's "faithful *& just* tribute to my *precious* Eddie, for he was indeed *very* precious, & his affection for me, is the most precious *memory* my heart holds."[19]

It seems that the emotional rapport between Poe and Annie Richmond would have clarified his relationship with Sarah Helen Whitman, who, probably because of the marriage proposal and the warnings that she had received, was more emotionally withholding. Still, Mrs. Richmond was not available. And Mrs. Whitman was. The Providence poet finally responded to Poe—ambiguously. She later wrote that her note to Poe "must have perplexed and agitated him." He replied, by mail, on Friday, November 3, that he would visit on the following evening.[20]

Annie encouraged him to continue his courtship of Whitman, even providing the language to employ (O 2:722). She must have imagined that marriage, which she could not offer, would yield the peace that Poe sought. He evidently made two promises to Annie (O 2:777–78), one of which was surely to stop drinking (O 2:753). And Annie made a promise to him—to come to him when he lay on his deathbed (O 2:722). Desperately conflicted, Poe would soon want Annie to fulfill her promise.

He parted from Annie in an "agony of grief," with "a dreadful horrible foreboding of ill" (O 2:721–22). He was, at this point, very fragile emotionally. And his back-and-forth travel—to Providence, back to Boston, and to Providence again—reflected his back-and-forth thinking. That is, as he wrote to Annie in the same letter of November 16, "I feel that I *must* die if I persist [in courting Sarah Helen Whitman], & yet, how can I now retract with honor?" (O 2:722). To do the honorable thing, he went to Providence, where he spent "a long, long hideous night of despair" (O 2:722). Not visiting Whitman, he initiated his plan to see Annie again, his true love. He bought two ounces of laudanum (comprising alcohol and morphine), and took the train back to Boston, where he wrote a letter to her stating, in part, that my "soul revolted from saying the words which were to be said" and imploring her to come to him, as she had promised she would, on his deathbed, giving his location in Boston. He then took half the laudanum. However, he became very sick, and he could not mail the letter at the post office. Recovering eventually, with the help of a friend, he took the train back to Providence, to honor his commitment.

He reported to Annie, "Here I saw *her*, & spoke, for *your* sake, the words which you urged me to speak." But he asked, "Ah *beloved*, think—think for *me* & for yourself—do I not *love* you Annie? do you not *love me*? Is not this *all*? Beyond this blissful thought, what other consideration *can* there be in this dreary world!" (O 2:722–23). And he confided his dream: "[M]y mother [his mother-in-law Maria Clemm] and myself would take a small cottage at Westford—oh *so* small—so *very* humble—I should be far away from the tumult[s] of the world—from the ambition which I loathe—I would labor day & night, and with industry, I could accomplish so much—Annie! it would be a Paradise beyond my wildest hopes—I could see some of your beloved family *every* day, & you often—oh VERY often" (O 2:723).

The dream would remain only a dream. But he would have one final visit with Annie and her family in May 1849, the year of his death.[21]

And so, Poe visited Sarah Helen Whitman for the third time, on Tuesday, November 7. It must have been very difficult for him to shift his attention from Mrs. Richmond to Mrs. Whitman. But he did call on the Providence poet in the early morning. She was not ready to see him, having slept poorly, worried about him. She suggested, by servant, meeting at noon. He wrote a short plaintive note, asserting his illness, seeking once again her expression of love and her hand in marriage (O 2:718–19). (Of course, he did not acknowledge the Annie Richmond visit.) Whitman agreed to meet him at the Providence Athenaeum in a half hour.[22]

Poe began again entreating Whitman to marry him, using some of the language that Annie had suggested (as he wrote to her [O 2:722]). He made his case on Tuesday and continued through Wednesday. According to a letter from Whitman to Ingram, she showed Poe letters that she had been sent from New York with accusations against him, including the accusation about which he had already been outraged and against which he had defended himself in his October 18 letter, that he had "*no* principle—*no* moral sense" (O 2:707–10). According to a letter from Whitman to S. E. R. (Sallie E. Robins) on the same incident, she read to Poe a letter from New York, cautioning against him. Whitman recalled, "He seemed deeply pained at the result of our interview, and left me abruptly, saying that, if we should meet again, it would be as strangers." She acknowledged in her letter to Ingram that he then wrote her "a note of renunciation & farewell." And he retreated, she reported in the earlier letter, to drink, experiencing "a night of delirious phrenzy." She referred to this night as "Ultima Thule," recalling Poe's lines in "Dream-Land," "I have reached these lands but newly / From an ultimate dim Thule—/ From a wild weird clime that lieth, sublime, / Out of Space—out of Time" (M 1:344). Of all the nadirs in a life of nadirs, this particular nadir is the most famous (after that of his death) because the next morning Poe would be daguerreotyped.[23]

A man who had been "very kind to Poe during the night" and "deeply interested in him," one Mr. MacFarlane, proposed the Thursday morning, November 9, visit from the hotel to Masury & Hartshorne, a local daguerreotype studio on the second floor of 25 Westminster Street (Market Street). An employee, Edwin H. Manchester, took the actual image, an icon of despair. Poe's ravaged visage is awry—the eyebrows slope to his left; the bags under his eyes hang uneven; the moustache slopes to his right. The gaze alone holds steady, fixed above the viewer. We may see here human "darkness visible."

Whitman commented, "And all the stormy grandeur of that via Dolorosa had left its sullen shadow on his brow. But it was *very* fine."[24]

From Masury & Hartshorne, Poe proceeded to the home on Benefit Street. Whitman recalled that he was "in a state of wild & delirious excitement, calling upon me to save him from some terrible impending doom." He was still suffering the effects of his night's agitation. She added, "The tones of his voice were appalling & rang through the house. Never have I heard anything so awful, even to sublimity."[25]

Her mother, Anna Marsh Power, spoke with Poe for two hours, having coffee made for him, before her daughter came into the room, and Poe held to her tightly, even causing the tearing of a piece of her dress. With Poe calm in the afternoon, Whitman or her mother called in Dr. O. H. Okie—he diagnosed "cerebral congestion" and suggested that William J. Pabodie take Poe to his own house. Pabodie offered Poe "the kindest care and attention," according to Whitman, and Poe later thanked him for his "considerate and gentlemanly attentions" (O 2:738).[26]

Anna Marsh Power objected unequivocally to the marriage of her daughter and Poe. Whitman declared, "My mother did say more than once in his presence that my death would not be regarded by her so great an evil as my marriage under circumstances of such ominous import."[27] However, before November 13, Whitman did agree to a "conditional engagement," depending on Poe's not drinking.[28] If Poe would remain sober, she would try to persuade her mother. Clearly, the possibility that Whitman could, through marriage, effectively end Poe's debilitating dependency was her motive and her hope.

On Monday, November 13, Poe returned to Masury & Hartshorne to have a daguerreotype of himself made for Whitman, a portrait considered to have been an engagement gift. Samuel W. Hartshorne took the image.[29] Here, Poe's countenance seems more composed and the lighting more gentle than in the "Ultima Thule" daguerreotype. Poe directly engages the viewer. Whitman later described the image as "sweet & serene in expression."[30]

Poe left Providence by the 6:00 p.m. train to Stonington, Connecticut. He arrived by boat in New York City at 5:00 a.m. and took the 7:00 a.m. train to Fordham (O 2:720). In departing, Poe had mentioned to Whitman the star Arcturus, and she thought that she saw that brilliant star after he was gone. That night she wrote the poem "To Arcturus," intimating her new fiancé as the "Star of resplendent front!" "thy resplendent sphere."[31]

Having written to Sarah Helen Whitman from the steamboat to New York City ("My own dearest Helen" [O 2:719]), Poe wrote to Annie two days later from Fordham ("Ah, Annie, Annie! *my* Annie!" [O 2:721]). He was caught in dual romances—neither sexual—unable to give up either one of them. Clearly, however, it was Annie whom he more deeply loved. Maria Clemm, who was so grateful that her son-in-law had returned—"But *how changed!*" (H 17:391–92)—wrote to Annie, "He raved all night about you, but is now more composed" (H 17:392). And Clemm herself preferred Annie. She wrote to her, "But I so much fear *she* [Whitman] is not calculated to make him happy. I fear I will not love her. I *know* I shall never love her as I do *you,* my own darling. I hope at all events they will not marry for some time."[32] Frances Sargent Osgood, on the other hand, visiting Whitman in Providence, expressed her "mingled joy & sorrow" at the match.[33]

In the coming weeks, Poe wrote to Sarah Helen Whitman frequently, and to Annie's sister Sarah and to Annie, once apiece (O 2:1261–63). But he also returned to his professional responsibilities, asking for an insertion in *Graham's Magazine* from staff member Bayard Taylor (O 2:726); seeking support for "The Stylus" from Frances Allan's cousin Edward Valentine (O 2:725), in a letter that he enclosed with another to the Richmond poet Susan Archer Talley (implied by her response [H 17:324]);[34] and requesting a copy of the July 1848 issue of the *Southern Literary Messenger*—with a poem titled "Genius," by Talley—from the editor John R. Thompson (O 2:739–40). It may well have been during this time that he went into New York City, visiting the office of the *Metropolitan Magazine,* on Broadway, and the studio of painter Frederic Church at the American Art Union, also on Broadway. He appeared at Church's studio as "a slender, nervous, vivacious, and extremely refined personage."[35]

Poe was then becoming focused on his approaching lecture in Providence. He wrote to T. L. Dunnell regarding the date (O 2:737)—it would eventually be determined to be December 20—and he wrote to Whitman for three of his critical essays, which he could incorporate in his talk (O 2:735–36).[36]

Poe made a fourth trip to Whitman after December 7, returning by December 12. On December 15, her mother, fearing that the marriage would indeed take place, made sure that her late sister's estate would devolve entirely upon her.[37] Concerned that something would prevent the marriage, Poe, visiting Mary E. Hewitt in New York, stated that the marriage would not take place.[38] (This became the basis for Rufus W. Griswold's slander that Poe had deliberately terminated the engagement.)[39] On December 20, Poe made his fifth and final visit to Whitman, in Providence, during which he would give his lecture "The Poetic Principle."

Poe arrived in the morning at the three-story brick hotel, Earl House, at 67 North Main Street in Providence. His lecture, in the Franklin Lyceum series, would be held at 7:30 p.m. at the elegant Howard's Hall. The event was advertised in Providence newspapers, the *Daily Journal,* the *Evening Transcript,* and the *Republican Herald*. The *Daily Journal* described Poe as "one of the most remarkable literary men of this country." Poe later judged that he had an audience of 1,800 people; William J. Pabodie estimated 2,000.[40]

"The poetic principle," as evident in a later version of the talk (published in August 1850), is "the Human Aspiration for Supernal Beauty" manifested in "*an elevating excitement of the Soul*" (L2 198). As the Poe scholars Stuart Levine and Susan Levine have noted, some of the ideas of the lecture may be traced backward to Poe's 1842 review of Longfellow's *Ballads and Other Poems* (L2 203n). (The April 1835 Drake-Halleck review is also relevant.) According to one member of the audience, Stephen H. Arnold, Poe read, among other works, "The Raven" and "The Bells" (the latter then unpublished in any version). And Arnold observed the interplay of expression between Poe and Whitman, who sat "just in front of him." Commenting on this interplay, Arnold wrote, "This had been very interesting but became intensely so when in closing he read Edward C. Pinkney's lines 'I fill this cup to one made up of loveliness alone'—all the while looking down into her eyes. You can imagine the emphasis he gave and how dramatic it was. I can never forget it." Poe's public performance was clearly also a private one, a part of his continuing courtship of Sarah Helen Whitman.[41]

Two evenings later, on Friday, December 22, matters finally seemed resolved. At her Benefit Street home, Whitman, who had agreed to an "immediate marriage," obtained the "reluctant consent" of her mother, on whom she relied financially, with Poe's signing a document affirming Power's transfer of property: "Whereas a Marriage is intended between the above named Sarah H. Whitman and the Subscriber Edgar A. Poe,—I hereby approve of and assent to the transfer of the property in the manner proposed in the papers of which the preceding [those of December 15] are copies— Providence December 22 1848 / EDGAR A. POE. / In presence of / WILLIAM J. PABODIE."[42] Doubtless Poe felt mistreated by Whitman's mother, but no doubt Power felt mistrustful and in need of legal protection. Poe also made "solemn promises" that evening to Whitman and to her friends—assuredly, promises not to drink.[43]

But Pabodie later stated that Poe had already been drinking. At the hotel, he had fallen in with "a set of somewhat dissipated young men, who often invited him to drink with them." That evening, though Poe was "very quiet," he was, Pabodie asserted, "in a state of partial intoxication" (H 17:413).

On the following day, Saturday, December 23, Poe apologized for his lapse (H 17:413). And he wrote to Reverend Nathan B. Crocker, asking him to publish the banns of marriage and to officiate at the event itself (O 2:744). The note, which Poe gave to a reluctant Pabodie, was never delivered (H 17:413–14). Poe also wrote to Maria Clemm, revealing the plan: he and Sarah Helen Whitman would be married on Monday, December 25 (Christmas), and would travel to Fordham, arriving on Tuesday, December 26 (O 2:744). Meanwhile, that Saturday morning, the couple shared a carriage, to arrange for their coming new life in Fordham. However, in the afternoon, at a local circulating library, Whitman received a note reliably reporting Poe's recent compromised behavior, including his having betrayed his pledge of the previous evening—that is, he had had a drink at the hotel that morning.[44] When they got back to Benefit Street, Whitman let Poe know what she had learned and directed that the note to Reverend Crocker not be delivered. She later recalled, "I felt utterly helpless of being able to exercise any permanent influence over his life."[45] So, she called off the engagement. She later explained to John H. Ingram, "If I had never seen Poe intoxicated, I should never have consented to marry him; had he kept his promise never again to taste wine, I should never have broken the engagement."[46]

Poe pled with Whitman but to no avail. She possessed, she later recalled, "that marble stillness of despair."[47] She had gained a hopeless certainty: "I knew that he had irrevocably lost the power of self-recovery."[48] Wishing to end the scene, she resorted to a handkerchief doused with ether. She took to the sofa and he to his knees, begging her to speak. She related their last conversation: "'What *can* I say?' 'Say that you love me, Helen.' '*I love you.*'"[49] He placed shawls on her cold and languid body and carried her closer to the fireplace. But all was lost. She felt "[a] merciful apathy."[50] And Anna Marsh Power and William J. Pabodie exhorted him to leave. Apparently, Power's words were especially harsh—Poe cried out, "Mr. Pabodie, you hear how I am insulted."[51] And Poe left. Pabodie accompanied him to the train station.[52] The rejected suitor began his long trip back to Fordham.

Poe had once again been defeated by his own great failing. He was, no doubt, humiliated and angry. Maria Clemm, a clear partisan of Annie Richmond, nonetheless later wrote to Sarah Helen Whitman, "You will never know how he loved you nor his agony at parting with you."[53] Whitman, who had endured much in the past three months, remembered her "intense sorrow thus to part from one whose sweet & gracious nature had endeared him to me beyond expression, and whose rare & peculiar intellect had given a new charm to my life."[54] She would never see him again, but she would devotedly defend Poe in the years to come. And Pabodie would defend him, as well.

Back home at Fordham, Poe readjusted. Very likely embarrassed about how things had ended with Whitman, Poe reached out to Annie Richmond. He wrote to Annie on December 28, "*All* is right! [. . .] I *hope* that I distinguished myself at the Lecture—I *tried* to do so, for your sake. There were 1800 people present, and such applause! I did so much better than I did at Lowell. If *you* had only been there" (O 2:745). His attitude toward Whitman was understandably bitter. He wrote to Annie on January 11, 1849, "[T]here is *nothing* in this world worth living for except love—love *not* such as I once thought I felt for Mrs. [Whitman] but such as burns in my very soul for *you*" (O 2:748).

And, probably with the encouragement of Maria Clemm, Poe was getting back to work. On January 11, she wrote to Annie that he was "writing most industriously," "from ten till four every day." He had even written a tale about "Darling Annie"—it would be the complement to "The Domain of Arnheim," "Landor's Cottage."[55] Writing to Annie that day, he echoed Clemm's estimate: "You can't think how industrious I am" (O 2:749). Two days later, he proposed to John R. Thompson, the editor of the *Southern Literary Messenger*, a continuation of the "Marginalia" series and added in a postscript, "I am about to bestir myself in the world of Letters rather more busily than I have done for three or four years past" (O 2:751). Once again, despite his personal difficulties, Poe would resume his literary labors.

There was one other piece of the badly ended saga of Poe and Whitman. Annie Richmond, through her husband (who had relatives in Providence), had heard unfavorable reports of Poe's final time with Whitman. She wrote to Poe, trying to understand—and thereby to let her family know—what had happened. He mentioned in a letter of January 21 "what I did in Providence on that terrible day" (O 2:753)—that is, that he had been drinking, which led to the end of the engagement. But he defended himself against false reports. He wanted to alleviate Annie's concerns by writing a formal letter to Sarah Helen Whitman ("Dear Madam"), asking her to deny these false reports, evident in an unattributed quotation (from Annie). And to reassure Annie, he sent her his letter to Whitman, requesting that Annie send it on from Boston to Whitman. Poe specifically asked Whitman to disavow the allegation that he had had the first banns of marriage published (O 2:757–58). In fact, they were never published. Pabodie wrote that he had delayed passing them on, and Poe stated that on the final day he himself had told Pabodie not to speak to Reverend Crocker about publishing them (O 2:757). Whitman did eventually receive Poe's letter, but "for his sake rather than my own" she did not respond to it directly, afraid that her response might reawaken for him the unhappy matter.[56] Yet she must have responded indirectly, for Annie wrote, "Mrs. W's reply exonerated him completely."[57] Annie trusted Poe's account and defended his honor, and she and Poe continued to maintain their close friendship. She later declared to John H. Ingram, "I do not think he was *capable* of a mean or dishonorable act toward any human being."[58]

Also in his January 21 letter to Annie, Poe confided, "I do not believe *that any one in the whole world fully understands me except your own dear self.*" And he added, "I am *so* busy now, and feel so full of energy." He had clearly returned to his writing—and to his reading. Particularly interesting is his recommendation of "'Percy Ranthorpe,' by Mrs. Gore." Even as Poe integrated his life in his work, he also found resonances of his life in another's work: "I have lately read it with deep interest, and derived great *consolation* from it also. It relates to the career of a literary man, and gives a just view of the true aims and the true dignity of the literary character. Read it for my sake." (O 2:754–55).

Percy Ranthorpe, a novel attributed in Poe's 1848 New York edition to Catherine Gore, was actually by George Henry Lewes, partner of George Eliot. Perhaps Poe had picked it up at Bartlett & Welford's Bookshop at the Astor House. He would readily have related to the eponymous character's sense of his own genius and his longing for fame, as well as his experiencing the dangers of fame. What is especially suggestive in the book is the highlighting of Dr. Neil Arnott, a friend of John Allan, who had written about the portrait of Edgar in 1821, and the remarkable chapter "Night of the Murder," with singular correspondences to "The Tell-Tale Heart."[59]

Poe continued to write steadily—he estimated, to Annie, on February 8, one page to three pages a day. He made specific reference to having written a long version of "The Bells" and a new story, "Hop-Frog" (O 2:766–67). He had just accepted an offer from the publisher Frederick Gleason to contribute to his weekly Boston newspaper, the *Flag of Our Union* (O 2:765)—he had left his poem "A Valentine" with Gleason's New York agent, Samuel French, at 293 Broadway, and he would soon place "Hop-Frog" and other pieces in that mammoth paper. Poe considered the *Flag* "not a *very* respectable journal, perhaps," but it paid well (O 2:767). And he had recently sent a roll of

"Marginalia" to editor John R. Thompson for publication in the *Southern Literary Messenger* (O 2:760–61). Poe would soon send the second version of "The Bells" to John Sartain for the *Union Magazine* (O 2:768–69) and a review of James Russell Lowell's *A Fable for Critics* to Thompson for the *Messenger* (O 2:771).[60] Poe was indeed bestirring himself in the world of letters.

He wrote to his old friend Frederick W. Thomas on February 14, "Depend on it, after all, Thomas, Literature is the most noble of professions. In fact, it is about the only one fit for a man." Comparing the benefits of the life of a writer to those of one who had joined the Gold Rush, he asked, "[D]id it ever strike you that all which is really valuable to a man of letters—to a poet in especial—is absolutely unpurchaseable? Love, fame, the dominion of intellect, the consciousness of power, the thrilling sense of beauty, the free air of Heaven, exercise of body & mind, with the physical and moral health which result—these and such as these are really all a poet cares for:—then answer me this—*why* should he go to California?" (O 2:770). Clearly, Poe had recovered his equanimity.

And to some degree he seems to have recovered his health again. He declared to Thomas, "You will be pleased to hear that I am in better health than I ever knew myself to be—full of energy and bent upon success" (O 2:771).

And so Poe attended to "Love, fame." He wrote to his beloved Annie on February 18, stating that he could not visit her, believing her husband to have been susceptible to the lies of the Lockes (and probably expecting that Mr. Richmond would read this letter). He is modulated in his address—"Dear—dearest Annie—my sweet friend & sister" (O 2:775)—and in his close—"Always your dear friend & brother / Edgar" (O 2:778). He affirms the "*purity*" of his love (O 2:777). His purpose in this letter was, no doubt, in part, to win back Charles B. Richmond so that he could visit Annie again. (But, understandably, Poe did harbor a jealousy of Annie's husband, as a later letter will indicate.) Poe's letter of February 18 would have the desired effect, and the writer would be welcomed by Annie and her husband in May.[61]

As for fame, Poe maintained his productivity, perhaps by this time beginning the short story "Von Kempelen and His Discovery." And his first piece appeared in the *Flag of Our Union*. Though he later termed the paper "vulgar and trashy" (O 2:781) and considered his sending his work there "consigning [it] to the tomb of the Capulets" (O 2:791), he welcomed the payment—which he termed "about 5$ a 'Graham page'" and "5$ for a Sonnet" (O 2:767)—and he appreciated the possibility of reprinting his work in more esteemed venues. That first piece, the poem "A Valentine," was described in the February 24 issue (appearing February 17) as "a very peculiar article, from our regular contributor, EDGAR A. POE." It was published in the March 3 issue (appearing February 24). This was the February 1848 corrected version of the progressive acrostic to Frances Sargent Osgood, with the originally misspelled "Sergeant" now appearing as "Sargent" (M 1:388–90). It may have been the publisher Frederick Gleason or editor M. M. Ballou who provided the asterisked note, "Should there be no solution furnished of the above, we will give the key next week." The solution to the acrostic was provided in the March 10 issue (appearing March 3), with an acknowledgment that several readers had worked it out.[62]

As his work began to appear in the *Flag of Our Union*, Poe's anonymous review of Lowell's satirical 1848 poem *A Fable for Critics* appeared in early March in the *Southern Literary Messenger*.[63] Writing to his friend Thomas, Poe had asserted, "Lowell is a ranting abolitionist and *deserves* a good using up" (O 2:771), and he mentions in his review "various criticisms" which "used up" Lowell (P 5:376). The phrase "ranting abolitionist" was also used in the review (P 5:377) and suggests the possibility of another kind of abolitionist—one who did not rant—perhaps such as the more moderate Harriet B. Winslow. Notably, Poe attacks in this review what he considers "fanaticism," either in an abolitionist or a slave owner (P 5:377).

Poe quotes Lowell's lines about him:

Here comes Poe with his Raven, like Barnaby Rudge—
Three-fifths of him genius, and two-fifths sheer fudge;
Who talks like a book of iambs and pentameters,
In a way to make all men of common sense d—n metres;
Who has written some things far the best of their kind;
But somehow the heart seems squeezed out by the mind. (P 5:377)

But Poe corrects Lowell, stating that it is precisely the absence of an adequate book on prosody that he has decried, relying on his own common sense. And he characterizes Lowell's supposed common sense as "*un*common nonsense" (P 5:377). Poe does not address the claim that he is "three-fifths of him genius, and two-fifths sheer fudge," presumably confident of his high literary reputation. But we may observe that Theodore Roosevelt later wrote, "If any man was ever about five fifths genius, that man was Poe."[64]

In light of a poem to come, it seems fitting to note that also appearing in the March 1849 issue of the *Southern Literary Messenger* was a poem titled "Castle by the Sea"—about a beloved young woman who has died.[65]

Poe's tale of revenge "Hop-Frog: or the Eight Chained Ourang-Outangs," was announced in the *Flag of Our Union* of March 10 (appearing March 3) and was published in a place of honor—at the upper left of page 2—in the *Flag* of March 17 (appearing March 10). There is evident pride in a squib titled "The Present Number," which states that this issue includes "some of the best writers in America."[66] In the tale, the fat, frivolous king—perhaps based on the detested King George IV—enlists his dwarf jester Hop-Frog to provide entertainment at a masquerade. Hop-Frog, especially susceptible to wine, is angry that the king compels him to drink and enraged that the king pushes his friend Trippetta and throws wine in her face when she pleads on his behalf. Hop-Frog therefore cunningly arranges, as supposed entertainment, the disguising of the king and his seven ministers as orangutans, chained together. He then hoists them above the guests with the chain of the removed chandelier and, climbing upon them, sets them on fire. He concludes, in his final speech to those below, "I am simply Hop-Frog, the jester—and *this is my last jest*" (M 3:1354), and he escapes through the sky-light to Trippetta on the roof.

Prompted by a translation of a passage about a similar but accidental conflagration, written by Jean Froissart and included in a piece by Evert A. Duyckinck in the *Broadway Journal*,[67] Poe again integrates his life in his work, blending the insult and intoxication he has experienced to yield a horrific devastation. Indeed, he acknowledged to Annie that the subject was "a terrible one" (O 2:767). Though "The Cask of Amontillado" is the greater tale of revenge, "Hop-Frog" does have an unmistakable intensity and a clear personal resonance.

At this time, of course, Poe had no Trippetta. But his former fiancée, Sarah Helen Whitman, published a poem "Stanzas for Music" (later "Our Island of Dreams") in mid-March, the last stanza of which was covertly addressed to Poe:

> When the clouds that now veil from us heaven's fair light,
> Their soft, silver lining turn forth on the night;
> When time shall the vapors of falsehood dispel,
> He shall know if I loved him; but never how well.[68]

Also, his adored Annie wrote to him, and Poe responded on March 23, sending a letter from Jane Ermina Locke to Maria Clemm, which confirmed Poe's allegation against the former (regarding her having warned him against Annie). He had already sent Annie "Hop-Frog" (as published in the *Flag of Our Union*) and asked if she had received it. And he had sent, as well, a manuscript poem called "For Annie," the final fifteen lines of the imminently-to-be-published "A Dream within a Dream."[69] He sent with this March 23 letter a second manuscript poem called "For Annie," soon to be published with this title. He acknowledged the distinction, referring to enclosing here "some other lines 'For Annie'" and "the lines 'For Annie' (those I now send)." He termed the lines of this new poem "much the *best* I have ever written" but asked "what my Annie *truly* thinks of them" (O 2:787–88).

The Flag of Our Union of March 31 (appearing March 24) featured Poe's poem "A Dream within a Dream" (the expansion of the first poem titled "For Annie"), already announced in the issue of March 24 (appearing March 17). Developed from his 1827 poem "Imitation" and his 1829 poem "To — —," "A Dream within a Dream" is an earnest lament about evanescence. It seems both loving and wise:

> Take this kiss upon the brow!
> And, in parting from you now,
> Thus much let me avow—
> You are not wrong, who deem
> That my days have been a dream;
> Yet if hope has flown away
> In a night, or in a day,
> In a vision, or in none,
> Is it therefore the less *gone?*
> *All* that we see or seem
> Is but a dream within a dream.
>
> I stand amid the roar
> Of a surf-tormented shore,
> And I hold within my hand
> Grains of the golden sand—
> How few! yet how they creep
> Through my fingers to the deep.
> While I weep—while I weep!
> O God! can I not grasp
> Them with a tighter clasp?
> O God! can I not save
> *One* from the pitiless wave?
> Is *all* that we see or seem
> But a dream within a dream? (M 1:451–52)

This work is focused and mature. And we may wonder if it implies an unspoken waking.

Poe was then publishing reviews of Sarah Anna Lewis's *The Child of the Sea and Other Poems* and the first of his new "Marginalia" series. And he continued to publish short stories, with "Von Kempelen and His Discovery" announced in the April 7 issue of the *Flag of Our Union* (appearing March 31) and featured in the place of honor in the *Flag* of April 14 (appearing April 7). Poe wrote that he was to be paid fifteen dollars for it (O 2:785). With shreds of the factual and dollops of faux certitude, he offers there fabulation as erudition. He had termed the work to Evert A. Duyckinck (who did not accept it for his magazine), "a kind of 'exercise', or experiment, in the plausible or verisimilar style" (O 2:785). Shifting from "Hop-Frog" to "Von Kempelen," Poe shifted from vengeance to fake news—indeed, fake news with a vengeance (and a twinkle).

An initial reference to "Silliman's Journal" (M 3:1357) intimates the comic tone of the whole. With pretended outrage at the false claim of Mr. Kissam, pretended regard for Sir Humphrey Davy's solemn description of the effects of laughing gas, and the pretended association of "the now immortal Von Kempelen" (M 3:1361) with the city of Utica, New York, home of the new insane asylum, Poe is in full wink. And he kids particular readers whom he knows with mention of Brunswick, Maine (George W. Eveleth); the *Home Journal* (N. P. Willis and George Pope Morris); and the *Literary World* (Evert A. Duyckinck). The culminating narrative concerns the Bremen police finding an imagined hidden apparatus of Von Kempelen—"two crucibles connected by a tube" (M 3:1362)—for converting lead into gold. Poe thereby pointedly deprecates the Gold Rush, imagining the inevitable depreciation of the hitherto precious metal. He was seeking to change the culture, however briefly—perhaps to unsettle California settlers, present and prospective. He wrote to Duyckinck earlier that "acting as a sudden, although of course a very temporary, *check* to the gold-fever, it [the tale] will create a *stir* to some purpose" (O 2:785).[70]

With yet another literary hoax, in the tradition of "The Balloon Hoax" and "The Facts in the Case of M. Valdemar," along with his celebrated tales of terror and tales of ratiocination, Poe was continuing to demonstrate his virtuosity—what he had termed, with regard to his tales, "the widest diversity of subject, thought, & especially *tone* & manner of handling" (O 1:596).

Announced in that same issue of the *Flag of Our Union*, April 14, was Poe's poem "Eldorado." The future classic, a mere four stanzas, employed the Gold

Rush trope of Eldorado as the City of Gold. It was published in the April 21 issue (appearing on April 14), on page 2, beneath the fold, in column five of eight columns. (Offered, by contrast, in places of honor at the top of the page were Frances Sargent Osgood's poems "The Soul's Appeal" and "The Rural Scene.") In Poe's poem, a hopeful lilt yields to a thoughtful lingering:

> Gaily bedight,
> A gallant knight,
> In sunshine and in shadow,
> Had journeyed long,
> Singing a song,
> In search of Eldorado.
>
> But he grew old—
> This knight so bold—
> And o'er his heart a shadow
> Fell, as he found
> No spot of ground
> That looked like Eldorado.
>
> And, as his strength
> Failed him at length
> He met a pilgrim shadow—
> "Shadow," said he,
> "Where can it be—
> This land of Eldorado?"
>
> "Over the Mountains
> Of the Moon,
> Down the Valley of the Shadow,
> Ride, boldly ride,"
> The shade replied,—
> "If you seek for Eldorado!" (M 1:463)

This poem is a song, characterized by the *"indefinitiveness"* that Poe had contended was needed for such a work (H 10:41, 42, 43; P 2:337, 338). Indeed, it was influenced by such songs as "Tom a-Bedlam Song" and Charles Lever's "The Man for Galway."[71] The poem's theme may be discerned, anticipated by Poe's having written years earlier of "the *earnest upward impulse of the soul*" (H 11:84–85) and the value of "an object of unceasing pursuit," especially a spiritual one (M 2:704 and, later, M 3:1269). If bliss is no longer the consequence (as it had been in "The Landscape-Garden" and "The Domain of Arnheim"), this may be because much time has passed and Poe knows that he is nearing his end. The quest for the soul's home—for Poe, often through "Supernal Beauty" (L2 198)—however unsuccessful, will endure. With "Eldorado," Poe was at his peak, writing a lyric of aspiration and inspiration, an allegory of man's greatest seeking. And with "Ride, boldly ride," Poe offered his greatest encouragement.

The lines that Poe had described to Annie as "much the *best* I have ever written" (O 2:788)—"For Annie" (the second piece so titled)—were announced as forthcoming in the same issue of the *Flag of Our Union* in which "Eldorado" appeared, that of April 21, where the work was termed "peculiar and characteristic."[72] The fifteen-stanza poem appeared in the April 28 issue (appearing on April 21), on page 2, occupying the upper two-thirds of column six.[73] The early stanzas of the poem relate the horrific recent illness of the resting speaker (who might seem dead but is not). A portion reads:

> The sickness—the nausea—
>   The pitiless pain—
> Have ceased with the fever
>   That maddened my brain—
> With the fever, called 'Living,'
>   That burned in my brain.
>
> The moaning and groaning,
>   The sighing and sobbing,
> Are quieted now; and the
>   Horrible throbbing
> At heart—O, that horrible,
>   Horrible throbbing![74]

The later stanzas of the poem concern Annie herself. Poe seems to be imagining the scene that he sought in early November 1848 but that never took place—Annie coming to him in Boston as he lay near death (O 2:722).[75] In the poem, she has helped him to recover. These stanzas read:

> And so it [his spirit] lies, happily
>   Bathing in many
> A dream of the love
>   And the beauty of Annie—

> Drowned in a bath
>   Of the tresses of Annie.
>
> She tenderly kissed me—
>   She fondly caressed—
> And then I fell gently
>   To sleep on her breast—
> Deeply to sleep from the
>   Heaven of her breast.
>
> When the light was extinguished,
>   She covered me warm;
> And she prayed to the angels
>   To keep me from harm—
> To the queen of the angels
>   To shield me from harm.
>
> And I lie so composedly
>   Now, in my bed—
> Knowing her love—
>   That you fancy me dead.
> And I rest so contentedly
>   Now, in my bed,
> With her love at my breast,
>   That you fancy me dead—
> That you shudder to look at me,
>   Thinking me dead.
>
> But my heart, it is brighter
>   Than all of the many
> Stars of the heaven,
>   For it sparkles with Annie—
> It glows with the fire
>   Of the love of my Annie—
> With the thought of the light
> Of the eyes of my Annie.[76]

With these words, Poe integrates into his work the loving and healing consolation that he must have felt from his beloved Annie. The latter portion of the poem seems a version of the much-cherished Thomas Moore song "Come Rest in This Bosom"—but from the perspective of the yearning man.

To be sure that "For Annie" received sufficient attention, Poe sent a manuscript of the poem to N. P. Willis for publication in the *Home Journal* (O 2:790–91) and sent a copy of the published poem from the *Home Journal* to E. H. N. Patterson for the work to be printed yet again (O 2:804). Furthermore, for the tenth edition of *Poets and Poetry of America,* Poe sent Rufus W. Griswold a copy of "For Annie" and an as-yet unpublished poem, one titled "Annabel Lee" (O 2:806).

24

"All May Yet Go Well"

1849

I<small>N RECENT MONTHS, POE HAD</small> informed John R. Thompson (O 2:740) and intimated to Annie (O 2:777) that he planned to travel to Richmond again. Richmond was home. In Richmond he could see his old friends—the Mackenzies especially, in both Duncan Lodge (where his sister Rosalie also lived) and Darby Town. He could visit Thompson himself and the young poet Susan Archer Talley. And he could see Elmira Shelton. This last was a possibility that would have taken on greater significance after the collapse of his engagement to Sarah Helen Whitman. Marie Louise Shew had warned him that he needed a caring woman in his life. And Elmira had been writing him love letters.[1]

Of course, Poe also wanted to visit Lowell and see Annie—perhaps by now he had set things right with her husband, persuading him of the *"purity"* of his love (O 2:777). Meanwhile, in Fordham, he was in the midst of his last great productive period.

And he had not given up his dream of editing his own literary magazine. Support for this dream arrived unexpectedly and belatedly in a letter, sent on December 18, 1848, and forwarded by George P. Putnam, from a young editor in Oquawka, Illinois, E. H. N. Patterson. In late April 1849, responding, at length and in detail, to Patterson's offer to publish a magazine that he would edit, Poe contended for the profitability of an elite five-dollar-per-year magazine, discussed a tour to build the needed subscription list, and referred to his partial list of future subscribers (O 2:792–94). He would continue to develop plans for "The Stylus" with Patterson in three subsequent letters. He would be planning the prospective magazine even a week before his death.[2]

Poe's work continued to be published in the *Flag of Our Union*. The May 5 issue of the *Flag* (appearing on April 28) announced, punningly, Poe's "'X-ing a Paragrab,' a capital prose sketch," and the May 12 issue (appearing on May 5) featured the work in the place of honor—where "Hop-Frog" and "Von Kempelen" had appeared—beginning at the top left of page 2. The comic tale concerns competing editors, the lately arrived Touch-and-go Bullet-Head and the established John Smith. Faulted by Smith for his overreliance on the letter "O," Bullet-Head doubles down, but the printer's devil finds that the type for the letter (in uppercase and lowercase) is used up, and he substitutes for the missing letter the type for the letter X (in uppercase and lowercase). The profusion of both versions of the letter X yields a profusion of X puns, culminating with a brilliant, climactic chiasmus: "X, everybody knew, was an unknown quantity; but in this case (as he [the town mathematician] properly observed), there was an unknown quantity of X" (M 3:1375). Chiasmus is the trope of crisscross; a diagram of this chiasmus may be useful:

$$X \qquad\qquad \text{an unknown quantity}$$
$$X$$
$$\text{an unknown quantity} \qquad\qquad X$$

And so we have a meta-chiasmus—an X about X. Poe is not so much solving for X as reconceiving it. An algebraic unknown has become knowably rhetoricized. Poe has varied the variable.[3]

But the buoyancy of this jeu d'esprit did not last. Poe became ill. Despite his reassuring comments to Annie (O 2:796), Maria Clemm wrote to her, "Do not believe Eddy; he has been very ill, but is now better. I thought he would *die* several times."[4] Furthermore, he became professionally discouraged. Though his work was getting published—not only in the *Flag of Our Union* but also in *Graham's Magazine* ("Fifty Suggestions") and the *Southern Literary Messenger* ("Marginalia")—and he had just written the extraordinary "Annabel Lee" (O 2:797), his prospects for selling future works had notably diminished, on account of the diminished number of paying periodicals, as he explained to Annie (O 2:796). Most significantly, he became afflicted again by an abiding melancholy. He wrote to her in his May 1849 letter, "[M]y sadness is *unaccountable,* and this makes me the more sad. I am full of dark forebodings. *Nothing* cheers or comforts me. My life seems wasted—the future looks a dreary blank; but I will struggle on and 'hope against hope'" (O 2:796–97). This echoes his September 1835 plaint to John P. Kennedy, "I am wretched, and know not why" (O 1:107). This must resonate also with three unlocated letters from Poe—one of them to William E. Burton in mid- to late May 1839, another to William Poe in mid-May 1843, and a third to Anne C. Lynch in June 1845—judging from the responses he received from his correspondents.[5] Perhaps today we would call Poe's condition intermittent depression. But whatever we call it, Poe was burdened. Perhaps unburdening himself to Annie helped. Whether he overcame his darkness or just put it to one side, Poe kept on with his life.

E. H. N. Patterson offered a speedy response to Poe's letter—the young editor's words must have been encouraging. He provided in his May 7 letter a confidence in his correspondent and a belief in the proposed magazine project. He would publish the five-dollar-per-year monthly, providing an office; Poe would edit the periodical; and the two men would enjoy the monies received on an equal basis. He supported the idea of Poe's subscription tour, judged that one thousand subscribers would be needed (of which his own "influence" might yield five hundred), and asked Poe to determine the magazine's name. He proposed meeting with Poe in New York in late July or early August, at which time they could elaborate the magazine's prospectus. And he suggested that publication could commence in January 1850.[6]

Poe seriously considered Patterson's second letter and responded on May 23, at first cautiously, and then with increasing approval: "[U]pon the whole, I say *Yes* to your proposition" (O 2:803). He enclosed a proposed title page "designed by myself about a year ago" (O 2:804), one featuring an image of a hand writing the Greek for "Truth" with an iron pen.[7] He stated that he would be traveling to Boston and Lowell, and later to Richmond, asking that Patterson forward fifty dollars, needed for his beginning the tour, to John R. Thompson at the *Southern Literary Messenger* office in Richmond. And he offered to meet Patterson in St. Louis, in the course of the tour (O 2:803–4).

This would have been a time of some promise for Poe. He would see Annie in Lowell. He would see his friends in Richmond. And finally embarking on his long-planned subscription tour, he would meet the potential publisher of his "Stylus" in St. Louis. There seemed to be some basis for hope.

Poe stayed with the Richmonds in Lowell for longer than a week in late May and early June. He copied out for Annie the third version of his as-yet-unpublished poem "The Bells," a masterpiece of onomatopoeia. He met the challenge of Reverend Warren H. Cudworth, readily decoding an alphabetical substitution cryptogram (about a patient with "spasms and acute pain in the hypogastric region"). He twice visited the Franklin Grammar School—where Annie's brother Bardwell Heywood was the principal—taking an interest in a young teacher, Eliza Jane Butterfield. And he sat for two daguerreotypes, one of them given to Annie and the other eventually to Sarah Anna Lewis ("Stella"). The Annie daguerreotype features the writer with tousled wavy hair, looking worn and perhaps questioning. The Stella daguerreotype, of which we have only a copy, is very similar, but, in its darker tonality, suggests less immediacy, less vulnerability.[8]

Especially touching was Poe's last farewell to Annie's nineteen-year-old sister Sarah. She recalled their final parting warmly: "He accompanied me nearly all the way [to school], taking leave of me at last in such a gentle, kindly manner that the thought of it brings tears now to the eyes that then looked their last upon that finished scholar, and winning, refined gentleman."[9] But Poe wrote to Annie on June 16, "I cannot tell you, darling, how sad I felt about parting with dear Sarah so coldly as I was forced to do. I did so long to kiss her and hold her to my heart—and I thought *she*, too, looked sad. Tell her I hope to see a great deal more of her when I return to Lowell" (O 2:810). He never did return to Lowell. It is telling that even as Annie's sister thought him "gentle" and "kindly," Poe wished he had been more expressive, more affectionate.

Poe returned to Fordham by June 4, writing then to Annie, anticipating his coming trip to Richmond by packet ship and sending her reviews of *Eureka* (O 2:807–8). Meanwhile, a sketch featuring Annie, "Landor's Cottage. A Pendant to 'The Domain of Arnheim,'" was announced in the *Flag of Our Union* in the June 2 issue (appearing May 26) and was published in the June 9 issue (appearing June 2). The new work, like the work with which it is paired, is an entrancing travelogue that explores the possibilities for beauty in an artist's fashioning of nature. Ellison's fashioning in "The Domain of Arnheim" involves "an intermedium between" the divine and the human, seeming to be "the handiwork of the angels" (O 3:1276). Landor's fashioning involves "a due medium between the neat and graceful on the one hand, and the *pittoresque*, in the true sense of the Italian term, on the other," also termed "variety in uniformity" and "combined novelty and propriety" (M 3:1330, 1335). But whereas the "intermedium" of "The Domain of Arnheim" culminates in Oriental splendor, the "due medium" of "Landor's Cottage" culminates in a rendering of a woman—an image that Poe had anticipated by stating that the work has "something about Annie in it" (O 2:754)—and the exterior and interior of a cottage, something akin to an idealization of the Fordham cottage and wholly consonant with the conclusion of "The Philosophy of Furniture."[10] It is fitting to note here that Sarah Helen Whitman offered in a scrapbook a moment that she remembered with Poe: "[W]hile sitting with me in a room whose arrangement & decoration seemed to charm his fancy, he expressed to me his intention of writing a pendant to the Domain of Arnheim in which the most beautiful effects should be attainable by artistic combinations of familiar & inexpensive materials." Poe evidently borrowed detail from that room—the pattern and coloring of the wallpaper—for that pendant.[11] Clearly, it is another work of integration. "The Domain of Arnheim" eventuates in a dream of the far; "Landor's Cottage" in a dream of the near.

Poe referred in the first printing of "Landor's Cottage"—the only printing in his lifetime—to a possible companion piece to this companion piece: "How he [Mr. Landor] made it [his residence] what it was—and *why,* with some particulars of Mr. Landon [*sic*] himself—may, *possibly* form the subject of another article" (M 3:1340v). Yet again, Poe might try to awaken the spiritual through the physical.

Published at this time were also the second installment of "Fifty Suggestions" in the June issue of *Graham's Magazine* and the third installment of the new "Marginalia" series in the June issue of the *Southern Literary Messenger.* It is interesting to observe that two works were then published related to Poe but never mentioning him or his work. In the same June issue of the *Messenger* in which that third installment appeared was Sarah Helen Whitman's poem "Lines," five stanzas characterized as "apparently intended as a reconciliatory message for Poe."[12] She takes all the blame ("The fault was mine, mine only"), evokes that final break ("those pleading eyes, / Those wild, sweet tones appealing / From heart to heart"), and closes in sorrow ("A love immortal and divine / Within my heart is waking—/ A dream of passion and despair / It owns not but in breaking").[13] Also at this time, John McLeod Murphy and W. N. Jeffers Jr. published *Nautical Routine and Stowage, with Short Rules in Navigation,* featuring two quoted passages in part 3, "Stowage," one of them concerning poorly stowed corn in the vessel *Firefly,* the other concerning the stowage of tobacco and poor stowage of cotton, the latter item attributed to "Am. Pub." As Joan Tyler Mead has shown, the American publication that was the source for both passages was Poe's 1838 novel *The Narrative of Arthur Gordon Pym.* Presumably the authors understood that Poe's book was a work of fiction, and they therefore did not name it. While Poe would certainly read Mrs. Whitman's poem in the *Messenger,* he may never have encountered the Murphy/Jeffers offering of two verisimilar passages from his only novel.[14]

Poe wrote to the *Messenger* editor John R. Thompson on June 9, asking him to forward to Fordham a letter to him—or, if it were not yet received, to hold on to it once it arrived. He planned to remain until he heard from Thompson and perhaps received the forwarded letter, from E. H. N. Patterson. Poe would be expecting that letter to bear importantly on his plans for "The Stylus." He imagined that he could leave for Richmond on "the 18th or 20th" (O 2:808–9). Meanwhile, during his time at Fordham in June, Poe probably wrote out another copy—or other copies—of his new poem "Annabel Lee," with slight variants.[15] And he continued his correspondence.

Poe wrote what would be his last letter to Annie, on June 16, expressing toward the end his regret over having asked her brother to "remember me to Miss B" [Eliza Jane Butterfield], reassuring her that "I thought it might have *pained* you in some measure—but indeed, darling Annie, no one in this whole world except your sweet self, is *more than a friend* to me." He closed, "And now Heaven forever bless you, my darling—/ Your own Eddie" (O 2:811). While he was waiting to hear from Thompson, Poe was also waiting a week (according to Mrs. Clemm) to hear from Annie. (Her response did not reach him before he left.)[16] On June 26, Poe wrote what would be his last letter to George W. Eveleth (responding to his of February 17), commenting on *Eureka;* noting with regard to "The Stylus," "I am now going to Richmond to 'see about it'" (presumably by receiving Patterson's letter there and lecturing to raise money for his magazine tour); and, relying on Patterson's estimate, adding, "& *possibly* I may get out the first number on next January" (O 2:813–14). He wrote again to John R. Thompson, contrasting his experience of women with that of men: "[T]hey [women] have been angels of mercy to me, and have tenderly led me from the verge of ruin while men stood aloof and mocked" (O 2:819). (There were, of course, important exceptions to this generalization.) And he requested a "favor" of Rufus Wilmot Griswold regarding publication of a longer notice of Sarah Anna Lewis for *Female Poets of America* (O 2:816–17).

Poe's last work to appear in the *Flag of Our Union* was "Sonnet—To My Mother." It was announced in the June 30 issue (appearing on June 23) and published in the July 7 issue (appearing on June 30). The poem was actually a tribute to his mother-in-law, Maria Clemm. The first printing of it was as follows:

Because I feel that, in the heavens above,
    The angels, whispering to one another,

> Can find, among their burning terms of love,
>   None so devotional as that of 'mother'—
> Therefore by that sweet name I long have called you—
>   You, who are more than mother unto me,
> And fill my heart of hearts, where Death installed you,
>   In setting my Virginia's spirit free.
> My mother—my own mother—who died early—
>   Was but the mother of myself; but you
> Are mother to the one I loved so dearly,
>   And thus are dearer than the mother I knew;
> By that infinity with which my wife
>   Was dearer to my soul than its soul-life.[17]

Clearly, in honoring his mother-in-law, Poe also honored his wife. The devotion and love that Poe expressed here to Maria Clemm are evident elsewhere, including his addressing her in his coming letters: "My *dear, dear* Mother" (O 2:820), "Oh, my darling Mother" (O 2:823), "My Own Beloved Mother" (O 2:825), "*My own darling, beloved Mother,*"[18] and "My own darling Muddy" (O 2:836, 837). The sonnet is faithful to his feeling.

Mayne Reid later wrote that Maria Clemm was "the ever-vigilant guardian of the house."[19] N. P. Willis later termed her Poe's "ministering angel."[20] True, we may question such matters as her sale of the borrowed Duane *Southern Literary Messenger,* her encouragement of Poe's advocacy of Sarah Anna Lewis, and her unfriendliness toward Poe's sister Rosalie. But it is important to add here that John H. Mackenzie strongly lauded Mrs. Clemm, as is evident in a letter written by his stepdaughter Flora Lapham Mack to William Lanier Washington on March 31, 1908: "Cousin John had nothing but praise and admiration for Mrs. Clemm. He considered her a miracle of patience & industry and a most dignified reticent & lady like person. He said he never saw such self-sacrificing affection lavished on any one as she gave to Edgar and his wife giving in equal measure to him and to her." Mack also comments, later in the letter (quoted in part earlier), "Mrs. Clemm had perfect patience undying love and a great and abiding faith always. She never gave Edgar a cross or unkind word or look under the most trying circumstances & Cousin John always said if anyone could have reclaimed him or altered him it would certainly have been Mrs. Clemm." Mack writes elsewhere, "Mrs. Clemm was his tower of strength his City of Refuge."[21] Perhaps Poe was too proud to admit his dependency on her publicly. And perhaps, in any case, a published sonnet would have been an inappropriate vehicle for the admission. But her yearslong devotion to, and love for, her nephew and son-in-law would surely have contributed to the feeling that prompted his "Sonnet—To My Mother" in the first place.

Even as Poe termed Maria Clemm "more than mother," she wrote in her prefatory "To the Reader" in the first volume of the Redfield edition of Poe's works that Poe was "more than a son to myself." And she went on to assert that before leaving New York on June 29, 1849, he "wrote . . . requests that the Rev. Rufus W. Griswold should act as his literary Executor, and superintend the publication of his works."[22] Perhaps this was true. Griswold had a significant reputation as an anthologist, and Poe's letter to him of June 28, regarding a notice of Sarah Anna Lewis, was forthright and proper. Perhaps Poe was simply too trusting, considering Griswold only his former enemy. But there is the other possibility—perhaps this was not true. Clemm wrote to Thomas Holley Chivers on December 13, 1852, "You ask why my dear Eddie, chose Griswold as his Executor. He did not."[23] Maybe, then, she made the decision herself, without Poe's approval. After all, Marie Louise Shew wrote, "Mr. Poe told me clearly that Griswold was his enemy," that he felt with Griswold "in the presence of a viper, who would sting him the first chance he got." But Clemm *"feared and asked favors of the man."*[24] And after Poe's drinking at dinner with Griswold in the spring of 1848, which Shew and Poe attributed to Griswold's enabling, Clemm overlooked Griswold's behavior, thinking it "unintentional."[25] So it is possible that Maria Clemm was the too-trusting one. She knew that Griswold was a powerful literary figure and may have believed—or wished to believe—that his enmity with Poe was only in the past and merely the result of "some unhappy misunderstanding."[26] Marie Louise Shew wrote to John H. Ingram, "I never liked the heartless way she [Mrs. Clemm] chose Griswold as Mr. Poe's biographer and I told her she was to blame[;] I do not consider her intentionally so but she forgot the power could be used to injure her beloved son."[27] Whether the decision to make Griswold the executor was Poe's or her own or both of theirs, Clemm would come to realize that it was a serious mistake.

Getting ready to leave New York, Poe visited a bookkeeper to whom he owed money, John W. Moore, at the publisher Pudney & Russell on John Street, and said, "Moore, I may never be able to repay you, but take this; some day it may be valuable." And he gave him a manuscript copy of "Annabel Lee."[28] Finally, on Friday, June 29, having had dinner with the Lewises in Brooklyn, Poe and his mother-in-law made their last trip together, to the steamboat that was headed south—presumably south to Perth Amboy, New Jersey, to the train.[29] Even as Maria Clemm was a vital support for Poe, so was he for her. She wrote to Annie later in the summer, "When I parted with him aboard of the steam boat, he was so dejected but still tried to cheer me. He said, 'God bless my own darling muddy [his pet name for her] do not fear for your Eddy see how good I will be while I am away from you, and will come back to love and comfort you.'"[30]

But she had good reason to fear, for now Poe was alone and—given his precarious health and his all-too-familiar susceptibility—very much at risk.

Precisely what happened next we do not know. We may infer that, at some point, he was drinking. What we do know is that in the early afternoon of Monday, July 2, Poe rushed into the engraving room of John Sartain, in the front of the first floor of 728 Sansom Street, between Seventh and Eighth Streets, just west of Independence Square, in Philadelphia. Sartain, who had known Poe since 1840, was the artist whose engraving in *Graham's Magazine* complemented, and was complemented by, Poe's short piece "The Island of the Fay," in 1841. Now, eight years later, the writer was "looking pale and haggard, with a wild and frightened expression in his eyes." Sartain—who would term Poe "one of my dearest friends"—shook his hand, asked him to sit down, and listened thoughtfully. Poe was there to ask for sanctuary.[31]

It was, of course, granted. And Poe recounted his experience on board a train—two men seated behind him had been quietly talking about murdering him and tossing his body from the car. Hearing their plans, Poe left the train and escaped the conspirators. Sartain doubted this story, wondering who would have the motive to kill him, and Poe said that it was revenge for "woman trouble." The writer was clearly suffering from some mental distress, as the engraver understood.[32] It was probably delirium tremens, a possible after-effect of drinking. Perhaps the origin for this particular irrational terror was the remembered threatened violent pursuit of Poe by Elizabeth Ellet's brother William H. Lummis back in early 1846.

Encouraging calm by continuing with his work—but very attentive to his visitor's words—Sartain sensed a turn to thoughts of suicide and deflected a request for a razor with which Poe might cut off his moustache (supposedly to elude identification), removing the moustache with a scissors himself instead. Sartain then accompanied Poe, through the settling darkness, to the writer's desired destination, the Schuylkill River. The two took the omnibus up Chestnut Street and made their way northwest toward the Fairmount area, not far from Poe's old Coates Street home. Discreetly pressing Poe away from the Fairmount Bridge, Sartain climbed with him up wooden steps to a landing with seats. And in the moonless night, Poe confided to his friend additional recent torments. There was darkness in that darkness.

Incarcerated in Moyemensing Prison, in the southern part of the city, Poe asserted, he had beheld from his cell a shining woman atop a tower, asking him questions to which anything but the correct answers meant death. And yet again, invited to drink from an enormous vat, he had declined, avoiding thereby immersion in the liquid and resulting death. And still yet again, having saved himself from the deadly traps, he had been forced to witness the cutting up of his mother-in-law—first Maria Clemm's feet were cut off, then her legs, then her thighs. Speaking of this final agony, Poe was, according to Sartain, in "a sort of convulsion."[33]

Sartain disbelieved what he heard, except for Poe's imprisonment, caused by "the drop too much."[34] But all the accounts that Poe offered were, at the time, real to him.

Sartain returned with his troubled friend, down the steps and back to the omnibus, riding up Chestnut Street and walking to Sansom Street. Attentive and protective, the artist engaged the writer in ongoing conversation. Poe slept on the couch in the dining room and Sartain, fully clothed, on three chairs near him. Two days later, well cared for by his host, Poe emerged from his desperate state, realizing that his terrors had been chimeras.[35] He would write to Maria Clemm on July 19, "For more than ten days I was totally deranged, although I was not drinking one drop; and during this interval I imagined the most horrible calamities.... All was hallucination, arising from an attack which I had never before experienced—an attack of *mania-à-potu*. May Heaven grant that it prove a warning to me for the rest of my days. If so, I shall not regret even the horrible unspeakable torments I have endured" (O 2:825–26). If there is some misremembering here ("more than ten days") and some exculpating, as well ("not drinking one drop"), at least Poe understood that he had been suffering from delusions. He had recovered his reason.

Borrowing some money, Poe left Sartain. He would have heard fireworks from dawn to midnight on the Fourth of July, but it was probably his health that preoccupied him. In response to the spreading cholera, Philadelphia's Board of Health had recommended foregoing the celebration, and President Zachary Taylor had recommended making August 3 "a day of fasting, humiliation, and prayer."[36] The disease was frightening. And Poe was sick—he wrote to Mrs. Clemm on July 7, "I have been *so* ill—have had the cholera, or spasms quite as bad, and can now hardly hold the pen." Freed from his delusions, he was not freed from his despair: "The very instant you get this, *come* to me. The joy of seeing you will almost compensate for our sorrows. We can but die together. It is no use to reason with me *now;* I must die. I have no desire to live since I have done 'Eureka.' I could accomplish nothing more. For your sake it would be sweet to live, but we must die together. You have been all in all to me, darling, ever beloved mother, and dearest, truest friend" (O 2:820). This letter was enclosed with a brief letter to Sarah Anna Lewis, with whom Poe must have believed Maria Clemm was still staying (O 2:822n). But Clemm had left and did not receive Poe's letter until she returned to Mrs. Lewis, in mid-July.[37]

Poe evidently tried to go about his life as well as he could. At the printing office of *Sartain's Union Magazine,* Poe talked with the editor John S. Hart and then explained to an eleven-year-old boy, who was holding a print, the background of that print. (We may recall Poe's fascination with Hogarth prints more than twenty years earlier in Charlottesville.) Poe accompanied young Henry Graham Ashmead to the boy's home on Walnut Street. Not knowing who this was at the time, Ashmead considered him a "gentleman of distinguished bearing but somewhat seedily attired," who offered "delightful conversation." (John Sartain soon clarified the gentleman's identity.) Poe also gave a manuscript copy of "Annabel Lee" to his old friend Henry B. Hirst, who lived on Sixth Street. But days passed, and Poe was running out of money. He was without resources and, increasingly, without resilience. On Thursday, July 12, he ascended the four flights to a printing office where his longtime admirer George Lippard, twenty-seven years old, was writing. (This was probably the office of Joseph Severns and Company, the printer of Lippard's weekly newspaper, *Quaker City,* at 72 Chestnut Street.) Poe was, Lippard later remembered, badly dressed, wearing only one shoe, and "He came stealthily up stairs, as if conscious that the world had forsaken him, and that he was an intruder anywhere."[38]

This was the man whom Lippard had described six years earlier, before his first Philadelphia lecture, as "perhaps, the most original writer that ever existed in America."[39] Eleven hundred people had attended that lecture, and hundreds had been turned away. Now, destitute and discouraged, Poe visited Philadelphia writers whose reputations he had helped make, and he was made to wait in the outer office, mocked by their assistants. Poe was worn-down, humiliated, plainly in need. And he said to Lippard, simply, "You are my last hope. If you fail me, I can do nothing but die."[40]

What he needed were food and a place to sleep. And what he wanted was a return to Virginia. Lippard recalled, in his obituary of Poe, that Poe had said, "I am sick—sick at heart. I have come to see you before I leave for Virginia. I am homesick for Virginia. I don't know why it is but when my foot is once in Virginia, I feel myself a new man. It is a pleasure to me to go into her woods—to lay myself upon her sod—even to breathe her air."[41] Lippard wanted to help, but he had no money, having just paid his rent. So, he set out in the hot, cholera-stricken city to seek funds from others in the newspaper district—but those he sought were gone. Sick himself, he went home. But Lippard returned to the printing office the following morning, Friday, July 13, and Poe was sitting in the corner, woeful, tearing up as he admitted, "I thought *you* had deserted me."[42]

Lippard would not desert him. He remembered Poe from better days. And as the obituary makes clear, he cherished him: "[H]e was a man of genius—a man of high honor—a man of good heart."[43] Lippard resumed his search and received contributions for Poe from publishers Louis A. Godey, Samuel D. Patterson, and the ever-supportive John Sartain, as well as Sartain's clerk Mr. Miskey and editor Charles Chauncey Burr (who also made his way to the printing office). This seems a kind of roll of honor.[44]

Lippard wrote that when he presented Poe with the small bounty—more than eleven dollars—"You should have seen the poet's face.... There was a grasp of the hand—and a look of the face—which said much more than words." We may imagine a transforming gratitude. The money was a relief—and a recognition. But there was also "a tremor of the poet's lip" as he heard of the publisher who had refused to offer him anything.

And then, Charles Chauncey Burr invited Poe and Lippard to visit with him at his home.[45] And so, perhaps, the consolation was complete. At Burr's home at Seventh Street south of Poplar, the three men talked—the still-young, shaggy Lippard; the slightly older, stolid Burr; and the worn but revived Poe. Lippard and Poe reminisced about their first meeting, at Poe's Spring Garden home, a place gladdened by Poe's wife Virginia, where Poe used to hold forth with Lippard, at ease. And Poe discussed his recent book *Eureka* and his anticipated future work.[46] Burr later wrote of Poe, "All who knew him well, bear this testimony, that he was, in private life, as gentle and refined as a woman, with a heart as tender and affectionate as a child."[47]

That evening, Lippard and Burr walked their rallying friend to the railroad depot, a few blocks away at Eleventh and Market Streets, where he was to take the 10:00 p.m. train to Baltimore. Perhaps they tried to help him find his lost valise. (Even if they found it, they did not find the lectures that the valise contained.) Poe gave Lippard a copy of *Eureka* and only reluctantly let go of his hand. Burr bought Poe the train ticket, and from Baltimore the writer would then proceed by boat to Richmond. Lippard later wrote of Poe at his departure, "[T]here was in his voice, look and manner something of a presentiment that his strange and stormy life was near its close."[48]

Poe knew that he had been rescued. He would later write to Maria Clemm, "To L[ippard] and to C[hauncey] B[urr] (and in some measure, also, to Mr. S[artain]) I am indebted for more than life. They remained with me (L[ippard] and B[urr]) all day on Friday last, comforted me and aided me in coming to my senses." As for drinking, he wrote that he had had "only a little Port wine" (perhaps as an anodyne) (O 2:826, 826n). And he reassured Mrs. Clemm, "All is not lost yet, and 'the darkest hour is just before daylight.' Keep up heart, my own beloved mother—all may yet go well. I will put forth all my energies. When I get my mind a little more composed, I will try to write something" (O 2:826).

On Saturday, July 14, on the boat approaching Richmond, Poe wrote to Maria Clemm, saying that he would never leave her again—"When I am with you I can bear anything, but when I am away from you I am too miserable to live" (O 2:823). She would finally have received Poe's earlier letter (from Mrs. Lewis) but could not afford to go to him in Philadelphia (although, she wrote to Annie, if she had received the letter in time, she would have gone "if I had to have *begged* my way").[49] That night, finally back in Richmond, Poe stayed at the new American Hotel, at Eleventh and Main, and wrote to Clemm, "I love you better than ten thousand lives" (O 2:823). Mentioning the lost lectures, he commented, "All my object here is over unless I can recover them or re-write one of them" (O 2:824). Clearly, he was still planning to lecture to raise funds for his trip on behalf of "The Stylus." Finding himself with two dollars remaining from the sum that Lippard had raised, he sent his mother-in-law one dollar. And he urged his devoted mother-in-law, "If possible, oh COME!" (O 2:824).

During the next two and a half months in his hometown, Poe would find a warm and heartening welcome. To those who had been following his career, his visit was both the return of the prodigal and the return of the prodigy. He had, after all, wrested fame from the cold and indifferent North. But he was still poor. And despite his presence in Virginia, he was not "a new man," for he was still vulnerable to the temptation of drink.

If Richmond had become to Poe, after many years, "a strange city,"[50] he still knew the lay of the land, from Duncan Lodge, in the suburbs to the west, to Darby Town, in the country to the south. He knew the churches, from Monumental Church to St. John's Church. He knew the buildings that had once been so important in his life, from the Allan House, Moldavia, to the old *Southern Literary Messenger* building. And he knew the nearby slave auctions and slave jails, clustered around Fifteenth Street. Much had not changed—yet. The Civil War, the Emancipation Proclamation, the burning of Richmond, the victory of the Union were still years in the future.

But in another sense, regarding his personal life, Poe was not at all sure of the lay of the land, for he did not know what might develop with his former sweetheart Elmira—now the wealthy widow Shelton—living on Church Hill, to the east. She had been writing him love letters, and he had been writing back. They had even met in the summer of 1848. Where this would all lead was a matter of uncertainty. According to Susan Archer Weiss (formerly Susan Archer Talley), it was Elmira whom Poe first visited.[51] He would have walked up Broad Street, climbing Church Hill to 2407 East Grace Street, between Twenty-Fourth and Twenty-Fifth Streets, opposite the grounds of St. John's Church.[52]

There is a backstory. After Virginia Poe's death in January 1847, Elmira had indicated an interest in Edgar Allan Poe, the love of her youth, to Tom Mackenzie, the second of the three Mackenzie brothers (born in 1821). Evidently Tom wrote to Poe of her interest and suggested Poe's possibly reciprocating it. (It was not John H. Mackenzie who made the suggestion.)[53] Elmira began sending Poe love letters, and he replied. Neither her letters to him nor his to her have survived. However, after Poe's death, second cousin Neilson Poe, of Baltimore, found Elmira's letters to Poe in Poe's trunk. And he stated to Eugene Didier, "They were as foolishly sentimental as those of a love-sick school girl." Neilson returned the letters to Elmira.[54] So, as Poe climbed Church Hill, we may imagine that although he was uncertain, he was also hopeful. There were the letters. And there was also his visit to Elmira in the summer of 1848. Perhaps this could work out.

Elmira said, in an interview many years later, that Poe greeted her that morning in her parlor enthusiastically, "Oh! Elmira is this you?" (We may note that in her daguerreotype she seems rather severe and that Susan Archer Weiss thought Elmira then looked like "a sensible, practical woman, the reverse of a poet's ideal," but that John H. Mackenzie considered her to have been, at this time, a still-attractive woman.) Elmira could not talk with Poe that morning because she was going to church, but she invited him to call again. When he did call again, he proposed marriage. She did not initially take him seriously, but when it became clear that he was indeed serious, she responded that if he could not accept "a positive denial," he must give her "time to consider of it." And so, there was at least a possibility.[55]

Poe certainly liked Elmira, but, as evidence will make clear, he saw his renewed relationship with her not so much as a romance as an opportunity.

At the other end of Broad Street, to the west, was the elegant Mackenzie home, Duncan Lodge. Poe had come to know it the previous summer, and it would again be a social center for him. Here he would see the matronly, beloved Jane Scott Mackenzie, as well as her second son, middle brother "Dr. Tom," of "[h]igh and [b]road" forehead, "the walking encyclopedia," and her third son, youngest brother Richard, who, lame from birth, was a great rider. Poe would see, too, Mrs. Mackenzie's daughter and son-in-law Martha and William P. Byrd, her heavy-set son-in-law Caleb Jones (he of leapfrog notoriety from the previous summer), and his own sister, often-unkempt but adoring Rosalie. Mrs. Mackenzie's oldest son and Poe's lifelong friend, hale and hearty John H. Mackenzie, and his petite, fragile wife Louisa, both living on their farm south of Richmond, Darby Town, would be frequent visitors.[56]

During one of his visits to Duncan Lodge, Poe gave a reading of "The Raven" and "Annabel Lee" to the family. Jane Scott Mackenzie, who had declined to lend Poe money, suggested that he give a public reading and raise funds that way. Such an event was scheduled at the Exchange Hotel, but—perhaps because many people were away on vacation—only thirteen people attended. And the profit, at fifty cents per person (not counting the usher), was only six dollars. Poe was, of course, disappointed. He did not cancel the reading (as he had canceled the lecture in New York in April 1845), but he did read his work without his customary expressiveness. Fortunately, his later lecture on "The Poetic Principle" would be well attended.[57]

Early on when Poe visited Duncan Lodge, Mrs. Mackenzie mentioned that young poet Susan Archer Talley lived nearby. Presumably she explained that Talley was deaf (owing to scarlet fever in her childhood), but that communication could still take place. Talley could, in fact, still speak. And we may conjecture that she could probably read lips. Alternatively, those around her could sign or spell with their hands or write something out.[58]

Poe had written briefly to Talley, in all likelihood on November 20, 1848, asking her to deliver a fundraising letter to Edward Valentine. Poe had also taken an interest in her poem "Genius," stating, in a December 8, 1848, letter to the *Southern Literary Messenger* editor John R. Thompson, that she herself had "real *genius*" (O 2:739–40), and later extolling her "*genius*" in a February 1849 *Messenger* review.[59]

With his sister Rosalie, Poe visited Talley at her family home, Talavera. The two-story farmhouse was set on twenty-five acres, which offered "greenhouses, orchard, vineyard." It was a retreat, an embowered home of "quiet seclusion." Susan Archer Talley—as Susan Archer Weiss—later wrote that Poe visited her "a day or two" after his arriving in Richmond, but she also wrote that she was introduced to Poe on a Friday, two days before she saw him at church. So that would suggest his visiting on Friday, July 20 (since he was not in Richmond on Friday, July 13).[60]

Talley was then a pretty, twenty-seven-year-old woman, relatively quiet on this first visit. She observed Poe as he talked with her mother and sister. She would later describe him as a man of "polish, courtesy, and refinement," "a refined, high-bred, and chivalrous gentleman" (recalling the description of Poe given by Annie's sister Sarah). Talley noted a detail that no daguerreotype can convey—she "saw his eyes suddenly brighten as I offered my hand." She would comment on this in her obituary of Poe, "It was touching to observe how his eye would brighten, his whole countenance cheer at the least display of friendly feeling." There was evidently a glad responsiveness, a lively luster in Poe's eyes. And these were extraordinary eyes—"Such eyes—large, deep, and luminous, with a strange depth and light—and yet, withal, I thought was a something of subtlety in their expression. I have never seen other such eyes."[61]

Often at Duncan Lodge in the evenings, Poe was also often at Talavera. Talley later left numerous reminiscences, which, if not always accurate, are nonetheless highly worthy of consideration.

Poe was feeling better. He wrote to Maria Clemm on July 19, "You will see at once, by the handwriting of this letter, that I am better—much better in health and spirits." Her recent letter to him had been a great relief. He promised to "try to write something" (O 2:825–26). Poe at some point asked George Lippard to seek the lost lectures, but Lippard and Burr could not locate them.[62] In the coming days, Poe evidently rewrote "The Poetic Principle" (perhaps at Duncan Lodge). He may then have worked on the never-to-be-finished "A Reviewer Reviewed" and "The Light-House." And Poe was still thinking about "The Stylus." Also on July 19, he wrote to the prospective "Stylus" publisher E. H. N. Patterson, mentioning his having had cholera and acknowledging the two letters and the fifty dollars (O 2:827–28).

The American Hotel—where Poe stayed when he arrived, at which he was seen with Dr. William Gibbon Carter on Monday, July 23—was too "expensive," and Poe shifted to the more modest Swan Tavern—indeed, past its prime—a two-story building between Eighth and Ninth Streets on Broad.

Weiss identified Poe's four reasons for the move there: "[I]t was cheap, well kept in 'the old Virginia style,' associated with many pleasant memories of his youth and, lastly and chiefly, nearest Duncan's Lodge, where most of his time was passed."[63]

Maria Clemm, having heard from Poe, let Annie know on July 30 that "he was going from Richmond in a few days, to stay with a friend in the country for a short time."[64] And so, Poe returned to John H. Mackenzie and his wife Louisa at Darby Town. He was back to the original setting for "Eleonora"—but without Eleonora. Still, he was with his lifelong friend and the wife whom Poe had considered "the sweetest creature in the world," she of the "heavenly smile" (O 2:683). The couple were devoted to Poe—had even named after him their one son, who had died in infancy. Like Duncan Lodge, Darby Town was a haven for Poe—until it was not.

There had been a significant change at Darby Town. The household of three (not including those enslaved)—John, Louisa, and Louisa's mother, Mary Lanier ("Aunt Polly")—had become seven. Although the three Mattox sisters whom John and Louisa had taken in back in April 1833 (Louisa's cousins Ann, Mary, and Eliza) had long ago grown up, married, and moved away, the couple had recently taken in the three Lanier sisters (Louisa's nieces—daughters of brother William Lewis Lanier, who had become a New Orleans merchant—Jane, Martha ["Mattie"], and Mary ["Mollie"]). Their mother, Virginia Armistead Lanier, had died on March 17, 1849, and the three sisters had traveled east and north from Holly Springs, Mississippi, to stay with their Aunt Louisa at Darby Town. The girls were, Flora Lapham Mack asserts, "the petted darlings of the entire household." And they had a live-in governess.[65]

Poe would certainly have seen the girls on his visits to Darby Town in the summer and fall of 1849. Indeed, William Lanier Washington wrote about Poe and his own mother Jane, when she was seven years old: "'Uncle Edgar' frequently took Jane upon his knee and amused her with such charming tales wrought extemporaneously out of his fertile imagination, while Jane gazed into his beautiful face and passed her fingers through his shiny black curly hair."[66] With the Mackenzies, whether at Duncan Lodge or Darby Town, Poe was part of the family.

When he sat with Jane on his knee, he was perhaps in one of the "cosy armchairs & rockers" in "the old huge square reception Hall at Darby [T]own" or on one of the Hall's "two long long old hair cloth sofas." This grand room had that memorable fireplace mantelpiece of "Pharoes [Pharoah's] host being drownded [sic]."[67] John and Louisa's abundance—in the house, on the

193 acres, even in John's tobacco warehouses and stables in the city—was made possible by the African Americans whom John "owned": in 1849, six of them over twelve years old, and another six over sixteen years old.[68] These were the Israelites who would be freed—the Mackenzies were the Egyptians, and although they would not drown, they would lose their old world. Or, to shift figures, turning from Exodus to Genesis, the Mackenzies would eventually lose their "Paradise" because of their culpability for America's Original Sin, slavery.

After a while, Poe returned to the Swan Tavern. Perhaps he was finishing the rewriting of "The Poetic Principle" or at work on "A Reviewer Reviewed" or "The Light-House." His lecture would be announced, as a coming "intellectual feast," in the *Richmond Daily Republican* of July 31.[69] During late July, Poe would have been visiting Elmira to continue his courtship and visiting Duncan Lodge and Talavera to enjoy his friendships. A topic of conversation would certainly have been his prospective magazine, "The Stylus." Mrs. Mackenzie promised to support it and provided detail for an article that Poe expected to publish there. Miss Talley, as Mrs. Weiss, later recalled that most of Poe's Richmond friends had pledged to support the magazine and that Poe had said, with regard to "The Stylus," "I must and will succeed!"[70] He would soon write again to Patterson—his last known letter to his prospective publisher (O 2:828–30).

August 1 might have recalled to Poe the death of his brother Henry eighteen years earlier, so honored at the center of his novel, begun in Richmond, *The Narrative of Arthur Gordon Pym*. And August 3 served as the "day of fasting, humiliation, and prayer," an effort, prompted by President Zachary Taylor, for the people to atone for the wrongs they had committed (unspecified), for which cholera was the evident punishment, and to ask for God's protection. The mayor of Richmond encouraged the observance of this day, and indeed, that Friday was more like a Sunday, for business ceased, and many attended church.[71] Whether Poe attended church then we do not know. What is particularly interesting is the public warning that Poe's reformist friend Lippard, in Philadelphia, had made: "God's Angel, whom men know by the name of Death, is in our midst. Fast for a little while; not merely for a day as Zachary Taylor advises in his Recommendation, but fast for a month or two, and fast not only from meats and wine, but fast from bank-stocks, politics, Saratoga balls—from everything but Brotherhood."[72]

Brotherhood Poe had. There were John, Tom, and Dick Mackenzie; Robert Sully; Robert Cabell; John R. Thompson; William Gibbon Carter;

John F. Carter; and others. But there was also, as always, a personal danger. Poe had acknowledged, in 1841, that during his time at the *Southern Literary Messenger* in Richmond, "I certainly did give way, at long intervals, to the temptation held out on all sides by the spirit of Southern conviviality. My sensitive temperament could not stand an excitement which was an everyday matter to my companions. In short, it sometimes happened that I was completely intoxicated" (O 1:263–64). Now that Poe was back in Richmond for an extended period of time, the problem could recur. And it did.

According to Weiss, after the first time that he "gave way" in the summer of 1849, he was cared for by the Mackenzies at the Swan Tavern. (An alternative recollection states that Dr. George W. Rawlins attended Poe there.) The second incident, however, was more severe, and it required both Dr. Tom Mackenzie and Dr. William Gibbon Carter to care for Poe at Duncan Lodge. Again Poe had been overcome by temptation. He was told by his doctors that "another such attack would prove fatal." At first he blamed his tempters. But later he confided to Dr. Carter that he had made repeated but ultimately unsuccessful efforts to resist. "Moved even to tears," he committed himself to total restraint, total abstinence. He would, in fact, in late August, join the Sons of Temperance.[73] Poe would try to do what his friend John H. Mackenzie had long ago concluded that he could not do.

Weiss reported that in the summer of 1849 Poe "had a pallid and careworn look, somewhat haggard, indeed—very apparent except in his moments of animation" and that after his first bout with drink he seemed "pale, tremulous and especially subdued." She considered him "rather distinguished-looking than handsome."[74] Yet Flora Lapham Mack wrote, "Mother [Mary Mattox Lapham] and Cousin John declared that he was handsomer then than at other time[s] and they both considered him very handsome."[75] Both characterizations—handsome, distinguished—were born out by descriptions of Poe as he appeared at the time from those outside his immediate circle. Seventeen-year-old Basil L. Gildersleeve saw him on Broad Street, "a poetical figure, if there ever was one, clad in black as was the fashion then—slender—erect—the subtle lines of his face fixed in meditation. I thought him wonderfully handsome, the mouth being the only weak point." And nearly twenty-year-old Oscar P. Fitzgerald observed him, as well: "There was a fascination about him that everybody felt. Meeting him in the midst of thousands a stranger would stop to get a second look, and to ask, 'Who is he?' He was *distingué* in a peculiar sense—a man bearing the stamp of genius and the charm of a melancholy that drew one toward him with a strange sympathy" (H 1:315–16).

Any stranger who saw Poe in Richmond in the summer of 1849 and wondered, "Who is he?" would soon have an opportunity to try to answer that question. On Friday, August 17, Poe would deliver his lecture "The Poetic Principle" at the Exchange Hotel, in its Concert Room. And the response to that talk would be mostly positive. Additionally, by that time, Poe would have answered his own question—regarding the possibility of a future with Elmira Shelton—in the negative.

But he would change his mind.

25

"Hope for a Wretch Like Me"

1849

THE EVENT WAS ADVERTISED ON August 15, 16, and 17: "EDGAR A. POE will lecture on '*The Poetic Principle*,' (with various recitations) at the Exchange Concert Room, on Friday evening, the 17th, at 8 o'clock. Tickets 25 cents; to be had at the various bookstores."[1] "The Poetic Principle" was the talk that Poe had previously presented, so successfully, at Howard's Hall in Providence, on December 20, 1848. (Given the loss or theft of his lectures, he must have rewritten the work.) Richmond's Exchange Concert Room—considered "the best hall in the city for the purpose"—was the expansive hall of the Exchange Hotel, the impressive three-story brick-and-granite building, of classical design, near the Capitol, at Franklin and Fourteenth Streets.[2] At 8:00 p.m., on August 17, 1849, the Exchange Concert Room was full. Poe later wrote that there was on that August evening "a crowded house (250 persons)," and he lamented having set the ticket price so low. And he was not there alone—he had come with Jane Clark, for whom he had given readings in the nearby Park Hotel the previous summer.[3]

One young man in attendance, the writer John Esten Cooke, recalled, "The lecturer stood in a graceful attitude, leaning one hand on a small table beside him, and his wonderfully clear and musical voice speedily brought the audience under its spell."[4] Poe offered his audience a succession of poems of transport—poems that reach to "Supernal Beauty" through a stirring of the soul (L2 198). Poe recited lines by Shelley on his beloved—"O, lift me from the grass! / I die, I faint, I fail! / Let thy love in kisses rain / On my lips and eyelids pale." Poe recited Longfellow on discontent—"A feeling of sadness and longing, / That is not akin to pain, / And resembles sorrow only / As the mist resembles the rain." And Poe recited lines by Bryant on death—"But if, around my place of sleep, / The friends I love should come to weep, / They might not haste to go. / Soft airs, and song, and light, and bloom / Should keep them lingering by my tomb" (L2 181, 186, 188). Cooke wrote to his brother of the lecture, "It was fine particularly the recitations." The *Richmond Times* stated, "These recitations were exceedingly well received by a large and appreciative audience."[5] Poe closed his talk by reciting "The Raven," his pleasurably painful, cathartic tribute to *"Mournful and Never-ending Remembrance"* (L2 70).

"The lecture ended," we are told, "in the midst of applause."[6] Poe later wrote, "I *never* was received with so much enthusiasm" (O 2:830). Never taken back by John Allan, Poe was now taken back by Richmond.

The reviews were mostly very favorable—the *Richmond Whig* reported that the lecture "was full of strong, manly sense"; the *Richmond Daily Republican* thought it "one of the richest intellectual treats we have ever had the good fortune to hear"; and the *Richmond Times* stated, "We do not know when we have enjoyed a more delightful evening—barring the heat—than in listening to Mr. Poe's lecture on the Poetic Principle, last Friday night."[7] Even the mixed review by John M. Daniel, in the *Richmond Semi-Weekly Examiner*, which faulted the recitations, acknowledged of Poe, "[H]is title to immortality would not and could not be surer than it is."[8]

Furthermore, despite the too-low ticket price, Poe did earn twenty-five dollars. He applied this to his significant bill from the Swan Tavern, thereby liberating his impounded trunk. (Still owing the Swan, he moved to the Madison House.)[9]

But even as his success with "The Poetic Principle" continued, his courtship of Elmira Shelton had temporarily ceased. According to Church Hill neighbors, by mid-August Poe was no longer visiting Elmira.[10] Once again, Poe could declare, however briefly, "And fame shall be my only bride."

What had happened? One problem with Poe and Elmira was pace. Poe wrote to Maria Clemm on August 29, "I got angry with her [Elmira] for wishing to defer it [their marriage] till January & wrote her a cross letter." And he mentioned, later in this same letter, "my marriage, which I will hurry as much as possible."[11] Probably Poe's impatience was due to his unending poverty. And perhaps Elmira's delay was owing to her family, especially her daughter and her brothers. Clearly, a critical problem was money. Elmira was an affluent widow, Poe an impoverished writer. Weiss stated, "Poe himself broke their engagement"—she contended that the issue was Elmira's initial reluctance to support "The Stylus." It is revealing that after the estrangement ended, Poe would write in his August 29 letter to Maria Clemm about the Mackenzies and his coming marriage, "They seem to think it a fortunate speculation for me."[12]

But John H. Mackenzie would disagree.

Following the lecture, Poe was much celebrated in Richmond but soon thereafter returned to Darby Town. Weiss observed, "[H]e did not appear to care for the formal parties, and declared that he found more enjoyment with his friends in the country."[13] Perhaps he sat again in the reception hall, telling stories to Jane on his knee. Perhaps he wandered the fields and woods with the Lanier sisters as he had done years earlier with Virginia and the Mattox sisters. Doubtless he talked of his recent lecture triumph and of his high hopes for "The Stylus" with John and Louisa. At this time, he probably wouldn't have discussed Elmira—after all, he had broken off with her. There was nothing to discuss.

During the rift with Poe, Elmira visited Jane Scott Mackenzie, John's mother, at Duncan Lodge. Weiss recalled seeing Elmira there, "a tall, rather masculine-looking woman, who drew her veil over her face as she passed us on the porch, though I caught a glimpse of large, shadowy, light blue eyes which must once have been handsome."[14] Elmira's mission, according to Weiss, was to ask Mrs. Mackenzie to help her retrieve her letters to Edgar. In his later response, Poe apparently requested the return of his own letters to Elmira—she said that they were "destroyed," but he was not sure that he should believe this.[15]

The issue with Elmira would soon be resolved. Meanwhile, Poe attended a lecture on Shakespeare by J. W. Taverner; only eight people were present, he reported (O 2:831), a fact that highlights the significance of the turnout at his own lecture. It may have been at this time that Poe made one of his visits to bookseller J. W. Randolph, on Main Street, and asked about the bookseller who had formerly been at that site, Richard D. Sanxay. Poe found the old bookman and reported back to Randolph that he and Sanxay had had "a pleasant meeting." There was an almost filial loyalty here that resonates with Poe's having repeatedly visited—years after his student days—his old teacher Joseph H. Clarke, in Baltimore.[16]

There was a possible new professional situation—Poe received an offer to edit the poetry of Mrs. Marguerite St. Leon Loud, of Philadelphia, and he accepted it (O 2:831).[17] And he continued to await the response from

E. H. N. Patterson to his recent letter about "The Stylus." The publisher would write his last known letter to Poe on August 21, proposing that the first issue of the five-dollar-per-year magazine appear in July 1850 (H 17:365–66).

Before long, the concern that Elmira had had about her letters to Poe vanished, for she wanted him back. And she let people know. Poe wrote, in his August 29 letter to Maria Clemm, "We made it up & she now sanctions my writing to you, announcing the marriage in a month. She went nearly frantic when I told her I would nt have her—went out to Mackenzie's after me & all about town—so that every body knows of our engagement."[18] Elmira returned to Duncan Lodge but must not have traveled to Darby Town. For John wouldn't learn of the new development until Poe visited again.

The engagement of Poe and Elmira was announced on August 28—she visited Rosalie at Duncan Lodge that day ("the Mackenzies are all very cordial"), and Poe and Rosalie visited Elmira on Church Hill the following day (O 2:830).[19] Poe introduced his fiancée to Maria Clemm in his letter of August 29—"And now let me tell you all about Elmira as well as I can in a letter."[20] He made clear that Elmira had agreed to his preferred timing and evidently his financial wishes, as well. Poe expounded on money matters to Mrs. Clemm:

> Her [Elmira's] property is not so large as I was told—but is ample for all our wants. Mr Shelton left property [when he died in 1844] to the amount of $60,000, and since his death it has much increased in value and is now worth at least 70,000. He left it to her sole charge and management so long as she remains his widow, but if she marries, she retains only a house, furniture, carriage &c, servants (slaves) and an income of from 12 to 1400$ [per year]. But she has had charge of the estate now for 9 [5] years; and as she is said to be a notable manager, no doubt she has laid by many thousand dollars in money. She says she is *quite* willing & eager to give up the charge of the estate for my sake.[21]

He went on to discuss the eventual inheritance for her ten-year-old son and his own possibly educating him (thus saving "about $500 a year"). And he mentioned that Elmira had been receptive to the idea of buying a cottage. Of course, wherever they would live, Maria Clemm would join them: "You are to live with us *always* & to take charge of the house."[22] Here we have a resuscitated Poe, anticipating a financial security that he had never before had as an adult. He could soon, he thought, carry on his literary projects—including "The Stylus"—in comfort and at ease.

Notably, a day before the engagement was announced, on the floor above a carpenter shop on Broad Street, near Brook Avenue, Poe joined the Shockoe Hill Division, Number 54, of the Sons of Temperance. Presumably he was thus trying to allay the legitimate concern of Elmira, and those around her, about his drinking—and to strengthen his resolve.[23]

The new arrangement was set. If it was not positively Ellisonian, it was certainly sufficient. And Poe even had the ring: "I have got the wedding ring.— and shall have no difficulty, I think, in getting a dress-coat" (O 2:832).[24] That gold ring survives today in the Susan Jaffe Tane Collection of the Poe Museum in Richmond. Engraved within the 5/8-inch band is simply the name "Edgar."[25]

There were still, not surprisingly, very substantial difficulties. However Poe may have responded to Elmira's love, his real love was for Annie. He wrote to Maria Clemm, in obvious conflict, "[B]ut I want to live *near Annie*" (O 2:831). And he later intimated his jealousy of Annie's husband: "Do not tell me anything about Annie—I cannot bear to hear it now—unless you can tell me that Mr. R. [Richmond] is dead" (O 2:832).[26] Additionally, even for those who didn't know about Annie, there were serious questions about Poe: Could he be a responsible husband? Was his motive merely mercenary? Poe wrote to Maria Clemm, "Since the report of my intended marriage, the McKenzies have overwhelmed me with attentions" (O 2:831).[27] Those at Duncan Lodge may have been approving, but one of them at Darby Town would not be.

Before Poe left for Norfolk by September 9 (and Elmira left for the country), he would have continued to visit Duncan Lodge and Talavera. Perhaps it was during this time that he repeated his remarkable "three flying leaps" for Mrs. Mackenzie and one Dr. George Watson, apparently setting a record.[28] Maybe it was also at this time that, with Susan Archer Talley, he visited the nearby well-remembered but now dilapidated old Mayo mansion, the Hermitage. Observing its fallen and abandoned state, he quoted Thomas Moore's "Oft, in the Stilly Night."[29] It could have been then, too, that Poe recited "The Raven" at Talavera. Toward the end of his performance, his sister Rosalie approached him and sat on his knee—the comic effect prompted Poe to say, when he had finished, that in the future "he would 'take Rose along, to act the part of the raven, in which she seemed born to excel.'"[30]

For those enslaved in the Talley household, Poe's recitation of "The Raven" was a thrilling event. Weiss's condescending, racist rendering reveals that they responded sympathetically to Poe's presentation and also to a later one, by Susan Archer Talley or her sister Eliza. Told of their response to the requested repetition, Poe was pleased.[31] It is fascinating to note that, sometime during the summer of 1849 in Richmond, Poe taught the former "body-servant" of John Allan, James Stirling—presumably enslaved or formerly enslaved—to recite "The Raven" and others of his poems. Even years later, Stirling offered an extraordinary performance of Poe's most famous work: "The 'Raven' was given in a mood of revery, until the first response of the bird, then jocularly, then with great seriousness, and, finally, exasperated to madness, the interpreter threw the box, that had served him as seat and rostrum, at the imaginary bird, and fell prostrate. His voice in the last lines weakened to a husky whisper, and his eyes wandered with the 'shadow on the floor.'" The writer adds, "I have seen [Italian actor Tommaso] Salvini in [the drama] 'Civil Death,' and can only instance him as an approach to that negro's abject terror and surrender."[32] And so, Poe's narrator, who yields to the emblem of *Mournful and Never-ending Remembrance*," was effectively brought to life by Poe's gifted student.

Poe soon traveled 125 miles southeast to Norfolk—probably by a James River steamer—to deliver again "The Poetic Principle." At the home of Susan Maxwell and as a guest of the Frenches at the Old Hygeia Hotel, Poe recited his own poetry. The hotel and nearby Fortress Monroe, where Poe had been stationed twenty years earlier, were on the small promontory of Old Point Comfort. Young Susan V. C. Ingram remembered her small group, including Poe, on the veranda of the Old Hygeia on Sunday evening, September 9. There were the girls in their white dresses, the moonlit sky, the glimmering ocean, and a bit of apt encouragement from Susan's aunt, "This seems to be just the time and place for poetry, Mr. Poe." And the others concurred.[33]

Mr. Poe obliged, reciting "The Raven," "Annabel Lee," and "Ulalume," all poems about a lost beloved. The second and third pieces were subtitled in some version "A Ballad"—indeed, they were potentially songs as well as poems.[34] The six-stanza "Annabel Lee," Poe's last poem, still unpublished at the time, begins with a tender lyric:

> It was many and many a year ago,
>   In a kingdom by the sea,
> That a maiden there lived whom you may know
>   By the name of Annabel Lee;—
> And this maiden she lived with no other thought
>   Than to love and be loved by me.
>
> *She* was a child and *I* was a child,
>   In this kingdom by the sea,

> But we loved with a love that was more than love—
>   I and my Annabel Lee—
> With a love that the wingéd seraphs of Heaven
>   Coveted her and me.

But the idyll could not endure for there were those who could not endure it:

> And this was the reason that, long ago,
>   In this kingdom by the sea,
> A wind blew out of a cloud by night
>   Chilling my Annabel Lee;
> So that her high-born kinsmen came
>   And bore her away from me,
> To shut her up, in a sepulchre,
>   In this kingdom by the sea.
>
> The angels, not so half so happy in Heaven,
>   Went envying her and me:—
> Yes! that was the reason (as all men know,
>   In this kingdom by the sea)
> That the wind came out of the cloud, chilling
>   And killing my Annabel Lee.

Still, the bereft lover never leaves his beloved:

> But our love it was stronger by far than the love
>   Of those who were older than we—
>   Of many far wiser than we—
> And neither the angels in Heaven above
>   Nor the demons down under the sea
> Can ever dissever my soul from the soul
>   Of the beautiful Annabel Lee:—
>
> For the moon never beams without bringing me dreams
>   Of the beautiful Annabel Lee;
> And the stars never rise but I see the bright eyes
>   Of the beautiful Annabel Lee;
> And so, all the night-tide, I lie down by the side
> Of my darling, my darling, my life and my bride
>   In her sepulchre there by the sea—
>   In her tomb by the side of the sea. (M 1:478–79)

(Other manuscript versions of the poem closed "In her tomb by the sounding sea" [M 1:478], and this would become the preferred final line.)

There are several notable literary sources for "Annabel Lee." For example, reading the March 1849 issue of the *Southern Literary Messenger,* which included his review of James Russell Lowell's *A Fable for Critics,* Poe would have encountered the poem "Castle by the Sea," translated from the German of Johann Ludwig Uhland, whom Poe had mentioned favorably in his 1842 review of Longfellow (H 11:65–66). "Castle by the Sea," with its suggestive title phrase, repeated in its first stanza, concerns the death of "[a] youthful daughter fair." It was translated by Charles Carter Lee.[35] This poem might have been a prompt for Poe's writing "Annabel Lee" (in May 1849) (O 2:797).[36] Furthermore, Poe would have read Frances Sargent Osgood's 1846 poetic allegory of Innocence and Truth, "The Life-Voyage," with its repeated phrase "the sounding sea."[37] Additionally, young Poe, while stationed at Fort Moultrie on Sullivan's Island in 1828, probably read earlier issues of the *Charleston Courier* for evidence of his mother's theatrical performances and would have found not only the March 22 and 23, 1811, listings of Theodore Hook's play *Tekeli,* featuring his mother in the role of the bride Christine (details importantly employed in *Pym*), but also D. M. C.'s December 4, 1807, poem "The Mourner," with its focus on the death of the beloved Anna and its refrain, "In the cot by the side of the sea."[38]

And there was a biographical background to the poem, too. Despite other claims, it is hard not to consider Annabel Lee to be Virginia, Poe's actual lost love. But perhaps the eponymous maiden is the romantic ideal, of which Virginia was for Poe the model. And a far-distant biographical background may have been at work, as well, also having shaped lines in "Tamerlane," "[My love] 'Twas such as angel minds above / Might envy" (M 1:30). Even as Edgar—before he left with the Allans for London in 1815—used to play at getting married to Mary Jane Dixon's "little sister whom he called his sweetheart" (M 1:470), he would also have known about the actual November 13, 1813, wedding, in Norfolk, of John Allan's partner Charles Ellis and the beloved Margaret Keeling Nimmo.[39] Ellis had written to Allan on August 10, 1813, "The Gods I am sure must begin to envy the happiness of your friend, The lovely Margaret has with that Frankness and candor which she is capable of given me her whole soul."[40] Perhaps Allan shared this remarkable expression with his family. Perhaps the heavenly envy of human love in 1813 shaped Poe's rendering of the heavenly envy of human love in 1827 and in 1849. We may recall, by way of analogy, the focus on the "emblematical" in Edgar's *Evenings at Home* in 1815 and his focus on the "emblematical" at the conclusion of "The Philosophy of Composition" in 1846 (L2 70). If Ellis's exultant comment was indeed related to and remembered by four-and-a-half-year-old Edgar, then in yet another way, Poe integrated his life in his art.

And the poem has become integrated into American culture, a renowned expression of romantic love, evident in a wide range of works, from a classic 1926 Buster Keaton film to a great 1965 Martin Luther King Jr. speech.[41]

Poe closed his recitation that Sunday evening with "Ulalume," including its possibly opaque last stanza, and he was pleased with the evident regard for the poem of young Susan V. C. Ingram. The following day, he wrote out a copy of the poem on five affixed sheets, and he left it beneath her door with a thoughtful note (O 2:834–35). She later saw him again when he visited her home. She added, "To me he seemed a good man, as well as a charming one, very sensitive and very high-minded." And Miss Ingram offered the memory of a memory: Poe had confided to her that the scent of orris root, which she had on her clothes, recalled to him that scent from his boyhood, in the opened bureau of his foster mother, Frances Allan.[42] Not all of Poe's remembrance was mournful.

On the evening of Monday, September 10, Poe wrote to Maria Clemm, concerned about not having heard from her—and uncertain about his having planned a future with Elmira: "So hold yourself in readiness as well as you can, my own darling mother—but do not sell off or anything of that kind yet, if you can avoid it—for 'there is many a slip between the cup & the lip'—& I confess that my heart sinks at the idea of this marriage. *I think,* however, that it will certainly take place & that immediately" (O 2:836). Practically, the marriage would be very beneficial, Poe knew, but he admits here that personally it might not be satisfying. After all, the original "boyish poet-love" (M 3:1122) was gone.

It was Friday, September 14, at 8:00 p.m., that Poe lectured at the Norfolk Academy (for fifty cents a ticket rather than twenty-five cents, as in Richmond in August).[43] The classical design of the Norfolk Academy, like that of the Exchange Hotel, was altogether fitting for the high theme of "The Poetic Principle." Poe again celebrated—and sought to elicit—the "pleasurable elevation, or excitement, *of the soul*" (L2 185). And he again won acclaim. According to the *Daily Southern Argus,* the "style" was "[c]haste and classic," the "delivery" "smooth and graceful," and the whole a "rich intellectual entertainment." The audience, small but genteel, offered "the profoundest attention" and "the warmest admiration." According to the *American Beacon,* there were "rounds of applause from the intelligent audience," which was described by Herbert M. Nash as "very fair and delighted."[44] Poe's literary reaching had reached his listeners.

Poe traveled back to Richmond on Monday, September 17, and saw Elmira that evening, presumably at her Church Hill home. On the following day, he responded to two letters from Maria Clemm, stating of Elmira, "I think she loves me more devotedly than any one I ever knew & I cannot help loving her in return." His own feeling for her did not equal hers for him. He added, "Nothing is yet definitely settled and it will not do to hurry matters." Anticipating his travel north, he made clear his continuing uncertainty: "*If possible* I will get married before I start—but there is no telling." And he tried to sustain and reassure his mother-in-law: "[K]eep up heart—I hope that our troubles are nearly over." Meanwhile, with the proceeds of his Norfolk lecture, Poe paid what he owed to the Madison House (O 2:837–38).

He wrote two more letters that day—one of them to Sarah Anna Lewis, expressing his appreciation for her help to Maria Clemm, and another to Marguerite St. Leon Loud, anticipating his belated visit to her in Philadelphia to edit her poetry (O 2:840–41). These are the last Poe letters for which the text survives.

It may well have been on the morning of that Tuesday, September 18, or shortly thereafter, that Poe, walking down Main Street, was invited by proprietor William A. Pratt (of 139 Main Street), to step upstairs, above Nash and Woodhouse's bookstore, to his own Daguerrean Gallery. Here Poe would likely have been seated on a chair on a riser, in a room full of light, with windows and a skylight. Pratt took the final two daguerreotypes of the writer, one of these to be known as the Thompson daguerreotype and the other as the Traylor daguerreotype. If viewed in person, the former daguerreotype, long held by Columbia University, is exceptionally vivid. The latter daguerreotype is lost. Although Poe seems a bit unkempt in the Thompson image, he also seems, in his direct gaze, to have a quiet energy. A photo of a tintype of the Traylor image offers a slightly more presentable Poe, with the same direct gaze.[45]

Probably by Thursday, September 20, or Friday, September 21, Poe made his final visit to John and Louisa Mackenzie at Darby Town. We know of Poe's visits to the Mackenzies' farm through Flora Lapham Mack, and we again turn to her for an account of what happened. She had heard the story from John H. Mackenzie himself. Poe and Mackenzie were a study in contrasts—the slender, sensitive, intellectual poet and the rugged, firm, practical businessman. Given the nature of their exchange, the conversation must have taken place—whether inside or outside—in private:

> He [Mackenzie] said Edgar came out to see him a week or two before his death and stayed several days at the Farm. During his visit he told cousin John of his engagement to Mrs. Shelton. Cousin John was surprised and rather indignant. He had known so much about Edgar's married life during Virginia's life time and deplored it so much that he did not think he ought to marry any woman & he could not believe at first that he had gone deliberately to work and selected as the victim of sheer cupidity the bright gay girl that they had both been so fond of when a school girl. But Edgar had been perfectly frank in declaring to him that while he had always liked Elmira very much he was influenced principally by the money with which he wanted to carry out a darling scheme he had long entertained & cherished as his life. They had the sharpest words they had ever had in their lives about this engagement. At least cousin John said Edgar had never said a sharp thing to him in his life & did not now but he [Mackenzie] had told him exactly what he thought of a man marrying a woman for such a motive and they parted less friends than they had ever been before never to meet again.[46]

The "darling scheme" was, of course, "The Stylus."

While once Poe had written "And fame shall be my only bride," it appears that now Poe thought that a bride could lead to further fame. John H. Mackenzie, however, could tolerate neither the possibility of Poe's again spending and spreeing, nor his taking advantage of Elmira for his own gain. Though the family of John H. Mackenzie may have thought the engagement "a fortunate speculation" for Poe, the eldest son clearly considered it an opportunistic mistreatment of their childhood friend. Poe responded to John H. Mackenzie with "wounded silence." And he left Darby Town, never to return.[47] Mack would write of her stepfather, "He always deplored . . . that after their long intimacy & friendship they should have parted this way for the last time."[48]

On Friday, September 21, the Richmond newspapers advertised Poe's second presentation of "The Poetic Principle," to be held on Monday, September 24. On Saturday, September 22, Elmira wrote to Mrs. Clemm, at Poe's request, expressing her readiness to love her and reassuring her that Edgar was "sober, temperate, moral, & much beloved." Soon after Poe's death, Elmira wrote again to Mrs. Clemm, with great pain at their loss, remembering that only weeks earlier, "[W]hen I told him I had written to you, his joy and delight were inexpressible." According to Susan Archer Weiss, writing many years later, "Mrs. Clemm, I heard, who had not favored Mrs. Whitman, was anxious for the match with Mrs. Shelton, whom she had known in Richmond, and with whom she anticipated a quiet and comfortable home."[49]

Soon, whether before or after Poe's last lecture, John H. Mackenzie made a clear warning to Elmira herself. Flora Lapham Mack writes, "He said a few days afterwards [after Poe's departure from Darby Town] as he was riding down Broad Street[,] Mrs Shelton who was driving towards him made her coachman stop at the corner of 7th and Broad Streets & called him to her." She had a "beautifully appointed and stylish carriage" with "beautiful cream colored carriage horses with their long flowing manes & tails & silver mounted harness." Contradicting the later judgment of Susan Archer Weiss, "Cousin John said she [Elmira] was still very pretty tho' a little artificial looking and that she retained all the winsome coquettish graces & frankness of address that had made her so irresistible in her youth." The exchange that Mack relates, based on Mackenzie's telling, is very revealing:

> After greeting him quite effusively she asked with an affectation of embarrassment and a girlish giggle "John has Edgar told you anything about us." Yes he has Elmira he replied but I did not believe you could be so deluded as to really mean it. Why John she cried I thought you liked Edgar. I do he said I love him as a friend but if I were a woman I would not like to marry him and you know why. He said she looked genuinely embarrassed now but said softly I always loved him John. Well he replied you know Edgar. He is as unstable as water. He will spend all your money and if you really do love him he will break your heart. He cannot help it. Tis his nature. Give him up Elmira and have no more to do with him. No John she said no. I've tried to do it and I cannot and I'll tell you plainly even if I knew I would be us'd as you say that he would spend my money & break my heart why I expect I would marry him just the same.[50]

Although she equivocated in later years as to whether she and Poe had been engaged, she subsequently admitted that they had been. Indeed, according to one reminiscence, she said, "I married another man, but the love of my life was Edgar Poe. I never loved anyone else."[51] Her response to John H. Mackenzie's warning makes evident the extent of her love for Poe. It was unconditional.

Poe gave his final lecture—his reprise of "The Poetic Principle" in Richmond—on Monday, September 24, at 8:00 p.m., again in the Concert Room of the Exchange Hotel. The attendance, though not as strong as on August 17, was still good. Again Poe offered his tribute to "[t]he struggle to apprehend the supernal Loveliness" (L2 184); recited exemplary poems; and closed with his signature poem, "The Raven." On the following day, John M. Daniel, referring to Poe's closing recitation, provided what he termed "the only correct copy ever published" (thanks to Poe's having furnished it to him). Daniel concluded of "The Raven," "It is stamped with the image of true genius—and genius in its happiest hour. It is one of those things that an author never does but once." The next day's newspaper reviews of the lecture were favorable, complimenting Poe's recitations and his voice.[52]

After Poe's death, Daniel—whose critique of Poe could be severe—characterized the two presentations of "The Poetic Principle" in Richmond as "worthy of his genius in his best moods." Sympathetic with Poe's argument, though not impressed with his recitations, he stated in his review of the first two volumes of the Griswold edition of Poe's works, "A large audience, we recollect, attended these lectures. Those who had not seen Edgar Poe since the days of his obscurity, came in crowds to behold their townsman then so famous."[53] A member of the audience at one of the two presentations, William Winston Valentine, conveyed to his brother Edward V. Valentine a notable insight about Poe's audience, which Edward reported in a letter to John H. Ingram: "There was little variation and much sadness in the intonations of his voice—yet this very sadness was so completely in harmony with his history as to excite on the part of the community a deep interest in him both as a lecturer and reader."[54] There was, evidently, some understanding in Poe's hometown, in August and September 1849, of the man behind the work—perhaps even of the boy behind the work.

Poe had two days left of his stay in Richmond. On Tuesday, September 25, he visited Susan Archer Talley at Talavera. He preferred the quiet sitting room to the crowded parlors, and here, whether signing or writing to her or enunciating so that she might read his lips, he confided to Talley his happiness during recent weeks. Of particular importance, of course, was "The Stylus." That morning, he had been writing a critique of Miss Talley's poetry for the second issue. (He had already begun to write the table of contents of the first issue and interviewed Mrs. Mackenzie for an article for a later issue.) He was now certain of the future of the magazine. Old friends had promised to support it. And we know, as well, Elmira had promised to support it. Furthermore, by then Poe would have received the August 21 letter from E. H. N. Patterson, who stated that with one thousand subscribers he would promise to publish a five-dollar-per-year magazine, edited by Poe, to commence in July 1850, and who suggested that Poe meet him in St. Louis on October 15. "The Stylus," Poe said, would be "the leading literary journal of the country."[55]

According to Weiss, Poe "declared that the last few weeks in the society of his old and new friends had been the happiest that he had known for many years." He shared with her that evening a letter from Rufus W. Griswold, in which the anthologist agreed with the writer's request that Griswold be his literary executor.[56] Perhaps both Poe and Mrs. Clemm were responsible for that very serious mistake.

At sunset, Poe left Talavera and walked to nearby Duncan Lodge. Flora Lapham Mack states that he was with his friends Tom and Dick Mackenzie that night, but Weiss stated that she was told (presumably by Tom Mackenzie) that Poe "sat late at his window, meditatively smoking, and seemingly disinclined for conversation."[57]

The following day, Wednesday, September 26, Poe left Duncan Lodge with Tom Mackenzie and William Gibbon Carter. Probably, whether with them or alone, he stopped at the Madison House. Later that day, he visited both John M. Daniel at the *Richmond Semi-Weekly Examiner* and John R. Thompson at the *Southern Literary Messenger*. Both journalists remembered him as hopeful—Daniel wrote on October 9 that Poe had departed "in high spirits, full of hope and in better health than he had been for years," and Thompson wrote on October 10 that Poe "spoke in the highest spirits of his resolves and prospects for the future." Perhaps Poe was heartened to imagine bringing Maria Clemm back to Richmond to live with him and Elmira and to anticipate finally editing his dream magazine, "The Stylus." Poe "borrowed" five dollars from Thompson and gave him a manuscript roll of "Annabel Lee." (This version of the poem would be published in the *Southern Literary Messenger* after the version that Poe had sent to Griswold appeared in the obituary in the *New York Tribune*.) Also, Poe agreed to give a letter from Thompson to Rufus W. Griswold in Philadelphia.[58]

Rosalie gave a note from her brother with a manuscript of "For Annie" to Susan Archer Talley, who was on her way to see a dying friend. And that evening Poe climbed Church Hill to say goodbye to Elmira. He was evidently willing to reveal to her what he had been unwilling to reveal to Daniel and Thompson. Elmira wrote to Maria Clemm, after Poe's death, about his last visit: "He was very sad, and complained of being quite sick. I felt his pulse, and found he had considerable fever, and did not think it probable he would be able to start the next morning, (Thursday) as he anticipated." But he continued with his plans.[59]

Poe walked down Church Hill to the office of Dr. John F. Carter at Seventeenth and Broad Streets at 9:30 p.m. They talked for a while—perhaps Poe read the papers—and Poe idly handled Carter's cane. He inadvertently took it with him, leaving his own cane and his copy of Thomas Moore's *Irish Melodies*, as he made his way to Sadler's Restaurant on Main Street between Fifteenth and Sixteenth Streets. He met Sadler and J. M. Blakey and others there and probably had supper. When he left the restaurant at midnight, he was "in good spirits and sober" (according to Sadler in Carter's telling) and "quite sober and cheerful to the last" (according to his acquaintances in Weiss's telling). It has been suggested that Poe may have returned to his hotel (probably the Madison House rather than the Swan Tavern), perhaps leaving Carter's cane. Whether or not he made this stop, he proceeded, with several others from Sadler's, to the steamboat and bade them farewell, promising to return. He had with him his trunk. The boat was later reported to have left at 4:00 a.m.[60]

At this point, on board the vessel, Poe needed someone with him—a friend and protector, someone who would watch out for him. He should not have been alone.

We lose sight of Poe for several days. There is uncertainty; there is mystery. But we may infer that, once in Baltimore, he was soon drinking. On October 7, the doctor who had tended him, John J. Moran, reported to the minister who would officiate at his funeral, William T. D. Clemm, that old friends had met Poe at the Baltimore dock when the Norfolk steamer arrived and invited him to have a drink. And the vulnerable writer had agreed, leading to "a terrible debauch."[61] We may recall Poe's earlier drinking, over the course of his life, in Charlottesville, Baltimore, Richmond, Philadelphia, New York, and Philadelphia again, where he had delirium tremens. And back in Richmond, in the summer of 1849, he had been warned, after a second bout, that another one would kill him. This was that one.

On October 9, the *New York Herald,* relying on an October 8 piece from its correspondent in Baltimore, specified as the cause of Poe's death "an attack of *mania à potu*" (madness from drink). On October 10, John Pendleton Kennedy, of Baltimore, attested to Poe's "debauch" and went on, "He fell in with some companion here who seduced him to the bottle."[62] And on November 8, John R. Thompson would write to E. H. N. Patterson, who might have published "The Stylus," that Poe had died "in delirium from drunkenness" (H 17:404).

This seems the likeliest explanation. But there are other possibilities—the subject is famously fraught. The most common alternative explanation, first provided by John R. Thompson, is that Poe was "cooped"—kept in a cellar, then given drinks for his repeatedly voting at various polling places. However, one of Poe's occasional drinking companions in Baltimore, Robert D'Unger, wrote a letter in 1899 asserting that this version of Poe's final days was "mere twaddle": "Poe was not a voter in Baltimore, being a nonresident; in addition Poe was never looked upon as a 'bum' although in them [bars] very frequently, *was not a bar-room* loafer. His drinking was that of a gentleman, if an unfortunate victim of alcohol can be rated a gentleman." Poe scholar T. O. Mabbott agreed that the "cooping" story was "twaddle" (M 1:569n).[63]

D'Unger was not present for Poe's final bout, but he had had firsthand experience of Poe's drinking. His comment about Poe as a drinker is worth quoting once again:

> The trouble with him was that he "*worked himself down*" and then became despondent. Drink was induced by this despondency, and he kept up the "drunk" as long as he had money; but without getting beastly drunk. He drank until his nerves were shattered, poured it down until he was actually sick. He ate very little whilst indulging. I suppose he told me a hundred times that *he was going to quit the habit,* and I am sure he was sincere in his wish to do so. All his drunks were followed by a weakening diarrhoea. That was what carried him off.[64]

There seems to be an authority here, an authenticity. And the account certainly seems to suggest that Poe had an addiction. Mabbott himself clearly believed D'Unger's explanation.[65] It is possible, of course, that Poe's response to his final spree was aggravated by other problems, such as those previously diagnosed, involving the heart and the brain.[66]

"[I]n high spirits" in Richmond on Wednesday September 26, Poe was "rather the worse for wear" in Baltimore on Wednesday, October 3. Joseph W. Walker—who saw the inebriated poet at Gunner's Hall, a tavern that also served as an election site—stated the case in a brief note to his former employer and Poe's friend, editor Joseph E. Snodgrass: "There is a gentleman, rather the worse for wear, at Ryan's 4th ward polls, who goes under the cognomen Edgar A. Poe, and who appears in great distress, & he says he is acquainted with you, and I assure you, he is in need of immediate assistance."[67] Years later, Snodgrass refuted an alternative narrative by Elizabeth Oakes Smith—that Poe was not drinking but was beaten—and he offered a memory of the woefully inert Poe, "stupefied by liquor": "His face was haggard, not to say bloated, and unwashed, his hair unkempt, and his whole physique repulsive. His expansive forehead, with its wonderful breadth between the points where the phrenologists locate the organ of ideality—the widest I ever measured—and that full-orbed and mellow, yet soulful eye, for which he was so noticeable when himself, now lusterless and vacant, as shortly I could see, were shaded from view by a rusty, almost brimless, tattered and ribbonless palmleaf hat."[68] Indeed, Poe's clothing was utterly shabby and not his own. Snodgrass wrote, in an earlier version of this essay, "[H]e had evidently been robbed of his clothing, or cheated in an exchange."[69] During his visit to the tavern on October 3, the concerned editor—to whom Poe had once defended his temperance (O 1:263–64)—remembered Poe under the influence on a previous occasion and ordered him a room. But Henry Herring, the husband of Poe's aunt Eliza, recommended the hospital, and so Poe was carried to a carriage and placed in a room at the Washington College Hospital.[70]

According to the physician at the hospital, John J. Moran, in his letter to Maria Clemm of November 15, Poe was "unconscious of his condition—who brought him or with whom he had been associating" from 5:00 p.m. on October 3 through 3:00 a.m. Poe then had delirium tremens—a "tremor of the limbs, and at first a busy, but not violent or active delirium—constant talking—and vacant converse with spectral and imaginary objects on the walls." This was, it would seem, the *"mania-à-potu,"* the consequence of withdrawal from drinking about which Poe had written to Maria Clemm in July, "May Heaven grant that it prove a warning to me for the rest of my days" (O 2:825–26). The doctor went on, "We were unable to induce tranquillity before the second day after his admission"—that would be Friday, October 5.[71]

Poe recovered consciousness, and Dr. Moran attended him, asking questions about his family but considering his patient's answers "incoherent & unsatisfactory." Poe mentioned "a wife in Richmond"—of course, he did have a fiancée there. And uncertain when he had departed Richmond, he also had no idea of the whereabouts of his trunk. The doctor, wishing to encourage the dying man, suggested that he would soon be able to see his friends. "At this he broke out with much energy," Moran wrote of Poe, "and said the best thing his best friend could do would be to blow out his brains with a pistol—that when he beheld his degradation he was ready to sink in the earth etc."[72] Poe slept, and the doctor stepped away.

The doctor's wife, Mary Moran, who characterized Poe at admission as "in a stupor," "overcome by drink," also later talked with the failing patient.

Perhaps Poe's conversation with her was his last. She stated, "I helped to nurse him here, and during an interval of consciousness he asked if there was any hope for him. Thinking he referred to his physical condition, I said, 'My husband thinks you are very ill, and if you have any directions to give regarding your affairs I will write them down.' He replied, 'I meant, hope for a wretch like me, beyond this life.'" (We may hear a touch of "Amazing Grace.") Mrs. Moran continued, "I assured him that the Great Physician said there was. I then read him the fourteenth chapter of St. John's Gospel, gave him a quieting draught, wiped the beads of perspiration from his face, smoothed his pillow, and left him" (H 1:337).

The chapter that she read begins, with Jesus speaking, "Let not your heart be troubled: ye believe in God, believe also in me. / In my Father's house are many mansions: if it were not so, I would have told you. I go to prepare a place for you" (John 14:1–2). This well-known passage resonates in tone with what Poe considered "the very noblest lines in all human poetry": "I know not—I ask not if guilt's in thy heart:—/ I but know that *I love thee* whatever thou art" (O 2:710). Familiar as he was with the Bible, Poe would certainly have recognized this chapter of John. Indeed, he had alluded to it in his short story "The Premature Burial"—the narrator, believing himself to be buried alive, writes, "And now the Comforter [Hope] fled for ever" (M 3:967). In John 14, the promise is of the coming of "the Comforter, which is the Holy Ghost" (John 14:26). Mrs. Moran had chosen well her passage of consolation.[73]

Poe lapsed into a "violent delirium," and then, from the evening of Saturday, October 6, through the early morning of Sunday, October 7, Poe called the name "Reynolds." Although the election judge Henry Reynolds and uncle-by-marriage Henry Herring have been offered as possibilities, neither person seems especially likely or sufficiently meaningful for Poe to have called for hours as he approached death.[74] However, J. N. Reynolds, cited in this context by such Poe biographers as James A. Harrison, Arthur Hobson Quinn, and Jeffrey Meyers—and whom Poe had probably met—may well be the right man.[75] Poe associated the South Sea explorer and advocate of South Sea exploration with intense interest in the unknown, including the hole at the South Pole that Reynolds had proposed, which is suggested at the end of Poe's novel *The Narrative of Arthur Gordon Pym*. And Poe linked that image of the unknown with the other world: the final paragraph of *Pym*, concerning the southern cataract and the white "shrouded human figure" in front of it, hermetically intimates Jesus in Revelation come to prophesy the New Jerusalem. In extremis as he was, Poe would fairly have called to Reynolds as a representation of someone approaching that other world. For years, Poe had integrated his life in his work—perhaps now, at the end, Poe was integrating his work in his life. Having reached toward the edge throughout his writing, he was finally there. Poe rested for a moment, and then, with a move of his head, implored, "*Lord help my poor Soul.*"[76]

And he died.

Conclusion
"A Dream within a Dream"

Mary Moran sewed the shroud and, with others, readied the body. Several people visited Poe's remains, some clipping locks of his hair. Henry Herring ordered the mahogany coffin. Neilson Poe arranged for the hearse and one carriage. In the carriage with him were Henry Herring, Reverend William T. D. Clemm, Joseph E. Snodgrass, and Z. Collins Lee (who had attended the University of Virginia when Poe was there). Fourteen-year-old art student Charles William Hubner saw the coffin carried to the hearse and asked a nearby gentleman, "Please sir, who are they going to bury?" And the man responded, "My son, that is the body of a great poet, Edgar Allan Poe, you will learn all about him some day." Twenty-three-year-old J. Alden Weston saw the slight funeral procession and asked the hearse driver, "Whose funeral is this?" And the driver replied, "Mr. Poe, the poet."[1]

Reverend Clemm officiated on that gloomy fall afternoon, Monday, October 8, at the Westminster Presbyterian Church cemetery, located on Green Street. Poe's gravesite was in the lot of his grandfather, David Poe. Herring later stated that also in attendance (besides those in the carriage and sexton George W. Spence and undertaker Charles Suter) were Poe's former teacher Joseph H. Clarke and Poe's cousin Elizabeth Rebecca Herring Smith and her husband, Edmund Morton Smith. Toward the back was young Weston. The ceremony for the great poet was brief and perfunctory. The eulogy was reportedly forsaken because few people were present. Snodgrass later stated that, hearing the sounds of "clods and stones" on the coffin, he felt "disappointment, mingled with disgust and something akin to resentment." Weston stated, "The burial ceremony, which did not occupy more than three minutes, was so cold-blooded and unchristianlike as to provoke on my part a sense of anger difficult to suppress." Perhaps, he conjectured, a delay of a day might have yielded a fuller turnout and a more fitting ceremony. But the actual event was meager and melancholy.[2]

The news of the death of Poe made its way from Baltimore to Richmond. Elmira Royster, having read the *Baltimore Sun*, wrote to Maria Clemm on October 11, "[Y]es, he was the *dearest object* on earth to me. . . . My heart is overwhelmed—yes, ready to burst!" Susan Archer Talley Weiss recalled, "Poe had made himself popular in Richmond. People had become interested in him, and his death cast a universal gloom over the city." One who had professional contact with Poe, his African American barber, reportedly reacted with great dismay, "Edgar A. Poe is dead, sir. The shock, sir, is too much for me. The greatest poet and kindest-hearted gentleman in America is dead. I cannot do any work to-day; I am too nervous, sir, to trust my hand."[3]

Obituaries were plentiful, offering in different proportions accolade and accusation.[4] Some of these obituaries commented on Poe's relationships with others. A writer in the October 9 *Richmond Whig* recalled Poe's "mingling with acquaintances in the sociability of friendships," and a New York correspondent for the *Philadelphia Public Ledger* (having heard of the death of Poe from Richmond) reported on October 8 for the issue of October 9 "a deep feeling of regret among his friends, and he had many of them here, even outside and away from literary circles."[5] But Horace Greeley, editor of the *New York Daily Tribune*, asked Rufus W. Griswold to write an obituary, and the malicious comments of one "Ludwig" (Griswold), also appearing on October 9, trumped the comments of the others: "[F]ew will be grieved by it [the death of Poe]. . . . [H]e had few or no friends." The hostile reverend presented Poe as a man of "unamiable character" who "walked the streets, in madness or melancholy, with lips moving in indistinct curses."[6] So commenced the myth of the demonic Poe. Poe's afterlife began as bleakly as his life had ended.

But soon there was pushback. Annie Richmond, writing to Maria Clemm on October 14, acknowledged the "kind notices," but added, "[I]t is so *cruel*, for those who envied him while living, to speak so harshly of him now that he is gone." Susan Archer Talley, writing an obituary in the *Richmond Republican* of October 15, faulted those comments on Poe's character that "represented it in so unjust and distorted a view as to be almost unrecognizable to those who best knew him." N. P. Willis in the *Home Journal* of October 20 countered "the disparaging portion" of Griswold's piece, and George Lippard in the *Quaker City* of October 20 cautioned, "And the men who now spit upon his grave; by way of retaliation for some injury which they imagine they have received from Poe living, would do well to remember, that it is only an idiot or a coward who strikes the cold forehead of a corpse." Also on that date, Henry B. Hirst corrected the record: "Unamiable he was not; he was otherwise to a fault; and always ready to forget and forgive." An appreciative anonymous writer in the *Daily Tribune* of November 13 and the *Semi-Weekly Tribune* of November 17 declared, in the opening of his or her poem "Edgar Allan Poe," "It is not true, 'the Poet had no friends.' / There's not a hamlet nor a way-side cot / Throughout the land, where misery has dwelt, / But furnished him a friend—warm heart-felt friend."[7]

Poe's posthumous work was beginning to appear—"Annabel Lee" in the Griswold obituary, the *Southern Literary Messenger* of November 1849, and *Sartain's Magazine* of January 1850, and the third version of "The Bells" in the *Home Journal* of October 27, 1849, and *Sartain's Magazine* of November 1849. In early 1850, the first two volumes of the Griswold edition of Poe's works (*Tales* and *Poems and Miscellanies*) came out, effectively discussed by George R. Graham and John Neal, with Poe well defended.[8] "The Poetic Principle" appeared in the *Home Journal* of August 31, 1850, and *Sartain's Magazine* of October 1850. And by September of the year, the third volume of Griswold's edition of Poe, *The Literati*, was published, with a pernicious "Memoir."

Griswold's "Preface" to the "Memoir" included distortions of Poe's letters, as the biographer Arthur Hobson Quinn has shown.[9] And the "Memoir" itself was not merely unsympathetic but, in places, outrageously false—as, for example, "Poe exhibits scarcely any virtue in either his life or his writings."[10] Envious of Poe's genius and probably still chafing at Poe's censure of his work, Griswold exacted his revenge and won for himself the ignominy of literary assassin.

Some believed the reverend's vilification—the *Boston Recorder,* for instance, stated that "Poor Poe was a genius without a conscience."[11] But others stood up for the defamed poet. Graham published a condemnatory letter to Griswold, stating, in part, "You should be sure that the vice of your brother is not his misfortune, and that the sin which taints your own fingers, may not turn crimson in contrast before the eyes of the gazers." A writer for the *Alta California* asserted, "The memory of this talented and admired child of genius has been most virulently assailed by one whose own life should have taught him a little charity" and went on to cite Graham's assessment and to offer a portion of Samuel Nichols's critique of Griswold's work (with a quotation from Samuel Johnson), which had appeared in the *New York Sunday Mercury:* "Altogether this memoir of Poe is the 'most contemptuous, insolent, petulant, selfish and brutal' that can be found in the English, or in any other language."[12]

Those close to Poe in Richmond handled Griswold's attack in different ways. Regarding Poe's friend John H. Mackenzie, William Lanier Washington wrote, "[H]is rage upon reading the Griswold Memoir was such that no one ever dared to refer to it again in his presence."[13] In after-years, Mackenzie would share his memories of Poe with his cousin's daughter—later his stepdaughter—Flora Lapham Mack. Poe's sister Rosalie, on the other hand, asked one whom she had known from his visits to Duncan Lodge, Parke Vanparke, to write a defense of her brother. Sixteen years later, Vanparke published that defense in *Discursions and Diversions*. He wrote, in part, "If the history of men since the days of Cain furnishes a more atrocious instance of human iniquity than the piece of writing in question, then I must confess it has not met my eye. It exhibits such a spirit of pointed hatred—such a singular and monstrous *acharn[e]ment* [relentlessness] of passion—such an explosion of hydrophobic fury—such malicious, gnashing, frantic madness—that we are inevitably led to the conclusion that the author of it was for the time saturated with the essence of seven devils." Vanparke closed by expressing his relief at having finally fulfilled his commitment.[14]

What more Poe might have accomplished had he not died so young we do not know. Perhaps he would have written additional remarkable tales and poems. But probably his primary effort would have been editing his long-planned literary magazine, "The Stylus," intended for publication in 1850. We may well wonder about the criticism he would have contributed, especially about the novels of Nathaniel Hawthorne and Herman Melville. Fittingly, through allusion, these novels paid tribute to Poe.

Hawthorne's 1850 classic *The Scarlet Letter* offers a transformation of Poe's "The Tell-Tale Heart," not only through its reimagining of the murder of a sleeping man as the spiritual violation of the sleeping Reverend Dimmesdale (by Roger Chillingworth), but also through the repetition of key language, including "old man," "awake," "chamber," "creak," "shadow," "cautious," "stealthily," "thrust," and "evil eye."[15] Hawthorne's 1851 *The House of the Seven Gables* intimates language about the *Flying Dutchman*, the Death Ship, in Poe's "MS. Found in a Bottle" with Holgrave's referring to "*A feeling which I cannot describe—an indefinite sense of some catastrophe,*" thus appropriately reinforcing the theme of mortality (here, that of Judge Pyncheon).[16] And Hawthorne's 1852 *The Blithedale Romance* features in its otherworldly Priscilla and the doomed Zenobia parallels with the raven and the lost Lenore of "The Raven," as well as resonant language—"creature, doomed to wander about," "a very slight tap," "a gentle tap at my chamber-door," and "just a coincidence—nothing more." In the years immediately following Poe's death, Hawthorne skillfully reworked Poe's treatment of death, thereby honoring his predecessor's achievement.[17]

Melville's extraordinary 1851 novel *Moby-Dick* offers allusions to Poe, from the aforementioned suggestion of Poe's "The Island of the Fay" to its "The Whiteness of the Whale," a seeming nod to the whiteness at the close of *Pym*.[18] And like Hawthorne's *The Blithedale Romance*, Melville's 1852 *Pierre; or, the Ambiguities* builds upon "The Raven," with not only the mysterious Isabel and themes of lost love and inevitable doom but also suggestive language—abundant instances of "nothing more" and "never more," as well as such phrases as "tapping at his mother's chamber door," "pierced into his bosom's core," and "all my soul looked up at thee."[19]

Hawthorne and Melville were Poe's equals—their allusions to Poe, suggesting respect, are both salient and enduring. And notably, even as the two men turned to "The Raven" as a key text in their work, later writers would critically employ it, too, as, for example, Walt Whitman in "Out of the Cradle Endlessly Rocking" and Elizabeth Bishop in "One Art."

In Richmond, shortly after Poe's death, John H. Mackenzie's twenty-eight-year-old brother Tom—"Dr. Tom"—honored Poe in another way: he gathered materials relating to Poe for a projected Poe biography. John contributed his letters from Poe and other Poe-related papers, and mother Jane Scott Mackenzie, foster sister Rosalie Poe, and brother-in-law Caleb Jones provided Tom with Poe materials, as well. When Mrs. Mackenzie sold Duncan Lodge in 1853 and moved, with Tom and Dick and Rosalie, to nearby Powhatan County, Tom relocated his beloved library—including classical works, medical works, and his singular Poe collection—to an office in the city. Over time, he did write his biography of Poe.[20]

Although Tom Mackenzie would have been on the right side of the Poe controversy, he was on the wrong side of history. After Abraham Lincoln was elected president in 1860, the South seceded from the Union in early 1861 over the issue of slavery, and most Virginians supported the Confederacy, including the Mackenzies.[21] Dr. Tom took a position as surgeon in the Confederate army. And his brother John, a slaveholder, served as quartermaster in Richmond, assisting Confederate soldiers from Louisiana who were stationed there. He sold Darby Town, moving to a smaller farm, Sedgemore, also near Richmond.[22]

Whether the carved mantelpiece of the drowning Egyptians at Darby Town was dismantled and reassembled in the new home or allowed to remain and eventually burned in a house fire we do not know. But we do know that the Israelites would escape the Egyptians—that is, the enslaved African Americans would be freed. Indeed, the Emancipation Proclamation would take effect on January 1, 1863. The Mackenzies, though not drowned, would eventually be significantly diminished, and John, after the war, would serve two weeks in Richmond's infamous Libby Prison.[23]

In early April 1865, when it became clear that the Union army would soon take Richmond, Confederate soldiers, in order to keep prized crops from the enemy, set ablaze the warehouses of tobacco. As people fled, the capital of the Confederacy burned. The Evacuation Fire of April 3, 1865, destroyed fifty-four blocks in the center of Richmond. Tom Mackenzie's cherished library there, including his incomparable Poe collection and his biography of Poe, was utterly consumed. Flora Lapham Mack wrote of Tom, "This loss of his library etc. was a blow from which he never recovered." He did not try to rewrite his biography. He died a few years later.[24]

Destroying the tobacco, the Confederate military had also inadvertently destroyed an irreplaceable part of southern literary history. Although Tom's stories were lost, his brother John's stories endured—John recounted his stories to Flora, who wrote them down for William Lanier Washington, who wrote and destroyed his own Poe biography but preserved Flora's letters, some of which were later acquired by the Poe Museum, some by the present author.[25] Extracts from these letters have been offered throughout this book.

Doubtless there would have been some overlap between Tom's narrative and John's narrative. But many of John's firsthand accounts of Poe would not have been experienced by Tom—from Edgar's telling John extraordinary fairy tales to his much later leaping into the Great Hall of John's Darby Town home to his even later suffering John's severe castigation about the engagement to Elmira. We lost much about Poe in Richmond's conflagration but learn much about him, too, from Flora's correspondence.

Flora and John had an unresolved disagreement about Poe. She faulted Poe strenuously for his not providing adequately for Virginia and Maria Clemm, for his drinking and gambling, for his borrowing money excessively without repaying it, and for his taking part in platonic liaisons that could prove embarrassing. John defended Poe: Flora wrote, "He would look miserable & declare that Edgar could not be judged by rules that applied to other people. He was[,] Cousin John said[,] of an entirely different order & organization from the generality of men. That he was his lifelong friend and he loved him & he was perfectly welcome to every penny he had ever loaned him or lost by him." John declared that regarding women, "[Poe] was as singularly pure in morals as far as these things were concerned as he was in conversation," and John explained that he and Maria Clemm considered Poe's platonic friendships with women to be "perfectly harmless and most ephemeral" though sometimes "misunderstood by others." Perhaps these friendships even protected Poe from his real susceptibilities, "drink and gambling." Mrs. Clemm did, though, chastise Poe and Mrs. Osgood on one occasion.[26]

We might remember, in this matter, that Flora also wrote about John H. Mackenzie, "[T]he truth is he died regarding Virginia as almost an angel and Poe's tender love & care for her as the most beautiful thing in his life."[27] And we might also remember that Virginia wrote an acrostic valentine for Poe that began "Ever with thee I wish to roam—/ Dearest my life is thine" (M 1:524). And we might recall, as well, that Virginia's time with Eddie as she lay on her deathbed was wholly loving.

This all does not seem that long ago. We can easily recover that boy who knew his own genius—that young man who began to prove that genius—that not quite middle-aged man who never gave up on that genius. We can readily recover Poe's steadfast aspiration, demonstrated so beautifully from "Israfel" to "Annabel Lee," from "MS. Found in a Bottle" to "The Domain of Arnheim," from *Pym* to *Eureka*. And we can effortlessly recover that other world that Poe offers, which so richly touches our own.

Like his last audience in Richmond, we understand something of the suffering that lay beneath his work, a noble pathos. And we may understand not only the recurrent theme of disintegration but also the recurrent process of the integration of his life in his work. Poe generously shared much, sometimes hermetically, sometimes not—for example, his birth and that of his brother Henry (*Pym*), his attending the Manor House School ("William Wilson"), his loss of Jane Stith Stanard ("To Helen"), his loss of Henry (*Pym*), his problem with alcohol ("The Man of the Crowd," "The Black Cat"), his joy with Virginia at Darby Town ("Eleonora"), his defense of his maligned mother ("The Purloined Letter"), his loss of Virginia ("Ulalume," "Annabel Lee"), his love for Annie Richmond ("For Annie," "Landor's Cottage"), his love for Maria Clemm ("To My Mother"), and his sense of his own mortality ("Eldorado"). Here was a man who, reaching inward, reached out, offering elements of his life, sometimes encoded, to the readers of his own time and to the readers of the future—that it, to us.

Often in need of consolation himself, Poe offered consolation to his readers. He provided the consolation of community through his sharing his own grief in "The Raven." He provided the consolation of Christian prophecy in the encrypted theophany at the ending of *Pym*. He provided the consolation of cosmological reverie in the rapturous ending of *Eureka*. And he suffused a consolation throughout his work through its sheer beauty—of language, of rhythm, and of form. There is indeed a heroism here.

The afternoon of Sunday, October 5, 2014, was a festive one in Edgar Allan Poe Square, at the corner of Boylston and Charles Streets, opposite the Boston Common. For it was then and there that Stefanie Rocknak's statue *Poe Returning to Boston* would be unveiled. A crowd of about 150 people had gathered, and in the roped-off center, near the covered statue, was a small group, including the chair of the Edgar Allan Poe Foundation of Boston, Paul Lewis; Poe collector *extraordinaire* Susan Jaffe Tane; Poe Studies Association president Philip E. Phillips; and former U.S. poet laureate Robert Pinsky. Thoughtful and fitting remarks were readily made for the occasion. And then, finally, the moment came—the covering was withdrawn, and the statue was revealed: a life-size Poe striding down the sidewalk, away from the Common and toward the site of the home of his birth, accompanied by a raven and a tell-tale heart, holding an open briefcase with his Boston-related compositions falling from it. Boston beheld this utterly approachable Poe—and then, with the velvet rope removed, the crowd converged on the figure in hilarious communion. Move over Big Papi—the man of the hour was Edgar Allan Poe.

It was a joyous photo-op—a rhapsody of cell phones and selfies as those in the crowd took turns posing with Poe. There was a celebratory intimacy—Poe was their guy. And as I remember that exhilarating coming together around Poe, I imagine that whether these people thought of the scary Poe or the analytical Poe or the lyrical Poe, they probably knew that this was a sorrowful man returning in triumph. And I imagine that perhaps they remembered their first reading Poe and felt grateful. It was not just that he was both otherworldly and accessible, but also that he reminded them of who they were. And, finally, I imagine that perhaps they felt—as I did—that he was a friend.

Acknowledgments

It is a pleasure to acknowledge the support that I have received for this work over the years. I am happy to acknowledge first my good friend Stephan Loewentheil, distinguished antiquarian book dealer, proprietor of The 19th Century Rare Book and Photograph Shop, who believed in this project from the beginning and contributed a generous subvention. Thank you, Stephan.

I am grateful for the Penn State DuBois Distinguished Professor funds, which supported my fall 2017 semester at the Manuscripts Division of the Library of Congress, where I read the Ellis & Allan Company Records. The dedicated staff at the Manuscripts Reading Room was very helpful—I am glad to mention, in particular, Frederick Augustyn, Jeffrey Flannery, Joseph Jackson, Patrick Kerwin, Bruce Kirby, Edith Sandler, and Lewis Wyman. I am grateful, as well, for a Virginia Humanities Fellowship for my work at the Library of Virginia in the fall of 2018. I am indebted to Jeanne Nicholson Siler and Matthew Gibson of Virginia Humanities and, at the Library of Virginia, to John G. Deal and his collegial crew, as well as Nancy Epperly, Kelley Ewing, Cassandra Farrell, Dave Grabarek, Cara Griggs, Joyce January, Audrey McElhinney, Dale L. Neighbors, Becky Schneider, and Errol S. Somay. During my fellowship, I visited the Albert & Shirley Small Special Collections Library at the University of Virginia in Charlottesville, where the staff, including Penny White and Anne Causey, invaluably assisted me in my research.

I appreciate, as well, the archival resources and helpful staffs of the American Antiquarian Society; the Birmingham Public Library; the Special Collections Department at the Boston Public Library; the Leventhal Center at the Boston Public Library; the Bostonian Society; the Bronx County Historical Society; the John Hay Library at Brown University; Butler Library at Columbia University; the Rare Book Library at Columbia University; the Danville, Virginia, Court House; the David M. Rubinstein Rare Book and Manuscript Library, Duke University; the Free Library of Philadelphia; the Grolier Club Library; the Harvard University Fine Arts Library; the Historical Society of

Philadelphia; the Houghton Library at Harvard University; the Huntington Library; the Lilly Library at Indiana University; the Thomas Ollive Mabbott Poe Collection in Special Collections and University Archives at the University of Iowa; the Thomas Jefferson Medical College; the Lowell Historical Society; the University of Massachusetts, Lowell; the Pattee/Paterno Library at the Pennsylvania State University; the National Archive of Philadelphia; the New-York Historical Society; the New York Public Library; the New York Public Library for the Performing Arts, Dorothy and Lewis B. Cullman Center; Newton Free Library; the Edgar Allan Poe Museum; the Enoch Pratt Free Library; the Providence Athenaeum; the Tappahannock (Virginia) Public Library; the Harry Ransom Center at the University of Texas at Austin; The Valentine in Richmond, Virginia; the Virginia Museum of History and Culture; and the United States Military Academy, West Point Library, including its Archives. And I am grateful to my friend Susan Tane for making her extraordinary Poe collection available to me.

Of the welcome responsiveness that I have received for this project from those in the Poe community, I would highlight in particular that of the late Kenneth Silverman, author of the important 1991 biography *Edgar Allan Poe Mournful and Never-ending Remembrance.* I visited him at his apartment near Washington Square in 2015. He was then already sick. He listened with great interest as I described my nascent work, asking questions and commenting thoughtfully. We eventually said our farewells at his doorway, knowing that we would never see each other again. And he added simply, "You're the man." I felt these words as a generous passing of the torch, one writer's blessing of another, an expression of confidence and encouragement that I have been glad to remember ever since. Thank you, Ken.

I would like to acknowledge various supportive friends, several of whom have also been active in the Poe Studies Association. Former president Paul Lewis, with whom I organized the Fifth International Edgar Allan Poe Conference, "Poe Takes Boston," is also the prime mover behind the Poe statue in Boston and my neighbor in Newton; he and I have had many lively and enjoyable conversations about Poe over the years. Current president Philip Phillips, who oversaw the program for the Boston Poe conference, has offered unfailing and welcome interest in this biography. Treasurer emerita Carole Shaffer-Koros and former president (and current treasurer) Amy Armiento have been enduring and devoted supporters, as well. Barbara Cantalupo, the founder and former editor of the *Poe Review,* listened appreciatively to passages I read over the telephone and responded to an early draft of the work.

I am happy to thank, as well, other friends who have importantly supported this work: Denise Bethel, photography expert and auctioneer, an enthusiast for archival discovery; Holt Edmunds, longtime Richmond Poe aficionado and Poe Museum supporter; Samantha Gilmore, my former Penn State undergraduate research intern and a recent recipient of the doctoral degree from the University of Nebraska, Lincoln; Sandra H. Petrulionis, Penn State Altoona professor and author, and her husband, Joe Petrulionis, retired instructor, Penn State Altoona, both discerning readers of an early draft of this work; and Michael Singer, former student and present pharmaceutical entrepreneur, an enduring Poe devotee. And I am pleased to mention my lifelong friend Bill Wrenn, teacher of tai chi and qigong, a willing listener to my tales of Poe.

Others who have contributed in various ways to my work include Jim Baggett, Mamadou Bah, Brianne Barrett, Jackson R. Bryer and Mary Hardig, Susan Brynteson, Reid Byers, Sean Casey, Andrea Cherenack, Erin Chiparo, David Clawson, Patricia Edwards Clyne, David Cody, Bridgett Cooley, David Cory, Bruce and Mary Crawford, Pastor Crespo Jr., Kelsey Duinkerken, Tom Edsall, James Gamble, Bryan A. Garner, Eleanor Gillers, Patricia Haile-McPhillips, Cathy Henderson, Maeve Jones, William L. Joyce, Carisa Kolias, John Hanson, Brian Lannery, Steven Lomazow, Elaine McConnell, F. Lawrence McFall Jr., Wesley Scott McMasters, Donald N. Mott, Howard Mott, Ed O'Shea, Steve Paul, Diane Ray, Jill Reichenback, Catherine Robertson, Carl Rollyson, Beth Rozskowski, Tony Sampos, Chris Semtner, Joseph Shemtov, Jane R. Siegel, David E. E. Sloane, Alyson L. Taylor-White, Crystal Toscano, Robert Travers, Troy Valos, Laura Wasowicz, Courtney Welu, Kate Wodehouse, and Robert Zinck. And thanks to Jeffrey A. Savoye, who told me of the owner of an unknown Poe collection.

During the years of COVID-19, I made new bookish friends online, including through the Grolier Club, the New England Grolier Club, and the BIO International literary biography group. My Poe musings and updates found a welcome reception on the screen and, sometimes, eventually, in person. I relished the rapport; thank you all. And I have been delighted with the heartening meetings of the Poe Museum's Scholarship Committee; thank you, fellow members.

I am grateful to Joel Myerson, the late dean of Transcendentalism studies, who set so wonderful an example for all students of the American Renaissance and who wisely recommended that I submit a proposal for my Poe biography to the University of Virginia Press. I took his advice and have enjoyed the great interest of editor Eric Brandt from the beginning. I am indebted to him for making possible the ideal home for this work. Thank you, Eric. Others of his superb staff who have been greatly helpful have been Fernando Campos, Jason Coleman, J. Andrew Edwards, Mary Kate Maco, Ellen Satrom, Jeffrey G. Shifflett, and Cecilia Sorochin. I am very fortunate to have worked with such an outstanding team. I have benefited from the reports of the Press's two anonymous readers (one of whom later identified himself—thank you, Philip Phillips). And I am glad to acknowledge the important assistance of my excellent copyeditor, Susan A. Murray, and my fine indexer, Enid Zafran.

And then there is my family. My daughter Emily, the author of a brilliant study, *Virginia Woolf and Poetry,* provided warm interest and keen commentary on the manuscript of this book. My son Gabe, a gifted manager in a tech company, has long cheered me on, eager to read the published book. My wife Amy, an accomplished Rembrandt scholar, read every word of the manuscript and furnished suggestions and complete belief in the work. And my mother, Irene Kopley, an early advocate of digital humanities and a devotee of biographies, has been my biggest fan and an appreciative (and appreciated) reader of the manuscript and listener to my reading of the latest passage. Thank you, beloved family.

Notes

Introduction

1. Francis Lieber, *Reminiscences of an Intercourse with Mr. Niebuhr the Historian during a Residence with Him in Rome, in the Years 1822 and 1823* (Philadelphia: Carey, Lea and Blanchard, 1835), 191.
2. D. H. Lawrence, *Studies in Classic American Literature*, ed. Ezra Greenspan, Lindeth Vasey, and John Worthen (Cambridge, UK: Cambridge University Press, 2003), 66.
3. Barbara Cantalupo, "Interview with Richard Wilbur (2003)," *Edgar Allan Poe Review* 4, no. 1 (2003): 79.
4. Arthur Hobson Quinn, *Edgar Allan Poe: A Critical Biography* (New York: D. Appleton-Century, 1941); Kenneth Silverman, *Edgar A. Poe: Mournful and Never-ending Remembrance* (New York: HarperCollins, 1991); Dwight Thomas and David K. Jackson, *The Poe Log: A Documentary Life of Edgar Allan Poe, 1809–1849* (Boston: G. K. Hall, 1987).
5. Richard Kopley, "Poe's Lives," in *The Oxford Handbook of Edgar Allan Poe*, ed. J. Gerald Kennedy and Scott Peeples (New York: Oxford University Press, 2019), 70–86; rpt., *Edgar Allan Poe Review* 22, no. 2 (2021): 241–59; "Edgar Allan Poe," in *Oxford Bibliographies in American Literature*, ed. Jackson R. Bryer and Paul Lauter (New York: Oxford University Press, 2012), https://www.oxfordbibliographies.com.
6. For the Mack letters in the Poe Museum's collection, see "Mackenzie Letters, 1908–1914," *Poe Messenger* 16, no. 1 (1986): 4–8.
7. The genealogical background is provided in Flora Lapham Mack to William Lanier Washington, January 11, 1908, Poe Museum; Mack to Washington, February 29, 1908, collection of the author; Mack to Washington, March 31, 1908, collection of the author; Washington on Susan Archer Weiss, April 12, 1908, collection of the author; Mack to Washington, July 7, 1909, Poe Museum; and the manuscript genealogy and question-and-answer between Washington and Mack, collection of the author. The dates of the Mackenzie-Lapham and Mack-Lapham marriages are noted on the marriage licenses and related documents at the Court House in Danville, Virginia.
8. *Mary Chesnut's Civil War*, ed. C. Vann Woodward (New Haven, CT: Yale University Press, 1981), 782.

9. Flora Lapham Mack, "Concerning Correspondence between Edgar Allan Poe & John H. Mackenzie," collection of the author.
10. William Lanier Washington to Mary M. Mack, September 4, 1933, Poe Museum.

1. "No Tie More Strong"

1. "Richmond New Theatre. Mrs. Wilmot's Benefit," *Virginia Gazette and General Advertiser,* March 19, 1806. They had performed this before, on September 1, 1805, when Mrs. Hopkins's first husband was still alive (Arthur Hobson Quinn, *Edgar Allan Poe: A Critical Biography* [New York: D. Appleton-Century, 1941], 709).
2. Henrico County Marriage Bonds, 1800–1830, Microfilm reel 103, Volume N–Re, 96, Library of Virginia.
3. "Richmond Theatre. For the Benefit of Mrs. Green," *Virginia Gazette and General Advertiser,* April 9, 1806.
4. "New Theatre," *Virginia Gazette and General Advertiser,* January 15, 1806, [3].
5. Meredith Henne Baker, *The Richmond Theater Fire: Early America's First Great Disaster* (Baton Rouge: Louisiana State University Press, 2012), 16.
6. Geddeth Smith, *The Brief Career of Eliza Poe* (Rutherford, NJ: Fairleigh Dickinson University Press, 1988), 20–25.
7. The miniature is widely reproduced (see, for example, Dwight Thomas and David K. Jackson, *The Poe Log: A Documentary Life of Edgar Allan Poe, 1809–1849* [Boston: G. K. Hall, 1987], 2). It also serves as the cover of Geddeth Smith's book. And it is included here.
8. Smith, *The Brief Career of Eliza Poe,* 81, 72–73. See also, for both Eliza and David Poe, Quinn, *Edgar Allan Poe: A Critical Biography,* 1–50.
9. For the Philadelphia and New York interim in 1806, see Quinn, *Edgar Allan Poe: A Critical Biography,* 24–25; and Smith, *The Brief Career of Eliza Poe,* 84–85.
10. Ellen Susan Bulfinch, ed., *The Life and Letters of Charles Bulfinch Architect with Other Family Papers* (Boston: Houghton Mifflin, 1896), 115. For accounts of Bulfinch and the first and second theater on Federal Street, see ibid., 93–97, 114–15; and Charles A. Place, *Charles Bulfinch Architect and Citizen* (Boston: Houghton Mifflin, 1925), 59–62. See also Donald C. King, *The Theatres of Boston: A Stage and Screen History* (Jefferson, NC: McFarland, 2004), 15–18.
11. "The Theatre" [re *Speed the Plough*], *New England Palladium,* October 17, 1806, [2]; "The Ordeal—No. 3" [re *The Romp*], *The Emerald, or, Miscellany of Literature,* November 8, 1806, 329; "Theatrical Retrospects, for December, 1806" [re *The Provoked Husband*], *Polyanthos* after December 26, 1806.
12. "The Ordeal—No. 2" [re *Lovers' Vows*], *The Emerald, or, Miscellany of Literature,* October 25, 1806, 305; "The Ordeal—No. 6" [re *John Bull*], ibid., November 29, 1806, 565; "Theatrical Communication" [re *The Provoked Husband*], *Columbian Centinel,* December 24, 1806, [2].
13. "The Young Roscius," *New England Palladium,* December 30, 1806, [3]. For a full discussion of Master Betty, see Jeffrey Kahan, *Bettymania and the Birth of Celebrity Culture* (Bethlehem, PA: Lehigh University Press, 2010). (Roscius had been a Roman actor [ibid., 18]. For a treatment of Roscius, see Anne Duncan,

Performance and Identity in the Classical World [Cambridge, UK: Cambridge University Press, 2006], 173–77).

14. See Poe-Allan-Ellis Papers, 1803–1881, MSC0033, The Valentine, Richmond VA. See also Quinn, *Edgar Allan Poe: A Critical Biography*, 30n.
15. [Joseph T. Buckingham], "The Drama," *Polyanthos*, March 1807, 281–82, 284.
16. "A Theatrical Communication," *New England Palladium*, November 18, 1806, [2]. For the full names of the Ushers, see M 2:393.
17. Joseph T. Buckingham, *Personal Memoirs and Recollections of Editorial Life*, 2 vols. (Boston: Ticknor, Reed, and Fields, 1852), 1:57.
18. "Theatrical," *Columbian Centinel*, March 18, 1807, [2].
19. "The Ordeal—No. 21," *The Emerald, or, Miscellany of Literature*, March 21, 1807, [137].
20. "Communication. Last Night's Insult," *Repertory* (Boston), April 7, 1807, 2 (America's Historical Newspapers). The note's date of "*Monday Evening, March 6*" is incorrect given that March 6, 1807, was a Friday, when *Venice Preserved* was performed. April 6, 1807, was a Monday and the date of the performance of *Julius Caesar.*
21. "[Among the new plays"], *Polyanthos,* April 1807, 67.
22. Bill Newton Dunn, *The Man Who Was John Bull: The Biography of Theodore Edward Hook, 1778–1841* (London: Allendale, 1996), 28.
23. George C. D. Odell, ed., *Annals of the New York Stage,* vol. 2 (New York: Columbia University Press, 1927), 294–95; "Theatre," *New England Palladium,* October 10, 1809, [2]; "TEKELI," *New England Palladium,* October 13, 1809, [2].
24. "The Drama No. 8," *The Emerald, or, Miscellany of Literature,* December 19, 1807, 99–100; "Memoranda Dramatica," ibid., October 3, 1807, 471–72.
25. "Communication. Benefit of Mr. & Mrs. Poe." *Boston Gazette,* March 21, 1808, [2] (America's Historical Newspapers).
26. "Theatrical Notice," *The Emerald, or, Miscellany of Literature,* April 16, 1808, 310.
27. Marie Louise Shew Houghton to John Ingram, April 3, [1875], in *Building Poe Biography,* ed. John Carl Miller (Charlottesville: University Press of Virginia, 1977), 121.
28. See also Smith, *The Brief Career of Eliza Poe,* 96. For elaboration of the embargo, see Burton Spivak, *Jefferson's English Crisis: Commerce, Embargo, and the Republican Revolution* (Charlottesville: University Press of Virginia, 1979), 102–36. See also Arthur Scherr, *Thomas Jefferson's Image of New England* (Jefferson, NC: McFarland, 2016), 139–44. William Cullen Bryant as a boy published a satirical poem in 1808, *The Embargo, or Sketches of the Times.* Poe would later mention this work in a notice of Bryant (H 10:86).
29. Houghton to Ingram, April 3, [1875], 121.
30. See Elizabeth Inchbald, ed., *The British Theatre,* vol. 4 (London: Longman, Hurst, Rees, and Orme, 1803), available through Google Books.
31. "The Ordeal—No. 21," *The Emerald, or, Miscellany of Literature,* March 21, 1807, 137.
32. William Bittner earlier made this suggestion (Bittner, *Poe: A Biography* [London: Elek, 1962], 12). Two quotations from Edgar in *King Lear* appear as epigraphs for

Jeffrey Meyers, *Edgar Allan Poe: His Life and Legacy* (New York: Charles Scribner's Sons, 1992).
33. "Theatre," *New England Palladium,* January 13, 1809, [3]. See also Quinn, *Edgar Allan Poe: A Critical Biography,* 718. For the date of Edgar's birth, see Poe-Allan-Ellis Papers, 1803–1811, MSC0033, The Valentine, Richmond, VA. See also Quinn, *Edgar Allan Poe: A Critical Biography,* 30n.
34. "Theatrical Communication," *Boston Gazette,* February 9, 1809, [3].
35. Maria Clemm to Neilson Poe, August 19, 1860, in *Building Poe Biography,* 46–47. Maria Clemm, Poe's aunt and later his mother-in-law, states that both of Poe's parents made the trip to Baltimore when Edgar was five weeks old, but this assertion is problematic since Eliza Poe was performing in Boston on February 3, 10, 15, 22, and 24, and March 6, 15, 17, 20, and 24 (Quinn, *Edgar Allan Poe: A Critical Biography,* 718–19). David Poe, who was in Stockerton, Pennsylvania, by February 22, was away from the Boston stage until mid-April. Perhaps a wet-nurse was provided for baby Edgar.
36. George Poe, Jr., to William Clemm, Jr., Stockerton, [PA], March 6, 1809, in *Edgar Allan Poe: Letters and Documents in the Enoch Pratt Free Library,* ed. Arthur H. Quinn and Richard H. Hart (New York: Scholars' Facsimiles & Reprints, 1941), 4–6.
37. "Theatre," *New England Palladium* March 17, 1809, [2].
38. "Theatre," *New England Palladium,* April 7, 1809, [3] [*Romeo and Juliet*]; "Boston Theatre," *Boston Mirror,* April 15, 1809, [3]; "Theatre," *New England Palladium,* April 21, 1809, [2] [*Hamlet*]; "Theatre," ibid., May 5, 1809, [2] [*King Lear*]. For further information on Payne, see Grace Overmyer, *America's First Hamlet* (New York: New York University Press, 1957).
39. "Theatrical Communication—MRS. POE'S Benefit," *New England Palladium,* April 18, 1809, [2].
40. Maria Clemm to Neilson Poe, August 19, 1860, in *Building Poe Biography,* 46–47.
41. Odell, *Annals of the New York Stage,* 2:8; Mary C. Henderson, *The City and the Theatre: New York Playhouses from Bowling Green to Times Square* (Clifton, NJ: James T. White, 1973), 32, 48.
42. "Theatrical Register, for 1809–10," *Ramblers' Magazine and New York Theatrical Register* 1, no. 1 (n.d.): 17–18. See also Odell, *Annals of the New York Stage,* 2:326–27.
43. "Theatrical Register, for 1809–10," *Ramblers' Magazine and New York Theatrical Register* 1, no. 1 (n.d.): 19, 26 [re *Hamlet* and *Othello*], 18 [re *The Romp*]; "Theatrical Register, for 1809–10," ibid., 1, no. 3 (n.d.): 211 [re *John Bull at Fontainbleau*].
44. "Theatrical Register, for 1809–10," *Ramblers' Magazine and New York Theatrical Register* 1, no. 1 (n.d.): 23 (pronunciation), 27 (*gravitas*); "Theatrical Register, for 1809–10," ibid. 1, no. 2 (n.d.): 92 (appearance), 94 (acting skills), 93 (character).
45. BAG-AND-TAIL, "Sur un *Poe* de Chambre," *Ramblers' Magazine and New York Theatrical Register* 1, no. 2 (n.d.): 88.
46. "Theatrical Register, for 1809–10," *Ramblers' Magazine and New York Theatrical Register* 1, no. 1 (n.d.): 27.
47. Nemo Nobody, "To Our Brother Editors of New-York," *Something* (Boston), vol. 1, December 16, 1809, 76.

48. "Theatrical Register, for 1809–10," *Ramblers' Magazine and New York Theatrical Register* 1, no. 2 (n.d.): 100.
49. Nemo Nobody, "To Our Brother Editors of New-York."
50. "Theatrical," *Lady's Weekly Miscellany*, March 10, 1810, 316 (American Periodicals).
51. Glum, "New-York Theatricals," *Mirror of Taste and Dramatic Censor*, May 1, 1810, 417.
52. "*A friend to female merit*," "Communication," *Columbian* (New York), July 2, 1810, [3] (America's Historical Newspapers).
53. "Richmond Theatre," *Virginia Patriot*, September 21, 1810, [3].
54. "Communication," *Virginia Patriot*, September 21, 1810, [3].
55. Letter to the editor, *Richmond Enquirer*, September 21, 1810, [3]; see also Martin Staples Shockley, *The Richmond Stage 1784–1812* (Charlottesville: University Press of Virginia, 1977), 318–19.
56. "Richmond Theatre," *Virginia Patriot*, November 6, 1810, [3].
57. Mackenzie Family Bible, "Births," Virginia Museum of History and Culture, Richmond. The language is qualified: "Rosalie Mackenzie Poe was delivered to the care of Wm & Jane Mackenzie 9th Dec 1811 (is said) was born 20 December 1810." The Norfolk information is provided in Quinn, *Edgar Allan Poe: A Critical Biography*, 40n.
58. See Mary E. Phillips, *Edgar Allan Poe—The Man*, 2 vols. (Chicago: John C. Winston, 1926), 1:219; see also Kenneth Silverman, *Edgar A. Poe: Mournful and Never-ending Remembrance* (New York: HarperCollins, 1991), 452n.
59. "*A friend to female merit*," "Communication."
60. ["A Letter Received This Day"], *Charleston Courier*, November 9, 1810, [3] (America's Historical Newspapers). Reprinted from *The Times* (Charleston).
61. W. Stanley Hoole, *The Ante-bellum Charleston Theatre* (Tuscaloosa: University of Alabama Press, 1946), 77.
62. Ibid., 5.
63. "Theatre," *Charleston Courier*, January 23, 1811, [3].
64. "Theatre," *Charleston Courier*, March 2, 1811, [3] (Lady Teazle); "Theatre," ibid., February 15, 1811 (Lydia Languish); and April 1, 1811, [2], April 17, 1811, [2] (Mopsa).
65. "Theatre," *Charleston Courier*, February 2, 1811, [3], February 4, 1811, [2], April 3, 1811 (nymph); ibid., April 26, 1811, [3] (Grace).
66. "Theatre," *Charleston Courier*, March 22, 1811, [2]; "Theatre," ibid., March 23, 1811, [3]. For the play itself, see Theodore Edward Hook, *Tekeli; or, The Siege of Montgatz: A Melo-drama, In Three Acts* (Literature Online).
67. "Theatre," *Charleston Courier*, April 29, 1811, [2]; "Theatre," ibid., May 20, 1811, [2].
68. Floretta, letter to the editor, *Norfolk and Portsmouth Herald*, July 26, 1811, [3]. Also on this page is "Theatre for the Benefit of Mrs. POE and Miss THOMAS." See also Quinn, *Edgar Allan Poe: A Critical Biography*, 41–42.
69. "Richmond Theatre," *Virginia Patriot*, September 20, 1811, [3]; "Richmond Theatre," ibid., October 8, 1811, [3]. See also Quinn, *Edgar Allan Poe: A Critical Biography*, 724; Shockley, *The Richmond Stage 1784–1812*, 331–39; and Thomas and Jackson, *The Poe Log*, 12.

70. Shockley, *The Richmond Stage 1784–1812*, 340. *The Hunters and the Milkmaid* was performed in Richmond not only on October 9, 1811, but also on September 6, 1811 ("Richmond Theatre," *Virginia Patriot*, September 6, 1811, [3]).
71. Thomas and Jackson, *The Poe Log*, 13.
72. Shockley, *The Richmond Stage 1784–1812*, 348–49; Thomas and Jackson, *The Poe Log*, 13–14.
73. Hervey Allen and Thomas Ollive Mabbott, *Poe's Brother: The Poems of William Henry Leonard Poe* (New York: George H. Doran, 1926), 41. The two other locks of hair are those of his father and his sister, whose illegitimacy is intimated.
74. Flora Lapham Mack to William Lanier Washington, February 29, 1908, collection of the author. See also Mack to Mackenzie, March 12, 1908, collection of the author. Thomas and Jackson's *The Poe Log* offers information on the last days of Eliza Poe drawn from previously published material by Susan Archer Weiss and T. O. Mabbott (14). Poe later wrote of his parents, "Both died . . . within a few weeks of each other" (O 1:116). But he seems to have been mistaken when he wrote that his mother had died "a few weeks before" his father (O 1:99).
75. Mack to Washington, February 29, 1908.
76. Mackenzie Family Bible, "Births" and "Deaths."
77. Mack to Washington, February 29, 1908. See also Mack to Washington, March 12, 1908.
78. Flora Lapham Mack [for William Lanier Washington], "Suggestions for the First Chapter of Your Book," collection of the author.
79. Flora Lapham Mack to William Lanier Washington, March 31, 1908, collection of the author.
80. Houghton, *Building Poe Biography* 121. See also Thomas and Jackson, *The Poe Log*, 14–15.
81. Thomas and Jackson, *The Poe Log*, 14–15.
82. "Died," *Richmond Enquirer*, December 10, 1811, [3]; Thomas and Jackson, *The Poe Log*, 15.
83. Marie Louise Shew Houghton to John Ingram, May 16, [18]75, in *Building Poe Biography*, 140.
84. Mack [for Washington], "Suggestions for the First Chapter of Your Book." I do not identify the residences of the Mackenzies and the Allans during 1811 to 1815 because they are not definitively known (see Mary Wingfield Scott: "Poe's Fourteenth Street Home" and "Where Did the McKenzies Live during Rosalie Poe's Childhood?," The Valentine, Richmond, VA).
85. Mack to Washington, March 31, 1908.

2. "From Childhood's Hour"

1. Flora Lapham Mack [for William Lanier Washington], "Suggestions for the First Chapter of Your Book," collection of the author. For the location of the Allan home, see Poe-Allan-Ellis Papers, 1803–1881 MSC0033, The Valentine, Richmond, VA. See also Arthur Hobson Quinn, *Edgar Allan Poe: A Critical Biography* (New York: D. Appleton-Century, 1941), 53; and Dwight Thomas and David K. Jackson, *The Poe Log: A Documentary Life of Edgar Allan Poe*,

1809–1849 (Boston: G. K. Hall, 1987), 14. Regarding Frances Allan's appearance, see the Thomas Sully portrait, reproduced here. Soon after he went to the Allans, Edgar was baptized ("Ellis Tells of Poe's Boyhood Days Here," *Richmond Times-Dispatch,* December 2, 1906, clipping at The Valentine). Thomas H. Ellis, a son of John Allan's partner Charles Ellis, wrote in a letter of April 22, 1881, "The name of Edgar Allan was given him in baptism, by the Rev. Dr. John Buchanan." That letter, reprinted in the article in the *Richmond Times-Dispatch,* originally appeared in Ellis's "Edgar Allan Poe," *Richmond Standard,* May 7, 1881, 2. See also Killis Campbell, ed., *The Poems of Edgar Allan Poe* (Boston: Ginn, 1917), 223–24; H 1:23; and Thomas and Jackson, *The Poe Log,* 15.

2. Mack [for Washington], "Suggestions for the First Chapter of Your Book," collection of the author. Mack states that the Allans and Mackenzies lived next door to one another at this time (Mack to Washington, February 29, 1908; Mack to Washington, March 12, 1908, collection of the author), but she later acknowledges that perhaps this was at a later date (Mack to Washington, March 31, 1908, collection of the author). I think it was 1825, when John Allan bought the home Moldavia at Fifth and Main Streets. Mary Wingfield Scott's "Where Did the Mackenzies Live during Rosalie Poe's Childhood?" ("Richmond Buildings Associated with Poe," The Valentine) does not definitively clarify the location for the earliest years. Mary E. Phillips states that the Mackenzies then lived "on Grace, between 5th and 6th Streets," crediting J. H. Whitty (Phillips, *Edgar Allan Poe—the Man,* 2 vols. [Chicago: John C. Winston, 1926] 1:92). For her Whitty source, see J. H. Whitty to Mary E. Phillips, November 4, 1919, MsAM 1200, Special Collections, Boston Public Library.

3. See "Ellis Tells of Poe's Boyhood Days Here" and also Poe-Allan-Ellis Papers, 1803–1881, MSC0033, The Valentine, Richmond, VA. Bowler Cocke's plantation was reported to comprise nine hundred acres, fifteen miles south of Richmond ("The Cocke Family of Virginia," *Virginia Magazine of History and Biography* 4, no. 4 [1897]: 446–48, JSTOR). Cocke was significantly indebted to the Ellis & Allan Company ("Statement of account," April 25, 1812, and "Indenture," May 5, 1812, Box 117, DLC-EA). See also the response of Bowler Cocke's son, Bowler F. Cocke, to Ellis & Allan's letter regarding the remaining indebtedness after his father's death in 1812 (Bowler F. Cocke to John Allan, August 13, 1812, Box 118, DLC-EA). Bowler F. Cocke, who would be the executor of his father's estate, later advertised an auction of those enslaved by his father (Bowler F. Cocke, Advertisement, *Virginia Patriot,* December 4, 1812, [America's Historical Newspapers]), and Allan bought a girl named Nancy ("Sundries Dr to Cash," December 19, 1812, Box 522, DLC-EA).

4. For Cocke as close friend of John Allan, see Poe-Allan-Ellis Papers, 1803–1881, MSC0033, The Valentine, Richmond, VA. For Cocke's invitation to Allan, see Bowler Cocke to John Allan, October 20, 1811, Box 113, DLC-EA.

5. This story and the quotations are drawn from Flora Lapham Mack to William Lanier Washington, March 31, 1908, collection of the author. John H. Mackenzie was born on March 28, 1806, in Richmond. See the annotation in *The New Testament of Our Lord and Saviour Jesus Christ,* Poe Museum; and Jane Mackenzie Byrd's handwritten Mackenzie genealogy accompanying letters to J. H. Whitty,

Poe Miscellany, Harry Ransom Center, University of Texas at Austin. Mack, in this same letter, mistakenly states that John H. Mackenzie was born in "January 1800" and therefore concludes that John and Edgar could not later have gotten into boyish mischief together, as Susan Archer Talley Weiss reports. In fact, John was not quite three years older than Edgar (not nine years older).
6. William Gray of Norfolk married a sister of Jane Scott Mackenzie. There were five Scott sisters; the remaining three married Michael Wall Hancock, Thomas Gilliat, and James Kirby, respectively (Poe-Allan-Ellis Papers, 1803–1881, MSC0033, The Valentine, Richmond, VA). Flora Lapham Mack mentions Mrs. Gray in Mack to Washington, May 26, 1908, collection of the author. Mack notes that Mrs. Gray had two sons, Alfred and Gilhette, and a daughter, Mary (Mack to Washington, February 1, 1909, collection of the author). In a question-and-answer format with William Lanier Washington, Mack mentions that William Gray "had some position under the English government" in Norfolk and that a third Scott sister was Sophia Scott, who married [Michael Wall] Hancock (collection of the author). (William Gray became British consulate in Norfolk.) The Poe Museum in Richmond, Virginia, holds a miniature of three of the Gray sisters.
7. "Overwhelming Calamity," *Richmond Enquirer,* December 28, 1811, [3].
8. Poe-Allan-Ellis Papers, 1803–1881, MSC0033, The Valentine Richmond, VA.
9. "Ellis Tells of Poe's Boyhood Days Here" and Poe-Allan-Ellis Papers, 1803–1881. MSC0033, The Valentine, Richmond, VA.
10. John Allan to White Matlock Jr., January 3, 1812, Box 521, DLC-EA.
11. White Matlock Jr. to John Allan, January 8, 1812, Box 438, DLC-EA.
12. Meredith Henne Baker, *The Richmond Theater Fire: Early America's First Great Disaster* (Baton Rouge: Louisiana State University Press, 2012), 31, 64, 73–74. For a novel based on the Richmond Theater Fire, see Rachel Beanland, *The House Is on Fire* (New York: Simon & Schuster, 2023).
13. Baker, *The Richmond Theater Fire,* 27–36.
14. Ibid., 40–41. See also "A Colored Hero," *Memphis Daily Eagle and Enquirer,* April 24, 1858 (America's Historical Newspapers). And consult, too, Philip Barrett, *Gilbert Hunt, the City Blacksmith* (Richmond, VA: James Woodhouse, 1859) and his story of Hunt in the collection *The Deaf Shoemaker* (New York: Dodd, Mead, 1859), 145–51. When Doctor McCaw himself dropped down from the window, he injured his leg, and Hunt bound it and set it with splints (Baker, *The Richmond Theater Fire,* 41).
15. Mack to Washington, March 31, 1908, collection of the author.
16. Ibid. Mary's middle name, Gallego, was clearly an honoring of her godfather.
17. Baker, *The Richmond Theater Fire,* 20, 30–31, 43–44, 115–16. John Allan wrote, "poor Mr. Gallego Miss Conyers & my little & much loved Nephew George Dixon are amongst the suffer[e]rs" (Allan to Matlock, January 3, 1812, Box 521, DLC-EA). A poem about the Richmond Theater Fire—a work written in 1812 and published in the *Southern Literary Messenger* of August 1835—included four lines about Joseph Gallego: "Yon man of woes, oh! Mark his furrowed cheek; / What deep-drawn sighs his misery bespeak: / Tis Gallego! Each bosom comfort flown, / In the dark vale of years he walks alone" (M. L. P., ["Whence the wild wail of agonizing woe"], in "Burning of the Richmond Theatre," *Southern*

Literary Messenger [August 1835]: 666–67). Perhaps Poe recalled such lines when he wrote the fire section of "The Bells" (M 1:436–37). Lieutenant James Gibbon Jr., the fiancé of Gallego's niece, tried to save her but failed and died in the attempt (Baker, *The Richmond Theater Fire*, 21–22, 28, 30–31, 58).

18. Mack to Washington, March 31, 1908, collection of the author. Isabelle Ritchie was the daughter of the *Richmond Enquirer* editor Thomas Ritchie.
19. Ibid.
20. See "Theatre," *Charleston Courier*, April 26, 1811, [3], for Mrs. Poe as a Grace in *Cinderella* in Charleston. See "Richmond Theatre," *Virginia Patriot*, September 20, 1811, [3], as well as Arthur Hobson Quinn, *Edgar Allan Poe: A Critical Biography* (New York: D. Appleton-Century 1941), 724; Martin Staples Shockley, *The Richmond Stage 1784–1812* (Charlottesville: University Press of Virginia, 1977), 332; and Dwight Thomas and David K. Jackson, *The Poe Log: A Documentary Life of Edgar Allan Poe, 1809–1849* (Boston: G. K. Hall, 1987), 12, for Mrs. Poe again as a Grace in *Cinderella* in Richmond. Shockley suggests that Edgar may have appeared as a Cupid in the September 20, 1811, performance (340).
21. Shockley, *The Richmond Stage 1784–1812*, 331.
22. Mack to Washington, March 31, 1908.
23. Ibid.
24. Edward M. Alfriend, "Unpublished Recollections of Edgar Allan Poe," *Literary Era* 8 (August 1901): 489.
25. Mack to Washington, March 31, 1908.
26. Poe-Allan-Ellis Papers, 1803–1881, MSC0033, The Valentine, Richmond, VA.
27. Receipt of Philip Thornton to John Allan, May 21–23, 1812, Box 438, DLC-EA; John Allan to Charles Ellis, May 27, 1812, Box 118, DLC-EA.
28. P. G. Meriwether (for John Allan) to Charles Ellis, June 7, 1812, Box 438, DLC-EA.
29. Eugene Didier wrote that "Edgar accompanied Mr. and Mrs. Allan to the White Sulphur in the summers of 1812, '13, '14, and '15" ("Memoir," in *The Life and Poems of Edgar Allan Poe* [New York: W. J. Widdleton, 1877], 28). However, Didier mistakenly stated that the Allans and Edgar traveled to Scotland in 1816 rather than in 1815 (28–29). Indeed, they were not in the United States during the summer of 1815. George E. Woodberry seems correct here: "He [Edgar] . . . spent the three summers following his mother's death at the White Sulphur Springs" (Woodberry, *Edgar Allan Poe* [Boston: Houghton Mifflin, 1885], 15–16).
30. "Bowyer's White Sulphur Springs, Greenbrier," *Richmond Enquirer*, July 16, 1811 [1]; July 19, 1811 [1]; and August 2, 1811 [1] (America's Historical Newspapers). John Allan later wrote to Edgar on May 18, 1829, pleased to hear from him (in a letter now lost) that Representative John J. Barber [Barbour] was supporting his application to West Point, "He perhaps remembered you when you were at the Springs in 1812" (Mary Newton Stanard, comp., *Edgar Allan Poe Letters till Now Unpublished in the Valentine Museum, Richmond, Virginia* [Philadelphia: J. B. Lippincott, 1925], 121–23). Edgar's letter to his foster father of November 18, 1829, indicates that Allan had returned to the springs for his health (O 1:51).
31. J. K. Paulding, *Letters from the South Written during an Excursion in the Summer of 1816*, 2 vols. (New York: James Eastburn, 1817), 1:195.

32. Didier, *The Life and Poems of Edgar Allan Poe*, 28.
33. See Poe-Allan-Ellis Papers, 1803–1881, MSC0033, The Valentine, Richmond, VA. For the September 6, 1812, letter, without the postscript, see Quinn, *Edgar Allan Poe: A Critical Biography*, 57–58. See also "Miscellaneous Poe Notes (answers to questions of Dr. Arthur H. Quinn, June 1939)" at the Valentine. Information on the Dixons is readily available in Thomas and Jackson, *The Poe Log*, xxii. Rosanna's brother George had died in the Richmond Theater Fire.
34. David S. Heidler and Jeanne T. Heidler, *The War of 1812* (Westport, CT: Greenwood, 2002), 30–35. For the Non-Intercourse Act itself, see 164–65.
35. For detail on the *Newburyport* incident, see especially Charles Ellis to John Allan, October 12, 1812, Box 120; John Allan to Charles Ellis, October 15, 1812, Box 121; Charles Ellis to John Allan, October 23, 1812, Box 121; William Galt to Charles Ellis, November 3, 1812, Box 121; Charles Ellis to John Allan, November 4, 1812, Box 121; Charles Ellis to John Allan, November 9, 1812, Box 121; Charles Ellis to John Allan, November 15, 1812, Box 122; John Allan to Charles Ellis, November 25, 1812, Box 122; Charles Ellis to John Allan, December 5, 1812, Box 122; and Calvin Goddard to Ellis & Allan, May 4, 1813, Box 126, DLC-EA.
36. John Allan to Charles Ellis, October 15, 1812, Box 121, DLC-EA.
37. George D. Fisher, *History and Reminiscences of the Monumental Church, Richmond VA., from 1814 to 1878* (Richmond, VA: Whittet & Shepperson, 1880), 20–29. For Gallego's leadership in the support of the Monumental Church, see Poe-Allan-Ellis Papers, 1803–1881, MSC0033, The Valentine, Richmond, VA. For the contribution of Allan and Ellis to the building of the church, see [Record of Payments], May 23, 1812, Box 522, DLC-EA.
38. "THE PLEASURE OF YOUR COMPANY . . . ," January 16, 1813, Box 124, DLC-EA.
39. Eliza Poe to Mrs. John Allan, February 8, 1813, Box 438, DLC-EA. I have corrected the name "Allen" with the spelling "Allan." Eliza Poe would marry Henry Herring in 1814 (Thomas and Jackson, *The Poe Log*, xxviii).
40. Poe-Allan-Ellis Papers, 1803–1881, MSC0033, The Valentine, Richmond, VA.
41. See John Ellis to Charles Ellis, February 16, 1813, Box 124, DLC-EA; and Charles Ellis to John Allan, April 22, 1813, Box 126, DLC-EA.
42. See John Allan to Charles Ellis, May 14, 17, and 18, 1813; Ellis to Allan, May 20, 1813, Box 127, DLC-EA (whooping cough); John Allan to Charles Goodall, July 12, 1813, Box 521, DLC-EA; and Edward Valentine Jr. to John Allan, July 26, 1813, Box 129, DLC-EA (measles).
43. See Charles Ellis to John Allan, June 20 and 27 and July 2, 1813, Box 129, DLC-EA; and John Allan to Charles Ellis, June 30, 1813, Box 129, DLC-EA. The rapes were attributed to French prisoners fighting for the British (John K. Mahon, *The War of 1812* [Gainesville: University of Florida Press, 1972], 120). But either Ellis or Allan wrote that "it can be no pal[l]iation to the British should it even appear that the French Troops committed such horrid and shocking Brutalities" (Ellis or Allan to Stephens & Ahearn, July 13, 1813, Box 521, DLC-EA).
44. John Allan to Charles Ellis, June 30, 1813, Box 129, DLC-EA. Ellis responded to Allan on Frances making Bounce on July 2, 1813, Box 129, DLC-EA.
45. For the departure of the British forces from the Norfolk area, see Thomas Owens & Co. to Ellis & Allan, July 12, 1813, Box 129, DLC-EA. John Ellis wrote to his

brother Charles that Richmonders have "got over their alarm" (July 13, 1813, Box 129, DLC-EA).

46. John Allan to Charles Ellis, September 23, 1813, Box 130, DLC-EA (Perry); John Allan to Charles Ellis, October 19, 1813, Box 131, DLC-EA (Harrison). For Allan's illness, see Josiah Ellis to Charles Ellis, September 27, 1813, Box 130, DLC-EA; and John Allan to John H. Cocke, October 1, 1813, Box 521, DLC-EA.
47. Charles Ellis to John Allan, August 10, 1813, Box 130, DLC-EA.
48. Ibid.
49. Margaret Nimmo to Mr. Williamson, September 2, 1813, Box 130, DLC-EA. That one of the Nancys is not Frances Allan is clear from John Allan's having written to Charles Ellis of "Frances and the two Nancys" (June 12, 1813, Box 128, DLC-EA).
50. Charles Ellis to John Allan, November 15, 1813, Box 131, DLC-EA.
51. John Allan to Joshua Fry, November 24, 1813, Box 521, DLC-EA; and see also John Allan to John Heathcote, December 3, 1813, Box 521, DLC-EA; and John Allan to Charles Ellis, November 18, 1813, Box 131, DLC-EA.
52. See "Sundries Dr to Cash," "John Allan pd ¼ tuition of Edgar 1 [pound] 4 [shillings]," July 31, 1813, Box 522, DLC-EA; and Clotilda Fisher to John Allan, receipt for "1 quarters Tuition for Edgar A Poe $4.00," January 20, 1814, Box 133, DLC-EA. Arthur Hobson Quinn comments on the Fisher family in an answer to a question in "Miscellaneous Poe Notes," The Valentine, Richmond, VA. See also Thomas and Jackson, *The Poe Log*, 21.
53. For this story of Allan's response to the punishment of his foster son, see M 1:534. Mabbott cites both R. H. Stoddard and Mary Jane Poitiaux Dixon as authorities for the story (R. H. Stoddard, "Life of Edgar Allan Poe," in *The Works of Edgar Allan Poe*, 6 vols. [New York: A. C. Armstrong, 1884], 1:13; Mary Jane Poitiaux Dixon to "Messrs. Editors," July 2, 1875, John Henry Ingram's Poe Collection, Albert & Shirley Small Special Collections Library, University of Virginia, Charlottesville, Item 237). Stoddard's story may be found earlier in Griswold's "Memoir" (Rufus Wilmot Griswold, "Memoir of the Author," in *The Works of the Late Edgar Allan Poe*, 4 vols. [New York: J. S. Redfield, 1850–56], 3:vii–viii; reprinted in Benjamin Franklin Fisher, ed., *Poe in His Own Time* [Iowa City: University of Iowa Press, 2010], 109).
54. Susan Archer Weiss, "Reminiscences of Edgar Allan Poe," *New York Independent* 57 (August 1904): 444 (https://www.eapoe.org); Susan Archer Weiss, *The Home Life of Poe* (New York: Broadway, 1907), 15–16.
55. Weiss, "Reminiscences," 444; Mack to Washington, March 31, 1908.
56. Burton R. Pollin, "Poe's Authorship of Three Long Critical and Autobiographical Articles of 1843 Now Authenticated," *American Renaissance Literary Report* 7 (1993): 164; Benjamin Franklin Fisher, "An Early Biography of Poe (1843): The Philadelphia Saturday Museum Sketch," in *Masques, Mysteries, and Mastodons: A Poe Miscellany*, ed. Fisher (Baltimore, MD: Edgar Allan Poe Society, 2006), 156; [Edgar A. Poe and Henry B. Hirst, or Poe alone], From "Poets and Poetry of Philadelphia," in *Poe in His Own Time*, ed. Benjamin F. Fisher (Iowa City: University of Iowa Press, 2010), 24.
57. Sarah Helen Whitman to John H. Ingram, March 27, 1874, in *Poe's Helen Remembers*, ed. John Carl Miller (Charlottesville: University Press of Virginia, 1979), 95.

58. Edgar Allan Poe, review of *Insubordination: An American Story of Real Life,* by T. S. Arthur, *Graham's Magazine* (June 1841): 296.
59. T. S. Arthur, *Insubordination: An American Story of Real Life* (Baltimore, MD: Knight & Colburn, 1841).
60. Mary Jane Poitiaux Dixon to "Messrs. Editors."
61. The consecration of Monumental Church took place on Wednesday, May 4 (George D. Fisher, *History and Reminiscences of the Monumental Church,* 34). The monument listed seventy-three victims (ibid., 39–40). For the names of pew-holders, see ibid., 35–38. It was Mary Brockenborough who remembered Mrs. Allan and Edgar attending Monumental Church (Phillips, *Edgar Allan Poe—the Man,* 1:108.)
62. Phillips, *Edgar Allan Poe—the Man,* 1:119. For further information, see James Penn, Indenture to Ellis & Allan, March 10, 1814, Box 134, DLC-EA. Penn owed money to the firm and promised to yield his property unless within a year he was able to pay. A subsequent letter indicated that "I shall this summer be in command of funds You shall honorably be paid with thankfulness for your politeness & indulgence" (James Penn to Ellis & Allan, March 12, 1815, Box 140, DLC-EA). Arthur Hobson Quinn comments on Penn in answer to a question in "Miscellaneous Poe Notes," The Valentine, Richmond, VA.
63. M. Randolph to John Allan, Misc. 1814 documents, Box 138, DLC-EA.
64. Mabbott places in 1814 Edgar's reading the newspaper to people he encountered on this horseback ride (M 1:534). See also William F. Gill, *The Life of Edgar Allan Poe,* 4th ed. (New York: W. J. Widdleton, 1878), 25; and Weiss, "Reminiscences," 16–17.
65. For Edgar's offering a toast and reciting poetry, see Woodberry, *Edgar Allan Poe,* 15. Woodberry mentions "Lay of the Last Minstrel" in his later *The Life of Edgar Allan Poe,* 2 vols. (Boston: Houghton, Mifflin, 1909), 1:18–19. See also John H. Ingram, *Edgar Allan Poe: His Life, Letters, and Opinions,* 2 vols. (London: John Hogg, 1880), 1:11–12; and Phillips, *Edgar Allan Poe—the Man,* 1:104.
66. James R. Nimmo to John Allan, August 17, 1814, Box 136, DLC-EA.
67. See Mahon, *The War of 1812,* 297–301; and Heidler and Heidler, *The War of 1812,* 114–16.
68. "Sundries Dr to Cash," October 8, 1814, Box 554, DLC-EA.
69. Margaret K. Nimmo (Ellis) to James Nimmo, September 1, 1814, Poe-Allan-Ellis Papers, 1803–1881, MSC0033, The Valentine, Richmond, VA.
70. Matthew S. Gottlieb, "Thomas Harding Ellis (1814–1898)," in *Dictionary of Virginia Biography,* Library of Virginia (1998–), published 2016, https://www.lva.virginia.gov/public/dvb/bio.asp?b=Ellis_Thomas_Harding.
71. Frances K. Allan to John Allan, September 11, 1814, Box 137, DLC-EA.
72. Mahon, *The War of 1812,* 308–11; Heidler and Heidler, *The War of 1812,* 116–17.
73. John Allan to John H. Cocke, September 19, 1814, Box 137, DLC-EA; John H. Cocke to John Allan, September 24, 1814, Box 137, DLC-EA. Charles Ellis, at this time, had received a leave of absence "to visit his sick family" (J. Ambler, ["Mr. Charles Ellis"], August 27, 1814; G. W. Gooch, "No. 15," September 10, 1814; and James Maurice, "No. 65," September 26, 1814, Box 137, DLC-EA).
74. John Allan to James Nimmo, October 14, 1814, Poe-Allan-Ellis Papers, 1803–1881, MSC0033, The Valentine, Richmond, VA. Allan mentions Margaret's new baby boy, Thomas H. Ellis.

75. Ellis & Allan [John Allan] to William Burgess, October 27, 1814, Box 521, DLC-EA.
76. "Treaty of Peace and Amity between His Britannic Majesty and the United States of America, Concluded at Ghent, December 24, 1814," in *The War of 1812: Writings from America's Second War of Independence,* ed. Donald R. Hickey (New York: Library of America, 2013), 621–30. For commentary on the treaty, see Mahon, *The War of 1812,* 381–86; and Heidler and Heidler, *The War of 1812,* 136–37.
77. Mahon, *The War of 1812,* 364–69; Heidler and Heidler, *The War of 1812,* 121–23.
78. Mahon, *The War of 1812,* 381; Heidler and Heidler, *The War of 1812,* 137.
79. Ellis and Allan [John Allan or Charles Ellis?] to William Holder, February 22, 1815, Box 521, DLC-EA; Ellis and Allan [John Allan or Charles Ellis?] to George Elwall, February 24, 1815, Box 521, DLC-EA.
80. Ellis & Allan [Charles Ellis] to George McIntosh, March 10, 1815, Box 521, DLC-EA. Ellis writes, "Our John Allan has serious thoughts of going to England in May next."
81. For the purchases, see "Sundries Dr to Robert Bell," February 13, 1815, Box 554, DLC-EA; and "Sundries Dr to Fitzwhylsoun & Potter," John Allan Sundries, February 18, 1815, Box 554, DLC-EA. I use here the third edition of *Evenings at Home* as published in Boston: Mrs. Barbauld and Dr. Aikin, *Evenings at Home, or the Juvenile Budget Opened: Consisting of a Variety of Miscellaneous Pieces for the Instruction and Amusement of Young Persons,* 2 vols. (Boston: Cummings and Hilliard, 1813). The tale of detection is "Trial: Of a Complaint Made against Sundry Persons for Breaking the Windows of DOROTHY CAREFUL, Widow and Dealer in Gingerbread" (1:275–88). The treatment of the emblematical is "On Emblems" (2:211–23). (For the word "emblematical," see 2:213, 217.) The account of the wayward university student (and another upright one) is "Good Company" (2:45–50). I draw from my essay *"Evenings at Home:* A Neglected Book of Poe's Childhood," *Edgar Allan Poe Review* 21, no. 1 (2020): 66–69.
82. Receipt from Fitzwhy[lsoun] & Potter to Ellis & Allan, March 10 and 13, 1815, Box 153, DLC-EA. Kevin Hayes clarifies that the volume *Olive Branch* was for John Allan (Hayes, "Poe's Earliest Reading," *English Language Notes* 32, no. 3 [1995]: 39).
83. "A Card," *Richmond Enquirer,* February 18, 1812, [3].
84. William Ewing to John Allan, November 27, 1817, Box 438, DLC-EA.
85. John Allan to William Ewing, March 21, 1818, Box 438, DLC-EA.
86. Ewing to Allan, November 27, 1817.
87. Allan to Ewing, March 21, 1818. For the printed text of the two letters, see Hervey Allen, *Israfel: The Life and Times of Edgar Allan Poe,* 2 vols. (New York: George H. Doran, 1926), 1:76–77. On February 25, 1814, Allan paid Daniel Ford for one-quarter tuition for Collier (Sundries, February 25, 1814, Box 554, DLC-EA).
88. Allen, *Israfel,* 1:42–43, 115, 357, Quinn, *Edgar Allan Poe: A Critical Biography,* 61; Bittner *Poe: A Biography,* 18, 36; Silverman, *Edgar A. Poe: Mournful and Never-ending Remembrance,* 14; Meyers, *Edgar Allan Poe: His Life and Legacy,* 9. Regarding Collier, Silverman allows for the possibility that Allan was "supporting the boy out of charity" (455). Allen states that at the time Edgar came to the Allans there was a second illegitimate child, a daughter (42).

89. John H. Cocke to Ellis & Allan, May 30, 1815, Box 142, DLC-EA.
90. That Allan was seeking passage as early as late May 1815 is evident from Ellis & Allan to Gordon, Trokes, Leitch & Co, May 24, 1815, Box 523, DLC-EA; and Gordon, Trokes, Leitch and Co. to John Allan, June 1, 1815, Box 142, DLC-EA. He had apparently wished to visit England earlier, in April 1814 (H. W. Evans to Charles Ellis, April 25, 1814, Box 135, DLC-EA). For the Ellis & Allan tobacco on board the *Lothair,* see John M. Foster, receipt, June 3, 1815; and John Stone, receipt, June 6, 1815, Box 142, DLC-EA. Allan purchased provisions, including bottles of liquor (John Stone, receipt from John Allan, June 16, 1815, Box 142, DLC-EA).
91. Moncure Robinson Pleasants for account of Mr. John Allan, June 16, 1815, Box 143, DLC-EA.
92. Andrew Hetherton to John Allan, receipt, June 11, 1815, Box 142, DLC-EA; Moses Myers & Sons to Ellis & Allan, June 15, 1815, Box 142, DLC-EA.
93. Phillips, *Edgar Allan Poe—the Man,* 1:120.
94. John Allan to Charles Ellis, June 22, 1815, Box 143, DLC-EA. He specifically names Scipio, of whom he wrote, "I wish you to sell Scipio for $600 he ought readily to command that price he is a good servant. I think him Honest, and never saw him Drunk." A day before, he had paid Scipio for a trip to Williamsburg (Sundries Dr to Cash, June 21, 1815, Box 554, DLC-EA). Yet Arthur St. Clair, citing the authority of Edward Ambler, Scipio's former owner, had warned Allan against Scipio as "one of the most cunning and accomplished villains on earth." St. Clair accused Scipio of forgery, treason, and theft. But he asks that Allan not make this information public in order to protect Ambler (Arthur St. Clair to John Allan, February 6, 1814, Box 135, DLC-EA). It is difficult to determine why Allan hid the accusations from his partner. Perhaps he did not believe them and was protecting Scipio. Or perhaps he did believe them but was protecting Ambler. Or perhaps he did believe them but was protecting the sale of his slave. He had bought Scipio, "a Mulatto man," for 150 pounds in January 1814 ("Sundries Dr to Cash," January 8, 1814, Box 554, DLC-EA). He had asked Ellis to sell Scipio for $600 in June 1815, and, indeed, Scipio was sold to William Pattison for $600 in December 1815 (Cash Dr to Sundries, December 11, 1815, Box 555, DLC-EA).
95. John Allan to Charles Ellis, June 22–23, 1815, Box 143, DLC-EA.
96. John Allan to Charles Ellis, July 29, 1915, Box 144, DLC-EA. Allan outlined the problems with the captain in a letter to Moses Myers & Sons. Allan had to sleep on the floor, Frances and Nancy were often prohibited from cooking on a fire, a fellow passenger was prevented from having sugar, and so forth. The captain also charged too much. That fellow passenger, Doctor G. L. Fontaine, wrote a letter supporting Allan, characterizing Captain Stone as "penurious, and fractious" (John Allan to Moses Myers & Sons, August 4, 1815, and October 26, 1815; followed by G. L. Fontaine to Moses Myers & Sons, Box 144, DLC-EA).
97. John Allan to Moses Myers & Sons, August 4, 1815, Box 144, DLC-EA. For the notice of the *Lothair,* see "Vessels Arrived," *Liverpool Mercury,* August 4, 1815.
98. John Allan to Charles Ellis, September 21, 1815, Box 438, DLC-EA.
99. Marie Louise Shew Houghton to John Ingram, ca. April 15, 1875, in *Building Poe Biography,* ed. John Carl Miller (Baton Rouge: Louisiana State University Press, 1977), 131–32.

3. "The Flap of Its Wings in My Ear"

1. Allan's last letter at this time from Liverpool was dated August 6 (John Allan to Charles Ellis, August 6, 1815, Box 144, DLC-EA). His first letter from London was dated October 10 and noted his arrival there on October 7 (John Allan to Charles Ellis, October 10, 1815, Box 147, DLC-EA). A thoughtful essay on Poe and England, which appeared after this chapter was written, is J. Gerald Kennedy's "The Realm of Dream and Memory: Poe's England," in *Poe and Place,* ed. Philip Phillips (Cham, Switzerland: Palgrave Macmillan, 2018), 71–96.

2. J. H. Whitty, "Edgar Allan Poe in England and Scotland," *Bookman* 44 (September 1916): 16–18; "Poe in Scotland," in *The Complete Poems of Edgar Allan Poe* (Boston: Houghton Mifflin, 1917), 202–5; Mary E. Phillips, *Edgar Allan Poe— The Man,* 2 vols. (Chicago: John C. Winston, 1926), 1:122–28, 132, and 2:931–32; Arthur Hobson Quinn, *Edgar Allan Poe: A Critical Biography* (New York: D. Appleton-Century, 1941), 65–66. The churchyard contains tombstones of the Allan family. In August 2014, the minister at Irvine Old Parish Church, Robert Travers, told me that the schoolboys used to practice their handwriting by copying the language on the tombstones. He also stated that young Edgar Allan would have known the local story that once, when a crypt at the church was opened, a skeleton was found out of its coffin.

3. Whitty: "Edgar Allan Poe in England and Scotland," 19–20, and "Poe in Scotland," 205–6; Lewis Chase, "Poe's Playmates in Kilmarnock," *Dial* 61 (October 19, 1916): 303; Phillips, *Edgar Allan Poe—the Man,* 1:132; Quinn, *Edgar Allan Poe: A Critical Biography,* 66–67. For the letter of August 22, 1815, see John Allan to Ellis & Allan, August 22, 1815, Box 145, DLC-EA. Allan does write to Ellis from Glasgow, where he is on business and by himself (John Allan to Charles Ellis, August 24, 1815, Box 145, DLC-EA). Letters to Allan were sent to Kilmarnock from August 5 through September 11 (letters to Allan from George Elwall, R. H. Gwathmey, James Maury, and Alex Kerr, Boxes 144 to 146, DLC-EA).

4. Whitty: "Edgar Allan Poe in England and Scotland," 20, and "Poe in Scotland," 206; Quinn, *Edgar Allan Poe: A Critical Biography,* 66. For Allan's letter, see John Allan to Charles Ellis, September 21, 1815, Box 438, DLC-EA.

5. John Allan to Charles Ellis, October 10, 1815, Box 147, DLC-EA. Margaret K. Ellis later reported that Allan's sister-in-law Nancy Valentine had written that the Allans were "miserably dissatisfied with London" (Margaret K. Ellis to James Nimmo, January 19, 1816, Poe-Allan-Ellis Papers, 1803–1881, MSC0033, The Valentine, Richmond, VA).

6. Edward Elwall addresses John Allan on October 10 at Blake's Hotel (Edward Elwall to John Allan, October 10, 1815, Box 147, DLC-EA). The Jermyn Street address of the hotel is given in *Leigh's New Picture of London,* 2nd ed. (London: Samuel Leigh, 1818), 422.

7. John Allan to John Richard, October 10, 1815, Box 523, DLC-EA.

8. John Allan to Charles Ellis, October 30, 1815, Box 147, DLC-EA. Noting those who had lived on Southampton Row in Poe's time, Lewis Chase suggested that the street was as upscale as nearby Russell Square (see "Poe's London" [20–21] in the Lewis Chase Papers, David M. Rubinstein Manuscript Library, Duke University,

Durham, NC). However, Rosemary Ashton observes that Russell Square was by no means the ultimate in wealth or status and was sometimes mocked (Ashton, *Victorian Bloomsbury* [New Haven, CT: Yale University Press, 2012], 131–41).

9. John Allan to Charles Ellis, November 7, 1815, Box 148, DLC-EA; John Allan to Charles Ellis, November 15, 1815, Box 148, DLC-EA.
10. Allan to Ellis, November 15, 1815.
11. Allan to Ellis, October 30, 1815; John Allan to Charles Ellis, November 20, 1815, Box 148, DLC-EA; Charles Ellis to John Allan, November 21, 1815, Box 524, DLC-EA.
12. John Allan to Charles Ellis, November 20, 1815, Box 148, DLC-EA.
13. Whitty: "Edgar Allan Poe in England and Scotland," 16, 21, and "Poe in Scotland," 206–7.
14. Charles Ellis to John Allan, December 18, 1815, Box 523, DLC-EA.
15. Edward Peticolas to John Allan, January 4, 1816, Box 151, DLC-EA. For a biographical sketch of Edward Peticolas, who became an accomplished artist, see "Edward F. Peticolas," in *Richmond Portraits in an Exhibition of "Makers of Richmond 1737–1860*," ed. Louise F. Catterall (Richmond: The Valentine, 1949), 150–51. He was the son of artist Philippe A. Peticolas, whom Joseph Gallego had invited to live in Richmond and to whom Margaret Ellis attributed the portrait of Frances Allan (228–30, 3–5).
16. John Allan to William Galt, January 26, 1816, Box 523, DLC-EA.
17. William Galt to John Allan, January 12, 1816, and January 14, 1816, Box 151, DLC-EA; Charles Ellis to John Allan, January 12, 1816, Box 524, DLC-EA.
18. John Allan to Charles Ellis, February 3, 1816, Box 523, DLC-EA; John Allan to Charles Ellis, February 12, 1816, Box 153, DLC-EA.
19. Charles Ellis to Allan & Ellis, February 2, 1816, February 6, 1816, February, 11, 1816, February 24, 1816, March 3, 1816, March 7, 1816, March 10, 1816, March 13, 1816, March 18, 1816, Box 524, DLC-EA.
20. Charles Ellis to Allan & Ellis, April 6, 1816, Box 524, DLC-EA; Charles Ellis to John Allan, April 15, 1816, Box 524, DLC-EA.
21. John Allan to Charles Ellis, April 23, 1816, May 4, 1816, Box 157, DLC-EA.
22. Charles Ellis to John Allan, April 19, 1816, May 6, 1816, Box 524, DLC-EA.
23. John Allan to William Galt, March 27, 1816, Box 523, DLC-EA ("Frances does not enjoy good health"); Josiah Ellis to Charles Ellis, March 13, 1816, Box 155, DLC-EA ("Mrs. Allan has been almost crazy").
24. Josiah Ellis to Jesse Higginbotham, March 19, 1816, Box 156, DLC-EA; Thomas Auldys to Allan & Ellis, April 10, 1816, Box 157, DLC-EA. That George Dubourg was the clerk in Allan's countinghouse is evident from C. S. Dubourg to John Allan, January 30, 1817, Box 172, DLC-EA. The older brother sought then and on July 26, 1817, to obtain a salary for his younger brother George (C. S. Dubourg, July 26, 1817, Box 179, DLC-EA).
25. Receipt from George Dubourg to John Allan, July 6, 1816, Box 161, DLC-EA. See also Payment to "Misses Dubourgs' a/c for Edgar," July 6, 1816, Box 571, DLC-EA. See Lewis Chase, "Poe's School in Chelsea," *Times Literary Supplement,* April 27, 1916, 201–2; and "More Notes on Poe's First School in London," *Dial* 60 (May 25, 1916): 499.

26. Receipt from George Dubourg to John Allan, July 6, 1816, Box 161, DLC-EA. For a discussion of the aforementioned books, see Kevin Hayes, *Poe and the Printed Word* (Cambridge, UK: Cambridge University Press, 2000), 3–5.
27. "Sales by Auction," *Morning Advertiser*, October 5, 1819, 4; see also "Sales by Auction," *London Times*, October 2, 1819, 4 (Times Digital Archive).
28. Catherine Poitiaux ["Lett"] to John Allan, May 18, 1816, Box 158, DLC-EA.
29. Lewis Chase proposes that Edgar had seen Piccadilly, Hyde Park, Russell Square, and Newington Green (Chase, "Poe's School in Chelsea," 202). See also Phillips, *Edgar Allan Poe—the Man*, 1:146. It is interesting to read a letter to John Allan from Thomas Nelson, who had moved to Richmond, comparing that city to London and adverting to the British Museum: "[W]e have no Museums of 40 Rooms none with Irish Giants & Egyptian Mummies" (Thomas Nelson to John Allan, September 28, 1818, Box 200, DLC-EA).
30. Allan Fowlds to John Allan, September 23, 1816, Box 165, DLC-EA.
31. Phillips, *Edgar Allan Poe—the Man*, 1:596, 631; Hervey Allen, *The Life and Times of Edgar Allan Poe*, 2 vols. (New York: George H. Doran, 1926), 2:515.
32. John Allan to Charles Ellis, August 31, 1816, Box 164 and Box 523, DLC-EA ("thin as a rasor"); John Allan to William Galt, October 2, 1816, Box 523, DLC-EA ("growing and of course thin"); William Galt to John Allan, December 9, 1816, Box 168, DLC-EA ("all fatt except Edgar").
33. Receipt from George Dubourg to John Allan, July 6, 1816, Box 161, DLC-EA; Payment to "Misses Dubourgs' a/c for Edgar," December 28, 1816, Box 571, DLC-EA.
34. C. S. Dubourg to John Allan, January 30, 1817, Box 172, DLC-EA.
35. John Allan to William Galt, October 2, 1816, Box 523, DLC-EA; John Allan to William Galt, October 23, 1816, Box 523, DLC-EA; William Galt to John Allan, December 28, 1816, Box 169, DLC-EA.
36. William Galt to John Allan, April 5, 1817, Box 174, DLC-EA.
37. For background, see John Stevenson, *Popular Disturbances in England 1700–1870* (London: Longman, 1979), 193–98; and David Worrall, *Radical Culture: Discourse, Resistance and Surveillance, 1790–1820* (Detroit, MI: Wayne State University Press, 1992), 97–112.
38. For references to the bells at the Richmond Theater Fire, see George D. Fisher, *History and Reminiscences of the Monumental Church* (Richmond, VA: Whittet & Shepperson, 1880), 4; and Meredith Henne Baker, *The Richmond Theater Fire: Early America's First Great Disaster* (Baton Rouge: Louisiana State University Press, 2012), 50.
39. Allan wrote "Edgar is at school" in a letter of March 6, according to Mary Newton Stanard, comp., *Edgar Allan Poe Letters till Now Unpublished in the Valentine Museum, Richmond, Virginia* (Philadelphia: J. B. Lippincott, 1925), 17; Quinn gives it as May 6 (*Edgar Allan Poe: A Critical Biography*, 70). For the August 28, 1817, payment for "Edgar's School a/c," see Receipt, August 28, 1817, Box 571, DLC-EA. See Phillips, *Edgar Allan Poe—the Man*, 1:149, for the judgment that this receipt was for the Dubourg school since the amount (24 pounds, 16 shillings) was similar to the amount for the previous receipt (23 pounds, 16 shillings).
40. John Allan to Charles Ellis, May 17, 1817, Box 175, DLC-EA.

41. H. W. Tabb to John Allan, June 10, 1817, Box 178, DLC-EA.
42. Phillips, *Edgar Allan Poe—the Man*, 1:133; Dwight Thomas and David K. Jackson, *The Poe Log: A Documentary Life of Edgar Allan Poe, 1809–1849* (Boston: G. K. Hall, 1987), 34.
43. John Richard to John Allan, April 14, 1817, Box 175, DLC-EA; Charles Ellis to John Allan, May 29, 1817, Box 524, DLC-EA.
44. John and Frances Allan and Nancy Valentine left for Cheltenham on August 2, 1817 (John Allan to Robert Gwathmey, August 1, 1817, Box 525, DLC-EA). George Dubourg's letters are addressed to John Allan at "Mr. Styles's" and the "Stiles's Hotel" (George Dubourg to John Allan, August 4, 6, 7, 8, 11, 13, 15, 16, 27, 1817, Boxes 180 and 181, DLC-EA). The Cheltenham newspaper listed "Mr. Allen" and "Miss Valentine" as having arrived ("Arrivals," *Cheltenham Chronicle and Gloucestershire Advertiser*, August 7, 1817, 3, https://www.newspapers.com).
45. John Allan to George Dubourg, August 9, 1817, Harry Ransom Center, University of Texas at Austin.
46. Dubourg to Allan, August 4 and 6, 1817, Box 180, DLC-EA ("Edgar is quite well"); Dubourg to Allan, August 7, 1817, Box 180, DLC-EA ("Edgar is quite well & desires his love"); Dubourg to Allan, August 9, 1817, Box 181, DLC-EA ("Edgar is perfectly well"); Allan to Dubourg, August 12, 1817, Harry Ransom Center, University of Texas at Austin ("Mrs. Allan desires her love to Edgar"); Allan to Dubourg, August 14, 1817, in Stanard, *Edgar Allan Poe Letters till Now Unpublished*, 17 ("Enclosed is a letter for Edgar"); Dubourg to Allan, August 15, 1817 Box 181, DLC-EA ("Edgar is quite well, & will I dare say be quite delighted"). For a piece on the French-speaking parrot of the Allans, see J. H. Whitty, "A Parrot," *Colophon*, n.s., vol. 2, no. 1 (1935): 188–90.
47. Allan returned to London from Cheltenham after August 14 (Stanard, *Edgar Allan Poe Letters till Now Unpublished*, 17) and returned to Cheltenham after August 26 (Allan to Ellis, August 26, 1817 Box 181, DLC-EA ["I start tomorrow"]). The Cheltenham newspaper listed "Mr. Allan" as having arrived ("Arrivals," *Cheltenham Chronicle and Gloucestershire Advertiser*, September 11, 1817, 3, https://www.newspapers.com). That Edgar was at Cheltenham is evident from the Stiles bill to John Allan for "Master A 4 days" (Bills, August 26 to September 2, 1817, Box 186, DLC-EA). See also "order for child," in Phillips, *Edgar Allan Poe—the Man*, 1:149.
48. For background on Cheltenham, see Phyllis Hembry, *British Spas from 1815 to the Present: A Social History* (Madison, NJ: Fairleigh Dickinson University Press, 1997), 33–53.
49. John Allan to Charles Ellis, September 26, 1817, Box 182, DLC-EA.
50. John Allan to William Galt, October 2, 1817, Box 525, DLC-EA. For Allan's having requested on September 12 that George Dubourg seek lodging for his family at 48 Southampton Row from September 20 for a month, see Thomas and Jackson, *The Poe Log*, 34.
51. William Galt Sr. to John Allan, December 2, 1817, Box 185, DLC-EA.
52. Phillips, *Edgar Allan Poe—the Man*, 1:142–43. The amount was 24 pounds, 16 shillings.

53. J. H. Whitty, *Complete Poems,* xxiii.
54. John Allan to Charles Ellis, January 31, 1818, Box 189, DLC-EA.
55. Thomas Rutherford & Son to Allan & Ellis, August 21, 1818, Box 199, DLC-EA.
56. John Allan to General John H. Cocke, March 23, 1818, Box 525, DLC-EA.
57. Thomas and Jackson, *The Poe Log,* 36.
58. This is according to Poe's mother-in-law, Maria Clemm (John Carl Miller, *Building Poe Biography* [Baton Rouge: Louisiana State University Press, 1977], 47).
59. John Allan to John Richard [?], January 22, 1818, Box 525, DLC-EA; John Allan to William Ewing, March 21, 1818, Boxes 438, 525, DLC-EA.
60. "Sundries Dr to Cash," January 22, 1818, Box 556, DLC-EA.
61. Phillips, *Edgar Allan Poe—the Man,* 2:936–37.
62. Burton R. Pollin, "Poe's Authorship of Three Long Critical and Autobiographical Articles of 1843 Now Authenticated," *American Renaissance Literary Report: An Annual* 7 (1993): 164; Benjamin F. Fisher, "An Early Biography of Poe (1843): The *Philadelphia Saturday Museum* Sketch," in *Masques, Mysteries, and Mastodons: A Poe Miscellany,* ed. Fisher (Baltimore, MD: Edgar Allan Poe Society, 2006), 156–57; [Edgar A. Poe and Henry B. Hirst or Poe alone], From "Poets and Poetry of Philadelphia," in *Poe in His Own Time,* ed. Benjamin F. Fisher (Iowa City: University of Iowa Press, 2010), 25.
63. William Elijah Hunter, "Poe and His English Schoolmaster," *Athenaeum* 2660 (October 19, 1878): 496–97; Phillips, *Edgar Allan Poe—the Man,* 1:157, 163. See also Lewis Chase, "John Bransby, Poe's Schoolmaster," *Athenaeum* 4605 (May 1916): 221–22 (later qualified by Chase, "Poe's School in Stoke Newington," *Athenaeum* 4606 [June 1916], 294); and M 2:449.
64. Phillips, *Edgar Allan Poe—the Man,* 1:153–55. See also M 2:449; and Thomas and Jackson, *The Poe Log,* 36. For Phillips's extended treatment of Stoke Newington, see *Edgar Allan Poe—the Man,* 1:150–64.
65. Hunter, "Poe and His English Schoolmaster," 496.
66. Ibid., 497.
67. John Allan to John Richard [?], January 22, 1818, Box 525, DLC-EA; John Allan to William Galt, January 31, 1818, Box 525, DLC-EA; John Allan to John Richard [?], February 11, 1818, Box 525, DLC-EA ("with a nervous attack"); Allan & Ellis to Ellis & Allan, March 14, 1818, Box 525, DLC-EA ("the croup"); John Allan to General John H. Cocke, March 23, 1818, Box 525, DLC-EA; John Allan to John Richard [?], March 23, 1818, Box 525, DLC-EA; John Allan to Charles Ellis, June 23, 1818, Box 525, DLC-EA ("catarrh").
68. John Allan to William Galt, May 29, 1818, Box 525, DLC-EA.
69. Thomas Nelson to John Allan, September 28, 1818, Box 200, DLC-EA.
70. John Allan to Charles Ellis, June 25, 1818, Box 195, DLC-EA. See also John Allan to Edmund F. Wickham, June 26, 1818, Box 525, DLC-EA.
71. John Allan to Charles Ellis, August 17, 1818, Box 199, DLC-EA.
72. John Allan to Charles Ellis, October 5, 1818, Box 201, DLC-EA; George Elwall to John Allan, October 7 and 15, 1818, Box 199, DLC-EA
73. Frances K. Allan to John Allan, October 15, 1818, The Valentine, Richmond, VA.
74. John Allan to William Galt, October 24, 1818, Box 527, DLC-EA.

75. Stanard, *Edgar Allan Poe Letters till Now Unpublished*, 319–27. For clarification of the textbook, see Kevin J. Hayes, "Poe's Earliest Reading," *English Language Notes* 32, no. 3 (1995): 41–42. See also Hayes, *Poe and the Printed Word*, 5–6.
76. Thomas and Jackson, *The Poe Log*, 39.
77. John Allan to Ellis & Allan, August 6, 1818, Box 198 and Box 527, DLC-EA.
78. John Allan to William Galt, October 24, 1818, Box 527, DLC-EA.
79. John Allan to Charles Ellis, December 28, 1818, Box 204 and Box 527, DLC-EA.
80. John Allan to Charles Ellis, January 29, 1819, Box 527, DLC-EA.
81. John Allan to Charles Ellis, January 9, 1819, Box 206, DLC-EA.
82. Stanard, *Edgar Allan Poe Letters till Now Unpublished*, 321.
83. Allan & Ellis to John F. Bowdoin, February 16, 1819, Box 527, DLC-EA.
84. John Allan to Charles Ellis, February 18, 1819, Box 527, DLC-EA; John Allan to Charles Ellis [?], n.d., Box 527, DLC-EA.
85. John Allan to Charles Ellis, March 3, 1819, Box 208, DLC-EA; Allan to Ellis, March 11, 1819, Box 208, DLC-EA; Allan to Ellis, March 29, 1819, Box 209, DLC-EA; Allan to Ellis, April 15, 1819, Box 210, DLC-EA.
86. Regarding the suicide of John Gilliat, see John Allan to Charles Ellis, April 19, 1819, Box 210, DLC-EA; Allan & Ellis [Edward Fayle] to Ellis & Allan, April 24, 1819, Box 210, DLC-EA; Allan to Ellis, April 27, 1819, Box 210, DLC-EA.
87. See, for example, John Allan to Charles Ellis, May 19 and May 29, 1819, Box 212, DLC-EA.
88. Allan & Ellis to Thomas Preston & Sons, May 22, 1819, Box 527, DLC-EA.
89. John Allan to William Galt, June 8, 1819, Box 527, DLC-EA; John Allan to Charles Ellis, June 17, 1819, Box 213, DLC-EA.
90. Phillips, *Edgar Allan Poe—the Man*, 1:168–69.
91. John Allan to Charles Ellis, July 3, 1819, Box 214, DLC-EA.
92. Allan & Ellis to Ellis & Allan, July 10 and 12, 1819, Box 214, DLC-EA, also Box 527 for the latter letter; Allan & Ellis to Ellis & Allan, July 16, 1819, Box 527, DLC-EA.
93. Allan & Ellis to Ellis & Allan, July 17, 1819, Box 214, DLC-EA; see also Boxes 228 and 527. For Allan's letter to William Galt advising of the firm's having suspended payment (noting that he has fifteen pounds left), see John Allan to William Galt, July 17, 1819, Box 527, DLC-EA.
94. For the date and place of the meeting, see Allan & Ellis to J. W. & R. Goulds, July 21, 1819, Box 527, DLC-EA; Allan & Ellis to Gough & Braithwaite, July 21, 1819, Box 528, DLC-EA; Allan & Ellis to Ellis & Allan, July 22, 1819, Box 215, DLC-EA; Allan & Ellis to Lionel Knowles & Sons, July 27, 1819, Box 528, DLC-EA; and John Allan to Charles Ellis, July 28, 1819, Box 215, DLC-EA. The allowance of twelve months is noted in the last of these letters. For information on the Baptist's Head Coffee House, which existed at both Aldermanbury and Chancery Lane, see Bryant Lillywhite, *London Coffee Houses: A Reference Book of Coffee Houses of the Seventeenth, Eighteenth and Nineteenth Centuries* (London: George Allen and Unwin, 1963), 106–7. For clarification that the deed precluded "danger of arrest," see John Allan to Ellis & Allan, December 8, 1819, Boxes 219 and 528, DLC-EA.
95. John Allan to Charles Ellis, August 12, 1819, Box 215, DLC-EA.
96. John Allan to Charles Ellis, September 8, 1819, Box 216, DLC-EA.

97. John Allan to Charles Ellis, October 15, 1819, Box 217 and Box 528, DLC-EA ("the distress of mind"); William Galt to John Allan, October 8, 1819, Box 217, DLC-EA ("a tender man").
98. For Allan's blaming his debtors, see John Allan to Charles Ellis, July 28, 1819, Boxes 215 and 528; and Allan & Ellis to Williams & Burgess, August 2, 1819, Box 215, DLC-EA. For Allan's blaming the bankers, see John Allan to Charles Ellis, August 12, 1819, Box 215 and Box 528, DLC-EA. For Allan's acknowledging his shared responsibility with his partner, see John Allan to Ellis & Allan, September 29, 1819, Boxes 217 and 528, DLC-EA.
99. John Allan to Ellis & Allan, October 18, 1819, Boxes 218 and 528, DLC-EA ("held Hostage"); John Allan to Charles Ellis, November 26, 1819, Box 528, DLC-EA; John Allan to Charles Ellis, December 4, 1819, Box 219, DLC-EA (asking for money); John Allan to Charles Ellis, November 26, 1819, Box 528, DLC-EA; John Allan to Ellis & Allan, November 29, 1819, Box 219, DLC-EA; John Allan to William Galt, December 3, 1819, Box 528, DLC-EA; Allan & Ellis to Ellis & Allan, December 6, 1819, Boxes 219 and 528, DLC-EA; John Allan to Ellis & Allan, December 8, 1819, Boxes 219 and 528, DLC-EA; John Allan to Charles Ellis, December 9, 1819, Boxes 219 and Box 528, DLC-EA (creditors reluctant to allow Allan to leave, then accepting his leaving).
100. John Allan to William Galt, September 28, 1819, Box 528, DLC-EA.
101. John Allan to William Galt, November 27 and 29, 1819, Box 528, DLC-EA.
102. John Allan to William Galt, October 29, 1819, Box 528, DLC-EA.
103. John Allan to Ellis & Allan, September 21, 1819, Box 217, DLC-EA; John Allan to Charles Ellis, December 4, 1819, Box 219, DLC-EA.
104. For a full narrative, see Donald Read, *Peterloo: The "Massacre" and Its Background* (Manchester, UK: Manchester University Press, 1958), 126–40. For the numbers given, see 140. See also John Stevenson, *Popular Disturbances in England, 1700–1832,* 2nd ed. (London: Longman, 1992), 281–88.
105. Percy Bysshe Shelley, "England in 1819," in *Shelley's Poetry and Prose,* 2nd ed., ed. Donald H. Reiman and Neil Fraistat (New York: W. W. Norton, 2002), 326–27. See also "The Mask of Anarchy Written on the Occasion of the Massacre at Manchester," 316–26.
106. John Allan to William Galt, August 28, 1819, Box 528, DLC-EA; John Allan to Ellis & Allan, September 21, 1819, Box 217, DLC-EA; Allan & Ellis to Ellis & Allan, September 21, 1819, Box 528, DLC-EA; John Allan to William Galt, September 28, 1819, Box 528, DLC-EA.
107. John Allan to William Galt, December 29. 1819, Box 528, DLC-EA.
108. Allan to Galt, September 28, 1819, Box 528, DLC-EA.
109. Allan to Galt, December 29, 1819.
110. John Allan to Charles Ellis, December 23, 1819, Box 219 and Box 528, DLC-EA.
111. John Allan to William Galt, January 28, 1818, The Valentine, Richmond, VA.
112. John Allan to Charles Ellis, February 1, 1820, Boxes 221 and 528, DLC-EA. The relationship is clarified in "Roderick Mackenzie," https://www.ancestry.com.
113. For the tuition payment, see Killis Campbell, "Unpublished Documents Relating to Poe's Early Years," *Sewanee Review* 20, no. 2 (1912): 206. For Allan's comments on Frances, see John Allan to William Galt, February 26, 1820, Box 528, DLC-EA.

114. Allan to Galt, February 26, 1820; John Allan to Charles Ellis, March 27, 1820, Box 222, DLC-EA.
115. John Allan to Charles Ellis, February 1, 1820, Box 221 and Box 528, DLC-EA. For more on Caroline, see Flora Foster, *The Unruly Queen: The Life of Queen Caroline* (Berkeley: University of California Press, 1996).
116. John Allan to Charles Ellis, April 13, 1820, Box 223, DLC-EA (on getting to the countinghouse); John Allan to Charles Ellis, April 28, 1820, Box 528, DLC-EA, and May 9, 1820, Box 223 and Box 528, DLC-EA (on working on the Holder business).
117. John Allan to Charles Ellis, April 13, 1820, Box 223, DLC-EA.
118. Campbell, "Unpublished Documents Relating to Poe's Early Years," 206.
119. Hunter, "Poe and His English Schoolmaster," 496–97.
120. John Allan to Joseph Fearon, May 31, 1820, Box 528, DLC-EA.
121. Phillips, *Edgar Allan Poe—the Man*, 1:171.
122. John Allan to Charles Ellis, June 9, 1820, Box 224, DLC-EA. The house at 39 Southampton Row was let to one Doctor Armstrong (Joshua Bates to John Allan, April 26, 1821, Box 230, DLC-EA).
123. Allan to Ellis, June 9, 1820.
124. Advertisement for *Martha, Liverpool Mercury*, June 2, 1820: 404, and June 9, 1820, 411. The phrase may also be found in Joseph C. Hart's novel *Miriam Coffin* (P 1:223).
125. John Allan to Charles Ellis, June 9, 1820, Box 224, DLC-EA.
126. John Allan to William Taylor, August 22, 1820, Box 526, DLC-EA; Phillips, *Edgar Allan Poe—the Man*, 1:171.
127. John Allan to Charles Ellis, July 27, 1820, Box 225, DLC-EA; Phillips, *Edgar Allan Poe—the Man*, 1:171.
128. Payment "By John Allan paid drayage of his Baggage from Steam Boat," Box 572, DLC-EA. It is said that Richmond, Virginia, was itself named after Richmond on the Thames, in England (Alyson L. Taylor-White, *Shockoe Hill Cemetery—A Richmond Landmark History* [Charleston, SC: History Press, 2017], 17).
129. Thomas H. Ellis, "Edgar Allan Poe," *Richmond Standard*, May 7, 1881, 2; George E. Woodberry, *The Life of Edgar Allan Poe* (Boston: Houghton Mifflin, 1909), 2:361. I also consult the M. Ellyson "Map of the City of Richmond" from 1856.
130. Charles Ellis to Margaret Ellis, August 7, 1820, Box 225, DLC-EA.
131. Charles Ellis to Margaret Ellis, August 10, 1820, Box 225, DLC-EA.
132. Neil Arnott to John Allan, May 15, 1821, Box 230, DLC-EA.

4. "With Many Cares and Toils Oppress'd"

1. G. Melvin Herndon, "From Scottish Orphan to Virginia Planter: William Galt, Jr., 1801–1851," *Virginia Magazine of History and Biography* 87, no. 3 (1979): 326–43, esp. 326–30 (the young William Galt); William Galt to John Allan, July 3, 1818, Box 196, DLC-EA (death of Gallego); William Galt to John Allan, August 17, 1818, Box 199, DLC-EA (fire); William Galt Jr. to John Allan, December 6, 1818, Box 204, DLC-EA (growth of Richmond).
2. For the fall in property values, see John Allan's stating, shortly after his return to Richmond, "We find an awful change here since we left it, the value of property

reduc'd even in the best situations to 1/4 & 1/3 of its former value" (John Allan to William Taylor, August 22, 1820, Box 526, DLC-EA).

3. Charles Ellis to Margaret Ellis, August 7, 1820, Box 225, DLC-EA; John Allan to James Ross, December 21, 1820, Box 526, DLC-EA.

4. Flora Lapham Mack disputes the Weiss telling, but Mack's argument is based on her erroneous belief that Mackenzie was born in January 1800 and therefore too old to play with Edgar. John H. Mackenzie was actually born in March 1806, and therefore at Edgar's return the older boy was fourteen and the younger eleven. Their proximate ages were fitting for young comrades in mischief (see also chapter 2, note 5).

5. Susan Archer Weiss, *The Home Life of Poe* (New York: Broadway, 1907), 21–22.

6. Ibid., 23.

7. John Allan to Charles Ellis, November 15, 1815, Box 148, DLC-EA.

8. Thomas H. Ellis, "Edgar Allan Poe," *Richmond Standard,* May 7, 1881. For a related story, see Charles Ellis, "Recollections of Poe by Various People Who Had Known Him," John Henry Ingram's Poe Collection, Albert & Shirley Small Special Collections Library, University of Virginia, Charlottesville, Item 361.

9. Dwight Thomas and David K. Jackson, *The Poe Log: A Documentary Life of Edgar Allan Poe, 1809–1849* (Boston: G. K. Hall, 1987), 47–48.

10. J. H. Whitty, ed., *The Complete Poems of Edgar Allan Poe,* 2nd ed. (Boston: Houghton Mifflin, 1917), 190; Mary E. Phillips, *Edgar Allan Poe—The Man,* 2 vols. (Chicago: John C. Winston, 1926), 1:118, 186.

11. E. L. Didier, "Life of Edgar A. Poe," in *The Life and Poems of Edgar Allan Poe* (New York: W. J. Middleton, 1877), 30. See also "Joseph Hanson Clarke," in *Richmond Portraits in an Exhibition of Makers of Richmond 1737–1860* (Richmond, VA: The Valentine, 1949), 43–44.

12. Dr. & Mrs. Ray Thomas, "Recollections of Poe by Various Persons Who Had Known Him," Ingram's Poe Collection, Item 361.

13. Didier, "Life of Edgar A. Poe," 30–31.

14. I. F. Allen, "Recollections of Poe by Various Persons Who Had Known Him," Ingram's Poe Collection, Item 361.

15. Whitty, *Complete Poems,* 2nd ed., 189.

16. Receipt for $27.20 for Pew 80 at Monumental Church for John Allan, December 1820, Box 227, DLC-EA.

17. Early on "[Fra]nces & Ann Edgar & myself are all well" (John Allan to Charles Ellis, September 4, 1820, Box 226, DLC-EA), but then John Allan became sick (John Allan to Charles Ellis, September 18, 1820, Box 226, DLC-EA). Frances was often sick from August through December 1820 (Ellis & Allan for Allan & Ellis to William Taylor, October 31, 1820, Box 526, DLC-EA ["much indisposed"]; R. S. Ellis to Charles Ellis, November 5 and 8, 1820, Box 227, DLC-EA ["the indisposition," "the continued indisposition"]; John Allan to James Ross, December 21, 1820, Box 526, DLC-EA ["a good deal indisposed since her return"]).

18. Thomas H. Ellis mentions the telescope in a letter to George E. Woodberry (Woodberry, *The Life of Edgar Allan Poe,* 2 vols. [Boston: Houghton Mifflin, 1909], 2:363–64). See receipt for $0.25 to "John Allan for 1 dog Collar," December 2, 1820, Box 557, DLC-EA. See receipt for 12 1/2 cents to John Allan for "1 Knife for Edgar," December 11, 1820, Box 557, DLC-EA.

19. Thomas H. Ellis, "Edgar Allan Poe," *Richmond Standard,* May 7, 1881, 2; Weiss, *The Home Life of Poe,* 20.
20. Receipt for eggs, ducks, pork to John Allan, December 24, 1820, Box 557, DLC-EA.
21. David K. Jackson, "Two Notes: A Joseph H. Clarke Manuscript and Something about a Mr. Persico," *Poe Studies* 9, no. 1 (1976): 22.
22. Didier, "Life of Edgar A. Poe," 30–31.
23. "Edgar Allan Poe: Some Reminiscences of the Poet by His Old School Teacher in Richmond," *Baltimore Sun,* February 14, 1896, 8. Susan Archer Weiss adapted Clarke's words in this piece for her *The Home Life of Poe,* 24–25.
24. Mary Jane Poitiaux Dixon to "Messrs. Editors," July 2, 1875, Ingram's Poe Collection, Item 237.
25. George Murn to John Allan, April 28, 1821, Box 230, DLC-EA.
26. "Sundries Dr to Cash," John Allan to Morgan Utz "for his expences while collecting," January 20, 1821, Box 557, DLC-EA; Charles Ellis to John Allan, March 27 and April 5 and 11, 1821, Box 229, DLC-EA.
27. Ellis & Allan to Arthur Saltmarsh, March 3, 1821, Box 526, DLC-EA; Ellis & Allan to John Ireland, May 4, 1821, Box 526, DLC-EA.
28. John Allan to John Noble, March 31, 1821, Box 526, DLC-EA; John Allan to Charles Ellis, April 2, 1821, Box 229, DLC-EA; Charles Ellis to John Allan, April 5, 1821, Box 229, DLC-EA.
29. J. H. Whitty, "Memoir," in *The Complete Poems of Edgar Allan Poe* (Boston: Houghton Mifflin, 1911), xxiv–xxv; Thomas and Jackson, *The Poe Log,* 46.
30. Ellis, "Edgar Allan Poe."
31. [Edgar Allan Poe]. "Ingenious Invention" in "A Chapter on Science and Art," *Burton's Gentleman's Magazine,* April 1840, 194. "A Chapter on Science and Art" is a four-part series that Charles F. Heartman and James R. Canny term "indubitably the work of Poe himself" in *A Bibliography of First Printings of the Writings of Edgar Allan Poe,* rev. ed., comp. Heartmen and Canny (Hattiesburg, MS: Book Farm, 1943), 84.
32. Ellis, "Edgar Allan Poe."
33. Sarah Elmira Shelton to George W. Eveleth, December 22, 1852, in *Building Poe Biography,* ed. John Carl Miller (Baton Rouge: Louisiana State University Press, 1977), 205; Edward M. Alfriend, "Unpublished Recollections of Edgar Allan Poe," *Literary Era* (August 1901): 490.
34. "Edgar A. Poe Conversation with Mrs. Shelton at Mr. Smith's Corner 8th and Leigh Streets Nov 19th 1875," The Valentine, Richmond, VA; John J. Moran, *A Defense of Edgar Allan Poe* (Washington, DC: William F. Boogher, 1885), 34. The view that Elmira lived on Second Street has been ably challenged (Mary Wingfield Scott, *Old Richmond Neighborhoods* [Richmond: Whittet & Shepperson, 1950], 198; and Arthur Hobson Quinn, *Edgar Allan Poe: A Critical Biography* [New York: D. Appleton-Century, 1941], 90–91).
35. For Elmira as "Myra," see Hervey Allen and Thomas Ollive Mabbott, *Poe's Brother: The Poems of William Henry Leonard Poe* (New York: George H. Doran, 1926), 28; and Hervey Allen, *Israfel: The Life and Times of Edgar Allan Poe,* 2 vols. (New York: George H. Doran, 1926), 1:134.

36. John Allan to Doctor—, July 25, 1821, Box 232, DLC-EA.
37. "Sociable Barbecue Club," August 4, 1821, Box 232, DLC-EA; "Sundries Dr to Cash," "[John Allan] paid drayage piano & Tub to House," July 28, 1821, Box 557, DLC-EA; "Sundries Dr to Cash," "John Allan paid for Bringing Turtle," July 30, 1821, Box 557, DLC-EA; John Allan to Charles Ellis ("We are Healthy here"), August 16, 1821, Box 232, DLC-EA; Charles Ellis to John Allan ("you will of course extend your protection"), August 10, 1821, Box 232, DLC-EA; Morgan Utz for Ellis & Allan to Charles Ellis, August 29, 1821, Box 232, DLC-EA. Samuel Mordecai mentions "The Barbacue Club"; see his *Richmond in By-Gone Days*, republished from the second edition of 1860 (Richmond, VA: Dietz, 1946), 261.
38. The coronation took place on July 19, 1821; the death of Queen Caroline occurred on August 7, 1821 (Flora Fraser, *The Unruly Queen: The Life of Queen Caroline* [1996; Berkeley: University of California Press, 1997], 1, 460–61). A correspondent writing to John Allan about the coronation of the king and the death of the queen concluded, "The King will now be happy" (Warwick to John Allan, August 8, 1821, Box 232, DLC-EA).
39. Charles Ellis for Ellis & Allan to George Elwall, October 5, 1821, Box 526, DLC-EA.
40. For Shepherd's initial series of letters, see William J. Shepherd to Ellis & Allan, October 24 and 30, 1821, and November 3, 1821, Box 233, DLC-EA; and November 19, 1821, Box 234, DLC-EA. Ellis & Allan responded on November 26, 1821. For the continuing letters, see Shepherd to Ellis & Allan, December 3, 1821, Box 234, DLC-EA; Shepherd to John Allan, December 18, 1821, Box 234, DLC-EA; and Shepherd to Ellis & Allan, January 7, 1822, Box 235, DLC-EA.
41. For the exchange of letters at the time between William Taylor and Arthur Saltmarsh and Ellis & Allan, see William Taylor to Ellis & Allan, August 20, 1821, Box 232, DLC-EA; Ellis & Allan to William Taylor and Arthur Saltmarsh, October 17, 1821, Box 233, DLC-EA; William Taylor to Ellis & Allan, November 29, 1821, Box 234, DLC-EA; Ellis & Allan to William Taylor and Arthur Saltmarsh, January 3, 4, 8, 10, 11, 1822, Box 235, DLC-EA; Charles Ellis to William Taylor and Arthur Saltmarsh, January 28, 1822, Box 235, DLC-EA.
42. For John Allan's payments to Joseph H. Clarke for Edgar's schooling, see "Sundries Dr to Cash," June 9, [1821], "[John Allan] paid him for Edgar school $12.50," and July 16, 1821, "paid Edgar's Tuition to 11th Septr next $12.50," Box 557, DLC-EA, and [Payment], July 24, [1821], "By John Allan pd Edgars Tuition to the 11th Sept next $12.50," Box 572, DLC-EA, and receipt from J. H. Clarke to John Allan, June 11, [1821], "To tuition of Son Edgar Poe from June 11th [1821] to Sept 11th," Box 438, DLC-EA; John Allan to J. H. Clarke, n.d., "To tuition of master Edgar Poe from Sept 11th to March 11th 1822 at $12.50 per qt. $25.00," (total $26.75), with receipt from J. H. Clarke, Box 438, DLC-EA, and [Payment], December 17, [1821], "By John Allan pd Clarkes for Edgars Tuition to 11th Dec $14" and [Payment], February 22 [1822], "By John Allan pd Mr Clarke his a/c for Edgars tuition to the 11th Mar 1822 $12.75," Box 572, DLC-EA, and [Payment], John Allan to J. H. Clarke, December 17, 1821, "To instruction of Edgar Poe 1 qtr from Sept 11th to December 11th 1821 $12.50," total $14.00, with receipt, Box 234, DLC-EA; "Sundries Dr to Cash," December 17, 1821, "John Allan

paid Clarke for Edgars Tuition to 11th December 1821 $14," Box 557, DLC-EA; [Payment], John Allan, "To present Quarter's tuition of master Poe from June 11th to Sept 11 1822 $12.50," with payment for Horace and Cicero and copybook, total 17.55, n.d., with receipt, Box 438, DLC-EA; John Allan to J. H. Clarke, "Yr Instructions of Edgar Poe from Sept 11th 1822 to Dec 11th @ 12 $12.50," total with "pens, ink & Paper, $13.25," n.d. with receipt, Box 438, DLC-EA; "Sundries Dr to Cash," November 5, 1822, "John Allan . . . paid Mr Clarke Edgars tuition to 11th December 1822 $13.25," Box 557, DLC-EA; [Payment], November 7, 1822, "By John Allan pd Mr Clarke Edgars Tuition to 11th Decr 1822," Box 572, DLC-EA.

43. Receipt to John Allan ("To making coat and pantaloons Edgar"), October 10, 1810, Box 234, DLC-EA. See also Box 557, DLC-EA.
44. Weiss, *The Home Life of Poe*, 23.
45. Ellis, "Edgar Allan Poe."
46. "Furniss Cutler & Stacey vs Allan & Ellis," n.d. 1821, Box 234, DLC-EA. For the calculation of inflation, see "Value of $1 from 1821 to 2023" (https://www.officialdata.org/us/inflation/1821). One dollar in 1821 equals $27.17 in 2023.
47. Ellis & Allan to William Taylor and Arthur Saltmarsh, January 24, 1822 (appended to January 10, 1822, letter), Box 234, DLC-EA; Ellis & Allan to Charles and John Adams, January 28, 1822, Box 526, DLC-EA; Ellis & Allan to William Taylor and Arthur Saltmarsh, February 2, 1822, Box 526, DLC-EA.
48. Ellis & Allan to William Taylor and Arthur Saltmarsh, January 24, 1822, Box 234, DLC-EA. The same sequence was repeated, with variation, in Ellis & Allan to Charles and John Adams, January 28, 1822, Box 526, DLC-EA; Ellis & Allan to William Taylor and Arthur Saltmarsh, February 2, 1822, Box 526, DLC-EA; and Ellis & Allan to Furniss, Cutler, and Stacey, [February 1822], Box 526, DLC-EA. These later letters indicate that the swearing out would be to the Insolvent Act. The letter to Furniss, Cutler, and Stacey refers to "Mr Galt who is Bail" but contends that he will not pay their debt.
49. Ellis & Allan to Charles & John Adams, January 28, 1822, Box 526, DLC-EA.
50. See Charles Ellis to William Taylor and Arthur Saltmarsh, February 4, 1822, Box 235, DLC-EA. Related documents include Charles Ellis to William Taylor and Arthur Saltmarsh, January 28, 1822, Box 235, DLC-EA; and John Forbes and John Richard to Charles Ellis, February 2, 1822, Box 235, DLC-EA.
51. "Memorandum," April 24, 1822, Box 236, DLC-EA; William Taylor and Arthur Saltmarsh to Allan & Ellis, April 27, 1822, Box 236, DLC-EA.
52. John R. Furniss to Ellis & Allan, May 1, 1822, Box 236, DLC-EA.
53. Furniss, Cutler and Stacey to Allan & Ellis, May 1, 1822, Box 236, DLC-EA.
54. Furniss, Cutler and Stacey v Ellis & Allan, *Reports of Cases Decided by The Honourable John Marshall, late Chief Justice of the United States, in the Circuit Court of the United States, for the District of Virginia and North Carolina from 1802 to 1833 Inclusive*, ed. John W. Brockenbrough, 2 vols. (Philadelphia: James Kay, Jun. & Brother, 1837), 2:14–19; Daniel Call to John Allan and Charles Ellis, June 18, 1822, Box 237, DLC-EA. Ellis & Allan wrote to Furniss, Cutler and Stacey that they were "disappointed that suit isn't dismissed" (Ellis & Allan to Furniss, Cutler and Stacey, June 26, 1822, Box 526, DLC-EA).

55. Ellis & Allan to Thomas Bennick, November 16, 1822, Box 526, DLC-EA. The other complainant was John Noble.
56. Issues included the discrepancy between John Allan's initial promise and the later offer (owing to lower real estate prices), the amount of payment per pound, the sale of real estate, and the sending of the books. Salient letters from midyear include Thomas Sheppard to Ellis & Allan, April 25, 1822, Box 236, DLC-EA; Ellis & Allan to William Taylor and Arthur Saltmarsh, June 5, 1822, Box 237, DLC-EA; Thomas Colquhoun to Ellis & Allan, June 8, 1822, Box 237, DLC-EA; Thomas Colquhoun to John Allan, June 18, 1822, Box 237, DLC-EA; Ellis & Allan to William Taylor and Arthur Saltmarsh, June 23, 1822, Box 237, DLC-EA; and John Sharpe to Ellis & Allan, June 24, 1822, Box 237, DLC-EA. Subsequent letters elaborate further.
57. [Charles Ellis to John Allan], August 20, 1822, Box 238, DLC-EA.
58. Weiss, *The Home Life of Poe,* 22.
59. Flora Lapham Mack to William Lanier Washington, March 31, 1908, collection of the author.
60. Ibid. For Mack's assertion about Mrs. Mackenzie's intercession, see Mack, "A Few More Words about Mr. & Mrs. Allan," collection of the author. Mack is clearly a partisan of John Allan in this piece and elsewhere.
61. J. T. L. Preston, "Some Reminiscences of Edgar A. Poe as a Schoolboy," in Sara Sigourney Rice, *Edgar Allan Poe: A Memorial Volume* (Baltimore, MD: Turnbull Brothers, 1877), 37–42.
62. "Edgar Allan Poe: Some Reminiscences of the Poet by His Old School Teacher in Richmond." Clarke said that "Edgar wasn't more than fourteen when he wrote that letter." I estimate Edgar to have been thirteen since by the summer of 1823, when he was fourteen, Edgar was at another school. Clarke would soon move to Baltimore.
63. Preston, "Some Reminiscences," 38.
64. Ibid., 40–41.
65. See Poe-Allan-Ellis Papers, 1803–1881, MSC0033, The Valentine, Richmond, VA; Phillips, *Edgar Allan Poe—The Man,* 1:187–88; Quinn, *Edgar Allan Poe: A Critical Biography,* 88–89. The Allans had not lived at Fourteenth Street and Tobacco Alley earlier in their stay in Richmond after their return from England (Quinn, *Edgar Allan Poe: A Critical Biography,* 53).
66. I take 1822 as the year of the school's founding because of an 1828 advertisement that indicated that Miss Mackenzie had been teaching for six years (Thomas and Jackson, *The Poe Log,* 54). That Miss Jane Mackenzie worked with Jane Scott Mackenzie is noted in Margaret Meagher's *History of Education in Richmond* (Richmond: Virginia Division of the Works Progress Administration, 1939), 59. Also given there is the location. Mack comments on Miss Mackenzie and her school in Flora Lapham Mack to William Lanier Washington, March 12, 1908; Mack [for William Lanier Washington], Suggestions for the Second Chapter—Break with the Allans; and Mack to Washington, [On Mr. Mackenzie and Miss Jane Mackenzie], collection of the author. See also Agnes M. Bondurant, *Poe's Richmond* (Richmond, VA: Garrett & Massie, 1942), 86–88. For the anecdote about Poe's rushing toward the group of schoolgirls, see John H. Ingram, "The

True Story of Edgar Allan Poe," Ingram's Poe Collection, Microfilm Roll 5. The Ingram manuscript was typed, briefly introduced, and lightly annotated by John Carl Miller in 1954–55.
67. See Martin S. Shockley, "*Timour the Tartar* and Poe's *Tamerlane,*" *PMLA* 56, no. 4 (1941): 1103–6.
68. See note 42 in this chapter.
69. Charles Marshall Graves, "Landmarks of Poe in Richmond," *Century Magazine*, n.s., vol. 45 (April 1904): 916.
70. Preston, "Some Reminiscences," 37.
71. "Married," Joseph H. Clarke to Jane Mupp, September 1, 1821, *Daily National Intelligencer*.
72. "Edgar Allan Poe: Some Reminiscences of the Poet by His Old School Teacher in Richmond."
73. John Allan, Notebook, April 1, 1823, Harry Ransom Center, University of Texas at Austin. Allan wrote, "Edgar was entered with Mr Burke for a session of 5 mos & $30 paid in advance." For comment on Burke's School, see Meagher, *History of Education in Richmond*, 58.
74. Weiss, *The Home Life of Poe*, 25–26.
75. For another story of Poe's waiting for his opponent to run out of breath, see Dr. & Mrs. Ray Thomas, "Recollections of Poe by Various Persons Who Had Known Him," Ingram's Poe Collection, Item 361.
76. Weiss, *The Home Life of Poe*, 28–29. Flora Lapham Mack disagrees with Weiss's description but again bases her views on her incorrect belief about John H. Mackenzie's age (Flora Lapham Mack to William Lanier Washington, March 31, 1908, collection of the author).
77. John Allan to Allan Fowlds, April 12, 1823, Box 240, DLC-EA.
78. For Edgar's swimming at this time, see "Edgar A. Poe's Swimming Powers," *New York Evening Post*, June 15, 1875 (America's Historical Newspapers); clippings at The Valentine; and Thomas and Jackson, *The Poe Log*, 56. For Edgar's visiting the Mackenzies and calling Mrs. Mackenzie "Ma," see Weiss, *The Home Life of Poe*, 21 ("Poe always called Mrs. Mackenzie 'Ma,' and was almost as much at home in her house as was his sister"). For Edgar's participation in the Thespian Society, see James A. Harrison, *New Glimpses of Poe* (New York: M. S. Mansfield, 1901), 30; and H 1:28–29. For Poe's reciting his poetry to a waiting audience, see Dr. and Mrs. Ray Thomas, "Recollections of Poe by Various Persons Who Had Known Him," Ingram's Poe Collection, Item 361.
79. For the address of Mrs. Stanard's house, see Mary Wingfield Scott, *Old Richmond Neighborhoods* (Richmond, VA: Whittet & Shepperson, 1950), 99, 101–2.
80. Sarah Helen Whitman, *Edgar Poe and His Critics* (New York: Rudd & Carleton, 1860), 49.
81. Maria Clemm to Sarah Helen Whitman, April 14, 1859, in *Building Poe Biography*, 42.
82. Whitman, *Edgar Poe and His Critics*, 49.
83. See, regarding waiting for satisfactory terms, Ellis & Allan to William Taylor and Arthur Saltmarsh, June 14, 1823, Box 529, DLC-EA. Regarding collecting, see Charles Ellis to John Allan, April 21, 1823, Box 240; July 14, 18, and 30, August 2,

5, and 14 [1823], Box 241, DLC-EA. And regarding working for the children who will later disdain working, see John Allan to Charles Ellis, August 4, 1823, Box 241, DLC-EA. For detail on the Sociable Club, see "The Clarke Spring Sociable Club," July 5, 1823, Box 241, DLC-EA. See also Mordecai, *Richmond in By-Gone Days,* 262–63.

84. For the burning of the penitentiary on August 8, 1823, see John Allan to Charles Ellis, August 11, 1823, Box 241, DLC-EA. For Gilbert Hunt's helping the prisoners escape from the fire and then fashioning their handcuffs the next day, see Philip Barrett, *Gilbert Hunt, the City Blacksmith* (Richmond, VA: J. Woodhouse, 1859), 9–11.

85. John Allan to Charles Ellis, September 5, 1823, Box 242, DLC-EA.

86. Ellis & Allan to William Taylor & Arthur Saltmarsh, November 8, 1823, Box 529, DLC-EA. The final settlement seems to have been twelve shillings, six pence on the pound. See [Ellis & Allan] to John Noble, August 8, 1822, Box 238, DLC-EA; [Ellis & Allan] to William Taylor and Arthur Saltmarsh, August 17, 1822, Box 238, DLC-EA; [Ellis & Allan] to William Taylor and Arthur Saltmarsh, Box 238, DLC-EA; John Forbes and John Richard to Arthur Saltmarsh and William Taylor, August 1822, Box 238, DLC-EA; Ellis & Allan to Gough & Braithewaite, September 6, 1822, Box 238, DLC-EA; and ["This agreement"], May 24, 1823, Box 241, DLC-EA

87. The first issue of the newspaper states, "The Office of the Phenix is on the street leading to Mayo's Bridge, called 14th Street, and between E or Main Street, and the street north of it called F Street [Franklin Street]—where, it is requested, all communications and advertisements intended for the paper may be left" ("Phenix Office," *Richmond Phenix,* December 19, 1823, [3]). See also December 22, [1], and December 29, 1823, [1]. The newspaper masthead features a picture of a phoenix, and, remarkably, the pages of the 1823 issues of the paper are singed in the lower right corner. The original is held by the Library of Congress and is on loan to the Library of Virginia. For brief bibliographical information, see Lester J. Cappon, *Virginia Newspapers 1821–1935* (New York: D. Appleton-Century, 1936), 181. The handwritten notation "Sec of State" or "Secy of State" at the top of some issues suggests the possibility that the subscription was for the office of the United States secretary of state, then John Quincy Adams.

88. "To the Patrons of the Va. Times," *Richmond Phenix,* December 19, 1823, [2].

89. Mordecai, *Richmond in By-Gone Days,* 239.

90. "Edgar A. Poe," Edward V. Valentine interviews Mrs. Shelton, November 19, 1875.

91. [Edgar Allan Poe], "To Myra," *Richmond Phenix,* December 22, 1823, [3]. Notably, in the next column to the right, somewhat below, is an advertisement for "The Exhibition of the Egyptian Mummy" (perhaps significant in light of Poe's 1845 "Some Words with a Mummy").

92. "Edgar A. Poe," Edward V. Valentine interviews Mrs. Shelton, November 19, 1875. If Elmira was born in 1810, then she would have been thirteen, not fifteen or sixteen, in 1823.

93. Didier, "Life of Edgar A. Poe," 33–34. The original letters by Andrew Johnston from which Didier quotes—one of them to J. T. L. Preston of April 29, 1876 and another to Didier of May 5, 1876—were later sold at auction (Anderson Auction Company, *Autographs Mainly American,* March 17, 1908).

94. John Allan to Allan Fowlds, October 4, 1823, Box 242, DLC-EA.
95. J. H. Whitty: *Complete Poems,* 2nd ed. (1917), "Memoir," xxv; "Appendix,"188. Whitty visited the Ellis & Allan building and wrote that Poe spent "so much time among the songs and periodicals" on the second and third floors (J. H. Whitty to Mary Elizabeth Phillips, April 3, 1918, Rare Books, Mary E. Phillips Collection, Boston Public Library [MsAM 1200 (446)]).
96. Harrison, *New Glimpses,* 31–32.
97. John Allan, "A General Note Book," January 23, 1824, Harry Ransom Center, University of Texas at Austin.
98. Arthur Saltmarsh and William Taylor to Ellis & Allan, January 30, 1824, Box 243, DLC-EA.
99. Thomas H. Ellis reports that the firm of Ellis & Allan "was dissolved by mutual consent in 1824" (Ellis, "Edgar Allan Poe," *Richmond Standard,* May 7, 1881, 2). For the document that set the terms of the dissolution, see "This Agreement," June 8, 1824, Box 244, DLC-EA.
100. For Allan's use of Edgar as a delivery boy, see John Allan to Charles Ellis, March 5, 1824, Box 243, DLC-EA ("If you have looked over the papers send them to me by Edgar"); "Sundries Dr to Cash," "John Allan sent you by Jacob $2 Ditto Do by Edgar [$]15," Box 557, DLC-EA; [Payment], "By John Allan sent him [Ellis?] by Edgar [$]10," March 16, 1824, Box 572, DLC-EA, and also "Sundries Dr to Cash," "John Allan sent him [Ellis?] by Edgar & Party[?] [$]10.21," March 16, 1824, Box 557, DLC-EA; [Payment], "By John Allan sent you [Ellis?] by Edgar [$]5," March 20, 1824, Box 572 and Box 557, DLC-EA.
101. See "Theatre—Richmond Astronomical Lectures," *Richmond Phenix,* March 22, 1824, [3]; "Theatre—Richmond Astronomical Lectures," ibid., March 23, 1824, [3]; "Theatre Richmond Astronomical Lectures," *Richmond Enquirer,* March 23, 1824, [3]; ["Mr. Goodacre"], *Richmond Family Visiter,* March 27, 1824, [2] [on "an overflowing assembly"]; "Mr. Goodacre," *Richmond Enquirer,* March 30, 1824, [3] (on "a crowd of near 1000 spectators"); ["Mr. Goodacre's Lectures"], *Richmond Family Visiter,* April 3, 1824, [2]; "Mr. Goodacre's Lectures Further Postponed," *Richmond Phenix,* April 5, 1824, [3]; "Mr. Goodacre's Lectures," ibid., April 9, 1824, [3]; "Mr. Goodacre's Lectures," *Richmond Enquirer,* April 9, 1824, [3]. For Cabell's comments, see William H. Cabell to Thomas Jefferson, May 10, 1824, Albert and Shirley Small Special Collections Library, University of Virginia, Charlottesville. For scholarly studies of Robert Goodacre's lectures on astronomy, see Robert Inkster: "Robert Goodacre (1777–1825) and Popular Astronomy," *Journal of the British Astronomical Association* 90 (1980): 245–51, and "Robert Goodacre's Astronomy Lectures (1823–25) and the Structure of Scientific Culture in Philadelphia," *Annals of Science* 35, no. 1 (1978): 353–63. The fourth edition of Goodacre's *A Brief Explanation of the Principal Terms Made Use of in Astronomy* was published in Richmond in 1824. And his *Outline of Eight Lectures in Astronomy* appeared in Washington earlier that year (WorldCat).
102. Weiss, *The Home Life of Poe,* 29.
103. Flora Lapham Mack to William Lanier Washington, February 29, 1908, collection of the author.

104. Maria Clemm to Sarah Helen Whitman, April 14, 1859, in *Building Poe Biography*, 42. Kenneth Silverman discusses Stanard's depression and insanity in *Edgar A. Poe: Mournful and Never-ending Remembrance* (New York: HarperCollins, 1991), 26, 458.
105. Phillips, *Edgar Allan Poe—The Man*, 1:204; Thomas and Jackson, *The Poe Log*, 59.
106. Weiss, *The Home Life of Poe*, 21.
107. Maria Clemm to Sarah Helen Whitman, April 14, 1859, in *Building Poe Biography*, 42. For Edgar's visiting Stanard's grave alone, see Sarah Helen Whitman to Maria Clemm, March 10, 1859, in *Edgar Allan Poe Letters and Documents in the Enoch Pratt Free Library*, ed. Arthur H. Quinn and Richard H. Hart (New York: Scholars' Facsimiles & Reprints, 1941), 42; Whitman, *Edgar Poe and His Critics* (New York: Rudd & Carleston, 1860), 49–50; and Whitman to John H. Ingram, April 2, 1874, in *Poe's Helen Remembers*, ed. John Carl Miller (Charlottesville: University Press of Virginia, 1979), 104.
108. John Allan, "Amicable Society," April 3, 1824, Box 243, DLC-EA; John Allan, "The Clark's Spring Barbecue Club," July 1824, Box 244, DLC-EA. The Amicable Society is mentioned in Mordecai, *Richmond in By-Gone Days*, 255–59, 262.
109. "This Agreement," June 8, 1824, Box 244, DLC-EA; John Forbes and John Richard to Ellis & Allan, July 8, 1824, Box 244, DLC-EA. See also Ellis & Allan to John Forbes and John Richard, July 8, 1824, Box 244, DLC-EA.
110. John Allan, "The Clark's Spring Barbecue Club," July 1824, Box 244, DLC-EA.
111. Accounts of Poe's swim are available in John Henry Ingram, *Edgar Allan Poe: His Life, Letters, and Opinions* (London: John Hogg, 1880), 1:27–29. Included there are reports by R. C. Ambler, Robert Mayo, and Robert G. Cabell. See also the manuscript letters of R. C. Ambler and Thomas G. Clarke and news clippings regarding Robert Mayo, all in the Ellis-Allan Papers at The Valentine. And see Thomas H. Ellis's record of the swim in James A. Harrison's *New Glimpses of Poe* (New York: M. F. Mansfield, 1901), 30; and H 1:25. According to the Mayo account in Ingram and the news clippings, Mayo himself stopped swimming at Tree Hill to avoid the hot sun. But another version suggests that he quit because Edgar was "furious that another should attempt to rival him" (Charles Marshall Graves, "Landmarks of Poe in Richmond Including Some Hitherto Unpublished Portraits of His Friends," *Century Magazine*, n.s., vol. 45 [April 1904]: 916). A variant of the Cabell account in Ingram is that Rob Stanard was not aboard a boat but, rather, walking along the river bank watching Edgar (Hervey Allen, *Israfel: The Life and Times of Edgar Allan Poe*, 2 vols. [New York: George H. Doran, 1926], 1:105–6). In yet another variant of the incident, offered by David Bridges (who said he had swum along), Edgar crawled over a shipwreck during his swim and did not walk home but returned home by boat with the others ("Poe the Poet: Recollection of Two Citizens Who Knew Him Well," *Richmond State*, November 29, 1885, Ingram's Poe Collection, Item 855). David Cody recently discovered a brief contemporary account of this swimming feat in "Abstract of Principal Occurrences," *Port Folio* (July 1824): 81 (David Cody, email message to author, January 2, 2020). For the comment on the swimming feat in the 1843 *Saturday Museum* piece—written by either Poe and Henry B. Hirst or Poe alone, see Burton R. Pollin, "Poe's Authorship of Three Long Critical and Autobiographical

Articles of 1843 Now Authenticated," *American Literary Renaissance Report* 7 (1993): 171; Benjamin F. Fisher, ed., *Masques, Mysteries, and Mastodons: A Poe Miscellany* (Baltimore, MD: Edgar Allan Poe Society, 2006), 188–89; and Benjamin F. Fisher, ed., *Poe in His Own Time: A Biographical Chronicle of His Life, Drawn from Recollections, Interviews, and Memoirs by Family, Friends, and Associates* (Iowa City: University of Iowa Press, 2010), 40.

112. Poe, "Poetry," 1824, Box 438, DLC-EA.

113. Weiss, *The Home Life of Poe*, 28. Of course, he was never legally adopted by John Allan.

114. R. H. Stoddard, "Life of Edgar Allan Poe," in *The Works of Edgar Allan Poe* (New York: A. C. Armstrong, 1884), 1:20. For the original statement about Edgar's giving Cassius's speech, see Mrs. Dixon, Letter to the Editor, July 2, 1875, Ingram's Poe Collection, Item 237.

115. Mrs. Dixon, Letter to the Editor, July 2, 1875, Ingram's Poe Collection, Item 237.

116. That Edgar was lieutenant of the Richmond Junior Volunteers is evident from his subsequent letters requesting permission to keep their arms. For these letters, the first in the edition of his letters, see O 1:3–5. There was also a group of boys known as the Morgan Legion or the Junior Morgan Riflemen, of which Edgar was said to have been a part. The two military groups are elsewhere listed separately (Robert D. Ward, comp., *General La Fayette in Virginia* [Richmond: West, Johnston, 1881], 51, 52).

117. For Lafayette's kissing the baby Walter Whitman in Brooklyn, see Joseph Jay Rubin, *The Historic Whitman* (University Park: Pennsylvania State University Press, 1975), 15. For Lafayette's asking for David Poe and seeing his widow in Baltimore, see J. Thomas Scharf, *The Chronicles of Baltimore; Being a Complete History of "Baltimore Town" and Baltimore City from the Earliest Period to the Present Time* (Baltimore, MD: Turnbull Brothers, 1874), 415.

118. For the elaborate tribute to Lafayette in Richmond over several days, see Ward, *General La Fayette in Virginia*.

119. The anecdote about Edgar's putting the clock two hours ahead is in "Recollections of Poe by Various Persons Who Had Known Him," Ingram's Poe Collection, Item 361.

120. Thomas Ellis is quoted in Harrison's *New Glimpses of Poe*, 30–31; and H 1:25–26. Ellis also mentions Edgar as a member of the Junior Morgan Riflemen.

121. John Allan to Henry Poe, November 1, 1824, Box 438, DLC-EA.

122. Ibid. For Mrs. Shelton on Ebenezer Burling, see "Edgar A. Poe," Edward V. Valentine interviews Mrs. Shelton, November 19, 1875.

123. William Henry Poe, "[In a Pocket Book]," *Poe's Brother: The Poems of William Henry Leonard Poe*, 41.

124. Marie Louise Shew Houghton to John Ingram, May 16, 1875, in *Building Poe Biography*, 140.

125. Thomas Ellis is quoted in Harrison's *New Glimpses of Poe*, 29–30.

126. Didier, "Life of Edgar A. Poe," 34; Woodberry, *The Life of Edgar Allan Poe*, 1:29–30.

127. For "Last Will and Testament of William Galt," see Allen, *Israfel*, 2:859–64. The quotations offered appear on page 860. For the estimate of the numbers attending

Galt's funeral, see "Died," *Richmond Constitutional Whig,* March 29, 1825. J. H. Whitty wrote, "Edgar must have attended the Galt funeral" (Whitty to Mary Elizabeth Phillips, November 27, 1918, Mary E. Phillips Collection, Rare Books and Manuscripts, Boston Public Library). There was apparently a death mask made of Galt ("Death Mask of William Galt," Ellis-Allan Papers, The Valentine).

128. For Allan's response to the charge that he had influenced the Galt will in his own favor, see John Allan to Doctor J. Black, August 19, 1825; John Allan to unknown correspondent, September 10, 1825; John Allan to unknown correspondents, September 1825, Box 249, DLC-EA. For Galt's estimate of the value of his estate, see "Died," *Richmond Constitutional Whig,* March 29, 1825. This highly positive obituary was followed by a correction to a perceived but unintended slight, in "The Late William Galt," *Richmond Constitutional Whig,* April 1, 1825. For the 1825 dollar equivalent, see "Value of $1 from 1825 to 2023" (https://www.officialdata.org/us/inflation/1825). One dollar in 1825 equals $31.01 in 2023.

129. For information on Moldavia, see Woodberry, *The Life of Edgar Allan Poe,* 1:30–31, 2:361–64 (Thomas H. Ellis's reminiscence); and Mary Wingfield Scott, *Houses of Old Richmond* (Richmond, VA: The Valentine, 1941), 46–49. That the Mackenzies lived next door is evident from Flora Lapham Mack to William Lanier Washington, March 31, 1908, collection of the author. For Nancy Valentine's observing William Mackenzie's moving his plants, see Anne Valentine to John Allan, April 23, 1826, Box 251, DLC-EA.

130. F. W. Thomas states that this was the second visit (Whitty [1911 and 1917], "Memoir," xxxi. For the information presented here on Henry Poe, see Allen and Mabbott's *Poe's Brother,* esp. 19–24. For further information on Henry Poe, see M 1:515–20; and Silverman, *Edgar A. Poe: Mournful and Never-ending Remembrance,* 82–85.

131. Edgar published *Tamerlane* in 1827, and Henry published poems in the Philadelphia *Saturday Evening Post* and poems and tales in the *North American* in that year. For bibliographies of Henry's publications, see Allen and Mabbott, *Poe's Brother,* 91–92; and M 1:516–20.

132. For Elmira's comment on seeing Henry, see Valentine, "Edgar A. Poe," The Valentine. See also Edward V. Valentine to John H. Ingram, "Conversation with Mrs. Shelton Nov. 22 1875," Ingram's Poe Collection, Item 263. Allen and Mabbott conjecture that Henry was a midshipman, in the navy or the merchant marine (23).

133. "Sundries Dr to Cash," May 14, [1825], Box 557, DLC-EA.

134. John Allan to Joseph Trent, bill paid, July 1, 1825 (covering services from June 1, 1824 to July 1, 1825), Box 249, DLC-EA; see also "Sundries Dr to Cash," July 5, 1825, Box 557, DLC-EA.

135. John Allan to Charles Ellis, September 12, 1825, Box 249, DLC-EA; John Allan to ?, September 1825, Box 249, DLC-EA; John Allan to Charles Ellis, October 3, 1825, Box 249, DLC-EA.

136. Allan to Ellis, October 3, 1825, Box 249, DLC-EA.

137. R. C. Ambler, December 14, 1874, Ellis-Allan Papers, The Valentine. See also Edward V. Valentine to John H. Ingram featuring an extract from the Ambler letter, May 18, 1875, Ingram's Poe Collection, Item 228. For further discussion, see M 1:6–7.

138. Mack to Washington, February 29, 1908, collection of the author.
139. Mack to Washington, March 31, 1908, collection of the author.
140. Mack to Washington, February 29, 1908. Mack identifies Robert Pitts's employer as Thomas R. Price, but Price was only nineteen years old at the time, unlikely to have had his own business and certainly not then the father of a young woman. Thomas Ollive Mabbott writes that Pitts worked for the dry goods company Robert & Hall Neilson & Co and then Hall & Moore (M 1:9). It was Hall & Moore that advertised in the fall of 1825 in the *Richmond Enquirer* (see "New Fall Goods," *Richmond Enquirer,* November 8, 11, 14, 18, 22, 25, 29, and December 2, 8, 10, 1825, Library of Virginia). For the two letters from Pitts that Mabbott mentions (1:9), see Robert Pitts to John Adams Smith, September 19, 1824, and March 3, 1825, The Valentine. The first of these letters indicates that Pitts was from Essex County, which was a farm county northeast of Richmond. Indeed, his family home was called Pittsville, near Loretto, and his father was Thomas Pitts (Jeffrey M. O'Dell, *Essex County Historic Site Survey,* Part III, Project of The Virginia Historic Landmarks Commission [n.p., n.d.], p. 484, Tappahannock Public Library). See also Wesley E. Pippenger, *Essex County, Virginia Will Abstracts 1751–1842 and Estate Records Index 1751–1799* (Tappahannock, VA: Barbour Printing Services, 2016), 205–6; and *Essex County, Virginia Newspaper Notices 1738–1938* (Tappahannock, VA: n.p., 2009), 25, 30–32.
141. Mack to Washington, February 29, 1908. It is probable that Pitts had had experience in participating in a fox hunt: James B. Slaughter writes that in the early nineteenth century, "Fox hunting was still the most fashionable game in Essex" (Slaughter, *Settlers, Southerners, Americans: The History of Essex County, Virginia 1608–1984* [Salem, WV: Don Mills, 1985], 95).
142. Mack to Washington, February 29, 1908.
143. Mack to Washington, September 12, 1908, collection of the author.
144. Significant scholarship on the poem, in addition to Mabbott's headnote, is Jay B. Hubbell, "'O, Tempora! O, Mores!' A Juvenile Poem by Edgar Allan Poe," in *Elizabethan Studies and Other Essays in Honor of George F. Reynolds,* University of Colorado Studies, ser. B, Studies in the Humanities, vol. 2, no. 4 (2012): 314–21; and Jeffrey A. Savoye, "Oh, Tempora! Oh, Mores! Oh, Didier!," *Edgar Allan Poe Review* 14, no. 1 (2013): 110–12. J. H. Whitty printed "Oh, Tempora! Oh, Mores!" in his 1911 *The Complete Poems of Edgar Allan Poe* and added a paragraph of commentary to the poem in the second edition of 1917: "The original manuscript of this poem in Poe's autograph was once in the possession of John H. MacKenzie. It was destroyed with other Poe papers by fire during the Civil War. A copy reading like the above verses is still preserved by a step-daughter of Mr. MacKenzie, with an account of how it came to be written by Poe in the year 1826" (171). Whitty had written to Flora Lapham Mack, but she had determined to tell Whitty nothing: "He is now wild to find some descendants of the Mackenzies or some papers to support his theories but I am now as silent and irresponsive as a tomb to these letters in every phase of the subject" (Mack to Washington, January 4, 1914, Poe Museum). Whitty visited Mack on July 26, 1915, but she was "a little evasive giving full information. I presume on Mr. Washington's account, who says has her recollection" (Whitty to Mary Elizabeth Phillips, July 28, 1915, Mary E. Phillips

Collection, Rare Books and Manuscripts, Boston Public Library). A letter from Mack to Washington reveals that the original manuscript of "Oh Tempora! Oh Mores!" was actually taken from Mackenzie's desk by Poe's sister Rosalie and sold for five dollars to Henry Pollard, the editor of *Southern Opinion*. Mackenzie was "really angry" with Rosalie, "furious"; he had "loved to show [the manuscript] to his friends, and tell the circumstance under which it was written." Mack at first mistakenly thought that the poem was never published (Mack to Washington, February 29, 1908).

145. Killis Campbell writes of Poe, "Clearly he had read Butler's *Hudibras*, however, as is attested by six quotations from that work and eleven references to it" (Campbell, "Poe's Reading," *University of Texas Studies in English* 5 [October 8, 1925]: 166–96, esp. 176).

146. In later years, "Counter-jumper" became a term associated with Walt Whitman and effeminacy (Robert J. Scholnick, "'An Unusually Active Market for Calamus': Whitman, Vanity Fair, and the Fate of Humor in War, 1860–63," *Walt Whitman Quarterly Review* 19, no. 3 [2002]: 148–81, esp. 159–61). See also Brian P. Luskey, "Homo Counter-Jumperii," in *On the Make: Clerks and the Quest for Capital in Nineteenth-Century America* (New York: New York University Press, 2010), 83–118.

147. Notably, Pitts, in his March 3, 1825, letter to John Adams Smith, refers to his dancing: "We are to have a splendid Ball at the Eagle Hotel tomorrow night—I wish it could have been on account of Jackson[']s Inauguration, instead of Adams' I think I should hop much more nimbly" (Pitts to Smith, March 3, 1825, The Valentine). (The inauguration of John Quincy Adams was to be on the following day, March 4, 1825.)

148. Mack to Washington, February 29, 1908.

149. Perhaps, in addition to Butler, a touch of Poe's hero, Byron, is here. The unusual rhyme at the climax of "Oh, Tempora! Oh, Mores!"—"himself" and "elf"—was the same as one at the climax of Byron's "Vision of Judgment" (Lord Byron, *The Complete Poetical Works*, vol. 6 [Oxford: Oxford University Press, 1991], 345).

150. Mack to Washington, February 29, 1908. But Pitts seems to have returned later: there is a receipt from Hall & Moore signed by Robert Pitts from 1827 (Robert Pitts, Receipt for Hall & Moore, June 9 [or later], 1827, The Valentine).

151. There was another satirical poem by Poe, "[Don Pompioso]," no longer extant, described by Dr. John F. Carter as written by Poe to get back at a young man who had scorned his parentage and poverty (Graves, "Landmarks of Poe in Richmond," 917). Susan Archer Weiss also described a satirical poem, titled "Don Pompiosa." In the case that she recounts, Edgar was ridiculing "a sprig of an aristocratic family" who had snubbed him (Weiss, *The Home Life of Poe*, 34). Perhaps she had heard the story from Carter or had read Graves. J. H. Whitty and Elizabeth Phillips believed "Don Pompioso" (or "Don Pompiosa") to be the same poem as "Oh, Tempora! Oh, Mores!," but Jay B. Hubbell and T. O. Mabbott thought it to be a different work since Pitts was not particularly pompous (Hubbell, 317n15; M 1:7). Flora Lapham Mack notes that "Oh, Tempora! Oh, Mores!" was not written to mock a son of the gentry. She considers the possibility that Edgar altered the original poem to apply to another target, but she does not

know (Mack to Washington, March 31, 1908, collection of the author). She later reasserts her uncertainty about whether the two poems were really one (Mack to Washington, September 12, 1908, collection of the author). I share the view of Hubbell and Mabbott that there were probably two different works. It is possible that "Don Pompioso" was an adaptation of "Oh, Tempora! Oh. Mores!" If, however, they were the same, I tend to have more confidence in Mack's recollection of John H. Mackenzie's one hundred tellings than I do of Graves's recollection of John F. Carter's telling. After all, Mackenzie had been at the reading and had been given the manuscript of the poem by Poe.

152. See "Edgar A. Poe," Edward V. Valentine interview with Mrs. Shelton, November 19, 1875, The Valentine; and Flora Lapham Mack to William Lanier Washington, March 31, 1908, collection of the author; September 17, 1908, Poe Museum; and September 18, [1908], collection of the author.

153. Flora Lapham Mack to William Lanier Washington, September 17, 1908, Poe Museum; "Edgar A. Poe," Edward V. Valentine interview with Mrs. Shelton, November 19, 1875, The Valentine.

154. Flora Lapham Mack to William Lanier Washington, September 17, 1908, Poe Museum. Mack believed that Edgar's love for Elmira was a mere fancy that he had for others as well (Flora Lapham Mack to William Lanier Washington, September 18, 1908 and February 1, 1909, collection of the author). But I believe that the evidence presented here suggests otherwise.

155. Whitty, *Complete Poems,* 1st and 2nd ed. (1911 and 1917), "Memoir," xxvii.

156. William Wertenbaker, "Statement about Poe," Ingram's Poe Collection, Item 92; see also Item 107.

5. "Mistakes for Manhood to Reform"

1. John Allan to Charles Ellis, August 4, 1823, Box 241, DLC-EA.
2. "The University of Virginia," December 15, 1825, *Richmond Enquirer.*
3. For information on the original buildings at the University of Virginia, see Philip Alexander Bruce, *History of the University of Virginia 1819–1919,* 5 vols. (New York: Macmillan, 1920), esp. 1:178–93. For general treatments of Poe at the university, see Charles W. Kent, "Poe's Student Days at the University of Virginia," in *The Unveiling of the Bust of Edgar Allan Poe* (Lynchburg, VA: J. P. Bell, 1901), 9–23; Bruce, *History of the University of Virginia 1819–1919,* 3:208–14; Floyd Stovall, "Edgar Poe and the University of Virginia," in *Edgar Poe the Poet: Essays New and Old on the Man and His Work* (Charlottesville: University Press of Virginia, 1969), 1–17; and Rex Bowman and Carlos Santos, "Tales of Horror," in *Rot, Riot, and Rebellion: Mr. Jefferson's Struggle to Save the University That Changed America* (Charlottesville: University of Virginia Press, 2013), 45–53.
4. For the detail here on Poe, see especially Kent, "Poe's Student Days at the University of Virginia." For information on the agreeable Professor Long, see Bruce, *History of the University of Virginia 1819–1919,* 2:4–9, 33–36; for that on the difficult Professor Blaetterman, see ibid., 2:157–60. See also Bowman and Santos, "Scholars amid Scoflaws," 56–59. For the pedagogical approach then practiced at the University of

Virginia, see Bruce, *History of the University of Virginia 1819–1919*, 2:128–30. For the subject of the lectures, see William Wertenbaker, "Edgar A. Poe," John Henry Ingram's Poe Collection, Albert & Shirley Small Special Collections Library, University of Virginia, Charlottesville, Item 107. Poe's name is listed as a student in Ancient Languages and Modern Languages in *A Catalogue of the Officers and Students of the University of Virginia*, Second Session, Commencing February 1st, 1826 (Charlottesville, VA: Chronicle Steam Book Printing House, 1880), [6].

5. George Long to John H. Ingram, April 15, 1875, Ingram's Poe Collection, Item 217 (published in "Poe at the University of Virginia: Unpublished Letters from the Ingram Collection," *University of Virginia Alumni Bulletin*, 3rd ser., vol. 16, no. 2 [April 1923]: 163–67); R. M. J. Hunter to H. Tutwiler, May 20, 1875, Ingram's Poe Collection, Item 267.

6. Robert S. Burkholder, "A Popular Error Concerning Poe," from the *South Atlantic* of August 1878 (373–75), Ingram's Poe Collection, Item 744. For other references to this incident, see William Wertenbaker's Statement about Poe, Ingram's Poe Collection, Item 92; and his "Edgar A. Poe," Ingram's Poe Collection, Item 107. The latter, published in the *Virginia University Magazine* (November/December 1868): 114–17, is also available at https://www.eapoe.org, the website of the Poe Society of Baltimore. See also "Poe as a Student," *New Glimpses of Poe*, ed. James A. Harrison (New York: M. F. Mansfield, 1901), 35–42. Blaetterman required translation of Tasso in his examination of students in the Italian class (*Minutes of the General Faculty 1825–1970*, 6–7, Albert and Shirley Small Special Collections Library, University of Virginia, Charlottesville). Regarding Poe's attendance, there is a countertradition, offered by Thomas G. Tucker by way of Douglas Sherley, that Poe and his group "were much given to non-attendance at lectures" (Sherley, "Edgar Allan Poe While a Student at the University of Virginia," "Old Oddity Papers—IV [Part 1]," *Virginia University Magazine* [March 1880]: 376–80, also available at https://www.eapoe.org). I trust Wertenbaker, for his was a firsthand account. Perhaps judgment on Poe's attendance was a matter of emphasis—"tolerably regular" also suggests that occasionally Edgar missed class. In an 1843 piece, Poe and Henry B. Hirst—or Poe himself—wrote, "He attended lectures at random" (Burton R. Pollin, "Poe's Authorship of Three Long Critical and Autobiographical Articles of 1843 Now Authenticated," *American Literary Renaissance Report* 7 [1993]: 139–71, esp. 164; Benjamin F. Fisher, ed., *Masques, Mysteries, and Mastodons: A Poe Miscellany* [Baltimore, MD: Edgar Allan Poe Society, 2006], 157; Benjamin F. Fisher, *Poe in His Own Time: A Biographical Chronicle of His Life, Drawn from Recollections, Interviews, and Memoirs by Family, Friends, and Associates* [Iowa City: University of Iowa Press, 2010], 23–40 ["Poets and Poetry in Philadelphia," esp. 25]).

7. Zu.lulu-Mo-zal, "Mr. William Wertenbaker—His Golden Wedding," *Virginia University Magazine* 14, no. 1 (October 1879): 42–47. For more on Poe's library borrowings, see Kenneth Walter Cameron, "Notes on Young Poe's Reading," *American Transcendental Quarterly* 24 (1974): Supplement, 33–34. *The List of Books Borrowed 1825–1827* is available at the Albert & Shirley Small Special Collections Library, University of Virginia, Charlottesville.

8. Bruce catalogues and describes minor and major offenses of the early students at the University of Virginia (Bruce, *History of the University of Virginia 1819–1919*, 2:266–311). For a more recent treatment, see Bowman and Santos, "'Vicious Irregularities.'"
9. William Wertenbaker, "Edgar A. Poe," Ingram's Poe Collection, Item 107; see also 92. Consult, alternatively, the piece in *Virginia University Magazine* or https://www.eapoe.org. Checking the university records myself (*Minutes of the General Faculty* and *Journals of the Chairmen of the Faculty*), I saw no evidence of censure of Edgar.
10. Wertenbaker, "Edgar A. Poe." See also Kenneth Walter Cameron, "Notes on Young Poe's Reading." A record of Edgar's fine of fifty-eight cents for an overdue library book was selected for Brendan Wolfe's *Mr. Jefferson's Telescope: A History of the University of Virginia in 100 Objects* (Charlottesville: University of Virginia Press, 2017), 28–29. The record of Edgar's six borrowings is available in *List of Books Borrowed 1825–1827,* Albert and Shirley Small Special Collections Library, University of Virginia, Charlottesville.
11. Sherley, "Edgar Allan Poe While a Student at the University of Virginia," 379. Notably, Edgar is reported to have been the secretary for the Jefferson Literary Society (H 1:60; Stovall, "Edgar Poe and the University of Virginia," 12).
12. Theodore Pease Stearns, "A Prohibitionist Shakes Dice with Poe," *Outlook* 126 (September–December 1920): 25–26.
13. Thomas Bolling to Edward V. Valentine, July 10, 1875, The Valentine (see also Edward V. Valentine to John H. Ingram, July 20, 1875, Ingram's Poe Collection, Item 239). For more on Poe's bookishness at the University of Virginia, see Kevin Hayes, *Poe and the Printed Word* (Cambridge, UK: Cambridge University Press, 2000), 8–16.
14. "Poe the Poet: Recollections of Two Citizens Who Knew Him Well," *Richmond State,* November 29, 1885, Ingram's Poe Collection, Item 855; Miles George to Edward V. Valentine, May 18, 1880, Ingram's Poe Collection, Item 351; and Miles George, "To the Editor of The State," *Richmond State,* May 22, 1880, Ingram's Poe Collection, Item 766. The letter to Valentine appears in "Poe at the University of Virginia: Unpublished Letters from the Ingram Collection."
15. Bolling to Valentine, July 10, 1875; Bolling to Ingram, July 20, 1875.
16. Douglass Sherley, extract from the "Oddity Papers," "Poe at the University," *Richmond State,* May 11, 1880, Ingram's Poe Collection, Item 765. See, alternatively, Sherley, "Edgar Allan Poe While a Student at the University of Virginia," "Old Oddity Papers IV—Concluded," *Virginia University Magazine* (April 1880): 426–45, also available at https://www.eapoe.org.
17. Miles George to Edward V. Valentine, Ingram Item 351; Miles George, "To the Editor of The State," Ingram Item 766. John Willis also remembered Poe's dorm room drawings (Sarah Helen Whitman to John H. Ingram, March 27, 1874, Ingram's Poe Collection, Item 137, included in John Carl Miller's *Poe's Helen Remembers* [Charlottesville: University Press of Virginia, 1979], 94). Poe and Hirst, or Poe alone, referred to his "covering the walls of his dormitory with crayon drawings, caricaturing the Faculty" (see Pollin, "Poe's Authorship," 164; Fisher, *Masques, Mysteries, and Mastodons,* 157; and Fisher, *Poe in His Own Time,* 25).

18. George to Valentine, Ingram's Poe Collection, Item 351; "Poe at the University of Virginia," 167; Bolling to Valentine and Valentine to Ingram's Poe Collection, Item 239; Wertenbaker, "Edgar A. Poe," Ingram's Poe Collection, Item 107.
19. Henry Tutwiler to John H. Ingram, December 3, 1875, Ingram's Poe Collection, Item 267. For Allan's sending Edgar at the university a copy of *Gil Blas*, see O 1:60. For Allan's negative comment on the book, see John Allan to Edgar Allan Poe, March 20 1827, in *Edgar Allan Poe Letters till Now Unpublished in the Valentine Museum Richmond, Virginia*, ed. Mary Stanard (Philadelphia: J. B. Lippincott, 1925), 67–70. For Poe's reading the first volume of *Gil Blas* under Professor Berard at West Point, see Melvin C. Helfers, "The Military Career of Edgar Allan Poe" (master's thesis, Duke University, 1949), 58.
20. For the relevant passage in *Gil Blas*, see *The Adventures of Gil Blas of Santillane. A New Translation by the Author of Roderick Random* [Tobias Smollett], 4 vols., 4th ed. (London: W. Strahan, 1773), 1:310. For the scholarly edition, see Alain René Le Sage, *The Adventures of Gil Blas of Santillane*, trans. by Tobias Smollett, ed. O. M. Brack Jr. and Leslie A. Chilton (Athens: University of Georgia Press, 2011), 147.
21. Wertenbaker, Ingram's Poe Collection, Item 92, Item 107. See also "Edgar A. Poe" in *Virginia University Magazine* and in Poe Society of Baltimore (https://www.eapoe.org).
22. George to Valentine, Ingram's Poe Collection, Item 351.
23. George E. Woodberry, *The Life of Edgar Allan Poe*, 2 vols. (Boston: Houghton Mifflin, 1909), 1:33. See also Douglass Sherley: "Poe at the University," Ingram's Poe Collection, Item 765, and "Edgar Allan Poe While a Student at the University of Virginia," "Old Oddity Papers IV—Concluded," *Virginia University Magazine* or Poe Society of Baltimore (https://www.eapoe.org).
24. Long to Ingram, Ingram's Poe Collection, Item 217. See also "Poe at the University of Virginia," *University of Virginia Alumni Bulletin* 16, no. 2 (April 1923): 164.
25. Sherley, "Poe at the University," Ingram's Poe Collection, Item 765. See, alternatively, Sherley's second piece on Poe at the university in the *Virginia University Magazine* or Poe Society of Baltimore (https://www.eapoe.org).
26. William Wertenbaker, Ingram's Poe Collection, Item 92, Item 107 (also Harrison's *New Glimpses of Poe*, 38); Tucker, "Poe at the University," Ingram's Poe Collection, Item 765; Sherley, "Edgar Allan Poe While at the University of Virginia," "Old Oddity Papers IV—Concluded," *Virginia University Magazine* (April 1880): 428, 430; William M. Burwell, "Edgar A. Poe and His College Contemporaries," *University of Virginia Alumni Bulletin* 16, no. 2 (April 1923): 169.
27. The account was originally published in the *Charlottesville Weekly Chronicle* of October 15, 1875, and is available online at https://tjrs.monticello.org/letter/38. It is mentioned in James A. Bear Jr., "The Last Few Days in the Life of Thomas Jefferson," *Magazine of Albemarle County* 32 (1974): 78; and Bowman and Santos, "Tales of Horror," 52.
28. See Kenneth Silverman, *Edgar A. Poe: Mournful and Never-ending Remembrance* (New York: HarperCollins, 1991), 35, 460. In his response to Edgar, Allan refers to his foster son's having "declared for your own Independence" (Stanard, *Edgar Allan Poe Letters till Now Unpublished*, 68).

29. In the 1843 *Saturday Museum* piece, Poe and Hirst—or Poe alone—made reference to the mountain walks that Poe took when he was in Charlottesville (see Pollin, "Poe's Authorship," 164; Fisher, *Masques, Mysteries, and Mastodons*, 157; or Fisher, *Poe in His Own Time*, 25).

30. See Dwight Thomas and David K. Jackson, *The Poe Log: A Documentary Life of Edgar Allan Poe, 1809–1849* (Boston: G. K. Hall, 1987), 72; and Lydia Sigourney, "Greece," *Central Gazette*, July 15, 1826, 1. For the corresponding lines in Poe's work, see M 1:65 ("Song") and 199 ("The Doomed City"). Writing in "A Reviewer Reviewed," Poe suggested a debt in "The City in the Sea" to Sigourney's "Musing Thoughts" (M 3:1385).

31. Spectator, "To the Editor of the Central Gazette," *Richmond Enquirer*, December 21, 1826. See also the university catalogue for 1826. It was thought that some of the students in the French class had secured the passages from which translation would be required, so the exam was delayed from December 5 to December 13. On the later date, the students were asked to translate "two short pieces of English" (*Minutes of the General Faculty 1825–1970*, 5).

32. See *Minutes of the General Faculty 1825–1970*, 2–3 (Latin) and 5–6 (French). There was one student above Poe's group in Latin, but no one above his group in French. For a slightly different report, see ["At a public examination"], *Richmond Enquirer*, December 27, 1826.

33. Regarding the clothing purchases, see "Mr. Edgar A. Powe [*sic*] / In Acct. With Samuel Leitch Jr. Dr.," December 4, [1826], Box 438, DLC-EA; and Thomas and Jackson, *The Poe Log*, 73. Regarding Poe's testifying, see Kent, "Poe's Student Days at the University of Virginia," 22. For the original record, see *Minutes of the General Faculty 1825–1970*, 13–15.

34. Wertenbaker, "Edgar A. Poe," Ingram's Poe Collection, Item 107; see also Item 92. As noted, the former piece is also available through *Virginia University Magazine* (November-December 1868): 114–17; and the Poe Society of Baltimore (https://www.eapoe.org). For the estimate of Poe's debt as $2,500, see T. H. Ellis in the *Richmond Standard* of May 7, 1881.

35. See "$1 in 1826 worth $31.09 today," https://www.officialdata.org/us/inflation/1826.

36. See Pollin, "Poe's Authorship" 164; Fisher, *Masques, Mysteries, and Mastodons*, 157; or Fisher, *Poe in His Own Time*, 25.

37. Flora Lapham Mack to William Lanier Washington, March 31, 1908, collection of the author.

38. See Ingram's Poe Collection, Item 107; and Thomas and Jackson, *The Poe Log*, 76.

39. Mack to Washington, March 31, 1908.

40. Ellis, *Richmond Standard*. In Poe's comic tale "The Business Man," the narrator writes that "my poor father put me, when I was about fifteen years of age, into the counting-house" (M 2:483).

41. Poe wrote to Allan on January 3, 1831, "Every day threatened with a warrant etc." (O 1:61). Among his other debts was one for $41.36 to Daniel S. Mosby and Company ("Edgar Allan Poe Note," The Valentine). Also at The Valentine are Bernard Peyton's letters to John Cochran and Company of Charlottesville regarding Poe's debts. And the Ellis & Allan Collection at the Library of

Congress includes Edward G. Crump's dunning letter of March 25, 1827. (See also Stanard, *Edgar Allan Poe Letters till Now Unpublished* 52; and Thomas and Jackson, *The Poe Log*, 78.)

42. See Whitty, "Memoir," in *The Complete Works of Edgar Allan Poe* (Boston: Houghton Mifflin, 1911), xxix–xxx. Mrs. Drew is mentioned in conjunction with Miss Jane Mackenzie—"Mrs. Drew and Miss MacKenzie have engaged a Lady to assist them" (in Socrates Maupin to Edgar Allan Poe, September 30, 1840, The Valentine). Thomas and Jackson refer to Drew as "an instructor in Miss Jane Mackenzie's school" (Thomas and Jackson, *The Poe Log*, 77). We do not know the name of the woman to whom Edgar wrote notes.

43. Edward V. Valentine to John H. Ingram, July 2, 1875, Ingram's Poe Collection, Item 236.

44. Frances K. Allan to John Allan, October 15–16, 1818, The Valentine.

45. "Mr. Reynolds," *Richmond Constitutional Whig*, March 2, 1827, 3. This piece may have been written by editor John Hampden Pleasants.

46. See, regarding the three additional lectures, "Card," *Richmond Enquirer*, March 3, 1827, 3. Reynolds later returned to the Virginia House of Delegates in January 1828 "to a crowded house of Members and Citizens" (Richard G. Woodbridge III, "J. N. Reynolds: Father of American Exploration," *Princeton University Library Chronicle* 45, no. 2 [1984]: 107–21, esp. 111).

47. "Stanzas on a View of the Sea," *Richmond Enquirer*, March 13, 1827, [4].

48. Stanard, *Edgar Allan Poe Letters till Now Unpublished*, 67–68.

49. "Edgar Allan Poe. Some Reminiscences of Him," *Cincinnati Daily Gazette*, January 12, 1869, 1, rpt. from *St. Louis Republican* (America's Historical Newspapers).

50. Woodberry, *The Life of Edgar Allan Poe*, 1:67.

51. See Pollin, "Poe's Authorship," 165; Fisher, *Masques, Mysteries, and Mastodons*, 157; and Fisher, *Poe in His Own Time*, 25. See also H 1:345.

52. Mack to Washington, March 23, 1908, collection of the author.

53. Stanard, *Edgar Allan Poe Letters till Now Unpublished*, 51–53.

54. Hervey Allen and Thomas O. Mabbott, *Poe's Brother: The Poems of William Henry Leonard Poe* (New York: George H. Doran, 1926), 91.

55. Mabbott earlier treated "To Margaret" in his edition of *Tamerlane* (Edgar Allan Poe, *Tamerlane and Other Poems,* reproduced in facsimile from the edition of 1827 with an introduction by Thomas Ollive Mabbott [New York: Facsimile Text Society, Columbia University Press, 1941], xvi–xvii). See also Mabbott's "Annals" (M 1:538–39). Mabbott includes, as well, "[To Octavia]" as canonical (*Tamerlane and Other Poems,* xiii–xiv; and M 1:16–17, 538–39), but it has since been shown to have been drawn from Horace Smith's "Song to Fanny" (Enrico Brandoli, "Two Stanzas for Octavia," *Edgar Allan Poe Review* 15, no. 2 [2014]: 247–49). Poe did not sign the poem in Walton's album. Brandoli notes that Smith's poem was then a popular song.

56. Peter Pindar Pease saw Poe in Boston in 1827 "one blustering March afternoon" (Stearns, "A Prohibitionist Shakes Dice with Poe," 25).

57. Marie Louise Shew Houghton to John H. Ingram, April 3, [1875], Ingram's Poe Collection, Item 35. See also John Carl Miller, ed., *Building Poe Biography* (Baton Rouge: Louisiana State University Press, 1977), 121.

6. "Abroad on the Wide Earth"

1. For the geography of Boston, I consult the "Plan of Boston—1828" in the Leventhal Center at the Boston Public Library. Also useful are *John Henry Stark's Antique Views of Boston,* ed. Theodore Thomte (Boston: Burdette, 1967); and Walter Muir Whitehill, *Boston: A Topographical History,* 2nd ed. (Cambridge: Belknap Press of Harvard University Press, 1973). Recent studies of Poe in Boston include Paul Lewis and Dan Currie, "The Raven in the Frog Pond: Edgar Allan Poe and the City of Boston," in *Born in the U.S.A.: Birth, Commemoration, and American Public Memory,* ed. Seth C. Bruggeman (Amherst: University of Massachusetts Press, 2012), 217–39; and Katherine J. Kim, "Poe and Boston," in *Poe and Place,* ed. Philip Edward Phillips (Cham, Switzerland: Palgrave Macmillan, 2018), 21–41. For the involvement of Charles Bulfinch in the design of several of the designated buildings, see Harold Kirker and James Kirker, *Bulfinch's Boston 1787–1817* (New York: Oxford University Press, 1964).
2. Theodore Pease Stearns, "A Prohibitionist Shakes Dice with Poe," *The Outlook: An Illustrated Weekly Journal of Current Events* 126 (September-December 1920): 125–26. Peter Pindar Pease apparently told the story to his nephew Judge Harlow Pease, who told it to his nephew Thomas Pease Stearns. T. O. Mabbott suggests that the "obscure paper" for which Poe worked (as a "market reporter") was P. P. F. De Grand's *Weekly Report* (Mabbott, introduction to *Tamerlane and Other Poems,* by Edgar Allan Poe, Publication no. 51 of The Facsimile Text Society [New York: Columbia University Press, 1941], xviii–xix and M 1:539).
3. For versions of the Greece/St. Petersburg story, see Poe's autobiographical memorandum to Rufus W. Griswold (H 1:345); Griswold's headnote concerning Poe in his *The Poets and Poetry of America* in *Poe in His Own Time,* ed. Benjamin F. Fisher (Iowa City: University of Iowa Press, 2010), 21; the Hirst/Poe (or solely Poe) biographical sketch in the *Saturday Museum* in Burton R. Pollin's "Poe's Authorship of Three Long Critical and Autobiographical Articles of 1843 Now Authenticated," *American Renaissance Literary Report: An Annual* 7 (1993): 139–71; Benjamin F. Fisher, ed., *Masques, Mysteries, and Mastodons: A Poe Miscellany* (Baltimore, MD: Edgar Allan Poe Society, 2006), 157; Fisher, ed., *Poe in His Own Time,* 25; and James Russell Lowell's biographical sketch of Poe (H 1:370).
4. Stearns, "A Prohibitionist Shakes Dice with Poe," 126.
5. Poe-Allan-Ellis Papers 1803–1881, MSC0033, The Valentine, Richmond, VA.
6. Arthur Hobson Quinn speculates on a possible performance: see *Edgar Allan Poe: A Critical Biography* (New York: D. Appleton-Century, 1941), 118–19. See also N. Bryllion Fagin, *The Histrionic Mr. Poe* (Baltimore, MD: Johns Hopkins Press, 1949), 37.
7. Walter K. Watkins, "An Historic Corner: Tremont Street and Temple Place," in *Days and Ways in Old Boston,* by William S. Rossiter (1915; Bedford, MA: W. E. Andrews, 1972), 91–132. See also news clippings and location notes at the Bostonian Society.
8. For a full treatment of Thomas, see Mabbott, introduction to *Tamerlane and Other Poems,* xx–xxx. Also of interest are Oscar Wegelin, "Poe's First Printer," *American Collector* 3, no. 1 (1926): 31; Oscar Wegelin, "The Printer of Poe's

Tamerlane," *New-York Historical Society Quarterly Bulletin* 24 (1940): 23–24; and Robert M. Davis, "The Quest for Calvin," *Poe Studies Association Newsletter* 16, no. 1 (1988): [8]. With regard to the nearby Washington Street offices, see Mary Elizabeth Phillips, *Edgar Allan Poe—The Man*, 2 vols. (Chicago: John C. Winston, 1926), 1:296–99. For the Broad Street location of enlistment, see A. Corbett Jr., "Edgar Allan Poe a Boston Boy," clipping at The Bostonian Society. For Robert P. and Charles Williams, see *The Boston Directory* (Boston: Hunt and Stimpson and John H. A. Frost, 1827), 285; for Jonathan P. Peaslee, see *Boston Directory*, 206.

9. George E. Woodberry, "Poe's Legendary Years," *Atlantic Monthly*, December 1884, 819; George E. Woodberry, *Edgar Allan Poe* (Boston: Houghton, Mifflin, 1885), 39.

10. For further information on Poe's joining the army, see Woodberry "Poe's Legendary Years" and his *Edgar Allan Poe*, as well as Quinn, *Edgar Allan Poe: A Critical Biography*, 119, 742–43. A valuable work regarding Poe's military career is William F. Hecker, introduction to *Private Perry and Mister Poe: The West Point Poems, 1831*, facsimile ed. (Baton Rouge: Louisiana State University Press, 2005), xvii–lxxv.

11. I rely here on both Carlisle Allan, "The Military Services of Edgar Allan Poe" (master's thesis, Columbia University, 1925), esp. 8–10, 12–14; and Melvin C. Helfers, "The Military Career of Edgar Allan Poe," (master's thesis, Duke University, 1949), esp. 14; as well as Hecker, introduction to *Private Perry and Mister Poe*, xxviii–xxxiii.

12. I consult here not only Mabbott's headnote in his edition but also his introduction to *Tamerlane and Other Poems*, by Edgar Allan Poe, v–lxvi. Mabbott estimated that two hundred copies of *Tamerlane* were printed (xxx). Notably, before Mabbott's introduction appeared, Charles F. Heartman and James R. Canny had estimated that forty copies were printed; after Mabbott's introduction appeared, they gave the figure as two hundred (Charles F. Heartman and James R. Canny, comps., *A Bibliography of First Printings of the Writings of Edgar Allan Poe* [Hattiesburg, MS: Book Farm, 1940], 14; *A Bibliography of First Printings of the Writings of Edgar Allan Poe*, rev. ed. [Hattiesburg, MS: Book Farm, 1943], 14). For the book's price, see Mabbott's 1941 introduction, xxxiii, xliv. The book is amply treated in the entry for Lot 213, *Fine Books and Manuscripts: Poe's Tamerlane* (New York: Sotheby's, 1988). See also *Evermore: The Persistence of Poe: The Edgar Allan Poe Collection of Susan Jaffe Tane* (New York: Grolier Club, 2014), 27–31, 156–57.

13. For the dates of composition, see Mabbott's introduction to *Tamerlane and Other Poems*, xlviii. For the comment on Poe and ambition, see Paul Lewis, "*Tamerlane and Other Poems*—Ambition," *Edgar Allan Poe in 20 Objects from the Susan Jaffe Tane Collection*, ed. Gabrielle Dean and Richard Kopley (Baltimore, MD: Johns Hopkins Sheridan Libraries, 2016), 48.

14. Flora Lapham Mack to William Lanier Washington, December 17, 1908, Poe Museum.

15. See also Mabbott's introduction to *Tamerlane and Other Poems*, lvii–lviii. The version of "To — —" in *Tamerlane and Other Poems* is reproduced on page 25. J. H. Whitty wrote that there was a copy of the 1826 *Saturday Evening Post* from

Ellis & Allan with Poe's notations (J. H. Whitty, ed., *The Complete Poems of Edgar Allan Poe* [Boston: Houghton Mifflin, 1911], 271).

16. The 1827 version of "Dreams" is reproduced in Mabbott, *Tamerlane and Other Poems,* 26–27. For Mabbott's comments, see lviii–lix.

17. See also Mabbott, introduction to *Tamerlane and Other Poems,* lix–lx. Consult, too, Killis Campbell, ed., *The Poems of Edgar Allan Poe* (New York: Ginn, 1917), 158–60; and Richard Wilbur, ed., *Poe* (New York: Dell, 1959), 120–21.

18. See Campbell, *The Poems of Edgar Allan Poe,* 160–61; and Mabbott, introduction to *Tamerlane and Other Poems,* lx; and M 1:73–74.

19. See Wilbur, *Poe,* 122. Mabbott summarizes Wilbur's reading (see M 1:76). For Mabbott's previous comments, see his introduction to *Tamerlane and Other Poems,* lxi–lxii. For an early acknowledgment of the Wordsworthian quality of the poem, see Campbell, *The Poems of Edgar Allan Poe,* 163.

20. For treatments of this work, see Campbell, *The Poems of Edgar Allan Poe,* 166; Mabbott, introduction to *Tamerlane and Other Poems,* lxii–lxiii; and M 1:79–80.

21. Mabbott originally thought "The happiest day—the happiest hour" to be about Elmira Royster (introduction to *Tamerlane and Other Poems,* lxiii) but later called into question this reading (1:80). Perhaps most perceptive is his stating, of lines 10 and 11, "A more general idea may be that Pride, renounced by the poet, may find another genius, equally unwise, to injure" (M 1:81n).

22. For considerations of "The Lake," see Campbell, *The Poems of Edgar Allan Poe,* 167–68; Mabbott, introduction to *Tamerlane and Other Poems,* lxiii–lxv; M 1:82–86; and Floyd Stovall, *Edgar Poe the Poet: Essays New and Old on the Man and His Work* (Charlottesville: University Press of Virginia, 1969), 206–7.

23. *Al Aaraaf by Edgar Allan Poe,* reproduced from the edition of 1829, with a bibliographical note by Thomas Ollive Mabbott (New York: Published for The Facsimile Text Society by Columbia University Press, 1933), 40.

24. For facsimiles of the two poems in the *North American,* see *Poe's Brother: The Poems of William Henry Leonard Poe,* by Hervey Allen and Thomas Ollive Mabbott (New York: George H. Doran, 1926), 43, 50; see also 78, 92. Mabbott suggested also that "some copies [of *Tamerlane*] reached friends in Virginia" (introduction to *Tamerlane and Other Poems,* xxxi–xxxii).

25. Allen and Mabbott, *Poe's Brother,* 30–31, 53–59, 78–79, 92. See also Mabbott, introduction to *Tamerlane and Other Poems,* xxxiv–xxxv. Lambert A. Wilmer, a friend of Poe and his brother, wrote a play titled *Merlin,* published in the *North American* of August 18, 25, and September 1, 1827, and this work adapted the story of Edgar and Elmira with Alphonse and Elmira, who are eventually happily reunited (see Allen and Mabbott, *Poe's Brother,* 79–80; Mabbott, introduction to *Tamerlane and Other Poems,* xxxv–xxxvi; and Thomas Ollive Mabbott, introduction to *Merlin Baltimore,1827, Together with Recollections of Edgar A. Poe,* by Lambert A. Wilmer, ed. Thomas Ollive Mabbott [1941; (Folcroft, PA): Folcroft Library Editions, 1973], v–xiii).

26. A contemporary periodical gave the history of the fort ("Fort Independence," *Juvenile Miscellany,* July 1827, 53–57). There is a story of a skeleton found behind a wall in the fort as a source for "The Cask of Amontillado," but Joel T. Headley's "A Man Built in a Wall" was the definitive, immediate source.

27. Richard Kopley, *The Threads of "The Scarlet Letter": A Study of Hawthorne's Transformative Art* (Newark: University of Delaware Press, 2003), 27–28, 128–29nn.
28. "Antarctic Expedition," *Columbian Centinel,* October 31, 1827, [3]; "Antarctic Expedition," *Boston Daily Advertiser,* November 1, 1827, [4]; "Antarctic Expedition," *Boston Traveller* (published as *American Traveller*), October 26, 1827, [2], and November 6, 1827, [2]. For a favorable editorial headnote and an extensive article by Reynolds, see "Antarctic Expedition" and "Communication Antarctic Expedition," *Columbian Centinel,* October 31, 1827, [1]. For comments on his lectures, see D., "Mr. Russell" ["Mr. Reynolds"], ibid., November 3, 1827, [2], and "Antarctic Expedition," ibid. November 10, 1827, [2]. Reynolds repeated his two lectures in Boston on November 10 and 13 (J. N. Reynolds, "A Card to the Citizens of Boston," ibid., November 10, 1827, [3]).
29. The First Regiment of the artillery switched with the Third Regiment to share the exposure to disease—especially malaria—more characteristic of the South. The order was made on October 12, 1827 (see "United States Artillery," *Columbian Centinel,* October 20, 1827, [2]; William L. Haskin, *The History of the First Regiment of Artillery* [Portland, ME: Thurston 1879], 41; Allan, "The Military Services of Edgar Allan Poe," 18–19; and Helfers, "The Military Career of Edgar Allan Poe," 20–21).
30. Flora Lapham Mack to William Lanier Washington, September 12, 1908, collection of the author.
31. See Marriage Bond of John H. Mackenzie, October 7, 1827, Petersburg City, Marriage Bonds and License, 1806–1822, Reel 109, Library of Virginia; "Family Record," Mackenzie Family Bible, Virginia Museum of History and Culture; and Jane Mackenzie Miller (Mrs. W. A. Miller) to J. H. Whitty, June 14, 1914, Harry Ransom Center, University of Texas at Austin. Louisa Lanier was born on June 16, 1808; she was therefore nineteen years old at the time of her marriage, and John H. Mackenzie was twenty-one. She was the daughter of William Sturtevant Lanier and Mary Simmons. John H. Mackenzie was then working as a clerk for the commercial firm of John and William Gilliat, in Richmond (see John H. Mackenzie, receipt for Charles Ellis, January 10, 1827, Box 254, and receipt for John Allan, June 16, 1827, Book 255, DLC-EA).
32. "Brig Waltham, Webb," *Columbian Centinel,* November 7, 1827, [2].
33. See "Ship News," *Charleston Courier,* November 19, 1827, [2]; H. W. Griswold, J. Howard, and James Mann, "A Card," *Charleston Courier,* November 20, 1827, [2]; H. C. Davis, "Poe's Stormy Voyage in 1827 Is Described," *Charleston News and Courier,* January 5, 1941, II, 3; and William Stanley Hoole, "Poe in Charleston, S.C.," *American Literature* 6, no. 1 (1934): 78–80.

7. "In the American Army"

1. Jim Stokeley, *Fort Moultrie Constant Defender* (Washington, DC: National Park Service, U.S. Department of the Interior, 1985), 30–31, 34.
2. H. W. Griswold, J. Howard, and James Mann, "A Card," *Charleston Courier,* November 20, 1827, 2 (America's Historical Newspapers).
3. Carlisle Allan, "The Military Services of Edgar Allan Poe" (master's thesis, Columbia University, 1925), 10.

4. For a thoughtful discussion of Poe and Sullivan's Island—and the island's having served in the eighteenth century as the landing place for imported enslaved people—see Liliane Weissberg, "Black, White, and Gold," in *Romancing the Shadow: Poe and Race,* ed. J. Gerald Kennedy and Liliane Weissberg (New York: Oxford University Press, 2001), 127–56.
5. Arthur Hobson Quinn, *Edgar Allan Poe: A Critical Biography* (New York: D. Appleton-Century, 1941), 129–30.
6. Robert Adger Law, "A Source for 'Annabel Lee,'" *Journal of English and Germanic Philology* 21, no. 2 (1922): 341–46.
7. Quinn, *Edgar Allan Poe: A Critical Biography,* 723–24.
8. For my earlier treatment of the March 22, 1811, scheduled performance of *Tekeli,* see "The Hidden Journey of *Arthur Gordon Pym,*" in *Studies in the American Renaissance 1982,* ed. Joel Myerson (Boston: Twayne, 1982), 29–51, esp. 43–44, 50–51; "The 'Very Profound Under-current' of *Arthur Gordon Pym,*" in *Studies in the American Renaissance 1987,* ed. Joel Myerson (Charlottesville: University Press of Virginia, 1987), 143–76, esp. 153, 169; and introduction to *The Narrative of Arthur Gordon Pym of Nantucket,* by Edgar Allan Poe (New York: Penguin, 1999), ix–xxix, esp. xxii, xxv–xxvi. See also my essay "Re-ordering Place in Poe's *Arthur Gordon Pym,*" in *Poe and Place,* ed. Philip Edward Phillips (Cham, Switzerland: Palgrave Macmillan, 2018), 193–213.
9. Thomas Bolling to Edward V. Valentine, July 10, 1875, Poe-Allan-Ellis Papers 1803–1881, MSC0033, The Valentine, Richmond, VA.
10. The manuscript of the excerpts, now held by the Poe Museum of Richmond, is discussed and presented in Burton R. Pollin, "Shakespeare in the Works of Edgar Allan Poe," in *Studies in the American Renaissance 1985,* ed. Joel Myerson (Charlottesville: University Press of Virginia, 1985), 181–86.
11. For this section on Poe as artificer, I rely on Carlisle Allan, "The Military Services of Edgar Allan Poe," 10–12; Melvin C. Helfers, "The Military Career of Edgar Allan Poe" (master's thesis, Duke University, 1949), 22–24; and William F. Hecker, introduction to *Private Perry and Mister Poe: The West Point Poems, 1831* (Baton Rouge: Louisiana State University Press, 2005), xxxiii–xxxv, esp. xxxiv.
12. "Fourth of July," *Charleston Courier,* July 7, 1828, 2 (America's Historical Newspapers).
13. See M. Foster Farley, *An Account of the History of Stranger's Fever in Charleston, 1699–1876* (Washington, DC: University Press of America, 1978), 86–88; and Samuel Henry Dickson, "Account of the Epidemic Which Prevailed in Charleston, etc. during the Summer of 1827," *American Journal of the Medical Sciences* 2, no. 3 (May 1828) (American Periodicals) (source for quoted symptoms). Dickson mentions the work on yellow fever by William Pym, the 1815 volume *Observations upon the Bulam Fever.* Poe wrote about yellow fever at the end of chapter 10 of *Pym* (P 1:126). For the parallels between this passage and the beginning of the "Note," see Kopley, "Hidden Journey," 44–46. It is possible that Poe was indebted for the last name of his eponymous protagonist to the same William Pym.
14. For mention of Samuel Leitch Jr.'s letter to Charles Ellis regarding Poe's debt for clothing, see Quinn, *Edgar Allan Poe: A Critical Biography,* 112, 112n. The original bill is in Book 438, DLC-EA. For the comment on Mrs. Allan's health, see Allan

to Ellis, September 7, 1828, Box 262, DLC-EA. For John H. Mackenzie and his wife Louisa's living at Mount Erin once they were married, I rely on Flora Lapham Mack to William Lanier Washington, March 23, 1908, collection of the author. Mack is incorrect in stating that the Mackenzies were married in 1829; they were actually married in 1827.

15. William Stanley Hoole, "Poe in Charleston, S.C.," *American Literature* 6, no. 1 (1934): 78–80; Helfers, "The Military Career of Edgar Allan Poe," 26, 27, 28. For information on Fortress Monroe, see John R. Weaver II, *A Legacy in Brick and Stone: American Coastal Defense Forts of the Third System, 1816–1867,* 2nd ed. (McLean, VA: Redoubt, 2018), 41, 58, 63, 165–66, 179–86.

16. Carlisle Allan, "The Military Services of Edgar Allan Poe," 5, 11–12, 14, 19; Dwight Thomas and David K. Jackson, *The Poe Log: A Documentary Life of Edgar Allan Poe 1809–1849* (Boston: G. K. Hall, 1987), 88; Hecker, introduction to *Private Perry and Mister Poe,* xli.

17. Hervey Allen, *Israfel; The Life and Times of Edgar Allan Poe,* 2 vols. (New York: George H. Doran, 1926), 1:230. Susan Archer Talley Weiss wrote a series of articles on Poe, as well as *The Home Life of Poe* (1907). For Poe and her uncle Robert Archer, see *The Home Life of Poe,* 52–53.

18. For Frances Allan's death by asthma, see Alyson L. Taylor-White, *Shockoe Hill Cemetery* (Charleston, SC: History Press, 2017), 37, 138.

19. For Frances Allan's epitaph, see ibid., 37–38. For the funeral's starting at Moldavia ("the late residence"), see Thomas and Jackson, *The Poe Log,* 89. For White's printing three hundred funeral tickets, see March 5, [1829], Cashbook 573 1824–1829, DLC-EA. For mention of the mourning clothes, see Killis Campbell, "New Notes on Poe's Early Years," *Dial* (February 17, 1916): 143–46; Mary Newton Stanard, *Edgar Allan Poe Letters till Now Unpublished* (Philadelphia: J. B. Lippincott, 1925), 97; and Thomas and Jackson, *The Poe Log,* 89. Sarah Helen Whitman wrote to John Henry Ingram in 1874 that "Poe spoke of the first Mrs. Allan with the tenderest affection" (John Carl Miller, ed., *Poe's Helen Remembers* [Charlottesville: University Press, of Virginia, 1979], 95).

20. Thomas H. Ellis to Charles Ellis, June 4, 1827, and Margaret K. Ellis to Charles Ellis, June 12, 1827, Box 255, DLC-EA.

21. See George E. Woodberry, "Poe's Legendary Years," *Atlantic Monthly* 54 (December 1884): 819–20; and Quinn, *Edgar Allan Poe: A Critical Biography,* 134–35. A reproduction of the letter is provided in Helfers, "The Military Career of Edgar Allan Poe," 29–30; and Kenneth Walter Cameron, "Young Poe and the Army—Victorian Editing," *American Transcendental Quarterly* 20 Supplement (1973): 155–56. I rely on the Cameron reproduction for quotations. Woodberry included material from "Poe's Legendary Years" in his *Edgar Allan Poe* (Boston: Houghton Mifflin, 1885) and *The Life of Edgar Allan Poe,* 2 vols. (Boston: Houghton, Mifflin, 1909).

22. Woodberry, "Poe's Legendary Years," 820. For the reproduction, see Helfers, "The Military Career of Edgar Allan Poe," 31.

23. Woodberry, "Poe's Legendary Years," 820; Carlisle Allan, "The Military Services of Edgar Allan Poe," 5; Quinn, *Edgar Allan Poe: A Critical Biography,* 742.

24. For House's characterization of the substitute, see Woodberry, "The Legendary Years," 820; Quinn, *Edgar Allan Poe,* 135; Helfers, "The Military Career of Edgar

Allan Poe," 30; and Cameron, "Young Poe and the Army," 156. I rely on the Cameron reproduction for the quotation. For the identification of the substitute, see Quinn, *Edgar Allan Poe: A Critical Biography*, 742.

25. Woodberry, "Poe's Legendary Years," 820; Helfers, "The Military Career of Edgar Allan Poe," 34–35; Cameron, "Young Poe and the Army," 158–59. I again rely on the Cameron reproduction for the quotations.

26. Woodberry, "Poe's Legendary Years," 820–21; Cameron, "Young Poe and the Army," 160–63, 166–67. See Cameron's reproductions for the quotations.

27. Woodberry, "Poe's Legendary Years," 821–22; Cameron, "Young Poe and the Army," 164–65. See Cameron's reproduction for the quotations. Floyd Stovall, commenting on Allan's restrained support of his foster son to the secretary of war, writes, "The tone of his letter was so cold and condescending that it would certainly have chilled the bearer [Poe] to the bone if he had seen it" (Stovall, *Edgar Poe the Poet: Essays New and Old on the Man and His Work* [Charlottesville: University Press of Virginia, 1969], 29).

28. John Allan to John H. Cocke, May 22, 1829, Papers of John H. Cocke, Box 59, MSS 640, Albert & Shirley Small Special Collections Library, University of Virginia, Charlottesville.

29. Woodberry, "Poe's Legendary Years," 821; Cameron, "Young Poe and the Army," 164–65. Consult Cameron's reproduction for quotations.

8. "Irrecoverably a Poet"

1. For President Adams's rubric for Baltimore, see John Dorsey and James D. Dilts, *A Guide to Baltimore Architecture* (Cambridge, MD: Tidewater, 1973), xx. Poe himself later used the term (O 1:339). For the Washington Monument's having had scaffolding, see J. H. B. Latrobe, "Reminiscences of Baltimore in 1824," *Maryland Historical Magazine* 1 (1906): 116; for its still not having been finished in August 1829, see "Baltimore's Centennial, 1829," *Maryland Historical Magazine* 24 (1929): 240. J. Thomas Scharf provides an excellent history of the monument in *History of Baltimore City and County* (1881; rpt., Baltimore, MD: Regional Publishing, 1971), 1:265–67. For early nineteenth-century views of Baltimore, see the 1831 T. Tanssen watercolor and the 1839 William H. Bartlett drawing in Mary Ellen Hayward and Frank F. Shivers Jr., *The Architecture of Baltimore: An Illustrated History* (Baltimore, MD: Johns Hopkins University Press, 2004), 100 and 68, respectively. See also 81–83 for discussion of the Washington Monument. Furthermore, Mary Newton Stanard provided an 1828 view of Baltimore in *Edgar Allan Poe Letters till Now Unpublished* (Philadelphia: J. B. Lippincott, 1925), facing 134.

2. For the Baltimore performances of David Poe Jr. and Elizabeth Arnold, see Arthur Hobson Quinn, *Edgar Allan Poe: A Critical Biography* (New York: D. Appleton-Century, 1941), 700–701, 703–5, 710. For church records of the Poe and Clemm families in Baltimore, see 725–26. For Poe's staying with his cousin, see Mary Elizabeth Phillips, *Edgar Allan Poe—The Man*, 2 vols. (Chicago: John C. Winston, 1926), 1:439; and M 1:541–42.

3. For Wirt's May 11, 1829, letter to Poe, see Stanard, *Edgar Allan Poe Letters till Now Unpublished*, 131–32.

4. Lea answered on May 27 (O 1:29), not returning the manuscript.
5. For mention of Poe's meeting Gwynn, see H 1:73; and George E. Woodberry, *The Life of Edgar Allan Poe,* 2 vols. (Boston: Houghton Mifflin, 1909), 1:55. The extracts of "Al Aaraaf" appearing in the *Baltimore Gazette and Daily Advertiser* are presented in Kenneth Rede, "Poe Notes: From an Investigator's Notebook," *American Literature* 5, no. 1 (1933): 51–53.
6. Stanard, *Edgar Allan Poe Letters till Now Unpublished,* 126, 135, 140.
7. The major early study of "Alone," which elaborates the presence of Byron's "Manfred," is Irby B. Cauthen Jr., "Poe's *Alone:* Its Background, Source, and Manuscript," *Studies in Bibliography* 3 (1950/1951): 284–91. Also helpful are M 1:145–47; and W. T. Bandy, *"Poe's* Alone: *The First Printing,"* Papers of the Bibliographical Society of America 70 (1976): 405–6. It is relevant to note that Poe compares his introductory sonnet for "Al Aaraaf" to Byron's introductory sonnet for "The Prisoner of Chillon" (O 1:27). Richard Wilbur rightly observes a resonance between "Alone" and Poe's short story "The Imp of the Perverse" (Wilbur, ed., *Poe* [New York: Dell, 1959], 132–33). Significantly, at some time in 1829, Poe also wrote in the album of Lucy Holmes three stanzas by his brother Henry (M 1:518–19).
8. Flora Lapham Mack states that Thomas G. Mackenzie planned to write a Poe biography, that John H. Mackenzie gave him all his Poe-related "letters & papers," and that "all his [Thomas's] Poe papers & pictures and the manuscript of his book already prepared" were destroyed in the Evacuation Fire of April 1865 (Mack, "Concerning Correspondence between Edgar Allen [*sic*] Poe & John H. Mackenzie," collection of the author). William Mackenzie's death at fifty-seven in Norfolk on June 7, 1829, is reported in "Died," *Richmond Enquirer,* June 12, 1829, 3. This paragraph was taken from the *Norfolk Beacon.* See also Dwight Thomas and David K. Jackson, *The Poe Log: A Documentary Life of Edgar Allan Poe, 1809–1849* (Boston: G. K. Hall, 1987), 94–95. Mack's explanation for William Mackenzie's death is in Mack [for William Lanier Washington], "Suggestions for the Third Chapter—Poe's Early Married Days"; John H. Mackenzie's explanation is in Mack, notes to Washington, "Mr. Mackenzie moved from his old home," collection of the author. For the naming of John and Louisa's baby boy, I draw on Flora Lapham Mack to William Lanier Washington, March 23, 1908, and March 31, 1908, collection of the author. For an alternative name, Edgar Allan Mackenzie, I consult Mack to Lanier, February 29, 1908, collection of the author.
9. An excellent book on Neal is Benjamin Lease's *That Wild Fellow John Neal and the American Literary Revolution* (Chicago: University of Chicago Press, 1972). See especially "The Long Visit—Poe and Other Discoveries," 123–36.
10. For Neal's first notice of Poe, see I. M. Walker, *Edgar Allan Poe: The Critical Heritage* (London: Routledge & Kegan Paul, 1986), 66–67.
11. Ibid., 67–68.
12. "Baltimore's Centennial, 1829," 241–45; Annie Leakin Sioussat, *Old Baltimore* (New York: Macmillan, 1931), 224; Robert I. Vexler, comp. and ed., *Baltimore: A Chronological & Documentary History, 1632–1970* (Dobbs Ferry, NY: Oceana, 1975), 32.
13. Thomas and Jackson, *The Poe Log,* 99.

14. See John C. Miller, "Did Edgar Allan Poe Really Sell a Slave?," *Poe Studies* 9, no. 2 (1976): 52–53. See also May Garrettson Evans, "When Edgar Allan Poe Sold a Slave," *Baltimore Evening Sun*, April 6, 1940, 4. For a facsimile of the letter of conveyance, see J. Gerald Kennedy, "'Trust No Man': Poe, Douglass, and the Culture of Slavery," in *Romancing the Shadow: Poe and Race*, ed. Kennedy and Liliane Weissberg (New York: Oxford University Press, 2001), 235.
15. For Poe and "average racism," see Terence Whalen, "Average Racism: Poe, Slavery, and the Wages of Literary Nationalism," in *Edgar Allan Poe and the Masses: The Political Economy of Literature in Antebellum America* (Princeton, NJ: Princeton University Press, 1999), 111–46.
16. For the date of the completion of the Washington Monument, see Scharf, *History of Baltimore City and County*, 1:266; and Vexler, *Baltimore: A Chronological & Documentary History, 1632–1970*, 32. The date of publication of *Al Aaraaf* is determined by Poe's having written a letter to John Neal to accompany the book on December 29 (O 1:52–53).
17. For the Saint-Pierre source, see Palmer C. Holt, "Notes on Poe's *To Science, To Helen*, and *Ulalume*," *Bulletin of the New York Public Library* 63 (1959): 568; and M 1:90. The fuller context is presented in George Monteiro, "Edgar Poe and the New Knowledge," *Southern Literary Journal* 4, no. 2 (1972): 37. In quoting from *Al Aaraaf, Tamerlane, and Minor Poems*, I rely on Poe's *Al Aaraaf*, with a bibliographical note by Thomas Ollive Mabbott (New York: Published for The Facsimile Text Society by Columbia University Press, 1933).
18. Poe, 1933 facsimile edition of *Al Aaraaf, Tamerlane, and Minor Poems*, [11]. For an alternative view of "To Science," according to which Poe is potentially sympathetic to science, see John Tresch, *The Reason for the Darkness of the Night: Edgar Allan Poe and the Forging of American Science* (New York: Farrar, Straus and Giroux, 2021), 47–49.
19. Poe, 1933 facsimile edition of *Al Aaraaf, Tamerlane, and Minor Poems*, 18, 14, 18, 21.
20. Ibid., 29, 34.
21. Ibid., 34n, 33.
22. Ibid., 14, 17, 15.
23. The fullest treatment of the complexities of "Al Aaraaf" is Floyd Stovall, "An Interpretation of 'Al Aaraaf,'" in *Edgar Poe the Poet: Essays New and Old on the Man and His Work* (Charlottesville: University Press of Virginia, 1969), 102–25. Poe did write to Isaac Lea about "Al Aaraaf," "I have imagined some well known characters of the age of the star's appearance, as transferred to Al Aaraaf—viz Michael Angelo—and others—of these Michael Angelo as yet, alone appears" (O 1:27). He then writes of sending three parts and withholding the fourth part. Quinn concludes that some part of the poem is missing; Mabbott argues that the additional part was never written (M 1:97). Eric Martin suggests that the first part is actually the opening sonnet (Martin, "'Al Aaraaf': A Poem in Three Parts," *Edgar Allan Poe Review* 10, no. 1 [2009]: 44–49).
24. Poe, 1933 facsimile edition of *Al Aaraaf, Tamerlane, and Minor Poems*, [7], [41].
25. Walker, *Edgar Allan Poe: The Critical Heritage*, 391–92.
26. Poe, 1933 facsimile edition of *Al Aaraaf, Tamerlane, and Minor Poems*, [57].

27. For the argument that the latter poem concerns Elmira Royster, see Killis Campbell, ed., *The Poems of Edgar Allan Poe* (Boston: Ginn, 1917), 194–95.
28. See M 1:142; and Stovall, "Poe as a Poet of Ideas," *Edgar Poe the Poet*, 178.
29. Walker, *Edgar Allan Poe: The Critical Heritage*, 69; [Edgar A. Poe and Henry B. Hirst (or solely Poe)], "Poets and Poetry of Philadelphia," in *Poe in His Own Time*, ed. Benjamin F. Fisher (Iowa City: University of Iowa Press, 2010), 35–36. See also Burton R. Pollin, "Poe's Authorship of Three Long Critical and Autobiographical Articles of 1843 Now Authenticated," *American Renaissance Literary Report: An Annual* 7 (1993): 166–67; and Benjamin F. Fisher, "An Early Biography of Poe (1843): The *Philadelphia Saturday Museum* Sketch," in *Masques, Mysteries, and Mastodons: A Poe Miscellany*, ed. Fisher (Baltimore, MD: Edgar Allan Poe Society, 2006), 171–72.
30. See Walker, *Edgar Allan Poe: The Critical Heritage*, 70.
31. Quinn, *Edgar Allan Poe: A Critical Biography*, 165.
32. See Walker, *Edgar Allan Poe: The Critical Heritage*, 72–74. For a satirical poem touching on Poe at this time, see Floyd Stovall, "Poe and 'The Musiad,'" in *Edgar Poe the Poet*, 64–101. Stovall thought the poem to be by Poe, but Mabbott disagreed (M 1: 505, 541).
33. See "The Herring Al Aaraaf," in *The Raven and Other Poems*, by Edgar Allan Poe, ed. Thomas Ollive Mabbott (New York: Published for The Facsimile Text Society by Columbia University Press, 1942), xxiii–xxv. See M 1:577 for mention of the Herring copy and the Neal copy.
34. Mabbott notes two versions of the Milford Bard story (M 1:501–2) (see William F. Gill, *The Life of Edgar Allan Poe* [New York: C. T. Dillingham, 1877], 46–50; and Phillips, *Edgar Allan Poe—The Man*, 1:457–61).
35. Thomas Bolling to Edward V. Valentine, July 10, 1875, The Valentine, Richmond, VA.
36. Thomas and Jackson, *The Poe Log*, 104.
37. When Poe was in Richmond in 1830, Allan bought him gloves, hose, and blankets (Quinn, *Edgar Allan Poe: A Critical Biography* 166n1).
38. Flora Lapham Mack to William Lanier Washington, March 31, 1908, collection of the author.
39. Mack [for Washington], "Suggestions for the Second Chapter—The Break with the Allans," collection of the author.
40. See Quinn, *Edgar Allan Poe: A Critical Biography*, 168–69.
41. Mack [for Washington], "Suggestions for the Second Chapter—The Break with the Allans," collection of the author.
42. See Kenneth Walter Cameron, "Young Poe and the Army—Victorian Editing," *American Transcendental Quarterly*, 20 Supplement Part Four (1973): 168, 170; Thomas and Jackson, *The Poe Log*, 104–5.
43. For William Galt Jr.'s two marriages, see Anne Waller Reddy and Andrew Lewis Riffe IV, comps., *Richmond City, Virginia Marriage Bonds, 1797–1853* (Baltimore, MD: Genealogical Publishing, 1976), 36, 43. The wedding to Taylor was on Tuesday, February 2, 1830.
44. See receipts, Charles Ellis to [Jane] Mackenzie, March 1 and August 1 1830; Charles Ellis to Margaret K. Ellis, March 25, 1830; and Margaret K. Ellis to Charles Ellis, March 30, 1830, Box 269, DLC-EA.

45. For the history of Duncan Lodge, which Poe would visit in 1848 and 1849, see Mary Wingfield Scott, *Houses of Old Richmond* (Richmond, VA: The Valentine, 1941), 215–17.

46. For information on Mount Erin, see "James Alexander Fulton of Mount Erin," https://www.brooklynmuseum.org/opencollection/objects/30367; Samuel Mordecai, *Richmond in By-Gone Days* (republished from the second edition of 1860; Richmond, VA: Dietz, 1946), 294–95; E. Raleigh Phillips, Title Book, 50–63, Virginia Museum of History and Culture; Phillips-Hargrove Family Papers 1873–1945, Personal Papers Collection, Manuscripts Division, Library of Virginia; Edward V. Valentine, "Landing Near C. & O. Wharf of Present Day, Belief of Historical Society Head: Old 'Mt. Erin,' on Location of Powhatan's Town, in All Probability, He Believes," *Richmond News-Leader*, December 29, 1924. The house burned down in 1868. For my brief earlier comments on Mount Erin, see "Mining the Manuscripts: Library Hosts Virginia Humanities Fellow, *Broadside: The Magazine of the Library of Virginia*, no. 1 (2018): 15. For the Fulton setting of Mount Erin, I draw on Flora Lapham Mack to William Lanier Washington, March 23, 1908, collection of the author. For Louisa Mackenzie's comment on naming her baby, I refer to Mack to William Lanier Washington, March 31, 1908, collection of the author. More on Mount Erin and on John and Louisa's son is offered in these two letters and Mack to Washington, February 25, 1908; there is also Mack [for Washington], "Suggestions for the Second Chapter—The Break with the Allans," collection of the author. There is evidence to suggest that John H. Mackenzie had been working at the Richmond post office (see receipts, John H. Mackenzie to Charles Ellis, December 31, 1829, and January 1, 1830, Box 268, DLC-EA).

47. For a dramatic early instance of the states' rights schism, which was covered in the newspapers, see Ted Widmer, *Martin Van Buren* (New York: Henry Holt, 2005), 81–82; and Jon Meacham, *American Lion: Andrew Jackson in the White House* (New York: Random House, 2009), 135–37.

48. For the *Richmond Enquirer*'s reprinting of pieces on the White murder, see "Daring Assassination" [from the *Boston Bulletin*], April 20, 1830, [3], and "The Murder" [from the *Salem Gazette*], May 18, 1830, [4]. For that newspaper's squib on the *Seraph* and *Annawan* [from the *U.S. Telegraph*], see ["We learn that the American discovery brigs"], May 14, 1830, [3].

49. For more on the voyage of the *Seraph*, *Annawan*, and *Penguin*, see William Stanton, *The Great United States Exploring Expedition of 1838–1842* (Berkeley: University of California Press, 1975), 26–28.

50. John Allan to Henry Poe, November 1, 1824, Box 438, DLC-EA.

9. "I Am a Cadet"

1. George E. Woodberry, *The Life of Edgar Allan Poe*, 2 vols. (Boston: Houghton Mifflin, 1909), 1:67; Eugene L. Didier, *The Poe Cult and Other Poe Papers* (New York: Broadway, 1909), 226. For a sketch of Nathan C. Brooks, see John H. Hewitt, *Shadows on the Wall or Glimpses of the Past, A Retrospect of the Past Fifty Years* (Baltimore, MD: Turnbull, 1877), 47–48.

2. I draw from Roswell Park's *A Sketch of the History and Topography of West Point and the U.S. Military Academy* (Philadelphia: Henry Perkins, 1840), available online. See esp. 14, 36, 49, 58–59, 72, 76, and 89–90. For the quoted passage, see 52.
3. For early mention of Hitchcock and Ross, see Park, *A Sketch of the History and Topography of West Point,* 81, 83. Discussion of the relationship of Poe and Hitchcock is offered in Melvin C. Helfers, "The Military Career of Edgar Allan Poe" (master's thesis, Duke University, 1949), 64–65. The date of Poe's formal admission to West Point is given in Order No. 82, U.S.M.A., June 25, 1830, *Post Orders U.S. Military Academy 1827–1832,* 5:446 (Archives of the West Point Library); see also *Cadets Admitted to the U.S.M.A.* (Archives of the West Point Library). For detail on the encampment, see Park, *A Sketch of the History and Topography of West Point,* 102–4; Carlisle Allan, "The Military Services of Edgar Allan Poe" (master's thesis, Columbia University, 1925), 21–24; and Helfers, "The Military Career of Edgar Allan Poe," 54–56. Information on the July Fourth celebration at West Point in 1830 is provided in B[attalion]. O[rders], no. 55, July 3, 1830, *Post Orders U.S. Military Academy 1827–1832,* 5: 451–43 (Archives of the West Point Library). For the July Fourth celebration and the masquerade ball at the encampment's end, see Karl E. Oelke, "Poe at West Point—A Revaluation," *Poe Studies* 6, no.1 (1973): 1–2; see also Park, *A Sketch of the History and Topography of West Point,* 104. The $4.25 withheld from a cadet's account is listed in "Statement of Payment for July & August 1830 & September & October 1830" (Archives of the West Point Library). I have consulted "A Map of West Point by Cadet W. Chapman" from 1830 (Archives of the West Point Library), as well as Park's consideration of the relevant locations (Park, *A Sketch of the History and Topography of West Point,* 112–14).
4. Both men left memoirs of Poe's time at West Point (see Thomas W. Gibson, "Poe at West Point," *Harper's New Monthly Magazine,* November 1867, 754–56, available also in H 1:85–94 and at https://www.eapoe.org; and Timothy Pickering Jones, *New York Sun,* May 10, 1903, and May 29, 1904, available in Woodberry, *The Life of Edgar Allan Poe,* 1:369–72). A complete version of the last piece is "At West Point with Poe," *New York Sun,* May 29, 1904, Poe file (Archives of the West Point Library). John H. Ingram contended that Poe did not share a room with Gibson but rather with John E. Henderson (Ingram, "The True Story of Edgar Allan Poe," transcribed and edited by John C. Miller, 1954–55, University of Virginia Library, 122). See also Carlisle Allan, "The Military Services of Edgar Allan Poe," 24–29. Neither Gibson nor Jones fared well at West Point (see ibid.; and Helfers, "The Military Career of Edgar Allan Poe," 57). For the original documents on Jones, see B.O. No 91, September 15, 1830; Order No 130, October 26, 1830; "Trial of Cadet Timothy P. Jones," November 13, 1830; and [Statement of Dismissal], November 15, 1830, *Post Orders U.S. Military Academy 1827–1832,* 5:480, 495 (Archives of the West Point Library).
5. John H. B. Latrobe, *Reminiscences of West Point for September, 1818 to Mar., 1882* (East Lansing, MI: Evening News, 1887), 4; Albert E. Church, *Personal Reminiscences of the Military Academy from 1824 to 1831* (West Point, NY: USMA Press, 1879), 22.
6. "Distribution of Studies, and Employment of Time, during the Day," in *General Regulations for the Army; or, Military Institutes* (Washington, DC: Davis &

Force, 1825), 389–90; "Distribution of Studies and Employment of Time during the Day," in *Regulations of the U.S. Military Academy of West Point* (New York: J. and J. Harper, 1832). See also Park, *A Sketch of the History and Topography of West Point,* 104–7.

7. [Edgar A. Poe and Henry B. Hirst (or Poe alone)], From "Poets and Poetry of Philadelphia," in *Poe in His Own Time,* ed. Benjamin F. Fisher (Iowa City: University of Iowa Press, 2010), 26; Woodberry, *The Life of Edgar Allan Poe,* 1:370. There is a contrary opinion, that Poe was not a serious student at West Point: Thomas W. Gibson wrote, "The Studies of the Academy Poe utterly ignored" (754). However, this seems at odds with other views, with Poe's background as a student, and with his academic success at West Point. Poe's paraphrase of a line from the first volume of *Gil Blas*—a volume he had known well and which was assigned in his West Point French class—in his third and last letter to John Allan from West Point also argues against Gibson's judgment. Perhaps the variety of opinion reflects the diminishing of Poe's academic focus over time.

8. Woodberry, *The Life of Edgar Allan Poe,* 1:370; "At West Point with Poe."

9. Arthur Hobson Quinn, *Edgar Allan Poe: A Critical Biography* (New York: D. Appleton-Century, 1941), 171.

10. Richard Henry Stoddard, "Edgar Allan Poe," *Harper's Monthly Magazine,* September 1872, 561n; see also https://www.eapoe.org.

11. See A. B. Magruder's comment, Woodberry, *The Life of Edgar Allan Poe,* 1:70. Magruder also recalled, "He was an accomplished French scholar."

12. For Poe's shyness and sensitivity, see Gibson, "Poe at West Point," 754; Woodberry, *The Life of Edgar Allan Poe,* 1:70; and Didier, *The Poe Cult and Other Poe Papers,* 253–54. See also Woodberry, *The Life of Edgar Allan Poe,* 1:370 ("a victim to the blues"); and Gibson, "Poe at West Point," 754 ("a worn, weary, discontented look"). This last phrase may owe a debt to Poe's "weary, way-worn wanderer" in the poem "To Helen," soon to be discussed.

13. Woodberry, *The Life of Edgar Allan Poe,* 1:70 ("great fault"); Evert A. Duyckinck and George L. Duyckinck, eds., *Cyclopædia of American Literature,* 2 vols. (New York: Charles Scribner, 1855), 2:537n ("visionary expedition"). See also Didier, *The Poe Cult and Other Poe Papers,* 253–54.

14. "At West Point with Poe."

15. Woodberry, *The Life of Edgar Allan Poe,* 1:70 ("devourer of books"); Gibson, "Poe at West Point," 754, 756 (critical judgments).

16. Gibson, "Poe at West Point," 755; Stoddard, "Edgar Allan Poe," 561n; Woodberry, *The Life of Edgar Allan Poe,* 1:370–71; "At West Point with Poe."

17. For more on this tavern, see Robert J. Wood, "Early Days of Benny Havens," *The Pointer,* February 26, 1937, 6–[13]. Jones discusses it in Woodberry, *The Life of Edgar Allan Poe,* 1:370–71; and "At West Point with Poe." See also Church, *Personal Reminiscences of the Military Academy,* 10, 19, 23.

18. Gibson, "Poe at West Point," 755–56.

19. Mary E. Phillips, *Edgar Allan Poe—The Man,* 2 vols. (Chicago: John C. Winston, 1926), 1:383–84; Latrobe, *Reminiscences of West Point,* 19–20; Church, *Personal Reminiscences of the Military Academy,* 71, 83–84. Phillips credits Lardon Bell

with the discovery that "Old K" was Kinsley. For another mention of Kinsley at West Point, see Park, *A Sketch of the History and Topography of West Point*, 84.

20. I have earlier made mention of this in "Re-ordering Place in Poe's *Arthur Gordon Pym*," in *Poe and Place*, ed. Philip Edward Phillips (Cham, Switzerland: Palgrave Macmillan, 2018), 201.

21. ["Science! meet daughter of Old Time thou art!"] appeared in September in Philadelphia's *Saturday Evening Post* and in October in the *Casket* as "Sonnet" (see Charles F. Heartman and James R. Canny, comps., *A Bibliography of First Printings of The Writings of Edgar Allan Poe*, rev. ed. [Hattiesburg, MS: Book Farm, 1943], 23, 170, 246; and M 1:90).

22. Flora Lapham Mack to William Lanier Washington, March 23, 1908, collection of the author. I estimate the timing of the baby's death based on Mack's stating that Poe's 1831 visit to Mount Erin—which I consider to have been in late February—was "about that time." Also relevant are Mack to Washington, February 19, 1908, and March 31, 1908, collection of the author.

23. Flora Lapham Mack, "Notes on Washington's Chapters," collection of the author; Mrs. William A. Miller (Jane Mackenzie Byrd Miller), statement of family genealogy for J. H. Whitty, June 16, 1914, Poe Miscellany, Harry Ransom Center, University of Texas at Austin.

24. "Merit Roll of the 4th Class—Mathematics" and "Merit Roll of the 4th Class—French," January 9, 1831, *Post Orders U.S. Military Academy 1827–1832*, vol. 5; "Cadets Arranged in Order of Merit, in Their Respective Classes, as Determined at the General Examination in January 1831," *Register of Merit 1817 to 1835*, no. 1, U.S. Military Academy (Archives of the West Point Library). See also Carlisle Allan, "The Military Services of Edgar Allan Poe," 36.

25. Poe's later, often unreliable, memorandum to Rufus Wilmot Griswold, though perhaps mixing chronology by first blaming the second Mrs. Allan for a precipitating argument, nonetheless accurately stated that Allan "wrote me an angry letter, to which I replied in the same spirit" (H 1:345). For a facsimile of Poe's furious response, see Mary Newton Stanard, *Edgar Allan Poe Letters till Now Unpublished* (Philadelphia: J. B. Lippincott, 1925), [259–62]. The claim that Poe had left West Point on hearing of the birth of a son to Allan's second wife seems a fabrication since Allan had married her in October (see James Russell Lowell, "Edgar Allan Poe," in *The Recognition of Edgar Allan Poe*, ed. Eric W. Carlson [Ann Arbor: University of Michigan Press, 1966], 7; and [Poe/Hirst (or Poe alone)], "From 'Poets and Poetry of Philadelphia,'" 26). Furthermore, John Allan Jr., the first child of John Allan and his second wife, was born on August 23, 1831 (Dwight Thomas and David K. Jackson, *The Poe Log: A Documentary Life of Edgar Allan Poe, 1809–1849* [Boston: G. K. Hall, 1987], 122).

26. Mack to Washington, March 31, 1908, collection of the author. Poe's letter to Mackenzie has not been found; it was probably destroyed in Richmond's Evacuation Fire of April 1865.

27. Military Academy, Engineer Department, Order No 7, February 8, 1831, in *Post Orders U.S. Military Academy 1827–1832* (Archives of the U.S.M.A.).

For treatment of this court-martial, see Carlisle Allan, "The Military Services of Edgar Allan Poe," 36–37. Poe's delayed dismissal on March 6 allowed Poe to earn more pay (Helfers, "The Military Career of Edgar Allan Poe," 71).

28. B.O. No 17, West Point, February 18, 1831 ("released from arrest"); Order No 14 U.S. Military Academy, February 20, 1831 ("name...will be dropped"). Both documents appear in *Post Orders U. S. Military Academy 1827–1832*, Archives of the West Point Library.

29. The arch features four lines from Poe's 1848 poem "To Helen [Whitman]" (M 1:446, lines 44–47).

30. "At West Point with Poe" (Jones); John Carl Miller, ed., *Building Poe Biography* (Baton Rouge: Louisiana State University Press, 1977), 47 (Clemm); John Carl Miller, ed., *Poe's Helen Remembers* (Charlottesville: University Press of Virginia, 1979), 454 (Whitman).

31. Susan Archer Weiss, *The Home Life of Poe* (New York: Broadway, 1907), 55–56.

32. For Jones's comment, see "At West Point with Poe"; and Woodberry, *The Life of Edgar Allan Poe*, 1:372.

33. "At West Point with Poe."

34. Weiss, *The Home Life of Poe*, 58–62; Woodberry, "Poe's Legendary Years," *Atlantic Monthly*, December 1884, 824 (https://www.eapoe.org); Woodberry, *The Life of Edgar Allan Poe*, 1:85, 95–96.

35. Theodore Pease Stearns, "A Prohibitionist Shakes Dice with Poe," *Outlook*, September 1, 1920, 25–26; https://www.eapoe.org.

36. Mary Wingfield Scott, *Houses of Old Richmond* (Richmond, VA: The Valentine, 1941), 215–17.

37. Mack to Washington, March 31, 1908, collection of the author. According to Mack, Louisa Mackenzie said that she had "always liked Edgar very much indeed," "but that she was glad when he decided to leave the city, because she was afraid of his influence on her brother [William Lewis Lanier]."

38. Nathaniel Holmes Morison to John H. Ingram, November 27, 1874, John Henry Ingram's Poe Collection, Albert & Shirley Small Special Collections Library, University of Virginia, Charlottesville, Item 184.

39. Weiss, *The Home Life of Poe*, 58–60. There is a specious version of this incident to which Rufus Wilmot Griswold later referred (Fisher, Griswold's "Memoir," in *Poe in His Own Time*, 113, 152).

40. Mack to Washington, March 23, 1908, collection of the author.

41. Mack [for Washington], "Suggestions for the Second Chapter—The Break with the Allans" / "Suggestions for the Third Chapter—Poe's Early Married Days," collection of the author.

42. See chapter 8, note 46—especially the E. Raleigh Phillips Title Book 50–63 at the Virginia Museum of History and Culture and the Phillips-Hargrove Family Papers 1873–1945 in the Personal Papers Collection of the Manuscripts Division of the Library of Virginia.

43. Mack [for Washington], "Suggestions for the Third Chapter—Poe's Early Married Days," collection of the author.

44. Stearns, "A Prohibitionist Shakes Dice with Poe."

45. A. B. Magruder wrote about Elam Bliss and *Poems*, "I think the publisher came up from New York and bargained with Poe for its publication" (Woodberry, *The Life of Edgar Allan Poe*, 1:78).
46. I rely on the facsimile edition of the 1831 volume. See either Edgar Allan Poe, *Poems*, reproduced from the edition of 1831, with a bibliographical note by Killis Campbell (New York: Published for The Facsimile Text Society for Columbia University Press, 1936); or the facsimile edition as appearing in *Private Perry and Mister Poe: The West Point Poems, 1831*, ed. William F. Hecker (Baton Rouge: Louisiana State University Press, 2005); or https://www.eapoe.org. Stuart and Susan Levine rely in *Critical Theory: The Major Documents* primarily on the slightly revised 1836 essay, appearing in the *Southern Literary Messenger*, appending the earlier variants, as well. The Levines' introduction and notes are excellent (see L2 1–19). For a relatively recent discussion of Poe's *Poems* and West Point, see Gina Claywell, "'A Worn, Weary, Discontented Look': The Influence of West Point and the Hudson River Valley on Poe," *Edgar Allan Poe Review* 19, no. 2 (2018): 141–48.
47. Timothy Pickering Jones claimed that "the major portion of this intervening time [that between the court-martial and Poe's departure] was utilized by Poe in writing poetry, the greater portion of which was printed in book form, dedicated to the United States Corps of Cadets." Jones does get wrong the date of the court-martial (here, January) and the date of Poe's departure (here, March 6) (see "At West Point with Poe." From January 23 to February 18, 1831, Poe was "in arrest").
48. Stoddard, "Edgar Allan Poe," 561n.
49. For the passages compared, see Floyd Stovall, "Poe's Debt to Coleridge," in *Edgar Poe the Poet: Essays New and Old on the Man and His Work* (Charlottesville: University Press of Virginia, 1969), 139 (see also L2 18–19).
50. See one of the facsimile editions of *Poems*, 21. The passage is not changed in Poe's 1836 light revision of the piece (L2 8).
51. See one of the facsimile editions of *Poems*, 39.
52. Sarah Helen Whitman, *Edgar Poe and His Critics* (New York: Rudd & Carleton, 1860), 49.
53. See one of the facsimile editions of *Poems*, 45; or M 1:174–75.
54. See one of the facsimile editions of *Poems*, 45; or M 1:174–75.
55. See one of the facsimile editions of *Poems*, 51; or M 1:200.
56. See the already cited poem "Greece," *Central Gazette*, July 15, 1826, 1.
57. Killis Campbell, ed., *The Poems of Edgar Allan Poe* (Boston: Ginn, 1917), 211.
58. Whitman, *Edgar Poe and His Critics*, 48. For a possible linking of "A Paean" with Jane Stith Stanard or Frances Allan, see M 1:207. For the passage from "Irene," see one of the facsimile editions of *Poems*, 62; or M 1:184. For the passage from "A Paean," see one of the facsimile editions of *Poems*, 68; or M 1:206.
59. For West Point's settlement with Poe, see "To Cash Received from Col. S. Thayer on account of the following Cadets the same being paid them on Settlement of their accounts during the months January & February 1831," March 16, 1831, [Cash Received] (Archives of the West Point Library). For the listing of cadet's subscriptions for Poe's *Poems*, see "Statement of Payment for March & April 1831," *Statement of Payments December 1828 to December 1833 Treasurer's Office U.S. Military*

Academy (Archives of the West Point Library). The check to "Mr. Edgar A. Poe," signed by Thos J. Leslie, is in the Archives of the West Point Library.

60. Woodberry, *The Life of Edgar Allan Poe,* 1:78; Gibson, "Poe at West Point," 755; Stoddard, "Edgar Allan Poe," 561n.
61. Notice in the *New-York Mirror,* May 7, 1831, in Walker, *Edgar Allan Poe: The Critical Heritage,* 75; Anonymous, [Review of *Poems of E. A. Poe*], *New-York American, for the Country,* May 6, 1831 (https://www.eapoe.org). Jeffrey Savoye credits Ton Fafianie with the discovery of this latter early review. For Poe's hope for the poems, see one of the facsimile editions of *Poems,* 13–14; and L2 12.
62. Lot 935, *The Stephen Wakeman Collection of Books of Nineteenth Century American Writers* (New York: American Art Association, [1924]).
63. [John Neal], Notice of *Poems, Morning Courier and New York Enquirer,* in *Edgar Allan Poe: The Critical Heritage,* ed. I. M. Walker (London: Routledge & Kegan Paul, 1986), 76.
64. Woodberry, *The Life of Edgar Allan Poe,* 1:89; Stanard, *Edgar Allan Poe Letters till Now Unpublished,* 277.
65. Flora Lapham Mack [for William Lanier Washington], "Suggestions for the Third Chapter—Poe's Early Married Days," collection of the author.
66. See Woodberry, *The Life of Edgar Allan Poe,* 1:375; Quinn, *Edgar Allan Poe: A Critical Biography,* 188.

10. "I Am Poor"

1. John Carl Miller, *Building Poe Biography* (Baton Rouge: Louisiana State University Press, 1977), 22. For identification of and commentary on the recipient of Maria Clemm's begging letter, see David K. Jackson, "The Identity of Maria Clemm's Friend, the Judge," *Poe Studies* 12, no. 1 (1979): 40.
2. For an early consideration of Poe's family, see George E. Woodberry, *The Life of Edgar Allan Poe,* 2 vols. (Boston: Houghton Mifflin, 1909), 1:86–87, 374–76. For Maria Clemm's doing "sewing, dress-making, or some similar work," see Augustus Van Cleef, "Poe's Mary," *Harper's New Monthly Magazine,* March 1889, 635. Susan Archer Weiss states that when Poe joined Maria Clemm's household in 1831, he was "ill—really ill" (Weiss, *The Home Life of Poe* [New York: Broadway, 1907], 64). The comment on Henry as "a dashing gay cavalier" was made by Marie Louise Shew Houghton, who had spoken with Poe about his brother (Miller, *Building Poe Biography,* 129).
3. W[illiam]. H[enry]. P[oe], "Monte Video," in Hervey Allen and Thomas Ollive Mabbott, *Poe's Brother: The Poems of William Henry Leonard Poe* (New York: George H. Doran, 1926), 46.
4. For a thoughtful discussion of Henry and Edgar and of Henry's publications in the *Baltimore North American,* see Allen and Mabbott, *Poe's Brother.*
5. [John Hill Hewitt], "William Henry Poe," Papers of Edgar Allan Poe 1826–1955, Box 1, Folder 4, Albert and Shirley Small Special Collections Library, University of Virginia, Charlottesville. Frank Luther Mott notes that Hewitt became editor of the *Baltimore Minerva* in 1830—see *A History of American Magazines 1741–1850* (Cambridge, MA: Harvard University Press, 1938), 380n. Another

associated with the *Baltimore Minerva* was Francis B. Davidge (John E. Reilly, *John Henry Ingram's Poe Collection at the University of Virginia*, 2nd ed. [Charlottesville: University of Virginia Library, 1994], 61).

6. Allen and Mabbott, *Poe's Brother*, 35.
7. Mukhtar Ali Isani, "Reminiscences of Poe by an Employee of the *Broadway Journal*," *Poe Studies* 6, no. 2 (1973): 33. See also the subsequent piece, "A Further Word on Poe and Alexander Crane," *Poe Studies* 7, no. 2 (1974): 40.
8. See Allen and Mabbott, *Poe's Brother*, 35; and "William Henry Poe."
9. Allen and Mabbott, *Poe's Brother*, 35. See also Mary Elizabeth Phillips, *Edgar Allan Poe—The Man*, 2 vols. (Chicago: John C. Winston, 1926), 1:430.
10. See Killis Campbell, "Gleanings in the Bibliography of Poe," *Modern Language Notes* 32, no. 5 (May 1917): 270–71; and M 2:5–6. For Henry's poems in the *Saturday Evening Post*, see Allen and Mabbott, *Poe's Brother*, 71–74. For the opposing view, that "A Dream" is not by Poe, see Burton R. Pollin, *Word Index to Poe's Fiction* (New York: Gordian, 1982), ix.
11. For background on McMichael, see John Wien Forney, *Memorial Address upon the Character and Public Services of Morton McMichael* (Philadelphia: Sherman, 1879); *Appleton's Cyclopaedia of American Biography; Biographical Dictionary of America;* Albert Mordell, *In Re Morton McMichael* (n.p.: privately printed, 1921); and *Dictionary of American Biography*. For information on Poe and the *Saturday Courier*, see John Grier Varner, *Edgar Allan Poe and the Philadelphia "Saturday Courier"* (Charlottesville: University of Virginia, 1933), esp. the introduction, iii–ix. See also Dwight Thomas and David K. Jackson, *The Poe Log: A Documentary Life of Edgar Allan Poe, 1809–1849* (Boston: G. K. Hall, 1987), 120–22; and Leon Jackson, *The Business of Letters: Authorial Economies in Antebellum America* (Stanford, CA: Stanford University Press, 2008), 220–21.
12. For my discussion of "Tales of the Folio Club," I rely primarily on the fine work of Alexander Hammond, including "A Reconstruction of Poe's 1833 *Tales of the Folio Club:* Preliminary Notes," *Poe Studies* 5, no. 2 (1972): 25–32; "Poe's 'Lionizing' and the Design of *Tales of the Folio Club*," *ESQ* 18 (1972): 154–65; "Further Notes on Poe's Folio Club Tales," *Poe Studies* 8, no. 2 (1975): 38–42; "Edgar Allan Poe's *Tales of the Folio Club:* The Evolution of a Lost Book," *University of Pennsylvania Library Chronicle* 41 (1976): 13–43, reprinted in *Poe at Work: Seven Textual Studies*, ed. Benjamin Franklin Fisher IV (Baltimore, MD: Edgar Allan Poe Society, 1978): 13–43; "Consumption, Exchange, and the Literary Marketplace: From the Folio Club Tales to *Pym*," in *Poe's Pym: Critical Explorations*, ed. Richard Kopley (Durham, NC: Duke University Press, 1992), 153–66, 314–15; "Literary Commerce and the Discourses of Gastronomy in Poe's 'Bon-Bon,'" *Poe Studies* 39–40 (2006–7): 38–45; "The Folio Club Collection and the Silver Fork School," *Edgar Allan Poe Review* 19, no. 2 (2018): 153–76; and "Early Experiments in Genre: Imitations, Burlesques, Satires," in *The Oxford Handbook of Edgar Allan Poe*, ed. J. Gerald Kennedy and Scott Peeples (New York: Oxford University Press, 2019), 139–56.
13. See Mary Newton Stanard, *Edgar Allan Poe Letters till Now Unpublished* (Philadelphia: J. B. Lippincott, 1925), 295; and Thomas and Jackson, *The Poe Log*, 123.
14. Varner, *Edgar Allan Poe and the Philadelphia "Saturday Courier,"* iii–iv, 6.

15. Ibid., 9–24. For the section on Lady Mary, see ibid., 11–12.
16. See Hammond: "A Reconstruction of Poe's 1833 *Tales of the Folio Club*," 29; "Edgar Allan Poe's *Tales of the Folio Club*," 22; and "Early Experiments in Genre," 142. For a relatively recent overview of the Delphian Club, see Jeffrey A. Savoye, "Poe and Baltimore: Crossroads and Redemption," in *Poe and Place*, ed. Philip Edward Phillips (Cham, Switzerland: Palgrave Macmillan, 2018), 104. The definitive early study is John Earle Uhler's "The Delphian Club: A Contribution to the Literary History of Baltimore in the Early Nineteenth Century," *Maryland Historical Magazine* 20, no. 4 (1925): 305–46.
17. For information on Wilmer and Poe, I rely in part on Wilmer's "Recollections of Edgar A. Poe," reprinted in Thomas Ollive Mabbott's edition of *Merlin Baltimore 1827* (1941; n.p. [Folcroft, PA]: Folcroft Library Editions, 1973), 29–34. See also Wilmer, *Our Press Gang* (Philadelphia: J. T. Lloyd, 1859), 23–29, 35–36, 39–40, 284–85, 385; Killis Campbell, "New Notes on Poe's Early Years," *Dial* 60 (February 17, 1916): 145–46; and "Lambert A. Wilmer," in Dwight Thomas's "Poe in Philadelphia, 1838–1844: A Documentary Record" (PhD diss., University of Pennsylvania, 1978), 2:942–44. For Wilmer's tribute, "Ode XXX.—To Edgar A. Poe," see Thomas, "Poe in Philadelphia, 1838–1844," 1:18–19.
18. Wilmer, "Recollections," 29–32.
19. For the text of "The Duke de L'Omelette" in the *Philadelphia Saturday Courier*, I rely on Varner, *Edgar Allan Poe and the Philadelphia "Saturday Courier*," 25–31. The critical studies I rely on are Kenneth L. Daughrity, "Poe's Quiz on Willis," *American Literature* 5, no. 1 (1933): 55–62; Ruth Leigh Hudson, "Poe and Disraeli," *American Literature* 8, no. 4 (1937): 402–16; and David H. Hirsch, "Another Source for Poe's 'The Duc de L'Omelette,'" *American Literature* 38, no. 4 (1967): 532–36, and "'The Duc De L'Omelette' as Anti-Visionary Tale," *Poe Studies* 10, no. 2 (1977): 36–39. The consumption of ortolans is depicted in the 2023 film *The Taste of Things*.
20. See Hammond: "A Reconstruction," 30; "Edgar Allan Poe's *Tales of the Folio Club*," 23; and "Early Experiments in Genre," 142.
21. Margaret K. Ellis to Charles Ellis, April 8, 1832, Box 281, DLC-EA ("confined to his room"); George William Hundley to Charles Ellis, April 20, 1832 Box 281, DLC-EA ("quite unwell"); Hervey Allen, *Israfel: The Life and Times of Edgar Allan Poe* (New York: Farrar & Rinehart, 1934), 684; Thomas and Jackson, *The Poe Log*, 126 (Allan's property and will); Charles Ellis to James N. Ellis, March 23, 1832, Box 280, DLC-EA ("change your room"); Charles Ellis to James N. Ellis, April 25, 1832, Box 281, DLC-EA (bank-shares); James N. Ellis to Charles Ellis, May 12, 1832, Box 282, DLC-EA (appreciation); Phillips, *Edgar Allan Poe—The Man*, 2:1496–97; Allen, *Israfel*, 267 (bookstore and oyster house); Weiss, *The Home Life of Poe*, 66–67 ("Bard").
22. For the tale's source in *Zillah*, see James Southall Wilson, "The Devil Was in It," *American Mercury* 24 (1931): 218; and M 2:41–42. For the tale's connection to Jewish history and the Talmud, see J. G. Varner, "Poe's *Tale of Jerusalem* and *The Talmud*," *American Book Collector* 6 (1935): 56–57. For the *Saturday Courier* version of the tale, see Varner, *Edgar Allan Poe and the Philadelphia "Saturday Courier*," 32–37.

23. T. O. Mabbott considered "A Tale of Jerusalem" to be a Folio Club tale; he originally thought it might have been by "Mr. Snap, the President" or Chronologos Chronology in "On Poe's 'Tales of the Folio Club,'" *Sewanee Review* 36 (1928): 175–76. He later assigned it definitively to Chronologos Chronology (M 2:42). James Southall Wilson also treated "A Tale of Jerusalem" as a Folio Club tale and believed it to have been written by Chronologos Chronology ("The Devil Was in It," 218). Alexander Hammond, on the other hand, has omitted "A Tale of Jerusalem" from the Folio Club tales, assigning to Chronologos Chronology instead "Epimanes" (see Hammond: "A Reconstruction," 31–32; and "Edgar Allan Poe's 'Tales of the Folio Club,'" 18, 19, 23). Hammond argues that "A Tale of Jerusalem" might have initially been a Folio Club tale but that it was superseded by "Epimanes," perhaps because the second tale relied on a later work by Horace Smith (Hammond, "Poe's 'Tales of the Folio Club,'" 24; Hammond, "Further Notes," 40).

24. For Poe and Kate Bleakley, see Phillips, *Edgar Allan Poe—The Man*, 1:421, 423. For Poe and Elizabeth Herring, see Woodberry, *The Life of Edgar Allan Poe*, 1:89–90; J. H. Whitty, ed., *The Complete Poems of Edgar Allan Poe* (Boston: Houghton Mifflin, 1911), xxxvi; and Phillips, *Edgar Allan Poe—The Man*, 1:423–26.

25. Van Cleef, "Poe's Mary," 634–40. Thomas and Jackson term the recollections "authentic but exaggerated" (Thomas and Jackson, *The Poe Log*, xliii). T. O. Mabbott relates that Mary's granddaughter said that the essay by Mary's nephew "was basically true but probably overcolored" (M 1:232).

26. Van Cleef. For Mary's street as Exeter Street rather than Essex Street, see May Garrettson Evans, "Poe in Amity Street," *Maryland Historical Magazine* 36 (1941): 377.

27. "Editorial in the Baltimore *Saturday Visiter*," in *Edgar Allan Poe: The Critical Heritage*, ed. I. M. Walker (London: Routledge & Kegan Paul), 77.

28. For Wilmer's account of his expulsion from the *Saturday Visiter* and his lawsuit, see *Our Press Gang*, 23–30. The suit was begun on August 10, 1832, according to Killis Campbell, "New Notes on Poe's Early Years," *Dial* 60 (February 17, 1916): 145. For Poe's later suggesting to Wilmer their co-editing an elite monthly magazine, see *Our Press Gang*, 35–36. Sandra Tomc discusses Wilmer in *Industry & the Creative Mind: The Eccentric Writer in American Literature and Entertainment, 1790–1860* (Ann Arbor: University of Michigan Press, 2012), 110–13.

29. For the time of cholera in Baltimore, see Robert I. Vexler, comp. and ed., *Baltimore: A Chronological & Documentary History 1632–1970* (Dobbs Ferry, NY: Oceana, 1975), 34. For Allan's comments on the cholera, see John Allan to Charles Ellis, August 10, 1832, Box 282, DLC-EA. George Whitlock soon wrote to Ellis, "It is with deep regret that I discover that the Cholera has beyond all doubt broken out in Richmond and that it is raging with violence" (Whitlock to Ellis, September 20, 1832, Box 283, DLC-EA). For Burling's death, see Phillips, *Edgar Allan Poe—The Man*, 1:440; 2:1083; and Thomas and Jackson, *The Poe Log*, 127.

30. The *Saturday Courier* tale "A Decided Loss" is available in both Varner, *Edgar Allan Poe and the Philadelphia "Saturday Courier"* 38–49; and Mabbott 2:52–59. For commentary, see Hammond: "A Reconstruction," 29–30; "Further Notes," 38–39; "Edgar Allan Poe's *Tales of the Folio Club*," 22; and "Early Experiments in

Genre," 142; as well as Hirsch, "'The Duc De L'Omelette,'" 36. For discussions of Poe and the *Blackwood's* tale, see Margaret Alterton, "Origins of Poe's Critical Theory," *University of Iowa Humanistic Studies* 2, no. 3 (1925): 7–45; and Michael Allen, *Poe and the British Magazine Tradition* (New York: Oxford University Press, 1969), 19–39.

31. The text of "The Bargain Lost" is available in both Varner, *Edgar Allan Poe and The Philadelphia "Saturday Courier,"* 50–63; and M 2:85–94. For an analysis of Poe's revision of "The Bargain Lost" to "Bon-Bon," see James W. Christie, "Poe's 'Diabolical' Humor: Revisions in 'Bon-Bon,'" in *Poe at Work: Seven Textual Studies,* ed. Benjamin Franklin Fisher IV (Baltimore, MD: Edgar Allan Poe Society, 1978), 44–55. For identification of the pseudonymous author of "Bon-Bon," see Hammond: "A Reconstruction," 27–28; "Edgar Allan Poe's *Tales of the Folio Club,*" 22; and "Early Experiments in Genre," 141. The earliest identification of the author is offered by T. O. Mabbott in "On Poe's 'Tales of the Folio Club,'" 175.

32. For commentary on the soul in these stories, see Hirsch, "'The Duc De L'Omelette' as Anti-Visionary Tale," 36.

33. Regarding Poe's writing to John H. Mackenzie from Baltimore, I rely on Flora Lapham Mack [for William Lanier Washington], "Suggestions for the Third Chapter—Poe's Early Married Days," collection of the author. Mack elsewhere explains that John H. Mackenzie's letters from Poe, given to brother Thomas Mackenzie for his prospective biography, were destroyed in the Richmond Evacuation Fire of 1865. I consult "Concerning Correspondence between Edgar Allan Poe and John H. Mackenzie," collection of the author. For Mack's recounting of the Mackenzies' trip west, I rely on Mack to Washington, April 2, 1908, collection of the author. For Allan's listing of debts, see "Arrivals that require attention & collection Feby 1833 [perhaps February 27 or 28]," Box 286, DLC-EA.

34. Burton R. Pollin, "Shakespeare in the Works of Edgar Allan Poe," in *Studies in the American Renaissance 1985,* ed. Joel Myerson (Charlottesville: University Press of Virginia, 1985), 157–86.

35. For a full study, see May Garrettson Evans, "Poe in Amity Street," *Maryland Historical Magazine* 36 (1941): 363–80.

36. I draw on letters from Flora Lapham Mack to William Lanier Washington, February 29, and March 23, 1908, collection of the author. In a letter from Mack to Washington of March 31, 1908, she refers to her mother and three sisters. The dates of the deaths of Robert Mattox and Susan (or Suzanna) Simmons are available at https://www.ancestry.com.

37. Flora Lapham Mack, genealogy, and letters throughout, collection of the author.

38. Thomas H. Ellis, extracts from "A paper prepared for Mrs. Margaret K. Ellis, in the 85th year of her age, from old letters in the possession of her son, T. H. E.—1875," Poe-Allan-Ellis Papers, 1803–1881, MSC0033, The Valentine, Richmond, VA.

39. For early treatment of these poems, see John C. French, "Poe and the Baltimore Saturday Visiter," *Modern Language Notes* 35 (1918): 264–67.

40. The location of the manuscript of the earliest version of "To One in Paradise" is not known, but Mabbott notes that the text of that version was published in the London *Spectator* in 1853 (M 1:213). For the early text, appearing in a false accusation of plagiarism, see "Letter to The Editor. American Plagiarism: Poe and

Tennyson," *The Spectator* [of London], January 1, 1853, 5. As Mabbott observes, Tennyson countered this on January 22, 1853.

41. "Book Table—The American Periodical Press—Magazines for March, etc," *New-York Magazine,* March 30, 1833, 310–11.
42. It is understandable if this submission did not get significant attention because Edwin Buckingham had tuberculosis and soon died (O 1:78). It is of note that in 1807 Joseph T. Buckingham had criticized the performances of Poe's parents, but most likely Poe did not know this.
43. See William Whipple, "Poe's Political Satire," *University of Texas Studies in English* 35 (1956): 83–84. The political convention that nominated Jackson for a second term met in Baltimore on May 21, 1832. As a second-term president, he visited Baltimore in June 1833 (Vexler, *Baltimore: A Chronological & Documentary History, 1632–1970,* 33, 34). (Worthy of mention, in light of Whipple's reference to Peggy Eaton, is that her husband had been Jackson's secretary of war, John H. Eaton, whom Poe had visited in Washington in 1829 to inquire about his possible cadetship. This was the same man after whom West Point's "Camp Eaton" was named. His wife's questionable reputation had forced Jackson to let his secretary of war resign in 1831.) Mabbott offers a later version of Poe's tale, with the 1833 variants. For photographs of Poe's original hand-printing of the tale, see *Evermore: The Persistence of Poe—The Edgar Allan Poe Collection of Susan Jaffe Tane* (New York: Grolier Club, 2014), 37–40.
44. Hammond: "A Reconstruction," 31–32, and "Edgar Allan Poe's *Tales of the Folio Club*," 23. As noted earlier, "Epimanes" replaced the earlier "A Tale of Jerusalem" in "Tales of the Folio Club."
45. See Thomas H. Ellis to Charles Ellis, May 6, 1833, Box 288, DLC-EA ("No No!"); John Allan to Charles Ellis, August 4, 1823, Box 241, DLC-EA ("boasting"); [John Allan], "[A]ccounts that may be pressed for pay," June 1833, Box 288, DLC-EA ("[$]4.63"); John Allan to Charles Ellis, July 27, 1833, Box 289, DLC-EA.
46. French, "Poe and the *Baltimore Saturday Visiter,*" 259–60.
47. Van Cleef, *Poe's Mary,* 637–38; Wilmer, "Recollections of Edgar A. Poe," 30.
48. Van Cleef, *Poe's Mary,* 638–40. For the comment on horsewhipping, see Bowman and Santos, *Rot, Riot, and Rebellion: Mr. Jefferson's Struggle to Save the University That Changed America* (Charlottesville: University of Virginia Press, 2013), 10.
49. We are fortunate to have two accounts by Latrobe of the judging of the contest (Jay B. Hubbell, "Charles Chauncey Burr: Friend of Poe," *PMLA* 69, no. 4 [1954]: 837–39; and John H. B. Latrobe, "Reminiscences of Poe by John H. B. Latrobe," in Sara Sigourney Rice, *Edgar Allan Poe: A Memorial Volume* [Baltimore, MD: Turnbull Brothers, 1877], 57–62). For the inclusion of "Lionizing" and "The Visionary" among the submitted tales, see [Thomas W. White], "To Readers and Correspondents," *Southern Literary Messenger* (August 1835): 716.
50. Latrobe, "Reminiscences of Poe," 60; see also Hubbell, "Charles Chauncey Burr," 838; and French, "Poe and the *Baltimore Saturday Visiter,*" 258–61. Although Latrobe states that the envelope for the poem "The Song of the Winds" indicated the author to be John H. Hewitt, Hewitt later corrected Latrobe, stating that the envelope gave the name "Henry Wilton." I have accepted Hewitt's correction (Hewitt, *Recollections of Poe,* ed. Richard Barksdale Harwell [Atlanta, GA: The

Library, Emory University, 1949], 18). Poe received the fifty dollars; Hewitt chose to receive a silver goblet. Hewitt published Poe's "The Coliseum" and his own "The Song of the Wind," to his disadvantage (John H. Hewitt, *Shadows on the Wall or Glimpses of the Past, a Retrospect of the Past Fifty Years* [Baltimore, MD: Turnbull Brothers, 1877], 154–59; Hewitt, *Recollections of Poe*, 25–28).

51. French, "Poe and the *Baltimore Saturday Visiter*," 260–61. The announcement of the results of the contest are given also in Arthur Hobson Quinn, *Edgar Allan Poe: A Critical Biography* (New York: D. Appleton-Century, 1941), 202–3; and Thomas and Jackson, *The Poe Log*, 132–33.

52. Hewitt, *Recollections of Poe*, 18.

53. Reviewing Captain Frederick Marryat's *The Phantom Ship* in the June 1839 issue of *Burton's Gentleman's Magazine*, Poe writes, "The old legend of the Flying Dutchman is one possessing all the rich *materiel* which a vigorous imagination could desire" (M 2:132). For an early assertion of Poe's authorship of the review, see William Doyle Hull II, "A Canon of the Critical Works of Edgar Allan Poe with a Study of Poe as Editor and Reviewer" (PhD diss. University of Virginia, 1941), [223–24].

54. I cite the later version of the text offered by Mabbott, but including the one *Saturday Visiter* variant ("operations"). The source for this passage is a passage concerning a gallows and a beheaded man appearing on a tarred sail in Sir David Brewster's *Letters on Natural Magic* (Burton R. Pollin, "'MS. Found in a Bottle' and Sir David Brewster's *Letters*: A Source," *Poe Studies* 15, no. 2 [1982]: 40–41).

55. I substitute the *Saturday Visiter* "shrieking" for the later "thundering" (see M 2:146v).

56. See Hammond, "A Reconstruction," 28–29. See also Hammond: "Edgar Allan Poe's *Tales of the Folio Club*," 22; and "Early Experiments in Genre," 142. For *Symzonia*, see J. O. Bailey, "An Early American Utopian Fiction," *American Literature* 14, no. 3 (1942): 285–93. For the Trelawney source, see George H. Soule Jr., "Another Source for Poe: Trelawney's *The Adventures of a Younger Son*," *Poe Studies* 8, no. 2 (1975): 35–37. A work that anticipates Poe's later "A Descent into the Maelström" anticipates, as well, the end of "MS. Found in a Bottle" (see David E. E. Sloane, "A Forerunner of 'A Descent into the Maelström,'" *Edgar Allan Poe Review* 21, no. 1 [2020]: 119).

57. I rely especially on Latrobe, "Reminiscences of Poe," 60–61. See also Hubbell, "Charles Chauncey Burr," 839. For Kennedy's journal entry from November 2, see Killis Campbell, "The Kennedy Papers (Second Article)," *Sewanee Review* 25, no. 2 (1917): 197.

58. Latrobe, "Reminiscences of Poe," 61. Pollin uses the Griswold text; for the relevant passage, see P 1:421–22. Though Latrobe's 1875 account has been questioned (William H. Gravely Jr., "A Note on the Composition of Poe's 'Hans Pfaall,'" *Poe Newsletter* 3, no. 1 [1970]: 2–5), I consider it reliable. Notably, Latrobe offered essentially the same account in 1852 (Hubbell, "Charles Chauncey Burr," 839). I accept as inevitable the occasional error in his accounts. And I accept the idea of a long period for the genesis of the work. At the time of his visiting Latrobe and telling the story of "Hans Pfaall," October 1833, "he [Poe] proposed to put [it] upon paper" (Hubbell, "Charles Chauncey Burr," 839). His later recollection of

the writing, six months before the June 1835 *Messenger* publication (H 15:127–28), does not seem to me to challenge seriously Latrobe's twice-recalled detailed recollection of Poe's storytelling. Latrobe's 1852 recollection is included in *The Poe Log* (132).

59. For the account of Poe's meeting Hewitt in the street, see Hewitt, "Reminiscences," 19. For Hewitt's expressed hostility to Poe, see both Hewitt's *Shadows on the Wall*, 40–43, 154–59; and his "Reminiscences," 10, 12–13, 17–21.

60. Lord Byron, *Manfred, The Major Works,* ed. Jerome J. McGann (New York: Oxford University Press, 2008), 310; "The Coliseum," *New-York Mirror,* July 28, 1832, [25]. The Fourth Canto of Byron's *Childe Harold's Pilgrimage,* from 1818, is less positive about the Coliseum (Byron, *Childe Harold's Pilgrimage, The Major Works,* 188–90). For Mabbott's comments, see M 1:226.

61. I rely on Mabbott's version of "The Coliseum," inserting appropriate variants for the earliest version (M 1:228–30).

62. Hammond, "Edgar Allan Poe's *Tales of the Folio Club,*" 26.

63. French, "Poe and the *Baltimore Saturday Visiter,*" 262; Hammond, "Edgar Allan Poe's *Tales of the Folio Club,*" 26–27.

64. John Allan to Charles Ellis, November 9, 1833, Box 290, DLC-EA; Allan to Ellis, December 16, 1833, Box 291, DLC-EA.

65. I rely on *The Lady's Book* version of the tale, available in Benjamin Franklin Fisher IV's "To 'The Assignation' from 'The Visionary' [Part One] and Poe's Decade of Revising," *Library Chronicle* 39 (1973): 90–100. For the response of the marchesa, see 93.

66. Fisher, "To 'The Assignation' from 'The Visionary' [Part One]," 97–98. For the text of the now-lost, circa 1833 manuscript of "To One in Paradise," mentioned by Mabbott (M 1:213, 214), see the false accusation of plagiarism, "Letter to the Editor: American Plagiarism: Poe and Tennyson," *Spectator* [of London], January 1, 1853, 5. As Mabbott notes, Tennyson countered this on January 22, 1853.

67. Fisher, "To 'The Assignation' from 'The Visionary' [Part One]," 100.

68. Ibid., 93.

69. Hammond: "A Reconstruction," 27, and "Edgar Allan Poe's *Tales of the Folio Club,*" 22. For suggestion of the saving of the baby in "The Visionary" as signifying resurrection, see David Ketterer, *The Rationale of Deception in Poe* (Baton Rouge: Louisiana State University Press, 1979), 184; as well as Edward W. Pitcher, "Poe's 'The Assignation': A Reconsideration," *Poe Studies* 13, no. 1 (1980): 3. One of the source studies for "The Visionary" identifies a source passage for the baby's fall in the water in Oliver Goldsmith's 1766 novel *The Vicar of Wakefield* (Jeannie B. Dixon, "Poe: A Borrowing from Goldsmith," *Notes and Queries* 163 [November 12, 1932]: 350). (It is of note that the introduction to the edition of *The Vicar of Wakefield* that Poe reviewed (H 11:8–10) was by John Aikin, one of the two authors of the children's book *Evenings at Home,* which John Allan had given Edgar.) For further commentary on the marchesa's response "Thou hast conquered," see David Ketterer, "Julian the Apostate and 'The Assignation': 'Thou Hast Conquered,'" in *Poe Writing / Writing Poe,* ed. Richard Kopley and Jana Argersinger (New York: AMS, 2013), 1–12. The Thomas Moore connection is suggested early on in Richard P. Benton, "Is Poe's 'Assignation' a Hoax?," *Nineteenth-Century Fiction* 18,

no. 2 (1963): 193–97. It is worth observing that Poe mentions "two large Etruscan vases" in the stranger's apartment, similar to "a curiously-fashioned vase" in the portrait (Fisher, "To 'The Assignation' from 'The Visionary' [Part One]," 39, 98), for they have been compared to vases perhaps belonging to John Allan in Moldavia (Nancy Hirschland Ramage and R. D. Cromey, "Two 'Etruscan' Vases and Edgar Allan Poe," *Metropolitan Museum Journal* 48, no. 1 [2013]: 175–77).

70. Fisher, "To 'The Assignation' from 'The Visionary' [Part One]," 92.
71. Edgar Allan Poe, *Poems* (New York: Published for The Facsimile Text Society for Columbia University Press, 1936), 39.
72. Fisher, "To 'The Assignation' from 'The Visionary' [Part One]," 92, 98.
73. Poe, *Poems*, 39. David Ketterer noted that the marchesa "is originally described, à la 'To Helen,' as an immobile statue" (Ketterer, *The Rationale of Deception in Poe*, 184).
74. Hammond, "Edgar Allan Poe's *Tales of the Folio Club*," 27, 41.
75. Hammond: "A Reconstruction," 28; "Further Notes," 39; "Edgar Allan Poe's *Tales of the Folio Club*," 22; "Early Experiments," 141. There is a manuscript fragment of "Siope" (M 2:194). For a facsimile of the fragment, see John W. Robertson, *Commentary on the Bibliography of Edgar A. Poe* (San Francisco: Russian Hill Private Press, 1934), between 114 and 115.
76. For the political reading of "King Pest," see William Whipple, "Poe's Political Satire," *University of Texas Studies in English* 35 (1956): 84–88; for the venereal reading, see Louis A. Renza, "Poe's King: Playing it Close to the Pest," *Edgar Allan Poe Review* 2, no. 2 (2001): 3–18. The Disraeli source is discussed in Ruth Leigh Hudson, "Poe and Disraeli," *American Literature* 8, no. 4 (1937): 402–6; and William Goldhurst, "Poe's Multiple King Pest: A Source Study," *Tulane Studies in English* 20 (1972): 107–21. For commentary on the imagined author of "King Pest," see Hammond: "A Reconstruction," 31–31; "Further Notes," 39–40; "Edgar Allan Poe's *Tales of the Folio Club*," 23; and "Early Experiments in Genre," 142. For another view, see Benjamin F. Fisher, "'King Pest' and the *Tales of the Folio Club*," in *Edgar Allan Poe: Beyond Gothicism*, ed. James M. Hutchisson (Newark: University of Delaware Press, 2011), 103–17.
77. For the story as it appeared in the *Philadelphia Saturday Courier*, see Varner, *Edgar Allan Poe and the Philadelphia "Saturday Courier*," 67–85. For the linking of "Raising the Wind" to "Mr. Snap," who is John Neal, see Hammond: "A Reconstruction," 26–27, "Further Notes," 41, "Edgar Allan Poe's *Tales of the Folio Club*," 22, and "Early Experiments in Genre," 141. For an early conjecture on the Snap-Neal connection, see French, "Poe's Literary Baltimore," *Maryland Historical Magazine*, June 1937, 111–12. Also relevant is Claude Richard, "Poe and the Yankee Hero: An Interpretation of 'Diddling Considered as One of the Exact Sciences,'" *Mississippi Quarterly* 21, no. 2 (1968): 93–109. Burton R. Pollin offers a contrary view in "Poe's 'Diddling': More on the Dating and the Aim," *Poe Studies* 9, no. 1 (1976): 11–13.
78. Hammond: "Poe's 'Lionizing'"; "A Reconstruction," 32; "Edgar Allan Poe's *Tales of the Folio Club*," 23; "Early Experiments in Genre," 142. Hammond eventually argues that Poe's "Folio Club" collection was critically influenced by the Silver Fork novel marketplace of London, manipulated by the powerful publisher of

Bulwer and Disraeli, among others, Henry Colburn (Hammond, "The Folio Club Collection and the Silver Fork School").

11. "Nothing Would Give Me Greater Pleasure"

1. Thomas H. Ellis, "Edgar Allan Poe," *Richmond Standard,* May 7, 1881, 2. Ellis was a partisan of the second Mrs. Allan, and I do not accept everything he wrote. But the incident he describes here seems credible. For commentary on Poe's possible lines of communication with Richmond from Baltimore, see Mary E. Phillips, *Edgar Allan Poe—The Man,* 2 vols. (Chicago: John C. Winston, 1926), 1:443.
2. Margaret K. Ellis to Charles Ellis, March 19, 1834, Box 292, DLC-EA; Thomas H. Ellis to Charles Ellis, March 20, 1834, Box 292, DLC-EA; Charles Ellis Jr. to Charles Ellis, March 27, 1834, Box 292, DLC-EA; and Thomas H. Ellis to Charles Ellis, Box 292, DLC-EA.
3. "Deaths," *Richmond Enquirer,* April 1, 1834; James N. Ellis to Charles Ellis Jr., April 15, 1834, Munford-Ellis Family Papers, David M. Rubinstein Rare Book & Manuscript Library, Duke University.
4. Flora Lapham Mack to William Lanier Washington, April 22, 1908, collection of the author.
5. "Deaths," *Richmond Enquirer,* April 1, 1834.
6. For Allan's will, see Hervey Allen, *Israfel: The Life and Times of Edgar Allan Poe,* 2 vols. (New York: George H. Doran, 1926), 2:865–69. For specific mention of Elizabeth Wills and her children, see 2:868. For comments on the will, see 2:870–73. Allen later notes that these comments were written by "an attorney-at-law of Washington D.C." (Allen, *Israfel: The Life and Times of Edgar Allan Poe* [New York: Farrar & Rinehart, 1934], 698).
7. For the relevant passage in the *Saturday Museum* biography, see Burton R. Pollin, "Poe's Authorship of Three Long Critical and Autobiographical Articles of 1843 Now Authenticated," *American Renaissance Literary Report: An Annual* 7 (1993): 164; Benjamin F. Fisher, "An Early Biography of Poe (1843): The *Philadelphia Saturday Museum* Sketch," in *Masques, Mysteries, and Mastodons: A Poe Miscellany,* ed. Fisher (Baltimore, MD: Poe Society, 2006), 159; and Benjamin F. Fisher, ed., "Poets and Poetry of Philadelphia," by Edgar Allan Poe and Henry B. Hirst (or Poe alone), in *Poe in His Own Time: A Biographical Chronicle of His Life Drawn from Recollections, Interviews, and Memoirs by Family, Friends, and Associates* (Iowa City: University of Iowa Press, 2010), 27.
8. Thomas H. Ellis, "Edgar Allan Poe."
9. Susan Archer Weiss, "Reminiscences of Edgar Allan Poe," *New York Independent,* August 25, 1904, 443.
10. Thomas H. Ellis, "Edgar Allan Poe"; Marie Louise Shew Houghton to John Ingram, March 28, 1875, in *Building Poe Biography,* ed. John Carl Miller (Baton Rouge: Louisiana State University Press, 1977), 116.
11. For background on Thomas W. White, see "New Printing Office," *Richmond Commercial Compiler,* December 6, 1823 (Library of Virginia); "From J. P. Kennedy," *Southern Literary Messenger* (August 1834): 1; Samuel Mordecai, *Richmond in By-Gone Days* (1860; Richmond, VA: Dietz, 1946), 240–41; David K. Jackson,

Poe and the Southern Literary Messenger (Richmond, VA: Dietz, 1934), 16–19; *Richmond Portraits in an Exhibition of Makers of Richmond* (Richmond, VA: The Valentine, 1949), 204–5; and "Thomas Willis White," in *American National Biography* (New York: Oxford University Press, 2019). For White's early life, see Thomas W. White to Beverly Tucker, November 17, 1834, Albert and Shirley Small Special Collections Library, University of Virginia, Charlottesville; as well as Beverly D. Tucker, *Nathaniel Beverley Tucker Prophet of the Confederacy 1784–1851* (Tokyo: Nan'un-Do, 1979), 265. The author of the prospectus for the *Southern Literary Messenger* was Robert Saunders, mathematics professor from the College of William & Mary (Tucker, *Nathaniel Beverly Tucker*, 266). A copy of the prospectus—"Prospectus of a Literary Paper to be Published in Richmond, VA by Thomas W. White to be Entitled The Southern Literary Messenger"—is available in Special Collections at the Library of Virginia.

12. R. T. P. Allen, "Edgar Allan Poe," *Scribner's Monthly Magazine,* November 1875, 142–43 (available at https://www.eapoe.org). See also "Poe a Bricklayer in 1834?," *American Notes & Queries* 3 (June 1943): 36.
13. For Carey's letters to Kennedy, see Killis Campbell, "The Kennedy Papers (Second Article) Letters from Dickens, Macaulay, Cooper, Holmes, Lowell, and Others," *Sewanee Review* 25, no. 2 (1917): 197–98. Poe later noted to Kennedy that he wished that "Siope" or "Epimanes" had appeared in *The Gift* instead (O ::108).
14. For the Kennedy letter, see Rufus Wilmot Griswold, "Memoir of the Author," in *The Literati: Some Honest Opinions about Autorial [sic] Merits and Demerits . . .* (New York: J. S. Redfield, 1850), xiii. (This is the third volume of Griswold's four-volume *Works of Edgar A. Poe.*) "The Doom," published anonymously, features a reference to Poe's boyhood swimming feat in the James River ("The Doom," *Southern Literary Messenger* 1 [January 1835]: 235). For references to it, see Benjamin Blake Minor, *The Southern Literary Messenger, 1834–1864* (New York: Neale, 1905), 23; and David K. Jackson, *Poe and "The Southern Literary Messenger,"* 40–41. For the dates of the appearance of the issues of the *Messenger,* I rely on Dwight Thomas and David K. Jackson, *The Poe Log: A Documentary Life of Edgar Allan Poe, 1809–1849* (Boston: G. K. Hall, 1987). The dates of appearance of the January and March 1835 issues are given in Thomas and Jackson, *The Poe Log,* 146, 149.
15. Arthur Hobson Quinn, *Edgar Allan Poe: A Critical Biography* (New York: D. Appleton-Century, 1941), 208.
16. For Poe's first tale in the *Messenger,* see Edgar A. Poe, "Berenice—A Tale," *Southern Literary Messenger* (March 1835): 333–36.
17. I quote from the *Messenger* text since Mabbott relies on the revised version in the Griswold edition (see, in the *Messenger* text, 335, 336).
18. "Editorial Remarks," *Southern Literary Messenger* (March 1835): 387. See also [James E. Heath], "Editorial Notices of Poe's Tales in the *Southern Literary Messenger,*" in *Edgar Allan Poe: The Critical Heritage,* ed. I. M. Walker (London: Routledge & Kegan Paul, 1986), 80.
19. Ronald B. Head, ed. "The Student Diary of Charles Ellis, Jr., March 10–June 25, 1835," *Magazine of Albemarle County History* 35 and 36 (1977/1978): 43.
20. Poe, "Berenice—A Tale," 333.
21. Ibid., 334.

22. Ibid., 333–34.
23. Ibid., 335.
24. For a fuller articulation of this argument, see my study *The Formal Center in Literature: Explorations from Poe to the Present* (Rochester, NY: Camden House, 2018), 20–24.
25. Flora Lapham Mack [for William Lanier Washington], "Suggestions for the Third Chapter—Poe's Early Married Days," collection of the author.
26. I rely on the *Messenger* version of the tale: Edgar A. Poe, "Morella—A Tale," *Southern Literary Messenger* (April 1835): 448–50. There was an earlier, incomplete manuscript version, which had been given to a generous Baltimore neighbor, Mrs. Sarah P. Simmons (M 2:224). For the date of publication of the April issue, see Thomas and Jackson, *The Poe Log*, 151.
27. James E. Heath, "Editorial Remarks," *Southern Literary Messenger* (March 1835): 460. See also Walker, *Edgar Allan Poe: The Critical Heritage*, 80.
28. "Personal Opinions," in *Edgar Allan Poe: The Critical Heritage*, ed. Walker, 118.
29. Review of *North American Review* and the *London Quarterly Review*, *Southern Literary Messenger* (April 1835): 457–58.
30. David K. Jackson, "Four of Poe's Critiques in the Baltimore Newspapers," *Modern Language Notes* 50, no. 4 (1935): 253–54.
31. Regarding Poe's pay, the Ostrom edition comments, "Poe probably received 80 cents per column, and $9.94 was payment in full for contributions to the May *SLM*" (O 1:90).
32. Thomas and Jackson, *The Poe Log*, 155.
33. "Editorial Remarks," *Southern Literary Messenger* (May 1835): 531.
34. Jackson, "Four of Poe's Critiques," 255.
35. Review of *Horse-Shoe Robinson*, *Southern Literary Messenger* (May 1835): 524.
36. Ibid., 523.
37. Jackson, "Four of Poe's Critiques," 255.
38. "Swimming," *Southern Literary Messenger* (May 1835): 468.
39. Thomas and Jackson, *The Poe Log*, 156–57.
40. Ibid., 159–60.
41. Edgar A. Poe, "Hans Phaall—A Tale," *Southern Literary Messenger* (June 1835): 565–80. For the scholarly edition, see volume 1 of the Pollin text. For Sparhawk's comment, see "Editorial Introduction," *Southern Literary Messenger* (June 1835): 533. Poe's anonymous comment on "Hans Phaall" appears in Jackson, "Four of Poe's Critiques," 256.
42. For Poe's reviews, see "Literary Notices," *Southern Literary Messenger* (June 1835): 594–95. For the appearance of the hole at the North Pole in "Hans Phaall," see 577.
43. Thomas and Jackson, *The Poe Log*, 159.
44. Ibid., 163–64.
45. E. A. P., "To Mary," *Southern Literary Messenger* (July 1835): 636. For a later version of the poem, "To F—," see M 1:236–37. It was also titled "To One Departed."
46. David K. Jackson, "An Uncollected Letter of James Kirke Paulding," *Poe Studies* 15, no. 2 (1982): 41; Thomas and Jackson, *The Poe Log*, 164.
47. Thomas and Jackson, *The Poe Log*, 164–65. Poe mentioned that "I shall go down to the Steamboat" (in Baltimore) in his July 20, 1835, letter to White (O 1:96).

12. "A Fair Prospect of Future Success"

1. David K. Jackson, *Poe and "The Southern Literary Messenger"* (Richmond, VA: Dietz, 1934), 98.
2. Mary Elizabeth Phillips, *Edgar Allan Poe—The Man*, 2 vols. (Chicago: John C. Winston, 1926), 1:503–4.
3. For the geography of Richmond at this time, I rely on Micajah Bates's 1835 "Plan of the City of Richmond Drawn from Actual Survey and Original Plans," available at the Library of Virginia. For detail on the *Southern Literary Messenger* building, see Charles Marshall Graves, "Landmarks of Poe in Richmond," *Century Magazine*, April 1904, 915–16; Benjamin Blake Minor, *The Southern Literary Messenger, 1834–1864* (New York: Neale, 1905), 13–14; Jackson, *Poe and "The Southern Literary Messenger*," 8; Mary Wingfield Scott, *Old Richmond Neighborhoods* (Richmond: Whittet & Shepperson, 1950), 132–33; and Keshia A. Case and Christopher P. Semtner, *Edgar Allan Poe in Richmond* (Charleston, SC: Arcadia, 2009), 45–46. For an account of the oil portrait of White, see Christopher P. Semtner, "Poe in Richmond: The New Face of Thomas Willis White," *Edgar Allan Poe Review* 18, no. 1 (2017): 77–87. The portrait was purchased and identified by Anders Rasmussen; images of it appear on pages 78 and 85 of the article. And the portrait is included in this volume. For an earlier copy held by the Poe Foundation, see *Richmond Portraits in an Exhibition of Makers of Richmond 1737–1860* (Richmond, VA: The Valentine, 1949), 204–5. For reference to Macfarlane and Fergusson, see Minor, *The Southern Literary Messenger, 1834–1864*, 14; and Jackson, *Poe and "The Southern Literary Messenger*," 8. For Frothingham, I consulted [Edward G. Frothingham], "Private Journal of E.G.F. No I," Special Collections, Library of Virginia. He began at the *Messenger* on Monday, March 30, 1835, somewhat intimidated to be working at a literary magazine and also somewhat resented. He noted, "About 11 workmen employed in the office—They dislike the idea of a "*Yankee*" coming to tell them what to do. I am determined to be decided, and whatever is correct do it, let the consequences be what they may." For Frothingham's having been a subscriber to the *Messenger* from Boston, see the back cover of the April 1835 issue. Poe, then still in Baltimore, was also listed there.
4. I draw on Flora Lapham Mack [for William Lanier Washington], "Suggestions for the Second Chapter—The Break with the Allans" and "Suggestions for the Third Chapter—Poe's Early Married Days," collection of the author.
5. See Richard Kopley, "John Neal on Hawthorne and Poe in the *New England Galaxy* of 1835," *Nathaniel Hawthorne Review* 42, no. 2 (2016): 27–29. For more on Neal, see Benjamin Lease, *That Wild Fellow John Neal* (Chicago: University of Chicago Press, 1972); and Benjamin Lease, "John Neal and Edgar Allan Poe," *Poe Studies* 7, no. 2 (1974): 38–41.
6. Bates, "Plan of the City of Richmond."
7. Jackson, *Poe and "The Southern Literary Messenger*," 98.
8. Ibid., 100. For White's later noting that he'd given Poe notice in September, see ibid., 110.
9. For the text of the license, see Hervey Allen, *Israfel: The Life and Times of Edgar Allan Poe*, 2 vols. (New York: George H. Doran, 1926), 2:880–81. For Mabbott's

opinion, see M 1:546; for Silverman's, see Kenneth Silverman, *Edgar A. Poe: Mournful and Never-ending Remembrance* (New York: HarperCollins, 1991), 124. For Quinn's dismissal of the idea of a marriage in Baltimore, see Arthur Hobson Quinn, *Edgar Allan Poe: A Critical Biography* (New York: D. Appleton-Century, 1941), 227–28. See also Arthur H. Quinn and Richard H. Hart, *Edgar Allan Poe: Letters and Documents in the Enoch Pratt Free Library* (New York: Scholars' Facsimiles & Reprints, 1941), 7–8.

10. Mack [for Washington], "Suggestions for the Third Chapter—Poe's Early Married Days," collection of the author. I consult also Mack to Washington, March 31, 1908, collection of the author. Mack incorrectly states that Mrs. Clemm and Virginia came to Richmond in the spring of 1836; they actually arrived in early October 1835.

11. Dwight Thomas and David K. Jackson, *The Poe Log: A Documentary Life of Edgar Allan Poe 1809–1849* (Boston: G. K. Hall, 1987), 172.

12. Elizabeth Oakes Smith claimed that Poe had had a romantic relationship with Eliza White (John Henry Ingram's Poe Collection, Albert & Shirley Small Special Collections Library, University of Virginia, Charlottesville, Items 196, 214, 233), but Sarah Helen Whitman denied it (Ingram's Poe Collection, Item 223); see also John Carl Miller, ed., *Poe's Helen Remembers* (Charlottesville: University Press of Virginia, 1979), 286. Susan Archer Weiss attested to the relationship (Weiss, *The Home Life of Poe* [New York: Broadway, 1907], 77–79). However, J. H. Whitty cited three people—*Messenger* assistant John W. Fergusson, T. W. White's other daughter Mrs. Bernard, and Maria Clemm—who stated that Poe and Eliza White were just friends (Whitty, *The Complete Poems of Edgar Allan Poe* [Boston: Houghton Mifflin, 1911], xxxix). Eliza White's niece Bell Lynes also denied the allegation (Semtner, "Poe in Richmond," 80–81). Eliza White remained a friend of Poe's, visiting in Philadelphia, and later, in Fordham, as Virginia lay dying.

13. See Jeffrey A. Savoye, "Some Updates on Poe's Correspondence, with a New Letter," *Edgar Allan Poe Review* 13, no. 1 (2012): 12–15, a corrected version of H 17:379–81; Thomas and Jackson, *The Poe Log*, 174–75; and O 1:118.

14. Savoye, "Some Updates," 13–14.

15. For Poe's having returned to the *Messenger* and worked on the December 1835 issue, see White's October 20, 1835, letter to Lucian Minor, in Jackson, *Poe and "The Southern Literary Messenger,"* 102–3. For White's caution to Minor, in a letter of October 24, see ibid., 104. White offered his introductory comments in "Publisher's Notice," *Southern Literary Messenger* (December 1835): 1. For White's pleasure in Poe's sobriety, expressed in a letter to Minor of December 25, see Jackson, *Poe and "The Southern Literary Messenger,"* 107.

16. Thomas and Jackson, *The Poe Log*, 177.

17. For Kennedy's comment, see Rufus Wilmot Griswold, "Memoir of the Author," in *The Literati: Some Honest Opinions about Autorial Merits and Demerits* [. . .] (New York: J. S. Redfield, 1850), xiii.

18. For the three scenes in the December 1835 issue, see "Scenes from an Unpublished Drama," *Southern Literary Messenger* (December 1835): 13–16. The line quoted, by Lalage, is on page 13. For Mabbott's comments on the full tragedy, "Politian," see M 1:241–47, 288–98. The play itself is on M 1:247–87; the line

quoted from it is on M 1:261. For Mabbott's early work on the play, see Thomas Ollive Mabbott, ed., *Politian: An Unfinished Tragedy*, by Edgar Allan Poe (Richmond, VA: Edgar Allan Poe Shrine, 1923). An important early study of Poe and the Bible is William Mentzel Forrest, *Biblical Allusions in Poe* (New York: Macmillan, 1928).

19. For the links among Gulielma Sands, *Norman Leslie*, and "The Mystery of Marie Rogêt," see Richard Kopley, *Edgar Allan Poe and the Dupin Mysteries* (New York: Palgrave Macmillan, 2008), 50–54. A useful treatment of Poe's review of *Norman Leslie* and the controversy that ensued is Sidney P. Moss, *Poe's Literary Battles: The Critic in the Context of His Literary Milieu* (Durham, NC: Duke University Press, 1963), 38–62.

20. Also appearing in the December 1835 issue of the *Messenger* is "To Mira," but it was noted to be by L. A. Wilmer and was originally titled "To Mary" (Thomas Ollive Mabbott, ed., *Merlin Baltimore, 1827* [1941; n.p. (Folcroft, PA): Folcroft Library Editions, 1973], viii–ix).

21. Beverly D. Tucker, *Nathaniel Beverly Tucker: Prophet of the Confederacy 1784–1851* (Tokyo: Nan'un-do, 1979), 285–88.

22. Kopley, "John Neal on Hawthorne and Poe," 29–30.

23. Lambert A. Wilmer, *Our Press Gang; or, A Complete Exposition of the Corruptions and Crimes of the American Newspapers* (Philadelphia: J. T. Lloyd, 1859), 36.

24. Flora Lapham Mack, "Poe's Appearance and Personality," collection of the author.

25. Francis Lieber, *Reminiscences of an Intercourse with Mr. Niebuhr the Historian during a Residence with Him in Rome, in the Years 1822 and 1823* (Philadelphia: Carey, Lea & Blanchard, 1835), 191.

26. Thomas and Jackson, *The Poe Log*, 187.

27. Ibid., 191.

28. Ibid., 190. White, who was writing to Beverly Tucker on February 6, had earlier had some reservation about Poe (according to Poe himself)—a reservation prompted partly by a letter from Tucker, whose sentiments Tucker then clarified on January 26 (Thomas and Jackson, *The Poe Log*, 189–90).

29. For contrasting views of the source of "Palaestine," see Burton R. Pollin (P 5:130–31); and J. V. Ridgely (P 5:131).

30. James L. Machor comments on Poe and the Art Novel in *Reading Fiction in Antebellum America: Informed Response and Reception Histories, 1820–1865* (Baltimore, MD: Johns Hopkins University Press, 2011), 114.

31. For a fuller discussion, see Richard Kopley, "The 'Very Profound Under-current' of *Arthur Gordon Pym*," in *Studies in the American Renaissance 1987*, ed. Joel Myerson (Charlottesville: University Press of Virginia, 1987), 143–47.

32. Samuel Taylor Coleridge, *Specimens of the Table Talk of the Late Samuel Taylor Coleridge*, 2 vols. (New York: Harper & Brothers, 1835), 2:26, 135. Coleridge had mentioned the Destruction of Jerusalem as the subject of a projected work as early as 1803 (R. C. Bald, "Coleridge and *The Ancient Mariner*: Addenda to *The Road to Xanadu*," *Nineteenth-Century Studies*, ed. Herbert Davis, William C. Devane, and R. C. Bald [1940; rpt., New York: Greenwood, 1968], 17).

33. I develop this argument in "The 'Very Profound Under-current,'" 146–47.

34. J. K. Paulding to T. W. White, March 3, 1836, in *The Letters of James Kirke Paulding*, ed. Ralph M. Aderman (Madison: University of Wisconsin Press, 1962), 173–75. Paulding did write directly to Poe on March 17 (H 17:31–32).
35. Quinn, *Edgar Allan Poe: A Critical Biography*, 250–51.
36. I rely for the date of the publication of the March 1836 of the *Messenger* on Thomas and Jackson, *The Poe Log*, 196.
37. A helpful biographical sketch of Frothingham is provided in *Genealogical and Personal Memoirs Relating to the Families of Boston and Eastern Massachusetts*, ed. William Richard Cutter (New York: Lewis Historical Publishing, 1908), 2:951–52. See also [Frothingham], "Private Journal." Frothingham writes there of seeing a slave auction. In fact, slaves were auctioned in front of the Bell Tavern, just across the street from the *Messenger* building. For the larger context, see Jack Trammell, *The Richmond Slave Trade: The Economic Backbone of the Old Dominion* (Charleston, SC: History Press, 2012).
38. Whalen's excellent work appears as "Average Racism: Poe, Slavery, and the Wages of Literary Nationalism," in *Edgar Allan Poe and the Masses: The Political Economy of Literature in Antebellum America* (Princeton, NJ: Princeton University Press, 1999), 111–46, 293–302. The essay is also available in a shorter version in *Romancing the Shadow: Poe and Race*, ed. J. Gerald Kennedy and Liliane Weissberg (New York: Oxford University Press, 2001), 3–40.
39. See "List of Payments," *Southern Literary Messenger* (March 1836): inside rear wrapper. A run of the *Messenger* with wrappers is available at the Virginia Museum of History and Culture. For the quotation on the theater fire, see "Virginia Gazetteer," *Southern Literary Messenger* (February 1835): 259. The story of Dr. James D. McCaw and Gilbert Hunt is told in Philip Barrett, *Gilbert Hunt, the City Blacksmith* (Richmond, VA: James Woodhouse, 1859), 27–31; and Philip Barrett, *The Deaf Shoemaker, to Which Are Added Other Stories for the Young* (New York: Dodd, Mead, 1859), 145–51; Samuel Mordecai, *Richmond in By-Gone Days* (1860; Richmond, VA: Dietz, 1946), 215–18; and Meredith Henne Baker, *The Richmond Theater Fire: Early America's First Great Disaster* (Baton Rouge: Louisiana State University Press, 2012), 40–41.
40. For an instance of the advertisement for the chess-automaton, see "Maelzel's Exhibition, of the Automaton Chess-player, The Automaton Trumpeter, the Melodium, etc. etc," *Richmond Whig and Public Advertiser*, March 17, 1836. According to this advertisement, the exhibition would close on March 19.
41. For discussion of Poe's essay, see W. K. Wimsatt Jr., "Poe and the Chess Automaton," *American Literature* 11, no. 2 (1939): 138–51. Wimsatt suggests Poe's having made an earlier visit to the chess-automaton, in December and January. Poe notes that Maelzel had offered his automata in Richmond "some years ago" (P 5:163). That would have been 1834 (P 5:181). See also Christopher M. Semtner, *Edgar Allan Poe's Richmond: The Raven in the River City* (Charleston, SC: History Press, 2012), 68–70.
42. For the Brewster source, see Wimsatt, "Poe and the Chess Automaton," 146–47; and P 5:178–80. John T. Irwin wrote, "[W]e should remember that the person who introduces mirrors into the mechanism of the chess-playing automaton is

Poe himself" (Irwin, "Handedness and the Self: Poe's Chess Player," *Arizona Quarterly* 45, no. 1 [1989]: 21). Burton R. Pollin and Joseph V. Ridgely write, "No contemporaneous exposé of the Turk [the automaton] mentions mirrors" (P 5:180).

43. The review of J. K. Paulding's *Slavery in the United States* and William Drayton's *The South Vindicated,* sometimes attributed to Poe, is actually by Beverly Tucker (P 5:153–54). "Supplement," featuring reviews of the *Messenger,* often paying tribute to Poe, closes out the April issue.

44. Flora Lapham Mack to William Lanier Washington, April 22, 1908, collection of the author. For the Weiss passage that Mack disputed, see Susan Archer Weiss, *The Home Life of Poe* (New York: Broadway, 1907), 222–26. John H. Mackenzie died in Danville, Virginia, in 1875, holding the hand of Flora Lapham Mack, according to Mack in a letter to Washington, March 31, 1908, collection of the author.

45. Flora Lapham Mack to William Lanier Washington, February 29, 1908, collection of the author.

46. Mack [for Washington], "Suggestions for the Third Chapter—Poe's Early Married Days," collection of the author. Virginia also had "two new calico dresses," two pieces of which Mary Mattox Lapham later used in a quilt. Years later, Mack sent these pieces to Washington; they are now in the collection of the author.

47. The marriage bond is reproduced in Thomas and Jackson, *The Poe Log,* 206. The comment about the customary nature of the marriage of very young brides is made by Mack to Washington, March 31, 1908.

48. I rely on Phillips, *Edgar Allan Poe—The Man,* 1:529–33; Allen, *Israfel,* 1:396–98; and Thomas and Jackson, *The Poe Log,* 207.

49. Phillips, *Edgar Allan Poe—The Man,* 1:532; Allen, *Israfel,* 1:398.

50. Mack [for Washington], "Suggestions for the Third Chapter—Poe's Early Married Days," collection of the author.

51. J. H. Whitty, *The Complete Poems of Edgar Allan Poe* (Boston: Houghton Mifflin, 1911), xxxix.

52. Robert D. Jacobs, *Poe: Journalist & Critic* (Baton Rouge: Louisiana State University Press, 1969), 180.

53. For Poe and Virginia in Petersburg, see Phillips, *Edgar Allan Poe—The Man,* 1:532–33. See also Poe's two letters to Haines and the related editorial commentary (O 1:156–57, 215–16), available originally in John Ward Ostrom, "Two Unpublished Poe Letters," *Americana* 36 (1942): 67–71. There is a brief discussion of Poe and Virginia in Petersburg in Jeffrey Abugel, *Edgar Allan Poe's Petersburg* (Charleston, SC: History Press, 2013), 100–107.

54. Frederick W. Coburn, "Poe as Seen by the Brother of 'Annie,'" *New England Quarterly* 16, no. 3 (1943): 471; Elizabeth Oakes Smith to John H. Ingram, January 18, 1875; Ingram's Poe Collection, Item 196.

55. Margaret Meagher, *History of Education in Richmond* (Richmond, VA: WPA, 1939), 59.

56. Flora Lapham Mack [for William Lanier Washington], "Poe's Appearance & Personality," collection of the author.

57. Quinn, *Edgar Allan Poe: A Critical Biography,* 634.

58. Thomas and Jackson, *The Poe Log,* 208.
59. For Virginia and Mrs. Clemm spending weekends at Darby Town, I consult Mack to Washington, March 31, 1908. Occasionally Virginia and Mrs. Clemm would spend weeks on the farm, with John H. Mackenzie and Poe leaving and returning every day. The same letter clarifies this. For John H. Mackenzie's vehicle and slaves, I consult "Henrico County Personal Property Tax Records," Microforms, Reel 173, 1831–1844. Flora Lapham Mack mentions John H. Mackenzie's slaves, as well as those of his mother-in-law, Mary Simmons Lanier (Aunt Polly), and identifies their work, and she names the overseer, Mr. Andrews, in Mack [for William Lanier Washington], "Suggestions for the Second Chapter—The Break with the Allans," collection of the author. For the association of Darby Town and Enroughty, see Mordecai, *Richmond in By-Gone Days,* 294. An 1853 map, "Smith's Henrico County Virginia," shows the Darby Town Road running south of Richmond, with a farm on the east side identified by the name "McKensy." Mack states that John H. Mackenzie was persuaded to buy the Darby Town farm by his wife Louisa and her mother, Mrs. Lanier. Mack does so in her "Suggestions for the Second Chapter—The Break with the Allans." Henrico Deed Books at the Library of Virginia reveal the sale of the land. Sarah M. Montague and Charles W. Montague sold 193 acres of land to Turner Sharpe on February 5, 1842 (Henrico Deed Book 42, pp. 369–70), and Turner and Eliza Sharpe sold it to John H. Mackenzie on April 17, 1844 (Henrico County Deed Book 47, p. 444). On August 3, 1844, owing Jane Mackenzie $900 for the purchase of the land, John H. Mackenzie promised to sell it to his brother Thomas G. Mackenzie for one dollar (who may put it up for auction), if he (John) failed to pay his aunt back in four payments over four years (Henrico County Trust Book 48, pp. 73–74). A corrected version of the sale by the Sharpes to John H. Mackenzie is made on December 1, 1844 (Henrico County Deed Book 48 1844–45, pp. 404–5). For women running plantations, see Catherine Clinton, *Plantation Mistress: Woman's World in the Old South* (New York: Pantheon, 1982). I rely for John H. Mackenzie's appearance on a daguerreotype, perhaps from the 1840s, held by the Poe Museum and reproduced here. (The museum also holds another of Mackenzie as an elderly man.) For his wife Louisa's appearance, I consult an ambrotype of her, in my collection, also reproduced here.
60. For Lincoln's October 16, 1854, comment, see *Collected Works of Abraham Lincoln,* ed. Roy P. Basler, 9 vols. (New Brunswick, NJ: Rutgers University Press, 1953–55), 2:255.
61. Mack to Washington, February 29, 1908. Mackenzie's comment about Poe's having found the woman "best suited" to him as a wife is in Mack [for Washington], "Suggestions for the Third Chapter—Poe's Early Married Days," collection of the author.
62. Weiss, *The Home Life of Poe,* 85.
63. Mack [for Washington], "Suggestions for the Third Chapter—Poe's Early Married Days," collection of the author.
64. Ibid. By contrast, Bardwell Haywood wrote that Poe and Virginia did not then share a bedroom (Coburn, "Poe as Seen by the Brother of 'Annie,'" 471).
65. Mack, "Poe's Appearance & Personality."

66. For an additional letter of solicitation from the period, see Paul Christian Jones, "A New Poe Letter—to Nicholas Biddle," *Edgar Allan Poe Review* 19, no. 1 (2018): 104–6.
67. Thomas and Jackson, *The Poe Log*, 211.
68. George E. Woodberry, *The Life of Edgar Allan Poe*, 2 vols. (Boston: Houghton Mifflin, 1909), 2:443.
69. Mack to Washington, March 31, 1908.
70. Mack [for Washington], "Poe's Appearance & Personality."
71. Mack notes that Rosalie disturbed her brother and that Mrs. Clemm protected him from her (Mack [for Washington], "Suggestions for the Third Chapter—Poe's Early Married Days," collection of the author).
72. Mack [for Washington], "Poe's Appearance & Personality."
73. Mack [for Washington], "Suggestions for the Third Chapter—Poe's Early Married Days," collection of the author.
74. *Facing Addiction in America: The Surgeon General's Report on Alcohol, Drugs, and Health* (Washington, DC: U.S. Department of Health & Human Services, 2016), 2–1.
75. Thomas and Jackson, *The Poe Log*, 214.
76. "From the Philadelphia Saturday News," "Supplement," *Southern Literary Messenger* (July 1836): rear cover. For my treatment of this important newspaper, see my booklet *Edgar Allan Poe and the Philadelphia Saturday News* (Baltimore, MD: Enoch Pratt Free Library and Poe Society of Baltimore, 1991); and my subsequent book *Edgar Allan Poe and the Dupin Mysteries* (New York: Palgrave Macmillan, 2008).
77. Thomas and Jackson, *The Poe Log*, 220.
78. Ibid., 221.
79. Ibid., 220.
80. Ibid., 221.
81. Silverman, *Edgar A. Poe: Mournful and Never-ending Remembrance*, 474.
82. For discussion of the contretemps between Poe and the *Richmond Compiler*, see P 5:273–76. See also Sidney P. Moss, *Poe's Literary Battles* (Durham, NC: Duke University Press, 1963), 56–58.
83. Jackson, *Poe and "The Southern Literary Messenger,"* 110.
84. Much of this paragraph is drawn from Mack's "Poe's Appearance and Personality," collection of the author. Also relevant is Mack [for Washington], "Suggestions for the Third Chapter—Poe's Early Married Days," collection of the author. The extravagance mentioned is Poe's dining well at a hotel. For Poe's requesting fifty dollars credit from John Allan's former partner Charles Ellis Senior, see Poe to Ellis, September 26, 1836, Edgar Allan Poe Society of Baltimore, https://www.eapoe.org. Poe's bankruptcy papers are available in Barbara Cantalupo, "Interview with Jefferson Moak (October 2007)," *Edgar Allan Poe Review* 8, no. 2 (2007): 92–98. These papers are held by the National Archives at Philadelphia. The bankruptcy document characterizes Poe's Richmond debts as "Note of Hand," "Book Debt," "Music Lesson" (presumably for Virginia), and "Money Lent."
85. See my essay "*Evenings at Home*: A Neglected Book from Poe's Childhood," *Edgar Allan Poe Review* 21, no. 1 (2020): 64–70.

86. Mack to Washington, March 31, 1908; Mack [for Washington]: "Suggestions for Second Chapter—The Break with the Allans" and "Suggestions for the Third Chapter—Poe's Early Married Days," collection of the author.
87. Mack [for Washington], "Suggestions for the Third Chapter—Poe's Early Married Days," collection of the author.
88. Ibid.
89. Ibid.
90. Ibid.
91. For an account of Fanny Elssler in the United States from 1840 to 1842, see Ivor Guest, *Fanny Elssler* (Middletown, CT: Wesleyan University Press, 1970), 126–85.
92. See especially Burton R. Pollin, "Poe and the Dance," in *Studies in the American Renaissance 1980,* ed. Joel Myerson (Boston: Twayne, 1980), 169–82.
93. Mack [for Washington], "Suggestions for the Third Chapter—Poe's Early Married Days," collection of the author.
94. Thomas and Jackson, *The Poe Log,* 230.
95. Ibid., 227.
96. Ibid., 233.
97. Ibid., 234, 235–36.
98. Jackson, *Poe and "The Southern Literary Messenger,"* 110.
99. See M 2:306; Benjamin Franklin Fisher IV, "Dickens and Poe: *Pickwick* and 'Ligeia,'" *Poe Studies* 6, no. 1 (1973): 14–16; and Edward Strickland, "Dickens' 'A Madman's Manuscript' and 'The Tell-Tale Heart,'" *Poe Studies* 9, no. 1 (1976): 22–23; and P 5:322.
100. Mack [for Washington], "Poe's Appearance and Personality," collection of the author. A guitar would not have cost very much, but, in any case, Miss Jane Mackenzie was wealthy, having large insurance policies left to her by her former lover, who had died (Mack [for Washington], "Suggestions for the Third Chapter—Poe's Early Married Days," collection of the author).
101. Mack [for Washington], "Suggestions for the Third Chapter—Poe's Early Married Days," collection of the author.
102. Jackson, *Poe and "The Southern Literary Messenger,"* 109–10.
103. Thomas and Jackson, *The Poe Log,* 240.
104. Ibid., 241.
105. Minor, *The Southern Literary Messenger, 1834–1864,* 64.
106. Jackson, *Poe and "The Southern Literary Messenger,"* 112.
107. Thomas and Jackson, *The Poe Log,* 242.
108. See Burton R. Pollin, "Poe's Authorship of Three Long Critical and Autobiographical Articles of 1843 Now Authenticated," *American Renaissance Literary Report: An Annual* 7 (1993): 165; Benjamin F. Fisher, "The *Saturday Museum* Sketch of Poe," in *Masques, Mysteries, and Mastadons; A Poe Miscellany,* ed. Fisher (Baltimore, MD: Edgar Allan Poe Society, 2006), 160; and [Edgar A. Poe and Henry B. Hirst (or Poe alone)], "From 'Poets and Poetry of Philadelphia,'" in *Poe in His Own Times,* ed. Benjamin F. Fisher (Iowa City: University of Iowa Press, 2010), 28.
109. Mack [for Washington], "Suggestions for the Third Chapter—Poe's Early Married Days," collection of the author.

110. "Contents / No. I—Vol. III—January, 1837," inside front wrapper. See the run at the Virginia Museum of History and Culture.
111. An association copy of Reynolds's *Address on the Subject of a Surveying and Exploring Expedition* features the inscription "T. W. White Esq. / With the sincere regards / of his old friend / J. N. Reynolds" (collection of the author). Perhaps this was even the copy that Poe read. However, White shortly came to learn "that Reynolds is suspected of being what he ought not be," and he wondered if this "most fascinating dog" was in fact "a corrupt man" (see his January 19, 1837, letter to Beverly Tucker, Jackson, *Poe and "The Southern Literary Messenger,"* 111). Taking his leave of the *Messenger,* Poe wrote, "With best wishes to the Magazine, and to its few foes as well as many friends, he is now desirous of bidding all parties a peaceable farewell" (P 5:325).
112. Thomas and Jackson, *The Poe Log,* 241.
113. Ibid., 242. Frederick Marryat was a British writer of sea fiction.
114. Ibid., 244.
115. I rely on the original version of the text: Edgar Allan Poe, "Arthur Gordon Pym," *Southern Literary Messenger,* no. 1 (January 1837): 12–16. I have published extensively on *Pym;* I would recommend, as an accessible overview, my introduction to Edgar Allan Poe, *The Narrative of Arthur Gordon Pym of Nantucket* (New York: Penguin, 1999), ix–xxix. For the Wilbur comment on "E. Ronald," see Richard Wilbur, introduction to *The Narrative of Arthur Gordon Pym* (Boston: David R. Godine, 1973), x–xi.
116. Whitty, *The Complete Poems of Edgar Allan Poe,* 282–83.

13. "A Flattering Invitation"

1. I take the quotation from William Gowans, *Catalogue of American Books,* vol. 28 (1870), 11. See also Mary E. Phillips, *Edgar Allan Poe—The Man,* 2 vols. (Chicago: John C. Winston, 1926), 1:549–56; and Roger E. Stoddard, *"Put a Resolute Hart to a Steep Hill": William Gowans Antiquary and Bookseller* (New York: Book Arts Press of the School of Library Service, Columbia University, 1990). Gowans's testimony to Poe's sobriety is even more impressive when we learn that "He [Gowans] was temperate in his habits—a cold water man through life" ("Obituary—William Gowans, Bibliopolist," *New York Tribune,* November 29, 1870, 8).
2. John H. Ingram, *Edgar Allan Poe: His Life, Letters, and Opinions,* 2 vols. (London: John Hogg, 1880), 1:144–45.
3. Burton R. Pollin, "Poe's Authorship of Three Long Critical and Autobiographical Articles of 1843 Now Authenticated," *American Renaissance Literary Report: An Annual 7* (1993): 165; Benjamin F. Fisher, "The *Saturday Museum* Sketch of Poe," in *Masques, Mysteries, and Mastodons; A Poe Miscellany,* ed. Fisher (Baltimore, MD: Edgar Allan Poe Society, 2006), 160; and [Edgar A. Poe and Henry B. Hirst (or Poe alone)], "From 'Poets and Poetry of Philadelphia,'" in *Poe in His Own Times* (Iowa City: University of Iowa Press 2010), 28.
4. Flora Lapham Mack [for William Lanier Washington], "Poe's Appearance & Personality," collection of the author.

5. Dwight Thomas and David K. Jackson, *The Poe Log: A Documentary Life of Edgar Allan Poe, 1809–1849* (Boston: G. K. Hall, 1987), 243.
6. Edgar Allan Poe, "Arthur Gordon Pym. No II," *Southern Literary Messenger* (February 1837): 111.
7. I detail the *Gil Blas* connection and the allegorical births of Henry and Edgar in "Re-ordering Place in Poe's *Arthur Gordon Pym*," *Poe and Place*, ed. Phillip Edward Philips (Cham, Switzerland: Palgrave Macmillan, 2018), 204–5, 194–95.
8. For Mr. Peterson, see Poe, "Arthur Gordon Pym," 109; for "*lying close*," see 114. Poe had written of Pym and Augustus in the first installment, "We occupied the same bed" (Poe, "Arthur Gordon Pym," 13). For "Goddin" and "Vredenburg," see 109. The latter name is spelled with an "h" in the first installment (13, 16). John Goddin is listed as a subscriber to the *Messenger* in the August 1834, April 1835, and January 1836 issues. Isaac A. Goddin is listed in the August 1834, November 1834, and January 1836 issues. Otis Vredenburgh appears as a subscriber in the April 1836 issue. The subscriber lists were published on the wrappers of the magazine, which are today available at the Virginia Museum of History & Culture.
9. Philip Hone, *The Diary of Philip Hone 1828–1851*, vols. 1 & 2 (1889; New York: Arno & New York Times, 1970), 251.
10. I take much of this detail from "The Booksellers' Dinner," *New York American* biweekly, April 7, 1837. I also consulted subsequent treatments of the event, including J. C. Derby, *Fifty Years among Authors, Books and Publishers* (New York: G. W. Carleton, 1884), 582–84; James Grant Wilson's *The Memorial History of the City of New York from Its First Settlement to the Year 1892* (New York: New-York History Co., 1893), 4:70–71; and Eugene Exman, *The Brothers Harper* (New York: Harper & Row, 1965), 87–92. I am grateful to have examined the remarkable menu for the dinner, kindly made available by two venerable bookmen—Howard S. Mott and, later, his son Donald N. Mott.
11. For Gowans's description of Poe's appearance, see *Catalogue of American Books*, no. 28 (1870), 11. His description of Poe's library is available in *Catalogue of American Books*, no. 27 (1869), 30, reprinted in Stoddard, "*Put a Resolute Hart to a Steep Hill*," 26.
12. For background, see William Charvat, "American Romanticism and the Depression of 1837," *Science and Society* 2 (1937): 67–82. For commentary on the Panic of 1837 and Harper and Brothers, see Exman, *The Brothers Harper*, 92–100.
13. For a facsimile of the copyright document, see Alexander Hammond, "The Composition of *The Narrative of Arthur Gordon Pym*: Notes toward a Re-examination," *American Transcendental Quarterly* 37 (1978): 11. Other compositional studies of *Pym* include J. V. Ridgely and Iola Haverstick, "Chartless Voyage: The Many Narratives of Arthur Gordon Pym," *Texas Studies in Literature & Language* 8, no. 1 (1966): 63–80; and Ridgely, "The Growth of the Text" (P 1:29–36).
14. The bankruptcy documents are included in Barbara Cantalupo, "Interview with Jefferson Moak (October 2007)," *Edgar Allan Poe Review* 8, no. 2 (2007): 92–98, and are available through the National Archives at Philadelphia. Poe owed Reynolds $10, Bryant $52, and Paulding $20. There were also a disputed rent payment of $40 and an unpaid rent security of $50. The other debts were "book debts"—debts recorded in account books—for $20 and $15, respectively.

15. The source is Charles Hemstreet's *Literary New York: Its Landmarks and Associations* (New York: G. P. Putnam's Sons, 1903). It features, as chapter 8, "Those Who Gathered about Poe" (145–66). For the passage on Poe in New York City in 1837, see 148–50. Mary E. Phillips cites the book in *Edgar Allan Poe—The Man*, 1:558–59.

16. Edgar Allan Poe, "Von Jung, the Mystific," *American Monthly Magazine*, June 1837, 562–71 (American Periodicals, ProQuest). The quoted passages appear on pages 564 and 571. For the contention that Poe's "Von Jung" was a response to a chapter in Theodore S. Fay's novel *Norman Leslie*, see Burton R. Pollin, "Poe's Mystification: Its Source in Fay's *Norman Leslie*," *Mississippi Quarterly* 25, no. 2 (1972), 11–30 (ProQuest). For the Mabbott edition's text of the tale, based on the *Broadway Journal* publication in 1845, see M 2:292–304. For the quoted passages there, sometimes revised, see M 2:295, 303.

17. Philip Hone, *The Diary of Philip Hone 1828–1851*, ed. Allan Nevins, 2 vols. (New York: Dodd, Mead, 1927), 1:267–68.

18. Sidney P. Moss comments on this possibility (Moss, *Poe's Literary Battles: The Critic in the Context of His Literary Milieu* [Durham, NC: Duke University Press, 1963], 61).

19. John Ward Ostrom, "Edgar A. Poe: His Income as Literary Entrepreneur," *Poe Studies* 15, no. 1 (1982): 2.

20. I take the date of the marriage from William Lanier Washington, "Untrustworthy Memorialists of Edgar Allan Poe, The Rev. Rufus W. Griswold and Mrs. Susan Archer Weiss," pp. 8–9, presented at Boston University on January 19, 1909 (the Poe centenary), and available in typescript at the Albert and Shirley Small Special Collections Library, University of Virginia, Charlottesville. The document was given to the University by Flora Lapham Mack's daughter, Mary Mackenzie Mack.

21. Flora Lapham Mack, "Concerning Correspondence between Edgar Allan Poe & John H. Mackenzie," collection of the author. Today, a copy of one letter from Poe to John H. Mackenzie is known, from April 1843 (O 1:398–99). A copy of one letter from Poe to Thomas G. Mackenzie is also known, from April 22, 1843 (O 1:396–98).

22. "The New York Review," in Frank Luther Mott, *A History of American Magazines 1741–1850* (Cambridge, MA: Harvard University Press, 1938), 669–71. This is volume 1 of the four-volume *A History of American Magazines*.

23. Burton R. Pollin, "Poe's Dr. Ollapod," *American Literature* 42, no. 1 (1970): 80–82 (JSTOR).

24. Phillips, *Edgar Allan Poe—The Man*, 1:556–57; M 1:547–48, 548n.

14. "I Shall Remain in Philadelphia Perhaps for a Year"

1. I discuss the presence of these places in *Pym* in "Re-ordering Place in Poe's *Arthur Gordon Pym*," in *Poe and Place*, ed. Philip Edward Phillips (Cham, Switzerland: Palgrave Macmillan, 2018), 193–213.

2. See John H. Ingram, *Edgar Allan Poe: His Life, Letters, and Opinions*, 2 vols. (London: John Hogg, 1880), 1:145; and William Gowans, *Catalogue of American*

Books, no. 28 (1870), 11. For Ingram's source, see Item 108 in John Henry Ingram's Poe Collection, Albert & Shirley Small Special Collections Library, University of Virginia, Charlottesville (T. C. Latto to Sarah Helen Whitman, July 8, 1870).

3. For the transformation of Reynolds's work in *Pym,* see my "The Secret of *Arthur Gordon Pym:* The Text and the Source," *Studies in American Fiction* 8, no. 2 (1980): 212–15.

4. J. H. Whitty, "Memoir," in *The Complete Poems of Edgar Allan Poe* (Boston: Houghton Mifflin, 1911), xli. Pedder was a specialist in making beet sugar (see *Appleton's Cyclopedia of American Biography, 1660–1889,* as well as A. S. W. Rosenbach, *A Catalogue of the Books and Manuscripts of Henry Elkin Widener* [Philadelphia: privately printed, 1918]).

5. Dwight Rembert Thomas, "Poe in Philadelphia 1838–1844: A Documentary Record" (PhD diss., University of Pennsylvania, 1978), 1:13, 2:825–28. See also Dwight Thomas and David K. Jackson, *The Poe Log: A Documentary Life of Edgar Allan Poe, 1809–1849* (Boston: G. K. Hall, 1987), 248.

6. I consulted the 1838 map of Philadelphia by Thomas G. Bradford, available at the Historical Society of Pennsylvania. Also useful was the 1836 map of Philadelphia by Henry S. Tanner. I consulted, as well, the Philadelphia directories for 1837, 1839, and 1840, published by A. M'Elroy, available online.

7. Frederick W. Coburn, "Poe as Seen by the Brother of 'Annie,'" *New England Quarterly* 16, no. 3 (1943): 471; Elizabeth Oakes Smith to John H. Ingram, January 18, 1875; Ingram's Poe Collection, Item 196.

8. For the story of the burning of Pennsylvania Hall, see Ellis Paxson Oberholtzer, *The Literary History of Philadelphia* (Philadelphia: George W. Jacobs, 1906), 319–26. John Sartain's engraving of the event is included in Barbara Cantalupo's *Poe and the Visual Arts* (University Park: Pennsylvania State University Press, 2014),

9. For McMichael's defense of the orphan asylum, see John W. Forney, *Memorial Address upon the Character and Public Services of Morton McMichael* (Philadelphia: Sherman, 1879), 6; and Albert Mordell, "The Literary Career of Morton McMichael," *In Re Morton McMichael,* ed. Albert Mordell (Philadelphia: privately printed, 1921), 13.

9. Thomas and Jackson, *The Poe Log,* 249 (date of publication); Alexander Hammond, "The Composition of *The Narrative of Arthur Gordon Pym:* Notes toward a Re-examination," *American Transcendental Quarterly,* no. 37 (1978): 11 (date of deposit).

10. Thomas and Jackson, *The Poe Log,* 254 (Burton); Richard Kopley, *Edgar Allan Poe and the Dupin Mysteries* (New York: Palgrave Macmillan, 2008), 30–31 (McMichael). For studies of the published contemporary response to *Pym,* see Burton R. Pollin, "Poe's *Narrative of Arthur Gordon Pym* and the Contemporary Reviewers," *Studies in American Fiction* 2, no. 1 (1974): 37–56; "Three More Early Notices of *Pym* and the Snowden Connection," *Poe Studies* 8, no. 2 (1975): 32–35; "*Pym's Narrative* in the American Newspapers: More Uncollected Notices," *Poe Studies* 11, no. 1 (1978): 8–10; "Poe 'Viewed and *Reviewed*': An Annotated Checklist of Contemporaneous Notices," *Poe Studies* 13, no. 2 (1980): 21–22; and J. Don Vann, "Three More Contemporary Reviews of *Pym,*" *Poe Studies* 9, no. 2 (1976): 43–44. See also I. M. Walker, ed., *Edgar Allan Poe: The Critical Heritage*

(London: Routledge & Kegan Paul, 1986), 91–108; and Graham Clarke, ed., *Edgar Allan Poe: Critical Assessments,* 4 vols. (Mountfield, UK: Helm Information, 1991), 2:73–91.

11. Richard Kopley, "Readers Write: Nineteenth-Century Annotations in Copies of the First American Edition of Poe's *The Narrative of Arthur Gordon Pym,*" *Nineteenth-Century Literature* 55, no. 3 (2000): 403, 405.
12. See my "Re-ordering Place in Poe's Arthur Gordon Pym," as well as my "The Hidden Journey of *Arthur Gordon Pym,*" in *Studies in the American Renaissance 1982,* ed. Joel Myerson (Boston: Twayne, 1982), 32–44.
13. See Philip Barrett [Thomas Ward White], *Gilbert Hunt, the City Blacksmith* (Richmond. VA: James Woodhouse, 1859) and his collection *The Deaf Shoemaker* (New York: Dodd, Mead, 1859), 145–51, as well as Samuel Mordecai, *Richmond in By-Gone Days* (1860; Richmond, VA: Dietz, 1946), 215–18. Also relevant are "A Colored Hero," *Memphis Daily Eagle and Enquirer,* April 24, 1858 (America's Historical Newspapers); and Meredith Henne Baker, *The Richmond Theater Fire: Early America's First Great Disaster* (Baton Rouge: Louisiana State University Press, 2012), 40–41. See, as well, Rachel Beanland's novel *The House is on Fire* (New York: Simon & Schuster, 2023). For Richmond's celebration of Hunt, see the welcome offered on Hunt's return from Africa (Barrett, *The Deaf Shoemaker,* 147). The issue of *Pym* and race has been widely treated (see, for example, Leslie Fiedler, *Love and Death in the American Novel,* rev. ed. [New York: Stein and Day, 1966], 391–429; Toni Morrison, *Playing in the Dark: Whiteness and the Literary Imagination* [New York: Vintage, 1992], 29–59; and Dana D. Nelson, *The Word in Black and White: Reading "Race" in American Literature, 1638–1867* [1992; rpt., New York: Oxford University Press, 1993], 90–108). For the issue of Poe and race in general, see Terence Whalen, *Edgar Allan Poe and The Masses: The Political Economy of Literature in Antebellum America* (Princeton, NJ: Princeton University Press, 1999), 111–46; and J. Gerald Kennedy and Liliane Weissberg, eds., *Romancing the Shadow: Poe and Race* (New York: Oxford University Press, 2001).
14. I elaborate here an autobiographical and religious interpretation of *Pym* that I have offered elsewhere in various studies. Most readily accessible are my introduction and notes for the Penguin edition of Poe's *The Narrative of Arthur Gordon Pym* (New York: Penguin, 1999).
15. John Allan to Charles Ellis, December 23, 1819, Box 219 and Box 528, DLC-EA.
16. William Lanier Washington, ["Of Rosalie Poe"], collection of the author.
17. For the location of the office of the *Saturday News,* I consult issues from July 29, 1837, and June 2, 1838. In the 1837 directory of Philadelphia, Godey is listed as "pub. *Lady's Book* and *Sat. News,* 100 Walnut."
18. For fuller detail on the *Saturday News* and "The Murders in the Rue Morgue," see my *Edgar Allan Poe and the Dupin Mysteries* (New York: Palgrave Macmillan, 2008), 29–44, 97–104.
19. Thomas, "Poe in Philadelphia," 1:18–19.
20. For the Sixteenth and Locust location, see Anne E. C. Clarke in John Sartain, *The Reminiscences of a Very Old Man, 1808–1897* (New York: D. Appleton, 1899), 217. She specifies "near Locust on Sixteenth, at that time named Schuylkill

Seventh Street." It was Amanda Harris who described the house as "rose covered" (Thomas, "Poe in Philadelphia," 2:789–90). For further discussion, see ibid., 1:25–27. The alternative view, "Christian street and Jefferson Avenue, formerly called the Moyamensing Road," is offered by Penn Junior [Lambert A. Wilmer] in "Edgar A. Poe," *Cincinnati Daily Gazette,* December 1859, vol. 70, no. 312, p. 1 (https://www.eapoe.org, courtesy Jeffrey A. Savoye, who credits Tom Fafianie and Dan Boudreau).

21. ["A brilliant *Soiree*"], *New York Evening Star,* September 7, 1838, 2.
22. "The Lady's Book," *Philadelphia Saturday News & Literary Gazette,* September 15, 1838, 2.
23. For George Palmer Putnam's comments on publishing *Pym,* see George Palmer Putnam, "Leaves from a Publisher's Letter-Book," *Putnam's Monthly,* October 1869, 470–71, https://www.eapoe.org, and J. C. Derby, *Fifty Years among Authors, Books and Publishers* (New York: G. W. Carleton, 1884), 302–3.
24. Ingram, *Edgar Allan Poe: His Life, Letters, and Opinions,* 1:155–56.
25. For the original version of the story, see Edgar A. Poe, "Ligeia," *The American Museum of Science, Literature, and the Arts* [Baltimore], September 1838, 25–37. The cited quotation appears on p. 27 (American Periodicals Series).
26. Sarah Helen Whitman, *Edgar Poe and His Critics* (New York: Rudd & Carleton, 1860), 70–71. For the quoted passage in the March 1846 marginalia entry, see P 2:258. Poe comments on "Ligeia" in a letter to Philip Pendleton Cooke on September 21, 1839 (O 1:193–94).
27. I discuss these sources in *Edgar Allan Poe and the Dupin Mysteries,* 31–44.
28. For the successor to the *Saturday News,* see "To the Subscribers to the 'Saturday News,'" *Philadelphia Saturday News and Literary Gazette,* January 5, 1838, 3; Winifred Gregory, ed, *American Newspapers 1821–1936* (New York: H. W. Wilson, 1937), 617; and *A Checklist of Pennsylvania Newspapers,* vol. 1: *Philadelphia County* (Harrisburg: Pennsylvania Historical Commission, 1944), 234.
29. For information on the Pedders, I have relied on *Appleton's Cyclopedia of American Biography, 1660–1889;* A. S. W. Rosenbach, comp., *A Catalogue of the Books and Manuscripts of Henry Elkins Widener,* 2 vols. (Philadelphia: privately printed, 1918), 2:56–57; Thomas, "Poe in Philadelphia," 2:865–66; and Thomas and Jackson, *The Poe Log,* 279. According to https://www.ancestry.com, the Pedder family arrived in the United States from England in 1833. Rosenbach mentions that James Pedder was writing of Poe in 1852. Amanda Bartlett Harris offers some similar detail in "Edgar A. Poe," *Hearth and Home* 8, no. 2 (January 29, 1875), 24 (https://www.eapoe.org).
30. Thomas and Jackson, *The Poe Log,* 260.
31. William Gowans, *Catalogue of American Books,* no. 28 (1870), 11.
32. For extensive treatment of Poe and *The Conchologist's First Book,* see Thomas, "Poe in Philadelphia," 1:40–41, 2:947–56, on which I relied. For the Thomas and Jackson quotation, see 630. Illustrations, they acknowledge, were taken from the Thomas Brown book that the *Post* had mentioned. Also of interest is Richard Johnson's "Edgar Allan Poe and Thomas Wyatt," *Occasional Papers on Mollusks* 4, no. 50 (November 15, 1974): 50–52. See, as well, Stephen Jay Gould, "Poe's Greatest Hit," *Natural History* 102, no. 7 (July 1993): 10, 12, 14–19. There was a

revised edition of *The Conchologist's First Book* in September 1839 with a new, two-paragraph preface by Poe. There has been conjecture regarding Poe's possible involvement with Wyatt's 1839 *A Synopsis of Natural History* (see Charles F. Heartman and James R. Canny, comps., *A Bibliography of First Printings of the Writings of Edgar Allan Poe* [Hattiesburg, MS: The Book Farm, 1943], 45–46; and Thomas, "Poe in Philadelphia," 1:41–42).

33. John Ward Ostrom, "Edgar A. Poe: His Income as a Literary Entrepreneur," *Poe Studies* 15, no. 1 (1982): 2.

34. The Burton letter is given in H 17:45–46 and with its correct date in Arthur Hobson Quinn, *Edgar Allan Poe: A Critical Biography* (New York: D. Appleton-Century, 1941), 277–78. For Poe's monthly salary at *Burton's* in 1840 of fifty dollars a month, see O 1:219.

35. For Burton's May 30, 1839, letter, see Quinn, *Edgar Allan Poe: A Critical Biography*, 279–82. Quinn offers, parallel to the actual letter, Rufus W. Griswold's manipulated and malicious version of it.

36. Thomas, "Poe in Philadelphia," 1:47.

37. Thomas Dunn English, "Reminiscences of Poe" II, *New York Independent*, October 22, 1896, 1415 (https://www.eapoe.org); and George E. Woodberry, *The Life of Edgar Allan Poe*, 2 vols. (Boston: Houghton Mifflin, 1909), 2:419.

38. See Edwin Wolf 2d, "Horace Wemyss Smith's Recollections of Poe," *Library Chronicle of the University of Pennsylvania* 17 (1951): 91–92; and William Fearing Gill, *The Life of Edgar Allan Poe* (New York: C. T. Dillingham, 1877), 96–97. Burton himself referred to Poe's "infirmities" (Thomas and Jackson, *The Poe Log*, 307). Quinn dismissed the Smith account but accepted the Alexander one (296–97). Thomas carefully assessed Smith's narrative ("Poe in Philadelphia," 2:889–94). Kenneth Silverman acknowledged some of the conflicting evidence (*Edgar A. Poe: Mournful and Never-Ending Remembrance* [New York: Harper-Collins, 1991], 158–59). I don't cite English here regarding his finding Poe intoxicated since English's biographer contends that English antedated the incident (William H. Gravely, "The Early Political and Literary Career of Thomas Dunn English" [PhD diss., University of Virginia, 1953], 287).

39. Gill, *The Life of Edgar Allan Poe*, 96–97.

40. Edgar Allan Poe, review of Thomas Wyatt, *A Synopsis of Natural History*, *Burton's Gentleman's Magazine*, July 1839, 61–62 (H 10:26–27); review of Henry Lord Brougham, *Sketches of Public Characters, Discourses, and Essays*, *Burton's Gentleman's Magazine*, July 1839, 62.

41. See Thomas, "Poe in Philadelphia," 1:51–54.

42. See Edgar Allan Poe, "The Man That Was Used Up," *Burton's Gentleman's Magazine*, August 1839, 66; and "Payments—Continued," inside rear wrapper, *Southern Literary Messenger* (March 1836), Virginia Museum of History and Culture. For consideration of a possible model for General A. B. C. Smith, see J. Gerald Kennedy, "Unwinnable Wars, Unspeakable Wounds: Locating 'The Man That Was Used Up,'" *Poe Studies* 39–40 (2006–7): 77–89.

43. For a brief biography of Fisher, see Thomas, "Poe in Philadelphia," 2:763–64. The letters from Fisher to Poe are provided in Heartman and Canny, *A Bibliography of First Printings of the Writings of Edgar Allan Poe*, 218–22.

44. Edgar Allan Poe, review of N. P. Willis, *Tortesa, the Usurer, Literary Examiner and Western Monthly Review* 1, no. 3 (July 1839): 212; Poe, "American Novel-Writing," *Literary Examiner and Western Monthly Review* 1, no. 4 (August 1839): 319. This periodical is available online in facsimile through ebscohost; the two Poe items are also available at https://www.eapoe.org. For more on the Browne quotation, see M 2:569n.

45. For the *Pelham* source, see my "Poe's Taking of *Pelham* One Two Three Four Five Six," *Poe Studies* 41 (2008): 113. For the *Ivanhoe* source, see Alexander Hammond, "Poe, Scott's Fiction, and the Holt Source Collection: The Example of *Ivanhoe* and 'The Fall of the House of Usher,'" *Resources for American Literary Study* 34 (2009): 57–66. For a review of German sources for "Usher," see Thomas S. Hansen with Burton R. Pollin, *The German Face of Edgar Allan Poe: A Study of Literary References in His Works* (Columbia, SC: Camden House, 1995), 60–66. We may recall the Washington Gardens in Boston, the site of the Usher mansion. Poe scholar J. H. Whitty remembered "the 'Usher' family house" in Old Town in Baltimore, and he suggested, "Poe must have known or heard of it in his day there" (J. H. Whitty to Mary Elizabeth Phillips, August 15, 1922, Whitty Collection, MsAm 1200 [446], Special Collections, Boston Public Library).

46. See Thomas and Jackson, *The Poe Log*, 275. Poe includes Irving's comment on "William Wilson" in the *Saturday Museum* biography of himself that he wrote with Henry B. Hirst or alone (see Benjamin F. Fisher, ed., *Poe in His Own Time* [Iowa City: University of Iowa Press, 2010], 29–30).

47. For Poe's earlier use of the term "well-doing" with Snodgrass, see O 1:197. For comment on the term, see O 1:198.

48. For the original review, see Edgar Allan Poe, review of *Hyperion, a Romance*, [by Henry Wadsworth Longfellow], *Burton's Gentleman's Magazine*, October 1839, 227.

49. For the original publication, consult Edgar Allan Poe, review of *An Address, Delivered before the Goethean and Diagnothian Societies of Marshall College*, *Burton's Gentleman's Magazine*, December 1839, 330.

50. Thomas, "Poe in Philadelphia," 1:89–91; Woodberry, *The Life of Edgar Allan Poe*, 2:375–76; Thomas, "Poe in Philadelphia," 1:79; Thomas and Jackson, *The Poe Log*, 274.

51. See also Heartman and Canny, *A Bibliography of First Printings of the Writings of Edgar Allan Poe*, 52.

52. Quinn, *Edgar Allan Poe: A Critical Biography*, 289.

53. The *Saint Louis Commercial Bulletin* offered this comment before September 11, 1839 (Thomas and Jackson, *The Poe Log*, 269). For the opinions appended to the second volume, see "'Personal' and 'Editorial Opinions,'" in *Edgar Allan Poe: The Critical Heritage*, ed. I. M. Walker (London: Routledge & Kegan Paul, 1986), 116–21.

54. See Heartman and Canny, *A Bibliography of First Printings of the Writings of Edgar Allan Poe*, 53; Thomas and Jackson, *The Poe Log*, 279, 280, 281, 311; Thomas, "Poe in Philadelphia," 1:92; *Evermore: The Persistence of Poe: The Edgar Allan Poe Collection of Susan Jaffe Tane* (New York: Grolier Club, 2014), 157.

55. For Poe's sending *Tales of the Grotesque and Arabesque* to Dickens, see Thomas and Jackson, *The Poe Log*, 361–62.

56. Respectively, these comments are by Joseph C. Neal in the *Pennsylvanian* on December 6 (Thomas and Jackson, *The Poe Log*, 280); Ezra Holden in the *Saturday Courier* on December 14 (Thomas, "Poe in Philadelphia," 1:96); and perhaps Louis F. Tasistro in the *New-York Mirror* on December 28 (Thomas and Jackson, *The Poe Log*, 284).
57. "Prejudice—A Good Joke!," *Philadelphia Public Ledger*, September 10, 1840, [2] (America's Historical Newspapers). The *Boston Notion* had commented severely on *Tales of the Grotesque and Arabesque* on December 14, 1839, and then published "The Fall of the House of Usher," from *Bentley's Miscellany*, on September 5, 1840 (Thomas and Jackson, *The Poe Log*, 282, 307).
58. For the advertisements for "Julius Rodman" and the premium scheme, see Thomas and Jackson, *The Poe Log*, 277–78. Thomas discussed the premium scheme in "William E. Burton and His Premium Scheme: New Light on Poe Biography," *University of Mississippi Studies in English*, n.s., vol. 3 (1982): 68–80. For other commentary, see Thomas S. Marvin, "'These Days of Double Dealing': Edgar Allan Poe and the Business of Magazine Publishing," *American Periodicals* 11 (2001): 88–90; and Leon Jackson, *The Business of Letters: Authorial Economies in Antebellum America* (Stanford, CA: Stanford University Press, 2008), 226.
59. Edgar Allan Poe, review of *Alciphron, a Poem*, by Thomas Moore, *Burton's Gentleman's Magazine*, January 1840, 53–55. (See also H 10:61–68.)
60. Edgar Allan Poe, review of *Voices of the Night*, by Henry Wadsworth Longfellow, *Burton's Gentleman's Magazine*, February 1840, 100, 102–3 (see also H 10:72, 76–80). For Longfellow's access to Tennyson's poem, see Sidney P. Moss, *Poe's Literary Battles: The Critic in the Context of His Literary Milieu* (Durham, NC: Duke University Press, 1963), 139–40.
61. ["On 'Our Club'"], Special Collections, Pattee/Paterno Library, Pennsylvania State University.
62. Charles M. McMichael to Mary E. Phillips, December 17, 1920, Rare Books and Manuscripts, Boston Public Library.
63. See Wolf, "Horace Wemyss Smith's Recollections of Poe," 91–92. Again, for Thomas's comment on the Horace Wemyss Smith recollection, see "Poe in Philadelphia," 2:889–94.
64. Burton R. Pollin, "*The Living Writers of America*: A Manuscript by Edgar Allan Poe," in *Studies in the American Renaissance 1991*, ed. Joel Myerson (Charlottesville: University Press of Virginia, 1991), 165.
65. For Poe at the Falstaff Hotel, see the comments of Isaac Winter Heysinger in Thomas, "Poe in Philadelphia," 2:805–8. See also Thomas and Jackson, *The Poe Log*, 284. However, Michael J. Deas rejects Heysinger's claim that Thomas Sully painted Poe's portrait (Deas, *The Portraits of Daguerreotypes of Edgar Allan Poe* [Charlottesville: University Press of Virginia, 1989], 120–22). For Poe with Hirst, Scott, and Smith, see Wolf, "Horace Wemyss Smith's Recollections of Poe," 92.
66. For more on Mitchell and Maelzel's Chess-Player, see Tom Standage, *The Turk: The Life and Times of the Famous Eighteenth-Century Chess-Playing Machine* (New York: Walker, 2002), 188–91.
67. Poe wrote in his review of the April 1840 issue of *Burton's Gentleman's Magazine* in *Alexander's Weekly Messenger*, "A fine engraving illustrates this chapter"

(Clarence S. Brigham, *Edgar Allan Poe's Contributions to Alexander's Weekly Messenger* [Worcester, MA: American Antiquarian Society, 1943], 66). However, the picture (Poe, "The Journal of Julius Rodman," chapter 4, *Burton's Gentleman's Magazine,* April 1840, 181) does not entirely correspond to Rodman's description, as Liliane Weissberg has noted (Weissberg, "Editing Adventures: Writing the Text of *Julius Rodman,*" *Modern Fiction Studies* 33, no. 3 [1987]: 423). For the image in Hawthorne's periodical, see the entry "Wild Horsemen," *American Magazine of Useful and Entertaining Knowledge* 2, no. 10 (June 1836): 432. The background missing in the "Rodman" image is present in "A Sioux on Horseback," as are the initials "GLF" or "GLE," perhaps those of the engraver. Probably the image circulated in a number of periodicals. Burton R. Pollin terms the woodcut that Poe used "a coarse little sketch" and considers Poe's comment on it "tongue in cheek" (P 1:629).

68. Thomas, "William E. Burton and His Premium Scheme"; Thomas and Jackson, *The Poe Log,* 292–93.
69. See Thomas, "William E. Burton and His Premium Scheme," 78. Lowell's poem "Callirhöe" was published in *Graham's,* and Peterson did offer payment. Lowell had submitted the poem under the pseudonym "Hugh Perceval."
70. Flora Lapham Mack, Family Chart, collection of the author. The date of the wedding is given as April 28, 1840, at https://www.ancestry.com. And Flora Lapham Mack gives the date as May 30, 1840, in her responses to William Lanier Washington's written questions ("Data," collection of the author). Mary Mattox was seventeen at the time of her wedding; her husband, Benjamin Byrene Lapham, thirty-nine. He died in 1865; seven years later, Mary Mattox married John H. Mackenzie, making her daughter his stepdaughter.
71. It is possible that this incident owes something to an incident appearing in the *Philadelphia Saturday News and Literary Gazette* concerning a bear and a hunter falling over the edge of a precipice (see the issue of July 7, 1838, 4).
72. David K. Jackson, "A Poe Hoax Comes before the U.S. Senate," *Poe Studies* 7, no. 2 (1974): 47–48; Joan Tyler Mead, "Poe's 'Manual of Seamanship,'" in *Poe's Pym: Critical Explorations,* ed. Richard Kopley (Durham, NC: Duke University Press, 1992), 29–32.
73. Edgar Allan Poe, "Some Account of Stonehenge, the Giant's Dance, a Druidical Ruin in England," *Burton's Gentleman's Magazine,* June 1840, 251. See J. O. Bailey, "Poe's 'Stonehenge,'" *Studies in Philology* 38, no. 4 (1941): 645–51.
74. [Conclusion of Volume Six], *Burton's Gentleman's Magazine,* June 1840, 294.
75. For treatment of this period, see Thomas, "Poe in Philadelphia," 1:121–38; and Thomas and Jackson, *The Poe Log,* 294–98.

15. "Fortune & Fame Must Go Hand in Hand"

1. Dwight Thomas and David K. Jackson, *The Poe Log: A Documentary Life of Edgar Allan Poe, 1809–1849* (Boston: G. K. Hall, 1987), 299–302.
2. The list may be found in Alexander G. Rose III and Jeffrey Alan Savoye, *Such Friends as These: Edgar Allan Poe's List of Subscribers and Contributors to His Dream Magazine* (Baltimore, MD: Enoch Pratt Free Library and Edgar Allan Poe Society, 1986).

3. Thomas and Jackson, *The Poe Log*, 306–7.
4. Ibid., 296.
5. Edward J. Balleisen, *Navigating Failure: Bankruptcy and Commercial Society in Antebellum America* (Chapel Hill: University of North Carolina Press, 2001), 103–5.
6. Frederick W. Thomas wrote Poe a very useful autobiographical letter (H 17:95–100), and Dwight Thomas provides a strong biographical sketch in "Poe in Philadelphia" (PhD diss., University of Pennsylvania, 1978), 2:913–17. Mary E. Phillips considers the correspondence between Poe and Thomas to date from 1836 (Phillips, *Edgar Allan Poe—The Man*, 2 vols. [Chicago: John C. Winston, 1926], 1:438). For an account of the 1840 campaign, see Richard G. Shafer, *The Carnival Campaign: How the Rollicking 1840 Campaign of "Tippecanoe and Tyler Too" Changed Presidential Elections Forever* (Chicago: Chicago Review Press, 2016).
7. For more on Poe, Thomas, and Dow, see Thomas and Jackson, *The Poe Log*, 295; and Thomas, "Poe in Philadelphia," 1:125–27. Poe recalled to Thomas "those literary and other disquisitions about which we quarrelld [*sic*] at Studevant's [John Sturdivant's Congress Hotel, at Chestnut and Third]" (O 1:248). For additional information, see J. Albert Robbins, "Edgar Poe and the Philadelphians: A Reminiscence by a Contemporary," *Poe Studies* 5, no. 2 (1972): 45–48. The "contemporary" was probably, according to Thomas, Thompson Westcott (Thomas. "Poe in Philadelphia," 2:935–38), who recalled Poe and Dow at Robert Harmer's Cornucopia restaurant, at North Third Street (47). For more on Sturdivant and Harmer, see ibid., 2:908, 787–88.
8. Thomas Dunn English, "Reminiscences of Poe II," *New York Independent*, October 22, 1896, 1415–16 (https://www.eapoe.org). See also Thomas, "Poe in Philadelphia," 2:757. I do not at this point include English's recollection of having found Poe drunk since the biographer William Henry Gravely asserts that English antedated the event (Gravely, "The Early Political and Literary Career of Thomas Dunn English" [PhD diss., University of Virginia, 1953], 286–87). Arthur Hobson Quinn believed that English's visits were to Poe's later Spring Garden house (Quinn, *Edgar Allan Poe: A Critical Biography* [New York: D. Appleton-Century, 1941], 349).
9. Augustus Van Cleef, "Poe's Mary," *Harper's New Monthly Magazine*, March 1889, 639 (https://www.eapoe.org). See also Thomas, "Poe in Philadelphia," 2:902. Mary Starr noted that "They lived in Seventh Street," and, according to Anne E. C. Clark, Poe then lived at "Locust Street on Sixteenth, at that time named Schuylkill Seventh Street" (John Sartain, *The Reminiscences of a Very Old Man* [New York: D. Appleton, 1899], 217). She wouldn't have been referring to the Seventh Street home to which the Poe family moved in 1842 since she mentions an event that occurred in 1842 as having taken place "A few years afterward." For the Moore song, see studylit.net.
10. Amanda Bartlett Harris, "Edgar A. Poe," *Hearth and Home*, January 9, 1875, 24 (https://www.eapoe.org); see also Thomas, "Poe in Philadelphia," 2:788–80; and George E. Woodberry, *The Life of Edgar Allan Poe*, 2 vols. (Boston: Houghton Mifflin, 1909), 297, 382. By the end of 1842, Poe had declared bankruptcy.

11. Lambert A. Wilmer, *Merlin Baltimore, 1827, together with Recollections of Edgar A. Poe*, ed. Thomas Ollive Mabbott (1941; rpt., n.p. [Folcroft, PA]: Folcroft Library Editions, 1973), 32.
12. George R. Graham, "The Late Edgar Allan Poe," *Graham's Magazine* 36, no. 3 (March 1850): 225 (ebscohost); reprinted H 1:406 and https://www.eapoe.org.
13. See Thomas and Jackson, *The Poe Log*, 309; and Thomas, "Poe in Philadelphia," 1:166–67 and 2:774–77. For more on *Graham's Magazine*, see Frank Luther Mott, *A History of American Magazines*, 4 vols. (Cambridge, MA: Harvard University Press, 1938–57), 1:545–55; and Arthur Wrobel, "Graham's Lady's and Gentleman's Magazine," *American Literary Magazines: The Eighteenth and Nineteenth Centuries*, ed. Edward E. Chielens (Westport, CT: Greenwood, 1986), 156–61. Also useful is J. Albert Robbins, "George R. Graham Philadelphia Publisher," *Pennsylvania Magazine of History and Biography* 75, no. 3 (1951): 279–94. The Ostrom source for the comment on Billy Barlow is Kenneth Silverman, *Edgar A. Poe Mournful and Never-ending Remembrance* (New York: HarperCollins, 1991), 158.
14. I quote from Sartain's "Poe's Last Days," reprinted in Richard Tuerk, "John Sartain and E. A. Poe," *Poe Studies* 4, no. 2 (1971): 22. See also John Sartain, "Reminiscences of Edgar Allan Poe," *Lippincott's Magazine* 17 (1889): 411–15; and *Reminiscences*, 199–217, 220–22, 226.
15. Thomas, "Poe in Philadelphia," 1:165. The notice was from the *St. Louis Commercial Bulletin* and was copied in the *Philadelphia Daily Chronicle*. F. W. Thomas later reversed the phrasing of this comment in a May 28, 1841, letter to Poe (see Thomas, "Poe in Philadelphia," 1:226; and Thomas and Jackson, *The Poe Log*, 327–28).
16. I take the publication date for the December issue of the *Casket* and the *Gentleman's Magazine* (as *Graham's Magazine*) from Thomas and Jackson, *The Poe Log*, 311.
17. I quote from the original: Edgar Allan Poe, "The Man of the Crowd," *Gentleman's Magazine* 7, no. 6 (December 1840) (also identified as *Graham's Magazine*), 268–69. See also M 2:511.
18. Edgar Allan Poe, "The Man of the Crowd," 270. See also M 2:515.
19. Edgar Allan Poe, "The Man of the Crowd," 267, 270. See also M 2:506, 515.
20. Edgar Allan Poe, "The Man of the Crowd," 268. See also M 2:510. For a fuller discussion of the structure of the tale, see my study *The Formal Center in Literature: Explorations from Poe to the Present* (Rochester, NY: Camden House, 2018), 19–20.
21. Edgar Allan Poe, "The Man of the Crowd," 267. See also M 2:506.
22. The translation is provided by Jerome McGann in his edition of *Pelham* (Edward George Bulwer-Lytton, *Pelham or The Adventures of a Gentleman*, ed. McGann [Lincoln: University of Nebraska Press, 1972], 168, 168n). See also Kopley, *The Formal Center in Literature*, 25, 135–36.
23. Poe, "The Man of the Crowd," *Gentleman's Magazine*, 268, 270. See also M 2:510, 515.
24. See Kopley, *The Formal Center in Literature*, 25–27, 136. Also pertinent is my "The Taking of *Pelham* One Two Three Four Five Six," *Poe Studies* 41 (2008): 112–13. The phrase "heart laid bare" occurs in *Pelham*, 365.

25. Thomas, "Poe in Philadelphia," 1:178; Balleisen, *Navigating Failure*, 104–5.
26. The *Philadelphia Public Ledger* offers a piece on the January issue of *Graham's Magazine* on December 17 ("Graham's Magazine," *Philadelphia Public Ledger*, December 17, 1840, 2).
27. The dinner party took place on December 24, 1840 (Thomas, "Poe in Philadelphia," 1:182–83). Curiously, Griswold's "To the Reader" in *The Biographical Annual* closes "New-York, Dec. 24, 1840" (Rufus W. Griswold, ed., *The Biographical Annual: Containing Memoirs of Eminent Persons Recently Deceased* [New York: Linen and Fennell 1841], x).
28. *Passages from the Correspondence and Other Papers of Rufus W. Griswold* (Cambridge, MA: W. M. Griswold, 1898), 47–52; Joy Bayless, *Rufus Wilmot Griswold: Poe's Literary Executor* (Nashville, TN: Vanderbilt University Press, 1943), 34–35; Thomas, "Poe in Philadelphia," 2:779–83. See also Richard J. Calhoun, "Rufus Wilmot Griswold," *American Literary Critics and Scholars, 1800–1850* (*DLB* 59), ed. John W. Rathbun and Monica M. Grecu (Detroit, MI: Gale Research, 1987), 153–58.
29. Edgar Allan Poe, "The Murders in the Rue Morgue," *Graham's Magazine* 18, no. 4 (April 1841): 166. See also M 2:528.
30. See Thomas, "Poe in Philadelphia," 1:193; and Alasdair Roberts, *America's First Great Depression: Economic Crisis and Political Disorder after the Panic of 1837* (Ithaca, NY: Cornell University Press, 2012), 46–47.
31. Thomas, "Poe in Philadelphia," 1:195–96; Thomas and Jackson, *The Poe Log*, 318–19.
32. See "Periodicals," in *M'Elroy's Philadelphia Directory for 1841*, 4th ed. (Philadelphia: Orrin Rogers, 1841), previous to the listing of names; and *M'Elroy's Philadelphia Directory for 1842*, 5th ed. (Philadelphia: Orrin Rogers, 1842), 348.
33. "Daily Newspapers," "Weekly Newspapers," and "Periodicals," in *M'Elroy's Philadelphia Directory* (1841, 1842).
34. See Sartain, *Reminiscences*, 200; Thomas, "Poe in Philadelphia," 1:202–4; and John Ward Ostrom, "Edgar A. Poe: His Income as Literary Entrepreneur," *Poe Studies* 15, no. 1 (1982): 3.
35. For the date, I consult Thomas and Jackson, *The Poe Log*, 320. For the final line, see Edgar Allan Poe, "The Murders in the Rue Morgue," *Graham's Magazine*, 179. See also M 2:568v.
36. W. T. Bandy, "Who Was Monsieur Dupin?," *PMLA* 79, no. 4 (1964): 509–10. The writer, Socrates Maupin, was asking Poe to convey the terms of the position to Dubouchet. John H. Mackenzie's aunt, Jane Mackenzie, head of the prestigious girls' school in Richmond, is twice referenced in the letter.
37. Frederick W. Thomas to Poe, May 11, 1841, in Thomas and Jackson, *The Poe Log*, 326; Thomas Wentworth Higginson, May 7, 1841 entry, manuscript diary, Houghton Library, MS Am 784, Thomas Wentworth Higginson Letters and Journals (discovered by Sandra H. Petrulionis); [Robert Morris], review of Poe's *The Prose Romances, Edgar Allan Poe: The Critical Heritage*, ed. I. M. Walker (London: Routledge & Kegan Paul, 1986), 133.
38. [Edgar Allan Poe], review of Edward Bulwer-Lytton's *Night and Morning*, *Graham's Magazine* 18, no. 4 (April 1841): 198. See also H 10:117.

39. [Thomas Dunn English or Edgar Allan Poe or English and Poe], review of Poe's *Tales*, in *Edgar Allan Poe*, ed. Walker, 197, 196. Poe introduced his 1846 essay "The Philosophy of Composition" with reference to Charles Dickens's having written to him about Bulwer's having composed *Caleb Williams* backward. Bulwer admitted as much in 1832 (L2: 60, 71).
40. Alan Gribben, "'That Pair of Spiritual Derelicts': The Poe-Twain Relationship," *Poe Studies* 18, no. 2 (1985): 17.
41. For Voltaire, Scott, and others, see M 2:521–25. For Bulwer-Lytton, see Kopley, "The Taking of *Pelham*," 110.
42. I draw from my own work on the *Saturday News* origins of "Rue Morgue" (see Kopley, *Edgar Allan Poe and the Dupin Mysteries* [New York: Palgrave Macmillan, 2008], 27–44, 95–105). For the quotation from "Rue Morgue," I rely on Edgar Allan Poe, "The Murders in the Rue Morgue," *Graham's Magazine*, 176; see also M 2:558.
43. Poe, "The Murders in the Rue, Morgue," *Graham's Magazine*, 175; see also M 2:555.
44. Poe, "The Murders in the Rue Morgue," *Graham's Magazine*, 174. The Mabbott edition of the tale is slightly different because the editor relies for copy-text on the J. Lorimer Graham copy of the 1845 *Tales* edition of the work, with manuscript alterations (see M 2:553). For my discussion of the symmetrical language of "Rue Morgue," see Kopley, *Edgar Allan Poe and the Dupin Mysteries*, 8–13.
45. See Poe, "The Murders in the Rue Morgue," *Graham's Magazine*, 166 (identification, sources), 167 (observation), and 172 (the unusual). For the relevant texts in the Mabbott edition, see M 2:529, 530, 548.
46. Kopley, *Edgar Allan Poe and the Dupin Mysteries*, 79–81.
47. Marie Louise Shew Houghton to John Ingram, May 16, [18]75, in *Building Poe Biography*, ed. John Carl Miller (Baton Rouge: Louisiana State University Press, 1977), 140.
48. Poe, review of Bulwer-Lytton's *Night and Morning*, 199. See also H 10:122.
49. Charles F. Heartman and James R. Canny, comps., *The Bibliography of First Printings of the Writings of Edgar Allan Poe*, rev. ed. (Hattiesburg, MS: Book Farm, 1943), 68; Thomas and Jackson, *The Poe Log*, 319.
50. See Thomas and Jackson, *The Poe Log*, 319, 323; and Balleisen, *Navigating Failure*, 105.
51. See Thomas, "Poe in Philadelphia," 2:898.
52. Joseph J. Moldenhauer, "Beyond the Tamarind Tree: A New Poe Letter," *American Literature* 42, no. 4 (1971): 477.
53. "Roderick Mackenzie" and "Jane Mackenzie," https://www.ancestry.com. Roderick was born about 1771 and died in London on October 19, 1854. Jane Mackenzie was born about 1772 and died in London on April 30, 1858.
54. For the first printing, see Edgar Allan Poe, "A Descent into the Maelström," *Graham's Magazine* 18, no. 5 (May 1841): 237. For the Mabbott edition, see M 2:583. For a related earlier work, see David E. E. Sloane, "A Forerunner of 'A Descent into the Maelström,'" *Edgar Allan Poe Review* 21, no. 1 (2020): 116–19.
55. For a thorough and thoughtful consideration of that added footnote, see Aldo Corcella, "Thomas Thomson's 'Sketch of the Progress of Physical Science," *Edgar Allan Poe Review* 20, no. 2 (2019): 173–99.

56. Edgar Allan Poe, review of Charles Dickens's *The Old Curiosity Shop, and Other Tales* and *Master Humphrey's Clock*, *Graham's Magazine* 18, no. 5 (May 1841): 250. See also H 10:150.
57. See Poe, review of *The Old Curiosity Shop*, 248; and Poe, "The Purloined Letter," *The Gift for 1845* (Philadelphia: Carey & Hart, 1845), 56–57. See also H 10:143–44; and M 3:989.
58. For Poe's lauding the "Confession," see review of *The Old Curiosity Shop*, 249. See also H 10:148. For the argument regarding "Confessions" and Poe's work, see Edith Smith Krappe, "A Possible Source for Poe's 'The Tell-Tale Heart' and 'The Black Cat,'" *American Literature* 12, no. 1 (1940): 84–88. See also M 3:791. For additional anticipatory passages in the Dickens review, see William Doyle Hull II, "A Canon of the Critical Works of Edgar Allan Poe with a Study of Poe as Editor and Reviewer" (PhD diss. University of Virginia, 1941), 329–31.
59. Edgar Allan Poe, review of *Barnaby Rudge*, by Charles Dickens, *Saturday Evening Post*, May 1, 1841 (https://www.eapoe.org). A classic assessment of the Poe-Dickens relationship is Gerald G. Grubb, "The Personal and Literary Relationships of Dickens and Poe (Part One: From 'Sketches by Boz' through 'Barnaby Rudge')," *Nineteenth-Century Fiction* 5, no. 1 (1950): 1–22; "(Part Two: 'English Notes' and 'The Poets of America')," *Nineteenth-Century Fiction* 5, no. 2 (1950): 101–20. Though he considers Poe to have been wrong with regard to some of his judgments, including that the raven would be prophetic, Grubb states that with regard to the identity of the murderer, Poe was right (see "Part One," 9–10). Mabbott briefly discusses *Barnaby Rudge* and "The Raven" (M 1:355–56).
60. William L. Keese, *John Keese, Wit and Littérateur. A Biographical Memoir* (New York: D. Appleton, 1883), 51.
61. Griswold related the circumstances of his meeting Poe in his "Memoir," in *Works of Edgar A. Poe*, 4 vols. (New York: J. S. Redfield, 1850–56), 3:v. For a convenient reprinting of the passage, see Griswold, "Memoir of the Author," in *Poe in His Own Time*, ed. Benjamin F. Fisher (Iowa City: University of Iowa Press, 2010), 103. For mention of the Jones Hotel, see Bayless, *Rufus Wilmot Griswold*, 36. For the name and address of Jones's hotel, see "Principal Hotels in the City of Philadelphia," in *M'Elroy's Directory for Philadelphia* (1841), 320. Burton R. Pollin discusses Griswold and the *Boston Notion* in "Poe and the *Boston Notion*," *English Language Notes* 8 (1970): 25–26.
62. B. Bernard Cohen and Lucian A. Cohen, "Poe and Griswold Once More," *American Literature* 34, no. 1 (1962): 97–101. Notably, probably in late May 1841, Griswold sought help from Poe in obtaining sketches of Edward Coote Pinkney and Amelia Welby for his anthology, and in early June, F. W. Thomas offered to assist (Thomas and Jackson, *The Poe Log*, 328–29). For the letter of Thomas to Griswold, June 8, 1841, see *Passages from the Correspondence and Other Papers of Rufus W. Griswold*, 66–67.
63. Thomas and Jackson, *The Poe Log*, 326.
64. For the date, see ibid., 327.
65. Burton R. Pollin, "Poe's Illustrations for 'The Island of the Fay': A Hoax Detected," in *The Mystery and Detection Annual*, ed. Donald K. Adams (Beverly Hills, CA: Donald Adams, 1972), 33–45. For a related piece, see Pollin, "*Undine* in the Works

of Poe," *Studies in Romanticism* 14, no. 1 (1975): 71–72. For the earlier view that Poe adapted the tale to the engraving, see F. DeWolfe Miller, "The Basis for Poe's 'The Island of the Fay,'" *American Literature* 14, no. 2 (1942): 135–40.

66. I rely on the first printing, Edgar Allan Poe, "The Island of the Fay," *Graham's Magazine* 18, no. 6 (June 1841): 253–55. For the Mabbott edition of the tale, based on the Griswold edition, see M 2:599–605.

67. Poe, "The Island of the Fay," *Graham's Magazine*, 254. For the passage in the Mabbott edition, see M 2:602–3.

68. Poe, "The Island of the Fay," *Graham's Magazine*, 254; and M 2:601.

69. For the date of the publication of the first two volumes of Griswold's edition of Poe, see Bayless, *Rufus Wilmot Griswold*, 175, 285. For the timing of Melville's beginning *Moby-Dick*, see Hershel Parker, *Herman Melville A Biography*, vol. 1: *1819–1851* (Baltimore, MD: Johns Hopkins University Press, 1996), 711.

70. Herman Melville, *Moby-Dick; or, The Whale*, ed. Harrison Hayford, Hershel Parker, and G. Thomas Tanselle (Evanston, IL: Northwestern University Press and Newberry Library, 1988), 7. Melville did later buy the 1859 edition of the *Works*, but his earlier borrowings from Poe suggest an earlier familiarity. For the 1859 set, see Merton M. Sealts Jr., *Melville's Reading*, rev. and enlarged ed. (Columbia: University of South Carolina Press, 1988), 205–6. The one modification in language from the center of the *Graham's* text of "The Island of the Fay" to the center of the Griswold text of that work (not affecting the identified parallels) is the shift from "fantastically verdured" to "profusely verdured" (M 2:602, 602v).

71. See Edgar Allan Poe, review of Thomas Macaulay's *Critical and Miscellaneous Essays*, *Graham's Magazine* 18, no. 6 (June 1841): 294–95; and H 10:156–60; Poe, review of T. S. Arthur's *Insubordination* and review of Pliny Earle's *Marathon, and Other Poems*, *Graham's Magazine* 18, no. 6 (June 1841): 296.

72. Edgar Allan Poe, review of J. H. Ingraham's *The Quadroon*, *Graham's Magazine* 18, no. 6 (June 1841): 296.

73. Cohen and Cohen, "Poe and Griswold Once More," 98–99. Griswold did not quote the portion of Poe's review of Earle that suggested plagiarism.

74. Ibid., 100–101.

75. Ibid., 101. See also Edgar Allan Poe, "A Chapter on Autography," *Graham's Magazine* 19, no. 2 (December 1841): 275; as well as H 15:215.

76. See Edgar Allan Poe, "A Few Words on Secret Writing," *Graham's Magazine* 19, no. 1 (July 1841): 33–38; and H 14:114–32. For the given quotations, see "A Few Words on Secret Writing," 35, 33 (H 14:121, 116). For the original December 18, 1839, invitation, see Clarence S. Brigham, *Edgar Allan Poe's Contributions to Alexander's Weekly Messenger* (Worcester, MA: American Antiquarian Society, 1943), 16. For Alexander's confirmation of Poe's assertions, see Thomas and Jackson, *The Poe Log*, 336. Poe's original claim regarding human ingenuity and ciphers, made on March 25, 1840, was "[H]uman ingenuity cannot concoct a proper cypher which we cannot resolve" (Brigham, *Edgar Allan Poe's Contributions to Alexander's Weekly Messenger*, 62).

77. For the challenge in the original review, see Edgar Allan Poe, review of R. M. Walsh's translation of *Sketches of Conspicuous Characters of Frances*, *Graham's Magazine* 18, no. 4 (April 1841): 203. See also H 10:136.

78. Michael J. Bielawa, "Unriddled: The Stonington Cipher Mystery and Who Is S. D. L.?," *Edgar Allan Poe Review* 20, no. 1 (2019): 144–50.
79. Poe, "A Few Words on Secret Writing," 36; H 14:124–27.
80. For mention of Poe's use of the *Encyclopaedia Britannica*, see W. K. Wimsatt Jr., "What Poe Knew about Cryptography," *PMLA* 58, no. 3 (1943): 767–69.
81. This passage appeared originally in Edgar Allan Poe, review of *Powhatan; a Metrical Romance, in Seven Cantos*, by Seba Smith, *Graham's Magazine* 19, no. 1 (July 1841): 46. See also H 10:165.
82. Cohen and Cohen, "Poe and Griswold Once More," 99; Poe, review of *Powhatan*, 47. See also H 10:166.
83. Edgar Allan Poe, review of James Bermingham's *A Memoir of the Very Reverend Theobald Mathew. With an Account of the Rise and Progress of Temperance in Ireland*, *Graham's Magazine* 19, no. 1 (July 1841): 48.
84. For Graham on Poe's devotion to Virginia and Maria Clemm, see "The Late Edgar Allan Poe," 225; for the epigraph from King Henry VIII, see ibid., 224. Poe's having visited Graham at his home is noted in Ellis Paxson Oberholtzer, *Philadelphia A History of the City and Its People A Record of 225 Years*, 4 vols. (Philadelphia: S. J. Clarke, 1912), 2:212; and J. Albert Robbins, "George R. Graham," 286. The common source was Graham's cousin, Katharine Rex (later Mrs. George H. Burgin Jr.), who then lived in Graham's home.
85. The newspaper was named after the personification of the New Englander, Brother Jonathan, the complement to the personification of the Englishman, John Bull.
86. Kopley, *Edgar Allan Poe and the Dupin Mysteries*, 57.
87. Ibid., 59.
88. See also ibid., 59–60. *Corrected Proofs* was Weld's 1836 collection of short periodical pieces.
89. Poe acknowledges in this letter that some of the review was drawn from a previous piece—his essay "American Novel Writing" in the *Pittsburgh Literary Examiner* (O 1:297–98).
90. Edgar Allan Poe, review of Lambert A. Wilmer's *The Quacks of Helicon*, *Graham's Magazine* 19, no. 2 (August 1841): 93; see also H 10:194.
91. For consideration of Poe and cryptography, see William F. Friedman, "Edgar Allan Poe, Cryptographer," *American Literature* 8, no. 3 (1936): 266–80; and Wimsatt, "What Poe Knew about Cryptography."
92. Balleisen, *Navigating Failure*, 105.
93. Edgar Allan Poe, "To Helen," *Graham's Magazine* 19, no. 3 (September 1841): 123. See also M 1:166.
94. Thomas and Jackson, *The Poe Log*, 340.
95. Edgar Allan Poe, review of Frederick Marryat's *Joseph Rushbrook, or the Poacher*, *Graham's Magazine* 19, no. 3 (September 1841): 143; see also H 10:201.
96. For the approximate date, see Thomas and Jackson, *The Poe Log*, 339.
97. Edgar Allan Poe, "Eleonora. A Fable," in *The Gift: A Christmas and New Year's Present for 1842* (Philadelphia: Carey & Hart, 1841), 155, 156–57. For the Mabbott edition, which features the 1845 *Broadway Journal* revision, see M 2:639, 640.
98. Poe, "Eleonora," 157. See also M 2:640–41.

99. Poe, "Eleonora," 157, 158–59, 161, 162. See also M 2:641n, 642–45.
100. Poe, "Eleonora," 155, 158. See also M 2:639v, 641v.
101. Burton R. Pollin has written, "Perhaps one may assume that regardless of the varied forms of the embodiment of love—Eleonora or Ermengarde—the disembodied spirit is fundamentally the same; hence there can be no real betrayal if the affections are sincere" (Pollin, "*Undine* in the Works of Poe," 73–74).
102. Poe, "Eleonora," 157–58. See also M 2:641v.
103. Poe, "Eleonora," 161–62. See also M 2:644v.
104. For Poe's faulting the end of "Eleonora," see Poe, review of *The Gift: A Christmas and New Year's Present for 1842, Graham's Magazine* 19, no. 5 (November 1841): 249.
105. See May Garrettson Evans, "Poe in Amity Street," *Maryland Historical Magazine* 36, no. 4 (December 1941): 379–80; John C. French, "The Maryland Scene and Poe's Eleonora [sic]," *Maryland Historical Magazine* 50, no. 1 (March 1955): 65–66.
106. Flora Lapham Mack [for William Lanier Washington], "Suggestions for the Third Chapter—Poe's Early Married Days," collection of the author.
107. Thomas and Jackson, *The Poe Log*, 347, 348.
108. Thomas wrote to Poe on October 14, 1841, about the new navy secretary, Abel Parker Upshur, "He could be of service to you in your views here" and renewed his invitation for Poe to visit Washington. He wrote again on November 23, noting that John Pendleton Kennedy's "Whig 'Manifesto'" (which had ousted Tyler from his own party) had eliminated his influence with the president, but Thomas added, "Cant you slip on here and see us—" (Thomas, "Poe in Philadelphia," 1:271, 291, and 1:262–63). See also Charles H. Bohner, *John Pendleton Kennedy: Gentleman from Baltimore* (Baltimore, MD: Johns Hopkins Press, 1961), 146–49; and Christopher J. Leahy, *President without a Party: The Life of John Tyler* (Baton Rouge: Louisiana State University Press, 2020), 189–90.
109. Note to "Review of New Books," *Graham's Magazine* 19, no. 4 (October 1841): 188.
110. Wimsatt, "What Poe Knew about Cryptography," 764.
111. Edgar Allan Poe, "Secret Writing," *Graham's Magazine* 19, no. 4 (October 1841): 192. See also H 14:138–39.
112. Poe, "Secret Writing," *Graham's Magazine*. See also H 14:139–40.
113. Thomas, "Poe in Philadelphia," 1:271–72; Thomas and Jackson, *The Poe Log*, 344.
114. Edgar Allan Poe, "A Chapter on Autography," *Graham's Magazine* 19, no. 5 (November 1841): 228, 229, 233. See also H 14:190, 191, 204.
115. Edgar Allan Poe, review of Samuel Warren's *Ten Thousand a Year, Graham's Magazine* 19, no. 5 (November 1841): 252. See also H 10:210.
116. For Mabbott's related comment, see M 3:803.
117. Thomas, "Poe in Philadelphia," 1:284; Thomas and Jackson, *The Poe Log*, 348. For the lyrics of "Oh! Blame Her Not," see Thomas, "Poe in Philadelphia," 1:305.
118. See Poe's response to Sigourney's positive response (O 1:316–17); Willis's letter to Poe (Thomas, "Poe in Philadelphia," 1:286); and Thomas and Jackson, *The Poe Log*, 348–49.
119. For Bolton's response to Poe, see Thomas, "Poe in Philadelphia," 1:309–10; and Thomas and Jackson, *The Poe Log*, 357.

120. "Graham's Magazine," *Salem Register,* November 25, 1841, 2 (America's Historical Newspapers).
121. Edgar Allan Poe, "A Chapter on Autography," *Graham's Magazine* 19, no. 6 (December 1841): 273; see also H 15:209.
122. Gerald E. Gerber, "E. P. Whipple Attacks Poe: A New Review," *American Literature* 53, no. 1 (1981): 113.
123. Graham himself acknowledged Poe's willingness to accede to a caution against critical acerbity: "[N]o man with more readiness would soften a harsh expression at the request of a friend" (Graham, "The Late Edgar Allan Poe," 226). John S. Du Solle of the *Spirit of the Times* did challenge Whipple's judgment, but the damage was done (Thomas and Jackson, *The Poe Log,* 355–57). Thomas later faulted Poe for yielding to Graham (H 17: 105–6; Thomas, "Poe in Philadelphia," 1:337; Thomas and Jackson, *The Poe Log,* 360).
124. Edgar Allan Poe, "A Chapter on Autography," *Graham's Magazine* 19, no. 6 (December 1841): 284; see also H 15:241.
125. T., "Graham's Magazine—John G. Whittier," *Hampshire Gazette* (Northampton, MA), December 7, 1841, 2 (America's Historical Newspapers). For Poe's comments on Whittier, see Poe's "A Chapter on Autography," *Graham's Magazine* 19, no. 6 (December 1841), 286. See also H 15:245.
126. Thomas and Jackson, *The Poe Log,* 346.
127. Edgar Allan Poe, "Secret Writing," *Graham's Magazine* 19, no. 6 (December 1841): 306–8; see also H 14:140–49.
128. See Terence Whalen, "Edgar Allan Poe and the Masses: The Political Economy of Literature in Antebellum American" (PhD diss. Duke University, 1991), 184–93; "The Code for Gold: Edgar Allan Poe and Cryptography," *Representations,* no. 46 (1994): 41–46; and *Edgar Allan Poe and The Masses: The Political Economy of Literature in Antebellum America* (Princeton, NJ: Princeton University Press, 1999), 208–16.
129. John A. Hodgson, "Decoding Poe? Poe, W. B. Tyler, and Cryptography," *JEGP* 92, no. 4 (1993): 523–34. For the argument that Tyler was Poe, see Louis A. Renza, "Poe's Secret Autobiography," in *The American Renaissance Reconsidered,* ed. Walter Benn Michaels and Donald E. Pease (Baltimore, MD: Johns Hopkins University Press, 1985), 87; Shawn Rosenheim: "The King of 'Secret Readers': Edgar Poe, Cryptography, and the Origins of the Detective Story," *ELH* 56, no. 2 (1989): 393–95; and *The Cryptographic Imagination: Secret Writing from Edgar Poe to the Internet* (Baltimore, MD: Johns Hopkins University Press, 1997), 34–41; and Whalen: "Edgar Allan Poe and the Masses," 184–93; "The Code for Gold," 41–46; and *Edgar Allan Poe and the Masses,* 208–16.
130. For Gil Broza's solution, see [Shawn Rosenheim], "Cipher Solved, But Mystery Remains," *Edgar Allan Poe Review* 1, no. 2 (2000): 77–79. See also Kristin Leutwyler, "A Cipher from Poe Solved at Last," *Scientific American,* November 3, 2000; S. Tomokiyo, "Solution to Tyler's Cryptograms Published in Poe's Article," cryptiana; and Raya Kuzyk, "A Piece of the Poe Puzzle Presents Itself!," *School Library Journal,* October 31, 2008. On December 6, 2008, George Monteiro posted to the Poe Studies Association listserv a transcription of a passage in the *Baltimore Sun* (of July 4, 1840) (see "Romantic," *Baltimore Sun,* July 4, 1840, 4

[America's Historical Newspapers], credited to the *Boston Post,* and *"Romantic," Boston Post,* July 1, 1840, 1, https://www.newspapers.com). In both the *Sun* and the *Post,* "sun" and "air" are italicized.

131. Edgar Allan Poe, "Secret Writing," *Graham's Magazine* 19, no. 6 (1841): 307. See also H 14:147.
132. Thomas and Jackson, *The Poe Log,* 353. For further information on the document with the tailor, see Joseph J. Moldenhauer, comp., *A Descriptive Catalog of Edgar Allan Poe Manuscripts in the Humanities Research Library, The University of Texas at Austin* (Austin: University of Texas at Austin, 1973), 79.
133. See Fannye N. Cherry, "The Source of Poe's 'Three Sundays in a Week,'" *American Literature* 2, no. 3 (1930): 232–35.
134. I quote from the *Saturday Evening Post* tale, held by the William H. Koester Collection of Edgar Allan Poe at the Harry Ransom Center at the University of Texas at Austin (Newspaper KPO Box 3), available online. See also the transcription at https://www.eapoe.org and, for the later "Three Sundays in a Week," M 2:649–57. Notably, Mabbott linked Uncle Rumgudgeon to John Allan (M 2:649).
135. Edgar Allan Poe, "A Chapter on Autography," 276; H 15:219.
136. [George Lippard], "Wirt Institute Lectures," *Citizen Soldier,* November 15, 1843, 301, collection of the author. See also Thomas, "Poe in Philadelphia," 2:639; and Thomas and Jackson, *The Poe Log,* 440. For a full study of Lippard, see Emilio de Grazia, "The Life and Works of George Lippard" (PhD diss., Ohio State University, 1969). For Lippard's possible subscribing or contributing to Poe's planned magazine, see Rose and Savoye, *Such Friends as These,* 18, 29. According to a note by a member of the Pratt staff, the planned magazine for which this list was relevant was the successor to "The Penn," "The Stylus" (see Rose and Savoye, *Such Friends as These,* 3). For other treatments of Lippard, see Emilio De Grazia, "Edgar Allan Poe, George Lippard, and the 'Spermaceti and Walnut-Coffin Papers,'" *Papers of the Bibliographical Society of America* 66 (1972): 58–60; and De Grazia, "Poe's Devoted Democrat, George Lippard," *Poe Studies* 6, no. 1 (1973): 6–8; Burton R. Pollin, "More on Lippard and Poe," *Poe Studies* 7, no. 1 (1974): 22–23; Thomas, "Poe in Philadelphia," 2:835–38; and David S. Reynolds, *George Lippard* (Boston: Twayne, 1982). (For Reynolds's discussion of Lippard and Poe, see ibid., 102–10.)
137. On January 1, 1842, Joseph E. Snodgrass commented on the January 1842 issue of the magazine in the *Baltimore Saturday Visiter* (Thomas, "Poe in Philadelphia," 1:307–8; Thomas and Jackson, *The Poe Log,* 356).
138. Edgar Allan Poe, "An Appendix of Autographs," *Graham's Magazine* 21, no. 1 (January 1842): 44. See also H 15:247.
139. Poe, "An Appendix of Autographs," *Graham's Magazine,* 48.
140. Edgar Allan Poe, ["Exordium"], *Graham's Magazine* 20, no. 1 (January 1842): 68–69. See also H 11:3 and L2 40–41.
141. Poe, ["Exordium"], *Graham's Magazine,* 69. See also H 11:8; and L2 44.
142. Edgar Allan Poe, review of *Stanley Thorn,* by Henry Cockton, *Graham's Magazine,* 20, no. 1 (January 1842): 69–70. See also H 11:10–15.
143. For the text of "A Critical Jack Ass" and my commentary, see Richard Kopley, "Poe as a Critical Jack Ass," *Edgar Allan Poe Review* 18, no. 2 (2017): 209–17.

144. Penn Junior (Lambert A. Wilmer?), "Edgar A. Poe," *Cincinnati Daily Gazette*, December 1859, 1 (https://www.eapoe.org). For the Bolton letter of January 10, 1842, see Thomas, "Poe in Philadelphia," 1:309–10; for the Thomas letter of January 13 and 14, see ibid., 1:314–15.

145. Amanda Bartlett Harris, "Edgar A. Poe." Harris explained in an 1896 letter that her source, who had lived near Poe, had told her the story in 1852 (George E. Woodberry, *The Life of Edgar Allan Poe*, 2 vols. [Boston: Houghton Mifflin, 1909], 1:297–98, 382; Thomas, "Poe in Philadelphia," 2:788). Poe's friend Thomas Holley Chivers later stated that Poe had said that the physician J. K. Mitchell had diagnosed Virginia with bronchitis (Chivers, *Chivers' Life of Poe*, ed. Richard Beale Davis [New York: E. P. Dutton, 1952], 43; see also 60, 108).

146. Miriam Allen deFord, "Cherry-tree Legend," *American Notes & Queries* 1 (August 1941): 69. The source for the story, deFord wrote, was Ida Jones Springer, the third cousin of deFord's mother. Apparently the little girl in the story was Springer's mother (whose maiden name was "Davis"). Miriam Allen deFord had elaborated the incident into a short short story, titled "A Forgotten Episode" (*Westminster Magazine* [Spring 1939]: 7).

16. "As Regards Myself—I Will Probably Succeed Too"

1. Edgar Allan Poe, review of Charles Dickens's *Barnaby Rudge*, *Graham's Magazine* 20, no. 2 (February 1842): 129. See also H 11:63. Another Dickens item in the February 1842 issue of *Graham's* was "Original Letter from Charles Dickens," written to John Tomlin (see 83–84). The Jackson, Tennessee, writer and postmaster had sent the letter to Poe (Dwight Thomas, "Poe in Philadelphia, 1838–1844" [PhD diss. University of Pennsylvania, 1978], 1:302; Dwight Thomas and David K. Jackson, *The Poe Log: A Documentary Life of Edgar Allan Poe, 1809–1849* [Boston: G. K. Hall, 1987], 353).

2. James Russell Lowell, "Rosaline," *Graham's Magazine* 20, no. 2 (February 1842): 90.

3. For a number of instances of the word "nevermore," and related words, in poetry, see Robert S. Forsythe, "'Nevermore': A Note," *American Literature* 7, no. 4 (1936): 439–52. For Forsythe's mention of "Rosaline," see ibid., 441. Poe mentioned "Rosaline" in his March 1842 review of Henry Wadsworth Longfellow's *Ballads and Other Poems* (H 11:68) and his March 1844 review of Lowell's *Poems* (where the poem is misidentified as "Rosalie" [H 11:249]). Poe also referred to "Rosaline" in his November 16, 1842, letter to Lowell (O 1:368). And he spoke admiringly of the poem with Charles J. Peterson in Philadelphia in 1842 and Thomas Holley Chivers in New York City in 1845 (Ann Prestwich, "Charles Jacob Peterson, Editor, and Friend of Lowell and Poe" [master's thesis, Columbia University, 1938], 55; *Chivers' Life of Poe*, ed. Richard Beale Davis [New York: E. P. Dutton, 1952], 45–46).

4. George R. Graham, "The Late Edgar Allan Poe," *Graham's Magazine* 36, no. 3 (March 1850): 225.

5. The Thomas dissertation (1:318–94) and Thomas and Jackson's *Poe Log* (358–70) report detail on Dickens's visit to the United States, from January 22 through June 7.

6. Edgar Allan Poe, notice of Nathaniel Hawthorne's *Famous Old People, Graham's Magazine* 20, no. 3 (March 1842): 192. It is interesting to see that the March 1842 issue of *Graham's* included writers whom Poe knew or would come to know, including Thomas Holley Chivers, Frances Sargent Osgood, Park Benjamin, George Pope Morris, and James Russell Lowell.
7. Ralph Waldo Emerson, "To the Humble-Bee," in *The Poets and Poetry of America*, ed. Rufus W. Griswold (Philadelphia: Carey and Hart, 1842), 238.
8. For Poe and Dickens, see Thomas, "Poe in Philadelphia," 1:318–94; and Thomas and Jackson, *The Poe Log*, 358–70; as well as Gerald G. Grubb, "The Personal and Literary Relationships of Dickens and Poe (Part One: From 'Sketches by Boz' through 'Barnaby Rudge')," *Nineteenth-Century Fiction* 5, no. 1 (1950): 1–22; "(Part Two: 'English Notes' and 'The Poets of America')," *Nineteenth-Century Fiction* 5, no. 2 (1950): 101–20; "(Part Three: Poe's Literary Debt to Dickens)," *Nineteenth-Century Fiction* 5, no. 3 (1950): 209–21. Also useful is Sidney P. Moss, "Poe's 'Two Long Interviews' with Dickens," *Poe Studies* 11, no. 1 (1978): 10–12. For a listing of the letters exchanged between Poe and Dickens in 1842, see O 2:1205, 1207, and 1211. For more recent treatments of Poe and Dickens, see Fernando Galván, "Plagiarism in Poe: Revisiting the Poe-Dickens Relationship," *Edgar Allan Poe Review* 10, no. 2 (2009): 11–24; and Tara Moore, "Charles Dickens" in *Edgar Allan Poe in Context*, ed. Kevin Hayes (New York: Cambridge University Press, 2013), 279–87.
9. Thomas, "Poe in Philadelphia," 1:467.
10. A Poe letter concerning the length of the manuscript of "The Pit and the Pendulum"—eighteen pages—includes in the return address "Office Graham's Magazine"; on the basis of that detail, the letter is tentatively estimated to be from April 1842 (see O 1:328–29). Given the "Thursday Morning" detail in the letter and Poe's April 1 resignation, I would suggest a possible date for the letter of March 31.
11. [Review of April 1842 issue of *Graham's Magazine*], *New Orleans Times-Picayune*, March 27, 1842, 2 (America's Historical Newspapers); [review of April 1842 issue of *Graham's Magazine*], *New York Tribune*, April 2, 1842 ("Addenda" to *The Poe Log*, https://www.eapoe.org); "Graham's Magazine," *Baltimore Saturday Visiter*, April 2, 1842, 2 (America's Historical Newspapers); Thomas, "Poe in Philadelphia," 1:360.
12. Edgar Allan Poe, "Life in Death," *Graham's Magazine* 20, no. 4 (April 1842): 201. Poe later revised the tale, titling it "The Oval Portrait." The phrase "*life-likeliness* of expression" appears in that version, too (M 2:664). I rely here on the first printing of the tale.
13. Mary E. Phillips, *Edgar Allan Poe—the Man*, 2 vols. (Chicago: John C. Winston, 1926), 1:691; M 1:660. T. O. Mabbott mentions the possibility of the influence of a story about Tintoretto (M 1:660), and Jeffrey A. Savoye develops this possibility (Savoye, "Tintoretto and 'The Oval Portrait,'" *Edgar Allan Poe Review* 14, no. 2 [2013]: 233–34). Perhaps Hawthorne's stories "The Prophetic Pictures" and "Edward Randolph's Portrait," in *Twice-Told Tales* stimulated Poe's imagination in the direction of a tale about an artwork.
14. Poe, "Life in Death," *Graham's Magazine* 20, no. 4 (April 1842): 200–201.
15. Ibid.

16. Ibid., 201.
17. Ibid.
18. Edgar Allan Poe, review of Henry Wadsworth Longfellow's *Ballads and Other Poems, Graham's Magazine* 20, no. 4 (April 1842): 248–49. See also H 11:71–72.
19. Poe, review of Henry Wadsworth Longfellow's *Ballads and Other Poems, Graham's Magazine,* 251; H 11:84–85.
20. Longfellow commented on "Excelsior" in an 1841 letter in a way that would have much interested Poe: "The idea of the poem is the Life of Genius" (Henry Wadsworth Longfellow to Samuel Cutler Ward, September 30, 1841, Catalog 190 of The 19th Century Rare Book and Photography Shop, *Magnificent Books and Photographs,* 168). Thanks to Stephan Loewentheil and Tom Edsall.
21. Prestwich, "Charles Jacob Peterson," 60.
22. Edgar Allan Poe, review of Nathaniel Hawthorne's *Twice-Told Tales, Graham's Magazine* 20, no. 4 (April 1842): 254 [252]. See also H 11:104.
23. See Thomas, "Poe in Philadelphia," 1:203, 357–59; and Thomas and Jackson, *The Poe Log,* 363. Poe wrote to Daniel Bryan on July 6, 1842, "My connexion with 'Graham's Magazine' ceased with the May number, which was completed by the 1rst of April" (O 1:346; see also O 1:333).
24. Thomas Cottrell Clarke, "Poe. What Those Say Who Knew Him Best," 1858, Ms, Columbia University Library.
25. John Ward Ostrom, "Edgar A. Poe: His Income as Literary Entrepreneur," *Poe Studies* 15, no. 1 (1982): 5.
26. Edgar Allan Poe, "The Mask of the Red Death. A Fantasy," *Graham's Magazine* 20, no. 5 (May 1842): 259. See also M 2:677.
27. For biblical resonance in "The Masque of the Red Death," see Jonathan A. Cook, "Poe and the Apocalyptic Sublime 'The Masque of the Red Death,'" *Religion and the Arts* 23 (2019): 489–515. For the Willis source, see Richard P. Benton, "'The Masque of the Red Death'—The Primary Source," *American Transcendental Quarterly* 1 (1969): 12–13. For considerations of the Poe-Hawthorne connection, see Robert Regan, "Hawthorne's 'Plagiary'; Poe's Duplicity," *Nineteenth-Century Fiction* 25, no. 3 (1970): 281–98; and D. M. McKeithan, "Poe and the Second Edition of Hawthorne's *Twice-Told Tales,*" in *The Nathaniel Hawthorne Journal 1974,* ed. C. E. Frazer Clark, Jr. (Englewood, CO: Microcard Editions, 1975), 257–69.
28. Poe, "The Mask of the Red Death," 257–59.
29. Edgar Allan Poe, review of Nathaniel Hawthorne's *Twice-Told Tales, Graham's Magazine* 20, no. 5 (May 1842): 300. See also H 11:113.
30. See Phillips, *Edgar Allan Poe—the Man,* 1:748.
31. See Edgar Allan Poe to Elizabeth Tutt, July 7, 1842, (https://www.eapoe.org). The text of this letter—only a portion of which is available in the Ostrom edition (O 1:351–52)—was found by Jeffrey A. Savoye in the J. H. Whitty Papers of the Rubinstein Library of Duke University. For his consideration of the abbreviated letter, as formerly known, see Savoye, "Some Updates on Poe's Correspondence, with a New Letter," *Edgar Allan Poe Review* 13, no. 1 (2012): 6–8. Elizabeth Tutt was the former Elizabeth Rebecca Herring, oldest daughter of Poe's aunt Elizabeth Herring, who was the sister of Poe's father David and the wife of Henry Herring. For a description of the neighborhood of Poe's new house on Coates Street,

see Ellis Paxson Oberholtzer, *Philadelphia A History of the City and Its People: A Record of 225 Years*, 4 vols. (Philadelphia: S. J. Clarke, [1912]), 2:213–14.

32. Dwight Thomas comments on this letter in "Poe in Philadelphia," 1:381–82.
33. Prestwich, "Charles Jacob Peterson," 64. The source for the phrase "unstable as water" is Genesis: Jacob terms his eldest son "unstable as water" because Reuben had slept with his father's concubine Bilhah (see Genesis 49:4 and 35:33).
34. See George R. Graham: "The Late Edgar Allan Poe," 226, and "The Genius and Characteristics of the Late Edgar Allan Poe," *Graham's Magazine* 44, no. 2 (February 1854): 220–21.
35. William H. Gravely states that English antedated his story of encountering Poe drunk; it would seem likeliest that it occurred in mid- to late 1842, after Peterson declared Poe "unstable as water" (Gravely, "The Early Political and Literary Career of Thomas Dunn English" [PhD diss., University of Virginia, 1953], 286–98). For English's account, see "Reminiscences of Poe II," *New York Independent*, October 22, 1896, 1415 (https://www.eapoe.org).
36. For Poe's reply to John H. Mackenzie in Richmond, see Flora Lapham Mack [for William Lanier Washington], "Suggestions for the Third Chapter—Poe's Early Married Days," collection of the author. For Graham's comment, see his "The Genius and Characteristics of the Late Edgar Allan Poe," 220. For love holding Poe, Virginia, and Mrs. Clemm together, see Amanda Bartlett Harris, "Edgar A. Poe," *Hearth and Home* 8, no. 2 (January 9, 1875): 24 (https://www.eapoe.org).
37. Prestwich, "Charles Jacob Peterson," 64.
38. Thomas and Jackson, *The Poe Log*, 370.
39. For Weld's taking a position at the *Saturday Evening Post*, see Charles J. Peterson to James Russell Lowell, on November 11, 1842, in Prestwich, "Charles Jacob Peterson," 27, 96. See also "H. Hastings Weld," *Philadelphia Public Ledger*, October 31, 1842, [2]; and "Newspaper Change," *Boston Evening Transcript*, November 2, 1842, [2] (America's Historical Newspapers). For Poe's queries regarding "Marie Rogêt," see my *Edgar Allan Poe and the Dupin Mysteries* (New York: Palgrave Macmillan, 2088), 62–63.
40. The title page and the table of contents of "Phantasy-Pieces" are reproduced in facsimile in M 2: [after 474]. A facsimile of the annotated first volume of *Tales of the Grotesque and Arabesque* was published in Paris by George Blumenthal, in 1927, according to WorldCat. See also Lot 2202, *The Library of H. Bradley Martin: Highly Important American and Children's Literature* (New York: Sotheby's, 1990), and Item 95, *Evermore: The Persistence of Poe: The Edgar Allan Poe Collection of Susan Jaffe Tane* (New York: Grolier Club, 2014), 77–78, 161.
41. Frederick W. Thomas recalled Poe's report of his failure (J. H. Whitty, ed., *The Complete Poems of Edgar Allan Poe* [Boston: Houghton Mifflin, 1911], xliv). For Poe's having visited New York on or shortly before June 24, I am guided by his having written a letter from New York on that date (O 1:343–44). And he did refer to his stay there as a "brief visit" (O 1:344, 346).
42. That Poe had sold "The Mystery of Marie Rogêt" to Robert Hamilton is evident from a letter of October 3, 1842 (O 1:365–66). The tale would appear in Snowden's *Ladies' Companion* in the November and December 1842 issues and the February 1843 issue. Dwight Thomas conjectures reasonably that Poe might

43. Whitty, *The Complete Poems of Edgar Allan Poe*, xliv.
44. For more on Wallace, see Thomas, "Poe in Philadelphia," 2:929–30.
45. Augustus Van Cleef, "Poe's Mary," *Harper's New Monthly Magazine,* March 1889, 639. For Poe's possibly visiting an area associated with the death of Mary Rogers, see John Walsh, *Poe the Detective: The Curious Circumstances behind "The Mystery of Marie Roget"* (New Brunswick, NJ: Rutgers University Press, 1968), 64; and Thomas, "Poe in Philadelphia," 2:904. The date of Poe's return home is clarified in his letter of June 30 to James Herron (O 1:344).
46. Edgar Allan Poe to Elizabeth Tutt, July 7, 1842 (https://www.eapoe.org).
47. Ibid. For more on Maffitt's preaching, see the obituary "John Newland Maffitt," *Eastern Star* (Easton, MD), October 8, 1850 (America's Historical Newspapers). For Edgar and John talking about religious matters, I rely on William Lanier Washington, "Notes on Washington's Chapters," ["Of Rosalie Poe"], collection of the author.
48. That he worked on the review of *Poets and Poetry of America* in the summer of 1842 is evident from his September 12 letter to Frederick W. Thomas indicating that Griswold had invited Poe to write the review "[a]bout two months since" (O 1:359). Despite the implicit offer of a bribe, Poe is clear that he wrote the review as he would have otherwise written it. Griswold received the review by August 12 (Thomas and Jackson, *The Poe Log*, 377). Jeffrey A. Savoye contends that "'The Gold-Bug' was started in earnest in August or September, and finished by the middle of October 1842" (Savoye, "Reconstructing Poe's 'The Gold-Bug': An Examination of the Composition and First Printing[s]," *Edgar Allan Poe Review* 8, no. 2 [2007]: 39). There is an account that Poe traveled to Saratoga Springs, New York, in the summer of 1842 and worked on the poem "The Raven" (see William Elliot Griffis, "Behind the Mystery of Poe's 'Raven,'" *New York Times Book Review,* January 20, 1924, 2; and Marjorie Peabody White, *Yaddo Yesterday and Today* [Albany, NY: Argus, 1933], 18–19). However, it seems that the visit actually took place in 1843 (M 1:358, 358n).
49. Frederick W. Thomas to Edgar Allan Poe, September 2, 1842, Rufus W. Griswold Papers, 1834–1857, Boston Public Library Rare Books and Manuscripts.
50. Whitty, *The Complete Poems of Edgar Allan Poe*, xliii–xliv.
51. Ibid., xliv.
52. Ibid., xliv. Reference to "a stout cane" may be found in Joseph H. Ingraham, "Francis [*sic*] William Thomas," *Southern Literary Messenger* 4, no. 5 (May 1838): 302 (Making of America). For Thomas's explanation of his lameness, see H 17:96.
53. Thomas to Poe, September 2, 1842.
54. With regard to Thomas on Poe's brother Henry, see H 17:96; and Whitty, *The Complete Poems of Edgar Allan Poe,* xxi, xxxi–xxxii. Concerning Thomas on Mary Starr (Mary Devereaux), see ibid., xxxiv.
55. "Frederick W. Thomas," *Constitutional Union* (Washington, DC), October 11, 1866, [2] (America's Historical Newspapers).
56. *The Gift for 1843* was listed in the *Alexandria Gazette* (Virginia) on September 22, 1843, 3 (America's Historical Newspapers).

57. See Poe review of *Twice-Told Tales, Graham's Magazine* (May 1842): 298–99. See also H 11:107–9.
58. For discussion of these *Blackwood's* sources for "The Pit and the Pendulum," see W. M. G., "Poe's 'The Pit and the Pendulum,'" *Critic* 14 (July 5, 1890): 7; David Lee Clark, "The Sources of Poe's 'The Pit and the Pendulum,'" *Modern Language Notes* 44 (June 1929): 349–51; Margaret Alterton, "Origins of Poe's Critical Theory," *University of Iowa Humanistic Studies* 2, no. 3 (1925): 27–29; Margaret Alterton, "An Additional Source for Poe's 'The Pit and the Pendulum,'" *Modern Language Notes* 48 (June 1933): 353–55; and David H. Hirsch, "Another Source for 'The Pit and the Pendulum,'" *Mississippi Quarterly* 23, no. 1 (1969–70): 35–43. Alterton stated, "Of all the foreign magazines which Poe knew, *Blackwood* is perhaps the one with which he was most familiar" ("Origins," 12). Other sources include Charles Brockden Brown's novel *Edgar Huntley* (Clark) and Juan Antonio Llorente's *History of the Spanish Inquisition* (Alterton). It is notable that the father in "On Emblems" in John Aikin and Anna Laetitia's collection *Evenings at Home* mentions the substitution of a pickaxe for the scythe in the Grim Reaper. For more on this book of Poe's childhood, see my "*Evenings at Home:* A Neglected Book from Poe's Childhood," *Edgar Allan Poe Review* 21, no. 1 (2020): 64–70. See the 1813 Boston edition of the volume, 2:213–15 (Internet Archive).
59. Poe wrote that *Blackwood's* tales "were relished by every man of genius" (see review of *Twice-Told Tales* in *Graham's Magazine* [May 1842]: 299; and H 11:109).
60. For the symmetrical phrases, see Edgar Allan Poe, "The Pit and the Pendulum," in *The Gift: A Christmas and New Year's Preset MDCCCXLIII* (Philadelphia: Carey & Hart, 1842), 133, 151. For the same passages in Mabbott's later version, see M 2:681, 697. For scholarly notice of these phrases, see David H. Hirsch, "The Pit and the Apocalypse," *Sewanee Review* 76, no. 4 (1968): 648; and David Ketterer, *The Rationale of Deception in Poe* (Baton Rouge: Louisiana State University Press, 1979), 204–5.
61. See Poe, "The Pit and the Pendulum," *The Gift*, 135, 145, 146; M 2:683, 692.
62. Poe, "The Pit and the Pendulum," *The Gift*, 138, 145; M 2:686. 691.
63. Poe, "The Pit and the Pendulum," *The Gift*, 140, 143; M 2:687, 690.
64. Poe, "The Pit and the Pendulum," *The Gift*, 143; M 2:689, 690.
65. Poe, "The Pit and the Pendulum," *The Gift*, 143; M 2:690.
66. Poe, "The Pit and the Pendulum," *The Gift*, 141; M 2:688.
67. Poe, review of Nathaniel Hawthorne's *Twice-Told Tales, Graham's Magazine* (May 1842): 299; H 11:108.
68. For the timing of the appearance of the October 1842 issue of Snowden's *Ladies' Companion*, I rely on an advertisement, "Graham's Magazine, Godey's Lady's Book, and Snowden's Ladies' Companion," *Philadelphia Public Ledger*, September 28, 1842, [3] (America's Historical Newspapers).
69. Edgar Allan Poe, "The Landscape-Garden," Snowden's *Ladies' Companion*, October 1842, 326. For a later printing, see M 2:711.
70. Poe, "The Landscape-Garden," 324 and 327 (four elements); 325 ("adaptation to the eyes" twice); 325 ("destiny as Poet"). See also M 2:703–4 and 711–12; 707. An actual recent version of Poe's Ellison was the late Frank Cabot, who was beautifully elaborated in the documentary film *The Gardener*.

71. Poe, "The Landscape-Garden," 324. I correct, in brackets, the error "unnecessary pursuit." For Poe's alarm at "[t]he typographical blunders" in the first printing of "The Landscape-Garden," see O 1:365–66. See also M 2:703–4.
72. Poe, "The Landscape-Garden," 324; M 2:704.
73. Poe, review of Longfellow's *Ballads and Other Poems, Graham's Magazine*, 249. See also H 11:73.
74. For Raymond's terming the review of Griswold's anthology (on October 21) "a good puff," see *Passages from the Correspondence and Other Papers of Rufus W. Griswold* (Cambridge, MA: W. M. Griswold, 1898), 125. For the review itself, I rely on Poe, review of *Poets and Poetry of America*, comp. Rufus W. Griswold, *Boston Miscellany* 2, no. 5 (November 1842): 218–21. See also H 11:147–60.
75. Poe, review of *Poets and Poetry of America*, 220, 221; H 11:153, 156.
76. *A Bibliography of First Printings of the Writings of Edgar Allan Poe*, rev. ed., comp. Charles F. Heartman and James R. Canny (Hattiesburg, MS: Book Farm, 1943), 157.
77. Thomas Dunn English offered an account of a conversation with Poe about the review of Griswold's anthology, claiming that Poe had said, "I abused the book and ridiculed him, and gave him the most severe using up he ever had, or ever will have, I fancy." This is so far from comporting with the actual review that I thoroughly distrust it, agreeing with the judgment of English's biographer William H. Gravely Jr. that English's recollections of Poe were "habitually biased" (see Thomas Dunn English, "Down among the Dead Men," *The Old Guard* (June 1870): 466; and Gravely, "The Early Political and Literary Career of Thomas Dunn English," 301, 299). For further comment relating to Poe's review of *Poets and Poetry of America*, see Joy Bayless, *Rufus Wilmot Griswold: Poe's Literary Executor* (Nashville, TN: Vanderbilt University Press, 1943), 70–71; Thomas, "Poe in Philadelphia," 1:405–6, 412–13, 427–28, 432–33, 436–38, 454–55; and Thomas and Jackson, *The Poe Log*, 372, 376, 377, 378, 384.
78. Each issue of Snowden's *Ladies' Companion* appeared late in the month previous to its date. The November 1842 issue was mentioned in the press as early as October 27, 1842 (see "*The Nov. Monthlies*," *Boston Post*, October 27, 1842, [2], https://www.newspapers.com). The December 1842 issue was noted as early as November 30, 1842. See review of the *Ladies' Companion*, December 1842, *Bangor Daily Whig and Courier*, November 30, 1842, [2], https://www.newspapers.com. The February 1842 issue was cited as early as January 28, 1843 (see ["Jordan & Co"], *Boston Evening Transcript*, January 28, 1843, [2] [America's Historical Newspapers]).
79. I am consulting the first printing of the tale. See Edgar Allan Poe, "The Mystery of Marie Rogêt," Snowden's *Ladies' Companion* 18 (November 1842): 15–20; (December 1842): 93–99; and (February 1843): 162–67. For the version in the J. Lorimer Graham copy of the 1845 *Tales*, see M 3:723–74. For the reference to the "naval officer" (suggested by the second extract) and "the secret lover," see the December installment, 98.
80. For a discussion of the revisions, see William K. Wimsatt Jr., "Poe and the Mystery of Mary Rogers," *PMLA* 56, no. 1 (1941): 242–48. See also Walsh, *Poe the Detective*, 69–71; and Richard Fusco, "Poe's Revisions of 'The Mystery of Marie

Rogêt': A Hoax?," in *Poe at Work Seven Textual Studies,* ed. Benjamin Franklin Fisher IV (Baltimore, MD: Edgar Allan Poe Society, 1978), 91–99. See also Mabbott's variant edition and his notes (M 3:723–88).

81. Available in addition to Wimsatt's 1941 piece is his 1950 addition, prompted by Samuel Copp Worthen's "Poe and the Beautiful Cigar Girl," *American Literature* 20, no. 3 (1948): 305–12 (see Wimsatt, "Mary Rogers, John Anderson, and Others," *American Literature* 21, no. 4 [1950]: 482–84). Books on the subject beyond Walsh include Raymond Paul, *Who Murdered Mary Rogers?* (Englewood Cliffs, NJ: Prentice-Hall, 1971); Amy Gilman Srebnick, *The Mysterious Death of Mary Rogers: Sex and Culture in Nineteenth-Century New York* (New York: Oxford University Press, 1995); and Daniel Stashower, *The Beautiful Cigar Girl: Mary Rogers, Edgar Allan Poe, and the Invention of Murder* (New York: Dutton, 2006).

82. See the November installment of "Marie Rogêt," 17, and the December installment of the tale, 27–28. See also M 3:728–29, 753–54.

83. See Walsh, *Poe the Detective,* 43 (also M 3:784); and Stashower, *The Beautiful Cigar Girl,* 270.

84. For my full argument, see my *Edgar Allan Poe and the Dupin Mysteries* (New York: Palgrave Macmillan, 2008), 48–50.

85. Ibid., 50–54.

86. Ibid., 56–60.

87. For the full argument, see ibid., 54–63, 106–9.

88. Poe, "The Mystery of Marie Rogêt," Snowden's *Ladies' Companion,* November 1842, 15, and February 1843, 167. See also M 3:723–24, 772–73.

89. Poe, "The Mystery of Marie Rogêt," Snowden's *Ladies' Companion* (November 1842), 17, and (February 1843), 164 (clothing) (M 3:730, 765), and (November 1842), 18, and (February 1843), 163 (thicket) (M 3:734, 762).

90. Poe, "The Mystery of Marie Rogêt," Snowden's *Ladies' Companion* (December 1842), 95, 97 (identity) (M 3:744, 751), and 96, 97 (M 3:748, 750) (questions about a newspaper).

91. Poe, "The Mystery of Marie Rogêt," Snowden's *Ladies' Companion* (December 1842), 96 (M 3:749–50).

92. Ibid. For a fuller treatment of the tale's symmetry, see Kopley, *Edgar Allan Poe and the Dupin Mysteries,* 13–18.

93. See Benjamin F. Fisher, ed., *Poe in His Own Time* (Iowa City: University of Iowa Press, 2010), 246 (Margaret E. Wilmer); and Lambert A. Wilmer, *Merlin Baltimore, 1827 Together with Recollections of Edgar A. Poe* (1941; [Folcroft, PA]: Folcroft Library Editions, 1973), 33.

94. For Graham's reading the manuscript of "The Gold-Bug" aloud, see Thomas, "Poe in Philadelphia," 2:723. The source for this information is an obituary of Graham's cousin Katharine Rex Burgin, "Mrs. Burgin Dead in Her 90th Year," *Germantown Independent-Gazette,* September 13, 1917.

95. For Peterson's letters to Lowell from 1841 and 1842, see Prestwich, "Charles Jacob Peterson," 46–66. For Poe to Lowell from mid-November to mid-December, see O 1:368 (November 16); and Gabriel McKee, "A New Letter from Poe to Lowell on the *Pioneer,*" *Edgar Allan Poe Review* 20, no. 1 (2019): 28 (November 24). For Lowell to Poe for that period, see George E. Woodberry, "Lowell's Letters to Poe,"

Scribner's Monthly 16, no. 2 (August 1894): 170–71 (November 19, December 17). See also H 17:120–21, 125. For Peterson on corresponding with Story, see Prestwich, "Charles Jacob Peterson," 58, 60. Story was a contributor to the *Pioneer* under his own name and under the pseudonym "I. B. Wright" (McKee, "A New Letter from Poe to Lowell on the *Pioneer*," 33). Willis's review of the January 1843 issue of the *Pioneer* was published in the *Brother Jonathan* on January 7, 1843 (Thomas and Jackson, *The Poe Log*, 395) and reprinted in the February 1843 issue of the magazine (see James Russell Lowell, ed., *The Pioneer: A Literary Magazine* [New York: Scholars' Facsimiles & Reprints, 1947], February 1843 issue, rear end-paper).

96. Edward J. Balleisen, *Navigating Failure: Bankruptcy and Commercial Society in Antebellum America* (Chapel Hill: University of North Carolina Press, 2001), esp. 2, 101–8, 119, 132.

97. For the bankruptcy document, see the National Archives at Philadelphia, the Bankruptcy Act of 1841 (File Unit 12089325-Case 1304, Edgar A. Poe). See also Barbara Cantalupo, "Interview with Jefferson Moak (October 2007)," *Edgar Allan Poe Review* 8, no. 2 (2007): 92–98; "Edgar A. Poe: 'possessed of no Property,'" *Prologue*, 47, no. 3 (2015); *National Archives' Today's Document Tumblr*; and Rebecca Onion, "A Melancholy List of Edgar Allan Poe's Debt's, From His Bankruptcy Petition of 1842." All the details regarding Poe's bankruptcy are drawn from the December 19, 1842, petition. The archivist who discovered it was Jefferson Moak.

98. A related document of January 28, 1843, at the National Archives, specifies how Poe's local creditors were served with notice of his bankruptcy.

99. Balleisen, *Navigating Failure*, 120, 152.

100. Oliver Hopkinson was one of four commissioners in bankruptcy in Philadelphia at the time; the others were Samuel Rush, John Swift, and James F. Macaully (see "Commissioners in Bankruptcy," *Pennsylvanian*, April 23, 1842, [2] [America's Historical Newspapers]). Hopkinson's office was at 65 S. Seventh Street; perhaps that is where Poe completed his petition (see *McElroy's Philadelphia City Directory* [Philadelphia: Orrin Rogers, 1842]). It is uncertain whether Poe knew that Oliver Hopkinson was the son of the writer Joseph Hopkinson, about whom Poe had written in "Autography" and "A Chapter on Autography" (see Poe, "Autography," *Southern Literary Messenger* 2, no. 3 [February 1836]: 212 [H 15:162–63]; and "A Chapter on Autography," *Graham's Magazine* 19, no. 5 [November 1841]: 232 [H 15:201]). Oliver Hopkinson's grandfather was Francis Hopkinson, a signer of the Declaration of Independence.

101. "Bankrupts," *Philadelphia Public Ledger*, December 20, 1842, [2] (America's Historical Newspapers); Sculley Bradley, "Introduction," *Pioneer: A Literary Magazine*, ix.

102. Balleisen, *Navigating Failure*, 2, 124. For an announcement of the publication of the January 1843 issue of the *Pioneer*, see "The Pioneer for January," *Boston Post*, December 27, 1842, [3], https://www.newspapers.com.

103. For the *Macbeth* connection, see Robert McIlvaine, "A Shakespearean Echo in 'The Tell-Tale Heart,'" *American Notes & Queries* 15, no. 3 (1976): 38–40; and Richard Wilbur, "Poe and the Art of Suggestion," *University of Mississippi Studies*

in English, n.s., vol. 3 (1982): 1–13. For the Bulwer-Lytton connection, see Burton R. Pollin, "Bulwer Lytton and 'The Tell-Tale Heart,'" *American Notes & Queries* 4 (1965): 7–9. Dickens tales are considered sources for the work (see Edith Smith Krappe, "A Possible Source for Poe's 'The Tell-Tale Heart' and 'The Black Cat,'" *American Literature* 12, no. 1 [1940]: 84–88; Laurence Senelick, "Charles Dickens and 'The Tell-Tale Heart,'" *Poe Studies* 6, no. 1 [1973]: 12–14; and Edward Strickland, "Dickens' 'A Madman's Manuscript' and 'The Tell-Tale Heart,'" *Poe Studies* 9, no. 1 [1976]: 22–23). I have recurred to the Webster, Shakespeare, and Dickens sources for "The Tell-Tale Heart" and posited as a source a Hawthorne sketch (see *The Threads of "The Scarlet Letter"* [Newark: University of Delaware Press, 2003], 24–29, 127–28). Lowell's February 1842 poem "Rosaline," which twice featured "nevermore," also included the line "The deathwatch tickt behind the wall," suggesting Poe's "death-watches in the wall" in "The Tell-Tale Heart" (see Lowell, "Rosaline," 89, and Poe, "The Tell-Tale Heart," 30 [M 3:794]).

104. I earlier elaborated the form of "The Tell-Tale Heart" in *The Threads of "The Scarlet Letter,"* 107.

105. This view has been suggested by scholars; see, for example, Marie Bonaparte, *The Life and Works of Edgar Allan Poe: A Psycho-Analytic Interpretation* (London: Imago, 1949), 491–504; and Daniel Hoffman, *Poe Poe Poe Poe Poe Poe Poe* (Garden City, NY: Doubleday, 1972), 226–32.

106. See Fisher, *Poe in His Own Time*, 40.

107. Poe's pocket watch was recently donated to the Poe Museum, of Richmond, by Poe collector Susan Tane. For more on the watch, see https://www.poemuseum.org; and Bob Frishman, "Poe's Pocket Watch Sells for $250,000," *Maine Antique Digest* (August 2019), 136.

108. Thomas and Jackson, *The Poe Log*, 395.

109. Ibid. The story appeared on January 6, 1843, in the *United States Gazette* and on January 25, 1843, in the *Dollar Newspaper*.

110. Kopley, *The Threads of "The Scarlet Letter,"* 130. *Narrative of the Life of Frederick Douglass* was published in May 1845 (see "Testimony in Relation to Slavery," *Boston Courier*, May 26, 1845, [1], America's Historical Newspapers).

111. The Poe review of the January 1843 issue of the *Pioneer* is reprinted at the end of the February issue of the *Pioneer*, just before the reprint of the Willis review. See also T. O. Mabbott, "A Review of Lowell's Magazine," *American Notes & Queries* 178 (June 29, 1940): 452–53. For the argument regarding the importance of *The Salem Belle* for *The Scarlet Letter*, see Kopley, *The Threads of "The Scarlet Letter,"* 64–96, 142–53. For the then anonymous 1842 novel, see Ebenezer Wheelwright, *The Salem Belle: A Tale of 1692*, ed. Richard Kopley (University Park: Pennsylvania State University Press, 2016).

112. "Bankruptcy," *Philadelphia Public Ledger*, January 14, 1843, [2] (America's Historical Newspapers); Balleisen, *Navigating Failure*, 124.

113. For a useful sketch of Clarke, see Thomas, "Poe in Philadelphia," 2:734–35. The characterization of Clarke is drawn from William Perrine's "Men and Things," *Philadelphia Evening Bulletin*, October 1, 1897, June 7, 1898, and June 11, 1898; as well as "Death of Thomas Cottrell Clarke," *Camden Democrat*, November 28, 1874. The June 7, 1898, installment of "Men and Things" also includes

brief reference to Poe's making the case to Clarke for "The Stylus." It is likely that Clarke had heard of Poe as early as 1837. A piece in his *American Monthly Magazine* suggests that Clarke may have attended the March 30, 1837, Booksellers' Dinner ("The New York Booksellers' Dinner," *American Monthly Magazine*, 9 [May 1837]: 521–24). And the June 1837 issue of the periodical contained Poe's "Von Jung, the Mystific" (M 2:292). During Poe's time in Philadelphia, Clarke is reported to have employed Poe "as a literary and art critic" on the *Philadelphia Saturday Courier* ("Thomas Cottrell Clarke," *Potter's American Monthly*, 4 [1875]: 80). Poe referred to his agreement with Clarke regarding "The Stylus" in a letter to Frederick W. Thomas of February 25, 1843: "The articles of copartnership have been signed & sealed for some weeks" (O 1:381). Clearly the Poe-Clarke agreement was established before the Poe-Clarke-Darley agreement of January 31, 1843. Noted on the verso side of the contract between Poe and Clarke and Darley is "Poe's Ms. This agreement was written by Mr. Poe" ("Agreement between Felix O. C. Darley and Thomas C. Clarke and Edgar A. Poe," HM2511, Huntington Library). For a consideration of Clarke's Poe collection, see Richard Kopley and Michael Singer, "Thomas Cottrell Clarke's Poe Collection: New Documents," *Poe Studies* 23, nos. 1 and 2 (1992): 1–5.

114. That the series was already planned in January 1843, with an expected installment on Poe, may be inferred from Frederick W. Thomas's February 1, 1843, letter to Poe, mentioning Poe's biography and Poe's notes for it (H 17:128–29). Thomas was responding to a letter from Poe that is unlocated and perhaps no longer extant (O 2:1212). Michael J. Deas dates the daguerreotype to "about 1842" (Deas, *The Portraits and Daguerreotypes of Edgar Allan Poe* [Charlottesville: University Press of Virginia, 1989], 12). The woodblock image was drawn by E. J. Pinkerton and engraved by Charles N. Parmelee (ibid., 16–17).

115. The critique of Griswold's *Poets and Poetry of America* in the January 28, 1843, issue of the *Philadelphia Saturday Museum* has been attributed to Poe (H 11:220–43; Burton R. Pollin, "Poe's Authorship of Three Long Critical and Autobiographical Articles of 1843 Now Authenticated," *American Renaissance Literary Report: An Annual 7* [Hartford, CT: Transcendental Books, 1993], 141–46), but I lean toward the judgment of T. O. Mabbott and Dwight Thomas that the piece was Hirst's work (M 1:553n; Thomas, "Poe in Philadelphia," 1:495–98). It is notable that the *Germantown Telegraph* of February 8, 1843, referred to it as Hirst's work (Thomas, "Poe in Philadelphia," 1:497, 504).

116. I infer the date of Poe's receiving the February issue of the *Pioneer* by noting that the magazine was to be published on the 20th of each month (Woodberry, "Lowell's Letters to Poe," 171) and that the February issue was probably received at the *New York Tribune* by January 26 since the newspaper's announcement of having received the issue appeared on January 27 ("The Pioneer for February," *New York Tribune*, January 27, 1843, [2], https://www.newspapers.com). For Hawthorne's comment on Poe in "The Hall of Fantasy," see Nathaniel Hawthorne, "The Hall of Fantasy," *Pioneer* (February 1843): 51. See also *The Centenary Edition of the Works of Nathaniel Hawthorne*, vol. 10, ed. William Charvat, Roy Harvey Pearce, and Claude M. Simpson (Columbus: Ohio State University Press, 1974), 636.

117. See Fisher, *Poe in His Own Time*, 30.

118. Poe must have indicated his plan to come to Washington in an unlocated January 1843 letter to Frederick W. Thomas since Thomas wrote back on February 1, "I hould be most glad to greet you in the Capital. Come on if possible" and "When you come to Washington stop at 'Fuller's Hotel' where you will find your friend / F. W. Thomas" (H 17:128–29).

17. "I Would Say to You, Without Hesitation, Aspire"

1. Thomas excused himself to Poe from writing the biography on the basis of his professional obligations while Congress was in session. And he added that his authorship might suggest that the piece merely reflected his friendship with Poe (H 17:128–29). Elsewhere, however, he indicated that his reluctance might have been owing in part to his far greater knowledge of Poe than the notes that Poe had sent him provided (J. H. Whitty, "Memoir," in *The Complete Poems of Edgar Allan Poe* [Boston: Houghton Mifflin, 1911], xlvii).
2. The traditional view is that Poe withdrew "The Gold-Bug" from *Graham's Magazine* after the *Dollar Newspaper* short story contest was announced on March 29, 1843 (see, for example, Dwight Thomas and David K. Jackson, *The Poe Log: A Documentary Life of Edgar Allan Poe, 1809–1849* [Boston: G. K. Hall, 1987], 409). However, Jeffrey A. Savoye has speculated that perhaps Poe requested the tale's return from Graham earlier, for inclusion in "The Stylus" (Savoye, "Reconstructing Poe's 'The Gold-Bug': An Examination of the Composition and First Printing[s]," *Edgar Allan Poe Review* 8, no. 2 [2007]: 35). For Poe's accounting of the purchase and return of "The Gold-Bug," see O 1:415. According to one source, Graham considered his relinquishing "The Gold-Bug" to Poe to be evidence of "love and friending" (Albert H. Smyth, *The Philadelphia Magazines and Their Contributors 1741–1850* [Philadelphia: Robert M. Lindsay, 1892], 218).
3. For Poe's February 4, 1843, submission of "Notes upon English Verse" to the *Pioneer*, see O 1:376–77; for his February 16 submission of "Eulalie," see O 1:379. Lowell wrote to Poe about the financial problems that led to the cessation of the *Pioneer* (George E. Woodberry, "Lowell's Letters to Poe," *Scribner's Monthly* 16, no. 2 [August 1894]: 171; see also H 17:138–39). Coeditor Robert Carter also discussed the end of the *Pioneer*, in a letter to contributor John Neal (Benjamin Lease, "Robert Carter, James Russell Lowell and John Neal: A Document," *Jahrbuch für Amerikastudien* 13 [1968]: 246–48). For two significant early studies of the *Pioneer*, see Sculley Bradley, "Introduction," *The Pioneer: A Literary Magazine*, ed. James Russell Lowell (New York: Scholars' Facsimiles & Reprints, 1947), v–xxix; and "Lowell, Emerson, and *The Pioneer*," *American Literature* 19, no. 3 (1947): 231–44.
4. The *Saturday Museum* biography is available in Benjamin F. Fisher's *Poe in His Own Time* (Iowa City: University of Iowa Press, 2010), 23–40. Poe credited it to Hirst (O 1:381, 441, 450). Fisher attributes the piece to Poe and Hirst (*Poe in His Own Time*, 23). Thomas and Jackson consider it "prepared by Poe in collaboration with Hirst" (*The Poe Log*, 398). However, Burton R. Pollin makes a case for Poe's sole authorship in "Poe's Authorship of Three Long Critical and Autobiographical Articles of 1843 Now Authenticated," *American Renaissance Literary*

Report: An Annual 7 (Hartford, CT: Transcendental Books, 1993), 139–71. This article also includes a facsimile publication of the biography in nine sections. We may note that Rufus W. Griswold, whose view should be considered despite his unquestionable nefariousness, wrote in his "Memoir," "In Philadelphia, in 1843, he [Poe] prepared with his own hands a sketch of his life for a paper called 'The Museum'" (Fisher, *Poe in His Own Time*, 144–45). Previous to this volume, Fisher wrote about the Poe biography in the *Saturday Museum* in "An Early Biography of Poe (1843): The *Philadelphia Saturday Museum* Sketch," in *Masques, Mysteries, and Mastodons: A Poe Miscellany,* ed. Fisher (Baltimore, MD: Edgar Allan Poe Society, 2006), 155–93; see esp. Fisher's afterword (191–93). Three installments of "The Poets and Poetry of Philadelphia" followed the Poe sketch in March and May 1843; they focused on J. K. Mitchell, Robert Conrad, and Robert Morris (Dwight Rembert Thomas, "Poe in Philadelphia, 1838–1844: A Documentary Record" [PhD diss., University of Pennsylvania, 1978], 1:508).

5. Gabriel Harrison, who knew Poe in New York in the 1840s, considered the McKee daguerreotype "the most characteristic of all the portraits of Poe known" (Michael J. Deas, *The Portraits and Daguerreotypes of Edgar Allan Poe* [Charlottesville: University Press of Virginia, 1989], 12). See also Amanda Pogue Schulte, "Portraits and Daguerreotypes of Edgar Allan Poe," *University of Virginia Record Extension Series* 10, no. 8 (1926): 51–52.

6. "Edgar A. Poe Esq," *Philadelphia Saturday Museum,* March 4, 1843; Fisher, *Poe in His Own Time,* 40; Thomas and Jackson, *The Poe Log,* 399 ("A very fair likeness"), 404 ("not very truthful").

7. For full discussion of the McKee daguerreotype and the *Saturday Museum* woodcut, see Deas, *The Portraits and Daguerreotypes of Edgar Allan Poe,* 12–18. Kevin J. Hayes offers an assessment in "Poe, the Daguerreotype, and the Autobiographical Act," *Biography* 25, no. 3 (2002): 477–92.

8. Whitty, "Memoir," xlvii.

9. For a discussion of the poems in the *Saturday Museum* biography, see Dudley Hutcherson, "The *Philadelphia Saturday Museum* Text of Poe's Poems," *American Literature* 5, no. 1 (1933): 36–48.

10. A shortened version of the *Saturday Museum* biography of Poe appeared in the *Boston Notion* of April 29, 1843 (Burton R. Pollin, "Poe in the *Boston Notion,*" *New England Quarterly* 42, no. 4 [1969]: 585–89).

11. Fisher, *Poe in His Own Time,* 29, 35.

12. For related studies, see Burton R. Pollin, "Poe's Iron Pen," in *Discoveries in Poe* (Notre Dame, IN: University of Notre Dame Press, 1970), 206–29, 289–95; and Alexander Hammond, "Poe, Scott's Fiction, and the Holt Source Collection: The Example of *Ivanhoe* and 'The Fall of the House of Usher,'" *Resources for American Literary Study* 34 (2009): 63–66.

13. See my "John Neal on Hawthorne and Poe in the *New England Galaxy* of 1835," *Nathaniel Hawthorne Review* 42, no. 2 (2016): 30–31, 28.

14. See Wilmer, *Merlin Baltimore, 1827,* ed. Thomas Ollive Mabbott (1941; rpt., n.p. [Folcroft, PA]: Folcroft Library Editions, 1973), 26. For Mabbott's source, see Lambert A. Wilmer, *Our Press Gang; or, A Complete Exposition of the Corruptions and Crimes of the American Newspapers* (Philadelphia: J. T. Lloyd, 1859), 36.

15. The address of the *Saturday Museum* and *Godey's Lady's Book* is given in *McElroy's Philadelphia City Directory* (Philadelphia: A. McElroy, 1843), 355. For Poe and Clarke at this time, see William Perrine ("Penn"), "Men and Things," *Philadelphia Evening Bulletin,* June 7, 1898, 4. For Poe's having visited Clarke's home, see John Sartain, *The Reminiscences of a Very Old Man, 1808–1897* (New York: D. Appleton, 1899), 217. For a photograph of Clarke's three-story home, see Mary E. Phillips, *Edgar Allan Poe—The Man,* 2 vols. (Chicago: John C. Winston, 1926), 1:810.
16. Perrine, "Men and Things," *Philadelphia Evening Bulletin,* June 7, 1898, 4.
17. Thomas, "Poe in Philadelphia," 1:516.
18. The best source of information for Poe's time in Washington is Jesse E. Dow's letter to Thomas Cottrell Clarke of March 12, 1843 (William F. Gill, *The Life of Edgar Allan Poe* [New York: D. Appleton, 1877], 120–22). See also Poe's letter to Clarke of March 11, 1843, and his letter to Thomas and Dow of March 16, 1843 (O 1:386–92). For the encounter with Hewitt, see John Hill Hewitt, *Recollections of Poe,* ed. Richard Barksdale Harwell (Atlanta, GA: The Library, Emory University, 1949), 19. More briefly, this encounter is mentioned in Hewitt's *Shadows on the Wall* (Baltimore, MD: Turnbull Brothers, 1877), 43. Thomas recalled of Poe, "He was sober when I saw him, but afterward in the company of old friends he drank to excess" (J. H. Whitty, "Memoir," in *The Complete Poems of Edgar Allan Poe* [Boston: Houghton Mifflin, 1911], xlvii). There is one account that Poe stayed with a widow Barrett and met Matthew Brady (John A. Joyce, *Edgar Allan Poe* [New York: F. Tennyson Neely, 1901], 78).
19. Gill, *The Life of Edgar Allan Poe,* 120–22. William H. Gravely contended that English was the person Dow had in mind who could harm Poe politically (Gravely: "The Early Political and Literary Career of Thomas Dunn English" [PhD diss., University of Virginia, 1953], 352–59, and "Poe and Thomas Dunn English: More Light on a Probable Reason for Poe's Failure to Receive a Custom-House Appointment," in *Papers on Poe Essays in Honor of John Ward Ostrom,* ed. Richard P. Veler [Springfield, OH: Chantry Music Press at Wittenberg University, 1972], 173–82).
20. For the chronology of Poe's visit to Washington, see Thomas, "Poe in Philadelphia," 2:525–37; and Thomas and Jackson, *The Poe Log,* 403–7.
21. Pollin lists "Original Conundrums" and "Conversation of Eiros and Charmion" in the *Saturday Museum* in "Poe's Authorship," 140–41. Jeffrey A. Savoye treats "The Business Man" in the *Saturday Museum* in "Poe's 1843 Text of 'The Business Man," *Edgar Allan Poe Review* 20, no. 2 (2019): 305–7. See also John E. Reilly, "The 'Missing' Version of Edgar Allan Poe's 'The Business Man,'" *American Periodicals* 9 (1999): 1–14.
22. Sartain, *Reminiscences,* 226; Thomas, "Poe in Philadelphia," 2:534; Thomas and Jackson, *The Poe Log,* 445.
23. Flora Lapham Mack to William Lanier Washington, "Concerning Correspondence between Edgar Allan Poe & John H. Mackenzie," collection of the author.
24. Peter D. Bernard was the husband of White's daughter Sarah. The couple knew Poe well (see "Death of Peter D. Bernard," *Richmond Daily Times,* December 21,

1889, 4; and [Obituary for Sarah Lloyd Bernard], *Alexandria Gazette,* April 24, 1897, 2 [Virginia Chronicle]). Sarah's sister was Elizabeth, or Eliza, a friend of Poe and Virginia. Eliza attended the Poes' marriage, visited Maria Clemm and Edgar and Virginia in Philadelphia, and would later visit the three of them in Fordham. For Eliza's visiting the Poes in Philadelphia, I consult "Mrs. Sarah Lloyd Bernard," from the *Baltimore Sun,* which appears in "Poeana," a scrapbook compiled by Eugene L. Didier, p. 31, collection of the author. Thomas G. Mackenzie had attended the College of William & Mary for one year (1839–40) ("Register of Students in William and Mary College," *William and Mary Quarterly,* 2nd ser., vol. 4, no. 1 [1924]: 63). According to Mack ("Concerning Correspondence"), he also studied in England. It was Thomas G. Mackenzie who would later collect Poe materials and write a biography, all of which would be destroyed in Richmond's Evacuation Fire of April 1865. For Minor's acquisition of the *Messenger,* see Benjamin Blake Minor, *The Southern Literary Messenger, 1834–1864* (New York: Neale, 1905), 103–6.

25. Thomas, "Poe and Philadelphia," 2:544.
26. For the estimated date of the move, see Thomas and Jackson, *The Poe Log,* 409. For detail on Poe's Coates Street home and his North Seventh Street home, see Ellis Paxson Oberholtzer, *Philadelphia: A History of the City and Its People, A Record of 225 Years,* 4 vols. (Philadelphia: S. J. Clarke, 1912), 2:213–14. For thoughtful treatments of the latter, Poe's Spring Garden home, see Arthur Hobson Quinn, *Edgar Allan Poe: A Critical Biography* (New York: D. Appleton-Century, 1941), 384–86; Alvin Holm, "Architecture," in *Edgar Allan Poe in Context,* ed. Kevin J. Hayes (Cambridge, UK: Cambridge University Press, 2013), 332–42; and Amy Branam Armiento, "Poe in Philadelphia," in *Poe and Place,* ed. Philip Edward Phillips (Cham, Switzerland: Palgrave Macmillan, 2018), 136–38.
27. Mayne Reid's "A Dead Man Defended," from *Onward* (April 1869), 1:305–8, is readily available in Thomas, "Poe in Philadelphia," 2:876–81; and at https://www.eapoe.org.
28. Phillips, *Edgar Allan Poe—the Man,* 1:827; Oberholtzer, *Philadelphia: A History of the City and Its People,* 2:214.
29. Susan Archer Weiss, *The Home Life of Poe* (New York: Broadway, 1907), 95–97; Thomas and Jackson, *The Poe Log,* 445.
30. Thomas, "Poe in Philadelphia," 2:558–59, 624–27; Thomas and Jackson, *The Poe Log,* 412.
31. Thomas, "Poe in Philadelphia," 2:626.
32. Sartain, *Reminiscences,* 215.
33. Quinn, *Edgar Allan Poe: A Critical Biography,* 401. See also Thomas, "Poe in Philadelphia," 2:559.
34. On August 9, 1843, a similar comment, following a manicule (a pointing hand), was made in the weekly Philadelphia newspaper the *Citizen Soldier:* "T. Cotrell C. shall be attended to at leisure. 'Imbecility is that protection which Heaven affords to fools.'" I quote from the *Citizen Soldier,* August 9, 1843, 188, collection of the author. The author of this comment was probably George Lippard, the editor of the newspaper. Poe may well have spoken to his friend Lippard about Clarke's withdrawal of support for "The Stylus."

35. Thomas Cottrell Clarke, "Poe: What Those Say Who Knew Him Best," ms., ca. 1858, Butler Library, Columbia University; Lambert Wilmer, "Recollections of Edgar A. Poe," in Wilmer, *Merlin Baltimore 1827,* 34.
36. Richard Kopley and Michael Singer, "Thomas Cottrell Clarke's Poe Collection: New Documents," *Poe Studies* 25, nos. 1 and 2 (1992): 1–5.
37. For the June 14 date of the announcement, see Thomas and Jackson, *The Poe Log,* 414. For the comment about the story's having been written backward, see Charles J. Peterson to John H. Ingram, March 3, 1880, Item 348, John Henry Ingram's Poe Collection, Albert & Shirley Small Special Collections Library, University of Virginia, Charlottesville, call number MSS 38-135, box 6.
38. George E. Woodberry, *The Life of Edgar Allan Poe,* 2 vols. (Boston: Houghton Mifflin, 1909), 2:2–3.
39. For this list, see Thomas, "Poe in Philadelphia," 2:570. For Poe's comment on Conrad, see Poe, "A Chapter on Autography," *Graham's Magazine* 19, no. 6 (December 1841): 281; see also H 15:232–33.
40. Savoye, "Reconstructing," 38–39. See also M 3:804. For images of the prints, see Phillips, *Edgar Allan Poe—the Man,* 1:790–91. For engaging commentary on these images, see Barbara Cantalupo, "Poe's Visual Legacy," in *The Oxford Handbook to Edgar Allan Poe,* ed. J. Gerald Kennedy and Scott Peeples (New York: Oxford University Press, 2019), 677–79. See also https://www.eapoe.org.
41. The story as it appeared in the *Dollar Newspaper* is available at https://www.eapoe.org. For a later version of the story, with variants from the original, see M 3:806–44.
42. For the initial publication of the story, see William Gilmore Simms, "The Lazy Crow," in *The Gift: A Christmas and New Year's Present for 1840,* ed. Miss Leslie (Philadelphia: Carey & Hart, 1839), 41–72. "William Wilson" appears on pp. 229–53. For an early linking of Poe's Jupiter with another Simms work, *The Yemassee,* see Elizabeth C. Phillips, "'His Right of Attendance': The Image of the Black Man in the Works of Poe and Two of His Contemporaries," in *No Fairer Land Studies in Southern Literature before 1900,* ed. J. Lasley Dameron and James W. Mathews (Troy, NY: Whitston, 1986), 172–84.
43. The cited comment on Jupiter appears in a review of Poe's *Tales, Aristidean* (October 1845): 317. The review has been attributed to Poe (see William Doyle Hull II, "A Canon of the Critical Works of Edgar Allen [sic] Poe with a Study of Poe as Editor and Reviewer" [PhD diss., University of Virginia, 1941], 699). The review appears in *Edgar Allan Poe: Essays and Reviews,* ed. G. R. Thompson (New York: Library of America, 1984), 868–73, see esp. 869. However, T. O. Mabbott considered the work to be by the editor Thomas Dunn English (M 2:395). Jeffrey A. Savoye discusses the ambiguous matter of the attribution of this piece in https://www.eapoe.org. For discussion of stereotyping in Poe and Simms, see Elizabeth C. Phillips, "'His Right of Attendance.'"
44. I follow the version in the *Dollar Newspaper,* offering the Mabbott edition page numbers, as well, with two variants. I treat these parallels earlier in *The Formal Center in Literature: Explorations from Poe to the Present* (Rochester, NY: Camden House, 2018), 29–30.
45. Kopley, *The Formal Center in Literature,* 30.

46. Ibid., 32.
47. Ibid.
48. Ibid., 31, 33. It was Kenneth Silverman who wrote that Poe "modeled [the letter of March 19, 1827] on the Declaration of Independence" (Silverman, *Edgar A. Poe: Mournful and Never-ending Remembrance* [New York: HarperCollins, 1991], 35).
49. Kopley, *The Formal Center in Literature,* 33.
50. Thomas and Jackson, *The Poe Log,* 414, 420, 424.
51. For Duffee, see ibid., 419–20 and 429; for Du Solle, see ibid., 422, 425. For Duffee's repeated false accusation against Poe years later through William Duane Jr., see W. T. Bandy, "Poe, Duane and Duffee," *University of Mississippi Studies in English,* n.s., vol. 3 (1982): 87–94. Duane's pseudonym was the anagrammatical "UNEDA."
52. Thomas and Jackson, *The Poe Log,* 420. For a consideration of the publication of "The Gold-Bug," including its reprintings, see Savoye, "Reconstructing Poe's 'The Gold-Bug.'"
53. See, for example, O 1:442; and Savoye, "Reconstructing," 38–39.
54. Thomas and Jackson, *The Poe Log,* 433–34.
55. Reid, "A Dead Man Defended," 308, 307, 306; Thomas, "Poe in Philadelphia," 2:881, 879, 878.
56. Thomas, "Poe in Philadelphia" 610. There is a facsimile edition of the volume: *Edgar Allan Poe Prose Romances,* prepared by George E. Hatvary and Thomas O. Mabbott (New York: St. John's University Press, 1968).
57. Poe also submitted a severe criticism of Longfellow's dramatic poem *The Spanish Student* by mid-August; it was bought but never published. Griswold referred to its having been submitted before he left *Graham's,* and George Lippard noted in the August 16 issue of the *Citizen Soldier* that Griswold was "discharged last week." For Griswold's comment, see Thomas, "Poe in Philadelphia," 2:656–57; and Thomas and Jackson, *The Poe Log,* 444. For Lippard's statement, see Thomas, "Poe in Philadelphia," 2:616. The original of that statement appears beside a manicule in the *Citizen Soldier,* August 16, 1843, 197. Poe refers to his review in a letter to Lowell of October 19, 1843 (O 1:413), and Graham mentions it in a letter to Longfellow of February 9, 1844 (Thomas, "Poe in Philadelphia," 2:679).
58. Woodberry, *The Life of Edgar Allan Poe,* 2:2–3; Thomas, "Poe in Philadelphia," 2:741.
59. The first version of "The Black Cat," that in the *United States Saturday Post,* is available at https://www.eapoe.org. The passages that I quote are identical in the Mabbott edition.
60. Brett Zimmerman, *Edgar Allan Poe: Rhetoric and Style* (Montreal: McGill-Queen's University Press, 2005), 43–44, 48–49; *Edgar Allan Poe: Amateur Psychologist* (New York: Peter Lang, 2019), 149–50.
61. The phrase is identical in the *Pioneer* version of the story (see Poe, "The Tell-Tale Heart," *Pioneer* 1, no. 1 [January 1843]: 30). The story is also available in the 1947 and 1977 Scholars' Facsimiles & Reprints versions of the *Pioneer.*
62. Marilynne Robinson, "On Edgar Allan Poe," *New York Review of Books,* February 5, 2015, 6.
63. See E. Kate Stewart, "Another Source for 'The Black Cat,'" *Poe Studies* 18, no. 2 (1985): 25; Edith Smith Krappe, "A Possible Source for Poe's 'The Tell-Tale Heart'

and 'The Black Cat,'" *American Literature* 12, no. 1 (1940): 84–88; and John E. Reilly, "A Source for the Immuration in 'The Black Cat,'" *Nineteenth-Century Literature* 48, no. 1 (1993): 93–95.

64. "Reminiscences of Poe," ca. November 4, 1880, copy by Reverend John Bannister Tabb, Ingram's Poe Collection, Item 361. Mabbott mentions this incident (M 3:848). The source for the incident is "Mr. Poiteaux"; the Poiteaux family of Richmond was close to the Allans.

65. William Elliot Griffis, "Behind the Mystery of Poe's 'Raven,'" *New York Times*, January 20, 1924, *Book Review*, 2 (ProQuest Historical Newspapers). See also Marjorie Peabody Waite, *Yaddo Yesterday and Today* (Saratoga Springs, NY: Argus, 1933), 20–22. There is also an account of a Poe visit to the Barhyte farm in 1842.

66. George E. Woodberry, *Edgar Allan Poe* (Boston: Houghton Mifflin, 1885), 221n; Woodberry, *The Life of Edgar Allan Poe*, 2:112–13. For Horace Wemyss Smith's asserting that Poe read "The Raven" at Graham's office and that the poem was "condemned," see Edwin Wolf 2nd, "Horace Wemyss Smith's Recollections of Poe," *Library Chronicle of the University of Pennsylvania* 17 (1951): 93–94. See also Thomas and Jackson, *The Poe Log*, 437. According to Smith's reminiscence, fifteen dollars was collected for the impoverished Poe, who then went to a nearby tavern and became intoxicated. For Pease's conveying Murdock's assertion, see Theodore Pease Stearns, "A Prohibitionist Shakes Dice with Poe," *Outlook* 126, no. 1 (1920): 26 (https://www.eapoe.org). For other comment on the Saratoga story, see Phillips, *Edgar Allan Poe—the Man*, 1:762–68; M 1:358; Thomas, "Poe in Philadelphia," 2:707–11, 778–79, 856–57; and Thomas and Jackson, *The Poe Log*, 435.

67. For more on Ide, see Kent P. Ljungquist, "'Fellowship with Other Poets': Lowell, Longfellow, and Poe Correspond with A. M. Ide Jr.," *Resources for American Literary Study* 28 (2003): 27–51.

68. The *Saturday Courier* version of "Diddling" is available in facsimile in J. G. Varner, *Edgar Allan Poe and The Philadelphia "Saturday Courier"* (Charlottesville: University of Virginia, 1933), 67–85. The Mabbott edition includes the *Opal* version of "Morning on the Wissahiccon" (M 3:861–66), which is the same as that in the Stedman and Woodberry edition of Poe's works. That "A Tale of the Ragged Mountains" was written, or at least begun, in 1843 is suggested by Poe's reference to that year in the first two versions of the work (M 3:942v).

69. Thomas and Jackson, *The Poe Log*, 440, 443.

70. "William Wirt Institute Lectures and Debates," *Philadelphia Public Ledger*, October 21, 1843, 2 (America's Historical Newspapers). One announcement of McMichael's victory was "The Sheriffalty," *Philadelphia Saturday Museum*, October 14, 1843, 2. See also the listing in the *Philadelphia Democratic Argus* of October 23 (Thomas, "Poe in Philadelphia," 2:635–36; Thomas and Jackson, *The Poe Log*, 439–40). Poe wrote to Clarke on March 11, 1843, from Washington, DC, that he was giving a lecture in two days (O 1:386), but there is no evidence for a lecture; indeed, Poe's condition mitigated against such an event. There is mention in Poe biography of Poe's giving a lecture in Baltimore in the summer of 1843, but there is no documentation (see Woodberry, *The Life of Edgar Allan Poe*, 2:48; and Phillips, *Edgar Allan Poe—the Man*, 2:841).

71. See Thomas, "Poe in Philadelphia," 2:639–40; and Thomas and Jackson, *The Poe Log*, 440–41. The original is in [George Lippard], "Wirt Institute Lectures," *Philadelphia Citizen Soldier*, November 15, 1843, 301, collection of the author.
72. Thomas, "Poe in Philadelphia," 2:641–42; Thomas and Jackson, *The Poe Log*, 441. For an early overview of Poe's lecturing, see Kathleen Edgerton, "The Lecturing of Edgar Allan Poe," *Southern Journal of Communication* 28, no. 4 (1963): 268–73.
73. For the attendance at Poe's lecture, see "American Poetry," *Dollar Newspaper*, January 10, 1844, 3 (America's Historical Newspapers). That hundreds were turned away, see Thomas, "Poe in Philadelphia," 2:642, 667; Thomas and Jackson, *The Poe Log*, 441, 447 (*United States Gazette*). For Poe's criticizing Griswold and "puffing" and sometimes criticizing with severity, even personally, see Thomas, "Poe in Philadelphia," 2:644–45, 648; and Thomas and Jackson, *The Poe Log*, 441–42, 443 (*Saturday Courier, Saturday Museum, Citizen Soldier*). Conrad lectured on American settlers and indigenous people on February 22, 1842 (*Pennsylvanian*, February 19, 1842, 2 [America's Historical Newspapers]). Morris recited his poetry on December 15, 1840 (*Pennsylvanian*, December 17, 1840, 2 [America's Historical Newspapers]). Poe wrote approvingly of Conrad and Morris in the 1841 "A Chapter on Autography" in *Graham's Magazine* 19, no. 6 (December 1841), 281, 274 (H 15:232–33, 211). Yet Poe noted in a February 3, 1842, letter to Frederick W. Thomas that he had written so positively of Conrad in part because of pressure from Graham (O 1:325–36). Conrad's poem "Sonnets on the Lord's Prayer" appeared in *Graham's Magazine* 22 (June 1843): 322–23. Poe mentioned it positively in "Robert T. Conrad," *Graham's Magazine* 25, no. 6 (June 1844): 242. Among Morris's poems was "The Student's Dream of Fame," which may well have particularly engaged Poe (*Graham's Magazine* 21, no. 2 [August 1842]: 101). I checked Griswold's *Poets and Poetry of America*, 3rd ed., rev. (Philadelphia: Carey and Hart, 1843). For my quotations, see Thomas, "Poe in Philadelphia," 2:645, Thomas and Jackson, *The Poe Log*, 442 ("a marked sensation," *Saturday Museum*); Thomas, "Poe in Philadelphia," 2:667, Thomas and Jackson, *The Poe Log*, 447 ("good sense," *The Spirit of the Times*); and Thomas, "Poe in Philadelphia," 2:667–68, Thomas and Jackson, *The Poe Log*, 447–48 ("one of the most brilliant," *Pennsylvania Inquirer*). Newspapers commented on Poe's November 21 lecture both shortly afterward and later, in early January, before his repeat performance in Philadelphia (see Thomas, "Poe in Philadelphia," 2:644–45, 648–49, 666–70; and Thomas and Jackson, *The Poe Log*, 441–42, 443, 447–48).
74. [George Lippard], ["The Rev. Rufus W. Griswold"], *Philadelphia Citizen Soldier*, August 16, 1843, 197, collection of the author; Thomas, "Poe in Philadelphia," 2:616. For Graham's assertion that Griswold had anonymously attacked Peterson, see Gill, *The Life of Edgar Allan Poe*, 111–12; and Hervey Allen, *Israfel: The Life and Times of Edgar Allan Poe*, 2 vols. (New York: George H. Doran, 1926), 2:532.
75. George R. Graham, "The Late Edgar Allan Poe," *Graham's Magazine* 36, no. 3 (March 1850): 225.
76. Thomas, "Poe in Philadelphia," 2:648; Thomas and Jackson, *The Poe Log*, 442–43.
77. Clarke explains in the *Philadelphia Saturday Museum* of January 6, 1844, the appearance of *The Doom of the Drinker* in two noncompeting magazines (Thomas,

"Poe in Philadelphia," 2:666). For a full analysis of the publication of English's *The Doom of the Drinker,* see Dwight Thomas, "Poe, English, and 'The Doom of the Drinker,'" *Princeton University Library Chronicle* 40, no. 3 (1979): 257–68. For English's portrayal of Poe, see Thomas and Jackson, *The Poe Log,* 443. Gravely comments on English's view of Poe in "The Early Political and Literary Career of Thomas Dunn English," 305–6, 315–16, 361.

78. See Ernest John Moyne, "Did Edgar Allan Poe Lecture at Newark Academy?," *Delaware Notes* (University of Delaware), 26th ser. (1953): 1–19; see 6, 15 (rain and mud); 6 (his too-tight coat); 7 ("dignified and well-bred"); 3, 6 (his drinking or not); 15 (audience); and 16 (length of lecture, audience "charmed").

79. The detail on the lecture is drawn from "Academicus" (perhaps principal William S. Graham), in a piece dated December 23, 1843, and published in the *Delaware State Journal* on January 2, 1844 (Moyne, "Did Edgar Allan Poe Lecture at Newark Academy?," 15–18). For the review of Longfellow, see Poe, review of Longfellow's *Ballads and Other Poems, Graham's Magazine* 20, no. 4 (April 1842): 248–49; as well as H 11:68–72. Poe's visit to Newark is today acknowledged, in part, through an association with Newark's Deer Park Tavern.

80. For the Lippard comment, see Thomas, "Poe in Philadelphia," 2:669; and Thomas and Jackson, *The Poe Log,* 448. For the Snodgrass comment, see Thomas, "Poe in Philadelphia," 2:676; and Thomas and Jackson, *The Poe Log,* 451.

81. See Deas, *The Portraits and Daguerreotypes of Edgar Allan Poe,* 18–23; Schulte, "Portraits and Daguerreotypes of Edgar Allan Poe," 43–44.

82. The parody was reprinted soon in the *Baltimore Republican and Daily Argus* and lightly revised for an 1848 issue of the *John Donkey.* For the former version, see Gravely, "The Early Political and Literary Career of Thomas Dunn English," 1:363–65; for the latter version, see Thomas Ollive Mabbott, "Poe and the Philadelphia Irish Citizen," *Journal of the American Irish Historical Society 1930–31* 29 (New York: American Irish Historical Society, 1931), 126–31.

83. William Charvat, *Literary Publishing in America 1790–1850* (Philadelphia: University of Pennsylvania Press, 1959), 23, 26–27.

84. Poe's letter of inquiry is inferred from Lowell's response of March 6. For an uncertain dating of Poe's letter to before February 9, see Thomas, "Poe in Philadelphia," 2:678; and Thomas and Jackson, *The Poe Log,* 452.

85. For the dating of the publication of the March 1844 issue of *Graham's,* I note that copies had already been received in Boston by February 17 (see ["Graham and Other Magazines"] and ["This Morning"], *Boston Evening Transcript,* February 17, 1844, 3 [America's Historical Newspapers]).

86. Such criticism may be found in Poe's treatment of the Transcendentalists (see my "Naysayers: Poe, Hawthorne, and Melville," in *The Oxford Handbook of Transcendentalism,* ed. Joel Myerson, Sandra Harbert Petrulionis, and Laura Dassow Walls [New York: Oxford University Press, 2010], 597–604).

87. Edgar Allan Poe, "Review of Orion," *Graham's Magazine* 25, no. 3 (March 1844): 140, 141. See also H 11:268, 275.

88. Thomas and Jackson, *The Poe Log,* 453.

89. Poe correspondent George E. Eveleth asked him on October 13, 1846, "Also in 'Graham's,' for March 1844, is the notice of Lowell's 'Legend of Brittany' by

yourself?" (*The Letters from George W. Eveleth to Edgar Allan Poe*, ed. Thomas Ollive Mabbott [New York: New York Public Library 1922], 8). And Poe responded on December 15, "The notice of Lowell's 'Brittany' *is* mine" (O 1:601; see also *The Letters of Edgar A. Poe to George W. Eveleth*, ed. James Southall Wilson [Charlottesville, VA, n.p., 1924], 9).

90. [Edgar Allan Poe], review of *Poems*, by James Russell Lowell, *Graham's Magazine* 25, no. 3 (March 1844): 142–43 (H 11:243, 246, 249). For Hawthorne's transformation of the organ passage in "A Legend of Brittany" for *The Scarlet Letter*, see my *The Threads of "The Scarlet Letter": A Study of Hawthorne's Transformative Art* (Newark: University of Delaware Press, 2003), 49–53. Doubtless Hawthorne would have been reading *Graham's Magazine* at this time, awaiting publication of his "Earth's Holocaust" (see Sophia Hawthorne and Nathaniel Hawthorne to Louisa Hawthorne, February 4, 1844, and Nathaniel Hawthorne to G. S. Hillard, March 24, 1844, in *Centenary Edition of the Works of Nathaniel Hawthorne*, vol. 16 [Columbus: Ohio State University Press, 1985], 13, 23). The tale appeared in the May 1844 issue of *Graham's Magazine*.

91. Goold Brown's *The Institutes of English Grammar* is available online at https://babel.hathitrust.org. The date of its publication is indicated by an announcement, ["We have received a copy of Goold Brown's Institutes of English Grammar"], *National Aegis* (Worcester, MA), February 28, 1844, 2 (America's Historical Newspapers). For more on Brown's book, see Bryan A. Garner, *Taming the Tongue in the Heyday of English Grammar (1711–1851)* (New York: Grolier Club, 2021), 123–24. For early mention of the Poe quotation in the Brown volume, see Charles F. Heartman and James R. Canny, comps., *A Bibliography of First Printings of the Writings of Edgar Allan Poe*, rev. ed. (Hattiesburg, MS: Book Farm, 1943), 87–88. I learned of the quotation from Garner in a Grolier Club Zoom "Happy Hour" and in an email of January 16, 2021. For the full context, in which Poe takes issue with a definition in Brown, see Lowell, *Pioneer: A Literary Magazine* 1, no. 3 (March 1843): 103; and L2:148.

92. J. Bennett Nolan, *Israfel in Berkshire: Edgar Allan Poe's Visit to Reading March 1844* (Reading: Pennsylvania Optical Company, 1948), 29–30.

93. For useful commentary, see *The Complete Works of Thomas Holley Chivers*, vol. 1: *The Correspondence of Thomas Holley Chivers 1838–1858*, ed. Emma Lester Chase and Lois Ferry Parks (Providence, RI: Brown University Press, 1957), 13nn4, 5, and 9. Poe acknowledged that he had done Chivers "injustice" in the December 1841 "A Chapter on Autography" piece (O 1:349). For the original entry, see H 15:241–42.

94. Thomas Holley Chivers, "The Heavenly Vision," *Graham's Magazine* 20, no. 6 (June 1842): 329.

95. Nolan, *Israfel in Berkshire* 30; Thomas and Jackson, *The Poe Log*, 455.

96. Valuable early studies of "A Tale of the Ragged Mountains" are Sidney E. Lind, "Poe and Mesmerism," *PMLA* 62, no. 4 (1947): 1077–94; and Doris V. Falk, "Poe and the Power of Animal Magnetism," *PMLA* 84, no. 3 (1969): 536–46.

97. See also Mukhtar Ali Isani, "Some Sources for Poe's 'Tale of the Ragged Mountains,'" *Poe Studies* 5, no. 2 (1972): 38–40.

98. Edgar Allan Poe, "A Tale of the Ragged Mountains," *Godey's Lady's Book* 28, no. 4 (April 1844): 178 ("steps," "sun," "agitation"), 179 ("arose and descended," "agitation," "sun"), 180 ("steps"); M 3:942 ("steps"), 943 ("sun"), 944 ("agitation"), 946 ("arose and descended"), 947 ("agitation," "sun"), 948 ("steps"). The *Godey's* publication is the first printing, and the Mabbott edition features the second printing, in which none of the language cited is changed.

99. For a fuller development of this reading, see my "Poe's *Pym*-esque 'A Tale of the Ragged Mountains,'" in *Poe and His Times: The Artist and His Milieu*, ed. Benjamin Franklin Fisher IV (Baltimore, MD: Edgar Allan Poe Society, 1990), 167–77. See also my study *The Formal Center in Literature*, 20–21, 22, 24.

100. Poe also sent the story "The Spectacles" to R. H. Orion in the hope that the poet would be able to place it in a British publication, but he could not (see O 1:429 [Poe's March 15, 1844, letter inquiring of Cornelius Mathews for Horne's address]; and H 17:167–69 [Horne's April 27, 1844, letter to Poe, mentioning that the manuscript of "The Spectacles" is in his "iron chest"]). For Horne's April 16, 1844, letter to Poe, noting the unlikelihood of his being able to help with the story's British publication, see Joseph J. Moldenhauer, "Poe's 'The Spectacles': A New Text from Manuscript," in *Studies in the American Renaissance 1977*, ed. Joel Myerson (Boston: Twayne, 1978), 182, 184. See also pages 184 and 186 for a partial reprinting of the April 27 letter.

101. I draw detail for their departure not only from Poe's April 7, 1844, letter to Maria Clemm (O 1:437) but also from an advertisement, "Camden and Amboy Rail Road Line, for New York and Intermediate Places, *via* South Amboy," *Philadelphia Public Ledger*, April 3, 1844, [1] (America's Historical Newspapers); and "Philadelphia" (map) by H. S. Tanner, 1845, collection of the author.

18. "A Certainty of Success"

1. The price, which John Ward Ostrom termed "probably exceptional" ("Edgar A. Poe: His Income as Literary Entrepreneur," *Poe Studies* 15, no. 1 [1982]: 7), was given by Thomas Low Nichols in *Forty Years of American Life, 1821–1861* (Doris V. Falk, "Thomas Low Nichols, Poe, and the 'Balloon Hoax,'" *Poe Studies* 5, no. 2 [1972]: 48).

2. Source studies include Horace H. Scudder, "Poe's 'Balloon Hoax,'" *American Literature* 21, no. 2 (1949): 179–90; and Richard Sterne Wilkinson, "'Balloon-Hoax' Once More," *American Literature* 32, no. 3 (1960): 313–17. Mabbott summarizes source studies for "The Balloon Hoax" in M 3:1063–65. A useful recent source study is Jeffrey A. Savoye, "Meanderings Here and There in Poe's 'Balloon Hoax,'" *Poe Studies* 18, no. 2 (2017): 257–63.

3. Edgar Allan Poe, *Doings of Gotham Poe's Contributions to The Columbia Spy*, ed. Jacob E. Spannuth and Thomas Ollive Mabbott (Pottsville, PA: Jacob E. Spannuth, 1929), 33.

4. Edgar Allan Poe, *The Works of Edgar Allan Poe*, ed. Rufus Wilmot Griswold, 4 vols. (New York: J. S. Redfield, 1850–56), 1:88. For Mabbott's suggesting that Poe wrote the note for the story used in *Works*, see *A Bibliography of First Printings*

of the Writings of Edgar Allan Poe, rev. ed., ed. Charles F. Heartman and James R. Canny (Hattiesburg, MS: Book Farm, 1943), 86.

5. Poe, *Doings of Gotham,* 33. Poe's "Hans Pfaall" preceded publication of Locke's "Moon Hoax," but Locke asserted that he had not then read it, and Poe stated that he believed the writer (H 15:129). See also H 15:259–60.

6. Falk, "Thomas Low Nichols, Poe, and the 'Balloon Hoax,'" 48–49.

7. "Beach's Balloon Humbug," *New York True Sun,* April 15, 1844, [2]. Microfilm obtained from the Library of Congress, Washington, DC.

8. "A Word about Balloons," *New York True Sun,* April 16, 1844, [2].

9. "Recipe for a Hoax," *New York True Sun,* April 17, 1844, [2]; "The New York Sun—Opinions of the Press," *New York True Sun,* April 20, 1844, [2].

10. Poe had asked Mrs. Clemm to return the borrowed second volume of the *Messenger* to Hirst, who would have returned it to its owner, William Duane Jr. She evidently instead sold it to Leary's Book Store of Philadelphia, and Duane blamed Poe. Poe wrote politely to Duane at first (O 1:461–62). It later turned out that the volume was sold to a bookseller in Richmond and then to the publishers of the *Messenger,* from whom it was bought by a friend of Duane and then returned to him. Poe wrote again to Duane with impatience and anger (O 1:480–81). For a full discussion of this incident, see W. T. Bandy, "Poe, Duane and Duffee," *University of Mississippi Studies in English,* n.s., vol. 3 (1982): 81–95.

11. See Mary E. Phillips, *Edgar Allan Poe—The Man,* 2 vols. (Chicago: John C. Winston, 1926), 2:882.

12. [George Lippard], "The Country Newspaper," *Citizen Soldier,* December 20, 1843, 340, collection of the author. The *Columbia Spy* began in June 1830 (WorldCat).

13. For Poe's contributions to the *Columbia Spy,* see Poe, *Doings of Gotham.* We may note the reference to the reservoir (40), the Bowling Green Fountain (26), the voyage around Blackwell's Island (40–41), a "villa" in Brooklyn (59–60; see also 65), "the spirit of Improvement" (25), the "street-cries" (60), and the relevance of the irrelevant (66–67).

14. Poe's *Doings of Gotham* includes Bulwer versus Dickens (42–43), the poetry of Willis (67–68, 74–75), the poetry of William Wallace (42) and Richard H. Horne (24–25, 75–76), "the great Seatsfield" (51–52), Bennett (32, 33), Nichols (32), Beach (32, 33), Greeley (33), Inman (41, 73), and Landor (68). For more on "the great Seatsfield," see Roger Forclaz, "Poe's *Doings of Gotham*: A Note on Charles Sealsfield," *Edgar Allan Poe Review* 19, no. 1 (2018): 107–12.

15. Poe, *Doings of Gotham,* 42.

16. For some of Poe's references to his own work in the *Columbia Spy,* see Poe's *Doings of Gotham* for the essay on Robert Conrad (35), "The Balloon Hoax" (33–34), and implicitly "The Purloined Letter" through reference to *The Gift for 1845* (68).

17. For Poe's mentioning "my next," see Poe, *Doings of Gotham,* 76. On June 4, 1844, Poe wrote a letter asking Bowen to send him "X by return of mail"—ten dollars (O 1:447–48). John Ward Ostrom infers that this would have been for four letters at $2.50 per letter. If Ostrom is correct, then Poe was paid $17.50 for the seven *Columbia Spy* letters (Ostrom, "Edgar A. Poe: His Income as Literary Entrepreneur," 4).

18. Poe, *Doings of Gotham*, 34.
19. Ibid., 32. Milton uses the phrase with regard to Satan in Hell (book 1, line 63). Poe had previously referred to the phrase in his "Pinakidia," in the August 1836 issue of the *Southern Literary Messenger* (P 2:49).
20. Poe, *Doings of Gotham*, 74–75.
21. "Poe and 'The Raven,'" *Augusta Chronicle,* April 30, 1900, 2 (America's Historical Newspapers), drawn from the *New York Mail and Express* of April 21, 1900 (see H 1:224–27; and https://www.eapoe.org).
22. Poe was referring to a line in Colley Cibber's edition of Shakespeare's *Richard III* (see O 1:458 and M 2:40n; see also Burton R. Pollin, "Shakespeare in the Works of Edgar Allan Poe," *Studies in the American Renaissance 1985,* ed. Joel Myerson [Charlottesville: University Press of Virginia, 1985], 175–76).
23. For an early identification of the source in the Colt-Adams story, see Clifford Carley Vierra, "Poe's 'Oblong Box': Factual Origins," *Modern Language Notes* 74, no. 8 (1959): 693–95 (see also M 3:920–21). Mabbott notes that the author's name was actually Clifford Vierra Carley (M 3:921n).
24. Edgar A. Poe, "The Purloined Letter," in *The Gift for 1845* (Philadelphia: Carey & Hart, 1844), 41–61.
25. Ibid., 58; see also M 3:990.
26. I. M. Walker, ed., *Edgar Allan Poe: The Critical Heritage* (London: Routledge & Kegan Paul, 1986), 188. Walker gives the author as Evert A. Duyckinck, but Thomas and Jackson give it as George H. Colton (Dwight Thomas and David K. Jackson, *The Poe Log: A Documentary Life of Edgar Allan Poe, 1809–1849* [Boston: G. K. Hall, 1987], 566).
27. T. O. Mabbott, introduction to *The Selected Poetry and Prose of Edgar Allan Poe* (New York: Modern Library, 1951), xiv.
28. For the fuller argument, see my *Edgar Allan Poe and the Dupin Mysteries* (New York: Palgrave Macmillan, 2008), 67–76, 109–15. With regard to the other sources, see ibid., 65–67.
29. Ibid., 72–73.
30. Ibid., 68–70. For the possible Brougham connection, see ibid., 73–76.
31. Ibid., 19–21. For the patterns in the original text, see Poe, "The Purloined Letter," in *The Gift for 1845,* 42 and 60, 48 and 52, and 50. Or see M 3:975 and 993, 981 and 985, and 983.
32. See Kopley, *Edgar Allan Poe and the Dupin Mysteries.* For the original passage, see Poe, "The Purloined Letter," in *The Gift for 1845,* 57; or M 3:989–90.
33. See Kopley, *Edgar Allan Poe and the Dupin Mysteries,* 21, 94. For the original passage, see Poe, "The Purloined Letter," in *The Gift for 1845,* 51–52; or M 3:984.
34. Kopley, *Edgar Allan Poe and the Dupin Mysteries,* 31. For the original examples of Poe's use of the word "odd," see Poe, "The Purloined Letter," in *The Gift for 1845,* 42; or M 3:975.
35. Kopley, *Edgar Allan Poe and the Dupin Mysteries,* 22. For the original examples of Poe's use of the word "even," see Poe, "The Purloined Letter," in *The Gift for 1845,* 55, 58; or M 3:987, 990, 991.
36. Kopley, *Edgar Allan Poe and the Dupin Mysteries,* 22–23.

37. Ibid., 23–24. For the original passage, see Poe, "The Purloined Letter," in *The Gift for 1845,* 58; or M 3:990.
38. Mary Douglas, *Thinking in Circles: An Essay on Ring Composition* (New Haven, CT: Yale University Press, 2007), 128–29.
39. F. O. Matthiessen, "Poe," *Sewanee Review* 54, no. 2 (1946): 205.
40. John Carl Miller, ed., *Building Poe Biography* (Baton Rouge: Louisiana State University Press, 1977), 140.
41. Kopley, *Edgar Allan Poe and the Dupin Mysteries,* 82–85. For the phrase "a partisan of the lady concerned," see Poe, "The Purloined Letter," in *The Gift for 1845,* 60; or M 3:993.
42. Mayne Reid, "A Dead Man Defended," *Onward* 1 (April 1869): 306–7 (https://www.eapoe.org).
43. Nathaniel P. Willis, "Death of Edgar A. Poe," in *Poe in His Own Time,* ed. Benjamin F. Fisher (Iowa City: University of Iowa Press, 2010), 97.
44. Nathaniel Parker Willis, "Letter about Edgar Poe," *Home Journal,* October 30, 1858, 2 (https://www.eapoe.org).
45. Francis P. Desmond, "Willis and Morris Add a Partner—and Poe," *Notes & Queries* 198 (1953): 253–54.
46. [Hiram Fuller], "A Reply for a Needful Purpose," *New York Weekly Mirror,* January 18, 1845, 227.
47. Thomas Dunn English, "Reminiscences of Poe," Part 1, *New York Independent,* October 15, 1896, 1382 (https://www.eapoe.org).
48. Laraine R. Fergensen, "Margaret Fuller as a Teacher in Providence: The School Journal of Ann Brown," *Studies in the American Renaissance 1991,* ed. Joel Myerson (Charlottesville: University Press of Virginia, 1991), 82.
49. [N. P. Willis], review of Elizabeth Barrett Barrett, *A Drama of Exile, and Other Poems, New York Evening Mirror,* October 8, 1844, [1]. For the date of the book's publication, see the advertisement for *The Drama of Exile, and Other Poems, New-York Commercial Advertiser,* October 4, 1844, [2] (America's Historical Newspapers).
50. [N. P. Willis], "Authors' Pay in America," *New York Evening Mirror,* October 10, 1844, [2]. For the deattribution to Poe of this piece, see Jeffrey A. Savoye, "A Reflection on the *Evening Mirror,*" *Edgar Allan Poe Review* 9, no. 1 (2008): 65–66.
51. [N. P. Willis], ["One of the regular allies"] and [Edgar Allan Poe], "The Swiss Bell-Ringers," *New York Evening Mirror,* October 10, 1844, [2]; *New York Weekly Mirror,* October 12, 1844, 13.
52. [N. P. Willis], "Jumping the Pew," *New York Evening Mirror,* October 19, 1844, [2]; *New York Weekly Mirror,* October 26, 1844, 34.
53. W. Penn-onas, "Our Correspondence," *New York Evening Mirror,* November 9, 1844, [2].
54. One exception is the brief introduction to "Taglioni's Application for a Divorce," which seems Poe's given the pun "lex talionis (query *legs Taglioni's*)" (see [Edgar Allan Poe], "Miscellany," [Introduction to "Taglioni's Application for a Divorce"], *New York Evening Mirror,* November 2, 1844, [1]; *New York Weekly Mirror,* November 9, 1844, 77).

55. For this anecdote, I rely on two Harrison recollections: "Edgar Allan Poe Some Reminiscences of His Old Friend Gabriel Harrison," *Brooklyn Daily Eagle*, November 17, 1875, 4; and "Edgar A. Poe Reminiscences of Gabriel Harrison, an Actor, Still Living in Brooklyn," *New York Times Saturday Review*, March 4, 1899, 144. Both are available at https://www.eapoe.org. For mention of the White Eagles during the campaign procession, see "The Town Democratic Torchlight Procession Reporter's Account," *New York Evening Mirror*, November 2, 1844, [2]. This would have been a climax to the campaign: Election Day was November 5. A possible antecedent of Thaddeus K. Peasley was the bookseller Jonathan P. Peaslee of 79 Washington Street, in 1827 Boston.
56. Arthur Hobson Quinn, *Edgar Allan Poe: A Critical Biography* (New York: D. Appleton-Century, 1941), 427. The letter may be found in the Harrison edition of Poe, H 17:193.
57. George E. Woodberry, *The Life of Edgar Allan Poe*, 2 vols. (Boston: Houghton Mifflin, 1909), 2:106–8.
58. See "Most Elegant and Popular Periodical in the World!," *New York Weekly Mirror*, December 21, 1844, 7. The only humorous piece that Poe would publish in *Graham's* in 1845 was "The System of Dr. Tarr and Professor Fether" in the November issue. Other writers noted as contributing humorous pieces to *Graham's* in 1845 were Joseph C. Neal and H. Hastings Weld. Other pieces that Poe published in the fall of 1844 were "Marginalia" (in the *Democratic Review*), "A Chapter of Suggestions" (in *The Opal for 1845*), "Puffing" (in the *Columbia Spy*), and "Byron and Miss Chaworth" (in the *Columbian Magazine*).
59. I rely primarily on "Poe and 'The Raven.'" See also M 1:358–59. Another source indicates that the landlady had had the signature painted over (Henry Collins Brown, ed., *Valentine's Manual of Old New York*, n.s., no. 7 [New York: Valentine's Manual, 1922], 283). Columbia University rare book librarian Jane R. Siegel could see no name on the mantelpiece in a recent examination (email to the author, March 3, 2021).
60. See Willis's response to Amelia Welby's "To the Editors of the Evening Mirror," *New York Evening Mirror*, November 28, 1844, [3]; and [Willis], ["Out of the 'Express'"], *New York Evening Mirror*, December 18, 1844, [2]. Regarding "Lenore" in the *Evening Mirror*, see Thomas Ollive Mabbott, "Unrecorded Texts of Two of Poe's Poems," *American Notes & Queries* 8, no. 5 (1948): 67–68.
61. [N. P. Willis and perhaps George Pope Morris], "We Copy the Following," *New York Evening Mirror*, November 29, 1844, [2]. For the wedding announcement, see "Married," ibid., November 8, 1844, [3].
62. Announcement of the coming *Aristidean* may be found at "T. D. English, Esq.," *New York True Sun*, November 23, 1844, [2]. The March number was described as "just issued" in "*The Aristidean*" (*Albany Argus*, February 28, 1845, [1] [America's Historical Newspapers]). For Poe's having visited Briggs, see Thomas and Jackson, *The Poe Log*, 479. A January 4, 1845, letter from the pseudonymous B notes that the first issue of the *Broadway Journal* has "come forth." See "From Our New-York Correspondent," *Albany Argus*, January 14, 1845, [1] (America's Historical Newspapers). For the December 12, 1844, letter from Lowell to Poe, see Woodberry, *The Life of Edgar Allan Poe*, 2:106–8. Alternatively, see H 17:194–95. For

the addresses of publications, see "Periodicals and Newspapers," in *Doggett's New York City Directory for 1845 & 1846* (New York: John Doggett Jr., 1845), 429–30. The February 1845 issue of *Graham's Magazine* was announced as received on January 7, 1845 (see "We Have Received," *Alexandria Gazette*, January 7, 1845, [2]; and "The February Number," *Sentinel of Freedom*, January 7, 1845, [2] [America's Historical Newspapers]).

63. See Poe's review of Elizabeth Barrett Barrett's *The Drama of Exile, and Other Poems*, *Broadway Journal*, January 4, 1845, 4–8, and January 11, 1845, 17–20; see also P 3:1–15. For the comparison of "Lady Geraldine's Courtship" with "Locksley Hall," see *Broadway Journal*, January 11, 1845, 17. For the earlier review by Christopher North, see *Blackwood's Edinburgh Review* (November 1844): 621–39.

64. Elizabeth Barrett Barrett, *A Drama of Exile, and Other Poems*, 2 vols. (New York: Henry G. Langley), 1:261; Poe, "The Raven," *New York Evening Mirror*, January 29, 1845; Quarles [Poe], "The Raven," *American Review* (February 1845): 143. (Interestingly, given Griswold's pseudonym for Poe's obituary, the printer of the Barrett volumes was H. Ludwig.)

65. For the early receipt of the February issue of *Graham's Magazine*, see "We Have Received a Copy," *Alexandria Gazette*, January 7, 1845, 2; and "Literary Notices," *Sentinel of Freedom*, January 7, 1845, [2] (America's Historical Newspapers). For the original essay, see James Russell Lowell, "Our Contributors.—No. XVII Edgar Allan Poe, with a Portrait," *Graham's Magazine* (February 1845): 49–53. For its inclusion in a scholarly collection, see James Russell Lowell, "Edgar Allan Poe," in *The Recognition of Edgar Allan Poe: Selected Criticism since 1829*, ed. Eric W. Carlson (Ann Arbor: University of Michigan Press, 1966), 5–16. Carlson clarifies Griswold's later distortions of this work. For specific quoted material, see "Our Contributors," 49–50 ("fearless critic," "prussic-acid"), 51 ("*genius*"), and 52 ("*x*"). Corresponding pages in Carlson are 6, 11, 13.

66. The Fuller, Briggs, and Duyckinck comments on Lowell's essay are available in Thomas and Jackson, *The Poe Log*, 491, 492, 494. An exception to the general praise is a reservation in the *New York Herald*: "Mr. J. Russell Lowell denies that Pope has any poetic merit. The same astute critic lately lauded Edgar A. Poe. There is no accounting for taste" ("Mr. J. Russell Lowell," *New York Herald*, February 24, 1845, 2, https://www.newspapers.com). This opinion may have been that of the editor James Gordon Bennett Sr.

67. For Briggs to Lowell, see Thomas and Jackson, *The Poe Log*, 486. Willis again refers to Poe as his "Sub-Editor" in a January 19[?], 1845, letter to Charles Sumner (bMSAm1, Houghton Library, Harvard University). Perhaps it was S. DeWitt Bloodgood who referred to Poe as "one of the associate editors of the Mirror" (see "The February Magazines," *New York True Sun*, January 21, 1845, [2]). It may have been Edmund Brewster Green who described Poe as "one of the editors of the Evening Mirror" (Kent P. Ljungquist, "'Mastodons of the Press': Poe, the Mammoth Weeklies, and the Case of the *Saturday Emporium*," in *Masques, Mysteries, and Mastodons: A Poe Miscellany*, ed. Benjamin Franklin Fisher [Baltimore, MD: Edgar Allan Poe Society, 2006], 83–84).

68. Nonliterary pieces included "The Cincinnati Telescope," *New York Evening Mirror*, January 10, 1845, [2]; "Lunar Atmosphere," *New York Evening Mirror*,

January 10, 1845, [2]; "The Alphadelphia Tocsin," ibid., January 11, 1845, [2]; and "Four Hundred Miles of Grasshoppers," ibid., January 23, 1845, [2].

69. For Poe's argument for a critical review in New York, see "Why Have the New Yorkers No Review?" *New York Evening Mirror,* January 8, 1845, [2]; and *New York Weekly Mirror,* January 11, 1845, 219. Willis invites a publisher to consider Poe as editor in "Sketch of Edgar Poe by Russell Lowell," *New York Evening Mirror,* January 20, 1845, [2]. Poe objected to the critic of *Blackwood's* in "Subserviency to British Criticism," *New York Evening Mirror,* January 8, 1845, [2]; and *New York Weekly Mirror,* January 11, 1845, 219. Regarding Poe on the quality of American drama, see "Does the Drama of the Day Deserve Support?" *New York Evening Mirror,* January 9, 1845; and *New York Weekly Mirror,* January 18, 1845, 229.

70. [Edgar Allan Poe], "Lowell's Conversations," *New York Evening Mirror,* January 11, 1845, [2]; *New York Weekly Mirror,* January 18, 1845, 239. For the response in the *New York Tribune,* see "The Mirror on Art," *New York Tribune,* January 14, 1845, [1]. For Poe's response, see "Nature and Art," *New York Evening Mirror,* January 17, 1845, [2]. Lowell mentioned the *Tribune* response in a letter to Briggs, who considered Poe's piece "extremely laudatory and discriminating" and blamed the inadequate understanding of the critic for the *Tribune,* intimating Margaret Fuller (Thomas and Jackson, *The Poe Log,* 488).

71. [Edgar Allan Poe], "Longfellow's Waif," *New York Evening Mirror,* January 13, 1845, [2], and January 14, 1845, [2]; *New York Weekly Mirror,* January 25, 1845, 250. For the Simms comment, see *The Letters of William Gilmore Simms,* ed. Mary C. Simms Oliphant, Alfred Taylor Odell, and T. C. Duncan Eames, vol. 2 (Columbia: University of South Carolina Press, 1953), 74.

72. For Willis, Hillard, and Poe, see "Longfellow's Waif," *New York Evening Mirror,* January 20,1845, [2]; and *New York Weekly Mirror,* January 25, 1845, 250–51. See also Thomas and Jackson, *The Poe Log,* 487–88, 491. For Willis's later account of his thinking about the publication of the Longfellow review by Poe ("a friend, who is a very fine critic") and Charles Sumner's response to the review, see "Longfellow's Waif," *New York Evening Mirror,* February 5, 1845, [2]; and *New York Weekly Mirror,* February 8, 1845, 287. See also Thomas and Jackson, *The Poe Log,* 499. The comment about Poe by Willis to Sumner occurs in another letter from Willis to Sumner in January 1845 (BMS AM1, Houghton Library, Harvard University).

73. [Edgar Allan Poe], "The Southern Literary Messenger," *New York Evening Mirror,* January 14, 1845, [2]. *Godey's Lady's Book* for February 1845 was available in Charleston, South Carolina, by January 20, 1845 ("Graham's Magazine and Godey's Lady's Book for February," *Charleston Courier,* January 20, 1845, [1] [America's Historical Newspapers]).

74. [N. P. Willis], "Sketch of Edgar Poe by Russell Lowell," *New York Evening Mirror,* January 20, 1845, [2].

75. See Arthur Hobson Quinn, *Edgar Allan Poe: A Critical Biography,* 443–50; and O 2:907–8

76. [Edgar Allan Poe], "Criticism," *New York Evening Mirror,* January 17, 1845, [2]; "A Mistake," ibid., January 18, 1845, [2]; "American Diffuseness—Objectionable

Concision," ibid., January 22, 1845, [2]; "Pay of American Authors," ibid., January 24, 1845, [2]; "Pay of Authors in America," ibid., January 25, 1845, [2]; "Pay of American Authors—The Magazines," ibid., January 27, 1845, [2]; "Pay of American Authors—Synopsis of the American Copy-Right Question," ibid., January 31, 1845, [2].

77. For Poe's encounter with Wallace about "The Raven," see Joel Benton, "Poe's Opinion of 'The Raven,'" *Forum* 22 (1897): 731–33; and Thomas and Jackson, *The Poe Log*, 495–96. For Colton's comment on the poem after reading it aloud, see Donald G. Mitchell, *American Lands and Letters* (New York: Charles Scribner's, 1898–99), 2:387–88; and Thomas and Jackson, *The Poe Log*, 484.

78. The variants, noted in the Mabbott edition, are "For we cannot help agreeing that no living human being" (for "For we cannot help agreeing that no sublunary being"); "Startled at the stillness broken by reply so aptly spoken," (for "Wondering at the stillness broken by reply so aptly spoken,"); and "Quaff, oh quaff this kind Nepenthe and forget this lost Lenore!" (for "Let me quaff this kind Nepenthe and forget this lost Lenore!") (M 1:369–70). Poe must have authorized the variants, all featured, as well, in the *New York Weekly Mirror* issue of February 8 (276).

79. [N. P. Willis], ["We are permitted to copy"]; Edgar Allan Poe, "The Raven," *New York Evening Mirror*, January 29, 1845, [4]. Willis's introductory comments appear also in M 1:361–62; and Thomas and Jackson, *The Poe Log*, 496. For the date of publication of the February 1845 issue of the *American Review*, see "The American Review," *Sentinel of Freedom*, January 21, 1845, [1] (America's Historical Newspapers). And see Quarles [Poe], "The Raven"; and George H. Colton, ["The following lines"], *American Review* (February 1845): 143–45. Colton's introduction appears also in M 1:360–61; and Thomas and Jackson, *The Poe Log*, 496. For discussion of Colton and "The Raven," see Cullen B. Colton, "George Hooker Colton and the Publication of 'The Raven,'" *American Literature* 10, no. 3 (1938): 319–30.

80. I quote from the *American Review*; a later version is quoted in Mabbott (1:364–69), which is nearly identical to the *American Review* version with regard to quoted passages. The famous phrase in the first stanza "quaint and curious" comes from Washington Irving's 1822 *Bracebridge Hall* (see my "New Traces in 'The Raven' and the Dedication to *The Raven and Other Poems*," *Edgar Allan Poe Review* 22, no. 2 [2021]: 379–80).

81. Thomas and Jackson, *The Poe Log*, 498, 499, 503.

82. Ibid., 497, 499.

83. Poe had written of Dickens's raven Grip, "Its croakings might have been prophetically heard in the course of the drama" (Poe, review of Charles Dickens's *Barnaby Rudge*, *Graham's Magazine* 20, no. 2 [February 1842]: 129; H 11:63.) For a contemporary recognition of Barrett's presence in "The Raven," see Thomas Dunn English, "Our Book-Shelves," *Aristidean* (November 1845): 400. See also Walker, *Edgar Allan Poe: The Critical Heritage* 231. Mabbott discusses Poe's debt in "The Raven" to Barrett, mentioning John H. Ingram's comment on a variant of her "purple curtain" line (see M 1:356–67); and Ingram, "Genesis," in *The Raven by Edgar Allan Poe* (London: George Redway, 1885), 12–13. For the dedication

to Barrett, see Edgar Allan Poe, *The Raven and Other Poems*, introduction by Thomas Ollive Mabbott (New York: Columbia University Press, 1942). For the full essay "The Philosophy of Composition," see L2 60–71.

84. See Henry E. Legler, *Poe's Raven: Its Origin and Genesis—A Compilation and a Survey* (Wausau, WI: Philosopher Press, 1907), 9–10; and L2 58.

85. For a fuller treatment of Poe and *Evenings at Home*, see my "*Evenings at Home*: A Neglected Book from Poe's Childhood," *Edgar Allan Poe Review* 21, no. 1 (2020): 64–70. For consideration of Poe and Francis Quarles, see William E. Engel, "Poe's Resonance with Francis Quarles: Emblems, Melancholy, and the Art of Memory," in *Deciphering Poe: Subtexts, Contexts, Subversive Meanings*, ed. Alexandra Urakova (Bethlehem, PA: Lehigh University Press, 2013), 1–11; as well as his *Early Modern Poetics in Melville and Poe: Memory, Melancholy, and the Emblematic Tradition* (Farnham, UK: Ashgate, 2012), 77–103. For Poe's early mention of Quarles in an 1836 book review, see H 9:91; and P 5:250. For Poe's recollection of the raven at Stoke Newington, see Phillips, *Edgar Allan Poe—the Man*, 2:936–37.

86. Susan Archer Weiss, *The Home Life of Poe* (New York: Broadway, 1907), 185. It is of note that Maria Clemm was reported to have said that Poe "had the idea [for 'The Raven'] in his mind for some years" (Legler, *Poe's Raven: Its Origin and Genesis*, 11).

87. Adam C. Bradford, *Communities of Death: Whitman, Poe, and the American Culture of Mourning* (Columbia: University of Missouri Press, 2014), 40–41, 46–51, 68–82.

88. For Lincoln's reading, I draw on David S. Reynolds, *Abe: Abraham Lincoln in His Times* (New York: Penguin, 2020), 747, 244.

19. "It Will Be a Fortune to Me If I Can Hold It"

1. Edgar Allan Poe, "The Raven," *Alexandria Gazette*, February 8, 1845, [1]; *Vermont Phoenix*, February 28, 1845, [1] (America's Historical Newspapers). For scholarly commentary on early publications of "The Raven," see G. Thomas Tanselle, "An Unknown Early Appearance of 'The Raven,'" *Studies in Bibliography* 16 (1963): 220–21; and Claude Richard, "Another Unknown Early Appearance of 'The Raven,'" *Poe Newsletter* 1, no. 2 (1968): 30.

2. George Vandenhoff's *A Plain System of Elocution*, 2nd ed. (New York: C. Shepherd, 1845) appeared on April 5, 1845, and Poe's *The Raven and Other Poems* on November 19, 1845 (see "This Day Published," *New-York Commercial Advertiser*, April 5, 1845, [2] [America's Historical Newspapers]; and Dwight Thomas and David K. Jackson, *The Poe Log: A Documentary life of Edgar Allan Poe, 1809–1849* [Boston: G. K. Hall, 1987], 591). For "The Raven" in Vandenhoff, see 264–67.

3. The instance of Poe's hearing "Nevermore" at the theater is reported by Elizabeth Oakes Smith in J. C. Derby, *Fifty Years among Authors, Books and Publishers* (New York: G. W. Carleton, 1884), 548 (also Thomas and Jackson, *The Poe Log*, 497). The Francis introduction of Poe is included in Thomas and Jackson, *The Poe Log*, 497–98. Poe's reading "The Raven" at an Anne C. Lynch reception and a Christmas party is mentioned ibid., 551–53, 607. The Murdock performance of "The Raven" is recounted by Alexander Crane, whose report is

featured in Mukhtar Ali Isani, "Reminiscences of Poe by an Employee of the *Broadway Journal*," *Poe Studies* 6, no. 2 (1973): 34 (also in Thomas and Jackson, *The Poe Log*, 500). A follow-up piece is Isani, "A Further Word on Poe and Alexander Crane," *Poe Studies* 7, no. 2 (1974): 48. For the reprints of "The Raven," see Tanselle, "An Unknown Early Appearance of 'The Raven'"; Richard, "Another Unknown Early Appearance of 'The Raven'"; as well as M 1:363. For the parodies of "The Raven," see Paul Lewis, "'The Raven': Imitated, Admired, and Sometimes Mocked," *Edgar Allan Poe Review* 22, no. 2 (2021): 274–311. For Poe's reciting "The Raven" to the seven-year-old boy in Brooklyn, related by Hayden Church in a 1905 article, see Isani, "Poe and 'The Raven': Some Recollections," *Poe Studies* 18, no. 1 (1985): 8.

4. For the snowstorm, see "The Storm," *New York Evening Mirror*, February 5, 1845, [2]; and "The Weather" and "The Storm," *New York Morning Courier and Enquirer*, February 5, 1845, [2]. For the fire, see "Disastrous Fire," *New York Evening Mirror*, February 5, 1845, [2]; "Extensive Fire—The Tribune Office Destroyed," *New York True Sun*, February 6, 1845, [2] (microfilm obtained from the Library of Congress, Washington, DC); and "The Fire," *New York Weekly Tribune*, February 8, 1845, 5 (drawn from the *Daily Tribune* of February 7, 1845). Graham lost his entire stock and was not insured. George E. Hatvary first suggested that the destruction of copies of *Prose Romances* in a fire might explain the pamphlet's rarity, but he placed the fire in Philadelphia (see his introduction to *Edgar Allan Poe Prose Romances: "The Murders in the Rue Morgue" and "The Man That Was Used Up*," photographic facsimile ed. prepared by George E. Hatvary and Thomas O. Mabbott [New York: St. John's University Press, 1968], ii).

5. For the faulting of moralistic poetry, see "Increase of Poetical Heresy—Didacticism," *New York Evening Mirror*, February 3, 1845, [2]; and *New York Weekly Mirror*, February 8, 1845, 281. For Poe's additional discussion of plagiarism, see "Imitation—Plagiarism," *New York Evening Mirror*, February 15, 1845, [2]; *New York Weekly Mirror*, February 22, 1845, 306; "Plagiarism," *New York Evening Mirror*, February 17, 1845, [2]; and *New York Weekly Mirror*, February 22, 1845, 310. See, as well, "The American Review," *New York Evening Mirror*, February 7, 1845, [2]; *New York Weekly Mirror*, February 15, 1845, 304; (for the *Aristidean*) "Magazine Literature," *New York Evening Mirror*, February 12, 1845, [2]; and *New York Weekly Mirror*, February 15, 1845, 299. Nathaniel Hawthorne is briefly discussed in "Literary Intelligence," *New York Evening Mirror*, February 7, 1845, [2], reprinted as "Literary," *New York Weekly Mirror*, February 15, 1845, 304. Robert Conrad is the focus in "The Hon. Robert T. Conrad," *New York Evening Mirror*, February 15, 1845, [2]; and *New York Weekly Mirror*, February 22, 1845, 320. Among the nonliterary pieces in the February 1845 *Mirror* are "Why Not Try a Mineralized Pavement?" *New York Evening Mirror*, February 8, 1845, reprinted as "Try a Mineralized Pavement," *New York Weekly Mirror*, February 15, 1845, 296; "New Views on the Theory of Color," *New York Evening Mirror*, February 8, 1845, [2], reprinted as "The Theory of Color," *New York Weekly Mirror*, February 15, 1845, 297; and "A Profitless Demonstration," *New York Evening Mirror*, February 11, 1845, [2]. Of note in this period is Willis's disavowal of support for any aspect of Poe's criticism of Longfellow's *The Waif* (prompted by pressure from

George R. Graham) (see ["To gratify a friend"], *New York Evening Mirror,* February 14, 1845, [2]; and *New York Weekly Mirror,* February 22, 1845, 317).

6. "New Magazine," *Town,* February 15, 1845, 4. See also Thomas and Jackson, *The Poe Log,* 502.

7. "Broadway Journal," *New York True Sun,* February 8, 1845, [2].

8. N. P. Willis, "Death of Edgar A. Poe," in *Poe in His Own Time,* ed. Benjamin F. Fisher (Iowa City: University of Iowa Press, 2010), 95.

9. For the full text of the contract, see Arthur Hobson Quinn, *Edgar Allan Poe: A Critical Biography* (New York: D. Appleton-Century, 1941), 751.

10. "Notices to Readers and Correspondents," *Broadway Journal,* February 22, 1845, 127 (P 3:24).

11. "Edgar A. Poe," *Town,* February 22, 1845, 24. See also Thomas and Jackson, *The Poe Log,* 505.

12. N. P. Willis, "Poets and Poetry of America," *New York Evening Mirror,* March 1, 1845, [2]; *New York Weekly Mirror,* March 8, 1845, 347. See also Thomas and Jackson, *The Poe Log,* 510.

13. I base my summary on contemporary responses, readily available in Thomas and Jackson, *The Poe Log,* 508–10, 512–14, 522.

14. See Rufus Wilmot Griswold, "Memoir of the Author," in *The Works of the Late Edgar Allan Poe,* 4 vols. (New York: J. S. Redfield, 1850–56), 3:xxxvi–xxxvii. See also Griswold, "Memoir of the Author"; Fisher, *Poe in His Own Time,* 147–48; as well as Thomas and Jackson, *The Poe Log,* 511–12. That Maria Clemm faulted the flirtatious but platonic relationship of Poe and Osgood is evident in Flora Lapham Mack, "Poe's Appearance and Personality," collection of the author.

15. Flora Lapham Mack, "Poe's Appearance and Personality," collection of the author; Frances Sargent Osgood to Rufus W. Griswold, 1850, *Passages from the Correspondence and Other Papers of Rufus W. Griswold* (Cambridge, MA: W. M. Griswold, 1898), 256.

16. Outis, "Plagiarism," *New York Evening Mirror,* March 1, 1845, [2]; *New York Weekly Mirror,* March 8, 1845, 346–47. For Willis's comments, see *New York Weekly Mirror,* March 8, 1845, 347.

17. For Briggs's comment, see Thomas and Jackson, *The Poe Log,* 518. For the argument that Outis was Felton, see Killis Campbell: "Who Was 'Outis'?," *University of Texas Studies in English,* no. 8 (1928): 107–9, and *The Mind of Poe and Other Studies* (Cambridge, MA: Harvard University Press, 1933), 229. For the view that Outis was Labree, see Kent Ljungquist and Buford Jones, "The Identity of 'Outis': A Further Chapter in the Poe-Longfellow War," *American Literature* 60, no. 3 (1988): 402–15; as well as Ljungquist, "A Further Note on Lawrence Labree," *Edgar Allan Poe Review* 10, no. 2 (2009): 122–25. For Outis as Poe himself, see Mary E. Phillips, *Edgar Allan Poe—The Man,* 2 vols. (Chicago: John C. Winston, 1926), 968; M 1:557; and Burton R. Pollin, "Poe as the Author of the 'O[u]tis' Letter and 'The Bird of the Dream,'" *Poe Studies* 20, no. 1 (1987): 10–15. Dwight Thomas, coeditor of *The Poe Log,* declared that no identification of Outis that had yet been presented was convincing (Thomas, "'Outis': A Gordian Knot Still Beckons," *Poe Studies Association Newsletter* 16, no. 2 [1988]: 3–4). For a subsequent exchange between Ljungquist and Thomas, see "Letter to the Editor," *Poe*

Studies Association Newsletter 17, no. 1 (1989): 6. Kenneth Silverman contended that Outis was Poe, but Jeffrey Meyers considered Outis "an unknown writer" (Silverman, *Edgar A. Poe: Mournful and Never-ending Remembrance* [New York: HarperCollins, 1991], 251; Meyers, *Edgar Allan Poe: His Life and Legacy* [New York: Charles Scribner's Sons, 1992], 172).

18. For the compelling argument against the identification of Tyler with Poe, see John A. Hodgson, "Decoding Poe? Poe, W. B. Tyler, and Cryptography," *Journal of English and Germanic Philology* 92, no. 4 (1993): 523–34.

19. "The Broadway Journal," broadside held by the Lilly Library, Indiana University.

20. Edgar Allan Poe, "Imitation—Plagiarism—Mr. Poe's Reply to the Letter of Outis—A Large Account of a Small Matter—A Voluminous History of the Little Longfellow War," *Broadway Journal*, March 8, 1845: 147–50; "A Continuation of the Voluminous History of the Little Longfellow War—Mr. Poe's Farther Reply to the Letter of Outis," *Broadway Journal*, March 15, 1845: 161–63; "More of the Voluminous History of the Little Longfellow War—Mr. Poe's Third Chapter of Reply to the Letter of Outis," *Broadway Journal*, March 22, 1845: 178–82; "Imitation—Plagiarism—The Conclusion of Mr. Poe's Reply to the Letter of Outis," *Broadway Journal*, March 29, 1845: 194–98; "Plagiarism—Imitation—Postscript to Mr. Poe's Reply to the Letter of Outis," *Broadway Journal*, April 5, 1845: 211–12. See also H 12:41–106 or P 3:28–33, 37–41, 45–53, 58–65, and 73–74. Poe again employed his argument from the "Postscript" in his July 1846 piece on James Aldrich in "The Literati of New York City" (H 15:62–63).

21. "Plagiarism," Item 497 in John Henry Ingram's Poe Collection, Albert & Shirley Small Special Collections, University of Virginia, Charlottesville, Item 497; *New Orleans Daily Picayune*, March 25, 1845 (https://www.eapoe.org, *The Poe Log* Addenda).

22. For a presentation of the ambiguous evidence for attribution of the Longfellow review in the April 1845 *Aristidean*, see Gravely, "The Early Political and Literary Career of Thomas Dunn English" (PhD diss., University of Virginia, 1953), 468–80. For the view that Poe "had more than a hand" in the attack on Longfellow in the *Aristidean*, see Sidney P. Moss, *Poe's Literary Battles: The Critic in the Context of His Literary Milieu* (Durham, NC: Duke University Press, 1963), 176–78. For the view that the piece was "his [Poe's], or at the very least written in very close collaboration with him [Poe]," see Silverman, *Edgar A. Poe: Mournful and Never-ending Remembrance*, 253. For the view that the piece "was written by the editor Thomas Dunn English, apparently after some consultation with Poe," see Thomas and Jackson, *The Poe Log*, 529.

23. Poe, review of Fauvel-Gouraud's *Phreneo-Mnemotechny*, *Broadway Journal*, April 12, 1845, 226, and April 19, 1845, 253 (P 3:83, 101). The two pieces were combined and expanded for the May 1845 *Southern Literary Messenger* (P 5:370–71). (With regard to these works, see my "Poe and Memory," in *Memory, Haunting, Discourse*, ed. Maria Holmgren Troy and Elisabeth Wennö [Karlstad, Sweden: Karlstad University Press, 2005], 45–58.) See also Poe, [On Margaret Fuller], *Broadway Journal*, March 8, 1845, 153 (P 3:34); and "The Democratic Review," *Broadway Journal*, April 12, 1845, 235–36 (P 3:88–89). Poe wrote that "*Grace* is Mrs. Osgood's queendom in which she reigns triumphant" ("The Magazines," April 5, 1845, 220

[P 3:78]). Poe features Osgood's "The Rivulet's Dream" (attributed to Kate Carol, a pen name) in the same issue, p. 215 (P 3:75), as well as "So Let It Be" (attributed to Violet Vane, another pen name), p. 217; and "Love's Reply" (attributed to Osgood) in the next issue, p. 231, and Violet Vane's "Spring," also p. 231.

24. Briggs reported in a letter to Lowell of March 8, 1845, that Wiley & Putnam had agreed to publish a book of Poe's tales (Thomas and Jackson, *The Poe Log*, 514).

25. "Mr. Poe on the Poets" (drawn from the *Express*), *Evening Post*, April 18, 1845, [2] (America's Historical Newspapers). See also Thomas and Jackson, *The Poe Log*, 526.

26. Isani, "Reminiscences of Poe," 33, 34.

27. Quinn, *Edgar Allan Poe: A Critical Biography*, 463; "Notice," *Broadway Journal*, May 3, 1845, 286.

28. Jeffrey A. Savoye, "A Forgotten Recollection," *Edgar Allan Poe Review* 12, no. 2 (2011): 123.

29. Thomas and Jackson, *The Poe Log*, 542, 551.

30. For Burton's letter, see Quinn, *Edgar Allan Poe: A Critical Biography*, 279–80.

31. Violet Vane [Frances Sargent Osgood], "To——," *Broadway Journal*, April 5, 1845, 217; [Edgar Allan Poe], "To——," *Broadway Journal*, May 24, 1845, 325; M 1:381–82. For a thoughtful overview of Poe's relationship to Osgood, see Mary G. De Jong, "Lines from a Partly Published Drama: The Romance of Frances Sargent Osgood and Edgar Allan Poe," in *Patrons and Protégées: Gender, Friendship, and Writing in Nineteenth-Century America*, ed. Shirley Marchalonis (New Brunswick, NJ: Rutgers University Press, 1988), 31–58. For the argument that "Impromptu: To Kate Carol" was written *by* Kate Carol—Frances Sargent Osgood—see John G. Varner, "Notes on a Poem Attributed to Poe," *American Literature* 8, no. 1 (1936): 66–68.

32. An item states, "A treatise on 'Aqua Pura,' its uses and abuses, by Edgar A. Poe, is to be issued at the Broadway Journal office" ("A Treatise," *Town*, April 26, 1845, 131). There is also a reference to "the perfect aquafortis of his [Poe's] satire" ("The 'Alleghanian,'" ibid., June 7, 1845, 203). And there is mention of an imagined Poe motto: "There is but one step from the sublime to the ridiculous. I know it by experience" (see "Edgar A. Poe," *Town*, May 17, 1845, 157).

33. Both comments by Lowell are available in I. B. Cauthen Jr., "Lowell on Poe: An Unpublished Comment, 1879," *American Literature* 24, no. 2 (1952): 230–33. For Maria Clemm's letter to Lowell about his visit, written on March 9, 1850, see Quinn, *Edgar Allan Poe: A Critical Biography*, 462.

34. Thomas and Jackson, *The Poe Log*, 542.

35. Thomas Holley Chivers, *Chivers' Life of Poe*, ed. Richard Beale Davis (New York: E. P. Dutton, 1952), 39–57 (conversation), 57–61 (Poe's drinking and avoiding presenting a poem) (particularly 59 ["d—dst amour"] and 60 [letter of invitation]). The inference about Poe's seeking Osgood's testimony is based on Poe's July 18, 1846, "Mr. Poe's Reply to Mr. English," in Sidney P. Moss, *Poe's Major Crisis: His Libel Suit and New York's Literary World* (Durham, NC: Duke University Press, 1970), 58 ("I left town to procure evidence"). But Chivers reported that Poe had asked him not to tell of his trip to Providence to his wife or mother-in-law (62). See also Thomas and Jackson, *The Poe Log*, 546; and O 1:514–15. For

Gravely's challenge to Chivers's assertions, see "The Early Political and Literary Career of Thomas Dunn English," 549–57. Mabbott maintained that Poe went to Providence to attend a lecture by Osgood (M 1:441).

36. "POH!" *Town,* July 5, 1845, 245.
37. Chivers to Poe, September 9, 1845, in *The Complete Works of Thomas Holley Chivers,* vol. 1, ed. S. Foster Damon and Charles H. Watts II (Providence, RI: Brown University Press, 1957), 54.
38. For Poe's reservation about the selection, see his review of *Tales, Broadway Journal,* July 12, 1845, 10 (also P 3:167); "Our Book-Shelves," *Aristidean,* September 1845, 238 (attributed to Poe by William Doyle Hull II, "A Canon of the Critical Works of Edgar Allan Poe with a Study of Poe as Editor and Reviewer" [PhD diss., University of Virginia, 1941], 36, 697–98; and by Mabbott in Charles F. Heartman and James R. Canny, *A Bibliography of First Printings of the Writings of Edgar Allan Poe,* rev. ed. [Hattiesburg, MS: Book Farm, 1943], 149); and O 1:595–96. For the presentation copies of *Tales* to Bisco, Lynch, and Gove, see Thomas and Jackson, *The Poe Log,* 540, 542, 608; for the presentation copy of *Tales* and *The Raven and Other Poems* to Whitman, see Heartman and Canny, *A Bibliography of First Printings of the Writings of Edgar Allan Poe,* 97. The first volume of Wiley and Putnam's Library of American Books was Hawthorne's *Journal of an African Cruiser.*
39. I. M. Walker's *Edgar Allan Poe: The Critical Heritage* (London: Routledge & Kegan Paul, 1986) includes Fuller (177), Duyckinck (190), and Simms (200). For the unidentified reviewer, see "Wiley and Putnam's Library of Choice Reading," *New-York Commercial Advertiser,* August 4, 1845, [2] (America's Historical Newspapers).
40. For Dana, see Walker, *Edgar Allan Poe: The Critical Heritage,* 179–80. For the unidentified reviewer, see "Notes on New Books—Recent Publications," *National Intelligencer,* July 15, 1845, [3] (Nineteenth Century U.S. Newspapers).
41. Poe wrote to Duyckinck on November 13, 1845, that "1500 of the Tales have been sold" (O 1:534). He had written in the October 4, 1845, *Broadway Journal* that "more than fifteen hundred copies have been sold here" (see [Poe], "Editorial Miscellany," *Broadway Journal,* October 4, 1845, 200; and P 3:276).
42. Edgar Allan Poe, "The Imp of the Perverse," *Graham's Magazine,* July 1845, [1]. See also M 3:1221. The July issue of *Graham's* was first listed on June 28. See "Literary Bulletin," *New-York Commercial Advertiser,* June 28, 1845, [2] (America's Historical Newspapers).
43. See Sarah Helen Whitman to George W. Eveleth, January 17, 1866, in *Building Poe Biography,* ed. John Carl Miller (Baton Rouge: Louisiana State University Press, 1977), 218.
44. I draw on [Poe], "Editorial Miscellany," *Broadway Journal,* August 23, 1845, 109; see also P 3:225 and P 4:178. The bookstore of James Munroe was then near Washington Street at 3 School Street (*Stimpson's Boston Directory* [Boston: Charles Stimpson, 1845]). For detail on the edition of Hawthorne's *Twice-Told Tales* that Poe saw, see C. E. Frazer Clark Jr., *Nathaniel Hawthorne: A Descriptive Bibliography* (Pittsburgh, PA: University of Pittsburgh Press, 1978), 20–21. The advertisement for Poe's book reads, "Library of American Books. No. 2. Tales of Edgar A.

Poe. This day received by W. D. Ticknor & Co. je 27 [June 27]," Boston *Evening Transcript,* July 3, 1845, [3] (America's Historical Newspapers).
45. Paul Lewis, "'The Raven': Imitated, Admired, and Sometimes Mocked," 290–94. See also Lewis, "The First Caricature of Poe Reconsidered," *Edgar Allan Poe Review* 23, no. 2 (2022): 228–31; and his subsequent "Letter to the Editor" in 24, no. 1 (2023): 127–28.
46. [Cornelia Wells Walter], ["The American Review, for July"], *Boston Evening Transcript,* July 14, 1845, [2]. For more on Walter, see Joseph Edgar Chamberlin, *The Boston Transcript: A History of Its First Hundred Years* (Boston: Houghton Mifflin, 1930): 68–83. Poe had been appreciative of Longfellow's poem "Excelsior," considering it to concern "the *earnest upward impulse of the soul*" (H 11:84–85).
47. For Poe's initial letter to Thomas, see O 1:514. Thomas's recantation is available also in Moss, *Poe's Major Crisis,* 58. For Poe's agreeing to serve on the committee for the literary competition of the Rutgers Female Institute, see O 1:511. For further information, see M 1:397–98; and Thomas and Jackson, *The Poe Log,* 548–49. Poe and the *Broadway Journal* are discussed in Heyward Ehrlich, "The *Broadway Journal (1):* Briggs's Dilemma and Poe's Strategy," *Bulletin of the New York Public Library* 73 (1969): 74–93, condensed in P 4:xii–xxxi.
48. John Bisco, "Our New Volume," *Broadway Journal,* July 12, 1845, [1]. See also P 3:161. For the July 14 contract between Poe and Bisco, see Quinn, *Edgar Allan Poe: A Critical Biography,* 751–52.
49. The Hirst review appeared in the July 12 issue of the *Broadway Journal,* and a Hood review as late as the August 30 issue. "Masque of the Red Death" was published on July 19 and "William Wilson" on August 30. "Sonnet—To Zante" was featured on July 19 and "The City in the Sea" on August 30. The advertisement for an investor appeared in the issues of August 16 and 23. The initials of the addressee ("E. S. T. G.") probably represent "Edward S. T. Grey," a Poe pseudonym, the last name of which would have been drawn from Frances Sargent Osgood's short story "Ida Grey" (Burton R. Pollin, "Poe as Edward S. T. Grey," *Ball State University Forum,* 14, no. 3 [1973]: 44–46). Poe mentioned his coming book of poems in the August 2 issue and the publication history of "Usher" in the August 30 issue. He paid tribute to his mother as an actress in the July 19 issue and discussed his recent visit to Boston in the August 23 issue.
50. Thomas and Jackson, *The Poe Log,* 555, 563, 564.
51. See both Richard H. Stoddard, "Edgar Allan Poe," *Harper's Monthly* 45 (1872): 564–65; and Stoddard, "Edgar Allan Poe," *Lippincott's Monthly Magazine* 43 (1889): 107–9. For the derivativeness of Stoddard's poem, see Burton R. Pollin, "Stoddard's Elegiac Sonnet on Poe," *Poe Studies* 19, no. 2 (1986): 32.
52. Isani, "Reminiscences of Poe," 33.
53. For Poe at Bartlett and Welford, I rely on both John D. Haskell, "Poe, Literary Soirées, and Coffee," *Poe Studies* 8, no. 2 (1975): 47 (some of which is included in John D. Haskell, "John Russell Bartlett [1805–1886]: Bookman" [PhD diss., George Washington University, 1977]; and Sarah Helen Whitman to John H. Ingram, November 30, 1874, in *Poe's Helen Remembers,* ed. John Carl Miller [Charlottesville: University Press of Virginia, 1979], 232). See also *Autobiography of John Russell Bartlett (1805–1886),* ed. Jerry E. Mueller (Providence, RI: John

Carter Brown Library, 2006), 90, 212. For the bookshop as "that cozy nook," see Haskell, "John Russell Bartlett," 61. See also the Bartlett and Welford advertisement for *Narrative of United States Exploring Expedition, New-York Commercial Advertiser,* April 10, 1845, [3]; and the Bartlett and Welford advertisement for *The Works of William Hogarth, New-York Commercial Advertiser,* May 16, 1845, [3] (America's Historical Newspapers). For Bartlett's living at 1 Amity Place, see the *Autobiography,* 35. He was there from 1844 to 1849. Notably, Bartlett helped found the Providence Athenaeum, and the John Russell Bartlett Society was an antiquarian book-collecting group in Rhode Island. The sale of the library of Charles Lamb by Bartlett and Welford in 1848 is ably treated in Denise Gigante, *Book Madness: A Story of Book Collectors in America* (New Haven, CT: Yale University Press, 2022).

54. Griswold, "Memoir of the Author," xxxviii; and "Memoir of the Author," in Fisher, *Poe in His Own Time,* 149; Frances Sargent Osgood, "Ida Grey," *Graham's Magazine* (August 1845): 83. J. H. Whitty and William H. Gravely note the resonance of language observed here (see Whitty, "Remarkable Find of New Poe Poems and Manuscripts," *New York Sun,* November 21, 1915, sec. VI, p. 3; Whitty, *The Complete Poems of Edgar Allan Poe* [Boston: Houghton Mifflin, 1917]; 150, 320–21; and Gravely, "The Early Political and Literary Career of Thomas Dunn English," 534). De Jong treats "Ida Grey" in "Lines from a Partly Published Drama," 38–39. Poe's "The Divine Right of Kings" has been taken to be a response to a passage in "Ida Grey" (see Whitty, "Remarkable Find," 3; and Whitty, *Complete Poems,* 320–21; as well as M 1:383).

55. Frances Sargent Osgood, ["Yes! 'lower to the level!'"], *New York Evening Mirror,* December 10, 1844, [1]. The phrase "literary alliance" is drawn from Mary G. De Jong, "Lines from a Partly Published Drama," 55. For the comment on the Samuel S. Osgood portrait of Poe, and the image itself, see Michael J. Deas, *The Portraits and Daguerreotypes of Edgar Allan Poe* (Charlottesville: University Press of Virginia, 1989), 24–25.

56. Poe annotated the table of contents for the September 1845 *Aristidean,* claiming "Our Book-Shelves" for himself (see *Magazines and the American Experience: Highlights from the Collection of Steven Lomazow, MD* [New York: Grolier Club, 2020], ix). See also Hull, "A Canon of the Critical Works of Edgar Allan Poe," 36, 697–98; and Heartman and Canny, *The Bibliography of First Printings of the Writings of Edgar Allan Poe,* 149.

57. [Edgar Allan Poe], "Editorial Miscellany," *Broadway Journal,* December 13, 1845, 358; P 3:338.

58. Poe mentions the new address in a letter to Duyckinck of November 13, but Laughton Osborn also mentions it in a letter to Poe of October 1 (O 1:533–35). Although Sarah Helen Whitman stated, "Mr. Bartlett knew Poe in New York. They lived in the same street during some portion of Poe's residence in the city" (Whitman to John H. Ingram, November 30, 1878, in *Poe's Helen Remembers,* ed. Miller, 232), Amity Street and Amity Place were two different, but proximate streets (see not only *Autobiography of John Russell Bartlett,* 35, but also Don Rogerson, *Manhattan Street Names Past and Present: A Guide to Their Origins* [Charleston, SC: Griffin Rose, 2013], 3–4). Bartlett later named his fourth and

last daughter Fanny Osgood Bartlett (Haskell, "John Russell Bartlett," 11; Mueller, introduction to *Autobiography*, 16).

59. Griswold, "Memoir of the Author," xxii; Fisher, *Poe in His Own Time*, 128; Thomas Dunn English, "Reminiscences of Poe IV," *New York Independent*, November 5, 1896, 1480 (4) (https://www.eapoe.org). For a contrast of English's early comment on the Lyceum event and his later assessment, see Gravely, "The Early Political and Literary Career of Thomas Dunn English," 504–6.

60. Griswold, "Memoir of the Author," xxii; Fisher, *Poe in His Own Time*, 128; see also O 1:527. I estimate the time of the invitation by a squib for Poe's appearance on September 24: "Boston Lyceum," *Daily Atlas*, September 24, 1845, [2]; and *Boston Evening Transcript*, September 24, 1845, [2] (America's Historical Newspapers). For the earliest full announcement of the fall 1845 lectures series, see "Boston Lyceum," *Boston Evening Transcript*, September 30, 1845, [2] (America's Historical Newspapers).

61. Griswold, "Memoir of the Author," xxii; Fisher, *Poe in His Own Time*, 153. For Osgood's poem, see "Lulin; or the Diamond Fay. A Fairy Legend, Sent by a Lover to His Mistress, with a Diamond Ring," *Union Magazine*, May 1848, 198, and July 1848, 6 (Google Books).

62. An early treatment of the location of the Boston Theatre, later the Odeon, is "A Historic Spot," *Vermont Phoenix*, June 20, 1882, [3] (America's Historical Newspapers). For the dense crowd at the Odeon, see "Boston Lyceum," *Charleston Courier* (from the *New York Courier & Enquirer*), October 22, 1845, [2] (America's Historical Newspapers). For a thoughtful consideration of Poe at the Boston Lyceum, see Philip Edward Phillips, "Poe's 1845 Boston Lyceum Appearance Reconsidered," in *Deciphering Poe: Subtexts, Contexts, Subversive Meanings*, ed. Alexandra Urakova (Bethlehem, PA: Lehigh University Press, 2013), 41–52. That someone in the audience read along in the 1831 *Poems* is stated in "'Quizzing the Bostonians,'" *Boston Evening Transcript*, October 30, 1845, [2] (America's Historical Newspapers). For the Higginson reminiscence, see Thomas Wentworth Higginson, in *Short Studies of American Authors* (Boston: Lee and Shepard, 1880), 12–21. He acknowledges his having been impressed by *Tales of the Grotesque and Arabesque* early on in "His Voice Like the 'Finest Golden Thread,'" *Boston Globe*, January 19, 1909, 9, https://www.newspapers.com.

63. See [Cornelia Wells Walter], "A Failure," *Boston Evening Transcript*, October 17, 1845, [2], (America's Historical Newspapers) and Thomas and Jackson, *The Poe Log*, 579; "Boston Lyceum," *Charleston Courier* (from the *New York Courier & Enquirer*), October 22, 1845, [2] (America's Historical Newspapers) and Thomas and Jackson, *The Poe Log*, 578. Remarkably, Buckingham had once criticized the performances of David and Eliza Poe at the same location.

64. For the documents regarding the sale of the *Broadway Journal*, see Joseph J. Moldenhauer, comp., *A Descriptive Catalog of Edgar Allan Poe Manuscripts in the Humanities Research Center Library, the University of Texas at Austin* (Austin: University of Texas, 1973), 79–81. Greeley mentioned his loan to Poe in his *Recollections of a Busy Life* (1868; New York: Tribune Association, 1873), 196–97. For the masthead with the new title for Poe, see *Broadway Journal*, October 25, 1845, 235.

65. For early pieces on Poe's Boston Lyceum appearance, see [Cornelia Wells Walter], "A Failure," *Boston Evening Transcript,* October 17, 1845, [2]; and "A Prodigy" and "Edgar A. Poe," ibid., October 18, 1845, [2] (America's Historical Newspapers). For Poe's lengthy pieces on his participation in the Boston Lyceum event, see ["We take the following paragraph"], *Broadway Journal,* November 1, 1845, 261–62 (P 3:297–99); and ["As we very confidently expected"], ibid., November 22, 1845, 309–11 (P 3:312–15). I tend to rely for quotations on the latter piece. For William Fairman's comment, see Thomas and Jackson, *The Poe Log,* 572. For Poe's later satirically jesting in the *Broadway Journal* that he planned to present "a fine poem that we wrote at seven months," see ["Mr. Edmund Burke"], *Broadway Journal,* December 6, 1845, 339 (P 3:325).

66. See ["Mrs. Kirkland's new book"], *Broadway Journal,* November 1, 1845, 264, and "New Works to Be Published by Messrs. Wiley & Putnam," November 8, 1845, 280. The *New York Tribune* listed *The Raven and Other Poems* as "this day published" on November 19 (see Thomas Ollive Mabbott, introduction to *The Raven and Other Poems by Edgar Allan Poe,* facsimile ed. [New York: Columbia University Press, 1942], xi).

67. I rely here on the aforementioned facsimile edition of *The Raven and Other Poems.* For Poe's revising Christopher North's reference to "one of the noblest of her sex," see my "New Traces in 'The Raven' and the Dedication to *The Raven and Other Poems,*" *Edgar Allan Poe Review* 22, no. 2 (2022): 380–83.

68. Walker, *Edgar Allan Poe: The Critical Heritage,* 236 (*Boston Post*), 238 (*Harbinger*).

69. Ibid., 225 (*New York Evening Mirror*), 240 (*Merchant's Magazine and Commercial Advertiser*). For the commendation to "lovers of song," see ("No. VIII of the same series"), *Baltimore Daily Commercial,* December 19, 1845, [2], https://www.newspapers.com.

70. Poe's copy of *The Raven and Other Poems* and *Tales,* bound as one, with his revisions, is known as the J. Lorimer Graham copy (named after one of its owners). Once held by the Century Club, it is now in the Harry Ransom Center Library of the University of Texas at Austin (Moldenhauer, *A Descriptive Catalog of Edgar Allan Poe Manuscripts,* 87–88).

71. See Thomas and Jackson, *The Poe Log,* 558–59; and William Gilmore Simms, *The Letters of William Gilmore Simms,* vol. 2: *1845–1849,* ed. Mary C. Simms Oliphant and T. C. Duncan Eaves (Columbia: University of South Carolina Press, 2012), 98–99.

72. See Thomas Dunn English, "Reminiscences of Poe," *New York Independent,* October 15, 1896, 1382 (https://www.eapoe.org); and Kenneth Rede, "Poe Notes: From an Investigator's Notebook," *American Literature* 5, no. 1 (1933): 53–54. English's early view of Poe's Lyceum appearance is in "Our Book-Shelves," *Aristidean* (November 1845): 399.

73. Richard Henry Stoddard, *Recollections Personal and Literary,* ed. Ripley Hitchcock (New York: A. S. Barnes, 1903), 151.

74. See Edgar Allan Poe, "Critical Notices," *Broadway Journal,* November 22, 1845, 307 (P 3:311) and ["The Office of the Broadway Journal"], *Broadway Journal,* November 29, 1845, 315. The lodgings of English and Lane were in the building at 304 Broadway (English, "Reminiscences," 1382).

75. Walter Whitman, "Art-Singing and Heart Singing," *Broadway Journal,* November 29, 1845, 318–19. For Poe's editorial comment, see 318n and P 3:315.
76. Thomas and Jackson, *The Poe Log,* 597.
77. Kent P. Ljungquist links "Valdemar" to Poe's experience at the Odeon in "'Valdemar' and the 'Frogpondians': The Aftermath of Poe's Boston Lyceum Appearance," in *Emersonian Circles: Essays in Honor of Joel Myerson,* ed. Wesley T. Mott and Robert E. Burkholder (Rochester, NY: University of Rochester Press, 1997), 181–206. The January 1846 issue of *Arthur's Ladies' Magazine* was out by December 15, as is evident from "New Publications," *Boston Evening Transcript,* December 15, 1845, [2] (America's Historical Newspapers).
78. Edgar Allan Poe, ["A New Volume of the Broadway Journal"], *Broadway Journal,* December 20, 1845, 376; and P 3:347.
79. English, "Reminiscences," 1382.
80. Flora Lapham Mack [for William Lanier Washington], "Suggestions for the Third Chapter—Poe's Early Married Days," collection of the author.
81. See [Edgar Allan Poe], review of *Hyperion, A Romance,* by Henry Wadsworth Longfellow, *Broadway Journal,* December 27, 1845, 387; and review of *Voltaire and Rousseau against the Atheists,* selected and translated by J. Akerly, *Broadway Journal,* December 27, 1845, 388 (P 3:351, 352).
82. Edgar Allan Poe, "Valedictory," *Broadway Journal,* January 3, 1846, 407 (P 3:360).

20. "There Is a Sweet *Hope* in the Bottom of My Soul"

1. The characterization "the observed of all observers" is taken from *Hamlet,* 3.1.154. For its application to Poe at the soirees, see Sarah Helen Whitman, "Introductory Letter," *The Life and Poems of Edgar Allan Poe,* ed. Eugene Didier (New York: W. J. Widdleton, 1877), 13. Whitman mentions that some of the evenings were held at the homes of Bartlett and Lynch (12); she mentions the homes of Dewey and Lawson, as well, in *Edgar Poe and His Critics* (New York: Rudd & Carleton, 1860), 23. See also Elizabeth Oakes Smith, "Autobiographic Notes: Edgar Allan Poe," in *Poe in His Own Times,* ed. Benjamin F. Fisher (Iowa City: University of Iowa Press, 2010), 224 (also available at https://www.eapoe.org); and Eugene L. Didier, *The Poe Cult and Other Poe Papers* (New York: Broadway, 1909), 245. For Poe's smile and his mystery, see Whitman, "Introductory Letter," 13. For Poe's sometimes attending these literary evenings with Virginia, see Whitman, *Edgar Poe and His Critics,* 26. For Poe's manners and his discussing Virginia, see Oakes Smith, "Autobiographic Notes," 224; for his delight in women, see ibid., 229. Poe's regard for Bryant is given in Dwight Thomas and David K. Jackson, *The Poe Log: A Documentary Life of Edgar Allan Poe, 1809–1849* (Boston: G. K. Hall, 1987), 608; his defense of a writer against Fuller is presented in Whitman, "Introductory Letter," 12; and Didier, *The Poe Cult,* 245–46.
2. George W. Eveleth to Edgar Allan Poe, December 21, 1845 and January 5, 1846, in *The Letters from George W. Eveleth to Edgar Allan Poe,* ed. Thomas Ollive Mabbott (New York: New York Public Library, 1922), 5, 6.
3. Michael J. Deas, *The Portraits and Daguerreotypes of Edgar Allan Poe* (Charlottesville: University Press of Virginia, 1989), 28–32.

4. S. Foster Damon, *Thomas Holley Chivers Friend of Poe* (New York: Harper & Brothers, 1930), 158.
5. Augustus Van Cleef, "Poe's Mary," *Harper's New Monthly Magazine,* March 1889, 639 (https://www.eapoe.org).
6. Osgood's recollection is presented in Rufus Wilmot Griswold, "Memoir of the Author," in *The Literati* (vol. 3 of *The Works of Edgar Allan Poe*) (New York: J. S. Redfield, 1850), xxxvii; see also *Poe in His Own Time,* ed. Benjamin F. Fisher (Iowa City: University of Iowa Press, 2010), 148.
7. Thomas and Jackson write that it was "probably Mrs. Elizabeth F. Ellet" (622). The source of the story is J. C. Derby, *Fifty Years among Authors, Books and Publishers* (New York: G. W. Carleton, 1884), 548.
8. For a discerning analysis of the literary flirtation of Osgood and Ellet with Poe, see Mary G. De Jong, "Lines from a Partly Published Drama: The Romance of Frances Sargent Osgood and Edgar Allan Poe," in *Patrons and Protégées: Gender, Friendship, and Writing in Nineteenth-Century America,* ed. Shirley Marchalonis (New Brunswick, NJ: Rutgers University Press, 1988), 41–44.
9. Along with Poe's account of the episode in his letter to Sarah Helen Whitman, Whitman's letter to John H. Ingram is also helpful (Whitman to Ingram, February 11, 1874, in *Poe's Helen Remembers,* ed. John Carl Miller [Charlottesville: University Press of Virginia, 1979], 20–22). For a careful evaluation of these incidents, see William H. Gravely Jr., "The Early Political and Literary Career of Thomas Dunn English" (PhD diss., University of Virginia, 1953), 558–75.
10. For English on the fight with Poe, see "A Card: Mr. English's Reply to Mr. Poe," in *Poe's Major Crisis: His Libel Suit and New York's Literary World,* ed. Sidney P. Moss (Durham, NC: Duke University Press, 1970), 37. See, too, Poe's response, "Mr. Poe's Reply to Mr. English and Others," in *Poe's Major Crisis,* ed. Moss, 52, and his letter to Henry B. Hirst (O 1:585). English later elaborated further his recollection in "Reminiscences of Poe, III," *New York Independent,* October 29, 1896, 1448 (https://www.eapoe.org). Poe mentions Ellet's "anonymous letters" (O 2:732). For Ellet's "*anonymous* letters" regarding Griswold, see John H. Ingram to Sarah Helen Whitman, September 4, 1874, in *Poe's Helen Remembers,* 207–8; and Joy Bayless, *Rufus Wilmot Griswold Poe's Literary Executor* (Nashville, TN: Vanderbilt University Press, 1943), 229.
11. Flora Lapham Mack, "Poe's Appearance and Personality," collection of the author.
12. Kelly Keener, "An Epistle Written by Frances Sargent Osgood to Elizabeth Ellet in Connection with the Poe-Osgood Scandal," *Edgar Allan Poe Review* 20, no. 2 (2019): 204.
13. For both affectionate nicknames, see O 1:104.
14. Flora Lapham Mack to William Lanier Washington, April 22, 1908, collection of the author.
15. For Osgood's assertion about Poe that Virginia was "the only woman whom he ever truly loved," see Griswold, "Memoir," xxxvii; or Fisher, *Poe in His Own Time,* 149.
16. J. H. Whitty, "Memoir," in *The Complete Poems of Edgar Allan Poe* (Boston: Houghton Mifflin, 1911), lvii; Mary E. Phillips, *Edgar Allan Poe—The Man,* 2 vols. (Chicago: John C. Winston, 1926), 2:1109–14, esp. 1111.

17. The letter is available in John E. Reilly, "Robert D'Unger and the Reminiscences of Poe in Baltimore," *Maryland Historical Magazine* (spring 1993): 66–69.
18. Ibid., 68.
19. Mary Elizabeth (Moore) Hewitt Stebbins to Edgar A. Poe, April 14, 1846, Rufus W. Griswold Collection, Rare Books and Manuscripts, Boston Public Library.
20. Sarah Helen Whitman to John H. Ingram, April 21, 1874, in *Poe's Helen Remembers*, 124; Whitty, "Memoir," lvii; Phillips, *Edgar Allan Poe—The Man*, 2:1113.
21. The original publication is Poe, "The Literati of New York City," *Graham's Magazine* (May 1846): 194–201.
22. Ibid., 200.
23. Lewis Gaylord Clark, "The Literary Snob," in Moss, *Poe's Major Crisis*, 5–7; Louis A. Godey, "Edgar A. Poe and the New York Writers—Lewis Gaylord Clark," ibid., 10–11. See also the 1956 essay "Poe and His Nemesis—Lewis Gaylord Clark," by Sidney P. Moss, reprinted in *On Poe: The Best from "American Literature*," ed. Louis J. Budd and Edwin H. Cady (Durham, NC: Duke University Press, 1993), 102–21.
24. Louis A. Godey, ["The first number"], *Godey's Lady's Book* (May 1846): 240; Godey, "Edgar A. Poe and the New York Writers—Lewis Gaylord Clark," 11.
25. Some of the detail provided here is drawn from Mary Gove Nichols, "Reminiscences of Edgar Poe (1863)," in *Poe in His Own Time*, 210–16; Reginald Pelham Bolton, *The Poe Cottage at Fordham, Transactions of the Bronx Society of Arts Sciences and History* 1, part 5 (1922); Phillips, *Edgar Allan Poe—the Man*, 2:1114–18; and Arthur Hobson Quinn, *Edgar Allan Poe: A Critical Biography* (New York: D. Appleton-Century, 1941), 506–8.
26. For Poe's April 28, 1846, letters on the University of Vermont invitation, see O 1:568–70; for his June 16, 1846, letter on the Dickinson College invitation, see O 1:583–84. For the April 1846 Barrett letter, see H 17:229–30; for the June 17, 1846, Hawthorne letter, see *The Centenary Edition of the Works of Nathaniel Hawthorne*, ed. William Charvat et al., 23 vols. (Columbus: Ohio State University Press, 1962–1997), 16:168–69. For Osgood's touching tribute, see "Ida's Farewell: From an Unpublished Novel," *Columbian Magazine*, June 1846, 246.
27. That Poe wrote other notes to Virginia is evident from Marie Louise Shew Houghton to John Ingram, February 16, 1875, in *Building Poe Biography*, ed. John Carl Miller (Baton Rouge: Louisiana State University Press, 1977), 111. He also included a line to Virginia in his August 29, 1835, letter to Maria Clemm (O 1:104).
28. The pieces by "Mustard Mace" and Hiram Fuller are available in Moss, *Poe's Major Crisis*, 13–20. For Field's printing Poe's letter, see ibid., 20–25. That the July issue of *Godey's Lady's Book* was published on June 20, 1846, is evident from "This Day Published," *New-York Commercial Advertiser*, June 20, 1846, [2] (America's Historical Newspapers). The second sentence of this advertisement begins, "This number contains eight of the literati of New York, by Edgar A. Poe."
29. The original publication of the third installment is "The Literati of New York City—No. III," *Godey's Lady's Book* (July 1846): 13–19; the English piece is on 17–18. See also Moss, *Poe's Major Crisis*, 26–30.
30. Sidney Moss provides "A Card: Mr. English's Reply to Mr. Poe" in *Poe's Major Crisis*, 34–39. Moss also furnishes "Mr. Poe's Reply to Mr. English and Others"

in *Poe's Major Crisis,* 49–59. For evidence of Fuller's not defending his wife when she was attacked by her father in the theater, see [N. P. Willis and perhaps George Pope Morris], "We Copy the Following," *New York Evening Mirror,* November 29, 1844, [2]. Poe offered the story of Fuller at the theater in a confidential letter of June 15, 1846, to Joseph M. Field (O 1:579), but Moss, not having found confirmation of the story, was doubtful (Moss, *Poe's Major Crisis,* 20–21). However, the *New York Evening Mirror* article, as well as other related articles of the time, makes clear the validity of the allegation that Poe restrained himself from making in his reply to English.

31. The "best men" probably included Evert A. Duyckinck and Cornelius Mathews, given Poe's letter of June 29, 1846 (O 1:587). Poe later commented on his reply to English in his January 4, 1848, letter to George W. Eveleth (O 2:640).

32. Moss reprints English "A Card: In Reply to Mr. Poe's Rejoinder," in Moss, *Poe's Major Crisis,* 61–63. Poe wrote, in his July 16 letter to Godey, "I have put this matter in the hands of a competent attorney, and you shall see the result" (O 1:588). He mentioned Fancher in a letter to John Bisco of July 17, 1846 (O 1:590). Moss includes the July 23, 1846, "Declaration of Grievances," in *Poe's Major Crisis,* 77–85, which concludes with the amount of damages sought. And Moss features, as well, Fuller's "A Sad Sight," ibid., 69–70. Moss plausibly conjectures about the appearance of Poe in the city, "Perhaps he had come to see his attorney" (69). For the *Morning News* defense, see "Mr. Poe," in Moss, *Poe's Major Crisis,* 71.

33. Susan Archer Weiss, *The Home Life of Poe* (New York: Broadway, 1907), 128, 130. For the final quotation, see Derby, *Fifty Years among Authors, Books and Publishers,* 547.

34. Weiss, *The Home Life of Poe,* 136.

35. Mary Gove Nichols, "Reminiscences of Edgar Poe," in *Poe in His Own Time,* ed. Fisher, 210–14.

36. Christopher M. Semtner, "A Young Girl's Recollections of Edgar Allan Poe," *Resources for American Literary Study* 38 (2016): 56.

37. Mary Gove Nichols, "Reminiscences of Edgar Poe," in *Poe in His Own Time,* ed. Fisher, 211; Semtner, "A Young Girl's Recollections of Edgar Allan Poe," 55.

38. John H. Birss, "Poe in Fordham: A Reminiscence," *Notes and Queries* 173 (December 18, 1937): 440.

39. For the fourth installment, see Edgar Allan Poe, "The Literati of New York City—No. IV," *Godey's Lady's Book* (August 1846): 72–78; or H 15:73–93. His comment on "the intention of the Deity" is evident in Poe, "Literati," 72; and H 15:74.

40. For the letter to which Poe is responding, see F. W. Thomas to Edgar Allan Poe, August 14, 1846 (https://www.eapoe.org).

41. William Gilmore Simms to Edgar Allan Poe, July 30, 1846, in Simms, *The Letters of William Gilmore Simms,* 6 vols. (Columbia: University of South Carolina Press, 1952–82), 2:175, 176.

42. T. O. Mabbott wrote of "The Cask of Amontillado," "Poe's story was probably written in the late summer or early fall of 1846" (M 3:1256).

43. For the original of the fifth installment, see Edgar Allan Poe, "The Literati of New York City—V," *Godey's Lady's Book* (September 1846): 126–33. For the passage on Osgood, see 127.
44. For the plea of Fuller and Clason on August 4, see Moss, *Poe's Major Crisis*, 95–98; for the postponement on September 7, see Moss, *Poe's Major Crisis*, 105. For English's move to Washington, DC, see Gravely, "The Early Political and Literary Career of Thomas Dunn English," 644. Poe claimed that English had fled prosecution (O 2:627).
45. For the original of the final installment, see Edgar Allan Poe, "The Literati of New York City—No. VI," *Godey's Lady's Book* (October 1846): 157–62. See also H 15:118–37.
46. Poe alleged that Godey was "badgered into giving up" in Burton R. Pollin, "*The Living Writers of America:* A Manuscript by Edgar Allan Poe," in *Studies in the American Renaissance 1991,* ed. Joel Myerson (Charlottesville: University Press of Virginia, 1991), 163. For Eveleth on Godey, see George W. Eveleth to Edgar Allan Poe, February 21, 1847, in *The Letters from George W. Eveleth to Edgar Allan Poe,* 14. Eveleth asked Poe if he had been right to respond to Godey thus, and Poe responded, "You were *perfectly* right in what you said to Godey" (O 2:627). Presentation and analysis of Poe's notes for the unpublished critical book are available in Pollin, "*The Living Writers of America.*"
47. For reprintings of the six sections of the novel that attack Poe, see Moss, *Poe's Major Crisis,* 98–104, 106–9, 113–15, 116–17, 117–21, 122–23. The abbreviation "S.F." stands for "Startled Falcon," an imagined clandestine political group.
48. Edgar Allan Poe, "The Cask of Amontillado," in *Godey's Lady's Book* (November 1846): 216. Variants in punctuation are evident in the version selected for the Mabbott edition, from Griswold's 1850 *Works* (M 3:1256).
49. Poe, "The Cask of Amontillado," *Godey's Lady's Book,* 218; M 3:1263.
50. Richard Dilworth Rust, "'Punish with Impunity': Poe, Thomas Dunn English, and 'The Cask of Amontillado,'" in *Poe Writing/Writing Poe,* ed. Richard Kopley and Jana Argersinger (New York: AMS, 2013), 13–29, esp. 20–21.
51. For "embedded" and "descended" and "descending," see Poe, "The Cask of Amontillado," *Godey's Lady's Book,* 217 (also M 3:1259, 1261). For my earlier treatment of these self-referential patterns, see Kopley, *Edgar Allan Poe and the Dupin Mysteries* (New York: Palgrave Macmillan, 2008), 10, 12, 18, 21, 25; and Kopley, *The Formal Center in Literature: Explorations from Poe to the Present* (Rochester, NY: Camden House, 2018), 20–24, 27. An earlier related study is David Ketterer, "'Shudder': A Signature *Crypt*-ogram in 'The Fall of the House of Usher,'" *Resources for American Literary Study* 35, no. 2 (1999): 192–205.
52. Mary Gove Nichols, "Reminiscences of Edgar Poe," in *Poe in His Own Time,* ed. Fisher, 214–15.
53. Ibid., 215. For a brief sketch of the life of Marie Louise Shew Houghton, see John Carl Miller, ed., *Building Poe Biography,* 88–89.
54. Dr. Alfred Freeman (1798–1861) is listed as living at 218 E. Broadway in the relevant directories: *Doggett's New York City Directory for 1845 & 1846* (New York: John Doggett, Jr, 1845); *Doggett's New-York City Directory for 1846 and 1847* (New York: John Doggett Jr., 1846); *Doggett's New-York City Directory for 1847 & 1848*

(New York: John Doggett Jr., 1847); and *Doggett's New York City Directory, Illustrated with Maps of New York and Brooklyn, 1848–1849* (New York: John Doggett Jr., 1848). In mid-1845, the Poe family had lived at 195 E. Broadway. For the quotation regarding the doctor's sympathy, see "The Late Dr. Alfred Freeman," *New York World,* February 18, 1861, 6 (America's Historical Newspapers).

55. Phillips, *Edgar Allan Poe—The Man,* 2:1243; Quinn, *Edgar Allan Poe: A Critical Biography,* 520.
56. "Illness of Edgar A. Poe," in Moss, *Poe's Major Crisis,* 126.
57. N. P. Willis, "Hospital for Disabled Labourers with the Brain," in Moss, *Poe's Major Crisis,* 129–32.
58. See also N. P. Willis to Edgar Allan Poe, [December 23, 1846], in Moss, *Poe's Major Crisis,* 129.
59. See also Poe to Willis, December 30, 1846, in Moss *Poe's Major Crisis,* 157. Poe mentioned a poem by Jane Ermina Locke (ibid., 156); it was probably "An Invocation for Suffering Genius," available in John E. Reilly, "Ermina's Gale: The Poems Jane Locke Devoted to Poe," in *Papers on Poe: Essays in Honor of John Ward Ostrom,* ed. Richard P. Veler (Springfield, OH: Chantry Music Press, 1971), 208. It was Walt Whitman who had reported that Poe and his wife were "without money and without friends" (Thomas and Jackson, *The Poe Log,* 673).
60. ["Mr. Poe Has a Letter"], *Washington Union* (Washington, DC), January 11, 1847, https://www.newspapers.com.
61. Shew raised sixty dollars for the Poes; she—or she and Mrs. Gove—provided "[a] featherbed and [an] abundance of bed-clothing and other comforts" (see Mary Gove Nichols, "Reminiscences of Edgar Poe"; Fisher, *Poe in His Own Time,* 215; as well as Moss, *Poe's Major Crisis,* 125). Oliver Leigh, author of *Edgar Allan Poe: The Man, The Master, The Martyr* (Chicago: Frank M. Morris, 1906), knew the Nichols in England and wrote that Mrs. Nichols had told him of "her chance discovery of his [Poe's] wife *in extremis* and alone, on which she stirred Mrs. Shew to raise the fund which set this household up for some months" (Oliver Leigh to William Lanier Washington, April 22, 1907, University of Iowa Libraries, Iowa City). Mary E. Hewitt wrote that she was "endeavoring to get up a contribution for them [the Poes] among the editors" (Mary E. Hewitt to Frances Sargent Osgood, in Thomas and Jackson, *The Poe Log,* 674). Willis forwarded an anonymous contribution to Poe and perhaps additional sums prompted by his editorial (Willis, "Hospital for Disabled Labourers with the Brain," in *Poe's Major Crisis,* ed. Moss, 130–31). Colton provided ten dollars to Poe from Charles Bristed, for which Poe wrote a letter of thanks to Bristed (O 2:617). The combative Cornelia Wells Walter noted that the weekly newspaper the *Bostonian* had, like the *Home Journal,* "opened a subscription for the relief of Mr. Poe" (see Thomas and Jackson, *The Poe Log,* 677, 675–76; and "Edgar A. Poe," Moss, *Poe's Major Crisis,* 126–27). The *Dollar Newspaper* of Philadelphia stated, "An effort is about to be made by his [Poe's] friends to contribute to the relief of his necessities. Mr. Poe has many friends in this city, and we have no doubt that they would willingly aid so benevolent a design" ("Lamentable," *Dollar Newspaper,* December 30, 1846, [2] [America's Historical Newspapers]).
62. Marie Louise Shew Houghton to John Ingram, January 23, 1875, in *Building Poe Biography,* 92.

63. For Mary Starr's presence at the Fordham cottage, see Augustus Van Cleef, "Poe's Mary," *Harper's New Monthly Magazine,* March 1889, 639 (https://www.eapoe.org). Shew mentioned her (Shew to John H. Ingram, January 23 and February 16, 1875, in *Building Poe Biography,* 97, 103). Mrs. Clemm notes that Eliza White was at Fordham at the time of Virginia's death (Maria Clemm to Sarah Helen Whitman, April 22, 1859, in James A. Harrison and Charlotte F. Dailey, "Poe and Mrs. Whitman: New Light on a Romantic Episode," *Century Magazine,* n.s., vol. 55 [January 1909]: 448). For cousin Elizabeth Herring's visiting the Poes in Fordham, see Phillips, 2:1202. Regarding Sylvanus D. Lewis's visiting the Poes there, see S. D. Lewis to Sara Sigourney Rice, in Sara Sigourney Rice, *Edgar Allan Poe: A Memorial Volume* (Baltimore, MD: Turnbull Brothers, 1877), 86. Sarah Anna Lewis (a.k.a. Stella Anna Lewis) was there, as well (Stella Anna Lewis to George W. Eveleth, November 6, 1854, in *Building Poe Biography,* 199).

64. Van Cleef, "Poe's Mary," 639 (https://www.eapoe.org).

65. The detail here is drawn from Marie Louise Shew Houghton to John Ingram, March 28, 1875, in *Building Poe Biography,* 116. Ingram relates Houghton's story to Sarah Helen Whitman in Ingram to Whitman, June 2, 1875, in *Poe's Helen Remembers,* 304.

66. Reilly, "Robert D'Unger and the Reminiscences of Poe in Baltimore," 68.

67. For a full treatment of the deathbed portrait of Virginia, see Deas, *The Portraits and Daguerreotypes of Edgar Allan Poe,* 168–70. He discusses, as well, two portraits that have been said to be of Virginia (170–72). For a consideration of "posthumous mourning paintings," see Phoebe Lloyd, "Posthumous Mourning Portraits," in *A Time to Mourn: Expressions of Grief in Nineteenth Century America,* ed. Martha V. Pike and Janice Gray Armstrong (Stony Brook, NY: Museum at Stony Brook, 1980), 70–89; and Jay Ruby, *Secure the Shadow: Death and Photography in America* (Cambridge, MA: MIT Press, 1995), 36–47.

68. Van Cleef, "Poe's Mary," 639; Marie Louise Shew Houghton to John Ingram, January 23, 1875, and February 16, 1875, in *Building Poe Biography,* 97, 103; Mary Gove Nichols, "Reminiscences of Edgar Poe," in *Poe in His Own Time,* ed. Fisher, 215; Phillips, *Edgar Allan Poe—the Man,* 2:1203; Thomas and Jackson, *The Poe Log,* 685; "Died," *New York Evening Post* and *New-York Commercial Advertiser,* February 1, 1847 (America's Historical Newspapers).

69. Marie Louise Shew Houghton to John Ingram, February 16, 1875, and E. Dora Houghton to John Ingram, March 29, 1875, in *Building Poe Biography,* 108, 113; S. D. Lewis to Sara Sigourney Rice, October 11, 1875, in *Edgar Allan Poe: A Memorial Volume,* 86; Van Cleef, "Poe's Mary," 639–40; Phillips, *Edgar Allan Poe—the Man,* 2:1202–05. See also Thomas and Jackson, *The Poe Log,* 686.

70. Nathaniel P. Willis, "Death of Mrs. Edgar A. Poe," in Moss, *Poe's Major Crisis,* 165.

21. "Then My Heart It Grew Ashen and Sober"

1. C. Chauncey Burr, "Character of Edgar A. Poe," *Nineteenth Century: A Quarterly Miscellany* 5, no. 1 (February 1852): 32–33.

2. For Poe's visiting Jane Stith Stanard's grave with her son, see Maria Clemm to Sarah Helen Whitman, April 14, 1859, in *Building Poe Biography,* ed. John Carl Miller

(Baton Rouge: Louisiana State University Press, 1977), 42. For his visiting the grave by himself, see Sarah Helen Whitman to Maria Clemm, March 10, 1859, in *Edgar Allan Poe: Letters and Documents in the Enoch Pratt Free Library,* ed. Arthur H. Quinn and Richard H. Hart (New York: Scholars' Facsimiles & Reprints, 1941), 42; Whitman, *Edgar Poe and His Critics* (New York: Rudd & Carleton, 1860), 49–50; and Whitman to John H. Ingram, April 2, 1874, in *Poe's Helen Remembers,* ed. John Carl Miller (Charlottesville: University Press of Virginia, 1979), 104. The quotation is drawn from the 1874 letter. Whitman commented, "I *know* that his report was *essentially* true. I cannot feel sure about anything else."

3. For Mrs. Shew's attending to Poe every other day after Virginia's death, with Mrs. Clemm caring for him on the other days, see Maria Clemm to Marie Louise Shew, ca. February 1847, in *Building Poe Biography,* 23–24; and Marie Louise Shew Houghton to John H. Ingram, January 23, 1875, ibid., 91–92. For Mrs. Shew's promises to Virginia, see Clemm to Shew, ca. February 1847, 23–24; and Houghton to Ingram, May 16, [18]75, ibid., 140. Mrs. Shew's advice to Poe is drawn from Marie Louise Shew Houghton to John H. Ingram, February 16, 1875, ibid., 102–3. For the story about the wine, see Clemm to Shew, ca. February 1847, ibid., 23.

4. Shew's asserting that she had saved Poe's life is in Marie Louise Shew Houghton to John H. Ingram, January 23, 1875, in *Building Poe Biography,* 92.

5. Ibid., 98.

6. The verdict, "rough minutes," and an immediate press report are provided in Sidney P. Moss, *Poe's Major Crisis: His Libel Suit and New York's Literary World* (Durham, NC: Duke University Press, 1970), 171–77.

7. "The Columbian Magazine," *New-York Commercial Advertiser,* February 20, 1847, [2] (America's Historical Newspapers). William Beckford's 1786 *Vathek* was a work of fantastic opulence and sensory intensity. Poe mentions Beckford's extraordinary gothic home Fonthill in "The Domain of Arnheim" (M 3:1278). See also Caroline Ticknor, *Poe's Helen* (New York: Charles Scribner's Sons, 1916), 273; and M 3:1266.

8. For the piece in the *Tribune* to which Poe objected, see "Genius and the Law of Libel," in Moss, *Poe's Major Crisis,* 188–89.

9. I draw on Shew Houghton to Ingram, January 23, 1875, in *Building Poe Biography,* 91–94. See also Shew Houghton to Ingram, April 9, 1875, ibid., 130. For Depau Row, see Christopher Gray, "High-Born Homes That Came and Went," *New York Times,* March 25, 2007 (online). "Beloved Physician" is St. Paul's term for St. Luke (Colossians 4:14). Marie Louise Shew married Roland S. Houghton on November 18, 1850 (see Patricia Cline Cohen, "Marie Louise Shew and Mrs. Maria Poe Clemm," *Poe Studies,* 42, no. 1 [2009]: 65).

10. John H. Ingram, *Edgar Allan Poe: His Life, Letters, and Opinions,* 2 vols. (London: John Hogg, 1880), 2:154. For the address "51 West 10th Street," see Mary E. Phillips, *Edgar Allan Poe—The Man,* 2 vols. (Chicago: John C. Winston, 1926), 2:1268. Phillips identifies Shew's uncle as Hiram Barney (2:1269). See also Miller, *Building Poe Biography* 100; and O 2:630–31. However, Patricia Cline Cohen maintains that Shew was referring to Henry D. Chapin (Cohen, "Marie Louise Shew and Mrs. Maria Poe Clemm," 65).

11. Edgar Allan Poe, "The Philosophy of Furniture," *Burton's Gentleman's Magazine*, May 1840, 243–45. For the quotations on the piano and the books, see 245. Mabbott provides the Griswold edition of the sketch, with textual variants, in M 2:495–503. John H. Ingram commented on parallels between Shew's music room and library and details of "The Philosophy of Furniture" in Ingram to Sarah Helen Whitman, April 22, 1875, in *Poe's Helen Remembers*, 280.
12. Ingram, *Edgar Allan Poe: His Life, Letters, and Opinions*, 2:154. For a discussion of the private bookroom in the nineteenth century, see Reid Byers, "The Nineteenth-Century Social Library," in *The Private Library: Being a More or Less Compendious Disquisition on the History of the Architecture and Furnishing of the Domestic Bookroom* (New Castle, DE: Oak Knoll, 2021), 267–325.
13. Carroll D. Laverty, "Poe in 1847," *American Literature* 20, no. 2 (1948): 165–66.
14. J. C. Derby, *Fifty Years among Authors, Books and Publishers* (New York: G. W. Carleton, 1884), 588–89.
15. Donald Yannella and Kathleen Malone Yannella, "Evert A. Duyckinck's 'Diary: May 29–November 8, 1847,'" in *Studies in the American Renaissance 1978*, ed. Joel Myerson (Boston: Twayne, 1978), 223.
16. Evert A. Duyckinck and George L. Duyckinck, eds., *Cyclopaedia of American Literature*, 2 vols. (New York: Charles Scribner, 1855), 2:536–39.
17. I rely on Laverty, "Poe in 1847," 166–67; and Michael J. Deas, *The Portraits and Daguerreotypes of Edgar Allan Poe* (Charlottesville: University Press of Virginia, 1989), 32–35.
18. Hiram Fuller, "Prenez Garde, Chrony," in Moss, *Poe's Major Crisis*, 208–9; Sarah Helen Whitman to John H. Ingram, February 20, 1874, in *Poe's Helen Remembers*, 37.
19. Rufus W. Griswold, *Passages from the Correspondence and Other Papers of Rufus W. Griswold* (Cambridge, MA: W. M. Griswold, 1898), 230.
20. Dwight Thomas and David K. Jackson, *The Poe Log: A Documentary Life of Edgar Allan Poe, 1809–1849* (Boston: G. K. Hall, 1987), 703.
21. Arthur Barksdale Kinsolving, *The Story of a Southern School: The Episcopal High School of Virginia* (Baltimore, MD: Norman, Remington, 1922), 35; "The Episcopal High School in Virginia," in Wm. A. R. Goodwin, *History of the Theological Seminary in Virginia and Its Historical Background*, 2 vols. (Rochester, NY: Du Bois, 1923–34), 2:420; Thomas and Jackson, *The Poe Log*, 703.
22. That Poe visited Godey is evident from George W. Eveleth to Edgar Allan Poe, January 11, 1848, in *The Letters from George W. Eveleth to Edgar Allan Poe*, ed. Thomas Ollive Mabbott (New York: New York Public Library, 1922), 16–17. That Poe visited Graham, encountered Conrad, and stayed at Arbuckle's hotel is evident from Poe's own August 10, 1847, letter to Conrad (O 2:632). For the name and address of that hotel, see *McElroy's Philadelphia Directory for 1847* (Philadelphia: Edward C. and John Biddle, 1847).
23. Eveleth to Poe, January 11, 1848, in *The Letters from George W. Eveleth to Edgar Allan Poe*, ed. Mabbott, 16–17.
24. Ibid.
25. Laverty, "Poe in 1847," 167.

26. John Ward Ostrom, "Edgar A. Poe: His Income as a Literary Entrepreneur," *Poe Studies* 15, no. 1 (1982): 6. See also Ostrom, "Poe's Literary Labors and Rewards," in *Myths and Reality: The Mysterious Mr. Poe*, ed. Benjamin Franklin Fisher IV (Baltimore, MD: Edgar Allan Poe Society, 1987), 41.
27. See also Laverty, "Poe in 1847," 167.
28. "Literary," *Boston Evening Transcript*, October 18, 1847, [2] (America's Historical Newspapers).
29. Edgar Allan Poe, "Tale-Writing—Nathaniel Hawthorne," *Godey's Lady's Book*, November 1847, 252–56. See esp. 252 ("*not* original in any sense"), 253 ("peculiar"), and 254 ("*very* profound under-current"). See also H 13:141–55.
30. See Sarah Helen Whitman to John H. Ingram, January 7, and February 14, 1875, in *Poe's Helen Remembers*, 246, 255. It was at the New Lebanon Springs Water Cure, in New York, where Mary Gove had been "resident physician" (Jean L. Silver-Isenstadt, *Shameless: The Visionary Life of Mary Gove Nichols* [Baltimore, MD: Johns Hopkins University Press, 2002], 75–76).
31. Sarah Helen Whitman to John H. Ingram, April 17, [18]74, in *Poe's Helen Remembers*, 124.
32. Sarah Helen Whitman to John H. Ingram, June 2, 1874, in *Poe's Helen Remembers*, 162.
33. Sarah Helen Whitman, *Edgar Poe and His Critics*, 30–32.
34. Laverty, "Poe in 1847," 167–68.
35. Derby, *Fifty Years among Authors, Books and Publishers*, 597.
36. Sarah Helen Whitman to John H. Ingram, February 16, 1874, in *Poe's Helen Remembers*, 27. Whitman added that many thought that Stoddard was jealous of Poe's reputation.
37. The story of the leaping contest is told in Mary Gove Nichols, "Reminiscences of Edgar Poe," in *Poe in His Own Time*, ed. Benjamin F. Fisher (Iowa City: University of Iowa Press, 2010), 212–13. The story's placement in Poe's chronology is given in Thomas and Jackson, *The Poe Log*, 707–8. Poe wrote that he took back from Colton "The Rationale of Verse" when "Ulalume" was accepted (O 2:639). Nichols states that "Ulalume" "bought the poet a pair of gaiters, and twelve shillings [a dollar and a half] over" (213). Ostrom estimated that Colton may have paid Poe twenty dollars for the poem (6). Mabbott contended that Poe may have been paid seventy-five or a hundred dollars for "The Rationale of Verse," which was then replaced by "Ulalume," (M 1:413).
38. For the timing of Poe's beginning his work on *Eureka*, I am guided, in part, by E. L. Didier, "Life of Edgar A. Poe," in *The Life and Poems of Edgar Allan Poe* (New York: W. J. Widdleton, 1877), 104. The length of Poe's cosmological work and the coming February 3 lecture argue for preliminary efforts by late fall.
39. Stuart and Susan Levine write, "It seems evident to us that although *Eureka* was published first, the story was written before it" (L2 119). It was probably "Mellonta Tauta" about which Poe inquired to Louis A. Godey on January 17, 1848 (O 2:645–46).
40. For Poe's negative reaction to Mrs. Lewis, see Marie Louise Shew Houghton to John H. Ingram, April 3, [1875], in *Building Poe Biography*, 120. Sylvanus D. Lewis left his thoughts on Poe in a letter to Sara Sigourney Rice (Lewis to Rice,

October 11, 1875, in Sara Sigourney Rice, *Edgar Allan Poe: A Memorial Volume* [Baltimore, MD: Turnbull Brothers, 1877], 86–87). He wrote, in part, of Poe, "He was one of the most affectionate, kind-hearted men I ever knew." Lewis's copy of the Rice volume includes the ownership notation "S. D. Lewis / 104 Dean St. / Brooklyn N.J. / Dec. 1876" (collection of the author).

41. J. P. [John Priestly?], "To the Patrons of the Review," *American Review* (December 1847): forematter. For the length of Colton's illness, see "Death of George H. Colton," *New-York Commercial Advertiser,* December 2, 1847, [2] (America's Historical Newspapers).

42. Poe offers criticism of Colton in his February 29, 1848, letter to George W. Eveleth (O 2:648) and in his May 1846 "Literati" sketch (H 15:7–9).

43. See Eveleth to Poe, March 9, 1848, *The Letters of George W. Eveleth to Edgar Allan Poe,* ed. Mabbott, 18.

44. Donald G. Mitchell, *American Lands and Letters* (New York: Charles Scribner's. 1898–99), 2:387–88 and Thomas and Jackson, *The Poe Log,* 484.

45. On December 7, 1847, the *New-York Commercial Advertiser* mentioned the December issue of the *American Review* as received ("The American Review for December," *New-York Commercial Advertiser,* December 7, 1847, [1] [America's Historical Newspapers]).

46. I quote the first printing of the poem in the *American Review:* Edgar Allan Poe, "To — — —. Ulalume: A Ballad," *American Review* (December 1847): 599–600. Mabbott offers a later version, with minor differences (M 1:415–19). He suggests that the three blanks in the title may represent "C. P. Bronson" or "M. E. Bronson" (M 1:420).

47. Among the sources suggested are N. P. Willis's "My Birth-Place" (K. L. Daughrity, "A Source for a Line of Poe's 'Ulalume,'" *Notes and Queries* 161 [July 11, 1931]: 27); W. G. C.'s "To the Autumn Leaf" (Nelson Adkins, "Poe's 'Ulalume,'" *Notes and Queries* 164 [January 14, 1933]: 30–31); Elizabeth Oakes Smith's "The Summons Answered" (M 1:411); and the *Blackwood's* poem "Ullaloo, Gol, or Lamentations over the Dead" (Burton R. Pollin, "Poe's 'Ulalume': Its Likely Source and Sound," *American Notes & Queries* 1, no. 1 [1988]: 17–20).

48. Whitman, *Edgar Poe and His Critics,* 48.

49. Ibid., 29. Mabbott mentions Poe's walk in Mamaroneck, north and east of Fordham in Westchester (M 1:410–11).

50. Sarah Helen Whitman to Maria Clemm, April 5, 1859, in Quinn and Hart, *Edgar Allan Poe: Letters and Documents in the Enoch Pratt Free Library,* 49.

51. John H. Ingram to Sarah Helen Whitman, April 28, 1874, in *Poe's Helen Remembers,* 132.

52. Sarah Helen Whitman to John H. Ingram, November 14, [18]76, in *Poe's Helen Remembers,* 457–58. For Whitman's earlier acknowledging that she had recommended that Poe omit the last verse, see Whitman to Ingram, March 30, [18]74, ibid., 98.

53. For the publication of the January 1848 issue of *Graham's Magazine* by December 21, 1847, see "Books for the Holidays" and "Now Is the Time," *New York Evening Post,* December 21, 1847, [2] (America's Historical Newspapers). For Poe's marginalia on "My Heart Laid Bare," see Edgar Allan Poe, "Marginalia," *Graham's*

Magazine (January 1848): 24; and P 2:322–23. For Bulwer-Lytton's early use of the phrase "heart laid bare," see Edward George Bulwer-Lytton, *Pelham or The Adventures of a Gentleman,* ed. Jerome J. McGann (Lincoln: University of Nebraska Press, 1972), 365. I offered a study of Poe's ongoing reliance on Bulwer-Lytton's *Pelham* in "Poe's Taking of *Pelham* One Two Three Four Five Six," *Poe Studies* 41 (2008): 109–16.

54. For Poe's notes for "Literary America," see "*The Living Writers of America:* A Manuscript by Edgar Allan Poe," transcribed, edited, and annotated by Burton R. Pollin, in *Studies in the American Renaissance 1991,* ed. Joel Myerson (Charlottesville: University Press of Virginia, 1991), 151–211. Mabbott estimated that the time of Poe's writing "To Marie Louise" was "a date in the period between December 1847 and January 1848" (M 1:406).

55. Poe wrote in his January prospectus for "The Stylus" that he had been working on "Literary America" "unremittingly for the last two years" (L2 33).

56. I draw from Marie Louise Shew Houghton to John Ingram, [ca. April 15, 1875], in *Building Poe Biography,* 132–33. See also Ingram, *Edgar Allan Poe: His Life, Letters, and Opinions,* 2:119–20.

57. Shew to Ingram, [ca. April 15, 1875], in *Building Poe Biography,* 133.

58. Didier, "Life of Edgar A. Poe," 104. According to a newspaper report, the coldest days of December 1847 were December 21, 26, and 27. (The low was 16°F.) The days in the month with the lowest mean temperature were December 26 and 27. (That mean was 18.75°F.) ("Observations on the Weather, for Dec. 1847, Made at the Institution for the Deaf and Dumb, New York," *New-York Commercial Advertiser,* January 4, 1848, [1] [America's Historical Newspapers]).

59. R. E. Shapley [probably Rufus E. Shapley] as quoted by George E. Woodberry, *The Life of Edgar Allan Poe,* 2 vols. (Boston: Houghton Mifflin, 1909), 2:236; Richard Henry Stoddard, *Recollections Personal and Literary* (New York: A. S. Barnes, 1903), 158.

60. Thomas and Jackson, *The Poe Log,* 715.

61. Poe had written to Nicholas Biddle in January 1841 of surprising support for his journal (then "The Penn") from the South and the West: "I have received a great many names from villages, in the South and West, of whose existence even I was not aware" (O 1:253–54). Writing in 1842 about his prospective journal to Thomas H. Chivers—whom he considered a possible partner—Poe mentioned his "many warm friends, especially in the South and West" (O 1:350). For Poe's eventual list of possible subscribers and contributors to his magazine, see *Such Friends as These: Edgar Allan Poe's List of Subscribers and Contributors to His Dream Magazine,* ed. Alexander G. Rose and Jeffrey Alan Savoye (Baltimore, MD: Enoch Pratt Free Library, Edgar Allan Poe Society, and Library of the University of Baltimore, 1986).

62. Richard Kopley, "John Neal on Hawthorne and Poe in the *New England Galaxy* of 1835," *Nathaniel Hawthorne Review* 42, no. 2 (2016): 30.

63. For Poe's list of those who might subscribe or contribute, see *Such Friends as These.*

64. The language is identical in Mabbott's 1933 facsimile edition (see *Al Aaraaf,* ed. Thomas Ollive Mabbott [New York: Published for The Facsimile Text Society by Columbia University Press, 1933], 33).

65. For a recent elaboration of the presence of science in Poe's life and work, see John Tresch, *The Reason for the Darkness of the Night: Edgar Allan Poe and the Forging of American Science* (New York: Farrar, Strauss and Giroux, 2021).
66. For Eveleth's initial response, see Eveleth to Poe, January 11, 1848, in *The Letters from George W. Eveleth to Edgar Allan Poe*, ed. Mabbott, 17–18. For Willis's notice, see Thomas and Jackson, *The Poe Log*, 720. For notices of Poe's coming lecture, see Burton R. Pollin, "Contemporary Reviews of *Eureka*: A Checklist," in *Poe as Literary Cosmologer: Studies on "Eureka" A Symposium*, ed. Richard P. Benton (Hartford, CT: Transcendental Books, 1975), 27–28. See also Thomas and Jackson, *The Poe Log*, 718–20.
67. Mukhtar Ali Isani, "Reminiscences of Poe by an Employee of the *Broadway Journal*," *Poe Studies* 6, no. 2 (1973): 34.
68. Maunsell B. Field, *Memories of Many Men and of Some Women* (New York: Harper & Brothers, 1874), 224.
69. For the *Philadelphia Saturday Gazette*'s view that Poe was half-crazy, see Pollin, "Contemporary Reviews of *Eureka*," 28. For the *New York Morning Courier*'s praise, see Arthur Hobson Quinn, *Edgar Allan Poe: A Critical Biography* (New York: D. Appleton-Century, 1941), 539. See also Pollin, "Contemporary Reviews of *Eureka*," 28; and Thomas and Jackson, *The Poe Log*, 724. For the *Herald*'s call for a lecture on common sense, see "Lectures and Lecturing," *New York Daily Herald*, February 12, 1848, [2] (America's Historical Newspapers). For the faulting of the *Morning Express* review, see "Hyperbolic Nonsense," *New-York Commercial Advertiser*, February 4, 1848, [2] (America's Historical Newspapers); see also Pollin, "Contemporary Reviews of *Eureka*," 27; and Thomas and Jackson, *The Poe Log*, 721.
70. John Henry Hopkins Jr., ["Report on Poe's Lecture on 'The Universe'"], *Evening Express*, February 4, 1848, [1] (https://www.eapoe.org), a reprint of the "Report" in the *Morning Express* (Thomas and Jackson, *The Poe Log*, 721).
71. George W. Eveleth to Edgar Allan Poe, March 9, 1848, in *The Letters from George W. Eveleth to Edgar Allan Poe*, 20.

22. "I Feel I Am Now a Prophet"

1. The earlier Valentine's Day poem to Marie Louise Shew was the 1847 "To M. L. S—." Marie Louise Shew Houghton wrote to John H. Ingram, "I have the origonal [sic] of the poem to M.L.S. and also the original of the valentine to Marie Louise." She later sent the valentines to Ingram (see Marie Louise Shew Houghton to John H. Ingram, February 16, 1875, and March 28, 1875, in *Building Poe Biography*, ed. John Carl Miller [Baton Rouge: Louisiana State University Press, 1977], 105, 115; for her further comments, see 125). Mabbott drew the text of "To Marie Louise" from the tracing of the manuscript that Houghton had sent to Ingram, in the Ingram Collection (M 1:406). The March 1848 issue of the *Columbian Magazine* is discussed on February 23 in the *Boston Evening Transcript* ("The Columbian Magazine," *Boston Evening Transcript*, February 23, 1848 [America's Historical Newspapers]). Mabbott asserts that the poem "was published by February 15, 1848" (M 1:406).

2. Juliet is compared to "a snowy dove trooping with crows" in Shakespeare's *Romeo and Juliet* (1.5.48). This line appears in a passage from which Poe copied a line, "O she doth teach the torches to burn bright," probably in 1829 (Burton R. Pollin "Shakespeare in the Works of Edgar Allan Poe," *Studies in the American Renaissance 1985*, ed Joel Myerson [Charlottesville: University Press of Virginia, 1985], 186).

3. For Poe's sending the 1831 "To Helen" to Sarah Helen Whitman on March 2, see Dwight Thomas and David K. Jackson, *The Poe Log: A Documentary Life of Edgar Allan Poe, 1809–1849* (Boston: G. K. Hall, 1987), 728. Whitman's poem to Poe was not published in the *Home Journal* on March 4 with the other valentines owing to Lynch's concerns about her guests' attitude toward him, but, because of Whitman's insistence, it did appear there later, on March 18. For relevant sections of the Lynch-Whitman correspondence, see Thomas and Jackson, *The Poe Log*, 726, 728. For Osgood's comment to Whitman on the published poem, see ibid., 729–30.

4. For treatment of this unpublished "Marginalia" piece, see Jeffrey A. Savoye, "A 'Lost' Roll of Marginalia," *Edgar Allan Poe Review* 3, no. 3 (2002): 52–72. See also Savoye, "Another 'Lost' Fragment of Poe's 'Marginalia,'" *Edgar Allan Poe Review* 24, no. 2 (2023): 232–40.

5. An advertisement for the March 1848 issue of *Graham's Magazine* appeared on February 22, 1848 (see "The Best Magazine Published," *New York Evening Post*, February 22, 1848, [2] [America's Historical Newspapers]). Also, an advertisement for the March 1848 issue of the *Union Magazine* appeared on February 24. See the listing of the March issue of the *Union Magazine* in the advertisement for Berford & Company, *New-York Commercial Advertiser*, February 24, 1848, [2] (America's Historical Newspapers).

6. The review that Isbell provided was by "Decius" and appeared in the *New World* on February 12 (O 2:660n).

7. An advertisement for the April 1848 issue of *Graham's Magazine* appeared in the *New York Evening Post* on March 17, 1848, [2], (America's Historical Newspapers). A fuller advertisement, mentioning Winslow's poem, appeared in that newspaper on March 20, 1848, [2] (America's Historical Newspapers). For the poem itself, see Harriet B. Winslow, "To the Author of 'The Raven,'" *Graham's Magazine* (April 1848): 203 (ProQuest). For Mabbott's comments on Poe and the poem, see M 1:492–93, 510. Poe's handwritten version of the poem was auctioned at Bangs & Company on April 11, 1896 (*Sale of Choice Literary Autographs and Manuscripts* [New York: Bangs & Company, 1896], 24–25 [American Antiquarian Society]). It is claimed incorrectly there that Poe wrote the poem. See also M 1:492. The poem, slightly revised and now titled "After Reading 'The Raven,'" is included in Harriet Winslow Sewall, *Poems by Harriet Winslow Sewall* (Cambridge, MA: Riverside, 1889), 47–50. This volume was published posthumously and features a memoir by Ednah D. Cheney.

8. "To the Unsatisfied" appeared, anonymously, as early as 1840 ("To the Unsatisfied," *Baltimore Sun*, October 23, 1840, [1] [America's Historical Newspapers]). It appeared, still anonymously, as "Why Thus Longing?" in Longfellow's *The Waif: A Collection of Poems* (Cambridge, MA: John Owen, 1845), 9–10. Although

sometimes incorrectly attributed to Longfellow, it was correctly given to Winslow in the March 22, 1845, issue of the *North American* (Nineteenth-Century U.S. Newspapers). "To the Authoress of the Unsatisfied" appeared in the *Pennsylvania Freeman,* April 2, 1846, [4] (America's Historical Newspapers).

9. Winslow, "To the Author of 'The Raven,'" 203. The relevant stanza was copied in an abolitionist paper; see "Graham's Magazine—April," *Anti-Slavery Bugle* (Salem, OH), March 31, 1848, 3, https://www.newspapers.com. It may be that the abolitionist poet John Greenleaf Whittier was addressing Harriet B. Winslow in "What the Quaker Said to the Transcendentalist" (see Thomas Franklin Currier, "Whittier's 'To—with a Copy of Woolman's *Journal*,'" *Quaker History: Bulletin of Friends Historical Association* 30, no. 2 [1941]: 69–74).

10. Paul Lewis, "'The Raven' Imitated, Admired, and Sometimes Mocked," *Edgar Allan Poe Review* 22, no. 2 (2021): 300.

11. See Mrs. Eliza Kurtz Starr to Samuel Henry Starr, April 21, 1848 (https://www.eapoe.org, "Addenda" to *The Poe Log*).

12. J. H. Hopkins to Marie Louise Shew Houghton, February 9, 1875, in *Building Poe Biography,* 101.

13. George Palmer Putnam, "Leaves from a Publisher's Letter-Book," *Putnam's Monthly* (October 1869): 471. There is another narrative, according to which Poe visited Putnam the day after the lecture and proposed the book, and the publisher merely lent Poe a shilling to get home to Fordham. However, this account is secondhand, published after Putnam's death, and does not include Putnam's commitment to publish the book (Maunsell R. Field, *Memories of Many Men and of Some Women* [New York: Harper & Brothers, 1874], 224–25).

14. I rely on Marie Louise Shew Houghton to John Ingram, February 16, 1875, in *Building Poe Biography,* 104; and John H. Hopkins to Marie Louise Shew Houghton, February 9, 1875, ibid., 101.

15. Marie Louise Shew Houghton to John Ingram, January 23, 1875, in *Building Poe Biography,* 95. Elsewhere, Mrs. Houghton wrote that Griswold's "hatred of Mr. Poe was a passion worthy of a *demon* instead of a man" (Marie Louise Shew Houghton to Sarah Helen Whitman, May 24, [1875], in *Poe's Helen Remembers,* ed. John Carl Miller [Charlottesville: University Press of Virginia, 1979], 299).

16. Houghton to Ingram, January 23, 1875, in *Building Poe Biography,* 98–99.

17. Ibid., 99.

18. Marie Louise Shew Houghton to John Ingram, February 16, 1875, in *Building Poe Biography,* 102–3.

19. For the May 15 Hopkins letter, see Thomas and Jackson, *The Poe Log,* 733. For Hopkins's later attack, see ibid., 745–46; for Poe's defense, see O 2:688–91. Facsimiles of the contract and the promissory note are provided in Roland W. Nelson, "Apparatus for a Definitive Edition of Poe's *Eureka,*" in *Studies in the American Renaissance 1978,* ed. Joel Myerson (Boston: G. K. Hall, 1978), 166, 168. Putnam, in an asterisked footnote, contended that Poe had threatened to take the manuscript to another publisher (Putnam, "Leaves from a Publisher's Letter-Book," 471). American magazine collector Dr. Steven Lomazow kindly provided Andrews's squib—["Edgar A. Poe at present resides"], *The Empire Ladies and Gentleman's Magazine,* May 28, 1848, 18.

20. Neither Mrs. Shew's letter nor Poe's letter in response survives, but fortunately Shew transcribed Poe's letter. For further detail, see O 2:680.
21. Marie Louise Shew Houghton to John Ingram, April 3, [1875], in *Building Poe Biography*, 124.
22. For Poe's conversation with Maria J. McIntosh, see Sarah Helen Whitman to John Ingram, March 6, 1874, and February 14, 1875, in *Poe's Helen Remembers*, 61, 255–56. For Whitman's receiving the second "To Helen" "[i]n the early summer of 1848," see Whitman to Ingram, March 6, 1874, in *Poe's Helen Remembers*, 60. Poe wrote to Whitman on November 24, 1848, "You had my poem about the first of June—was it not?" (O 2:733).
23. For Locke's visit to Poe in Fordham, see Annie Richmond to John Ingram, March 13, 1877, in *Building Poe Biography*, 166; and Sarah Helen Whitman to John H. Ingram, June 2, 1874, and October 25, 1875, in *Poe's Helen Remembers*, 162, 346. For a study of Poe and Mrs. Locke, see John E. Reilly, "Ermina's Gales: The Poems Jane Locke Devoted to Poe," in *Papers on Poe: Essays in Honor of John Ward Ostrom*, ed. Richard P. Veler (Springfield, OH: Chantry Music Press, 1972), 206–20.
24. For Bristed's address, see *Doggett's New York City Directory [. . .] 1848–1849* (New York: John Doggett Jr., 1848). For Poe's query on his calling card, see *A Descriptive Catalog of Edgar Allan Poe Manuscripts in the Humanities Research Center Library, the University of Texas at Austin*, ed. Joseph J. Moldenhauer (Austin: University of Texas at Austin, 1973), 68; or O 2:670. It has been suggested that the "distant connexion near Richmond, Va" "is probably John R. Thompson, or possibly John Mackenzie" (O 2:670n), but Poe had not yet met Thompson at this time, so it seems unlikely that Poe would consider Thompson his "last hope."
25. Nelson, "Apparatus for a Definitive Edition of Poe's *Eureka*," 166.
26. Annie Richmond to John Ingram, March 13, 1877, in *Building Poe Biography*, 166.
27. Reilly, "Ermina's Gales," 211, 212.
28. Richmond to Ingram, March 13, 1877, in *Building Poe Biography*, 166. "Annie" was Poe's name for Mrs. Richmond.
29. See Thomas and Jackson, *The Poe Log*, 455, 506, 507.
30. Ibid., 739–42.
31. The two responses to Poe's lecture are drawn from Frederick W. Coburn, "Poe as Seen by the Brother of 'Annie,'" *New England Quarterly* 16, no. 3 (1943): 470; and William F. Gill, *The Life of Edgar Allan Poe* (New York: D. Appleton, 1877), 210. For the latter, see also H 1:304. For Poe's discussion of the meter in Byron's "The Bride of Abydos" in "The Rationale of Verse," see L2:104–8. It is possible that before his lecture, Poe wrote "[Lines on Ale]" at the Washington Tavern in Lowell (M 1:449–50).
32. Coburn, "Poe as Seen by the Brother of 'Annie,'" 470–71.
33. For an early listing of *Eureka*, see Notice of *Eureka A Prose Poem, New-York Commercial Advertiser*, July 12, 1848, [2] (America's Historical Newspapers). For the advertisement on publication day, see "The Material and Spiritual Universe," which states "Published This Day, *Eureka; or the Universe, a Prose Poem*, by Edgar A. Poe," in *New-York Commercial Advertiser*, July 15, 1848, [2] (America's Historical Newspapers). Also on this day, a notice appeared in the *New York Evening Post* regarding

the book that "has just been published" (Notice of *Eureka, A Prose Poem, New York Evening Post,* July 15, 1848, [2], https://www.newspapers.com).

34. I rely on the Levines' scholarly edition of *Eureka,* which is based on the Hurst-Wakeman copy of Poe's work, a volume that includes Poe's 1849 revisions. The Levines' introduction to their edition is valuable, as is Roland Nelson's "Apparatus for a Definitive Edition of Poe's *Eureka.*" Notably, Poe's asking that his "Book of Truths" be judged as a "Poem" suggests a development in his thinking since his 1842 reference to "the obstinate oils and waters of Poetry and Truth" (H 11:70).

35. Reversibility in action is apparent in the *"bouleversement"* of "Hans Pfaall" (P 1:422). Reversibility in language is apparent in "Berenice," *The Narrative of Arthur Gordon Pym,* "The Man of the Crowd," "The Gold-Bug," "A Tale of the Ragged Mountains," and the Dupin tales. (For more on this pattern, see my *The Formal Center in Literature: Explorations from Poe to the Present* [Rochester, NY: Camden House 2018].) Reversibility in expectation is clear in "The Murders in the Rue Morgue" (murderer is an ape) and "The Purloined Letter" (the letter is hidden in plain sight). Reversibility in interpretation is notable in "Maelzel's Chess-Player" (the machine as a person) and "The Swiss Bell-Ringers" (the synchronized musicians as a machine).

36. Poe, in his April 1835 Drake-Halleck review, wrote about "the *intention* of the Deity" as inferred from human reverence and the sense of the beautiful (P 5:165–66). He referred in his August 1846 "Literati" piece on Margaret Fuller to "the intention of the Deity as regards sexual differences" (H 15:74–75). He considered "the intention of the Deity" as evidenced from the limits of Human Progress in his 1846/1847 manuscript for "The Living Writers of America" (Burton R. Pollin, transcriber, editor, and annotator, "*The Living Writers of America:* A Manuscript by Edgar Allan Poe," in *Studies in the American Renaissance 1991,* ed. Joel Myerson [Charlottesville: University Press of Virginia, 1991], 169). For Poe's discussion of "the providential plan of the Deity" and biblical prophecy, see his 1837 review of John L. Stephens's *Incidents of Travel in Egypt, Arabia Petrea, and Palestine* (H 10:9). The angel Agathos, in Poe's 1845 "The Power of Words," contends that matter exists so that "the soul may allay the thirst *to know*" (M 3:1212).

37. Poe, *Al Aaraaf, Tamerlane, and Minor Poems,* with a bibliographical note by Thomas Ollive Mabbott (New York: Published for The Facsimile Text Society by Columbia University Press, 1933), [11]. See also M 1:91, with 1829 variants.

38. The reviews in the *Literary World* (July 29), the *Daily Tribune* (August 3), and the *Evening Transcript* (July 20) may be found in I. M. Walker, ed., *Edgar Allan Poe: The Critical Heritage* (London: Routledge & Kegan Paul, 1986), 281–85, 286–87, 280–81. For the selected quotations, see 284, 286, 280. For the *John-Donkey* note, see Thomas and Jackson, *The Poe Log,* 752. The full text of this note is available in [Thomas Dunn English], "Great Literary Crash," *John-Donkey,* August 12, 1848, 67 (ProQuest American Periodicals). The *Merchants' Magazine* review (August) is also provided in Thomas and Jackson, *The Poe Log,* 747. The *Illustrated Monthly Courier* review is furnished in the issue of August 1, 1848, p. 30 (EBSCOhost American Literary Periodicals). The periodical, edited by Andrew M'Makin and Henry B. Hirst, ran from July through December 1848. For M'Makin's negative response to Poe's lecture on the universe, see Thomas and Jackson, *The Poe Log,*

725. The review of *Eureka* in the *Illustrated Monthly Courier* offers an entirely different tone from M'Makin's earlier comments. In all likelihood, it was the prospectus for the *Illustrated Monthly Courier* that Poe was seeking in his letter to Hirst of May 3 (O 2:663–65). Other Poe-related items in the magazine include Hirst's "Berenice" (in the July issue), Christopher Cryptograph's (Hirst's?) "Speculations in Autography" (in the July and August issues), a reprint of "Ligeia" (in the August issue), and a reprint of "The Coliseum" (in the December issue). The first of the two installments of "Speculations" includes Poe's signature and the corresponding analysis. Relevant archives include the American Antiquarian Society and the Boston Public Library. For more information on Hirst, including letters relating to the unidentified *Illustrated Monthly Courier*, see Helen Lucille Watts, "The Life and Writings of Henry Beck Hirst of Philadelphia" (master's thesis, Columbia University, 1925), esp. 24–29.

39. Discussing the Mackenzies' having taken in the Lanier sisters in 1849, Flora Lapham Mack wrote that the Mattox sisters—whom the Mackenzies had taken in years earlier—had by then left, "my mother and her sister's [sic] having married and gone away long before this time" (Flora Lapham Mack to William Lanier Washington, February 29, 1908, collection of the author).

40. I draw here on the advertisement for the auction of the Darby Town farm. See ["Very Valuable and highly Productive Farm of 193 acres"], *Richmond Daily Dispatch,* October 13, 1862, [3] (Virginia Chronicle). The overseer, Andrews, is mentioned in the question-and-answer portion of the correspondence between Flora Lapham Mack and William Lanier Washington (collection of the author). Here further information on the Darby Town farm is provided.

41. For Mackenzie's "owning" eleven slaves, see John H. Mackenzie, Henrico County Personal Property Tax Records, 1848, Reel 175 (Lower District of Henrico County, Book A). Five of the enslaved were above twelve years old; six more were above sixteen years old. For the use of the phrase "average racism" as applied to Poe, see Terence Whalen, *Edgar Allan Poe and the Masses: The Political Economy of Literature in Antebellum America* (Princeton, NJ: Princeton University Press, 1999), 111–46.

42. For information on Duncan Lodge, see Mary Wingfield Scott, *Houses of Old Richmond* (Richmond, VA: The Valentine Museum, 1941), 215–17. Particularly useful early items are "Duncan Lodge for Sale," *Richmond Enquirer,* April 25, 1851, [3] (America's Historical Newspapers); and the July 4, 1853, document of purchase of Duncan Lodge from Miss Jane Mackenzie (Jane Scott Mackenzie's sister-in-law) by Alexander R. Holladay and Henry P. Poindexter, with a plat, a surveyor's sketch of the property (Library of Virginia). The most substantial collection of material relating to the Mackenzies and Duncan Lodge is held by the Poe Museum of Richmond.

43. A listing of members of the Duncan Lodge household is in the *1850 United States Federal Census* (available online). For Tom Mackenzie's graduation from the Thomas Jefferson Medical College in Philadelphia in 1848, I rely on Andrea Cherenack, university registrar, in an email of February 11, 2014. Tom wrote a graduation thesis on "The Use of Sulphuric Ether," according to Kelsey Duinkerken by way of David R. Clawson, senior associate university registrar, in an email of March 10, 2014. Tom was listed as one of Virginia's new doctors from the Jefferson

Medical College in "More Doctors," *Richmond Enquirer*, April 11, 1848, [1] (America's Historical Newspapers). Martha Mackenzie's marriage to William P. Byrd took place on October 5, 1848. Mary Mackenzie Jones died, with her infant, on September 21, 1844. (I rely on the Mackenzie Family Bible at the Virginia Museum of History & Culture.) Susan Archer Weiss tells the story of the leapfrog incident in *The Home Life of Poe* (New York: Broadway, 1907), 166. The quoted passage on Duncan Lodge is drawn from Flora Lapham Mack to William Lanier Washington, January 27, 1908, collection of the author. The mention of Poe's writing at the round desk in the hall of Duncan Lodge is offered by Edward Byrd Armistead in an unpublished interview, conducted by Denise B. Bethel and Bruce English, available on audiotape through the Poe Museum.

44. According to the *1850 U. S. Federal Census* "Slave Schedules," Mrs. Jane Mackenzie had five female slaves (https://www.ancestry.com).

45. Parke Vanparke, *Discursions and Diversions* (Philadelphia: Jas. B. Rogers, 1866), 263. That this recitation took place in 1848 rather than 1849 is clear from the author's specifying a time "shortly after the appearance of 'Ulalume.'" Presumably this chapter in the Vanparke book, "Edgar A. Poe," is the same as "Van Park's Defense of Edgar A. Poe," a copy of which was owned by J. H. Whitty (Mary E. Phillips, *Edgar Allan Poe—The Man*, 2 vols. [Chicago: John C. Winston, 1926], 2:1309). Discussing "Ulalume," T. O. Mabbott offered in brief the same story as Vanparke but added in a note, "I do not recall seeing the Mackenzie story in print; I was told it in Richmond" (M 1:415n). Nonetheless, a copy of the print source is in the Mabbott Poe Collection at the University of Iowa Libraries.

46. "Reminiscences of E. A. Poe. A Louisville Lady Who Thirty Years Ago Was His Intimate Friend—His Life in Richmond, His Readings and His Behavior in Society," *New Orleans Times* (from the *New York World*), March 25, 1878, 2 (America's Historical Newspapers). See also John Henry Ingram's Poe Collection, Albert & Shirley Small Special Collections Library, University of Virginia, Charlottesville, Item 730.

47. "Reminiscences of E. A. Poe."

48. For Whitman's writing in 1859 that Poe had visited Royster in 1848, see Sarah Helen Whitman to Julia Deane Freeman, January 20, 1859, in *The Correspondence of Sarah Helen Whitman to Julia Deane Freeman: Writer to Writer, Woman to Woman*, ed. Catherine Kunce (Newark: University of Delaware Press, 2014), 69–70. Whitman states here that Poe was then planning to propose to Royster. For Whitman's writing in 1872 that Poe had visited Royster in 1848, see R. H. Stoddard, "Life of Edgar Allan Poe," in *The Works of Edgar Allan Poe*, 6 vols. (New York: A. C. Armstrong, 1884), 1:155–56. Elmira Royster, in her recollection, did not specify an 1848 visit (see Edward V. Valentine's 1875 transcription of his interview with her, "Edgar A. Poe," at The Valentine in Richmond, partially quoted in Arthur Hobson Quinn, *Edgar Allan Poe: A Critical Biography* [New York: D. Appleton, 1941], 628–29). However, there seems little reason to doubt Whitman. Thomas and Jackson accept the 1848 visit (746), and so does Kenneth Silverman in *Edgar A. Poe: Mournful and Neverending Remembrance* (New York: HarperCollins, 1991), 352–53.

49. For the subscription list itself, see Alexander G. Rose III and Jeffrey Alan Savoye, eds., *Such Friends as These: Edgar Allan Poe's List of Subscribers and Contributors*

to His Dream Magazine (Baltimore, MD: Enoch Pratt Free Library, Edgar Allan Poe Society, and Library of the University of Baltimore, 1986).

50. Quinn, *Edgar Allan Poe: A Critical Biography*, 568.
51. For the 1849 version, see ibid., 569–70. For the 1860 version, see Thomas Dimmock, "Notes on Poe," *Century Magazine*, June 1895, 316. It is possible that in the late summer of 1848 Poe shared quarters with the *Richmond Whig* editor Hugh Pleasants (see George E. Woodberry, *The Life of Edgar Allan Poe*, 2 vols. [Boston: Houghton Mifflin, 1909], 2:271; Phillips, *Edgar Allan Poe—The Man*, 2:1306; and Thomas and Jackson, *The Poe Log*, 749).
52. Dimmock, "Notes on Poe," 316.
53. As Poe notes, "The Rationale of Verse" drew in part upon his 1843 "Notes upon English Verse" (L2 80n); it would appear in the October and November 1848 issues of the *Southern Literary Messenger*. The review of the Lewis book appeared in the August 1848 *Democratic Review* and would appear in the September 1848 issue of the *Southern Literary Messenger*. Poe mentioned Thompson's acceptance of both pieces in his August 5, 1848, letter to Maria Clemm (O 2:683). Thompson noted in his October 17, 1848, letter to Philip Pendleton Cooke having taken Poe's "The Rationale of Verse" but wrote that he considered the acceptance "an act of charity" given that the piece was "too bizarre and too technical for the general reader" (Quinn, *Edgar Allan Poe: A Critical Biography*, 568).
54. For Poe's acknowledgment of his challenge of Daniel in his August 29, 1849, letter to Maria Clemm, see O 2:830. The full letter is available at https://www.eapoe.org. For Thomas and Jackson's inference about the duel, based on Daniel's January 1849 announcement of the engagement of Poe and Sarah Helen Whitman, see Thomas and Jackson, *The Poe Log*, 750.
55. For Whitman's response to Poe's comments about her and his poem to her, see Sarah Helen Whitman to John H. Ingram, March 6, 1874, in *Poe's Helen Remembers*, 61. See also her September 30, 1872, letter to R. H. Stoddard in Stoddard, "Life of Edgar Allan Poe," in *Works of Edgar Allan Poe*, 1:155. The former letter mentions six lines; the latter letter mentions two stanzas. She quotes the full two stanzas in a letter to Julia Deane Freeman (Sarah Helen Whitman to Julia Deane Freeman, January 20, 1859, in *The Correspondence of Sarah Helen Whitman and Julia Deane Freeman*, ed. Kunce, 70). Mrs. Whitman again recounts her meeting with Maria J. McIntosh in Sarah Helen Whitman to John H. Ingram, February 14, 1875, in *Poe's Helen Remembers*, 255–56.
56. Whitman mentions Poe's poem as "Lines to Helen" in her September 30, 1872, letter to Stoddard.
57. For the history of Poe's use of the pseudonym "Edward S. T. Grey," see Burton R. Pollin, "Poe as Edward S. T. Grey," *Ball State University Forum* 14, no. 3 (1973): 44–46.

23. "The Passionate Throbbings of My Heart"

1. See Richard H. Stoddard, "Life of Edgar Allan Poe," in *The Works of Edgar Allan Poe*, 6 vols. (New York: A. C. Armstrong, 1884), 1:156; and Dwight Thomas and

David K. Jackson, *The Poe Log: A Documentary Life of Edgar Allan Poe, 1809–1849* (Boston: G. K. Hall, 1987), 754.

2. For the dates, see Stoddard, "Life of Edgar Allan Poe," 1:156; and O 2:697. The evening gathering of her friends is mentioned in Sarah Helen Whitman to John H. Ingram, February 14, 1875, in *Poe's Helen Remembers*, ed. John Carl Miller (Charlottesville: University Press of Virginia, 1979), 256. For the account of the embrace and the kiss, see John W. Robertson, *Edgar A. Poe: A Study* (San Francisco: n.p., 1921), 393–94. For the visit to the Providence Athenaeum, see Sarah Helen Whitman to John H. Ingram, April 10, 1874, in *Poe's Helen Remembers*, 116–17. The visit to Swan Point Cemetery is in Mary E. Phillips, *Edgar Allan Poe—The Man* (Chicago: John C. Winston, 1926), 2:1317. See also Poe's October 1, 1848, letter to Whitman (O 2:692–93).

3. Sarah Helen Whitman mentions the gift of the double volume (Whitman to John H. Ingram, April 21, [18]74, in *Poe's Helen Remembers*, 122–23). The inscription to her is provided in *The Stephen H. Wakeman Collection of Books of Nineteenth Century American Writers* (New York: American Art Association, 1924), Lot 948. The volumes of the *Broadway Journal* are noted by Whitman to John H. Ingram, February 11, 1874, in *Poe's Helen Remembers*, 22. For more on the *Broadway Journal*, see Whitman to Ingram, February 16, 1874, ibid., 28, and Whitman to Ingram, 27 March [18]74, ibid., 93–94. For the argument that not all of Poe's contributions to the *Broadway Journal* were marked with a "P," see William Doyle Hull II, "A Canon of the Critical Works of Edgar Allan Poe with a Study of Poe as Editor and Reviewer" (PhD diss., University of Virginia, 1941), 518–19. For Poe's showing Whitman the manuscript of his July lecture in Lowell, see Sarah Helen Whitman to Maria Clemm, February 3, [1852–54?], in *Edgar Allan Poe Letters and Documents in the Enoch Pratt Free Library*, ed. Arthur H. Quinn and Richard H. Hart (New York: Scholars' Facsimiles & Reprints, 1941), 39–40. Poe gave her pages of the manuscript that referred to her.

4. That Poe told Mrs. Whitman the story of his life may be inferred from her letters to Maria Clemm (H 17:422–30) and to Ingram (see, for example, Sarah Helen Whitman to John H. Ingram, March 27, [18]74 and April 2, 1874, in *Poe's Helen Remembers*, 95, 104). With regard to Poe's reading "Ulalume" aloud, see Sarah Helen Whitman to John H. Ingram, August 18, 1874, ibid., 205.

5. Sarah Helen Whitman to John H. Ingram, January 7, 1875, in *Poe's Helen Remembers*, 246.

6. Stoddard, "Life of Edgar Allan Poe," 156.

7. Whitman wrote to Ingram that Poe had sent her a lock of his hair in "one [letter] written after his first visit to Providence" (Sarah Helen Whitman to John H. Ingram, May 14, [18]74, in *Poe's Helen Remembers*, 156). This suggests the October 1 letter, which Thomas and Jackson stipulate in *The Poe Log* (759–60). However, Burton R. Pollin and Jeffrey A. Savoye suggest that the lock accompanied the October 18 letter (O 2:715n). Whitman made reference to sending Ingram passages from both letters (Whitman to Ingram, March 20, [18]74 and March 23, [1874], in *Poe's Helen Remembers*, 87–90). The letter with reference to Mrs. Stanard, which Whitman mentions to Ingram, is that of October 1 (see O 2:694). According to the Lilly Library, however, the lock of hair is associated with

an envelope sent by Poe to Whitman on November 8 (email from Erin Chiparo, March 10, 2022).

8. The italics have been added by Poe. Also, he substitutes "thy heart" for "that heart."
9. For Poe's private disparagement of Sarah Anna Lewis, see Marie Louise Shew Houghton to John Ingram, April 3, 1875, in *Building Poe Biography*, ed. John Carl Miller (Baton Rouge: Louisiana State University Press, 1977), 120.
10. I rely on Sarah Helen Whitman to John H. Ingram, October 25, 1875, in *Poe's Helen Remembers*, 346. See also her quoted letter to Richard H. Stoddard in Stoddard, "Life of Edgar Allan Poe," 156.
11. *Lincoln Day by Day: A Chronology 1809–1865*, ed. Earl Schenk Miers, vol. 1: *1809–1848*, ed. William E. Barringer (Washington, DC: Lincoln Sesquicentennial Commission, 1960), 320.
12. Sarah Helen Whitman to John H. Ingram, June 25, 1875[?], in *Poe's Helen Remembers*, 311–12. See also 346.
13. Frederick W. Coburn, "Poe as Seen by the Brother of 'Annie,'" *New England Quarterly* 16, no. 3 (1943): 471. A related piece is Fred B. Freeman Jr., "Poe's Lowell Trips," *Poe Studies* 4, no. 2 (1971): 23.
14. William F. Gill, *The Life of Edgar Allan Poe* (New York: D. Appleton, 1877), 211–12.
15. Coburn, "Poe as Seen by the Brother of 'Annie,'" 473–74.
16. See Sarah Helen Whitman to John H. Ingram, October 25, 1875, in *Poe's Helen Remembers*, 346–47. Whitman mentions that Mrs. Locke told her that Poe was "nervous & abstracted" while he waited for her letter (347).
17. Annie Richmond to John Ingram, February 5, 1877, in *Building Poe Biography*, 163.
18. See Annie Richmond to John Ingram, January 1, 1877, in *Building Poe Biography*, 157; and Richmond to Ingram, December 30, [18]77, ibid., 181.
19. Annie Richmond to John Ingram, February 12, 1878, in *Building Poe Biography*, 185. She soon came to resent Ingram's publishing her letters from Poe.
20. Sarah Helen Whitman to John H. Ingram, October 25, 1875, in *Poe's Helen Remembers*, 346–47.
21. Ostrom conjectures that Poe may have visited Lowell in December, based on a fragmentary letter from Poe to Maria Clemm (O 2:1263; see also John Ward Ostrom, "Revised Check List of the Correspondence of Edgar Allan Poe," in *Studies in the American Renaissance 1981*, ed. Joel Myerson [Boston: Twayne, 1981], 241). However, I find more persuasive that this fragment relates to Poe's October/November visit to Lowell, as Thomas and Jackson have inferred (763).
22. Whitman to Ingram, October 25, 1875, in *Poe's Helen Remembers*, 347; O 2:718–19.
23. Whitman left two reminiscences of this experience. One of these is Whitman to Ingram, October 25, 1875, in *Poe's Helen Remembers*, 347–48; the other one is Whitman to S. E. R. [Sallie E. Robins], 1860, included in a letter from Whitman to George W. Eveleth, January 17, 1866, in *Building Poe Biography*, 220–21.
24. On Mr. MacFarlane, see Whitman to Ingram, October 25, 1875, in *Poe's Helen Remembers*, 348. For scholarly treatment of this image, see Michael J. Deas, *The Portraits and Daguerreotypes of Edgar Allan Poe* (Charlottesville: University Press of Virginia, 1988), 36–41. The phrase "darkness visible," as aforementioned, comes

from book 1 (line 63) of John Milton's *Paradise Lost*. For Whitman's remarks on the daguerreotype, see Sarah Helen Whitman to John H. Ingram, February 11, 1874, in *Poe's Helen Remembers*, 22.

25. Whitman to Ingram, October 25, 1875, in *Poe's Helen Remembers*, 348.
26. Ibid. Stoddard, "Life of Edgar Allan Poe," 157.
27. Whitman to Ingram, March 20, 18[74], in *Poe's Helen Remembers*, 88.
28. Stoddard, "Life of Edgar Allan Poe," 157. See also Stanley T. Williams, "New Letters about Poe," *Yale Review*, n.s., vol. 14, no. 4 (1925): 761–62.
29. For full treatment of the "Whitman daguerreotype," see Deas, *The Portraits and Daguerreotypes of Edgar Allan Poe*, 42–45.
30. Sarah Helen Whitman to John H. Ingram, February 11, 1874, in *Poe's Helen Remembers*, 22.
31. Sarah Helen Whitman to John H. Ingram, March 16, 18[74], in *Poe's Helen Remembers*, 76–78. For "To Arcturus," see John E. Reilly, "Poe in Imaginative Literature: A Study of American Fiction, Drama, and Poetry Devoted to Edgar Allan Poe or His Works" (PhD diss., University of Virginia, 1965), 190. For a recent edition of Sarah Helen Whitman's works, see *Break Every Bond: Sarah Helen Whitman in Providence*, ed. Brett Rutherford (Pittsburgh, PA: Yogh & Thorn, 2019). See also Rutherford's *Last Flowers: The Romance and Poems of Edgar Allan Poe & Sarah Helen Whitman*, 4th ed., expanded and revised (Pittsburgh, PA: Poet's Press, 2011).
32. Maria Clemm to Annie Richmond, [November-December 1848], in *Building Poe Biography*, 25.
33. Sarah Helen Whitman to John H. Ingram, May 11, 1874, in *Poe's Helen Remembers*, 154–55; Sarah Helen Whitman to Mary E. Hewitt, October 10, 1850, in Williams, "New Letters," 769.
34. For recent scholarly treatment of the Poe letter to Valentine, see Jeffrey A. Savoye, "Some Updates on Poe's Correspondence, with a New Letter," *Edgar Allan Poe Review* 13, no. 1 (2012): 9–10; Christopher P. Semtner, "Poe in Richmond: Poe's Appeal to Edward Valentine," *Edgar Allan Poe Review* 20, no. 2 (2019): 329–36; and Jeffrey A. Savoye, "Letter to the Editor," *Edgar Allan Poe Review* 21, no. 1 (2020): 169–70. A note by Valentine makes clear that he wasn't going to offer Poe the requested support for "The Stylus." For Susan Archer Talley Weiss's comment, see "Reminiscences of Edgar Allan Poe," *New York Independent*, August 25, 1904, 1013 (https://www.eapoe.org).
35. For Poe at the office of the *American Metropolitan Magazine*, see Sarah Helen Whitman to Mary E. Hewitt, October 4, 1850, in Williams, "New Letters," 768; for Poe at the studio of Frederic Church, see William James Stillman, *The Autobiography of a Journalist*, 2 vols. (Boston: Houghton, Mifflin, 1901), 1:116.
36. Poe asked for "The Philosophy of Composition," the November 1847 *Godey's* review of Hawthorne, and the April 1845 *Aristidean* review of Longfellow. The last was, I believe, co-written with Thomas Dunn English. For Poe's effort to distance himself somewhat from this work, see P 3:108.
37. For the legal document that Mrs. Power had created, see James A. Harrison and Charlotte F. Dailey, "Poe and Mrs. Whitman: New Light on a Romantic Episode," *Century Magazine*, n.s., vol. 55 (1909): 446.

38. Thomas and Jackson, *The Poe Log*, 778.
39. For the slander, see Rufus Wilmot Griswold, "Memoir of the Author," in *Poe in His Own Time: A Biographical Chronicle of His Life, Drawn from Recollections, Interviews, and Memoirs by Family, Friends, and Associates,* ed. Benjamin Franklin Fisher (Iowa City: University of Iowa Press, 2010), 138. For Whitman's comment, see Whitman to Ingram, October 25, 1875, in *Poe's Helen Remembers*, 348–49. For William J. Pabodie's comment, see H 17:413.
40. I rely on Thomas and Jackson, *The Poe Log*, 776–78, for the newspaper advertisements and comment; O 2:745 for Poe's judgment of the number of people in his audience; and H 17:413 for Pabodie's judgment. For an image of the Earl Hotel, see Phillips, *Edgar Allan Poe—the Man*, 2:1393.
41. Stephen H. Arnold to Mrs. Henry R. Chace, May 28, 1907, in Harrison and Dailey, "Poe and Mrs. Whitman," 447. We do not have the manuscript of the Providence lecture, but it is interesting to note that in the publication of a later version of "The Poetic Principle," Pinkney's poem, "Health," was followed by Thomas Moore's "Come Rest in This Bosom" (L2 189–91).
42. For Whitman's agreeing to an "immediate marriage," see Stoddard, "Life of Edgar Allan Poe," 158; as well as H 17:413. Her financial reliance on her mother and her mother's "reluctant consent" are mentioned in Sarah Helen Whitman to Mary E. Hewitt, [August-September] 1850, in Williams, "New Letters," 762. The signed December 22, 1848, document regarding transfer of property is in Harrison and Dailey, "Poe and Mrs. Whitman," 446. Poe would have understood well Power's enmity ahead of this trip, as his December 16, 1848, letter to Whitman makes clear (O 2:741).
43. Sarah Helen Whitman to Hewitt, [August-September] 1850, in Williams, "New Letters about Poe," 762.
44. Ibid.
45. Ibid.
46. Sarah Helen Whitman to John H. Ingram, July 21, 1874, in *Poe's Helen Remembers*, 193.
47. Sarah Helen Whitman to Mary E. Hewitt, [August-September] 1850, in Williams, "New Letters about Poe," 762.
48. Sarah Helen Whitman to John H. Ingram, May 1, 1874, in *Poe's Helen Remembers*, 145.
49. Ibid.
50. Ibid.
51. Ibid.
52. Harrison and Dailey, "Poe and Mrs. Whitman," 447.
53. Sarah Helen Whitman to John H. Ingram, December 31, 1876, in *Poe's Helen Remembers*, 464–65.
54. Sarah Helen Whitman to Mary E. Hewitt, [August-September] 1850, in Williams, "New Letters about Poe," 763.
55. John H. Ingram, *Edgar Allan Poe His Life, Letters, and Opinions*, 2 vols. (London: John Hogg, 1880), 2:201–2.
56. Thomas and Jackson, *The Poe Log*, 790; Sarah Helen Whitman to John H. Ingram, February 20, 1874, in *Poe's Helen Remembers*, 35.

57. Annie Richmond to John Ingram, January 14, [18]77, in *Building Poe Biography*, 159.
58. Annie Richmond to John Ingram, March 13, 1877, in *Building Poe Biography*, 165.
59. George Henry Lewes, *Ranthorpe*, edited, introduced, and annotated by Barbara Smalley (Athens: Ohio University Press, 1974), 173 (Dr. Neil Arnott) and 206–14 ("Night of the Murder"). For a brief consideration of other correspondences between *Ranthorpe* and Poe's life, see Selma B. Brody, "Percy Ranthorpe and Edgar Allan Poe: Surprising Parallels," *George Eliot, George Henry Lewes Newsletter* 10 (1987): 8–10.
60. Poe had also sent the first version of "The Bells," a substantially different poem than the longer version, to the *Union Magazine*.
61. Perhaps Poe's March 1 letter to Annie's sister Sarah helped his effort to persuade the Richmonds to resist the allegations of the Lockes (see O 2:779).
62. For the anticipation of "A Valentine," see "To Our Correspondents," *Flag of Our Union*, February 24, 1849, [3]. For the poem itself, see Edgar A. Poe, "A Valentine," ibid., March 3, 1849, [2]. The asterisked note immediately follows. The solution to the acrostic was provided in "The Key to the Valentine," ibid., March 10, 1849, [3], and successful decrypters were "H. C. B., Emma H., and some other correspondents" as reported in "The Valentine by Edgar A. Poe," ibid., March 10, 1849, [3]. I rely for my discussion of Poe's works in the *Flag of Our Union* on my own run of the newspaper and the online run available through the Library of Congress website. There was some question about the publication of "A Valentine" in the March issue of *Sartain's Union Magazine*, but Frederick Gleason, who had requested an explanation from Poe, considered it "full and satisfactory." Poe had given the poem to a Mr. De Graw, who had planned a magazine but who left for California—leaving Poe to infer that the poem was his again. But unbeknownst to Poe, De Graw had passed it on to Sartain ("That Valentine, by Poe," *Flag of Our Union*, March 17, 1849, [3]). See also Poe to Annie Richmond, March 1 [?], 1849 (O 2:780). The earlier version of "A Valentine" had been published in the *New York Evening Mirror* of February 21, 1846, but Poe may not have known this (M 1:387).
63. Early mention of the March 1849 issue of the *Southern Literary Messenger* is "Southern Literary Messenger," *Richmond Whig*, March 6, 1849, [4] (America's Historical Newspapers). The review of *A Fable for Critics* is listed here.
64. Quoted by Burton R. Pollin, "Theodore Roosevelt to the Rescue of the Poe Cottage," *Mississippi Quarterly* 34, no. 1 (1980): 57 (ProQuest).
65. "Castle by the Sea," *Southern Literary Messenger* (March 1849): 147–48. The work was translated from John Ludwig Uhland by one "C. C. L." of Staunton, Virginia—presumably Charles Carter Lee (Benjamin Blake Minor, *The Southern Literary Messenger 1834–1864* [New York: Neale, 1905], 240).
66. "The Present Number," *Flag of Our Union*, March 17, 1849, [3]. Also appearing in this issue was Frances Sargent Osgood; her contribution was "A Love Song of Scotland."
67. The Duyckinck piece, discussed by Mabbott (M 3:1343–44), was titled "Barbarities of the Theatre" and appeared in the *Broadway Journal* on February 1, 1845.
68. Sarah Helen Whitman, *Poems* (Boston: Houghton, Osgood, 1879), 77. The poem first appeared in the *American Metropolitan Magazine* for February 1849 (Sarah

Helen Whitman to John H. Ingram, February 20, 1874, in *Poe's Helen Remembers*, 35–36). See also Stoddard, "Life of Edgar Allan Poe," 1:159; and Williams, "New Letters about Poe," 769–70.

69. For a facsimile of the manuscript, see "For Annie," *Bookman* (London) 35 (1909): 190. Annie Richmond discussed this manuscript in Annie Richmond to John Ingram, January 8, 1878, and February 5, 1878, in *Building Poe Biography*, 182–84.

70. For an interesting consideration of "Von Kempelen and His Discovery," see Burton R. Pollin, "Poe in 'Von Kempelen and His Discovery,'" in *Discoveries in Poe* (Notre Dame, IN: University of Notre Dame Press, 1970), 166–89, 277–84.

71. See M 1:461–63; as well as Burton R. Pollin, "Poe's 'Eldorado' Viewed as a Song of the West," *Prairie Schooner* 46 (1972): 228–35; and "Poe as a Writer of Songs," *American Renaissance Literary Report: An Annual* 6 (1992): 58–66.

72. "To Our Correspondents," *Flag of Our Union*, April 21, 1849, [3].

73. For a facsimile of the poem "For Annie" from the *Flag of Our Union* (with the first half appearing side by side with the second half), see John W. Robertson, *Commentary on the Bibliography of Edgar A. Poe* (the first volume being *Bibliography of the Writings of Edgar A. Poe*) (San Francisco: Russian Hill Private Press, 1934), facing 272.

74. I quote the stanzas as they appeared in the *Flag of Our Union;* their order was reversed in subsequent versions (M 1:455–59).

75. Sarah Helen Whitman wrote that Annie actually tended Poe after a lapse in Lowell (Sarah Helen Whitman to John H. Ingram, January 7, 1875, John Henry Ingram's Poe Collection, Albert & Shirley Small Special Collections Library, University of Virginia, Charlottesville, Item 193). Whether this was only her inference we do not know.

76. I quote the text from the *Flag of Our Union;* modest revisions are evident in subsequent versions (M 1:455–59).

24. "All May Yet Go Well"

1. Eugene L. Didier to Sarah Helen Whitman, June 26, 1876, Manuscripts Department, Lilly Library, Indiana University, Bloomington.

2. For information on E. H. N. Patterson, see *Some Letters of Edgar Allan Poe to E. H. N. Patterson of Oquawka, Illinois, With Comments by Eugene Field* (Chicago: Caxton Club, 1898); as well as Francis Higgins, "The Man from Oquawka," *Americana* 20 (1926): 519–33; Higgins, "'Sniktau,' Pioneer Journalist," *Colorado Magazine* 5 (1928): 102–8; and M. D. McElroy, "Poe's Last Partner: E. H. N. Patterson of Oquawka, Illinois," *Papers on Language and Literature* 7 (1971): 252–71. For Poe's list of subscribers to "The Stylus," see Alexander G. Rose III and Jeffrey Alan Savoye, eds., *Such Friends as These: Edgar Allan Poe's List of Subscribers and Contributors to His Dream Magazine* (Baltimore, MD: Enoch Pratt Free Library, Edgar Allan Poe Society, and the Library of the University of Baltimore, 1986). For Poe's planning "The Stylus" in his final week, see Susan Archer Talley Weiss, "The Last Days of Edgar A. Poe," *Scribner's Magazine*, March 1878, 713–14 (https://www.eapoe.org).

3. For an early comment on reversibility in Poe's sentences, see William Carlos Williams, *In the American Grain* (1925; New York: New Directions, 1956), 221–22. For scholarly comment on the quoted chiastic sentence from "X-ing a Paragrab," see Leroy Perkins and Joseph A. Dupras, "Mystery and Meaning in Poe's 'X-ing a Paragrab,'" *Studies in Short Fiction* 27, no. 4 (1990): 491–92; Tom Quirk, "What If Poe's Humorous Tales Were Funny? Poe's 'X-ing a Paragrab' and Twain's 'Journalism in Tennessee,'" *Studies in American Humor*, n.s., vol. 3, no. 2 (1995): 45; Richard Kopley, *The Threads of "The Scarlet Letter"* (Newark: University of Delaware Press, 2003), 109; William E. Engel, *Early Modern Poetics in Melville and Poe: Memory, Melancholy, and the Emblematic Tradition* (Farnham, Surrey, UK: Ashgate, 2012), 141–42; and Henri Justin, "'X-ing a Paragrab': *Guess What* That *Is About If You Can!*" *Poe Studies* 53 (2020): 109–10.
4. John H. Ingram, *Edgar Allan Poe His Life, Letters, and Opinions*, 2 vols. (London: John Hogg, 1880), 2:215.
5. The mid- to late May 1839 letter to Burton is listed in O 2:1184. For Burton's response, see Arthur Hobson Quinn, *Edgar Allan Poe: A Critical Study* (New York: D. Appleton Century, 1941), 279–81. Quinn effectively demonstrates Griswold's distortion of this letter. The mid-May 1843 letter to William Poe is listed in O 2:1215. For the response by William Poe, see H 17:145–46. The June 1845 letter to Anne C. Lynch is listed in O 2:1230. For the response from Lynch, see H 17:258–59.
6. See *Some Letters of Edgar Allan Poe*, 15–21; or H 17:352–55.
7. For a beautiful facsimile of this title page, see *Some Letters of Edgar Allan Poe*, facing p. 16. An image is also available in Dwight Thomas and David K. Jackson, *The Poe Log: A Documentary Life of Edgar Allan Poe, 1809–1849* (Boston: G. K. Hall, 1987), 806.
8. For the length of Poe's third visit, see Frederick W. Coburn, "Poe as Seen by the Brother of 'Annie,'" *New England Quarterly* 16, no. 3 (1943): 474. Annie herself stated that Poe copied out "The Bells" for her during this visit (Annie Richmond to John Ingram, November 21, 1876, in *Building Poe Biography*, ed. John Carl Miller [Baton Rouge: Louisiana State University Press, 1977], 155). For the full cryptogram, see Rev. Warren H. Cudworth, "Cryptography—Mr Poe as a Cryptographer," *Lowell Weekly Journal*, April 19, 1850, 2 (https://www.eapoe.org). For Poe's visit to the school, see Coburn, "Poe as Seen by the Brother of 'Annie,'" 474–75; and for Miss Butterworth, see Fred B. Freeman Jr., "The Identity of Poe's 'Miss B.,'" *American Literature* 39, no. 3 (1967): 389–91; "A Note on Poe's 'Miss B.'" *American Literature*, 43, no. 1 (1971): 115–17; and "Poe's 'Miss B.' and 'Annie,'" *American Notes and Queries*, 12 (1974): 79–80. Also relevant is Freeman's "Poe's Lowell Trips," *Poe Studies* 4, no. 2 (1971): 23–24. As always, the authority on Poe portraiture is Michael J. Deas (see his *The Portraits and Daguerreotypes of Edgar Allan Poe* [Charlottesville: University Press of Virginia, 1989], 47–54).
9. William F. Gill, *The Life of Edgar Allan Poe* (New York: D. Appleton, 1877), 213. Although the time markers in Sarah Heywood's sketch allow for a reader to place the incident in the fall ("A few months later" [than his July lecture] [211], "in the early autumn evening" [212], "Later in the evening" [212], and "The next morning" [213]), the reference to "the eyes that then looked their last upon that

finished scholar, and winning, refined gentleman" suggests the June farewell that Poe related. Given his comments, Sarah couldn't have had her last look at Poe in the fall of 1848. Gill published Sarah Richmond's sketch despite her indicating to him that she wished to adapt it herself for magazine publication (see Annie Richmond to John Ingram, October 8, 1877, in *Building Poe Biography*, 173).

10. For a perceptive appreciation of "Landor's Cottage," see Barbara Cantalupo, *Poe and the Visual Arts* (University Park: Pennsylvania State University Press, 2014), 80–85.
11. Alvin Rosenfeld, "Description in Poe's 'Landor's Cottage,'" *Studies in Short Fiction* 4, no. 2 (1967): 265.
12. Thomas and Jackson, *The Poe Log*, 808.
13. Sarah Helen Whitman, "Lines," *Southern Literary Messenger* (June 1849): 362.
14. For the cited stowage passages, see John McLeod Murphy and W. N. Jeffers Jr., *Nautical Routine and Stowage, with Short Rules in Navigation* (New York: Henry Spear, 1849), part 3, "Stowage," 39, 40. For the date of this book's publication, see "Notice to Mariners. / Published This Day," *New York Evening Post*, June 5, 1849, [2] (America's Historical Newspapers). The inclusion of these passages from *Pym* is presented in Joan Tyler Mead, "Poe's 'Manual of "Seamanship,"'" in *Poe's Pym: Critical Explorations*, ed. Richard Kopley (Durham, NC: Duke University Press, 1992), 29–32, 283.
15. For the timing of Poe's writing his various manuscripts of "Annabel Lee," I rely on Jeffrey A. Savoye's presentation "'In Her Tomb by the Sounding Sea': A Radical Reconsideration of the Manuscripts of 'Annabel Lee,'" "Poe and Manuscripts" session, Fifth International Edgar Allan Poe Conference, "Poe Takes Boston," Boston, MA, April 9, 2022. The published version, by the same title, appears in *Edgar Allan Poe Review* 25, no. 1 (2024): 15–36.
16. Maria Clemm to Annie Richmond, August 4, [1849], in *Building Poe Biography*, 29.
17. Edgar Allan Poe, "Sonnet—To My Mother," *Flag of Our Union*, July 7, 1849, [2]. For the two subsequent versions, see M 1:466–67.
18. Edgar Allan Poe to Maria Clemm, August 29, 1849 (https://www.eapoe.org). The letter as it appears in the Ostrom edition (O 2:830–32) is incomplete.
19. Mayne Reid, "A Dead Man Defended," *Onward* (April 1869), 306 (https://www.eapoe.org).
20. N. P. Willis, "Death of Edgar A. Poe," in *Poe in His Own Time: A Biographical Chronicle of His Life, Drawn from Recollections, Interviews, and Memoirs by Family, Friends, and Associates*, ed. Benjamin F. Fisher (Iowa City: University of Iowa Press, 2010), 98.
21. Flora Lapham Mack to William Lanier Washington, March 31, 1908, collection of the author; [Mack for Washington], "Suggestions for the Third Chapter—Poe's Early Married Days," ibid.
22. Maria Clemm, "To the Reader," in *The Works of the Late Edgar Allan Poe*, 4 vols. (New York: J. S. Redfield, 1850–1856), 1:[iii].
23. Maria Clemm to Thomas Holley Chivers, December 13, 1852, *Chivers' Life of Poe*, ed. Richard Beale Davis (New York: E. P. Dutton, 1952), 71.
24. Marie Louise Shew Houghton to John Ingram, January 23, 1875, in *Building Poe Biography*, 95.

25. Marie Louise Shew Houghton to John Ingram, February 16, 1875, *Building Poe Biography,* 104.
26. Clemm, "To the Reader."
27. Houghton to Ingram, February 16, 1875, in *Building Poe Biography,* 105. For one negative assessment of Mrs. Clemm, see Burton R. Pollin, "Maria Clemm, Poe's Aunt: His Boon or His Bane," *Mississippi Quarterly* 48, no. 2 (1995): 211–24.
28. This incident involving Moore is presented in M 1:475, where the *New York Times* source is mentioned; I find it also in "'Annabel Lee' in the Handwriting of Poe," *Minneapolis Journal,* January 24, 1909, 13, https://www.newspapers.com.
29. In his April 1844 trip from Philadelphia to New York, Poe had taken a train to Perth Amboy and then a steamboat the rest of the way (O 1:437).
30. Maria Clemm to Annie Richmond, August 4, [1849], in *Building Poe Biography,* 29.
31. For iterations of Sartain's story, see John Sartain: "Reminiscences of Edgar Allan Poe," *Lippincott's Magazine,* March 1889, 411–15; *The Reminiscences of a Very Old Man* (New York: D. Appleton, 1899), 205–12; and "Poe's Last Days," in Richard Tuerk, "John Sartain and E. A. Poe," *Poe Studies* 4, no. 2 (1971): 21–23. For the specific location of the engraving room, see Joseph Jackson, *Literary Landmarks of Philadelphia* (Philadelphia: David McKay, 1939), 274.
32. I rely primarily on Sartain, *Reminiscences,* 206–7. He refers to Poe's "mental overstrain" in "Poe's Last Days."
33. I draw from all three versions of Sartain's reminiscence. The quotation is from *Reminiscences,* 210.
34. Sartain, *Reminiscences,* 210. Poe stated that he was thought to have tried to pass a counterfeit bill, but Sartain states that the cause for imprisonment was "the drop too much." When Poe appeared before the mayor, he was recognized as "Poe, the poet," and, without the exacting of any financial penalty, he was released. Poe referred to his imprisonment in a letter to Maria Clemm (O 2:821) but maintained that he had not been drunk—that the cause had involved Virginia. No prison record has been found indicating that Poe was in fact there.
35. I draw primarily on Sartain, *Reminiscences,* 211–12.
36. For the unceasing fireworks, see "The Celebration of the Fourth," *North American,* July 6, 1849 (Nineteenth Century U.S. Newspapers). The advice of the Board of Health is noted in "Timely Recommendations," *Philadelphia Public Ledger,* June 30, 1849, [2], https://www.newspapers.com. For the president's proclamation, see "A Recommendation," *North American,* July 6, 1849; and "Public Humiliation," ibid., July 7, 1849 (Nineteenth Century U.S. Newspapers).
37. Maria Clemm to Annie Richmond, August 4, 1849, in *Building Poe Biography,* 29.
38. For Poe's walk with eleven-year-old Henry Graham Ashmead, see Mary Elizabeth Phillips, *Edgar Allan Poe—The Man,* 2 vols. (Chicago: John C. Winston, 1926), 2:1296–97. For the gift of "Annabel Lee" to Hirst, see M 1:475–76. For Poe's visit to George Lippard, I rely on T. C. Duncan Eaves, "Poe's Last Visit to Philadelphia," *American Literature* 26, no. 1 (1954): 44–51; as well as Emilio De Grazia, "The Life and Works of George Lippard" (PhD diss., Ohio State University, 1969). See also De Grazia's "Poe's Devoted Democrat, George Lippard," *Poe Studies* 6, no. 1 (1973): 6–8. For background on Lippard, see David S. Reynolds, *George Lippard* (Boston: Twayne, 1982).

39. [George Lippard], "Wirt Institute Lectures," *Philadelphia Citizen Soldier*, November 15, 1843, 301.
40. I rely here on Eaves, "Poe's Last Visit to Philadelphia," 46–47.
41. This passage is reprinted in De Grazia's "The Life and Works of George Lippard," 370; and his "Poe's Devoted Democrat, George Lippard," 8.
42. Eaves, "Poe's Last Visit to Philadelphia," 47.
43. De Grazia: "The Life and Works of George Lippard," 370, and "Poe's Devoted Democrat, George Lippard," 8.
44. George Lippard to Rufus W. Griswold, November 22, 1849, Griswold Papers, Rare Books Department, Boston Public Library (digital version). Lippard wrote, "It is but just to state, that C. C. Burr, John Sartain, L. A. Godey, S. D. Patterson, were the only persons in this city, whom (last summer), I could induce to give one cent to save Poe from Starvation. These gentlemen (and Mr. Miskey clerk of Sartain's I may add) aided in the most honorable manner."
45. Eaves, "Poe's Last Visit to Philadelphia," 48.
46. I draw primarily on De Grazia, "The Life and Works of George Lippard," 370; see, alternatively, his "Poe's Devoted Democrat, George Lippard," 8.
47. C. Chauncey Burr, "Character of Edgar A. Poe," *Nineteenth Century* (February 1852): 26 (https://www.eapoe.org).
48. I rely on De Grazia—especially the obituary as furnished in "Life and Works" and "Poe's Devoted Democrat"—as well as Thomas and Jackson, *The Poe Log*, 817. Poe wrote to Maria Clemm about finding his lost valise at the depot in Philadelphia, though his lectures were stolen (O 2:824); Eaves contends that the date of the search was July 13 ("Poe's Last Visit to Philadelphia," 49–50). Oddly, Lippard referred to looking for Poe's lost valise at the Philadelphia depot after Poe's death, and without success (Lippard to Griswold, November 22, 1849). Eaves suggests that perhaps the valise was never recovered but Poe did not want to worry Mrs. Clemm further. For the gift of *Eureka*, see Reynolds, *George Lippard*, 103. With regard to the purchase of the train ticket, Poe wrote to Maria Clemm, "B[urr] procured me a ticket as far as Baltimore" (O 2:826).
49. Maria Clemm to Annie Richmond, August 4, 1849, in *Building Poe Biography*, 29.
50. Edgar Allan Poe to Maria Clemm, August 29, 1849 (https://www.eapoe.org).
51. Susan Archer Weiss referred to Poe's attending to Elmira "immediately upon his arrival" in "Last Days of Edgar A. Poe," 710 (https://www.eapoe.org) and later wrote, "Poe's first visits on his arrival in Richmond had been to Mrs. Shelton" in her *Home Life of Poe* (New York: Broadway, 1907), 194.
52. "Poe and Elmira," The Valentine, Richmond, VA.
53. Thomas G. Mackenzie was born January 2, 1821 (Jane Mackenzie Miller [Mackenzie Family Vital Information], Harry Ransom Center, University of Texas at Austin). Susan Archer Weiss wrote, "After his [Poe's] wife's death she [Mrs. Shelton] was continually inquiring about him of Mr. Thos. Mackenzie" (Weiss, "Reminiscences of Edgar Allan Poe," *New York Independent*, August 25, 1904, 445 [https://www.eapoe.org]). She had earlier written, "Shortly after the death of his wife, an intimate friend wrote to him [Poe] that Mrs. Shelton often inquired after him, and suggested the plan which he somewhat later, when so much in need of money, came seriously to consider" (Weiss, "Last Days of

Edgar A. Poe," 710 [https://www.eapoe.org]). She later referred to "Dr. Gibbon Carter and Dr. Mackenzie" and "others of his intimate friends" (714). However, in her 1907 *Home Life of Poe*, Weiss stated that John H. Mackenzie had counseled Poe's approaching Elmira (158, 196, 197). Flora Lapham Mack was outraged by this contention, knowing that the eldest Mackenzie brother (later her stepfather) had been fiercely opposed to the match (Mack to Washington, March 31, 1908).

54. Eugene Didier to Sarah Helen Whitman, June 26, 1876, Manuscripts Department, Lilly Library, Indiana University, Bloomington.

55. Edward V. Valentine, "Edgar A. Poe Conversation with Mrs. Shelton," November 19, 1875, The Valentine, Richmond, VA. Regarding Elmira's appearance in 1849, see Weiss, *The Home Life of Poe*, 200. Mrs. Shelton was then thirty-nine years old.

56. For background on Duncan Lodge, see Mary Wingfield Scott, *Houses of Old Richmond* (Richmond, VA: Valentine Museum, 1941), 215–17. The 1850 Census for the Western District of Henrico County, Virginia, lists Tom as "Physician," Dick as "Farmer," William P. Byrd as "Lawyer," and Caleb Jones as in the "Woolen business." Also listed is the Byrds' baby daughter Jane (https://www.ancestry.com). Images of Mrs. Mackenzie and John H. Mackenzie are held by the Poe Museum, and Tom's appearance is given in his May 5, 1851, passport, also held by the Poe Museum. Flora Lapham Mack described Tom as "the walking encyclopedia," and she mentioned Richard as lame from birth (Mack to Washington, March 31, 1908).

57. John F. Carter, "Poe's Last Night in Richmond," *Lippincott's Magazine*, November 1902, 562–63.

58. Flora Lapham Mack felt competitive with Susan Archer Weiss—the younger woman had published extensively on Poe as Mack herself had not—and Mack argued to William Lanier Washington against Weiss's authority (Mack to Washington, April 15 and 22, 1908, collection of the author). Weiss can sometimes be unreliable, but scholars have disagreed about this matter, with Kenneth Silverman, for example, doubting her (*Edgar A. Poe Mournful and Never-ending Remembrance* [New York: HarperCollins, 1991], 516n) and T. O. Mabbott trusting her (M 1:353–54, 567). But it is clear that communication with Talley/Weiss was possible (see, in particular, "Miss Susan Archer Talley," *Greensboro Times*, December 3, 1859, 4, https://www.newspapers.com). William Lanier Washington visited Susan Archer Weiss in 1908, communicating with her by writing his questions, while she answered in a voice that was "unnatural and mechanical" and difficult to understand. He considered her unreliable in [Statement about a visit to Susan Archer Weiss], April 12, 1908, collection of the author, and "Untrustworthy Memorialists of Edgar Allan Poe: The Rev. Rufus Wilmot Griswold and Mrs. Susan Archer Weiss" [Poe Centenary Address], Special Collections, University of Virginia Library. He was, in part, conveying the views of his correspondent, Flora Lapham Mack. I do not share the dismissive attitude of Mack and Washington toward Weiss.

59. For Poe's cover letter to Weiss, see Weiss, "Reminiscences of Edgar A. Poe," *New York Independent*, May 5, 1904, 1013 (https://www.eapoe.org). For his comments on Weiss in the *Southern Literary Messenger*, see his review of *The Female Poets*

of America, by Rufus Wilmot Griswold, *Southern Literary Messenger* (February 1849): 126–27. See also H 11:157–59.

60. See Scott, *Houses of Old Richmond,* 190–92; and Weiss: "Edgar Allan Poe," *New York Weekly Review,* October 6, 1866, 2 (https://www.eapoe.org); "Last Days of Edgar A. Poe," 708; and "Reminiscences of Edgar A. Poe," August 25, 1904, 446.

61. See Weiss: "Edgar Allan Poe," 2; and "Last Days of Edgar A. Poe," 708. For her obituary of Poe, see "Edgar A. Poe," *Richmond Republican,* October 15, 1849, John Henry Ingram's Poe Collection, Albert & Shirley Small Special Collections Library, University of Virginia, Charlottesville, Item 65. For Susan Archer Talley's age at the time of Poe's visit, see John C. Miller, "The True Birthdate and the Hitherto Unpublished Deathdate of Susan Archer Talley Weiss," *Poe Studies* 10, no. 1 (1977): 29.

62. George Lippard to R. W. Griswold, November 22, 1849, Rare Books Department, Boston Public Library (online).

63. For Weiss's observation of Poe and Dr. Gibbon Carter at the American Hotel, see her "Reminiscences," August 25, 1904, 446. Poe identified the American Hotel as "expensive" in his August 29, 1849, letter to Maria Clemm (https://www.eapoe.org). For Poe's four reasons for his move to the Swan Tavern, see Weiss, "Last Days of Edgar A. Poe," 708. For the Swan Tavern in its glory days, see Samuel Mordecai, *Richmond in By-Gone Days* (1860; Richmond, VA, Dietz, 1946), 249–50.

64. Maria Clemm to Annie Richmond, July 30, 1849, in *Building Poe Biography,* 26–27. This information does not appear in the extracts published of Poe's letter to Maria Clemm of July 19, 1849, but it may have been in the full letter (no longer extant) or another letter from Poe to her in mid-July (see Burr, "Character of Edgar A. Poe," 30–31; and O 2:825–27).

65. Flora Lapham Mack to William Lanier Washington, February 29, 1908, collection of the author. The live-in governess is mentioned in "Data" ([Question-and-Answer Exchange of William Lanier Washington and Flora Lapham Mack], collection of the author). There was a "Miss Coen" at one time and a "Miss Yerby" at another time. Of the seven residents of Darby Town in 1849 whom I name here, only three—John, Louisa, and her mother Mary Lanier—are listed in the 1850 Census (https://www.ancestry.com). For the location of the home of William Lewis Lanier and Virginia Armistead Lanier, for the latter's death date, and for her daughter Jane Britney Lanier's birthdate, I rely on William Lanier Washington, "Untrustworthy Memorialists," 8–9.

66. William Lanier Washington, "Untrustworthy Memorialists," 9–10.

67. [Flora Lapham Mack for William Lanier Washington], "Suggestions for the Third Chapter—Poe's Early Married Days," collection of the author.

68. Henrico County Personal Property Tax Records—Reel 175, Lower District of Henrico Co. (Book A) (online).

69. Thomas and Jackson, *The Poe Log,* 820–21.

70. For Mrs. Mackenzie's promise of support for "The Stylus," see Weiss, "Reminiscences of Edgar A. Poe," May 5, 1904, 1013 (https://www.eapoe.org). Among those Poe knew in Richmond, Mrs. Mackenzie and Mrs. Julia Mayo Cabell were the first to make this promise. For Mrs. Mackenzie's furnishing detail for a piece

that Poe anticipated publishing in "The Stylus," see Weiss, *The Home Life of Poe*, 198. (T. O. Mabbott suggested that this might have been a sequel to "Landor's Cottage" [M 3:1327–28].) Poe evidently began a table of contents for the first issue of "The Stylus." Poe's statement of confidence in "The Stylus" to Mrs. Weiss is in her "Last Days of Edgar A. Poe," 709.

71. For the mayor's edict, see [Statement of Mayor William Lambert], *Richmond Whig*, August 3, 1849, [2] (America's Historical Newspapers). For the response of Richmonders to the president and the mayor urging a day of fasting, see "Friday Last," *Richmond Enquirer*, August 7, 1849, [2] (America's Historical Newspapers). There were, in fact, only five cases of cholera in Richmond at the time ("The Cholera," *Richmond Enquirer*, August 3, 1849, [2] [America's Historical Newspapers]).

72. George Lippard, [Cholera and Poverty in America, Oppression in Europe], *Quaker City Weekly*, July 21, 1849, rpt., David S. Reynolds, ed., *George Lippard, Prophet of Protest: Writings of an American Radical, 1822–1854* (New York: Peter Lang, 1986), 157.

73. For Poe's having been cared for by the Mackenzies after the first incident, see Weiss, "Last Days of Edgar A. Poe," 712. For the alternative story, that Poe was tended by Dr. George W. Rawlins (or Rawlings), see H 1:311–12; and J. H. Whitty, "Memoir," in *The Complete Poems of Edgar Allan Poe* (Boston: Houghton Mifflin, 1911), lxxiii. For Poe's having been tended by Dr. Tom Mackenzie and Dr. William Gibbon Carter at Duncan Lodge after the second incident and his having later made his pledge to resist drink to Dr. Carter, see Weiss, "Last Days of Edgar A. Poe," 712.

74. Weiss, "Last Days of Edgar A. Poe," 711, 712.

75. Flora Lapham Mack to William Lanier Washington, August 24, 1908, collection of the author.

25. "Hope for a Wretch Like Me"

1. The notice, which appeared in the *Richmond Daily Republican* and the *Richmond Whig*, appears in Dwight Thomas and David K. Jackson, *The Poe Log: A Documentary Life of Edgar Allan Poe, 1809–1849* (Boston: G. K. Hall, 1987), 825. I quote "Edgar A. Poe," *Richmond Republican*, August 17, 1849, 3, https://www.newspapers.com.

2. My sources on the Exchange Hotel are Mary Wingfield Scott, *Old Richmond Neighborhoods* (Richmond, VA: Whittet & Shepperson, 1950), 127, 129–30; and, for the quotation, "Reminiscences of E. A. Poe. A Louisville Lady Who Thirty Years Ago Was His Intimate Friend—His Life in Richmond, His Readings and His Behavior in Society," *New Orleans Times*, March 25, 1878, 2 (from the *New York World*) (America's Historical Newspapers). See also John Henry Ingram's Poe Collection, Albert & Shirley Small Library, University of Virginia, Charlottesville, Item 730.

3. John M. Daniel wrote, "A large audience was in attendance. Indeed, the concert room was completely filled" (Thomas and Jackson, *The Poe Log*, 827). For Poe's own comment, see Edgar Allan Poe to Maria Clemm, August 29, 1849 (https://www.eapoe.org). That Poe was accompanied by Mrs. Jane Clark is evident from "Reminiscences of E. A. Poe."

4. John Esten Cooke, *Poe as a Literary Critic,* ed. N. Bryllion Fagin (Baltimore, MD: Johns Hopkins Press, 1946), 2.
5. For John Esten Cooke's comment to his brother Philip Pendleton Cooke, see Thomas and Jackson, *The Poe Log,* 828. For the comment in the *Times,* see "Mr. Poe on the Poetic Principle," *New Orleans Crescent,* September 5, 1849, [2] (reprinted from the *Richmond Times* of August 21, 1849), https://www.newspapers.com.
6. Cooke, *Poe as a Literary Critic,* 3.
7. The reviews of Poe's lecture in the *Richmond Whig* and the *Richmond Daily Republican* appear in Thomas and Jackson, *The Poe Log,* 826. For the review in the *Richmond Times,* see "Mr. Poe on the Poetic Principle."
8. For the review in the *Richmond Semi-Weekly Examiner,* see Thomas and Jackson, *The Poe Log,* 826–27. Notably, an unknown writer stated in a contemporary newspaper piece on Thomas Moore, "We could not help reflecting upon the mournful vicissitudes of Time on hearing Mr. Poe recite at his recent lecture, those exquisite lines, 'Come rest in this bosom,' which, more than any other single composition of the author, have fastened themselves upon the memory of thousands" ("Thomas Moore," *Alexandria Gazette,* August 22, 1849, [1] [reprinted from the *Richmond Whig*] [America's Historical Newspapers]). A few months later, a writer stated of the lines of this song, "[T]heir tenderness is scarcely surpassed by any thing in the language; and there are states of mind with every one in which their repetition would bring tears" ("Gems from Moore's Irish Melodies. No. III.—Come Rest in This Bosom," *Graham's Magazine* 36, no. 3 [March 1850]: 221). Since the previous two installments in the short series were attributed to T. S. A., this item, too, may have been by T. S. A.—presumably T. S. Arthur.
9. Poe to Clemm, August 29, 1849 (https://www.eapoe.org).
10. For Poe's no longer visiting Elmira on Church Hill in mid-August, see Susan Archer Weiss, *The Home Life of Poe* (New York: Broadway, 1907), 195–96. See also Weiss: "Edgar A. Poe," *New York Herald,* April 26, 1876, 4; and "Reminiscences of Edgar Allan Poe," *New York Independent,* August 25, 1904, 444 (https://www.eapoe.org). Weiss tells the story of Poe's ignoring Elmira at his "last lecture in Richmond" "during the period of their estrangement." However, during the last lecture, Poe and Elmira were reconciled (Weiss, "Reminiscences," August 25, 1904, 445; see also *The Home Life of Poe,* 200). Perhaps Poe ignored Elmira at the earlier lecture.
11. Poe to Clemm, August 29, 1849 (https://www.eapoe.org).
12. Weiss, *The Home Life of Poe,* 196–97. See also Weiss, "Last Days of Edgar A. Poe," *Scribner's Magazine,* March 1878, 710 (https://www.eapoe.org). Poe writes to Maria Clemm on August 29, "Her [Elmira's] relations—her married daughter especially—are opposed to it [the marriage]—because their pecuniary interests will be injured—but she defies them & seems resolved" (https://www.eapoe.org). Flora Lapham Mack comments, "Her [Elmira's] brothers disapproved of Edgar to the end" (Mack to William Lanier Washington, September 17, 1908, Poe Museum). For Poe's mention of the "fortunate speculation," see, again, Poe to Clemm, August 29, 1849 (https://www.eapoe.org).
13. Weiss, "Last Days of Edgar A. Poe," 711. See also Weiss, *The Home Life of Poe,* 197.
14. Weiss, *The Home Life of Poe,* 197.

15. Weiss, "Edgar A. Poe," 4. See also Weiss: "Reminiscences of Edgar Allan Poe," 444; and *The Home Life of Poe,* 197. Poe's letters to Elmira have not survived. Her letters to Poe were returned to her by Neilson Poe (see Eugene Didier to Sarah Helen Whitman, June 26, 1876, Manuscripts Department, Lilly Library, Indiana University, Bloomington). These letters have also not survived; presumably, she destroyed them.
16. For the full letter in which Poe mentions the Shakespeare lecture, see Poe to Clemm, August 29, 1849 (https://www.eapoe.org). His meeting with Richard D. Sanxay is noted in J. H. Whitty, "Memoir," in *The Complete Poems of Edgar Allan Poe* (Boston: Houghton Mifflin, 1911), lxxxii–lxxxiii. Poe's visiting Joseph H. Clarke in Baltimore is given in "Edgar Allan Poe—Some Reminiscences of the Past by His Old School Teacher in Richmond," *Baltimore Sun,* February 14, 1896, 8 (America's Historical Newspapers).
17. For the full letter, see Poe to Clemm, August 29, 1849 (https://www.eapoe.org).
18. Ibid.
19. Ibid.
20. Ibid.
21. Ibid.
22. Ibid.
23. "Edgar A. Poe, Esq.," *Raleigh Times,* September 7, 1849, [3] (reprint from Richmond's weekly *The Banner of Temperance,* August 31, 1849), https://www.newspapers.com. See also Thomas and Jackson, *The Poe Log,* 829, 830. William J. Glenn left an account of Poe's joining the Sons of Temperance (Glenn to Edward V. Valentine, June 29, 1899, The Valentine, Richmond, VA). It is interesting to note that George Lippard critiqued the Sons of Temperance, arguing that the plight of the working class was the real cause of much intemperance (see "[The Social Roots of Intemperance]," *Quaker City Weekly,* November 3, 1849, reprinted in George Lippard, *George Lippard—Prophet of Protest: Writings of an American Radical, 1822–1854,* ed. David S. Reynolds [New York: Peter Lang, 1986], 187–88).
24. For the full letter, see Poe to Clemm, August 29, 1849 (https://www.eapoe.org). Perhaps Poe borrowed money for the ring from Mrs. Mackenzie, or Dr. Tom or Dick, or even Caleb Jones. Flora Lapham Mack states, in "Poe's Appearance and Personality" (collection of the author), that Poe sometimes borrowed from John, Tom, and Dick Mackenzie, as well as Caleb Jones. But John wouldn't have contributed in this case since he didn't even know of the engagement when the ring was bought—and he would have objected had he known.
25. See Philip Edward Phillips, "Engagement Ring—Elmira Royster Shelton," in *Edgar Allan Poe in 20 Objects from the Susan Jaffe Tane Collection,* ed. Gabrielle Dean and Richard Kopley (Baltimore, MD: Johns Hopkins Sheridan Libraries, 2016), 38–43; and *The Susan Jaffe Tane Collection at the Poe Museum Richmond, Virginia* (Richmond: Poe Museum, 2022), 14. See also Christopher P. Semtner, "Poe in Richmond: A Gift from Poe to Elmira Shelton," *Edgar Allan Poe Review* 22, no. 1 (2021): 206–12; and the website of the Poe Museum at https://www.poemuseum.org.
26. For the full letter, see Poe to Clemm, August 29, 1849 (https://www.eapoe.org).

27. Ibid.
28. Mary E. Phillips, *Edgar Allan Poe—The Man*, 2 vols. (Chicago: John C. Winston, 1926), 2:1448–49.
29. Weiss, "Last Days of Edgar A. Poe," 712.
30. Ibid., 713.
31. Susan Archer Weiss, "Edgar Allan Poe," *New York Weekly Review*, October 6, 1866, 2 (https://www.eapoe.org).
32. "Poe's Wonderful Interpreter. The Old Richmond Negro Whom the Poet Taught to Recite His Lines," *New York Sun*, August 1879, John H. Ingram's Poe Collection, Item 758. I infer that Poe taught James Stirling in the summer of 1849 rather than the summer of 1848 since other poems that were included, "Annabel Lee" and the final version of "The Bells," were not completed in 1848. "Poe's Wonderful Interpreter" was reprinted in the *Inter Ocean* on September 30 and October 9, 1879 (America's Historical Newspapers.)
33. I draw on "She Lives over an Evening with Poe," *New York Herald*, February 19, 1905, sec. 3, p. 4, and a slightly different version, "Was a Friend of Poe," *New York Herald*, about February 19, 1905, 4 (https://www.eapoe.org); as well as Charles W. Kent and John S. Patton, eds., *The Book of the Poe Centenary: A Record of the Exercises at the University of Virginia January 16–19, 1909, in Commemoration of the One Hundredth Birthday of Edgar Allan Poe* (Charlottesville: University of Virginia, 1909), 27–28; and Phillips, *Edgar Allan Poe—The Man*, 2:1467–76 and O 2:836. For detail on the Old Hygeia Hotel, see Thomas J. Wertenbaker and Marvin W. Schlegel, *Norfolk: Historic Southern Port*, 2nd ed. (Durham, NC: Duke University Press, 1962), 294; and John V. Quarstein and Julia Steere Clevenger, *Old Point Comfort Resort: Hospitality, Health and History on Virginia's Chesapeake Bay* (Charleston, SC: History Press, 2009), 23–36.
34. See M 1:419, 480. Poe in his correspondence refers to both "Ulalume" and "Annabel Lee" as "a ballad" (O 2:638, 797). See also Burton R. Pollin, "Poe as a Writer of Songs," *American Renaissance Literary Report* 6 (1992): 58–66. "Annabel Lee" is the Poe text most frequently made the basis for a song (63).
35. See [Johann Ludwig] Uhland, "Castle by the Sea," trans. C[harles] C[arter] Lee, *Southern Literary Messenger* (March 1849): 147–48. The poem was also translated by Longfellow.
36. The criticism of the translation of the title "The Castle by the Sea" in the review of Longfellow in the April 1845 issue of the *Aristidean* is yet another detail suggesting the partial authorship of Thomas Dunn English (see "Longfellow's Poems," *Aristidean* [April 1845]: 138). For the dating of Poe's writing "Annabel Lee," see Jeffrey Savoye, "In Her Tomb by the Sounding Sea: A Radical Reconsideration of the Manuscripts of 'Annabel Lee,'" *Edgar Allan Poe Review* 25, no. 1 (2024): 15–36.
37. Buford Jones and Kent Ljungquist, "Poe, Mrs. Osgood, and 'Annabel Lee,'" in *Studies in the American Renaissance 1983*, ed. Joel Myerson (Charlottesville: University Press of Virginia, 1983), 275–80.
38. Robert Adger Law, "A Source for 'Annabel Lee,'" *Journal of English and Germanic Philology* 21, no. 2 (April 1922): 341–46. See also M 1:471. Mabbott also gives Sarah Helen Whitman's "Stanzas for Music" as a possible source (M 1:472). For a consideration of the order of Poe's writing the manuscripts of "Annabel Lee," see

Savoye, "In Her Tomb by the Sounding Sea," originally given at the Fifth International Edgar Allan Poe Conference, "Poe Takes Boston," Boston, MA, April 9, 2022.

39. Charles Ellis to John Allan, November 15, 1813, Box 131, DLC-EA. See also Thomas and Jackson, *The Poe Log*, 20.

40. Charles Ellis to John Allan, August 10, 1813, Box 130, DLC-EA. Also, the words "The Gods will envy my happiness" are written on the envelope of a letter that Charles Ellis received (John Tunis to Charles Ellis, June 14, 1813, Box 128, DLC-EA).

41. "Annabelle Lee" is the romantic interest of Buster Keaton's character Johnnie Gray in the 1926 movie *The General*. Martin Luther King Jr. mentions "Annabelle Lee" when discussing romantic love in his January 25, 1965, speech in Selma, Alabama. King also refers to William Shakespeare's Sonnet 116, reciting a portion of it. A recording of the speech is held by the Montgomery Public Library in Alabama. The speech ("A Long, Long Way to Go") is included in *Ripples of Hope: Great American Civil Rights Speeches,* ed. Joshua Gottheimer (New York: Basic Civitas Books, 2004), 258–65, see esp. 263. Notably, in his early dating, King recited Poe's poem "To Helen" (see Jonathan Eig, *King: A Life* [New York: Farrar, Straus and Giroux, 2023], 69).

42. "She Lives over an Evening with Poe" and "Was a Friend of Poe" (https://www.eapoe.org).

43. Thomas and Jackson, *The Poe Log*, 834–35.

44. Ibid., 836; Kent and Patton, *The Book of the Poe Centenary,* 28.

45. For more on the Thompson and Traylor daguerreotypes, see Michael Deas, *The Portraits and Daguerreotypes of Edgar Allan Poe* (Charlottesville: University Press of Virginia, 1989), 54–61. For the interior of Pratt's Daguerrean Gallery, I note the image that appeared with the advertisement (see, for example, "The Celerotypes," *Richmond Enquirer,* July 17, 1849, [3]; and "Eureka," ibid., October 12, 1849, [3] [America's Historical Newspapers]). For recent commentary on the image of the lost Traylor daguerreotype, see Gabrielle Dean, "The Players Club Daguerreotype Final Portrait," in *Edgar Allan Poe in 20 Objects from the Susan Jaffe Tane Collection,* ed. Dean and Richard Kopley (Baltimore, MD: Johns Hopkins Sheridan Libraries, 2016), 108–13; and Christopher P. Semtner, "Poe in Richmond: Tane Gift Brings Poe's Story to Life," *Edgar Allan Poe Review* 23, no. 1 (2022): 101–2. Flora Lapham Mack maintained that Poe sat twice for his picture in September 1849, once for Elmira and once for Rosalie. She added that while Elmira's picture of Poe was placed in a case, Rosalie's was mounted by Mrs. Mackenzie in a brooch, which Poe's sister wore pinned to her collar. Rosalie later sold copies of an image of Poe in Richmond, Petersburg, and Baltimore. Mack offers her comments in Mack to Washington, February 29, 1908 and March 31, 1908 (longer letter and shorter letter) and on the verso of pages of his Rosalie chapter (collection of the author). Rosalie presented a copy of the Oscar Halling portrait of Poe (based on the Thompson daguerreotype) to Mack (collection of the author) (see Deas, *The Portraits and Daguerreotpes of Edgar Allan Poe,* 78–79). Edward V. Valentine wrote in 1875 about having seen "a locket with [a] daguerreotype of Poe, which I think belonged to his sister" (Edward V. Valentine to John H. Ingram, October 1, 1875, Ingram's Poe Collection, Item 246). (Rosalie had died the previous year.)

46. Flora Lapham Mack to William Lanier Washington, March 31, 1908 (longer letter, collection of the author).
47. For the phrase "wounded silence," I cite Flora Lapham Mack to William Lanier Washington, September 18, [1908] (collection of the author). Also relevant are Flora Lapham Mack to William Lanier Washington, February 1, 1909, and the fragment beginning "She was a little child" (collection of the author).
48. Flora Lapham Mack to William Lanier Washington, March 31, 1908 (longer letter, collection of the author).
49. For the Richmond newspaper advertisements, see Thomas and Jackson, *The Poe Log*, 838. For Elmira's September 22, 1849, letter to Maria Clemm, see H 17:396–97; for the complete version, see Arthur Hobson Quinn, *Edgar Allan Poe: A Critical Biography* (New York: D. Appleton-Century, 1941), 634–35; or *Edgar Allan Poe: Letters and Documents in the Enoch Pratt Free Library*, ed. Arthur H. Quinn and Richard H. Hart (New York: Scholars' Facsimiles & Reprints, 1941), 26–27. Elmira wrote to Maria Clemm again on October 11; her memory of Poe's elation is in Elmira Shelton to Maria Clemm, October 11, 1849, in "The Poe-Chivers Papers," ed. George E. Woodberry, *Century Magazine*, n.s., vol. 43 (February 1903): 552. For Weiss's comment on Maria Clemm and Elmira Shelton, see Weiss, "Reminiscences," August 25, 1904, 445. Hearing from Whitman but not Shelton years after Poe's death, Mrs. Clemm then wrote to Whitman, "She [Shelton] has not been the friend to me that you have, and she is *rich too,* but I will not blame her, for she I suppose is entirely estranged from me" (Maria Clemm to Sarah Helen Whitman, April 14, 1859, in *Building Poe Biography*, ed. John Carl Miller [Baton Rouge: Louisiana State University Press, 1977], 42).
50. Flora Lapham Mack to William Lanier Washington, March 31, 1908 (longer letter, collection of the author). (Minor errors, of spelling and capitalization, are silently corrected.)
51. Elmira spoke of a "partial understanding" rather than an engagement in Edward V. Valentine, "Edgar A. Poe Conversation with Mrs. Shelton," November 19, 1875, Valentine Center, Richmond, VA. However, she acknowledged the engagement to John J. Moran (see his *A Defense of Edgar Allan Poe* [Washington, DC: William F. Boogher, 1885], 50). For her stating that Poe was the love of her life, see Edward M. Alfriend, "Unpublished Recollections of Edgar Allan Poe," *Literary Era* (August 1901): 490 (https://www.eapoe.org).
52. For Daniel's September 25 piece in the *Semi-Weekly Examiner,* "Edgar A. Poe," see Thomas and Jackson, *The Poe Log,* 841–42; or *Poe in His Own Time: A Biographical Chronicle of His Life, Drawn from Recollections, Interviews, and Memoirs by Family, Friends, and Associates,* ed. Benjamin F. Fisher (Iowa City: University of Iowa Press, 2010), 68–69. For the September 26 notices of the lecture in the *Richmond Daily Republican* and the *Richmond Daily Times,* see Thomas and Jackson, *The Poe Log,* 842.
53. John M. Daniel, [Obituary of Edgar A. Poe], *Richmond Semi-Weekly Examiner,* October 12, 1849, [2] (https://www.eapoe.org); review of *The Works of the Late Edgar Allan Poe,* 2 vols., *Southern Literary Messenger* (March 1850): 177.
54. Thomas and Jackson, *The Poe Log,* 841.

55. See, primarily, Weiss, "Last Days of Edgar A. Poe," 709, 713–14; as well as her "Edgar Allan Poe"; "Edgar A. Poe"; "Reminiscences of Edgar Allan Poe," May 5, 1904, 1013; and "Reminiscences," August 25, 1904, 446. For Poe's having begun to write a table of contents for the first issue and interviewed Mrs. Mackenzie for a subsequent issue, see Weiss, *The Home Life of Poe*, 198. For Patterson's commitment to Poe, see E. H. N. Patterson to Edgar Allan Poe, August 21, 1849, in *Some Letters of Edgar Allan Poe to E. H. N. Patterson of Oquawka, Illinois, with Comments by Eugene Field* (Chicago: Caxton Club, 1898), 26–28, or H 17:365–66.
56. Weiss, "Last Days of Edgar A. Poe," 713–14.
57. For the time of day, see Weiss, "Edgar Allan Poe." Flora Lapham Mack wrote "[T]he intimate connection [with the Mackenzies] lasted as long as his life his last night in Richmond being spent with Dr. Tom & Mr. Richard Mackenzie at their lovely country home 'Duncan Lodge'" (Mack to William Lanier Washington, February 29, 1908, collection of the author). For Poe at Duncan Lodge, smoking, in solitary thought, see Weiss "Last Days of Edgar A. Poe," 714.
58. That Poe left Duncan Lodge on that last day with Tom Mackenzie and Gibbon Carter is noted by Weiss, "Last Days of Edgar A. Poe," 714. For Daniel and Thompson's comments on Poe's attitude during his last visit, see Thomas and Jackson, *The Poe Log*, 851, 854. Daniel later shifted his view: "Mr. Poe was indisposed when he left Richmond—complained of chilliness and exhaustion" (Daniel, "Edgar Allan Poe," *Southern Literary Messenger* [March 1850]: 178 [https://www.eapoe.org]). For other detail regarding Poe's last visit to Thompson, see Thomas and Jackson, *The Poe Log*, 854; Thompson, "The Late Edgar A. Poe," *Southern Literary Messenger* (November 1849): 696–97; "Editor's Table," *Southern Literary Messenger* (February 1854): 124 (Making of America); and William Fearing Gill, *The Life of Edgar Allan Poe* (New York: D. Appleton, 1877), 231.
59. Weiss mentioned Rosalie's giving her the note and manuscript poem in "Last Days of Edgar A. Poe," 714. Elmira described Poe's last visit to her in her October 11, 1849, letter to Maria Clemm, in Woodberry, "The Poe-Chivers Papers" (February 1903), 551.
60. I rely on John F. Carter, "Poe's Last Night in Richmond," *Lippincott's Monthly Magazine*, November 1902, 565–66; Weiss: "Last Days," 714; and *The Home Life of Poe*, 203–4. Also useful is Whitty, "Memoir," in *The Complete Poems of Edgar Allan Poe* (Boston: Houghton Mifflin, 1911), lxxxiii. For commentary on Carter's cane and Poe's trunk, see Jeffrey A. Savoye, "Two Biographical Digressions: Poe's Wandering Trunk and Dr. Carter's Mysterious Sword Case," *Edgar Allan Poe Review* 5, no. 2 (2004): 15–42. Notably, the Weiss piece does not state that Poe had then been drinking, and, according to Whitty, both Sadler and Blakey, who saw Poe at the restaurant, did not think he was drinking. However, the Carter piece claims that Sadler said that Poe was drinking. I take the view of Weiss and Whitty because the Sons of Temperance considered Poe to have maintained his pledge while in Richmond and because it is unlikely that, if he had been drinking, he would have been sober (as both Weiss and Carter report that he was).
61. Thomas and Jackson, *The Poe Log*, 846–47.
62. Ibid., 850, 852; see also Charles H. Bohner, *John Pendleton Kennedy: Gentleman from Baltimore* (Baltimore, MD: Johns Hopkins University Press, 1961), 194.

63. Robert D'Unger to Chevalier Reynolds, October 29, 1899, University of Iowa Libraries, Iowa City (also Item 402 in Ingram's Poe Collection). For the published letter, see John E. Reilly, "Robert D'Unger and His Reminiscences of Edgar Allan Poe in Baltimore," *Maryland Historical Magazine,* 88, no. 1 (1993): 66–69. For treatments of Poe's final days, see Matthew Pearl, "A Poe Death Dossier: Discoveries and Queries in the Death of Edgar Allan Poe, Part I," *Poe Review* 7, no. 2 (2006): 4–29, and 8, no. 1 (2007): 8–31, and Jeffrey A. Savoye, "The Mysterious Death of Edgar Allan Poe" (https://www.eapoe.org). For versions of the cooping story, see William F. Gill, *The Life of Edgar Allan Poe* (New York: D. Appleton, 1877), 237–38; Phillips, *Edgar Allan Poe—The Man,* 2:1500–1501; and John R. Thompson, *The Genius and Character of Edgar Allan Poe* (n.p.: n.p., 1929), 42. A recent biography of Poe focusing on his death is Mark Dawidziak, *A Mystery of Mysteries: The Death and Life of Edgar Allan Poe* (New York: St. Martins, 2023). A recent study of Poe's last days in Baltimore is David F. Gaylin, *The Final Days of Edgar Allan Poe: Nevermore in Baltimore* (Bethlehem, PA: Lehigh University Press, 2024).

64. Robert D'Unger to Chevalier Reynolds. D'Unger added later in the letter, "He died, as I understood at the time from inflammation of the intestines, the diarrhoea preceding the fever." See Reilly 68. Mabbott quotes this passage (M 1:569n).

65. Mabbott wrote below the close of the letter, "Isn't this an item?" And his assistant, Patricia Edwards Clyne, wrote, "Like you, I think this man (Unger) is telling the truth," adding, "I think this is really important, Tom, and will be a 'feather in your cap'" (see the file on D'Unger to Reynolds, including [Clyne] to Mabbott, November 27, 1962, at the University of Iowa Libraries, Iowa City).

66. Poe had been diagnosed with heart disease (Thomas and Jackson, *The Poe Log,* 732), a brain lesion (ibid., 694), and "cerebral congestion" (ibid., 766). Recently, Patricia Edwards Clyne stated, "Neither Tom [Mabbott] nor I was ever fully convinced that the cause of Poe's death was solely alcohol-related" (email to the author, August 8, 2022).

67. Joseph W. Walker to Joseph E. Snodgrass, October 3, 1849, in *Building Poe Biography,* 85–86.

68. J. E. Snodgrass, "The Facts of Poe's Death and Burial," *Beadle's Monthly* 3 (March 1867): 283–84.

69. Joseph E. Snodgrass, "Edgar A. Poe's Death and Burial," *New York Reformer,* July 26, 1855, 2 (https://www.eapoe.org).

70. Snodgrass, "The Facts of Poe's Death and Burial," 283–84. While Poe was at the hospital, its name changed to Baltimore City Marine Hospital (see W. T. Bandy, "Two Notes on Poe's Death," *Poe Studies* 14, no. 2 [1981]: 32).

71. John J. Moran to Maria Clemm, November 15, 1849, Quinn and Hart, *Edgar Allan Poe: Letters and Documents in the Enoch Pratt Free Library,* 32. I do not cite Moran's 1875 "Official Memoranda of the Death of Edgar A. Poe" or his 1885 *A Defense of Edgar Allan Poe* regarding Poe's death since neither account is reliable.

72. Quinn and Hart, *Edgar Allan Poe: Letters and Documents in the Enoch Pratt Free Library,* 33.

73. For recognition of Poe's allusion to John 14 in "The Premature Burial," see William Mentzel Forrest, *Biblical Allusions in Poe* (New York: Macmillan, 1928),

164. Notably, Poe had written in the 1835/1836 "Politian" that sorrowful Lalage requested from the library "The Holy Evangelists" (Matthew, Mark, Luke, and John) because, she says, "If there be balm / For the wounded spirit in Gilead it is there!" (M 1:261).

74. Quinn and Hart, 33. Sources for Henry Reynolds are mentioned by Matthew Pearl, "A Poe Death Dossier, Part II," 14, 28. For the proposal that Poe was really calling Henry Herring, see W. T. Bandy, "Dr. Moran and the Poe-Reynolds Myth," in *Myths and Reality: The Mysterious Mr. Poe,* ed. Benjamin Franklin Fisher IV (Baltimore, MD: Edgar Allan Poe Society, 1987), 26–36. Kenneth Silverman lends credence to Bandy's view in *Edgar A. Poe: Mournful and Never-ending Remembrance* (New York: HarperCollins, 1991), 435. Pearl is sympathetic to the view, too (part 2, 14–15). The argument is based on *A Defense of Edgar Allan Poe,* published thirty-six years after Poe's death, a work of considerable imagination that does not even mention Poe's calling out at the end. It is interesting to note that during his time at the *Southern Literary Messenger,* Poe referred to Henry Herring as "a man of unprincipled character" (O 1:99).

75. H 1:336n; Quinn, *Edgar Allan Poe: A Critical Biography* 640; Jeffrey Meyers, *Edgar Allan Poe His Life and Legacy* (New York: Charles Scribner's Sons, 1992), 255. The likelihood of Poe's having met Reynolds is indicated by Poe's commenting in his review of Reynolds's 1836 *Address,* "Gentlemen have impugned his motives—have these gentlemen ever seen him or conversed with him half an hour?" (P 5:356). Poe might have met Reynolds through his employer, Thomas W. White. And Poe was indebted to Reynolds for ten dollars in New York City (see the bankruptcy document in [Barbara Cantalupo], "Interview with Jefferson Moak [October 2007]," *Edgar Allan Poe Review* 8, no. 2 [2007]: 97).

76. Quinn and Hart, *Edgar Allan Poe: Letters and Documents in the Enoch Pratt Free Library,* 33.

Conclusion

1. James A. Harrison quotes Mary Moran in H 1:338. For further information, see Neilson Poe to Maria Clemm, October 11, 1849, in *Edgar Allan Poe: Letters and Documents in the Enoch Pratt Free Library,* ed. Arthur H. Quinn and Richard H. Hart (New York: Scholars' Facsimiles & Reprints, 1941), 30–31; John J. Moran to Maria Clemm, November 15, 1849, in *Edgar Allan Poe: Letters and Documents,* 32–34; William Elliott Jr., "The History of the Movement [for a Poe Monument]," in Sara Sigourney Rice, *Edgar Allan Poe: A Memorial Volume* (Baltimore, MD: Turnbull Brothers, 1877), 44–45; George E. Woodberry, *The Life of Edgar Allan Poe,* 2 vols. (Boston: Houghton Mifflin, 1909), 2:448–49; Mary E. Phillips, *Edgar Allan Poe—The Man* (Chicago: John C. Winston, 1926), 2:1510–11; M 1:569; and George P. Clark, "Two Unnoticed Recollections of Poe's Funeral" [by Hubner and Weston], *Poe Studies* 3, no. 1 (1970), 1–2. See also J. E. Snodgrass, "The Facts of Poe's Death and Burial," *Beadle's Monthly* (March 1867): 283–87. For a series of well-chosen excerpts, see Dwight Thomas and David K. Jackson, *The Poe Log: A Documentary Life of Edgar Allan Poe, 1809–1849* (Boston: G. K. Hall, 1987), 847–49.

2. For a consideration of the date of the burial, see W. T. Bandy, "The Date of Poe's Burial," *Poe Studies* 4, no. 2 (1971): 47–48. For treatment of the ceremony, see Neilson Poe to Maria Clemm; Elliott, "The History of the Movement [for a Poe Monument]"; Snodgrass, "The Facts of Poe's Death and Burial"; Woodberry, *The Life of Edgar Allan Poe*, 2:448–49; Phillips, *Edgar Allan Poe—The Man*, 2:1510–11; M 1:569; and Clark, "Two Unnoticed Recollections of Poe's Funeral." Again, Thomas and Jackson offer useful excerpts (848–49). Both Matthew Pearl and Christopher Scharpf mention, in their helpful analytical essays, that the funeral oration was not given (Pearl, "A Poe Death Dossier: Discoveries and Queries in the Death of Edgar Allan Poe, Part I," *Edgar Allan Poe Review* 7, no. 2 (2006): 20, 28; Scharpf, "Where Lies a Noble Spirit?—An Investigation into the Curious Mystery of Edgar Allan Poe's Grave in Baltimore," in *Masques, Mysteries, and Mastodons: A Poe Miscellany*, ed. Benjamin F. Fisher [Baltimore, MD: Edgar Allan Poe Society, 2006], 198).

3. Susan Archer Talley Weiss, "The Last Days of Edgar A. Poe," *Scribner's Magazine*, March 1878, 715 (https://www.eapoe.org); Elmira Shelton to Maria Clemm, October 11, 1849, in "The Poe-Chivers Papers," ed. George E. Woodberry, Second Paper, *Century Magazine*, n.s., vol. 43 (February 1903): 551–52; "Edgar Allan Poe—Some Reminiscences by One Who Knew Him," *The State*, February 26, 1878, John Henry Ingram's Poe Collection, Albert & Shirley Small Library, University of Virginia, Charlottesville, Item 728.

4. For a useful overview of commentary on Poe after his death, see Burton R. Pollin, "A Posthumous Assessment: The 1849–1850 Periodical Press Response to Edgar Allan Poe," *American Periodicals* 2 (1992): 6–50.

5. "Death of Edgar A. Poe, Esq." *Richmond Whig*, October 9, 1849, [3]; "Things in New York," *Philadelphia Public Ledger*, October 9, 1849, [3] (America's Historical Newspapers).

6. Ludwig [Rufus W. Griswold], "Death of Edgar A. Poe," *New York Daily Tribune*, October 9, 1849, [2]. It was widely reprinted, including in the *Richmond Enquirer*. The obituary is reproduced in *Poe in His Own Time*, ed. Benjamin F. Fisher (Iowa City: University of Iowa Press, 2012), 73–80, and at https://www.eapoe.org.

7. Annie Richmond to Maria Clemm, October 14, [1849], in Quinn and Hart, *Edgar Allan Poe: Letters and Documents in the Enoch Pratt Free Library*, 55; Susan Archer Talley, "Edgar A. Poe," *Richmond Republican*, October 15, 1849, Ingram's Poe Collection, Item 65; N. P. Willis, "Death of Edgar Poe," *Home Journal*, October 20, 1849, [2] (https://www.eapoe.org); George Lippard, "[Edgar Allan Poe]," *Quaker City*, October 20, 1849, [2] (https://www.eapoe.org); Henry B. Hirst, "Edgar Allan Poe," in Dwight Thomas, "Poe in Philadelphia, 1838–1844: A Documentary Record" (PhD diss., University of Pennsylvania, 1978), 2:815 (and https://www.eapoe.org); Anonymous, "Pen-Etchings from Prairie-Land," "Edgar Allan Poe," *New York Daily Tribune*, November 13, 1849, [1]; *New York Semi-Weekly Tribune*, November 17, 1849, [1] (https://www.eapoe.org).

8. George R. Graham, "The Late Edgar Allan Poe," *Graham's Magazine* (March 1850): 224–26 or H 1:399–410; John Neal, "Edgar A. Poe," *Portland Daily Advertiser*, April 26, 1850 (https://www.eapoe.org).

9. See Arthur Hobson Quinn, *Edgar Allan Poe: A Critical Biography* (New York: D. Appleton-Century 1941) for evidence of Griswold's forgeries and other distortions in these works (444–50, 646–47, 668–76).
10. Rufus Wilmot Griswold, "Memoir," in *The Literati*, by Edgar Allan Poe (vol. 3 of *The Works of Edgar A. Poe*) (New York: J. S Redfield, 1850), xxxi; see also Griswold, "Memoir," in *Poe in His Own Time*, 140.
11. Review of *The Literati*, *Boston Recorder*, September 26, 1850, 156 (America's Historical Newspapers).
12. See George R. Graham, "To Rev. Rufus Wilmot Griswold," *Graham's Magazine* (November 1850): 327 (https://www.eapoe.org); and "Edgar A. Poe," *Alta California*, November 30, 1850 (Nineteenth Century U.S. Newspapers).
13. William Lanier Washington, "Untrustworthy Memorialists of Edgar Allan Poe: The Rev. Rufus W. Griswold and Mrs. Susan Archer Weiss," Accession 2996, Special Collections, University of Virginia Library, University of Virginia, Charlottesville.
14. Parke Vanparke, "Edgar A. Poe," *Discursions and Diversions* (Philadelphia: James B. Rodgers, 1866), 264. For Vanparke's commitment to Rosalie, see 266. For comment on Vanparke, see J. H. Whitty in Mary E. Phillips, *Edgar Allan Poe—The Man*, 2:1309.
15. See my *The Threads of "The Scarlet Letter": A Study of Hawthorne's Transformative Art* (Newark: University of Delaware Press, 2003), 22–35, 125–30. See also my brief summary in "Hawthorne and Poe," in *Nathaniel Hawthorne in Context*, ed. Monika M. Elbert (Cambridge, UK: Cambridge University Press, 2018), 281.
16. Kopley, *Threads*, 34–35; see also Kopley, "Hawthorne and Poe," 281–82.
17. See my "Poe at Blithedale," *Edgar Allan Poe Review* 10, no. 3 (2009): 53–59, as well as "Hawthorne and Poe," 282.
18. See Patrick F. Quinn, *The French Face of Edgar Poe* (Carbondale: Southern Illinois University Press, 1957), 205–15, 291–92; Harold Beaver, "Poe and Melville," in *The Narrative of Arthur Gordon Pym of Nantucket*, by Edgar Allan Poe, ed. Harold Beaver (1975; London: Penguin, 1986), 278–81; and Burton R. Pollin, "Traces of Poe in Melville," *Melville Society Extracts*, no. 109 (1997): 10–12.
19. See my "'The Raven' and Melville's *Pierre*," *Edgar Allan Poe Review* 20, no. 2 (2019): 210–18.
20. Flora Lapham Mack, "Concerning Correspondence between Edgar Allan Poe & John H. Mackenzie," collection of the author. Tom Mackenzie was born January 2, 1821 (Mackenzie Family Bible, Virginia Museum and History and Culture) and died July 13, 1867 (Flora Lapham Mack to William Lanier Washington, March 23, 1908 [collection of the author] and June 8, 1908 [Poe Museum]). Tom's death is also given in the *Richmond Daily Dispatch*, July 18, 1867 (Virginia Chronicle). More on the move from Duncan Lodge is in Flora Lapham Mack to William Lanier Washington, February 29, 1908 (collection of the author).
21. Exceptions were Virginian Winfield Scott, who served as a Union general, and Richmonder Elizabeth Van Lew, who served as a Union spy.
22. Tom's serving as a surgeon for the Confederacy is noted in Mack, "Concerning Correspondence." John's serving on behalf of Louisiana troops in Richmond is noted in "Louisiana Depot," *Richmond Daily Dispatch*, November 13, 1861, [4]

(Chronicling America); and *Louisiana Soldiers' Relief Association and Hospital, in the City of Richmond, Virginia* (Richmond: Enquirer Book and Job Press, 1862), 31. John's Darby Town farm was auctioned on October 20, 1862 ("Very Valuable and Highly Productive Farm," *Richmond Daily Dispatch*, October 13, 1862 [Virginia Chronicle]). Flora Lapham Mack estimated that John H. Mackenzie left Darby Town "in 1863 I think or about that time" ("Data" [Questions and Answers between William Lanier Washington and Flora Lapham Mack], collection of the author). The deed for the purchase of Sedgemore was dated June 1, 1864 (Library of Virginia).

23. The burning of the Darby Town farmhouse is noted in "Data" [Questions and Answers between William Lanier Washington and Flora Lapham Mack], collection of the author. John's time in Libby Prison is mentioned in Flora Lapham Mack to William Lanier Washington, March 31, 1908, and April 2, 1908 (collection of the author).

24. Mack, "Concerning Correspondence." For treatment of the Evacuation Fire, see Ernest B. Furgurson, *Ashes of Glory: Richmond at War* (1996; New York: Vintage, 1997), 326–40. President Lincoln visited the burned, defeated city of Richmond on April 4, 1865 (341–48).

25. For an article on the Poe Museum's acquiring its Flora Lapham Mack letters, see A. B. M. [Agnes Bondurant Marcuson], "Mackenzie Letters, 1908–1914," *Poe Messenger* 16, no. 1 (1986): 4–8.

26. Flora Lapham Mack, "Poe's Appearance and Personality," collection of the author.

27. Flora Lapham Mack to William Lanier Washington, April 22, 1908, collection of the author.

Index

Illustrations are indicated by italicized gallery page numbers preceded by a "g" (e.g., g1, g2).

Adam and Eve (biblical), 103
Adams, John Quincy, 97, 519n147
Addison, Joseph: *Cato* (play), 257
aesthetic standards, 65, 186, 223, 252, 266, 276, 295, 303, 333
afterlife, 149, 190, 249–50, 254, 358, 404, 470, 474. *See also* metempsychosis
Aikin, John. See *Evenings at Home*
Albright, J. W., 282, 283
Aldrich, James, 335; "A Death-Bed," 324, 614n20
Alexander, Charles W., 221, 247
Alexander's Weekly Messenger, 225–27, 247
Alfriend, Edward M., 47
Allan, Frances (foster mother): at Cheltenham resort (England), 32–33; death of, impact on Poe, 93, 362; funeral of (1829), 80, 93, 154; grave epitaph of, 93; health issues of, 29, 30, 32–33, 35–36, 38, 40–41, 45, 46, 52, 62, 92, 507n17; Ingram associated with memory of, 461; in London, 30, 32–33; Poe alluding to in "A Paean," 125, 541n58; Eliza Poe and, 14; Poe raised by and relationship with, 15–16, 19, 22–23, 50, 92–93, 106, 153, 531n19; on Poe's profligate life at University of Virginia, 77; Poe's purported killing of pet fawn of, 298; Poe's visits to grave of, 108; portrait of, 500n15, *g1*; as *Pym* character, 194; in Scotland, 28; during War of 1812, 21–22, 24. *See also* London stay of Allan family

Allan, Jane (John Allan's sister in Scotland), 28
Allan, John (foster father): accusing Poe of theft, in letters to Poe at West Point, 111; anxiety of Poe about their relationship, 99–100, 115; arrest for nonpayment of debt, 48; buried next to Frances, 153; Byrd Plantation inherited by, 61, 62, 77, 141; at Cheltenham resort (England), 32–33, 502n47; cholera (1832) and, 136; death of, 153; drunkenness of, 62, 95, 109, 116, 153; Ellis relationship affected by debt issues, 49; extramarital affairs and children of, 25, 59, 107, 109, 153, 154, 497n88; final encounter with Poe prior to Allan's death, 152; financial and business problems, 29–30, 32, 36–38, 46, 47–48, 52, 53, 56, 58, 511n56; funeral of Frances as rapprochement with Poe, 93–94; on George IV and his wife Caroline, 40, 314; health of, 40, 45, 52, 133, 141, 147, 152; Henry Poe receiving letter from, complaining about Edgar, 59–60, 67; inadequate support for Poe at University of Virginia and at West Point, 66, 67, 72, 75, 115–16, 118, 153; inheritance and wealth from uncle William Galt, 61, 76; Moldavia home purchased by (1825), 61; negativity about Edgar's placement in his home and disavowal of kinship with, 15, 16,

665

Allan, John (foster father) (*continued*): 67, 96, 106; ordering Poe to leave Moldavia after altercation with second Mrs. Allan, 120; in Poe's "A Succession of Sundays" as Rumgudgeon character, 258; Poe's correspondence with (1831), 130–31, 139; Poe's Declaration of Independence letter to and Allan's response (1827), 74, 78–79, 295, 523n28, 598n48; Poe's early childhood poetry, possible publication of, 45, 53; Poe's exchange of last letters with (1833), 139; Poe's final visit to, 152, 283; Poe's letters from University of Virginia (1826 & 1827), 74; Poe's request for discharge from military and, 94; Poe's requests for forgiveness and acceptance, 76, 98–99, 100, 102, 131, 139; portrait of, *91*; public sentiment on harsh treatment of Poe by, 79–80, 134, 153; in *Pym*, 194, 198, 210; refusal to acknowledge any fault in his relationship with Poe, 107, 116, 139, 154, 367; refusing to support Poe's publication of his poetry, 98–99; relationship with Poe, 19–20, 22, 25, 34, 38, 49–50, 57, 58–60, 69, 92–93, 106–7, 511n60; Richmond homes' locations, 16, 45, 47, 51, 491n2, 511n65; Richmond social life of, 20, 23, 26, 43, 45, 58, 60; sale of enslaved people by, 26, 498n94; Scotland visit with relatives, 25–26, 28; second marriage to Louisa Gabriella Patterson, 107, 115; slandering Eliza Poe for Rosalie as possible issue of illicit union, 60, 153, 240; in "The Tell-Tale Heart," 283; temperament as severe and punitive, 22–23, 52, 59, 106–7, 141, 284; Thomas Ellis complaining to his father Charles Ellis about, 141; threatening to disinherit Poe, 135; War of 1812 and, 24–25; West Point cadet appointment of Poe and, 94, 96, 107, 532n27; West Point letters from Poe to (1831), 72, 74, 75, 76, 109, 116, 139; whipping Poe, 22, 59, 153; will of, 154, 551n6. *See also* London stay of Allan family

Allan, Louisa Gabriella Patterson (second wife of John Allan), 107, 115, 152, 154, 367, 551n1

Allan, Mary (John Allan's sister in Scotland), 28, 35, 36

Allan & Ellis (British firm), 29, 36–37, 39, 504n93; arrest of Allan and Ellis for nonpayment of debt, 48; Deed of Conditional Release (1823), 53, 56; Deed of Inspection (1819) and allowance of twelve months, 37, 46, 504n94; legal proceedings by creditors of, 49

allegory, in Poe's work: analysis of Poe and, 2; "Epimanes" and, 140; "King Pest" and, 167; *Pym* and, 9, 130, 134, 171, 172, 194, 198, 209–10, 377, 563n7; "Some Words with a Mummy" and, 74, 140; "Tamerlane" and, 84–85; "William Wilson" and, 34, 223

Allen, Hervey, 129

Ambler, Edward, 498n94

Ambler, R. C., 62

American Magazine, 218

American Monthly Magazine: absorption of *New England Magazine*, 169; Poe publishing in, 199, 592n113; Poe's poetry rejected by, 102; "Von Jung, the Mystific" published in, 200, 201

American Museum: "The Haunted Palace" published in, 219; "Ligeia" published in, 217

American Review, 314, 320, 321; "The Facts in the Case of M. Valdemar" published in, 349; "The Raven" published in and attributed to "Quarles," 326, 328; "Some Words with a Mummy" published in, 336; "Ulalume" published in, 379, 630n37

Anderson, James, 28

Andrews, M. Harbin, 395

"Annabel Lee" (poem): associated with Virginia Poe, 460; as ballad, 656n34; in Griswold obituary for Poe, 466, 475;

666 · Index

Hirst receiving copy from Poe, 443; integration of life and work in, 479; Moore receiving manuscript copy from, 440; Poe reciting at Duncan Lodge, 447; Poe reciting in Norfolk, 458–60; Poe's aspiration and, 479; posthumous publication of, 475; sources for, 90, 460; submitted to Griswold's *The Poets and Poetry of America*, 432, 466; Thompson given manuscript roll of, 466; writing of, 434, 438
Anthon, Charles, 200, 203, 319–20, 358
Anthony, John Gould, 219
Ariel (Norfolk shipwreck), 173, 194, 207, 212
Aristidean (magazine), 321, 349, 607n62, 614n22; "Our Book-Shelves" published in, 344
Armistead, Lucy Eliza Virginia (wife of William Lewis Lanier), 202
Arnott, Neil, 42, 423
Arthur, T. S.: *Insubordination*, 23; Poe's review of, 245
Arthur's Ladies' Magazine: "The Sphinx" published in, 349
art novel, 172, 174, 194, 207, 209, 212, 215
Ashmead, Henry Graham, 443
Ashton, Rosemary, 500n8
aspiration (ambition): for acclaim of literary world, 199; conflict with love, 55, 84, 104, 123; for launch of his own literary magazine, 136, 170, 223, 229, 433; in "Ligeia," 217; for publication, 155; for readers, 157, 283–84; resilience and, 361, 384–85, 386; resurgence with "Ulalume," 382; seeking to reach the divine through art, 276, 362, 624n39; summary of, 479; tensions in Poe's life and, 259–60, 267; uniting with consolation, 217; writing of grief ("The Raven," "Ulalume," and *Pym*) and, 382. *See also* "Penn Magazine"; "Stylus, The"
Atkinson's Evening Post and Saturday News (successor to *Philadelphia Saturday News*), 218

Aunt Pollie/Polly. *See* Lanier, Mary Simmons

Bacon, Delia S.: "Love's Martyr," 131
Baltimore, Poe's residence in (1829–1830), 97–105; correspondence with John Mackenzie, 99; locating paternal grandparents in, 97–98; visiting brother Henry, 129
Baltimore, Poe's residence in (1831–1835): Poe residing with Maria Clemm's family (Amity Street), 62, 126–29, 138, 154, 253, 542n2; Poe's correspondence with John Mackenzie, 138; Poe's courtship of Mary Starr (a.k.a. Mary Devereaux), 134–35, 141–42; Poe's debt and arrest, 130–31; Poe's plan to return to, 120, 121, 126; Poe's productivity, 150; Poe working in brick-yard, 155
Baltimore, Poe's return to (1849), 467; drinking spree leading to death in, 467–71, 660n64
Baltimore Book with Poe's contribution (1837), 197, 204
Baltimore Gazette and Daily Advertiser: extract from Poe's "Al Aaraaf" published in (1829), 98
Baltimore Minerva, 105, 129
Baltimore Republican and Commercial Advertiser: Poe writing anonymous review of his tale "Lionizing" in, 160; positive review of *Messenger*'s April issue (1835), 159
Baltimore Saturday Visiter, 129, 132, 135, 136, 138, 140; Hewitt winning poetry prize for "The Song of the Wind" by using pseudonym, 143, 146; literary contest (1833), 141–44; "MS. Found in a Bottle" as contest winner for story, 143–44, 165, 548n50; Poe criticizing for Hewitt's association with, 146; Poe's announcement of forthcoming book "The Folio Club," 147
Baltimore Sun's review of Poe's lecture at Academy Hall, 304

Index · 667

bankruptcy reform and Bankruptcy Act of 1841, 231, 235, 241, 251, 281, 282, 284
Barbauld, Anna Letitia. See *Evenings at Home*
Barbour/Barber, John J., 493n30
Barhyte Farm (Saratoga Springs, NY), 298, 313, 320, 599n65
Barrett, Elizabeth Barrett: "Consolation," 223; *A Drama of Exile, and Other Poems*, 318–19; influence on Poe, 299, 327; "Lady Geraldine's Courtship," 299, 318, 322, 327; Poe's admiration and defense of, 322, 323, 358; Poe's dedication of *The Raven and Other Poems* to, 347; Poe's review of *A Drama of Exile, and Other Poems*, 148, 318, 319, 321
Bartlett, John Russell, 343, 345, 351, 618n53
Bartlett and Welford (booksellers), 343
Bassett, Margaret, 80
Battle of New Orleans (1815), 24–25
Beach, Moses Y., 310
Beauchamp, Jeroboam O., 168
beauty as theme: in "Al Aaraaf," 103–4; *Al Aaraaf, Tamerlane, and Minor Poems* and, 105; in "Berenice," 157; in "Letter to B—," 104; letter to John Neal on, 101; in "Ligeia," 217; Poe on Coleridge's distinction between "Fancy" and "Imagination," 226; in Poe's review of Longfellow's *Ballads and Other Poems*, 266; in "The Poetic Principle," 104, 124, 175; in *Pym*, 195, 215; in "Tamerlane," 123; in "To Helen," 123
Beckford, William: *Vathek*, 628n7
Bell, Henry Glassford: "The Dead Daughter," 159
Bell, Landon, 538–39n19
Benjamin, Park, 583n6
Bennett, James Gordon, 310
Bermingham, James: *A Memoir of the Very Reverend Theobald Mathew. With an Account of the Rise and Progress of Temperance in Ireland*, Poe's review of, 248

Betty, William Henry West, 7
Bible, Poe's knowledge and use of, 173, 200, 203, 213–14, 268, 383, 470, 556n18
Bickerstaffe, Isaac: *The Romp*, 6, 11, 12
Biddle, Nicholas, 224, 236, 632n61
Bielawa, Michael J., 247
Bielfeld, Jacob Friedrich, 400
Bird, Robert Montgomery: *The Hawks of Hawk-Hollow*, Poe's review of, 169; influence on Poe, 294; *Sheppard Lee*, Poe's review of, 187, 294; *Southern Literary Messenger* and, 186
Bisco, John, 321, 333, 340, 342, 346, 348. See also *Broadway Journal*
Bishop, Elizabeth: "One Art," 477
Blackwell, Anna, 377
Blackwood's Edinburgh Magazine: influence on Poe, 136–37, 222, 274, 587nn58–59; review of Elizabeth Barrett Barrett by John Wilson published in, 322–23. See also Poe, Edgar Allan, works by: "How to Write a Blackwood Article"
Blaetterman, George, 68–69, 521n6
Bleakley, Kate, 134
Bliss, Elam, 121, 122, 541n45
Bolles, William: *An Explanatory and Phonographic Pronouncing Dictionary of the English Language*, Poe's review of, 338
Bolling, Thomas, 70, 71–72, 105–6
Bolton, Richard, 256, 260
Booksellers' Dinner (March 30, 1837), 198–99, 201, 563n10
Boston, Poe's criticism of literary culture, 333, 334, 341, 345; animus of Boston press to Poe, 341, 348
Boston, Poe's move to (1827), 79–84; association with his mother and his place of birth, 80, 617n49; military enlistment, 82, 83–84; possessions with Poe, 80; publication of first book, 82–83; theater performances (possibly), 82; troubles in, 82
Boston Lyceum lecture (October 1845), 77, 341, 345–47, 619n62

Bowen, Eli, 311, 414
Bowman, Rex, 142
Boyd, Joseph B., 231
Bradford, Adam C., 329
Brainard, John G. C.: *Poems*, Poe's review of, 262
Bransby, John, 34, 40, 50
Brennan, Martha Susannah, 320
Brennan, Mary, 312, 320, 378
Brewster, David: *Letters on Natural Magic*, 175
Bridges, David, 515n111
Briggs, Charles F.: agreeing with Lowell on Poe's lack of character, 342; in "The Literati of New York City," 357; Longfellow's plagiarism dispute and, 335, 613n17; on Lowell's biography of Poe, 323; on Poe's drinking, 337, 339, 342; relationship with Poe, 321, 357. See also *Broadway Journal*
Bristed, Charles Astor, 396, 404
British novels, influence on Poe, 132. See also Dickens, Charles
Broadway Journal: Briggs launching, 320, 321; cessation of publication, 349, 350; critical reception of, 332; "The Facts in the Case of M. Valdemar" published in, 349; final issue, 350; "Four Beasts in One—The Homo-Cameleopard" published in, 349; Lane's purchase of interest in, 349; "Loss of Breath" published in, 350; Poe as contributor, 319, 321, 332, 338, 344, 347; Poe as editor, 129, 332, 342; Poe removed as editor, 339; Poe's purchase of, 346; "The Spectacles" published in, 349; "A Tale of the Ragged Mountains" published in, 349; valedictory remarks from Poe, 350
Brockenborough, Mary, 496n61
Bronson, Cotesworth P., 373, 376–78
Bronson, Mary Elizabeth. *See* LeDuc, Mary Elizabeth Bronson
Brooks, James, 327
Brooks, Nathan C., 111, 126, 216

brotherhood, bond of, 5, 62, 101, 128, 210
Brother Jonathan (newspaper), 249–50, 279, 283; name of, 578n85; "Never Bet Your Head" published in, 251; review of *Pioneer*, 590n95
Brougham, Henry Lord, 314; *The Critical and Miscellaneous Writings of Henry Lord Brougham*, Poe's review of, 263; *Historical Sketches of Statesmen Who Flourished in the Time of George III*, Poe's review of, 222; *Opinions of Lord Brougham*, Poe's review of, 223; *Sketches of Public Characters, Discourses, and Essays*, Poe's review of, 221
Brown, Charles Brockden: *Edgar Huntly*, 305
Brown, Goold: *The Institutes of English Grammar*, 304
Browne, Thomas: *Urn-Burial*, Poe's review of, 222
Broza, Gil, 257
Bruce, Alexander, 522n8
Bryant, William Cullen, 122, 198, 200, 246, 250, 333, 351, 487n28; "June," 454; Poe's "A Notice of William Cullen Bryant," 228
Buckingham, Edwin, 140, 547n42
Buckingham, Joseph T., 7, 140, 346, 547n42, 619n63
Bulwer-Lytton, Edward: influence on Poe, 235, 239, 283; *Ismael; An Oriental Tale*, 122; "Literary Small Talk," Poe's criticism of, 219–20; "Monos and Daimonos, A Legend," 149; *Night and Morning*, Poe's review of, 238, 240; *Pelham*, 169, 222, 235, 382, 632n53; Poe comparing to Dickens, 242, 310; *Rienzi, The Last of the Tribunes*, Poe's review of, 172; *Weeds and Wild Flowers*, 122
Burke, William, 58; school of, 52, 56, 61, 512n73
Burling, Ebenezer, 46, 60, 80, 136, 210
Burr, Charles Chauncey, 370, 444–45, 448

Burton, William E., 182, 204, 209, 226, 228–29, 251; literary contest proposed by, 225, 227, 570n58; Poe's criticism of, 241; portrait of, *g4*; relationship with Poe, 220–21, 229, 233. See also *Burton's Gentleman's Magazine*

Burton's Gentleman's Magazine: "A Chapter on Science and Art" published in, 227, 256–57; "The Conversation of Eiros and Charmion" published in, 223; "Fairyland" published in, 221; "The Fall of the House of Usher" published in, 222; "Julius Rodman" (six chapters of unfinished narrative, published serially), 225–29; "Peter Pendulum the Business Man" published in, 226; "The Philosophy of Furniture" published in, 373; Poe as editor, 46, 204, 206, 220–23; Poe's firing and dispute with Burton, 229; Poe's job duties, 226; sold to Graham, 227, 233; "Some Account of Stonehenge, the Giant's Dance, A Druidical Ruin in England" published in, 228–29; "Spirits of the Dead" published in, 221; "To—" (formerly "To Elizabeth") published in, 221; "To Ianthe in Heaven" published in, 221; "To the River—" published in, 221; "William Wilson" published in, 223

Burwell, William M., 73
Butler, Samuel: *Hudibras*, 64, 519n145, 519n149
Butterfield, Eliza Jane, 436, 438
Byrd Plantation, 61, 62, 77, 141
Byron, Lord: "Bride of Abydos," 398, 636n31; "The Dream," 86; "English Bards and Scotch Reviewers," 167; "The Giaour," 84; "Manfred," 84, 86, 99, 146, 533n7; Poe's emulation of, 45, 55–56, 58, 70, 84, 86, 99, 149, 519n149, 533n7; "The Prisoner of Chillon," 99, 533n7; "Vision of Judgment," 519n149

Cabell, Julia Mayo, 120
Cabell, William H., 57

Campbell, John, 95, 96
Campbell, Killis, 125, 129–30, 519n145
Carey, John L., 224
Carey, Lea & Blanchard (publishers), 145, 147, 149, 154, 173
Carey, Lea & Carey (publishers), 98, 100, 155
Carey, Matthew, 186
Carey & Hart (publishers), 235–36, 243, 270
Caroline (queen of England), 40, 41, 47, 314–15, 316, 509n38
Carroll, Charles, 101
Carter, John F., 467, 519n151
Carter, Robert, 288
Carter, William Gibbon, 451, 466
Caulfield, Thomas, 7, 9
Central Gazette (Charlottesville), influence on Poe, 74, 125
Chambers, Robert: *Vestiges of the Natural History of Creation*, 390
Champollion (decipherer of Egyptian hieroglyphics), 204
Chandler, Joseph R., 226; *An Address, Delivered before the Goethean and Diagnothian Societies of Marshall College*, Poe's review of, 224
Channing, William Ellery, Poe's review of, 297
Chapin, Henry D., 385, 386
Chapman, J. G., 299
Charleston Courier, 12, 214; "Fourth of July" published in, 91; "The Mourner" published in, 90
Charleston Theatre, 12, 90
Chase, Lewis, 499n8, 501n29
Chaworth, Mary, 149
Cheltenham resort (England), 32–33, 502n47
Chesnut, Mary, 3
Chivers, Thomas Holley, 231, 256, 312, 339–40, 344, 348, 360, 398, 582n145, 583n6, 602n93, 615n35, 632n61; "The Heavenly Vision," 304, 333
cholera (1832), 136, 268, 545n29
cholera (1849), 442, 450

Chorley, Henry F.: *Conti the Discarded*, Poe's review of, 172, 209
Christianity, 122, 125, 129–30, 168, 203, 213–15, 313, 329, 383, 403, 470, 480, 566n14
Church, Frederic, 419
Cibber, Colley *The Provoked Husband* (with Vanbrugh), 6
Cicero, 64
ciphers. *See* puzzles
Civil War: Mackenzies on Confederate side, 477–78, 663n22; Richmond fire set by retreating Confederates (1865), 3, 99, 203, 478, 533n8, 539n26, 546n33, 596n24
Clark, Anne E. C., 572n9
Clark, Jane, 407, 453
Clark, Lewis Gaylord, 339, 348, 357, 363
Clarke, James A., 70; *The Christian Keepsake and Missionary Annual for 1840*, Poe's review of, 223
Clarke, Joseph G., 58
Clarke, Joseph H., 44–45, 51, 53, 455, 473, 511n62. *See also* Poe, Edgar Allan, education of, Clarke's academy (Richmond)
Clarke, Thomas C., 284, 287–89, 292, 384, 592n113, 596n34. *See also* "Stylus, The"
Clarke, William. *See* Lewis, Meriwether
Clason, Augustus A., Jr., 360, 363, 371
Cleland, Thomas W., 163, 176
Clemm, Henry, 127, 128, 172
Clemm, Josephine, 164
Clemm, Maria (aunt, mother-in-law): Annie Richmond and, 414, 419, 421, 422, 434, 441, 449, 457, 474; on Baltimore trip of David Poe to take Edgar to his grandparents, 488n35; boarders to supplement income, 181, 196, 200, 202, 377; calling on publishers to seek job for Poe in New York City, 317; Darby Town visits of, 179–80, 186–90, 559n59; description of, 316–17; Elmira Shelton and, 456, 462, 463–64, 466, 474, 658n49; Gove on, 361; Griswold and, 440; health issues of, 128, 167, 191; Henry Poe living with and dying at home of, 127, 129, 193, 212; as household guardian for Poe and Virginia, 200, 260, 377, 439; John Mackenzie's relationship with, 183, 191, 193, 202–3, 361, 376, 439; last parting from Poe, 440–41; letter to Allan on Poe's behalf (1831), 131; move to New York City, 309; move to Philadelphia, 204, 205; move to Richmond, 167, 491n2; on Osgood's relationship with Poe, 334–35, 354, 479, 613n14; photograph of, *g3*; Poe declaring his intention to marry Elmira Shelton to, 456, 462; Poe declaring his love for Virginia to, 158; Poe living in home of (1831–1834), 62, 126–29, 138, 154, 542n2; Poe's drinking sprees and, 132–33, 182–83, 191, 271, 289, 338–39; on Poe's illness (1849), 434; on Poe's pressure of grief, 195, 212; on Poe's relationship with Jane Stanard, 53, 57; Poe's response to Neilson Poe's offer to Virginia, 164–65; on Poe's unhappiness at West Point, 117–18; possibility of opening boardinghouse in Richmond, 171; poverty of, 98, 128, 164, 202, 206, 299, 355; relationship with Poe, 167–68, 173, 180, 181, 184, 185, 232, 249, 296, 316, 383–84, 438–39; Sarah Helen Whitman and, 407, 419, 421, 658n49; as seamstress, 102, 128, 202, 206, 220; selling enslaved man, 102; "Sonnet—To My Mother" as tribute to, 438–39; *Southern Literary Messenger* volume sold by, 309, 604n10; as strict mother to Virginia, 178–79; at Virginia's marriage to Poe (1835), 176–77
Clemm, Virginia. *See* Poe, Virginia Clemm (Poe's wife)
Clemm, William (husband of Maria Clemm), 164
Clemm, William T. D. (minister), 467, 473

Index · 671

Cleveland, John, 104
closeness: bond of brotherhood, 5, 62, 101, 128, 210; brotherhood as standard for, 128–29. *See also* Mackenzie, John H.
close reading, 2, 182, 201, 209, 259
Cloud, Charles F., 141
Cocke, Bowler, 16, 19, 491n3
Cocke, Bowler F. (son of Bowler), 491n3
Cocke, John H., 24, 74, 96
Cockton, Henry: *Stanley Thorn*, Poe's review of, 259
Cody, David, 515n111
Coleman, Edward and Ann, 239–40
Coleridge, Henry, 159
Coleridge, Samuel Taylor: *Biographia Literaria*, 122; "Kubla Khan," 123; *Letters, Conversations and Recollections of S. T. Coleridge*, Poe's review of, 182; Poe emulating, 123, 159; Poe on Coleridge's distinction between "Fancy" and "Imagination," 225–26; Poe's praise of, 122; self-acknowledged failure to write epic about Jerusalem's destruction, 173, 204, 212; substance problems of, 290; *Table Talk*, Poe's review of, 159, 173
Collier, Edward, 25, 107, 497nn87–88
Colman the Younger, George: *John Bull*, 6; *Love Laughs at Locksmiths*, 13
Colt, John C., 313
Colton, George H., 320, 321, 325–26, 357, 366, 378, 379, 396, 630n37, 631n42. *See also* American Review
Columbian Magazine: "The Angel of the Odd" published in, 320; "The Domain of Arnheim" published in, 371; "Mesmeric Revelation" published in, 312; "Some Words with a Mummy" published in, 325
Columbia Spy, topical letters from Poe published in, 310–11, 604n17
Conrad, Robert T., 300, 332, 594n4; Poe acknowledging himself as author of biography of, 310; "Sonnets on the Lord's Prayer" published in *Graham's Magazine*, 600n73

consolation: Boston in association with Poe's mother as, 80; Chivers's "The Heavenly Vision" and, 304; in "The Coliseum," 147; in "Eldorado," 431; in "Eleonora," 253; in *Eureka*, 362, 403–4; health crisis of Virginia precipitating Poe's need for, 267; in "The Lake," 86; in "Ligeia," 217; literary consolation for Poe, 4, 39; Poe's need to find, 166, 330, 480; in *Pym*, 39, 147, 195, 215, 304, 329, 362; in "The Raven," 329, 330; in "Tamerlane," 85; in "To Mary," 162; uniting with aspiration, 217
Conyers, Sally, 18, 23
Cook, Ann, 168
Cooke, John Esten, 453
Cooke, Philip Pendleton, 224, 238–39, 304, 356, 363, 384; "Florence Vane," 333
Cooper, James Fenimore, 246, 285; *Ned Myers*, Poe's review of, 302; *Wyandotté*, Poe's review of, 299
copyright issues, 200, 205, 207, 219, 227, 264. *See also* plagiarism
corporal punishment, 22, 35, 52, 59
correspondence. *See specific correspondents for letters to and from Poe*
cosmology, 31, 313, 382–87, 390, 392, 480. *See also Eureka: A Prose Poem*
Cousin John. *See* Mackenzie, John H.
Cowley, Hannah: *Belle's Stratagem*, 12
Cowper, William, 84
Cox, John C., 217–18, 224
Crane, Alexander T., 129, 336, 342–43, 611n3
Crawford, Samuel, 53
cryptographs. *See* puzzles
Cudworth, Warren H., 435
Cullum, George W., 113, 122, 126
Cushing, Caleb, 345
Custom House job as possibility. *See* Philadelphia, Poe's residence in

Daniel, John M., 409, 465, 466, 653n3
Dante, 2, 171

672 · Index

Darby Town (John Mackenzie's farm), 165, 178–80, 186–90, 202, 228, 253–54, 312, 353, 397, 404–5, 433, 449, 455, 457, 462, 478, 559n59, 638n40, 652n65, 664nn22–23
Darley, Felix O. C., 284, 292, 297
Davis, Andrew Jackson, 352
Dawes, Rufus: poetry, Poe's review of, 276, 281
Dearborn, George, 198, 200
Deas, Michael J., 344, 570n65
Death-Bed Confessions of the Late Countess of Guernsey, to Lady Anne H*******, The, 314
decoding and encoding, 201, 204, 225, 247, 254–55, 257, 435
Defoe, Daniel: *Robinson Crusoe*, Poe's review of, 171
deFord, Miriam Allen, 582n146
de la Motte Fouqué, Friedrich: *Undine: A Miniature Romance*, Poe's review of, 222
Delphian Club of Baltimore, 132
Democratic Review: "The Power of Words" published in, 338
desolation: biblical, 204; Poe's ability to deal with, 151
detective stories, 204. *See also* Dupin tales
Devereaux, James, 142
Devereaux, Mary. *See* Starr, Mary
devil as character in Poe's fiction, 133, 136, 137, 166, 251, 337, 347
Dew, Thomas: "Address," 174
Dial (magazine), 251–52
Dick, Thomas: *Christian Philosopher*, 401
Dickens, Charles: *Barnaby Rudge*, 327; *Barnaby Rudge*, Poe's review of, 242–43, 262, 610n83; "The Clock-Case: A Confession Found in a Prison in the Time of Charles the Second," 242, 298; "The Drunkard's Death," 235; "Gin-Shops," 235; influence on Poe, 235, 283, 298, 327, 575n39, 576n59, 591n103, 610n83; *The Life and Adventures of Nicholas Nickleby*, Poe's review of, 223; "*A Madman's MS*," 191; *Master Humphrey's Clock*, Poe's review of, 242; *The Old Curiosity Shop, and Other Tales*, Poe's review of, 242; *Pickwick Club*, Poe's review of, 191; Poe comparing to Bulwer-Lytton, 242, 310; Poe meeting in Philadelphia with (1842), 263–64, 576n59; Poe's desire to secure British publisher and, 264; Poe sending *Tales of the Grotesque and Arabesque* to, 224
Dickson, Samuel Henry, 530n13
Didier, Eugene, 20, 99, 446, 493n29, 513n93
Didier, Henry, 62
disintegration as theme, 2, 222, 479
Disraeli, Benjamin: as influence on Poe, 132; Poe praising, 132; Poe satirizing, 133, 150; *Vivian Grey*, 132, 150; *The Young Duke*, 133
Dixon, Mary Jane Poitiaux, 23, 46
Dixon, Rosanna (first wife of William Galt, Jr.), 20, 62, 108
Dollar Newspaper: contest, 286, 291–93, 296; "The Premature Burial" published in, 312; "The Spectacles" published in, 305
Doucet, Edward, 365
Douglass, Frederick, 284
Dow, Jesse E., 229, 231, 232, 235, 254, 257, 270, 285, 289, 595nn18–19
Downing, Jack. *See* Smith, Seba
Drake, Joseph Rodman: *The Culprit Fay, and Other Poems*, Poe's review of, 175, 333
Drake-Halleck review by Poe, 175, 333, 362, 405, 637n36
Drayton, William, 90, 224; *The South Vindicated*, Beverly Tucker's review of, 558n43
Drew, Mrs. Juliet J., 77, 525n42
Dubouchet, C. Auguste, 237
Dubourg, C. S., 31–32, 500n24
Dubourg, George, 30, 32, 33, 500n24
Dubourg boarding school (London), 30–33, 45, 57, 61, 385, 501n39

dueling, 201, 409, 640n54
Duncan, Henry: *Sacred Philosophy of the Seasons*, Poe's review of, 227
Duncan Lodge, 108, 119, 165, 404, 405–6, 433, 447, 450, 451, 457, 466, 477, 536n45, 638–39nn42–43, g9
D'Unger, Robert, 356, 368, 468
Dunnell, Thomas L., 414, 419
Dupin tales (short stories): compared to "The Gold-Bug," 295; creation of Dupin character, 216; reversibility of language in, 637n35; single solution requiring only one perspective in, 204; symmetry around central point in, 240, 280, 315. See also "Murders in the Rue Morgue, The" (Dupin tale); "Mystery of Marie Rogêt, The" (Dupin tale); "Purloined Letter, The" (Dupin tale)
Du Solle, John S., 237, 258, 287, 303, 580n123
Duyckinck, Evert A.: *Broadway Journal* article by, 426; *Edgar Allan Poe: The Critical Heritage* and, 605n26; Fordham visit by, 374; on Lowell's profile of Poe, 323; Poe considering one of the "best men," 624n31; Poe on "Von Kempelen and His Discovery," 428; in Poe's "The Literati of New York City," 359; Poe's response to essays of, 325; selection of tales in *American Review* by, 340; sketch of Poe in *Cyclopaedia of American Literature* by, 375; *Tales* and *The Raven and Other Poems* and, 336, 344, 348

Earle, Pliny, 231, 248; *Marathon, and Other Poems*, Poe's review of, 243, 245–46
Eaton, John H., 95–96, 99, 107, 112, 547n43
Ellet, Elizabeth F., 353–54, 359, 389, 441, 622n7
Ellis, Charles: on Allan family's return to Richmond, 41, 43; Allan's final illness and death, news of, 152–53; arrest for nonpayment of debt, 48; correspondence with John Allan during his years in England, 26, 28, 32, 36; financial and business issues with Allan, 49, 53; funeral of Frances Allan and, 94; marriage to Margaret Keeling Nimmo, 22, 460; Poe's debts, handling inquiries about 92, 56; Poe visiting home of, 56; Richmond business and social life of, 20–22, 23, 47–48; Richmond Theater fire (1811) and, 17; supportive treatment of son James at West Point, 133–34
Ellis, Frances (daughter of Charles), 108
Ellis, James N. (son of Charles), 133–34, 153
Ellis, Margaret (Keeling Nimmo), 21, 22, 24, 94, 496n74
Ellis, Powhatan (brother of Charles Ellis), 107
Ellis, Thomas H.: on Allan family on return from England, 51; birth of, 24, 496n74; on fire at Richmond Theater, 17, 29; funeral of Frances Allan and, 94; illness of, 29; on John Allan, 141, 152, 153; on Poe in Boston, 82; on Poe's possible employment in Ellis & Allan counting room, 76; on Poe's practical jokes, 56; on Poe's volunteer role in Richmond reception for Lafayette, 59; relationship with Poe, 24, 44–48; on second Mrs. Allan's noninterference between John Allan and Poe, 154, 551n1; as source on Poe's childhood, 19
Ellis & Allan, 16, 20, 491n3, 496n62; Allan's return from London to, 39; arrest of Allan and Ellis for nonpayment of debt, 48; British debts and, 47–48; debt collection issues, 46; Deed of Release, 58; dissolution, 56, 58, 514n99; legal proceedings by creditors of, 49; London market and, 29–30; Poe as delivery boy for Allan, 56, 514n100; Poe possibly later employed in counting room, 76; Poe visiting shop and reading British

magazines, 56, 132, 136, 514n95. *See also* Allan & Ellis (British firm)

Elwall, George, 35, 47

Emancipation Proclamation, 478

Emerson, Ralph Waldo: in Hawthorne's literary pantheon, 285; in Longfellow's *The Waif*, 324; Poe's review of, 258–59; "To the Humble-Bee," 264

encoding. *See* decoding and encoding

Encyclopaedia Britannica, 247

English, Thomas Dunn: *1844, or, the Power of the "S.F.,"* 363–64, 625n47; *Aristidean*'s publication of harsh piece on Longfellow, 336; "Ben Bolt," 344; *Broadway Journal* and, 349; *The Doom of the Drinker* mentioning Poe in negative light, 301, 600n77; Ellet scandal and, 359; feud with Poe, 220, 289, 290, 321, 359–60, 588n77; on Fuller's dislike of Poe, 317; *Graham's Magazine* and, 235; planning new monthly *Aristidean*, 321; Poe's Boston Lyceum talk and, 345, 348; Poe's "The Cask of Amontillado" and, 2, 65, 279, 364; on Poe's drinking, 568n38, 572n8; Poe's *Eureka*, review of, 404; on Poe's family, 232; Poe's lecture tour on cosmology and, 386; Poe's "The Murders in the Rue Morgue" and, 238; Poe's "The Black Cat," parody of, 302; politics and, 231, 235, 289

Eureka: A Prose Poem: compared to and recalling *Pym*, 403; compared to "Sonnet—To Science," 403; compared to "The Mystery of Marie Rogêt," 250; consolation and, 215, 362, 403–4; cosmology and, 31, 39, 313, 379, 403, 480; critical reception of, 404, 436, 637–38n38; dedication of, 398; Hopkins's reaction to, 393–95, 402; Hurst-Wakeman copy with Poe's penciled note, 403; "The Island of the Fay" and, 245; Lippard receiving copy from Poe, 444; longing for divine and, 276; memory in, 4; notice in anticipation of, 395; pantheism in, 391; Poe considering as his ultimate accomplishment, 387, 443; Poe's aspiration and, 479; Poe's proposal for publication of, 392; Poe's writing about, 408, 438; publication of (1848), 387, 392, 394, 397, 398–99, 636–37n33; summary of, 399–403; symmetry and, 146, 157–58, 295, 401, 403; writing of, 383, 630nn38–39

evanescence, 427

Eveleth, George W.: on Colton, 379; correspondence with Poe, 260, 269, 352, 368, 438; Godey and, 363, 625n46; on "Literati" series, 363; Poe explaining Mary Rogers's death to, 278; Poe's defense of charge of plagiarism to, 219, 372; Poe's health and, 372, 384, 389–90; on Poe's intoxication, 376, 408; Poe's last letter to, 438; Poe's lectures and, 387; "The Stylus" and, 384, 386, 438; "Von Kempelen and His Discovery" referencing, 428

Evening Mirror: Fuller-Poe and English-Poe exchanges in, 359, 360; Fuller's father-in-law's altercation with his daughter reported in, 321, 360; launch of, 318; Longfellow review by Poe and its responses, 324–25; pieces attributed to Poe in, 318, 321; Poe's deciding to end employment by, 332; Poe's role change, 323, 325, 608n67; "The Raven" published in variant form in, 326, 610n78

Evenings at Home (Aikin & Barbauld), 25, 328, 460–61, 549n69; "On Emblems," 328, 587n58; "The Transmigrations of Indur," 187

Ewing, William, 25

Fafianie, Ton, 542n61

Fairman, William, 347

Fancher, E. L., 360, 624n32

Fauvel-Gouraud, Francis: *Phreno-Mnemotechny; or The Art of Memory*, 336, 614n23

Fay, Theodore S.: *Norman Leslie*, 279, 564n16; Poe's review of, 168–69, 171, 202, 333, 556n19
Felton, C. C., 335
Fergusson, John W., 163, 176, 177, 182
fiction, Poe writing of, 129–30, 135, 154–58. *See also specific titles*
Field, Joseph M., 359
Field, Maunsell B., 386
First Artillery Regiment, Poe's military service in, 83–84, 89, 529n29
First International Conference on Edgar Allan Poe (Richmond 1999), 4
Fitzgerald, Oscar P., 451
Flag of Our Union, 424–25, 434; "Eldorado" published in, 430; "For Annie" published in, 430; "Hop-Frog: or the Eight Chained Ourang-Outangs" published in, 426; "Landor's Cottage" published in, 436; "Sonnet—To My Mother" published in, 438
Flying Dutchman legend, 144, 208, 476, 548n53
Forbes, John, 48, 58
Fordham residence, *97*; Blackwell as boarder at Poe cottage, 377; Clemm nursing Poe, 393; Clemm receiving Whitman letter for Poe at, 409; move to cottage for Virginia's health, 356–58; Poe's drinking, 393; Poe's financial straits, 371, 396, 408; Poe's health issues, 372, 394; Poe's need for "womanly love" to save him, 370, 396, 409; Poe's relationships with women as possible mates, 394, 408; Poe's return from Lowell trip (1849), 436; Starr visiting Poes, 367; Virginia's death at, 368; visitors to Poe's cottage, 373–74, 377, 378, 391, 394
Fort Independence, Poe's military service at (1827), 81, 83, 87, 89
Fort McHenry, 24
Fort Moultrie, Poe's military service at (1827–1828), 87–91, 460; consulting newspaper for his mother's performances in Charleston, 214; discharge requiring reconciliation of Poe with Allan, 92; "The Gold-Bug" recalling, 295; Poe's desire for discharge, 92; promotion to artificer, 91
Fortress Monroe, Poe's military service at (1828–1829), 92–95, 458; correspondence with John Mackenzie, 99; letters of recommendation given to Poe, 95; Poe's discharge granted (April 15, 1829), 94; Poe's promotion to regimental sergeant major, 93
Fowlds, Allan, 28, 31
fox hunting, 63, 518n141
Frailey, Charles S., cryptograph of, 250, 254–55, 256
Francis, John W., 331, 357, 394
Franklin Lyceum lecture by Poe (November 1843), 301
fraud, exposure of, 221. *See also* Poe, Edgar Allan, works by: "Maelzel's Chess-Player"
Froissart, Jean, 426
Frothingham, Edward G., 163, 174, 554n3, 557n37
Fuller, Hiram, 317, 321, 323; father-in-law's altercation with his daughter reported in *Evening Mirror*, 321, 624n30; Poe's libel suit against, 360, 363, 371, 374
Fuller, Margaret, 323, 324, 336, 351, 362, 609n70, 637n36; *Woman in the Nineteenth Century*, 362
Furniss, Cutler, and Stacey, 48, 49, 510n54

Gallego, Joseph, 18, 20, 43, 61, 492n17
Gallego, Mary. *See* Mackenzie, Mary Gallego
Galt, James (adopted son of William Galt, Sr.), 45, 53, 61, 75, 94
Galt, John: *Continuation of the Diary Illustrative of the Times of George IV*, Poe's review of, 222
Galt, William (John Allan's uncle), 30–33, 37, 38, 40, 43, 51, 504n93; death

of, 61, 517n128; estate distribution by, 56, 61
Galt, William, Jr. (adopted son of William Galt, Sr.), 43, 61, 62, 94, 108
Garrigues, Lydia Hart, 291
George III (king of England), 39, 40, 74, 295
George IV (king of England), 40, 47, 314, 426
George, Miles, 70, 71, 72–73
Germanic tradition of short stories, 132, 298. *See also* Gothic genre
Germanism, 224–25
Gibbon, Edward, 219
Gibson, Thomas W., 112–13, 117, 125–26, 210, 537n4, 538n7
Gift, The: A Christmas and New Year's Present for 1836, 155, 552n13; Poe's review of, 165, 167
Gift for 1840, The: Poe's review of, 223; Simm's "The Lazy Crow" published in, 294; "William Wilson. A Tale" first published in, 219, 223, 224, 294, 617n49
Gift for 1842, The: "Eleonora" published in, 241, 252, 254
Gift for 1843, The: "The Pit and the Pendulum" published in, 274
Gift for 1845, The: "The Purloined Letter" published in, 305, 310, 313
Gildersleeve, Basil L., 451
Glass, Francis: *A Life of George Washington, in Latin Prose*, Poe's review of, 169
Gleig, G. R.: *Memoirs of the Life of the Right Hon. Warren Hastings*, Macaulay's review of, 305
Godey, Louis A., 185, 215, 216, 226, 256, 444, 625n46, 629n22
Godey's Lady's Book, 148, 215, 217, 237; "The Literati of New York City," 351, 357, 362–64; "The Oblong Box" published in, 312; Poe contributing to, 342, 344, 354, 377; "A Tale of the Ragged Mountains" published in, 305; "Thou Art the Man" published in, 320; "The Thousand-and-Second Tale of Scheherazade" published in, 325

"Gold-Bug, The" (short story): commencement of writing, 273, 275, 280, 586n48; integration of Poe's life in, 295; John Allan and, 295; plot of, 293–94; popular reception of, 296, 340; reversibility of language in, 637n35; secret writing in, 247; on single point of view in, 204–5; sources for, 87, 89, 294; submitted to *Graham's* but withdrawn by Poe, 281, 286, 292, 593n2; as success for Poe, 296; symmetry in, 294–95; theme of, 255; as winning entry in *Dollar Newspaper* contest, 286, 291–93, 296; written backwards, 292; written on self-fashioned roll, 292, 297
Gold Rush, 424, 428
Goldsmith, Oliver: *The Vicar of Wakefield*, 549n69
Gooch, Richard: *Nuts to Crack*, 314
Goodacre, Robert, 57
Gothic genre, 131, 132, 156, 222, 265, 274, 372
Gove, Mary, 340, 358, 359, 361–62, 364–66, 377–79, 630n30
Gowans, William, 196–202, 205, 218, 562n1
Graham, George R.: advising Poe to write more positive reviews, 600n73; Griswold and, 300, 475; on Poe's devotion to Virginia and Maria Clemm, 249, 263, 578n84; on Poe's posthumous publications, 475; on Poe's reversion to drinking in times of despair, 269, 270; portrait of, *g4*; purchase of *Burton's Gentleman's Magazine*, 227, 233; relationship with Poe, 233, 236, 241, 243, 246, 249, 254, 267, 580n123, 593n2. *See also Graham's Magazine*
Graham, William H., New York Tribune building fire and, 332, 612n4

Index · 677

Graham's Magazine, 235–51, 254–81, 419; "An Appendix of Autographs" published in, 258; Chivers's "The Heavenly Vision" published in, 304; "The Colloquy of Monos and Una" published in, 248, 249–50; combining *Casket* and *Burton's Gentleman's Magazine*, 234; Conrad's "Sonnets on the Lord's Prayer" published in, 600n73; "A Descent into the Maelström" published in, 242; Dickens's work featured in, 263; enhancing Poe's reputation, 260, 264, 300, 323; "Exordium" as introduction to the reviews, 259; favorable reviews of, 264; "A Few Words on Secret Writing," published in, 247, 250; "Fifty Suggestions" published in, 434, 437; first issue of, 235; "The Gold-Bug" offered to and withdrawn, 292; Griswold as editor, 270, 300; "The Imp of the Perverse" published in, 340; "The Island of the Fay" published in, 233, 441; "Israfel" published in, 254; "Life in Death" published in, 265; Lowell's biography of Poe published in, 321–22; "The Man of the Crowd" published in, 233, 234; "Marginalia" installments published in, 382, 389; "The Mask of the Red Death" published in, 268; "The Murders in the Rue Morgue" published in, 236; "Never Bet Your Head" published in, 249, 251; "The Philosophy of Composition" published in, 327, 357; Poe as editor, 51, 204, 206, 236–37, 254, 262; Poe as freelance reviewer and contributor, 276, 302, 303, 344; Poe listed as humorous contributor (1845), 320; Poe's drinking problem and, 268; Poe's job duties, 254; Poe's pay for work on, 237, 267; Poe's resignation from, 267, 584n23; Poe's unhappiness with, 246, 267; "Secret Writing" published in, 254; Smith's watercolor portrait of Poe published in, 302; "Sonnet—To Science" published in, 244; success of, 236, 241, 251, 260, 263, 267–68; "The System of Dr. Tarr and Professor Fether" published in, 347, 607n58; "To Helen" published in, 251; "To One Departed" published in, 263; "To the Author of 'The Raven'" (Winslow with editing by Poe), 390

Gravely, William Henry, 572n8, 588n77; on English's hostility to Poe, 301, 595n19; as publisher of *The Prose Romances of Edgar A. Poe*, 296–97

Graves, Samuel (Poe's army substitute), 94–95, 109, 116, 153

Grays of Norfolk, 17, 492n6

Greeley, Horace, 235, 283, 310, 334, 346, 372, 474, 619n64

Grey, Edward S. T. (Poe pseud.), 410, 617n49

grief and bereavement: "A Dream" and, 130; Eliza Poe, Edgar's devotion to, 5, 9, 26–27, 60, 62, 109, 217, 240, 304, 617n49; Frances Allan's death and, 93, 362; Henry Poe's death and, 1, 129, 195, 200, 212, 263, 274, 306, 328, 362, 365, 368, 450; Isaiah's treatment of, 383; *Pym* and, 382; "The Raven" and, 382; recurring topic for Poe, 1, 125, 195; "To One in Paradise" and, 146; "Ulalume" and, 380, 382; Virginia Poe's death and, 370, 377, 388, 398, 407, 479

Griswold, H. W., 89, 95, 96

Griswold, Rufus Wilmot, 540n39, 568n35, 576n61; "Annabel Lee" published in Poe obituary by, 466, 475; antagonistic relationship with Poe, 236, 243, 246–47, 288, 301, 304, 325, 392–93, 419, 440, 475, 635n15; compared to Poe, 270; condemned for his vilification of Poe, 475–76, 647n5; Earle and, 245, 248; Ellet and, 354; *Female Poets of America*, 438; as literary executor for Poe, 440, 466; *The Literati* published with "Memoir" by, 475; loan to Poe, 346; meetings

with Poe, 325, 392–93; on Poe as author of *Saturday Museum* biography, 594n4; Poe's Declaration of Independence letter and, 78; Poe's New York lecture on American poetry omitting attack on, 334; politics and, 235; portrait of, *g4*; *Prose Works of John Milton*, Poe's review of, 344; *Prose Writers of America*, 325; slander that Poe terminated engagement with Whitman, 419; succeeding to editor of *Graham's Magazine* after Poe's departure, 270; vicious obituary of Poe by, 236, 246, 372, 474. See also *Poets and Poetry of America, The* (Griswold, ed.)
grotesque, the, 137, 150, 157, 201, 218, 224. See also Poe, Edgar Allan, works by: *Tales of the Grotesque and Arabesque*
Grubb, Gerald G., 576n59
Guiccioli, Countess, 149
Gwynn, William, 98, 126

Haines, Hiram, 178, 186, 227, 228
Hale, David E., 113, 115, 125
Hale, Sarah Josepha: *Alice Ray: A Romance in Rhyme*, Poe's review of, 347; *The Lady's Book* (later *Godey's Lady's Book*), 148; *Southern Literary Messenger* and, 186
Hall, Harrison, 186
Halleck, Fitz-Greene, 198, 246, 319, 333, 348, 359; *Alnwick Castle, with Other Poems*, Poe's review of, 175
Hamilton, Robert, 271, 277
Hammond, Alexander, 134, 545n23
Harper, Fletcher, 199
Harper and Brothers (publishers), 121, 173–74, 182, 199, 203, 207, 319
Harris, Amanda Bartlett, 232, 260, 567n20, 567n29, 582n145
Harrison, Gabriel, 318–19
Harrison, James A.: *Complete Works of Edgar Allan Poe*, 2
Harrison, William Henry, 22, 229, 231, 235, 241, 247

Hatch & Dunning (Baltimore publishers), 100, 102, 105
Hawks, Francis L., 193, 203
Hawthorne, Nathaniel: *American Magazine of Useful and Entertaining Knowledge*, 227; *The Blithedale Romance*, 477; *Broadway Journal* review by Poe, 336; "Earth's Holocaust," 602n90; *Famous Old People*, Poe's review of, 263; "The Hall of Fantasy" giving literary pantheon of eminent writers, 285; *The House of the Seven Gables*, 476–77; "Howe's Masquerade," 268; influence on Poe, 283, 320, 583n13; "Lady Eleanore's Mantle," 268; *Mosses from an Old Manse*, Poe's review of, 377; "Mr. Higginbotham's Catastrophe," 320; Poe's influence on, 476–77; Poe's review of *Twice-Told Tales*, 267, 268–69, 274, 275, 365, 377, 583n13; *The Scarlet Letter*, 284, 304, 476; *Twice-Told Tales*, 332, 341
Headley, Joel T.: "A Man Built in a Wall," 528n26
"heart laid bare," 235, 382, 573n24, 632n53
Heath, James E., 156, 159, 163; *Edge-Hill*, 154
Hecker, William F., 91
Henderson, John E., 125, 537n4
Herring, Elizabeth Rebecca (cousin), 99, 105, 134, 167, 366, 368
Herring, Henry, 469, 473, 494n39, 661n74
Herron, James, 269, 272
Herschel, John: *Treatise on Astronomy*, 161
Hewitt, John Hill, 105, 129, 136, 142–43, 289, 595n18; "Song of the Wind" written under pseudonym, 143, 146, 547–48n50
Hewitt, Mary E., 356, 363, 365, 419, 626n61
Hewitt, Mary L.: *The Songs of Our Land and Other Poems*, Poe's review of, 347
Heysinger, Isaac Winter, 570n65

Heywood, Bardwell, 178, 206, 397, 398, 415, 436, 559n64
Heywood, Susan H., 397–98
Higginson, Thomas Wentworth, 238, 345, 347
Hillard, George S., 324
Hirst, Henry B., 220, 226, 227, 285, 286, 443, 475, 617n49; *The Coming of the Mammoth, and Other Poems*, Poe's review of, 342, 617n49; review of Poe's *Eureka*, 404. See also *Saturday Museum* (biography)
Hobbs, Tabitha, 3
Hodgson, John A., 257
Hoffman, Charles Fenno, 198, 200, 327, 363
Hogarth prints, 70, 82, 343, 443
Holder, William, 30–31, 36, 40, 47
Holmes, Lucy, 99, 533n7
Home Journal: "The Bells" published in, 475; "For Annie" published in, 432; Poe's letter to Willis published in, 366; "The Poetic Principle" published in, 475; promoting Poe's lecture tour, 386; "To M. L. S—" published in, 371; "Ulalume" republished in, 379, 384; Virginia Poe's death noted in, 369
Hone, Philip, 198, 199, 201
Hood, Thomas: "Bridge of Sighs," 324; "The Death-Bed," 324; *Prose and Verse*, Poe's review of, 342
Hook, Theodore: *Magpie Castle*, Poe's review of, 165; *Tekeli; or, The Siege of Montgatz*, 8, 12–13, 90, 165, 214, 460
Hopkins, Charles (first husband of Eliza Arnold Poe), 6
Hopkins, John Henry, Jr., 387, 391, 393–95, 402, 404
Horne, R. H., 310; *Orion*, Poe's review of, 302–4, 332
Houghton, Marie Louise Shew. See Shew, Marie Louise
House, James, 83–84, 94, 95
Howard, Joshua, 89, 92, 94–95
Humboldt, Alexander von, 398, 401
Hunt, Freeman, 404

Hunt, Gilbert, 17, 53, 174, 210–11, 492n14, 513n84, 566n13
Hunter, R. M. T., 68, 177–78
Hunter, Robert, 24

Ide, Abijah M., Jr., 299, 323
imagination: Poe on Coleridge's distinction between "Fancy" and "Imagination," 225–26; as soul of "Intellectual Happiness," 175
Ingraham, J. H., Poe's review of, 245–46
Ingram, John H., 205, 217, 373, 381, 395, 415, 417, 421, 423, 465, 537n4, 629n11, 633n1, 642n19
Ingram, Susan V. C., 458, 461
Inman, John, 310
integration of life and work, 479; in "Annabel Lee," 479; in "The Black Cat," 298, 479; in "Eldorado," 431, 480; in "Eleonora," 252, 479; in "The Fall of the House of Usher," 222; in "For Annie," 479; in "The Gold-Bug," 295; in "Landor's Cottage," 479; in "The Man of the Crowd," 479; Poe's death and, 471; Poe's method of, 2, 4; in "The Purloined Letter," 316, 479; in *Pym*, 209–10, 252, 382, 479; in "The Raven," 382; in "Sonnet—To My Mother," 480; in "A Succession of Sundays," 258; in "A Tale of the Ragged Mountains," 305–6; in "The Tell-Tale Heart," 283; in "To Helen," 479; in "Ulalume," 381–82, 479; in "William Wilson," 479
intuition, 86, 387, 399, 400, 403
Irvine, Scotland: Allan family visiting relatives living in, 28, 29, 37, 499n2; Allan's birthplace, 28; Poe attending Old Grammar School, 28–29, 34
Irving, Washington: *Astoria*, 194, 225; *Bracebridge Hall*, 610n80; in *The Gift . . . for 1836*, 167; in Hawthorne's literary pantheon, 285; influence on Poe, 235; "King Pest" and, 150; Poe's "Penn Magazine" proposal and, 246; Poe's "Usher," response to, 223; Poe's

"William Wilson" and, 223, 569n46; "Rip Van Winkle," 235; "An Unwritten Drama of Lord Byron," 34; "Wolfert Webber," 294
Irwin, John T., 557–58n42
Isbell, George, 387, 390

Jackson, Andrew, 24–25, 140, 201, 547n43
Jackson, David K. *See* Thomas, Dwight, and David K. Jackson
Jefferson, Thomas: death of, 73; Declaration of Independence and, 295–96; design of University of Virginia by, 68; rules set for University of Virginia by, 69; trade embargo with Britain, 8, 10
Jerusalem: Coleridge's lament of inability to write epic about destruction of, 173, 182, 204, 212; destruction of, 69, 125, 134, 172, 173, 194; *Pym*'s referencing destruction of, 212; Smith's novel *Zillah, a Tale of Jerusalem* as influence on Poe, 134; tale of siege set in ("A Tale of Jerusalem"), 134, 213; Tasso's "Jerusalem Delivered," 69
John-Donkey, 386, 404
Johnston, Andrew, 56
Jones, Caleb, 406, 447, 655n24
Jones, Timothy Pickering, 112–13, 114, 117, 118, 541n47
Justin, Henri, 295

Keats, John: "On First Looking into Chapman's Homer," 144
Keith, Alexander: *Evidence of the Truth of the Christian Religion, Derived from the Literal Fulfilment of Prophecy*, 203
Kennedy, John Pendleton: as *Baltimore Saturday Visiter* contest judge, 141–43, 166; *Horse-Shoe Robinson*, 159–60; inheritance for Maria Clemm's children investigated by, 172; inquiry to Carey, Lea & Blanchard on publishing "Tales of the Folio Club," 149, 155; loan to Poe, 181–82, 346; as Poe mentor and advocate, 155–56, 166, 172, 552n13; Poe promoting launch of "Penn Magazine" to, 236; on Poe's final drinking spree in Baltimore, 467; Poe writing of his unhappiness to, 435; *Southern Literary Messenger* and, 155; *Swallow Barn*, 145
Kenney, James: *Matrimony, or the Test of Love*, 12
Kepler, Johannes, 399
Key, Francis Scott: "The Star-Spangled Banner," 24, 319
King, Martin Luther, Jr., 461, 657n41
Kinsley, Zebina J. D., 114, 539n19
Kirkland, Caroline M., 362, 378; *Western Clearings*, Poe's review of, 349
Kunstromanen (art novel), 172. *See also* art novel

Labree, Lawrence, 335
La Bruyère, 235
Ladies Companion: "The Landscape-Garden" published in, 276; "The Mystery of Marie Rogêt" published in installments in, 277, 585n42; publication schedule, 588n78
Lady's Book, The (later *Godey's Lady's Book*): "The Visionary" published in, 147
Lafayette, Marquis de, 59, 60, 97, 121
Lamb, Charles, 618n53; *Specimens of English Dramatic Poets*, Poe's review of, 347
Landor, William, 248
Lane, Thomas H., 349–50
Langley, James and Henry G. (publishers), 271
Lanier, Jane Bretney, 3, 202, 449
Lanier, Louisa. *See* Mackenzie, Louisa Lanier
Lanier, Lucy Eliza Virginia Armistead, 202
Lanier, Mary Simmons (Aunt Pollie/Polly, mother of Louisa Lanier Mackenzie), 108, 119–20, 165, 177, 180, 187, 191, 405

Lanier, William Lewis (brother of Louisa Lanier Mackenzie), 202, 449, 540n37
Lanier sisters (nieces of Louisa Lanier Mackenzie), 3, 449
Lapham, Benjamin Byrene, 139, 228
Lapham, Mary Mattox (second wife of John Mackenzie), 3, 170, 190, 228, 254, 571n70. *See also* Mattox sisters taken in by Mackenzies
Laplace, Pierre Simon, 401
Latrobe, John H. B., 114; as *Baltimore Saturday Visiter* contest judge, 141–43, 145, 166, 547n49
Latto, Thomas C., 197, 205
Law, Robert Adger, 90
Lawson, James, 351, 362
Lea, Isaac, 98, 534n23
Lea & Blanchard (publishers), 100, 223, 224, 250
LeDuc, Mary Elizabeth Bronson, 373, 375–78
Lee, Z. Collins, 473
Le Sage, Alain-René: *Gil Blas*, 72, 198, 523nn19–20, 538n7, 563n7
Leslie, Eliza, 155; *Pencil Sketches*, Poe's review of, 162. See also *Gift, The: A Christmas and New Year's Present for 1836*
letters. *See specific correspondents for letters to and from Poe*
Lever, Charles: *Charles O'Malley*, Poe's review of, 263
Levine, Stuart and Susan, 2, 122, 420, 541n46, 630n39, 637n34
Lewes, George Henry, 423
Lewis, Meriwether and William Clarke: *History of the Expedition*, 225
Lewis, Paul, 84, 390, 480
Lewis, Sarah Anna (a.k.a. Stella), 379, 397, 414, 436, 443, 462; *Child of the Sea*, 397, 409, 428; in *Female Poets of America*, 438
Lewis, Sylvanus D., 366, 368, 379
libel suit by Poe against Fuller and Clason, 360, 363, 371, 374

Lieber, Francis: *Reminiscences of an Intercourse with Mr. Niebuhr*, Poe's review of, 2, 171; *Southern Literary Messenger* and, 186
Lincoln, Abraham, 180, 329–30
Lippard, George: anti-Dickens writing, 258, 263; assisting Poe in looking for lost lectures, 448; on cholera epidemic (1849), 450; on *Columbia Spy*, 310; obituary of Poe, 443–44, 475; with Poe in his last days, 443–45; Poe's correspondence with, 303; as Poe's friend, 258; on Poe's lecture series, 300, 302; on Sons of Temperance, 655n23; at *Spirit of the Times*, 237, 258
Literary Examiner and Western Monthly Review, Poe's writings published in, 221–22
literary hoax, 56, 89, 114, 161
literary magazine, Poe's desire for his own, 136, 170, 223, 229. See also "Penn Magazine"; "Stylus, The"
Locke, Jane Ermina, 372, 394, 396, 397, 414; "Ermina's Tale," 397; "The True Poet," 396
Locke, Joseph, 113
Locke, Richard Adams, 363; "Moon Hoax," 308, 604n5
"Loco-Focos" (Democrats), 231
Lofland, John: influence on Poe, 74, 85; poetry writing competition with Poe, 105; "The Bride," 74
London stay of Allan family (1815–1820), 28–41, 493n29; Allan's business problems, 29–30, 32, 36–38; final year in London, 39–40; influence on Poe's writing, 42; planning and preparation to go, 25–26, 497n80, 498n90; Poe at Dubourg boarding school (London), 30–33, 45, 57, 61, 501n39; Poe at Manor House School (Stoke Newington), 34–36, 38, 40, 223; portrait of Poe left behind in London, 42; return to Richmond, 41; visit to Allan family in Scotland, 25–26, 28, 29, 37, 499n2

Long, George, 68–69, 73
Longfellow, Henry Wadsworth: *Ballads and Other Poems*, Poe's review of, 263, 266–67, 276, 302, 303, 420; "The Day Is Done," 454; "Excelsior," 266–67, 584n20, 617n46; in Hawthorne's literary pantheon, 285; *Hyperion, a Romance*, Poe's review of, 223, 350; influence on Poe, 584n20; "Midnight Mass for the Dying Year," 226; *Outre-Mer*, Poe's review of, 161; plagiarism accusations against, 226, 243, 255, 324, 333, 335–36, 613n17; Poe asking for contribution to *Graham's*, 243–44; Poe's assessment in *Graham's Magazine*, 255; Poe's "Penn Magazine" proposal and, 246; "Proem," 324; *The Spanish Student*, Poe's review of, 598n57; *Visions of the Night*, Poe's review of, 226; *The Waif: A Collection of Poems*, Poe's review of, 324–25, 335, 612–13n5; "Why Thus Longing?" from *The Waif*, 390; Willis and, 335
Lord, William W.: *Poems*, Poe's review of, 338
Lothair (transatlantic ship), 26; criticisms of captain of, 26, 498n96
Loud, Marguerite St. Leon, 455, 462
Lowell, James Russell: biography of Poe by, 311, 321–22, 384; Briggs-Poe relationship facilitated by, 321; Burton's contest and, 227; "Callirhöe," published in Graham's, 571n69; *Conversations on Some of the Old Poets*, Poe's review of, 324; critical reception of biography of Poe by, 608n66; *A Fable for Critics*, Poe's review of, 424, 425, 460; influence on Poe, 262, 582n3; "A Legend of Brittany," 303, 324, 601–2n89; *Poems*, Poe's review of, 303; on Poe's drinking, 338; on Poe's lack of character, 342; Poe's opinion of, 304; relationship and correspondence with Poe, 281, 290, 292, 303, 306, 311–13, 319, 320, 583n6, 593n3;

"Rosaline," 262, 582n3, 591n103; *Saturday Museum* and, 284; "The Stylus" and, 384
Lowell, Massachusetts: lecture by Poe (1848), 397, 411; visits to Richmonds in, 414–15, 433, 435–36
Lucretius: *De Rerum Natura*, 137
Lummis, William M., 354, 441
Lynch, Anne C., 337–38, 340, 351, 354, 363, 389, 397, 634n3

Mabbott, Thomas Ollive: on *Al Aaraaf, Tamerlane, and Minor Poems*, 90; on "The Balloon Hoax" sources, 603n2; on "The Cask of Amontillado," 364; on "cooping" story, 468; on Dismal Swamp as "The Lake," 86; first poems by Poe to "young female friends" not extant, 53; on missing part of "Al Aaraaf," 534n23; on "The Murders in the Rue Morgue," 575n44; "Oh, Tempora! Oh, Mores!" as first substantial poem by Poe, 64; "Oh, Tempora! Oh, Mores!" as separate poem from "Don Pompioso," 520n151; on Pitts's identity, 518n140; on Poe brothers in Clemm's home, 129; on Poe in Boston, 526n2; on *Poems* opening letter to Bulwer, 122; on Poe's death, 468; on Poe's fiction, 129–30; on Poe's marriage to Virginia Clemm (1835), 167; on Poe's poetry about Elmira Royster, 85; on Poe's relationship with Shew, 633n1; on "The Purloined Letter," 314; on Scottish influence in "The Valley Nis," 125; as source on Poe, 2, 77; on Starr-Poe relationship, 545n25; on *Tamerlane and Other Poems*, 84, 527n12; on "Ulalume," 639n45; on Weiss as trustworthy source, 651n58; on young Edgar reading aloud on horseback rides, 23–24, 496n64
Macaulay, Thomas: Poe's review of essays by, 245

Mack, Flora Lapham (stepdaughter of John Mackenzie): on Allan's desire for second marriage to his sister-in-law Nancy Valentine, 107; competitive with Weiss, 651n58; critical of Poe, 478–79; on Duncan Lodge, 406; on Edgar Poe Mackenzie, 108, 115, 120; on "Edgar the immortal climbing the trees for fruit," 188, 261; on Eliza Poe, 14; on enslaved people at Darby Town, 180; genealogical background of, 139, 228, 485n7, 491–92n5; on her mother, Mary Mattox Lapham, 190; on Jane Scott Mackenzie's opinion of Poe as child, 50; on John and Louisa Mackenzie's western trip, 138; on John Mackenzie and Maria Clemm's relationship, 183, 184, 193, 203, 439; on John Mackenzie-Poe friendship, 18–19, 88, 99–100, 119, 120, 126, 137–38, 183, 184; on John Mackenzie's encounter with Elmira Shelton (1849), 464; John Mackenzie sharing his memories of Poe with, 3–4, 476, 478–79; on John Mackenzie's opposition to Poe's match with Shelton, 651n53; on John Mackenzie's regard for Clemm, 439; on Lanier sisters at Darby Town, 449; letters as source of Poe information, 3–4, 23, 478, 492n6; on Mattox sisters at Maria and Virginia Clemm's house, 181; on Mount Erin, 108, 120; on Mrs. Lanier and her daughter Louisa, 120; on "Oh, Tempora! Oh, Mores!," 63, 518–19n144, 519–20n151; on Poe as source of "strain and unrest" in Allan household, 23, 57; on Poe at Darby Town, 187–89, 190, 254; on Poe at Duncan Lodge, 406; on Poe daguerreotypes, 657n45; on Poe's appearance, 170–71, 192, 451; on Poe's childhood, 16–19, 50; on Poe's drinking and gambling, 182–83, 187; on Poe's final visit to Mackenzies and last days in Richmond (1849), 462–63, 659n57; on Poe's letters to John Mackenzie, 99–100; on Poe's living with Maria Clemm, 126–27, 137–38; on Poe's marriage to Virginia Clemm, 167, 175–77, 188, 191; on Poe's relationships with women, 120; on Poe's relationship with Elmira Shelton, 65–66, 520n154; on Poe's relationship with Frances Allan, 50, 106; on Poe's relationship with Frances Sargent Osgood, 334–35, 354; on Poe's relationship with John Allan, 15, 19, 50, 75–76, 106, 119, 120, 153; on Poe's relationship with Maria Clemm, 183, 184, 439; on Poe's relationship with Robert Pitts, 63–65; on Poe's relationship with Rosalie Poe, 57, 119; on Poe's return to Richmond following dismissal from West Point, 118, 120–21; on Poe's story of travel abroad, 80; on Richard Mackenzie's disability, 651n56; on Richmond school for young ladies started by Jane Mackenzie, 51; on Richmond Theater fire, 18; on Thomas Mackenzie and loss of Poe biography and source letters, 203, 478, 651n56; on Virginia Poe's education, 158, 178–79, 191; on Virginia Poe's personality, 180, 181; Whitty's relationship with, 518n144; William Lanier Washington as correspondent of, 3, 63–64, 202, 215, 406, 439; on William Mackenzie, 100

Mackenzie, Edgar Poe (son of John and Louisa Mackenzie), 100, 108, 115, 120, 405, 449, 539n22

Mackenzie, Jane (William Mackenzie's sister, John's aunt): Allan family socializing in Richmond with, 47; brother Roderick and, 40; guitar gifted to Virginia Poe by, 191, 561n100; Richmond school for young ladies started by, 32, 51, 108, 139, 178, 187, 242, 511n66, 525n42; visit to London, 32, 38

Mackenzie, Jane Scott (Mrs. William Mackenzie): on Allan's desire to marry

684 · Index

Nancy Valentine as his second wife, 107; Duncan Lodge and, 406; Poe announcing his marriage to Virginia to, 176; Poe reciting "Ulalume" and, 407; on Poe's agitated state on return from West Point dismissal, 119; on Poe's childhood, 50; on Poe's earliest poems, 45; Eliza Poe and, 14; Poe's relationship with, 52, 108, 165, 447; on Poe's relationship with John Allan, 58–59, 75–76, 106; on Poe's university debts as final straw for John Allan, 75–76, 106; portrait of, *g2*; Richmond school for young ladies started with sister-in-law, 51, 511n66; Rosalie Poe living with, 15, 57, 108, 178, 406; Elmira Shelton visiting, 455; sisters of, 492n6; as source on Poe, 3, 19, 22–23. *See also* Duncan Lodge

Mackenzie, John H. (Cousin John, Poe's best friend): appearance of, 179–80, 559n59; as Confederate quartermaster in Civil War, 478, 663n22; conversion to Methodism, 272; correspondence with Poe given to brother Tom, 99, 203, 477, 533n8, 546n33; death of (1875), 558n44; as defender of Poe after Poe's death, 479; enslaved persons working for, 180, 559n59; falling out with Poe, 19, 66, 463; financial assistance provided to Poe family by, 197, 200, 202, 361, 376, 397, 655n24; Griswold's Memoir of Poe, reaction to, 476; intervening with Allan on Poe's behalf, 93, 117; on John Allan's relationship with adolescent Poe, 49–50, 52; Lanier nieces of his wife residing with, 3, 202; as lifelong friend of Poe, 16–17, 18–19, 43–44, 88, 165, 492n5, 507n4, 512n76; as Mack's source, 3–4, 476, 478–79; Maria Clemm and Virginia visiting at Darby Town, 179–80, 186–90; Maria Clemm's relationship with, 183, 191, 193, 202–3, 361, 376, 439; marriage to Louisa Lanier, 53, 88, 531n14; Mattox orphan girl cousins residing with his wife residing with, 3, 138–39, 165, 178; Mount Erin as residence, 92, 94, 100, 108, 119, 138, 531n14; move from Mount Erin to Darby Town farm, 108, 165; occupation and employment of, 179, 185, 405, 536n46; opposed to Poe's engagement to Elmira Shelton, 463, 651n53; on Poe's appearance, 170–71; Poe's correspondence while in Baltimore (1831), 138; on Poe's drinking and gambling, 182, 184–85, 270, 290, 350, 356; on Poe's marriage, 175–77, 180, 184, 355, 463, 479; on Poe's possible correspondence with Elmira Royster, 66, 85; Poe staying with at Mount Erin after ejectment from Allan home, 120–21; Poe's visits to (1848 & 1849), 404–5, 447, 449–50, 462–63; portrait of, *g2*; refusal to visit Allan home with Poe, 52; religious discussions with Poe, 215, 586n47; repeating Poe's poem "Oh, Tempora! Oh, Mores!," 64; second marriage to Mary Mattox Lapham, 571n70; on Stanard's death's effect on Poe, 49–50, 57; visits with Poe to Elmira Royster, 65; westward move to assert property rights and return after failure, 138. *See also* Darby Town

Mackenzie, Louisa Lanier (first wife of John Mackenzie): appearance of, 180, 559n59; background of, 529n31; fondness for Poe, 165, 540n37; marriage to John, 53, 88, 531n14; Mattox orphan girl cousins residing with, 138–39, 165, 178; Mount Erin as residence with husband John, 92, 94, 100, 108, 119, 138, 531n14; nursing Poe after ejectment from Allan home, 119–20; photograph of, *g3*; as source on Poe, 3. *See also* Darby Town

Mackenzie, Martha (sister of John Mackenzie, later wife of William P. Byrd), 406, 447

Mackenzie, Mary (sister of John Mackenzie), 192, 406

Mackenzie, Mary Gallego, 18, 23, 405

Index · 685

Mackenzie, Mary Mattox Lapham (second wife of John Mackenzie). *See* Lapham, Mary Mattox

Mackenzie, Richard (brother of John), 3, 406, 447, 466, 651n56, 655n24

Mackenzie, Roderick, 242

Mackenzie, Thomas G. (brother of John): birth and death recorded in Mackenzie Family Bible, 663n20; caring for intoxicated Poe, 451; as Confederate physician in Civil War, 477, 663n22; Elmira Shelton and, 446; financial assistance to Poe from, 655n24; living at Duncan Lodge, 406; medical education of, 638n43; Poe's biography and all source letters, loss to fire, 3, 99, 203, 477, 533n8, 546n33, 596n24; Poe's visits with, 447, 466; on subscription list of *Southern Literary Messenger*, 290–91

Mackenzie, William, 23, 61, 99–100, 533n8

"Maelzel's Chess-Player" (automaton), 175, 226, 557nn40–41

Maffitt, John Newland, 272

Magruder, A. B., 113, 125–26, 193

malaria, 529n29

Manchester, Edwin H., daguerreotype of, 417–18

Marshall, John: *Life of George Washington*, 70, 162

Martha (ship), 41, 92

Martin, Eric, 534n23

Mason, Monck, 308

Masury & Hartshorne (daguerreotype studio), 417, 418

Mathews, Cornelius, 374, 624n32; *Wakondah*, Poe's review of, 262

Matthiessen, F. O., 316

Mattox, Mary. *See* Lapham, Mary Mattox

Mattox sisters taken in by Mackenzies (Ann, Mary, & Eliza), 3, 138–39, 165, 178, 181, 187–88, 228, 254, 404, 449, 638n39

Mattson, Morris: *Paul Ulric*, Poe's review of, 172

Maupin, Socrates, 574n36

Mayo, Joseph, 79–80

Mayo, Robert, 58, 515n111

McCabe, John Collins, 193

McCaw, James D., 17, 174, 210, 492n14

McDougall, John A., portrait of Poe by, 352

McHenry, James, 286

McKee daguerreotype of Poe, 284, 286–87, 594n5

McMasters, Wesley, 295

McMichael, Morton, 130, 136, 185, 207, 209, 215–17, 226, 239, 300

McMurtrie, Henry, 219

Mead, Joan Tyler, 437

Mechanics Institute of Reading, Pennsylvania, Poe's lecture at (1844), 304

Melville, Herman: *Moby-Dick*, 245, 477; *Pierre; or, the Ambiguities*, 477; Poe's influence on, 477, 577n70

Memorials of Mrs. Hemans, Poe's review of, 190

memory: *Eureka* and, 4; of Frances Allan, scent associated with, 461; Poe's grief for Virginia and, 398; Poe's interest in Fauvel-Gouraud's *Phreno-Mnemotechny; or The Art of Memory*, 336, 614n23; *Pym* and, 4, 39, 185, 380, 381; "The Raven" and, 328, 336, 380, 381; "Ulalume" and, 380, 382

Messenger. *See Southern Literary Messenger*

metempsychosis, 131, 158–59, 187, 217, 222, 297, 305

Methodism, 272

military service of Poe, 527n10; correspondence with John Mackenzie during, 99; discharge requiring reconciliation of Poe with Allan, 92; in First Artillery Regiment, 83–84, 89, 529n29; at Fort Independence (1827), 81, 83, 87, 89; at Fort Moultrie (1827–1828), 87–91, 214, 294, 295, 308; at Fortress Monroe (1828–1829), 92–95, 99; Graves as Poe's substitute,

94–95, 109, 116, 153; letters of recommendation given to Poe, 95; Poe's desire for discharge, 92; Poe's discharge granted (April 15, 1829), 94; promotion to artificer, 91; promotion to regimental sergeant major, 93
Millar, Albert E., Jr., 4
Miller, James H., as *Baltimore Saturday Visiter* contest judge, 141, 142, 166
Millington, John H., 356
Milton, John: influence on Poe, 103, 231; "L'Allegro," 353; *Paradise Lost*, 311, 605n19, 643n25; Poe copying out excerpts from, 90; Poe denigrating, 132
Miner's Journal, interested in Poe writing letters for, 311
Minor, Benjamin B., 193, 291
mirrors, 175, 201, 208, 211–12, 328, 380, 557–58n42
Miss Jane Mackenzie's School (for young ladies), 32, 51, 108, 139, 178, 187, 242, 511n66, 525n42; Rosalie Poe teaching at, 32, 51, 178
Mitchell, John Kearsley, 226, 582n145, 594n4
Moldavia (John Allan's Richmond house): Frances Allan's funeral at, 93; Henry Poe's visit to, 62; photograph of, *g2*; Poe's conflict with second Mrs. Allan upon arrival from West Point dismissal, 120; Poe staying at, for Frances Allan's funeral, 94; Poe staying at, upon return from Baltimore (1830), 105–6; purchase of, 61; second Mrs. Allan refusing Poe entry to, 152, 154; vases in, 550n69
Moldenhauer, Joseph J., 241
Moore, John W., 440
Moore, Thomas: *Alciphron, a Poem*, Poe's review of, 225; as Byron biographer, 149; "Come Rest in This Bosom" (song), 232, 271, 367, 409–10, 413, 431, 644n41, 654n8; *The History of Ireland*, Poe's review of, 162; influence on Poe, 103, 549n69; *Irish Melodies*, 467;

"I Wish I Was by That Dim Lake," 86; "Oft, in the Stilly Night," 457; "When Gazing on the Moon's Light," 86
Moran, John J., 47, 467, 469
Moran, Mary, 469–70, 473
Mordecai, Samuel, 13–14, 54, 509n37
Morford, Harry, 243
Morgan, Susan Rigby: *The Swiss Heiress*, Poe's review of, 190
Morrell, Benjamin: *A Narrative of Four Voyages*, 211
Morris, George Pope, 317, 348, 368, 583n6, *g7*
Morris, P. H.: "The Evil Effects of Drunkenness Physiologically Explained," 248
Morris, Robert, 235, 238, 300, 594n4, 600n73; "The Student's Dream of Fame," Poe's review of, 600n73
Morton, Thomas: *Speed the Plough*, 6
Mott, Valentine, 372–73, 394
Mount Erin, 53, 108, 121, 126, 536n46. See also Mackenzie, John H.
"*Mournful and Never-ending Remembrance*," 1, 212, 328, 380, 454, 458
Moxon, Edward, 264
Muhlenberg, William Augustus, 383
"Murders in the Rue Morgue, The" (Dupin tale): Browne's *Urn-Burial* and, 222; compared to "Life in Death," 265; considered for inclusion in other formats, 236, 250, 271; correspondence concerning, 365; critical reception, 238–39; Dubourg character named for Poe's London school, 33; Dupin's first appearance in, 237; first modern detective story, 25, 236, 238; influences on, 25; link with other Dupin tales, 280, 315; manuscript extant, 237; pay from *Graham's* for, 237; *Philadelphia Saturday News* as source for, 185, 216, 218; plot of, 237–38; in *The Prose Romances of Edgar A. Poe*, 296; published in *Graham's Magazine*, 236, 237; reversibility of language in, 637n35; written backwards, 238

Murdock, James E., 331
"Musiad" (poem touching on Poe), 535n32
"Mystery of Marie Rogêt, The" (Dupin tale), 277–80; based on death of Mary Rogers, 249, 250, 278; compared to *Eureka* and *Pym*, 250; conflict with Griswold and, 248; extensive time to write, 251, 257, 260; included in proposed "Phantasy-Pieces," 271; link with other Dupin tales, 315; plot of, 278–79; publication queries sent by Poe, 270; published in installments, 277, 585n42; selling possibility on New York City trip (1844), 271, 585n42; as sequel to "The Murders in the Rue Morgue," 278, 280; sources for, 169, 240; Weld-Poe feud leading to covert attack on Weld in, 279

Narrative of Arthur Gordon Pym, The (novel): allegory in, 9, 130, 134, 171, 172, 194, 198, 209–10, 377, 563n7; analysis of, 209–15; anticipating publication of, 204; "Ariel" name signifying Jerusalem and, 173, 194, 212–13; *Ariel* shipwreck as prompt for, 173, 194, 207, 212; as art novel (Kunstromanen), 172, 174, 194, 207, 209, 212, 215; Augustus-Henry Poe character, 1, 9, 194, 195, 198, 210, 212, 479, 563n8; Augustus's death, 208, 210, 212; author surrogate of Arthur Gordon Pym, 194; birth allegories of Augustus-Henry and Pym-Poe in, 9, 194, 198; cannibalism as seemingly sole alternative for survival, 208; characters based on figures from Poe's life, 194, 198; Christianity and, 122, 168, 213–15, 276, 329, 403, 480, 566n14; Clarke's academy at beginning of, 44; Coleridge's inability to write epic about Jerusalem's destruction as prompt for, 159, 212; commencement of writing, 174, 186, 190; compared to *Eureka*, 403; compared to "The Mystery of Marie Rogêt," 250; compared to "The Premature Burial," 313; compared to "The Raven," 328–29; consolation and, 39, 147, 195, 215, 304, 329, 362; countermutiny, 208; critical response to, 209, 215, 229, 239, 300; death of Poe's brother Henry and, 1, 195, 212, 306, 328, 450; *dénouement* constantly in view when writing, 190; "A Dream" and, 130; etymology and, 186; final journal entry, 210, 211, 214, 267; *Flying Dutchman*'s appearance in, 208; Frances Allan and, 194; Harper and Brothers as publishers, 174, 207, 219, 319; Hunt as possible model for character Peters in, 53, 210–11; integration of life and work in, 209–10, 252, 382, 479; *Jane Guy*'s voyage and arrival at island of Tsalal, 208; Jerusalem in, 69, 125, 172, 173, 194; Jesus, crucifixion, and other biblical imagery referenced in, 213–14; John Allan as character of Pym's maternal grandfather, 135, 194, 198, 210; memory and, 4, 39, 185, 380, 381; mirrors and, 175, 208, 211–12, 328; Murphy and Jeffers's *Nautical Routine and Stowage, with Short Rules in Navigation* treating as if authoritative, 228, 437; Nu-nu and, 186, 209; as one of Poe's greatest achievements, 182, 207; "other" in character of Dirk Peters, 174, 208, 210; "partly allegorical, partly metaphysical," 172, 194, 209, 215; *Penguin* (ship) role in, 41, 109, 194, 207, 211; penguins and, 211, 214, 328; Poe as ghost at Ellis home's whist game linked to Pym's appearance as dead man on *Grampus*, 114, 210, 309; Poe continuing to edit even as book going to press, 205; Poe's aspiration and, 479; Eliza Poe (Poe's mother) and, 194, 210, 214, 306, 460; Poe's escape from Richmond linked to Pym's escape on *Grampus*, 210; Poe's own writing standards applied to, 252; Poe's practical joke at West Point as foreshadowing of, 114, 210; Poe working on while living in New York City (1837–1838), 196, 197, 200; preface, 207; Pym and Peters' adventures on island of Tsalal, 208–9; race and, 102, 174, 208, 210, 566n13; Ragged Mountains' link to "mountains of ragged ice," 78, 210; reversibility of language in, 637n35; Reynolds and, 78, 205, 470; ship details and, 41; "shrouded human figure" at conclusion, 209, 211, 214, 403, 470, 477; *Southern Literary Messenger* publishing installments of, 193–94, 197, 207–8; *Southern Literary Messenger*'s subscriber names used in, 198, 563n8; Symmes's Hollow Earth theory and, 145, 161, 242; symmetry in, 211, 328, 403; "A Tale of Jerusalem" as precursor to, 213; *Tekeli* and, 90, 214; Too-Wit (native chief) in scene with mirrors, 208, 211, 212, 328; twelve shipmates similar to twelve tribes of Israel, 213; "unity of effect" and, 182; verbal pattern encoded in, 201; White perplexed by, 194; Wiley & Putnam publishing in London (October 1838), 217; written in response to Harper and Brothers' request for "single and connected story," 174, 182; yellow fever and, 530n13

nature, Poe's response to, 86. *See also* cosmology

Neal, John: as advocate of "respectable and independent journal," 288; as champion of Poe, 100–101, 104–5, 106, 126, 169, 288, 385; Poe dedication of "Tamerlane" to, 165; Poe's assessment in *Graham's Magazine*, 255; on Poe's character, 475; Poe sending prospectus for "Penn Magazine" to, 230; Poe's reviews and, 284; Poe telling no tie stronger than between brothers, 5, 62; *Rachel Dyer*, 101; "Raising the Wind" reference to, 150, 550n77; on *Southern Literary Messenger*, 167, 169–70

Neal, Joseph C., 185, 215, 217, 226

Nelson, Thomas, 35, 58

"nevermore": drawn from Poe for a contemporary play, 331, 611n3; in Lowell's "Rosaline," 262, 582n3; in Poe's "The Raven," 262, 298, 326, 327, 329, 330, 390

Newark Academy lecture by Poe (1843), 301–2, 601n79

Newburyport (ship), 20

New England Galaxy, 165, 170, 288

New England Magazine, 140, 169

New York City, Poe's residence in (1837–1838), 196–204; Booksellers' Dinner (March 30, 1837), 198–99, 201, 563n10; departure for Philadelphia (early 1838), 204; household income, 202, 204; July Fourth celebration, 201–2; modest time for Poe, 196, 198, 204; move to (February 1837), 193, 196; pay received for literary contributions, 202; Poe, Virginia, and Maria Clemm living on Carmine Street, 200; Poe, Virginia, and Maria Clemm living on Sixth Avenue with boarder Gowans, 196–97; Poe's not drinking, 562n1

New York City and environs, Poe's residence in (1844–1849, intermittent): boardinghouse on Greenwich Street as residence for Poe and Virginia, 307; Boston trip (1845), 341; Brennan farmhouse as country home of Poe and Virginia, 312, 319, 320–21, g5; Clemm moving to New York to reside with Poe and Virginia, 309; financial troubles, 307, 337, 348, 350, 358, 360, 626n59; forgery allegations against Poe, 339, 341, 359, 360, 615n35; move near Turtle Bay, 355; move to Amity Street apartment, 344–45, 618n58; Nassau Street as heart of New York publishing, 307–8; New York

Index · 689

New York City and environs, Poe's residence in (1844–1849, intermittent) (*continued*): Tribune building fire, 332, 612n4; Poe as member of literary aristocracy, 352; Poe's drinking, 337–40, 349–50, 360–61; Poe's illness, 360; Poe's sobriety upon initial move, 312; Providence trip by Poe, 339, 341, 615n35; returning to city (Greenwich Street) from country home, 325; Rosalie's visit to Fordham cottage, 361; Starr visiting Poes in, 367; St. Johns College, Poe's visit to, 365; at Twentieth Street Free Church for Christmas Eve, 382–83; Virginia's illness (tuberculosis), 307, 312, 319, 350

New York City excursions: Poe looking for job and/or publisher (1844), 271–72, 585n41; Poe seeking to secure publication of his poetry (1831), 121

New York Daily Tribune: Poe's obituary in, 474; review of *Eureka* in, 404; review of *Tales* in, 340

New-York Mirror, anonymous poem "The Coliseum" in, 146

New York Review, Poe's association with, 193, 197, 199, 200, 203, 227

New York Society Library, Poe's lectures at (1845), 333, 336–37, 385, 386; critical reviews of, 387

New York Sun: Locke's "Moon Hoax" published in, 308; Poe's "Balloon Hoax" published in, 308–9

New York Tribune, obituary for Poe in, 466

New York True Sun on Balloon Hoax, 309

Nichols, Mary Gove. *See* Gove, Mary

Nichols, Samuel, 476

Nichols, Thomas Low, 308–9, 310

Niebuhr, Barthold Georg: "Essay on the Allegory in the First Canto of Dante": Poe's review of, 2, 171

Nimmo, James, 24

Nimmo, Margaret Keeling. *See* Ellis, Margaret

Noah, Mordecai M., 140, 198, 199, 279, 347

No Name Magazine (1889), "Oh, Tempora! Oh, Mores!" published in, 63–64

Non-Intercourse Act (1809), 20

Norfolk: Norfolk Academy lecture of "The Poetic Principle," 461; Old Hygeia Hotel lecture of "The Poetic Principle," 458–60

North, Christopher. *See* Wilson, John

North American reprinting "The Happiest Day" and "Dreams" (1827), 87, 528n24

O'Neil, Augustine, 362

onomatopoeia, 435

Opal, The (annual), "Morning on the Wissahiccon" published in, 299

originality, 140, 143, 230, 236, 258, 296, 297, 316, 443

Osgood, Frances Sargent, 583n6; Clemm chastising for relationship with Poe, 334–35, 354, 479, 613n14; Ellet and, 353–54; husband of, 341, 343–44; "Ida Grey," 343, 358, 617n49, 618n54; "Ida's Farewell," 358; "The Life-Voyage," 460; "Love's Reply," 615n23; "Lulin; of the Diamond Fay," 345; *Poems*, Poe's review of, 349; Poe's acrostic valentine to, 388; Poe's high regard for, 333, 336, 354, 363, 374; in Poe's lecture "Poets and Poetry of America," 397; Poe's poem in *Broadway Journal* to, 338; Poe's relationship with, 334–35, 339, 341, 343, 344, 345, 352, 396, 583n6, 613n14; portrait of, *g5*; "The Rivulet's Dream" (pseud. Kate Carol), 615n23; scandal associated with Poe and, 353–54; "So Let It Be" (pseud. Violet Vane), 615n23; "Spring" (pseud. Violet Vane), 615n23

Osgood, Samuel S., 343–44, *g6*

Ostrom, John Ward, 376, 630n37; *The Collected Letters of Edgar Allan Poe* (3d ed., with Pollin and Savoye), 2, 219, 220, 237

"Our Club" of Philadelphia literati, 226

Pabodie, William J., 408, 411, 418, 420–23
Panic of 1819, 43
Panic of 1837, 200, 231, 281
Panic of 1839, 231, 281
pantheism, 391–92, 394
Patterson, E. H. N., 433–35, 448, 450, 456, 465–66
Patterson, Louisa Gabriella (second wife of John Allan). *See* Allan, Louisa Gabriella Patterson
Paulding, J. K.: at Booksellers' Dinner (March 30, 1837), 198, 199; *A Life of Washington*, Poe's review of, 179; Poe imploring for job, 206; Poe's debt to, 200; *Slavery in the United States*, Beverly Tucker's review of, 558n43; *Southern Literary Messenger* and, 186; on "Tales of the Folio Club," 173–74, 182; on White Sulphur Springs resort, 19
Payne, John Howard, 10
Pease, Harlow, 526n2
Pease, Peter Pindar, 70, 82, 83, 84, 118–19, 121, 299, 525n55, 526n2
Peasley, Thaddeus K. (Poe pseud.), 319, 607n55
Pedder, Anna and Bessie, 218, 224, 565n4
Pedder, James, 205, 218, 225, 567n29; *Farmer's Cabinet*, 237
Penguin (ship). *See Narrative of Arthur Gordon Pym, The*
Penn, James, 23, 496n62
"Penn Magazine": delay of launch due to Poe's illness, 235; dim prospects due to financial crisis, 236; Graham not fulfilling promise to support, 267; never published, 229; newspaper articles anticipating, 234; planning and writing to friends about, 234–36, 275, 632n61; Poe's hopes for and ongoing commitment to idea of, 233, 246, 247, 254, 260, 263, 272, 281; prospectus for, 229–31, 233; renamed "The Stylus," 284. *See also* "Stylus, The"

Perry, Edgar A. (Poe pseud. for military enlistment), 83–84, 94
Perry, Oliver Hazard, 22
Peterloo massacre (1819), 38
Petersburg, Virginia, as honeymoon location of Poe and Virginia, 178
Peterson, Charles J., 227, 243, 254, 267, 270, 281, 300, 571n69
Philadelphia, Poe's residence in (1838–1844): bankruptcy of Poe, 281–82, 284; Custom House position as possibility, 269, 272, 273, 275, 277, 288, 302; departing for New York City (1844), 303, 306; financial straits of Poe, 217–19, 232–33, 263, 268, 273, 281–83; friendships developed, 229, 231, 233, 258, 299, 583n6; Harper & Brothers's publication of *Pym*, 207; move to east side Fairmount area (North Seventh Street), 291, 596n26; New York City excursion, Poe looking for job and/or publisher (1842), 271–72, 585n41; "Our Club" of literati, 226; periodicals district, 205; Poe family living at Mr. Jones's boardinghouse, 205; Poe family living in northeast neighborhood, 269; Poe family living near Locust on Sixteenth Street, 216, 232, 566–67n20, 572n9; Poe living "miserable life of literary drudgery," 206; Poe's debt to his tailor (J. W. Albright), 282, 283; Poe's drinking, 220–21, 241, 263, 269–70, 274, 275; Poe's unemployment (1840), 233; pro-slavery mob burning down Pennsylvania Hall (1838), 206; Washington excursion from, 288–89. *See also Burton's Gentleman's Magazine*; *Graham's Magazine*
Philadelphia Museum lecture (1844), 302, 443
Philadelphia Saturday Chronicle, "The Devil in the Belfry" published in, 219
Philadelphia Saturday Courier, 207, 219; "Raising the Wind" published in, 150, 299

Philadelphia Saturday Museum. See
  Saturday Museum (biography)
*Philadelphia Saturday News and
  Literary Gazette* (*Saturday News*),
  207; cessation of publication, 218;
  Poe adapting stories from, 185, 216,
  218, 239; *Pym* review in, 215; *Southern
  Literary Messenger* review in, 185
Phillips, Elizabeth, 519n151
Phillips, Mary E., 491n2, 538n19, 572n6
Phillips, Philip E., 480
Pinsky, Robert, 480
Pioneer (magazine): critical reception of,
  590n95; "Lenore" published in, 285;
  "Notes upon English Verse" published
  in, 286, 304; Poe's anonymous review
  of, 284, 591n111; publication schedule,
  592n116; "The Tell-Tale Heart"
  published in, 281, 282, 285
Pitts, Robert, 63–65, 357, 518n140,
  519n147
plagiarism: Aldrich accused of, 324,
  614n20; in classical competition at
  University of Virginia, 69; English
  accusing Poe, 359–60; Outis defending Longfellow, 335, 613n17; Poe
  accused of, for *The Conchologist's First
  Book*, 219, 372; Poe accusing English,
  359; Poe accusing Longfellow, 226,
  243, 255, 324, 333, 335–36; Poe's
  defense of Keith, 203; Poe's discussion of, 172, 223, 332, 344; in Poe's
  review of Clarke's *The Christian
  Keepsake and Missionary Annual for
  1840*, 223; Poe's review of Earle and,
  577n73
Pleasants, Hugh, 640n51
Pleasants, John Hampden, 162, 525n45
pleasure as poetry's purpose, 122, 124
Pliny, Earle: *Marathon, and Other Poems*,
  Poe's review of, 243, 245–46
Poe, David, Sr. (paternal grandfather),
  9–10, 59, 62, 97–98, 162, 473
Poe, David, Jr. (father): acting career of,
  5–8, 9–10, 82, 90, 97; critical reviews
  of performances, 6–8, 11–12, 619n63;

death of, 14, 490n74; family relationships, 10
Poe, Edgar Allan
  athletic abilities, 46, 50, 52, 58, 72, 160,
    226, 378, 630n37
  bankruptcy of, 187, 200, 204, 257, 269,
    281, 284, 560n84, 563n14, 572n10
  baptism of, 491n1
  biography clarifying works of, 2
  birth of (1809), 9
  burial in gravesite of grandfather
    David Poe, 473–74
  charisma of, 134–35
  confidence in literary future, 92–93,
    231
  critical reception of fiction by, 135–36,
    159, 160, 162, 244, 297, 340. *See also
    specific works*
  critical reception of lectures by, 304,
    346–47, 387, 397, 420, 461–62, 465.
    See also specific location of lecture
  critical reception of poetry by, 65, 98,
    100–101, 104–5, 106, 126, 325–26,
    327, 330, 348. *See also specific titles of
    poems*
  critical reception of reviews by. *See*
    Poe, Edgar Allan: "as harsh and
    controversial critic of literature"
  death of, 467–71, 660n64
  depression and melancholic, dark side
    of, 1, 71–72, 85, 86, 113, 124, 135, 160,
    166, 183, 220, 269, 287, 311, 337–38,
    348, 361, 412, 434–35, 443
  devotion to mother Eliza, 5, 9, 26–27,
    60, 62, 109, 217, 240, 304, 617n49
  drawing ability of, 70, 522n17
  drinking problems, 66, 69, 70, 72–73,
    75, 113–14, 132–33, 141, 177, 182–85,
    187, 191–92, 195, 235, 241, 248, 268,
    269–70, 271–72, 287, 289–90, 291,
    338–40, 349–50, 356, 389–90,
    408–9, 420–21, 441, 451, 467–70,
    572n8, 647n34
  effeminacy of, 46, 132, 519n146
  facing coming death of Virginia,
    364–65

fame attained by, 330, 331, 474
financial problems and poverty of, 66, 69, 70, 72–73, 75–76, 106, 182–85, 187, 217–19, 232–33, 263, 268, 273, 281–82, 360, 371, 396, 408
gambling and related financial problems of, 66, 69, 70, 72–73, 75, 182–85, 187
genius and intelligence recognized in, 1, 46, 48, 52, 122, 126, 169, 175, 216, 234, 288, 296, 300, 322, 323, 465, 475
as harsh and controversial critic of literature, 175, 186, 190, 192, 200, 203, 220, 248, 249, 252, 255, 256, 259, 279, 281, 285, 292, 300, 301, 302, 359, 580n123, 600n73
in Hawthorne's literary pantheon, 285
health/illness of, 365–66, 372, 418, 424, 434, 441–42, 448, 451, 466, 660nn64–65
homesick for Richmond, 444
humor, jokes, satire of, 44, 56, 62–65, 113, 122, 133, 136, 160, 169, 201, 218, 248, 249, 285, 347, 434, 519n151, 620n65
imagination of, 18, 27, 69, 101, 145, 209
last correspondence of, 462
literary intentions of, 4, 248. *See also* aspiration
lock of his hair given to Sarah Helen Whitman, 412, 641n7
locks of his hair taken after his death, 473
marriage to Virginia Clemm (1835), 166–68, 175–76. *See also* Poe, Virginia Clemm
name of, 8–9, 491n1
nervousness of, 23, 73, 226, 233, 263, 283
not adopted by Allans, 19, 51
obituaries for, 474–75
overseas travel, made-up tales of, 80, 82
parodies of his works by others, 331, 338, 341, 359, 615n32
personality of, 20, 28, 35, 44, 45–46, 48, 50–52, 56, 71, 113, 135, 145, 221, 241, 248, 269, 292, 317, 336, 342–43, 360, 365, 371, 407, 412, 448, 585n33, 631n40
physique (looks) of, 31, 46, 48, 83, 132, 134–35, 163, 170–71, 197, 199, 286, 386, 448, 449, 451, 563n11
pictures (portraits, engravings, etc.) of, ii, 284–85, 286–87, 302, 321, 344, 352, 417, 436, 462, 592n114, *g6, g9*
pocket watch of, 283, 591n107
productivity of, 150, 185, 248, 280, 312, 422–24, 433
regret for not vindicating his mother's good name, 240, 316
reputation after his death, 474
resilience of, 361, 384–85, 386
self-assessment and self-confidence of, 1, 27, 45, 67, 81, 84, 85, 122, 150, 212, 374
sensitivity of, 71, 125, 182, 222, 226, 263, 345, 451
slavery and ("an average racist"), 102, 163, 174, 405, 534n15
voice of, 135, 346, 362, 397–98, 407, 412, 465
"womanly love" and care needed after Virginia's death, 370, 394, 396, 409, 433, 440, 628n9
See also University of Virginia; West Point; *and specific locations of residence*
Poe, Edgar Allan, childhood of: adolescence in Richmond (1820–1825), 43–66; adolescent romance with Elmira Royster, 47; as baby with paternal grandfather and grandmother in Baltimore, 9–10, 97–98; early years in Richmond (1811–1815), 13, 15–27; Ebenezer Burling as friend, 46; illnesses, 21; John Mackenzie as friend, 16–17, 18–19, 43–44, 492n5; Richmond Junior Volunteers membership, 59, 60, 516n116; Robert Sully as friend, 46, 48; swimming feat in James River, 58, 226, 515n111, 552n14. *See also* London stay of Allan family; Poe, Edgar Allan, education of

Poe, Edgar Allan, education of: academic achievement of, 44–45, 46, 48, 52, 56; Burke's school (Richmond), 52, 56, 61, 512n73; Clarke's academy (Richmond), 44–45, 46, 48, 50–51, 53, 194; classical education, 44, 45, 50, 68–69, 74; Dubourg boarding school (London), 30–33, 45, 57, 61, 385, 501n39; earliest education in Richmond, 22, 25; Manor House School (Stoke Newington), 34–36, 38, 40, 223, 479; Old Grammar School (Irvine, Scotland), 28–29; poetry written by Poe while in Clarke's academy, 45, 50, 53; relationship with classmates, 51, 52; social class issues at schools, 51; Thespian Society membership, 52. *See also* University of Virginia; West Point

Poe, Edgar Allan, reviews by
  Arthur, T. S.: *Insubordination*, 245
  Barrett, Elizabeth Barrett: *A Drama of Exile, and Other Poems*, 148, 318, 319, 321
  Bermingham, James: *A Memoir of the Very Reverend Theobald Mathew. With an Account of the Rise and Progress of Temperance in Ireland*, 248
  Bird, Robert Montgomery: *The Hawks of Hawk-Hollow*, 169
  Bird, Robert Montgomery: *Sheppard Lee*, 187
  Brainard, John G. C.: *Poems*, 262
  Brougham, Henry Lord: *The Critical and Miscellaneous Writings of Henry Lord Brougham*, 263
  Brougham, Henry Lord: *Historical Sketches of Statesmen Who Flourished in the Time of George III*, 222
  Brougham, Henry Lord: *Opinions of Lord Brougham*, 223
  Brougham, Henry Lord: *Sketches of Public Characters, Discourses, and Essays*, 221
  Browne, Thomas: *Urn-Burial*, 222
  Bulwer-Lytton, Edward: *Night and Morning*, 238, 240
  Chandler, Joseph R.: *An Address, Delivered before the Goethean and Diagnothian Societies of Marshall College*, 224
  Channing, William Ellery, 297
  Chorley, Henry F.: *Conti the Discarded*, 172, 209
  Clarke, James A. *The Christian Keepsake and Missionary Annual for 1840*, 223
  Cockton, Henry: *Stanley Thorn*, 259
  Coleridge, Samuel Taylor: *Letters, Conversations and Recollections of S. T. Coleridge*, 182
  Coleridge, Samuel Taylor: *Table Talk*, 159, 173
  Cooper, James Fenimore: *Ned Myers*, 302
  Cooper, James Fenimore: *Wyandotté*, 299
  Dawes, Rufus: poetry, 276, 281
  Defoe, Daniel: *Robinson Crusoe*, 171
  de la Motte Fouqué, Friedrich: *Undine: A Miniature Romance*, 222
  Dickens, Charles: *Barnaby Rudge*, 242–43, 262, 610n83
  Dickens, Charles: *The Life and Adventures of Nicholas Nickleby*, 223
  Dickens, Charles: *Master Humphrey's Clock*, 242
  Dickens, Charles: *The Old Curiosity Shop, and Other Tales*, 242
  Dickens, Charles: *Pickwick Club*, 191
  disparaging pretenders to literary elite, 65
  Drake, Joseph Rodman: *The Culprit Fay, and Other Poems*, 175, 333
  Duncan, Henry: *Sacred Philosophy of the Seasons*, 227
  Emerson critique, 258–59
  Fay, Theodore S.: *Norman Leslie*, 168–69, 171, 202, 333, 556n19

Galt, John: *Continuation of the Diary Illustrative of the Times of George IV*, 222
Gift, The: A Christmas and New Year's Present for 1836, 165, 167
Gift for 1840, The, 223
Glass, Francis: *A Life of George Washington, in Latin Prose*, 169
Griswold, Rufus Wilmot: *The Poets and Poetry of America*, 272–73, 276–77, 300, 302, 586n48, 588n77
Griswold, Rufus Wilmot: *Prose Works of John Milton*, 344
Hale, Sarah Josepha: *Alice Ray: A Romance in Rhyme*, 347
Halleck, Fitz-Greene: *Alnwick Castle, with Other Poems*, 175
Hawthorne, Nathaniel: *Famous Old People*, 263
Hawthorne, Nathaniel: "Howe's Masquerade," 268
Hawthorne, Nathaniel: *Mosses from an Old Manse*, 377
Hawthorne, Nathaniel: *Twice-Told Tales*, 267, 268–69, 274, 275, 365, 377, 583n13
Hewitt, Mary L.: *The Songs of Our Land and Other Poems*, 347
Hirst, Henry B.: *The Coming of the Mammoth, and Other Poems*, 342, 617n49
Hood, Thomas: *Prose and Verse*, 342
Hook, Theodore: *Magpie Castle*, 165
Horne, R. H.: *Orion*, 302, 303, 332
Ingraham, J. H., 245–46
Irving, Washington: *Astoria*, 194
Kennedy, John P.: *Horse-Shoe Robinson*, 160
Kirkland, Caroline M.: *Western Clearings*, 349
Lamb, Charles: *Specimens of English Dramatic Poets*, 347
Leslie, Eliza: *Pencil Sketches*, 162
Lever, Charles: *Charles O'Malley*, 263
Lewis, Sarah Anna: *Child of the Sea*, 409, 428

Lieber, Francis: *Reminiscences of an Intercourse with Mr. Niebuhr*, 2, 171
Longfellow, Henry Wadsworth: *Ballads and Other Poems*, 263, 266–67, 276, 302, 303, 420
Longfellow, Henry Wadsworth: "Excelsior," 617n46
Longfellow, Henry Wadsworth: *Hyperion, a Romance*, 223, 350
Longfellow, Henry Wadsworth: *Outre-Mer*, 161
Longfellow, Henry Wadsworth: *Visions of the Night*, 226
Longfellow, Henry Wadsworth: *The Waif: A Collection of Poems*, 324–25, 335, 612–13n5
Lowell, James Russell: *Conversations on Some of the Old Poets*, 324
Lowell, James Russell: *A Fable for Critics*, 424, 425, 460
Lowell, James Russell: *Poems*, 303
Macaulay, Thomas: essays, 245
Marshall, John: *Life of George Washington*, 162
Mathews, Cornelius: *Wakondah*, 262
Mattson, Morris: *Paul Ulric*, 172
Memoirs and Letters of Madame Malibran, 228
Memorials of Mrs. Hemans, 190
Moore, Thomas: *Alciphron, a Poem*, 225
Moore, Thomas: *The History of Ireland*, 162
Morgan, Susan Rigby: *The Swiss Heiress*, 190
Morris, Robert: "The Student's Dream of Fame," 600n73
Niebuhr, Barthold Georg: "Essay on the Allegory in the First Canto of Dante," 2, 171
Osgood, Frances Sargent: *Poems*, 349
Paulding, J. K.: *A Life of Washington*, 179
Pioneer (anonymous review), 284, 591n111
Pliny, Earle: *Marathon, and Other Poems*, 243, 245–46

Poe, Edgar Allan, reviews by (*continued*)
Poe, Edgar Allan: "Lionizing," 160
Prescott, William H.: *Biographical and Critical Notices*, 349
Reynolds, Jeremiah N.: *Address*, 194
Reynolds, Jeremiah N.: *Report on the Committee on Naval Affairs*, 186
Reynolds, Jeremiah N.: *Voyage of the United States Frigate Potomac*, 161–62
Richardson, Charles: *A New Dictionary of the English Language*, 186, 214
Roszel, S. A.: *Address*, 190
Sigourney, Lydia: *Letters to Young Ladies*, 185
Simms, William Gilmore: *The Damsel of Darien*, 223
Simms, William Gilmore: *The Wigwam and the Cabin*, 344
Slidell, Alexander: *Spain Revisited*, 179
Smith, Seba: *Powhatan; A Metrical Romance, in Seven Cantos*, 248, 249, 279, 578n81
Stephens, John Lloyd: *Incidents of Travel in Egypt, Arabia Petræa, and the Holy Land*, 200–203, 215, 637n36
Stone, William Leete: *Ups and Downs in the Life of a Distressed Gentleman*, 182
Thomas, F. W.: *Clinton Bradshaw*, 169
Tyler, Robert: "Death," 299
Walsh, R. M.: *Sketches of Conspicuous Living Characters of France* translation, 247
Warren, Samuel: *Ten Thousand a Year*, 255
Williams, Robert Folkestone: *Mephistopheles in England*, 167
Willis, N. P.: *Inklings of Adventure*, 186
Willis, N. P.: *Tortesa, the Usurer*, 221–22
Wilmer, Lambert A.: *The Confessions of Emilia Harrington*, 172
Wilson, John (pseud. Christopher North): *Genius and Character of Burns*, 344
Wyatt, Thomas: *A Synopsis of Natural History*, 221
Poe, Edgar Allan, works by
acrostic poems composed for cousin Elizabeth Rebecca Herring, 99
"Al Aaraaf" (poem), 98, 101, 102–4, 122, 276, 345–47, 385, 533n7
Al Aaraaf, Tamerlane, and Minor Poems (book title), 87, 90, 97, 102, 105, 534n17
"Alone" (poem, a.k.a. "From Childhood's Hour"), 86, 99, 533n7
"American Novel-Writing" (essay), 222, 578n89
"American Parnassus" (essay), 337
"Angel of the Odd, The" (short story), 313, 320, 325
"Annabel Lee" (poem). *See* "Annabel Lee"
"Appendix of Autographs, An" (essay), 258
"Article on Beet-Root" (newspaper article), 225
"Autography" (handwriting and character analysis), 172, 186, 215, 255, 590n100
"Ballad" (poem), 193
"Balloon Hoax, The" (newspaper article), 89, 303, 308–9, 310, 603n2
"Bargain Lost, The" (short story), 130, 136, 137, 149, 158, 167
"Bells, The" (poem), 207, 377, 393–94, 420, 423, 424, 435, 475, 493n17, 645n60, 647n8
"Berenice" (short story, a.k.a. "The Teeth"), 154, 156–58, 222, 234, 271, 283, 295, 336, 637n35, 638n38
"Black Cat, The" (short story), 204, 242, 280, 297–98, 302, 479
"Bon-Bon—A Tale" (short story, rewriting of "The Bargain Lost"), 137, 165, 222, 546n31

"Business Man, The" (short story, a.k.a. "Peter Pendulum, the Business Man"), 226, 250, 271, 290, 524n40, 595n21
"Byron and Miss Chaworth" (essay), 55, 607n58
canon of, 122, 222, 274, 314, 326
"Cask of Amontillado, The" (short story), 2, 65, 132, 279, 363, 364, 426, 528n26, 624n42
"Chapter of Suggestions, A" (essay), 299, 607n58
"Chapter on Autography, A" (essay), 246, 249, 255, 256–57, 281, 376, 590n100
"Chapter on Science and Art, A" (essay), 227
"City in the Sea, The" (poem, "The City of Sin" and formerly "The Doomed City"), 186, 244–45, 342, 617n49
"Coliseum, The" (poem), 143, 146–47, 165, 270, 548n50, 638n38
"Colloquy of Monos and Una, The" (imaginary dialogue), 248, 249–50, 271
Columbia Spy, topical letters published in, 310–11
Conchologist's First Book, The (largely by Thomas Wyatt), 219, 241, 320, 372, 567–68n32
"Conversation of Eiros and Charmion, The" (imaginary dialogue), 223, 290, 595n21
"Decided Loss, A" (short story), 130, 136–37
"Descent into the Maelström, A" (short story), 242, 250, 271, 385, 548n56
"Devil in the Belfry. An Extravaganza, The" (short story), 219, 347
"Domain of Arnheim, The" (short story), 276, 365, 371–72, 415, 422, 436–37, 479, 628n7
"Don Pompioso" (poem, possibly same as "Oh, Tempora! Oh, Mores!"), 519–20n151

"Doomed City, The" (poem, later "The City in the Sea"), 74, 122, 124–25, 126, 244, 524n30
"Dream, A" (poem, formerly without title), 86, 104
"Dream, A" (short story), 55, 58, 85, 123, 129, 214
"Dream-Land" (poem), 417
"Dreams" (poem), 27, 85–86, 87, 528n16
"Dream within a Dream, A" (poem), 427
"Duke de L'Omelette, The" (short story, a.k.a. "The Duc de L'Omelette"), 130, 133, 137, 149, 158, 172, 222
Dupin tales. See Dupin tales
"Eldorado" (poem), 430–31, 480
"Eleonora" (short story), 188, 206, 241, 250, 252–54, 265, 271, 381, 449, 479
"Eleven Tales of the Arabesque" (unpublished collection of tales), 140
"Enigma [on Shakespeare]" (poem), 138
"Enigmatical and Conundrum-ical" (newspaper article), 225
"Epimanes" (short story), 134, 140, 149, 151, 174, 547n44, 552n13
"Eulalie" (poem), 286, 341
Eureka. See *Eureka: A Prose Poem*
"Evening Star, The" (poem), 86
"Facts in the Case of M. Valdemar, The" (short story), 349, 352, 365, 379, 384, 621n77
"Fairyland" (poem, previously "Heaven"), 101, 102, 104, 122, 126, 221, 344
"Fall of the House of Usher, The" (short story), 40, 204, 219, 222, 225, 241–42, 253, 288, 569n45
"Fanny" (poem), 55, 140
"Few Words on Secret Writing, A" (essay), 247, 250, 254–55
"Fifty Suggestions" (brevities), 434, 437

Poe, Edgar Allan, works by (*continued*)
"For Annie" (poem), 430–31, 432, 466, 479
"Four Beasts in One—The Homo-Cameleopard" (short story), 349
"Hans Pfaall" or "Hans Phaall—A Tale," 145, 157, 161, 162, 309, 363, 385, 548n58, 604n5, 637n35
"Happiest Day, The" (poem), 87, 528n21
"Haunted Palace, The" (poem), 219, 222, 270
"Heaven" (poem, retitled "Fairy-land"), 101, 104
"Hop-Frog: or the Eight Chained Ourang-Outangs" (short story), 423, 426, 434
"How to Write a Blackwood Article" (short story), 204, 218, 274
"Imitation" (poem), 86–87, 104, 427
"Imp of the Perverse, The" (short story), 191, 340, 400, 533n7
"Impromptu: To Kate Carol" (poem), 338, 615n31
"Introduction" (poem), 122
"In Youth Have I Known One" (poem, "[Stanzas]"), 86
"Irene" (poem, later "The Sleeper"), 122, 125, 126, 179, 193, 270
"Island of the Fay, The" (short story), 244–45, 250, 271, 441, 477, 577n70
"Israfel" (poem), 122, 123–24, 175, 186, 254, 266, 276, 332, 479
"Journal of Julius Rodman, The" (six chapters of unfinished narrative, published serially), 225–29, 287
"King Pest" (short story), 149–50, 167
"Lake, The" (poem), 86
"Lake — To —, The" (poem, formerly "The Lake"), 104
"Landor's Cottage" (short story), 358, 397, 414, 422, 436–37, 479
"Landscape-Garden, The" (sketch), 268, 271, 272, 276, 287, 365, 415
"Lenore" (poem), 125, 285, 321
"Letter to Mr. ———"/"Letter to B—" (essay), 104, 122, 126, 185

"Life in Death" (short story, later "The Oval Portrait"), 265–66, 271, 583nn12–13
"Ligeia" (short story), 191, 216, 217, 222, 344, 567n26, 638n38
"Light-House, The" (unfinished short story), 448, 450
"Lines on Joe Locke" (poem), 65
"Lines Written in an Album" (poem), 167
"Lionizing" (short story), 65, 142, 149, 150, 151, 160, 336, 547n49
"Literary America" (projected book), 382
"The Literary Life of Thingum Bob, Esq., The" (short story), 65, 320, 325
"Literary Small Talk" (essays), 218–19
Literati, The (published by Griswold with "Memoir"), 475
"Literati of New York City, The" (series of essays), 351, 352, 357, 359, 362–64, 637n36
"Living Writers of America, The" (manuscript), 637n36
"Loss of Breath" (short story), 136–37, 149, 158, 167, 222, 350
"Maelzel's Chess-Player" (essay), 175, 211, 221, 318, 637n35
"Man of the Crowd, The" (short story), 31, 233, 234–35, 250, 271, 340, 479, 637n35
"Man That Was Used Up, The" (short story), 221, 296–97, 318
"Marginalia" (brevities, published in installments), 235, 313, 382, 389, 396, 422, 424, 434, 437, 607n58
"Mask/Masque of the Red Death, The" (short story), 33, 91, 136, 264, 271, 342, 617n49
"Mellonta Tauta" (short story), 379, 399, 630n39
"Mesmeric Revelation" (short story), 312, 313, 385–86
"Messenger Star" (poem), 102
"Metzengerstein" (short story, later subtitled "A Tale in Imitation of the

German"), 130, 132, 133, 137, 149, 150, 158, 171, 217, 222, 271, 297
"Miscellaneous Poems," 104
"Morella" (short story), 154, 158–59, 160, 217, 222, 223, 297
"Morning on the Wissahiccon" (sketch), 299
"MS. Found in a Bottle" (short story), 142–44, 150, 155, 162, 168, 169, 242, 344, 476, 479, 548n56
"Murders in the Rue Morgue, The" *See* "Murders in the Rue Morgue, The" (Dupin tale)
"Mystery of Marie Rogêt, The" *See* "Mystery of Marie Rogêt, The"
"Mystification" (short story, early version titled "Von Jung, the Mystific"), 350
Narrative of Arthur Gordon Pym, The. See *Narrative of Arthur Gordon Pym, The*
"Never Bet Your Head. A Moral Tale" (short story), 249, 250, 251, 271
"Notes upon English Verse" (essay), 286, 304, 640n53
"Notice of William Cullen Bryant, A" (essay), 228
"Oblong Box, The" (short story), 312
"Oh, Tempora! Oh, Mores!" (poem), 63–65, 518–19n144, 519n149, 519n151
"Omniana" (brevities), 227
"Original" (poem, later titled "Alone"), 99
"Original Conundrums" (newspaper article), 290, 595n21
"Our Book-Shelves" (magazine article), 344
"Paean, A" (poem, later fully revised as "Lenore"), 122, 125, 171, 541n58
"Palaestine" (essay), 172
"Peter Pendulum the Business Man" (short story), 226
"Phantasy-Pieces" (proposed collection of tales), 270–71, 585n40

"Philosophy of Composition, The" (essay), 25, 125, 190, 212, 327, 357, 461, 575n39, 643n36
"Philosophy of Furniture, The" (essay), 228, 373, 437
"Pinakidia" (brevities), 186, 605n19
"Pit and the Pendulum, The" (short story), 264, 271, 274, 583n10
Poems (book title, 1831), 65, 121–27, 345, 541n45, 541n47, 618n62
Poems and Miscellanies (Griswold's posthumous publication), 475
"Poetic Principle, The" (essay), 104, 124, 175, 266, 276, 382, 409, 413–14, 448, 450, 475, 644n41
"Poetic Principle, The" (lecture), 409, 419–20, 447, 452, 453–54, 458, 461, 464–65
"Poetry" (first extant manuscript), 58–59
"Poets and Poetry of America, The" (lecture), 337, 396, 397
"Politian," 55
posthumous work, publication of, 475
"Power of Words, The" (imaginary dialogue), 338, 637n36
"Preface" (poem, later "Romance"), 104
"Premature Burial, The" (short story), 312, 313, 470
Prose Romances of Edgar A. Poe, The (book title), 296–97
"Psyche Zenobia, The" (short story, later "How to Write a Blackwood Article"), 218
"Puffing" (essay), 607n58
"Purloined Letter, The." *See* "Purloined Letter, The (Dupin tale)"
Pym. See *Narrative of Arthur Gordon Pym, The*
"Raising the Wind; or, Diddling Considered as One of the Exact Sciences" (short story), 149, 150, 299, 344
"Rationale of Verse, The" (essay), 363, 409, 630n37, 636n31, 640n53

Index · 699

Poe, Edgar Allan, works by (*continued*)
"Raven, The" (poem). *See* "Raven, The"
Raven and Other Poems, The (book title), 344, 347–48, 389
Raven and Other Poems, The, bound with *Tales* (J. Lorimer Graham copy), 348, 357, 411, 620n70, 641n3
"Reviewer Reviewed, A" (essay), 124, 448, 450, 524n30
"Romance" (poem), 104
"Scenes from an Unpublished Drama" (verse drama), 171
"Scythe of Time, The" (short story, later "A Predicament"), 218
"Secret Writing" (essay), 250, 254
"Serenade" (poem), 140
"Shadow. A Fable" (short story), 167
"Silence. A Sonnet" (poem), 227
"Siope—A Fable" (short story, later "Silence—A Fable"), 149–50, 197, 202, 204, 552n13
"Some Account of Stonehenge, the Giant's Dance, A Druidical Ruin in England" (essay), 228–29
"Some Secrets of the Magazine Prison-House" (essay), 332
"Some Words with a Mummy" (short story), 74, 140, 313, 325, 336, 347, 379, 513n91
"Song" (poem), 54, 74, 524n30
sonnet in honor of Sarah Anna Lewis, 379, 389
"Sonnet" or "Sonnet—To Science" (poem), 78, 102–3, 122, 126, 179, 244, 245, 385, 403, 534n18, 539n21
"Sonnet—To My Mother" (poem), 438, 480
"Sonnet. To Zante" (poem), 193, 234, 342, 617n49
"Spectacles, The" (short story), 302, 305, 306, 349, 603n100
"Sphinx, The" (short story), 349
"Spirits of the Dead" (poem, formerly "Visit of the Dead"), 86, 104, 221
"Spiritual Song" (poem), 194–95

stolen or lost lectures during Poe's visit to Philadelphia, 444–45, 448, 453, 650n48
"Succession of Sundays, A" (short story, based on "Three Thursdays in a Week"), 257–58, 271
"Swiss Bell-Ringers, The" (essay), 318, 637n35
"System of Dr. Tarr and Professor Fether, The" (short story), 347, 607n58
"Tale of Jerusalem, A" (short story), 130, 134, 175, 213, 271, 545n23, 547n44
"Tale of the Ragged Mountains, A" (short story), 74, 299, 302, 305, 349, 599n68, 637n35
Tales (book title, 1845), 238, 242, 314, 336, 337, 340, 344, 348, 351, 616n41
Tales (Griswold's posthumous publication), 475
"Tales of the Folio Club" (unpublished collection of short stories). *See* "Tales of the Folio Club"
Tales of the Grotesque and Arabesque (collection of short stories). *See* *Tales of the Grotesque and Arabesque*
"Tamerlane" (poem), 1, 27, 51, 54–55, 62, 66, 84–87, 101, 104, 122–23, 165, 173, 252, 341, 391, 460, 479
Tamerlane and Other Poems (book title), 81, 83, 85–86, 87, 129, 525n55
"Tell-Tale Heart, The" (short story). *See* "Tell-Tale Heart, The"
"Thou Art the Man" (short story), 320
"Thousand-and-Second Tale of Scheherazade, The" (short story), 325, 347
"To——" (poem, formerly "To Elizabeth"), 221
"To ——" (poem, "I saw thee on the bridal day"), 85, 87, 104, 527n15
"To——" (poem, possibly "To [Elmira]"), 54
"To ——" (poem, "Should my early life seem"), 101, 104, 427

700 · Index

"To——" (poem, "Sleep on, sleep on"), 55, 140
"To — — —" (Valentine's Day poem), 388
"To F—" (poem, a.k.a. "To Mary" and "To One Departed"), 263, 553n45
"To Helen" (poem), 1, 53, 55, 122–23, 126, 149, 162, 174, 251, 304, 348, 389, 396–97, 409, 479, 538n12, 540n29, 550n73, 657n41
"To Ianthe in Heaven" (poem, a.k.a. "To One in Paradise"), 221
"To M—" (poem), 55, 90, 104
"To Margaret" (poem), 80, 525n55
"To Marie Louise" (poem), 382, 388–89, 632n54
"To Mary" (poem), 162
"To M. L. S—" (poem), 371, 633n1
"To Myra" (poem), 54–55, 85
"To Octavia" (poem), 525n55
"To One Departed" (formerly "To Mary"), 263
"To One in Paradise" (poem), 140, 148, 546n40
"To Readers and Correspondents," 165–66
"To the River —" (poem), 104, 221, 344
"To [Violet Vane]" (poem), 338, 344
"Ulalume" (poem). *See* "Ulalume"
untitled poem (later "A Dream"), 81, 86, 104
"Valentine, A" (poem), 424–25, 645n62
"Valley Nis, The" (poem, later "The Valley of Unrest"), 122, 125, 172
"Visionary, The" (short story, later "The Assignation"), 142, 148–49, 150, 158, 162, 222, 547n49, 549n69
"Von Jung, the Mystific" (short story), 200, 201–2, 204, 564n16, 592n113
"Von Kempelen and His Discovery" (short story), 424, 428, 434
West Point poems (published as *Poems*), 65, 121–27
"Why the Little Frenchman Wears His Hand in a Sling" (short story), 33, 224, 225

"William Wilson" (short story), 34–35, 73, 219, 223–24, 268, 294, 298, 342, 479, 569n46, 617n49
See also specific correspondents for letters to and from Poe
Poe, Eliza (mother, née Arnold): acting career of, 5–12, 18, 82, 90, 97, 460; Allan accusing of illicit affair, 60, 109; benefit performances to raise funds for, 12, 13–14; birth of daughter Rosalie, 12; birth of first son Henry, 7; birth of second son Edgar (1809), 9; *Boston Harbour Morning 1808* (painting), 8, 15, 80, 81; Boston move of Poe, association with his mother and place of birth, 80; Charleston move of Poe, association with his mother, 90; critical reviews of performances, 6–8, 10–12, 13, 619n63; death of, 15, 305, 329, 490n74; devotion of Edgar to, 5, 9, 26–27, 60, 62, 109, 217, 240, 304, 617n49; jewel case of, 367; last performance and illness of, 13–14; "Metzengerstein" allusion to, 132; miniature of, 6, 26, 217, 486n7, *g1*; Poe's regret for not vindicating good name of, 240, 316; *Pym* and, 194, 210, 214, 306, 460
Poe, Elizabeth (aunt, later married to Henry Herring), 9–10, 21, 97, 469, 494n39
Poe, Elizabeth Cairnes (paternal grandmother), 10, 62, 97–98, 127, 128, 138, 154, 162
Poe, George, Jr. (cousin of Poe's father), 10, 171, 173, 348
Poe, George W. (son of George Poe, Jr.), 221
Poe, Henry (brother, William Henry Leonard Poe): Allan's letter complaining about Edgar to, 59–60, 67, 109; birth of, 7; childhood with paternal grandparents in Baltimore, 14, 21, 62, 97; as "dashing gay cavalier," 128, 542n2; death of, impact on Poe, 1, 129, 195, 200, 212, 263, 274, 362, 365, 368,

Index · 701

Poe, Henry (brother, William Henry Leonard Poe) (*continued*): 450; debt shared with Edgar, 130–31; drinking and health problems of, 98, 128, 129; Edgar's poems from *Tamerlane* and, 87; Edgar's relationship with, 5, 128; Edgar writing Henry's verses in Holmes's album, 533n7; Hewitt on, 129; "Jacob's Dream" (poem), 80; living in Clemm's home, 127, 129; "The Pirate" (short story), 87, 129; "Psalm 139th" (poem), 80; publishing career of, 80, 129; *Pym* and, 1, 9, 194, 195, 198, 210, 212, 479, 563n8; "Recollections" (short story), 129; shared love with Edgar for mother Eliza, 5, 62; visiting Edgar in Richmond, 61–62, 129

Poe, Neilson, 105, 120, 164, 446, 473

Poe, Rosalie (sister): Allan calling Poe's half-sister, 60, 109; asking Vanparke to write defense of Poe, 476; birth of, 12, 489n57; brother Edgar's relationship with, 26, 57, 60, 560n71; brother Henry's relationship with, 60, 87; care during mother's final illness, 14; conversion to Methodism, 272; Elmira Shelton and, 456; giving Talley note from Poe with manuscript of "For Annie," 466; illness of, 20; living with Jane Scott Mackenzie, 15, 57, 108, 165, 406; Poe reciting "The Raven" at Talavera with, 457; Poe's picture, copies sold by, 657n45; in poetry of Henry Poe, 87; Poe visiting while in Richmond, 407, 447; portrait of, *g10*; sale of original manuscript of "Oh, Tempora! Oh, Mores!," 519n144; teaching at Miss Jane Mackenzie's school for girls, 32, 51, 178; visiting Talley with Poe, 448

Poe, Virginia Clemm (Poe's wife): age at marriage to Poe, 176, 178, 558n47; appearance of, 176, 197, 273; Darby Town visits of, 179–80, 186–90, 253–54, 404, 559n59; death of, 142, 260, 368; described by Flora Lapham Mack, 180; described by Frederick Thomas, 273; described by Mayne Reid, 296; education of, 32, 51, 158, 178; "Eleonora" referring to, 252; emotional encounter with funeral when walking with Wilmer and Poe, 132; expenses of final illness and death, 376; facing her coming death, 361, 364–65, 367; first encounter with Poe at her mother's home, 127, 128; Fordham village move and, 356–57; gift of fawn offered by Haines, 228; guitar lessons and playing, 191, 561n100; illness (tuberculosis) of, 204, 252, 253, 260–61, 265, 269, 273, 280, 290, 291, 319, 350, 361, 365–66, 582n145; "Life in Death" and, 265–66; marriage to Poe (1835), 4, 166–68, 175–78, 398, 479; Neilson Poe's offer to, 164–65; obituary of, 368; Osgood and, 334, 354–55; personality of, 180, 181, 197, 232; piano and, 191, 232–33; Poe declaring his love for, 158; poem she wrote to Poe, 354–55, 479; Poe's drinking and, 220, 272, 290; Poe's mourning and response to death of, 370, 377, 388, 398, 407, 479; Poe's notes to, 358–59, 623n27; Poe's relationship with, 180, 232, 249, 260, 273, 362, 479, 578n84; portrait of, 368, *g8*; singing and musical interests, 191, 232–33, 255–56; "Ulalume" written on death of, 1

Poe, Washington, 231, 233

Poe, William (cousin to Maria Clemm), 164, 167, 231, 233, 291

Poe, William Henry Leonard. *See* Poe, Henry (brother)

Poe Museum, 3; Susan Jaffe Tane Collection, 457

Poets and Poetry of America, The (Griswold, ed.): "Annabel Lee" submitted to, 432, 466; Dickens, Poe bringing prepublication copy to, 264; "For Annie" submitted to, 432; Hirst's

review of, 285; notable omissions from, 300; Poe helping with, 251; Poe's desire to challenge, 288, 333; Poe's inclusion in, 243, 270; Poe's review of, 272–73, 276–77, 300, 302, 586n48, 588n77; publication by Carey & Hart, 270; success of, 235–36
Poitiaux, Catherine Elizabeth, 26, 31
Polk, James K., 319
Pollin, Burton R., 204, 262, 571n67, 579n101, 593n4, 641n7; *The Collected Letters of Edgar Allan Poe* (3d ed., with Ostrom and Savoye), 2, 219, 220, 237; *Collected Writings of Edgar Allan Poe*, 2
Pouder, William P., 141
Power, Anna Marsh, 418, 421
practical jokes, 44, 56, 59, 210, 308–9; Poe as ghost at Ellis home's whist game, 114, 210, 309; Poe's ruse of supposed killing of unpopular professor at West Point, 114, 210, 309
Pratt, William A., 462
Prescott, William H.: *Biographical and Critical Notices*, Poe's review of, 349
Preston, James P., 95
Preston, J. T. L., 50, 65
prophecy, 203, 227, 480, 637n36
Providence: Poe's lecture in (1848), 419–20, 453; Poe's visits to Sarah Helen Whitman in (1848), 411, 416–17, 419
Public Ledger, Poe's writings in, 312
puffing, Poe's critique of, 300–301, 333, 334, 397
"Purloined Letter, The" (Dupin tale): Brougham and, 221, 222, 263; Caroline, English queen, and, 41, 314–15, 316; commencement of writing, 303, 305; as detective story, 38–39; Dickens and, 242; Galt (John) and, 222; games within, 315–16; integration of life and work in, 479; link with other Dupin tales, 280, 315, 316; plot of, 313–16; published in *The Gift for 1845*, 305, 310, 313; reversibility of language in, 637n35; sources for and influences on, 28, 314
Putnam, George P., 392, 394, 433, 635n13, 635n19
puzzles, 226, 227, 247, 250, 254, 256–57, 435–36, 577n76. *See also* decoding and encoding
Pym (novel). See *The Narrative of Arthur Gordon Pym*
Pym, William, 530n13

Quarles, Francis: *Emblems*, 328
Quinn, Arthur Hobson: *Edgar Allan Poe: A Critical Biography*, 2, 107, 167, 475, 495n52, 496n62, 534n23, 647n5

race and racism, 102, 163, 174, 208, 210, 239, 390, 534n15, 566n13. *See also* slavery
Ragged Mountains (near Charlottesville), 74, 210, 305, 524n29
"Raven, The" (poem), 1; *American Review* publishing, 321, 326, 328; attributed to "Quarles," 326, 328; balm in Gilead and, 168, 329; Brennan farmhouse as site of revision, 95; Brennan farmhouse as writing site, 320–21, 378; compared to Barrett's poetry, 322; compared to *Pym*, 328–29; compared to "Ulalume," 381; consolation and, 329, 330; critical reception of, 325–26, 327, 379, 384; description of structure, 326; Dickens and, 243, 327, 576n59, 610n83; foreshadowing in "To Myra," 55; included in *The Raven and Other Poems*, 347; influence on later works, 477; James Stirling's recitation of, 458; Lincoln's fondness for, 330; Melville's *Pierre* and, 477; multiple printings of, 331; narrative of, 326–27; "nevermore" and, 262, 298, 326, 327, 329, 330, 390, 611n3; Osgood quoting in "Ida Grey," 343; parodies of, 331, 341; Poe commenting on writing of ("The Philosophy of Composition"), 190,

"Raven, The" (poem) (*continued*) 212, 327, 357; Poe continuing to work on, 313, 320; Poe having idea for some years prior to composing, 329, 611n86; Poe reciting at Duncan Lodge, 447; Poe reciting at Richmond's Exchange Concert Room, 454, 465; Poe reciting at Talavera, 457; Poe reciting during Lowell talk (1848), 397; Poe reciting during Richmond visit to Mackenzies (1848), 407; Poe reciting during visit to Heywoods, 415; Poe reciting early version at Barhyte Farm, 298, 313, 320, 599n65; Poe reciting in Norfolk, 458; Poe reciting in Providence lecture, 420; Poe working on in Saratoga Springs, 298–99, 586n48; sources for and influences on, 25, 34, 262, 318, 327; trochaic octameter in, 322, 326, 327; Winslow's "To the Author of 'The Raven'" and, 390, 634n7

Ravenel, Edmund, 90

Reid, Mayne, 291, 296, 316, 439

religion: Poe and, 4, 129, 168, 203, 215, 382–83, 586n47; Poe on atheism, 350. *See also* Christianity

resurrection, 149, 371, 549n69

revenge: in Bulwer-Lytton's *Pelham*, 382; in "The Cask of Amontillado," 2, 364, 426; Griswold's writings on Poe as, 475; "Hop-Frog" as story of, 426; "Morella" as story of, 217

Reynolds, Jeremiah N.: *Address*, Poe's review of, 194; Boston lectures by, 87, 529n28; "Leaves from an Unpublished Journal," 205; *A Life of George Washington, in Latin Prose* (ed.), Poe's review of, 169; likelihood of Poe having met, 470, 661n75; Poe calling out name "Reynolds" prior to dying, 470, 661n74; Poe's debt to, 200; Poe's regard for, 310, 470; possibly corrupt, 562n111; *Report on the Committee on Naval Affairs*, Poe's review of, 186; Richmond lectures by, 77–78, 144, 525n46; on South Pacific voyage, 109;

Voyage of the United States Frigate Potomac, Poe's review of, 161–62; Wilkes writing book on voyage initially proposed by, 343

Richard, John, 48, 58

Richardson, Charles: *A New Dictionary of the English Language*, Poe's review of, 186, 214

Richmond: American Hotel, Poe staying at (1849), 445, 448, 652n63; brother Henry visiting Poe in, 61–62, 129; Evacuation Fire (1865) and loss of Poe's letters and Thomas Mackenzie's biography, 3, 99, 203, 478, 533n8, 539n26, 546n33, 596n24; Exchange Concert Room, Poe's lectures at (1849), 453, 464–65; Exchange Hotel, Poe's reading at (1848), 447; Madison House, Poe staying at (1849), 454, 462, 467; Monumental Church, 20, 23, 45, 107, 215, 496n61; named after England's Richmond on the Thames, 506n128; Poe's death, reaction to, 474; Poe's drinking sprees in (1848 & 1849), 408–9, 451; Poe's return after military discharge (1829), 95; Poe's return from Baltimore (1830), 105–10; Poe's return to (1849), 433, 445; Poe's trip to see John Mackenzie (1848), 404–9; Swan Tavern, Poe staying at (1849), 448–49, 450, 451, 454. *See also* Moldavia; Poe, Edgar Allan, childhood of

Richmond, Poe's residence in (1835–1837): Clemms and Poe living at Mrs. James Yarrington's boardinghouse, 167; Darby Town visits with Mackenzies, 179–80, 186–90; domestic contentment, 162, 180; drinking problems and, 162, 163, 166, 177, 182–85, 187, 191–92, 195, 196, 241; move to New York City (1837), 193; Poe, Virginia, and Maria Clemm living in rental tenement, 181; Poe's anxieties, 166; Poe's arrival (August 1835), 162; Poe's circle of friends, 165,

189; Poe working at *Southern Literary Messenger*, 163, 165–92; residing solo at Mrs. Poore's boardinghouse, 163; Virginia and Maria Clemm arriving in Richmond, 167, 555n10. See also *Southern Literary Messenger*

Richmond, Annie (Nancy Locke Heywood Richmond): "The Bells" sent to prior to publication, 435; Clemm and, 414, 419, 421, 422, 434, 441, 449, 474; as defender of Poe's honor, 423; description of, 414–15; "For Annie" and, 427, 430–31; integration of life and work (Poe's love for Annie), 430–31, 479; Jane Ermina Locke and, 394, 397, 414; "Landor's Cottage" as Poe's tale about, 422, 436; Poe giving his daguerreotype to, 436; Poe on his parting from Annie's younger sister Sarah, 436; Poe's desire to visit in Lowell, 433; Poe's final letter to, 438; Poe's love for, 178, 394, 410, 415, 416, 419, 422, 424, 430–31, 457, 479; on Poe's negative obituaries, 474; Poe's relationship with Elmira Shelton vs., 457; Poe's relationship with Sarah Helen Whitman vs., 415–19, 422; Poe's telling plans and unburdening his fears to, 433–35; Poe's visits to, 414–15, 416, 424, 435; portrait of, *g8*; Sarah Anna Lewis and, 414; as unattainable married woman, 408, 415

Richmond, Charles B. (husband of Annie Richmond), 397, 414, 424, 433, 457

Richmond Compiler, Poe's letter to, 186

Richmond Enquirer: on death of Eliza Poe (1811), 15; on John Allan, 153–54; on murder of Joseph White (1830), 108; review of Eliza Poe's performance in Richmond (1810), 12; on Richmond Theater fire (1811), 17; "Stanzas on a View of the Sea" (March 13, 1827), 78

Richmond Junior Volunteers, 59, 60, 516n116

Richmond Phenix, 54, 513n87; "To Myra" published in (1823), 54–55

Richmond Theater: appearances of Eliza and David Poe, 5–6; benefits held for Eliza Poe, 12–14; fire (1811), 16–18, 20–21, 43, 53, 174, 210, 405, 492n14, 492n17; *Timour the Tartar* performance (1822), 51

Ridgely, J. V., 205

Ridgway, Henry, 102

Ritchie, Thomas, 108–9

Rocknak, Stefanie: *Poe Returning to Boston* (statue), 480

Rogers, Mary, mystery of death of, 249, 278, 280, 316

Roszel, S. A.: *Address*, Poe's review of, 190

Royster, Sarah Elmira. *See* Shelton, Elmira Royster

Rust, Richard Dilworth, 364

Rutgers Female Institute, Poe as judge of student writing at, 341, 617n47

Saint-Pierre: "Pleasures of Ignorance," 102, 385

Sale, George: *Koran*, 103

Saltmarsh, Arthur, and William Taylor, 48, 49, 56

Sands, Gulielma, murder of, 169, 279

Santos, Carlos, 142

Sanxay, Richard D., 105–6, 108, 455

Saratoga Springs visit by Poe (September 1843), 298, 586n48, 599n65

Sargent, Epes, 404

Sartain, John, 233, 235, 243, 244, 424, 441–44, 565n8, 647n34

Sartain's Magazine: "Annabel Lee" published in, 475; "The Bells" published in, 475; "The Poetic Principle" published in, 475

Saturday Courier: contest for "best American tale," 130, 131; McMichael as editor, 130; publication of Poe's tales in, 131, 133, 134, 136–37, 141, 224

Saturday Evening Post: Graham as owner of, 233, 237; Henry Poe publishing poems in, 80, 539n21; influence on Poe, 74; plagiarism accusation against Poe

Index · 705

Saturday Evening Post (continued): in, 219; Poe acclaimed in "Ode XXX.—To Edgar A. Poe" in, 216; Poe publishing fiction in, 129; Poe's prospectus for "Penn Magazine" in, 230

Saturday Museum (biography): 23, 34, 75, 80, 112, 154, 286–88, 515n111, 521n6, 524n29, 569n46; attribution of authorship, 593–94n4; commencement by Clarke, 284; English's *The Doom of the Drinker* published in, 301, 600n77; "The Poets and Poetry of Philadelphia" series, 284–85, 286, 288, 594n4shortened version published in *Boston Notion*, 594n10

Saunders & Otley (publishers), 190

Savoye, Jeffrey A., 262, 542n61, 584n31, 593n2, 595n21, 603n2, 641n7, 656n36; *The Collected Letters of Edgar Allan Poe* (3d ed., with Ostrom and Pollin), 2, 219, 220, 237

Schlegel, Friedrich, 157

scientific topics, 386, 399, 403. *See also* cosmology; *Eureka: A Prose Poem*; Poe, Edgar Allan, works by: "Sonnet—To Science"

Scott, Andrew, 226

Scott, Sir Walter, 150, 169; *Ivanhoe*, 222; "Lay of the Last Minstrel," 24; "On the Supernatural in Fictitious Composition," 224

Scott, William, 192, 194

Scott, Winfield, 115, 371

Scott sisters, 492n6

Seaborn, Adam: *Symzonia: A Voyage of Discovery*, 144–45

Shakespeare, William: Allan's admiration of, 139; *Hamlet*, 10, 295–96, 621n1; *Henry VIII*, 249; *Julius Caesar*, 7–8, 59; *King Lear*, 7, 8; *Macbeth*, 232, 236, 259, 283, 298, 329–30, 591n103; *The Merchant of Venice*, 140; Poe copying out excerpts from, 90, 138; Poe denigrating, 132; Poe writing in praise of ("Engima [on Shakespeare]"), 138; *Richard III*, 312, 605n22; *Romeo and Juliet*, 10, 634n2; Sonnet 116, 657n41; Taverner's lecture on, 455; *The Winter's Tale*, 12

Sharp, Solomon P., murder of, 168

Shelley, Percy Bysshe: "England in 1819," 38; "The Indian Serenade," 453–54; "To—," 266

Shelton, Alexander B. (husband of Elmira), 66, 77, 85, 179

Shelton, Elmira Royster "Myra": adolescent romance with Poe, 47, 55, 61, 65–66, 520n154; appearance of, 455, 464; on Burling and Poe, 60; Clemm and, 463–64, 466, 474, 658n49; engagement to Poe, 456; engagement to Shelton, 77, 85; family opposition to marriage to Poe, 654n12; finances of, 454–55, 456, 463; first meeting of Poe, 47, 508n34; Henry Poe, encounter with, 62; on learning of Poe's death, 474; Poe alluding to in "Tamerlane" and other poems, 85, 87, 528n21; Poe's correspondence with, 455; Poe's courtship and marriage proposal to (1848 & 1849), 446–47, 450, 452, 454, 654n10; on Poe's final visit, 466; on Poe's marriage to Virginia, 179; Poe's wedding ring for, 457, 655n24; portrait of, *g10*; Tom Mackenzie and, 446; as widow, interested in relationship with Poe, 66, 179, 407–8, 433, 446–47, 639n48, 650–51n53

Shepherd, William J., 48–49

Sheridan, Richard: *The Rivals*, 12; *School for Scandal*, 12

Sherley, Douglass, 70, 71, 73, 521n6

Shew, Marie Louise: "The Bells" and, 393–94; compared to Jane Stith Stanard, 395; forsaking Poe, 395; on Griswold's animosity to Poe, 392–93, 635n15; on Henry Poe, 542n2; John H. Hopkins, Jr. and, 391–93, 395; as nurse of Virginia and Poe, 365–68, 370–73, 394, 626n61, 628n9; with Poe at Christmas Eve service, 382–83; Poe's loan countersigned by, 394; on Poe's need for caring woman in his life, 370, 396, 440, 628n9; Poe's poems for, 388, 633n1; Poe telling about his regret over not defending his mother's honor, 60, 240, 316

Sigourney, Lydia: contributing poem to *Graham's*, 256; "Greece," 74, 124–25; influence on Poe, 74, 124, 524n30; *Letters to Young Ladies*, Poe's review of, 185; "Musing Thoughts," 124, 524n30; Poe's opinion on, 333; *Southern Literary Messenger* and, 186

Silverman, Kenneth, 2, 167, 233, 598n48, 614n17, 651n58

Simmons, Susan (aunt of Louisa Lanier Mackenzie), 138

Simmons, William, 3

Simms, William Gilmore: *The Damsel of Darien*, Poe's review of, 223; in *The Gift . . . for 1836*, 167; influence on Poe, 294, 597n42; "The Lazy Crow," 294; on Longfellow's *The Waif*, 324; offering advice to Poe, 362; on Poe's lecture in Boston, 347; on Poe's *Tales* (1845), 294; in *Southern Literary Messenger*, 186; *The Wigwam and the Cabin*, Poe's review of, 344

Sioux on Horseback, A (image in Poe's "Julius Rodman"), 227, 571n67

slavery: abolitionists and, 425; Allan's sale of enslaved people, 26, 498n94; Clemm's sale of enslaved man, 102; Dew's defense of, 174; Mackenzie family's enslaved persons, 180, 190, 405, 406, 450, 559n59, 638n41; Poe and, 102, 163, 174, 534n15; slave auctions in Richmond, 174, 557n37; Talavera's enslaved persons hearing Poe's recitation of "The Raven," 457–58

Slidell, Alexander: *Spain Revisited*, Poe's review of, 179

Smith, A. C., watercolor portrait of Poe by, 302, 321

Smith, Andrew K., 73

Smith, Edmund Morton, 473

Smith, Elizabeth Oakes, 178, 206, 333, 351, 361, 468, 555n12

Smith, Elizabeth Rebecca Herring, 473

Smith, Horace: influence on Poe, 134; "Song to Fanny," 80, 525n55; *Tales of Early Ages*, 140; *Zillah, a Tale of Jerusalem*, 134

Smith, Horace Wemyss, 226, 568n38, 599n66

Smith, Seba (a.k.a. Jack Downing): *Powhatan; A Metrical Romance, in Seven Cantos*, review by Poe, 248, 249, 279, 578n81

Smith, Thomas S., 277, 288

Smith, William Penn, 226

Snodgrass, Joseph E., 147, 182, 223–25, 227, 230, 236, 241, 242, 249–51, 270, 287, 288, 302, 408, 468–69, 473–74, 581n137

Snodgrass, W. D., 341

social class: Poe's allegiance to social distinction, 63, 64–65; Poe's class issues at school, 51, 65, 118

Sons of Temperance, 451, 457, 655n23, 659n60

soul in Poe's work: in "The Bargain Lost" (later "Bon-Bon"), 136, 137, 158, 222; in "Berenice," 222; "bi-part soul," allegory of, 34; in "A Decided Loss," 136; in Drake-Halleck review by Poe, 175; in "The Duke de L'Omelette," 133, 149, 158, 222; in "Eleonora," 253; in *Eureka*, 399, 403; in "The Fall of the House of Usher," 222, 253; in Fouqué's *Undine: A Miniature Romance*, Poe's review of, 222; in "Ligeia," 217, 222; in "Loss of Breath," 136, 137, 149, 158, 222; in "Metzengerstein," 131, 133, 149, 158, 217, 222; in "Morella," 158, 159, 217, 222; in "Never Bet Your Head," 251; Poe seeking something akin to home of, 276; in "The Poetic Principle," 175; in "Politian," 55; in *Pym*, 403; in *Tales of the Grotesque and Arabesque*, 220; in "Tamerlane," 84; in "To Helen," 122–23; in "To Myra," 55, 85; "The

soul in Poe's work (*continued*):
Visionary" (later "The Assignation"), 148–49, 158, 222. *See also* metempsychosis

Southern Literary Messenger: "Annabel Lee" published in, 466, 475; "Autography" published in, 172, 255; "Ballad" published in, 193; "Bon-Bon" published in, 165; "The City in the Sea" published in, 186; Clemm selling volume of, prior to move to NYC, 309, 604n10; "The Doom" published anonymously in, 155, 552n14; "The Duc de L'Omelette" published in, 172; "Epimanes" published in, 174; farewell from Poe published in, 194, 562n111; "Hans Phaall—A Tale" published in, 161; "Irene" published in, 125, 179; "Israfel" published in, 186; Kennedy suggesting Poe contact, 155; "King Pest" published in, 167; launch of, 154–55; "Letter to Mr. —— —" (later "Letter to B—") published in, 185; "Lines Written in an Album" published in, 167; "The Literary Life of Thingum Bob, Esq." published in, 320; "Loss of Breath" published in, 136, 167; "Marginalia" published in, 424, 434, 437; "Metzengerstein" published in, 171; Neal on, 167, 169–70; "Palaestine" published in, 172; *Philadelphia Saturday News and Literary Gazette* favorably reviewing, 185, 215; "Pinakidia" published in, 605n19; Poe fired from position and rehired on promise to cease drinking, 166–68; Poe in editing role in Richmond, 163–65, 171, 173, 185; Poe praising Reynolds in, 78; Poe's association with, 136, 145, 155, 158; Poe's drinking problem and, 166–68, 177–78, 187, 191–92, 350, 408; Poe's illness resulting in delayed issue, 186–87; Poe's pay for contributions, 194, 553n31; *Pym* installments in, 193–94, 197, 207; "Scenes from an Unpublished Drama" published in, 171; "Shadow. A Fable" published in, 167; "Sonnet" or "Sonnet—To Science" published in, 179; "Sonnet. To Zante" published in, 193; subscribers' names used in *Pym* (Goddin and Vredenburgh), 198, 563n8; subscription list, Poe attempting to purchase for "The Stylus," 290–91; "A Tale of Jerusalem" published in, 175; termination of Poe's time at, 191–92; "To Helen" published in, 174; "To Mira" (Wilmer) published in, 556n20; "The Valley Nis" published in, 172; "The Visionary" published in, 162; White expecting to wind up, 191

Southern Opinion (1863): publication of Poe poem "Oh, Tempora! Oh, Mores!," 63

Spa Fields Riot (England 1816), 32

Sparhawk, Edward V., 160–61, 163

Spirit of the Times, 230, 237, 258, 301, 303, 360

Stanard, Jane Stith: compared to Marie Louise Shew, 395; illness and death of, effect on Poe, 57, 58, 71, 304, 329, 362, 370; as inspiration for "To Helen," 1, 53, 123, 149, 162; language of Poe used to describe, 149; Poe alluding to in "A Dream," 86; Poe alluding to in "A Paean," 125, 541n58; Poe alluding to in "Tamerlane," 85; as Poe's confidant and first "purely ideal love," 52–53, 101, 123, 413; Poe's visits to grave of, 58, 86, 108; recognizing Poe's worth, 101, 123

Stanard, Robert, 52, 58, 370

Starr, Eliza Kurtz, 390, 394

Starr, Mary (a.k.a. Mary Devereaux): close to Poe in later years, 142; love for Poe, 271; Poe's courtship of, 134–35, 141–42, 258, 274, 545n25; on Poe's Philadelphia home, 232; Poe visiting (1844), 271, 367; singing "Come Rest in This Bosom" for Poe, 232, 271, 367, 409; at Virginia Poe's funeral, 368; visit to Poe's home in New York City, 352

Stearns, Thomas Pease, 526n2
Stephens, Ann S., 359, 368
Stephens, John Lloyd: *Incidents of Travel in Egypt, Arabia Petræa, and the Holy Land*, Poe's review of, 200–203, 215, 637n36
Stevenson, Andrew, 95, 96
Stirling, James, 458, 656n32
St. Johns College, Poe's visit to, 365
Stoddard, Richard Henry, 233–34, 349, 378, 383–84, 630n36; "Ode on a Grecian Flute," 342
Stoke Newington. *See* Poe, Edgar Allan, education of
Stone, William Leete, 199; *Ups and Downs in the Life of a Distressed Gentleman*, Poe's review of, 182
Stovall, Floyd, 104, 532n27, 535n32
"Stylus, The": biography of *Saturday Museum* to generate interest in, 287; Clarke as backer and his later withdrawal, 284, 292, 592n113, 596n34; Eveleth and, 386; lecture tour to raise funds for, 385, 388, 408–9, 433, 435, 445; never published, 319; Patterson as possible publisher, 433–35, 448, 456, 465–66; Poe's drafting reviews for, 465; Poe's drinking problems and, 292; Poe's hope for and commitment to, 313, 323, 332, 344, 350, 363, 384, 408, 419, 438, 450; Poe's realization of failure to launch, 302; Poe's Richmond friends pledging support for, 450, 465, 652n70; Poe's table of contents for first issue, 465, 653n70; prospectus for, 287–88, 382, 384, 388, 389; Shelton's reluctance to support Poe in, 455; as successor of planned magazine "The Penn," 284, 581n136; Valentine and, 419, 643n34
Sullivan's Island, 87, 89, 91, 530n4
Sully, Robert, 44, 48, 265
Sully, Thomas, 570n65
Sumner, Charles, 324
Symmes, John Cleves, 144–45

Symmes's Hollow Earth theory, 77–78, 144–45, 161, 242
symmetry: in "Berenice," 157–58, 295; in "The City of Sin," 245; in Dupin tales, 240, 280, 315; in *Eureka*, 146, 157–58, 295, 401, 403; in "The Gold-Bug," 294–95; in "The Landscape-Garden," 276; in "Life in Death," 265; in "The Man of the Crowd," 239–40; in "The Mask of the Red Death," 268; in "The Murders in the Rue Morgue," 240; in "The Mystery of Marie Rogêt," 280; in "The Pit and the Pendulum," 274–75; in "The Purloined Letter," 314–16; in *Pym*, 211, 328, 403; in "A Tale of the Ragged Mountains," 305

Tabb, H. W., 32
Talavera (Talley family home), 448, 450, 457, 465, 466
"Tales of the Folio Club" (unpublished collection of short stories): announcement in *Baltimore Saturday Visiter* of forthcoming book, 147; Carey, Lea & Blanchard's slow-coming rejection of, 149, 155; contents of, 130; critical reception of, 143, 145; Harper and Brothers' rejection of, 182; host in introduction, 133, 150; influenced by Silver Fork novel marketplace (London), 550n78; never published, 147, 186, 287; Poe continuing to write, 135–37; rejected for publication, 173; as satirical works, 65, 132–33; stories included in, 134, 136–37, 140, 149, 160, 162, 175; winning tale in *Baltimore Saturday Visiter* contest (1833), 143
Tales of the Grotesque and Arabesque (collection of short stories): *Alexander's Weekly Messenger* articles and, 226; contents of, 218, 224; critical reception of, 224–25, 345; Dickens agreeing to help find British publisher for, 264; introduction, 220, 224; personal and editorial encomia at end of second volume, 224; Poe proposing

"Tales of the Folio Club" (unpublished collection of short stories) (*continued*): collection called "Phantasy-Pieces" from, 270–71; Poe's distribution of his complementary copies, 224; possibility of new edition, 250; publication by Lea & Blanchard, 100, 223, 224; reprinted, 159; sending Dickens copy of, 263

Talley, Susan Archer, 93, 419, 433, 447–48, 450, 457, 465, 466; "Genius," 447; Poe's obituary in *Richmond Republican* by, 474. See also Talavera

Tane, Susan Jaffe, 480

Tasso, Torquato, 521n6; "Jerusalem Delivered," 69

Taverner, J. W., 455

Taylor, Mary Bell (wife of William Galt, Jr.), 108

Taylor, William. *See* Saltmarsh, Arthur, and William Taylor

Taylor, Zachary, 442, 450

telescopes, 31, 45, 57, 61, 385

"Tell-Tale Heart, The" (short story): based on White's murder in Salem, Massachusetts, 108; commencement of writing, 280; critical reception of, 283–84; Dickens and, 242; essay by Poe on calm manner of insane man and, 227; Hawthorne's *The Scarlet Letter* and, 476; John Allan as character in, 283; *Macbeth* allusion, 298; "A Madman's MS" and, 191; "old man" in, 77, 94; plot of, 282–83; Poe's nervousness in narrator of, 283; publication in *Pioneer*, 281, 282; rejected for publication by Tuckerman, 281; reprinting of, 284; sources for and influences on, 283, 423; writing of, 204

Temperance Reformation, 248; English's *The Doom of the Drinker* as temperance novel, 301, 600n77. *See also* Sons of Temperance

Tennyson, Alfred: "The Death of the Old Year," 226; "Locksley Hall," 322; Poe praising, 132

Thayer, Sylvanus, 111, 115, 118, 121

Thomas, Calvin F. S., 82–83, 87, 295

Thomas, Dwight: "Poe in Philadelphia," 572n6, 585–86n42

Thomas, Dwight, and David K. Jackson: *The Poe Log: A Documentary Life of Edgar Allan Poe, 1809–1849*, 2, 205, 219, 409, 570n58, 593n4, 613n17

Thomas, Frederick W.: autobiographical letter for Poe, 572n6; *Clinton Bradshaw*, Poe's review of, 169; *Howard Pinckney*, 231, 234; job possibility for Poe in Washington, D.C., 244, 246–47, 249, 251, 254, 260, 285, 290, 579n108; "Oh! Blame Her Not" (song), 255–56; "Penn Magazine" plan and, 254; on Poe's drinking, 338; on Poe's education in London, 33; Poe's "The Murders in the Rue Morgue," response to, 238; on Poe's visit to Washington, 595n18; refusing to write biography of Poe, 593n1; relationship and correspondence with Poe, 229, 231–32, 244, 251, 260, 269, 271, 273–74, 284, 285, 286, 289, 312, 337, 362, 368, 424, 593n118; "'Tis Said That Absence' &c" ["Conquers Love"] (song), 255; visit to Poe in Philadelphia (1844), 273–74

Thompson, John R., 408–9, 419, 433, 438, 447, 466, 636n24

Tomlin, John, 231, 233, 234, 275

"To the Authoress of The Unsatisfied" (author unknown), 390

Transcendentalism, 251, 301, 332, 333, 334, 601n86

Travers, Robert, 499n2

Treaty of Ghent (1815), 24–25

Trelawney, Edward John: *The Adventures of a Younger Son*, 145

tuberculosis, 14. *See also* Poe, Virginia Clemm

Tucker, Nathaniel Beverly, 169, 192, 193, 556n28

Tucker, Thomas G., 70, 71, 73, 521n6

Tuckerman, Henry T., 281, 341

Tutt, Elizabeth (Poe's cousin), 271–72, 584n31
Tutwiler, Henry, 72
Twain, Mark, 239
Tyler, John, 241, 246–47, 251, 290, 579n108
Tyler, Robert, 272, 277, 289, 290; "Death," Poe's review of, 299
Tyler, W. B., cryptographs of, 256–57
typhus fever (London 1817), 33, 91, 136, 268

Uhland, Johann Ludwig: "Castle by the Sea," 460, 656n36
"Ulalume" (poem), 377–82, 630n37; acknowledgment of authorship, 411; as ballad, 656n34; compared to *Pym*, 381; compared to "The Raven," 381; integration of life and work in, 1, 381–82, 479; memory and, 380, 382; Moore's "When Gazing on the Moon's Light" and, 86; Poe reciting during Duncan Lodge visit, 406, 639n45; Poe reciting during visit to Heywoods, 415; Poe reciting in Norfolk, 458, 461; Poe reciting to Sarah Helen Whitman, 411–12; published in *American Review*, 379; rejected by *Union Magazine*, 378; reprinted in *Home Journal*, 379, 384; shift from forgetting to recovered memory, 380; structure of, 380; substituted for "The Rationale of Verse," 630n37; writing of, 378
Union Magazine, 389, 424, 443; "The Bells" published in, 424; "To Helen" published in, 397; "Ulalume" rejected by, 378
"unity of effect," 157, 160, 182, 223, 226, 274, 324
University of Virginia, Poe attending (1826), 67–77; Allan's insufficient financial support, 66, 67, 72, 75; Allan visiting Poe, 69; Ancient Languages, classes in, 68, 70, 74; attendance at lectures, 521n6; campus and Rotunda of, 68; classical education, 68–69, 74; drawings by Poe while attending, 70, 522n17; drinking, gambling, and rowdiness as common vices of student body, 69, 73, 522n8; drinking and gambling as Poe's downfall, 66, 69, 70, 72–73, 75; exams, Poe's distinction in, 74–75, 95–96, 524nn31–32; financial worries and debts, 66, 67–68, 72, 73, 75–76, 106, 524n41; forced to leave due to debts, 73–77; Jefferson Literary Society, Poe as secretary for, 522n11; Jefferson's funeral, Poe in attendance, 73; library borrowings by Poe, 70, 522n10; Modern Languages, classes in, 68, 69, 74; poem published in Charlottesville's *Central Gazette*, 124–25; Poe's blaming Allan for his troubles, 75–77; Poe's expressions of and denials of responsibility and regret, 75, 77; Poe's letters to Allan from (1826 & 1827), 74; Poe's preparation for attending, 61; Poe writing poetry and fiction, 70, 129
Upton, John, 226
Usher, Luke Noble and Harriet Ann L'Estrange, 7

Valentine, Edward, Jr., 22–23, 419, 643n34, 657n45
Valentine, Nancy (sister of Frances Allan, a.k.a. Ann): correspondence about London, 499n5; fondness for Poe, 16, 80, 107, 153; funeral of Frances and, 94; John Allan's interest in second marriage to, 107; in London with Allans, 31, 32, 38, 133; at Moldavia with Allans, 61; as nurse to Allans, 35, 40, 41; in Richmond with Allans, 46, 52, 56; taking Poe's part against second Mrs. Allan after John Allan's death, 154
Valentine, William Winston, 465
Van Buren, Martin, 231
Van Cleef, Augustus, 134
Vane, Violet. *See* Osgood, Frances Sargent
Vanparke, Parke, 406, 476

Index · 711

verbal patterning, in Poe's work, 2, 157–58, 201, 234
von Kotzebue, August: *The Stranger*, 13

Walker, Joseph W., 468
Wallace, Horace Binney: *Stanley*, 314
Wallace, William Ross, 271, 310, 325
Walpole, Horace: *Castle of Otranto*, 132
Walsh, R. M.: *Sketches of Conspicuous Living Characters of France* translation, Poe's review of, 247
Walsh, Robert, 98
Walter, Cornelia Wells, 346, 626n61
Walton, Octavia, 80
War of 1812, 21–22, 24, 494n43, 494–95n45
Warren, Samuel: *Ten Thousand a Year*, Poe's review of, 255
Washington, D.C., Poe's job prospects in, 244, 246–47; Poe's travel to Washington, 288–89, 595n18
Washington, William Lanier, 3, 63–64, 202, 215, 406, 439, 449, 476, 492n6, 651n58
Washington College Hospital, 469
Webster, Daniel, 108, 283, 591n103
Weiss, Susan Archer, 43, 45, 49, 118, 120, 175, 181, 328–29, 361, 446, 448, 449, 451, 455, 464, 474, 507n4, 512n76, 519n151, 542n2, 555n12, 611n86, 639n43, 650–51n53, 651n58
Welby, Amelia B., 321, 333
Weld, H. Hastings, 248, 251, 270, 279; *Corrected Proofs*, 249, 279, 578n88. See also *Brother Jonathan*
Wertenbaker, William, 69–70, 72, 73, 75, 76, 118
West, Charles E., 358
Weston, J. Alden, 473–74
West Point (1830–1831), 111–21; academic achievement and good standing, 112, 116, 538n7, 538n11; admission granted to Poe for June 1830, 107, 110; Allan giving permission as Poe's guardian for Poe to enter, 107; Allan severing his relationship with Poe (1831), 116; Kinsley as unpopular instructor, 114; letters in support of Poe for, 95–96; mathematics as academic weakness of Poe, 112–13; memorial arch to Poe in West Point's library, 117, 540n29; Poe attending for one semester, 110; Poe on West Point campus and in barracks, 112; Poe's court-martial for gross neglect of duty and dismissal, 117, 540n27; Poe's departure and return to Richmond, 118, 119; Poe's desire to obtain admission, 93, 94, 99, 100–102, 493n30; Poe's desire to resign, requiring Allan's permission, 116–17; Poe's drinking problem while attending, 113–14; Poe's finances and incurred debts, 115–16, 118, 125, 541n59; Poe's letters to John Allan, 72, 74, 75, 76, 109, 116; Poe's practical joke of supposedly murdered professor, 210, 309; Powhatan Ellis's letter of support for, 107; purchase of Poe's *Poems* by cadets, 125; West Point poems, 65, 121–27
West Point letters to John Allan (1831), 72, 74–76, 109, 116, 139
Whalen, Terence, 174, 257, 405
Whigs, 231, 235, 241, 579n108
Whipple, Edwin P., 256
White, Eliza (daughter of Thomas), 167, 176, 555n12, 596n24, 627n63
White, Joseph, murder of, 108, 283
White, Thomas W.: background of, 154–55; death of, 290; funeral of Frances Allan and, 93, 531n19; Kennedy recommending Poe to, 155; Poe family seeking to rent house from, 181, 182; on Poe's drinking, 165, 555n15; Poe seeking loan from, 193; at Poe's wedding to Virginia, 176; portrait of, *g4*; relationship with Poe, 160–61, 167, 172, 185, 191–92, 270, 283, 556n28; reservations about "Berenice," 156; *Southern Literary Messenger* as periodical of, 154–55; Tucker correspondence, 169, 192, 193, 556n28. See also *Southern Literary Messenger*

712 · Index

White Eagle Club, 319, 607n55
Whitelock, William, 219
White Sulphur Springs (resort), 19–20, 22, 23, 141, 493nn29–30
Whitman, Sarah Helen: on Allan's temperament, 23; on Blackwell, 377; breaking off engagement due to Poe's drinking, 421; Clemm and, 407, 419, 421, 658n49; conditional engagement to Poe, 418; on Eliza White's relationship with Poe, 555n12; on Ellet's persecution of Poe, 353–54; on Frances Allan's funeral, 531n19; on Gowans, 205; on Jane Stith Stanard, 52, 53, 123, 370; loyalty to Poe in years after breakup, 422; mother's objections and reluctant consent to marriage to Poe, 418–20, 644n42; Poe asking her to confirm to Annie Richmond how their relationship ended, 422–23; on Poe at West Point, 118; Poe presenting copy of *Tales* to, 340, 348; Poe's courtship and proposal to, 408–9, 411–13, 417–18; in Poe's lecture "Poets and Poetry of America," 397; on Poe's pity and sorrow for the dead, 125, 381; Poe's relationship with Annie Richmond vs., 415–16, 418–19, 422; on Poe's relationship with Osgood, 341, 353; Poe's response to accusations against him, 413; Poe's "To Helen" and, 341, 389, 409; Poe using pseudonym Edward S. T. Grey in correspondence with, 410, 617n49; portrait of, *g8*; relationship sought by Poe with hope of marriage, 396, 407–23; on Shelton-Poe relationship, 407–8; on Stoddard's jealousy of Poe, 630n36; on *Ulalume*, 382; Wyatt visiting and telling of his regard for Poe, 219
Whitman, Sarah Helen, works by: "Lines," 437; "Stanzas for Music" (later "Our Island of Dreams"), 426, 656n38; "To Arcturus," 418; "To Edgar A. Poe," 389, 396, 409, 634n3

Whitman, Walt, 59, 349, 516n117, 519n146; "Out of the Cradle Endlessly Rocking," 477
Whittier, John Greenleaf, 256, 344, 635n9
Whitty, J. H., 514n95, 517n127; on Eliza White and Poe, 555n12; Mack's relationship with, 518n144; on "Oh, Tempora! Oh, Mores!," 518n144, 519n151; on Poe family move to Philadelphia, 205; on Poe leaving Allans to go to University of Virginia, 66; on "Spiritual Song," 194–95; on Usher family house in Baltimore, 569n45
Wilbur, Richard, 2, 86, 194, 528n19, 533n7
Wiley & Putnam (publishers), 217, 336, 340, 344, 347, 348, 357; Library of American Books, 340, 347, 616n38
Wilkes, Charles: *Narrative of the United States Exploring Expedition*, 343
Williams, Robert Folkestone: *Mephistopheles in England*, Poe's review of, 167
William Wirt Institute Lectures and Debates, Poe's lecture at (Philadelphia 1843), 300
Willis, N. P.: at Booksellers' Dinner (March 30, 1837), 198; "The Cherokee's Threat," 186; Clemm and, 317, 439; declining to contribute article to *Graham's*, 256; defense of Poe's review of Longfellow, 324; hiring Poe, 317; *Inklings of Adventure*, Poe's review of, 186; Longfellow and, 335, 612–13n5; negative reaction to Poe's poem, 102, 104; "Pencillings by the Way," 268; Poe ending employment with, 332; Poe's assessment of poetry of, 255–56, 310; Poe satirizing, 133, 150; in Poe's "Autography," 186; Poe's correspondence with, 311, 365–66, 432; Poe seeking aid with speaking tour on cosmology, 385; on Poe's illness and poverty, 365; in Poe's lecture at

Willis, N. P. (*continued*):
Mechanics Institute of Reading, Pennsylvania, 304; on Poe's lecture at New York Society Library, 333; in Poe's "The Literati of New York City," 357; Poe's obituary in *Home Journal* by, 475; on Poe's "The Tell-Tale Heart," 281, 283, 285; portrait of, *g7*; *Tortesa, the Usurer*, Poe's review of, 221–22; "Unseen Spirits," 311, 333; at Virginia Poe's funeral, 368; Wilmer and, 250

Wills, Elizabeth, 107, 154

Wilmer, Lambert A.: *Baltimore Saturday Visiter* editor, 129, 132, 136, 545n28; *The Confessions of Emilia Harrington*, Poe's review of, 172; departure from Baltimore, 136; friendship with Poe, 132, 170; *Merlin*, 132, 528n25; "Ode XXX.—To Edgar A. Poe," 216, 250; on Poe's care of Virginia, 280; on Poe's drinking problems, 292; on Poe's genius, 216; on Poe's offering excuse of supper and drinks with friends, 141; on Poe's piano for Virginia, 232; Poe's proposal to coedit magazine, 288; on Poe's tales, 135–36; *The Quacks of Helicon*, 250; *Saturday Evening Post* editor, 129; on Shakespeare, 138; "To Mira" published in *Southern Literary Messenger*, 556n19

Wilmer, Margaret E., 280

Wilson, John (pseud. Christopher North), 125, 224, 322–23; *Genius and Character of Burns*, Poe's review of, 344

Wilton, Henry (pseud. John H. Hewitt), 143, 146, 547n50

Wimsatt, William K., Jr., 254

Winfree, Mary, 162

Winslow, Harriet B., 425; "To the Author of 'The Raven'" (with Poe's editing, later "After Reading 'The Raven'"), 390, 634n7; "To the Unsatisfied" (or "Why Thus Longing?"), 390, 634n8

Wirt, William, 98

women writers, Poe's opinion of, 333. *See also specific women's names*

Woodberry, George E., 118, 298–99, 493n29

Wordsworth, William: influence on Poe, 86, 528n19; Intimations Ode, 389; Poe disagreeing with, 122

Worth, W.J., 95, 96

Wyatt, Thomas, 241; *The Conchologist's First Book*, published under Poe's name, 219, 241, 320, 567–68n32; high regard for Poe, 219; *A Synopsis of Natural History*, Poe's review of, 221

Yankee, Poe's poetry published in, 100–101

Yarrington, Mrs. James, 167, 176

yellow fever (Charleston 1828), 91, 136, 268, 530n13

Zimmerman, Brett, 297

Also by the Author

The Formal Center in Literature: Explorations from Poe to the Present
Edgar Allan Poe and the Dupin Mysteries
The Threads of "The Scarlet Letter": A Study of Hawthorne's Transformative Art